McGraw-Hill's
American
Idioms
Dictionary

Richard A. Spears, Ph.D.

New York Chicago San Francisco Lisbon London Madrid Mexico City
Milan New Delhi San Juan Seoul Singapore Sydney Toronto

Library of Congress Cataloging-in-Publication Data

Spears, Richard A.
    McGraw-Hill's American idioms dictionary / Richard A. Spears. — 4th ed.
        p.   cm.
    Previously published as: NTC's American idioms dictionary. Chicago, Ill. : NTC Pub.
Group, © 2000.
    Includes index.
    ISBN-13: 978-0-07-147893-9 (pbk. : alk. paper)
    ISBN-10: 0-07-147893-0 (pbk. : alk. paper)
    1. English language—United States—Idioms—Dictionaries.   2. Figures of
speech—Dictionaries.   3. Americanisms—Dictionaries.   I. Title.   II. Title:
American idioms dictionary.

PE2839.S64   2007
423'.130973—dc22   2006046933

2 3 4 5 6 7 8 9 10 11 12 13 14 15 16 17 18   DOC/DOC   0 9 8 7

ISBN-13: 978-0-07-147893-9
ISBN-10:   0-07-147893-0

Interior design by Terry Stone

McGraw-Hill books are available at special quantity discounts to use as premiums and
sales promotions, or for use in corporate training programs. For more information, please
write to the Director of Special Sales, Professional Publishing, McGraw-Hill, Two Penn
Plaza, New York, NY 10121-2298. Or contact your local bookstore.

This book is printed on acid-free paper.

Contents

What Is an Idiom?

A phrase or sentence linked to a meaning that is different from the literal meanings of its component words is described as idiomatic and is called an idiom. Most idioms are found embedded in sentences and are sometimes difficult to isolate and extract.

English, like other languages, has many of these phrases or sentences that cannot be understood literally. Even if you know the meaning of all the words in a phrase and understand all the grammar of the phrase completely, the meaning of the phrase may still be puzzling. Many proverbs, informal phrases, and common sayings offer this kind of problem. This dictionary is a collection of the idiomatic phrases and sentences that occur frequently but not exclusively in American English. A large percentage of the idioms listed here are also found in other national varieties of English.

Quick-Start Guide

A. If you are confident that you know the exact wording of the idiom you are seeking, simply look it up directly in the dictionary. *The*, *A*, and *An* at the beginning of the idiom are ignored in alphabetizing. Consult the next section, "How the Dictionary Works," for instructions on how to interpret the entries.

B. If you are uncertain about the exact wording of an idiom, look up any major word (i.e., verb, adjective, adverb, or noun) in the Key Word Index. Do the exercise (see #15 on page xxi) to gain skills in isolating the idiom from the rest of the sentence. Search the index until you find a sequence that matches the idiom you are seeking. Then look up that idiom in the dictionary. There is more information at the beginning of the index on page 591.

How the Dictionary Works

The following sections are numbered sequentially, since there is cross-referencing between the sections. Here is a directory:

1. Terms, Symbols, and Type Styles
2. Fixed and Variable Idioms
3. Optional Elements
4. Variable Elements
5. Movable Elements and the Dagger
6. Someone vs. One
7. The Asterisk, Swung Dash, and Shared Idiomatic Core
8. Brackets and Extra Information
9. Alphabetization, Organization, and Synonym Clusters
10. The Key Word Index and Search Strategies
11. Origins
12. Taboo and Proscribed Words
13. Slang vs. Idiom
14. Illustrations
15. Exercise
16. New in the Fourth Edition
17. Reference Works Mentioned

1. Terms, Symbols, and Type Styles

□ (a square) is found at the beginning of an example. Examples are printed in *italic type*. Words emphasized within an example are printed in roman (not italic) type.

† (a dagger) follows a **movable element**. (See #5.)

* (an asterisk) stands for a short list of words or phrases that are part of an entry head, as with ***above suspicion** where the * stands for **be, keep, remain**. (See #7.)

~ (a swung dash) stands for any entry head at the beginning of the entry block in which the swung dash is used. (See #7.)

( ) (parentheses) enclose **optional elements** and explanatory comments such as origins, etymologies, cross-referencing, and additional entry heads formed with the swung dash. (See #3.)

[ ] (brackets) enclose information in a definition that is necessary for the understanding of the entry head. (See #8.)

AND introduces **synonymous** entry heads or additional entry heads after a sense number. Additional synonymous entry heads are separated by semicolons (;). (See #9.)

entry block refers to a paragraph starting with a boldface word or phrase and including all the senses and examples. This replaces *entry*, which is ambiguous.

entry head refers to the phrase(s) found starting an entry block. An entry head is what the definition explains. An entry head is printed in **boldface type**.

Fig. means figurative or nonliteral.

Euph. means euphemism or euphemistic.

Go to means to locate and move to the entry head named after **Go to**. This does not indicate synonymy. An entry head being pointed to by a **Go to** is in sans serif type.

Inf. means informal.

Lit. means literal.

movable element is an adverb or other particle that can either follow or precede a direct object. In entry heads movable elements follow the direct object and are followed by the dagger (†). (See #5.)

optional element is a word, phrase, or **variable element** that may or may not be present in an entry head. Optional elements are enclosed in parentheses. (See #3.)

Rur. means rural.

See also means to consult the entry head named after **See also** for additional information or to find expressions similar in form or meaning. An entry head being pointed to by a **See also** is in sans serif type.

sense is the definition of an entry head. Some entry heads have two or more senses, and in this case, the senses are numbered. Some senses have *additional* entry heads for that sense only. These appear after the sense number and are preceded by the word AND in light type. (See #9.)

Sl. means slang or highly informal.

synonymous means having the same meaning. **Synonymy** is the quality of having the same meaning.

typeface: bold is used for the introduction of entry heads.

typeface: italic is used for examples and to single out individual words for comment.

typeface: sans serif is used for entry heads that are referred to, such as with cross-referencing.

typeface: light, condensed sans serif is used for variable elements.

variable element is a "word" in an entry head that can stand for an entire list or class of words or phrases. Variable elements are in light, condensed sans serif type. (See #4.)

2. Fixed and Variable Idioms

Although idioms are usually described as "fixed phrases," most of them exhibit some type of variation. Only about one-third of the entries in this dictionary are fixed in the sense that they occur with exactly the same words in exactly the same order, as with **above the fray, out of season**, and **You and what army?** This kind of idiom is very easy to find in the dictionary. Just look it up in its normal alphabetical order. Generally, it is not usually possible to identify an invariable idiom by sight unless it constitutes a complete sentence.

A much larger number of idioms present various kinds of variation, and much of the symbolic and typographic apparatus used here describes the details of this variation. The majority of the idioms found in this dictionary—and in the real world—allow four kinds of variation, as represented by optional elements, variable elements, movable elements, and grammatical variation. Optional elements are enclosed in parentheses within an entry head. Variable elements are printed in a light, condensed sans serif typeface in an entry head. Movable elements, mostly in idiomatic phrasal verbs, are followed by the dagger (†). Grammatical variation—as with differences in tense, aspect, voice, irregular forms, number, and pronoun case and gender—can cause some confusion in identifying the dictionary form of the idiom. A knowledge of basic English grammar provides the ability to reduce nouns to their singular form, verbs to their infinitive or bare form, and passive voice to active.

3. Optional Elements

An example of an optional element is the word *two* in the following entry head:

alike as (two) peas in a pod.

This idiom is actually two variant forms:

alike as peas in a pod
alike as two peas in a pod

Idioms of this nature are fairly easy to locate in the dictionary, except when the optional element is the first word in the entry head. When the first word is an optional element, cross-referencing is used to make sure you can find the idiom. It is possible to locate the short form and then be directed to the full form. For instance, an entry head **for the best** will tell you to go to **(all) for the best** where you will find the definition and example.

Some optional elements in parentheses represent ellipsis. A phrase may seem difficult to understand simply because it is really just a shortened form of a longer, more easily understood phrase. This dictionary shows as full a form of an idiom as reasonable, with the frequently omitted parts in parentheses. For example: **back down (from** so/sth**)**; **at loggerheads (with** so**) (over** sth**)**. The optional elements are generally known to the native speaker but not usually known by the learner, nor can this information always be found in learner's dictionaries.

4. Variable Elements

Variable elements stand for the classes or lists of the possible words or phrases that can occur in entry heads. They are sort of wild cards. The most common variable elements used here are: so = someone; sth = something; so/sth = someone or something; one = the same person as the agent of the utterance (see #6); some place = a location. There are others that are more specific, such as an amount of money; some quality; some time; doing sth; etc. These are straightforward and easy to understand. If you quickly scan a few pages of the dictionary, you will see that the use of variable elements is quite common. This means that in the example **age out of** sth, the **age out of** is fixed, but there are many things that can be "something."

5. Movable Elements and the Dagger

The use of the dagger (†) is a bit more complicated. The dagger will be found in the following sequence, typically called a phrasal verb:

Verb + Object + Particle†
Put + your hat + on.
Take + the trash + out.

The dagger indicates that the particle can also occur before the object. This means that there is an alternate form of the idiom:

Verb + Particle + Object
Put + on + your hat.
Take + out + the trash.

Study these examples: **Beef the engine up, beef up the engine; belt a song out, belt out a song; iron the difficulty out, iron out the difficulty**. Notice that **beef** sth **up**† also stands for **beef up** sth. There is a special rule that says that the movable element cannot be moved if the direct object is a pronoun. Thus **beef it up** is fine, but X **beef up it** is wrong. Almost all of these particles look like prepositions (*at, in, on, up*, etc.), but they do not have objects of their own. They are essentially adverbs and are typically found in phrasal verbs. Phrasal verb reference works following the same organization as this dictionary are: *NTC's Dictionary of Phrasal Verbs and Other Idiomatic Verbal Phrases* and *McGraw-Hill's Dictionary of American Idioms and Phrasal Verbs*.

6. Someone vs. One

Two of the variable elements discussed above, so and one, are quite distinct from one another and need further explanation. The use of the word *one* in a sentence seems very stilted, and many people would feel uncomfortable using it in the company of their peers. Do not worry about that; it is just a stand-in for a class of variables. Used as a variable element here, it refers to the same human being that is named as the agent or subject of the sentence in which the variable element one is found. The variable element oneself works the same way. For an example, look at the following idiom:

able to do sth **standing on** one's **head**

Here are some sentences containing this idiom:

<u>He</u> is able to bake cookies standing on <u>his</u> head.
<u>She</u> is able to bake cookies standing on <u>her</u> head.
<u>Those guys</u> are able to bake cookies standing on <u>their</u> heads.

Notice how the underlined sets of words in each sentence refer to the very same person or persons: <u>He</u> and <u>his</u> refer to the same person, as do <u>She</u> and <u>her</u> and <u>Those guys</u> and <u>their</u>. The variable element **one** must coordinate with an agent or subject, even if the agent or subject is not displayed as part of the entry head. Now look at this incorrect representation of the idiom:

X able to do sth **standing on** so's **head**

Here are some sentences containing this incorrect representation:

X <u>He</u> is able to bake cookies standing on <u>her</u> head.
X <u>She</u> is able to bake cookies standing on <u>Tom's friends'</u> head.

These two sentences simply sound silly and do not even suggest the idiomatic meaning. Since **so's** can stand for any human possessive noun or pronoun, there is an indefinite number of things that it can stand for, and all but one or two fail to coordinate with the subject or agent of the sentence. Native speakers of English know instinctively that the **X**-marked sentences are wrong, but language learners do not have this knowledge and require these details to be spelled out. This dictionary spells out the required knowledge by showing the difference between *one* and *someone*. Now study this idiom:

take sth **out of** so's **hands**

Here are some sentences containing this framework:

<u>He</u> took the project out of <u>her</u> hands.
<u>They</u> took the project out of <u>John's</u> hands.
<u>Those guys</u> took the project out of <u>my</u> hands.
<u>I</u> took the project out of <u>my</u> hands.

These sentences are perfectly reasonable and are good representations of the idiom. The idiom shows that there is no requirement that the possessor refer to the exact same person as the subject of the sentence, although it can in the appropriate context (e.g., "You were in charge of the project. Who took it out of your hands?" "<u>I</u> took the project out of my hands."). In the dictionary, the *someone* usually includes *oneself*, and that can be determined from the context of the definition. The significance of the use of one is extremely important, and you should keep it in mind while using the dictionary.

7. The Asterisk, Swung Dash, and Shared Idiomatic Core

Examine the following idiomatic expressions:

be against the grain
cut against the grain
go against the grain
run against the grain
saw against the grain

They all share a common idiomatic core, **against the grain**. In this dictionary, the shared idiomatic core (in this case, **against the grain**) is defined one time in one place, and the words that enhance the meaning are represented by an asterisk (*). Look up ***against the grain** in the dictionary to see how this is done. The asterisk (*) in the entry head is explained within the entry block at "***Typically:**," where the variant phrases **be against the grain, cut against the grain, go against the grain, run against the grain,** and **saw against the grain** are listed. To save space, the swung dash (~) is used as an abbreviation for the entry head, so that ~ = **against the grain**. The shared idiomatic core is defined only once, and the variants are listed at the same place. This saves space, displays variation, and brings all the related forms together in one place. Similarly, "***Also**" is used to explain a variant of the entry head.

8. Brackets and Extra Information

In compiling the dictionary, one goal has been to make certain that the entry head, definition, and example(s) within each sense match one another in syntax and semantics. Occasionally, it is useful to add additional contextual information to the definition to make it more specific. This added information appears within brackets because it is not actually present in the wording of the entry head. Look up **age out (of sth)** for an example. Brackets are used in a similar fashion for other similar purposes, which should be clear from the context. The bracketed information adds to or alters the information that is found in the entry head, providing context and specificity that is not otherwise evident in the entry head. Basically, brackets alert you to a point that needs some additional study. Of course, the major source for additional context is the example provided for each sense.

9. Alphabetization, Organization, and Synonym Clusters

In alphabetizing, an initial *the, a,* or *an* is ignored, and the entry head is alphabetized on the second word. All punctuation is ignored, as are the major variable element symbols.

Many of the entry blocks contain more than a single sense. In that case, the senses are numbered. Often, sense number one is more literal than the others and is listed first. When the subsequent senses are figuratively based on the first sense, that is noted with **Fig.** In some instances, one of the senses may have one or more variants *in addition to* the entry head at the top of the entry block. In that case, the additional sense(s) are listed after the sense number preceded by AND. This means *in addition to* the entry head, not *instead of* the entry head. Look up **kick off**, sense 2, for an example.

Some idioms, about 15 percent of this collection, are synonyms of other idioms. These synonym clusters are grouped together in a single entry block. This allows writers to select from synonymous forms of an idiom and allows the learner to assimilate the cluster as a group. Some dictionaries are organized according to key word. That means that a selected word heads a section of the dictionary with all the idioms that contain the word defined below. This usually separates the synonym clusters. In longer idioms, there is some problem in knowing which key word to look under. In this dictionary, the Key Word Index (see #10) shows all the idioms that share a particular word, and the entries themselves show all the idioms that share a particular meaning.

10. The Key Word Index and Search Strategies

A few idioms can stand alone as a separate sentence, but most of them are found embedded in a spoken or written sentence. Only in classroom exercises do we find idioms already extracted from their contexts. It's easy to find **age out of** sth in a dictionary, because it has already been extracted from its context.

The new-to-English user is faced with the difficulty of isolating an idiomatic expression from the rest of the sentence and determining where to find it in a dictionary of idioms. If the user fails to extract the essential idiomatic expression, the likelihood of finding it in *any* dictionary is reduced considerably. One way to improve your skills in isolating the idiom from the rest of the sentence is to do the exercise in #15.

In the sentence "At about 35 years of age, even the most recalcitrant criminal will have aged out of most of his wrongdoings and will be on the way to productive citizenship," it will take a bit of skill to extract the idiom **age out (of** sth**)**. Using the Key Word Index to look up the verb in the confusing area of the sentence will locate the form of the idiom quickly. The learner will benefit greatly by working through the senses of the entries, looking for the common thread to be found in the entry head, the definition, and the example(s).

The consequence of the large amount of variation in the form of idioms is that they are hard to find in any dictionary. Basically, you can *never* find the idiom by basing your search on one of the words covered by a variable element. The problem is that you may not be able to tell the difference between the variable element and the rest of the terms in the idiom. For that reason, you are encouraged to use the Key Word Index and do the exercise in #15. Since most of the variable elements stand for nouns, look up verbs first and then adjectives and adverbs.

11. Origins

Many of these phrases have their origins as figurative uses of literal phrases. In fact, virtually one-half of the senses here are marked **Fig.** In some cases, it is possible to link the figurative allusion to some sort of mental picture suggested by the words in an idiom. In other instances, the idiom is simply a metaphorical extension of the literal meaning. A few well-known idioms listed here are from the Bible (21) or the works of Shakespeare (13). Many other idioms are really just the "first and best choice" phrases for expressing something.

The number of idioms that have really intriguing stories of origins attached to them is quite small. The number of those with stories that have *any* supporting evidence is very small indeed. The mere sight of a square wooden plate immediately suggests to some (especially tour guides) the "square meal." A bed with ropes strung across the frame to support a mattress seems to suggest that one ought to be encouraged to "sleep tight" in such a bed. The fact that these unsupported tales are so readily believed by the public is a constant source of grief to lexicographical scholars who prize evidence rather than creativity in explaining phrase origins. It is not the role of this dictionary to debunk popular language myths or provide the true origins that have often been sought by many and found by none. For that, the reader might consult *Word Myths* by David Wilton. Although the book deals mainly with words, it is a good example of rigorous linguistic forensics. Another well-researched book of interest is *Ballyhoo, Buckaroo, and Spuds* by Michael Quinion. Quinion also has a website. Search for "quinion worldwide words" to locate its URL. Of course, other researchers dispute some of the findings in these resources, but they do so with evidence, not myth. This dictionary is concerned primarily with form and meaning and deals with origins only to the degree that knowing the origin, allusion, or literal source contributes to the understanding of the idiom.

12. Taboo and Proscribed Words

Some of the traditionally proscribed words are used in some of the more informal idioms, specifically *piss, shit, fuck, fart, ass,* and milder words like *crap*. These are used in the dictionary with a cautionary note. It is worth noting, especially for learners of English, that many people find the public use of expressions containing these words (and others) out of place and objectionable. For many, these words are second nature. For others, they represent a coarseness that they do not wish to be associated with. There are still others who object that anyone should be averse to these words.

To be completely safe and inoffensive, it is probably better not to use them if you do not understand the protocol of their use. That said, *butt* is in widespread use when it is necessary to refer to the posterior. Many people announce that they are *pissed off* instead of *angry* or *mad* but are not likely to use *piss* to mean *urine* or *urinate*, and they are much less likely to use the term in raising young children.

13. Slang vs. Idiom

Although there are some entries that are very casual or informal English, slang and idioms should not be confused. Some slang is also idiomatic, and some idioms are also slang, but generally, they refer to different aspects of language.

Idiomatic refers to the way a phrase is linked to a unique meaning rather than to the literal meanings of its component words.

Slang refers to expressions that are informal, often humorous synonyms for widely known standard words as well as specialized words with limited use in the general population.

There are a few slang terms in this dictionary, because they are also fairly commonly known idioms. For other specific varieties of vocabulary, such as slang, common phrases, or phrasal verbs, it is best to consult a dictionary compiled for those kinds of vocabulary. There is a slang dictionary companion to this, *McGraw-Hill's Dictionary of American Slang and Colloquial Expressions, Fourth Edition*, that follows the format used here.

14. Illustrations

Some idioms are entertaining because they can have literal interpretations that allow us to paint funny mental pictures. Phrases like **at the crack of dawn**, **come to a pretty pass**, **in hog heaven**, **pie in the sky**, and **stick to** one's **ribs** seem to beg for illustrations. This edition includes a number of classic illustrations that underline one of the more fascinating aspects of idioms. Although they have funny literal meanings, we still use them every day with a straight face, having long forgotten the literal meanings and their entertaining ambiguities.

15. Exercise

There is an exercise you can do with little more than an opaque sheet of paper and your own brain power.

Isolating Idioms: Open the dictionary at random and cover the entry head of the last entry block on a page. Study the examples and try to figure out what the entry head is. Try to figure out which words will be represented by variable elements and which belong to the fixed part of the idiom. Check yourself by looking at the entry head. Move the opaque paper up to the next entry block in the column and repeat. It will take a while to catch on, but with practice it will get easier.

Some of the examples are complex, challenging, off-the-wall, lengthy, erudite, or informal. Others are very informal, and a few contain nonstandard grammar. Some are in the passive voice or exhibit complicated verbal aspects. A few show the movable elements in their "moved" position. They provide highly varied examples of the ways the idiom is embedded in a complete sentence. This exercise in isolating or extracting the idiom from a longer context will develop a useful skill in the study of the puzzling phrases in English. If the user can identify the common thread linking the entry head, definition, and example, then the dictionary has done its job. If you master this skill, it will be easy to pick out a key word and look it up in the Key Word Index.

16. New in the Fourth Edition

The first edition of this work appeared as *NTC's American Idioms Dictionary* in 1987. It has grown from about 8,000 expressions to more than 12,500. Although it has increased in complexity, the original goals are still in place: (a) to show the idiom in its complete proper form without inverting parts of it for alphabetizing purposes, (b) to show the difference between human (someone) and nonhuman (something) variable elements, (c) to show as many optional elements of the idiom as possible, (d) to design a dictionary structure that recognizes that it is difficult to extract the idiom from the complete utterance, (e) to make sure that the entry head can be matched to the definition and example(s) in meaning and syntax, (f) to aim the dictionary at people who do not already know the material (learners), giving them more details than the native speaker needs, (g) to use multiple entry heads, rather than slashes (house/hut/barn), to show variant forms, (h) to provide two or more examples per sense.

The original Phrase-Finder Index, a KWIC (key word in context) index, has become the more familiar Key Word Index, even though it is the same kind of index. Changes in typography and abbreviation have reduced the amount of space required by the common variable elements, such as *someone* and *something*. The alphabetizing scheme has been altered to ignore the most common of the variable elements as well as the initial *a*, *an*, and *the*. Point (g) has been compromised by the use of the abbreviation so/sth and perhaps by the use of the asterisk at the beginning of the entry head. (See #7.) Point (h) has been abandoned in favor of one or two examples, showing more contexts, style, and register where needed. The examples are, as before, designed to aid in the understanding of the entry head and the definition as well as to supply context. The user should try to identify what is semantically identical in the entry head, the definition, and the example. See the exercise in #15.

17. Reference Works Mentioned

Quinion, Michael. *Ballyhoo, Buckaroo, and Spuds: Ingenious Tales of Words and Their Origins.* 2006. New York: Collins.

Spears, Richard A. *McGraw-Hill's Dictionary of American Idioms and Phrasal Verbs.* 2005. New York: McGraw-Hill.

Spears, Richard A. *McGraw-Hill's Dictionary of American Slang and Colloquial Expressions, Fourth Edition.* 2006. New York: McGraw-Hill.

Spears, Richard A. *NTC's Dictionary of Phrasal Verbs and Other Idiomatic Verbal Phrases.* 1993. New York: McGraw-Hill.

Wilton, David. *Word Myths: Debunking Linguistic Urban Legends.* 2004. New York: Oxford.

*an A for effort *Fig.* an acknowledgement for having tried to do something, even if it was not successful. (*Typically: **get** ~; **give** so ~.) □ *The plan didn't work, but I'll give you an A for effort for trying.*

abandon ship 1. to leave a sinking ship. □ *The captain ordered the crew and passengers to abandon ship.* **2.** *Fig.* to leave a failing enterprise. □ *A lot of the younger people are abandoning ship because they can get jobs elsewhere easily.*

abandon oneself **to** sth *Fig.* to accept the comforts or delights of something. □ *The children abandoned themselves to the delights of the warm summer day.*

the **ABCs of** sth *Fig.* the basic facts or principles of something. □ *I have never mastered the ABCs of car maintenance.*

abide by sth to follow the rules of something; to obey someone's orders. □ *John felt that he had to abide by his father's wishes.*

abide with so to remain with someone; to stay with someone. (Old and stilted. Primarily heard in the church hymn *Eventide.*) □ *You are welcome to abide with me for a while, young man.*

able to do sth **blindfolded** AND **able to** do sth **standing on** one's **head; able to** do sth **with** one's **eyes closed** *Fig.* able to do something very easily, possibly without even looking. (*Able to* is often *can.*) □ *Bill boasted that he could pass his driver's test blindfolded.* □ *It's easy. I can do it with my eyes closed.*

able to breathe (easily) again AND **able to breathe (freely) again 1.** able to breathe clean, fresh air with no restriction or obstruction. (*Able to* is often *can.*)

□ *After I got out of the dank basement, I was able to breathe easily again.* **2.** *Fig.* able to relax and recover from a busy or stressful time; able to catch one's breath. (*Able to* is often *can.*) □ *Final exams are over, so I can breathe easily again.*

able to breathe (freely) again Go to previous.

able to cut sth *Inf.* to be able to manage or execute something. (Often negative. *Able to* is often *can.*) □ *We thought he could handle the new account, but he is simply not able to cut it.*

able to fog a mirror *Inf.* alive, even if just barely. (Usually jocular. Refers to the use of a small mirror placed under the nose to tell if a person is breathing or not. *Able to* is often *can.*) □ *Look, I don't need an athlete to do this job! Anybody able to fog a mirror will do fine!*

able to make an event *Fig.* able to attend an event. (*Able to* is often *can.*) □ *I don't think I'll be able to make your party, but thanks for asking me.*

able to sit up and take (a little) nourishment *Fig.* well; [feeling] good. (Also a response to "How are you?") □ *Q: How are you doing? A: Oh, I'm able to sit up and take nourishment.*

able to do sth **standing on** one's **head** Go to able to do sth blindfolded.

able to take a joke *Fig.* to be able to accept ridicule good-naturedly; to be able to be the object or butt of a joke willingly. (*Able to* is often *can.*) □ *Better not tease Ann. She can't take a joke.*

able to take just so much AND **able to take only so much** *Fig.* able to endure only a limited amount of discomfort or unpleasantness. (*Able to* is often *can*.) □ *Please stop hurting my feelings. I'm able to take just so much.*

able to take only so much Go to previous.

able to do sth **with** one's **eyes closed** Go to able to do sth blindfolded.

***about** sth *Fig.* in the process of doing something. (*Typically: **be** ~; **get** ~.) □ *I'd better be about my yard work.*

***about** one's **business** busy doing something. (*Typically: **be** ~; **get** ~; **go** ~.) □ *Why are you still in the house? It's time to be about your business.*

about to (do sth**)** almost ready to do something; on the verge of doing something. □ *I was about to leave for home when the telephone rang.*

***above and beyond (the call of duty)** AND ***above and beyond (what is expected)** *Fig.* more than is required; greater than the required amount. (*Typically: **be** ~; **go** ~.) □ *The English teacher helped students after school every day, even though it was beyond the call of duty.*

above (doing) sth *Fig.* [of someone] too mature or honorable to do something. □ *I thought you were above doing something so thoughtless.*

above par *Fig.* better than average or normal. □ *His work is above par, so he should get paid better.*

above reproach *Fig.* not deserving of blame or criticism. □ *Some politicians behave as though they are above reproach.*

***above suspicion** *Fig.* [for one] to be honest enough that no person would suspect one; in a position where one could not be suspected. (This is a translation of words attributed to Julius Caesar, who divorced his wife, Pompeia, on the grounds of her possible involvement in a public scandal; Caesar stated, "Caesar's wife must be above suspicion." *Typically: **be** ~; **keep** oneself ~; **remain** ~.) □ *The general is a fine old man, completely above suspicion.*

above the fray *Fig.* not involved in the fight or argument; aloof from a fight or argument. □ *The president tried to appear above the fray, but he couldn't keep out of things, no matter how nasty they got.*

above the law *Fig.* not subject to the law; immune to the law. □ *None of us is above the law. We have to obey all of them.*

aboveboard *Fig.* in the open; visible to the public; honest. (See also honest and aboveboard.) □ *Don't keep it a secret. Let's make certain that everything is aboveboard.*

an **absent-minded professor** *Fig.* a bumbling professor who overlooks everyday things. □ *Fred is such an absent-minded professor. He'd forget his head if it wasn't screwed on.*

acceptable damage AND **acceptable losses** *Euph.* death or destruction inflicted by an enemy that is considered minor or tolerable. □ *The general indicated that the two thousand casualties were within the range of acceptable losses.*

acceptable losses Go to previous.

accidentally-on-purpose *Inf.* deliberate, but meant to look like an accident. □ *Then, I accidentally-on-purpose spilled water on him.*

according to Hoyle *Fig.* according to the rules; in keeping with the way something is normally done. (Refers to the rules for playing games. Edmond Hoyle wrote a widely used book with rules for card games.) □ *That's wrong. According to Hoyle, this is the way to do it.*

according to one's **own lights** *Fig.* according to the way one believes; according to the way one's conscience or inclinations lead one. □ *John may have been wrong, but he did what he did according to his own lights.*

ace in the hole AND so's **ace in the hole** *Fig. Inf.* something important held in reserve. □ *The twenty-dollar bill I keep in my shoe is my ace in the hole.*

ace in(to sth**)** *Fig.* to be lucky in getting admitted to something. □ *I aced into the history class at the last minute.*

ace out *Inf.* to be fortunate or lucky. □ *Freddy aced out at the dentist's office with only one cavity.*

ace so **out**† *Inf.* to maneuver someone out; to win out over someone. □ *Martha aced out Rebecca to win the first place trophy.*

ace out (of sth) *Inf.* to get out of something through luck; to evade or avoid something narrowly. □ *I just aced out of having to take the math test!*

ache for so/sth AND **hurt for** so/sth *Fig.* to desire someone or something very much. (So much that it "hurts.") □ *Jim ached for the sight of Mary, whom he loved deeply.* □ *Sometimes I just hurt for chocolate.*

Achilles' heel *Fig.* a weak point or fault in someone or something otherwise perfect or excellent. (From the legend of the Greek hero Achilles, who had only one vulnerable part of his body, his heel. As an infant his mother had held him by one heel to dip him in the River Styx to make him invulnerable.) □ *He was very brave, but fear of spiders was his Achilles' heel.*

aching heart *Fig.* the feeling of pain because of love that is lost or has faded away. (Described as being in the heart, where love is said to reside.) □ *I try to tell my aching heart that I don't love him.*

the **acid test** *Fig.* a test whose findings are beyond doubt or dispute. □ *The senator doesn't look too popular just now, but the acid test will be if he gets reelected.*

acquire a taste for sth Go to a taste for sth.

across the board *Fig.* [distributed] equally for everyone or everything. □ *The school board raised the pay of all the teachers across the board.*

an **act of faith** *Fig.* an act or deed demonstrating religious faith; an act or deed showing trust in someone or something. □ *For him to trust you with his safety was a real act of faith.*

an **act of God** *Fig.* an occurrence or an event for which no human is responsible; an act of nature such as a storm, an earthquake, or a wildfire. □ *Will your insurance company pay for damage caused by earthquakes and other acts of God?*

an **act of war 1.** *Fig.* an international act of warlike violence for which war is considered a suitable response. □ *To bomb a ship is an act of war.* **2.** *Fig.* any hostile act between two people. □ *"You just broke my stereo!" yelled John. "That's an act of war!"*

act out *Euph.* to behave badly. (Usually used to describe young people.) □ *Your son has been acting out in the classroom, and his teacher feels that professional intervention is desirable.*

Act your age! *Fig.* Behave more maturely! (A rebuke for someone who is acting childish. Often said to a child who is acting like an even younger child.) □ *Child: Aw, come on! Let me see your book! Mary: Be quiet and act your age. Don't be such a baby!*

add fuel to the fire AND **add fuel to the flame** *Fig.* to make a problem worse; to say or do something that makes a bad situation worse; to make an angry person get even angrier. □ *Shouting at a crying child just adds fuel to the fire.*

add fuel to the flame Go to previous.

add insult to injury *Fig. Cliché* to make a bad situation worse; to hurt the feelings of a person who has already been hurt. □ *My car barely started this morning, and to add insult to injury, I got a flat tire in the driveway.*

add sth **up**† to sum or total a set of figures. □ *Please add these figures up again.*

add up (to sth) **1.** [for a set of figures] to equal a total. □ *These figures don't add up to the right total!* **2.** *Fig.* [for facts or explanations] to make sense. (Fig. on ①. Considering facts as if they were figures.) □ *Your explanation just doesn't add up!*

add up to the same thing Go to amount to the same thing.

advanced in years Go to up in years.

*the **advantage of** so AND *the **advantage over** so; *an **advantage over** so; *the **edge on** so; *the **edge over** so a position superior to that of someone else; a status wherein one controls or has superiority or authority over someone else.

(*Typically: **get** ~; **give** so ~; **have** ~.) □ *She'd gotten an advantage over me at the start of the competition.* □ *I got an edge on Sally, too, and she came in second.*

afraid of one's **own shadow** *Fig.* easily frightened; always frightened, timid, or suspicious. □ *After Tom was robbed, he was even afraid of his own shadow.*

after a fashion *Fig.* in a manner that is just barely adequate; poorly. □ *He thanked me—after a fashion—for my help.*

after all 1. anyway; in spite of what had been decided. (Often refers to a change in plans or a reversal of plans.) □ *It looks like Tom will go to law school after all.* **2.** remember; consider the fact that. □ *Don't punish Tommy! After all, he's only three years old!*

after all is said and done AND **when all is said and done** *Fig.* Cliché when everything is settled or concluded; finally. □ *After all is said and done, it will turn out just as I said.* □ *When all is said and done, this isn't such a bad part of the country to live in after all.*

after hours *Fig.* after the regular closing time; after any normal or regular time, such as one's bedtime. □ *John got a job sweeping floors in the library after hours.*

after the fact *Fig.* after something has happened; after something, such as a crime, has taken place. □ *John is always making excuses after the fact.*

after the fashion of so/sth AND **after the style of** so/sth *Fig.* in the manner or style of someone or something. □ *He sang after the fashion of a whiskey tenor.* □ *The parish church was built after the style of a French cathedral.*

after the style of so/sth Go to previous.

After while(, crocodile). *Inf.* Good-bye till later.; See you later. (The word *crocodile* is used only for the sake of the rhyme. It is the response to See you later, alligator.) □ *Mary: See you later, alligator. Bill: After while, crocodile.*

After you. *Fig.* Please go ahead of me.; Please pass through ahead of me. □ *Bob stepped back and made a motion with his hand indicating that Mary should go first. "After you," smiled Bob.*

*oneself **again** *Fig.* showing signs of being healthy again or restored. (*Typically: **act like** ~; **be** ~; **feel like** [one's old self] ~; **seem like** ~.) □ *After such a long illness, it's good to be myself again.*

again and again repeatedly; again and even more [times]. □ *He knocked on the door again and again until I finally answered.*

Again(, please). *Fig.* Say it one more time, please. □ *Tom: I need some money. I'll pay you back. Bill (pretending not to hear): Again, please. Tom: I said I need some money. How many times do I have to say it?*

against all odds AND **against the odds** *Fig.* despite very low probability; despite opposing forces. □ *Against all odds, she managed to win the trophy.*

against one's **better judgment** despite one's doubts. □ *I came here against my better judgment, and I am pleasantly surprised at how nice it is.*

***against the grain 1.** across the alignment of the fibers of a piece of wood. (*Typically: **be** ~; **cut** ~; **go** ~; **run** ~; **saw** ~.) □ *You sawed it wrong. You sawed against the grain when you should have cut with the grain.* **2.** *Fig.* running counter to one's feelings or ideas. (Fig. on ①. *Typically: **be** ~; **go** ~.) □ *The idea of my actually taking something that is not mine goes against the grain.*

Age before beauty. *Fig.* a jocular way of encouraging someone to go ahead of oneself; a comical, teasing, and slightly grudging way of indicating that someone else should or can go first. □ *"No, no. Please, you take the next available seat," smiled Tom. "Age before beauty, you know."*

age out (of sth) *Fig.* [for an adult] to grow [mentally or in years] out of certain behavior or out of a group or classification that is based on age. □ *Most of the offenders age out of criminality at about 35.*

agree to disagree *Fig.* [for two or more parties] to calmly agree not to come to an agreement in a dispute. □ *We have accomplished nothing except that we agree to disagree.*

***ahead of schedule** *Fig.* having done something before the time given on a schedule or before the expected time. (*Typically: **be** ~; **finish** ~.) □ *I want to be able to finish the job ahead of schedule.*

***ahead of the game** *Fig.* being early; having an advantage in a competitive situation; having done more than necessary. (*Typically: **be** ~; **get** ~; **keep** ~; **remain** ~; **stay** ~.) □ *Without the full cooperation of my office staff, I find it hard to stay ahead of the game.*

***ahead of the pack** *Fig.* at the front of a group of people; ahead of other competitors. (*Typically: **be** ~; **keep** ~; **stay** ~.) □ *I work hard to stay ahead of the pack so I can make the best sales first.*

***ahead of time** *Fig.* beforehand; before the announced time. (*Typically: **arrive** ~; **get there** ~; **leave** ~; **show up** ~.) □ *If you show up ahead of time, you will have to wait.*

***ahead of** one's **time** *Fig.* having ideas or attitudes that are too advanced to be acceptable in the present. (*Typically: **be** ~; **think** ~.) □ *Sue's grandmother was ahead of her time in wanting to study medicine.*

aid and abet so *Cliché* to help someone; to incite someone to do something, possibly something that is wrong. □ *He was scolded for aiding and abetting the boys who were fighting.*

aim for the sky Go to reach for the sky.

aim to do sth *Fig. Rur.* to intend to do something. □ *I didn't aim to hurt your feelings, sugar, you know I didn't.*

Ain't it the truth? AND **Tell me about it!** I agree.; That is true.; Isn't that true? (Jocular. Used to agree with a statement someone has made.) □ *Jane: I swear, life can be a trial sometimes. Bill: Ain't it the truth?*

***the **air** *Fig.* a dismissal. (*Typically: **get** ~; **give** so ~.) □ *Whenever I get around Tom, I end up getting the air.*

air one's **belly** *Fig. Sl.* to empty one's stomach; to vomit. □ *I had a bad case of food poisoning and was airing my belly for most of the night.*

air one's **dirty linen in public** AND **wash** one's **dirty linen in public** *Fig.* to discuss private or embarrassing matters in public, especially when quarreling. (This *linen* probably refers to underwear or other soiled cloth.) □ *They are arguing again. Why must they always air their dirty linen in public?* □ *Let's not wash our dirty linen in public!*

air one's **grievances** *Fig.* to complain; to make a public complaint. □ *I know how you feel, John, but it isn't necessary to air your grievances over and over.*

air one's **pores** *Sl.* to undress oneself; to become naked. □ *Me and Wilbur, that's my brother, both fell in the creek and had to air our pores awhile so our pants could dry out.*

***alike as (two) peas in a pod** very similar. (Compare this with like (two) peas in a pod. *Also: **as** ~.) □ *These two books are as alike as peas in a pod.*

alive and kicking AND **alive and well** *Fig.* well and healthy. □ *Jane: How is Bill since his illness last month? Mary: Oh, he's alive and kicking.*

alive and well Go to previous.

alive with people/things *Fig.* covered with, filled with, or active with people or creatures. (Fig. on the image of a place covered with moving creatures.) □ *Look! Ants everywhere. The floor is alive with ants!*

all agog *Fig.* surprised and amazed. □ *He sat there, all agog, as the master of ceremonies read his name as the winner of first prize.*

all along throughout the whole time in question. □ *I looked all over for her, but she was right there at home all along.*

all and sundry *Cliché* everyone; one and all. □ *Cold drinks were served to all and sundry.*

all around Robin Hood's barn going somewhere by an indirect route; going way out of the way [to get somewhere]; by a long and circuitous route. □ *We had to go all around Robin Hood's barn to get to the little town.*

all at once 1. *Fig.* all at the same time. □ *The entire group spoke all at once.* **2.** *Fig.* suddenly. □ *All at once the little girl fell out of her chair.*

(all) at sea (about sth**)** *Fig.* to be confused; to be lost and bewildered. (Fig. on being lost at sea.) □ *When it comes to higher math, John is totally at sea.*

*(all) balled up *Fig. Inf.* troubled; confused; in a mess. (*Typically: **be** ~; **get** ~.) □ *John is all balled up because his new hybrid van was stolen last night.*

(all) beer and skittles *Fig. Inf.* all fun and pleasure; easy and pleasant. (Skittles is the game of ninepins, a game similar to bowling. Fixed phrase.) □ *For Sam, college was beer and skittles. He wasted a lot of time and money.*

all better (now) *Fig.* improved or cured. (Juvenile.) □ *I fell off my tricycle and bumped my knee. Mommy kissed it, and it's all better now.*

all by one's **lonesome** *Rur.* all alone; by oneself. □ *Mary's folks went out and left her all by her lonesome.*

all day long throughout the day; during the entire day. □ *We waited for you at the station all day long.*

*(all) dolled up *Fig.* dressed up and well-groomed. (Usually used of females. *Typically: **be** ~; **get** ~.) □ *I have to get all dolled up for the dance tonight.*

*(all) dressed up dressed in one's best clothes; dressed formally. (*Typically: **be** ~; **get** ~; **get** so ~.) □ *I really hate to get all dressed up just to go somewhere to eat.*

all dressed up and nowhere to go AND **all dressed up with nowhere to go** *Fig. Lit.* completely ready for something that has been postponed or has failed to materialize. □ *The space shot was cancelled, so all the astronauts are all dressed up with nowhere to go.*

all ears *Fig.* listening eagerly and carefully. □ *Well, hurry up and tell me. I'm all ears.*

all eyes and ears *Fig.* listening and watching eagerly and carefully. □ *Be careful what you say. The children are all eyes and ears.*

all eyes are on so/sth *Fig.* everyone is looking at someone or something. □ *All eyes were on Melinda as she nonchalantly stepped out of her half slip, which had worked its way down to her ankles.*

all for so/sth *Fig.* (completely) in favor of someone or something; supporting someone or something. (Vocal emphasis on *for*.) □ *I'm all for your candidacy.*

all for nothing AND **all for naught** for no purpose or benefit. □ *The project was canceled and our hard work was all for naught.*

(all) for the best *Fig.* good in spite of the way it seems; better than you think or than it appears to be. (Often said when someone dies after a painful illness.) □ *I'm very sorry to hear of the death of your aunt. Perhaps it's for the best.* □ *I didn't get into the college I wanted, but I couldn't afford it anyway. It's probably all for the best.*

all hell broke loose *Fig.* all sorts of wild or terrible things happened. □ *When the boss left early for the weekend, all hell broke loose.*

*all hours (of the day and night) *Fig.* very late in the night or very early in the morning. (*Typically: **until** ~; **till** ~; **at** ~.) □ *Why do you always stay out until all hours of the day and night?* □ *I like to stay out till all hours.*

all in *Fig.* completely tired. □ *I'm all in. I need some rest.*

all in a day's work *Fig.* part of what is expected; typical or normal. □ *I don't particularly like to cook, but it's all in a day's work.*

all in all AND **in total** *Fig.* considering everything that has happened; in summary and in spite of any unpleasantness. □ *All in all, I'm glad that I visited New York City.*

all in fun only for the purpose of making fun; not serious or meant to be harmful. □ *I'm sorry. It was all in fun. I didn't mean to hurt your feelings.*

(all) in good time Go to in due course.

(all) in one breath *Fig.* spoken very rapidly, usually while one is very excited. □ *Jane was in a play, and she was so excited that she said her whole speech in one breath.*

(all) in one piece *Fig.* safely; without damage. □ *Her son come home from school all in one piece, even though he had been in a fight.* □ *The package was handled carelessly, but the vase inside arrived all in one piece.*

(all) in the family *Fig.* restricted to one's own family or closest friends, as with private or embarrassing information. □ *Don't tell anyone else. Please keep it all in the family.*

(all) joking aside AND **(all) kidding aside** *Fig.* being serious for a moment; in all seriousness. □ *I know I laugh at him but, joking aside, he's a very clever scientist.* □ *Kidding aside, I know you tried your best.*

(all) kidding aside Go to previous.

all manner of so/sth *Fig.* all types of people or things. □ *We saw all manner of people there. They came from every country in the world.*

all so **needs** *Fig.* the thing that someone needs the least. □ *Look, he just slipped and fell. That's all he needs, a broken leg.*

all night long *Fig.* throughout the whole night. □ *John was sick all night long.*

(all) of a piece each one [is] part of the same type. □ *These chairs are all of a piece. They are painted differently, but they are the same.*

all of a sudden *Fig.* suddenly. □ *All of a sudden lightning struck the tree we were sitting under.*

all of the above everything named in the list of possibilities just listed or recited. □ *Q: What's wrong, Sally? Are you sick, tired, frightened, or what? A: All of the above. I'm a mess!*

all or nothing everything or nothing at all. □ *Sally would not accept only part of the money. She wanted all or nothing.*

all over 1. AND **(all) over with** *Fig.* finished. □ *Dinner is all over with. I'm sorry you didn't get any.* **2.** *Fig.* everywhere. □ *Oh, I just itch all over.* □ *She's spreading the rumor all over.*

all over again repeated; again for another time. □ *It was done wrong so I had to do it all over again.*

all over creation AND **all over hell and half of Georgia; all over the earth; all over the world; all over the map; all over hell and gone; to hell and gone** *Rur.* everywhere. □ *Little Billy had his toys spread out all over creation. It took forever to clean up after him.* □ *Tom has traveled all over hell and half of Georgia trying to find the man who done him wrong.* □ *Our grandchildren are spread all over the world.*

all over hell and gone Go to previous.

all over hell and half of Georgia Go to all over creation.

all over the earth Go to all over creation.

all over the map Go to all over creation.

all over the place 1. everywhere. □ *The car hit the ice and then skidded all over the place.* **2.** *Fig.* widely variant; of uneven distribution. □ *The estimates we got were all over the place.*

all over the world Go to all over creation.

all over town 1. *Fig.* in many places in town. □ *Jane looked all over town for a dress to wear to the party.* **2.** *Fig.* known to many; widely known. □ *In a short time the secret was known all over town.*

(all) over with Go to all over.

all right 1. *Fig.* an indication of agreement or acquiescence. (Often pronounced *aright* in familiar conversation.) □ *Tom: Please remember to bring me back a pizza.*

Sally: *All right, but I get some of it.* **2.** *Inf.* a shout of approval or encouragement. (Usually **All right!**) □ *"That's the way to go! All right!" shouted various members of the audience.* **3.** *Fig.* well, good, or okay, but not excellent. (This phrase has all the uses that *okay* has.) □ *His work is all right, but nothing to brag about.* **4.** *Fig.* beyond a doubt; as the evidence shows; as someone just asserted. □ *The dog's dead all right. It hasn't moved at all.*

all right by so Go to fine by so.

All right for you! *Fig.* That's the end of being friendly with you!; That's the last chance for you! (Usually said by a child who is angry with a playmate.) □ *All right for you, John. See if I ever play with you again.*

All righty. *Inf.* All right.; OK. □ *Tom: Let's go to the state fair. Bill: All righty, let's do that.*

All right(y) already! *Inf.* an impatient way of indicating agreement or acquiescence. □ *Bill: Come on! Get over here! Bob: All righty already! Don't rush me!*

(all) rolled into one [of items] joined together to create a single whole. □ *Today was a mixture of fear, anxiety, and indigestion all rolled into one!*

*(all) set (to do sth**) 1.** *Inf.* prepared or ready to do something. (*Typically: **be** ~**; get** ~.) □ *Yes, the fire is ready, and I'm all set to start.* **2.** ready to order a meal in a restaurant. (Not used where ③ is used.) □ *The waitress asked us if we were set to order.* **3.** finished with a restaurant meal in a restaurant and ready to receive the bill. (Used in the northeast U.S.) □ *When we finished eating, the waitress asked if we were set.*

*(all) shook up *Sl.* excited and confused. (See also shook up. *Typically: **be** ~**; get** ~. Popularized by Elvis Presley. Sort of jocular. Not used with *shaken*.) □ *She stole my heart, and I'm all shook up.*

all show and no go *Sl.* equipped with good looks but lacking action or energy. (Used to describe someone or something that looks good but does not perform as promised.) □ *He's mighty handsome, but I hear he's all show and no go.*

(all) skin and bones Go to nothing but skin and bones.

*(all) spruced up freshened up; tidied up; cleaned up. (*Typically: **be** ~**; get** ~**; get** so/sth ~.) □ *Let's get the yard all spruced up for spring.*

all sweetness and light *Fig. Cliché* very kind, innocent, and helpful. □ *At the reception, the whole family was all sweetness and light, but they argued and fought after the guests left.*

All systems (are) go. *Fig.* Everything is ready. (Originally said when preparing to launch a rocket.) □ *The rocket is ready to blast off—all systems are go.*

all talk (and no action) *Fig.* talking often about doing something, but never actually doing it. (See also all show and no go.) □ *The car needs washing, but Bill is all talk and no action on this matter.*

All the best to so. Go to Give my best to so.

all the livelong day *Fig.* all day long. (Dated.) □ *Well, of course you get to feeling stiff, sitting in front of a computer all the livelong day.*

*all the marbles *Fig.* all the winnings, spoils, or rewards. (*Typically: **end up with** ~**; get** ~**; win** ~**; give** so ~.) □ *Somehow Fred always seems to end up with all the marbles. I don't think he plays fair.*

all the more reason for doing sth AND **all the more reason to** do sth *Fig.* with even better reason or cause for doing something. (Can be included in a number of grammatical constructions.) □ *Bill: I don't do well in calculus, because I don't like the stuff. Father: All the more reason for working harder at it.*

all the rage *Fig.* in current fashion; being a current fad. (Dated.) □ *Wearing a rope instead of a belt was all the rage in those days.*

all the same AND **just the same** *Fig.* nevertheless; anyhow. □ *They were told not* *to bring presents, but they brought them all the same.* □ *Just the same, you should have done as you were told.*

all the same (to so) AND **just the same (to so)** *Fig.* of no consequence to someone—one way or the other; [of a choice] immaterial to someone. □ *It's all the same to me whether we win or lose.* □ *If it's just the same to you, I'll leave now.*

all the time 1. *Fig.* throughout a specific period of time. □ *Bill was stealing money for the last two years, and Tom knew it all the time.* **2.** *Fig.* at all times; continuously. □ *Your blood keeps flowing all the time.*

all the way 1. from the beginning to the end; the entire distance, from start to finish. □ *I walked all the way home.* **2.** *Fig.* with everything on it, as with a hamburger with pickles, onion, catsup, mustard, lettuce, etc. □ *I'd like one double cheeseburger—all the way.*

all the way live *Sl.* very exciting; excellent. □ *Oh, Tiffany is just, like, all the way live!*

all there *Fig.* [of a person] alert, aware, and mentally sound. (Usually negative.) □ *After talking with Larry today, I get the feeling that he's not quite all there.*

all things being equal Go to other things being equal.

all things considered Go to when it comes right down to it.

all things must pass AND **all things will pass** *Fig.* everything comes to an end eventually. □ *You'll get over this setback. All things must pass.*

all things to all men AND **all things to all people** *Fig.* [for someone or something] liked or used by all people; [for someone or something] everything that is wanted by all people. (The phrase with *men* is biblical.) □ *The candidate set out to be all things to all men and came off looking very wishy-washy.* □ *The party's philosophy tries to be all things to all people.*

all thumbs *Fig.* very awkward and clumsy, especially with one's hands. □ *Poor Bob can't play the piano at all. He's all thumbs.* □ *Mary is all thumbs when it comes to gardening.*

all to the good *Fig.* for the best; to one's benefit. □ *He missed the train, but it was all to the good because the train had a wreck.*

all told *Fig.* totaled up; including all parts. □ *All told, he earned about $700 last week.* □ *All told, he has many fine characteristics.*

all too sth much too something, such as hard, easy, disgusting. □ *Leaving there was all too easy.*

***all tore up (about** sth) *Inf.* very upset and sorry about something. (*Typically: **be** ~; **get** ~. Of course, *tore* ought to be *torn*.) □ *I'm all tore up about denting your car like that. I'd be more than happy to pay for fixing it.*

***(all) tuckered out** *Rur.* tired out; worn out. (*Typically: **be** ~; **get** ~.) □ *Look at that little baby sleeping. She's really tuckered out.*

all walks of life *Fig.* all social, economic, and ethnic groups. □ *The people who came to the street fair represented all walks of life.*

(all) well and good *Fig.* good; desirable. □ *It's all well and good that you're passing English, but what about math and science?*

all wet *Inf. Fig.* mistaken; wrongheaded; on the wrong track. □ *That's not the correct answer, John. You're all wet.*

all wool and a yard wide *Fig.* trustworthy and genuinely good. (A description of good quality wool cloth.) □ *I won't hear another word against Bill. He's all wool and a yard wide.*

(all) year round *Fig.* throughout all the seasons of the year; during the entire year. □ *The public swimming pool is enclosed so that it can be used all year round.*

***an all-out effort** *Fig.* a very good and thorough effort. (*Typically: **begin** ~; **have** ~; **make** ~; **start** ~.) □ *We need to make an all-out effort to get this job done on time.*

all-out war *Fig.* total war, as opposed to limited military actions or threats of war.

□ *Threats of all-out war caused many tourists to leave the country immediately.*

allow for sth Go to provide for sth.

Allow me. AND **Permit me.** *Fig.* Please let me help you. (Typically said by someone politely assisting another person, as by opening a door or providing some personal service. In Allow me, the emphasis is usually on *me*. In Permit me, the stress is usually on *-mit*.) □ *Tom and Jane approached the door. "Allow me," said Tom, grabbing the doorknob.* □ *You look like you need help. Permit me.*

the **almighty dollar** *Fig.* the U.S. dollar, or the acquisition of money, when viewed as more important than anything else. □ *It's the almighty dollar that drives Wall Street thinking.*

(almost) jump out of one's **skin** AND **nearly jump out of** one's **skin** *Fig.* to react strongly to shock or surprise. □ *The noise had us jumping out of our skin.* □ *Oh! You really scared me. I nearly jumped out of my skin.*

almost lost it *Inf. Fig.* to nearly lose one's temper, composure, or control, as out of anger. □ *I was so mad, I almost lost it.*

along in years Go to up in years.

along the line(s) of sth *Fig.* similar to or patterned like something. □ *I would like to shop for a house along the lines of those we saw in the magazine I showed you.*

along those lines AND **along these lines; along similar lines** *Fig.* similarly; in nearly the same way. □ *We will deal with the other students along similar lines.*

alpha and omega *Fig.* the essentials, from the beginning to the end; everything, from the beginning to the end. □ *He was forced to learn the alpha and omega of corporate law in order to even talk to the lawyers.*

alphabet soup initialisms and acronyms, especially when used excessively. □ *Just look at the telephone book! You can't find anything, because it's filled with alphabet soup.*

also-ran *Fig.* someone of no significance. (From horse racing, used of a horse that finishes a race but that does not finish among the money winners.) □ *Oh, he's just another also-ran.*

(always) chasing rainbows *Fig.* tending to look for something (more) exciting and (more) rewarding but without realistic expectations. □ *He can't seem to settle down and enjoy life. He's always chasing rainbows.*

Am I glad to see you! *Inf.* I am very glad to see you! (Not a question. There is emphasis on *I* and emphasis on *you*.) □ *Tom (as Bill opens the door): Here I am, Bill. What's wrong? Bill: Boy, am I glad to see you! I need your help right now.*

Am I right? *Inf.* Isn't that so? Right? (A way of demanding a response and stimulating further conversation.) □ *Fred: You want to make something of yourself. Am I right? Bob: I suppose.*

ambulance chaser *Inf.* a lawyer who hurries to the scene of an accident to try to get business from injured persons. □ *The insurance companies are cracking down on ambulance chasers.*

***American as apple pie** Cliché* quintessentially American. (*Also: as ~.) □ *A small house with a white picket fence is supposed to be as American as apple pie.*

the **American dream** *Fig.* financial stability as well as physical and emotional comfort. (From the notion that Americans are preoccupied with obtaining certain materialistic goals.) □ *The American dream of home ownership in the garage and a chicken in every pot started in the early 1930s.*

amount to sth **1.** *Fig.* [for someone or something] to become worthwhile or successful. □ *I hope Charles amounts to something someday.* **2.** *Fig.* [for something] to be the equivalent of something. □ *Your comments amount to treason.* **3.** AND **amount (up) to** sth [for a sum of money] to increase [to a large amount]. □ *Is that everything you want to buy? That all amounts up to twenty dollars.*

amount to much *Fig.* to be as good as something; to be any good. (Usually negative.) □ *She's a nice girl, but she'll never amount to much.*

amount to the same thing AND **come to the same thing; add up to the same thing** *Fig.* to be the same [as something]. □ *Borrowing can be the same as stealing. If the owner does not know what you have borrowed, it amounts to the same thing.* □ *Red or green, it comes to the same thing.*

ancient history *Fig.* someone or something from so long ago as to be completely forgotten or no longer important, as a former relationship. □ *Bob? I never think about Bob anymore. He's ancient history.*

sth **and a half** *Fig.* a thing (or kind of person) that seems bigger or more important than other similar things or persons. □ *This is not just a common wrench. It's a wrench and a half! It will do anything!*

and all that jazz *Inf.* and all that stuff; and all that nonsense. □ *She told me I was selfish, hateful, rude, ugly, and all that jazz.*

and change *Fig.* plus a few cents; plus a few hundredths. (Used in citing a price or other decimal figure to indicate an additional fraction of a full unit.) □ *The New York Stock Exchange was up seven points and change for the third broken record this week.*

And how! Yes!; Definitely! □ *Q: Did you like the meal I cooked? A: And how!*

and so forth AND **and so on; and so on and so forth** *Fig.* with additional related or similar things mentioned (but not specified). □ *He told me about all his health problems, including his arthritis and so on.*

and so on and so forth Go to previous.

and that's a fact *Fig.* and that is true. (Used to emphasize a statement.) □ *John ain't no friend of mine, and that's a fact.*

And that's that. That is the end of it!; There is no more to say about it. *Inf.* □ *I refuse to go with you and that's that!*

and the like *Fig.* and other similar things. □ *Whenever we go on a picnic, we take potato chips, hot dogs, soda pop, and the like.*

and them Go to and those.

and then some *Fig.* and even more; and more than has been mentioned. □ *John is going to have to run like a deer and then some to win this race.*

and this and that *Fig.* and more; and other miscellaneous things. □ *The repairman tightened some screws, fiddled with some bolts, and this and that.*

and those AND **and them** *Rur.* and some other people; and other friends or family members. □ *But if we invite Jill, Mary and them will want to come.* □ *Jim and those was sayin' nasty things about me.*

and sth **to spare** AND **with** sth **to spare** *Fig.* with extra left over; with more than is needed. □ *We got a loan big enough to pay off the car and something to spare.* □ *I had as much flour as I needed with some to spare.*

and what have you *Fig.* and more things; and other various things. □ *The merchant sells writing paper, pens, string, and what have you.*

angle for sth **1.** to fish for something, as with a fishhook and line. □ *Fred was angling for a big bass.* **2.** *Fig.* to scheme or plan to get something; to "fish" for something. (Fig. on ①.) □ *Are you angling for a raise in pay?*

angry enough to chew nails Go to mad enough to chew nails (and spit rivets).

another country heard from *Fig.* yet another person adds to the conversation. (Fig. on the image of yet another international delegate addressing other delegates. Used when someone joins a discussion other people are having, especially unexpectedly. Used sarcastically, implying that the new speaker is not welcome in the discussion.) □ *Alan: You ought to take a vacation tomorrow. You really look tired. Fred: I am not tired and I don't need a vacation. Jane: But you do* *seem awfully short-tempered. Fred: Well, well, another country heard from!*

another pair of eyes AND a **fresh pair of eyes** *Fig.* another person to examine something closely in addition to anyone previously. □ *Another pair of eyes would be a help in finding the needle.* □ *As soon as we can get a fresh pair of eyes on this manuscript, we will find the last of the typos.*

answer back (to so) AND **answer so back** *Fig.* to talk back (to someone); to argue (with someone). (Fixed phrase.) □ *Don't answer back or I'll ground you for a week!*

answer for so 1. *Fig.* to vouch for someone; to tell of the goodness of someone's character. □ *Mr. Jones, who had known the girl all her life, answered for her. He knew she was innocent.* **2.** to speak for another person; to speak for oneself. □ *I can't answer for Chuck, but I do have my own opinion.*

answer for so/sth *Fig.* to explain or justify the actions of someone or something; to take responsibility or blame for someone or something. □ *I will answer only for my own misdeeds.*

answer so's purpose AND **serve so's purpose** *Fig.* to fit or suit someone's aim or goal. □ *This piece of wood will answer my purpose quite nicely.* □ *This one will serve my purpose just fine.*

answer the call 1. *Euph.* to die. □ *Our dear brother answered the call and has gone to his eternal rest.* **2.** AND **answer the call (of nature)** *Euph.* to find and use the toilet. □ *We stopped the car long enough for Jed to answer the call of nature.*

answer the door *Fig.* [after hearing the doorbell or a knock] to go to the door to see who is there. □ *Would you please answer the door. I am busy.*

answer to so 1. to explain or justify one's actions to someone. (Usually with *have to.*) □ *If John cannot behave properly, he'll have to answer to me.* **2.** *Fig.* [in the hierarchy of the workplace] to be under the supervision of someone; to report to someone. □ *I answer only to the boss.*

so's **answer to** so/sth someone serving in the role of someone or something; someone acting as a (poor) substitute for someone or something. □ *The funny-looking "sandwich" with a chunk of meat between slices of bread was the old lady's answer to the hamburger.*

the **answer to** so's **prayer(s)** *Fig.* a person or thing that seems to be just what someone has wished or prayed for. □ *She was so beautiful and perfect. She was the answer to his prayers.*

answer to the description of so AND **answer to** so's **description** *Fig.* to match a particular set of physical or facial characteristics. □ *The men in police custody answer to the description of the burglar.*

answer to the name (of) sth to respond to a particular name. □ *I answer to the name Walter.*

***ants in** one's **pants** *Fig.* the imaginary cause of nervousness and agitation. (From the image of someone suffering great discomfort as if having actual ants in the pants. *Typically: **get** ~; **have** ~; **give** one ~.) □ *I always get ants in my pants before a test.*

any fool thing *Fig.* any ridiculous thing; anything that should be viewed as unimportant. □ *Bill can get distracted by any fool thing.*

Any friend of so('s) (is a friend of mine). *Cliché.* I am always pleased to meet a friend of someone I know. (A pleasant response when meeting or being introduced to a friend of a friend.) □ *Fred: Well, nice to meet you, Tom. Any friend of my brother is a friend of mine. Tom: Thanks, Fred. Nice to meet you too.*

any number of so/sth *Fig.* a large number; a sufficiently large number. (Used when the exact number is not important.) □ *I can give you any number of reasons why I should join the army.*

any old thing *Fig.* just anything, not necessarily old. □ *Just give me one. I don't care which. Just give me any old thing.*

any port in a storm *Fig.* any solution, whether one likes it or not. □ *He hates his* *job, but he can't get another. Any port in a storm, you know.*

any Tom, Dick, and Harry Go to (every) Tom, Dick, and Harry.

Anybody's guess is as good as mine. Go to Your guess is as good as mine.

Anyone I know? AND **Anybody I know?** *Inf.* a coy way of asking "Who?" □ *Bill: I've got a date for the formal next month. Henry: Anybody I know?*

anything but any choice but that choice; any conclusion but that one. □ *You think my idea was wrong. Anything but. I was right on target.*

Anything you say. *Fig.* Yes.; I agree. □ *Mary: Will you please take these blouses over to the cleaners? Bill: Sure, anything you say.*

Anytime you are ready. *Fig.* a phrase indicating that the speaker is waiting for the person spoken to to make the appropriate move or action. □ *Surgeon: Shall we begin the operation? Nurse: Anytime you're ready, doctor.*

appear as sth **1.** to act a certain part in a play, opera, etc. □ *Madame Smith-Franklin appeared as Carmen at the City Opera last season.* **2.** [for something] to be seen or occur in a particular form or with particular characteristics. □ *The first signs of the disease appear as a fever and a rash.*

appear in court to go to a court of law as a participant. □ *I have to appear in court for my traffic violation.*

appear under the name (of) some name *Fig.* [for an actor] to perform under a special name. □ *She is appearing under the name of Fifi.*

the **apple of** so's **eye** *Fig.* someone's favorite person or thing; a boyfriend or a girlfriend. □ *Tom is the apple of Mary's eye. She thinks he's the greatest.*

apple-polisher *Fig.* a flatterer. □ *Doesn't that wimpy apple-polisher know how stupid he looks?*

apply within *Fig.* to ask about something [inside some place]. (Usually part of a sign or announcement posted outside a place.) □ *If you are interested in working here, please apply within.*

(Are) things getting you down? *Inf.* Are everyday issues bothering you? □ *What's the matter, Bob? Things getting you down?*

(Are you) doing okay? AND **You doing okay? 1.** *Inf.* How are you? □ *Mary: Doing okay? Bill: You bet! How are you?* **2.** *Inf.* How are you surviving this situation or ordeal? □ *Tom: Wow, that was some turbulence we just hit! Are you doing okay? Mary: I'm still a little frightened, but I'll make it.*

(Are you) going my way? *Fig. Inf.* If you are traveling in the direction of my destination, could I please go with you or can I have a ride in your car? □ *Mary: Are you going my way? Sally: Sure. Get in.*

(Are you) ready for this? *Inf.* a way of presenting a piece of news or information that is expected to excite or surprise the person spoken to. □ *Boy, do I have something to tell you! Are you ready for this?*

(Are you) ready to order? *Inf.* Would you please tell me what you want as your meal? (A standard phrase used in eating establishments to find out what a customer wants to eat.) □ *The waitress came over and asked, "Are you ready to order?"*

(Are you) sorry you asked? *Inf.* Now that you have heard (the unpleasant answer), do you regret having asked the question? □ *Father: How are you doing in school? Bill: I'm flunking out. Sorry you asked?*

arguing for the sake of arguing AND **arguing for the sake of argument** arguing simply to be difficult or contrary. □ *You are just arguing for the sake of arguing. You don't even know what the issue is.*

*****an **arm and a leg** *Fig.* a great amount of money; more money than the value of the purchase warrants. (*Typically: **charge** ~; **cost** ~; **pay** ~.) □ *I had to pay an arm and a leg for these seats.* □ *They charge an arm and a leg for a gallon of gas these days!*

*****arm in arm** *Fig.* [of persons] linked or hooked together by the arms. (*Typically:

go ~; **stroll** ~; **walk** ~.) □ *The two lovers walked arm in arm down the street.*

*armed and dangerous *Cliché* [of someone who is suspected of a crime] having a gun or other lethal weapon and not being reluctant to use it. (This is part of a warning to police officers who might try to capture an armed suspect. *Typically: **be** ~; **be regarded as** ~; **be presumed to be** ~.) □ *The murderer is at large, presumed to be armed and dangerous.*

armed to the teeth *Fig.* heavily armed with deadly weapons. (Armed so heavily that even a knife was carried in the teeth.) □ *The bank robber was armed to the teeth when he was caught.*

*(a)round the bend 1. *Fig. Inf.* crazy; having lost sanity. (*Typically: **be** ~; **go** ~.) □ *I think this job is sending me around the bend.* **2.** *Inf.* intoxicated from alcohol or drugs. (*Typically: **be** ~; **go** ~.) □ *From the glassy look in her eyes, I'd say she is completely round the bend now.*

(a)round the clock *Fig.* continuously for twenty-four hours at a time. □ *The priceless jewels were guarded around the clock.*

around the corner *Fig.* in the very near future. □ *Wow, my retirement is just around the corner, and I haven't saved a penny.*

arrive at a decision AND **reach a decision** to make a decision; decide. □ *Have you arrived at a decision yet?* □ *We have not yet reached a decision.*

arrive on the scene Go to come on the scene.

article of faith *Fig.* a statement or element of strong belief. (Refers to a religious tenet.) □ *With Chuck, believing that the oil companies are cheating people is an article of faith.*

as a duck takes to water *Cliché* easily and naturally. □ *She took to singing just as a duck takes to water.*

as a (general) rule *Fig.* usually; almost always. □ *As a rule, things tend to get less busy after supper time.*

as a last resort as the last choice; if everything else fails. □ *Call me at home only as a last resort.*

as a matter of course *Fig.* normally; as a normal procedure. □ *You are expected to make your own bed as a matter of course.*

as a matter of fact *Fig.* actually; in addition to what has been said; in reference to what has been said. □ *I'm not a poor worker. As a matter of fact, I'm very efficient.*

as a rule *Fig.* in general; usually. □ *As a rule, men should wear tuxedos at formal dinners.*

as a token (of sth**)** *Fig.* symbolic of something, especially of gratitude; as a memento of something. □ *Here, take this gift as a token of my appreciation.*

as a whole considered as a unit or a single body. □ *We need to meet with the committee as a whole after the subcommittees have had a chance to meet.*

as all get out *Rur.* very much; as much as can be. □ *I'm tired as all get out.*

as an aside *Fig.* [said] as a comment that is not supposed to be heard by everyone. □ *At the wedding, Tom said as an aside, "The bride doesn't look well."*

as bad as all that *Fig.* as bad as reported; as bad as it seems. (Usually expressed in the negative.) □ *Stop crying. It can't be as bad as all that.*

as easy as shooting fish in a barrel Go to like shooting fish in a barrel.

as easy as taking candy from a baby Go to like taking candy from a baby.

as far as anyone **knows** AND **so far as** anyone **knows; to the best of** one's **knowledge** *Fig.* to the limits of anyone's knowledge. (The *anyone* can be replaced with a more specific noun or pronoun.) □ *As far as anyone knows, this is the last of the great herds of buffalo.*

as far as sth **goes** as much as something does, covers, or accomplishes. (Usually said of something that is inadequate.) □

Your plan is fine as far as it goes. It doesn't seem to take care of everything, though.

as far as I can see AND **so far as I can see** *Fig.* as best as I can figure out. □ *As far as I can see, you have to study harder and attend class.*

as far as so **is concerned** AND **so far as** so **is concerned** *Fig.* from the point of view of someone. □ *As far as we are concerned, anything at all would be fine for dinner.*

as far as sth **is concerned** AND **so far as** sth **is concerned** *Fig.* having to do with something; pertaining to something; as for something. □ *As far as the roof's concerned, it will just have to last another year.*

as far as possible AND **so far as possible** *Fig.* as much as possible; to whatever degree is possible. □ *As far as possible, the police will issue tickets to all speeding drivers.*

as for so/sth AND **as to** so/sth *Fig.* regarding someone or something. □ *As for the mayor, he can pay for his own dinner!*

as good as done *Fig.* almost completed; essentially completed; certain to be completed. (Requires a past participle.) □ *The house is as good as painted. I'll just be a few more minutes.*

as good as one's **word** obedient to one's promise; dependable in keeping one's promises. □ *She said she would babysit, and she was as good as her word.*

***as Gospel** AND ***as the Gospel truth** *Fig.* as if [something] were absolutely true. (*Typically: **accept** sth ~; **believe** sth ~; **take** sth ~. Refers to the belief that the Bible is literally true, metaphors and all.) □ *I wouldn't take anything he says as Gospel. He's a liar.*

As I live and breathe! *Fig.* How amazing! (Said on seeing or experiencing something surprising.) □ *Well, as I live and breathe, it's Harry Smith!*

as I see it AND **in my opinion; in my view** *Fig.* the way I think about it. □ *Tom: This matter is not as bad as some would make*

it out to be. Alice: Yes. This whole affair has been overblown, as I see it. □ *In my view, it's a waste of time.* □ *It's great, in my opinion.*

as I was saying AND **like I was saying** *Fig.* to repeat what I've been saying; to continue with what I was saying. (The first form is appropriate in any conversation. The second form is colloquial, informal, and familiar.) □ *Bill: Now, Mary, this is one of the round ones that attaches to the wire here. Bob (passing through the room): Hello, you two! I'll talk to you later. Bill: Yeah, see you around. Now, as I was saying, Mary, this goes here on this wire.*

as if one **owned the place** Go to like one owned the place.

as if there's no tomorrow Go to like there's no tomorrow.

as is a state of goods for purchase wherein there may or may not be concealed or unknown defects in the goods. □ *I purchased this car "as is" and so far, everything has been all right.*

as it is AND **as it stands; as things stand; the way things stand** *Fig.* the way things are; the way it is now. □ *"I wish I could get a better job," remarked Tom. "I'm just getting by as it is."*

as it stands Go to previous.

as it were *Fig.* as one might say; as could be said. (Sometimes used to qualify an assertion that may not sound reasonable.) □ *He carefully constructed, as it were, a huge submarine sandwich.*

as long as 1. AND **so long as** *Fig.* since; because. □ *As long as you're going to the bakery, please buy some fresh bread.* **2.** AND **so long as** *Fig.* if; only if. □ *You may have dessert so long as you eat all your vegetables.* **3.** for a specified length of time. □ *I didn't go to school as long as Bill did.*

as luck would have it *Fig.* by good or bad luck; as it turned out; by chance. □ *As luck would have it, the check came in the mail today.*

as some quality **as they come** [of someone or something] as extreme a quality as possible. (Qualities such as: dumb, ugly, fat, strong, weak, sweet, sour, polite, rude, etc. *They* is used indicating that there is a group, among which this is the most extreme of the type.) □ *I like this black puppy. It's just as cute as they come.*

as much fun as a barrel of monkeys AND **more fun than a barrel of monkeys; funnier than a barrel of monkeys** *Cliché* a great deal of fun. □ *Roger always makes me laugh! He is as much fun as a barrel of monkeys.* □ *Sally is more fun than a barrel of monkeys.*

***as one** *Fig.* as if acting or moving as a single person. (*Typically: **act** ~; **move** ~; **speak** ~.) □ *All the dancers moved as one.*

as opposed to sth in contrast to something; unlike something. □ *I usually wear sandals, as opposed to athletic shoes or leather shoes.*

as regards so/sth Go to with regard to so/sth.

as soon as at the moment that; at the time that; when. □ *I fell asleep as soon as I lay down.*

as such in the way something is; as someone or something is. □ *You are new to this job, and as such, I will have to train you.*

as the crow flies [of a route] straight. □ *Yes, the old cemetery is about two miles west, as the crow flies. There ain't no proper road, though.*

as things stand Go to as it is.

as one **think(s) best** in whatever way that one thinks is best. □ *I can't advise you. Just do as you think best.*

as to so/sth Go to as for so/sth.

as usual as is the normal or typical situation. □ *John ordered eggs for breakfast, as usual.*

as we speak Go to (even) as we speak.

as well also; in addition. □ *I'm feeling tired, and dizzy as well.*

aside from sth without considering something; ignoring something. □ *Aside from the small dent on the driver's door, this car is in excellent condition.*

ask after so *Fig.* to inquire about the health and well-being of someone. □ *Hermione asked after you when I saw her today.*

ask so **back 1.** [for a host or hostess] to invite someone to come again (at a later time or to another similar event). □ *After the way you behaved, they'll never ask us back.* **2.** [for someone who has been a guest] to invite a previous host or hostess to come to an event. □ *We've had the Smiths to dinner five times. I think it's time they asked us back.*

ask so **(for) a favor** to ask a person to do something special for oneself. □ *I have to ask you a favor: Will you lend me $100?*

ask for sth bad to act badly, such that one will bring on bad consequences. □ *If you keep misbehaving, you'll be asking for punishment.*

ask for it to do something that brings on the (unpleasant) results now being experienced. (Usually in the past tense.) □ *Yes, the guy struck you, but after all, you asked for it.*

ask for the moon *Fig.* to make outlandish requests or demands for something, such as a lot of money or special privileges. □ *She's asking for the moon, and she's not going to get it.*

ask for trouble AND **look for trouble** *Fig.* to seem to be trying to get into trouble; to do something that would cause trouble; to do or say something that will cause trouble. □ *Stop talking to me that way, John. You're just asking for trouble.* □ *Are you jerks looking for trouble?*

Ask no questions and hear no lies. AND **Ask me no questions, I'll tell you no lies.** *Fig.* If you ask me that, my answer might not be the truth. □ *Maybe I like Greg, and maybe I don't. Ask me no questions, I'll tell you no lies.*

ask so **out (to** sth) AND **ask** so **out**† **(for** sth) *Fig.* to invite someone to go out (to something or some place) [on a date]. □ *He asked her out to dinner, but she had other plans.*

ask so **over** *Fig.* to invite someone who lives close by to come to one's home [for a visit]. (Either to a house or apartment.) □ *He has been asked over a number of times.*

asking price the price that someone puts on an item being offered for sale. □ *I think your asking price is a little high.*

*asleep at the switch *Fig.* not attending to one's job; failing to do one's duty at the proper time. (Fig. on the image of a technician or engineer on a train sleeping instead of turning whatever switches are required. *Typically: **be** ~; **fall** ~.) □ *If I hadn't been asleep at the switch, I'd have noticed the car being stolen.*

*asleep at the wheel asleep while behind the steering wheel of a car or other vehicle. (*Typically: **be** ~; **fall** ~.) □ *He fell asleep at the wheel and crashed.*

assault and battery a violent attack [upon someone] followed by a beating. (A technical legal charge.) □ *Ricky was charged with two counts of assault and battery for the beating he gave Charlie.*

assault the ear *Fig.* [for sound or speech] to be very loud or persistent. □ *I can't hear you with all that traffic noise assaulting my ears.*

at so *Fig.* being argumentative or contentious with someone. □ *She is always at him about something.*

at a cost Go to at a price.

at a crossroad(s) AND **at the crossroad(s)** *Fig.* at the point where a decision or choice must be made. □ *We are at the crossroads and need to decide what our plan is before we go on.*

at a dead end *Fig.* having reached an impasse; able to go no further forward. □ *We are at a dead end; the project is hopelessly stalled.*

*at a disadvantage in a situation where everyone else has an advantage. (*Typically: **be** ~; **have** so ~; **put** so ~. See also You have me at a disadvantage.) □ *Since I have no car, I am at a disadvantage and must depend on someone else to offer me a ride.*

*at a good clip AND ***at a fast clip** *Fig.* rapidly. (*Typically: **go** ~; **move** ~; **run** ~; **travel** ~.) □ *We were moving along at a good clip when a state trooper stopped us.* □ *The cop was chasing the car at a fast clip.*

at a loss (for words) AND **lost for words** *Fig.* unable to speak; speechless or befuddled. □ *I was so surprised that I was at a loss for words.*

at a low ebb *Fig.* at a low or nearly inactive point or level of activity. □ *Things are at a low ebb at the office because everyone is on vacation.*

at a moment's notice AND **on a moment's notice** with very little advance notice; with just a little bit of warning. □ *They are always asking us to produce reports at a moment's notice.* □ *You can't expect me to be ready on a moment's notice.*

at a premium *Fig.* at a high price; priced high because of something special. □ *This new sports car sells at a premium because so many people want to buy it.*

*at a price AND ***at a cost** *Fig.* with some "cost" or sacrifice. (Fig. on an actual monetary price. *Typically: **only** ~; **come** ~; **have** sth ~.) □ *Good health in one's old age comes at a price. You can't eat as much as you want.*

at a set time *Fig.* at a particular time; at an assigned time. □ *Do I have to be there at a set time, or can I come whenever I want?*

at a sitting AND **at one sitting** *Fig.* at one time; during one period. (Usually refers to an activity that takes place while a person is seated.) □ *I can read about three hundred pages at a sitting.*

at a snail's pace AND **at a snail's gallop** very slowly. □ *Things are moving along at a snail's pace here, but we'll finish on time—have no fear.* □ *The old ladies* *moved along at a snail's gallop, blocking the hallway.*

at a stretch *Fig.* continuously; without stopping. □ *We all had to do eight hours of duty at a stretch.*

at all without qualification. □ *It really wasn't very cold at all.* □ *Tom will eat anything at all.*

at all costs AND **at any cost; at any price** *Fig.* regardless of the difficulty or cost; no matter what. □ *Mary was going to get that job at any cost.*

at all times *Fig.* constantly; continuously. □ *You must keep your passport handy at all times when you are traveling in a foreign country.*

at an early date *Fig.* soon; someday soon. □ *You are expected to return the form to the office at an early date.*

at an end *Fig.* having come to a stop; having reached the end. □ *It's over between us. It's at an end. Good-bye.*

at any cost Go to at all costs.

at any one time in the same deed or action. □ *I can't carry too much at any one time.* □ *She tries to keep from owing too much money at any one time.*

at any rate *Fig.* in any case; anyway. □ *At any rate, I don't think you should quit your job.*

*at bay *Fig.* at a distance; away from oneself. (*Typically: **be** ~; **keep** so/sth ~; **hold** so/sth ~; **remain** ~.) □ *I have to keep the bill collectors at bay until I get my paycheck.*

at so's **beck and call** *Fig.* ready to obey someone. □ *What makes you think I wait around here at your beck and call? I have to leave for work, you know!*

at best AND **at most** *Fig.* in the most favorable view; in the most positive judgment; as the best one can say. □ *At best we found their visit pleasantly short.*

at one's best 1. AND **at its best** *Fig.* to the utmost; to the highest degree possible. □ *This restaurant serves gourmet food at its best.* **2.** *Fig.* in the best of health; dis-

playing the most civilized behavior. (Often in the negative.) □ *He's at his best after a good nap.*

at close range *Fig.* very near; in close proximity. (Usually used in regard to shooting.) □ *The powder burns tell us that the gun was fired at close range.*

at cross-purposes *Fig.* with opposing viewpoints; with goals that interfere with each other. □ *Bill and Tom are working at cross-purposes. They'll never get the job done right.*

at death's door *Fig.* very near the end of one's life. (Often an exaggeration.) □ *I was so ill that I was at death's door for three days.*

*at so's **disposal** *Fig.* to make someone or something available to someone; to offer someone or something to someone. (*Typically: **be** ~; **have** so/sth ~; **put** so/sth ~.) □ *I'd be glad to help you if you need me. I put myself at your disposal.*

at each other's throats AND **at one another's throats** *Fig.* arguing and squabbling. (Fig. on grabbing someone's throat with the intent of strangulation.) □ *They just can't get along. They are always at each other's throats.*

at so's **earliest convenience** *Fig.* as soon as it is possible for someone to do something. □ *Please stop by my office at your earliest convenience.*

at ease *Fig.* without worry or anxiety. □ *The performer is at ease on the stage.*

at every turn *Fig.* everywhere; everywhere one looks. □ *Life holds exciting adventures at every turn.*

at so's/sth's **expense** Go to at the expense of so/sth.

at fault to blame [for something]; serving as the cause of something bad. □ *I was not at fault in the accident. You cannot blame me.*

at one's fingertips *Fig.* very close to one's hands; within one's immediate reach. (Usually a bit of an exaggeration.) □ *I* *had my pen right here at my fingertips. Now where did it go?*

at first initially; at the very beginning. □ *He was shy at first. Then he became more friendly.*

at first blush *Fig.* when first examined or observed. □ *At first blush, the whole idea appealed to us all. Later on we saw its flaws.*

at first glance AND **at first sight** *Fig.* when first examined; at an early stage. □ *At first glance, the problem appeared quite simple. Later we learned just how complex it really was.* □ *At first glance, he looked like Albert Turner.*

at first hand *Fig.* by direct experience or observation. □ *We observe at first hand the suffering the hurricane victims endured.*

at first light *Fig.* at dawn; when the first light of dawn appears. □ *We will be ready to leave at first light.*

at first sight Go to at first glance.

*****at full blast** *Fig.* using full power; as loudly as possible. (*Typically: **be on** ~; **play** ~; **play** sth ~; **run** ~; **run** sth ~.) □ *The car radio was on at full blast. We couldn't hear what the driver was saying.*

at full speed AND **at full tilt; at full throttle** *Fig.* as fast as possible. □ *The motor was running at full speed.* □ *Moving at full throttle, the red car pulled ahead.*

at full strength *Fig.* at the strongest amount, dilution, power, loudness, etc. □ *You should use this medicine at full strength, even if it tastes bad.*

at full tilt Go to at full speed.

*****at great length** *Fig.* for a long period of time. (*Typically: **explain** ~; **question** so ~; **speak** ~.) □ *The lawyer questioned the witness at great length.*

at half-mast AND **at half-staff** *Fig.* [of a flag] less than all the way up its flagpole. □ *The flag was flying at half-mast because the general had died.* □ *The president ordered all flags flown at half-staff.*

at hand *Fig.* very close by in time or space. (See also at one's **fingertips**.) □ *With the holiday season at hand, everyone is very excited.*

at hazard *Fig.* in danger; at risk. □ *He is not willing to have much of his money at hazard in the stock market.*

at home (with so/sth**) 1.** *Lit.* in one's home with someone or something. □ *Bob's not alone. He's at home with the cats.* **2.** *Fig.* comfortable with someone or something; comfortable doing something. □ *Tom is very much at home with my parents.*

at it again *Fig.* doing something again (regrettably). □ *I asked Tom to stop playing his trumpet, but he's at it again.*

at its best Go to at one's best.

at large 1. *Fig.* free; uncaptured. (Usually said of criminals not in custody.) □ *At noon, the day after the robbery, the thieves were still at large.* **2.** *Fig.* in general; according to a general sample. □ *Truck drivers at large don't like the new speed restriction on the highway.* **3.** *Fig.* representing the whole group rather than its subsections. (Always refers to a special kind of elective office.) □ *She represented shareholders at large on the governing board.*

at least *Fig.* anyway; in spite of difficulties. □ *At least we had a good evening, even though the afternoon was rainy.*

at least so many *Fig.* no less than; no fewer than. □ *There were at least four people there that I knew.*

at (one's) leisure *Fig.* at one's convenience. □ *Choose one or the other at your leisure.*

at length 1. *Fig.* after some time; finally. □ *At length, the roses bloomed, and the tomatoes ripened.* **2.** AND **at some length** *Fig.* for quite a long time. □ *He spoke to us about the problem at some length.*

at liberty 1. *Fig.* free; unrestrained. □ *You're at liberty to go anywhere you wish.* **2.** [of an actor] unemployed. □ *I'm an actor, but at the moment, I'm at liberty.*

at loggerheads (with so) (over sth) AND **at loggerheads (with so) (about sth)** *Fig.* in conflict with someone; having reached an impasse with someone about something. □ *The twins were at loggerheads over who should take the larger room.*

at (long) last after a long wait; finally. □ *Sally earned her diploma at long last after six years in college.* □ *At last, I finally got my chance to play on the team.*

*__at loose ends__ *Fig.* restless and unsettled; unemployed. (*Typically: **be** ~; **leave** so ~.) □ *Just before school starts, all the children are at loose ends.* □ *Jane has been at loose ends ever since she lost her job.*

at so's mercy Go to at the mercy of so.

at most Go to at best.

at one's mother's knee *Fig.* from one's mother, when one was very young. □ *I learned most of my moral training at my mother's knee.*

at no time never; not at any time. □ *At no time did I enter the room where the murder took place.*

at odds (with so) AND **at odds over sth** *Fig.* in opposition to someone; at loggerheads (with so) (over sth). □ *Mary is always at odds with her father about how late she can stay out.*

at once *Fig.* immediately; right now. □ *You must come here at once; it is an emergency.*

at one blow AND **at one stroke; in one stroke; in a single stroke** *Fig.* in one act of doing or trying. □ *I landed three sales in one stroke today.*

at one fell swoop AND **in one fell swoop** *Fig.* in a single incident; as a single event. (This phrase preserves the old word *fell*, meaning "terrible" or "deadly.") □ *The party guests ate up all the snacks at one fell swoop.* □ *In one fell swoop, the teacher flunked half the class.*

at one stroke Go to at one blow.

at one time 1. at a particular time in the past. □ *At one time, we visited the museum each Sunday, but we no longer do that.* **2.** at one instance; during one period of time; at the same time. □ *There were two people in the room at one time, but it was not crowded.*

at one time or another Go to at some time or another.

at peace 1. *Fig.* relaxed and happy. □ *When the warm breeze is blowing, I am at peace.* **2.** *Euph.* dead. □ *It was a long illness, but she is at peace now.*

at play *Fig.* [at this moment] involved in playing. □ *Whether I am at work or at play, I try to be pleasant to people.*

at present AND **at the moment** *Fig.* now; at this point in time. □ *We are not able to do any more at present.*

at random *Fig.* by chance; haphazard. □ *As a prank, the children dialed phone numbers at random.*

at regular intervals *Fig.* [of things in a series] at points that are equally distant from each other. □ *You will find service stations at regular intervals along the highway.*

at so's request *Fig.* in response to someone's request; on being asked by someone. □ *At his mother's request, Tom stopped playing his saxophone.*

at rest 1. *Fig.* not moving; not active. □ *After the hectic day, the office was finally at rest at 8:00 P.M.* **2.** *Euph.* dead. □ *After a long, weary life, Emily is at rest.*

*__at risk__ AND *__at stake__ *Fig.* in a situation where there is risk or hazard; in danger. (*Typically: **be** ~; **put** so/sth ~.) □ *I refuse to put my family's welfare at risk by quitting my job.*

at sea 1. *Fig.* on the sea; away on a voyage on the ocean. □ *The ship is at sea now, and you can't disembark.* **2.** Go to (all) at sea (about sth).

at sea level *Fig.* at the level of the surface of the ocean. □ *It is easier to breathe at sea level than in the mountains.*

at so's service *Fig.* ready to help someone in any way. □ *The count greeted me warmly and said, "Welcome to my home.*

Just let me know what you need. I'm at your service."

at some time **sharp** *Fig.* exactly at the time named. □ *The plane is expected to arrive at 7:45 sharp.*

at short notice Go to on short notice.

at sixes and sevens *Fig.* lost in bewilderment; at loose ends. □ *Bill is always at sixes and sevens when he's home by himself.*

at some length Go to at length.

at some point (in the future) Go to somewhere down the line.

at some point (in the past) Go to somewhere along the line.

at some time or another AND **at one time or another** at some unspecified time or instance in the past or future. □ *I was supposed to meet her at one time or another, but I forgot when.*

at that 1. because of something; upon hearing something. □ *She heard the bell, and at that, she went to the door.* **2.** so stated; in the way indicated after all. □ *I thought there were three cats, but you said there were four. Now that I look again, I can make out four at that.*

at that rate *Fig.* in that manner; at that speed. □ *At that rate we'll never get the money that is owed us.*

at the appointed time *Fig.* at the expected or assigned time. □ *We all met at the hotel at the appointed time.*

at the bottom of the hour *Fig.* on the half hour; the opposite of at the top of the hour. (Fig. on the image of the big hand of a clock pointing to the 6. Typically heard on television or the radio.) □ *We will have an interview with Harry Kravitz at the bottom of the hour.*

at the bottom of the ladder AND **on the bottom rung (of the ladder)** *Fig.* at the lowest level of pay and status. (Fig. on the lowness of the bottom rung of a ladder.) □ *Most people start work at the bottom of the ladder.*

at the break of dawn Go to next.

at the crack of dawn AND **at the break of dawn** *Fig.* at the earliest light of the day. □ *Jane was always awake at the crack of dawn.* □ *All the birds began to sing at the break of dawn.*

at the drop of a hat *Fig.* immediately; instantly; on the slightest signal or urging. (Fig. on the dropping of a hat as a signal.) □ *John was always ready to go fishing at the drop of a hat.*

at the eleventh hour *Fig.* at the last possible moment. (Just before the last clock hour, 12) □ *She always turned her term papers in at the eleventh hour.*

at the end of one's **rope** AND **at the end of** one's **tether** *Fig.* at the limits of one's endurance. (*Tether* is more U.K. and U.S.) □ *I'm at the end of my rope! I just can't go on this way!* □ *I can't go on! I'm at the end of my tether.*

at the end of the day 1. at the time when work or one's waking hours end. (Very close to by the end of the day. See also late in the day.) □ *Will this be finished at the end of the day or before?* **2.** *Fig.* when everything else has been taken into consideration. □ *The committee interviewed many applicants for the post, but at the end of the day made no appointment.*

at the expense of so/sth AND **at** so's/sth's **expense** *Fig.* to the detriment of someone or something; to the harm of someone or something. □ *He had a good laugh at the expense of his brother.*

at the forefront (of sth**)** AND **in the forefront (of** sth**)** *Fig.* at the place of greatest activity; vital or important to some activity. □ *The university I go to is at the forefront of computer technology.*

at the hand(s) of so AND **at the** so's **hand(s)** *Fig.* with someone in particular as the cause [of something unpleasant]. □ *He was tortured at the hands of the terrorists.*

at the helm (of sth**)** *Fig.* in the position of being in control of something. (Fig. on the helmsman of a ship, who is responsible for steering the ship.) □ *Things will go well with Anne at the helm.*

at the end of one's rope

at the last gasp *Fig.* at the very last; at the last chance; at the last minute. (Fig. on the idea of someone's last breath before death.) □ *She finally showed up at the last gasp, bringing the papers that were needed.*

at the last minute *Fig.* at the last possible chance; in the last few minutes, hours, or days. □ *Please don't make reservations at the last minute.*

at the latest *Fig.* not beyond the time mentioned. □ *I'll be home by midnight at the latest.*

at the mercy of so AND **at** so's **mercy** *Fig.* under the control of someone; without defense against someone. □ *We were left at the mercy of the arresting officer.*

at the moment Go to at present.

at (the) most *Fig.* no more than the amount mentioned. □ *At the most, there were only 15 people in the audience.*

at the outset *Fig.* at the very beginning. □ *At the outset, we were told everything we had to do.*

at the outside [of an amount] as much as the maximum estimate [and no more]. □ *The repairs should cost $400 at the outside.*

at the point of doing sth Go to on the point of doing sth.

at the present time AND **at this point (in time)** *Cliché* now; at present; as of now. (Used often as a wordy replacement for *now*.) □ *We don't know the location of the stolen car at the present time.* □ *At this point in time, we think we have caught the thief.*

at the ready ready to do something. □ *The doctors are at the ready, waiting for the ambulance to arrive at the hospital.*

at the same time 1. during the same moment; simultaneously. □ *Too many things are happening at the same time, and I am confused.* **2.** *Fig.* nevertheless; however; along with that. □ *We agree to your de-*

mands. At the same time, we object strongly to your methods.

at the top of one's **game** *Fig.* good and as good as one is likely to get. (Usually of sports.) □ *I guess I was at the top of my game last year. This year, I stink.*

at the top of the hour *Fig.* at the exact beginning of an hour. (Fig. on the big hand on a clock pointing to the 12. Often heard on television or the radio. See also at the bottom of the hour.) □ *Our next newscast will be at the top of the hour.*

at the top of one's **voice** AND **at the top of** one's **lungs** *Fig.* very loudly. □ *Imagine 20 kids all screaming at the top of their voices. □ How can I drive safely when you're all screaming at the top of your lungs?*

at the very least at the very minimum. □ *You seemed to be grasping for something polite to say. At the very least, you could have said, "Thank you."*

at the (very) outside *Fig.* at the very most. □ *The car repairs will cost $300 at the very outside.*

at the wheel 1. operating the wheel that turns a ship's rudder; at the helm. □ *The cabin boy was at the wheel with the captain close by.* **2.** AND **behind the wheel** operating the steering wheel of a car. □ *Bobby was at the wheel when the car went off the road.*

at (the) worst the worst that could happen; from the most unfavorable point of view. □ *At worst, the rains could wash out the bridge, but we are safe here.*

at the zenith of sth AND **at** sth's **zenith** *Fig.* at the highest point of something; at the pinnacle of something. □ *The scientist was at the zenith of his career when he made his discovery.*

at this juncture *Fig.* at this point; at this pause. □ *There is little more that I can say at this juncture.*

at this point (in time) Go to at the present time.

at this rate *Fig.* at this speed; if things continue in the same way. (Usually of a pessimistic view.) □ *Hurry up! We'll never get there at this rate.*

at this stage (of the game) *Fig.* at the current point in some event or situation; currently. □ *We'll have to wait and see. There isn't much we can do at this stage of the game.*

at times *Fig.* sometimes; occasionally. □ *At times, I wish I had never come here.*

at will *Fig.* whenever one wants; freely. □ *You're free to come and go at will. □ The soldiers were told to fire their guns at will.*

at one's **wit's end** *Fig.* at the limits of one's mental resources. □ *I'm at my wit's end with this problem. I cannot figure it out.*

at work 1. at one's place of work. □ *I'm sorry to call you at work, but this is important.* **2.** *Fig.* working [at something]; busy [with something]. (See also at play.) □ *Tom is presently at work on his project. He'll be finished in a half hour.*

attach importance to sth Go to give weight to sth.

*an **attack (of** an illness) *Fig.* a bout of some sickness; an instance or acute case of some disease. (*Typically: **have** ~; **produce** ~; **suffer** ~.) □ *Mr. Hodder had an attack of stomach upset that forced him to stay at home.*

attain one's **stride** Go to reach one's stride.

the **author of** one's **own** problem the cause of one's own unfortunate problem such as: downfall, fate, doom, failure, demise, etc. □ *I bring all my problems on myself. I am always the author of my own doom.*

avail oneself **of** sth to take advantage of something. □ *You would be wise to avail yourself of the resources offered to you.*

avenue of escape *Fig.* the pathway or route along which someone or something escapes. □ *Bill saw that his one avenue of escape was through the back door.*

average out to a figure to be an average of a certain amount. □ *All the figures average out to 37.*

avoid so/sth **like the plague** *Fig.* to avoid someone or something completely. (As if contact would transmit the plague.) □ *I hate candied sweet potatoes and avoid them like the plague.*

(Aw) shucks! AND **(Ah) shoot!** *Rur.* Darn! (A mild oath.) □ *Ah, shucks! I forgot to call Grandma.* □ *Shoot! I'm late again.*

*****away from** one's **desk** *Fig.* not available for a telephone conversation; not available to be seen or spoken to. (Sometimes said by the person who answers a telephone in an office. It means that the person whom the caller wants is not immediately available due to personal or business reasons. *Typically: **be** ~; **step** ~.) □ *I'm sorry, but Ann is away from her desk just now. Can you come back later?* □ *Tom has stepped away from his desk, but if you leave your number, he will call you right back.*

*****away from it all** *Fig.* at a place where one can avoid completely what one is leaving behind. (*Typically: **be** ~; **get** ~.) □ *Everyone needs to get away from it all every now and then.*

*****awkward as a cow on a crutch** AND *****awkward as a cow on roller skates** very clumsy or off balance. (*Also: **as** ~.) □ *He runs like a cow on a crutch.* □ *Tom will never be a gymnast. He's as awkward as a cow on roller skates!*

awkward as a cow on roller skates Go to previous.

the **ax** Go to the sack.

B

a **babe in arms 1.** *Fig.* a very young baby that is carried by an adult. □ *I have known that since I was a babe in arms!* **2.** *Fig.* an innocent or naive person. (Informal.) □ *Mary has no idea how to win the election. Politically she's a babe in arms.*

a **babe in the woods** *Fig.* a naive or innocent person; an inexperienced person. (Like a child lost in the woods.) □ *Bill is a babe in the woods when it comes to dealing with plumbers.*

back and fill *Fig.* to act indecisively; to change one's direction repeatedly; to reverse one's course. (Originally nautical, referring to trimming the sails so as to alternately fill them with wind and release the wind, in order to maneuver in a narrow space.) □ *The president spent most of his speech backing and filling on the question of taxation.*

back and forth *Fig.* in one direction and then the other repeatedly; from one place to another repeatedly, facing forward in each case. □ *The tiger paced back and forth in its cage.*

***back (at so)** *Fig.* repaying someone for a bad deed. (*Typically: **get** ~; **have** ~.) □ *Tom called me a jerk, but I'll get back at him.* □ *I don't know how I'll get back for her insult, but I will.*

back at it (again) *Fig.* doing something again. (Usually said in criticism.) □ *I thought you stopped smoking, but I see you are back at it again.*

back away (from so/sth) AND **back off (from so/sth)** *Fig.* to begin to appear uninterested in someone or something; to withdraw one's interest from someone or something. □ *The board of directors be-* gan to back away from the idea of taking over the rival company. □ *I sort of backed off when I saw how dull the class was going to be.*

back down (from so/sth) to yield to a person or a thing; to fail to carry through on a threat. □ *Jane backed down from her position on the budget.*

back down (on sth) *Fig.* to lessen or drop an earlier rigid position on something; to yield something in an argument. □ *She backed down on her demands.*

back East *Fig.* to or from the eastern U.S., especially the northeastern or New England states. □ *Tom went to school back East, but his brother attended college in the Midwest.*

back so for sth to support or endorse someone for something, such as a public office. □ *We all back Tom for president.*

***back in business** *Fig.* operating as usual again. (As if one were operating one's business again. *Typically: **be** ~; **get** ~.) □ *I was sick for a week, but I'm back in business again now.*

back in the game 1. back playing the game with the other members of the team. □ *After a bit of a rest, I was back in the game again.* **2.** *Fig.* back doing things as one was before; in action again; back in circulation. □ *Now that final exams are over, I'm back in the game. Wanna go out tonight?*

***back in (the) harness** *Fig.* back doing one's job. (*Typically: **be** ~; **get** ~.) □ *I don't look forward to getting back in the harness next Monday.*

back in the saddle (again) *Fig.* back in control again; back into a routine again.

(In a cowboy song made famous by Gene Autry in the 1940s.) □ *Vacation was great, but it's good to be back in the saddle again.*

*back in time *Fig.* a previous period in time. (*Typically: **go** ~; a **step** ~; **step** ~; **take a step** ~.) □ *Let us step back in time and experience these scenes showing typical Victorian Sunday clothing.*

back so **into a corner** AND **paint** so **into a corner; hem** so **in** *Fig.* to manage to get someone into a position where there is limited escape. □ *He tells different stories to different people. Finally he backed himself into a corner and had to admit his lies.*

*back in(to) circulation *Fig.* back enjoying one's social contacts; back continuing to make new friends and develop a new social life. (*Typically: **be** ~; **get** ~.) □ *After her illness, Kristine looked forward to getting back into circulation.* □ *Now that you're divorced, are you going to get back into circulation?*

the **back of the beyond** *Fig.* the most remote place; somewhere very remote. □ *Mary likes city life, but her husband likes to live in the back of the beyond.*

back off (from so/sth) Go to **back away (from** so/sth).

*back on one's **feet 1.** *Fig.* recovered from an illness and out of one's sickbed. (*Typically: **be** ~; **get** ~.) □ *I will go back to work as soon as I get back on my feet.* **2.** *Fig.* recovered from financial problems. (*Typically: **be** ~; **get** ~.) □ *I can't afford to buy a car until I get a job and get back on my feet.*

*back on track *Fig.* running according to schedule again. (*Typically: **get** ~; **get** sth ~; **have** sth ~; **put** sth ~.) □ *I hope we can have this project back on track by the end of the week.*

back out (of sth) *Fig.* [for someone] to withdraw from something, such as an agreement, negotiations, an argument, etc. □ *Are you going to try to back out of our agreement?*

back the wrong horse AND **bet on the wrong horse** *Fig.* to support someone or

something that cannot win or succeed. (Fig. on a bettor who has picked the wrong horse to win.) □ *I don't want to back the wrong horse, but it seems to me that Jed is the better candidate.*

back to basics *Fig.* return to basic instruction; start the learning process over again. □ *Class, you seem to have forgotten the simplest of facts, so it's back to basics for the first week of classes.*

back to square one *Fig.* back to the beginning. (As with a board game.) □ *Negotiations have broken down, and it's back to square one.*

back to the drawing board *Fig.* time to start from the start; it is time to plan something over again. (Plans or schematics are drawn on a drawing board.) □ *It didn't work. Back to the drawing board.*

back to the salt mines *Cliché* time to return to work, school, or something else that might be unpleasant. (The phrase implies that the speaker is a slave who works in the salt mines.) □ *School starts in the fall, so then it's back to the salt mines again.*

back so **up**† to support someone; to provide support and agreement for someone. □ *I hope you'll back me up on this, but I am pretty sure that Bob is wrong.*

back up 1. [for objects] to obstruct and accumulate in a pathway or channel. □ *Something clogged the sewer and it backed up.* **2.** to refuse to go through with something; to **back out (of** sth). □ *Fred backed up at the last minute, leaving me to do the job alone.*

back up (to sth) *Fig.* to go back to something said in a conversation. (Fig. on reversing a recording device.) □ *Let's back up to what you just said and go over that point again.*

backfire on so *Fig.* [for something, such as a plot] to fail unexpectedly; to fail with an undesired result. (Fig. on the image of an explosion coming out of the breech of a firearm, harming the person shooting rather than the target.) □ *I was afraid that my scheme would backfire on me.*

backhanded compliment AND **left-handed compliment** *Fig.* an unintended or ambiguous compliment. □ *Backhanded compliments are the only kind he ever gives!* □ *I'd rather have criticism than a left-handed compliment.*

back-order sth [for a merchant] to order something that is not in stock and make a delivery to the customer when the goods become available. □ *The store didn't have the replacement part for my vacuum cleaner, so the manager back-ordered it for me.*

the **backroom boys** Go to the boys in the backroom.

backseat driver *Fig.* an annoying passenger who tells the driver how to drive; someone who tells others how to do things. □ *Stop pestering me with all your advice. Nobody likes a backseat driver!*

back-to-back 1. adjacent and touching backs. □ *Two people who stand back-to-back can manage to see in all directions.* **2.** *Fig.* following immediately. (Actually such things are front to back, with the "end" of one event followed in time by the beginning of another.) □ *I have three lecture courses back-to-back every day of the week.*

*bad blood (between people) *Fig.* unpleasant feelings or animosity between people. (*Typically: **be** ~; **have** ~.) □ *There is no bad blood between us. I don't know why we should quarrel.*

a **bad egg** Go to a rotten egg.

a **bad hair day** *Inf.* a bad day in general. (As when one's inability to groom one's hair in the morning seems to color the events of the day.) □ *I'm sorry I am so glum. This has been a real bad hair day.*

a **bad penny** *Fig.* a worthless person. □ *Wally is a bad penny. Someday he'll end up in jail.*

a **bad time** Go to a hard time.

bad times AND **difficult times; trying times; hard times; tough times** *Fig.* a period that offers difficulties, such as when there is not enough food, money, or work. □ *We went through trying times*

when Perry was out of work, but we all bounced back. □ *These are difficult times, but we'll survive.*

bag and baggage AND **part and parcel** *Fig.* [with] one's luggage; with all one's possessions. □ *Sally showed up at our door bag and baggage one Sunday morning.* □ *I want you out of here, part and parcel, by noon!*

bag of bones *Inf.* an extremely skinny person or animal with bones showing. (The skin is the figurative bag.) □ *I've lost so much weight that I'm just turning into a bag of bones.*

bag of tricks *Fig.* a collection of special techniques or methods. □ *What have you got in your bag of tricks that could help me with this problem?*

bag on so *Sl.* to criticize someone. □ *If you are going to bag on everyone all the time, I don't want to hear it.*

bag some rays Go to catch some rays.

Bag that! *Sl.* Forget that! □ *There are four—no, bag that!—six of the red ones and three blue ones.*

bail so **out**† to deposit a sum of money that allows someone to get out of jail while waiting for a trial. □ *John was in jail. I had to go down to the police station to bail him out.*

bail so/sth **out**† *Fig.* to rescue someone or something from trouble or difficulty. (Fig. on bailing someone out of jail.) □ *The proposed law was in trouble, but Senator Todd bailed out the bill at the last minute.*

bail sth **out**† **1.** to remove water from the bottom of a boat by dipping or scooping. □ *Tom has to bail the water out before we get in.* **2.** to empty a boat of accumulated water. □ *Would you bail this boat out?*

bail out (of sth) **1.** to jump out of an airplane with a parachute. □ *When we get to 8,000 feet, we'll all bail out and drift down together. We'll open our parachutes at 2,000 feet.* **2.** *Fig.* AND **pull out (of** sth) to abandon a situation; to get out of something. (Fig. on ①.) □ *John got tired of school, so he just bailed out.*

*the **bait** *Fig.* a temptation or attraction to which people respond positively. (Fig. on the image of a fish coming up from deep water to seize bait. *Typically: **rise to** ~; **swallow** ~; **take** ~.) □ *He rose to the bait and I am sure we will hear from him soon, ready to agree to our offer.*

bait and switch *Fig.* a deceptive merchandising practice where one product is advertised at a low price to get people's attention [the bait], but pressure is applied to get the customer to purchase a more expensive item. □ *Wilbur accused the merchant of bait-and-switch practices and stalked out of the store.*

a **baker's dozen** *Fig.* thirteen. (Bakers often added an extra item to an order for a dozen.) □ *We ended up with a baker's dozen each of socks and undershirts on our shopping trip.*

the **balance of power** the situation where the power held by one governing body or adversary is balanced by the power of another. □ *The balance of power was threatened when China captured our airplane.*

balance out to equal out; to become even or fair. □ *These things all balance out in the end.*

balance the accounts 1. AND **balance the books** to determine through accounting that accounts are in balance, that all money is accounted for. □ *Jane was up all night balancing the accounts.* **2.** *Fig.* to get even [with someone]. (Fig. on ①.) □ *Tom hit Bob. Bob balanced the accounts by breaking Tom's toy car.*

balance the books Go to previous.

bald as a baby's backside Go to next.

***bald as a coot** AND ***bald as a baby's backside** completely bald. (*Also: **as** ~.) □ *If Tom's hair keeps receding like that, he'll be bald as a coot by the time he's 30.* □ *My grandfathers were as bald as a baby's backside.*

***baleful as death** promising evil; very threatening. (*Also: **as** ~.) □ *The wind's moan was as baleful as death.*

balk at sth to resist and object to something; to shy away from doing something. □ *I hope they don't balk at finishing their work.*

ball and chain 1. *Inf.* a wife. (Mostly jocular.) □ *I've got to get home to my ball and chain.* **2.** *Inf.* a person's special burden; a job. (Prisoners sometimes were fettered with a chain attached to a leg on one end and to a heavy metal ball on the other.) □ *Tom wanted to quit his job. He said he was tired of that old ball and chain.*

the **ball is in** so's **court** *Fig.* someone is responsible for the next move in some process; someone has to make the next response. □ *There was no way that Liz could avoid responding. The ball was in her court.*

ball of fire *Fig.* an energetic and ambitious person; a go-getter. □ *I was a real ball of fire until my heart attack.*

ball so/sth **up**† *Inf.* to interfere with someone or something; to mess someone or something up. □ *Who balled this television up?*

ball sth **up**† to roll something up into a ball. (Alluding to something, such as rope, being tangled up and so useless.) □ *She balled the putty up and stuck it to the clown's face as a nose.*

a **ballpark figure** *Fig.* an estimate; an off-the-cuff guess. □ *I don't need an exact number. A ballpark figure will do.*

the **balls of** one's **feet** the bottom part of the feet just behind the toes. □ *Mary got blisters on the balls of her feet from playing tennis.*

bandy sth **about** to spread information or gossip around; to discuss something informally. (*Bandy* = to chatter; to trade words back and forth.) □ *Now that you know my secret, I hope you don't bandy it about.*

(bang) dead to rights *Inf.* in the act; (guilty) without question. □ *There he was, bang dead to rights with the smoking gun still in his hands.*

bang for the buck AND **bang for** one's **buck** *Inf.* value for the money spent; excitement for the money spent; a favorable cost-to-benefit ratio. (Expressed as an amount of bang for the buck.) □ *How much bang for the buck did you really think you would get from a 12-year-old car—at any price?*

bang one's **head against a brick wall** Go to beat one's head against the wall.

bang sth **out**† *Fig.* to play something on the piano, loudly, banging on the keys; to type something on a keyboard by pounding on the keys. □ *Let me bang this melody out and see if you can guess who wrote it.* □ *I banged out the newspaper story and just barely made my deadline.*

bang the drum for so/sth Go to beat the drum for so/sth.

bank on sth *Fig.* to be so sure of something that one can trust it as one might trust a bank with one's money. (See also can take it to the bank.) □ *I will be there on time. You can bank on it.*

banker's hours *Fig.* short work hours: 10:00 A.M. to 3:00 P.M. □ *There aren't many bankers who keep banker's hours these days.*

baptism of fire *Fig.* a first experience of something, usually something difficult or unpleasant. □ *My son's just had his first visit to the dentist. He stood up to this baptism of fire very well.*

bar none *Fig.* with no exceptions. (Follows an assertion of fact.) □ *This is the best of all, bar none.*

the **bare** sth *Fig.* the smallest or least possible. □ *Bob did the bare minimum of work to pass the class.*

bare one's **soul (to** so**)** *Fig.* to reveal one's innermost thoughts to someone; to tell another person exactly how one feels about someone or something. □ *You don't have to bare your soul to me. Just tell me what I can do to help.*

bare one's **teeth** Go to show one's teeth.

bare sth **to** so to reveal or disclose something to someone. □ *I have to know a guy pretty well before I will bare my innermost thoughts to him.*

bare-bones *Cliché* limited; stripped down; lacking refinements or extras. □ *This one is the bare-bones model. It has no accessories at all.*

bargaining chip *Fig.* something to be used (traded) in negotiations. □ *I want to use their refusal to meet our terms as a bargaining chip in future negotiations.*

barge in (on so/sth**)** AND **burst in (on** so/sth**)** *Fig.* to break in on someone or something; to interrupt someone or something. □ *Oh! I'm sorry. I didn't mean to barge in on you.*

barge in(to some place**)** *Fig.* to go or come rudely into some place. □ *He just barged right into the room without knocking.* □ *Don't barge in like that, without letting us know you're here!*

bark at so *Fig.* to speak harshly to someone. □ *Don't bark at me like that over such a trivial mistake!*

One's **bark is worse than** one's **bite.** *Fig.* a person's manner is more severe than the actual harm the person may do. (Alludes to the dog whose bark is more threatening than its bite is harmful.) □ *Don't worry about the boss. His bark is worse than his bite.*

bark sth **out at** so AND **bark** sth **at** so; **bark** sth **to** so; **bark** sth **out**† **(to** so**)** *Fig.* to say something harshly to someone. (Fig. on the barking of an angry dog.) □ *The sergeant barked the orders out at the recruits.* □ *Don't bark commands at me!*

bark up the wrong tree *Fig.* to make the wrong choice; to ask the wrong person; to follow the wrong course. (Fig. on the image of a dog in pursuit of an animal, where the animal is in one tree and the dog is barking at another tree.) □ *If you think I'm the guilty person, you're barking up the wrong tree.*

barrel along *Fig.* to move along rapidly. □ *The car was barreling along at a fairly rapid clip.*

a **barrel of fun** *Fig.* a tremendous amount of fun. □ *Jill is just a barrel of fun in class.*

bask in sth *Fig.* to enjoy or revel in something, such as praise, fame, etc. (Fig. on the image of a person or animal resting in the warming rays of the sun.) □ *Alice enjoyed basking in her newfound fame.*

a **basket case** *Fig.* a person who is a nervous wreck. (Formerly referred to a person who is physically disabled and must be transported in a basket on wheels.) □ *After that all-day meeting, I was practically a basket case.*

bat sth **around** *Fig.* to discuss something informally; to negotiate a matter. □ *Let's bat this idea around and see if we can't reach an agreement.*

batch (it) *Fig.* to live alone like a bachelor. □ *I tried to batch it for a while, but I got too lonely.*

batten down the hatches 1. to seal a ship's deck hatches against storm damage. □ *Batten down the hatches, lads! She's blowing up a good one!* **2.** *Fig.* to prepare for difficult times. (Fig. on ①. Fixed order.) □ *Batten down the hatches; Congress is in session again!*

battle of the bulge *Inf.* the attempt to keep one's waistline slim. (Jocular here. This is the U.S. name for the German Ardennes Offensive, December 16, 1944, to January 25, 1945, involving over a million men.) □ *She appears to have lost the battle of the bulge.*

a **battle royal** *Fig.* a classic, hard-fought battle or argument. (The word order is typical of French order, as is the plural, **battles royal.** *Battle Royale* with an *e* is the name of a film.) □ *The meeting turned into a battle royal, and everyone left angry.*

be a slave to sth Go to a slave to sth.

the **be all (and) (the) end all** to be everything that could be required. □ *This medicine is useful, but it's not the be-all-end-all pill that we hoped it might be.*

be all smiles Go to grin from ear to ear.

be at the head of the pack Go to lead the pack.

be at the point of (doing**)** sth Go to on the point of (doing) sth.

be big on sth to be interested in something; to be concerned with or intrigued by something. □ *Fred is really big on jazz.*

be one's **brother's keeper** *Fig.* to be responsible for someone else. (Used of others besides just real brothers.) □ *I can't force these kids to go to school and get an education so they can get jobs. I am not my brother's keeper.*

be conspicuous by one's **absence** Go to conspicuous by one's absence.

be crazy about so/sth AND **be mad about** so/sth; **be wild about** so/sth *Fig.* to be very fond of someone or something; to just love someone or something with enthusiasm. □ *I'm just crazy about chocolate doughnuts!* □ *Bob's crazy about me!*

be for so/sth AND **be for** doing sth supporting or in favor of someone or something. □ *Mary is running for office, and the whole family is for her.*

be game (for sth**)** *Fig.* to be ready for action; to be agreeable to participating in something. □ *We're going to the park to play football. Are you game?*

be in aid of *Fig.* to be intended to help, cure, or resolve [something]. (Stilted.) □ *I don't understand what your comments are in aid of.*

be in with so Go to in with so.

be mad about so/sth Go to be crazy about so/sth.

Be my guest. *Fig.* Help yourself.; After you. (A polite way of indicating that someone else should go first, take a serving of something, or take the last one of something.) □ *Mary: I would just love to have some more cake, but there is only one piece left. Sally: Be my guest. Mary: Wow! Thanks!*

be of a (good) mind to do sth Go to have a (good) mind to do sth.

be on a losing streak Go to a losing streak.

be on the same page Go to read from the same page.

be on the same screen Go to read from the same page.

be one's **own boss** to run one's own business and to report to no one but oneself. □ *I started my own plumbing business, and I love being my own boss.*

be one's **own man** AND **be** one's **own master** *Fig.* to be someone who is not controlled by other people; to be an independent person. (Other number and gender combinations are in use.) □ *Bert longed to be his own master, but at the same time feared losing the security he had as the employee of a large company.*

be one's **own worst enemy** Go to one's own worst enemy.

be short with so Go to short with so.

be so Go to be too.

be that as it may *Cliché* even if what you say is true. □ *Be that as it may, I still cannot help you.*

Be there or be square. *Sl.* Attend or be at some event or place or be considered uncooperative or not "with it." (Older. Mid-20th century.) □ *There's a bunch of people going to be at John's on Saturday. Be there or be square!*

be too AND **be so** to be something [despite any information to the contrary]. (An emphatic form of *is, am, are, was, were.*) □ *Mother: Billy, you aren't old enough to be up this late. Billy: I am too!*

be (up)on so Go to (up)on so.

be wild about so/sth Go to be crazy about so/sth.

be within one's **rights** Go to within one's rights.

Beam me up, Scotty! *Inf.* Get me out of here!; Take me away from this mess! (From the late 1960s television program *Star Trek.*) □ *This place is really crazy! Beam me up, Scotty!*

beam up *Sl.* to die. (Alluding to the television program *Star Trek.*) □ *I was so exhausted after climbing four flights that I was afraid I would beam up.*

bear so/sth Go to put up with so/sth.

bear a grudge (against so) AND **have a grudge (against** so); **hold a grudge**

(against so) *Fig.* to continue feeling an old resentment for someone; to harbor continual anger for someone. □ *I have a grudge against my landlord for not fixing the leaky faucet.*

bear arms to carry and display weapons, usually firearms. □ *He claims that he has the right to bear arms any place at any time.*

bear one's **cross** AND **carry** one's **cross** *Fig.* to handle or cope with one's burden; to endure one's difficulties. (This is a biblical theme. It is always used figuratively except in the biblical context.) □ *I just carry my cross and try not to complain.* □ *It's a very painful disease, but I'll bear my cross.*

bear fruit *Fig.* to yield results. □ *We've had many good ideas, but none of them has borne fruit.*

bear sth **in mind** Go to keep sth in mind.

bear in mind that . . . *Fig.* to remember something; to consider something. □ *I asked the teacher to bear in mind that I am just a beginner.*

bear sth **out**† *Fig.* to demonstrate or prove something. (Often in the passive voice.) □ *Our earlier suspicions have been borne out by the evidence you just presented.*

bear the brunt (of sth) to experience and endure the major force of something. □ *The car's bumper bore the brunt of the crash.* □ *Bill bore the brunt of the criticism of the committee because he was chairman.*

bear up (under sth) AND **stand up (under** sth) to manage to cope with emotional distress; to survive under certain conditions; to withstand adverse conditions. □ *How well did he bear up under the news of the death?*

bear watching *Fig.* to need close, attentive observation or monitoring. (Note that this is verb + nominal. Typically in the present or future tense.) □ *This is a very serious disease, and it will bear watching for further developments.*

bear with so/sth to wait until further news or action has come from or about someone or something. □ *Please bear with me until we have the final word from the mayor.*

bear witness to sth to state or indicate that one has witnessed something. □ *I can bear witness to the fact that John left the office at noon.*

***one's bearings** *Fig.* the knowledge of where one is; the knowledge of how one is oriented to one's immediate environment. (*Typically: **get** ~; **have** ~; **tell** one ~.) □ *After he fell, it took Ted a few minutes to get his bearings.*

beat a dead horse Go to flog a dead horse.

beat a (hasty) retreat *Fig. Cliché* to withdraw from a place very quickly. □ *We went out into the cold weather, but quickly beat a retreat to the warmth of our fire.*

beat a path to so's **door** *Fig.* [for people] to arrive (at a person's place) in great numbers. (The image is that so many people will wish to come that they will wear down a pathway to the door.) □ *I have a new product so good that everyone will beat a path to my door.*

beat around the bush AND **beat about the bush** *Fig.* to avoid answering a question; to stall; to waste time. □ *Stop beating around the bush and answer my question.*

beat one **at** one's **own game** *Fig.* to outwit someone by using their own strategies. □ *He thought he could trick Mrs. Edwards into picking him for the job, but I beat him at his own game, and she picked me. After all, Jane Edwards is my sister.*

beat so's **brains out** AND **beat** so **to a pulp 1.** *Inf. Fig.* to hit or batter someone severely. □ *Those thugs nearly beat his brains out.* **2.** *Inf. Fig.* to drive oneself hard (to accomplish something). □ *I beat my brains out all day to clean this house, and you come in and get dirt on the carpet!*

beat one's **brains out**† **(to** do sth**)** *Inf.* to try very hard to do something. □ *If you think I'm going to beat my brains out to do this, you are crazy.*

beat city hall Go to fight city hall.

beat so **down**† *Fig.* to defeat or demoralize someone. □ *The constant bombing finally beat them down.*

beat one's **gums** *Inf.* to waste time talking a great deal without results. (As if one were toothless.) □ *You're just beating your gums. No one is listening.*

beat one's **head against the wall** AND **bang** one's **head against a brick wall** *Inf.* to waste one's time trying hard to accomplish something that is completely hopeless. □ *You're banging your head against a brick wall trying to get that dog to behave properly.*

Beat it! AND **Get lost!** *Inf.* Go away!; Get out! □ *"Beat it, you kids! Go play somewhere else!" yelled the storekeeper.*

beat the bushes for so/sth *Fig.* to look everywhere for someone or something. (Fig. on the way that a hunter might seek out prey.) □ *I beat the bushes for a date for Friday night and came up with Gloria.*

beat the clock *Fig.* to do something before a deadline; to finish before the time is up. (Fig. on accomplishing something before a clock reaches a specific time.) □ *Sam beat the clock, arriving a few minutes before the doors were locked.*

beat the drum for so/sth AND **bang the drum for** so/sth *Inf.* to promote or support someone or something. (As if one were beating a drum to get attention.) □ *I spent a lot of time beating the drum for our plans for the future.*

beat the gun *Fig.* to manage to do something before the ending signal. (Originally from sports, referring to scoring in the last seconds of a game just before the signal for the end of the game. See also beat the clock.) □ *Tom kicked and tried to beat the gun, but he was one second too slow.*

beat the hell out of so AND **beat the living daylights out of** so; **beat the pants off (of)** so; **beat the shit out of** so; **beat all hell out of** so; **beat the socks off (of)** so; **beat the stuffing out of** so; **beat the tar out of** so **1.** *Inf. Fig.* to defeat someone very badly. (Caution with *shit. Of* is usually retained before pronouns.) □ *Our team beat the hell out of the other side.* □ *We beat the stuffing out of the other team.* **2.** *Inf.* to batter someone severely. (Refers to physical violence, not the removal of someone's pants. *Of* is usually retained before pronouns.) □ *The thugs beat the living daylights out of their victim.* □ *If you do that again, I'll beat the pants off of you.*

beat the living daylights out of so Go to previous.

beat the pants off (of) so Go to beat the hell out of so.

beat the rap *Sl.* to evade conviction and punishment [for a crime]. □ *The police hauled Tom in and charged him with a crime. His lawyer helped him beat the rap.*

beat the shit out of so Go to beat the hell out of so.

beat the socks off (of) so Go to beat the hell out of so.

beat the stuffing out of so Go to beat the hell out of so.

beat the system Go to fight city hall.

beat the tar out of so Go to beat the hell out of so.

beat so **to a pulp** Go to beat so's brains out.

beat so **to the draw** Go to next.

beat so **to the punch** AND **beat** so **to the draw** *Fig.* to do something before someone else does it. □ *I planned to write a book about using the new software program, but someone else beat me to the draw.*

beat oneself **up** *Fig.* to be overly critical of one's behavior or actions; to punish oneself with guilt and remorse over past actions. (Fixed order.) □ *It's over and done with, and it wasn't your fault. There's no need to beat yourself up.*

the **beauty of** sth *Fig.* the cleverness or ingenuity of something. □ *The beauty of my plan is that it does much and costs little.*

become of so/sth to happen or occur to someone or something. □ *Whatever became of Joe and his friends?*

become rooted to sth Go to rooted to sth.

***becoming on** so [of clothing] complimentary to someone; [of clothing] enhancing one's good looks. (Refers to clothing and other personal ornaments that can be worn. *Typically: be ~; look ~.) □ *The dress you wore last night is not becoming on you.*

bed down some place *Fig.* to sleep somewhere; to find a place to sleep somewhere. □ *I need to bed down somewhere for the night.*

bed down (for sth) *Fig.* to lie down to sleep for a period of time. □ *After she had bedded down for the night, the telephone rang.*

a **bed of roses** *Inf. Fig.* a luxurious situation; an easy life. (Fig. on a soft mattress made of rose petals.) □ *Who said life would be a bed of roses?*

bed-and-breakfast a type of lodging for travelers or tourists that offers a place to sleep and breakfast the next morning, typically in a small inn or private home. □ *We visited six European countries and stayed in a bed-and-breakfast every night.*

*a **bee in** one's **bonnet** *Fig.* a single idea or a thought that remains in one's mind; an obsession. (*Typically: get ~; have ~; give one ~; put ~.) □ *I have a bee in my bonnet over that cool new car I saw, and I can't stop thinking about it.*

beef about so/sth *Sl.* to complain about someone or something. □ *He is always beefing about his working conditions.*

beef sth **up**† *Inf.* to add strength or substance to something. □ *They beefed up the offer with another thousand dollars.*

been around *Fig.* have had many experiences in life. (Sometimes meant to include sexual experiences.) □ *You don't need to warn me about anything! I've been around.*

been had AND **was had; have been had 1.** *Inf.* (of a woman) been copulated with; been made pregnant. □ *She was had and is going to have the baby.* **2.** *Inf.* been mistreated, cheated, or dealt with badly. □ *Look at this cheap shirt that I paid $30 for! I was had!*

Been there(, done that). Go to (I've) been there(, done that).

beer and skittles Go to (all) beer and skittles.

some time **before last** at a period of calendar time just before the last period of the time named. (Such as *week, day, month, year,* and even *fortnight.*) □ *I saw him day before last, and he was fine then.*

before long soon. □ *Billy will be grown-up before long.*

before one's **time** before one might be expected to experience something, such as aging or death. □ *If you don't eat better, you'll die before your time.*

*****before** so's **time** *Fig.* happening before someone was born or old enough to know what was going on. (*Typically: **be** ~; **happen** ~; **occur** ~.) □ *Of course I don't remember it. It was before my time.*

before you can say Jack Robinson AND **quicker than you can say Jack Robinson** *Fig.* almost immediately. □ *I'll catch a plane and be there quicker than you can say Jack Robinson.*

before you know it *Fig.* almost immediately. □ *If you keep spending money like that, you'll be broke before you know it.*

beg off (on sth**)** *Fig.* to ask to be released from something; to refuse an invitation. □ *I have an important meeting, so I'll have to beg off on your invitation.*

beg so's **pardon** *Fig.* to ask someone for indulgence or forgiveness for either a major or minor offense. □ *Whoops. I didn't see you there. I beg your pardon.*

beg the question 1. *Fig.* to carry on a false argument where one assumes as proved the very point that is being argued, or more loosely, to evade the issue at hand. (Essentially a criticism of someone's line of argument.) □ *Stop arguing in circles. You're begging the question.* □ *A: Why do two lines that are equidistant from one another never meet? B: Because they are parallel. A: You are begging the question.* **2.** to invite the (following) question. (This misunderstanding of beg the question is heard frequently.) □ *His complaints beg the question: Didn't he cause all of his problems himself?*

beg to differ (with so**)** *Fig.* to disagree with someone; to state one's disagreement with someone in a polite way. (Usually used in a statement made to the person being disagreed with.) □ *If I may beg to differ, you have not expressed my position as well as you seem to think.*

begin by doing sth to start out by doing something first. □ *We will begin by painting the house.*

begin to see daylight *Fig.* to begin to see the end of a long task. □ *I've been so busy. Only in the last week have I begun to see daylight.*

(begin to) see the light (at the end of the tunnel) Go to see the light.

beginner's luck *Fig.* absolute luck; the luck of an inexperienced person. (Referring to surprisingly good luck.) □ *I could never have accomplished this if I had practiced a lot. My win was just beginner's luck.*

the **beginning of the end** *Fig.* the start of the termination of something or of someone's death. □ *When he stopped coughing and grew still, I knew it was the beginning of the end.* □ *The enormous debt we ran up marked the beginning of the end as far as our standard of living was concerned.*

*****behind** so/sth *Fig.* supporting and advocating someone or something. (*Typically: **be** ~; **get** ~; **stand** ~.) □ *I hope you are behind the building of the new city hall. We need your support.*

behind sth *Fig.* planning or leading something in secret; causing something. □ *I think that the Morlocks are behind all these disappearances.* □ *Who is behind the plot to take over the production of mushrooms?*

behind so's **back** *Fig.* without someone's knowledge; secret from someone. □ *Please don't talk about me behind my back.*

*****behind bars** *Fig.* in jail. (*Typically: **be** ~; **put** so ~.) □ *Very soon, you will be behind bars for your crimes.*

behind closed doors *Fig.* in secret; away from observers, reporters, or intruders, usually in a closed room. □ *They held the meeting behind closed doors, as the law allowed.*

*behind schedule *Fig.* having failed to do something by the appointed time, especially the time given on a written plan. (*Typically: **be** ~; **fall** ~; **get** ~.) □ *We have to hurry and finish soon or we will fall behind schedule.*

*behind the eight ball 1. *Inf.* in trouble; in a weak or losing position. (Referring to the eight ball in billiards, which in certain games cannot be touched without penalty. *Typically: **be** ~; **get** ~; **have** so ~; **put** so ~.) □ *John is behind the eight ball because he started writing his term paper far too late.* **2.** *Inf.* broke. (*Typically: **be** ~; **get** ~; **have** so ~; **put** so ~.) □ *I was behind the eight ball again and couldn't make my car payment.*

behind the scenes *Fig.* out of public view. □ *I'm always there, behind the scenes, doing my thankless job!*

behind the times *Fig.* old-fashioned. □ *Sarah is a bit behind the times. Her clothes are quite old-fashioned.*

behind the wheel Go to at the wheel.

Behind you! *Inf.* Look behind you!; There is danger behind you! □ *Alice shouted, "Behind you!" just as the pickpocket made off with Fred's wallet.*

belabor the point *Fig.* to spend too much time on one item of discussion. □ *If the speaker would agree not to belabor the point further, I will place it on the agenda for resolution at the next meeting.*

belch out *Fig.* to burst, billow, or gush out. □ *Smoke belched out of the chimney.*

believe it or not *Fig.* (you may) choose to accept something as true or not; it may seem amazing but it is true. □ *I'm over 50 years old, believe it or not.*

Believe you me! *Inf.* You really should believe me!; You'd better take my word for it! □ *Sue: How do you like my cake? John: Believe you me, this is the best cake I've ever eaten!*

bell, book, and candle the trappings of magic and witchcraft. (Alluding originally to the items used when performing the rite of excommunication from the Roman Catholic Church.) □ *Look, I can't work miracles! Do you expect me to show up at your house with bell, book, and candle, and make everything right? You have to take charge of your own destiny!*

bells and whistles *Fig.* extra, fancy add-ons or gadgets. (Fig. on steam locomotives enhanced with added bells and whistles.) □ *I like cars that are loaded with all the bells and whistles.*

belly up 1. *Inf.* intoxicated by alcohol. (Like a dead fish that floats belly up.) □ *After four beers, I was belly up, for sure.* **2.** *Sl.* (of a business) bankrupt; dead. □ *After the fire the firm went belly up.*

belly up (to sth**)** *Inf.* to move up to something, often a bar. (Usually in reference to nudging one's way to a bar.) □ *The man swaggered in and bellied up to the counter and demanded my immediate attention.*

below par *Fig.* not as good as average or normal. □ *His work is below par, and he is paid too much money.*

below so's **radar (screen)** *Fig.* outside of the consciousness or range of observation of someone. (Fig. on flying lower than can be seen on radar.) □ *It's not important right now. It's completely below my radar.*

belt a drink **down**† *Fig.* to drink an alcoholic drink rapidly. □ *She belted a couple of drinks down and went out to face her guests.*

belt sth **out**† *Fig.* to sing or play a song loudly and with spirit. □ *She really knows how to belt out a song.*

belt the grape *Sl.* to drink wine or liquor heavily and become intoxicated. □ *He has a tendency to belt the grape—every afternoon after work.*

bend so's **ear** *Fig.* to talk to someone, perhaps annoyingly. (As if talking so much that the other person's ear is moved back.) □ *I'm sorry. I didn't mean to bend your ear for an hour.*

bend one's **elbow** AND **bend the elbow; lift** one's **elbow** *Inf.* to take a drink of an alcoholic beverage; to drink alcohol to excess. □ *He's down at the tavern, bending his elbow.*

bend so **out of shape** *Fig.* to make someone angry. □ *Why do you let yourself get bent out of shape? Chill, man, chill.*

bend over backwards (to do sth**)** Go to **fall over backwards (to** do sth**)**.

bend the law AND **bend the rules** *Fig.* to cheat a little bit without breaking the law. (Jocular.) □ *I didn't break the rules. I just bent the rules a little.* □ *Nobody ever got arrested for bending the law.*

bend the rules Go to previous.

beneath so *Fig.* too shameful for a polite person to do. □ *That kind of thing is beneath Fred. I'm appalled that he did it.*

beneath contempt *Fig.* exceedingly contemptible. □ *Your rude behavior is beneath contempt.*

beneath one's **dignity** *Fig.* too rude or coarse for a polite person to do. □ *That kind of thing is beneath my dignity, and I hope yours as well.*

*the **benefit of the doubt** *Fig.* a judgment in one's favor when the evidence is neither for one nor against one. (*Typically: **get** ~; **have** ~; **give** so ~.) □ *I thought I should have had the benefit of the doubt, but the judge made me pay a fine.*

bent on doing sth *Fig.* determined to do something. □ *I believe you are bent on destroying the entire country!*

bent out of shape 1. *Inf.* angry; insulted. □ *I'm bent out of shape because of the way I was treated.* **2.** *Inf.* intoxicated by alcohol or drugs. □ *I've been drunk, but never as bent out of shape as this.*

beside the point AND **beside the question** *Fig.* irrelevant; of no importance; [of a] tangential [issue]. (The second form is less common.) □ *That's very interesting, but beside the point.*

beside the question Go to previous.

beside oneself **(with** sth**)** *Fig.* in an extreme state of some emotion. □ *I was beside myself with joy.* □ *Sarah could not speak. She was beside herself with anger.*

*****best as** one **can** as well as one can. (*Also **as** ~.) □ *I will do it as best as I can.*

best bet best choice. □ *Your best bet is to take the main highway to the lake, and then turn off at the first road to the right.*

one's **best bib and tucker** *Rur.* one's best clothing. □ *Put on your best bib and tucker, and let's go to the city.*

*the **best of both worlds** *Fig.* a situation wherein one can enjoy two different opportunities. (*Typically: **enjoy** ~; **have** ~; **live in** ~.) □ *When Don was a fellow at the university, he had the privileges of a professor and the freedom of a student. He had the best of both worlds.*

the **best of the best** the very best. □ *I am very particular. I want only the best of the best.*

the **best of the lot** the best one of all of them. □ *This one is supposed to be the best of the lot, but even this one isn't very good.*

*the **best of times** *Fig.* when things are good; when things are going well. (*Typically: **(even) at** ~.) □ *John had difficulty getting a loan even in the best of times because of his poor credit record.*

the **best part of** sth Go to the **better part of** sth.

one's **best shot** *Fig.* one's best attempt (at something). □ *That was his best shot, but it wasn't good enough.* □ *I gave the project my best shot.*

the **best-case scenario** *Cliché* the optimum outcome of those being considered. (Compare this with the **worst-case scenario**.) □ *In the best-case scenario, we're all dead eventually—but then that's true of the worst-case scenario also.*

bet one's **bottom dollar** AND **bet** one's **life** *Fig.* to be quite certain (about something). (A *bottom dollar* is the last dollar.) □ *I bet my bottom dollar you can't swim across the pool.* □ *You bet your life I can't swim that far.*

bet so **dollars to doughnuts** *Inf.* to bet something of value against something worth considerably less. □ *I bet you dollars to doughnuts that the train is on time.*

bet one's **life** Go to bet one's bottom dollar.

bet on the wrong horse Go to back the wrong horse.

bet the farm (on sth**)** Go to sell the farm.

bet the ranch (on sth**)** Go to sell the farm.

one's **better half** *Fig.* one's spouse. (Usually refers to a wife.) □ *I think we'd like to come for dinner, but I'll have to ask my better half.*

Better late than never. It is better to do something late than to never do it at all. □ *You were supposed to be here an hour ago! Oh, well. Better late than never.*

*****better left unsaid** *Fig.* [refers to a topic that] should not be discussed; [refers to a thought that] everyone is thinking, but would cause difficulty if talked about in public. (*Typically: sth **is** ~.) □ *Bill: I had such a terrible fight with Sally last night. I can't believe what I said. Bob: I don't need to hear all about it. Some things are better left unsaid.*

Better luck next time. 1. *Fig.* an expression that comforts someone for a minor failure. (Said with a pleasant tone of voice.) □ *Bill: That does it! I can't run any farther. I lose! Bob: Too bad. Better luck next time.* **2.** *Fig.* an expression that ridicules someone for a failure. (Said with rudeness or sarcasm. The tone of voice distinguishes ② from ①.) □ *Sue: You thought you could get ahead of me, you fool! Better luck next time! Joan: I still think you cheated.*

better off (doing sth**)** AND **better off (if** sth **were done)** *Fig.* in a better position if something were done. □ *She'd be better off if she sold her house.* □ *They are better off flying to Detroit than driving.*

better off (some place**)** AND **better off (if** one **were** some place else**)** in a better position somewhere else. □ *They would be better off in a cheaper apartment.* □ *We'd all be better off if we were in Florida.*

the **better part of** sth AND the **best part of** sth the larger part of something. □ *I've been waiting for you for the better part of an hour! Where have you been?*

better safe than sorry better to take extra precautions than to take risks and suffer the consequences. □ *I know I probably don't need an umbrella today, but better safe than sorry.*

between a rock and a hard place AND **between the devil and the deep blue sea** *Fig.* in a very difficult position; facing a hard decision. □ *I couldn't make up my mind. I was caught between a rock and a hard place.* □ *He had a dilemma on his hands. He was clearly between the devil and the deep blue sea.*

between jobs AND **between projects** *Euph.* unemployed. □ *Interviewer: Tell me about your current position. Job candidate: I'm between jobs right now.* □ *When Jill was between projects, she took a computer class at the community college.*

between projects Go to previous.

between the devil and the deep blue sea Go to between a rock and a hard place.

between you (and) me and the bedpost AND **between you and me and these four walls; (just) between you and me** *Fig.* a way of signaling that you are about to tell a secret. (Also heard commonly is "between you and I.") □ *Alan: What's wrong with Ellen these days? She seems so touchy. Jane: Between you and me and the bedpost, I've heard that her boyfriend is seeing someone else.* □ *Jill: How much did you get for your used car? Jane: Well—between you and me and these four walls—$5,000.*

between you and me and these four walls Go to previous.

betwixt and between 1. *Fig.* between (people or things). □ *I liked the soup and the dessert and all that came betwixt and between.* **2.** *Fig.* undecided about someone or something. □ *I wish she would choose. She has been betwixt and between for three weeks.*

a **bevy of beauties** *Cliché* a group of very attractive women, as found in a beauty contest. □ *A whole bevy of beauties waltzed past the old man, but he didn't even notice.*

*****beyond** so/sth finished with someone or something; having solved the problems relating to someone or something. (*Typically: **be** ~; **get** ~; **move** ~.) □ *Things will be better when we get beyond this financial crisis.* □ *When the country moves beyond the current situation, things will have to get better.*

beyond a reasonable doubt *Fig.* almost without any doubt. (A legal phrase.) □ *The jury decided beyond a reasonable doubt that she had committed the crime.*

beyond caring AND **beyond feeling; past caring** *Fig.* in too extreme a state to feel or care. □ *Do what you want. You have hurt me so much, I am beyond caring.* □ *The dying patient is beyond feeling. It doesn't matter now.*

beyond one's **depth** AND **out of** one's **depth 1.** in water that is too deep. □ *Jane swam out to get her even though it was beyond her depth.* **2.** *Fig.* beyond one's understanding or capabilities. (Fig. on ①.) □ *I'm beyond my depth in calculus class.*

beyond feeling Go to beyond caring.

beyond help *Fig.* unable to be helped. □ *The poor dog that was hit by a truck is beyond help.*

beyond one's **ken** *Fig.* outside the extent of one's knowledge or understanding. □ *Why she married that shiftless drunkard is beyond my ken.*

beyond me *Fig.* completely exceeding or surpassing my understanding. (There is usually a heavy stress on *me*.) □ *I'm confused. All this is beyond me.*

beyond one's **means** *Fig.* more than one can afford. □ *They feel that a Caribbean cruise is beyond their means.*

beyond measure *Fig.* in an account or to an extent more than can be quantified; in a very large amount. □ *They brought in hams, turkeys, and roasts, and then they brought vegetables and salads beyond measure.*

beyond question unquestionably true. □ *His honesty is beyond question.*

beyond repair *Fig.* not able to be fixed. □ *This old car is beyond repair.*

beyond reproach so good as to not be vulnerable to criticism or reproach. □ *Her credentials are superb—beyond reproach.*

beyond the pale *Fig.* unacceptable; outlawed. (Fig. on a *pale* as a barrier made of wooden stakes.) □ *Your behavior is simply beyond the pale.*

beyond the shadow of a doubt Go to without a shadow of a doubt.

*****beyond words** *Fig.* more than one can say. (*Typically: **grateful** ~; **shocked** ~; **thankful** ~.) □ *Sally was thankful beyond words.* □ *His declaration left us shocked beyond words.*

bid adieu to so/sth *Cliché* to say good-bye to someone or something. (The word *adieu* is French for *good-bye* and should not be confused with *ado*.) □ *Now it's time to bid adieu to all of you gathered here.* □ *He silently bid adieu to his favorite hat as the wind carried it down the street.*

bide one's **time** *Fig.* to wait patiently. □ *He's not the type to just sit there and bide his time. He wants some action now.*

big and bold large and capable of getting attention. (Usually refers to things, not people.) □ *She wore a brightly colored dress. The pattern was big and bold, and the skirt was very full.*

the **Big Apple** *Fig.* New York City. (Originally a nickname used of New York area racetracks as being the best. Much has been written on the origin of this expression. There are entire websites devoted to advocating and demolishing new and old theories of origin.) □ *We spent the weekend in the Big Apple.*

*****big as all outdoors** *Cliché* very big, usually referring to an indoor space of some kind. (*Also: **as** ~.) □ *You should see Bob's living room. It's as big as all outdoors!*

*big as life (and twice as ugly) AND ***large as life (and twice as ugly); bigger than life (and twice as ugly)** *Cliché* a colorful way of saying that a person or a thing has appeared, often surprisingly or dramatically, in a particular place. (*Also: **as** ~.) □ *The little child just stood there as big as life and laughed very hard.* □ *I opened the door, and there was Tom as large as life.* □ *I came home and found this cat in my chair, as big as life and twice as ugly.*

a **big break** Go to a lucky break.

big bucks *Fig.* a very large amount of money. □ *He earns big bucks for doing almost nothing.*

a **big drink of water** AND a **tall drink of water 1.** *Fig.* a very tall person. □ *Tim is sure a big drink of water.* □ *Kelly grew into a tall drink of water.* **2.** *Fig.* a boring person or thing. (A pun on *hard to take* or *hard to swallow*.) □ *She is a big drink of water, but she could be worse.* □ *The lecture was a big drink of water.*

*the big eye 1. *Fig.* a flirtatious look or gaze; a long look to get another person's attention. (*Typically: **get** ~; **give** so ~.) □ *Look at that pretty girl. She is giving you the big eye.* **2.** *Fig.* obvious eye contact with someone. (*Typically: **get** ~; **give** so ~.) □ *Tom gave me the big eye to let me know he wanted to talk to me.*

a **big frog in a small pond** *Fig.* an important person in the midst of less important people. (Fig. on the idea of a large frog that dominates a small pond with few challengers.) □ *The trouble with Tom is that he's a big frog in a small pond. He needs more competition to make him do even better.*

*a big hand for sth *Fig.* lots of applause for something. (*Typically: **get** ~; **have** ~; **give** so ~.) □ *She got a big hand for singing so well.*

*a (big) head 1. *Inf.* a hangover. (*Typically: **get** ~; **have** ~; **give** so ~.) □ *Oh, man, that booze gave me a big head!* □ *Tom has a head this morning and won't be coming into work.* **2.** Go to a swelled head.

big man on campus *Sl.* an important male college student. (Often derisive or jocular.) □ *Hank acts like such a big man on campus.*

the **big moment** AND the **moment everyone has been waiting for** the special time that everyone has been waiting for. □ *The big moment has come. I will now announce the winner.* □ *This is the moment everyone has been waiting for. Now we will learn the name of the big winner.*

big of so *Fig.* generous; kind or forgiving. (Sometimes sarcastic.) □ *He gave me some of his apple. That was very big of him.* □ *It was big of Sally to come over and apologize like that.*

*the big picture AND ***the whole picture** *Fig.* the whole story of something; a complete view of something. (*Typically: **get** ~; **have** ~; **give** so ~; **know** ~; **see** ~; **show** so ~.) □ *The sales manager gave us all the big picture this morning, and I'm more confused than ever.*

*a big send-off a happy celebration before departing. (*Typically: **get** ~; **have** ~; **give** so ~.) □ *I had a wonderful send-off before I left.*

big with so *Fig.* famous with or desired by someone or some group. □ *This kind of pizza is supposed to be big with people in Chicago.*

bigger than life Go to larger than life.

bigger than life (and twice as ugly) Go to big as life (and twice as ugly).

binge and purge *Fig.* to overeat and vomit, alternatively and repeatedly. (A symptom of the condition called bulimia.) □ *She had binged and purged a number of times before she finally sought help from a doctor.*

A bird in the hand (is worth two in the bush). *Fig.* □ *I prefer the other one, but I already have this one. Oh, well. A bird in the hand is worth two in the bush.*

a **bird's-eye view 1.** *Fig.* a view seen from high above. □ *From the top of the church tower you get a splendid bird's-eye view of the village.* **2.** *Fig.* a brief survey of something; a hasty look at something. (Fig. on

①. Alludes to the smallness of a bird's eye.) □ *The course provides a bird's-eye view of the works of Mozart, but it doesn't deal with them in enough detail for your purpose.*

the **birds and the bees** *Euph.* sex and reproduction. (See also the facts of life.) □ *He's twenty years old and doesn't understand about the birds and the bees!*

a **bit much** *Fig.* beyond what is needed or tolerable. □ *The speech she gave in acceptance of the award was a bit much. She went on and on.*

a **bit of the action** Go to a piece (of the action).

*a **bit off** AND *a **little off** *Fig.* a little crazy; a little out of whack. (*Typically: **be** ~; **think** so ~; **find** so ~.) □ *This guy's a little off, but he is harmless.*

bitch about so/sth *Inf.* to complain about someone or something. □ *Stop bitching about your job so much!*

a **bitch of a** so/sth *Inf.* a really difficult person or thing. □ *He is really a bitch of a boss.*

bitch so **off**† *Sl.* to make someone angry. □ *You really bitch me off, do you know that?*

bitch so/sth **up**† *Inf.* to mess someone or something up. □ *Who bitched these cards up?*

bite back (at so/sth) **1.** to defend an attack by biting at someone or something. (Usually an animal.) □ *I threatened the dog, and the dog bit back.* **2.** *Fig.* to fight back at someone; to return someone's anger or attack; to speak back to someone with anger. (Fig. on ①.) □ *She is usually tolerant, but she will bite back if pressed.*

bite so's **head off** *Fig.* to speak sharply and with great anger to someone. (Fixed order.) □ *I'm very sorry I lost my temper. I didn't mean to bite your head off.*

bite one's **nails 1.** to use one's teeth to remove parts of one's fingernails as a means of shortening them. □ *Stop biting your nails! Use clippers!* **2.** *Fig.* to be nervous or anxious, perhaps actually biting one's

nails. □ *I spent all afternoon biting my nails, worrying about you.*

bite off more than one **can chew 1.** to take a larger mouthful of food than one can chew easily or comfortably. □ *I bit off more than I could chew and nearly choked.* **2.** *Fig.* to take (on) more than one can deal with; to be overconfident. (Fig. on ①.) □ *Ann is exhausted again. She's always biting off more than she can chew.*

bite on so *Sl.* to copy something that someone else has done; to dress the same way someone else does. □ *Nobody will bite on Sally. She has terrible taste.*

bite the big one Go to buy the big one.

bite the bullet *Sl.* to accept something difficult and try to live with it. □ *You are just going to have to bite the bullet and make the best of it.*

bite the dust 1. *Sl.* to die. □ *A shot rang out, and another cowboy bit the dust.* **2.** *Sl.* to break; to fail; to give out. □ *My old car finally bit the dust.*

bite the hand that feeds one *Fig.* to do harm to someone who does good things for you. (Does not involve biting.) □ *She can hardly expect sympathy when she bites the hand that feeds her.*

Bite the ice! *Sl.* Go to hell! □ *If that's what you think, you can just bite the ice!*

*a **bite (to eat)** *Fig.* to get something to eat; to get food that can be eaten quickly. (*Typically: **get** ~; **grab** ~; **have** ~.) □ *I need a few minutes to grab a bite to eat.*

bite one's **tongue** *Fig.* to struggle not to say something that you really want to say. □ *I had to bite my tongue to keep from telling her what I really thought.* □ *I sat through that whole silly conversation biting my tongue.*

bitten by the same bug *Fig.* having the same need, desire, or obsession. □ *Bob and I were both bitten by the same bug and ended up getting new cars at the same time.*

a **bitter pill (to swallow)** *Fig.* an unpleasant fact that has to be accepted. (Does not involve pills or swallowing.) □ *We found his deception a bitter pill to swallow.*

blab sth **around**† *Inf.* to gossip something to others; to spread some news or secret. □ *Did you blab around everything I told you to keep to yourself?*

black and blue *Fig.* "bruised," physically or emotionally. □ *I'm still black and blue from my divorce.*

black and white *Fig.* [describing] a clear choice; this one or that one. □ *It's not just black and white. It's a hard, complex choice.*

*black as a skillet AND ***black as a stack of black cats; *black as coal; *black as night; *black as pitch; *black as the ace of spades** completely dark or black. (*Also: **as** ~.) □ *I don't want to go down to the cellar. It's as black as a skillet down there.* □ *The stranger's clothes were all black as pitch.*

black as a stack of black cats Go to previous.

black as coal Go to black as a skillet.

*black as one **is painted** as evil as described. (Usually negative. *Also: **as** ~.) □ *The landlord is not as black as he is painted. He seems quite generous to me.*

black as night Go to black as a skillet.

black as pitch Go to black as a skillet.

black as the ace of spades Go to black as a skillet.

*a black eye 1. *Fig.* a bruise near the eye from being struck. (*Typically **have** ~; **get** ~; **give** so ~.) □ *I have a black eye where John hit me.* **2.** *Fig.* harm done to one's character. (Fig. on ①. *Typically **have** ~; **get** ~; **give** so ~.) □ *The whole group now has a black eye, and it will take years to recover our reputation.*

*a black mark beside one's **name** *Fig.* something negative associated with a person. (*Typically: **get** ~; **have** ~; **give** one ~.) □ *I did it wrong again! Now I've got still another black mark beside my name!*

black out 1. [for lights] to go out. □ *The power went dead and everything blacked out.* **2.** *Fig.* to pass out; to become unconscious. (Fig. on ①.) □ *After I fell, I must have blacked out.*

black sth **out**† **1.** to cut or turn out the lights or electric power. □ *The manager blacked out the whole building during the emergency to prevent an explosion.* **2.** *Fig.* to prevent the broadcast of a specific television or radio program in a specific area. (Fig. on ①. Usually refers to a sports event.) □ *Will they black the game out around here?*

the **black sheep of the family** *Fig.* the worst member of the family. □ *He keeps making a nuisance of himself. What do you expect from the black sheep of the family?*

a **blank check** freedom or permission to act as one wishes or thinks necessary. □ *He's been given a blank check with regard to reorganizing the workforce.*

a **blast from the past** *Fig.* something out of the past. □ *Wow, all that retro kitchen furniture is a real blast from the past.*

blaze a trail 1. *Fig.* to make and mark a trail. □ *The scout blazed a trail through the forest.* **2.** *Fig.* to do early or pioneering work that others will follow up on. (Fig. on ①.) □ *Professor Williams blazed a trail in the study of physics.*

bleed so **dry** Go to bleed so white.

bleed for so *Fig.* to feel the emotional pain that someone else is feeling; to sympathize or empathize with someone. (See also one's heart bleeds for so.) □ *I just bled for him when I heard his sad story.*

bleed to death to die from the loss of blood. □ *If something isn't done, he will bleed to death!*

bleed so **white** AND **bleed** so **dry** *Inf.* to take all of someone's money; to extort money from someone. □ *The creeps tried to bleed me white.* □ *Richard got a picture of Fred and Joan together and tried to bleed both of them dry by threatening to show it to their spouses.*

bleeding heart *Fig.* someone, usually considered politically liberal or leftist, who is very emotional about certain political issues, such as endangered species, down-trodden people, the suffering poor, etc. □ *Bob is such a bleeding heart. No cause is extreme for him.*

bleep sth **out**† *Fig.* to replace a word or phrase in a radio or television broadcast with some sort of covering tone. (This is sometimes done to prevent a taboo word or other information from being broadcast.) □ *He tried to say the word on television, but they bleeped it out.*

Bless so's **heart!** May God bless your heart! □ *You brought me these lovely flowers. Bless your heart!*

blessed event *Fig.* the birth of a child. □ *The young couple anxiously awaited the blessed event.*

blessed with sth providentially provided with something. □ *We are blessed with three wonderful children and a fine town to raise them in.*

a **blessing in disguise** *Fig.* something that at first seems bad but later turns out to be beneficial. □ *Dad's illness was a blessing in disguise; it brought the family together for the first time in years.*

blimp out (on sth**)** AND **pig out (on** sth**); scarf out (on** sth**); oink out (on** sth**); pork out (on** sth**)** *Inf.* to overeat; to eat too much and gain weight. □ *If I could stop blimping out, I could lose some weight.*

***blind as a bat 1.** completely blind. (Bats are not really blind. *Also: **as** ~.) □ *He lost his sight in an accident and is as blind as a bat.* **2.** *Fig.* not able to see well. □ *I'm as blind as a bat without my glasses.* **3.** *Fig.* unwilling to recognize problems or bad things. □ *Connie is blind as a bat when it comes to her daughter's disgraceful behavior.*

blind luck Go to pure luck.

bliss out *Sl.* to be overcome with happiness. □ *She blissed out at the concert, because she loves that kind of music.*

bliss so **out**† *Sl.* to cause someone to be overcome with happiness. □ *This kind of sunny weather just blisses me out.*

blitz so **out**† *Sl.* to shock or disorient someone. □ *The accident blitzed her out for a moment.*

blitzed out *Sl.* shocked or disoriented. □ *Ann was totally blitzed out by the events of the day.*

block sth **out**† **1.** to obscure a clear view of something. □ *The bushes blocked out my view of the car that was approaching.* **2.** AND **map** sth **out**†; **sketch** sth **out**† to describe a plan for something; to explain the details of something. □ *She blocked it out for us, so we could understand.* **3.** AND **blot** sth **out** *Fig.* to attempt to erase something from one's memory or consciousness. □ *The sight was so horrible. I did everything I could to blot it out, but it even haunted me in my dreams.*

block so **up**† *Fig.* to constipate someone. □ *That food always blocks me up.*

blood and guts 1. *Inf. Fig.* strife; acrimony. □ *There is a lot of blood and guts around here, but we get our work done anyway.* **2.** *Inf. Fig.* acrimonious. (This is hyphenated before a nominal.) □ *Old blood-and-guts Albert is making his threats again.*

blood, sweat, and tears *Fig.* the signs of great personal effort. □ *After years of blood, sweat, and tears, Timmy finally earned a college degree.*

bloody but unbowed *Fig.* showing signs of a struggle, but not defeated. (Originally referring to the head. From the poem *Invictus* by William Earnest Henley.) □ *Liz emerged from the struggle, her head bloody but unbowed.* □ *We are bloody but unbowed and will fight to the last.*

blossom (forth) 1. [for a plant] to burst into flower. □ *All the trees blossomed forth at the same time.* **2.** *Fig.* [for someone or a concept] to develop or grow quickly. (Fig. on ①.) □ *That summer she suddenly blossomed forth into a young woman.*

blossom (out) into sth **1.** [for a plant] to develop into full bloom. □ *Imagine this brown old bulb blossoming out into a lovely flower.* **2.** *Fig.* [for someone or a concept] to develop into something. (Fig.

on ①.) □ *She blossomed into a lovely young lady.*

a **blot on the landscape** AND a **blight on the land** *Fig.* a sight that spoils the look of a place. □ *That monstrosity you call a house is a blot on the landscape. You should have hired a real architect!*

blot sth **out** Go to block sth out†.

blow sth *Sl.* to ruin or waste something. □ *I had a chance to do it, but I blew it.*

blow a bundle (on so**)** Go to drop a bundle (on so).

blow a fuse 1. to burn out the fuse on an electrical circuit and lose power. □ *You'll blow a fuse if you use too many appliances at once.* **2.** AND **blow** one's **fuse; blow a gasket; blow** one's **cork; blow** one's **lid; blow** one's **top; blow** one's **stack** *Inf.* to explode with anger; to lose one's temper. □ *Come on, don't blow a fuse.* □ *Go ahead, blow a gasket! What good will that do?*

blow a gasket Go to previous.

blow so **a kiss** *Fig.* to pantomime the sending of a kiss to a person visible nearby by kissing one's hand and "blowing" the kiss off the hand toward the person. □ *As she boarded the train she blew him a kiss, and he waved back.*

blow so **away 1.** *Sl.* [for something shocking or exciting] to overwhelm a person; to excite a person very much. □ *The amount of the check blew me away.* **2.** *Sl.* to murder someone, usually by gunfire. □ *Mr. Big ordered Lefty to blow Max away.*

blow so's **brains out**† *Sl.* to kill someone with a gun. □ *Careful with that gun, or you'll blow your brains out.*

blow one's **cookies** Go to blow (one's) lunch.

blow one's **cool** Go to lose one's cool.

blow one's **cork** Go to blow a fuse.

blow so's **cover** *Sl.* to reveal someone's true identity; to ruin someone's scheme for concealment. □ *I didn't mean to blow your cover by calling out to you.*

blow so's **doors off**† *Sl.* [for a driver] to speed past another vehicle. □ *Wow, he almost blew my doors off when he went by!*

blow one's **groceries** Go to blow (one's) lunch.

blow hot and cold *Fig.* to be changeable or uncertain (about something). □ *He blows hot and cold about this. I wish he'd make up his mind.*

blow in(to some place**) (from** some place**)** *Sl.* [for someone] to arrive at a place suddenly, or surprisingly, or with a casual air. □ *We blew into town about midnight from Detroit.*

Blow it out your ear! *Sl.* Go away!; Leave me alone! □ *You are not cool, you're just weird! Blow it out your ear!*

blow itself out *Fig.* [for a storm or a tantrum] to lose strength and stop; to subside. (Fixed order.) □ *Eventually, the hurricane blew itself out.*

blow one's **lid** Go to blow a fuse.

blow one's **lines** Go to fluff one's lines.

blow (one's**) lunch** AND **lose** one's **lunch; blow** one's **cookies; blow** one's **groceries** *Sl.* to vomit. □ *I almost lost my lunch, I ran so hard.* □ *I wanted to blow my lunch, that's how rotten I felt.* □ *He got carsick and blew his cookies all over the front seat.*

blow so's **mind 1.** *Sl.* to disturb or distract; to destroy the function of one's brain. □ *It was a terrible experience. It nearly blew my mind.* **2.** *Sl.* to overwhelm someone; to excite someone. □ *It was so beautiful, it nearly blew my mind.*

blow one's **nose** to expel mucus and other material from the nose using air pressure from the lungs. □ *Bill blew his nose into his handkerchief.*

blow off 1. [for something] to be carried off something by moving air. □ *The leaves of the trees blew off in the strong wind.* **2.** [for a valve or pressure-maintaining device] to be forced off or away by high pressure. □ *The safety valve blew off and all the pressure escaped.* □ *The valve blew off, making a loud pop.* **3.** *Fig.*

[for someone] to become angry; to lose one's temper. (Fig. on ②.) □ *I just needed to blow off. Sorry for the outburst.* **4.** *Sl.* to goof off; to waste time; to procrastinate. □ *You blow off too much. Settle down and get to work.* **5.** *Sl.* a time-waster; a goof-off. (Usually **blow-off.**) □ *Get busy. I don't pay blow-offs around here.* **6.** *Sl.* something that can be done easily or without much effort. (Usually **blow-off.**) □ *Oh, that is just a blow-off. Nothing to it.* □ *The test was easy—a blow-off.* **7.** AND **blow** so/sth **off**† *Sl.* to ignore someone or something; to skip an appointment with someone; to not attend something where one is expected. □ *He decided to sleep in and blow this class off.* □ *It wasn't right for you to just blow off an old friend the way you did.* **8.** AND **blow** so **off**† *Sl.* to ignore someone in order to end a romantic or other relationship. □ *She knew that he had blown her off when he didn't even call her for a month.* **9.** *Sl.* the final insult; an event that causes a dispute. (Usually **blow-off.**) □ *The blow-off was a call from some girl named Lulu who asked for Snookums.* **10.** *Sl.* a dispute; an argument. (Usually **blow-off.**) □ *There was a big blow-off in the office today.*

blow so/sth **off**† Go to previous.

blow off (some) steam Go to let off (some) steam.

Blow on it! *Sl.* Cool it!; Take it easy! □ *It's all right, Tom. Blow on it!*

blow so **out** *Sl.* to kill someone, especially with gunshots. (Fixed order.) □ *Lefty set out to blow Max out once and for all.*

blow so/sth **out of the water** *Fig.* to destroy utterly someone or something, such as a plan. (Fig. on a torpedo or other weapon striking a ship and causing a great explosion that makes pieces of the ship fly out of the water.) □ *The boss blew the whole idea out of the water.*

blow over *Fig.* [for something] to diminish; to subside. (As with a storm or a temper tantrum.) □ *Her display of temper finally blew over.* □ *The storm will blow over soon, I hope.*

blow so **over**† *Fig.* to surprise or astound someone. (Fixed order.) □ *Her announcement just blew me over.*

blow one's **own horn** AND **toot** one's **own horn** *Fig.* to brag. □ *Gary sure likes to toot his own horn.* □ *"I hate to blow my own horn," said Bill, "but I am always right."*

blow one's **stack** Go to blow a fuse.

blow the joint *Sl.* to get out of a place, usually in a hurry or without delay. □ *Come on, let's blow the joint before there's trouble.*

blow the lid off (sth) *Sl.* to expose something to public view. □ *The police inspector blew the lid off the work of the gang of thugs.*

blow the whistle (on so/sth**) 1.** *Fig.* to report someone's wrongdoing to someone (such as the police) who can stop the wrongdoing. (Fig. on blowing a whistle to attract the police.) □ *The citizens' group blew the whistle on the street gangs by calling the police.* **2.** to report legal or regulatory wrongdoing of a company, especially one's employer, to authorities. □ *She was fired for blowing the whistle on the bank's mismanagement of accounts, but she then sued the bank.*

blow so **to** sth *Sl.* to pay for something or someone, such as a meal, a movie, a drink, etc. □ *I think I'll blow myself to a fancy dessert.*

blow so/sth **to bits** Go to blow so/sth to smithereens.

blow so/sth **to kingdom come** *Fig.* to destroy someone or something by means of an explosion. □ *You'd better get that gas leak fixed, or it will blow you and your car to kingdom come.*

blow so/sth **to pieces** Go to next.

blow so/sth **to smithereens** AND **blow** so/sth **to bits; blow** so/sth **to pieces 1.** to explode someone or something into tiny pieces. □ *The bomb blew the ancient church to smithereens.* □ *The explosion blew the tank to bits.* **2.** to destroy an idea or plan by exposing its faults. (Fig. on ①.) □ *The opposing lawyer blew my case to smithereens.*

blow one's **top** Go to blow a fuse.

blow so/sth **up**[†] **1.** to destroy someone or something by explosion. □ *The terrorists blew the building up at midday.* **2.** *Fig.* to exaggerate something [good or bad] about someone or something. □ *The press blew the story up unnecessarily.*

blow sth **up**[†] **1.** to inflate something. □ *He didn't have enough breath to blow the balloon up.* **2.** to have a photograph enlarged. □ *How big can you blow this picture up?*

blow up 1. [for something] to explode. □ *The bomb might have blown up if the children had tried to move it.* **2.** *Fig.* to burst into anger. (Fig. on ①.) □ *I just knew you'd blow up.* **3.** *Fig.* a fight or spectacular argument. (Usually **blowup.**) □ *After the third blowup, she left him.* **4.** *Fig.* an enlarged version of a photograph, map, chart, etc. (Usually **blowup.**) □ *Here's a blowup of the scene of the crime.* **5.** *Fig.* the ruination of something; the collapse of something. (Usually **blowup.**) □ *The blowup in the financial world has ruined my chances for early retirement.* **6.** *Fig.* to fail or get ruined. (Fig. on ①.) □ *The whole project blew up. It will have to be canceled.* **7.** [for a storm] to arrive accompanied by the blowing of the wind. □ *A terrible storm blew up while we were in the movie theater.*

blow up in so's **face** AND **explode in** so's **face** *Fig.* [for something] to get ruined while someone is working on it. □ *All my plans blew up in my face.*

blow sth **wide open** AND **bust** sth **wide open** *Sl.* to expose corrupt practices or a secret plan; to put an end to corruption. □ *The press is trying to blow the town wide open, and the cops are trying to hush them up so they can move about in secret.* □ *I'm going to bust this racket wide open.*

a **blow-by-blow account** AND a **blow-by-blow description** *Fig.* a detailed description (of an event) given as the event takes place. (This referred originally to reporting on boxing.) □ *The lawyer got the witness to give a blow-by-blow description of the argument.*

a **blow-by-blow description** Go to previous.

blown (up) *Sl.* intoxicated. □ *I guess I'm a little too blown up to drive.*

blue around the gills Go to pale around the gills.

blue blood 1. *Fig.* the blood [heredity] of a noble family; aristocratic ancestry. □ *The earl refuses to allow anyone who is not of blue blood to marry his son.* **2.** *Fig.* a person of aristocratic or wealthy ancestry. □ *Because his great-grandparents made millions, he is regarded as one of the city's blue bloods.*

blue-collar *Fig.* of the lower class or working class; of a job or a worker, having to do with manual labor. (Compare this with **white-collar.** Refers to the typical color of work shirts worn by mechanics, laborers, etc.) □ *His parents were both blue-collar workers. He was the first person in his family to go to college.*

*the **blues** *Fig.* **1.** sadness; a mood of depression. (*Typically: **get** ~; **have** ~.) □ *I get the blues every time I hear that sad song.* **2.** a traditional style of popular music characterized by lyrics expressing hardship, lost love, etc. □ *Buddy had been singing the blues ever since the Depression.*

bluff one's **way in(to** sth**)** to make entry to a place or group through deception or bluffing. □ *The robbers bluffed their way into the bank and held up a teller.*

bluff one's **way out (of** sth**)** to evade, avoid, or escape something through deception or bluffing. □ *They asked me a question I should have known the answer to, but I couldn't bluff my way out of the situation.*

bodily functions *Euph.* anything the body does automatically or as a normal occurrence, especially urinating and defecating. □ *It is not polite to discuss bodily functions at the dinner table.*

the **body politic** *Fig.* the people of a country or state considered as a political unit. □ *The body politic was unable to select between the candidates.*

bog so/sth **down**[†] *Fig. Lit.* [for a difficulty or complication] to slow down a person or a process. (See also **bogged down**.) □ *All the paperwork bogged down the project, but we finally got it finished.*

*bogged down 1. to become encumbered and slow. (*Typically: **become** ~; **find** oneself ~; **get** ~.) □ *The truck got bogged down in the mud soon after it started.* **2.** *Fig.* stuck; prevented from making progress. (As if one were walking through a bog and getting stuck in the mud. *Typically: **become** ~; **find** oneself ~; **get** ~.) □ *The students became bogged down with the algebra problems.* □ *The Smiths really got bogged down in decorating their house.*

boggle so's **mind** AND **boggle the mind** to confuse someone; to overwhelm someone. □ *She said that his arrogance boggled her mind.*

boil sth **down**† **1.** to condense or thicken something, such as a liquid. □ *I have to boil this stock down for a while before I can use it.* **2.** *Fig.* to reduce a problem to its simple essentials. (Fig. on ①.) □ *We don't have time to boil down this matter. This is too urgent.*

boil down to sth **1.** AND **boil down** [for a liquid] to be condensed to something by boiling. □ *Boil this mixture down to about half of what it was.* **2.** *Fig.* [for a complex situation] to be reduced to its essentials. (Fig. on ①.) □ *It boils down to the question of who is going to win.*

*bold as brass very bold; bold to the point of rudeness. (*Also: **as** ~.) □ *The tiny kitten, as bold as brass, began eating the dog's food right under the dog's nose.*

bolster so **up**† *Fig.* to give someone emotional support and encouragement. □ *We bolstered her up the best we could, but she was still unhappy.*

bolt sth **down**† *Fig.* to eat something too rapidly. □ *She bolted down her dinner and ran out to play.*

a **bolt from the blue** *Fig.* a sudden surprise. (Fig. on the image of a stroke of lightning from a cloudless sky.) □ *The news that Mr. and Mrs. King were getting a divorce struck all their friends as a bolt from the blue.*

bomb out (of sth**)** *Sl.* to flunk out of or fail at something, especially school or a job. □ *She was afraid she would bomb out of school.*

bone of contention *Fig.* the subject or point of an argument; an unsettled point of disagreement. □ *We've fought for so long that we've forgotten what the bone of contention is.*

bone up (on sth**)** *Fig.* to study something thoroughly; to review the facts about something. □ *I have to bone up on the state driving laws because I have to take my driving test tomorrow.* □ *I take mine next month, so I'll have to bone up, too.*

boo so **off the stage** AND **boo** so **off**† to jeer and hoot, causing a performer to leave the stage. □ *The rude audience booed the performer off the stage.*

booby prize *Fig.* a mock prize given to the worst player or performer. □ *Bob should get the booby prize for the worst showing in the race.*

boogie down (to some place**)** *Sl.* to hurry (to somewhere); to go (somewhere). (Fig. on the popular musical style called *boogie* or *boogie-woogie*.) □ *So, why don't you boogie down to the store and load up with goodies for the weekend?*

book (on) out *Sl.* to leave in a hurry; to depart very suddenly and rapidly. □ *I'm in a hurry, so I've got to book out right now.* □ *Let's book on out of this place as soon as we can.*

boom sth **out**† [for someone] to say something very loud; to shout. □ *The announcer boomed out the names of the players.*

*the boot *Inf.* dismissal from employment or from a place that one is in. (*Typically: **get** ~; **give** so ~.) □ *I guess I wasn't dressed well enough to go in there. They gave me the boot.*

boot so/animal **out**† AND **kick** so/animal **out**† **1.** to send or remove someone or some creature from a place forcefully, often by kicking. □ *I kicked the cat out and then went to bed.* **2.** *Fig.* to force someone or something to leave some place. (Fig. on

①.) □ *We booted out the people who didn't belong there.*

boot up 1. *Fig.* [of a computer] to begin operating. □ *He turned on the computer and it booted up.* **2.** *Fig.* to start up one's computer. □ *He booted up and got to work.*

boot sth **up**† *Fig.* to start up a computer. □ *Please go boot up your computer so we can get started.*

booze (it) up *Sl.* to drink heavily; to drink to get drunk. (Fixed order.) □ *She wanted to get home and booze it up by herself.*

border on sth **1.** [for an area] to reach as far as and touch another place. □ *Nebraska borders on Kansas.* **2.** *Fig.* [for a deed] to be almost as bad as a more extreme deed. □ *Your remarks are quite harsh, and during wartime would border on treason.*

border (up)on sth **1.** [for something] to touch upon a boundary. (*Upon* is more formal and less commonly used than *on*.) □ *Our property borders on the lakeshore.* □ *The farm borders upon the railroad tracks.* **2.** *Fig.* [for some activity or idea] to be very similar to something else. (Fig. on ①. Not usually physical objects. *Upon* is formal and less commonly used than *on*.) □ *This notion of yours borders upon mutiny!* □ *That plan borders on insanity.*

bore one **out of** one's **mind** Go to next.

bore so **stiff** AND **bore** so **to death; bore one out of** one's **mind; bore the pants off of** so; **bore** so **to tears** *Fig.* to be exceedingly dull and uninteresting. (*Stiff* means "dead.") □ *The play bored me stiff.* □ *The lecture bored everyone to death.*

bore the pants off of so Go to previous.

bore through so *Fig.* [for someone's gaze] to seem to penetrate the person being gazed or stared at. □ *Her stare bored right through me.*

bore so **to death** Go to bore so stiff.

bore so **to tears** Go to bore so stiff.

bored out of one's **mind** Go to next.

bored silly AND **bored to distraction; bored stiff; bored to death; bored out of** one's **mind; bored to tears** very bored; extremely dull and uninteresting (Usually an exaggeration.) □ *I was bored silly at the lecture.* □ *The dull speaker left me bored to distraction.* □ *I am bored to tears. Let's go home.*

bored stiff Go to previous.

bored to distraction Go to bored silly.

bored to tears Go to bored silly.

born and bred some place Go to next.

born and raised some place AND **born and bred** some place *Fig.* born and nurtured through childhood in a specific place. □ *She was born and raised in a small town in western Montana.* □ *Freddy was born and bred on a farm and had no love for city life.*

born lazy very lazy indeed. (This means the same as *bone lazy* to which it could be related, but there is no evidence for any such derivation.) □ *You are not suffering from any sickness at all! You're just born lazy!*

born out of wedlock *Fig.* born to an unmarried mother. □ *In the city many children are born out of wedlock.*

born to do sth *Fig.* to be destined to do something because of devotion and talent; to be utterly and totally devoted to doing something. □ *Look how she glides over the ice. She was born to skate in the Olympics.*

born to be so/sth *Fig.* to be destined to become someone or a type of person because of devotion and talent. □ *Look how she glides over the ice. She was born to be an Olympic skater.*

born with a silver spoon in one's **mouth** *Fig.* born into wealth and privilege. □ *James doesn't know anything about working for a living; he was born with a silver spoon in his mouth.*

borrow trouble *Fig.* to worry needlessly; to make trouble for oneself. □ *Do not get involved with politics. That's borrowing trouble.*

bosom buddy AND **bosom pal** *Fig.* a close friend; one's closest friend. □ *Of course I know Perry. He is one of my bosom pals.*

bosom pal Go to previous.

boss so **around** to give orders to someone; to (rudely) treat a person as an employee. □ *I don't work for you! You can't boss me around!*

both sheets in the wind *Inf.* intoxicated. (A ship's sheets are the ropes or lines that control the sails.) □ *She's not just both sheets in the wind—they're all in the wind.*

bother one's **(pretty little) head about** so/sth *Rur.* to worry about something. (Stereotypically polite Southern talk to a woman; typically said facetiously or patronizingly.) □ *Now, don't bother your pretty little head about all this.*

the **bottle** *Fig.* [the habit of drinking] alcohol. □ *His friends thought he was a bit too fond of the bottle.* □ *She tried to stay away from the bottle, but she never could manage it for long.*

bottle sth **up**† AND **bottle** sth **up**† **(inside (oneself))** *Fig.* to hold one's feelings within; to keep from saying something that one feels strongly about. □ *Let's talk about it, John. You shouldn't bottle it up.* □ *Don't bottle up your problems. It's better to talk them out.*

the **bottom fell out (of** sth**)** *Fig.* a much lower limit or level of something was reached. □ *The bottom fell out of the market and I lost a lot of money.*

the **bottom line 1.** the last figure on a financial profit-and-loss statement or on a bill. □ *Don't tell me all those figures! Just tell me the bottom line.* **2.** *Fig.* the result; the final outcome. (Fig. on ①.) □ *I know about all the problems, but what is the bottom line? What will happen?*

the **bottom of the barrel** AND the **bottom of the heap;** the **bottom of the pile** *Inf.* the location of persons or things of the very lowest quality; someone or something of the lowest quality. (The fruit at the bottom of a barrel of apples is likely to be bruised from the weight of the other apples.) □ *That last secretary you*

sent me was really the bottom of the barrel.

the **bottom of the heap** Go to previous.

the **bottom of the pile** Go to the bottom of the barrel.

bottom out *Fig.* to reach the lowest or worst point of something. (Fig. on a car making a loud noise when going over a bump because the bottom of the car or its suspension gets hit.) □ *Interest rates bottomed out last February.*

Bottoms up! AND **Here's looking at you.; Here's mud in your eye.; Here's to you.** *Inf.* an expression said as a toast when people are drinking together. (Refers to the bottoms of the drinking glasses, that they should be up so that the glasses are emptied.) □ *Bill: Bottoms up. Tom: Here's mud in your eye. Bill: Ah, that one was good. Care for another?*

bounce sth **around**† **(with** so**)** *Inf.* to discuss something with a number of people; to move an idea from person to person like a ball. □ *I need to bounce this around with my family.*

bounce back (from sth**)** AND **bounce back (after** sth**)** *Fig.* [for someone] to recover after a disability, illness, blow, or defeat. (See also rebound from sth.) □ *She bounced back from her illness quickly.*

bounce for sth Go to spring for sth.

bounce sth **off (of)** so/sth AND **bounce** sth **off**† *Fig.* to try an idea or concept out on someone or a group, hoping that comments will "bounce back" in return. (*Of* is usually retained before pronouns.) □ *Let me bounce off this idea, if I may.* □ *Can I bounce something off of you people, while you're here?*

bound and determined *Cliché* very determined; very committed or dedicated (to something). □ *We were bound and determined to get there on time.*

bound for some place headed for a specific goal or destination. □ *Bill accidentally got on a bus bound for Miami.* □ *Our baseball team is bound for glory.*

bound hand and foot *Fig.* with hands and feet tied up. □ *We remained bound hand and foot until the police found us and untied us.*

bound to do sth *Fig.* certain to do something; destined to do something. □ *We are bound to tell the truth.*

***bound up in** sth *Fig.* devoted to something; deeply involved with something. (*Typically: **be** ~; **get** ~.) □ *He's bound up in his work and pays little attention to his family.*

bound up with sth *Fig.* linked to or dependent on something; coordinated with the fate of something else. □ *My ability to earn a living is bound up with the financial success of the company I work for.*

bow and scrape *Fig.* to be very humble and subservient. □ *The salesclerk came in, bowing and scraping, and asked if he could help us.*

bow before so/sth *Fig.* to submit to someone or something; to surrender to someone or something. □ *Our country will never bow before a dictator's demands.*

bow down to so/sth *Fig.* to defer to someone or something; to show homage to someone or something. (Often sarcastic.) □ *I am supposed to bow down to Mrs. Buff-Orpington and all her money? Not likely!*

bow out (of some place**)** to bow as one departs from a place. □ *The servant bowed out of the room.*

bow out (of sth**)** *Fig.* to retire or resign as something. (Fig. on **bow out (of** some place**)**.) □ *I think I will bow out and leave this job to someone else.* □ *He had been head of the department for years and finally decided to bow out before he was invited to leave.*

bow to sth *Fig.* to yield to some kind of pressure. □ *Fred felt obliged to bow to the many requests for his explanation.*

bowl so **over 1.** to knock someone over. (Fixed order.) □ *Bob hit his brother and bowled him over.* **2.** *Fig.* to surprise or overwhelm someone. (Fixed order. Fig.

on ①.) □ *The details of the proposed project bowled everyone over.*

box so's **ears** to strike someone on the ears. □ *The child claimed that the teacher had boxed her ears, and the parents went immediately to the police.*

box so/sth **in**† to trap or confine someone or something. □ *He boxed her in so she could not get away from him.*

boxed in *Fig.* in a bind; having few alternatives. □ *I got him boxed in. He'll have to do it our way.*

boxed (up) 1. *Sl.* intoxicated. □ *I am way boxed, and I feel sick.* **2.** *Sl.* in jail. □ *Pat was boxed up for two days till we got bond money.*

the **boys in the backroom** AND the **backroom boys** *Fig.* any private group of men who make decisions, usually political decisions. □ *The boys in the backroom picked the last presidential candidate.*

brace oneself **for** sth **1.** to hang onto something or prop oneself against something in preparation for something that might cause one to fall, blow away, wash away, etc. □ *Hold onto the rail. Brace yourself. Here comes another huge wave.* **2.** *Fig.* to prepare for the shock or force of something. (Fig. on ①.) □ *Brace yourself for a shock. I have very bad news.*

brace up *Fig.* to take heart; to be brave. □ *I told John to brace up because things would probably get worse before they got better.*

brain so *Fig.* to strike a person hard on the skull as if to knock out the person's brains. (Often said as a vain threat.) □ *I thought he was going to brain me, but he only hit me on the shoulder.*

the **brains behind** sth *Fig.* the originator of the plans for something; the operator or manager of a complex matter. □ *Fred was the brains behind the scheme and made sure that all went well.*

branch out (from sth**) 1.** *Lit.* [for a branch] to grow out of a branch or trunk. (Having to do with plants and trees.) □ *A twig branched out of the main limb and grew straight up.* **2.** *Fig.* to expand away from something; to diversify away from narrower interests. (Fig. on ①.) □ *The speaker branched out from her prepared remarks.*

branch out (into sth) *Fig.* to diversify and go into new areas. □ *I have decided to branch out into some new projects.*

brand spanking new *Fig.* very new; just purchased and never before used. □ *Look at that brand spanking new car!*

brass so **off**† *Sl.* to make someone angry. (Primarily military. As angry as the "brass," or officers, might get about something.) □ *You really brass me off!*

brave sth **out**† *Fig.* to endure something; to put up with something courageously. □ *I don't know if all the men can brave the attack out.*

so's **bread and butter** *Fig.* the source of someone's basic income; someone's livelihood—the source of one's food. □ *I can't miss another day of work. That's my bread and butter.*

bread and water *Fig.* the most minimal meal possible; the meal that was once given to prisoners. (Usually used in reference to being in prison or jail.) □ *Wilbur knew that if he got in trouble again it would be at least a year on bread and water.*

bread-and-butter letter *Fig.* a letter or note written to follow up on a visit; a thank-you note. □ *I got sort of a bread-and-butter letter from my nephew, who wants to visit me next summer.*

*a **break** *Fig.* a chance; another chance or a second chance. (*Typically: **get** ~; **have** ~; **give** so ~.) □ *I'm sorry. Please don't send me to the principal's office. Give me a break!*

break a code *Fig.* to figure out a code; to decipher a secret code. □ *When they broke the code, they were able to decipher messages.*

break a habit AND **break the habit; break** one's **habit** *Fig.* to end a habit. □ *It's hard to break a habit that you have had for a long time.*

break a law AND **break the law** *Fig.* to fail to obey a law; to act contrary to a law. □ *Lisa broke the law when she drove the wrong way on a one-way street.*

Break a leg! *Inf.* Good luck! (A special theatrical way of wishing a performer good luck. Saying "good luck" is considered by actors to be a jinx.) □ *"Break a leg!" shouted the stage manager to the heroine.*

break a record *Fig.* to destroy a previously-set high record by setting a new one. □ *The athlete broke a record in swimming every time he entered a competition.*

break a story *Fig.* [for a media outlet] to be the first to broadcast or distribute the story of an event. □ *The Tribune broke the story before the Herald could even send a reporter to the scene.*

break away (from so/sth**)** AND **break free (from** so/sth**); break loose (from** so/sth**)** *Fig.* to sever a relationship with another person, especially the parent-child relationship or to leave home. □ *He found it hard to break away from his mother.* □ *She was almost 30 before she finally broke free.*

break one's **back (to** do sth**)** Go to break one's neck (to do sth).

break (so's**) balls** AND **break (**so's**) stones; bust (**so's**) balls; bust (**so's**) stones 1.** *Sl.* to wreck or ruin (someone); to overwork someone; to overwhelm someone. (Used among men, but not necessarily.) □ *The boss acts like he's trying to break everybody's balls all the time.* **2.** *Sl.* to kid or tease (someone). □ *Don't sweat what I said—I was just busting balls.*

break one's **balls to** do sth Go to bust (one's) ass (to do sth).

break bread with so *Fig.* to eat a meal with someone. (Stilted or religious.) □ *Please come by and break bread with us sometime.*

break camp *Fig.* to close down a campsite; to pack up and move on. □ *Okay, everyone. It's time to break camp. Take those tents down and fold them neatly.*

break down 1. [for something] to fall apart; [for something] to stop operating. □ *The air-conditioning broke down, and* *we got very warm.* **2.** *Fig.* [for one] to lose control of one's emotions; [for one] to have an emotional or psychological crisis. (*Fig.* on ①.) □ *He couldn't keep going. He finally broke down.*

break so **down**† *Fig.* to force someone to give up and tell secrets or agree to do something. □ *After threats of torture, they broke the spy down.*

break sth **down**† *Fig.* to destroy a social or legal barrier. □ *They had to break down many social prejudices to succeed.*

break sth **down**† **(for** so**)** *Fig.* to explain something to someone in simple terms or in an orderly fashion. (*Fig.* on the image of breaking a complex problem into smaller segments that can be explained more easily.) □ *I can help. This is a confusing question. Let me break down the problem for you.*

break sth **down**† **(into** sth**) 1.** to reduce a compound or its structure to its components. □ *Heat will break this down into sodium and a few gases.* **2.** to reduce a large numerical total to its subparts and explain each one.

break even *Fig.* for income to equal expenses. (This means that money was not made or lost.) □ *Unfortunately my business just managed to break even last year.*

break so's **fall** *Fig.* to cushion a falling person; to lessen the impact of a falling person; to catch or intercept a falling person. □ *When the little boy fell out of the window, the bushes broke his fall.* □ *The old lady slipped on the ice, but a snow bank broke her fall.*

break for sth **1.** to stop working and do something else, such as lunch, coffee, etc. □ *We should break now for lunch.* **2.** to run suddenly toward something; to increase dramatically one's speed while running. □ *At the last moment, the deer broke for the woods.*

break free (from so/sth**)** Go to break away (from so/sth).

break ground (for sth**)** *Fig.* to signal the building of a new structure by a ceremony in which an important person digs out the first shovelful of earth. □ *When do they expect to break ground at the new site?*

break so's **heart** *Fig.* to cause someone great emotional pain. □ *It just broke my heart when Tom ran away from home.* □ *Sally broke John's heart when she refused to marry him.*

break so **in**† *Fig.* to train someone to do a new job; to supervise someone who is learning to do a new job. □ *Who will break the new employee in?*

break sth **in**† **1.** to crush or batter something (such as a barrier) to pieces. □ *Why are you breaking the door in? Here's the key!* □ *Who broke in the barrel?* **2.** *Fig.* to use a new device until it runs well and smoothly; to wear shoes, perhaps a little at a time, until they feel comfortable. □ *I can't drive at high speed until I break this car in.* □ *Her feet hurt because her new shoes were not yet broken in.*

break in (on so**) 1.** *Fig.* to burst into a place and violate someone's privacy. □ *The police broke in on him at his home and arrested him.* **2.** *Fig.* to interrupt someone's conversation. □ *If you have urgent news, just break in on me.*

break in (on sth**)** to interrupt something; to intrude upon something. □ *I didn't mean to break in on your discussion.*

break into sth *Fig.* to begin to perform or utter suddenly, especially with song, speech, chattering, tears, etc. □ *As soon as the movie started, the people behind me broke into loud chattering.*

break into a gallop *Fig.* [for a horse] to begin to gallop; [for a horse] to speed up to a gallop. □ *Near the stables, the horse broke into a fast gallop.*

Break it up! *Inf.* Stop fighting!; Stop arguing! (Fixed order.) □ *When the police officer saw the boys fighting, he came over and hollered, "Break it up! You want me to arrest you?"*

break loose (from so/sth**)** Go to break away (from so/sth).

break one's **neck (to** do sth**)** AND **break** one's **back (to** do sth**)** *Fig.* to work very hard to accomplish something. □ *I broke my neck to get here on time.* □ *There is no point in breaking your back. Take your time.*

break new ground *Fig.* to begin to do something that no one else has done; to pioneer [in an enterprise]. □ *Dr. Anderson was breaking new ground in cancer research.*

break so/sth **of** sth *Fig.* to cause someone or something to stop practicing a habit. □ *We worked hard to break the dog of making a mess on the carpet.*

break off (with so/group**)** AND **break with** so/group *Fig.* to end communication with someone or a group; to end a relationship with someone, especially a romantic relationship, or to create a break between adult members of a family. □ *Terri has broken off with Sam.* □ *We thought she would break with him pretty soon.*

break out 1. to burst forth suddenly, as with a fire, a riot, giggling, shouting, etc. □ *A fire broke out in the belfry.* □ *A round of giggling broke out when the teacher tripped.* **2.** *Sl.* to leave. □ *It's late, man. Time to break out.*

break out in a cold sweat *Fig.* to become frightened or anxious and begin to sweat. □ *I was so frightened, I broke out in a cold sweat.*

break out in a rash *Fig.* [for the skin] to erupt with a rash. (See also break out in a cold sweat; break out (with a rash).) □ *I knew Dan had the chicken pox, because he broke out in a rash and had a dry cough.*

break out (in pimples) *Fig.* [for the skin] to erupt with pimples. □ *Chocolate makes me break out in pimples.*

break out in(to) tears AND **break in(to) tears** *Fig.* to start crying suddenly. □ *I was so sad that I broke out into tears.*

break out (of sth**) 1.** to escape from something, often by destructive means, especially from prison. □ *The convicts plotted to break out of prison.* **2.** *Fig.* to escape from something in one's life that is too confining. (Fig. on ①.) □ *She just*

couldn't break out of her old patterns of behavior.

break out with sth *Fig.* to utter or emit laughter, a shout, or a cry. □ *They broke out with laughter every time they saw the pale lady with the red wig.*

break out (with a rash**)** *Fig.* [for the skin] to erupt with pimples, hives, or lesions, from a specific disease such as measles, chicken pox, rubella, etc. □ *They both broke out with hives at the same time.*

break ranks with so/sth *Fig.* to disagree with or dissociate oneself from a group in which one is a member. (Fig. on leaving a line or rank of soldiers.) □ *I hate to break ranks with you guys, but I think you are all completely wrong.*

break silence *Fig.* to give information about a topic that no one was mentioning or discussing. □ *The press finally broke silence on the question of the plagiarized editorial.*

break one's **stride** to deviate from a rhythmic stride while walking, running, or marching. □ *After I broke my stride, I never could pick up enough speed to win the race.*

break the back of sth AND **break** sth's **back** *Fig.* to end the domination of something; to reduce the power of something. □ *The government has worked for years to break the back of organized crime.*

break the bank *Fig.* to use up all one's money. (Fig. on the image of casino gambling, in the rare event that a gambler wins more money than the house [bank] has on hand.) □ *It will hardly break the bank if we go out to dinner just once.* □ *Buying a new dress at a discount price won't break the bank.*

break the habit Go to break a habit.

break the ice *Fig.* to initiate social interchanges and conversation; to get something started. □ *It's hard to break the ice at formal events.* □ *Sally broke the ice at the auction by bidding $20,000 for the painting.*

break the law Go to break a law.

break the bank

break the news (to so) *Fig.* to tell someone some important news, usually bad news. □ *The doctor had to break the news to Jane about her husband's cancer.*

break the silence *Fig.* to make a noise interrupting a period of silence. □ *The wind broke the silence by blowing the door closed.*

break the spell 1. *Fig.* to put an end to a magic spell. □ *The wizard looked in his magic book to find out how to break the spell.* **2.** *Fig.* to do something that ends a desirable period of [figurative] enchantment. □ *At the end of the second movement, some idiot broke the spell by applauding.*

break through (sth) *Fig.* to overcome something; to penetrate a [figurative] barrier. □ *Tom was able to break through racial barriers.* □ *The scientists broke through the mystery surrounding the disease and found the cause.*

break sth to so *Fig.* to disclose some news or information to someone. (Often said of unpleasant news.) □ *I hate to be the one to break this to you, but there is trouble at home.* □ *We broke the bad news to Ken gently.*

break up 1. *Fig.* [for a marriage] to dissolve in divorce. □ *Their marriage finally broke up.* **2.** *Fig.* to begin laughing very hard. (It is one's composure that is "breaking.") □ *The comedian told a particularly good joke, and the audience broke up.* **3.** Go to break up (with so).

break so up† *Fig.* to cause a person to laugh, perhaps at an inappropriate time. □ *The comedian's job was to break up the audience by telling awesome jokes.*

break sth up† **1.** to destroy something. □ *The police broke up the gambling ring.* **2.** *Fig.* to put an end to something. □ *Walter's parents broke up the party at three in the morning.*

break up (with so) *Fig.* to end a romantic relationship with someone. □ *Tom broke up with Mary and started dating Lisa.*

break wind *Euph.* to expel gas from the anus. □ *Someone on the bus broke wind. It smelled terrible.*

break with so/group Go to break off (with so/group).

break with tradition 1. *Fig.* to deviate from tradition; to cease following tradition. □ *The media broke with tradition and completely ignored Groundhog Day to devote more space to serious news.* **2.** *Fig.* a deviation from tradition. □ *In a break with tradition, Groundhog Day was totally ignored by the media.*

break one's **word** *Fig.* not to do what one said one would do; not to keep one's promise. (Compare this with keep one's word.) □ *If you break your word, she won't trust you again.*

break sth **off**† *Fig.* to end a relationship abruptly. □ *After a few long and bitter arguments, they broke off their relationship.*

break sth **out** *Fig.* to bring out and open something. □ *Bob asked the host if he could break out another bottle of wine.*

breaking and entering *Fig.* the crime of forcing one's way into a place. □ *Wilbur was charged with four counts of breaking and entering.*

the **breaking point** *Fig.* the point at which nerves or one's mental state can endure no more. □ *My nerves are at the breaking point.*

*a **breath of fresh air 1.** *Fig.* a portion of air that is not "contaminated" with unpleasant people or situations. □ *You people are disgusting. I have to get out of here and get a breath of fresh air.* **2.** *Fig.* a new, fresh, and imaginative approach (to something). (*Typically: like ~.) □ *Sally, with all her wonderful ideas, is a breath of fresh air.*

breathe a sigh of relief 1. *Fig.* to sigh in a way that signals one's relief that something has come to an end. □ *At the end of the contest, we all breathed a sigh of relief.* **2.** *Fig.* to express relief that something has ended. (Fig. on ①.) □ *With the contract finally signed, we breathed a sigh of relief as we drank a toast in celebration.*

breathe down so's **neck 1.** *Fig.* to keep close watch on someone; to watch someone's activities intently. (Fig. on the image of someone standing very close behind a person.) □ *I will get through my life without your help. Stop breathing down my neck.* **2.** *Fig.* [for someone or something] to represent an approaching deadline. (Fig. on ①.) □ *The project deadline is breathing down my neck.*

breathe easy *Fig.* to assume a relaxed state after a stressful period. □ *After this crisis is over, I'll be able to breathe easy again.*

breathe one's **last** *Euph.* to die. □ *She breathed her last at about two o' clock that afternoon.*

breathe new life into sth *Fig.* to revive something; to introduce something new or positive into a situation. □ *Her positive attitude breathed new life into the company.*

breathe sth **(of** sth**) (to** so**)** *Fig.* to tell something to someone. (Usually in the negative.) □ *Don't breathe a word of this to anyone!*

breeze along *Fig.* to travel along casually, rapidly, and happily; to go through life in a casual and carefree manner. □ *We just breezed along the highway, barely paying attention to what we were doing.*

breeze away to leave quickly or abruptly. □ *She said nothing more. She just breezed away.*

breeze in(to some place**)** to enter a place quickly, in a happy and carefree manner. □ *She breezed into the conference room and sat down at the head of the table.*

breeze off to leave quickly or abruptly. □ *Don't just breeze off! Stay and talk.*

breeze out (of some place**)** to leave a place quickly. □ *She was here for a moment and then suddenly breezed out.*

breeze through (sth**) 1.** *Fig.* to complete some task rapidly and easily. □ *I breezed through my calculus assignment in no time at all.* **2.** *Fig.* to travel through a place rapidly. □ *They breezed through every little town without stopping.*

brew a plot *Fig.* to plot something; to make a plot. □ *The children brewed an evil plot to get revenge on their teacher.*

brew up *Fig.* to build up; [for something] to begin to build and grow. (Typically said of a storm or some other threat.) □ *A bad storm is brewing up in the west.* □ *Something serious is brewing up in the board room.*

brew sth **up**† *Fig.* to cause something to happen; to foment something. □ *I could see that they were brewing some kind of trouble up.*

bricks and mortar *Fig.* buildings; the expenditure of money on buildings rather than something else. (The buildings referred to can be constructed out of anything.) □ *Sometimes people are happy to donate millions of dollars for bricks and mortar, but they never think of the additional cost of annual maintenance.*

brick(s)-and-mortar [of businesses] based in buildings rather than relying on online sales over the Internet. □ *Many of the dot-com business owners have never been involved in a brick-and-mortar business.*

bridge the gap *Fig.* to do or create something that will serve temporarily. (The "gap" is temporal.) □ *We can bridge the gap with a few temporary employees.*

bridle at so/sth *Fig.* to show that one is offended by someone or something. □ *She bridled at the suggestion that she should go.*

bright and breezy *Fig.* cheery and alert. □ *Bright and breezy people on a gloomy day like this make me sick!*

bright and early *Fig.* very early in the morning or the workday. □ *I want to see you here on time tomorrow, bright and early, or you're fired!*

***bright as a button** intelligent; quick-minded. (Usually used to describe children. *Also: **as** ~.) □ *You can't fool Jane. She may be only six years old, but she's bright as a button.*

***bright as a new pin** bright and clean; shiny. (*Also: **as** ~.) □ *My kitchen floor is bright as a new pin since I started using this new floor wax.*

***a **bright idea** *Fig.* a clever thought or new idea. (*Typically: **have** ~; **get** ~; **give** so ~.) □ *Now and then I get a really bright idea!*

bright-eyed and bushy-tailed *Fig.* awake and alert. (The idea is that one is like a frisky animal, such as a squirrel.) □ *Despite the early hour, Dennis was bright-eyed and bushy-tailed.*

brim with sth Go to next.

brimming over (with sth) AND **brim with** sth to overflow with something. □ *The basket was brimming over with flowers.* □ *I was brimming with confidence after my recent success.*

bring a verdict in† [for a jury] to deliver its decision to the court. □ *Do you think they will bring a verdict in today?* □ *The jury brought in its verdict around midnight.*

bring sth **about**† *Fig.* to make something happen. □ *Is he clever enough to bring it about?*

bring so **around**† **1.** AND **bring** so **around (to consciousness)** *Fig.* to bring someone to consciousness. □ *The boxer was knocked out, but his manager brought him around.* **2.** AND **bring** so **around (to** one's **way of thinking); bring** so **around (to** one's **position)** *Fig.* to persuade someone (to accept something); to manage to get someone to agree (to something). □ *I knew I could bring her around if I just had enough time to talk to her.*

bring so **around (to consciousness)** Go to previous.

bring so **around (to** one's **way of thinking)** Go to bring so around†.

bring sth **back**† *Fig.* to restore an earlier style or practice. □ *Please bring the good old days back, so we can relax and have fun.*

bring so **back out** [for an applauding audience] to succeed in bringing a performer back onto the stage for a curtain call or encore. □ *They brought her back*

out about seven times, cheering and applauding.

bring sth **back**† **(to** so**)** *Fig.* to remind someone of something. □ *The funeral brought
lots of memories back to the grandmother.*

bring sth **back to life** *Fig.* to restore vitality to something, such as a performance,
a story, etc. □ *The third act of the play had
a clever twist that brought the whole
drama back to life.*

bring sth **crashing down (around** one**) 1.**
to cause a structure to collapse and fall
(on oneself). □ *He hit the tent pole and
brought the tent crashing down around
him.* **2.** *Fig.* to destroy something, such as
one's life and well-being, that one has a
special interest in; to cause someone's basic orientation to collapse. □ *She brought
her whole life crashing down around her.*

bring so **down**† **1.** *Fig.* to restore someone
to a normal mood or attitude. (After a
period of elation or, perhaps, drug use.)
□ *The bad news brought me down quickly.*
2. Go to bring so down (to earth).

bring sth **down**† **1.** to lower something,
such as prices, profits, taxes, etc. □ *The
governor pledged to bring taxes down.*
2. *Fig.* to defeat or overcome something,
such as an enemy, a government, etc. □
*The events of the last week will probably
bring the government down.*

bring so **down a peg (or two)** Go to take
so down a peg (or two).

bring sth **down**† **on** one**('s head)** *Fig.* to
cause the [figurative] collapse of some-
thing or some enterprise onto oneself. □
*Your bumbling will bring everything down
on your head!*

bring so **down (to earth)** *Fig.* to help
someone face reality; to help someone
who is euphoric become more realistic.
□ *The events helped bring us all down to
earth.* □ *I hate to be the one to bring you
down to earth, but things aren't as good
as you think.*

bring home the bacon *Inf.* to earn a
salary; to bring home money earned at a
job. □ *I've got to get to work if I'm going
to bring home the bacon.*

bring sth **home to** so *Fig.* to cause someone to realize something. □ *My weakness
was brought home to me by the heavy work
I had been assigned to do.*

bring so **in**† **(on** sth**)** *Fig.* to include someone in some deed or activity. □ *I'm go-
ing to have to bring a specialist in on this.*

bring sth **into being** *Fig.* to cause something to be; to create something. □ *How
can I bring my new scheme into being?*

bring sth **into blossom** *Fig.* to make a plant
or tree bloom. □ *The special plant food
brought the rosebush into blossom.*

bring sth **into focus** *Fig.* to make something clear and understandable. □ *Please
try to bring your major point into focus
earlier in the essay.*

bring sth **into line (with** sth**)** *Fig.* to make
someone or something conform to some-
one or something. □ *Sam brought his proposal into line with the company standards.*

bring sth **into play 1.** *Fig.* [in a ball game]
to put the ball into the action of the
game, such as after a timeout. □ *Fred
brought the ball into play when he bounced
it in from the sidelines.* **2.** *Fig.* [for the
shares of a company] to become the subject of a takeover bid. (Fig. on ①.) □ *The
recent drop in the value of that stock
brought the company into play.* □ *The
company was brought into play by a news
story about their new product line.* **3.** *Fig.*
to cause something to become a factor
in something. □ *Now, this recent development brings some other factors into play.*

bring sth **into question** Go to call sth into
question.

bring so **into the world 1.** *Fig.* to deliver
a baby; to attend the birth of someone. □
*I was brought into the world by a kindly
old doctor.* **2.** *Fig.* to give birth to a baby.
□ *Son, when I brought you into the world,
you weighed only five pounds.*

bring money **in**† *Fig.* to earn an amount of
money; to draw or attract an amount of
money. □ *My part-time job brings $50 in
every week.*

bring sth **off**[†] *Fig.* to cause something to happen; to carry out a plan successfully. □ *He brought off his plan without a hitch!*

bring so **on**[†] **1.** *Fig.* to bring someone out onto the stage. □ *Now, for the next act, I'm going to bring a chorus on, and I'm sure you'll love them.* **2.** *Fig.* to arouse someone romantically or sexually. □ *Ted sought to bring Sally on, but she was uninterested.*

bring sth **on**[†] **1.** *Fig.* to cause something to happen; to cause a situation to occur. □ *What brought this event on?* **2.** *Fig.* to cause a case or an attack of a disease. □ *What brought on your coughing fit?*

bring sth **on** so to cause something to go wrong for someone. □ *You brought it on yourself. Don't complain.*

bring sth **out**[†] *Fig.* to issue something; to publish something; to present something [to the public]. □ *I hear you have brought out a new edition of your book.*

bring sth **out**[†] **(in** so**)** *Fig.* to cause a particular quality to be displayed by a person, such as virtue, courage, a mean streak, selfishness, etc. □ *This kind of thing brings out the worst in me.*

bring people/animals **out in droves** *Fig.* to lure or draw out people or animals in great number. □ *The availability of free drinks brought people out in droves.* □ *The fresh grass sprouts brought the deer out in droves.*

bring sth **out of mothballs 1.** to remove something from storage in mothballs. □ *He brought his winter coat out of mothballs to wear to the funeral in Canada. Wow, did it stink!* **2.** *Fig.* to bring something out of storage and into use; to restore something to active service. (Fig. on ①.) □ *They were going to bring a number of ships out of mothballs, but the war ended before they needed them.*

bring out the best in so *Fig.* to cause someone to behave in the best manner. □ *This kind of situation doesn't exactly bring out the best in me.*

bring the curtain down[†] **(on** sth**)** Go to ring the curtain down[†] (on sth).

bring the house down[†] **1.** to cause a house to collapse or at least be heavily damaged. □ *The most severe earthquake in years finally brought the house down.* **2.** *Fig.* [for a performance or a performer] to excite the audience into making a great clamor of approval. (Fig. on ①. House = audience.) □ *Karen's act brought the house down.*

bring so **to** *Fig.* to help someone return to consciousness. □ *We worked to bring him to before he went into shock.*

bring one **to** oneself *Fig.* to cause one to become conscious or rational; to cause one to act normally. □ *I was brought to myself by some smelling salts.*

bring so **to** do sth *Fig.* to cause someone to do something; to encourage someone to do something. □ *What brought you to do this?*

bring so **to a boil** *Fig.* to make someone very angry. □ *This really brought her to a boil. She was fit to be tied.*

bring sth **to a climax** Go to next.

bring sth **to a close** AND **bring** sth **to a climax** *Fig.* to end something; to cause something to reach its final point and stop. □ *I think it is time to bring this matter to a close.* □ *The incident has been brought to a climax.*

bring sth **to a dead end** *Fig.* to cause something to reach a point from which it can go no further. □ *The study was brought to a dead end by the loss of federal funding.*

bring sth **to a head** *Fig.* to cause something to come to the point when a decision has to be made or action taken. □ *The latest disagreement between management and the union has brought matters to a head. There will be an all-out strike now.*

bring sth **to a standstill** to cause a process or a job to reach a point at which it must stop, possibly temporarily. □ *The strike brought construction to a standstill.*

bring so **to account** *Fig.* to confront someone with a record of misdeeds and errors. □ *The committee decided to bring Martha to account.*

bring so/sth **to** so's **attention** to make someone aware of someone or something; to mention or show someone or something to someone. □ *Thank you for bringing this to my attention.* □ *I am grateful for your bringing her to my attention.*

bring sth **to bear on** sth to apply some kind of information to a problem. □ *I have some new information to bring to bear on the current problem.*

bring an audience **to its feet** Go to next.

bring one **to** one's **feet** AND **bring** an audience **to its feet** *Fig.* to make someone or an audience rise up applauding or cheering in approval or in salute to someone or something. □ *The finale brought the audience to its feet.* □ *Liz was brought to her feet by the playing of the national anthem.*

bring sth **to fruition** *Fig.* to make something come into being; to achieve a success. □ *The plan was brought to fruition by the efforts of everyone.*

bring a dog **to heel** to make a dog heel; to make a dog stand or follow close to one's heels. □ *A quiet command from his owner brought Fido to heel.*

bring so **to heel** *Fig.* to cause someone to act in a disciplined fashion; to force someone to act in a more disciplined manner. (Fig. on bring a dog **to heel**.) □ *She tried to bring her husband to heel, but he had a mind of his own.*

bring one **to** one's **knees** *Lit.* to defeat or humble someone, perhaps to the point of bowing to pray. □ *An experience like that really brings a person to his knees.*

bring so/sth **to life** *Fig.* to give vigor or vitality to someone or something; to reactivate someone or something. □ *A little singing and dancing would have brought the play to life.*

bring so/sth **to light** *Fig.* to present or reveal someone or something to the public. □ *The newspaper story brought the problem to light.*

bring sth **to light** *Fig.* to make something known. □ *The scientists brought their findings to light.*

bring sth **to mind** Go to call sth to mind.

bring sth **to rest** *Fig.* to cause a machine, vehicle, or process to stop. □ *Jill brought the car to rest against the curb.*

bring one **to** one's **senses** *Fig.* to cause someone to return to normal [after being out of control or irrational]. □ *A gentle slap in the face brought him to his senses.*

bring sth **to the fore** to move something forward; to make something more prominent or noticeable. □ *All the talk about costs brought the question of budgets to the fore.*

bring sth **to the party** Go to next.

bring sth **to the table** AND **bring** sth **to the party** *Fig.* [for someone or something] to contribute something useful to an event or process. □ *Joel brings a lot of talent to the table. I hope he will participate.* □ *A little fresh ginger brings a bit of punch to the party. Add only a little to the mixing bowl.*

bring so/sth **to trial** to bring a crime or a criminal into court for a trial. □ *At last, the crooks were brought to trial.*

bring so **together** *Fig.* to attempt to get people to agree with one another. □ *I tried to bring them together on a fair price, but they were too stubborn.*

bring so/sth **up**† **1.** *Fig.* to mention someone or something. □ *Why did you have to bring that up?* **2.** *Fig.* to raise someone or something; to care for someone or something up to adulthood. □ *We brought up the puppies carefully and sold them for a good profit.*

bring sth **up**† **1.** *Euph.* to vomit something up; to cough something up. □ *See if you can get him to bring the penny up.* **2.** *Fig.* to mention something. □ *Why did you have to bring that problem up?*

bring so **up**† **for** sth **1.** *Fig.* to suggest someone's name for something. □ *I would like to bring Beth up for vice president.* **2.** *Fig.* to put someone's name up for promotion, review, discipline, etc. □ *We brought Tom up for promotion.*

bring so **up**† **on** sth *Fig.* to provide something while raising a child to adulthood. □ *She brought her children up on fast food.*

bring so **up sharply** AND **bring** so **up short** *Fig.* to surprise or shock someone; to make someone face something unpleasant, suddenly. □ *The slap in the face brought me up sharply.* □ *The loud bang brought me up short.*

bring so **up short** Go to previous.

bring up the rear *Fig.* to move along behind everyone else; to be at the end of the line. (Originally referred to marching soldiers. Fixed order.) □ *Hurry up, Tom! Why are you always bringing up the rear?*

bring so/sth **up-to-date** *Fig.* to modernize someone or something. □ *We brought the room up-to-date with a little paint and some modern furniture.*

bring so **up-to-date (on** so/sth**)** *Fig.* to inform someone of the latest information about something. □ *Let me bring you up-to-date on what is happening in the village.*

bring sth **(up)on** oneself *Fig.* to be the cause of one's own trouble. (*Upon* is more formal and less commonly used than *on.*) □ *It's your own fault. You brought it upon yourself.*

bring sth **with** *Inf.* to carry something along with [oneself]. (Informal or regional.) □ *Are you going to bring your umbrella with?*

bristle at sth *Fig.* to show sudden anger or other negative response to something. (Fig. on the image of a dog or cat raising the hair on its back in anger or as a threat.) □ *She bristled at the suggestion.*

bristle with anger Go to bristle with rage.

bristle with indignation Go to next.

bristle with rage AND **bristle with anger; bristle with indignation** *Fig.* to demonstrate one's anger, rage, or displeasure with a strong negative response. (Fig. on the image of a dog or cat raising the hair on its back in anger or as a threat.) □ *She was just bristling with anger. I don't know what set her off.* □ *Walter bristled with rage as he saw the damage to his new car.*

*broad as a barn door very broad or wide. (*Also: as* ~.) □ *Jim's backside is as broad as a barn door.*

broad in the beam 1. [of a ship] wide at amidships. □ *This old tub is broad in the beam and sits like a ball in the water, but I love her.* **2.** *Inf.* with wide hips or large buttocks. (Fig. on ①.) □ *I am getting a little broad in the beam. It's time to go on a diet.*

broken dreams *Fig.* wishes or desires that cannot be fulfilled. □ *We all have our share of broken dreams, but they were never all meant to come true anyway.*

a **broken reed** an unreliable or undependable person. (On the image of a useless, broken reed in a reed instrument.) □ *Mr. Smith is a broken reed. His deputy has to make all the decisions.*

*brown as a berry very brown from the sun; quite suntanned. (*Also: as* ~.) □ *She was out in the sun so much that she became as brown as a berry.*

brown so **off**† *Sl.* to make someone angry. □ *You really brown me off!*

brown out 1. *Fig.* [for the electricity] to diminish in power and dim the lights, causing a brownout. (Something less than a *blackout,* when there is no power.) □ *The lights started to brown out, and I thought maybe there was a power shortage.* **2.** *Fig.* a period of dimming or fading of the electricity. (Spelled **brownout.**) □ *They keep building all these expensive power stations, and then we still have brownouts!*

browned (off) *Sl.* angry. □ *I am really browned off at you!* □ *The boss really got browned—to say the least; he fired me!*

brush so/sth **aside**† *Fig.* to rid oneself of someone or something; to ignore or dismiss someone or something. □ *The clerk brushed aside the old man and moved on to the next person in line.*

brush so **off**† **1.** to remove something, such as dust or lint, from someone by brushing. □ *The bathroom attendant brushed Mr. Harris off and was rewarded with a small tip.* **2.** *Fig.* to reject someone; to dis-

59

miss someone. (As if someone were mere lint.) □ *He brushed her off, telling her she had no appointment.*

brush over so/sth *Fig.* to deal lightly with an important person or matter; to just barely mention someone or something. □ *I want to hear more. You only brushed over the part I was interested in.*

brush sth **up**† *Fig.* to improve one's knowledge of something or one's ability to do something. □ *I need to brush my French up a little bit.* □ *I need to brush up my French.*

brush up (on sth**)** *Fig.* to improve one's knowledge of something or one's ability to do something. □ *I need to brush up on my German.* □ *My German is weak. I had better brush up.*

a **brush with death** *Fig.* an instance of nearly dying. □ *After a brush with death in an automobile accident, Claire seemed more friendly and outgoing.*

*the **brush-off** *Fig.* rejection; being cast aside and ignored. (*Typically: **get** ~; **give** so ~.) □ *Don't try to talk to Tom. He'll just give you the brush-off.*

bubble over 1. [for boiling or effervescent liquid] to spill or splatter over the edge of its container. □ *The pot bubbled over and put out the flame on the stove.* **2.** *Fig.* [for someone] to be so happy and merry that the joy "spills over" onto other people. (Fig. on ①.) □ *She was just bubbling over, she was so happy.*

buck for sth *Sl.* to work ambitiously for something, such as a promotion. □ *I'm just bucking for recognition, and of course, a 20 percent raise.* □ *You can tell by her attention to the boss that she's bucking for promotion.*

The **buck stops here.** *Fig.* The need to act or take responsibility, that other people pass on to still other people, ultimately ends up here. (An expression made famous by U.S. President Harry Truman, about the decisions a president must make. See also **pass the buck**.) □ *After everyone else has avoided making the de-*cision, I will have to do it. The buck stops here.*

buck the system *Fig.* to oppose or fight the system. (See also **(You) can't fight city hall**.) □ *I like nothing better than bucking the system! Let's go down to the bank and raise a little hell!*

buck up *Fig.* to cheer up; to perk up. □ *Come on, now, buck up. Things can't be all that bad.*

buckle down (to sth**)** *Fig.* to settle down to something; to begin to work seriously at something. □ *If you don't buckle down to your job, you'll be fired.*

buckle under (sth**)** to collapse under or from the weight of something. □ *The bridge buckled under the weight of the truck and collapsed.*

a **budding genius** *Fig.* a very bright and promising young person. □ *Harry is a budding genius, and he seems like a fairly normal teenager.*

buddy up (to so**)** *Fig.* to become overly familiar or friendly with someone. □ *Don't try to buddy up to me now. It won't do any good.*

buddy up (with so**)** *Fig.* to join with another person to form a pair that will do something together or share something. □ *Carl and I buddied up, and we shared a canoe.*

bug so *Inf.* to irritate someone; to bother someone. □ *Leave me alone. Go bug somebody else.*

bug out 1. *Sl.* to pack up and leave or retreat; to get out. (Military.) □ *Orders are to bug out by oh-nine-hundred.* **2.** *Sl.* to become very upset; to **freak out (over** so/sth**).** □ *What a terrible experience. I almost bugged out!*

build a better mousetrap *Fig.* to develop or invent something superior to a device that is widely used. (From the old saying, "If you build a better mousetrap, the world will beat a path to your door.") □ *Harry thought he could build a better mousetrap, but everything he "invented" had already been thought of.*

build castles in Spain Go to next.

build castles in the air AND **build castles in Spain** *Fig.* to daydream; to make plans that can never come true. □ *Ann spends most of her waking hours building castles in Spain.* □ *I really like to sit on the porch in the evening, just building castles in the air.*

build one's **hopes on** so/sth AND **place** one's **hopes on** so/sth *Fig.* to make plans or have aspirations based on someone or something. □ *I have built my hopes on making a success of this business.*

build sth **into** sth AND **build** sth **in**† **1.** to integrate a piece of furniture or an appliance into a building's construction. □ *We will build this cupboard into the wall about here.* **2.** to make a particular quality a basic part of something. □ *We build quality into our cars before we put our name on them.* **3.** to make a special restriction or specification a part of the plan of something. □ *The lawyer built in the requirement that payments be by certified check.*

build sth **to order** *Fig.* to build an individual object according to a special set of specifications. □ *The car will be built to order.*

build so/sth **up**† *Fig.* to advertise, praise, or promote someone or something. □ *Advertising can build a product up so much that everyone will want it.*

build sth **up**† **1.** to add buildings to an area of land or a neighborhood. □ *They are really building this area up. There is no more open space.* **2.** *Fig.* to develop, accumulate, or increase something, such as wealth, business, goodwill, etc. □ *I built this business up through hard work and hope.* **3.** *Fig.* to praise or exalt something; to exaggerate the virtues of something. □ *The master of ceremonies built the act up so much that everyone was disappointed when they saw it.*

build so **up**† **(for** sth**)** *Fig.* to prepare someone for something; to bring a person into a state of mind to accept some informa-

tion. □ *We built them up for the challenge they were to face.*

build so/sth **up**† **(from** sth**)** to transform someone or something from a lowly start to a higher state. □ *I built up this business from nothing.*

build up to sth **1.** *Fig.* [for a person] to lead up to something or advance to doing or saying something. □ *I can tell you are building up to something. What is it?* **2.** *Fig.* [for a situation] to develop into something. □ *The argument is building up to something unpleasant.*

build sth **(up)on** sth *Fig.* to add to and develop something that already exists. □ *We have a good reputation, and we must build on it.*

build (up)on sth **1.** to construct something on a particular space. (*Upon* is more formal and less commonly used than *on*.) □ *Are you going to build upon this land?* □ *Yes, we will build on it.* **2.** to start with something and add to it. (*Upon* is more formal and less commonly used than *on*.) □ *Our progress has been good so far. Let's build on it.* □ *We will build upon the success of our forebears.*

built like a brick outhouse AND **built like a brick shithouse** *Inf.* well-built—either strong or full-sized. (Built more strongly than is typical. Caution with *shit*.) □ *Look at that guy's muscles—he's built like a brick shithouse.* □ *This garage is built like a brick outhouse. It'll last for years.*

built like a brick shithouse Go to previous.

bulk so **up**† to add bulk or weight to someone. □ *Dario ate and ate, trying to bulk up for the football season.*

bulldoze into sth *Fig.* to move clumsily into something. □ *Don't just bulldoze into me! Watch where you are going!*

bulldoze through sth *Fig.* to push clumsily and carelessly through something. □ *Don't just bulldoze through your work!*

Bully for you! 1. *Inf.* an expression that praises someone or someone's courage. (Dated.) □ *The elderly audience shouted,*

"Bravo! Bully for you!" **2.** *Inf.* a sarcastic phrase belittling someone's statement or accomplishment. □ *Bob: I managed to save three dollars last week. Bill: Well, bully for you!*

bum around (with so**)** *Inf.* to spend or waste a lot of time with a particular person. □ *He used to bum around with Ted a lot.*

bum sth **off** so *Sl.* to beg or borrow something from someone. □ *Can I bum a cigarette off you?*

bum out *Sl.* to have a bad experience. (Originally referred to a bad experience with drugs.) □ *Are you going to bum out again tonight?*

bum so **out**† *Sl.* to disappoint someone. □ *The plotless and tasteless movie bummed out the entire audience.*

*the **bum's rush** *Inf.* the act of hurrying someone out of a place. (As someone might quickly escort a vagrant from a fancy restaurant. *Typically: **get** ~; **give** so ~.) □ *The young customer in the jewelry store was getting the bum's rush until he pulled out an enormous roll of bills.*

*a **bum steer** *Inf.* misleading instructions or guidance; a misleading suggestion. (*Bum* = false; phony. *Steer* = guidance, as in the steering of a car. *Typically: **get** ~; **have** ~; **give** so ~.) □ *Wilbur gave Ted a bum steer, and Ted ended up in the wrong town.*

bummed (out) *Sl.* discouraged; depressed. □ *I feel so bummed! I think I need a nice hot bath.*

bump into so AND **run into** so; **run across** so *Fig.* to chance on someone; to meet someone by chance. (Not normally with physical contact.) □ *Guess who I bumped into downtown today?* □ *I ran into Bill Jones yesterday.*

bump so **off**† AND **knock** so **off**† *Sl.* to kill someone. □ *They tried to bump him off, but he was too clever and got away.* □ *The crooks threatened to knock off the witness to the crime.*

Bump that! *Sl.* Forget that! □ *Bump that! I was wrong.*

bump so/sth **up**† **1.** *Fig.* to raise someone or something to a higher category or level. (As if pushing someone into a higher category.) □ *I wanted to fly first class, but they wouldn't bump me up.* **2.** to damage or batter someone or something. □ *The crash into the wall bumped the race driver up a little.*

bumper to bumper *Fig.* [of traffic] close together and moving slowly. □ *The traffic is bumper to bumper from the accident up ahead.*

a **bunch of fives** *Sl.* a punch from a closed fist. □ *How would you like a bunch of fives right in the kisser?*

bunch up to pack together or cluster. □ *Spread out. Don't bunch up!*

bunch so/sth **up**† to pack or cluster things or people together. □ *Bunch them up so you can squeeze them into the sack.* □ *Kelly bunched up the roses and put them in a vase.*

bundle from heaven Go to next.

bundle of joy AND **bundle from heaven** *Fig.* a baby. □ *We are expecting a bundle of joy next September.* □ *When your little bundle from heaven arrives, things will be a little hectic for a while.*

a **bundle of nerves** a very nervous person. □ *I was a bundle of nerves before my dental appointment.*

bung sth **in**† *Fig.* to cram or bang something into something. □ *He bunged the cork into the barrel.*

bung sth **up**† *Inf.* to damage someone or something by blows. □ *Last time I put up the storm windows, I really bunged up my hands.*

bunged up battered or bruised. □ *It used to be a nice table, but it got all bunged up.*

bunk down (for the night) to bed down for the night; to go to bed. □ *Where are you going to bunk down for the night?*

bunk (up) with so to share a bed, a bedroom, or a tent with someone. □ *Are you going to bunk up with Fred?*

buoy so **up**† *Fig.* to support, encourage, or sustain someone. □ *The good news* *buoyed her up considerably.* □ *Her good humor buoyed up the entire party.*

burden so **with** so/sth *Fig.* to bother or "weigh down" someone with someone or something. □ *Please don't burden us with the bad news at this time.* □ *I don't want to burden the school with a troublesome child.*

burn so **at the stake 1.** to set fire to a person tied to a post as a form of execution. □ *They used to burn witches at the stake.* **2.** *Fig.* to chastise or denounce someone severely or excessively. (Fig. on ①.) □ *Stop yelling! I made a simple mistake, and you're burning me at the stake for it!*

burn one's **bridges (behind** one) **1.** *Fig.* to cut off the way back to where you came from, making it impossible to retreat. □ *By blowing up the road, the spies had burned their bridges behind them.* **2.** *Fig.* to act unpleasantly in a situation that you are leaving, ensuring that you'll never be welcome to return. (Fig. on ①.) □ *If you get mad and quit your job, you'll be burning your bridges behind you.* □ *No sense burning your bridges. Be polite and leave quietly.* **3.** *Fig.* to make decisions that cannot be changed in the future. (Fig. on ①.) □ *If you drop out of school now, you'll be burning your bridges behind you.*

burn one's **bridges in front of** one *Fig.* to create future problems for oneself. (A play on **burn** one's **bridges (behind** one).) □ *I accidentally insulted a math teacher whom I will have to take a course from next semester. I am burning my bridges in front of me!*

burn so **down**† *Sl.* to humiliate someone. □ *You just want to burn down everybody to make yourself seem better.*

burn one's **fingers** Go to **get** one's **fingers burned.**

burn sth **in**† *Fig.* to run a piece of new electronic equipment for a while, making certain that all the electrical parts will last a long time. □ *Please burn this computer in for a couple of hours before you deliver it.*

burn so **in effigy** to burn a dummy or other figure that represents a hated person. □ *For the third day in a row, they burned the king in effigy.*

burn sth **into** sth AND **burn** sth **in**† *Fig.* to implant something firmly in someone's head, brain, memory, etc. □ *She burned the information into her head.*

burn out 1. [for a motor or electronics] to fail. □ *All the lights in the kitchen burned out in a week!* **2.** to get really tired of something, such as a job. □ *I taught for many years, then I burned out. I went into sales and made a lot of money.*

burn so **out**† *Fig.* to make someone ineffective through overuse or overwork. (*Someone* includes oneself.) □ *Facing all these problems at once will burn Tom out.* □ *I burned myself out as a competitive swimmer. I just cannot stand to practice anymore.* □ *Tom burned himself out in that boring job.*

burn the candle at both ends *Fig.* to work very hard and stay up very late at night. (Figuratively, one end of the candle is work done in the daylight, and the other end is work done at night.) □ *No wonder Mary is ill. She has been burning the candle at both ends for a long time.*

burn the midnight oil *Fig.* to stay up working, especially studying, late at night. (Fig. on working by the light of an oil lamp late in the night.) □ *I have a big exam tomorrow, so I'll be burning the midnight oil tonight.*

burn sth **to a crisp** to burn something totally or very badly. □ *The cook burned the meat to a crisp.*

burn so **up**† *Fig.* to make someone very angry; to make someone endure the "heat" of rage. □ *You really burn me up! I'm very angry at you!*

burn sth **up**† *Fig. Inf.* to use up a lot of something. □ *We sure burn up a lot of paper towels around here.*

burn with a low blue flame 1. *Lit.* [of a properly adjusted gas burner] to burn and put off heat. □ *Each burner on the stove burns with a low blue flame giving the maximum amount of heat.* **2.** *Fig.* to be quietly and intensely angry. (Fig. comparing the heat of the anger to the heat of the low blue flame.) □ *She accidentally dumped her whole plate in her lap, and just sat there, burning with a low blue flame.* **3.** *Fig.* to be heavily intoxicated with alcohol. (Fig. on the amount of flammable alcohol ingested.) □ *He's not just drunk, he's burning with a low blue flame.*

burned to a cinder *Fig. Lit.* burned very badly. □ *I stayed out in the sun too long, and I am burned to a cinder.* □ *This toast is burnt to a cinder.*

burned up *Fig.* very angry. □ *My new assistant's mistakes are so maddening! I've never been so burned up in my life.*

a **burning question** AND the **burning question** *Fig.* a question whose answer is of great interest to everyone; a question that needs very much to be answered, as a fire needs to be extinguished. □ *There's a burning question that needs to be answered: Why did you leave your wife of only one month?*

burst See also entries at bust.

burst at the seams *Fig.* [for someone] to strain from holding in pride or laughter as if one might burst. □ *We laughed so hard we just about burst at the seams.*

burst so's **bubble** *Fig.* to destroy someone's illusion or delusion; to destroy someone's fantasy. □ *I hate to burst your bubble, but Columbus did not discover Canada.*

burst forth to come forth explosively. □ *The blossoms burst forth in the first warm days of the year.*

burst in (on so/sth**)** Go to barge in (on so/sth).

burst into sth to suddenly display a characteristic or a behavior. (See nearby entries.) □ *Bob burst into laughter and frightened the horse.* □ *Dario burst into a coughing fit and disrupted the meeting.*

burst into flame(s) [for something] to catch fire and become a large fire quickly. □ *The two cars burst into flames soon after the collision.*

burst into sight *Fig.* to come into view suddenly. □ *Suddenly, a tiger burst into sight and caught the hunter off guard.*

burst into tears AND **burst out crying** *Fig.* to begin to cry suddenly. □ *After the last notes of her song, the audience burst into tears, such was its beauty and tenderness.*

burst onto the scene *Fig.* to appear suddenly in a location. □ *The police suddenly burst onto the scene and arrested everyone in the room.*

burst out doing sth *Fig.* to begin to do something suddenly, such as cry, laugh, shout, etc. □ *Suddenly, she burst out singing.* □ *Ted burst out laughing when he read the joke.*

burst out crying Go to burst into tears.

burst out with sth *Fig.* to utter something loudly and suddenly. □ *The child burst out with a scream.*

burst with sth *Fig.* to be full to the bursting point with some expression of an emotion, such as excitement, joy, pride.) □ *Joe was just bursting with excitement because of his triumph.* □ *When I got my grades, I could have burst with joy.* □ *I almost burst with pride when I was chosen for the first prize.*

bury one's **head in the sand** AND **hide** one's **head in the sand; have** one's **head in the sand; stick** one's **head in the sand** *Fig.* to ignore or hide from obvious signs of danger. (Fig. on the image of an ostrich, which is believed incorrectly to hide its head in a hole in the ground when it sees danger.) □ *Stop burying your head in the sand. Look at the statistics on smoking and cancer.*

bury oneself **in** sth *Fig.* to become very busy with something. (Fig. on being covered in the materials of one's work.) □ *She stopped taking phone calls and buried herself in her work.*

bury the hatchet *Fig.* to make peace. (Fig. on the image of warring tribes burying a tomahawk as a symbol of ending a war.) □ *Let's stop arguing and bury the hatchet.*

*the **business 1.** *Fig.* harassment; a scolding; general bad treatment. (*Typically: **get** ~; **give** so ~.) □ *The guys have been giving me the business about my new hairstyle.* **2.** *Sl.* an execution. (Underworld. *Typically: **get** ~; **give** so ~.) □ *The mob wanted to give him the business for confessing to the federal prosecutor.*

business as usual *Fig.* having things go along as usual. □ *Even right after the flood, it was business as usual in all the stores.* □ *Please, everyone, business as usual. Let's get back to work.*

the **business end of** sth *Fig.* the part or end of something that actually does the work or carries out the procedure. □ *Keep away from the business end of the electric drill so you won't get hurt.* □ *Don't point the business end of that gun at anyone. It might go off.*

a **busman's holiday** leisure time spent doing something similar to what one does at work. (*Fig.* on the notion of a bus driver going on a bus tour for his vacation or on a day off.) □ *Tutoring students in the evening is a busman's holiday for our English teacher.*

bust a bronco *Fig.* to ride and thus tame a wild horse so that it can be ridden. (*Bust* is a nonstandard form of *burst*.) □ *That was the meanest bronco I ever seen. Nobody could bust 'im.*

bust a gut Go to split a gut.

bust a move *Sl.* to leave [a place]. □ *Let's go. Time to bust a move.*

bust ass out of some place *Sl.* to get out of someplace in a hurry. (Caution with *ass*.) □ *I had to bust ass out of the house and run all the way to school.*

bust (one's) ass (to do sth**) AND break** one's **balls to** do sth; **bust** one's **butt to** do sth; **bust** one's **nuts to** do sth *Sl.* to work very hard to do something. (The expressions with *balls* and *nuts* are said typically, but not necessarily, of a male. Caution with *ass*.) □ *I've been busting my ass to get this thing done on time, and now they don't want it!* □ *The new boss expects you to bust your nuts every minute you are at work at the warehouse.*

bust (so's**) balls** Go to break (so's) balls.

bust one's **butt to** do sth Go to bust (one's) ass (to do sth).

bust one's **nuts to** do sth Go to bust (one's) ass (to do sth).

bust so **one** *Sl.* to punch someone; to give someone a punch, probably in the face. (*Bust* is a nonstandard form of *burst* = "hit" here.) □ *You better shut up, or I'll bust you one!*

bust out laughing *Inf.* to start laughing suddenly. (See also burst out doing sth. *Bust* is a nonstandard form of *burst*.) □ *The bridegroom was so nervous, it was all he could do not to bust out laughing.*

bust out (of some place**)** *Sl.* to break out of some place, especially a prison. (*Bust* is a nonstandard form of *burst* = "break" here.) □ *Somehow the gangsters busted out of prison and left the country.*

bust so **out of** some place AND **bust** so **out**† **1.** *Sl.* to help someone escape from prison. (*Bust* is a nonstandard form of *burst* = "break" here.) □ *Lefty managed to bust Max out of prison.* **2.** *Sl.* to expel or force someone to withdraw from school. (*Bust* is a nonstandard form of *burst* = "break" here.) □ *The dean finally busted Bill out of school for low academic performance.*

bust (some) suds 1. *Sl.* to drink some beer. (*Bust* is a nonstandard form of *burst*.) □ *Let's go out and bust some suds.* **2.** *Sl.* to wash dishes. (*Bust* is a nonstandard form of *burst*.) □ *I don't want to spend the rest of my life busting suds.*

bust (so's**) stones** Go to break (so's) balls.

bust up 1. *Sl.* [for lovers] to separate or break up. (*Bust* is a nonstandard form of *burst* = "break" here.) □ *Tom and Alice busted up for good.* **2.** *Sl.* [for something] to break up due to natural causes. (*Bust* is a nonstandard form of *burst* = "break (apart)" here.) □ *The rocket busted up in midair.*

bust so **up**† **1.** *Sl.* to cause lovers to separate; to break up a pair of lovers, including married persons. (*Bust* is a nonstandard form of *burst* = "break (apart)" here.) □ *Mary busted Terri and John up by spreading gossip.* **2.** *Sl.* to beat someone up; to batter someone. (*Bust* is a nonstandard form of *burst* = "hit" here.) □ *Max busted up Lefty pretty badly.*

bust sth **up**† **1.** *Inf.* to break or ruin something; to break something into smaller pieces. (*Bust* is a nonstandard form of *burst* = "break" here.) □ *Who busted this plate up?* **2.** *Sl.* to ruin a marriage by coming between the married people. (See also **bust** so **up.** *Bust* is a nonstandard form of *burst* = "break" here.) □ *He busted their marriage up by starting rumors about Maggie.*

bust sth **wide open** Go to **blow** sth **wide open.**

***busy as a beaver (building a new dam)** AND ***busy as a bee;** ***busy as a one-armed paperhanger;** ***busy as Grand Central Station;** ***busy as a cat on a hot tin roof;** ***busy as a fish peddler in Lent;** ***busy as a cranberry merchant (at Thanksgiving);** ***busy as popcorn on a skillet** very busy. (*Also: **as** ~.*) □ *My boss keeps me as busy as a one-armed paperhanger.* □ *I don't have time to talk to you. I'm as busy as a beaver.* □ *When the tourist season starts, this store is busy as Grand Central Station.* □ *Sorry I can't go to lunch with you. I'm as busy as a beaver building a new dam.*

busy as a bee Go to previous.

busy as a cat on a hot tin roof Go to **busy as a beaver (building a new dam).**

busy as a cranberry merchant (at Thanksgiving) Go to **busy as a beaver (building a new dam).**

busy as a fish peddler in Lent Go to **busy as a beaver (building a new dam).**

***busy as a hibernating bear** not busy at all. (*Also: **as** ~.*) □ *He lounged on the sofa all day, busy as a hibernating bear.*

busy as a one-armed paperhanger Go to **busy as a beaver (building a new dam).**

busy as Grand Central Station Go to **busy as a beaver (building a new dam).**

busy as popcorn on a skillet Go to **busy as a beaver (building a new dam).**

but for so/sth *Fig.* if it were not for someone or something. □ *But for the children, Mrs. Smith would have left her husband years ago.*

but good *Fig.* severely; thoroughly. □ *She told him off but good.*

butt in (on so/sth**)** to interrupt a conversation; to enter a place where people are conversing and interrupt. □ *I wish you wouldn't keep butting in!*

the **butt of a joke** *Fig.* the reason for or aim of a joke, especially when it is a person. (*Butt* = target.) □ *Poor Fred was the butt of every joke told that evening.*

butt out *Inf.* to exit [as abruptly as one has intruded]. (Compare this with **butt in (on** so/sth**).** Usually a command.) □ *Butt out! Leave me alone!*

one's **(butter and) egg money** *Fig.* money that a farm woman earns. (Farm women would often sell butter and eggs for extra money that would be stashed away for an emergency.) □ *Jane was saving her butter and egg money for a new TV.*

butter so **up**† AND **butter up to** so *Fig.* to flatter someone; to treat someone especially nicely in hopes of receiving special favors. □ *A student tried to butter the teacher up.*

***butterflies in** one's **stomach** *Fig.* a nervous feeling in one's stomach. (*Typically: **get** ~; **have** ~; **give** one ~.*) □ *Whenever I have to speak in public, I get butterflies in my stomach.*

button up *Fig.* to get silent and stay silent. (See also **button (up)** one's **lip.**) □ *Hey, button up! That's enough out of you.*

button (up) one's **lip** *Fig.* to stop talking. (Fixed order.) □ *Will you button your lip? I don't want the news to get out.*

buttress sth **up**† *Fig.* to provide extra support, often financial support, for something. □ *We rounded up some money to buttress the company up through the sales slump.*

buy sth AND **fall for** sth *Fig.* to believe someone; to accept something to be a fact. □ *It may be true, but I don't fall for it.* □ *I* *just don't buy the idea that you can swim that far.*

buy a pig in a poke *Fig.* to buy something without looking inside first. (Fig. on the notion of buying a pig in a sack [*poke* is a folksy word for a sack or bag], without looking at it to see how good a pig it is.) □ *If you don't get a good look at the engine of a used car before you buy it, you'll wind up buying a pig in a poke.*

buy a round (of drinks) AND **buy the next round (of drinks)** *Fig.* to buy a drink for each person present, with the expectation that one or more of those persons will later do likewise. □ *Which one of you guys is going to buy the next round?*

buy sth **for a song** Go to for a song.

buy in(to sth) **1.** *Fig.* to purchase shares of something; to buy a part of something the ownership of which is shared with other owners. □ *I bought into a company that makes dog food.* □ *Sounds like a good company. I would like to buy in.* **2.** *Fig.* to agree with; to accept an idea as worthwhile. (Fig. on ①.) □ *The committee liked my proposal and decided to buy into my plan.*

buy it Go to buy the farm.

buy so **off**† *Fig.* to bribe someone to ignore what one is doing wrong. □ *Do you think you can buy her off?*

buy sth **on time** *Fig.* to buy something on credit. □ *I bought the sofa on time, but I paid cash for the chairs.*

buy sth **sight unseen** *Fig.* to buy something without seeing it first. □ *I bought this land sight unseen. I didn't know it was so rocky.*

buy the big one AND **bite the big one** *Sl.* to die. □ *I don't plan to buy the big one for at least another thirty years.*

buy the farm AND **buy it** *Sl.* to die; to get killed. (Possibly, to buy a grave site. Other proposed origins involve buying an actual farm, such as with a dead pilot's insurance money.) □ *I'll pass through this illness; I'm too young to buy the farm.*

buy the next round (of drinks) Go to buy a round (of drinks).

buy time *Fig.* to postpone an event hoping that the situation will improve. □ *You are just stalling to buy time.* □ *Maybe I can buy some time by asking the judge for a continuance.*

buy trouble *Fig.* to encourage trouble; to bring on trouble. □ *Saying something insulting to him is just buying trouble. He already hates you.*

buy one's **way in(to** sth) *Fig.* to achieve entry or membership in something often by paying money. □ *Do you think you can buy your way into this fraternity?*

buy one's **way out (of** sth) *Fig.* to get out of trouble by bribing or influencing someone to ignore what one has done wrong. □ *You can't buy your way out of this mess, buster!*

buy so's **wolf ticket** *Sl.* to challenge someone's boast or taunt. □ *He wants me to buy his wolf ticket bad.*

Buy you a drink? Go to (Could I) buy you a drink?

buzz along to move or drive along fast. □ *The cars were buzzing along at a great rate.*

buzz for so to sound a signal for someone. □ *I buzzed for my secretary and waited for a reply.*

buzz in(to some place) *Fig.* to come into a place rapidly or unexpectedly. □ *The child buzzed into the shop and bought a nickel's worth of candy.*

buzz so **into** some place AND **buzz** so **in**† *Fig.* to push a button that opens a door latch electrically, allowing someone to use the door and enter. (The process creates a buzz while the latch is open.) □ *Oh, hello. I will buzz you into the lobby. Then take the elevator to apartment 310.*

buzz off *Fig.* to leave quickly. □ *I've got to buzz off. Bye.*

buzz with sth *Fig.* [for a place] to be busy or filled with something. □ *The room buzzed with excitement.*

by a hair('s breadth) AND **by a whisker** *Fig.* just barely; by a very small distance.

□ *I just missed getting on the plane by a hair's breadth.* □ *I made it onto the last flight by a hair!*

by a mile *Fig.* by a great distance. (Usually an exaggeration.) □ *You missed the target by a mile.* □ *Your estimate of the budget deficit was off by a mile.*

by a show of hands *Fig.* [of a vote taken] expressed by people raising their hands. □ *Bob wanted us to vote on paper, not by a show of hands, so that we could have a secret ballot.*

by a whisker Go to by a hair('s breadth).

by all appearances *Fig.* apparently; according to what one sees or how things seem. □ *She is, by all appearances, ready to resume work.*

by all means *Fig.* certainly; yes; absolutely. □ *Bob: Can you come to dinner tomorrow? Jane: By all means. I'd love to.*

by all means of sth *Fig.* trying to do something by the use of every possible manner of something. □ *People will be arriving by all means of transportation.*

by and by *Fig.* at some time in the future; as time passes. □ *You may think your heart is broken, but you'll feel better by and by.*

by and large *Fig.* generally; usually. (Originally a nautical expression.) □ *I find that, by and large, people tend to do what they are told to do.*

by ankle express *Inf.* on foot. □ *After my horse was stolen, I had to go by ankle express.*

by any means *Fig.* by any way possible. □ *I need to get there soon by any means.*

by brute strength *Fig.* by great muscular strength. □ *The men moved the heavy door by brute strength.*

by chance *Fig.* accidentally; randomly; without planning. □ *I found this book by chance at a book sale.*

by coincidence *Fig.* by an accidental and strange similarity; by an unplanned pairing of events or occurrences. □ *By coincidence, the circus was in town when I was there. I'm glad because I love circuses.*

by day AND **by night** *Fig.* during the day; during the night. □ *By day, Mary worked in an office; by night, she took classes.* □ *Dave slept by day and worked by night.*

by degrees little by little. □ *I got into the cold, cold water by degrees. I couldn't bring myself to dive in.*

by dint of sth *Fig.* because of something; due to the efforts of something. (*Dint* is an old word = "force," and it is never used except in this phrase.) □ *They got the building finished on time by dint of hard work and good organization.*

by fits and starts Go to fits and starts.

by force of habit *Fig.* owing to a tendency to do something that has become a habit. □ *After I retired, I kept getting up and getting dressed each morning by force of habit.*

By Godfrey! *Inf.* By God! (A mild, minced oath, based on *By God!*) □ *By Godfrey, Jim's brother is a big man!* □ *Those cats sure do make a lot of noise, by Godfrey.*

by guess and by golly Go to next.

by guess and by gosh AND **by guess and by golly** *Rur.* by estimating; without careful planning. □ *Jane: Did you have a plan for putting up that tool shed? Tom: Nope, we just sort of did it by guess and by golly.*

by halves partially; in an incomplete manner; without complete attention. □ *You need to devote your full attention to this problem. You will not be able to solve it by halves.*

by hand *Fig.* made by human hands and handheld tools as opposed to a machine. □ *This fine wooden cabinet was made by hand.*

*by heart *Fig.* completely memorized. (*Typically: **know** sth ~; **learn** sth ~; **play** sth ~; **recite** sth ~.) □ *I went over and over it until I knew it by heart.* □ *I know the words by heart.*

by hook or (by) crook *Inf.* by any means, legal or illegal. □ *I must have that house. I intend to get it by hook or crook.*

*by leaps and bounds *Fig.* rapidly; at a high rate of change. (*Typically: **grow** ~;

gain ~**; increase** ~**; expand** ~.) □ *The profits of my company are increasing by leaps and bounds.*

by main strength and awkwardness *Rur.* by force or brute strength. □ *By main strength and awkwardness, we got all the luggage crammed into the car.*

by mistake *Fig.* in error; accidentally. □ *I chose the wrong road by mistake. Now we are lost.*

by night Go to by day.

by no means AND **not by any means** *Fig.* absolutely not; certainly not. □ *Bob: Did you put this box here? Tom: By no means. I didn't do it, I'm sure.*

by return mail AND **by return post** *Fig.* by a subsequent mailing (back to the sender). (A phrase indicating that an answer is expected very soon, by mail.) □ *Since this bill is overdue, would you kindly send us your check by return mail?*

by return post Go to previous.

by rote *Fig.* [of learning or memorizing] done as habit and without thinking. □ *The student learns everything by rote and doesn't really understand the concepts.*

by shank's mare *Fig.* by foot; by walking. (*Shank* refers to the shank of the leg.) □ *My car isn't working, so I'll have to travel by shank's mare.*

*by the book AND ***by the numbers** *Fig.* following the rules exactly. (Refers to a book of (numbered) rules. *Typically: **go** ~; do sth ~; **play** ~; **run** sth ~.) □ *The judge of the contest ran things strictly by the rules and disqualified us on a small technicality.*

by the by Go to by the way.

by the day *Fig.* [for] one day at a time. □ *I don't know when I'll have to leave town, so I rent this room by the day.*

by the dozen *Fig.* in groups of 12. (Compare this with **by the dozens.**) □ *Eggs are normally sold by the dozen.*

by the dozens *Fig.* many; by some fairly large, indefinite number. (Similar to but implying less than *hundreds.* Compare

this with **by the dozen.**) □ *Just then people began showing up by the dozens.*

by the end of the day by the time when the workday is over; by the time that the sun goes down. □ *We have to do all these things by the end of the day.*

by the grapevine Go to through the grapevine.

by the handful *Fig.* in amounts equal to a handful; in quantity. □ *Billy is eating candy by the handful.*

by the hour *Fig.* at each hour; once each hour. □ *It kept growing darker by the hour.*

by the month *Fig.* one month at a time. □ *I needed a car for a short while, so I rented one by the month.*

by the nape of the neck by the back of the neck. (Mostly said in threats.) □ *If you do that again, I'll pick you up by the nape of the neck and throw you out the door.*

by the same token *Cliché* a phrase indicating that the speaker is introducing parallel or closely contrasting information. □ *Tom: I really got cheated! Bob: You think they've cheated you, but, by the same token, they believe that you've cheated them.*

*by the seat of one's **pants** *Fig.* by sheer luck and use of intuition. (*Typically: **fly** ~; **make it** ~.) □ *I got through school by the seat of my pants.*

by the skin of one's **teeth** *Fig.* just barely. (By an amount equal to the thickness of the [imaginary] skin on one's teeth.) □ *I got through calculus class by the skin of my teeth.*

by the sweat of one's **brow** *Fig.* by one's efforts; by one's hard work. □ *Tom raised these vegetables by the sweat of his brow.*

*by the throat with hands on someone's throat, intending to do harm. (*Typically: **grab** so ~; **hold** so ~; **seize** so ~; **take** so ~.) □ *She grabbed him by the throat and began to shake some sense into him.*

by the way AND **by the by 1.** *Fig.* a phrase indicating that the speaker is adding information. (*By the by* is not as frequent.) □ *Tom: Is this one any good? Clerk: This is the largest and, by the way, the most expensive one we have in stock.* **2.** a phrase indicating that the speaker is casually opening a new subject. □ *Jane: By the by, don't you owe me some money? Sue: Who, me?*

by the week *Fig.* one week at a time. □ *Where can I rent a room by the week?*

by the year *Fig.* one year at a time. □ *Most apartments are available by the year.*

by virtue of sth *Fig.* because of something; due to something. □ *They are members of the club by virtue of their great wealth.*

by way of sth **1.** *Fig.* passing through something (as a place); via something. □ *He came home by way of Toledo.* **2.** *Fig.* in illustration; as an example. □ *He read them a passage from Shakespeare by way of example.*

by word of mouth *Fig.* by speaking rather than writing. □ *I need it in writing. I don't trust things I hear about by word of mouth.*

Bye for now. Go to Good-bye for now.

cadge sth **from** so AND **cadge** sth **off** so *Sl.* to beg or borrow something from someone. □ *I cadged this jacket off a friendly guy I met.*

cage so/sth **in**† *Fig.* to confine someone or something. □ *Please don't cage me in this tiny room!*

call a halt (to sth**)** to demand that something be stopped. □ *We must call a halt to this childish behavior.*

call a meeting *Fig.* to ask that people assemble for a meeting; to request that a meeting be held. □ *The mayor called a meeting to discuss the problem.*

call a meeting to order AND **call the meeting to order** *Fig.* to announce that a meeting is about to begin. □ *The meeting will be called to order at noon.*

call a spade a spade *Fig.* to call something by its right name; to speak frankly about something, even if it is unpleasant. (This, in its history and origins has no racial connotations but has recently been misinterpreted as relating to the slang pejorative *spade* = Negro.) □ *Well, I believe it's time to call a spade a spade. We are just avoiding the issue.*

Call again. *Fig.* Please visit this shop again sometime. (Said by shopkeepers and store clerks.) □ *"Thank you," said the clerk, smiling, "Call again."*

call (all) the shots *Fig.* to decide on the course of action; to be in charge. □ *Why do you have to call all the shots?*

call at some place **1.** to visit some place. □ *I called at the druggist's for some medicine.* **2.** [for a ship] to put into port at a place. □ *Our ship will call at seven ports during the voyage.*

call attention to so/sth to cause someone, including oneself, or something to be noticed or observed. □ *I think he dresses like that simply to call attention to himself.*

call so's **attention to** sth AND **call** sth **to** so's **attention** *Fig.* to bring something to someone's notice; to make someone recognize some fact. □ *He called to our attention the notice on the wall.*

call back 1. to call [someone] again on the telephone at a later time. □ *Call back later, please.* □ *I will call back when you are not so busy.* **2.** to return a telephone call received earlier. □ *The note says I am to call back. What did you want?* □ *This is Bill Wilson calling back.*

call so's **bluff** *Fig.* to demand that someone prove a claim or is not being deceptive. □ *Tom said, "You've made me really angry, and I'll punch you if you come any closer!" "Go ahead," said Bill, calling his bluff.*

call so **by** a name to address someone by a particular kind of name. □ *They call me by my first name.* □ *Don't call me by my nickname!*

call so **down**† *Fig.* to reprimand a person. □ *"I wish you wouldn't call me down in public," cried Sally.*

call sth **down**† **(on** so**)** *Fig.* to invoke some sort of divine punishment onto someone. □ *The preacher sounded as though he was calling down the wrath of God on us.* □ *Moses called down a plague on the Pharaoh.*

call for so/sth **1.** *Fig.* to need, require, or demand something or the services of someone. □ *The recipe calls for two cups of flour.* □ *This job calls for someone with ex-*

perience. **2.** to arrive to collect or pick up a person or a thing. (Used especially when you are to pick someone up and are acting as an escort.) □ *I will call for you about eight this evening.* □ *The messenger will call for your reply in the morning.* **3.** to shout for or request someone or something. □ *I stood on the porch and called for the dog.*

call hogs to snore. □ *I couldn't sleep at all last night, with Cousin Joe calling hogs in the next room.* □ *Joe calls hogs so loudly the windows rattle.*

call so **in (on** sth**)** to invite another person to come and help with a problem, such as calling in another doctor for a second opinion. □ *My doctor called in a specialist on this matter.*

call in sick *Fig.* to call one's place of work to say that one is ill and cannot come to work. □ *I have to call in sick today. I have a fever.*

call sth **into question** AND **bring** sth **into question** *Fig.* to cause something to be evaluated; to examine or reexamine qualifications or value. □ *We called Dr. Jones's qualifications into question.*

call it a day *Fig.* to quit work and go home; to say that a day's work has been completed. □ *I'm tired. Let's call it a day.*

call it a night *Fig.* to end what one is doing at night and go [home] to bed. □ *Guest after guest called it a night, and at last we were alone.*

call it quits *Fig.* to quit; to resign from something; to announce that one is quitting. □ *Time to go home, John. Let's call it quits.*

Call my service. *Fig.* Please don't call me directly, but through my answering service. (Not a friendly or encouraging invitation.) □ *Good to talk to you, but I gotta go now. Call my service.*

call so **names** to call someone by an abusive or insulting name. □ *Billy cried when the other kids called him names.*

the **call of nature** *Euph.* the need to go to the lavatory. □ *There was no break in the agenda, not even for the call of nature.*

call sth **off**† to cancel an event. □ *It's too late to call the party off. The first guests have already arrived.*

call the dogs **off**† **1.** to order hunting or watch dogs to abandon their quarry. □ *The robber gave up, and the guard called the dogs off.* **2.** *Fig.* to stop threatening, chasing, or "hounding" [a person]. (Fig. on ①.) □ *Tell the sheriff to call off the dogs. We caught the robber.*

call on so to court someone. □ *In the old days, a boy had to ask a girl's father for permission to come call on her.*

call on sth *Fig.* to draw on something, such as a particular quality or talent. □ *This project calls on all the creative skills you can gather together.*

call so **on the carpet** AND **haul** so **on the carpet** *Fig.* to reprimand a person. (When done by someone of clear superiority. *Haul* is stronger than *call.*) □ *One more error like that and the big boss will call you on the carpet.* □ *I'm sorry it went wrong. I really hope the regional manager doesn't haul me on the carpet again.*

call so **out**† *Fig.* to challenge someone to a fight. □ *Why did you call that guy out? He used to be a prize fighter!*

call sth **square** *Fig.* to pronounce a debt or obligation to have been paid, balanced, or ended. □ *Thanks for the hundred bucks. I think we can call it square now.*

call (the) roll AND **take (the) roll** *Fig.* to call the names of people from a list of those enrolled, expecting them to reply if they are present. □ *After I call the roll, please open your books to page 12.* □ *I will take roll, and then we will do arithmetic.*

call the tune Go to call (all) the shots.

call so **to account** *Fig.* to ask one to explain and justify one's behavior, policy, performance, etc. □ *The sergeant called the police officer to account.*

call so **to attention** *Fig.* to demand that someone assume the formal military stance of attention. □ *The sergeant called us to attention.*

call sth **to mind** AND **bring** sth **to mind** *Fig.* to bring something into someone's mind; to cause something to be remembered. □ *This photo album calls our vacation to mind.*

the **calm before the storm** Go to the lull before the storm.

camp it up *Fig.* [for performers] to over-act or behave in an affected manner. (Fixed order.) □ *The cast began to camp it up in the second act, and the critics walked out.*

camp out (some place) **1.** to camp in a place as in a tent or camper. □ *We love to camp out in the mountains.* **2.** *Fig.* to locate near someone from whom one is trying to get attention. (This can mean actually stay-ing at a place literally or just monitoring a place for activity.) □ *I guess we'll have to camp out on his doorstep until he agrees to talk to us.*

Can do. *Inf.* I can definitely do it. (The op-posite of No can do.) □ *Jane: Will you be able to get this finished by quitting time to-day? Alice: Can do. Leave it to me.*

one **can (just) get** oneself **another boy** *Fig.* the dissatisfied party can simply find someone else. (Typically said by males. More U.K. than U.S.) □ *If they don't like the way I am doing this stinking job, they can just get themselves another boy.*

Can I be excused? Go to Could I be ex-cused?

(Can I) buy you a drink? Go to (Could I) buy you a drink?

Can I call you? Go to Could I call you?

Can it! *Inf.* Shut up! □ *That's enough com-plaining from you! Can it!*

can (just) see the wheels turning *Fig.* able to imagine [that someone is] think-ing carefully [and figuring something out]. □ *The little boy looked up at the cookies on the table, and I could just see the wheels turning.*

can (just) whistle for sth *Fig.* can just for-get about having something. □ *The last time Mary came over for dinner, she was* downright rude. If she wants dinner at my house again, she can just whistle for it!

*a **can of worms** *Fig.* a very difficult issue or set of problems; an array of difficul-ties. (*Typically: **be** ~; **open (up)** ~.) □ *This political scandal is a real can of worms.* □ *Let's not open that can of worms!*

can take it to the bank *Fig.* able to depend on the truthfulness of the speaker's state-ment: it is not counterfeit or bogus. □ *Be-lieve me. What I am telling you is the truth. You can take it to the bank.*

Can you imagine? Can you believe that?; Imagine that! □ *She wore jeans to the wedding. Can you imagine?* □ *Billy was eating the houseplant! Can you imagine?*

cancel so's **Christmas** *Sl.* to kill someone; to destroy someone. (Underworld or joc-ular; the idea is that the threatened per-son will not live until Christmas.) □ *If he keeps bugging me, I'm gonna cancel his Christmas!*

cancel each other out† [for the opposite effects of two things] to balance each other. □ *The cost of the meal you bought and what I owed you cancel each other out, so we're even.*

cancel out (of sth**)** to withdraw from something. □ *I hate to cancel out of the event at the last minute, but this is an emergency.*

cancel so **out of** sth AND **cancel** so **out**† *Sl.* to eliminate someone; to kill someone. □ *The drug lord threatened to cancel out his former partner for testifying against him.*

*a **candidate for a pair of wings** *Euph.* someone who is likely to die; someone who is close to death. (Jocular. *Typi-cally: **be** ~; **look like** ~.) □ *Tom: How's Bill doing? I heard he was sick. Jane: Not good, I'm afraid. He looks like a candidate for a pair of wings.*

cannot hack it *Inf.* unable to do the job. □ *I thought delivering papers would be an easy job, but I just can't hack it.*

cannot hear oneself **think** *Fig.* [a person] cannot concentrate. (Often following an expression something like *It's so loud*

can't carry a tune (in a bushel basket)

here. . . .) □ *Quiet! You're so loud I can't hear myself think!*

cannot see (any) further than the end of one's **nose** Go to see no further than the end of one's nose.

cannot stomach so/sth Go to not able to stomach so/sth.

can't be bothered to do sth AND **can't be troubled to** do sth will not take the trouble to do something. □ *No, I won't stop my work and take you to the bank. I can't be bothered to do that.*

can't be troubled to do sth Go to previous.

can't call one's **soul** one's **own** *Fig.* working for other people all the time. (Also with *cannot.*) □ *Jane has to work two jobs and take care of both her aging parents. She can't call her soul her own.*

can't carry a tune in a bucket Go to next.

can't carry a tune (in a bushel basket) AND **can't carry a tune in a bucket; can't carry a tune in a paper sack** *Rur.*

unable to sing or hum a melody. (Also with *cannot.*) □ *I don't know why Mary's in the choir. She can't carry a tune in a bushel basket.* □ *I'd try to hum the song for you, but I can't carry a tune in a paper sack.*

can't carry a tune in a paper sack Go to previous.

can't do anything with so/sth not [to be] able to manage or control someone or something. (Also with *cannot.*) □ *Bill is such a discipline problem. I can't do anything with him.*

can't find one's **butt with both hands (in broad daylight)** *Sl.* is stupid or incompetent. (Also with *cannot.*) □ *Why did they put Jim in charge? He can't find his butt with both hands!*

can't help doing sth *Fig.* not able to refrain from doing something; not able not to do something. (Also with *cannot.*) □ *Anne is such a good cook, I can't help eating everything she serves.*

can't help but do sth *Fig.* [to be] unable to choose any but one course of action. (Also with *cannot.*) □ *Her parents live nearby, so she can't help but go there on holidays.*

can't hit the (broad) side of a barn *Rur.* cannot aim something accurately. (Also with *cannot.*) □ *Please don't try to throw the paper into the wastebasket. You can't hit the side of a barn.*

can't say (a)s I do, (can't say (a)s I don't) *Rur.* I am not sure. (Also with *cannot.*) □ *Jane: What do you think of my cousin? Do you like him? Mary: Can't say's I do, can't say's I don't.*

can't see a hole in a ladder *Inf.* stupid or drunk. (Also with *cannot.*) □ *After the big party, Joe needed someone to drive him home. He couldn't see a hole in a ladder.*

can't see beyond the end of one's **nose** Go to see no further than the end of one's nose.

can't see one's **hand in front of** one's **face** *Fig.* [to be] unable to see very far, usually due to darkness or fog. (Also with *cannot.*) □ *Bob said that the fog was so thick he couldn't see his hand in front of his face.*

can't see straight *Fig.* cannot function (often because of strong emotion). (Also with *cannot.*) □ *I am so mad I can't see straight.*

can't stomach so/sth *Fig.* [to be] unable to tolerate someone or something; disliking someone or something extremely. (Also with *cannot.*) □ *Mr. Jones can't stomach the sight of blood.*

can't unring the bell *Fig.* cannot undo what's been done. □ *I wish I wasn't pregnant, but you can't unring the bell.*

Can't win them all. Go to (You) can't win them all.

cap and gown the academic cap or mortarboard and the robe worn in formal academic ceremonies. □ *We all had to rent a cap and gown for graduation.*

capitalize on sth *Fig.* to build on something; to exploit something, such as an opportunity or talent, to one's own ben-

efit. □ *Let's try to capitalize on the strength of the economy and invest for the future.*

captain of industry *Fig.* a high-ranking corporation officer; a wealthy and successful capitalist. □ *The captains of industry manage to hang on to their money no matter what.*

capture so's **imagination** *Fig.* to intrigue someone; to interest someone in a lasting way; to stimulate someone's imagination. □ *The story of the young wizard has captured our imagination no matter what our ages.*

***a card** *Fig.* an entertaining and clever person who says or does funny things. (*Typically: **act like ~; be ~.**) □ *Mary is a card, and she has to learn to take things seriously sometimes.*

card-carrying member *Fig.* an official member of some group, originally, the U.S. Communist Party. □ *Bill is a card-carrying member of the electricians union.*

the cards are stacked against so *Inf.* luck is against one. (See also stack the deck (against so/sth).) □ *I have the worst luck. The cards are stacked against me all the time.*

care for sth to like the taste of some kind of food or drink. (Usually used with a negative.) □ *I don't care for sweet desserts.*

carry (a lot of) weight (with so/sth) *Fig.* to be very influential with someone or some group of people. □ *Your argument does not carry a lot of weight with me.*

carry a secret to the grave AND **carry a secret to** one's **grave** *Fig.* to never reveal a secret, even to the day of one's death. □ *John carried our secret to his grave.*

carry a torch (for so) AND **carry the torch (for** so) *Fig.* to be in love with someone who is not in love with you; to brood over a hopeless love affair. □ *Is John still carrying a torch after all this time?*

carry one's **cross** Go to bear one's cross.

carry on 1. to continue with what one was doing. □ *Don't mind me. Carry on.* **2.** *Inf.* to behave badly or mischievously. □ *The children always carry on when the* *teacher's out of the room.* □ *Stop carrying on and go to sleep!*

carry on (about so/sth**)** *Fig.* to make a great fuss over someone or something; to cry (especially for a long time or uncontrollably) about someone or something. (Note the variation in the examples.) □ *Billy, stop carrying on about your tummy ache like that.* □ *Calm down. There's no need to carry on about it.*

carry sth **out** *Fig.* to complete an assignment; to complete a task. □ *It was a hard task, Charles, and I'm glad you carried it out so well.*

carry one's **(own) weight** AND **pull** one's **(own) weight** *Fig.* to do one's share; to earn one's keep. (The *weight* is the burden that is the responsibility of someone.) □ *Tom, you must be more helpful around the house. We each have to carry our own weight.*

carry the ball *Fig.* to be in charge; to be considered reliable enough to make sure that a job gets done. □ *We need someone who knows how to get the job done. Hey, Sally! Why don't you carry the ball for us?*

carry the day AND **win the day** *Fig.* to be successful; to win a competition, argument, etc. (Originally meaning to win a battle.) □ *Our team didn't play well at first, but we won the day in the end.* □ *Good preparation carried the day, and James passed his exams.*

carry the torch 1. *Fig.* to lead or participate in a (figurative) crusade. □ *If Jane hadn't carried the torch, no one would have followed, and the whole thing would have failed.* **2.** Go to **carry a torch (for** so**)**.

carry the weight of the world on one's **shoulders** *Fig.* to appear or behave as if burdened by all the problems in the whole world. □ *Look at Tom. He appears to be carrying the weight of the world on his shoulders.*

carry so **through** sth *Fig.* to support and sustain someone during an ordeal. □ *She had an inner strength that carried her through her illness.*

carry weight (with so**)** *Fig.* to have influence with someone; [for an explanation] to amount to a good argument to use with someone. □ *That carries a lot of weight with the older folks.*

*carte blanche *Fig.* freedom or permission to act as one wishes or thinks necessary. (*Typically: **get** ~; **have** ~; **give** so ~.) □ *He's been given carte blanche with the reorganization of the workforce.* □ *The manager has been given no instructions about how to train the staff. He has carte blanche from the owner.*

carve sth **in stone** *Fig.* to fix some idea permanently. (See also **carved in stone**.) □ *No one has carved this one approach in stone. We have several options.*

carve out a niche *Fig.* to have developed and mastered one's own special skill. □ *John, you have carved out a niche for yourself as the most famous living scholar on the Akadian language.*

carve out a reputation *Fig.* to have developed a reputation for doing something well. □ *I worked for years to carve out a reputation as a careful and thoughtful scholar.*

carved in stone AND **engraved in stone; set in concrete; set in cement; set in stone; etched in stone; written in stone** *Fig.* permanent or not subject to change. (Often in the negative.) □ *Now, this isn't carved in stone yet, but this looks like the way it's going to be.*

a case in point *Fig.* a specific example of what one is talking about. □ *Now, as a case in point, let's look at 19th-century England.*

*a case of sth **1.** *Fig.* an instance of something. (*Typically: **be** ~; **have** ~.) □ *This is a case of police brutality. They should not have injured the suspect.* **2.** *Fig.* an occurrence of a disease. (*Typically: **be** ~; **look like** ~; **treat** ~.) □ *I am suffering from a case of the flu.*

a case of mistaken identity *Fig.* the incorrect identification of someone. □ *I am not the criminal you want to arrest! This is a case of mistaken identity!*

a case of the blind leading the blind *Fig.* a situation where people who don't know how to do something try to teach other people. □ *Tom doesn't know anything about cars, but he's trying to teach Sally how to change the oil. It's a case of the blind leading the blind.*

case so/sth **out**† AND **check** so/sth **out**†; **scope** so/sth **out**† *Sl.* to look someone or something over; to check someone or something out. (See also **case the joint.**) □ *Hey, scope the new car out!*

case the joint 1. *Sl.* to look over someplace to figure out how to break in, what to steal, etc. (Underworld.) □ *You could see he was casing the joint the way he hung around.* **2.** *Sl.* to look a place over. □ *The dog came in and cased the joint, sniffing out friends and foes.*

cash one's **checks in**† Go to next.

cash (one's **chips**) **in**† **1.** to turn in one's gaming tokens or poker chips when one quits playing. □ *Cash in your chips before you go.* **2.** *Fig.* to quit [anything], as if one were cashing in gaming tokens; to leave or go to bed. (Fig. on ①.) □ *I guess I'll cash my chips in and go home.* □ *I'm really tired. I'm going to cash in.* **3.** AND **cash** one's **checks in**† *Euph.* to die; to finish the "game of life." □ *Poor Fred cashed in his chips last week.*

cash flow problem *Fig.* a lack of hard currency. □ *Due to his cash flow problem, he was unable to pay his employees that month.*

cash in (on sth**)** *Fig.* to earn a lot of money at something; to make a profit at something. □ *This is a good year for drug stocks, and you can cash in on it if you're smart.*

cash on the barrelhead AND **cash on the line** *Rur.* cash at the time of purchase. □ *They offered me $50,000 cash on the line for Aunt Nancy's old house.*

cash on the line Go to previous.

cash or credit *Fig.* [a purchase made] either by paying cash or by putting the charges on a credit account. □ *When Fred had all his purchases assembled on the counter, the clerk asked, "Cash or credit?"*

cash-and-carry *Fig.* a method of buying and selling goods at the retail level where the buyer pays cash for the goods and carries the goods away. (As opposed to paying on credit or with the cost of delivery included.) □ *Sorry, we don't accept credit cards. This is strictly cash-and-carry.*

cast a pall on sth AND **cast a pall over** sth *Fig.* to make an event less enjoyable; to place an unpleasant aura on an event. □ *The death of the bride's grandmother cast a pall over the wedding.*

cast so **as** sth *Fig.* to decide or fantasize that someone is going to follow a particular pattern of behavior in real life. □ *I'm afraid my teachers cast me as hopeless when I was very young.*

cast aspersions on so to make a rude and insulting remark. □ *It is rude to cast aspersions on people you haven't even met!*

cast doubt on so/sth AND **throw doubt on** so/sth *Fig.* to imply someone is to be doubted or something is doubtful. □ *The new evidence casts doubt on Tom's explanation.*

cast in the same mold *Fig.* [of two or more people or things] very similar. □ *The two sisters are cast in the same mold—equally mean.*

cast one's **lot with** so/sth AND **throw in** one's **lot with** so/sth *Fig.* to join a people or a group and be willing to share in whatever good and bad might be experienced. □ *I cast my lot with an amateur rock band, and we were all millionaires within two years.*

cast (one's**) pearls before swine** *Fig.* to waste something good on someone who doesn't care about it. (From a biblical quotation.) □ *To serve them French cuisine is like casting one's pearls before swine.*

cast the first stone *Fig.* to make the first criticism; to be the first to attack. (From a biblical quotation.) □ *John always casts the first stone. Does he think he's perfect?*

cast one's **vote** *Fig.* to vote; to place one's ballot in the ballot box. □ *The wait in line to cast one's vote was almost an hour.*

cast-iron stomach AND **strong stomach** *Inf.* a very strong stomach that can withstand bad food or anything nauseating.

□ *If I didn't have a cast-iron stomach, I couldn't eat this stuff.*

Cat got your tongue? *Inf.* Why are you not saying anything? (Often said by adults to children.) □ *Hi, Lisa! How are you? How's your husband? Are you surprised to see me? What's the matter, cat got your tongue?*

the **cat is out of the bag** *Fig.* the secret has been made known. (See also let the cat out of the bag.) □ *Now that the cat is out of the bag, there is no sense in pretending we don't know what's really happening.*

catch sth *Fig.* to see or listen to something. □ *I will try to catch that new movie this weekend.*

catch a whiff of sth Go to a whiff of sth.

catch (a)hold of so/sth to grasp or seize someone or something. □ *See if you can catch hold of the rope as it swings back and forth.*

catch as catch can [finding what one needs] in whatever manner works; however it is possible. □ *Welcome to the party. Better late than never. There's not much food left. It's sort of catch as catch can.*

catch one's **breath** *Fig.* to struggle for normal breathing after strenuous activity. □ *It took Jimmy a minute to catch his breath after being punched in the stomach.*

catch so **by surprise** Go to take so by surprise.

catch cold AND **take cold** *Fig.* to contract a cold (a common respiratory infection). (Use with *catch* is more frequent.) □ *Please close the window, or we'll all catch cold.*

catch one's **death (of cold)** *Fig.* to contract a cold, a common respiratory infection; to catch a serious cold. (See also catch cold.) □ *If I go out in this weather, I'll catch my death of cold.*

catch so's **drift** Go to get so's drift.

catch so's **eye** AND **get** so's **eye 1.** *Fig.* to establish eye contact with someone; to attract someone's attention. □ *The shiny red car caught Mary's eye.* **2.** *Fig.* to appear and attract someone's interest. □ *One of*

the books on the top shelf caught my eye, and I took it down to look at it.

catch so's **fancy** Go to strike so's fancy.

catch so **flat-footed** Go to catch so redhanded.

catch forty winks AND **take forty winks; have forty winks** *Fig.* to take a nap; to get some sleep. □ *I'll just catch forty winks before getting ready for the party.* □ *I think I'll go to bed and take forty winks. See you in the morning.*

catch hell Go to hell.

catch it *Fig.* to get into trouble and receive punishment. □ *I know I'm going to catch it for denting Mom's car when I get home.*

Catch me later. AND **Catch me some other time.** *Inf.* Please try to talk to me later. □ *Bill (angry): Tom, look at this phone bill! Tom: Catch me later.*

Catch me some other time. Go to previous.

catch so **napping** AND **catch** so **off balance; catch** so **up short** *Fig.* to come upon someone who is unprepared; to surprise someone. (See also asleep at the switch.) □ *The thieves caught the security guard napping.* □ *I didn't expect you so soon. You caught me off balance.*

catch so **off balance** Go to previous.

catch so **off guard** AND **catch** one **off (one's) guard** *Fig.* to catch a person at a time of carelessness. □ *She caught me off my guard, and my hesitation told her I was lying.*

catch on (to so/sth**)** AND **wise up (to** so/sth**)** *Fig.* to see what someone or something is doing or meaning. (*Wise* is informal.) □ *I finally caught on to what she was talking about.* □ *It takes a while for me to wise up.*

catch on (with so**)** *Fig.* [for something] to become popular with someone. □ *I hope our new product catches on with children.*

catch onto so Go to onto so.

catch so **out†** *Fig.* to discover the truth about someone's deception. □ *The investigator tried to catch me out, but I stuck to my story.*

catch so **out in the open** Go to out in the open.

catch so **red-handed** AND **catch** so **flat-footed** to catch a person in the act of doing something wrong. (See also caught red-handed.) □ *Mary tried to cash a forged check at the bank, and the teller caught her red-handed.*

catch some rays AND **bag some rays** *Inf.* to get some sunshine; to tan in the sun. □ *We wanted to catch some rays, but the sun never came out the whole time we were there.*

catch some Zs AND **cop some Zs; cut some Zs** *Inf.* to get some sleep. (In comic strips, Zs are used to show that someone is sleeping or snoring.) □ *I gotta catch some Zs before I drop.*

catch the next wave AND **wait for the next wave** *Fig.* to follow the next fad. □ *He has no purpose in life. He sits around strumming his guitar and waiting to catch the next wave.*

a **catch to it** *Fig.* a hidden problem associated with it. □ *It sounds good at first, but there's a catch to it. You have to pay all costs up front.*

catch up (on so/sth**)** to learn the news of someone or something. □ *I need a little time to catch up on the news.*

catch up (on sth**)** to bring one's efforts with something up-to-date; to do the work that one should have done. □ *I need a quiet time so I can catch up on my work.*

catch so **up short** Go to catch so napping.

catch wind of sth Go to get wind of sth.

catch one **with** one's **pants down** *Fig.* to discover someone in the act of doing something that is normally private or hidden. (Figurative, although literal uses are possible.) □ *Some council members were using tax money as their own. But the press caught them with their pants down, and now the district attorney will press charges.*

catch-as-catch-can *Fig.* the best one can do with whatever is available. □ *There were ten children in our family, and every meal was catch-as-catch-can.*

cater to so/sth **1.** to provide for or care for someone or something. □ *I believe that we can cater to you in this matter.* **2.** *Fig.* to provide special or favorable treatment for someone or something. (Fig. on ①.) □ *We do not have the time to cater to special requests.*

caught between life and death AND **hovering between life and death** *Fig.* being in a position where living or dying is an even possibility. □ *And there I was on the operating table, hovering between life and death.* □ *The mountain climber hung by his rope, caught between life and death.*

caught in the act AND **caught red-handed** *Fig.* seen doing something illegal or private. (See also catch so red-handed.) □ *Tom was caught in the act and cannot deny what he did.*

caught in the crossfire 1. trapped between two lines of enemy fire. □ *I was caught in the crossfire and dove into a ditch to keep from getting killed.* **2.** AND **caught in the middle** *Fig.* caught between two arguing people or groups, making it difficult to remain neutral. (Fig. on ①.) □ *Bill and Ann were arguing, and poor Bobby, their son, was caught in the middle.*

caught in the middle Go to previous.

caught red-handed Go to caught in the act.

caught short 1. *Fig.* left without any money temporarily. □ *I'm caught a little short. Can I borrow a few bucks?* **2.** *Sl.* pregnant and unmarried. □ *Both of Jane's sisters got caught short before they graduated high school.*

caught unaware(s) surprised and unprepared. □ *The clerk was caught unawares, and the robber emptied out the cash register before the clerk could sound the alarm.*

caught up in sth AND **caught up with** sth *Fig.* deeply involved with something; participating actively or closely in something. □ *Wallace is caught up in his work and has little time for his son, Buxton.*

cause a commotion Go to cause (quite a) stir.

cause so's **hair to stand on end** Go to make so's hair stand on end.

cause (quite a) stir AND **cause a commotion; create a commotion** *Fig.* to cause people to become agitated; to cause trouble in a group of people; to shock or alarm people. □ *When Bob appeared without jacket and tie, it caused a stir at the dean's dinner.*

cause (some) eyebrows to raise AND **cause some raised eyebrows; raise a few eyebrows; raise some eyebrows** *Fig.* to shock people; to surprise and dismay people. □ *John caused eyebrows to raise when he married a woman half his age.*

cause (some) tongues to wag *Fig.* to cause people to gossip; to give people something to gossip about. □ *The way John was looking at Mary will surely cause some tongues to wag.*

a **caution** *Fig.* someone or something that seems out of the ordinary. □ *Bob is a real caution—the jokes that he tells!*

cave in (to so/sth**)** *Fig.* to give in to someone or something. □ *Finally, the manager caved in to the customer's demands.*

cease and desist *Fig.* to completely stop doing something and not resume doing it. (A legal phrase.) □ *The judge ordered the merchant to cease and desist the deceptive practices.*

center around so/sth *Fig.* to focus broadly on the details related to someone or something; to **center on** so/sth. (A seeming contradiction.) □ *The novel centers around the friends and activities of an elderly lady.*

the **center of attention** *Fig.* the focus of people's attention; the thing or person who monopolizes people's attention. □ *She had a way of making herself the center of attention wherever she went.*

center on so/sth *Fig.* to focus or fix one's interest or concern on someone or something. □ *The biography centers on an elderly lady and her success in life.*

a **certain party** *Fig.* someone you know but whom I do not wish to name. □ *If a certain party finds out about you-know-what, what on earth will you do?*

Certainly not! Go to Definitely not!

the **chain of command** *Fig.* the series or sequence of holders of responsibility in a hierarchy. □ *The only way to get things done in the military is to follow the chain of command. Never try to go straight to the top.*

chain of events *Fig.* a sequence of things that happened in the past, in order of occurrence. □ *An odd chain of events led up to our meeting on the plane. It was like some unseen force planned it.*

chalk sth **out**† *Fig.* to explain something carefully to someone, as if one were talking about a chalk drawing. □ *She chalked out the details of the plan over the phone.*

chalk sth **up**† *Fig.* to add a mark or point to one's score. □ *Chalk another goal up for Sarah.*

chalk sth **up to** sth *Fig.* to attribute (the cause of) a deed to something. □ *I chalked up her rude behavior to trouble at home.*

champ at the bit AND **chomp at the bit 1.** [for a horse] to bite at its bit, eager to move along. □ *Dobbin was champing at the bit, eager to go.* **2.** *Fig.* to be ready and anxious to do something. (Fig. on ①.) □ *The kids were champing at the bit to get into the swimming pool.*

chance (up)on so/sth *Fig.* to find someone or something by accident; to happen on someone or something. (*Upon* is formal and less commonly used than *on*.) □ *I chanced upon a nice little restaurant on my walk today.*

chances are *Fig.* the likelihood is (followed by a clause stating what is likely). □ *Chances are that she would have been late even if she had left on time.*

change for the better Go to for the better.

change hands *Fig.* [for something] to be sold or passed from an old owner to a new owner. □ *How many times has this lot changed hands in the last ten years?*

change horses in midstream AND **change horses in the middle of the stream** *Fig.* to make major changes in an activity that has already begun; to choose someone or something else after it is too late. (Fig. on the image of someone trying to move from one horse to another while crossing a stream.) □ *The house is half-built. It's too late to hire a different architect. You can't change horses in midstream.* □ *Jane: I've written a rough draft of my research paper, but the topic doesn't interest me as much as I thought. Maybe I ought to pick a different one. Jill: Don't change horses in the middle of the stream.*

change horses in the middle of the stream Go to previous.

change so's **mind** to cause a person to think differently (about someone or something). □ *Tom thought Mary was unkind, but an evening out with her changed his mind.* □ *I will change my mind if you convince me that you are right.*

the **change (of life)** *Fig.* menopause. □ *The change of life affects each woman differently.* □ *Jill started the change when she was 47.*

a **change of pace** an addition of some variety in one's life, routine, or abode. □ *Going to the beach on the weekend will be a change of pace.*

a **change of scenery** a move to a different place, where the surroundings are different. □ *I thought I would go to the country for a change of scenery.* □ *A change of scenery would help me relax and organize my life.*

change off *Fig.* [for people] to alternate in doing something. □ *Tom and I changed off so neither of us had to answer the phone all the time.*

change out of sth to take off a set of clothing and put on another. □ *You should change out of your casual clothes and put on something more formal for dinner.*

change places (with so) Go to trade places (with so).

change the channel *Sl.* to switch to some other topic of conversation. (Fig. on changing to a different television channel or station.) □ *Just a minute. I think you changed the channel. Let's go back to the part about you owing me money.*

change the subject to begin talking about something different. □ *They changed the subject suddenly when the person whom they had been discussing entered the room.*

change one's **tune** Go to sing a different tune.

change so's **tune** to change someone's manner or attitude, usually from bad to good, or from rude to pleasant. □ *The teller was most unpleasant until she learned that I'm a bank director. Then she changed her tune.*

change one's **ways** Go to mend one's ways.

change with the times to adopt and adapt to new and modern ways of thinking and doing. □ *If you don't change with the times, you will feel out of place and old-fashioned.*

chapter and verse *Fig.* very specifically detailed, in reference to sources of information. (A reference to the method of referring to biblical text.) □ *He gave chapter and verse for his reasons for disputing that Shakespeare had written the play.*

character assassination *Fig.* an act of seriously harming someone's reputation. □ *The review was more than a negative appraisal of his performance. It was total character assassination.*

*the **charge (of** so/sth) *Fig.* control of someone or something; the responsibility for caring for someone or something. (*Typically: **take** ~; **have** ~; **give** so ~.) □ *How long have you had charge of this office?*

*a **charley horse** *Fig.* a painful, persistent cramp in the arm or leg, usually from strain. (*Typically: **get** ~; **have** ~; **give** so ~.) □ *Don't hike too far or you'll get a charley horse.*

charm the pants off so *Inf.* to use very charming behavior to persuade someone to do something. □ *He will try to charm the pants off you, but you can still refuse to take the job if you don't want to do it.*

chase so/sth **down**† Go to track so/sth **down**†.

chasing rainbows Go to (always) chasing rainbows.

cheap at half the price nicely priced; fairly valued; bargain priced. (This is the way that many people seem to use this phrase. The meaning does not follow logically from the wording of the phrase. There are other interpretations, but none is clearly correct. One thought is that it is a play on "cheap at twice the price" = if the price were doubled, it would still be cheap for the value received.) □ *I only paid $12 for this ring. Wow! It would be cheap at half the price!*

cheat on so Go to two-time so.

check sth **at the door 1.** to leave something with an appointed custodian near the entrance of a place. (Coats, parcels, umbrellas, and hats are dealt with in this manner. In the Old West, guns were likewise checked at the door.) □ *Please check your wraps at the door.* **2.** *Fig.* to set aside a thought or an attitude when undertaking serious thinking. □ *You need to check those old ideas at the door and look deeper for more relevant things.*

check so's **bags through (to** some place) AND **check** so's **luggage through (to** some place) to have one's luggage sent directly to one's final destination. □ *Please check these bags through London to Madrid.*

check sth **in**† **1.** to make a record that someone has returned something. □ *I asked the librarian to check the book in for me.* **2.** to take something to a place, return it, and make sure that its return has been recorded. □ *Did you really check in the book on time?* **3.** to examine a shipment or an order received and make certain that everything ordered was received. □ *Tim checked in the order from the supplier to make sure that everything was there.*

check into sth Go to look into sth.

check so's **luggage through (to** some place) Go to check so's bags through (to some place).

check so/sth **out**† Go to case so/sth out†.

check out the plumbing AND **visit the plumbing** *Euph.* to go to the bathroom.

(Fixed order.) □ *I think I'd better check out the plumbing before we get on the highway.*

Check, please. AND **Could I have the bill?; Could I have the check?** Could you give me the check or the bill for this food or drink? □ *Bill: That meal was really good. Waiter! Could I have the check, please. Waiter: Right away, sir.*

check that *Inf.* cancel that; ignore that (last remark). □ *At four, no, check that, at three o'clock this afternoon, the shipment arrived and was signed for.*

check so/sth **through (sth)** to allow one to pass through something after checking one's identification, tickets, passes, etc. (Fixed order.) □ *The guard checked us through the gate, and we went about our business.*

checks and balances *Fig.* a system, as in the U.S. Constitution, where power is shared between the various branches of government. □ *The newspaper editor claimed that the system of checks and balances built into our Constitution has been subverted by party politics.*

***a **checkup** a physical examination by a physician. (*Typically: **get** ~; **have** ~; **give** so ~.) □ *I'm going to have a checkup in the morning. I hope I'm okay.*

cheek by jowl *Fig.* side by side; close together. □ *The pedestrians had to walk cheek by jowl along the narrow streets.*

cheese so **off**† *Sl.* to make someone very angry. □ *You sure know how to cheese Laurel off.*

***cheesed off** *Sl.* angry; disgusted. (*Typically: **be** ~; **get** ~; **get** so ~.) □ *Clare was really cheesed off at the waiter.*

cherry pick sth *Fig.* to choose something very carefully. (As if one were closely examining cherries on the tree, looking for the best.) □ *We have to cherry pick the lumber we want to use for the cabinetry. Nothing but the best will do.*

chew one's **cud** to think deeply; to be deeply involved in private thought. (Fig. on the cow's habit of bringing food back from the stomach to chew it further. The cow appears to be lost in thought while doing this.) □ *He's chewing his cud about what to do next.*

chew on sth Go to chew sth over†.

chew so **out**† AND **eat** so **out**† *Inf.* to scold someone. □ *The sergeant chewed the corporal out; then the corporal chewed the private out.*

chew sth **over**† AND **mull** sth **over**† **1.** to talk something over; to discuss something. (*Chew* is less formal than *mull*. *Mull* = grind or mix.) □ *We can chew it over at lunch.* **2.** AND **chew on** sth to think something over. (*Chew* is less formal than *mull*.) □ *I have to chew on all this stuff for a day or two. Then I'll get back to you.*

chew the fat AND **chew the rag** *Inf.* to chat or gossip. □ *Sit yourself down and let's chew the fat for a while.*

chew the rag Go to previous.

chew so/sth **up**† to damage or ruin someone or something by pinching, grinding, biting, etc. □ *Stay away from the mower blade or it will chew you up.*

chicken feed *Fig.* a small amount of anything, especially of money. (See also for chicken feed.) □ *It may be chicken feed to you, but that's a month's rent to me!*

chicken out (of sth**)** AND **chicken out on** so *Inf.* to decide not to do something for or with someone, usually because of fear or cowardice. □ *Freddy chickened out of the drag race at the last minute.*

chicken-hearted cowardly. □ *Yes, I'm a chicken-hearted softie. I never try anything too risky.*

chief cook and bottle washer *Fig.* the person in charge of practically everything (such as in a very small business). □ *I'm the chief cook and bottle washer around here. I do everything.*

child's play *Fig.* something very easy to do. □ *The test was child's play to those who took good notes.*

chill out AND **cool out** *Sl.* to calm down. □ *Before we can debate this matter, you're* all gonna have to chill out. So sit down and stop bickering.

*chilled to the bone *Fig.* very cold. (*Typically: **be** ~; **get** ~.) □ *The children were chilled to the bone from their swim in the ocean.*

chime in (with sth**)** *Fig.* to add a comment to the discussion. □ *Billy chimed in with a suggestion.*

chin music *Inf.* talk; conversation. □ *Whenever those two get together, you can be sure there'll be plenty of chin music.*

a **chink in** one's **armor** *Fig.* a special weakness that provides a means for attacking or impressing someone otherwise invulnerable. (*Fig.* on the image of an opening in a suit of armor that allows a weapon to penetrate.) □ *The boss seems mean, but the chink in his armor is that he is easily flattered.*

chip in (on sth**)** AND **chip** sth **in**† **(on** sth**)** **1.** *Fig.* to contribute a small amount of money to a fund that will be used to buy something. **2. chip in (on** sth**) (for** so**)** to contribute money toward a gift for someone. □ *Would you please chip in on the present for Richard?*

chip in (with sth**) (on** sth**) (for** so**)** AND **chip in (with** sth**) (for** sth**) (for** so**); chip** sth **in**† **(on** sth**) (for** so**)** to contribute money for a gift for someone. □ *Would you like to chip in with a little cash on a gift for Carol?* □ *Yes, I'd be happy to chip in.*

a **chip off the old block** *Fig.* a person (usually a male) who behaves in the same way as his father or who resembles his father. □ *John looks like his father—a real chip off the old block.*

*a chip on one's **shoulder** *Fig.* a bad attitude that tends to get someone easily upset. (*Typically: **get** ~; **have** ~; **give** one ~.) □ *Why did you get so angry at the slightest criticism? You seem to have a chip on your shoulder.*

chisel in (on so/sth**)** *Sl.* to use deception to get a share of something. □ *I won't chisel in on your deal.*

chisel so **out of** sth AND **chisel** sth **out of** so**; chisel** sth **from** so to get something away from someone by cheating. □ *The crook tried to chisel pension money out of retired people.*

chock full of sth *Fig.* very full of something. □ *These cookies are chock full of big chunks of chocolate.*

choke up *Fig.* to become emotional or saddened so that one cannot speak. □ *I choked up when I heard about the disaster.*

chomp at the bit Go to champ at the bit.

choose (up) sides *Fig.* to select from a group to be on opposing sides for a debate, fight, or game. (Fixed order.) □ *Let's choose up sides and play basketball.*

chow (sth**) down** *Sl.* to eat something, usually quickly or without good manners. □ *I found a box of cookies and chowed it down before anybody knew what I was doing.*

chuck it in *Inf.* to quit; to give up. (Fixed order.) □ *If I didn't have to keep the job to pay my bills, I'd have chucked it in long ago.*

chuck so **under the chin** to tap someone, as a child, lightly under the chin, as a sign of affection. □ *Please don't chuck me under the chin! I am not a child, you know!*

a **chunk of change** *Fig.* a lot of money. □ *Tom's new sports car cost a real big chunk of change!*

church key *Inf.* a two-ended device used to remove bottle tops and to pierce a hole in can lids. □ *I'm looking for the church key so I can open this beer.*

churn sth **out**† Go to crank sth out†.

city slicker *Inf.* someone from the city who is not familiar with country ways. □ *Them city slickers think we're stupid just because we talk different.*

claim a life *Fig.* [for something] to take the life of someone. □ *The killer tornado claimed the lives of six people at the trailer park.*

so's **claim to fame** *Fig.* someone's reason for being well-known or famous. □ *Her claim to fame is that she can recite the entire works of Shakespeare from memory.*

clam up *Inf.* to say nothing. (Closing one's mouth in the way that a clam closes tight.) □ *The minute they got him in for questioning, he clammed up.*

clamp down on so AND **come down (hard) on** so *Fig.* to apply stricter discipline to someone. □ *After the trouble in the cafeteria, the principal decided to clamp down on the students for a few weeks.*

clamp down on sth AND **come down (hard) on** sth *Fig.* to limit some kind of activity. □ *The cops are beginning to clamp down on speeding, at long last.*

clap so **in(to)** some place *Inf.* to shove or push someone into a place, usually jail. □ *Be good or the sheriff will clap you into jail.*

claw one's **way to the top** *Fig.* to climb to the most prestigious level of something ruthlessly. (Fig. on climbing up a treacherous cliff.) □ *He was the type of hard-hitting guy who claws his way to the top.*

one's **claws are showing** *Inf.* one is acting catty; one is saying spiteful and cruel things. □ *Gloria: Did you see what she was wearing? I wouldn't be caught dead in it! Sally: Gloria, my dear, your claws are showing.*

clean one's **act up**† to reform one's conduct; to improve one's performance. □ *I cleaned up my act, but not in time. I got kicked out.*

*clean as a hound's tooth AND ***clean as a whistle 1.** very clean. (*Also: **as** ~.) □ *After his mother scrubbed him thoroughly, the baby was as clean as a hound's tooth.* **2.** *Rur. Fig.* innocent and free from sin or wrong. (*Also: **as** ~.) □ *Jane's record was clean as a whistle; she had never committed even the smallest infraction.*

clean as a whistle Go to previous.

*a clean bill of health *Fig.* a physician's determination that a person is in good condition, especially following an illness, surgery, etc. (*Typically: **get** ~; **have** ~; **give** so ~.) □ *Now that Sally has a clean bill of health, she can go back to work.*

clean so **out**† **1.** *Fig.* to clear out one's digestive tract. □ *Wow, all that fresh fruit really cleaned me out!* **2.** *Fig.* to steal everything from someone. □ *While we were away, some thieves came and cleaned us out.*

clean one's **plate (up**†**)** *Fig.* to eat all the food on one's plate. □ *You have to clean up your plate before you can leave the table.*

a **clean sweep** *Fig.* a broad movement clearing or affecting everything in its pathway. (See also make a clean sweep.) □ *The manager and everybody in accounting got fired in a clean sweep of that department.*

clean the floor up† **with** so AND **mop the floor up**† **with** so *Inf.* to beat someone up. □ *If you don't shut up, I'll clean up the floor with you.*

clean up good Go to clean up well.

clean up (on sth**)** *Fig.* to make a lot of money on something. □ *If we get this invention to market soon, we can clean up on it.*

clean up well AND **clean up good; scrub up well; scrub up good** *Jocular* appears decent and well-groomed after a little effort. (A parody of what a country person might use as a compliment for someone who looks neat and tidy, as for a date.) □ *Hey, you scrub up pretty good, Maude!*

clean-cut having to do with a person (usually male) who is neat and tidy. □ *He's sort of clean-cut looking, but with curly hair.*

cleaned out 1. *Inf.* broke; with no money. □ *I'm cleaned out. Not a cent left.* **2.** *Inf.* [of the bowels] emptied. □ *That medicine really left me cleaned out.*

*clear as a bell very clear, as with the sound of a bell. (*Also: **as** ~.) □ *Through the wall, I could hear the neighbors talking, just as clear as a bell.*

*clear as crystal 1. *Cliché* very clear; transparent. (*Also: **as** ~.) □ *The stream was as clear as crystal.* **2.** *Cliché* very clear;

easy to understand. (*Also: **as** ~.) □ *The explanation was as clear as crystal.*

*clear as mud 1. *Cliché* not clear at all. (*Also: **as** ~.) □ *Your swimming pool needs cleaning; the water is clear as mud.* **2.** *Cliché* not easy to understand. (*Also: **as** ~.) □ *This physics chapter is clear as mud to me.*

a **clear conscience (about** so/sth**)** AND a **clean conscience (about** so/sth**)** *Fig.* complete lack of guilt about someone or something. □ *I'm sorry that John got the blame. I have a clean conscience about the whole affair.* □ *I have a clear conscience about John and his problems.* □ *I didn't do it. I can swear to that with a clean conscience.*

clear so's **name** *Fig.* to prove that someone is not guilty of a crime or misdeed. □ *I was accused of theft, but the real thief confessed and I cleared my name.*

*clear of sth *Fig.* without touching something; away from something. (*Typically: **keep** ~; **move** ~; **remain** ~; **stand** ~.) □ *Make sure the dog moves clear of the driveway before you back the car up.*

clear off ((of some place**))** to depart; to get off someone's property. □ *Clear off my property!*

clear out (of some place**)** *Fig.* to get out of some place. □ *Will you all clear out of here?*

*clear sailing AND ***smooth sailing** *Fig.* a situation, nautical or otherwise, where progress is made without any difficulty. (*Typically: **be** ~; **have** ~.) □ *Once you've passed that exam, it will be clear sailing to graduation.*

clear the air 1. to get rid of stale or bad air. □ *Open some windows and clear the air. It's stuffy in here.* **2.** *Fig.* to get rid of doubts or hard feelings. (*Fig.* on the notion of removing unpleasantness from the environment.) □ *All right, let's discuss this frankly. It'll be better if we clear the air.*

clear the decks 1. [for everyone] to leave the deck of a ship and prepare for action. (A naval expression urging seamen to stow gear and prepare for battle or other action.) □ *An attack is coming. Clear the decks.* **2.** *Fig.* get out of the way; get out of this area. (Fig. on ①.) □ *Clear the decks! Here comes the teacher.*

clear the table to remove the dishes and other eating utensils from the table after a meal. (Compare this with **set the table**.) □ *Will you please help clear the table?*

Clear the way! *Fig.* Please get out of the way, because someone or something is coming through and needs room! □ *The movers were shouting, "Clear the way!" because they needed room to take the piano out of the house.*

clear one's **throat** to vocalize in a way that removes excess moisture from the vocal cords and surrounding area. □ *I had to clear my throat a lot today. I think I'm coming down with something.*

click with so **1.** [for something] to be understood or comprehended by someone suddenly. □ *His explanation clicked with Maggie at once.* **2.** [for someone or something new] to catch on with someone; to become popular or friendly with someone very quickly. □ *The new product clicked with consumers and was an instant success.*

climb on the bandwagon Go to on the bandwagon.

climb the wall(s) *Fig.* to be very agitated, anxious, bored, or excited. (Fig. on the image of a nervous wild animal trying to climb up a wall to escape.) □ *He was home for only three days; then he began to climb the wall.*

clip so's **wings** *Fig.* to restrain someone; to ground someone; to reduce or put an end to someone's privileges. (Fig. on the image of clipping a bird's wings to keep it from flying away.) □ *My mother clipped my wings. I can't go out tonight.*

cloak so/sth **in secrecy** *Fig.* to hide or conceal someone or something in secrecy. □ *Patrick cloaked his activities in secrecy.*

cloak-and-dagger *Fig.* involving secrecy and plotting. □ *A great deal of cloak-and-dagger stuff goes on in political circles.*

clock in to record one's time of arrival, usually by punching a time clock. □ *What time did she clock in?*

clock out to record one's time of departure, usually by punching a time clock. □ *Jim clocked out early Tuesday to go to the doctor.*

clock watcher someone—a worker or a student—who is always looking at the clock, anticipating when something will be over. □ *People who don't like their jobs can turn into clock watchers.*

clog so **up**† [for some kind of food] to constipate someone. □ *This cheese clogs me up. I can't eat it.*

close a deal AND **close the deal** *Fig.* to formally conclude bargaining; to bring negotiating to an end by reaching an agreement. □ *We negotiated the terms of the agreement, and this afternoon we will close the deal.*

close a sale AND **close the sale** *Fig.* to complete the sale of something; to seal a bargain in the sale of something. □ *The salesman closed the sale, and the customer drove off in a brand new car.*

*close as two coats of paint *Cliché* close and intimate. (*Also: **as** ~.) □ *All their lives, the cousins were close as two coats of paint.*

close at hand *Fig.* within reach; handy. □ *When you're cooking, you should keep all the ingredients close at hand.*

Close, but no cigar. *Cliché* Some effort came close to succeeding, but did not succeed. (Fig. on the idea of failing to win a contest for which a cigar is a prize.) □ *Jill: How did you do in the contest? Jane: Close, but no cigar. I got second place.*

a **close call** Go to a close shave.

close down AND **shut down** [for someone] to close a business, office, shop, etc., permanently or temporarily. □ *This shop will have to close down if they raise taxes.*

close enough for government work AND **good enough for government work** *Inf.* sufficiently close; done just well enough. (Fig. on the notion that work for the government is not done with care or pride.) □ *I didn't do the best job of mending your shirt, but it's close enough for government work.*

close one's **eyes to** sth AND **shut** one's **eyes to** sth **1.** to close one's eyes to avoid seeing something unpleasant. □ *I had to close my eyes to the carnage about me. I couldn't bear to look.* **2.** *Fig.* to ignore something; to pretend that something is not happening. (Fig. on ①.) □ *Maria simply shut her eyes to the terrible morale in her department.*

close in for the kill AND **move in for the kill 1.** to move in on someone or something for the purpose of killing. □ *When the lions closed in for the kill, the zebras began to stampede.* **2.** *Fig.* to get ready to do the final and climactic part of something. (Fig. on ①.) □ *The car salesman closed in for the kill with contract and pen in hand.*

close in (on so/sth) **1.** to move inward on someone or something. □ *The cops were closing in on the thugs.* **2.** *Fig.* [for threats or negative feelings] to overwhelm or seem to surround someone or something. (Fig. on the image of walls pressing on someone.) □ *My problems are closing in on me.*

close ranks *Fig.* to move closer together in a military formation. □ *The soldiers closed ranks and marched on the enemy in tight formation.*

close ranks (behind so/sth) to support someone or something; to back someone or something. (Fig. on the image of soldiers moving in behind their leader.) □ *Let's close ranks behind her and give her the support she needs.*

a **close shave** AND a **close call** a narrow escape. (See also have a close shave.) □ *The speeding car passed only a few inches from us—a real close call.*

close the books on so/sth *Fig.* to declare that a matter concerning someone or something is finished. (The *books* here originally referred to financial accounting records.) □ *It's time to close the books on Fred. He's had enough time to apologize to us.*

close the door on so/sth Go to shut the door (up)on so/sth.

*****close to** so *Fig.* friendly or intimate with someone. (*Typically: be ~; get ~.) □ *She is very shy and really won't let anyone get close to her.*

*****close to** so/sth *Fig.* approximating someone or something in some quality or measure. (*Typically: be ~; get ~.) □ *This brand of frozen fish does not even get close to that brand in flavor and freshness.* □ *Tom doesn't even get close to Nancy when it comes to artistic ability.*

close to one's **heart** Go to dear to one's heart.

close to home *Fig.* affecting one personally and intimately. □ *Her remarks were a bit too close to home. I took her review as a personal insult.*

close to the bone Go to (too) close to the bone.

close up 1. [for an opening] to close completely. □ *The wound will close up completely in a day or so.* **2.** *Fig.* [for a place of business] to close for business. □ *The store closed up and did not open until the next day.*

close up shop to quit working, for the day or forever. (Fixed order.) □ *It's five o'clock. Time to close up shop.*

closefisted (with money) Go to tightfisted (with money).

cloud up *Fig.* [for someone] to grow very sad, as if to cry. □ *Whenever Mary got homesick, she'd cloud up. She really wanted to go home.*

clown around (with so) *Fig.* to join with someone in acting silly; [for two or more people] to act silly together. □ *The kids are having fun clowning around.*

clue so **in**† **(on** sth) *Fig.* to inform someone of something. □ *Please clue me in on what's been going on.*

clutch (up) *Inf.* to become very tense and anxious; to freeze with anxiety. □ *Just relax, play your best game, and you won't clutch!*

clutching at straws Go to grasping at straws.

The **coast is clear.** *Fig.* There is no visible danger. □ *I'm going to stay hidden here until the coast is clear.*

coast-to-coast *Fig.* from the Atlantic to the Pacific oceans (in the continental U.S.); all the land between the Atlantic and Pacific oceans (considered in either direction). □ *My voice was once heard on a coast-to-coast radio broadcast.*

coat and tie [for men] a jacket or sports coat and necktie. (A respectable but less than formal standard of dress.) □ *My brother was not wearing a coat and tie, and they would not admit him into the restaurant.*

cock of the walk *Fig.* someone who acts more important than others in a group. □ *He loved acting cock of the walk and ordering everyone about.*

cock-and-bull story *Fig.* a hard-to-believe, made-up story; a story that is a lie. □ *I asked for an explanation, and all I got was your ridiculous cock-and-bull story!*

*cocky as the king of spades boastful; overly proud. (*Also: **as** ~.) □ *He'd challenge anyone to a fight. He's as cocky as the king of spades.*

coffee and *Inf.* coffee and a doughnut or a pastry. □ *We stopped at a little shop for coffee and.*

coffee and Danish *Fig.* a cup of coffee and a Danish sweet roll. □ *Coffee and Danish is not my idea of a good breakfast!*

coffee, tea, or milk *Fig.* a choice of beverage. (Originally used by airline personnel when offering something to drink to the passengers.) □ *Would you prefer coffee, tea, or milk to go with your meal?*

coffee-table book *Fig.* a book that is more suitable for display than for reading, typically, an oversize, illustrated book left on the coffee table for visitors to examine. □ *This book is more of a coffee-table book than an art book. I prefer something more scholarly.*

coin a phrase *Fig.* to create a new expression that is worthy of being remembered and repeated. (Often jocular.) □ *He is*

"worth his weight in feathers," to coin a phrase.

*cold as a well digger's ass (in January) AND ***cold as a well digger's feet (in January); *cold as a witch's caress; *cold as marble; *cold as a witch's tit; *cold as a well digger's ears (in January)** very, very cold; chilling. (*Also: **as** ~. Caution with *ass*.) □ *Bill: How's the weather where you are? Tom: Cold as a well digger's ass in January.* □ *By the time I got in from the storm, I was as cold as a well digger's feet.* □ *The car's heater broke, so it's as cold as a well digger's ears to ride around in it.*

cold as a well digger's ears (in January) Go to previous.

cold as a well digger's feet (in January) Go to cold as a well digger's ass (in January).

cold as a witch's caress Go to cold as a well digger's ass (in January).

cold as a witch's tit Go to cold as a well digger's ass (in January).

cold as marble Go to cold as a well digger's ass (in January).

cold cock so *Fig.* to knock someone unconscious. □ *He hit him once and looks like he cold cocked him.*

cold comfort *Fig.* no comfort or consolation at all. □ *She knows there are others worse off than her, but that's cold comfort.*

*cold feet *Fig.* fear of doing something; cowardice at the moment of action. (*Typically: **get** ~; **have** ~; **give** so ~.) □ *The bridegroom got cold feet on the day of the wedding.*

*a cold fish *Fig.* a person who is distant and unfeeling. (*Typically: **act like** ~; **be** ~.) □ *Bob is so dull—a real cold fish.*

cold, hard cash *Inf.* cash, not checks or credit. □ *I want to be paid in cold, hard cash, and I want to be paid now!*

cold shoulder to ignore someone; to give someone a cool reception. (See also the cold shoulder.) □ *Tiffany cold shouldered the guy who was trying to flirt with her.*

*the **cold shoulder** *Fig.* an attitude of rejection. (*Typically: **get** ~; **give** so ~.) □ *If you greet her at a party, you'll just get the cold shoulder.*

cold sober Go to stone (cold) sober.

cold turkey immediately; without tapering off or cutting down gradually. (Slang. See also go cold turkey. Originally drug slang. Now used of breaking any habit.) □ *She gave up her drinking habit cold turkey and had no ill effects.*

collect one's **thoughts** *Fig.* to take time to think through an issue; to give some thought to a topic. □ *I'll speak to the visitors in a moment. I need some time to collect my thoughts.*

come a cropper *Fig.* to have a misfortune; to fail. (Meaning "fall off one's horse." More U.K. than U.S.) □ *Bob invested all his money in the stock market just before it fell. Boy, did he come a cropper.*

come about 1. to happen. □ *How did this damage come about?* **2.** *Fig.* [for a ship or boat] to turn. □ *Look how easily this boat comes about.*

come across 1. to be compliant. □ *Oh, she'll come across, just you wait; she'll do what we want.* **2.** AND **come across (with** sth**)** to deliver or give something to someone, even if reluctantly. □ *You had better come across with the money you owe me.*

come across so/sth Go to come (up)on so/sth.

come across like so/sth **(to** so**)** AND **come across as** so/sth **(to** so**)** to appear or seem like someone or something to other people. □ *She comes across like the Queen of the Nile to most people who meet her.*

come across (to sth**)** Go to come across.

come across (with sth**)** Go to come across.

Come again. 1. Please come back again sometime. □ *Mary: I had a lovely time. Thank you for asking me. Sally: You're quite welcome. Come again.* **2.** Go to Say what?

Come an(d) get it! *Inf.* Dinner's ready. Come eat! □ *The camp cook shouted, "Time to eat! Come an' get it!"*

come apart (at the seams) Go to fall apart (at the seams).

come (a)round 1. *Fig.* finally to agree or consent (to something). □ *I thought he'd never agree, but in the end he came around.* **2.** *Fig.* to return to consciousness; to wake up. □ *The boxer was knocked out, but came round in a few seconds.*

come around (again) Go to roll around (again).

come around (to doing sth**)** *Fig.* to agree to do something eventually, after a long wait. □ *Finally, she came around to painting the kitchen.*

come as no surprise *Fig.* will not be surprising [for someone] to learn [something]. □ *It will come as no surprise for you to learn that the company is losing money this year.*

come at a price Go to at a price.

come away empty-handed *Fig.* to return without anything. □ *All right, go gambling. Don't come away empty-handed, though.*

Come back and see us. AND **Come back and see me.** *Inf.* Come visit us [or me] again. (Often said by a host or hostess to departing guests.) □ *Bob: I enjoyed my visit. Good-bye. Mary: It was very nice of you to pay me a visit. Come back and see me.*

Come back anytime. *Inf.* Please come and visit us again. You're always welcome. (Often said by a host or hostess to departing guests.) □ *Mary: So glad you could come. Bill: Thank you. I had a wonderful time. Mary: Come back anytime.*

come back (to so/sth**)** *Fig.* [for a memory] to return to someone's consciousness. □ *Everything you said suddenly came back to me.*

come back to haunt one AND **return to haunt** one *Fig.* [for a bad memory] to recur; for the consequences of a bad decision to affect one negatively later. □ *I never dreamed that a little thing like a traffic ticket could come back to haunt me years later.*

Come back when you can stay longer. *Inf.* Come back again sometime when your visit can be longer. (Often said by a host or hostess to departing guests.) □ *John: I really must go. Sue: So glad you could come. Please come back when you can stay longer.*

come before so/sth **1.** [of persons or things in an order or a line] to be in front of or in advance of someone or something. □ *This one comes before that one.* □ *She comes before me.* **2.** [for one] to present oneself in the presence of someone or a group. □ *Thank you for coming before this committee with your testimony.* **3.** [for an issue] to be raised before someone, a board, committee, etc.; [for an issue] to appear on the agenda of someone or a deliberative body. □ *The matter of the broken windows came before the school board at last.*

come by sth *Fig.* to find or get something. □ *How did you come by that haircut?*

come by sth **honestly 1.** *Fig.* to acquire something honestly. (See also **come by** sth.) □ *I have a feeling she didn't come by it honestly.* **2.** *Fig.* to inherit something—such as a character trait—from one's parents. (Fig. on ①.) □ *I know I'm mean. I came by it honestly, though.* □ *She came by her kindness honestly.*

come clean (with so**) (about** sth**)** *Fig.* to be honest with somebody about something. □ *I want you to come clean with me about your financial status.*

come close (to so/sth**)** *Fig.* to approximate someone or something in a specific quality. □ *You don't come close to the former owners in caring for your property.*

come down 1. *Sl.* to happen. □ *Hey, man! What's coming down?* **2.** *Inf.* a letdown; a disappointment. (Usually **comedown.**) □ *The loss of the race was a real comedown for Willard.* **3.** *Sl.* to begin to recover from the effects of alcohol or drug intoxication. □ *She came down slow from her ad-*

diction, which was good. **4.** *Fig.* [for something] to descend (to someone) through inheritance. □ *All my silverware came down to me from my great-grandmother.*

come down (from sth**)** to move from a higher status to a lower one. (See also **come down in the world.**) □ *He has come down from his original position. Now he is just a clerk.*

come down (hard) on so Go to clamp down on so.

come down (hard) on sth Go to clamp down on sth.

come down in the world *Fig.* to lose one's social position or financial standing. □ *Mr. Jones has really come down in the world since he lost his job.*

come down on the side of so/sth AND **come down on** so's/sth's **side** *Fig.* [for a person] to be in favor of someone or something; to judge in favor of someone or something; to state agreement with someone's or something's position. (Often in the context of a contest or a court trial.) □ *The judge came down on our side and we won the case.*

come down to sth *Fig.* to be reduced to something; to amount to no more than something. □ *It comes down to whether you want to go to the movies or stay at home and watch television.*

come down to earth 1. *Lit.* to arrive on earth from above. □ *An angel came down to earth and made an announcement.* **2.** *Fig.* to become realistic; to become alert to what is going on around one. (Fig. on ①.) □ *You are having a spell of enthusiasm, John, but you must come down to earth. We can't possibly afford any of your suggestions.*

come forward with sth to present oneself voluntarily to offer evidence or ideas, especially in regard to legal proceedings. □ *Why did you not come forward earlier in the trial?* □ *Colleen came forward with a new idea.*

come from behind to advance from a losing position. (Refers to being behind in a score or in a race.) □ *Our team came* from behind to win the game. □ *The horse I bet on came from behind and almost placed second.*

come from far and wide Go to far and wide.

come from nowhere to come as a surprise with no warning. □ *The dogs came from nowhere and attacked my cat.* □ *The whole set of problems came from nowhere. There was no way we could have foreseen them.*

come full circle *Fig.* to return to the original position or state of affairs. □ *The family sold the house generations ago, but things have come full circle and one of their descendants lives there now.*

come hell or high water *Inf.* no matter what happens. □ *I'll be there tomorrow, come hell or high water.*

come home (to so) *Fig.* [for a fact] to be recognized suddenly by someone. □ *Suddenly, it came home to me that you thought I was Ronald.*

come home (to roost) 1. [for a fowl or other bird] to return to its home, as for a night's rest. □ *The chickens come home to roost in the evening.* **2.** *Fig.* [for a problem] to return to cause trouble [for someone]. (Fig. on ①. See also come home (to so). □ *As I feared, all my problems came home to roost.*

come in *Fig.* [for a broadcast signal] to be received satisfactorily. □ *Can you hear me? How am I coming in?* □ *You are coming in all right.*

Come in and get some weight off your feet. Go to Come in and sit a spell.

Come in and make yourself at home. *Fig.* Please come into my home and make yourself comfortable. □ *Sue: Oh, hello, Tom. Come in and make yourself at home. Tom: Thanks. I will.*

Come in and sit a spell. AND **Come in and set a spell.; Come in and get some weight off your feet.; Come in and sit down.; Come in and take a load off your feet.** *Rur.* Please come in and have a seat and a visit. (The variant with *set* is informal or folksy.) □ *"Hi,*

Fred," smiled Tom, "Come in and sit a spell." □ *Tom: I hope I'm not intruding. Bill: Not at all. Come in and set a spell.*

Come in and sit down. Go to previous.

Come in and take a load off your feet. Go to Come in and sit a spell.

come in for sth *Fig.* to be eligible for something; to be due something. □ *You are going to come in for a nice reward.* □ *Your report came in for a lot of criticism at the last board meeting.*

come in handy *Fig.* [for something] to be useful. □ *I think that this gadget will come in handy in the kitchen.*

come in on a wing and a prayer Go to on a wing and a prayer.

come in out of the cold Go to next.

come in out of the rain AND **come in out of the cold; come in from the rain; come in from the cold** *Fig.* to wake up to reality; to come down to earth. (See also not know enough to come in out of the rain.) □ *Hey, man! Come in out of the rain! Don't you see that your boss is taking advantage of you!*

come in useful *Fig.* to be useful. □ *Your report has come in useful a number of times.*

come into (some) money AND **come into a fortune** *Fig.* to get some money unexpectedly, usually by inheritance. (See also a small fortune.) □ *She came into a lot of money when she turned 20.* □ *I hope I can come into some money some day.*

come into a fortune Go to previous.

come into being to begin existence. □ *This idea came into being during the last decade.*

come into bloom AND **come into blossom** [for a plant, bush, or tree] to begin to have many blossoms. □ *When do these bushes come into bloom?* □ *They come into blossom in June.*

come into blossom Go to previous.

come into so's hands AND **fall into so's hands** *Fig.* to become someone's possession as if by accident. □ *This old map* *came into my hands as part of an inheritance from an uncle.*

come in(to) heat AND **come in(to) season** *Fig.* [for a female animal] to enter into the breeding season. □ *This animal will come into heat in the spring.*

come into one's or **its own** *Fig.* to become independent; to be recognized as independent and capable, usually after much effort or time. □ *Maria is coming into her own as a concert pianist.*

come into play *Fig.* to become an important factor in something; to go into force. □ *All your hard practice and preparation will now come into play in the finals.*

come into season 1. *Fig.* [for a game animal] to be subject to legal hunting. □ *When do ducks come into season around here?* **2.** Go to come in(to) heat.

come into service AND **go into service** *Fig.* to begin to be used; to begin to operate and function as designed. (See also put sth in(to) service; press sth into service.) □ *When did this elevator come into service?* □ *I think that this machine went into service during World War II.*

come into the world *Fig.* to be born. □ *Little Timmy came into the world on a cold and snowy night.*

come Monday *Rur.* when Monday comes. (Can be used with other expressions for time, as in *come next week, come June, come five o'clock.*) □ *Joe plays so hard on the weekend that come Monday, he's all worn out.* □ *You may think that putting up storm windows is a bother, but come December, you'll be glad you did it.*

come naturally (to so**)** *Fig.* to be natural and easy for someone. □ *Her ability to deal easily with people comes naturally to her.*

come of age Go to of age.

come off *Inf.* to happen; to take place. □ *What time does this party come off?* □ *How did your speech come off?*

come off as so/sth *Inf.* to make an impression as someone or as a type of person. □ *You always come off as a quick-tem-*

pered person. Of course, I know you better.

Come off it! 1. *Inf.* Stop acting arrogantly! □ *Come off it, Tiff. You're not the Queen of England.* **2.** *Inf.* Abandon your incorrect point of view! □ *Come off it! You're wrong, and you know it!*

come off second best *Fig.* to be second to someone or something; to get the poorer end of a bargain. □ *As usual, he came off second best with a little less prize money than the winner.*

come on 1. *Inf.* Stop it!; Stop doing or saying that. (Usually **Come on!**) □ *Mary: Are you really going to sell your new car? Sally: Come on! How dumb do you think I am?* **2.** *Inf.* please oblige me. □ *Mother: Sorry. You can't go! Bill: Come on, let me go to the picnic!* □ *"Come on," whined Jimmy, "I want some more!"* **3.** *Inf.* to hurry up; to follow someone. □ *If you don't come on, we'll miss the train.* **4.** [for electricity or some other device] to start operating. □ *After a while, the lights came on again.* □ *I hope the heat comes on soon.* **5.** to walk out and appear onstage. □ *You are to come on when you hear your cue.* **6.** *Fig.* [for a pain] to begin hurting; [for a disease] to attack someone. □ *The pain began to come on again, and Sally had to lie down.* **7.** *Fig.* [for a program] to be broadcast on radio or television. □ *The news didn't come on until an hour later.*

come on as sth *Fig.* to appear to be something; to project one's image as something. □ *The senator comes on as a liberal, but we all know better.*

come on (duty) to begin to work at one's scheduled time. □ *When did you come on duty tonight?*

Come on in. *Inf.* Enter.; Come into this place. (A polite invitation to enter someone's home, office, room, etc.) □ *Bob: Hello, you guys. Come on in. We're just about to start dinner.*

Come on in, the water's fine! 1. *Fig.* Get into the water and swim! (Usually a polite command.) □ *As Todd swam along, he said to Rachel, "Come on in. The water's fine."* **2.** *Fig.* to begin to do anything.

(Fig. on ①. A phrase that encourages someone to join in doing something.) □ *I think you would like working here, and I'm happy to offer you the job. Come on in, the water's fine.*

come on like gangbusters Go to next.

come on strong AND **come on like gangbusters** *Inf.* to seem aggressive; to impress people initially as very aggressive and assertive. □ *She has a tendency to come on strong, but she's really a softie.*

come on the scene AND **arrive on the scene** *Fig.* to become part of a situation. □ *She thought she was in love with Harry until Bob came on the scene.*

come on (to so) *Sl.* to attempt to interest someone romantically or sexually. □ *He was trying to come on to me, but I found him unappealing.*

come on(to) so/sth to find someone or something by accident; to happen onto someone or something. □ *When I was out on my walk, I came on a little shop that sells leather goods.*

come out 1. *Fig.* to result; to succeed; to happen. □ *I hope everything comes out fine.* **2.** *Fig.* to come before the public; [for a book] to be published; [for a report] to be made public. □ *When will your next book come out?* **3.** *Fig.* [for a young woman] to make a social debut. (Now only done in certain U.S. regions.) □ *Does your daughter plan to come out this year?* **4.** *Fig.* to reveal one's homosexuality. (See also out of the closet.) □ *Herbie finally came out when he was 45.*

come out against so/sth to announce or reveal that one is opposed to someone or something. □ *Our governor came out against the new tax bill.*

come out at an amount AND **come out to** an amount *Fig.* to result in a certain amount, as the result of mathematical computation. □ *The total charges came out at far more than we expected.*

come out fighting Go to come out swinging.

come out for so/sth AND **come out in favor of** so/sth *Fig.* to announce or reveal that one supports someone or something. □ *Roger came out for Lynn, who was running for mayor.* □ *I thought the mayor would come out in favor of more public housing.*

come out in favor of so/sth Go to previous.

come out in the wash *Fig.* to work out all right. (Fig. on the image of a clothing stain that can be removed by washing.) □ *Don't worry about that problem. It'll all come out in the wash.*

come out in(to) the open AND **come (out) into the open** *Fig.* [for someone who has been hiding] to appear in public. □ *The thief came out into the open and was recognized by one of the witnesses to the crime.* □ *The FBI agents finally came into the open.*

come out in(to) the open with sth *Fig.* to make something known publicly. □ *After much fuss about its secret dealings, the city council came out in the open with the whole story.*

come out (of sth) *Fig.* to result from something. □ *Nothing at all came out of our discussions.*

come out of a clear blue sky AND **come out of the clear blue sky; come out of the blue** suddenly; without warning. □ *Then, out of a clear blue sky, he told me he was leaving.* □ *My sister Mary appeared on my doorstep out of the blue, after years with no word from her.*

come out of left field AND **come from left field** [for a problem or dilemma] to come from an unexpected place. (See also out of left field.) □ *This new problem came out of left field. We were really surprised.*

come out of nowhere Go to out of nowhere.

come out of one's **shell** Go to out of one's shell.

come out of the closet Go to out of the closet.

come out on sth [for someone] to do well or poorly on a business venture. □ *We came out ahead on the Adams project, but* *for the quarter we came out with a loss overall.*

come out on top *Fig.* to end up being the winner. □ *I knew that if I kept trying, I would come out on top.* □ *Harry came out on top as I knew he would.*

come out smelling like a rose AND **come up smelling like a rose** *Fig.* to succeed; to do better than anyone else in some situation. □ *Everyone else in the firm lost money in the real estate deal, but Bob came out smelling like a rose.*

come out swinging AND **come out fighting 1.** [for a boxer] to come from his corner punching at his opponent. □ *Come on Willie! Come out swinging! Show them you're still semiconscious.* **2.** *Fig.* to come into a discussion, sports contest, or any activity ready to play or perform actively. □ *You make the presentation at the board meeting, Charlie. You have to impress them with your eagerness. Come out fighting, and they'll pay attention.*

come out with sth **1.** *Fig.* to publish something. □ *When are you going to come out with a new edition?* **2.** *Fig.* to express or utter something. □ *It was over an hour before the president came out with an explanation.*

come over so *Fig.* [for something] to affect a person, perhaps suddenly. □ *I just don't know what came over me.* □ *Something came over her just as she entered the room, and she suddenly turned pale.*

come rain or (come) shine AND **rain or shine** *Inf.* no matter whether it rains or the sun shines; in any sort of weather. □ *Don't worry. I'll be there come rain or shine.* □ *We'll hold the picnic—rain or shine.*

Come right in. *Inf.* Come in, please, you are very welcome here. □ *Fred (opening the door): Well, hi, Bill. Bill: Hello, Fred. Good to see you. Fred: Come right in. Bill: Thanks.*

come (right) on top of sth *Fig.* [for something] to happen immediately after something else. □ *The accident expenses came right on top of the costs of her illness.*

come short of sth *Fig.* to do something almost; to fail to achieve something completely. □ *We came short of our goal for the year.*

come through 1. *Fig.* [for someone] to do what one is expected to do, especially under difficult conditions. □ *Tom came through at the last minute with everything we needed.* **2.** *Fig.* [for something] to be approved; [for something] to gain approval. □ *Your papers came through, and you can be sure that the matter has been taken care of.*

come through sth **(with flying colors)** *Fig.* to survive something quite well. (See also **with flying colors.** *Colors* here refers originally to flags.) □ *Mr. Franklin came through his operation with flying colors.*

come to *Fig.* to become conscious; to wake up. □ *We threw a little cold water in his face, and he came to immediately.*

come to oneself *Fig.* to begin acting and thinking like one's normal self. □ *I began to come to myself and realize the wrong I had done.*

come to sth *Fig.* [for something] to end up being helpful or significant. □ *Do you think this work will come to anything?*

come to a bad end *Fig.* to have a disaster, perhaps one that is deserved or expected; to die an unfortunate death. □ *The dirty crook came to a bad end!*

come to a boil 1. *Fig.* [for a problem or situation] to reach a critical or crucial stage. (Fig. on the image of water reaching an active boil.) □ *Everything came to a boil after Mary admitted her guilt.* **2.** *Fig.* [for someone] to get very angry. (Fig. on the heat of anger.) □ *Fred was coming to a boil, and clearly he was going to lose his temper.*

come to a conclusion 1. to reach a decision after discussion. □ *We talked for a long time but never came to any conclusion.* **2.** [for a process] to reach the end and be finished. □ *At last, the yearlong ordeal of buying a house came to a conclusion.*

come to a dead end 1. to reach a point where one can go no farther and can turn in no new direction. □ *The road comes to a dead end about a mile farther.* **2.** *Fig.* to have run out of possible ideas, solutions, energy, etc. (Fig. on ①.) □ *The committee came to a dead end on the matter and tabled the whole business.*

come to a head *Fig.* [for a problem] to reach a critical or crucial stage. □ *At the end of the week, everything came to a head and Sam was fired.*

come to a pretty pass *Fig.* to encounter a difficult situation. (Older. Here *pretty* expresses irony.) □ *This project has come to a pretty pass. I don't know how we can possibly finish on time.*

come to an untimely end *Fig.* to come to an early death. □ *Poor Mr. Jones came to an untimely end in a car accident.*

come to attention *Fig.* to assume a formal military posture, standing very straight. □ *Almost immediately, the soldiers came to attention.*

come to so's **attention** AND **come to** so's **notice** *Fig.* to be told to, revealed to, or discovered by someone. □ *It has come to my attention that you are not following the rules.*

come to blows (over so/sth**)** AND **come to blows (about** so/sth**)** *Fig.* to reach the point of fighting about someone or something. □ *Let's not come to blows over this silly disagreement.*

come to one's **feet** *Fig.* to stand up. □ *The audience came to its feet, cheering.*

come to grief *Fig.* to experience something unpleasant or damaging. □ *In the end, he came to grief because he did not follow instructions.*

come to grips with so/sth *Fig.* to begin to deal with someone or something; to face the challenge posed by someone or something. □ *I found it hard to come to grips with Crystal and her problems.*

come to life *Fig.* [for someone or something] to become vigorous or lively. □ *About midnight, the party really came to life.*

come to light *Fig.* [for something] to become known or to be discovered. □

Nothing new has come to light since we talked last.

come to mind *Fig.* [for a thought or idea] to enter into one's consciousness or be remembered. □ *Another idea comes to mind. Why not check in the phone book?*

come to much 1. *Fig.* to amount to a large amount of money. (Usually used with a negative.) □ *The bill did not come to much, considering what we had for dinner and drinks.* **2.** *Fig.* to count for much; to be important or meaningful. (Usually negative.) □ *No one thought he would come to much.*

come to naught Go to come to nothing.

come to no good *Fig.* to end up badly; to come to a bad end. □ *The street gang leaders came to no good in the end.*

come to nothing AND **come to naught; count for naught** *Fig.* to amount to nothing; to be worthless. □ *So all my hard work counts for naught.* □ *Yes, the whole project comes to naught.*

come to so's **notice** Go to come to so's attention.

come to pass *Fig.* to happen; to take place. □ *And when do you think all these good things will come to pass?*

come to one's **senses** *Fig.* to begin thinking sensibly. □ *I'm glad he finally came to his senses and went on to college.*

come to terms (with so/sth**) 1.** *Fig.* to come to an agreement with someone. □ *I finally came to terms with my lawyer about his fee.* **2.** *Fig.* to learn to accept someone or something. (Fig. on ①.) □ *She couldn't come to terms with her estranged husband.*

come to the same thing Go to amount to the same thing.

come to think of it *Fig.* I just remembered. □ *Come to think of it, I know someone who can help.*

come to this *Fig.* to result in this situation. □ *Who would believe it would come to this?* □ *So, it has come to this?*

come true *Fig.* to materialize as expected or hoped. □ *Jane's wishes had come true at last!*

come under sth *Fig.* to be classed in the category of something. □ *Your proposal comes under the heading of new business and is out of order.*

come under the hammer AND **go under the hammer** *Fig.* [for something] to be auctioned. □ *The house at the corner is coming under the hammer next week.*

come unglued *Inf.* to lose emotional control; to break out into tears or laughter. □ *When Sally heard the joke, she almost came unglued.*

come up 1. to come near; to approach. □ *He came up and began to talk to us.* **2.** *Fig.* to come to someone's attention. □ *The question of what time to be there never came up.*

come up for sth *Fig.* to be eligible for something; to be in line or sequence for something. □ *She comes up for reelection in April.* □ *How soon does your driver's license come up for renewal?*

come up for air 1. *Fig.* to stop what one is doing for a different activity or rest. □ *Whenever you get off the phone and come up for air, I have a question for you.* **2.** *Fig.* to stop kissing for a moment and breathe. (Fig. on ①.) □ *Don't those kids ever come up for air?*

come (up) from behind to advance in competition; to improve one's position relative to the positions of other things or people. □ *Lee was losing in the election, but he began to come from behind in the last week.*

come up heads AND **come up tails** *Fig.* [for a tossed coin] to turn out to be either heads or tails. □ *We tossed a coin, and it came up heads.*

come up in the world Go to move up in the world.

come up smelling like a rose Go to come out smelling like a rose.

come up tails Go to come up heads.

come up through the ranks AND **rise from the ranks** *Fig.* to rise to a position of leadership by working up through the sequence of lower positions. □ *The general came up through the ranks. There is no other way to become a general.*

come up to so's **expectations** *Fig.* to be as good as someone expected. □ *Sorry, but this product does not come up to my expectations, and I want to return it.*

come up to so's **standards** *Fig.* to meet or be equal to someone's standards or requirements. □ *Does this ice cream come up to your standards?*

come up with so/sth *Fig.* to find or supply someone or something; to manage to find or improvise something. □ *My mom is always able to come up with some yummy snack for me in the afternoon.*

come (up)on so/sth AND **happen (up)on** so/sth; **come across** so/sth to meet with or discover someone or something, as if by accident. □ *I just happened upon a strange little man in the street who offered to sell me a watch.* □ *I came on this little store near Maple Street that has everything we need.*

come what may *Cliché* no matter what might happen. □ *I'll be home for the holidays, come what may.*

come with the territory AND **go with the territory** *Fig.* to be expected under circumstances like this. (Refers to the details and difficulties attendant on something like the assignment of a specific sales territory to a salesperson. When one accepts the assignment, one accepts the problems.) □ *There is a lot of paperwork in this job. Oh, well, I guess it comes with the territory.*

come within an ace of sth *Inf.* to come very close to [doing] something. □ *I came within an ace of leaving school. I'm glad you talked me out of it.*

come within an inch of doing sth *Fig.* almost to do something; to come very close to doing something. (Can also be literal.) □ *I came within an inch of going into the army.* □ *I came within an inch of falling off the roof.*

come-hither look *Fig.* an alluring or seductive look or glance, usually done by a woman. □ *She had mastered the come-hither look, but was not ready for the next part.*

***comes down the pike** *Fig.* makes an appearance; happens. (*Typically: **anything that** ~; **whoever** ~; **whatever** ~; **who knows what** ~; **the next thing that** ~.) □ *We are ready to deal with anything that comes down the pike.*

***comfortable as an old shoe** *Cliché* very comfortable; very comforting and familiar. (*Also: **as** ~.) □ *My old house may seem small to you, but I think it's cozy. It's as comfortable as an old shoe.*

coming out of one's **ears** *Fig.* very numerous or abundant. (As if people or things were coming in great numbers from many sources including unlikely ones.) □ *We are very busy at the factory. We have orders coming out of our ears.*

commit to so to marry or enter into an exclusive relationship with another person. □ *Jane says she loves me, but she's not ready to commit to any one person.*

commit to sth to make a promise about something. □ *Tuesday is the best time, but I can't commit to it yet.*

commit sth **to memory** *Fig.* to memorize something. □ *The dress rehearsal of the play is tomorrow night. Please make sure you have committed all your lines to memory by that time.*

commode-hugging drunk *Sl.* heavily alcohol intoxicated; drunk and vomiting. □ *Willie got commode-hugging drunk in the space of two hours.*

***common as an old shoe** AND ***common as dirt** low class; uncouth. (*Also: **as** ~.) □ *That ill-mannered girl is just as common as an old shoe!* □ *Despite Mamie's efforts to appear to be upper class, most folks considered her common as dirt.*

common as dirt Go to previous.

a **common thread (to all this)** *Fig.* a similar idea or pattern to a series of events. □ *All of these incidents are related. There is a common thread to all this.*

compare apples and oranges *Fig.* to compare two entities that are not similar. (Used especially in reference to comparisons of unlike things.) □ *Talking about her current book and her previous best-seller is like comparing apples and oranges.*

comprised of so/sth made up of someone or something. (The use of *of* after *comprise* is regarded as bad grammar by some.) □ *The committee was comprised of representatives from all areas.*

conk out 1. *Sl.* [for something] to break down; to quit running. □ *My car conked out finally.* **2.** *Sl.* to fall asleep. □ *I conked out about midnight.*

connect (with so**)** *Fig.* to meet with someone as for a date or a discussion; to talk to someone on the telephone. □ *We finally connected and discussed the matter fully over dinner.*

***conspicuous by** one's **absence** *Cliché* noticeably absent (from an event). (*Typically: **be** ~; **made** ~.) □ *How could the bride's father miss the wedding? He was certainly conspicuous by his absence.*

a **contradiction in terms** *Fig.* a statement containing a seeming contradiction. □ *A straight-talking politician may seem to be a contradiction in terms.*

control the purse strings AND **hold the purse strings** *Fig.* to be in charge of the money in a business or a household. □ *Mr. Williams is the treasurer. He controls the purse strings.*

cook so's **goose** *Inf.* to damage or ruin someone. □ *I cooked my own goose by not showing up on time.*

cook the accounts AND **cook the books** to cheat in bookkeeping; to make the accounts appear to balance when they do not. □ *Jane was charged with cooking the accounts of her mother's store.*

cook the books Go to previous.

cook sth **up**† **(with** so**)** *Fig.* to arrange or plan to do something with someone. □ *I tried to cook something up with Karen for Tuesday.* □ *I want to cook up something with John.*

cooking with gas *Inf.* doing [something] exactly right. □ *I knew she was finally cooking with gas when she answered all the questions correctly.*

*cool as a cucumber extremely calm; imperturbable. (*Also: **as** ~.) □ *The politician kept cool as a cucumber throughout the interview with the aggressive journalist.*

cool, calm, and collected *Cliché* [of a person] very calm and poised. □ *The bad news didn't seem to distress Jane at all. She remained cool, calm, and collected.*

cool down Go to cool off.

cool so **down**† AND **cool** so **off**† **1.** *Fig.* to reduce someone's anger. (Reducing the "heat" of anger.) □ *I just stared at him while he was yelling. I knew that would cool him down.* **2.** *Fig.* to reduce someone's passion or love. (Reducing the "heat" of passion.) □ *When she slapped him, that really cooled him down.*

cool one's **heels** *Inf.* to wait (for someone); to wait for something to happen. □ *I spent an hour cooling my heels in the waiting room while the doctor saw other patients.*

Cool it! *Inf.* Calm down!; Take it easy! □ *Cool it, you guys! No fighting around here.*

cool off AND **cool down 1.** *Fig.* to let one's anger die away. (As the "heat" of anger declines.) □ *I'm sorry I got angry. I'll cool off in a minute.* □ *Cool off, Tom. There is no sense in getting so excited.* **2.** *Fig.* to let one's passion or love die away. (As the "heat" of passion declines.) □ *Ted: Is Bob still in love with Jane? Bill: No, he's cooled off a lot.*

cool so **off**† Go to cool so down†.

cool out Go to chill out.

cooler heads prevail *Fig.* the ideas or influence of less-emotional people prevail in a tense situation. □ *One hopes that cooler heads will prevail and soon everything will calm down.*

cop a packet *Fig.* to become badly injured; to be wounded severely. (Originally military. More U.K. than U.S.) □ *If you want to cop a packet or worse, just stand up in that shallow trench, son.*

cop a plea *Inf.* to plead guilty to a lesser charge to avoid a more serious charge or lessen time of imprisonment. □ *He copped a plea and got off with only two months in the slammer.*

cop a squat *Sl.* to sit down. □ *Hey, man! Come in and cop a squat here next to me.*

cop an attitude *Sl.* to take a negative or opposite attitude about something. □ *My teenage son copped an attitude when I asked why he seemed to be sneaking around.*

cop onto sth *Sl.* to understand or become aware of something. □ *I think I'm copping onto the significance of this at last.* □ *Try to cop onto what I'm saying, Otto.*

cop out 1. *Sl.* to plead guilty (to a lesser charge). □ *Frank copped out and got off with a night in the cooler.* **2.** *Sl.* a poor excuse to get out of doing something. (Usually **cop-out** or **copout**. See also cop out (of sth) ②.) □ *This is a silly copout.*

cop out (of sth**)** AND **cop out (on** sth**) 1.** *Sl.* to withdraw from doing something. □ *Are you copping out of this job?* **2.** *Sl.* to break one's promise about doing something. □ *You said you would and now you are copping out of it.*

cop some Zs Go to catch some Zs.

cope with so/sth Go to reckon with so/sth.

corner the market (on sth**)** AND **have a corner on the market (for** sth**) 1.** to manipulate a market (for good) so that one controls it. □ *Circumstances allowed our company to corner the market on granite widgets.* **2.** *Fig.* to be especially guilty of some sort of negative behavior. (Fig. on ①.) □ *Yes, you are a bit selfish, but you certainly haven't cornered the market on greed.*

cost a pretty penny AND **cost the earth** *Fig.* to be expensive; to cost a lot of money. □ *Mary's dress is real silk. It must have cost a pretty penny.* □ *It cost the earth, so I didn't buy it.*

cost an arm and a leg Go to an arm and a leg.

cost sth **out**[†] *Fig.* to figure out the total cost of some set of costs or a complex purchase of goods or services. □ *Give me a minute to cost this out, and I will have an estimate for you.*

cost the earth Go to cost a pretty penny.

couch sth **in** sth *Fig.* to express something in carefully chosen or deceptive words. □ *She couched her words in an overly polite manner.*

a **couch potato** a lazy individual, addicted to television-watching. □ *All he ever does is watch TV. He's become a real couch potato.*

cough one's **head off** *Fig.* to cough long and hard. □ *I had the flu. I nearly coughed my head off for two days.*

cough sth **up**[†] **1.** *Euph.* to vomit something. □ *The dog coughed up the food it had eaten.* **2.** *Sl.* to produce or present something, such as an amount of money. □ *You had better cough up what you owe me, if you know what's good for you.*

could do with so/sth to want or need someone or something; to benefit from someone or something. □ *I could do with a nice cool drink right now.*

Could I be excused? AND **Can I be excused?; May I be excused?** Would you give me permission to leave?; Would you give me permission to leave the table? □ *Bill: I'm finished, Mom. Could I be excused? Mother: Yes, of course, when you use good manners like that.*

(Could I) buy you a drink? AND **(Can I) buy you a drink?; (May I) buy you a drink? 1.** Could I purchase a drink for you? (An offer by one person—usually in a bar—to buy a drink for someone else.) □ *When Bill and Mary met by accident in the hotel bar, Bill said to Mary, "Could I buy you a drink?"* **2.** *Fig.* Could I make you a drink? (A slightly humorous way of offering to prepare and serve someone a drink, as in one's home.) □ *Bill: Come in, Fred. Can I buy you a drink? I've got wine and beer. Fred: Great. Beer would be fine, thanks.*

Could I call you? AND **Can I call you? 1.** *Fig.* I am too busy to talk to you now. Do you mind if I telephone you later on? □ *Sally: I can't talk to you right now. Could I call you? Tom: Sure, no problem.* **2.** *Fig.* Do you mind if I call you and ask for another date sometime?; Do you mind if I call you sometime (in order to further our relationship)? □ *Mary: I had a marvelous time, Bob. Bob: Me, too. Can I call you? Mary: Sure.*

Could I come in? AND **May I come in?; Can I come in?** Do you mind if I enter? □ *Tom (standing in the doorway): Hello, I'm with the Internal Revenue Service. Could I come in?*

Could I have the bill? Go to Check, please.

Could I have the check? Go to Check, please.

one **could (just) kick** oneself *Fig.* I think I should punish myself. □ *He could just kick himself for not thinking of this solution sooner.*

Couldn't ask for more. *Inf.* Everything is fine, and there is no more that one could want. □ *Bill: Are you happy? Sue: Oh, Bill. I couldn't ask for more.*

could(n't) care less *Inf.* [one is] unable to care at all; it does not matter at all. □ *John couldn't care less whether he goes to the party or not.*

count so **among** sth *Fig.* to consider someone as a particular type of person or part of a particular group. □ *I count her among my closest friends.*

count one's **blessings** to recognize and appreciate one's good fortune and providential gifts. □ *Whenever I see someone really in need, I always count my blessings.*

count one's **chickens before they hatch** *Fig.* to plan how to utilize good results of something before those results have occurred. □ *You may be disappointed if you count your chickens before they hatch.*

count for naught Go to come to nothing.

count heads AND **count noses** *Fig.* to count people. □ *I'll tell you how many people are here after I count heads.*

count so in *Fig.* someone wishes to join the group or participate. □ *Q: Who wants to play poker? A: Count me in.*

count noses Go to count heads.

count on so/sth *Fig.* to depend on someone or something. □ *Can I count on your being there on time?*

count so out *Fig.* someone wishes not to join the group or to leave the group. □ *Q: Who wants to play poker? A: Not me. Count me out.*

a **country mile** *Rur.* a great distance. □ *The batter knocked that ball a country mile.*

a **couple (of)** AND a **couple three** about two; two or three; a few; some; not many. (Informal *couple* instead of *couple of* is gaining ground. *Couple three* is very informal.) □ *Bill grabbed a couple of beers from the refrigerator.* □ *The camp is 16 miles up Broadway, a couple three hours at most.*

a **couple three** Go to previous.

course of action *Fig.* the procedures or sequence of actions that someone will follow to accomplish a goal. □ *I plan to follow a course of action that will produce the best results.*

cover a lot of ground 1. to travel over a great distance; to investigate a wide expanse of land. □ *The prospectors covered a lot of ground, looking for gold.* **2.** *Fig.* to deal with much information and many facts. (Fig. on ①.) □ *The history lecture covered a lot of ground today.*

cover a multitude of sins *Fig.* to include many kinds of sins or errors. □ *The term offensive covers a multitude of sins.*

cover all the bases AND **make sure all the bases are covered** *Fig.* to make sure that all details have been dealt with and all vulnerabilities have been protected. (Alludes to guarding or monitoring the bases in baseball.) □ *I think I have a good solution and that I have covered all the bases.*

cover one's **ass** *Fig. Inf.* to protect oneself; to develop a strategy in advance that provides protection in some future activity. (Caution with *ass*.) □ *Your plan is a good one, but you need to cover your ass in case of questioning by the lawyers.*

cover for so **1.** *Fig.* to make excuses for someone; to conceal someone's errors or absence. □ *If you're late, I'll cover for you.* **2.** *Fig.* to handle someone else's work. □ *Dr. Johnson's partner agreed to cover for him during his vacation.*

cover the territory 1. to travel or deal with a specific large area. □ *The sales manager was responsible for all of the eastern states and personally covered his territory twice each year.* **2.** *Fig.* to deal with all matters relating to a specific topic. (Fig. on ①.) □ *That lecture really covered the territory in only an hour.*

cover the waterfront to deal with every detail concerning a specific topic. □ *Her talk really covered the waterfront. By the time she finished, I knew much more than I wanted to know.*

cover so's **tracks (up)**† *Fig.* to conceal one's trail; to conceal one's past activities. □ *She was able to cover her tracks up so that they couldn't pin the charges on her.*

cover sth **up**† *Fig.* to conceal a wrongdoing; to conceal evidence. □ *They tried to cover the crime up, but the single footprint gave them away.*

cover (up) for so *Fig.* to conceal someone's wrongdoing by lying or concealing the evidence of wrongdoing. □ *Are you covering up for the person who committed the crime?*

cow juice *Inf.* milk. □ *Here's a little cow juice to pour on your cereal.*

crack a book *Inf.* to open a book to study. (Typically in the negative.) □ *Sally didn't crack a book all semester and still passed the course.*

crack a bottle open† *Inf.* to open a bottle of liquor. □ *Let's crack open a bottle and celebrate.*

crack a joke *Fig.* to tell a joke. □ *Every time Tom cracked a joke, his buddies broke up laughing.*

crack a smile *Fig.* to grin; to smile. □ *I was tellin' my best jokes, but Jim never cracked a smile.*

a **crack at** so Go to a try at so.

a **crack at** sth Go to a try at sth.

crack down (on so/sth) *Fig.* to put limits on someone or something; to become strict about enforcing rules about someone or something. □ *The police cracked down on the street gangs.* □ *I wish they would crack down on speeding violations.*

crack some suds *Sl.* to drink some beer. □ *Let's go out tonight and crack some suds.*

crack the door (open)† AND **crack the window (open)**† *Fig.* to open the door or window a very small amount. □ *I cracked open the door to peek out.*

crack the window (open)† Go to previous.

crack under the strain *Fig.* to have a mental or emotional collapse because of continued work or stress. □ *He worked 80-hour weeks for a month and finally cracked under the strain.*

crack up 1. *Inf.* to have a wreck. □ *A car full of people cracked up on the expressway.* **2.** *Inf.* to break out in laughter. □ *The whole audience cracked up when the scenery fell.* **3.** *Inf.* to have a mental or emotional breakdown. □ *You would crack up like John did, if you had been through all he went through.* **4.** *Fig.* an accident; a wreck. (Usually **crack-up**.) □ *There was a terrible crack-up on the expressway.*

crack so **up**† *Inf.* to make someone laugh very hard; to make someone break out laughing. □ *You and your jokes really crack me up.*

crack sth **(wide) open** to expose and reveal some great wrongdoing. □ *The police cracked the drug ring wide open.*

*cracked *Fig.* solved; understood. (*Typically: **get** sth ~; **have** sth ~.) □ *I've got the mystery cracked!*

cracked up to be sth AND **cracked up as** sth *Fig.* alleged or understood to be something. □ *She was cracked up to be a pretty good player.* □ *She was cracked up as a pretty good golfer.*

cram for an exam(ination) *Fig.* to study very hard for an examination, trying to make up for a failure to study regularly.

□ *If you would study during the school term, you would not have to cram for the final exam.*

cramp so's **style** *Fig.* to limit someone in some way. □ *I hope this doesn't cramp your style, but could you please not hum while you work?* □ *To ask Bob to keep regular hours would cramp his style.*

crank sth **out**† AND **churn** sth **out**† *Inf. Fig.* to produce something quickly or carelessly; to make something in a casual and mechanical way. □ *John can crank a lot of work out in a single day.*

crank so **up**† *Fig.* to motivate; to get someone started. (Fig. on crank sth up† ①.) □ *Some mornings, I can't crank myself up enough to get to work on time.*

crank sth **up**† **1.** *Fig.* to get a machine or a process started. (Fig. on the image of someone turning the starting crank of an early automobile.) □ *Please crank the machinery so the workers can start working.* **2.** *Fig.* to increase the volume of an electronic device. □ *He cranked the stereo up a little more and CRACK, there went both speakers!*

crap out *Sl.* to die. □ *Spike almost crapped out from the beating he took.*

crap out (of sth) *Inf.* to lose on a roll of the dice in a dice game called craps and leave the game and the other players. □ *Wally crapped out of the game early in the evening.*

crap out (of sth) **(on** so) **1.** *Sl.* to withdraw from doing something with someone, unexpectedly, perhaps because of fear or cowardice. □ *Are you going to crap out of this game on me?* **2.** *Sl.* to quit doing something with someone or withdraw because of exhaustion. □ *Don't crap out of this on me! Pull yourself together!*

crash and burn 1. [for a plane or car] to crash and burst into flames. □ *The small plane crashed and burned just after it took off.* **2.** *Fig.* to fail spectacularly. (Fig. on ①.) □ *Poor Chuck really crashed and burned when he made his presentation at the sales meeting.*

a **crash course in** sth *Fig.* a short and intense training course in something. □ *I* took a crash course in ballroom dancing so we wouldn't look stupid on the dance floor.

crash down (around so/sth**)** AND **crash down (about** so/sth**)** *Fig.* [for the structure and stability of one's life] to fall apart. □ *Her whole life crashed down around her.*

crash with so *Sl.* to spend the night at someone's place. □ *I don't need a hotel room. I can crash with Tom.*

crawl out of the woodwork Go to out of the woodwork.

crawling with so *Fig.* [of a surface] covered with many people or members of a class of people moving about. □ *The city was crawling with tourists, making it almost impossible to go from place to place in a reasonable amount of time.*

crawling with some kind of creature [of a surface] covered with insects or animals, moving about. □ *The basement was crawling with rats!* □ *We came home and found the kitchen floor crawling with ants.*

***crazy as a betsy bug** AND ***crazy as a peach-orchard boar; ***crazy as a loon** *Rur.* acting as if insane. (*Also: **as** ~.) □ *Tom: Susan says she's really the Queen of England. Bill: She's crazy as a betsy bug.* □ *Jill: David's a little eccentric, isn't he? Jane: Crazy as a loon, I'd say.* □ *What's wrong with Jim? He's acting as crazy as a peach-orchard boar.*

crazy as a loon Go to previous.

crazy as a peach-orchard boar Go to crazy as a betsy bug.

crazy bone Go to funny bone.

crazy in the head *Inf.* stupid or insane. □ *Am I crazy in the head, or did I just see someone walking a leopard on a leash?*

the **cream of the crop** *Fig.* the best of all. □ *These three students are very bright. They are the cream of the crop in their class.*

create a commotion Go to cause (quite a) stir.

create a scene Go to make a scene.

create a stink (about sth**)** AND **make a stink (about** sth**); raise a stink (about** sth**); kick up a stink (about** sth**)** *Inf.* to make a major issue out of something; to make much over something; to make a lot of complaints and criticisms about something. □ *Tom raised quite a stink about Bob's remarks.*

create an uproar AND **make an uproar** to cause an outburst or sensation. □ *Her spoiled poodle created an uproar in the restaurant.*

creature comforts *Fig.* things that make people comfortable. □ *The hotel room was a bit small, but all the creature comforts were there.*

a **credit to** so/sth *Fig.* of value or benefit to someone or something; of enough value or worth to enhance someone or something. □ *I always want to be a credit to my school.* □ *John is not exactly what you would call a credit to his family.*

credit so **with** sth to acknowledge that someone has accomplished something. □ *We credit Thomas Edison with the invention of the electric lightbulb.*

creep across sth *Fig.* [for light, fog, etc.] to move slowly across a place or an area. □ *A heavy fog crept across the coastal areas.* □ *The spotlight crept across the stage from one side to the other, as if looking for the performer.*

***the **creeps** AND ***the **willies** *Inf.* a state of anxiety or uneasiness. (*Typically: **get** ~; **have** ~; **give** so ~.) □ *I get the creeps whenever I see that old house.* □ *I really had the willies when I went down into the dark basement.*

crib sth **from** so/sth *Fig.* to cheat by copying something from someone or something. □ *It appears that you cribbed this directly from the person sitting next to you.*

a **crick in** one's **back** a twisted or cramped place in the back that causes pain or immobility. □ *I had a crick in my back all night and I couldn't sleep.*

a **crick in** one's **neck** a twisted place or a cramp in the neck that causes pain. □ *I got a crick in my neck from sleeping in a draft.*

*crooked as a barrel of fish hooks AND ***crooked as a fish hook; *crooked as a dog's hind leg** *Inf.* very dishonest. (**Also: **as** ~.*) □ *Don't play cards with him. He's as crooked as a barrel of fish hooks.* □ *Mary says that politicians are all crooked as a dog's hind leg.*

crooked as a dog's hind leg Go to previous.

crooked as a fish hook Go to crooked as a barrel of fish hooks.

crop up *Fig.* [for something] to appear almost as a surprise. □ *A few problems may crop up along the way, but we can solve them.*

cross so to oppose someone. □ *You best not cross Jim. He has a very bad temper.* □ *This is the last time you cross me! Do you understand that?*

cross bridges before one **comes to them** Go to cross that bridge before one comes to it.

cross one's **fingers** Go to keep one's fingers crossed (for so/sth).

cross one's **heart (and hope to die)** *Fig.* a phrase said to pledge or vow that the truth is being told. □ *What I told you is true, cross my heart and hope to die.*

cross so's **mind** Go to pass through so's mind.

cross so/sth **off (of)** sth AND **cross** so/sth **off**[†] to eliminate a name from a list or record. (*Of* is usually retained before pronouns.) □ *We will have to cross her off of our list.* □ *I crossed the sweater off the list of what I needed to buy.*

cross so/sth **out**[†] to draw a line through the name of someone or something on a list or record. □ *You can cross me out. I'm not going.* □ *I crossed the sweater out. It was an error.*

cross over 1. to change sides, from one to another. □ *Some players from the other team crossed over and joined ours after the tournament.* **2.** *Euph.* to die. □ *Uncle Herman crossed over many years before Aunt Helen died.*

cross (over) the line *Fig.* to cross a threshold of behavior into an area where one's behavior is unacceptable. □ *When Jim greeted the hostess and failed to even speak to the host, he crossed the line and was never welcomed in the house again.*

cross so's **palm with silver** *Fig.* to pay money to someone in payment for a service. (Fig. on a fortune-teller asking a customer to cross [fill] her palm with silver.) □ *You will find that things happen much faster in hotels if you cross the workers' palms with silver fairly often.*

cross paths (with so**)** *Fig.* to meet someone by chance and not by choice. □ *The last time I crossed paths with Fred, we ended up arguing about something inconsequential.*

cross swords (with so**)** *Fig.* to become the adversary of someone. □ *Gloria loved an argument and was looking forward to crossing swords with Sally.*

cross that bridge before one **comes to it** AND **cross bridges before** one **comes to them** *Fig.* to worry excessively about something before it happens. □ *There is no sense in crossing that bridge before you come to it.* □ *She's always crossing bridges before coming to them. She needs to learn to relax.*

cross that bridge when one **comes to it** *Fig.* to delay worrying about something that might happen until it actually does happen. □ *Alan: Where will we stop tonight? Jane: At the next town. Alan: What if all the hotels are full? Jane: Let's cross that bridge when we come to it.*

cross the Rubicon *Fig.* to do something that inevitably commits one to following a certain course of action. (Based on the crossing of the River Rubicon by Julius Caesar with his army, which involved him in a civil war in 49 B.C. See also the die is cast.) □ *Jane crossed the Rubicon by signing the contract to purchase the house.*

cross so **up**[†] to give someone trouble; to defy or betray someone; to spoil someone's plans. (Also without *up*.) □ *You really crossed up Bill when you told Tom what he said.* □ *Please don't cross me up again.*

cross-examine SO **1.** to question someone in court who has already been questioned by the opposing side. □ *The lawyer plans to cross-examine the witness in court tomorrow morning.* **2.** to question someone in great detail, persistently. □ *There is no need to cross-examine me about the loss of the account. It was my fault, and I can't say any more.*

crow about sth AND **crow over** sth *Fig.* [for someone] to brag about something. (Fig. on the cry of a rooster.) □ *Stop crowing about your successes!*

crow bait *Rur.* some living creature that is likely to die; a useless animal or person. □ *That old dog used to hunt good, but now he's just crow bait.*

crow over sth Go to crow about sth.

crown SO **with** sth *Fig.* to strike someone on the head with something. (Fig. on placing a heavy crown on someone's head with force.) □ *The carpenter crowned himself with a board he knocked loose.*

cruisin(g) for a bruisin(g) *Sl.* asking for trouble. □ *You are cruising for a bruising, you know that?*

crum(b) sth **up**† *Sl.* to mess something up. □ *Now don't crum up this deal. Just do what I tell you.*

*a **crush on** SO *Fig.* infatuation with someone. (*Typically: **get** ~; **have** ~.) □ *Mary thinks she's getting a crush on Bill.* □ *Sally says she'll never have a crush on anyone again.*

crushed by sth *Fig.* demoralized; having hurt feelings. □ *The whole family was completely crushed by the news.* □ *I was just crushed by your attitude. I thought we were friends.*

*the **crux of the matter** AND *the **root of the matter**; *the **heart of the matter** the central issue of the matter. (*Crux* is an old word meaning "cross." *Typically: **be at** ~; **get at** ~; **go to** ~; **look at** ~.) □ *All right, this is the crux of the matter. You are irresponsible.* □ *It's about time that we got to the heart of the matter.*

cry all the way to the bank *Inf.* to make a lot of money on something that one

ought to be ashamed of. □ *Jane: Have you read the new book by that romance novelist? They say it sold a million copies, but it's so badly written that the author ought to be ashamed of herself. Alan: I'm sure she's crying all the way to the bank.*

cry before one **is hurt** *Fig.* to cry or complain needlessly, before one is injured. □ *There is no point in crying before one is hurt.*

cry bloody murder AND **holler bloody murder; scream bloody murder; yell bloody murder** *Fig.* to complain bitterly; to complain unduly, exaggerating the affront. □ *When we put him in an office without a window, he screamed bloody murder.*

cry crocodile tears Go to shed crocodile tears.

cry one's **eyes out** *Fig.* to cry very hard. □ *When we heard the news, we almost cried our eyes out with joy.*

cry one's **heart out** AND **sing** one's **heart out; play** one's **heart out; sob** one's **heart out** *Fig.* to do something (such as crying, singing, playing, or sobbing) with vigor or intensity. □ *She suffered such grief—alone and sobbing her heart out.* □ *The bird sang its little heart out each morning.*

cry in one's **beer** *Inf.* to feel sorry for oneself, possibly while intoxicated. □ *She calls up, crying in her beer, and talks on and on about her problems.*

cry out for sth *Fig.* [for something or a place] to need something obviously. □ *This room just cries out for new carpeting.*

cry over spilled milk *Fig.* to be unhappy about what cannot be undone. □ *He is always crying over spilled milk. He cannot accept reality.* □ *It can't be helped. Don't cry over spilled milk.*

cry oneself **to sleep** to weep until sleep overtakes one. □ *The baby finally cried herself to sleep.*

cry uncle Go to holler uncle.

cry wolf *Fig.* to cry or complain about something when nothing is really wrong. (From the story wherein a child sounds the alarm frequently about a wolf when there is no wolf, only to be ignored when there actually is a wolf.) □ *Pay no attention. She's just crying wolf again.*

a **crying need (for so/sth)** *Fig.* a definite or desperate need for someone or something. □ *There is a crying need for someone to come in and straighten things out.*

a **crying shame** *Fig.* a very unfortunate situation; a real shame. □ *It's a crying shame that people cannot afford adequate housing.*

cuddle up with a (good) book AND **curl up (with a (good) book); snuggle up (with a (good) book)** to snuggle into a chair or bed comfortably to read a book. □ *I want to go home and cuddle up with a good book.* □ *She went home and curled up with a good book.*

cue so in† *Fig.* to tell someone what is happening. □ *I want to know what's going on. Cue me in.*

cunning as a fox Go to sly as a fox.

cup one's **hands together** to put one's hands together to form a sort of cup. □ *He cupped his hands together and scooped up the water.*

curdle so's **blood** *Fig.* to frighten or disgust someone severely. □ *The story was scary enough to curdle your blood.*

curl so's **hair** AND **make** so's **hair curl** *Fig.* to frighten or alarm someone; to shock someone with sight, sound, or taste. □ *Don't ever sneak up on me like that again. You really curled my hair.*

curl up and die 1. to die. □ *The cat was very old, and one day she just curled up and died.* **2.** to suffer from extreme embarrassment. □ *When I heard you say that, I could have curled up and died.*

curl up (with a (good) book) Go to cuddle up with a (good) book.

curly dirt AND **house moss** *Inf.* a stringy bunch of dirt and dust. □ *How long has it been since you swept under this bed? There's a mountain of curly dirt under here!* □ *She was a terrible housekeeper. House moss collected in all the corners of her rooms.*

curry favor with so to try to win favor from someone. □ *The lawyer tried to curry favor with the judge.*

curtain falls on sth *Fig.* something comes to an end like a play when the stage curtain comes down. □ *At the end of the president's term, the curtain falls on a presidency loved by some and hated by others—like all presidents.*

cushion the blow Go to soften the blow.

cuss so **out**† *Fig.* to curse at someone. □ *Dad cussed me out for losing the money he gave me.*

cut a big swath Go to cut a wide swath.

cut so **a break** AND **cut** so **some slack** *Sl.* to give someone a chance or opportunity; to allow someone a reprieve from the consequences of an action. □ *Come on, cut me a break! I'm a good guy!* □ *I was only a few minutes late! Cut me a break! Don't dock my pay!*

cut (so) a check *Fig.* to write a check; to have a computer print a check. (Used in business especially of machine-made checks.) □ *We will cut a check for the balance due you later this afternoon.*

cut a dashing figure AND **cut a fine figure** *Fig.* [usually of a male] to have a nice build and profile; to move and act in a manly fashion. (A little stilted or flowery.) □ *Reginald cuts a dashing figure considering his age and dental issues.*

cut a deal *Fig.* to arrange a deal; to negotiate an agreement. □ *Maybe we can cut a deal. Let's talk.*

cut a fine figure Go to cut a dashing figure.

cut a long story short Go to make a long story short.

cut a rug *Fig.* to dance. (Older. Strange, because people do not normally dance on carpets.) □ *Come on, let's get out there and cut a rug.*

cut a wide swath AND **cut a big swath** *Fig.* to seem important; to attract a lot of attention. □ *In social matters, Mrs. Smith cuts a wide swath.*

a **cut above** sth AND a **cut above average**
Fig. a measure or degree better than
something else or better than typical,
normal, or average. (The *cut* is a degree
or notch.) □ *John isn't the best mechanic
in town, but he's a cut above average.* □
*Your shirt is beautiful, but mine is a cut
above yours.*

a **cut above average** Go to previous.

cut across sth **1.** AND **cut across** to travel
across a particular area; to take a shortcut across a particular area. □ *Please don't
cut across the neighbor's yard anymore.*
2. *Fig.* to reach beyond something; to
embrace a wide variety; to slice across a
figurative boundary or barrier. (Fig. on
①.) □ *His teaching cut across all human
cultures and races.* □ *This rule cuts across
all social barriers.*

cut against the grain Go to against the
grain.

cut and dried *Fig.* fixed; determined beforehand; usual and uninteresting. (Can
be hyphenated before nominals.) □ *I find
your writing quite boring. It's too cut and
dried.* □ *The lecture was, as usual, cut and
dried.*

cut and paste 1. to cut something out of
paper with scissors and paste it onto
something else. □ *The teacher told the little children that it was time to cut and
paste, and they all ran to the worktables.*
2. *Fig.* something trivial, simple, or childish. (Fig. on ①.) □ *I don't mind doing
things that have to be done, but I hate to
waste my time on cut and paste.* **3.** to
move computer data section by section in
a document. □ *It's simple to cut and paste.
Just highlight this section and move it to
where you want it.*

cut and run *Sl.* to run away quickly. (Fig.
on the image of cutting loose a ship's or
boat's anchor and sailing away in a
hurry.) □ *As soon as I finish what I am doing here, I'm going to cut and run. I've got
to get home by six o'clock.*

cut both ways AND **works both ways** *Fig.*
to affect both sides of an issue equally.
□ *Remember that your suggestion that
costs should be shared cuts both ways. Your*

*division will have to reduce its budgets as
well.*

cut class AND **cut school** *Fig.* to skip a
school class or a day of school without an
excuse. □ *As a joke, one day all the students cut their math class and went to
lunch.*

cut corners *Fig.* to take shortcuts; to save
money or effort by finding cheaper or
easier ways to do something. □ *I won't cut
corners just to save money. I put quality
first.*

cut sth **down**† **1.** *Fig.* to destroy someone's
argument; to destroy someone's position
or standing. □ *The lawyer cut the testimony down quickly.* **2.** AND **roll** sth **back**
to reduce the price of something. □ *They
cut the prices down to sell the goods off
quickly.*

cut down (on sth**)** *Fig.* to reduce the
amount of something or of doing something; to use or buy less of something. □
*You will have to cut down on the time it
takes you to get ready in the morning.* □
*The doctor told him to cut down on his
drinking.*

cut so **down to size** Go to whittle so down
to size.

cut one's **(eye)teeth on** sth *Fig.* to grow up
experiencing something; to have had the
experience of dealing with something
[successfully] at a very early age. □ *My
grandfather taught me how to fish, so I cut
my eyeteeth on fishing.*

cut from the same cloth AND **made from
the same mold** *Fig.* sharing a lot of similarities; seeming to have been created,
reared, or fashioned in the same way. □
*She and her brother are cut from the same
cloth. They both tell lies all the time.* □ *Father and son are made from the same mold
and even sound alike on the telephone.*

cut in to signal to a dancing couple that
someone wishes to replace and retire one
of the dancers. □ *Pardon me, may I cut
in?*

Cut it out! *Inf.* Stop doing that!; Stop saying that! □ *Sue: Why, I think you have a
crush on Mary! Tom: Cut it out!* □ *"Cut*

it out!" yelled Tommy as Billy hit him again.

cut loose (with sth**)** Go to let go (with sth).

cut one's **losses** *Fig.* to do something to stop a loss of something. □ *I knew I had to do something to cut my losses, but it was almost too late.*

cut no ice (with so**)** *Sl.* to have no influence on someone; to fail to convince someone. □ *So you're the mayor's daughter. It still cuts no ice with me.*

cut so **off**† **at the pass** *Fig.* to block someone's effort to get away; to thwart someone's efforts. □ *They are ahead now, but we'll cut them off at the pass.*

cut off one's **nose to spite** one's **face** *Fig.* to harm oneself while attempting to harm someone else. □ *Why do you want to fire your best worker? That's just cutting off your nose to spite your face.*

cut so **off**† **without a penny** *Fig.* to end someone's allowance; to fail to leave someone money in one's will. □ *We learned, when Uncle Sam's will was read, that he cut off his own flesh and blood without a penny.*

cut out (for some place**)** AND **light out (for** some place**)** *Fig. Inf.* to leave quickly for some place. □ *When they heard their mother call, the Wilson kids cut out for home.*

cut out to be sth AND **cut out for** sth destined to be something or a particular type of person. □ *I don't think I was cut out for this.* □ *We weren't cut out to be laborers.*

cut one's **(own) throat** *Fig.* [for someone] to bring about one's (own) failure. □ *If I were to confess, I'd just be cutting my throat.*

cut school Go to cut class.

cut so **some slack** Go to cut so a break.

cut some Zs Go to catch some Zs.

cut teeth [for a baby or young person] to have new teeth emerging through the gums. □ *Billy is cranky because he's cutting teeth.*

Cut the comedy! AND **Cut the funny stuff!** *Inf.* Stop acting silly and telling jokes!; Be serious! □ *John: All right, you guys! Cut the comedy and get to work!*

cut the deadwood out† *Fig.* to remove unproductive persons from employment. (Fig. on pruning trees and bushes.) □ *When we cut the deadwood out, all our departments will run more smoothly.*

cut the dust *Fig.* to take a drink of liquor. □ *I need to cut the dust. Can I have a drink out of your whisky bottle?*

Cut the funny stuff! Go to Cut the comedy!

cut the ground out† **from under** so *Fig.* to destroy the foundation of someone's plans or someone's argument. □ *The politician cut the ground out from under his opponent.*

cut the pie up† *Fig.* to divide something up. (Can refer to an actual pie or anything that can be divided into varying portions.) □ *It all depends on how you cut the pie up.*

cut the (umbilical) cord *Fig.* to become independent, especially from one's parents. □ *I decided to cut the cord, so I'm moving out of my parents' house into my own apartment.*

cut through red tape *Fig.* to eliminate or neutralize something complicated, such as bureaucratic rules and procedures. (Fixed order.) □ *I will try to cut through all the red tape for you so you get your visa on time.* □ *I am sure someone can help us cut through all this red tape.*

cut to so/sth *Fig.* to shift the radio, movie, or television audience's attention abruptly to someone or something new. □ *The technical director cut to a remote unit that was covering an accident.* □ *The camera cut to scenes of Atlanta burning.*

cut so/sth **to ribbons** *Fig.* to criticize someone severely. □ *The critics just cut her acting to ribbons!*

cut so **to the bone** Go to cut so to the quick.

cut sth **to the bone 1.** *Lit.* to slice something deep to the bone. □ *Cut each slice of ham to the bone. Then each slice will* *be as big as possible.* **2.** *Fig.* to cut down severely (on something). (Fig. on ①.) □ *We cut our expenses to the bone and are still losing money.*

cut to the chase *Sl.* to focus on what is important; to abandon the preliminaries and deal with the major points. □ *After a few introductory comments, we cut to the chase and began negotiating.*

cut so **to the quick** AND **cut** so **to the bone 1.** to slice the flesh of someone or some animal clear through to the underlying layer of flesh or to the bone. □ *He cut his finger to the quick with the sharp knife.* **2.** *Fig.* to injure someone emotionally. (Fig. on ①. See also cut sth to the bone.) □ *Her remarks cut him to the bone.*

cut up 1. *Fig.* to act wildly; to show off and be troublesome; to act like a clown. □ *If you spent more time studying than cutting up, you'd get better grades.* **2.** Go to cut up (about so/sth).

cut up (about so/sth**)** *Sl.* emotionally upset about someone or something. □ *She was all cut up about her divorce.*

cut so's **water off**† *Fig.* to squelch someone; to thwart someone. □ *Well, I guess that cuts your water off!* □ *That sure cuts off my water!*

cut one's **wolf loose** *Sl.* to go on a drinking bout; to get drunk. □ *I'm gonna go out and cut my wolf loose tonight.*

*cute as a bug's ear very cute. (*Also: **as** ~.) □ *That little baby is cute as a bug's ear.*

the **daddy of them all** AND the **grand-daddy of them all** *Fig.* the biggest or oldest of all; the patriarch. □ *This old fish is the granddaddy of them all.*

daily dozen *Fig.* physical exercises done every day. □ *My brother always feels tired after his daily dozen.*

the **daily grind** [someone's] everyday work routine. □ *When my vacation was over, I had to go back to the daily grind.*

a **(damn) sight better** *Inf.* much better. □ *You look a sight better with your hair cut short.*

damn so/sth **with faint praise** *Fig.* to criticize someone or something indirectly by not praising enthusiastically. □ *The critic did not say that he disliked the play, but he damned it with faint praise.*

dance at so's **wedding** *Fig.* to celebrate in honor of someone at someone's wedding. □ *I will dance at your wedding—if you invite me, of course.*

dance on air *Fig.* to be very happy; to be euphoric enough as if to dance on air. □ *She was just dancing on air, she was so happy.*

dance to a different tune Go to next.

dance to another tune AND **dance to a different tune** *Fig.* to shift quickly to different behavior; to change one's behavior or attitude. □ *A stern talking-to will make her dance to a different tune.*

dance with death *Fig.* to attempt to do something that is very risky. □ *The crossing of the border into enemy territory was like dancing with death.*

a **dark cloud (looming) on the horizon** *Fig.* a looming threat; a threat or a prob-lem in the near future. □ *The approaching tax-preparation season is a dark cloud on the horizon. I owe plenty and have nothing.*

dark horse *Fig.* someone or something whose abilities, plans, or feelings are little known to others. (From a race horse about which little or nothing is known.) □ *It's difficult to predict who will win the prize—there are two or three dark horses in the tournament.*

the **dark side of** so/sth *Fig.* the negative and often hidden aspect of someone or something. □ *I had never seen the dark side of Mary before, and I have to tell you that I was horrified when she lost her temper.*

darken so's **door** *Fig.* [for an unwelcome person] to come to someone's door seeking entry. (As if the visitor were casting a shadow on the door. Formal, or even jocular.) □ *She pointed to the street and said, "Go and never darken my door again!"*

darn tootin(g) *Fig. Inf.* absolutely. □ *You're darn tooting I'll be there. I wouldn't miss it for the world.*

dart a glance at so/sth to shoot a quick look at someone or something. □ *She darted a glance at him and looked quickly away.*

dash a letter off† Go to next.

dash a note off† AND **dash a letter off**† to write a note or letter quickly and send it off. □ *I have to dash this letter off, then I will be with you.* □ *I'll dash off a note to her.*

dash away AND **dash off** to run away; to leave in a hurry. □ *Jane had to dash away to an appointment.* □ *Ken dashed off and* *left me behind to deal with the angry customer.*

dash cold water on sth Go to pour cold water on sth.

dash so's **hopes** *Fig.* to ruin someone's hopes; to put an end to someone's dreams or aspirations. □ *Mary dashed my hopes when she said she wouldn't marry me.*

dash off Go to dash away.

dash sth **to pieces** to break something into small pieces. □ *She dashed the glass to pieces on the floor—she was that mad.*

Davy Jones's locker *Fig.* the bottom of the sea, especially when it becomes a grave. □ *Most of the gold from that trading ship is in Davy Jones's locker.*

dawn (up)on so *Fig.* [for a fact] to become apparent to someone; [for something] to be suddenly realized by someone. (*Upon* is formal and less commonly used than *on.*) □ *On the way home, it dawned on me that I had never returned your call, so when I got home I called immediately.*

day after day *Fig.* every day; daily; all the time. (See time period **after** time period.) □ *She visits her husband in the hospital day after day.*

day and night AND **night and day** *Fig.* all the time; around the clock. □ *The house is guarded night and day.*

day by day every day. (See time period **after** time period.) □ *The doctor will check on your progress day by day until it looks like the worst is over.*

day in and day out AND **day in, day out** *Fig.* on every day; for each day. □ *She watches soap operas day in and day out.*

a **day late and a dollar short** *Fig.* late and ill-prepared. □ *Tommy, you seem to show up a day late and a dollar short all the time. You need to get organized.*

*the **day off** AND *a **day off** *Fig.* a day free from working. (*Typically: **get** ~; **have** ~; **give** so ~; **take** ~.) □ *I have the day off. Let's go hiking.*

day one *Fig.* the very beginning; the very first day. (*Typically: **from** ~; **since** ~.)

□ *You haven't done anything right since day one! You're fired!*

a **day person** *Fig.* a person who prefers to be active during the daytime. (Compare this with a night person.) □ *I am strictly a day person. Have to be in bed early.*

daylight robbery 1. robbery fearlessly done in the daylight. □ *The thief was charged with daylight robbery and assault.* **2.** AND **highway robbery** *Fig.* outrageous overpricing; a bill that is much higher than normally acceptable but must be paid. (As if one had been accosted openly and robbed on the open road or in broad daylight.) □ *It's daylight robbery to charge that amount of money for a hotel room!* □ *Four thousand dollars! That's highway robbery for one piece of furniture!*

one's **days are numbered** *Fig.* one is facing death or dismissal. □ *If I don't get this contract, my days are numbered at this company.*

days running AND **weeks running; months running; years running** days in a series; months in a series; etc. (Follows a number.) □ *I had a bad cold for five days running.* □ *For two years running, I brought work home from the office every single night.*

day-to-day *Fig.* daily; everyday; common. □ *They update their accounts on a day-to-day basis.*

day-tripper *Fig.* a tourist who makes excursions lasting just one day. □ *At about 4:00 P.M. the day-trippers start thinning out.*

dead ahead *Fig.* straight ahead; directly ahead. □ *The farmer said that the town we were looking for was dead ahead.*

dead and buried 1. dead and interred, and soon to be forgotten. □ *Now that Uncle Bill is dead and buried, we can read his will.* **2.** *Fig.* gone forever. (Fig. on ①.) □ *That kind of old-fashioned thinking is dead and buried.*

dead and gone 1. [of a person] long dead. □ *When I'm dead and gone, I hope folks remember me at my best.* **2.** *Fig.* [of a thing] gone long ago. (Fig. on ①.) □ *The horse-and-buggy days are dead and gone.*

*dead as a dodo AND ***dead as a doornail; *deader than a doornail** dead; no longer in existence. (*Also: **as** ~.) □ *That silly old idea is dead as a dodo.* □ *When I tried to start my car this morning, I discovered that the battery was deader than a doornail.*

dead as a doornail Go to previous.

dead broke *Fig.* completely broke; without any money. □ *I'm dead broke—not a nickel to my name.*

dead center *Fig.* at the exact center of something. (See also **on dead center**.) □ *The arrow hit the target dead center.*

dead certain *Fig.* very sure. (*Dead* means *absolutely*.) □ *I didn't believe the rumor at first, but Bill's dead certain that it's true.*

dead drunk very intoxicated; totally inebriated. □ *They were both dead drunk. They could only lie there and snore.*

a dead duck *Fig.* someone or something that is certain to die or fail. □ *If I fail that test, I'm a dead duck.*

dead easy *Inf.* very easy. □ *It was so dead easy, Frank did it with one hand.*

dead from the neck up 1. *Fig.* stupid. (With a "dead" head.) □ *She acts like she is dead from the neck up.* **2.** *Fig.* no longer open to new ideas. □ *Everyone on the board of directors is dead from the neck up.*

a dead giveaway *Fig.* something that reveals a fact or an intention completely. □ *The car in the driveway was a dead giveaway that someone was at home.*

dead in the water *Fig.* stalled; immobile. (Originally nautical.) □ *The project is out of funds and dead in the water for the time being.*

dead letter 1. *Fig.* a piece of mail that is returned to the post office as both undeliverable and unreturnable. □ *At the end of the year, the post office usually has bushels of dead letters.* **2.** *Fig.* an issue, law, or matter that is no longer important or that no longer has force or power. (Fig. on ①.) □ *His point about the need for ed-*

ucation reform is a dead letter. It is being done now.

a dead loss *Fig.* a total loss. □ *This car is a dead loss after the accident.*

dead meat *Fig.* dead; as good as dead. (Usually an exaggeration.) □ *If you don't do exactly as I say, you are dead meat!*

dead on *Fig.* exactly right; on target. □ *That's a good observation, Tiffany. You are dead on.*

dead on arrival AND **D.O.A. 1.** dead at the time of arrival at a hospital. (Abbreviated D.O.A.) □ *The drug user was dead on arrival by the time his parents got to the hospital.* **2.** inadequate, obsolete, defunct, or failed at the time of introduction. (Fig. on ①.) □ *You may have worked a long time on that plan, but it was dead on arrival when you presented it.*

dead on one's **feet** AND **dead on its feet** *Fig.* exhausted; worn out; no longer useful. □ *Ann is so tired. She's really dead on her feet.* □ *This inefficient company is dead on its feet.*

*a (dead) ringer (for so**)** *Fig.* very closely similar in appearance to someone else. (There are a few entertaining origins made up for this phrase, all of which include a person who has rigged a coffin with a device that will ring a bell in case of burial before death. The concern was real and such devices were invented, but they have no connection with this phrase. *Typically: **be** ~; **look like** ~.) □ *You are sure a dead ringer for my brother.*

dead serious *Fig.* absolutely serious; not joking. □ *Tom: You're funning me. Bill: No, I'm dead serious.*

dead set against so/sth *Fig.* totally opposed to someone or something. □ *I'm dead set against the new tax proposal.*

dead to rights Go to **(bang) dead to rights**.

dead to the world 1. sound asleep. □ *He's dead to the world, and I can't rouse him.* **2.** *Inf.* intoxicated. □ *Six beers and he was dead to the world.*

dead wrong *Fig.* completely wrong. □ *I'm sorry. I was dead wrong. I didn't have the facts straight.*

dead-end kid *Fig.* a poor youth with no prospects for the future, usually a male. □ *Wilbur was a dead-end kid from the day he was born.*

deader than a doornail Go to dead as a dodo.

deadly dull *Fig.* very dull. □ *Her story was really deadly dull. I am sorry I was awake for part of it.*

deaf and dumb *Fig.* unable to hear or speak. (Sometimes euphemized as "hearing and speech impaired.") □ *Fred objected to being called deaf and dumb.* □ *Aunt Clara—she was deaf and dumb, you know—lived to be over 100.*

*deaf as a post deaf. (*Also: **as** ~.) □ *When my cousin was a teenager, she played her drum set without ear protection, and she was as deaf as a post by the age of 25.*

deal so/sth **a death blow** AND **deal** so/sth **a fatal blow; deal** so/sth **the fatal blow** to perform the final act that terminates or kills someone or something. □ *Fred gave the project the death blow by voting against the needed funding.*

deal so/sth **a fatal blow** Go to previous.

deal so **in 1.** to bring someone into a card game (poker) by dealing them a hand of cards. □ *I want to play. Deal me in.* **2.** *Fig.* to allow someone to join in. (Fig. on ①.) □ *If it's not too late to participate in the negotiations, please deal me in.*

deal sth **out**† AND **parcel** sth **out**† *Fig.* to distribute something. (See also **mete** punishment **out.**) □ *Let's deal out the remaining food the best we can, and hope no one is terribly hungry.*

deal so **out of** sth AND **deal** so **out**† *Fig.* to remove someone from participation in something. (Fig. on card playing.) □ *They dealt me out at the last minute.*

deal with so **1.** *Lit.* to transact business with someone; to manage or accommodate someone. □ *I'll deal with Jane as soon as I get this other matter tended to.* **2.** *Sl.* to kill someone. □ *The secret agent planned how best to deal with the rebel leader without getting caught.*

dear departed *Euph.* a dead person, as referred to at a funeral. □ *Let's take a moment to meditate on the life of the dear departed.*

a **Dear John letter** a letter a woman writes to her boyfriend telling him that she does not love him anymore. □ *Bert got a Dear John letter today from Sally. He was devastated.*

Dear me! *Fig.* an expression of mild dismay or regret. □ *Sue: Dear me, is this all there is? Mary: There's more in the kitchen.*

dear to one's **heart** AND **close to** one's **heart** held in fond regard by someone. □ *All those wonderful memories of home are still dear to my heart. I wish I could bring them all back.*

death on sth **1.** *Fig.* very harmful; very effective in acting against someone or something. □ *This road is terribly bumpy. It's death on tires.* **2.** *Fig.* accurate or deadly at doing something requiring skill or great effort. □ *The boxing champ is really death on those fast punches.*

decked out (in sth**)** dressed or decorated nicely in or with something. □ *The room was decked out in flowers and candles.* □ *She was decked out in her best dress and brand new shoes.*

deep in thought Go to lost in thought.

deep-six so/sth *Inf.* to get rid of someone or something; to dispose of someone or something. (Refers originally to burying someone or something six feet deep, the standard depth of a grave.) □ *Take this horrible food out and deep-six it.* □ *That guy is a pain. Deep-six him so the cops will never find him.*

Definitely not! AND **Certainly not!** No, without any doubt at all. □ *Bill: Will you lend me some money? Bob: No way! Definitely not!*

deliver the goods *Fig.* to do something as promised. (Not necessarily actually to deliver something.) □ *If he says he will* *paint your house in a week, he will. He always delivers the goods.*

a **den of iniquity** *Fig.* a place filled with criminal activity or wickedness. □ *The town was a den of iniquity, and vice was everywhere.*

depart this life *Euph.* to die. □ *He departed this life on April 20, 1973.*

desert a sinking ship AND **leave a sinking ship** *Fig.* to leave a place, a person, or a situation when things become difficult or unpleasant. (Rats are said to be the first to leave a ship that is sinking.) □ *There goes Tom. Wouldn't you know he'd leave a sinking ship rather than stay around and try to help?*

*the **devil** *Fig.* a severe scolding. (*Typically: **get** ~; **catch** ~; **give** so ~.) □ *Bill is always getting the devil about something.*

a **devil of a job** AND the **devil's own job** *Fig.* the most difficult task. □ *We had a devil of a job fixing the car.*

a **devil of a time** AND the **devil's own time** *Fig.* a very difficult time. □ *I had a devil of a time with my taxes.* □ *Fixing the car was going to be easy, but I had the devil's own time doing it.*

devil-may-care attitude AND **devil-may-care manner** *Fig.* a very casual attitude; a worry-free or carefree attitude. □ *You must get rid of your devil-may-care attitude if you want to succeed.*

devil-may-care manner Go to previous.

the **devil's own job** Go to a devil of a job.

dialogue with so *Inf.* to talk with someone. □ *I look forward to dialoguing with you tomorrow.* □ *The supervisor sets aside time to dialogue with each and every person in the department once a week.*

a **diamond in the rough** *Fig.* a person who has good qualities despite a rough exterior; a person with great potential. □ *Sam looks a little scruffy, but he's a diamond in the rough.*

diarrhea of the jawbone Go to next.

diarrhea of the mouth AND **diarrhea of the jawbone** *Fig.* a tendency to constant

talking. □ *Wow, does he ever have diarrhea of the mouth!* □ *You're getting diarrhea of the jawbone again.*

dibs on sth *Fig.* a claim on something. (See also *have dibs on* sth; *put* one's *dibs on* sth.) □ *I've got dibs on the yellow one!*

did everything he could 'cept eat us *Rur.* acted very hostilely. □ *When it came time to pass sentence on the criminal, the judge did everything he could 'cept eat him.*

didn't care a whit AND **don't care a whit** *Fig.* didn't care at all. □ *Sally thought Joe liked her, but he didn't care a whit about her.*

didn't exchange more than three words with so to say hardly anything to someone. (The number may vary.) □ *I know Tom was there, but I am sure that I didn't exchange more than three words with him before he left.*

die a natural death 1. [for someone] to die by disease or old age rather than by violence or foul play. □ *The police say she didn't die a natural death, and they are investigating.* **2.** *Fig.* [for something] to fade away or die down. (Fig. on ①.) □ *I expect that all this excitement about the scandal will die a natural death.*

die away *Fig.* to fade away. □ *The sound of the waterfall finally died away.*

die behind the wheel *Fig.* to die in an automobile accident in a car that one is driving. □ *Poor Fred died behind the wheel in a horrible collision.*

die by one's **own hand** AND **end it (all); do away with** oneself; **take** one's **own life** *Euph.* to commit suicide. □ *She died at the age of 50, by her own hand.*

die for so/sth *Fig.* to experience great physical or emotional desire for someone or something. □ *Freddie was dying for a glass of water—he was so thirsty.*

die from curiosity Go to die of curiosity.

die in one's **boots** AND **die with** one's **boots on** *Fig.* to die in some fashion other than in bed; to die fighting. (Popularized by western movies. Heroes and villains of these movies said they preferred death in a gunfight to showing cowardice or giving up.) □ *I won't let him get me. I'll die in my boots.*

The **die is cast.** *Fig.* An irrevocable move has been made. (Originated in Latin at the crossing of the River Rubicon by Julius Caesar with his army, which involved him in a civil war in 49 B.C. See also can't unring the bell; cross the Rubicon; When the chips are down. This has nothing to do with metal casting. It is one of a pair of dice.) □ *It is done. The die is cast. Matters are settled.*

die laughing 1. to meet one's death laughing—in good spirits, revenge, or irony. □ *Sally is such an optimist that she'll probably die laughing.* **2.** *Fig.* to laugh very long and hard. (Fig. on ①. An exaggeration.) □ *The play was meant to be funny, but the audience didn't exactly die laughing.*

die of a broken heart *Fig.* to die of emotional distress. □ *I was not surprised to hear of her death. They say she died of a broken heart.*

die of boredom *Fig.* to be very bored. □ *We sat there and listened politely, even though we almost died of boredom.*

die of curiosity AND **die from curiosity** *Fig.* to experience a strongly felt need to know about something. □ *I almost died from curiosity to finish the book and see how the mystery was solved.*

die on so **1.** *Fig.* [for a patient] to die under the care of someone. □ *Get that saline over here fast, or this guy's gonna die on me.* **2.** *Fig.* [for something] to quit running for someone. (Fig. on ①.) □ *My car died on me, and I couldn't get it started.*

die with one's **boots on** Go to die in one's boots.

a **difference of opinion** *Fig.* a disagreement treated lightly. □ *Your father and I weren't fighting. We simply had a difference of opinion.*

***different as night and day** *Cliché* completely different. (*Also: **as** ~.) □ *Although Bobby and Billy are twins, they are as different as night and day.*

difficult times Go to bad times.

dig at so/sth *Fig.* to make a cutting remark about someone or something. □ *She is always digging at her husband's laziness.*

dig deep Go to dig down.

dig ditches Go to flip burgers.

dig down AND **dig deep** *Fig.* to be generous; to dig deep into one's pockets and come up with as much money as possible to donate to something. (As if digging into one's pocket.) □ *Please dig down. We need every penny you can spare.* □ *Dig down deep. Give all you can.*

dig for sth *Fig.* to go to great pains to uncover information of some kind. □ *The police were digging for some important information while they questioned Mike "Fingers" Moran.*

dig one's **heels in**[†] *Fig.* to refuse to alter one's course of action or opinions; to be obstinate or determined. □ *The student dug her heels in and refused to obey the instructions.*

dig in one's **heels** *Fig.* to maintain one's position or mind-set with determination. □ *He dug in his heels and refused to reason with anyone.*

dig in(to sth) **1.** *Fig.* to begin to process something; to go to work on something. □ *I have to dig into all these applications today and process at least half of them.* **2.** *Fig.* to begin to eat food. □ *We dug into the huge pile of fried chicken.*

dig sth **out**[†] *Fig.* to work hard to locate something and bring it forth. □ *I dug out an old dress and wore it to the fifties party.*

dig one's **own grave** *Fig.* to be responsible for one's own downfall or ruin. □ *Those politicians have dug their own grave with their new tax bill. They won't be reelected.*

dig some dirt up[†] **(on** so) *Fig.* to find out something bad about someone. □ *If you don't stop trying to dig some dirt up on me, I'll get a lawyer and sue you.*

dig so/sth **up**[†] AND **scare** so/sth **up**[†]; **scrounge** so/sth **up**[†] *Fig. Inf.* to work hard to find someone or something. □ *I don't*

dip into one's savings

have a red one, but I thing I can scare one up.

Dig up! *Sl.* Listen carefully! □ *John: All right, you guys! Dig up! You're going to hear this one time and one time only!*

a **dime a dozen** *Fig.* abundant; cheap and common. □ *People who can write good books are not a dime a dozen.*

dine out Go to eat (a meal) out.

dinged out *Sl.* intoxicated. □ *Gary is dinged out and can't drive.*

Dinner is served. It is time to eat dinner. Please come to the table. (As if announced by a butler; often jocular.) □ *"Dinner is served," said Bob, rather formally for a barbecue.*

dip into one's **savings** *Fig.* to use part of the money one has been saving. □ *I had to dip into my savings in order to pay for my vacation.*

dirt cheap *Fig.* extremely cheap. □ *Buy some more of those plums. They're dirt cheap.*

dirty crack *Inf.* a rude remark. □ *Another dirty crack like that and I'll leave.*

dirty deal *Inf.* an unfair deal. □ *I got a dirty deal at that shop, and I won't go back.*

dirty dog *Inf.* a low and sneaky person. □ *That dirty dog tried to cheat in the card game!*

dirty one's **hands** Go to get one's hands dirty.

so's **dirty laundry** *Fig.* someone's unpleasant secrets. □ *I don't want to hear about her dirty laundry. Why do you feel it necessary to gossip about things like that?*

*a **dirty look** *Fig.* an angry face or a frown. (*Typically: **draw** ~; **get** ~; **give** so ~.) □ *I got a dirty look from the teacher when I cracked a joke in class.*

dirty old man *Inf.* a lecherous old man. (Usually jocular.) □ *Jimmy, what you call flirting will make some girls call you a dirty old man!*

a **dirty word 1.** a swearword; an obscene or blasphemous word; a four-letter word. □ *You are not allowed to use dirty words* *in your school essays.* **2.** something that is disliked or disapproved of. □ *Since Tom broke off his engagement, his name is a dirty word in the village.*

dirty work 1. unpleasant or uninteresting work. □ *My boss does all the traveling. I get all the dirty work to do.* **2.** *Fig.* dishonest or underhanded actions; treachery. (Fig. on ①.) □ *The company seems respectable enough, but there's a lot of dirty work that goes on.*

disagree with so *Fig.* [for food or drink] to upset someone's stomach. □ *Onions disagree with my husband, so he never eats them.*

disappear into thin air Go to vanish into thin air.

disappointed at so/sth AND **disappointed in** so/sth becoming sad because of someone or something. □ *I am very disappointed in you. That was a terrible thing to do.*

a **disaster of epic proportions** *Cliché* a very large disaster. (Often jocular.) □ *The earthquake was responsible for a disaster of epic proportions.*

the **disease to please** an obsessive need to please people. □ *I, like so many, am afflicted with the disease to please. I am just too nice for my own good.*

dish on so *Sl.* to gossip about or slander someone. □ *Stop dishing on her. She never hurt you!*

dish sth **out**† **1.** *Fig.* to distribute information, news, etc. □ *The press secretaries were dishing reports out as fast as they could write them.* **2.** *Fig.* to give out trouble, scolding, criticism, etc. □ *The teacher dished out a scolding to each one who was involved in the prank.*

dish the dirt *Sl.* to spread gossip; to gossip. □ *Let's sit down, have a drink, and dish the dirt.*

dispense with so/sth *Fig.* to eliminate someone or something. □ *I think we will have to dispense with Bob and his services. We simply must cut expenses.* □ *We will dispense with the reading of the minutes this week.*

dispose of so *Sl.* to kill someone. □ *Max suggested that he would dispose of Lefty if Lefty continued to be a pest.*

dis(s) (on) so *Sl.* to belittle someone; to show disrespect for someone. (From either the transitive verb *disrespect* or from *dismiss [as insignificant]*.) □ *Please stop dissing my little sister. She didn't do any of those things.*

dissolve into sth *Fig.* to change quickly into another state of behavior. (The *something* can be tears, laughter, chattering, giggles, a state of boredom, etc.) □ *The little girls saw the struggling puppy and dissolved into tears.*

distance oneself **from** so/sth to "separate" oneself ideologically from someone or something. □ *She felt that he would want to distance himself from her radical politics.*

dive in (with both feet) AND **jump in (with both feet)** *Fig.* to become completely involved with something quickly, especially something new. □ *I had never done anything like this before, but I just jumped in with both feet and learned it in no time.*

dive in(to sth**)** *Fig.* to start immediately on some business or activity with energy. □ *I can't wait to dive into the next project.*

divide and conquer *Fig.* to cause the enemy to divide and separate into two or more factions, and then move in to conquer all of them. □ *Sam led his men to divide and conquer the enemy platoon, and his strategy succeeded.*

divorce oneself **from** sth *Fig.* to separate oneself from something, such as an idea, policy, philosophy, etc. □ *She was not able to divorce herself from long-held prejudice.*

do a double take *Fig.* to react with surprise; to have to look twice to make sure that one really saw correctly. □ *When the boy led a goat into the park, everyone did a double take.* □ *When the nurse saw that the man had six toes, she did a double take.*

do a dump on so/sth Go to dump on so/sth.

do a fade *Sl.* to leave; to sneak away. □ *Richard did a fade when he heard the police siren.*

do oneself **a favor** *Fig.* to do something positive to benefit oneself. □ *I suggested that he do himself a favor and at least try to do some of the math problems.*

do a flip-flop (on sth**)** AND **do an about-face** *Fig.* to make a total reversal of opinion. □ *The candidate had done an about-face on the question of tax deductions last year.*

do a job on so/sth **1.** *Sl.* to damage someone or something; to mess up someone or something. □ *The robbers really did a job on the bank guard. They beat him when they robbed the bank.* **2.** *Fig.* to defecate on someone or something. (Note the variation in the second example.) □ *The puppy did a job on the living-room carpet.*

do a land-office business *Fig.* to do a large amount of buying or selling in a short period of time. □ *The tax collector's office did a land-office business on the day that taxes were due.*

do a number on so/sth *Sl.* to damage or harm someone or something. □ *The teacher did a number on the whole class by giving them a pop quiz.*

do a one-eighty AND **turn one hundred and eighty degrees 1.** *Fig.* to turn around and go in the opposite direction. □ *When I hollered, the dog did a one-eighty and headed back to its own yard.* **2.** *Fig.* to radically reverse a decision or opinion. □ *His political philosophy turned one hundred and eighty degrees when he grew a little older.*

do a slow burn *Fig.* to be quietly angry. (See also burn with a low blue flame.) □ *I did a slow burn while I was waiting in line for a refund.*

do a snow job on so *Sl.* to deceive or confuse someone. □ *She thought she did a snow job on the teacher, but it backfired.*

do a takeoff on so/sth *Fig.* to perform a parody on someone or something. (As if to blind someone with snow.) □ *The co-median did a takeoff on the president, and everyone thought it was terribly funny.*

do a three-sixty AND **turn three hundred and sixty degrees 1.** *Fig.* to turn completely around. □ *I was really lost. I did a three-sixty in the middle of the street because I couldn't make up my mind which way to go.* **2.** *Fig.* to reverse a decision or an opinion and then return to one's original stance. □ *Over time, he did a three-sixty in his thinking about integration.*

do a world of good (for so/sth**)** Go to make a world of difference (in so/sth).

do an about-face Go to do a flip-flop (on sth).

do an errand Go to run an errand.

do away with oneself Go to die by one's own hand.

do away with so/animal *Fig.* to kill someone or some creature. (See also do away with oneself; do away with sth.) □ *The crooks did away with the witness.*

do away with sth *Fig.* to get rid of something. □ *This chemical will do away with the stain in your sink.*

do battle with so/sth *Fig.* to confront someone or something that is a threat or challenge. □ *I know I will end up doing battle with the boss in the board meeting. Why can't I just keep quiet?* □ *Sally is doing battle with cancer, and we all wish her well.*

do so's **bidding** to do what someone demands. □ *Why do you think I should do your bidding? I'm not your slave.*

do one's **bit** to do one's share of work. □ *Each of us has to do his bit. We all need to cooperate.*

do one's **business** *Euph.* to defecate or urinate. □ *Do you need to do your business before we get in the car?*

do sth **by hand** *Fig.* to do something with one's hands rather than with a machine. □ *The calculator was broken so I had to do the calculations by hand.*

do so **credit** Go to next.

do credit to so AND **do** so **credit** *Fig.* to add positively to the reputation of someone. □ *Your new job really does credit to you.*

do so **damage** *Fig.* to harm someone. □ *I hope she doesn't plan to do me damage.*

do one's **damnedest** *Fig.* to do as well as one can, not sparing energy or determination. □ *I know you can win the contest. Just get out there and do your damnedest.*

do so **dirt(y)** *Rur.* to do something bad or dishonest to someone. □ *He sure did his wife dirty, leaving her like that.*

do dope Go to next.

do drugs AND **do dope** *Inf.* to take illegal drugs; to use illegal drugs habitually. □ *Sam doesn't do drugs, and he doesn't drink.* □ *Ron started doing dope when he was very young.*

do for so *Fig.* to suffice for someone; to be sufficient for someone. □ *Will this amount of sweet potatoes do for you?*

do so's **heart good** *Fig.* to make someone feel good emotionally. □ *When she sent me a get-well card, it really did my heart good.*

do one's **homework** *Fig.* to do what is necessary to become well prepared for something. (Fig. on preparing school homework.) □ *Since Reggie had done his homework, he was able to participate in all the discussions.*

Do I have to paint (you) a picture? Go to next.

Do I have to spell it out (for you)? AND **Do I have to paint (you) a picture?; Do I need to paint you a picture?** *Fig.* What do I have to do to make this clear enough for you to understand? (Shows impatience.) □ *Sally: Would you please go over the part about the square root again? Mary: Do I have to paint you a picture? Pay attention!*

Do I make myself (perfectly) clear? *Fig.* Do you understand exactly what I mean? (Very stern.) □ *Sue: No, the answer is no! Do I make myself clear?*

do so **in 1.** *Fig.* to make someone tired. □ *That tennis game really did me in.* **2.** *Fig.*

to cheat someone; to take so in. □ *The scam artists did the widow in by talking her into giving them all the money in her bank account.* **3.** *Sl.* to kill someone. □ *The crooks did the bank guard in.*

do sth **in**† to destroy something. □ *The huge waves totally did in the seaside community.*

do it *Euph.* to have sex. □ *I hear that Bill and Jane did it in the back of his car.*

do justice to sth **1.** *Fig.* to do something well; to represent or portray something accurately. (Often negative.) □ *This photograph doesn't do justice to the beauty of the mountains.* **2.** *Fig.* to eat or drink a great deal. □ *The party didn't do justice to the roast pig. There were nearly 10 pounds left over.*

do one's **(level) best** *Fig.* to do something as well as one can. □ *Just do your level best. That's all we can ask of you.*

do more harm than good [of a remedy] hurting more than helping. □ *Please stop giving the child advice. You are doing more harm than good.*

do so **one better** Go to go (so) one better.

do one **one better (than that)** AND **go** one **one better (than that)** to report or tell of an accomplishment or event even better or more extreme than the one previously told. □ *He thought he had told the funniest joke in the world, but I knew I could do him one better.*

do or die *Fig.* trying as hard as one can. □ *I was determined to get there—do or die.*

do so **out of** sth *Fig.* to swindle something away from someone; to defraud someone of a right or of property. □ *Spike tried to do her out of everything she had.* □ *I did myself out of a week's vacation by quitting when I did.*

do sth **out of the goodness of** one's **heart** Go to out of the goodness of one's heart.

do so **over**† AND **make** so **over**† *Fig.* to buy a new wardrobe for someone; to redo someone's hairstyle, makeup, etc. □ *Sally's mother did Sally over for the play tryouts.*

do one's **(own) thing** *Fig.* to do what one wants; to do what pleases oneself no matter what others think. □ *She's going to start doing her own thing for a change.*

do oneself **proud** *Fig.* to have done a very fine job. □ *I feel like I've done myself proud by earning high honors.*

do so **proud** *Fig.* to make someone proud. □ *Bill's kids sure did him proud at the boat race.*

do's and don'ts *Fig.* the rules; the things that should be done and those that should not be done. □ *I must admit that a lot of do's and don'ts at this company are hard for me to understand.*

do so Go to do too.

Do tell. *Fig.* a response to one of a series of statements by another person. (The expression can indicate disinterest. Each word has equal stress.) □ *Bill: The Amazon basin is about 10 times the size of France. Mary: Do tell.*

do the dishes *Fig.* to wash the dishes; to wash and dry the dishes, knives, forks, glasses, etc., after a meal. □ *Bill, you cannot go out and play until you've done the dishes.*

do the honors *Fig.* to act as host or hostess and serve one's guests by pouring drinks, slicing meat, making (drinking) toasts, etc. □ *All the guests were seated, and a huge juicy turkey sat on the table. Jane turned to her husband and said, "Bob, will you do the honors?" Bob smiled and began slicing thick slices of meat from the turkey.*

do the trick *Fig.* to do exactly what is needed. □ *This new paint scraper really does the trick.*

do the unspeakable AND **do the unthinkable** *Fig.* to do something extreme that normally would not be done. (An exaggeration.) □ *Jethro did the unspeakable and used his fish knife to butter his bread!*

do the unthinkable Go to previous.

do time Go to serve time.

do too AND **do so** *Fig.* to do something (despite anything to the contrary). (An emphatic way of saying *do.*) □ *Bob: You don't have your money with you. Bill: I do too!* □ *She did too take a cookie. I saw her do it.*

do so/sth **up**† *Fig.* to make someone or something attractive; to decorate or ornament someone or something. □ *Would you do up this present for Jane? It's her birthday.*

do sth **up brown** *Fig.* to do something just right or with great effect. (Fixed order.) □ *Whenever they put on a party, they do it up brown.*

Do what? *Fig.* What did you say?; You want me to do what? □ *Charlie: My mama's coming to visit, so I want you to cook a fancy dinner. Mary: Do what?*

do without Go to go without.

do without (so/sth**)** to manage or get along without someone or something that is needed or expected. □ *I guess I will have to do without dinner.* □ *Yes, you'll do without.*

(Do) you eat with that mouth? AND **(Do) you kiss your momma with that mouth?** *Sl.* Do you actually eat with the mouth you use to talk that filth?; Do you actually use that filthy mouth to kiss your mother? (A phrase said to someone who talks dirty all the time.) □ *That's a lot of foul talk. Do you eat with that mouth?* □ *After the suspect finished swearing at him, the police officer said, "Do you kiss your momma with that mouth?"*

Do you follow? *Fig.* Do you understand what I am saying?; Do you understand my explanation? □ *Mary: Keep to the right past the fork in the road, then turn right at the crossroads. Do you follow? Jane: No. Run it by me again.*

(Do you) get my drift? *Inf.* Do you understand what I mean?; Do you understand what I am getting at? □ *Father: I want you to settle down and start studying. Get my drift? Bob: Sure, Pop. Whatever you say.*

(Do) you hear? *Rur.* Do you hear and understand what I said? □ *John: I want you to clean up this room this instant! Do you hear? Sue: Okay. I'll get right on it.*

(Do) you kiss your momma with that mouth? Go to (Do) you eat with that mouth?

Do you mind? 1. *Fig.* You are intruding on my space!; You are offending me! (Impatient or incensed. Essentially, "Do you mind stopping what you are doing?") □ *The lady behind her in line kept pushing against her every time the line moved. Finally, Sue turned and said sternly, "Do you mind?"* **2.** *Fig.* Do you object to what I am about to do? □ *Mary had her hand on the lovely silver cake knife that would carry the very last piece of cake to her plate. She looked at Tom, who stood next to her, eyeing the cake. "Do you mind?" she asked coyly.*

Do you read me? 1. *Fig.* an expression used by someone communicating by radio, asking if the hearer understands the transmission clearly. □ *Controller: This is Aurora Center, do you read me? Pilot: Yes, I read you loud and clear.* **2.** *Fig.* Do you understand what I am telling you? (Said sternly, as when giving an instruction, and used in general conversation, not in radio communication.) □ *Mother: Get this place picked up immediately. Do you read me? Child: Yes, ma'am.*

Do you want to know something? AND **Want to know something?; Know something?** *Inf.* Can I tell you something that you probably need to know? (Usually just a prelude to telling someone something in an informal conversation.) □ *A: Want to know something? B: Unh huh. A: I think we're lost.*

(Do you) want to make something of it? AND **You want to make something of it?** *Inf.* Do you want to start a fight about it? (Rude and contentious.) □ *Bob: Please be quiet. You're making too much noise. Fred: Do you want to make something of it?*

(Do) you want to step outside? *Inf.* an expression inviting someone to go outdoors to settle an argument by fighting. □ *John: Drop dead! Bob: All right, I've had enough out of you. You want to step outside?*

Doctor Livingstone, I presume? *Jocular* You are who I think you are, are you not? □ *Oh, there you are. Doctor Livingstone, I presume?*

doctor's orders *Fig.* something that one is strongly advised to do as ordered or as if ordered by a doctor. □ *I'm doing this on doctor's orders, but I don't like it.*

Does it work for you? *Inf.* Is this all right with you?; Do you agree? (Answered with **(It) works for me.**) □ *Bill: I'll be there at noon. Does it work for you? Bob: Works for me.*

dog and pony show *Fig.* a display, demonstration, or exhibition of something— such as something one is selling. (As in a circus act where trained dogs leap onto and off of trained ponies.) □ *Gary went into his standard dog and pony show, trying to sell us on an upgrade to our software.*

The **dog ate my homework.** a poor excuse for something that someone has failed to do on time. (From an excuse a student might give for failing to turn in homework on time. Occurs in many variations.) □ *The dog ate my homework, so I have nothing to turn in.*

dog days *Fig.* the hottest days of summer, usually during July and August. (Named for *Sirius*, the "dog star.") □ *Bill spent the dog days lying out in his hammock.*

dog in the manger *Fig.* one who unreasonably prevents other people from doing or having what one does not wish them to do or have. (From one of Aesop's fables in which a dog—which cannot eat hay—lay in the hayrack [manger] and prevented the other animals from eating the hay.) □ *If Martin were not such a dog in the manger, he would let his brother have that dinner jacket he never wears.*

dog-eat-dog *Fig.* a situation in which one has to act ruthlessly in order to survive or succeed; ruthless competition. □ *It is* *dog-eat-dog in the world of business these days.*

a **doggy bag** *Fig.* a bag or other container used to carry uneaten food home from a restaurant. (As if it is for the dog.) □ *I can't eat all of this. Can I have a doggy bag, please?*

dollar for dollar *Fig.* considering the amount of money involved; considering the cost or value. (Often seen in advertising.) □ *Dollar for dollar, this laundry detergent washes cleaner and brighter than any other product on the market.*

domestic partner *Fig.* a person, often a lover, with whom one shares a household. □ *Domestic partners are covered under our health care plan.*

domestic worker a person who cleans houses. □ *Experienced domestic workers are wanted for our cleaning service.*

done by mirrors AND **done with mirrors** *Fig.* illusory; purposefully deceptive. □ *The company's self-review was done by mirrors and didn't come off too bad, despite our falling stock price.*

a **done deal** *Fig.* a completed deal; something that is settled. □ *The sale of the property is a done deal. There is nothing that can be done now.*

done for *Fig.* finished; dead. □ *The goldfish looked as if it was either done for or sunning its tummy.*

***done in** *Fig.* exhausted. (*Typically: **be** ~; **get** ~.) □ *I'm really done in! I think I'll go to bed.*

done over *Sl.* beat; outscored. □ *The other team was done over, and they showed it in their lackluster play.*

done to a T *Fig.* cooked just right. □ *I like it done to a T, not overcooked and not too raw.*

done to a turn 1. *Fig.* well-cooked; nicely cooked. □ *The turkey was done to a turn.* **2.** *Inf.* beaten. □ *When Wilbur's opponent was done to a turn, Wilbur was declared the winner.*

done with mirrors Go to done by mirrors.

Don't ask. *Inf.* It is so bad, I do not wish to be reminded or talk about it, so do not ask about it. □ *Tom: What was your calculus final exam like? Mary: Don't ask.*

Don't ask me. Go to How should I know?

Don't be a stranger. Please come back to visit often. □ *It was really good to see you, Fred. Don't be a stranger. Come back and see us.*

Don't be too sure. *Fig.* I think you are wrong, so do not sound so certain.; You may be wrong. □ *Bill: I think I've finally saved up enough money to retire. John: Don't be too sure. Inflation can ruin your savings.*

Don't bet on it! *Fig.* Do not be at all sure! □ *So, you think I will be at your house at 5:00 A.M.? Don't bet on it!*

Don't bother. *Inf.* Please don't do it. It is not necessary, and it is too much trouble. □ *Mary: Should I make some dinner for you? Bill: No, don't bother; it's late.*

Don't bother me! *Inf.* Go away!; Leave me alone! □ *"Don't bother me! Leave me alone!" the child shouted at the dog.*

Don't breathe a word of this to anyone. *Fig.* This is a secret or secret gossip. Do not tell it to anyone. (*Breathing a word* is fig. on whispering.) □ *Bill: Have you heard about Mary and her friends? Sally: No. Tell me! Tell me! Bill: Well, they all went secretly to Mexico for the weekend. Now, don't breathe a word of this to anyone.*

Don't call us, we'll call you. *Cliché* a formulaic expression said to applicants who have just interviewed or auditioned for a job or part. □ *Stupendous, Gloria, just stupendous. What glamour and radiance! Don't call us, we'll call you.*

don't care who knows it *Fig.* does not try to conceal something from people. (Also with *doesn't. Don't* used with all persons is folksy.) □ *Jane dyes her hair, and she doesn't care who knows it.*

Don't do anything I wouldn't do. *Inf.* an expression said when two friends are parting. □ *Bill: See you next month, Tom.*

Tom: *Yeah, man. Don't do anything I wouldn't do.*

Don't do me any favors! *Fig.* Your attempt to help me (after my unpleasant experience) is not welcome. (Usually with a touch of sarcasm.) □ *Don't do me any favors! Haven't you done enough already? I know you hate me!*

Don't even look like sth! *Fig.* Do not even appear to be doing something! (The *something* can be thinking about something or actually doing something.) □ *Mary: Are you thinking about taking that last piece of cake? Bob: Of course not. Mary: Well, don't even look like you're doing it!*

Don't even think about (doing) it. *Fig.* Do not do it, and do not even think about doing it. □ *John reached into his jacket for his wallet. The cop, thinking John was about to draw a gun, said, "Don't even think about it."*

Don't even think about it (happening). *Fig.* Do not think about something like that happening, as the mere thought of it is so bad. □ *Sally: If the stock market crashes, we'll lose everything we have. Sue: Don't even think about it!*

Don't get your bowels in an uproar! *Inf.* Do not get so excited! □ *Bill: What have you done to my car? Where's the bumper? The side window is cracked! Bob: Calm down! Don't get your bowels in an uproar!*

Don't give me any of your lip! *Fig.* Don't talk back! □ *Do as I tell you and don't give me any of your lip!*

Don't give me that (line)! AND **Don't hand me that (line)!** *Fig.* Don't tell me those lies!; Don't try to deceive me! □ *Don't give me that line! I know the truth! You're lying to me!*

Don't give up! Do not stop trying!; Keep trying! □ *John: Get in there and give it another try. Don't give up! Bill: Okay. Okay. But it's hopeless.*

Don't give up the ship! *Fig.* Do not give up yet!; Do not yield the entire enterprise! (Fixed order. Based on the words on a flag made by Captain Oliver Hazard Perry in the Battle of Lake Erie during the War of 1812.) □ *Bill: I'm having a devil of a time with calculus. I think I want to drop the course. Sally: Keep trying. Don't give up the ship!*

Don't give up without a fight! *Fig.* Do not yield easily.; Keep struggling and you may win.; Do not give up too soon. □ *Sue: She says no every time I ask her for a raise. Mary: Well, don't give up without a fight. Keep after her.*

Don't give up your day job. Go to Don't quit your day job.

Don't hand me that (line)! Go to Don't give me that (line)!

Don't have a cow! *Inf.* Calm down!; Don't get so excited! (Made famous in the television show *The Simpsons*.) □ *Chill out, man! Don't have a cow! □ Aw, don't have a cow, Dad!*

don't have a pot to piss in (or a window to throw it out of) *Fig.* doesn't have anything of value; very poor. (Caution with *piss*.) □ *Jane's folks don't have a pot to piss in or a window to throw it out of.*

Don't hold your breath. *Fig.* Do not stop breathing waiting for something to happen that won't happen. (Meaning that it will take longer for it to happen than you can possibly hold your breath.) □ *Sally: Someone said that gasoline prices would go down. Bob: Oh, yeah? Don't hold your breath.*

Don't I know it! *Inf.* I know that very well! □ *Mary: Goodness gracious! It's hot today. Bob: Don't I know it!*

Don't knock it. *Fig.* Don't criticize it. □ *You don't want any okra? Don't knock it.*

don't know one's **ass from a hole in the ground** AND **don't know** one's **ass from** one's **elbow** doesn't know anything; acts ignorant. (Caution with *ass*. Also with *doesn't*. Don't used with all persons is folksy.) □ *That teacher doesn't know his ass from a hole in the ground. □ She's supposed to be an expert, but she doesn't know her ass from her elbow.*

don't know one's **ass from** one's **elbow** Go to previous.

don't know beans (about sth) *Fig.* does not know anything about something. □ *Bill doesn't know beans about car engines.*

Don't let so/sth **get you down.** *Fig.* Do not allow yourself to be overcome or disappointed by someone or something. □ *Don't let Tom get you down. He's not always unpleasant.*

Don't let it go any further. AND **Don't let it out of this room.** Don't tell this secret to anyone else. (Also lit.) □ *I'll tell you what you what to know, but don't let it go out of this room.*

Don't let it out of this room. Go to previous.

Don't let the bastards wear you down. *Fig.* Don't let those people get the best of you. □ *Bill: The place I work at is really rough. Everybody is rude and jealous of each other. Tom: Don't let the bastards wear you down.*

Don't make me laugh! *Inf.* That is a stupid suggestion! □ *Don't make me laugh. Tom could never do that.*

Don't mention it. Go to Think nothing of it.

Don't mind me. *Fig.* Don't pay any attention to me.; Just ignore me. (Sometimes sarcastic.) □ *Bill and Jane were watching television when Jane's mother walked through the room, grabbing the newspaper on the way. "Don't mind me," she said.*

Don't quit trying. Go to Keep (on) trying.

Don't quit your day job. AND **Don't give up your day job.** Don't quit your regular job in hopes that you can support yourself doing this task that you do not do very well. □ *I saw your comedy act at the nightclub. Don't quit your day job!*

Don't speak too soon. I think you may be wrong. Don't speak before you know the facts. (Compare this with Don't be too sure.) □ *Bill: It looks like it'll be a nice day. Mary: Don't speak too soon. I just felt a raindrop.*

Don't stand on ceremony. *Fig.* Do not wait for a formal invitation.; Please be at ease and make yourself at home. (Some people read this as "Don't remain standing because of ceremony," and others read it "Don't be totally obedient to the requirements of ceremony.") □ *Come in, Tom. Don't stand on ceremony. Get yourself a drink and something to eat and introduce yourself to everyone."*

Don't start (on me)! *Fig.* Do not complain! □ *Yes, I know it's a mess. Don't start!*

Don't that (just) beat all! Go to If that don't beat all!

Don't waste your breath. *Inf.* You will not get a positive response to what you have to say, so don't even say it.; Talking will get you nowhere. □ *Alice: I'll go in there and try to convince her otherwise. Fred: Don't waste your breath. I already tried it.*

door-to-door 1. having to do with movement from one door to another or from one house to another. □ *John is a door-to-door salesman.* **2.** by moving from one door to another or one house to another. □ *Anne is selling books door-to-door.*

dope sth **out**† **1.** AND **puzzle** sth **out**† *Inf.* to figure something out. □ *He spent a lot of time trying to dope the assignment out so he could understand it.* **2.** *Sl.* to explain something carefully. □ *He doped it all out to them very carefully so that no one would be confused.*

a **dose of** one's **own medicine** Go to a taste of one's own medicine.

dote on so/sth to exhibit great fondness and caring for someone or something. □ *Mrs. Grant just dotes on her grandchildren. She is always doing something nice for them.*

double in brass (as sth) *Fig.* to serve in two capacities. (As with a musician who can play the brass instruments as well as other instruments.) □ *Wally was our bookkeeper and doubled in brass as a clerk.*

a **double whammy** *Fig.* a double dose of something; a strong or powerful helping of something. □ *When the Federal Reserve Board raised the interest rates, I got a double whammy. My stocks went down and my bonds did too.*

double-check *Fig.* to check something and check it again. □ *Please, double-check this carefully to make sure it's right.*

a **double-edged sword** Go to a two-edged sword.

doubting Thomas *Fig.* someone who will not easily believe something without strong proof or evidence. (Can be said of a man or a woman. From the biblical account of the apostle Thomas, who would not believe that Jesus had risen from the dead until he actually touched the risen Christ.) □ *Mary won't believe that I have a dog until she sees it. She's such a doubting Thomas.*

down and dirty 1. *Fig.* crude and carelessly done. (Used as an attributive.) □ *The last time he painted the kitchen, it was a down and dirty job because he thought we were moving.* **2.** *Fig.* coarse; mean-spirited. □ *The campaign for governor really got down and dirty in the final week.*

down and out *Fig.* having no money or means of support. □ *There are many young people down and out in the city.*

*down at the heels 1. *Lit.* [of shoes] worn on the bottom of the heels. (*Typically: **be** ~; **get** ~.) □ *This pair is a little down at the heels, but I only use them for gardening.* **2.** *Fig.* worn down; showing signs of use or age. (Fig. on ①. *Typically: **be** ~; **get** ~.) □ *He is a little down at the heels, but give him a new suit of clothes and he'll look just great.*

down by some amount *Fig.* having a score that is lower, by the specified amount, than someone else's score or the other team's score. □ *Down by one run, the team scored two runs in the ninth inning and won the game.*

*down for the count 1. AND ***out for the count** *Fig.* [of a boxer] knocked down by an opponent's punching and remaining down until the last count, or even beyond. (*Typically: **be** ~; **go** ~.) □ *Wally is down for the count. Chris is the winner.* **2.** *Fig.* eliminated from something or an activity for a period of time, perhaps permanently. (Fig. on ①. *Typically: **be** ~;

go ~.) □ *I can't continue with this course. I'm down for the count.*

*down in the dumps *Fig.* sad or depressed. (*Typically: **be** ~; **get** ~.) □ *Try to cheer Jane up. She's down in the dumps for some reason.*

down in the mouth *Fig.* sad-faced; depressed and unsmiling. □ *Since her dog died, Barbara has been down in the mouth.*

*down on so/sth *Fig.* against someone or something. (*Typically: **be** ~; **get** ~.) □ *You've been down on us all lately.*

down on one's **luck** *Fig.* without any money; unlucky. □ *The gambler had to get a job because he had been down on his luck and hadn't won enough money to live on.*

*down pat *Fig.* learned or memorized perfectly. (*Typically: **get** sth ~; **have** sth ~.) □ *Tom has his part in the play down pat. He won't make any mistakes.*

down South *Fig.* to or at the southeastern United States. □ *I used to live down South.* □ *We are going down South for the winter.*

down the chute *Fig.* gone; wasted; ruined. □ *A lot of money went down the chute on that deal, and all for nothing.*

down the drain *Fig.* gone; wasted. □ *A lot of money went down the drain in that Wilson deal.*

Down the hatch. I am about to drink this.; Let's all drink up. (Said as one is about to take a drink, especially of something bad-tasting or potent. Also used as a jocular toast.) □ *Let's toast the bride and groom. Down the hatch!*

down the little red lane *Fig.* down someone's throat; down a child's throat. □ *This really tasty medicine has to go down the little red lane.*

down the road 1. *Fig.* farther along on this same road. □ *Just continue down the road until you come to a little church. Turn left there.* **2.** *Fig.* in the future. □ *We don't know what things will be like a few months down the road.*

down the road a piece AND **down the road a stretch** *Rur.* a short distance farther on this road. □ *Smith's Dry Goods Store? It's down the road a piece, on the left-hand side.*

down the road a stretch Go to previous.

down the street *Fig.* a short distance away on this same street. □ *There is a drugstore down the street. It's very convenient.*

down the tube(s) *Inf.* ruined; wasted. □ *His political career went down the tubes after the scandal. He's lost his job.*

down time 1. *Fig.* the time when a computer or some other system is not operating. (Computer jargon.) □ *I can't afford a lot of down time in the system I buy.* **2.** *Fig.* a time for rest and relaxation. (Fig. on ①.) □ *This has been a terrible day, and I need some down time.*

down to a gnat's eyebrow *Fig.* down to the smallest detail. □ *No use trying to sneak anything out of the refrigerator. Mom knows what's in there, down to a gnat's eyebrow.*

down to earth *Fig.* practical; not fanciful; businesslike; honest and frank. (Hyphenated before nominals.) □ *Her ideas for her new boutique are always very down to earth.* □ *If Ann said that, I would believe it. She is very down to earth.*

***down to the last** bit of money *Fig.* having only a small amount of money left. (*Typically: **be** ~; **get** ~.) □ *I'm down to my last nickel.*

down to the last detail *Fig.* considering all of the details. □ *Mary wanted to be in charge of everything right down to the last detail.*

***down to the wire** *Fig.* waiting until the very last moment; right up to the deadline. (*Typically: **be** ~; **get** ~.) □ *It came down to the wire before I turned the proposal in.*

down under Australia and New Zealand. □ *We spent Christmas down under.*

***down (with so)** *Sl.* friends with someone; okay or on good terms with someone. (*Down* = okay. *Typically: **be** ~; **get** ~.)

□ *It's okay. I'm down with Chuck.* □ *Chuck and I are down.*

***down with** sth *Fig.* sick in bed with some illness. (*Typically: **be** ~; **come** ~; **go** ~.) □ *Susan came down with a bad cold and had to cancel her trip.* □ *I didn't go to work, because I had come down with the flu.*

***down with** a disease *Fig.* ill; sick at home. (Can be said about many diseases. *Typically: **be** ~; **get** ~.) □ *Tom isn't here. He's down with a cold.*

Down with so/sth! *Fig.* Do away with someone or something!; I am opposed to someone or something! □ *Down with higher taxes! Down with corporate tax breaks!*

downhill all the way *Fig.* easy the entire way. □ *Don't worry about your algebra course. It's downhill all the way after this chapter.*

downhill from here on *Fig.* easy from this point on. □ *The painful part of this procedure is over. It's downhill from here on.*

drag one's **feet (on** or **over** sth) AND **drag** one's **heels (on** or **over** sth) *Fig.* to progress slowly or stall in the doing of something. □ *Why is she taking so long? I think she is just dragging her feet on this matter.* □ *If the planning department had not dragged their heels, the building would have been built by now.*

drag one's **heels (or** or **over** sth) Go to previous.

drag on AND **drag out** to go on slowly for a very long time; to last a very long time. □ *The lecture dragged on and on.*

a **drag (on** so) *Inf.* a burden (to someone). □ *I wish you wouldn't be such a drag on your friends.*

drag on sth *Fig.* to pull or suck on something such as a cigarette, pipe, cigar, etc. □ *He dragged again on his pipe, which was beginning to sound like a bubble pipe and smell like a garbage incinerator.*

*a **drag (on** sth) *Sl.* a puff on any kind of cigarette. (*Typically: **have** ~; **take** ~.)

□ *She had a drag on her cigarette and crushed it out on the sidewalk.*

drag out Go to drag on.

drag so **through the mud** *Fig.* to insult, defame, and debase someone. □ *The newspapers dragged the actress through the mud week after week.*

dragged out *Sl.* exhausted; worn out. □ *I feel so dragged out. I think I need some sleep.*

draw a blank 1. *Fig.* to get no response; to find nothing. □ *We looked in the files for an hour, but we drew a blank.* **2.** *Fig.* to fail to remember something. □ *I tried to remember her telephone number, but I could only draw a blank.*

draw a line in the sand AND **draw a battle line** *Fig.* to create or declare an artificial boundary and imply that crossing it will cause trouble. □ *Todd drew a line in the sand by giving his roommate an ultimatum about his sloppiness—he had to start cleaning up after himself or move out.*

draw blood 1. to remove blood from a person using a hypodermic needle as for a medical laboratory test. □ *A nice lady came into my hospital room at dawn to draw blood for some tests.* **2.** to injure someone severely enough to cause bleeding. □ *It was a nasty bite and it drew blood, but not a lot.* **3.** *Fig.* to anger or insult a person. □ *Sally screamed out a terrible insult at Tom. Judging by the look on his face, she really drew blood.*

draw so's **fire 1.** to do something that will attract an attack from someone firing a weapon. □ *I will make a move with my gun that will draw their fire; then you can see where the shots are coming from.* **2.** *Fig.* to do or say something that will bring criticism or condemnation from someone. (Fig. on ①.) □ *I knew when I wrote the last paragraph that I would draw your fire, but it had to be said anyway.*

draw in one's **horns** AND **pull in** one's **horns** *Fig.* to back down from a fight. □ *For a minute it looked like they was gonna start sluggin' each other, but then they drew in their horns.*

draw on sth *Fig.* to utilize a supply or reserve of something. □ *I will have to draw on my savings to pay for the car repairs.* □ *She drew on her boundless supply of energy to get through the day.*

draw so **out** to try to get information from a person; to get an opinion or a hint from someone. □ *I attempted to draw her out on the way things were going in the board meetings, but she would reveal nothing.*

draw sth **out** *Fig.* to make something last longer than it needs to. □ *Why did the speaker draw the thing out so much? He said everything that needed to be said in the first hour.*

draw one **out (of** oneself) *Fig.* to encourage someone to become more open and sociable. □ *I talked with him in private hoping to draw him out, but he remained quiet and kept to himself.*

draw straws for sth *Fig.* to decide who gets something or must do something by choosing straws from an unseen set of straws of different lengths. (The person who gets the shortest straw is chosen.) □ *We drew straws for the privilege of going first.*

draw the line (at sth) AND **draw the line (on** sth) *Fig.* to set a limit at something; to decide when a limit has been reached. □ *It's hard to keep young people under control, but you have to draw the line somewhere.*

draw the line between sth **and** sth (else) *Fig.* to distinguish between something and something else. (Usually the two things represent kinds of behavior.) □ *I am afraid I draw the line between happy informality and just plain rudeness, and you, sir, are plainly rude!*

a **drawing card** *Fig.* an attraction that helps bring patrons to a place of entertainment. □ *The comedian was a real drawing card at the night club.*

***drawn and quartered** *Fig.* to be dealt with very severely. (Now fig. except in historical accounts; refers to a former practice of torturing someone guilty of treason, usually a male, by disemboweling and then dividing the remaining body into four parts. *Typically: **be** ~; **have so** ~. Fixed order.) □ *Todd was practically drawn and quartered for losing the Wilson contract.*

drawn like a moth to a flame *Fig.* attracted [to someone or some event] instinctively or very strongly, as a moth is drawn to the light of a flame. □ *Customers were drawn to the sale like a moth to a flame. They came from all over and bought up everything in the store.*

a **dream come true** *Fig.* a wish or a dream that has become a reality. □ *My vacation to Hawaii was like a dream come true.*

Dream on. *Fig.* What you are expecting or wanting to happen is nothing but fantasy. □ *You want to get promoted to general manager? Dream on.*

dredge so/sth **up**† *Fig.* to use some effort to seek and find someone or something. □ *I don't have a wrench here, but I'll see if I can dredge one up from the basement.*

dress so **down**† **(for** sth**)** Go to read so out† (for sth).

dressed to kill AND **dressed (up) fit to kill** *Fig.* dressed in fancy or stylish clothes. □ *Wow, look at Sally! She's really dressed to kill.* □ *When Joe came to pick Mary up for the movie, he was dressed up fit to kill and carrying a dozen roses.*

dressed to the nines AND **dressed to the teeth** *Fig.* dressed very stylishly with nothing overlooked. □ *She showed up for the picnic dressed to the nines.* □ *Clare is usually dressed to the teeth in order to impress people.*

dressed to the teeth Go to previous.

dressed (up) fit to kill Go to dressed to kill.

a **dressing down** *Fig.* a harsh scolding. □ *The boss gave the entire sales crew a powerful dressing down for missing their forecast.*

drift off to sleep *Fig.* to fall asleep gradually. □ *At last, he drifted off to sleep.* □ *During that boring lecture, I drifted off to sleep a number of times.*

drill sth **into** so Go to drum sth into so.

drink like a fish *Fig.* to drink alcohol excessively; to be in the habit of drinking alcohol excessively. □ *Jeff really drank like a fish at the party on Saturday.* □ *I worry about Nancy; she drinks like a fish.*

drink to excess *Euph.* to drink too much alcohol; to drink alcohol continually. □ *Some people drink to excess only at parties.*

drink so **under the table** *Fig.* to be able to drink more alcohol than someone else. □ *I bet I can drink you under the table.*

Drink up! *Fig.* Finish your drink!; Finish that drink, and we'll have another! □ *Okay, drink up! It's almost closing time.* □ *Drink up, and let's get going.*

drive a coach and horses through sth *Fig.* to expose weak points or "wide gaps" in an argument, alibi, or criminal case by "driving a horse and carriage through" them. (Emphasizes the large size of the holes or gaps in the argument.) □ *The opposition will drive a coach and horses through the wording of that government bill.*

drive a hard bargain *Fig.* to work hard to negotiate prices or agreements in one's own favor. □ *All right, sir, you drive a hard bargain. I'll sell you this car for $12,450.*

drive so **around the bend** *Fig.* to make someone angry or very frustrated. □ *Gert will drive us all around the bend with her constant complaining.*

drive so **batty** AND **drive** so **bonkers; drive** so **nuts** *Fig.* to annoy or irritate someone. □ *You are certainly annoying! You're going to drive me batty.* □ *This cold is driving me bonkers.* □ *These tax forms are driving me nuts.*

drive so **bonkers** Go to previous.

drive so **crazy** AND **drive** so **insane; drive** so **mad 1.** *Fig.* to force someone into a state of insanity or mental instability. □ *The sound of the wind howling almost drove me crazy.* **2.** *Fig.* to annoy or irritate someone. (Fig. on ①.) □ *This itch is driving me crazy.* □ *All these telephone calls are driving me mad.*

drive sth **home**† **(to** so**)** *Fig.* to emphasize an important point about something (to someone). □ *The teacher repeated the point three times just to drive it home.* □ *I hope this really drives the importance of safety home to you.*

drive so **insane** Go to drive so crazy.

drive so **mad** Go to drive so crazy.

drive so **nuts** Go to drive so batty.

drive one **out of** one's **mind** *Fig.* to make someone go crazy; to frustrate someone. □ *You are driving me out of my mind with your nagging.*

drive so **to distraction** *Fig.* to confuse or perplex someone. □ *The problems I am having with my boss are driving me to distraction.*

drive so **to drink** *Fig.* [for someone or something] to cause someone to turn to alcohol as an escape from frustration. □ *She was driven to drink by the problems she had with her teenage son.*

drive so **to the wall** Go to force so to the wall.

drive so **up the wall** Go to up the wall.

*the **driving force (behind** so/sth**)** *Fig.* the person or a thing that motivates or directs someone or something. (*Typically: **be** ~; **become** ~; **serve as** ~.) □ *Making money is the driving force behind most businesses.*

drop so **1.** *Sl.* to knock someone down; to punch and knock down a person. □ *Fred dropped Willie with one punch to the jaw.* **2.** *Fig.* to stop being friends with someone, especially with one's boyfriend or girlfriend. □ *Bob finally dropped Jane. I don't know what he saw in her.*

drop a bomb(shell) AND **explode a bombshell** *Fig.* to announce shocking or startling news. □ *They really dropped a bombshell when they announced that the mayor would resign.* □ *They must choose their words very carefully when they explode a bombshell like that.*

drop a brick *Fig.* to commit a social error. □ *When he ignored the hostess, he really dropped a brick!*

drop a bundle (on so**)** AND **blow a bundle (on** so**)** *Inf.* to spend a lot of money pleasing or entertaining someone. □ *I blew a bundle on the candidate, and it didn't help me at all.*

drop a bundle (on sth**)** *Inf.* to pay a lot of money for something. □ *Pete dropped a bundle on this car.*

drop a hint *Fig.* to give a tiny or careful hint about something. □ *Mary dropped a hint that she wanted a new ring for her birthday.*

drop so **a line** AND **drop** so **a few lines; drop** so **a note** to write a letter or a note to someone. (The **line** refers to lines of writing.) □ *I dropped Aunt Jane a line last Thanksgiving.* □ *She usually drops me a few lines around the first of the year.*

drop so **a note** Go to previous.

drop by Go to drop over.

drop by the wayside AND **fall by the wayside 1.** to leave a march or procession in exhaustion to recover beside the pathway. □ *A few of the marchers dropped by the wayside in the intense heat.* **2.** *Fig.* to fail to keep up with others. (Fig. on ①.) □ *Many of the students will drop by the wayside and never finish.*

drop dead 1. to die suddenly. □ *I understand that Tom Anderson dropped dead at his desk yesterday.* **2.** *Inf.* Go away and stop bothering me. (Usually **Drop dead!**) □ *If you think I'm going to put up with your rudeness all afternoon, you can just drop dead!*

drop one's **drawers** *Fig.* to lower one's pants or underpants. □ *The boys dropped their drawers and jumped in the creek.*

drop everything *Fig.* to stop doing whatever you are doing. □ *Drop everything and go outside. The house is on fire.*

drop so/sth **from** sth *Fig.* to exclude someone or something from something. □ *The professor was forced to drop the failing students from the course.*

drop one's **guard** Go to let one's guard down†.

Drop in sometime. *Fig.* Visit my home or office sometime when you are nearby. □

Bob: Bye, Bill, nice seeing you. Bill: Hey, drop in sometime. Bob: Okay.

a **drop in the bucket** AND a **drop in the ocean** *Fig.* an insignificant contribution toward solving a large problem. □ *Many companies donated food and medicine to help the survivors of the earthquake, but it was just a drop in the ocean of what was needed.*

a **drop in the ocean** Go to previous.

drop in one's **tracks 1.** to collapse from exhaustion. □ *Kelly almost dropped in her tracks from overwork.* **2.** to die instantly. □ *I know that someday I will just drop in my tracks.*

drop into one's **lap** Go to fall into one's lap.

Drop it! Go to Drop the subject!

drop so/sth **like a hot potato** *Fig.* to dissociate oneself with someone or something instantly. □ *I dropped the idea like a hot potato when the big boss said he didn't like it.*

drop like flies *Fig.* to faint, sicken, collapse, or die in great numbers like houseflies dying in a large group. □ *It was a terrible year for the flu. People were dropping like flies.*

drop so's **name** Go to next.

drop names AND **drop** so's **name** *Fig.* to mention a name or the names of important or famous people as if they were personal friends. □ *Bill's such a snob. Leave it to him to drop the names of all the local gentry.*

drop off *Fig.* to decline. □ *Attendance at the meetings dropped off after Martin became president.*

drop so/sth **off**† **(some place) 1.** to let someone or a group out of a vehicle at a particular place; to deliver someone or something some place. □ *Let's drop off Tom and Jerry at the hamburger joint.* **2.** *Fig.* to give someone or a group a ride to some place. □ *Can I drop you off somewhere in town?*

drop off the face of the earth AND **fall off the face of the earth; drop off the map; fall off the map** *Fig.* [for some-one] to disappear altogether. □ *I don't know where he is. It's like he dropped off the face of the earth.*

drop off the map Go to previous.

drop off (to sleep) *Fig.* to go to sleep without difficulty; to fall asleep. □ *I sat in the warm room for five minutes, and then I dropped off to sleep.*

drop sth **on** so *Fig.* to give someone some bad news. (Fig. on the image of dropping a burden on someone.) □ *Sally dropped some really bad news on Walter.*

drop out (of sth**)** *Fig.* [for someone] to resign from or cease being a member of something; [for someone] to leave school. □ *Sally dropped out of school for some unknown reason.*

drop out of sight AND **drop from sight** *Fig.* to disappear from public view; [for someone] to go into hiding. □ *The robbers dropped out of sight, and the crime was never solved.*

drop over AND **drop by; swing by** to come for a casual visit. (See also **pop around (for a visit)**.) □ *We would love for you to drop over.* □ *I would really like to drop over soon.*

drop one's **teeth** *Fig.* to react with great surprise. □ *They dropped their teeth when I told them I was married.*

drop the ball *Fig.* to make a blunder; to fail in some way. □ *Everything was going fine in the election until my campaign manager dropped the ball.*

drop the other shoe *Fig.* to do the deed that completes something; to do the expected remaining part of something. (See also **wait for the other shoe to drop**.) □ *Tommy has just failed three classes in school. We expect him to drop the other shoe and quit altogether any day now.*

Drop the subject! AND **Drop it!** *Fig.* Do not discuss it further! □ *Bill: Sally, you're gaining a little weight. I thought you were on a diet. Sally: That's enough! Drop the subject!*

drop-dead date *Fig.* the absolutely last possible date (by which something must be done). (Widely used as jargon in the workplace.) □ *What's the drop-dead date for these designs to reach the manufacturing department?*

drop-dead gorgeous *Sl.* very good looking. □ *Perry's girlfriend is drop-dead gorgeous. How can a twit like him hold onto a looker like that?*

drown in sth *Fig.* to experience an overabundance of something. □ *We are just drowning in cabbage this year. Our garden is full of it.*

drown so **in** sth *Fig.* to inundate someone with something. □ *I will drown you in money and fine clothes.* □ *Mike drowned the nightclub singer in fancy jewels and furs.*

drown sth **out** *Fig.* to make so much noise that something cannot be heard. □ *The sound of the passing train drowned out the child's sobbing.*

drown one's **sorrows** Go to next.

drown one's **troubles** AND **drown** one's **sorrows** *Fig.* to try to forget one's problems by drinking a lot of alcohol. □ *Bill is in the bar, drowning his troubles.*

a **drug on the market** AND a **glut on the market** something that is on the market in great abundance. □ *Right now, small computers are a drug on the market.* □ *Thirty years ago, small transistor radios were a glut on the market.*

drum sth **into** so AND **drum** sth **into** so's **head; drill** sth **into** so; **drum** sth **in**† *Fig.* to teach someone something intensely. □ *Her mother had drummed good manners into her.*

drum sth **into** so's **head** Go to previous.

drum so **out of** sth AND **drum** so **out**† *Fig.* to expel or send someone away from something, especially in a formal or public fashion. □ *They drummed Bill out of the bridge club for having a bad attitude.*

drunk and disorderly *Fig.* a criminal charge for public drunkenness accompanied by bad or offensive behavior. □ *In addition to being convicted for driving while intoxicated, Roscoe was found guilty of being drunk and disorderly.*

*drunk as a lord AND ***drunk as a skunk** very drunk. (*Also: **as** ~.) □ *James bought himself a case of beer and proceeded to get as drunk as a skunk.*

drunk as a skunk Go to previous.

dry as a bone Go to next.

*dry as dust AND ***dry as a bone 1.** *Cliché* very dry. (*Also: **as** ~.) □ *When the leaves are dry as a bone, they break into powder easily.* **2.** *Cliché* very dull; very boring. (*Also: **as** ~.) □ *Her lecture was dry as dust—just like her subject.*

dry out *Fig.* to allow alcohol and the effects of drunkenness, especially if habitual, to dissipate from one's body. □ *He required about three days to dry out completely.*

dry so **out**† *Fig.* to cause someone to become sober; to cause someone to stop drinking alcohol to excess. □ *If the doctor at the clinic can't dry him out, no one can.*

dry run *Fig.* an attempt; a practice or rehearsal. □ *The children will need another dry run before their procession in the pageant.*

dry spell a period with no rain. □ *The dry spell killed the crops.*

dry-gulch so *Inf.* to ambush someone. □ *The posse planned to dry-gulch the outlaw by waiting outside his favorite saloon.*

sth **du jour** Go to flavor of the month.

duck and cover 1. *Fig.* to bend down and seek protection against an attack. □ *When the gunfire started, we had to duck and cover or get killed.* **2.** *Fig.* to dodge something, such as an issue or a difficult question, and attempt to shield oneself against similar issues or questions. (Fig. on ①.) □ *The candidate's first reaction to the question was to duck and cover.*

duck soup *Fig.* very easy; an easy thing to do. □ *For Maria, knitting a sweater is duck soup.*

duded up *Sl.* dressed up. □ *He hates fancy clothes. He didn't even get duded up for his own wedding.*

duke it out *Sl.* to have a fistfight. □ *John told George to meet him in the alley so they could duke it out.*

*dull as dishwater AND ***dull as ditchwater** very uninteresting. (*Also: **as** ~.) □ *I'm not surprised that he can't find a partner. He's as dull as dishwater.*

dull as ditchwater Go to previous.

dummy up *Sl.* to refuse to talk. □ *John dummied up right away when the police arrived.*

dump a load Go to dump one's load.

dump all over so/sth Go to dump on so/sth.

dump one's **load 1.** *Sl.* to empty one's stomach; to vomit. □ *He's had too much to drink and is dumping his load.* **2.** AND **dump a load** *Sl.* to defecate. □ *He dumped his load and settled back down to work.*

dump on so/sth AND **do a dump on** so/sth; **dump all over** so/sth *Sl.* to criticize someone or something; to destroy someone or something. □ *There is no need to do a dump on me. I didn't wreck your car.*

dump sth **on** so *Fig.* to pour out one's troubles to someone. □ *I wish you wouldn't dump all your problems on me.*

dumped on *Sl.* maligned; abused. □ *The jerk who designed this stupid congested stairway hasn't been dumped on enough.*

a dust bunny AND **a dust kitten; a turkey's nest** *Fig.* a clump of dust and lint. □ *She swept the dust bunnies out from under the bed.* □ *He hasn't cleaned in weeks. There are turkey's nests in every corner.*

a dust kitten Go to previous.

dust so's **pants** *Sl.* to spank someone, usually a child. □ *My dad will dust my pants if he hears about this.*

Dutch auction *Fig.* an auction or sale that starts off with a high asking price that is then reduced until a buyer is found. (Viewed by some as insulting to the Dutch.) □ *My real estate agent advised me to ask a reasonable price for my house rather than get involved with a Dutch auction.*

Dutch courage *Fig.* unusual or artificial courage arising from the influence of alcohol. (Viewed by some as insulting to the Dutch.) □ *It was Dutch courage that made the football fan attack the policeman.*

Dutch treat *Fig.* a social occasion where one pays for oneself. (Viewed by some as insulting to the Dutch.) □ *"It's nice of you to ask me out to dinner," she said, "but could we make it a Dutch treat?"*

Dutch uncle *Fig.* a man who gives frank and direct advice to someone. (In the way an uncle might, but not a real relative.) □ *I would not have to lecture you like a Dutch uncle if you were not so extravagant.*

duty bound to do sth obliged to do something because it is one's duty. □ *You are duty bound to attend the meetings if you are elected an officer.*

dwell on so/sth *Fig.* to talk about or concentrate on someone or something. □ *I wish you wouldn't dwell on my faults so much!*

dyed-in-the-wool *Fig.* [of someone] permanent or extreme. □ *My uncle was a dyed-in-the-wool farmer. He wouldn't change for anything.*

dying to do sth AND **dying to have** sth *Fig.* very eager to do something, such as to have, get, or ingest something. □ *After a long hot day like this one, I'm just dying to drink a cold beer.* □ *After a long hot day, I'm just dying to have a cold beer.*

E

eager beaver *Fig.* someone who is very enthusiastic; someone who works very hard. □ *The young assistant gets to work very early. She's a real eager beaver.*

eagle eye *Fig.* acute eyesight; an intently watchful eye. (From the sharp eyesight of the eagle.) □ *The students wrote their essays under the eagle eye of the headmaster.*

*****an **earful** *Fig.* a great amount of discussion, criticism, gossip, or complaint. (*Typically: **get** ~; **have** ~; **give** so ~.) □ *Sue was standing around the corner while Jim and Mary were arguing and got an earful.*

early bird 1. *Fig.* a person who gets up early. □ *I never miss sunrise. I'm an early bird.* **2.** *Fig.* a person who arrives early. □ *The early birds get the best seats.* **3.** *Fig.* having to do with early arrival. □ *The early-bird special this week is a free six-pack of iced tea for the first 100 visitors.*

early on *Fig.* early; at an early stage. □ *We recognized the problem early on, but we waited too long to do something about it.*

earn one's **keep** *Fig.* to help out with chores in return for food and a place to live; to earn one's pay by doing what is expected. □ *Tom hardly earns his keep around here. He should be fired.*

one's **ears are red** *Fig.* [for someone's ears] to be red from embarrassment. □ *My ears are red! I can't believe I said that.*

one's **ears are ringing** *Fig.* [for someone's ears] to have a ringing sound because of an illness or other condition; very loud music, or some other very loud sound. □ *After the explosion, my ears were ringing for hours.*

ease so's **burden** Go to lighten so's load.

easier said than done *Cliché* said of a task that is easier to talk about than to do. □ *Finding a really good job is easier said than done.*

*****easy as A, B, C** AND *****easy as falling off a log; *****easy as rolling off a log; *****easy as (apple) pie; *****easy as duck soup** very easy. (*Also: **as** ~.) □ *If you use a cake mix, baking a cake is easy as A, B, C.* □ *Getting out of jail is as easy as rolling off a log when you have a good lawyer.*

easy as (apple) pie Go to previous.

easy as duck soup Go to easy as A, B, C.

easy as falling off a log Go to easy as A, B, C.

easy come, easy go *Cliché* said to explain the loss of something that required only a small amount of effort to acquire in the first place. □ *John spends his money as fast as he can earn it. With John it's easy come, easy go.*

Easy does it. 1. *Fig.* Move slowly and carefully. □ *Bill (holding one end of a large crate): It's really tight in this doorway. Bob (holding the other end): Easy does it. Take your time.* **2.** *Fig.* Calm down.; Don't lose your temper. □ *Sue (frantic): Where is my camera? My passport is gone too! Fred: Easy does it, Sue. I think you have someone else's purse.*

easy money Go to soft money.

easy pickings *Fig.* [of things] easy to get or steal; [of people] easy to get or persuade. □ *The pickpockets found lots of easy pickings at the state fair.*

easy to come by *Fig.* easily found; easily purchased; readily available. □ *Please be*

eat crow

careful with that phonograph record. It was not easy to come by.

eat (a meal) out AND **dine out** *Fig.* to eat a meal at a restaurant. □ *I like to eat a meal out every now and then.* □ *It costs a lot of money to dine out often.*

eat so **alive** *Fig.* [for insects] to bite someone many times. □ *These mosquitoes are just eating me alive!*

eat and run *Fig.* to eat a meal or a snack quickly and then leave. □ *Well, I hate to eat and run, but I have to take care of some errands.*

eat (away) at so *Fig.* [for a problem] to trouble someone constantly. □ *The nasty situation at work began to eat away at me.*

eat one's **cake and have it too** Go to have one's cake and eat it too.

eat crow 1. *Fig.* to display total humility, especially when shown to be wrong. □ *Well, it looks like I was wrong, and I'm going to have to eat crow.* **2.** *Fig.* to be shamed; to admit that one was wrong. □

When it became clear that they had arrested the wrong person, the police had to eat crow.

eat one's **fill** *Fig.* to eat as much as one can hold; to eat as much as one wants. □ *Please eat your fill. There's plenty for everyone.*

eat so **for breakfast** AND **have** so **for breakfast** *Fig.* to defeat someone thoroughly. (Usually future tense.) □ *Watch out! Those guys are incredibly aggressive. They will eat you for breakfast!*

eat one's **hat** *Fig.* a phrase telling the kind of thing that one would do if a very unlikely event really happens. □ *I'll eat my hat if you get a raise.*

eat one's **heart out 1.** *Fig.* to grieve; to be sorrowful. (Fixed order.) □ *She has been eating her heart out over that jerk ever since he ran away with Sally.* **2.** *Fig.* to suffer from envy or jealousy. (Usually a command.) □ *Yeah, the reward money is all mine. Eat your heart out!*

eat humble pie *Fig.* to act very humble when one is shown to be wrong. (*Umbles* is an old generic term for edible animal innards and does not necessarily involve humility. Nonetheless some writers tell us that only the humble poor ate such things—without regard to the elegant yuletide boar's head. The similarity between *umbles* and *humble* may then have given rise to the "pie of humility," *humble pie*, the expression being essentially a pun.) □ *I think I'm right, but if I'm wrong, I'll eat humble pie.*

eat like a bird *Fig.* to eat only small amounts of food; to peck at one's food. □ *Jane is very slim because she eats like a bird.*

eat like a horse *Fig.* to eat large amounts of food. □ *John works like a horse and eats like a horse, so he never gets fat.*

eat so's **lunch** *Inf.* to best someone; to defeat, outwit, or win against someone. (Like a school bully taking away children's lunches and eating them.) □ *The upstart ABC Computer Company is eating IBM's lunch.*

eat so **out**† Go to chew so **out**†.

eat out of so's **hand** AND **eat from** so's **hand** *Fig.* to do exactly as someone says; to grovel to someone. □ *He will be eating out of your hand before you are finished with him.*

eat so **out of house and home** *Fig.* to eat everything that someone has in the house. □ *The entire football team came over and ate poor Sally out of house and home.*

eat (pretty) high off the hog Go to live (pretty) high off the hog.

eat so **up**† **1.** *Fig.* [for an idea] to consume a person. □ *The obsession to own a car was eating up my brother and his friends.* **2.** *Fig.* [for insects] to bite a person all over. (Fig. on ①.) □ *These mosquitoes are just eating me up!*

eat sth **up**† **1.** *Fig.* to consume something rapidly, such as money. □ *Running this household eats my income up.* **2.** *Inf.* to believe something. □ *Those people really eat that stuff up about tax reduction.* **3.** *Inf.* to appreciate something. □ *The audience liked my singing. They really ate it up.*

eat one's **words** *Fig.* to have to take back one's statements; to confess that one's predictions were wrong. □ *John was wrong about the election and had to eat his words.*

eat(en) up with sth *Fig.* consumed with something, such as jealousy. □ *Jed was so eaten up with hatred that he couldn't see straight.*

ebb and flow *Fig.* to decrease and then increase, as with tides; a decrease followed by an increase, as with tides. □ *The fortunes of the major political parties tend to ebb and flow over time.*

economical with the truth *Euph.* untruthful. □ *The mayor was known to be economical with the truth.*

egg so **on** *Fig.* to encourage, urge, or dare someone to continue doing something, usually something unwise. □ *The two boys kept throwing stones because the other children were egging them on.*

eighty-six sth *Sl.* to throw something away. □ *Let's eighty-six this stew and go out and get some decent pizza.*

***(either) feast or famine** *Fig.* either too much (of something) or not enough (of something). (*Typically: **be** ~; **have** ~.) □ *This month is very dry, and last month it rained almost every day. Our weather is either feast or famine.*

elbow grease *Fig.* hard scrubbing. □ *Tom: What did you use to get your car so shiny? Mary: Just regular wax and some elbow grease.*

electronic superhighway AND **information superhighway** *Fig.* the World Wide Web; the computer Internet. □ *Most of my communications travel on the electronic superhighway.*

an **elegant sufficiency** Go to a gracious plenty.

eleventh-hour decision *Fig.* a decision made very late in a process, or at the last possible moment. □ *The president's eleventh-hour decision was made in a great hurry, but it turned out to be correct.*

*an **end in itself** *Fig.* existing for its own sake; existing for no clear purpose. (*Typically: **be** ~; **become** ~.) □ *For Bob, art is an end in itself. He doesn't hope to make any money from it.*

end it (all) Go to die by one's own hand.

End of story. *Inf.* That completes the story, and I will say no more. □ *I did it because I wanted to. End of story.*

the **end of the ball game** *Fig.* the end of some process; the end of life. □ *It looked like the end of the ball game as we sped too fast around the curve.*

the **end of the line** Go to next.

the **end of the road** AND the **end of the line**; the **end of the trail** **1.** the place where the road or pathway stops; the end of the route, such as a bus, train, or subway route. □ *We drove to the end of the road and began our hike into the mountains.* **2.** *Fig.* the end of the whole process. (Fig. on ①.) □ *You've come to the end of the line. I'll not lend you another penny.* **3.** *Euph.* death. □ *When I reach the end of the road, I wish to be buried in a quiet place, near some trees.* □ *She was nearly 90 when she came to the end of the line.*

the **end of the trail** Go to previous.

end up some place Go to wind up some place.

end up somehow Go to wind up somehow.

end up (by) doing sth Go to wind up (by) doing sth.

end up on the cutting room floor *Fig.* to end up excluded or left out. (Fig. on the idea that pieces of film edited out of films are traditionally dropped on the floor of the room in which the film is edited. Some good scenes are sometimes eliminated that way, as well as the sole appearances of minor actors.) □ *Some of my best moments in life end up on the cut-*

ting room floor, unlived and unremembered.

end up with all the marbles Go to all the marbles.

engraved in stone Go to carved in stone.

Enough is enough! I had enough of what you are doing!; That is enough of that, (so stop)! □ *I am so tired of your really bad jokes. Enough is enough! Stop it!*

enough to keep body and soul together *Fig.* very little; only enough to survive. (Usually refers to money.) □ *When he worked for the library, Marshall only made enough to keep body and soul together.*

enter the fray Go to join the fray.

enter the lists *Fig.* to begin to take part in a contest or argument. □ *He had decided not to stand for Parliament, but entered the lists at the last minute.*

err on the side of sth good *Fig.* to allow range of judgment to include more generosity or tolerance than not. □ *When I am distributing clothes to the needy, I tend to err on the side of generosity rather than follow the guidelines rigorously.* □ *If I err, I err on the side of fairness and the American Way!*

sth **escapes me** *Fig.* I cannot quite remember a certain fact or name. □ *Sorry, but your name escapes me.*

the **eternal triangle** a sexual or emotional relationship involving two women and one man or two men and one woman. (Typically, a couple [man and woman] and another man or woman.) □ *Henry can't choose between his wife and his mistress. It's the eternal triangle.*

evacuate one's **bowels** *Euph.* to defecate. □ *After taking a jog around the block, Jill felt the need to evacuate her bowels.*

(even) as we speak *Cliché* just now; at this very moment. □ *"I'm sorry, sir," consoled the agent at the gate, "the plane is taking off as we speak."*

*an **even break** *Fig.* a fair chance; a fair judgment. (*Typically: **get** ~; **have** ~;

give so ~.) □ *Please give me an even break! I need some help here!*

even if it kills me *Fig.* [pledging to do something] even if [doing it] is very difficult. □ *Don't worry. I will get it done even if it kills me.*

even so even if something is so or accurately reported. □ *A: I am the one who saw this car first, so I have the first rights to buy it. B: Even so, I am here right now with the cash to buy it.*

even steven *Inf.* to be even (with someone or something) by having repaid a debt, replied in kind, etc. □ *Bill hit Tom; then Tom hit Bill. Now they are even steven.*

***even (with** so) *Fig.* not being indebted to someone for money; no longer needing to retaliate against someone. (*Typically: **be** ~; **get** ~.) □ *I will get even with you for breaking my baseball bat!*

the **evening of life** *Euph.* old age. □ *As she approached the evening of life, Sarah looked back on her accomplishments with satisfaction.*

ever and anon *Fig.* now and then; occasionally. (Literary and archaic.) □ *Ever and anon the princess would pay a visit to the sorcerer in the small walled garden directly behind the castle.*

every fool thing *Inf.* every ridiculous or insignificant thing. □ *I don't want to hear about every fool thing you did on your vacation.*

every inch a sth AND **every inch the** sth *Fig.* completely; in every way. (Usually strengthening a following adjective. The *something* can be a type of person.) □ *Mary is every inch the schoolteacher.*

every last one *Fig.* every one; every single one. □ *You must eat all your peas! Every last one!*

every living soul *Fig.* every person. □ *This is the kind of problem that affects every living soul.*

Every man for himself! Every person must fend for himself. (This generic, common gender phrase is fixed and means person, not male.) □ *The boat is turning over! Every man for himself!*

every minute counts AND **every moment counts** *Fig.* time is very important. (Used especially in situations where time is very limited.) □ *Doctor, please try to get here quickly. Every minute counts.* □ *When you're trying to meet a deadline, every moment counts.*

every moment counts Go to previous.

every mother's son (of them) *Fig.* every one of them. □ *The scout leader said that unless the scouts told him who had stolen the money, he would punish every mother's son of them.*

every nook and cranny *Fig.* every small, out-of-the-way place or places where something can be hidden. □ *We looked for the tickets in every nook and cranny. They were lost. There was no doubt.*

(every) now and again Go to next.

(every) now and then AND **(every) now and again; every so often; (every) once in a while** *Fig.* occasionally; infrequently. □ *We eat lamb every now and then.* □ *We eat pork now and then.* □ *I read a novel every now and again.*

(every) once in a while Go to previous.

every other person or thing every second or alternate person or thing. □ *The magician turned every other card over.*

every single each [one]. (Emphatic.) □ *You need to take one of these pills every single day!*

every so often Go to (every) now and then.

every time one **turns around** *Fig.* frequently; at every turn; with annoying frequency. □ *Something goes wrong with Bill's car every time he turns around.*

(every) Tom, Dick, and Harry AND **any Tom, Dick, and Harry** *Fig.* everyone, without discrimination; ordinary people. (Not necessarily males.) □ *The golf club is very exclusive. They don't let any Tom, Dick, or Harry join.*

every trick in the book *Fig.* every deceptive method known. □ *I used every trick* *in the book, but I still couldn't manage to get a ticket to the game Saturday.*

every walk of life *Fig.* every status and occupation. □ *We invited people from every walk of life, but only those who could afford the long drive could possibly come.*

ever(y) which way *Rur.* in all directions. □ *That mountain road kind of turns you ever which way before it finally gets you to the top.*

everybody and his brother AND **everybody and his uncle** *Fig.* everybody; lots of people. □ *Everybody and his uncle was asking me where you were today.*

everybody and his uncle Go to previous.

everything but the kitchen sink AND **everything under the sun** *Cliché* almost everything one can think of. □ *John orders everything but the kitchen sink when he goes out to dinner, especially if someone else is paying for it.*

everything from A to Z Go to next.

everything from soup to nuts AND **everything from A to Z** *Cliché* almost everything one can think of. □ *For dinner we had everything from soup to nuts.*

everything humanly possible *Fig.* everything that is in the range of human powers. □ *The doctor tried everything humanly possible to save the patient.*

everything under the sun Go to everything but the kitchen sink.

Everything's coming up roses. *Fig.* Everything is really just excellent. Life is prosperous. □ *Life is wonderful. Everything is coming up roses.*

exchange places (with so**)** Go to trade places (with so).

***exciting as watching (the) paint dry** very, very dull. (Sarcastic. *Also: **about as** ~**; as** ~.) □ *This book is about as exciting as watching paint dry.*

excuse oneself to make polite apologies or explanations before leaving a place. □ *I will have to excuse myself from this meeting, since I have a vested interest in the outcome.*

Excuse my French. Go to Pardon my French.

exercise a firm hand Go to a firm hand.

expand one's **horizons** *Fig.* to experience and learn new things. □ *Read more! Travel! Go out and expand your horizons!*

expectant mother *Fig.* a pregnant woman. □ *The doctor's waiting room was filled with expectant mothers.*

expecting (a child) *Fig.* to be pregnant. □ *Tommy's mother is expecting a child.*

expense is no object Go to money is no object.

explain sth **away**† *Fig.* to explain something so that it is no longer a problem. □ *You can't just explain away all your problems.*

explode a bombshell Go to drop a bomb(shell).

explode in so's **face** Go to blow up in so's face.

explode with sth **1.** *Fig.* to burst out saying something; to be about to burst with eagerness to say something. □ *The children exploded with protests when their parents told them it was bedtime.* **2.** *Fig.* to produce a sudden abundance of something. (Fig. on the notion of buds bursting or a sudden blooming or sprouting of vegetation.) □ *The fields exploded with an enormous crop of wildflowers.*

extenuating circumstances *Fig.* special (but otherwise unspecified) circumstances that account for an irregular or improper way of doing something. □ *Mary was permitted to arrive late because of extenuating circumstances.*

the eye of the hurricane AND **the eye of the storm 1.** the area of calm in the center of a hurricane. □ *It is calm and peaceful in the eye of the storm.* **2.** *Fig.* a temporary peaceful time amidst more trouble and strife yet to come. (Fig. on ①.) □ *Don't relax. This is the eye of the storm. The lunch hour rush is over, but the dinner rush will start soon.*

the eye of the storm Go to previous.

eyeball to eyeball *Fig.* face-to-face and often very close; in person. □ *They approached each other eyeball to eyeball and frowned.*

*an **eyeful (of** so/sth**)** *Fig.* a shocking or surprising sight. (*Typically: **get** ~; **have** ~; **give** so ~.) □ *The office door opened for a minute, and I got an eyeful of the interior.*

one's **eyes are bigger than** one's **stomach** *Fig.* one has taken more food than one can eat. □ *I can't eat all this. I'm afraid that my eyes were bigger than my stomach.*

eyes like saucers *Fig.* eyes opened widely as in amazement. □ *Our eyes were like saucers as we witnessed another display of the manager's temper.*

one's **eyes pop out of** one's **head** *Fig.* someone is showing extreme surprise. □ *When I saw the bill, my eyes nearly popped out of my head.*

face off *Fig.* to prepare for a confrontation. □ *The opposing candidates faced off and the debate began.*

a **face (that) only a mother could love** AND a **face that could stop a clock** *Fig.* a very ugly face. (Usually jocular.) □ *The poor baby has a face only a mother could love.* □ *Look at that guy. That's a face that could stop a clock.*

face the consequences Go to suffer the consequences.

face (the) facts *Fig.* to confront the (unpleasant) truth about someone or something; to confront and accept the consequences of something. □ *Eventually, you will have to face the facts. Times are hard.*

face the music *Fig.* to receive punishment; to accept the unpleasant results of one's actions. □ *Mary broke a dining-room window and had to face the music when her father got home.*

face-to-face 1. *Fig.* in person; in the same location. (Said only of people. An adverb.) □ *Let's talk about this face-to-face. I don't like talking over the telephone.* **2.** *Fig.* facing one another; in the same location. (Used as an attributive.) □ *I prefer to have a face-to-face meeting.*

the **facts of life 1.** *Euph.* the facts of sex and reproduction, especially human reproduction. (See also the **birds and the bees.**) □ *My parents told me the facts of life when I was nine years old.* **2.** *Fig.* the truth about the unpleasant ways that the world works. □ *Mary really learned the facts of life when she got her first job.*

fagged out *Sl.* exhausted. □ *I'm really fagged out after all that running.*

faint dead away *Fig.* to faint and fall unconscious. □ *David will faint dead away when he reads this.*

the **faint of heart** *Fig.* people who are squeamish; someone who is sickened or disturbed by unpleasantness or challenge. □ *The pathway around the top of the volcano, near the crater, is not for the faint of heart.*

fair and impartial *Fig.* just and unbiased. (Usually referring to some aspect of the legal system, such as a jury, a hearing, or a judge.) □ *We demand that all of our judges be fair and impartial in every instance.*

fair and square *Fig.* completely fair(ly); justly; within the rules. □ *The division of the money should be fair and square.*

do sth **fair and square** *Fig.* to do something fairly. □ *He always plays the game fair and square.*

fair enough *Fig.* agreed; agreeable. □ *A: I think we should divide the pizza right down the middle. B: Fair enough.*

*a **fair shake** *Fig.* an instance of fair treatment. (*Typically: **get** ~; **have** ~; **give** so ~.) □ *He's unpleasant, but we have to give him a fair shake.*

fair to middlin' *Rur.* mediocre; not bad but not good. (*Middling* = of average quality.) □ *Tom: How are you feeling today? Bill: Fair to middlin'.*

fair-haired boy *Fig.* a favored person. (Not necessarily young or a boy.) □ *The supervisor's son was the fair-haired boy on the construction site.*

fair-weather friend *Fig.* someone who is your friend only when things are pleasant or going well for you. □ *Bill stayed for* *lunch but he wouldn't help me with the yard work. He's just a fair-weather friend.*

fake it *Inf.* to pretend (to do something). □ *I can't fake it anymore. I've got to be honest with you.*

fall (all) over oneself **(to** do sth) *Fig.* to attempt to do something with much energy and activity. □ *Bob fell all over himself to get on the right side of Tiffany so he could open the door for her.*

fall apart (at the seams) AND **come apart (at the seams) 1.** [for something] to break apart where its parts are joined. □ *The dress fell apart at the seams.* **2.** AND **fall apart** *Fig.* [for someone] to break down emotionally or mentally. (Fig. on ①.) □ *Poor Ralph simply fell apart at the seams.*

fall asleep at the switch Go to asleep at the switch.

fall behind schedule Go to behind schedule.

fall between two stools *Fig.* to come somewhere between two possibilities and so fail to meet the requirements of either. □ *The material is not suitable for an academic book or for a popular one. It falls between two stools.*

fall by the wayside Go to drop by the wayside.

fall down on the job *Fig.* to fail to do something properly; to fail to do one's job adequately. □ *The team kept losing because the coach was falling down on the job.*

fall (flat) on one's **face 1.** *Lit.* to fall down, face first. □ *Bobby fell flat on his face and skinned his nose.* **2.** AND **fall (flat) on its face** *Fig.* to fail miserably, usually in a performance. (Fig. on ①.) □ *She was terrible in the play. She fell flat on her face.* □ *The whole play fell on its face.*

fall for so Go to fall in love (with so).

fall for sth Go to buy sth.

fall for sth **hook, line, and sinker** Go to swallow sth hook, line, and sinker.

fall from grace 1. *Fig.* to sin and get on the wrong side of God. (A Christian con-

cept.) □ *It was either fall from grace or starve from lack of money. That's how thieves are made.* **2.** *Fig.* to do something wrong and get in trouble with someone other than God. (Fig. on ①.) □ *I hear that Ted lost the Wilson contract and has fallen from grace with the boss.*

fall from power *Fig.* to go out of power; to go out of office. □ *The dictator fell from power after the riots.*

fall head over heels *Fig.* to fall down, perhaps turning over or rolling. □ *Fred tripped on the rug and fell head over heels into the center of the room.*

fall head over heels in love (with so) *Fig.* to fall in love with someone, especially deeply and suddenly. □ *Roger fell head over heels in love with Maggie, and they were married within the month.*

fall heir to sth *Fig.* to end up with having to take care of something that no one else wants; to be placed in charge of something unexpectedly. □ *Bob fell heir to the Wilson project and has to complete what Jane failed to do.*

fall ill *Fig.* to become ill. □ *Tom fell ill just before he was to perform.*

fall in love (with so) AND **fall for** so *Fig.* to develop the emotion of love for someone. □ *Tom fell in love with Mary, but she only wanted to be friends.*

fall in love (with sth) *Fig.* to become enamored of something. □ *I simply fell in love with the dress. I had to have it.*

fall into a trap AND **fall into the trap; fall into** so's **trap** *Fig.* to become caught in someone's scheme; to be deceived into doing or thinking something. □ *We fell into a trap by asking for an explanation.*

fall into decay *Fig.* to degenerate; to rot. □ *The house was very old and had fallen into decay.*

fall into disfavor *Fig.* to lose one's influence; to be preferred less and less. □ *This style of government fell into disfavor some years ago.*

fall into disgrace *Fig.* to become without honor. □ *The mayor fell into disgrace because of his financial dealings.*

fall into disuse *Fig.* to be used less and less. □ *The pump had fallen into disuse, and the joints had rusted solid.*

fall into so's **hands** Go to come into so's hands.

fall into one's **lap** AND **drop into** one's **lap** *Fig.* [for something of great value or usefulness] to be given or granted to someone without having been requested. □ *Some valuable antique jewelry just fell into his lap. His late mother had kept it hidden for years.*

fall in(to) line 1. *Fig.* to line up so that each person (except the first person) stands behind someone. □ *The teacher told the students to fall in line for lunch.* **2.** *Fig.* to conform; to fall in(to) place. (Fig. on ①.) □ *All the parts of the problem finally fell into line.* **3.** *Fig.* to behave in a manner similar to someone or something. (Fig. on ①.) □ *You are expected to fall into line with the other people.*

fall in(to) place 1. *Fig. Lit.* [for something] to go into the place that it belongs. □ *The puzzle was easy. After a few minutes, all the pieces just fell into place.* **2.** *Fig.* [for the elements of a complicated issue] to begin to make sense and reveal the structure of the issue. □ *Once we had established the motive, the sequence of events of the murder fell into place.*

fall in(to) step *Fig.* to get into the same marching pattern as everyone else as regards which foot moves forward. (Everyone should be moving the same foot forward at the same time.) □ *I just can't seem to fall into step. I am very uncoordinated.*

fall into the habit of doing sth AND **fall into the trap of** doing sth; **fall into the rut of** doing sth *Fig.* to surrender to the practice of doing something so that it becomes habitual. □ *I fell into the habit of sleeping late and found it hard to give up.* □ *John fell into the trap of eating chocolate before going to bed and could never give it up.*

fall into the rut of doing sth Go to previous.

fall into the trap of doing sth Go to fall into the habit of doing sth.

fall into the wrong hands *Fig.* to become associated with the wrong person; to become the possession of the wrong person. □ *I don't want these plans to fall into the wrong hands.*

fall off the face of the earth Go to drop off the face of the earth.

fall off the wagon Go to off the wagon.

fall on deaf ears *Fig.* [for talk or ideas] to be ignored by the persons they were intended for. □ *Her pleas for mercy fell on deaf ears; the judge gave her the maximum sentence.*

fall on hard times *Fig.* to experience difficult times, especially financially. □ *We fell on hard times during the recession.*

fall on one's **knees** AND **fall to** one's **knees** *Fig.* to kneel down, usually in respect. □ *The people fell on their knees and prayed in gratitude for their salvation from the flood.*

fall on one's **sword** *Fig.* to accept defeat; to go to extremes to indicate one's defeat. (From the ancient practice of a military commander committing suicide this way rather than being captured.) □ *So, because I lost the contract, I am supposed to fall on my sword or something?*

fall out 1. *Fig.* to happen; to result. □ *What fell out of our discussion was a decision to continue.* **2.** *Fig.* to leave one's place in a formation when dismissed. (Usually in scouting or the military. The opposite of fall in.) □ *All the soldiers fell out and talked among themselves.*

fall out of bed *Inf.* [for a measurement] to drop very low very fast. □ *The major stock averages fell out of bed today as the market suffered its second severe crash in two months.*

fall out of favor (with so**)** AND **fall from favor (with** so**); lose favor (with** so**)** *Fig.* to lose someone's approval or acceptance. □ *This style of house has fallen out of favor with most people lately.*

fall out of love (with so) *Fig.* to stop being in love with someone. □ *She claimed she had fallen out of love with him.*

fall out with so AND **have a falling-out with so** *Fig.* to have a disagreement with a friend that ruins the friendship. □ *She had a falling-out with her boyfriend, and they stopped talking to each other.*

fall over backwards (to do sth) AND **bend over backwards (to do sth); lean over backwards (to do sth)** *Fig.* to do everything possible to please someone. □ *The taxi driver fell over backwards to be helpful.* □ *The teacher bent over backwards to help the students understand.* □ *You don't have to lean over backwards to get me to help. Just ask.*

fall overboard to fall from a boat or a ship into the water. (See also **go overboard.**) □ *Someone fell overboard, and they had to stop the boat and go back.*

fall prey to so/sth AND **fall victim to so/sth** *Fig.* to become a victim of the deception, lawlessness, or temptation created by someone or something. (Fig. on becoming the prey of an animal.) □ *Jon fell prey to Tiffany's charms.* □ *We fell victim to a pickpocket.*

fall short *Fig.* to lack something; to lack enough of something, such as money, time, etc. □ *Tom fell short of cash and had to borrow from me.*

fall short of one's goal(s) AND **fall short of the goal(s); fall short of the record** *Fig.* to fail to achieve a goal. □ *We fell short of our goal of collecting $1,000.* □ *Ann ran a fast race but fell short of the record.*

fall short of the goal(s) Go to previous.

fall short of the record Go to fall short of one's **goal(s)**.

fall through *Fig.* to fail; not to get approved; [for an agreement] to be rescinded. □ *Our mortgage fell through, so I had to withdraw my offer to buy the house.*

fall through the cracks Go to through the cracks.

fall to *Fig.* to begin doing something; to prepare to do something and go to work on it. □ *She asked for help, and everyone fell to.*

fall to so *Fig.* to become the responsibility of someone. □ *It always falls to me to apologize first.*

fall to one's knees Go to fall on one's knees.

fall to pieces Go to go to pieces.

fall victim to so/sth Go to fall prey to so/sth.

a falling-out *Fig.* a disagreement that leads to an estrangement. □ *They had a falling-out years ago and have never spoken since.*

a false move AND **one false move** *Fig.* [even] a single movement that indicates that one is disobeying an order to remain still or in a nonthreatening posture. □ *The robber threatened to shoot us if we made one false move.*

famous last words *Fig.* assertions that are almost immediately countered. (Sarcastic.) □ *A: I said I would never speak to her again in my entire life! B: Famous last words! You just said hello to her.*

*****a fan of so** to be a follower of someone; to idolize someone. (*Typically: **be** ~; **become** ~.) □ *My mother is still a fan of the Beatles.*

fan the breeze *Fig.* to chat or gossip. □ *We're just fanning the breeze, so you didn't interrupt anything.*

fan the flames (of sth) *Fig.* to make something more intense; to make a situation worse. □ *The riot fanned the flames of racial hatred even more.*

fancy so's chances *Fig.* to have confidence in someone's [including one's own] ability to be successful. (Informal.) □ *We all think she will refuse to go out with him, but he certainly fancies his own chances.*

fancy footwork 1. *Fig.* clever and intricate dance steps. □ *The old man was known for his fancy footwork when he was on Broadway.* **2.** *Fig.* adroit movements of the feet that help someone retain balance or move through treacherous territory. □ *It took some fancy footwork to get down the mountain carrying the injured child.*

3. *Fig.* a clever and intricate strategy that helps someone get out of trouble. □ *The governor did some fancy footwork to keep from getting blamed for the scandal.*

Fancy meeting you here! *Fig.* I am very surprised to meet you here! □ *"Fancy meeting you here," said Mr. Franklin when he bumped into the company president at the racetrack.*

Fancy that! AND **Imagine that!** *Fig.* I am very surprised to hear that.; That is hard to imagine or believe. □ *Sue: This computer is 10 times faster than the one we had before. Jane: Imagine that! Is it easy to operate? Sue: Of course not.*

far and away the best AND **far and away the worst; far and away the greatest; far and away the** most extreme *Fig.* unquestionably the most extreme examples of something or some type of person, such as ugliest, prettiest, fattest, skinniest. □ *Sally is good, but Ann is far and away the best artist in our school.* □ *You are far and away the most tedious person I have ever met.*

far and away the greatest Go to previous.

far and away the worst Go to far and away the best.

*far and wide *Fig.* to arrive from everywhere; to arrive from many directions and great distances. (*Typically: **scattered** ~; **come from** ~; **found** ~.) □ *People came from far and wide to attend the annual meeting.*

far be it from me (to do sth**)** It is probably not my place to do something. (The origin of the *far be it from me* part is biblical, 2 Samuel 20:20. "Far be it, far be it from me, that I should swallow up or destroy." Also misstated as *far be it for me*.) □ *Far be it from me to try to tell you how to lead your life, but why don't you take that damn ring out of your nose?*

a **far cry from** sth *Fig.* a thing that is very different from something else. □ *What you did was a far cry from what you said you were going to do.*

far from doing sth *Fig.* unlikely to do something. □ *I'm far from quitting my job and running off with Miss Gilbert, but I do really get tired of all this nonsense.*

far from it *Fig.* not it at all; not at all. □ *Jane: Does this hat look strange? Tom: Far from it. It looks good on you.*

far from the madding crowd *Fig.* in a quiet, restful place. (From Thomas Gray's poem, "Elegy Written in a Country Churchyard.") □ *Julia sat daydreaming at her desk, wishing she were far from the madding crowd.*

far gone *Inf.* in an extreme state, usually an irrational or intoxicated state. □ *He was too far gone to make any sense.* □ *Larry's far gone and looking sick.*

far into the night *Fig.* late into the night; until very late. □ *She sat up and read far into the night.*

far-away look AND **far-off look** *Fig.* an appearance on one's face of having one's mind in another place. □ *Lisa's face had a far-off look indicating that she was daydreaming.*

far-off look Go to previous.

far-out 1. great; extraordinary. (Older.) □ *You want to hear some far-out heavy metal?* **2.** *Inf.* very hard to understand; arcane; highly theoretical. □ *This physics chapter is too far-out for me.*

fart around *Inf.* to waste time playing around. (Caution with *fart*.) □ *Stop farting around and get the job started!*

fast and furious *Cliché* very rapidly and with unrestrained energy. □ *Everything was going so fast and furious at the store during the Christmas rush that we never had time to eat lunch.*

fast friends *Fig.* good, loyal friends. □ *The two of them had been fast friends since college.*

a **fast one** *Fig.* a clever and devious trick. (Compare this with pull a fast one (on so).) □ *That was a fast one. I didn't know you were so devious.*

faster and faster *Fig.* at an increasing rate of speed; fast and then even faster. □ *The* *car went faster and faster, and I was afraid we would crash.*

fast-talk so **into** sth *Fig.* to use deceitful talk to get someone to do something. □ *You can't fast-talk me into giving you money. How dumb do you think I am?*

fast-talk so **out of** sth *Fig.* to use deceitful talk to get someone not to do something or to give something up. □ *Don't try to fast-talk me out of my share.*

fat and happy *Fig.* content, as if from being well-fed. □ *Since all the employees were fat and happy, there was little incentive to improve productivity.*

fat and sassy *Fig.* in good health and spirits. □ *She came back from her vacation all fat and sassy.*

*fat as a pig exceptionally fat; grotesquely fat. (*Also: **as** ~.) □ *You really ought to go on a diet. You're as fat as a pig.*

fat cat 1. *Fig.* someone who is ostentatiously and smugly wealthy. □ *I like to watch the fat cats go by in their BMWs.* **2.** *Fig.* having to do with wealth or a wealthy person. (Hyphenated. Used as an attributive.) □ *You'll never see me driving any of those fat-cat cars.* □ *I just have a bank account. No fat-cat investments.*

fat chance *Fig.* very little likelihood. □ *You think she'll lend you the money? Fat chance!*

*the fat hit the fire *Fig.* a situation that suddenly becomes frantic and unpleasant. (*Typically: **suddenly** ~; **then** ~; **when** ~.) □ *Things were looking bad in the stock market; then the fat hit the fire and I lost everything.*

so's **fate is sealed** *Fig.* the destiny of someone has been determined. □ *When the driver finally saw that the bridge was out, he knew his fate was sealed.*

a **fate worse than death** *Fig.* a terrible fate. (Usually an exaggeration.) □ *Having to sit through one of his lectures is a fate worse than death.*

father sth **on** so *Fig.* to regard someone as the author or originator of something. □

Do not attempt to father that stupid idea on me!

feast one's **eyes ((up)on** so/sth) *Fig.* to enjoy the sight of someone or something. (*Upon* is formal and less commonly used than *on.*) □ *Just feast your eyes on that beautiful beach.*

a **feast for the eyes** AND a **feast for** one's **eyes** *Fig.* a delight for someone to look at. (Can be used to describe a fine-looking display of prepared food or anything that looks good.) □ *Ah, my dear, you are a feast for the eyes!*

a **feather in** one's **cap** *Fig.* an honor; a reward for something. □ *John earned a feather in his cap by getting an A in physics.*

feather one's **(own) nest** *Fig.* to use power and prestige to provide for oneself selfishly. (Said especially of politicians who use their offices to make money for themselves.) □ *The mayor seemed to be helping people, but she was really feathering her own nest.*

fed up (with so/sth) *Fig.* disgusted with someone or something. □ *I am so fed up with her nonsense that I could scream.*

feed so **a line** Go to give so a line.

feed one's **face** *Inf.* to put food in one's mouth; to eat (something). □ *You're always feeding your face. You're going to get fat.*

feed the kitty *Fig.* to contribute money. (A *kitty* here is a small collection of money.) □ *Please feed the kitty. Make a contribution to help sick children.*

a **feeding frenzy 1.** *Fig.* [of sharks] a vicious, competitive feeding attack on prey animals. □ *One of the sharks was fatally bitten during a feeding frenzy amongst his own kind.* **2.** *Fig.* a vicious attack on someone or something. □ *It wasn't an office argument, it was a feeding frenzy led by the head accountant!*

feel a draft *Inf.* to sense that one is being rejected; to sense that someone is cool toward one, possibly for racial reasons. □ *Oh, man, I feel a draft in here. Let's leave.*

feel one's **age** to feel the aches and pains of old age. □ *It's these cold mornings that I really feel my age.*

feel at home to feel as if one belongs; to feel as if one were in one's home; to feel accepted. □ *I liked my dormitory room. I really felt at home there.*

feel blue *Fig.* to feel sad. □ *You look like you feel blue. What's wrong?*

feel for so *Fig.* to feel the emotional pain that someone else is feeling; to empathize or sympathize with someone. □ *I really feel for you. I'm so sorry it turned out this way.*

*a **feel for** sth *Fig.* a natural or learned ability to do something. (*Typically: **get** ~; **have** ~.) □ *He doesn't have a feel for this kind of careful work.*

feel free (to do sth**)** *Fig.* to feel like one is permitted to do something or take something. □ *Please feel free to stay for dinner.* □ *If you see something you want in the refrigerator, please feel free.*

feel one's **hair stand on end** AND **feel the hair on the back of** one's **neck stand on end; raise the hair on the back of** one's **neck** to feel a creepy feeling on one's scalp or neck during fright. □ *That movie was so scary! I felt my hair stand on end!*

feel sth **in** one's **bones** AND **know** sth **in** one's **bones** *Fig.* to sense something; to have an intuition about something. □ *The train will be late. I feel it in my bones.*

feel (sth**) in** one's **heart of hearts** AND **know (**sth**) in** one's **heart of hearts** *Fig.* to have the good feeling of being very certain of something. (The *something* can become a clause at the end of the phrase.) □ *I feel in my hearts of hearts that you are right, but others still have doubts.*

feel (kind of) puny AND **feel a little puny** *Inf.* to feel weak or ill. □ *I'm feeling kind of puny. Think I might be coming down with a cold.*

feel like a million (dollars) Go to like a million (dollars).

feel like a new person *Fig.* to feel refreshed and renewed, especially after getting well or getting dressed up. □ *I bought a new suit, and now I feel like a new person.*

feel like oneself **again** Go to oneself again. (The first entry in "A.")

feel like (having) sth *Fig.* to want to have something. □ *I feel like a cold beer about now.*

feel one's **oats** *Fig.* to be lively and full of energy. (Like a young horse, perhaps.) □ *What a glorious spring day. All the kids around here are really feeling their oats. Look at them go!*

*the **feel of** sth *Fig.* a sense for how something feels when it is being used correctly. (*Typically: **get** ~; **have** ~; **give** so ~.) □ *I can drive better now that I have the feel of this car's steering.*

feel on top of the world *Fig.* to feel very good, as if one were ruling the world. (See also sitting on top of the world.) □ *I do not actually feel on top of the world, but I have felt worse.*

feel so **out**† Go to sound so out†.

feel out of place Go to out of place.

feel the hair on the back of one's **neck stand on end** Go to feel one's hair stand on end.

feel the pinch *Fig.* to experience the problem of not having enough money. □ *I have been out of a job for a year now, and we are beginning to feel the pinch.*

feel one's **way 1.** *Fig.* to move along a route in the dark by feeling the walls, etc. □ *I felt my way to the light switch and turned it on.* **2.** *Fig.* to work though [something] difficult and unfamiliar. (Fig. on ①.) □ *I am unfamiliar with legal language and the contracts were complicated, so I had to feel my way.*

feeling no pain *Inf.* numbed by alcohol and feeling nothing; intoxicated. □ *He drank the whole thing, and he's feeling no pain.*

*a **feeling (that** sth **is the case)** AND *a **feeling about** sth a premonition that [something might happen or be the case]; an intuition about something.

(*Typically: **get** ~; **have** ~; **give** so ~.) □ *I had a feeling that you might be dropping by this afternoon.*

fence an animal **in**† to enclose an animal and its area within a fence or barrier. □ *We fenced the dog in to keep it at home.*

fend for oneself Go to shift for oneself.

fender bender *Fig.* a minor car accident. □ *A small fender bender tied up traffic on the expressway for hours!*

ferret sth **out 1.** *Fig.* to remove something from some narrow place. (Fig. on a ferret's being able to enter small spaces.) □ *I found a silver dollar, but I had to ferret it out of a crack in the floor.* **2.** *Fig.* to manage to get a bit of information from someone. □ *I managed to ferret out the location of the place where she bought that dreamy pair of shoes.*

fetch up at some place *Rur.* to reach a place; to end up at a place. □ *We fetched up at Sam's house at about midnight.*

few and far between *Fig.* very few; few and widely scattered. □ *Get some gasoline now. Service stations on this highway are few and far between.*

a **few bricks short of a load** Go to next.

a **few bricks shy of a load** AND a **few bricks short of a load;** a **few cards shy of a full deck;** a **few cards short of a deck; not playing with a full deck; two bricks shy of a load** *Fig.* lacking in intellectual ability. □ *Tom: Joe thinks he can build a car out of old milk jugs. Mary: I think Joe's a few bricks short of a load.* □ *Ever since she fell and hit her head, Jane's been a few bricks short of a load, if you know what I'm saying.* □ *You twit! You're two bricks shy of a load.*

a **few cards short of a deck** Go to previous.

fiddle about (with so) Go to next.

fiddle around (with so) AND **fiddle about (with** so) *Fig.* to tease, annoy, or play with someone; to waste someone's time. □ *All right, stop fiddling around with me and tell me how much you will give me for my*

car. □ *Now it's time for all of you to quit fiddling around and get to work.*

fiddle around (with sth) AND **fiddle about (with** sth) *Fig.* to play with something; to tinker with something ineptly. □ *My brother is outside fiddling around with his car engine.*

fiddle while Rome burns *Fig.* to do nothing or something trivial while knowing that something disastrous is happening. (From a legend that the Roman emperor Nero played the lyre while Rome was burning.) □ *The lobbyists don't seem to be doing anything to stop this tax bill. They're fiddling while Rome burns.*

field questions AND **field a question** *Fig.* to answer a series of questions, especially from reporters. □ *After her speech, Jane fielded questions from reporters.*

a **fifth wheel** *Fig.* an unwelcome or extra person. □ *I don't like living with my son and daughter-in-law. I feel like a fifth wheel.*

fifty-fifty *Fig.* even or equal. (See also go fifty-fifty (on sth).) □ *The chances of success are about fifty-fifty.*

fight a losing battle *Fig.* to struggle in a hopeless struggle; to fight a hopeless fight. □ *I know I am fighting a losing battle, but I hope to have my plan accepted.*

fight against time *Fig.* to hurry to meet a deadline or to do something quickly. □ *The ambulance sped through the city to reach the accident, fighting against time.*

***fight city hall** AND ***beat city hall;** ***beat the system** *Fig.* to battle against and overcome a bureaucracy. (*Typically: **You can't** ~; **There's no point trying to** ~.) □ *Bill: I guess I'll go ahead and pay the tax bill. Bob: Might as well. You can't fight city hall.*

fight sth **down**† **1.** to struggle to hold something back; to struggle to keep from being overwhelmed by something. □ *She fought her anger down and managed to stay calm.* **2.** *Fig.* to struggle to swallow something; to fight to get something down one's throat. □ *It tasted terrible, but I managed to fight it down.*

fight fire with fire *Fig.* to respond to an attack or a threat with the same "weapons" or tools that the attacker uses. (Fig. on the idea of fighting the spread of a raging fire by burning an area before the fire gets to it, thereby robbing the raging fire of fuel.) □ *They are suing us for breach of contract. We've got to defend ourselves by suing them back. We've got to fight fire with fire!*

fight so/sth **hammer and tongs** AND **fight** so/sth **tooth and nail; go at it hammer and tongs; go at it tooth and nail** *Fig.* to fight against someone or something energetically and with great determination. □ *They fought against the robber tooth and nail.* □ *The dogs were fighting each other hammer and tongs.*

fight so/sth **off**† Go to stand so/sth off†.

fight sth **out**† Go to slug it out.

fight the good fight *Fig.* to fight a noble and well-intentioned battle. □ *He fought the good fight and left the meeting with a clear conscience.*

fight to the death *Fig.* to engage in a battle that isn't finished until one opponent is dead. □ *The two men looked as though they were going to fight to the death.*

fight so/sth **tooth and nail** Go to fight so/sth hammer and tongs.

a **fighting chance** a good possibility of success, especially if every effort is made. □ *They have at least a fighting chance of winning the race.*

a **figment of** one's **imagination** AND a **figment of the imagination** an imaginary thing or event; something that one has imagined. □ *You're not sick. Your symptom is just a figment of your imagination.*

figure in sth [for someone or something] to play a role in something. □ *Tom figures in our plans for future office management.* □ *I don't wish to figure in your future.*

fill a void AND **fill the void** to supply what is needed in a place that had none. (This also includes the jocular **fill a much needed void**, which is said in criticism of someone or something.) □ *Your pres-*

ence fills a void in my life. I'm glad you're here. □ *This book fills a void in the literature of the pipe organ in 15th-century Europe.*

fill one's **face** AND **stuff** one's **face** *Sl.* to eat food fast; to stuff food into one's face. □ *Every time I see you, you are stuffing your face. No wonder you're overweight!*

fill so **full of lead** *Sl.* to shoot someone. □ *The shopkeeper bought a gun and swore the next time someone broke into the shop, he'd fill him full of lead.*

fill in for so Go to pinch-hit for so.

fill so **in on** sth *Fig.* to give someone the information about something. □ *Please fill me in on the new procedure you are using for e-mail.*

Fill in the blanks. *Fig.* You can figure out the rest.; You can draw a conclusion from that. (Fig. on the idea of filling in blank spaces on a form. Fixed order.) □ *John: They had been lost for two days, then the wolves came, and the rest is history. Jane: Yes, I think I can fill in the blanks.*

*one's **fill of** so/sth *Fig.* as much of someone or something as one needs or can tolerate. (*Typically: **get** ~; **have** ~.) □ *You'll soon get your fill of Tom. He can be quite a pest.*

fill so's **shoes** AND **step into** so's **shoes** *Fig.* to take the place of some other person and do that person's work satisfactorily. (As if you were wearing the other person's shoes.) □ *I don't know how we'll be able to do without you. No one can fill your shoes.*

fill the bill AND **fit the bill** *Fig.* to be acceptable. □ *Jane: I need some string. Tom: Here's some twine. Will it fill the bill?*

fill the gap *Fig.* to serve temporarily. □ *I think that the temporary employee will fill the gap until a new person can be hired.*

filled to the brim *Fig.* filled all the way full; filled up to the top edge. □ *I like my coffee cup filled to the brim.*

filthy lucre *Inf.* money. □ *I sure could use a little of that filthy lucre.*

filthy rich 1. *Fig.* very wealthy. □ *I wouldn't mind being filthy rich.* **2.** *Fig.* people who are very wealthy. □ *The filthy rich can afford that kind of thing, but I can't.*

a **final fling** *Fig.* the last act or period of enjoyment before a change in one's circumstances or lifestyle. □ *Mary's going out with her girlfriends for a final fling. She's getting married next week.*

final touch(es) Go to finishing touch(es).

the **final word** Go to the last word.

financially embarrassed *Euph.* broke. □ *Gary found himself financially embarrassed when the time came to pay the bill.*

find oneself *Fig.* to discover what one's talents and preferences are. □ *John tried a number of different jobs. He finally found himself when he became a cook.*

find a happy medium Go to strike a happy medium.

find enough time to do sth Go to find the time to do sth.

find one's **feet** *Fig.* to become used to a new situation or experience. □ *It takes time to learn the office routine, but you will gradually find your feet.*

find for so/sth *Fig.* [for a jury or a judge] to announce a decision in favor of one side of a lawsuit. □ *The judge found for Mrs. Franklin, and that made her family quite happy.*

find it in one's **heart (to** do sth**)** AND **find it in** oneself **(to** do sth**)** *Fig.* to have the courage or compassion to do something. □ *She couldn't find it in herself to refuse to come home to him.*

find (sth) out the hard way Go to learn (sth) the hard way.

find one's **own level** *Fig.* to find the position or rank to which one is best suited. □ *You cannot force new clerks to be ambitious. They will all find their own level.*

find the time to do sth AND **find enough time to** do sth; **have the time to** do sth; **have enough time to** do sth *Fig.* to manage to schedule enough time to do something. (Often negative.) □ *It's difficult to find enough time to do all the things I want to do.*

find one's **tongue** *Fig.* to be able to talk; to figure out what to say. □ *Tom was speechless for a moment. Then he found his tongue.*

fine and dandy *Inf.* nice; good; well. □ *Well, that's just fine and dandy. Couldn't be better.*

fine by so AND **okay by** so; **all right by** so satisfactory as far as someone is concerned. (*Someone* is usually *me*.) □ *It's fine by me. I don't care at all.*

a **fine how-do-you-do** *Fig.* an unpleasant situation. (Said with surprise.) □ *This is a fine how-do-you-do! Someone left a big puddle of motor oil in my driveway.*

a **fine kettle of fish** *Fig.* a troublesome situation; a vexing problem. □ *What a fine kettle of fish! My husband is not here to meet me at the train station, and there's no phone here for me to call him.* □ *Alan: Oh, no! I've burned the roast. We don't have anything to serve our guests as a main dish. Jane: But they'll be here any minute! This is a fine kettle of fish.*

fine print Go to small print.

a **fine state of affairs** Go to a pretty state of affairs.

Fine weather for ducks. Go to Lovely weather for ducks.

fine-tune sth *Fig.* to make small alterations in a plan or procedure. □ *We need to spend some time fine-tuning the scheme, then we will seek approval.*

finger so **as** so *Sl.* to identify someone as a certain person. (As if one were pointing a finger at someone.) □ *The accountant fingered the bookkeeper as the one who fixed the books.*

finishing touch(es) AND **final touch(es)** *Fig.* a final adjustment of something; some effort or action that completes something. □ *Norm is in his workshop putting the finishing touches on his latest project.*

fire a shot across the bow *Fig.* to warn or threaten [someone] sternly. (Fig. on the firing of a warning shot in front of the bow of a ship.) □ *Don't worry, John always fires a shot across the bow before he starts a major argument in public.*

fire sth **off**† **1.** to launch a rocket or mortar. □ *The enemy fired off mortars at the walls of the castle, but the walls held.* **2.** *Fig.* to send something, such as a letter, quickly and with anger or urgency. □ *When I heard what he had done, I fired off a letter to him telling him just what I thought of him!*

*a **fire under** so *Fig.* something that makes someone start doing something. (*Typically: **build** ~; **light** ~; **start** ~.) □ *The teacher built a fire under the students, and they really started working.* □ *You had better light a fire under your staff. Either that or we will lay off some of them.*

fired up *Fig.* excited; enthusiastic. □ *How can you be so fired up at this time of the morning?*

firing on all cylinders AND **hitting on all cylinders 1.** [of an internal combustion engine] having all its cylinders working and thus providing the maximum amount of power. □ *This thing's not hitting on all cylinders.* **2.** *Fig.* working at full strength; making every possible effort. (Fig. on ①.) □ *The team is firing on all cylinders under the new coach.*

*a **firm hand** *Fig.* [someone's] a strong sense of management; a high degree of discipline and direction. (*Typically: **exercise** ~; **have** ~; **need** ~; **use** ~.) □ *I had to use a firm hand with Perry when he was a child. He had a problem with discipline.*

first and foremost *Cliché* first to be dealt with and most important. □ *First and foremost, I think you should work harder on your biology.*

first and ten *Fig.* [in football] the first down [of four] with 10 yards needed to earn another first down. □ *It is first and ten on the 40-yard line, and Army has the ball.*

***first crack at** sth *Fig.* the first opportunity at doing, fixing, or having something. (*Typically: **get** ~; **have** ~; **give** so ~; **take** ~; **want** ~.) □ *I'll take the first crack at it, and if I can't do it, you can try.*

the **first leg (of** a journey**)** AND the **first leg (of** the journey**)** *Fig.* the first segment of a journey; the first flight of a multiflight trip. □ *The first leg of the journey got me to London.*

first of all *Fig.* as the very first thing; before anything else. □ *First of all, put your name on this piece of paper.*

first off *Fig.* first; the first thing. (Almost the same as first of all.) □ *First off, we'll find a place to live.*

first see the light of day 1. *Fig.* to be born. □ *My grandfather has taken care of me since I first saw the light of day.* **2.** *Fig.* to come into being. □ *Bob's collection of short stories first saw the light of day in a privately printed edition three years ago.*

first thing (in the morning) *Fig.* before anything else is done in the morning. □ *Please call me first thing in the morning. I can't help you now.*

the **first thing that comes into** one's **head** AND **whatever comes into** one's **head (first)** *Fig.* whatever one thinks of first. □ *She has a tendency to say the first thing that comes into her head when she meets someone. It can be embarrassing.*

First things first. The important [scheduled] matters [have to be dealt with] first. □ *We will discuss that in a minute. We need to follow the agenda. First things first.*

the **firstest with the mostest** *Inf.* the earliest and in the largest numbers; the earliest with more of what's needed. □ *Pete got the prize for being the firstest with the mostest.*

fish for sth *Fig.* to seek some kind of information. □ *You could tell the lawyer was fishing for something from the vague way she asked the questions.* □ *The telephone caller was fishing for too much information, so I hung up.*

fish for a compliment *Fig.* to try to get someone to pay oneself a compliment. □ *When she showed me her new dress, I could tell that she was fishing for a compliment.*

fish in troubled waters *Fig.* to involve oneself in a difficult, confused, or dangerous situation, especially with a view to gaining an advantage. □ *Frank is fishing in troubled waters by buying more shares of that company. They are supposed to be in financial difficulties.*

fish or cut bait *Fig.* either perform the task at hand or withdraw to a supporting position so that someone else can do the job unhampered. □ *You're not doing a good job, Tom. Get going. You need to fish or cut bait!*

fish story AND **fish tale** *Fig.* a great big lie. (As with a fisherman who exaggerates the size of the fish that got away.) □ *That's just a fish story. Don't try to fool me.*

fish tale Go to previous.

a **fishing expedition** a search for information without knowledge of whether such information exists. (This involves asking questions with no preconceived notion of what the answers might reveal.) □ *We are going to have to go on a fishing expedition to try to find the facts.*

fit and trim *Fig.* slim and in good physical shape. □ *Jean tried to keep herself fit and trim at all times.*

*fit as a fiddle *Cliché* in very good health. (*Also: **as** ~.) □ *You may feel sick now, but after a few days of rest and plenty of liquids, you'll be fit as a fiddle.*

fit for a king AND **fit for the gods** *Fig.* very nice; luxurious. □ *Our room at the hotel was fit for a king.*

fit for the gods Go to previous.

fit like a glove *Fig.* to fit very well; to fit snugly. □ *My new coat is a little tight. It fits like a glove.*

fit the bill Go to fill the bill.

fit so **to a T** Go to suit so to a T.

fit to be tied *Fig.* angry and agitated. (As if needing to be restrained.) □ *Joe was fit to be tied when his wife told him she was leaving.*

fit to kill *Rur.* a great deal; to the highest possible degree. □ *I had my car gussied up fit to kill.*

*fits and starts *Fig.* with irregular movement; with much stopping and starting. (*Typically: **by** ~; **in** ~; **with** ~.) □ *By fits and starts, the old car finally got us to town.*

five-finger discount *Inf.* shoplifting. □ *Sam used his five-finger discount to get the kind of ring Jane wanted.*

*a fix 1. *Sl.* a dose of a drug or narcotic. (*Typically: **get** ~; **have** ~; **give** so ~; **need** ~.) □ *The addict badly needed a fix and was very fidgety.* **2.** *Fig.* an appropriate repair. □ *Do you have a good fix for a leaky faucet?*

fix an animal *Fig.* to remove the uterus or testicles of a pet animal. □ *We took Fluffy to the veterinarian to have her fixed.*

fix sth *Fig.* to pay money in secret to have something turn out the way you want. □ *After the gun-control bill failed to pass, there were rumors that the gun lobby had fixed the legislature.*

*a fix on sth **1.** *Fig.* the exact location of something distant. (*Typically: **get** ~; **have** ~; **give** so ~.) □ *I can't get a fix on your location. Where are you?* **2.** *Fig.* an understanding of the direction of a discussion. (Fig. on ①. *Typically: **get** ~; **have** ~; **give** so ~.) □ *I can't get a fix on where you're going with this argument.*

fix so's **wagon** *Fig.* to punish someone; to get even with someone; to plot against someone. □ *If you ever do that again, I'll fix your wagon!* □ *Tommy! You clean up your room this instant, or I'll fix your wagon!*

fix sth **with** so **1.** *Fig.* to get someone's agreement or permission for something. □ *Don't worry, I'll fix it with your boss.* **2.** *Fig.* to apologize or make amends to someone for something. □ *She is upset at you, but you can fix it with her, I'm sure.*

fixed up *Fig.* provided with a date. □ *Okay, Sam is fixed up with a date for Saturday.*

fixin(g) to do sth *Rur.* getting ready to do something; getting ready to start something. □ *I'm fixin' to go to the store. Need anything?*

flake down *Sl.* to go to bed and go to sleep. □ *I've got to go home and flake down for a while.*

flame with sth *Fig.* [for someone's eyes] to "blaze" or seem to communicate a particular quality or excitement, usually a negative feeling, such as resentment, lust, vengeance, rage, etc. □ *His eyes flamed with resentment when he heard Sally's good news.*

flare up 1. *Fig.* [for a pain or medical condition] to get worse suddenly. (Fig. on the image of bursting into flame.) □ *My arthritis flares up during the damp weather.* **2.** *Fig.* [for a dispute] to break out or escalate into a battle. (Fig. on the image of bursting into flame.) □ *A war flared up in the Middle East.* **3.** AND **flare up at** so/sth *Fig.* to lose one's temper at someone or something. (Fig. on the image of bursting into flame.) □ *I could tell by the way he flared up at me that he was not happy with what I had done.*

flare up at so/sth Go to previous.

flash sth **around**† *Fig.* to display something so everyone can see it. (Usually something one would hold in one's hand.) □ *She flashed around the pictures of her grandchildren every chance she got.*

flash sth **at** so/sth *Fig.* to show something, such as a badge, to someone or a group quickly. □ *The cop flashed his badge at the suspect.*

a **flash in the pan** *Fig.* someone or something that draws a lot of attention for a very brief time. □ *Tom had hoped to be a major film star, but his career was only a flash in the pan.*

flash through one's **mind** *Fig.* [for an idea or image] to move quickly through one's mind. □ *The same idea flashed through all of our minds at once.*

flash with sth [for someone's eyes] to "glimmer" or seem to communicate a particular quality or excitement, such as anger, recognition, eagerness, etc. □ *His green eyes flashed with anger.* □ *Ellen's eyes flashed with recognition when she saw me.*

*flat as a board AND ***flat as a pancake** *Cliché* very flat. (Also used to describe someone's chest or abdomen, referring to well-developed abdominal muscles or small or nearly absent breasts or pectoral muscles—in either sex. **Also: as ~.*) □ *Jane was flat as a board until she was 16, when she suddenly blossomed.* □ *Lucy can mash an aluminum can flat as a pancake with one blow from her heel.*

flat as a pancake Go to previous.

flat broke AND **flat busted** *Fig.* having no money at all. □ *You may be flat broke, but you will find a way to pay your electricity bill or you will live in the dark.* □ *Mary was flat busted, and it was two more weeks before she was due to get paid.*

flat busted Go to previous.

flat on one's **ass 1.** *Inf.* completely exhausted. (Caution with *ass.*) □ *After the day of the marathon, Pete was flat on his ass for a week.* **2.** *Inf.* broke; financially destroyed. (An elaboration of **flat broke.** Caution with *ass.*) □ *Sorry, I can't help you. I'm broke—flat on my ass.*

(flat) on one's **back** *Fig.* ill in bed. □ *I've been on my back with the flu for two weeks.*

flat out 1. *Fig.* clearly and definitely; holding nothing back. □ *I told her flat out that I didn't like her.* **2.** *Inf.* at top speed. □ *How fast will this car go flat out?*

flatter one's **figure** *Fig.* [for clothing] to make one look thin or to make one's figure look better than it is. □ *The lines of this dress really flatter your figure.*

Flattery will get you nowhere. *Fig. Cliché* Flattering me will not increase your chances of success. □ *A: Gee, you can do almost anything, can't you? B: Probably, but flattery will get you nowhere.*

flavor of the month AND sth **du jour;** the **latest rage** *Fig.* a popular choice or fad that is certain not to last long. (Alludes to a featured ice-cream flavor of the month, or some other kind of food choice that is the special for the day. *Du jour* is French.) □ *Having designs painted on one's teeth seems to be the flavor of the* *month amongst the trendy set. How do you brush 'em?* □ *Crystal's boyfriend du jour looks like he's seen better days.*

fleet of foot *Fig.* able to run fast. □ *Frederick, who was notably fleet of foot, outran all the other boys and won the prize.*

a **fleeting glance** *Fig.* a quick glance; a very brief look. □ *I had a fleeting glance at the car as it sped by, but I couldn't read the license plate number.*

flesh and blood 1. *Fig.* a living human body, especially with reference to its natural limitations; a human being. □ *This cold weather is more than flesh and blood can stand.* **2.** *Fig.* the quality of being alive. □ *The paintings of this artist are lifeless. They lack flesh and blood.* **3.** AND **own flesh and blood** *Fig.* one's own relatives; one's own kin. □ *That's no way to treat one's own flesh and blood.*

flesh sth out *Fig.* to add details to a basic idea, sketch, or outline. (As if one were adding flesh to a skeleton.) □ *I have a great idea; I will flesh it out a little more before trying to explain it to you.*

flex so's/sth's muscles *Fig.* to do something that shows potential strength, power, or ability. (Fig. on someone demonstrating muscular development, and presumably strength, by displaying tensed or pumped muscles, usually biceps.) □ *The music committee is flexing its muscles again by threatening to make the choir wear robes even during the summer months.*

flexed out of shape *Sl.* very angry; bent out of shape. □ *The boss was completely flexed out of shape.*

flight of fancy an idea or suggestion that is out of touch with reality or possibility. □ *What is the point in indulging in flights of fancy about exotic vacations when you cannot even afford the rent?*

flimflam artist *Fig.* someone who practices confidence tricks or deceptions on someone else. □ *I don't trust that flimflam artist at all.*

fling oneself at so Go to throw oneself at so.

flip burgers AND **dig ditches** to be employed in a low-paying job. (Digging im-

plies manual labor and flipping implies a low-wage job in fast-food preparation.) □ *So drop out of school and spend the rest of your life flipping burgers. See if I care!*

flip one's lid Go to flip one's wig.

flip so off† AND **flip so out**†; **flip so the bird** *Sl.* to give someone the finger—that is, raise the middle finger, a rude sign. (The *digitus impudicus.*) □ *The youth flipped the police officer off. Not a good idea.*

the **flip side 1.** *Fig.* the "other" side of a phonograph record. □ *On the flip side, we have another version of "Love Me Tender" sung by Sandy Softly.* **2.** *Fig.* another aspect of a situation. (Fig. on ①.) □ *On the flip side, if we lower the taxes it may stimulate consumer spending.*

flip so the bird Go to flip so off†.

flip one's wig AND **flip one's lid** *Sl.* to suddenly become angry, crazy, or enthusiastic. □ *Whenever anyone mentions taxes, Mr. Jones absolutely flips his wig.*

flirt with disaster *Fig.* to take a great risk; to tempt fate. (Fig. on flirting with a person.) □ *Building a city below sea level is just flirting with disaster.*

flirt with the idea of doing sth *Fig.* to think about doing something; to toy with an idea; to consider something, but not too seriously. □ *I flirted with the idea of going to Europe for two weeks.*

float a loan *Fig.* to get a loan of money; to arrange for a loan of money. □ *I couldn't afford to pay cash for the car, so I floated a loan.*

float on air *Fig.* [for someone] to feel free and euphoric. □ *I was so happy, I was floating on air.*

flog a dead horse AND **beat a dead horse** *Fig.* to insist on talking about something that no one is interested in, or that has already been thoroughly discussed. □ *Jill: I think I'll write the company president another letter asking him to prohibit smoking. Jane: There's no use beating a dead horse, Jill; he's already decided to let people smoke.*

flog sth **to death** *Fig.* to dwell on something so much that it no longer has any interest. □ *Walter almost flogged the whole matter to death before we stopped him.*

flood in(to sth**)** *Fig.* [for large amounts or numbers of people or things] to pour or rush into something or some place. □ *The people flooded into the hall and took their seats.*

flood out (of sth**)** *Fig.* [for people] to rush out of something or some place. □ *The people flooded out of the theater, totally disgusted with the performance.*

*****the floor** *Fig.* the exclusive right to address the audience. (*Typically: **get** ~; **have** ~; **hold** ~; **grant** so ~.) □ *The last time you had the floor, you talked for an hour.*

floor so *Fig.* to surprise and astound someone. □ *His brashness simply floored me!*

floor it *Fig.* to press down hard and fast on the accelerator of a vehicle. □ *She floored it and sped off over the hill.*

flora and fauna *Fig.* plants and animals. □ *We went for a hike in the Finnish wilderness hoping to learn all about the local flora and fauna.*

floral tribute *Fig.* flowers sent to a funeral. □ *Did you wish to make any arrangements for floral tributes at your grandmother's funeral?*

flotsam and jetsam 1. the floating wreckage of a ship and its cargo, or floating cargo deliberately cast overboard to stabilize a ship in a rough sea. □ *All sorts of flotsam and jetsam washed up on the beach.* **2.** *Fig.* worthless matter; worthless encumbrances. (Fig. on ①.) □ *His mind is burdened with the flotsam and jetsam of many years of poor instruction and lax study habits.*

fluff one's **lines** AND **blow** one's **lines; muff** one's **lines** *Inf.* to speak one's speech badly or forget one's lines when one is in a play. □ *The actress fluffed her lines badly in the last act.* □ *I was in a play once, and I muffed my lines over and over.*

fly by *Fig.* [for time] to go quickly. □ *Time flew by so fast that it was dark before we knew it.*

fly by the seat of one's **pants** Go to by the seat of one's pants.

fly in the face of sth *Fig.* to flout something; to challenge or ignore social norms or order. □ *What you have done flies in the face of public opinion and my own personal convictions!*

a **fly in the ointment** *Fig.* a small, unpleasant matter that spoils something; a drawback. □ *We enjoyed the play, but the fly in the ointment was not being able to find my hat afterward.*

fly into a rage *Fig.* to become enraged suddenly. □ *When he heard the report, he flew into a rage.*

fly into the face of danger *Fig.* to take great risks; to threaten or challenge danger, as if danger were a person. (This may refer to flying, as in an airplane, but not necessarily.) □ *John plans to go bungee jumping this weekend. He really likes flying into the face of danger.*

fly off *Fig.* to leave in a hurry. □ *Well, it's late. I must fly off.*

fly off the handle *Fig.* to lose one's temper. □ *Every time anyone mentions taxes, Mrs. Brown flies off the handle.*

fly off with so/sth *Fig.* to leave in a hurry with someone or something. □ *She flew off with her packages before she got her change.*

fly out (of some place**)** *Fig.* to leave a place quickly. □ *We flew out of there as fast as we could.*

fly the coop *Fig.* to escape; to get out or get away. (Refers to a chicken escaping from a chicken coop.) □ *The prisoner flew the coop at the first opportunity.*

fly the nest Go to leave the nest.

fly-by-night *Fig.* irresponsible; untrustworthy. (Refers to a person who sneaks away secretly in the night.) □ *The carpenter we hired was a fly-by-night worker who did a very bad job.*

flying high 1. *Fig.* very successful in one's ambitions; in an important or powerful position. (Often with the implication that this is not the usual situation or will change.) □ *He's flying high these days, but he comes from a very poor family.* **2.** *Fig.* in a state of euphoria. (From good news, success, or drugs.) □ *Wow! Todd is really flying high. Did he discover a gold mine?*

foam at the mouth 1. *Lit.* to create froth or foam around the mouth, as with some diseases. □ *The poor dog was foaming at the mouth and looked quite dangerous.* **2.** *Fig.* to be extraordinarily angry. (Fig. on ①.) □ *She was almost foaming at the mouth when she heard about the cost of the car repairs.*

the **foggiest (idea)** AND the **foggiest (notion)**; the **faintest (idea)**; the **faintest (notion)** *Fig.* (even) a hazy idea. (Usually in the negative.) □ *I don't have the foggiest idea of how to do this.*

fold one's **hands** *Fig.* to bring one's hands together, palm to palm, with the fingers interlocking; to grasp one's hands together, palm to palm, perpendicular to one another. □ *Please fold your hands and put them on the table while the teacher reads you a story.*

fold, spindle, or mutilate *Fig.* to harm or disfigure. (Referring to a once-standard line printed on machine-readable documents, such as computer punch cards. Such a document, if folded, placed on a bill spike, or otherwise punctured, would no longer be machine-readable. Pertains to obsolescent technology, but still heard.) □ *At the bottom of the bill, it said "do not fold, spindle, or mutilate," and Jane, in her anger, did all three.*

fold sth **up**† *Fig.* to put an end to something; to close a money-losing enterprise. □ *Mr. Jones was going broke, so he folded his business up.*

fold up 1. *Fig.* [for someone] to faint. □ *She folded up when she heard the news.* **2.** *Fig.* [for a business] to cease operating. □ *Our shop finally folded up because of the recession.*

folding money *Inf.* bills of various dollar denominations. □ *You got any folding money with you?*

follow one's **heart** *Fig.* to act according to one's feelings; to obey one's sympathetic or compassionate inclinations. □ *I trust that you will follow your heart in this matter.*

follow in so's **footsteps** Go to next.

follow in so's **tracks** AND **follow in** so's **footsteps** to follow someone's example; to assume someone else's role or occupation. □ *She followed in her father's footsteps and went into medicine.*

follow so's **lead** *Fig.* to do as someone else does; to accept someone's guidance; to follow someone's direction. □ *Just follow my lead and you will not get lost.*

follow one's **nose 1.** *Fig.* to go straight ahead, the direction that one's nose is pointing. □ *The chief's office is right around the corner. Turn left and follow your nose.* **2.** *Fig.* to follow an odor to its source. □ *The kitchen is at the back of the building. Just follow your nose.*

follow on (after so/sth**)** *Euph.* to die at a date later than someone or a group. □ *She followed on after her husband a few years later.*

follow orders to do as one has been instructed. □ *I didn't do anything wrong. I was only following orders.*

follow suit to follow in the same pattern; to follow someone else's example. (From card games.) □ *Mary went to work for a bank, and Jane followed suit. Now they are both head cashiers.*

follow the crowd *Fig.* to do what everyone else is doing. □ *I am an independent thinker. I could never just follow the crowd.*

follow the line of least resistance Go to the line of least resistance.

foment trouble *Fig.* to cause trouble. □ *I wasn't fomenting trouble, just expressing my opinion!*

***fond of** so/sth liking someone or something. (*Typically: **be** ~; **become** ~.) □ *Mary isn't fond of me, but I'm fond of her.*

food for thought *Fig.* something for someone to think about; issues to be considered. □ *Your essay has provided me with some interesting food for thought.*

fool around *Fig.* to waste time doing something unnecessary or doing something amateurishly. □ *I wish you didn't spend so much time fooling around.*

fool (around) with so/sth **1.** *Fig.* to waste time in the company of someone or a group. □ *Stop fooling around with those guys. They're up to no good most of the time.* **2.** *Fig.* to have dealings with or tamper with someone or something. □ *Don't fool with that thing!* **3.** *Fig.* to challenge or threaten someone or something. □ *You had better not fool around with me, if you know what's good for you.*

a **fool's paradise** *Fig.* a state of being happy for foolish or unfounded reasons. □ *Fred is confident that he'll get a big raise this year, but I think he's living in a fool's paradise.*

*a **foot in both camps** *Fig.* an interest in or support for each of two opposing groups of people. (*Typically: **get** ~; **have** ~; **give** so ~.) □ *Mr. Smith has a foot in both camps in the parent-teacher dispute. He teaches math, but he has a son at the school.*

foot the bill (for sth**)** *Fig.* to pay for something; to pay for a bill. □ *My boss took me out for lunch, and the company footed the bill.*

*a **foothold (**some place**)** *Fig.* an initial position of support; a starting point. (*Typically: **get** ~; **have** ~; **help** so **get** ~.) □ *It's difficult to get a foothold in the education market when schools are laying off teachers.*

foot-in-mouth disease *Inf.* the tendency to say the wrong thing at the wrong time. □ *I suffer a lot from foot-in-mouth disease.*

footloose and fancy-free *Fig.* without long-term responsibilities or commitments. □ *All the rest of them have wives, but John is footloose and fancy-free.*

for a change for something different; as an opportunity for someone else. □ *You have driven the new car every day this week. Let me drive for a change.*

for a lark AND **on a lark** *Fig.* for a joke; as something done for fun. □ *For a lark, I wore a clown's wig to school.* □ *On a lark, I skipped school and drove to the beach.*

do sth **for a living** to do some kind of work to earn enough money to live. □ *John paints houses for a living.*

for a price for a (large) amount of money. □ *Of course you can have the best chocolate in the world, for a price.*

*for a song** *Fig.* cheaply. (As if the singing of a song were payment. *Typically: **buy** sth ~; **get** sth ~; **pick up** sth ~.) □ *No one else wanted it, so I picked it up for a song.* □ *I could buy this house for a song, because it's so ugly.*

*for a spin** AND *for a ride**; *for a drive** *Fig.* to take a ride in a vehicle or on a bicycle. (*Typically: **go** ~; **go out** ~; **take** sth ~.) □ *Let's get out our bikes and go for a spin.*

for all I care *Fig.* I don't care if (something happens). □ *They can all starve for all I care.*

for all I know *Fig.* according to the information I have; I think; probably. (Usually implies uncertainty.) □ *For all I know, the mayor has resigned already.*

for all intents and purposes *Cliché* seeming as if; looking as if. □ *Mary: Is the car washed now? John: For all intents and purposes, yes, but I didn't dry it yet.*

for all it's worth AND **for what(ever) it's worth** *Fig.* if it has any value. (Usually implies lack of confidence.) □ *My idea—for all it's worth—is to offer them only $300.*

for all practical purposes *Fig.* as might be reasonably expected; essentially. □ *This should be considered final, for all practical purposes.*

for all so's **problems** *Fig.* in spite of a person's problems (as specified). □ *For all her complaining, she still seems to be a happy person.* □ *For all my aches and pains, I'm still rather healthy.*

for all that in spite of all that; after all that. □ *We argued, but for all that we are still friends.*

for all the world 1. *Fig.* everything. (Usually in the negative.) □ *I wouldn't give up my baby for all the world.* **2.** AND ***for all the world like** so/sth *Fig.* exactly or precisely like someone or something. (*Typically: **act** ~; **feel** ~; **look** ~; **seem** ~.) □ *He looks for all the world like his uncle.*

for (all) one's **trouble** *Fig.* in spite of one's efforts; in return for one's efforts. (Implies that the effort was not worth taking, or was harmful.) □ *For her trouble, she got only honorable mention.*

for better or (for) worse *Fig.* under any conditions; no matter what happens. □ *For better or for worse, I'm going to quit my job.* □ *I know I married you for better or worse, but I didn't really know how bad worse could be!*

for chicken feed AND **for peanuts** *Fig.* for nearly nothing; for very little money. (Also used without *for.*) □ *Bob doesn't get paid much. He works for chicken feed.* □ *I won't do that kind of work for peanuts!*

For crying in a bucket! Go to next.

For crying out loud! AND **For crying in a bucket!** *Inf.* an exclamation of shock, anger, or surprise. □ *Fred: For crying out loud! Answer the telephone! Bob: But it's always for you!* □ *John: Good grief! What am I going to do? This is the end! Sue: For crying in a bucket! What's wrong?*

for days on end *Fig.* for many days. □ *We kept on traveling for days on end.*

for (some) days running AND **for (some) weeks running; for (some) months running; for (some) years running** *Fig.* days in a series; months in a series; etc. (The *some* can be any number.) □ *I had a bad cold for five days running.*

for free *Fig.* for no charge or cost; free of any cost. □ *They let us into the movie for free.*

for giggles Go to for kicks.

for good *Fig.* forever; permanently. □ *They tried to repair it many times before they fixed it for good.*

for good measure *Fig.* as extra; (adding) a little more to make sure there is enough. □ *I always put a little extra salt in the soup for good measure.*

For goodness sake(s)! Go to For Pete's sake!

For heaven('s) sake(s)! Go to For Pete's sake!

for hours on end *Fig.* for many hours. □ *The children were happy to play video games for hours on end.*

for instance for example. □ *Jane is very generous. For instance, she volunteers at the hospital and gives money to charities.*

for keeps *Inf.* forever. □ *This is yours for keeps. Enjoy it.*

for kicks AND **for laughs; for giggles** *Fig.* for fun; just for entertainment; for no good reason. □ *They didn't mean any harm. They just did it for kicks.* □ *We drove over to the next town for laughs.*

for laughs Go to previous.

for life *Fig.* for the remainder of one's life. □ *The accident caused me to become blind for life.*

for miles on end *Fig.* for many miles. □ *The huge field of wheat extends for miles on end.*

for (some) months running Go to for (some) days running.

for my money *Fig.* in my opinion (as regards value or worth). □ *That's the best brand of tools there is, for my money.*

for old time's sake *Fig.* [to do something] because of memories of better times and relationships in the past. □ *I stopped and had a drink with him for old time's sake, even though he was no longer a good friend.*

for openers AND **for starters** *Fig.* to start with. □ *For openers, they played a song everyone knows.*

for one's **(own) part** *Fig.* as far as one is concerned; from one's point of view. □ *For my own part, I wish to stay here.*

for one's **(own) sake** *Fig.* for one's good or benefit; in honor of someone. □ *I have to earn a living for my family's sake.*

for so's **part** as someone's position or opinion; from someone's point of view. □ *For my part, I think she ought not to go there.*

for peanuts Go to for chicken feed.

For Pete's sake! AND **For pity's sake!; For the love of Mike!; For goodness sake(s)!; For gosh sake(s)!; For heaven('s) sake(s)** *Inf.* a mild exclamation of surprise or shock. □ *For Pete's sake! How've ya been?* □ *For pity's sake! Ask the man in out of the cold!*

For pity's sake! Go to previous.

for real *Inf.* genuine; not imaginary. □ *Ken is really strange. Is he for real?*

for safekeeping *Fig.* for the purpose of keeping someone or something safe. □ *I put my jewelry in the vault for safekeeping.*

for so's/sth's **sake** AND **for the sake of** so/sth for the purpose or benefit of someone or something; to satisfy the demands of someone or something. □ *The teacher repeated the assignment for the sake of the slower students.*

for sale *Fig.* available for purchase; buyable. □ *How long has this house been for sale?*

For shame! *Fig.* That is shameful! (Usually mock serious.) □ *Mary: I've decided not to go to the conference. John: For shame! Who will represent us?*

for short *Fig.* as an abbreviation or shortening. □ *The Internal Revenue Service is known as the IRS for short.*

for starters Go to for openers.

for sure *Fig.* for certain. □ *I will be there for sure.* □ *Sally: Are you ready to go? Bob: For sure. Sally: Then, let's go.*

for that matter *Fig.* besides; in addition. □ *I don't like this house. The roof leaks. For that matter, the whole place is falling apart.*

for the asking Go to (free) for the asking.

one's **for the asking** Go to (free) for the asking.

for the best Go to (all) for the best.

***for the better** *Fig.* to be an improvement. (*Typically: be ~; be a change ~.) □ *A change of government would be for the better.*

for the birds *Inf.* worthless; undesirable. (Older.) □ *Winter weather is for the birds.*

for the devil of it AND **for the heck of it; for the hell of it** *Inf.* because it is slightly evil; for no good reason. □ *The kids broke the window just for the devil of it.*

for the duration *Fig.* for the whole time that something continues; for the entire period of time required for something to be completed; for as long as something takes. □ *We are in this war for the duration.* □ *However long it takes, we'll wait. We are here for the duration.*

for the fun of it *Fig.* just for the entertainment value of doing it. □ *We went on a picnic just for the fun of it.*

for the good of so/sth for the benefit, profit, or advantage of someone or something. □ *The president said the strict drug laws were for the good of the country.*

for the heck of it Go to for the devil of it.

for the hell of it Go to for the devil of it.

for the life of me *Fig.* at all; even one little bit. (Used with a negative.) □ *For the life of me, I can't figure this out.*

for the long haul Go to over the long haul.

for the long term Go to over the long haul.

For the love of Mike! Go to For Pete's sake!

for the moment AND **for the time being** *Fig.* for the present; for now; temporarily. □ *This is all right for the time being. It'll have to be improved next week, however.*

for the most part AND **in large part** mostly; in general. □ *For the most part, the class is enjoying geometry.*

for the record *Fig.* so that (one's own version of) the facts will be known; for open, public knowledge. (This often is said when there are reporters present.) □ *For the record, I've never been able to get anything done around city hall without bribing someone.*

for the short haul Go to over the short haul.

for the taking Go to (free) for the taking.

one's **for the taking** Go to (free) for the taking.

for the time being Go to for the moment.

For two cents I would do sth. *Fig.* If someone would give me two cents, I would do something. □ *What a jerk. For two cents I'd poke him in the nose.*

for (some) **weeks running** Go to for (some) days running.

for what(ever) it's worth Go to for all it's worth.

for (some) **years running** Go to for (some) days running.

for your information *Fig.* a phrase that introduces or follows a piece of information. (Can be spoken with considerable impatience.) □ *Bob: How long do I have to wait here? Bill: For your information, we will be here until the bus driver feels that it is safe to travel.*

forbidden fruit *Fig.* someone or something that one finds attractive or desirable partly because having the person or thing is immoral or illegal. (Biblical: from the apple in the Garden of Eden that was forbidden to Adam by God.) □ *The boy watches that program only when his parents are out. It's forbidden fruit.*

force so's **hand** to force a person to reveal plans, strategies, or secrets. (Refers to a handful of cards in card playing.) □ *We didn't know what she was doing until Tom forced her hand.*

a **force to be reckoned with** AND a **force to reckon with** *Fig.* someone or something that is important and powerful and must not be ignored. □ *Walter is a force to be reckoned with. Be prepared to deal with him.*

force so **to the wall** AND **drive** so **to the wall** *Fig.* to push someone to an extreme position; to put someone into an awkward position. □ *He wouldn't tell the truth until we forced him to the wall.* □ *They don't pay their bills until you drive them to the wall.*

fore and aft *Fig.* at the front and the back, usually of a boat or ship. □ *They had to attach new lights fore and aft because the old ones were not bright enough to meet the new regulations.*

foreclose on sth to take the property on which a mortgage is held; to satisfy an unpaid loan by taking ownership of the property put up for security on the loan. □ *If you don't pay, we will be forced to foreclose on your house.*

a **foregone conclusion** *Cliché* a conclusion already reached; an inevitable result. □ *That the company was moving to California was a foregone conclusion.*

forever and a day Go to next.

forever and ever AND **forever and a day** *Fig.* forever. □ *I will love you forever and ever.* □ *We have enough money to last forever and a day.*

forget oneself *Fig.* to forget one's manners or training. (Said in formal situations in reference to belching, bad table manners, and, in the case of very young children, pants-wetting.) □ *John, we are going out to dinner tonight. Please don't forget yourself.*

Forget (about) it! 1. *Inf.* Drop the subject!; Never mind!; Don't bother me with it. □ *Jane: Then, there's this matter of the unpaid bills. Bill: Forget it! You'll have to pay them all!* **2.** *Inf.* Nothing. □ *Tom: Now I'm ready to go. Sue: Excuse me? Tom: Oh, nothing. Just forget it.* **3.** *Inf.* You're welcome.; It was nothing. □ *John: Thank you so much for helping me! Bill: Oh, forget it!*

forget one's **manners** *Fig.* to do something ill-mannered. □ *Jimmy! Have we forgotten our manners?*

forgive and forget to end a disagreement in a friendly fashion with mutual forgiveness and no further animosity. □ *We were both mad, but we decided to forgive and forget.*

fork some money **out**† **(for** sth) *Fig.* to pay (perhaps unwillingly) for something. (Often mention is made of the amount of money.) □ *Do you think I'm going to fork $20 out for that book?*

fork sth **out**† **(to** so) *Fig.* to give out something to someone. □ *We forked the coupons out to everyone who asked for them.*

fork sth **over**† **(to** so) *Inf.* to give something to someone. (Usually refers to money.) □ *Come on! Fork the money over to me!*

form an opinion *Fig.* to think up or decide on an opinion. □ *I don't form opinions without careful consideration.*

form and substance *Fig.* structure and meaningful content. □ *The first act of the play was one screaming match after another. It lacked form and substance throughout.*

forty winks *Fig.* a nap; some sleep. □ *I could use forty winks before I have to get to work.*

foul out (of sth) *Fig.* [for a basketball player] to be forced out of a game because of having too many fouls. □ *The center fouled out in the first 15 minutes.*

foul one's **own nest** *Fig.* to harm one's own interests; to bring disadvantage upon oneself. (Fig. on the image of a bird excreting into its own nest.) □ *He tried to discredit a fellow senator with the president but just succeeded in fouling his own nest.*

foul play *Fig.* illegal activity; bad practices. □ *Each student got an A on the test, and the teacher imagined it was the result of foul play.*

foul up *Inf.* to blunder; to screw up (on sth). □ *Please don't foul up this time.*

foul so/sth **up**† to cause disorder and confusion for someone or something; to tangle up someone or something; to **mess** so/sth up. □ *You've fouled up my whole day.*

fouled up *Inf.* messed up; ruined; tangled up. (Usually as **fouled-up** when attributive.) □ *This is sure a fouled-up mess.* □ *You sure are fouled up, you know.*

found money *Fig.* money that has come to someone with such ease or surprise that one might have just as well found it by accident. □ *The money he got from his uncle's estate is all found money except for the taxes. He did nothing to earn it.*

found sth **(up)on** sth to establish something on some kind of basis or justification. (*Upon* is formal and less commonly used than *on*.) □ *We founded our business on practically no money.*

four sheets in the wind AND **four sheets (to the wind)** *Inf.* intoxicated. (See comments at three sheets in the wind.) □ *After only three beers, Gary was four sheets to the wind.*

frame sth **in** sth *Fig.* to express something in a particular way. □ *He framed his comments in very simple language.*

one's **frame of mind** *Fig.* one's mood or mental state. □ *My frame of mind is sort of low at the moment. I've had a very bad day.*

fraught with danger *Fig.* Cliché [of something] full of something dangerous or unpleasant. □ *My escape from the kidnappers was fraught with danger.*

freak so **out**† *Inf.* to shock or disorient someone. □ *The whole business freaked me out.*

freak out (on sth) *Inf.* to lose control of one's mind because of something, usually a drug. □ *She freaked out on the stuff she was smoking.*

freak out (over so/sth) AND **freak out (at** so/sth) to become very angry or lose control of one's mind because of someone or something that has happened. □ *I absolutely freaked out over the whole business!*

free and clear *Fig.* without encumbrance, particularly in regard to the ownership of something. □ *After the last payment, Jane owned the car free and clear.*

free and easy *Fig.* casual. □ *Now, take it easy. Just act free and easy. No one will know you're nervous.*

***free as a bird** AND ***free as (the) air** *Cliché* carefree; completely free and unhindered. (*Also: **as** ~.) □ *The convict escaped from jail and was as free as a bird for two days.*

free as (the) air Go to previous.

free for all AND **free-for-all** *Fig.* a brawl; a general fight. □ *A free for all started on the beach over near the concession stand.*

(free) for the asking AND one's **for the asking** given if one just asks (for something); given on request. (Almost the same as **(free) for the taking**.) □ *Do you want to use my car? It's yours for the asking.*

(free) for the taking AND one's **for the taking** available and granted if one simply takes [it]. (Almost the same as **(free) for the asking**.) □ *It's yours if you want it. It's free for the taking.*

free gift something extra given to you when you buy something else. □ *When you order your magazine subscription, this book is yours to keep as our free gift.*

***a **free hand (with** so/sth**)** *Fig.* freedom to exercise complete control over something. (*Typically: **get** ~; **have** ~; **give** so ~.) □ *I didn't get a free hand with the last project.*

a free ride *Fig.* an easy time; participation without contributing anything. □ *You've had a free ride long enough. You have to do your share of the work now.*

a free translation AND **a loose translation** a translation or restatement that is not completely accurate and not well thought out; a translation or restatement done casually. □ *John gave a free translation of what our Japanese client asked for, and we missed the main issue.*

freeze so/sth **in** one's **memory** *Fig.* to preserve the image of someone or something in one's memory. □ *I tried to freeze her in my memory so I would have her with me always.*

a freeze on doing sth *Fig.* a policy that put a temporary end to something. □ *The company put a freeze on hiring as soon as they took us over.*

freeze so **out**† AND **squeeze** so **out**† *Fig.* to lock someone out socially; to isolate someone from something or a group. □ *We didn't want to freeze you out. You failed to pay your dues, however.*

freeze one's **tail off** *Inf.* to freeze; to get very cold. □ *It's as cold as a well digger's nose today. I about froze my tail off walking to work.*

freeze so/sth **to death 1.** [for extreme cold] to kill someone or something. □ *I was afraid that the cold snap would freeze the dog to death.* **2.** *Fig.* to make someone or something very cold. (Fig. on ①.) □ *This weather is going to freeze us all to death.*

freeze up *Fig.* [for someone] to become frightened and anxious and be unable to move, speak, or continue with something. □ *I froze up and couldn't say anything more.*

freeze so's **wages** *Fig.* to hold someone's pay at its current level. □ *The company froze everyone's wages as soon as the economy went sour.*

fresh and sweet 1. very clean and fresh smelling. □ *Now the baby is changed and she is all fresh and sweet.* **2.** *Inf.* just out of jail. □ *Mary is fresh and sweet and back on the street.*

***fresh as a daisy** *Cliché* very fresh; [of a person] always alert and ready to go. (*Also: **as** ~.) □ *How can you be fresh as a daisy so early in the morning?*

fresh blood Go to (some) new blood.

fresh from some place *Fig.* just arrived from a place. □ *Bob is fresh from California, where he has a factory that makes homemade avocado ice cream.*

fresh out of sth **1.** *Fig.* just now released from something. □ *Bob is fresh out of jail.* **2.** *Fig.* just now having exhausted the supply of something. □ *I'm sorry, but we are fresh out of roast beef. Can I get you something else?*

a **fresh pair of eyes** Go to another pair of eyes.

*a **fresh start** *Fig.* a new start; an act of starting over. (*Typically: **get** ~; **get off to** ~; **give** so ~; **have** ~; **make** ~.) □ *After our apologies and a little discussion, we decided to make a fresh start.*

*fresh (with so)** *Fig.* overly bold or impertinent with someone. (*Typically: **be** ~; **get** ~.) □ *When I tried to kiss Mary, she slapped me and shouted, "Don't get fresh with me!"*

Fret not! *Inf.* Don't worry!; Do not fret about it! □ *Mary: Oh, look at the clock! I'm going to be late for my appointment! Bob: Fret not! I'll drive you.*

A **friend in need is a friend indeed.** A true friend is a person who will help you when you really need help. □ *When Bill helped me with geometry, I really learned the meaning of "A friend in need is a friend indeed."*

friend or foe *Fig.* a friend or an enemy. □ *I can't tell whether Jim is friend or foe.* □ *"Who goes there? Friend or foe?" asked the sentry.*

*friends with** so a friend of someone. (*Typically: **be** ~; **become** ~.) □ *Mary and Bill are friends with one another.*

frighten so **out of a year's growth** Go to frighten one out of one's wits.

frighten one **out of** one's **mind** Go to next.

frighten one **out of** one's **wits** AND **scare** one **out of** one's **wits; frighten** so **out of a year's growth; scare** so **out of a year's growth; frighten** one **out of** one's **mind; scare** one **out of** one's **mind** *Fig.* to frighten one very badly. □ *Oh! That loud noise scared me out of my wits.* □ *I'll give him a good scolding and frighten him out of his wits.* □ *Oh, you frightened me out of a year's growth!* □ *You frightened Bob out of his mind.*

frighten the hell out of so AND **frighten the pants off** so; **frighten the living daylights out of** so; **scare the living daylights out of** so; **scare the shit out of** so; **scare the wits out of** so to frighten someone badly, suddenly, or both. (Caution with *shit*.) □ *These figures frighten the hell out of me.* □ *The door blew shut and scared the shit out of me.* □ *It takes a lot to scare the pants off a hardened criminal.*

frighten the living daylights out of so Go to previous.

frighten the pants off so Go to frighten the hell out of so.

frighten so **to death** AND **scare** so **to death 1.** *Lit.* to cause someone to die by terrifying them. □ *It was so horrible. It almost frightened me to death.* **2.** *Fig.* to frighten someone very badly. □ *Youch! You scared me to death! Make a little noise when you come into the room, okay?*

frightened to death AND **scared to death 1.** *Lit.* frightened to the point of dying. □ *This poor animal has been frightened to death by the attacking dogs.* **2.** *Fig.* frightened or anxious. (*Fig.* on ①.) □ *I don't want to go to the dentist today. I'm frightened to death.*

fritter sth **away** *Fig.* to waste all of something, usually money or time, carelessly and without any thought for the consequences. □ *You frittered away all your study time watching television, and now it's time for bed.* □ *Billy frittered away the family fortune on fast cars and gold chains.*

*a **frog in** one's **throat** *Fig.* a feeling of hoarseness or a lump in one's throat. (Often regarded as a sign of fear. *Typically: **get** ~; **have** ~.) □ *I feel like I'm getting a frog in my throat when I have to speak in public.*

from A to Z *Fig.* of a complete and wide variety. □ *We have just about everything from A to Z.*

from all corners of the world AND **from the four corners of the earth** *Fig.* from all places in the world. □ *People came from all corners of the world to attend the conference.*

from cover to cover [of a book] from beginning to end. □ *I read this book from cover to cover and still don't know what it is about.*

from dawn to dusk *Fig.* during the period of the day when there is light; from the rising of the sun to the setting of the sun. □ *I have to work from dawn to dusk on the farm.*

from day to day *Fig.* on a daily basis; for one day at a time; occasionally. □ *We face this kind of problem from day to day.*

from door to door *Fig.* moving from one door to another—typically, from one house to another. □ *The candidate went from door to door, campaigning for town council.*

from far and near AND **from near and far** *Fig.* from all around, both close by and farther away. (In either order.) □ *All the young people from far and near gathered at the high school for the game.*

from hand to hand *Fig.* from one person to a series of other persons. □ *The book traveled from hand to hand until it got back to its owner.*

(from) head to toe *Fig.* from the top of one's head to one's feet. □ *She was decked out in flowers from head to toe.*

so/sth from hell *Inf.* someone or something very intense, annoying, or challenging. (As if the person or thing were a demon from hell.) □ *She is the nurse from hell and just loves to give shots.* □ *I worked for three years at that job from hell, and I'm glad to be gone.*

from here on (in) AND **from here on (out)** from this point forward. □ *From here on in we do it my way.*

from Missouri *Fig.* requiring proof; needing to be shown something in order to believe it. (From the nickname for the state of Missouri, the Show Me State.) □ *You'll have to prove it to me. I'm from Missouri.*

from my perspective AND **from where I stand; from my point of view; the way I see it** *Fig.* a phrase used to introduce one's own opinion. □ *Mary: What do you think of all this? Tom: From my perspective, it is just terrible.* □ *Bob: From my point of view, this looks like a very good deal.*

from my point of view Go to previous.

from near and far Go to from far and near.

from now on at all times; from now until well into the future. □ *From now on, you will do exactly as I tell you.*

from on high from high in the hierarchy. □ *Orders have come down from on high that we are to work this weekend until the report is done.*

from pillar to post *Fig.* from one place to a series of other places; from person to person, as with gossip. □ *My father was in the army, and we moved from pillar to post year after year.*

from rags to riches *Fig.* from poverty to wealth; from modesty to elegance. □ *The princess used to be quite poor. She certainly moved from rags to riches.*

*from scratch *Fig.* [making something] by starting with the basic ingredients. (*Typically: **bake** sth ~; **do** sth ~; **make** sth ~.) □ *We made the cake from scratch, using no prepared ingredients.*

from sea to shining sea *Fig.* from coast to coast. (From the lyrics of the song "America the Beautiful.") □ *The new insect pest spread from sea to shining sea in a matter of months.*

from start to finish *Fig.* entirely; throughout. □ *I disliked the whole business from start to finish.*

from stem to stern 1. from the front of a boat or ship to the back. □ *He inspected the boat from stem to stern and decided he wanted to buy it.* **2.** *Fig.* from one end to another. (Fig. on ①.) □ *I polished my car carefully from stem to stern.*

from the (bottom of one's**) heart** *Fig.* sincerely. □ *When I returned the lost kitten to Mrs. Brown, she thanked me from the bottom of her heart.*

from the cradle to the grave *Fig.* from birth to death. □ *The government promised to take care of us from the cradle to the grave.*

from the four corners of the earth Go to from all corners of the world.

from the git-go *Inf. Rur.* from the starting point; from the very first. (Also **get-go**.) □ *I was sort of suspicious of him from the git-go.*

from the ground up *Fig.* from the very beginning. (Lit. in reference to building a house or other building.) □ *We must plan our sales campaign carefully from the ground up.*

from the old school AND **of the old school** *Fig.* holding attitudes or ideas that were popular and important in the past, but which are no longer considered relevant or in line with modern trends. □ *Grammar is not taught much now, but fortunately my son has a teacher from the old school.*

from the outset *Fig.* throughout, from the very beginning. □ *I felt from the outset that Lisa was the wrong one for the job.*

from the sublime to the ridiculous *Fig.* from something fine and uplifting to something ridiculous or mundane. □ *After Mr. Jones had introduced my wife to his wife, he jokingly turned to introduce me and said, "From the sublime to the ridiculous."*

from the top *Fig.* from the beginning of something, such as a song or a script. □ *Okay, let's try it again from the top.*

from the word go *Cliché* from the very beginning. □ *I knew about the problem from the word go.*

from this day forward Go to next.

from this day on AND **from this day forward** *Fig.* from today into the future. □ *We'll live in love and peace from this day on.*

from time to time *Fig.* irregularly; now and then; occasionally; sometimes; not predictably. □ *From time to time, I like to go fishing instead of going to work.*

from tip to toe AND **from top to toe** *Fig.* from the top to the bottom; from one end to the other. □ *She is wearing all new clothes from tip to toe.*

from top to bottom *Fig.* from the highest point to the lowest point; throughout. □ *We need to replace our elected officials from top to bottom.*

from way back *Fig.* from far in the past; from a much earlier time. □ *This antique clock is from way back.*

from where I stand Go to from my perspective.

front so some amount of money *Fig.* to provide an advance payment of some amount to someone. □ *The buyer fronted me half the purchase price as a favor.*

front for so/sth *Inf.* to serve as the public contact or public "face" for someone or something. □ *Her publicity agent fronted for her most of the time.*

front off (about sth) *Sl.* to be brash and resentful about something. □ *Todd was fronting off about his assignment and got a detention for it.*

front on sth *Fig.* [for a building or a piece of land] to face out on something. □ *The property fronts on a lovely boulevard that has very little traffic.*

the **front runner** the person or thing thought most likely to win or succeed. □ *The press found out some juicy secrets about the front runner and made them all public.*

frosted (over) *Sl.* angry; annoyed. □ *The clerk was really frosted over when I asked for a better one.*

the **fruits of** one's **labor(s)** *Fig.* the results of one's work. □ *What have you accomplished? Where is the fruit of your labors?*

Fuck you! a strong condemnation. (Taboo.) □ *Fuck you! I don't care anymore!*

fudge factor *Fig.* a margin of error. □ *I never use a fudge factor. I measure correctly, and I cut the material exactly the way I measured it.*

*full as a tick very full of food or drink. (Refers to a tick that has filled itself full of blood. See also **tight as a tick**. *Also: **as ~**.) □ *Little Billy ate and ate until he was as full as a tick.*

*full of oneself *Fig.* conceited; self-important. (*Typically: **act ~; be ~**.) □ *She doesn't care about other people's feelings. She's too full of herself.*

full of beans Go to full of hot air.

full of bull Go to full of hot air.

full of crap AND **full of shit** *Fig.* full of nonsense and deception. (Caution with *crap, shit*.) □ *Don't pay any attention to her. She's just full of crap.*

full of holes *Fig.* [of an argument or plan] that cannot stand up to challenge or scrutiny. (See also **not hold water**; **pick holes in** sth.) □ *This plan is full of holes and won't work.*

full of hot air AND **full of beans; full of bull; full of it; full of prunes** *Fig.* full of nonsense; talking nonsense. □ *Oh, shut up, Mary. You're full of hot air.* □ *Don't pay any attention to Bill. He's full of beans.* □ *My English professor is full of bull.* □ *You're full of it.*

full of it Go to previous.

full of Old Nick Go to full of the devil.

full of prunes Go to full of hot air.

full of shit Go to full of crap.

full of the devil AND **full of Old Nick** *Inf.* always making mischief. □ *Little Chuckie is sure full of the devil.* □ *Toward the end of the school year, the kids are always full of Old Nick.*

full steam ahead *Fig.* onward with determination. □ *We started moving full steam ahead on the project.*

full up *Rur.* full. □ *I can't get any more gas in the tank. It's full up.*

a full-blown sth *Fig.* a full-size, completely active disease, disorder, crisis, etc. □ *Three days after I was exposed to the virus, I developed a full-blown case of the flu.*

fun and games *Fig.* playing around; doing pointless things. □ *All right, Bill, the fun and games are over. It's time to get down to work.*

*funny as a crutch not funny at all. (Sarcastic. *Also: **as ~**.) □ *Your trick is about as funny as a crutch. Nobody thought it was entertaining.*

funny bone AND **crazy bone** *Fig.* a spot near the elbow bone that is very sensitive to being struck. □ *Effie bumped her crazy bone and made a horrendous face.*

funny business Go to monkey business.

funny ha-ha *Fig.* amusing; comical. (As opposed to **funny peculiar**.) □ *I didn't mean that Mrs. Peters is funny ha-ha. She's weird—funny peculiar, in fact.*

funny money 1. *Fig.* counterfeit money. □ *The bank teller spotted the funny money in the man's deposit almost immediately.* **2.** *Fig.* temporary or substitute money, good only in certain places. □ *What am I going to do with all this funny money when I leave here? It's no good anywhere else.* **3.** *Fig.* foreign currency. (Jocular.) □ *We had better buy some gifts and get rid of some of this funny money before our flight.*

funny peculiar *Fig.* odd; eccentric. (As opposed to **funny ha-ha**.) □ *I didn't mean that Mrs. Peters is funny ha-ha. She's weird—funny peculiar, in fact.*

Funny thing is that . . . Go to It's a funny thing, but . . .

furthermore AND **what's more** and in addition [to what was just said]. □ *I'm tired of your complaining. Furthermore, you leave this place in a mess all the time!* □ *You are sweet and loveable. What's more, I can't live without you.*

a **furtive glance** *Fig.* a secret or quick glance, quickly averted. □ *He made a furtive glance in the direction of the closet when the robbers asked where the jewelry was hidden.*

One's **future looks bright.** *Fig.* One has a promising future. □ *Tom's future looks bright, and he will do well if he keeps working hard.*

futz around *Sl.* to waste time. □ *Stop futzing around and get the job done.*

futz sth **up**† AND **screw** sth **up**† *Sl.* to mess something up. □ *I don't want to futz up the deal, so I will be quiet.*

G

gad around AND **gad about** *Fig.* to go from place to place, having fun. □ *She wastes too much time gadding about with her friends.*

gag on sth to choke on something; to retch on something. □ *This fish is good, but I hope I don't gag on a bone.*

gain from sth to benefit from something. □ *I hope you gain from this experience.*

gain ground (on so/sth**)** to advance further; to become more important or popular than someone or something else. □ *Since the government announced its new policies, the opposition has been gaining ground.*

gales of laughter *Fig.* repeated choruses of laughter. □ *As the principal strode down the hall, she could hear gales of laughter coming from Mrs. Edwards's room.*

gallivant around *Fig.* to travel around aimlessly. □ *Why don't you stop gallivanting around and come home for a while?*

gallop through sth *Fig.* to go through something quickly; to do or perform something rapidly and perhaps carelessly. □ *Mike galloped through his song and left the stage in a hurry.*

galumph around *Fig.* to move around looking for someone or something or transporting someone or something. □ *I am so tired of galumphing around, dropping off and picking up kids.*

galvanize so **into action** *Fig.* to stimulate someone into some activity. □ *The explosion galvanized Martha into action.*

gamble sth **away**† to lose all of something by gambling. □ *He gambled all his money away.*

gamble on so/sth *Fig.* to run a risk by choosing or depending on someone or something. □ *I wouldn't gamble on Ted's being able to come. I don't think he can.*

The **game is up.** AND The **jig is up.** *Fig.* The illegal activity has been found out or has come to an end. □ *When the police were waiting for them inside the bank vault, the would-be robbers knew that the game was up.* □ *"The jig is up!" said the cop as he grabbed the shoulder of the pickpocket.*

a **game that two can play** *Fig.* a manner of competing that two competitors can use; a strategy that competing sides can both use. (Said when about to use the same ploy that an opponent has used.) □ *The mayor shouted at the city council, "Politics is a game that two can play."*

gang up (on so**)** to form into a group and attack someone. (Usually a physical attack, but it can also be a verbal attack.) □ *All right, you guys, don't gang up on me. Play fair!*

garbage sth **down**† *Sl.* to gobble something up; to quickly swallow something down. □ *Don't garbage your food down!*

gather dust *Fig.* [for something] to sit unused for a long time. □ *Most of my talent is just gathering dust because I don't really have an opportunity to perform.*

***gaudy as a butterfly** fancy; colorful. (*Also: as ~.) □ *Marie looked as gaudy as a butterfly in her new dress.*

Generation X(er) *Fig.* people reaching puberty during the 1970s and 1980s. □ *Three or four Generation Xers were in the antique store looking eagerly at some of* *those horrible old dinette chairs from the 1950s.*

generous to a fault *Cliché* too generous; overly generous. □ *Sally—always generous to a fault—gave away her lunch to a homeless man.*

*gentle as a lamb *Cliché* [of someone] very gentle. (*Also: **as** ~.) □ *Don't be afraid of Mr. Schaeffer. He may look fierce, but he's as gentle as a lamb.*

the **genuine article** *Fig.* the real thing rather than a substitute. □ *Is this the genuine article or some cheap imitation substitute?*

get sth AND **get it 1.** *Fig.* to receive punishment. □ *John got it for arriving late at school.* **2.** *Fig.* to receive the meaning of a joke; to understand a joke. □ *Bob laughed very hard, but Mary didn't get it.*

get a bee in one's **bonnet** Go to a bee in one's bonnet.

get a bright idea Go to a bright idea.

get a charge out of so/sth AND **get a charge from** so/sth; **get a kick out of** so/sth; **get a kick from** so/sth *Fig.* to get some excitement from someone or something. □ *We always get a charge out of visiting the theme park.*

get a foothold (some place**)** Go to a foothold (some place).

get a grip on oneself Go to a grip on oneself.

get a handle on sth Go to a handle on sth.

get a head start (on so**)** Go to a head start (on so).

get a kick out of so/sth Go to get a charge out of so/sth.

get a licking Go to a licking.

Get a life! *Inf.* Change your life radically! Find something interesting to do or say! □ *You are such a twit! Get a life!*

get a load of so/sth *Inf.* to get a good look at someone or something. □ *Wow! Get a load of that car!*

get a lot of mileage out of sth AND **get a lot of mileage from** sth *Fig.* to get a lot of use from something, as if it were a car.

□ *Bob always got a lot of mileage out of his favorite joke.*

Get a move on. *Fig.* to hurry up; to start doing what one is supposed to do. □ *Come on. Get a move on. We're going to be late.*

get a reputation (as a sth**)** Go to a reputation (as a sth).

get a reputation (for doing sth**)** Go to a reputation (for doing sth).

get a rise from so AND **get a rise out of** so *Fig.* to make someone react, usually angrily. □ *Tease Joe about his girlfriend. That generally gets a rise from him.*

get a ticket *Fig.* to receive a traffic ticket. □ *If you keep racing along at this speed, you will get a ticket!*

get a word in edgewise AND **get a word in edgeways** *Fig.* to manage to say something when other people are talking and ignoring you. (Often in the negative. *Fig.* on the image of trying to "squeeze" a word into a running conversation.) □ *It was such an exciting conversation that I could hardly get a word in edgewise.*

get aboard sth to get onto a ship or an airplane. □ *What time should we get aboard the ship?*

get so **across (**in a good way**)** Go to put so across (in a good way).

get sth **across (to** so**)** Go to put sth across (to so).

get one's **act together** *Inf.* to get oneself organized and on schedule. □ *I've got to get my act together and start getting my work done.*

get after so **1.** to begin to chase someone. □ *The other boys got after him and almost caught him.* **2.** *Fig.* to bother someone about doing something; to scold someone about something. □ *I will get after Fred about his behavior.*

get ahead (in sth**)** to advance in one's employment, school, or life in general. □ *I work hard every day, but I can't seem to get ahead in my job.*

get ahead of the game Go to ahead of the game.

get (a)hold of so *Fig.* to make contact with someone, especially on the telephone. □ *I kept calling him, but couldn't get hold of him at all.*

get (all) spruced up Go to (all) spruced up.

get so **(all) wrong** to misunderstand someone's intentions or character. □ *I think you've got me all wrong. I want to be your friend, not your enemy.*

get along 1. [for people or animals] to be amiable with one another. □ *Those two just don't get along.* **2.** *Fig.* to leave; to be on one's way. □ *It's time for me to get along. See you later.*

get along on sth *Fig.* to manage to survive with just something. □ *I think we can get along on what I earn.*

get along (on a shoestring) AND **get by (on a shoestring)** *Fig.* to be able to afford to live on very little money. □ *With so many expenses, it's hard to get by on a shoestring.*

get along (with so**)** Go to get on (with so).

get along without (so/sth**)** to manage without someone or something; to do without someone or something. □ *I don't think I can get along without my secretary.*

get ants in one's **pants** Go to ants in one's pants.

get around so/sth *Fig.* to avoid or elude an authority or regulation that constitutes a barrier; to circumvent someone or something in order to get one's way. □ *I know I can find a way to get around the rule.*

get so **around the table** *Fig.* to collect people together for discussion or bargaining. □ *We have to get everyone around the table on this matter.*

get one's **ass in gear** AND **get** one's **tail in gear** *Sl.* to get moving; to get organized and get started. (Caution with *ass.*) □ *Come on, you guys. Get moving. Get your ass in gear!*

get at so *Fig.* to find a way to irritate someone; to manage to wound someone, physically or emotionally. □ *Mr. Smith found a way to get at his wife.*

get at sth **1.** *Fig.* to explain or understand something. □ *We spent a long time trying to get at the answer.* **2.** *Fig.* begin doing something. □ *I won't be able to get at it until the weekend.*

get so's **attention** Go to grab so's attention.

get away from it all Go to away from it all.

get away with sth *Fig.* to do something bad and not get punished for it. (See also get away with murder.) □ *Don't do it! You won't get away with it!*

get away with murder 1. to commit murder and not get punished for it. □ *Don't kill me! You can't get away with murder!* **2.** *Fig.* to do something very bad and not get punished for it. (Fig. on ①.) □ *You will spoil your son if you let him get away with murder. You should punish him for his backtalk.*

get axed *Fig.* to get fired. □ *Betty and two of her friends got axed today.*

get back (at so**)** Go to back (at so).

get back in (the) harness Go to back in (the) harness.

get back in(to) circulation Go to back in(to) circulation.

get back on one's **feet** Go to back on one's feet.

get sth **back on track** Go to back on track.

get so's **back up** Go to get so's dander up.

get one's **bearings** Go to one's bearings.

get behind schedule Go to behind schedule.

get so's **blood up** *Fig.* to get someone or oneself angry. (Fixed order.) □ *That kind of language really gets my blood up.*

get busy to start working; to work or appear to work harder or faster. □ *I've got to get busy and clean this house up.*

get butterflies in one's **stomach** Go to butterflies in one's stomach.

get by (on a small amount of money**)** to survive with only a small amount of money. □ *I can't get by on that much money.*

get by (with sth**)** *Fig.* to satisfy the minimum requirements. □ *I was failing geometry, but managed to get by with a D.* □ *I took the bar exam and just barely got by.*

get carried away *Fig.* to be overcome by emotion or enthusiasm (in one's thinking or actions). □ *Here, Bill. Take this money and go to the candy store, but don't get carried away.*

get close to so Go to close to so.

get cold feet Go to cold feet.

get one's **comeuppance** *Fig.* to get a deserved punishment. □ *I can't wait till that snobbish girl gets her comeuppance.*

get so's **dander up** AND **get** so's **back up; get** so's **hackles up; raise** so's **hackles; get** so's **Irish up; put** so's **back up** *Fig.* to make someone get angry. (Fixed order. An animal's dander [dandruff] becomes airborne when the animal is active. A cat gets its back up when it is angry. A dog's hackles are the hairs around its neck, which are raised up when it is angry. *Irish* is an Irish temper, relating to the alleged temper of redheads.) □ *Now, don't get your dander up. Calm down.* □ *I insulted him and really got his hackles up.* □ *Now, now, don't get your back up. I didn't mean any harm.*

get down 1. *Sl.* to lay one's money on the table. (Gambling.) □ *Get down, and let's get going!* **2.** *Sl.* to concentrate; to do something well. (As with **get down to business.**) □ *Come on, Sam, pay attention. Get down and learn this stuff.*

get so **down** *Fig.* to depress a person; to make a person very sad. □ *Oh, that's too bad. Don't let it get you down.*

get sth **down**† *Fig.* to manage to swallow something, especially something large or unpleasant. □ *It was the worst food I have ever had, but I got it down somehow.*

get sth **down (in black and white)** AND **get** sth **down (on paper); get** sth **down**† *Fig.* to record some important information in writing. (Refers to the black of ink and the white of paper.) □ *I'm glad we have agreed on a price. I want to get it down in black and white.* □ *This is important. Please get it down on paper.*

get (down) off one's **high horse** *Fig.* to become humble; to be less haughty. □ *It's about time that you got down off your high horse.*

get down on so/sth Go to down on so/sth.

get down (on all fours) *Fig.* to position oneself on one's hands and knees. □ *He got down on all fours and played with the children.*

get sth **down (on paper)** Go to get sth down (in black and white).

get down to doing sth *Fig.* to begin to do something in earnest. □ *Okay, let's get down to sweeping this place out.*

get sth **down to a science** Go to make sth into a fine art.

get down to brass tacks *Fig.* to begin to talk about important things; to get down to business. □ *Let's get down to brass tacks. We've wasted too much time chatting.*

get down to business AND **get down to work** *Fig.* to begin to get serious; to begin to negotiate or conduct business. □ *All right, everyone. Let's get down to business. There has been enough chit-chat.*

get down to cases *Fig.* to begin to discuss specific matters; to get down to business. □ *When we've finished the general discussion, we'll get down to cases.*

get down to the facts *Fig.* to begin to talk about things that matter; to get to the truth. □ *Let's get down to the facts, Mrs. Brown. Where were you on the night of January 16?*

get down to the nitty-gritty *Inf.* to get down to the basic facts. □ *Stop messing around and get down to the nitty-gritty.*

get down to the nuts and bolts *Fig.* to get down to the basic facts. (See also nuts and bolts.) □ *Stop fooling around. Get down to the nuts and bolts.*

get down to work Go to get down to business.

get so's **drift** AND **catch** so's **drift** *Fig.* to understand what someone is saying or implying. (Akin to if you get my drift.) □ *I don't want to hear any more about her or you. Do you get my drift?*

get one's **ducks in a row** *Fig.* to get one's affairs in order or organized. □ *You can't hope to go into a company and sell something until you get your ducks in a row.*

get one's **ears lowered** Go to get one's ears set out.

get one's **ears pinned back** *Fig.* to experience a severe scolding. □ *Jimmy was ordered to report to the principal's office and got his ears pinned back.*

get one's **ears set out** AND **get** one's **ears lowered** *Inf.* to get one's ears made more visible by getting a haircut. □ *Better get my ears lowered because I'm getting a little shaggy.*

get enough courage up[†] **(to** do sth**)** Go to get enough nerve up[†] (to do sth).

get enough guts up[†] **(to** do sth**)** Go to next.

get enough nerve up[†] **(to** do sth**)** AND **get enough courage up**[†] **(to** do sth**); get enough guts up**[†] **(to** do sth**); get enough pluck up**[†] **(to** do sth**); get enough spunk up**[†] **(to** do sth**); get the nerve up**[†] **(to** do sth**); get the courage up**[†] **(to** do sth**); get the guts up**[†] **(to** do sth**); get the pluck up**[†] **(to** do sth**); get the spunk up**[†] **(to** do sth**)** *Fig.* to work up enough courage to do something. □ *I hope I can get enough nerve up to ask her for her autograph.* □ *I wanted to do it, but I couldn't get up enough nerve.* □ *I thought he would never get up the courage to ask me for a date.*

get enough pluck up[†] **(to** do sth**)** Go to previous.

get enough spunk up[†] **(to** do sth**)** Go to get enough nerve up[†] (to do sth).

get euchred out of sth *Fig.* to get cheated out of something. (Refers to losing in the card game euchre.) □ *Joe's dad left him a farm, but he got euchred out of it by some city slicker real estate agent.*

get even (with so**)** Go to even (with so).

get so's **eye** Go to catch so's eye.

get one's **feet wet** *Fig.* to get a little first-time experience with something. □ *Of course he can't do the job right. He's hardly got his feet wet yet.*

get one's **fingers burned** AND **burn** one's **fingers** *Fig.* to receive harm or punishment for one's actions. □ *I had my fingers burned the last time I questioned the company policy.*

get one's **foot in the door** *Fig.* to complete the first step in a process. (Fig. on the image of people selling things from door-to-door and blocking the door with a foot so it cannot be closed on them.) □ *I think I could get the job if I could only get my foot in the door.*

get so's **goat** *Fig.* to irritate someone; to annoy and arouse someone to anger. □ *I'm sorry. I didn't mean to get your goat.* □ *Jean got Sally's goat, and Sally made quite a fuss about it.*

get going *Fig.* to start moving, especially to depart. □ *Let's get going! We can't stand here all day.* □ *What time should we get going in the morning?*

get so **going** AND **get** so **started (talking); get** so **talking** *Fig.* to allow someone to start talking (passionately and endlessly). □ *Of course, I'm mad at her, but don't get me started!* □ *Don't get me started unless you got all day to listen to me.*

get sth **going with** so *Fig.* to start a romance or affair with someone. □ *Todd got something going with Amy, and they both look pretty happy.*

get so's **hackles up** Go to get so's dander up.

get one's **hands dirty 1.** to get closely involved in a difficult task where you may actually get dirty. □ *You have to get your hands dirty if you expect to get the gutters cleaned out.* **2.** AND **dirty** one's **hands; soil** one's **hands** *Fig.* to become involved with something illegal; to do a shameful thing; to do something that is beneath one. □ *The mayor would never* *get his hands dirty by giving away political favors.*

get one's **hands on** so/sth/animal Go to put one's hands on so/sth/animal.

get one's **head above water** Go to keep one's head above water.

get one's **head together** *Inf.* to get one's thoughts or attitude properly organized. □ *I've got to get my head together and get going.*

get home free Go to home free.

get sth **home to** so/sth *Fig.* to carry something home [quickly] to someone or something. □ *I have to get this pizza home to my parents before it gets cold.*

get one's **hooks in(to)** so/sth AND **get** one's **hooks in**† *Fig.* to obtain a strong and possessive hold on someone or something. □ *She just can't wait to get her hooks into him.*

get one's **house in order** Go to put one's house in order.

get sth **in black and white** Go to in black and white.

get in deeper *Fig.* to get in more and more trouble; to get more deeply involved with someone or something. □ *Every time he opened his mouth to complain, he just got in deeper.*

get inside sth **1.** to go inside of something or some place. □ *Get inside the car so you won't get wet.* **2.** *Fig.* to learn about the inner workings of something or some organization. □ *I can't wait to get inside that company and see what makes it tick.*

get into sth *Sl.* to become involved in something; to develop an interest in something. □ *No matter how hard I try, I can't get into basketball.*

get into a jam Go to next.

get into a mess AND **get into a jam** *Fig.* to get into difficulty; to get into trouble. □ *Now you have really gotten into a mess.*

get (oneself) into a stew (over so/sth**)** *Fig.* to be worried or upset about someone or

something. □ *Liz is the kind of person who gets into a stew over little problems.*

get into bed with so *Fig.* to work closely with as business partners; to merge businesses. □ *Have you heard? The company's getting into bed with Acme Industries.*

get sth **in(to) print** Go to put sth in(to) print.

get into one's **stride 1.** [for a runner] to reach a comfortable and efficient pace. □ *I got into my stride right away, and that helped win the race.* **2.** *Fig.* to reach one's most efficient and productive rate of doing something. (Fig. on ①.) □ *Amy will be more efficient when she gets into her stride.*

get in(to) the act *Fig.* to participate in something; to try to be part of whatever is going on. (As if someone were trying to get onstage and participate in a performance.) □ *Everybody wants to get into the act! There is not room here for everyone.*

get in(to) the swing of things *Fig.* to join in with people and their activities; to become more social and up-to-date. □ *Come on, Bill. Try to get into the swing of things.*

get sth **into** so's **(thick) head** Go to get sth through so's thick skull.

get so's **Irish up** Go to get so's dander up.

get it Go to get sth.

get it (all) together *Fig.* to become fit or organized; to organize one's thinking; to become relaxed and rational. (Fixed order.) □ *Bill seems to be acting more normal now. I think he's getting it all together.*

get it in the neck *Sl.* to receive trouble or punishment. □ *You are going to get it in the neck if you are not home on time.*

get it off *Sl.* to achieve sexual release; to copulate. □ *Harry kept saying he had to get it off or die. What's wrong with Harry?*

get it on 1. *Sl.* [for people] to copulate. □ *I don't want to get it on with you or any other creep.* **2.** *Sl.* to undertake to enjoy oneself. □ *I can really get it on with that slow jazz.*

get it out *Fig.* to tell someone about a problem; to pour out one's grief. (Fixed order.) □ *Come on, get it out. You'll feel better.*

get one's **just deserts** AND **get** one's **just reward(s)** *Fig.* to get what one deserves. □ *The criminal who was sent to prison got his just rewards.* □ *You'll get yours!*

get one's **just reward(s)** Go to previous.

get one's **kicks (from** so/sth**)** *Fig. Inf.* to get pleasure from someone or something. □ *Do you get your kicks from this sort of thing?*

get one's **knuckles rapped 1.** to get one's knuckles struck with a ruler as a punishment. □ *I got my knuckles rapped for whispering too much.* **2.** *Fig.* to receive a minor punishment. □ *The lawyer only got his knuckles rapped for talking back to the judge.*

get laid *Fig.* to have sexual intercourse; to receive sexual intercourse. □ *Tommy wanted nothing more out of life than to get laid.*

Get lost! Go to Beat it!

get one's **lumps** *Inf.* to get the result or punishment one deserves. (See also take one's lumps.) □ *We will see that Dave gets his lumps!*

get mad (at sth**)** *Fig. Inf.* to muster all one's physical and mental resources in order to do something difficult. □ *Come on, Bill. If you're going to lift your end of the piano, you're going to have to get mad at it.*

get some kind of **mileage out of** sth AND **get** some kind of **mileage from** sth **1.** *Fig.* to achieve some level of efficiency with a vehicle. (*Some kind of* typically includes *more, better, good*, etc.) □ *Do you get good mileage out of a vehicle like this?* **2.** *Fig.* to get [sufficient] use or service from something. (Fig. on ①.) □ *I wish I could get better mileage out of this car.*

get one's **mind off (of)** so/sth; AND **keep** one's **mind off (of)** so/sth; **take** one's **mind off (of)** so/sth *Fig.* no longer thinking about someone or something con-

stantly. □ *She is so beautiful. I can't get my mind off of her.*

get mixed up in sth Go to mixed up in sth.

get one's **money's worth** Go to one's money's worth.

get moving *Fig.* to get busy; to get started; to work harder or faster. □ *The director is coming. You had better get moving.*

Get my drift? Go to (Do you) get my drift?

get one's **nose out of** so's **business** *Fig.* to stop interfering in someone else's business; to mind one's own business. □ *Go away! Get your nose out of my business!*

get one's **nose out of joint** AND **have** one's **nose out of joint; put** one's **nose out of joint** *Fig.* to resent that one has been slighted, neglected, or insulted. □ *You get your nose out of joint too easily about stuff like that.*

get nowhere fast AND **go nowhere fast** *Fig.* not to make progress; to get nowhere. □ *I can't seem to make any progress. No matter what I do, I'm just getting nowhere fast.*

get off 1. *Fig.* to start off (on a friendship). (See other entries beginning with *get off* below.) □ *Tom and Bill had never met before. They seemed to get off all right, though.* **2.** *Fig.* to leave; to depart. □ *We have to get off early in the morning before the traffic gets heavy.*

get so **off 1.** *Fig.* to get someone cleared of a criminal charge. □ *I hope someone can get her off. She is innocent no matter how it looks.* **2.** *Fig.* to get someone freed from a responsibility. □ *What do I need to do to get myself off?*

get off a few good ones *Fig.* to tell a few good jokes; to land a few good punches; to manage to make a few strong criticisms. □ *The comedian managed to get off a few good ones, but most of his material was old or obscene.*

get off one's **ass** AND **get off** one's **rear; get off** one's **butt** *Sl.* to get up and get busy; to stop loafing and get to work. □ *It's* *time you got off your butt and started to work.*

Get off so's **back!** Go to Get off so's **case!**

get so **off** so's **back** *Fig.* to manage to stop someone from bothering or nagging someone. (*Someone's* can be *oneself's.*) □ *I've been trying to get Martha off Bob's back about his smoking.*

get off one's **butt** Go to get off one's **ass.**

Get off so's **case!** AND **Get off** so's **back!** *Fig. Inf.* Leave someone alone!; Stop picking on someone! (Usually a command.) □ *I'm tired of your criticism, Bill. Get off my case!*

get sth **off** one's **chest** *Fig.* to unburden oneself; to confess something; to criticize or make a personal complaint to someone. □ *I have to get this off my chest. I'm tired of your rudeness to me!*

get off (easy) AND **get off (lightly)** to receive very little punishment (for doing something wrong). □ *It was a serious crime, but Mary got off easy.* □ *Billy's punishment was very light. Considering what he did, he got off lightly.*

Get off it! 1. *Inf.* Stop acting so arrogant! □ *Get off it, you jerk!* **2.** *Inf.* You're lying! □ *Get off it! That can't be true.*

get off (lightly) Go to get off (easy).

Get off my back! *Inf.* Stop harassing me!; Leave me alone about this matter! □ *Alice: I'm tired of your constant criticism! Get off my back! Jane: I was just trying to help.*

get off (of) sth AND **get off** *Inf.* to stop discussing the topic that one is supposed to be discussing [and start discussing something else]; to stray from the topic at hand. (*Of* is usually retained before pronouns.) □ *I wish you wouldn't get off the subject so much.*

get off (on sth**)** Go to off (on sth).

get off on the wrong foot Go to off on the wrong foot.

get off one's **rear** Go to get off one's **ass.**

get off scot-free Go to go scot-free.

get off so's **tail 1.** *Fig.* to stop following someone closely, usually in an automobile. □ *Get off my tail! Keep your distance!* **2.** *Fig.* to stop bothering someone; to stop monitoring someone's actions. □ *Who needs your help? Get off my tail!*

get off the dime *Sl.* to start moving; to get out of a stopped position. □ *As soon as the board of directors gets off the dime on this proposal, we will have some action.*

get sth **off the ground** *Fig.* to get something started. (Fig. on the image of an airplane beginning a flight.) □ *It is my job to get the celebration plans off the ground.*

get off to sleep *Fig.* to manage to get to sleep finally. □ *I wasn't able to get off to sleep until dawn.*

get off with sth *Fig.* to receive only a light punishment for something. □ *Let's hope John gets off with a light sentence.*

get on *Fig.* to get along; to thrive. □ *Well, how are you two getting on?* □ *We are getting on okay.*

get on so *Fig.* to pester someone (about something); to pressure someone. □ *John is supposed to empty the trash every day. He didn't do it, so I will have to get on him.*

get on so's **case** Go to on so's **case.**

get one on one's feet AND **put one on one's feet** *Fig.* to get someone back to normal, financially, medically, mentally, etc. □ *We will put him on his feet and help him along.*

get on one's **horse** *Sl.* to prepare to leave. (Usually fig., with no horse present.) □ *It's time to get on my horse and get out of here.*

get on (in years) *Fig.* to grow older; to be aged. □ *Aunt Mattie is getting on in years.*

get sth **on its feet** Go to on its feet.

get on so's **nerves** Go to on so's nerves.

get on the stick Go to on the stick.

get on (with so**)** AND **get along (with** so**)** *Fig.* to be friends with someone; to have a good relationship with someone. (The friendship is always assumed to be good unless it is stated to be otherwise.) □ *I get along with John just fine.*

get on with sth to continue with something from this point in time onward. (See also **get on with** one's **life**.) □ *Okay, we've had a little rest. Let's get on with the job.*

get on with one's **life** AND **move on** to ignore recent problems and attempt to live the rest of one's life normally. □ *Now that the divorce is over with, it's time for me to get on with my life.* □ *Yes, it's time to move on.*

get on(to) so **(about** sth**)** *Fig.* to remind someone about something. □ *I'll have to get onto Sarah about the deadline.*

get sth **out**† *Fig.* to manage to get something said. □ *He tried to say it before he died, but he couldn't get it out.*

get sth **out of** so *Fig.* to cause or force someone to give specific information. □ *We will get the truth out of her yet.* □ *They got a confession out of him by beating him.*

get sth **out of** sth *Fig.* to get some kind of benefit from something. □ *I'm always able to get something helpful out of our conversations.*

get out of a jam *Fig.* to get free from a problem or a bad situation. □ *Would you lend me $500? I need it to get out of a jam.*

get so **out of a jam** *Fig.* to get someone out of trouble. □ *Thanks for getting my brother out of that jam.*

get out of a mess *Fig.* to get free of a bad situation. (Also with *this, such a,* etc.) □ *How can anyone get out of a mess like this?*

get sth **out of** doing sth *Fig.* to get some sort of reward or benefit from doing something. □ *I get a lot of pleasure out of singing in the church choir.*

get out of one's **face** *Inf.* to stop bothering or intimidating someone. □ *Look, get out of my face, or I'll poke you in yours!*

get out of so's **hair** *Inf.* to stop annoying someone. □ *Will you get out of my hair! You are a real pain!*

get so **out of** one's **hair** *Inf.* to cause someone to stop annoying oneself. □ *What do I have to do to get this guy out of my hair?*

Get out (of here)! Go away!; Leave this place! □ *John: I've heard enough of this! Get out of here! Bill: I'm going! I'm going!*

Get out of my sight! *Fig.* Go away immediately! (Usually said in anger.) □ *Get out of my sight!*

get so/sth **out of** one's **sight** *Fig.* to remove someone or something from one's presence. (Often said in anger.) □ *Get that child out of my sight!*

get sth **out of** one's **system 1.** to get something like food or medicine out of one's body, usually through natural elimination. □ *He'll be more active once he gets the medicine out of his system.* **2.** *Fig.* to be rid of the desire to do something; to do something that you have been wanting to do so that you aren't bothered by wanting to do it anymore. (Fig. on ①.) □ *I bought a new car. I've been wanting to for a long time. I'm glad I finally got that out of my system.* **3.** *Fig.* to do so much of something that one does not want or need to do it anymore. (Fig. on ①.) □ *I got riding roller coasters out of my system when I was young.*

get out of the way Go to out of the way.

get out of the wrong side of bed Go to get up on the wrong side of bed.

Get out of town! *Inf.* Beat it!; Get out of here! □ *You'd better get out of town, my friend. You are a pest.*

get (out) while the gettin(g)'s good AND **get (out) while the goin(g)'s good** *Inf.* to leave while it is still safe or possible to do so. □ *I could tell that it was time for me to get while the gettin's good.*

Get out with it! *Fig. Inf.* to manage to get something said. (Usually a command.) □ *Get out with it! I don't have all day to wait for you to get it said!*

get out with one's **life** *Fig.* to survive a serious or life-threatening incident or an accident without dying. □ *We were lucky to get out with our lives.*

get over so/sth *Fig.* to recover from difficulties regarding someone or something. ☐ *I almost never got over the shock.*

get over sth *Fig.* to recover from a disease. ☐ *It took a long time to get over the flu.*

Get over it! *Fig.* Forget about it and be done with it! (Said to someone who is fretting and stewing over some kind of problem.) ☐ *Forget about her. She's gone. Get over it!*

get sth **over (to** so) *Fig.* to make someone understand something; to succeed in explaining something to someone. ☐ *I finally got the basic concepts of trigonometry over to him.*

get one's **own house in order** Go to put one's own house in order.

get sth **past** so/sth AND **get** sth **past** *Fig.* to get someone or a group to approve something; to work something through a bureaucracy. ☐ *I will never get this size increase past the board.*

get physical (with so) Go to physical (with so).

Get real! *Inf.* Start acting realistically! ☐ *Hey, chum! You are way off base! Get real!*

get religion Go to religion.

get rid of so/sth Go to rid of so/sth.

get one **right here** *Inf.* to affect one deeply in a specific way. (Usually accompanied with a hand gesture showing exactly where one is affected: over the heart: lovingly; over the stomach or bowels: sickeningly.) ☐ *Pete clasped his hand to his chest and said, "That sort of thing gets me right here."*

get right on sth *Fig.* to do something immediately. ☐ *I know it has to be done today. I'll get right on it.*

get one's **rocks off (on** sth) **1.** *Sl.* [for a male] to ejaculate. (Considered coarse.) *Boys normally don't talk about getting their rocks off.* **2.** *Sl.* to enjoy something. (Fig. on ①. Fixed order.) ☐ *I really get my rocks off on heavy metal.*

get rolling *Fig.* to get started. ☐ *Come on. It's time to leave. Let's get rolling!*

get screwed 1. *Sl.* to have sexual intercourse. (Considered a crude usage.) ☐ *A lot of the college kids on spring break in Florida do nothing but get drunk and get screwed.* **2.** *Sl.* to get cheated. ☐ *I really got screwed on that last deal.*

get one's **sea legs** Go to one's sea legs.

get one's **second wind** Go to one's second wind.

Get serious! *Inf.* Get realistic!; Stop horsing around! ☐ *Oh, come on! Get serious! You don't really mean that!*

get shed of so/sth Go to get shut of so/sth.

get shet of so/sth Go to get shut of so/sth.

get one's **shit together** Go to get one's stuff together.

get shut of so/sth AND **get shed of** so/sth; **get shet of** so/sth *Rur.* to get rid of someone or something. ☐ *I can't wait to get shut of that old refrigerator.*

get sidetracked Go to sidetracked.

get smart (with so) *Fig.* to become fresh with someone; to talk back to someone. ☐ *Don't you get smart with me!*

get some shut-eye Go to some shut-eye.

get (some) steam up† **1.** [for a steam engine] to build up steam pressure and become more powerful. ☐ *As the engine got up steam, it began to move faster.* **2.** *Fig.* to begin to be stronger and more powerful. (Fig. on ①.) ☐ *The movement to cut taxes is getting up some steam.*

get one's **start** Go to one's start.

get so **started (talking)** Go to get so going.

get sth **straight** *Fig.* to understand something clearly. ☐ *Let me get this straight. I'm supposed to go there in the morning?*

get one's **stuff together** AND **get** one's **shit together 1.** *Fig.* to get one's possessions organized. (Caution with *shit*.) ☐ *Will you all please get your stuff together so we can get going?* **2.** *Idiomatic* to get oneself mentally organized. (Caution with *shit*.) ☐ *As soon as I get my shit together, I can be of more help.*

get one's teeth into something

get one's **tail in gear** Go to get one's ass in gear.

get one's **teeth into** sth AND **sink** one's **teeth into** sth; **get** one's **teeth in**; **sink** one's **teeth in**† *Fig.* to begin to do something; to get completely involved in something. □ *I can't wait to get my teeth into that Wallace job.* □ *Here, sink your teeth into this and see if you can't manage this project.*

get the advantage of so Go to the advantage of so.

get the best of so Go to next.

get the better of so AND **get the best of** so *Fig.* triumph over someone. (*Typically: **get** ~; **have** ~.) □ *Bill got the best of John in the boxing match.* □ *I tried to get the better of Tom in the golf match, but he won anyway.*

get the big picture Go to the big picture.

get the draw on so *Fig.* to be faster than one's opponent in a fight. (Alludes originally to an Old West gunfight.) □ *The sheriff got the draw on Arizona Slim and shot him in the arm.*

get the drift of sth *Fig.* to understand the general idea of something. □ *I know enough German to get the drift of this article.*

get the drop on so **1.** *Sl.* [for person A] to manage to get a gun aimed at person B before person B can aim back at person A. (The gun is then "dropped" by person B.) □ *Fred got the drop on Wilbur in a flash.* **2.** *Sl.* to succeed in getting an advantage over someone. □ *I guess I got the drop on you because I was early.*

get the edge on so Go to the edge on so.

get the facts straight AND **have the facts straight** *Fig.* to have an understanding of the real facts. □ *Ask a lot of questions, and get all of your facts straight.*

get the feel of sth Go to the feel of sth.

get the gate *Inf.* to be sent away; to be rejected. □ *I thought he liked me, but I got the gate.*

get the go-by *Inf.* to be ignored or passed by. □ *Tom stood on the road for 15 minutes trying to get a ride, but all he could get was the go-by.*

get the goods on so Go to the goods on so.

get the hang of sth Go to the hang of sth.

get the hell out (of some place**)** *Inf.* to depart as rapidly as possible. □ *Time for us all to get the hell out of here, I think. The cafe is closing now.*

get the inside track Go to the inside track.

get the jitters Go to the jitters.

get the jump on so Go to the jump on so.

get the kinks (ironed) out *Fig.* to fix a problem associated with something. □ *That'll be a right nice car, when you get the kinks ironed out in the engine.*

get the last laugh (on so**)** Go to the last laugh (on so).

get the lead out AND **shake the lead out** *Inf.* to hurry; to move faster. (This originally refers to getting lead weights [used in exercise] off so you can move faster.) □ *If you're going to sell cars, you're going to have to shake the lead out.*

get the lowdown (on so/sth**)** Go to the lowdown (on so/sth).

Get the message? AND **Get the picture?** *Inf.* Do you understand?; Are you able to figure out what is meant? □ *Things are tough around here, and we need everyone's cooperation. Get the picture?* □ *We don't need lazy people around here. Get the message?*

get the most out of so/sth AND **get the most from** so/sth *Fig.* to achieve the greatest output of work, effort, production, etc., out of someone or something. □ *I try to get the most out of my employees.*

get the nod Go to the nod.

Get the picture? Go to Get the message?

get the point (of sth**)** *Fig.* to understand the purpose, intention, or central idea of something. □ *I wish he would stop telling jokes and get to the point of his speech.*

get the runaround Go to the runaround.

get the shock of one's **life** Go to the shock of one's life.

get the short end (of the stick) Go to the short end (of the stick).

get the show on the road AND **get this show on the road** *Fig.* to get (something) started. □ *Let's get started! Get the show on the road!* □ *Get this show on the road. We don't have all day.*

get the third degree Go to the third degree.

get the word *Fig.* to receive an explanation; to receive the final and authoritative explanation. □ *I'm sorry, I didn't get the word. I didn't know the matter had been settled.*

get the worst of sth Go to the worst of sth.

get the wrinkles out (of sth**)** *Fig.* to eliminate some initial, minor problems with an invention, a procedure, a computer program, or a mechanical device. □ *I need more time working with this system to get the wrinkles out.*

get through (sth**) 1.** *Fig.* to complete something; to manage to finish something. □ *I'll get through college in five years instead of four.* **2.** *Fig.* to survive something; to go through sth. □ *This is a busy day. I don't know how I'll get through it.*

get sth **through** so's **thick skull** AND **get** sth **into** so's **(thick) head** *Fig.* to manage to get someone, including oneself, to understand something. □ *He can't seem to get it through his thick skull that he has to study to pass the exam.*

get through (to so**) 1.** *Fig.* to reach someone; to manage to communicate to someone. □ *I called her on the telephone time after time, but I couldn't get through to her.* □ *I tried every kind of communication, but I couldn't get through.* **2.** to pass through (something) to reach someone. □ *The crowd was so thick that I couldn't get through to him.* **3.** *Fig.* to make someone understand something. □ *Why don't you try to understand me? What do I have to do to get through to you?*

get through (to sth**)** to make contact by radio or telephone with a company, organization, or group. □ *I could not get through to the police, because the telephone line was down.*

get one's **ticket punched** *Sl.* to die; to be killed. (Literally, to be cancelled.) □ *Poor Chuck got his ticket punched while he was waiting for a bus.*

get to so **1.** *Fig.* [for someone or something] to annoy someone. □ *The whole business began to get to me after a while.* **2.** *Fig.* [for someone or something] to please or entice someone. □ *Lovely flowers and things like that get to me.*

get to sth **1.** *Fig.* to arrive at a topic of discussion. □ *Money? We will get to that in a minute.* **2.** *Fig.* to start on [doing] something; to begin doing something. □ *I'll get to it as soon as possible.*

get to one's **feet** *Fig.* to stand up. □ *On a signal from the teacher, the students got to their feet.* □ *I was so weak, I could hardly get to my feet.*

get to first base (with so/sth**)** AND **reach first base (with** so/sth**)** *Fig.* to make a major advance with someone or something. (Fig. on the notion that arrival at first base is the first step to scoring in baseball.) □ *I wish I could get to first base with this business deal.* □ *John adores Sally, but he can't even reach first base with her. She won't even speak to him.*

get to the bottom of sth *Fig.* to get an understanding of the causes of something. □ *There is clearly something wrong here, and I want to get to the bottom of it.*

get to the point (of sth**)** *Fig.* to arrive at a discussion or explanation of the purpose of something. □ *Please get to the point of all this.* □ *Will you kindly get to the point?*

get to the root of the problem Go to the root of the problem.

get to the top (of sth**)** *Fig.* to work up to the highest status in something. □ *She got to the top of her field in a very short time.* □ *It takes hard work to get to the top.*

get sth **together** Go to pull sth together.

get sth **together (for a** particular time**)** *Fig.* to arrange a party or other gathering for a certain time. (Fixed order.) □ *I'll try to get a meeting together for Friday afternoon.*

get together (with so**) (on** so/sth**)** *Fig.* to agree with someone about someone or something. □ *I would like to get together with you on this, but we are still nowhere near agreement.*

get tough (with so**)** *Fig.* to become firm with someone; to use physical force against someone. □ *The teacher had to get tough with the class because the students were acting badly.*

get under so's **skin** *Fig.* to bother or irritate someone. □ *John is so annoying. He really gets under my skin.*

get sth **under way** Go to under way.

get up to wake up and get out of bed. □ *What time do you usually get up?*

get sth **up**† *Fig.* to organize, plan, and assemble something. □ *Let's get a team up and enter the tournament.*

get up a (full) head of steam 1. *Fig.* [for a steam engine] to build steam pressure in order to start operating. □ *It took nearly 30 minutes to get up a full head of steam so that the locomotive could start moving.* **2.** *Fig.* to develop sufficient energy, enthusiasm, commitment, or determination to undertake something. □ *It's nearly noon before I can get up a full head of steam and accomplish something.*

get up a thirst AND **work up a thirst** *Fig.* to do something that will make one thirsty. (Fixed order.) □ *Doing this kind of work always gets up a thirst with me.*

get up an appetite *Fig.* to do something to make one very hungry. (Fixed order.) □ *Whenever I jog, I really get up an appetite.*

get so **up (for** sth**)** *Fig.* to get someone into peak condition for something; to prepare someone for something. □ *I hope we can get Walter up for the race.*

get up on one's **hind legs** *Fig.* to get angry and assertive. (Refers to the action of a horse when it is excited or frightened.) □ *She got up on her hind legs and told them all to go to blazes.*

get up on the wrong side of bed AND **get out of the wrong side of bed; wake up on the wrong side of bed** *Fig.* to seem grouchy on a particular day. □ *Did you get out of the wrong side of bed this morning? You are a real grouch.*

get up to sth *Fig.* to arrive as far as something. □ *We got up to the halfway point and stopped.*

get up to speed on so/sth Go to up to speed.

get upside down Go to upside down.

get one's **walking papers** Go to one's walking papers.

get what's coming to one Go to what's coming to one.

get wind of sth AND **catch wind of** sth *Fig.* to learn of something; to hear about something. □ *John caught wind of the gossip being spread about him.*

get wise to so/sth Go to wise to so/sth.

get with it 1. *Inf.* to modernize one's attitudes and behavior. □ *Get with it, Martin. Go out and buy some new clothes!* **2.** *Inf.* to hurry up and get busy; to be more industrious with something. □ *Let's get with it. There's a lot of work to be done.*

get with the program *Fig.* follow the rules; do what you are supposed to do. (Implies that there is a clearly known method or "program" that is usually followed.) □ *Jane just can't seem to get with the program. She has to do everything her way, right or wrong.*

get word (from so/sth**)** Go to word (from so/sth).

get worked up (over sth**)** Go to worked up (over sth).

get so **wrong** Go to take so wrong.

Get your ass over here! AND **Get your buns over here!; Get your butt over here!** *Sl.* Get yourself over here, now! (Caution with *ass*.) □ *Get your butt over here and help me move this trunk.*

Get your buns over here! Go to previous.

Get your butt over here! Go to Get your ass over here!

Get your head out of the clouds! *Inf.* Stop daydreaming! □ *Get your head out of the clouds and watch where you are driving! You're going to kill us all.*

Get your nose out of my business. Go to Mind your own business.

Getting there is half the fun. *Fig.* The time spent traveling and the route taken is a major part of the entertainment of the entire journey. (Often sarcastic.) □ *The road is rough, the air-conditioning is broken, and the kids are fighting. Sure, getting there is half the fun!*

get-up-and-go *Fig.* energy; motivation. □ *A good breakfast will give you lots of get-up-and-go.*

a **ghost of a chance** even the slightest chance. (Usually negative.) □ *There is just a ghost of a chance that I'll be there on time.*

gild the lily *Fig.* to add ornament or decoration to something that is pleasing in its original state; to attempt to improve something that is already fine the way it is. (Often refers to flattery or exaggeration.) □ *Your house has lovely brickwork. Don't paint it. That would be gilding the lily.*

Gimme a break! Go to Give me a break!

gird up one's **loins** *Fig.* to get ready, especially for hard work; to prepare oneself (for something). □ *Well, I guess I had better gird up my loins and go to work.*

give so **a bang** AND **give** so **a charge; give** so **a kick** *Inf.* to give someone a bit of excitement. □ *The whole afternoon, with all its silliness, gave me a charge anyway.*

give so **a big hand for** sth Go to a big hand for sth.

give so **a (big) head** Go to a (big) head.

give so **a big send-off** Go to a big send-off.

give so **a blank check** AND **give a blank check to** so *Fig.* to give someone freedom or permission to act as one wishes or thinks necessary. (See also **carte blanche**.) □ *He's been given a blank check with regard to reorganizing the workforce.*

give so **a blank look** AND **give** so **a blank stare** *Fig.* to look back at someone with a neutral look on one's face. □ *After I told her to stop smoking, she just gave me a blank look and kept puffing.*

give so **a blank stare** Go to previous.

give so **a break** Go to a break.

give so **a bum steer** Go to a bum steer.

give so **a buzz** Go to give so a ring.

give so **a call** Go to give so a ring.

give so **a charge** Go to give so a bang.

give so **a clean bill of health** Go to a clean bill of health.

give so **a dig** *Fig. Sl.* to insult someone; to say something that will irritate a person. □ *The headmaster's daughter gets tired of people giving her digs about favoritism.*

give so **a dirty look** Go to a dirty look.

give so **a fair shake** Go to a fair shake.

give so **a fat lip** *Inf.* [for someone] to punch someone in the face; [for something] to strike someone in the face. □ *How would you like a knuckle sandwich? Or maybe I should give you a fat lip!*

give so **a free hand** Go to a free hand (with so/sth).

give sth **a go** Go to give sth a try.

give a good account of oneself *Fig.* to do (something) well or thoroughly. □ *John gave a good account of himself when he gave his speech last night.*

give so **a (good) bawling out** *Fig.* to bawl someone out; to chastise someone. □ *The the teacher caught Billie; he gave him a good bawling out.*

give so **a (good) dressing-down** Go to a (good) dressing-down.

give so **a (good) talking to** Go to a (good) talking to.

give so **a (good) working over** Go to a (good) working over.

give so **a hand with** sth Go to lend so a hand with sth.

give so **a heads up** to give someone advance notice or warning (about something). □ *I gave Charlie a heads up that the auditors were coming next week.*

give so **a kick** Go to give so a bang.

give so **a leg up** Go to a leg up.

give so **a lift 1.** AND **give** so **a ride** *Fig.* to provide transportation for someone. □ *I've got to get into town. Can you give me a lift?* **2.** *Fig.* to raise someone's spirits; to make a person feel better. □ *It was a good conversation, and her kind words really gave me a lift.*

give so **a line** AND **feed** so **a line** *Fig.* to lead someone on; to deceive someone with false talk. □ *Don't pay any attention to John. He gives everybody a line.*

give a little 1. *Fig.* to move a slight amount. □ *When he pressed on the wall, it gave a little where the water had soaked in.* **2.** *Fig.* to yield a little bit on a point to someone. □ *She is so stubborn. If she would just give a little, she could get more cooperation from other people.*

give so **a pain** *Inf.* to annoy or bother someone. □ *Please don't give me a pain. I've had a hard day.* □ *She's such a pest. She really gives me a pain.*

give so **a pat on the back** Go to pat so on the back.

give so **a perspective on** sth Go to a perspective on sth.

give so **a piece of** one's **mind** *Fig.* to bawl someone out; to tell so off. □ *I've had enough from John. I'm going to give him a piece of my mind.*

give so **a red face** *Fig.* to make someone visibly embarrassed. □ *We really gave him a red face when we caught him eavesdropping.*

give sth **a rest 1.** *Fig.* to stop talking about a subject. □ *I'm tired of hearing about it. Give it a rest!* **2.** *Fig.* to stop using one's mouth to talk incessantly. □ *I've been listening to your constant jabber for the entire afternoon! Now, shut up! Give it a rest!*

give so **a ride** Go to give so a lift.

give so **a ring** AND **give** so **a buzz; give** so **a call** *Fig.* to call someone on the telephone. □ *Nice talking to you. Give me a ring sometime.*

give sth **a shot** Go to give sth a try.

give so **a start** *Fig.* to startle someone. □ *Gee, you gave me a start! I almost spilled my coffee.*

give sth **a try** AND **give something a go; give** sth **a whirl; give** sth **a shot** *Fig.* to make a try at something. □ *Why don't you give it a go and see if you like it?*

give sth **a whirl** Go to previous.

give so/sth **a wide berth** AND **steer clear of** so/sth *Fig.* to keep a reasonable distance from someone or something; to go around someone or something. (Both originally referred to sailing ships.) □ *The dog we are approaching is very mean. Better give it a wide berth.*

give oneself **airs** Go to put on airs.

give so **an A for effort** Go to an A for effort.

give an account of so/sth **(to** so**)** AND **give** so **an account of** so/sth *Fig.* to tell a narrative about someone or something to someone. □ *You are going to have to give an account of yourself to your parole officer.*

give (an) ear to so/sth AND **give** one's **ear to** so/sth *Fig.* to listen to someone or to what someone is saying. □ *I gave an ear to Mary so she could tell me her problems.* □ *She wouldn't give her ear to my story.* □ *He gave ear to the man's request.*

give so **an earful** Go to an earful.

give so **an even break** Go to an even break.

give so **an eyeful** Go to an eyeful (of so/sth).

Give one **an inch and** one **will take a mile.** *Fig.* Yield just a small amount to a person and that person will demand even more. □ *When I agreed to pay an advance of 10 percent, he suddenly wanted 25 percent. Give some people an inch and they'll take a mile.*

give so **an out** Go to an out.

give as good as one **gets** *Fig.* to give as much as one receives; to pay someone back in kind. (Usually in the present tense.) □ *John can take care of himself in a fight. He can give as good as he gets.*

give so/sth **away**† to reveal a secret about someone or something. □ *I thought no one knew where I was, but my loud breathing gave me away.* □ *We know that Billy ate the cherry pie. The cherry juice on his shirt gave him away.*

give so **away (to** so**) 1.** *Fig.* [for the bride's father] to give the bride away to the groom. (Customarily done just prior to the actual marriage ceremony.) □ *Mr. Franklin gave Amy away to Terry just as he had done in the rehearsal.* **2.** *Fig.* to reveal something secret about someone to someone else. □ *Alice did everything she could to keep from giving herself away.*

give sth **away**† **(to** so**)** *Fig.* to reveal the answer to a question, riddle, or problem to someone. □ *Don't give the answer away to them!*

give birth to sth *Fig.* to bring forth a new idea, an invention, a nation, etc. □ *The basic idea of participatory democracy gave birth to a new nation.*

give so **carte blanche** Go to carte blanche.

give cause for sth *Fig.* to serve as a just cause for something; to warrant something. □ *Your comments give cause for further investigation.*

give chase (to so/sth**)** *Fig.* to chase someone or something. □ *A mouse ran by, but the cat was too tired to give chase.*

give credence to so/sth *Fig.* to consider someone or something as believable or trustworthy. □ *How can you give credence to a person like Henry?* □ *He tells lies. Don't give credence to what he says.*

give currency to sth *Fig.* to grant acceptance to a story or idea; to believe something. (With a negative if there is doubt about what is said.) □ *His actions gave currency to the rumor that he was about to leave.*

give evidence of sth *Fig.* to show signs of something; to give proof of something.

□ *You are going to have to give evidence of your good faith in this matter. A nominal deposit would be fine.*

give one's **eyeteeth (for** so/sth**)** Go to give one's right arm (for so/sth).

give forth with sth AND **give out with** sth *Fig.* to say or shout something. □ *The kids in the street gave forth with cries of excitement.*

give free rein to so AND **give** so **free rein** *Fig.* to allow someone to be completely in charge (of something). □ *The boss gave the manager free rein with the new project.*

give one one's **freedom** *Fig.* to set someone free; to agree to a divorce. □ *Mrs. Brown decided to give her husband his freedom.*

give so **gray hair(s)** Go to gray hair(s).

give so **grief (over** so/sth**)** *Fig.* to cause someone distress about someone or something. □ *I hope she doesn't give me grief over the money I owe her.*

give ground *Fig.* to "retreat" from an idea or assertion that one has made. □ *When I argue with Mary, she never gives ground.*

give so **Hail Columbia** *Inf.* to scold someone severely. □ *The teacher gave her students Hail Columbia over their poor test scores.*

give so/sth **half a chance** *Fig.* to give someone or something an opportunity to be heard, seen, tried, or proved. □ *Just give me half a chance, and I'll show you how well I can sing.*

give one's **heart to** so *Fig.* to pledge one's eternal and exclusive love to someone. (Similar to lose one's heart to so/animal.) □ *I saw her and loved her at once. I gave my heart to her on the spot.*

give her the gun Go to give it the gun.

give in (to so/sth**)** to yield to someone or something; to give up to someone or something. □ *He argued and argued and finally gave in to my demands.*

Give it a rest! *Inf.* Stop talking so much. Give your mouth a rest. (Compare this with Give me a rest!) □ *Mary: So, I really think we need to discuss things more and*

go over all our differences in detail. *Bill: Stop! I've heard enough. Give it a rest!*

Give it all you've got! *Inf.* Do your very best! □ *Go out there and try. Give it all you've got!*

give it the gun AND **give her the gun** *Fig.* to make a motor or engine run faster; to rev up an engine. (The *her* is often pronounced "er.") □ *Bill: How fast will this thing go? Bob: I'll give it the gun and see.*

Give it time. Be patient.; In time, things will change. (Usually said to encourage someone to wait or be patient.) □ *Things will get better. Don't worry. Give it time.*

give it to so **(straight)** *Fig.* to tell something to someone clearly and directly. □ *Quit wasting time and tell me. Give it to me straight.*

Give it up! *Inf.* Stop trying!; You are wasting your time! (Fixed order.) □ *Tom: I'm just not a very good singer, I guess. Sue: It's no good, Tom. Give it up! Tom: Don't you think I'm doing better, though? Sue: Give it up, Tom!*

Give me a break! AND **Gimme a break!**
1. *Inf.* Don't be so harsh to me!; Give me another chance! □ *I'm sorry! I'll do better! Give me a break!* **2.** *Inf.* That is enough, you're bothering me!; Stop it! □ *Do you have to go on and on? Give me a break!* **3.** *Inf.* I don't believe you!; You don't expect anyone to believe that! □ *You say a gorilla is loose in the city? Gimme a break!*

Give me a call. AND **Give me a ring.** *Fig.* Please call me (later) on the telephone. □ *Mary: See you later, Fred. Fred: Give me a call if you get a chance.*

Give me a chance! *Fig.* Please give me a fair chance and enough time to complete the task. □ *Alice: Come on! I need more time to finish the test. Give me a chance! Teacher: Would another 10 minutes help?*

Give me a rest! *Inf.* Stop being such a pest!; Stop bothering me with this problem! (Compare this with Give it a rest!) □ *"Go away and stop bothering me!" moaned Bob. "Give me a rest!"*

Give me a ring. Go to Give me a call.

Give me five! AND **Give me (some) skin!; Skin me!; Slip me five!; Slip me some skin!** *Sl.* Slap my hand! (As a greeting or to show joy, etc.) □ *"Yo, Tom! Give me five!" shouted Henry, raising his hand.* □ *Bob: Hey, man! Skin me! Bill: How you doing, Bob?*

Give me (some) skin! Go to previous.

Give my best to so. AND **All the best to** so. *Fig.* Please convey my good wishes to a particular person. (The *someone* can be a person's name or a pronoun.) □ *Tom: See you, Bob. Bob: Give my best to Jane. Tom: I sure will. Bye.* □ *Bill: Bye, Rachel. All the best to your family. Rachel: Thanks. Bye.*

Give so **my love.** AND **Send** so **my love.** *Fig.* Please convey my love or kind regards to someone. (The person to whom the second entry head is addressed is really being asked to carry the sentiment rather than send it.) □ *Good-bye. Please send my love to your family.*

give so **no quarter** Go to grant so no quarter.

give (one's) notice AND **give notice to** so *Fig.* to formally tell one's employer that one is quitting one's job. □ *Lisa gave notice today. She got a job offer from another company.*

give notice that . . . to announce something in advance. □ *The mayor gave notice that she planned to appoint a new assistant.*

give notice to so Go to give (one's) notice.

give so **odds that . . .** *Fig.* to bet or postulate that. . . . (Often with a negative.) □ *I'll give you odds that you won't be able to order a decent steak at this restaurant.*

give of oneself *Fig.* to be generous with one's time and concern. □ *If you want to have more friends, you have to learn to give of yourself.*

give or take an amount within a numerical range. □ *I think I paid about $20, give or take a few bucks.*

give out 1. *Fig.* to wear out and stop; to quit operating. □ *I think that your shoes* are about ready to give out. **2.** *Fig.* to become depleted. □ *The eggs gave out, and we had to eat cereal for breakfast for the rest of the camping trip.*

give sth **out**† *Fig.* to make something known to the public. □ *The president gave out the news that the hostages had been released.*

give out with sth Go to give forth with sth.

give oneself **over to** so/sth to surrender to the influence or control of someone or something. □ *Finally, he gave himself over to his habit and drank from dawn to dusk.*

give so **pause (for thought)** *Fig.* to cause someone to stop and think. □ *When I see a golden sunrise, it gives me pause for thought.* □ *Witnessing a severe accident is likely to give all of us pause.*

give one's **right arm (for** so/sth**)** AND **give** one's **eyeteeth (for** so/sth**)** *Fig.* to be willing to give something of great value for someone or something. □ *I'd give my right arm for a nice cool drink.* □ *I'd give my eyeteeth to be there.*

give rise to sth *Fig.* to cause something; to instigate something. □ *The attack gave rise to endless arguments.*

give so **some lip** *Inf.* to speak rudely or disrespectfully to someone; to sass someone. □ *Jane is always giving the teacher some lip.*

give some thought to sth *Fig.* to think about something; to devote some time to thinking about something. □ *After I have had time to give some thought to the matter, I will call you.*

give so **static** *Fig.* to argue with someone; to give someone back talk. □ *I want you to do it and do it now! Don't give me any static!*

give so **the air** Go to the air.

give so **the benefit of the doubt** Go to the benefit of the doubt.

give so **the big eye** Go to the big eye.

give so **the boot** Go to the boot.

give so **the brush-off** Go to the brush-off.

give so the bum's rush Go to the bum's rush.

give so the business Go to the business.

give so the cold shoulder Go to the cold shoulder.

give so the devil Go to the devil.

give the devil his due AND **give the devil her due** *Fig.* to give your foe proper credit (for something). (This usually refers to a person who has been evil—like the devil.) □ *She's very messy in the kitchen, but I have to give the devil her due. She bakes a terrific cherry pie.*

give so the edge on so Go to the edge on so.

give so the eye *Fig.* to look at someone in a way that communicates romantic interest. □ *Tom kept giving Sally the eye. She finally got disgusted and left.*

give so the finger 1. *Fig.* to display the middle finger upright as a sign of derision. (The gesture is derisive and offensive. See also flip so off, flip so the bird.) □ *Did one of you guys give Ted the finger?* **2.** *Inf.* to mistreat someone; to insult someone. □ *You've been giving me the finger ever since I started working here. What's wrong?*

give the game away *Fig.* to reveal a plan or strategy. □ *Now, all of you have to keep quiet. Please don't give the game away.*

give so the gate *Sl.* to get rid of someone. □ *He threatened to give me the gate, so I left.*

give so the glad hand Go to the glad hand.

give so the go-by *Fig.* to bypass someone; to ignore someone. □ *Gert gave us all the go-by when she took up with that rich boyfriend.* □ *I didn't mean to give you the go-by. I'm preoccupied, that's all.*

give so the high sign Go to the high sign.

give the lie to sth AND **put the lie to** sth *Fig.* to show that something is a lie; to label something as a lie. □ *Your own admission of your part in the conspiracy gives the lie to your earlier testimony.*

give so the (old) heave-ho Go to the (old) heave-ho.

give so the once-over Go to the once-over.

give so/sth the once-over Go to look so/sth over†.

give so the raspberry *Inf.* to make a rude noise with the lips at someone. □ *The audience gave him the raspberry, which gave him some second thoughts about his choice of career.*

give so the sack Go to the sack.

give so the shaft Go to the shaft.

give so the shirt off one's **back** *Fig.* to give anything that is asked for, no matter the sacrifice required. □ *You can always count on Mark when you're in trouble. He'd give you the shirt off his back.*

give so the slip *Sl.* to escape from a pursuer. □ *I can give her the slip in no time at all.*

give so the works Go to the works.

give so tit for tat *Fig.* to give someone something equal to what was given you; to exchange a series of very similar things, one by one, with someone. □ *They gave me the same kind of difficulty that I gave them. They gave me tit for tat.*

give so/sth to talk about to do something that will cause gossip. □ *I think I'll have another drink and really give them something to talk about.*

give so to understand sth *Fig.* to explain something to someone; to imply something to someone. (Possibly misleading someone, accidentally or intentionally. See also given to understand.) □ *Mr. Smith gave Sally to understand that she should be home by midnight.*

give so up† for dead 1. *Fig.* to give up hope for someone who is dying; to abandon a dying person as already dead. □ *The cowboys gave up their comrade for dead and rode off.* **2.** *Fig.* to abandon hope for someone to appear or arrive. (Fig. on ①.) □ *We were delighted to see you. We had almost given you up for dead.*

give so/sth up† (for lost) *Fig.* to abandon someone or something as being lost; to quit looking for someone or something that is lost. □ *After a week we had given* *the cat up for lost when suddenly she appeared.*

give up the fight AND **give up the struggle 1.** *Fig.* to quit fighting; to stop trying to do something. □ *Don't give up the fight. Keep trying.* **2.** *Fig.* to give up and die. (Fig. on ①.) □ *In the end, he lost interest in life and just gave up the struggle.*

give up the ghost *Fig. Euph.* to die; [for something] to break down. (Fixed order. Biblical, Acts 12.) □ *The old man gave up the ghost.* □ *My poor old car finally gave up the ghost.*

give up the struggle Go to give up the fight.

give vent to sth *Fig.* to express anger. (The *something* is usually anger, ire, irritation, etc.) □ *Bill couldn't give vent to his frustration, because he had been warned to keep quiet.*

give voice to sth *Fig.* to express a feeling or an opinion in words; to speak out about something. □ *The protesters gave voice to their anger at Congress.*

give weight to sth AND **attach importance to** sth *Fig.* to respect or believe something. □ *I give a lot of weight to your opinion.* □ *Kelly attached no importance at all to the comments by Betty.*

give so **what for** Go to what for.

give with sth *Inf.* to give something to someone; to tell something to someone. □ *Come on! Give with the money!*

give-and-take *Fig.* the cooperation between two sides who are bargaining for something; the essence of negotiation. □ *The union asked for a little give-and-take from management.*

a **given** a fact that is taken for granted; a fact that is assumed. □ *It is a given that the earth revolves around the sun.*

given half a chance *Fig.* [if one were] given even just a slight opportunity. □ *Given half a chance, I would tell her exactly what I thought of her.*

given to doing sth *Fig.* likely to do something; inclined to do something habitu-

ally. □ *Bob is given to shouting when things don't go his way.*

given to understand *Fig.* [of someone] made to believe [something]. (See also give so to understand.) □ *They were given to understand that there would be no tax increase, but after the election taxes went up.*

*the **glad hand** *Fig.* an overly friendly welcome; a symbol of insincere attention. (*Typically: **get** ~; **give** so ~.) □ *I hate to go to a party and get the glad hand and then be ignored.*

glaze over *Fig.* [for one's eyes] to assume a dull, bored appearance, signifying an inability to concentrate or a lack of sleep. □ *My eyes glaze over when I hear all those statistics.*

glean sth **from** so/sth *Fig.* to figure something out from bits of gossip. □ *I was able to glean some important news from Tommy.*

gloom and doom *Fig.* unpleasant predictions, statements, or atmosphere. □ *All we hear these days from the government is gloom and doom. Isn't there any good news?*

Glory be! *Inf.* an exclamation expressing surprise or shock. (A bit old-fashioned.) □ *Mary: Glory be! Is that what I think it is? Sue: Well, it's a kitten, if that's what you thought.*

glory in sth *Fig.* to take great pleasure in something; to revel in something. □ *He just glories in all the attention he is getting.*

gloss over sth *Fig.* to rush by something, in speech or writing, hoping no one will take much notice. □ *The president bragged about his successes and glossed over his major failures.*

The **gloves are off.** *Fig.* There is going to be a serious dispute. (As if boxers had removed their gloves in order to inflict more damage. See also take one's gloves off.) □ *Bob got mad and yelled, "Okay, the gloves are off!" and started cussing and pounding the table.*

glow with sth *Fig.* [for someone's face, eyes, etc.] to display some quality, such as pride, pleasure, rage, health. □ *Her healthy face glowed with pride.*

glued to so *Fig.* following someone everywhere. □ *His little sister was glued to him all afternoon. Finally he sent her home.*

glued to sth *Fig.* to sit and stare at something as if stuck to it. (Usually about a television set or a book.) □ *Those kids are glued to that set all day! They should go out and play.*

a **glut on the market** Go to a drug on the market.

a **glutton for punishment** *Fig.* someone who is eager for a burden or some sort of difficulty; someone willing to accept a difficult task. □ *I enjoy managing difficult projects, but I am a glutton for punishment.*

gnash one's **teeth** *Fig.* to grind or bite noisily with one's teeth. □ *Bill clenched his fists and gnashed his teeth in anger.*

a **gnashing of teeth** *Fig.* a show of anger or dismay. (Biblical: "weeping/wailing and gnashing of teeth.") □ *After a little gnashing of teeth and a few threats, the boss calmed down and became almost reasonable.*

gnaw (away) at so *Fig.* to worry someone; to create constant anxiety in someone. □ *The thought of catching some horrible disease gnawed away at her.*

go a long way toward doing sth AND **go a long way in** doing sth *Fig.* almost to satisfy specific conditions; to be almost right. □ *Your plan went a long way in helping us with our problem.*

go about AND **go around 1.** [for a rumor] to go from person to person. □ *What is this story about you that I hear going about?* **2.** [for a disease] to spread. □ *There is a lot of this flu going about these days.*

go about one's **business** Go to about one's business.

go above and beyond one's **duty** AND **go above and beyond the call of duty** *Fig.* to exceed what is required of one. □

Doing what you ask goes above and beyond my duty.

go above and beyond (what is expected) Go to above and beyond (what is expected).

go after so to investigate someone or something for possible criminal prosecution. □ *The prosecutor went after Spike first, knowing that Spike was the gang leader.* □ *The police detectives went after the whole gang.*

go after so/sth/animal *Fig.* to charge or attack someone or some creature. □ *The bear went after the hunters and scared them off.*

go against the grain Go to against the grain.

(Go ahead,) make my day! 1. *Fig. Inf.* Just try to do me harm or disobey me. I will enjoy punishing you. (From a phrase said in a movie by someone holding a gun on a villain and wanting the villain to do something that would justify firing the gun.) □ *As Bill pulled back his clenched fist to strike Tom, who is much bigger and stronger than Bill, Tom said, "Make my day!"* **2.** *Fig. Inf.* Go ahead, ruin my day!; Go ahead, give me the bad news. (A sarcastic version of ①.) □ *Tom (standing in the doorway): Hello, I'm with the Internal Revenue Service. Could I come in? Mary: Go ahead, make my day!*

go all out *Fig.* to try as hard as possible; to do a great deal. □ *She went all out to make sure we would have a good time.*

go all out (for so/sth) *Fig.* to do everything possible for someone or something. □ *We went all out for George and threw a big party on his return.*

go all the way (with so) AND **go to bed (with** so) *Euph.* to have sexual intercourse with someone. □ *If you go all the way, you stand a chance of getting pregnant.* □ *I've heard that they go to bed all the time.*

go along with so/sth **1.** *Fig.* to agree with someone or agree to something. □ *I will go along with Sharon's decision, of course.* **2.** *Fig.* to play along with someone or something; to pretend that you are party to someone's scheme. □ *I went along with the gag for a while.*

go along (with so**) for the ride** *Fig.* to accompany someone. □ *I'll just go along for the ride to the beach. I don't want to bask in the sun all day.*

go ape (over so/sth**)** *Sl.* to become very excited over something. □ *I just go ape over chocolate.*

go around Go to go about.

go around so *Fig.* to avoid dealing with someone. □ *We will want to go around the boss. He will say no if asked.*

go around and around (about so/sth**)** AND **go round and round (about** so/sth**)** *Fig.* to argue or discuss something over and over. □ *We went round and round about her grade, but she still doesn't study enough.*

go (a)round in circles 1. *Fig.* to act in a confused and disoriented manner. □ *I've been going around in circles all day and really need a break.* **2.** *Fig.* to keep going over the same ideas or repeating the same actions, often resulting in confusion, without reaching a satisfactory decision or conclusion. □ *We're just going round in circles discussing the problem. We need to consult someone else to get a new point of view.*

go (a)round the bend Go to (a)round the bend.

go around (with so**)** Go to hang around (with so).

go astray 1. *Fig.* [for something] to get lost or misplaced. □ *Mary's book went astray or maybe it was stolen.* **2.** *Fig.* to turn bad or wander from the way of goodness; to make an error. □ *I'm afraid your son has gone astray and gotten into a bit of trouble.*

go at it hammer and tongs Go to fight so/sth hammer and tongs.

go at it tooth and nail Go to fight so/sth hammer and tongs.

go at one another tooth and nail *Fig.* to fight one another like animals. (*One another* can also be *each other*. See also fight so/sth **hammer and tongs.**) □ *The man and his wife went at one another tooth and nail.*

Go away! Leave me!; Get away from me! □ *"Go away!" yelled the child at the bee.*

go away empty-handed *Fig.* to depart with nothing. □ *They came hoping for some food, but they had to go away empty-handed.*

go AWOL 1. to become absent without leave. (Military.) □ *Private Smith went AWOL last Wednesday. Now he's in a military prison.* **2.** *Fig.* absent without permission from anything. □ *Tom was AWOL at too many meetings, and finally we had to fire him.*

go back a long way Go to go back quite a way(s).

go back on one's **pledge** Go to go back on one's word.

go back on one's **promise** Go to next.

go back on one's **word** AND **go back on** one's **promise; go back on** one's **pledge** *Fig.* to break a promise that one has made. □ *I hate to go back on my word, but I won't pay you $100 after all.* □ *Going back on your promise makes you a liar.*

go back quite a way(s) AND **go back a long way** [our friendship] extends far back in time. □ *Tom and I go back a long way. We went to grade school together.*

go back to square one *Fig.* to return to the starting point. (Refers to the squares of a board game.) □ *It's back to square one. We have to start over.*

go back to the drawing board *Fig.* to return to the planning stage, so that a failed project can be planned again. (Fig. on the image of a designer returning to the drawing board to correct design mistakes.) □ *These plans have to go back to the drawing board.*

go back to the salt mines *Fig.* to return to one's work. (Jocular. Fig. on the image of menial labor working in salt mines.) □ *It's late. I have to go back to the salt mines.*

go bad *Fig.* to become rotten, undesirable, evil, etc. □ *I'm afraid that this milk has gone bad.*

go ballistic AND **go postal** *Fig.* to become irrationally enraged. (*Ballistic* refers to a missile launching. *Postal* refers to an enraged post office employee attacking those at his place of work. See also **go into orbit**.) □ *The boss went ballistic when he saw my expense report.*

go bananas *Sl.* to go mildly crazy. □ *Sorry, I just went bananas for a minute.*

go begging *Fig.* to be left over, unwanted, or unused. (As if a thing were begging for an owner or a user.) □ *There is still food left. A whole lobster is going begging. Please eat some more.*

go behind so's **back** *Fig.* to do something that is kept a secret from someone affected by it. □ *I hate to go behind her back, but she makes so much trouble about things like this.*

go belly up Go to turn belly up.

go beyond sth to do more of something than the expected amount; to go further with something than was required. □ *You clearly went beyond what was required of you.*

go blank *Fig.* to forget what one was talking about. □ *Suddenly I went blank and just stood there like a jerk.*

go broke *Fig.* to completely run out of money and other assets. □ *This company is going to go broke if you don't stop spending money foolishly.*

go by sth **1.** to follow the rules, recipe, instructions, guidelines, etc. □ *If you go by the rules, no one will give you any problems.* **2.** to be called by a particular name. □ *I usually go by Roe. That's from Jethro.*

go by the board *Fig.* to get ruined or lost. (This is originally a nautical expression meaning "to fall or be washed overboard.") □ *I hate to see good food go by the board. Please eat up so we won't have to throw it out.*

go by the book Go to by the book.

go by the name of sth *Fig.* to be known by a specific name. □ *She goes by the name of Gladys George.*

Go chase yourself! AND **Go climb a tree!; Go fly a kite!; Go jump in the lake!** *Inf.* Go away and stop bothering me! □ *Bill: Dad, can I have 10 bucks? Father: Go climb a tree!* □ *Stop pestering me, John. Go jump in the lake!*

Go climb a tree! Go to previous.

go cold turkey 1. to stop taking an addictive drug without tapering off. □ *She tried to break her heroin habit by going cold turkey.* **2.** *Fig.* to stop (doing something) without tapering off. □ *I had to stop eating chocolate, so I went cold turkey. It's awful!*

go crazy AND **go nuts** *Fig.* to become crazy, disoriented, or frustrated. □ *It is so busy here that I think I will go crazy.* □ *Bob went nuts because his car got a flat tire.*

go down 1. *Sl.* to happen. □ *Hey, man! What's going down?* **2.** *Sl.* to be accepted. □ *We'll just have to wait awhile to see how all this goes down.* **3.** *Sl.* to be arrested. (Underworld.) □ *Lefty didn't want to go down for a crime he didn't do.*

go down fighting *Fig.* to continue the struggle until one is completely defeated. □ *Sally, who is very determined, went down fighting.*

go down for the third time *Fig.* to be just on the verge of failing. (From the notion that a boxer who is knocked down three times in one round normally loses the fight.) □ *I was going down for the third time when I thought of a plan that would save my job.*

go down in defeat AND **go down to defeat** *Fig.* to submit to defeat; to be defeated. □ *The team went down in defeat again.*

go down in flames *Fig.* to fail spectacularly. (See also shoot so down in flames.) □ *Todd went down in flames in his efforts to win the heart of Marsha.*

go down (in history) (as so/sth**)** *Fig.* to be recorded for history as a significant person or event. □ *You will go down in his-*

tory as the most stubborn woman who ever lived.

go down in the annals of history AND **go down in the history books** *Fig.* [of sufficient significance] to be recorded in history books. □ *His remarks will go down in the annals of history.*

go down in the history books Go to previous.

go down on one's **knees** *Fig.* to kneel down, usually for prayer. □ *Larry went down on his knees and asked for forgiveness.*

go down that road Go to go there.

go down the chute AND **go down the drain; go down the tube(s)** *Sl.* to fail; to be thrown away or wasted. □ *Everything we have accomplished has gone down the chute.*

go down the drain Go to previous.

go down the line *Fig.* to go from person to person or thing to thing in a line of people or things. □ *She went down the line, asking everyone for a dollar for a cup of coffee.*

go down the tube(s) Go to go down the chute.

go downhill *Fig.* [for something] to decline and grow worse and worse. □ *This industry is going downhill. We lose money every year.*

go Dutch *Fig.* [for each person in a pair or a group] to pay for himself or herself. □ *I don't want you to pay for my ticket. Let's go Dutch.*

go easy on so/sth *Fig.* to be gentle on someone or something; not to be too critical of someone or something; to take it easy on someone or something. □ *Go easy on Sherri. She's my friend.*

go easy on sth *Fig.* to use something sparingly. □ *Please go easy on the onions in the stew. I don't like them very much.*

go fifty-fifty (on sth**)** *Fig.* to divide the cost of something in half with someone. □ *Todd and Jean decided to go fifty-fifty on dinner.*

Go figure. *Fig.* It's really strange.; Just try to figure it out. □ *She says she wants to have a conversation, but when I try, she does all the talking. Go figure.*

Go fly a kite! Go to Go chase yourself!

go for so/sth **1.** *Fig.* to find someone or something interesting or desirable. □ *I really go for chocolate in any form.* □ *Tom really goes for Gloria in a big way.* **2.** *Fig.* to believe or accept something or something that someone says. □ *It sounds pretty strange. Do you think they'll go for it?*

go for a spin Go to for a spin.

go for broke *Inf.* to risk everything; to try as hard as possible. □ *Okay, this is my last chance. I'm going for broke.*

Go for it! *Inf.* Go ahead! Give it a good try! □ *Sally: I'm going to try out for the basketball team. Do you think I'm tall enough? Bob: Sure you are! Go for it!*

go for nothing AND **go for naught 1.** [for something] to be done for no purpose. □ *All our hard work went for nothing.* **2.** *Fig.* [for something] to be sold for a very low price. □ *This merchandise can go for nothing. Let's just clear it out at 90 percent off.*

go for the jugular (vein) Go to next.

go for the throat AND **go for the jugular (vein)** *Fig.* to aim for a person's vulnerable points when attacking. □ *The drama critic was insulting and went straight for the playwright's jugular. Such cruelty.*

go from bad to worse *Fig.* to progress from a bad situation to one that is worse. □ *Things went from bad to worse in a matter of days.*

go from one extreme to the other *Fig.* to change from one thing to its opposite. □ *You go from one extreme to another about Tom—one day angry, the next day perfectly happy.*

go from strength to strength *Fig.* to get more and more successful in stages. □ *Our company has gone from strength to strength because of our founder's foresight.*

Go fry an egg! Go away and stop bothering me! □ *Go away and stop bothering me. Go fry an egg!*

go haywire to go wrong; to malfunction; to break down. □ *I was talking to Mary when suddenly the telephone went haywire. I haven't heard from her since.* □ *There we were, driving along, when the engine went haywire. It was two hours before the tow truck came.*

go head to head with so AND **go one on one with** so *Fig.* to confront someone directly, face-to-face. (See also lock horns (with so).) □ *I had to go head to head with the boss, but finally I got my way.*

go hog wild *Rur.* to behave wildly. □ *Have a good time at the party, but don't go hog wild.*

go home in a box *Sl.* to be shipped home dead. (Often said in exaggeration.) □ *You had better be careful on this camping trip, or you'll go home in a box.*

go home to mama *Inf.* to give up something—such as a marriage—and return to one's mother's home. □ *I've had it. I'm going home to mama.*

go hungry *Fig.* to miss a meal and end up hungry. □ *The kids were late for dinner so they had to go hungry.*

go in so's **favor** *Fig.* [for something] to change to someone's benefit. (Refers to very changeable things like game scores, wind direction, or chance in general.) □ *Things appear to be going in our favor—finally.*

go in for sth *Fig.* to be interested in something; to indulge in something. □ *I don't go in for loud music and hard drinking.*

go in one ear and out the other *Cliché Fig.* [for something] to be heard and then soon ignored or forgotten. □ *Everything I say to you seems to go in one ear and out the other. Why don't you pay attention?*

go in with so **(on** sth**)** *Fig.* to join together with someone to work on a project; to pool financial resources with someone to buy something. □ *I would be happy to go in with you on the charity ball. I'll find a hall.*

go into sth **1.** *Fig.* to enter some line of business or a profession. □ *He went into accounting when he got out of college.* **2.** *Fig.* to examine or study something; to discuss and explain something. □ *When we have time, we need to go into this question more thoroughly.*

go into a huddle *Fig.* [for people] to group together to talk and decide what to do. □ *Top-level management needs to go into a huddle and come up with a good plan.*

go into a nosedive AND **take a nosedive** **1.** *Fig.* [for an airplane] suddenly to dive toward the ground, nose first. □ *The small plane took a nosedive. The pilot was able to bring it out at the last minute, so the plane didn't crash.* **2.** *Fig.* [for someone] to fall to the ground face first. (Fig. on ①.) □ *She took a nosedive and injured her face.* **3.** *Fig.* to go into a rapid emotional or financial decline, or a decline in health. (Fig. on ①.) □ *Our profits took a nosedive last year.* □ *After he broke his hip, Mr. Brown's health went into a nosedive, and he never recovered.*

go into a song and dance (about sth**)** AND **go into the same old song and dance (about** sth**)** *Fig.* to start repeating excuses or stories about something. □ *He always goes into the same old song and dance every time he makes a mistake.*

go into a tailspin 1. [for an airplane] to lose control and spin to the earth, nose first. □ *The pilot was not able to bring the plane out of the tailspin, and it crashed into the sea.* **2.** *Fig.* [for someone] to become disoriented or panicked; [for someone's life] to fall apart. (Fig. on ①.) □ *Although John achieved great success, his life went into a tailspin. It took him a year to get straightened out.*

go into one's **act** AND **go into** one's **song and dance** *Fig.* to begin one's act or performance; to begin to behave in a way typical to oneself. □ *I go into my song and dance with each customer just to get them talking.*

go into detail(s) *Fig.* to give all the details; to present and discuss the details. □ *The* *clerk went into detail about the product with the customer.*

go into effect AND **take effect** *Fig.* [for a law or a rule] to become effective. □ *When does this new law go into effect?*

go into hiding *Fig.* to conceal oneself in a hidden place for a period of time. □ *After robbing the bank, the bandits went into hiding for months.*

go into hock *Fig.* go into debt. □ *We will have to go into hock to buy a house.*

go into orbit *Inf.* [for someone] to get very excited. □ *Todd went into orbit when he heard the price.*

go into service Go to come into service.

go into one's **song and dance** Go to go into one's act.

go into the same old song and dance (about sth**)** Go to go into a song and dance (about sth).

go into the service *Fig.* to enter one of the military services. □ *I chose not to go into the service.*

go it alone *Fig.* to do something by oneself. □ *I think I need a little more experience before I go it alone.*

Go jump in the lake! Go to Go chase yourself!

go like clockwork *Fig.* to progress with regularity and dependability. □ *The elaborate pageant was a great success. It went like clockwork from start to finish.*

go native to start, on purpose, to live like the local population in the community where one is a visitor. (That is, to pick up habits, dress, and behavioral patterns.) □ *I decided to go native, so I cast off my shirt and left my shoes behind.*

go near (to) so/sth to approach someone or something. □ *Don't go near Sue. She's got chicken pox.*

go nowhere fast Go to get nowhere fast.

go nuts Go to go crazy.

go off 1. [for an explosive device] to explode. □ *The fireworks all went off as scheduled.* **2.** [for a sound-creating de-

vice] to make its noise. □ *The alarm went off at six o'clock.* **3.** *Fig.* [for an event] to happen or take place. □ *Did your medical examination go off as well as you had hoped?*

go off half-cocked *Fig.* to go into action too early or without thinking. (Originally refers to a flintlock or matchlock gun firing prematurely, before the trigger was pulled.) □ *Bill went off half-cocked and told everybody he was running for the state legislature.*

go off on so *Sl.* to berate someone. □ *Don't go off on me! I'm not the cause of your problems!*

go off the deep end AND **jump off the deep end 1.** *Fig.* to become deeply involved (with someone or something) before one is ready. (Applies especially to falling in love.) □ *Look at the way Bill is looking at Sally. I think he's about to go off the deep end.* **2.** *Fig.* to act irrationally, following one's emotions or fantasies. □ *Now, John, I know you really want to go to Australia, but don't go jumping off the deep end. It isn't all perfect there.*

Go on. 1. Please continue. □ *Jane: Don't turn here. Go on. It's the next corner. Bill: Thanks. I didn't think that was where we should turn.* **2.** to happen. □ *What went on here last night?* **3.** *Fig.* That's silly!; You don't mean that! (Usually **Go on!**) □ *John: Go on! You're making that up! Bill: I am not. It's the truth!*

go on sth *Fig.* to start acting on some information. □ *We can't go on this! We need more information before we can act on this matter!*

go on a binge *Fig.* to do too much of something, especially to drink too much. □ *Jane went on a binge last night and is very sick this morning.* □ *Bill loves to spend money on clothes. He's out on a binge right now—buying everything in sight.*

go on a fool's errand Go to on a fool's errand.

go on a rampage *Fig.* to get very disturbed or angry. □ *The angry bull went on a rampage and broke the fence.*

go on and on *Fig.* to (seem to) last or go forever. □ *The road to their house is very boring. It goes on and on with nothing interesting to look at.*

go on (and on) (about so/sth**)** to talk endlessly about someone or something. □ *Albert went on about the book for a long time.*

go on before so AND **go on before** *Euph.* to die before someone. □ *Uncle Herman went on before Aunt Margaret by a few years.*

go on for an age AND **go on for ages** *Fig.* to continue for a very long time. □ *The symphony seemed to go on for an age.*

go on to a better land *Euph.* to die. □ *When I finally go on to a better land, I hope there is enough money for a proper funeral.*

Go on (with you)! *Inf.* Go away! (Always a command. No tenses.) □ *It's time you left. Go on with you!*

go (so) one better AND **do so one better** *Fig.* to do something superior to what someone else has done; to top someone. □ *That was a great joke, but I can go you one better.*

go one **one better (than that)** Go to do one one better (than that).

go one on one with so Go to go head to head with so.

go out 1. to become extinguished. □ *The lights went out and left us in the dark.* **2.** *Fig.* to become unfashionable; to become obsolete. (See also out of style.) □ *That kind of furniture went out years ago.*

go out (for sth**)** *Fig.* to try out for something. (Usually refers to sports.) □ *Tom went out for baseball.*

go out for a spin Go to for a spin.

go out in search of so/sth to leave to find someone or something. □ *I went out in search of someone to help me.*

go out like a light *Fig.* to pass out totally and quickly. □ *Henry fell and went out like a light.*

go out of business *Fig.* to stop doing commerce or business. □ *The new shop will probably go out of business if sales don't get better.*

go out of one's **mind** Go to out of one's mind.

go out of play *Fig.* [for a ball] to roll away out of the playing area so that the game stops. □ *When the ball went out of play, the referee blew the whistle.*

go out of one's **skull** Go to out of one's skull.

go out of one's **way (to** do sth**) 1.** *Fig.* to travel an indirect route or an extra distance in order to do something. □ *I'll have to go out of my way to give you a ride home.* **2.** *Fig.* to make an effort to do something; to accept the bother of doing something. (Fig. on ①.) □ *We went out of our way to please the visitor.*

go (out) on strike AND **go out (on strike)** *Fig.* [for a group of people] to quit working at their jobs until certain demands are met. □ *If we don't have a contract by noon tomorrow, we'll go out on strike.*

go out to so *Fig.* [for one's sympathy, heart, gratitude, etc.] to be aimed toward someone. □ *All of my sympathy went out to her. I knew just how she felt.*

go out (with so**) 1.** to go out with someone for entertainment. □ *The Smiths went out with the Franklins to a movie.* **2.** *Fig.* to go on a date with someone; to date someone regularly. □ *Is Bob still going out with Sally?*

go over sth *Fig.* to study or read through something, perhaps leading a group of students. (Fixed order.) □ *I haven't had time to go over this material, so we will go over it together.*

go over big (with so**)** *Fig.* to be very much appreciated by someone. □ *We hope that the musical will go over big with the audience.*

go over like a lead balloon *Fig.* to fail completely; to go over badly. □ *Your joke went over like a lead balloon.* □ *Her suggestion went over like a lead balloon.*

go over (well) *Fig.* [for someone or something] to be accepted or well received. □ *The play really went over with the audience.*

go over sth **(with** so) *Fig.* to review or explain something. □ *The teacher went over the lesson with the class.*

go over with a bang 1. *Inf.* [for something] to be funny or entertaining. □ *That's a great joke. It went over with a bang.* **2.** *Inf.* to succeed spectacularly. □ *The play was a success. It really went over with a bang.*

go over sth **with a fine-tooth(ed) comb** AND **search** sth **with a fine-tooth(ed) comb; go through** sth **with a fine-tooth(ed) comb.** *Fig.* to search through something very carefully. □ *I can't find my calculus book. I went over the whole place with a fine-tooth comb.* □ *I searched this place with a fine-tooth comb and didn't find my ring.*

go overboard 1. to fall out of a boat or off of a ship; to fall overboard. □ *Be careful or you will go overboard.* **2.** *Fig.* to do too much; to be extravagant. □ *Look, Sally, let's have a nice party, but don't go overboard. It doesn't need to be fancy.*

go places *Inf.* to become very successful. □ *I knew that Sally, with all her talent, would go places.*

Go play in the traffic. Go to Take a long walk off a short pier.

go postal Go to go ballistic.

go public (with sth) **1.** *Fig.* to sell to the public shares of a privately owned company. (Securities markets.) □ *The company decided not to go public, because the economy was so bad at the time.* **2.** *Fig.* to reveal something to the public. □ *It's too early to go public with the story.*

go (right) through so AND **go through** so **like a dose of the salts** *Inf.* [for something] to be excreted very soon after being eaten; [for something] to go immediately through the alimentary canal of a person. □ *The coffee went through me like a dose of salts.*

go scot-free AND **get off scot-free** *Fig.* to go unpunished; to be acquitted of a crime. (This *scot* is an old word meaning tax or tax burden.) □ *The thief went scot-free.* □ *Jane cheated on the test and got caught, but she got off scot-free.*

go sky-high *Fig.* to go very high. □ *Prices go sky-high whenever there is inflation.*

go so far as doing sth AND **go so far as to** do sth; **go as far as** doing sth; **go as far as to** do sth *Fig.* to go to the extremes of doing a particular thing; to risk doing something. □ *I think that Bob is dishonest, but I wouldn't go so far as to say he's a thief.*

go sour *Inf.* to turn bad or unpleasant. □ *It looks like all my plans are going sour.*

go South AND **head South 1.** *Inf.* to make an escape; to disappear. (Not necessarily in a southerly direction.) □ *Lefty went South the minute he got out of the pen.* **2.** *Inf.* to fall; to go down. (Securities markets.) □ *The market headed South today at the opening bell.* **3.** *Inf.* to quit; to drop out of sight. □ *Fred got discouraged and went South. I think he gave up football permanently.*

go stag *Fig.* to go to an event (which is meant for couples) without a member of the opposite sex. (Originally referred only to males.) □ *Is Tom going to take you, or are you going stag?*

go (steady) with so *Fig.* to have a romantic relationship with someone. □ *Sally has been going with Mark for two months now.* □ *My parents went steady with each other during the fifties.*

go stir crazy Go to stir crazy.

go straight *Fig.* to stop breaking the law and lead a lawful life instead. □ *After Bob was arrested, he promised his mother he would go straight.*

go (straight) to the top *Fig.* to attempt to confer with the person at the top of the chain of command, bypassing the intermediate people. □ *When I want something, I always go straight to the top. I don't have time for a lot of bureaucracy.*

go that route Go to go there.

go the distance *Fig.* to do the whole amount; to play the entire game; to run the whole race. (Originally sports use.) □ *This is going to be a long, hard project. I hope I can go the distance.*

go the extra mile AND **walk the extra mile** to try harder to please someone or to get the task done correctly; to do more than one is required to do to reach a goal. □ *I like doing business with that company. They always go the extra mile.*

go the limit *Fig.* to do as much as possible; to get as much as possible. □ *Let's plan to do everything we can. Let's go the limit.*

go the way of the dodo AND **go the way of the horse and buggy** *Fig.* to become extinct; to become obsolete. □ *The floppy disc has gone the way of the horse and buggy.*

go the way of the horse and buggy Go to previous.

go their separate ways AND **go our separate ways** [for two or more people] to separate and become independent of each other. □ *After the divorce, they went their separate ways.* □ *We said good-bye and went our separate ways.*

go there AND **go down that road; go that route** *Fig.* to begin a discussion of something; to take up a certain topic. (Often in the negative. This has nothing to do with traveling or going to a place.) □ *We don't have time to discuss your health problems, so let's not go there.*

go through to be approved; to succeed in getting through the approval process. □ *I sent the board of directors a proposal. I hope it goes through.*

go through so/sth *Fig.* to work through someone or something; to use someone or something as an intermediary. □ *I can't give you the permission you seek. You will have to go through our main office.* □ *I have to go through the treasurer for all expenditures.*

go through sth **1.** to search through something. □ *She went through his pants pock-*ets, looking for his wallet. **2.** to use up all of something rapidly. □ *How can you go through your allowance so fast?* **3.** to work through something, such as an explanation or story. □ *I went through my story again, carefully and in great detail.* **4.** to experience or endure something. □ *You can't believe what I've gone through.* □ *Mary has gone through a lot lately.* **5.** to rehearse something; to practice something for performance. □ *They went through the second act a number of times.*

go through so **like a dose of the salts** Go to go (right) through so.

go through the changes *Fig.* to experience life's changes. □ *A good day, a bad day—it's all part of going through the changes.*

go through the mill Go to through the mill.

go through the motions *Fig.* to make a feeble effort to do something; to do something insincerely or in cursory fashion. □ *Jane isn't doing her best. She's just going through the motions.*

go through (the proper) channels to use the proper procedure, working through the correct people and offices to get something done; to cooperate with a bureaucracy. □ *I'm sorry. I can't help you. You'll have to go through the proper channels.*

go through the roof 1. *Inf.* to become very angry. □ *She saw what had happened and went through the roof.* **2.** *Inf.* [for prices] to become very high. □ *These days, prices for gasoline are going through the roof.*

go through with sth to complete something, the outcome of which is troubling or doubtful; to do something in spite of problems and drawbacks. □ *I have to go through with it, no matter what.*

go through sth **with a fine-tooth(ed) comb** Go to go over sth with a fine-tooth(ed) comb.

Go to! *Fig. Inf.* Be damned to hell! (See also go to hell.) □ *Oh, you're terrible. Just go to!*

go to any length *Fig.* to do whatever is necessary. (See also go to great lengths (to do sth).) □ *I'll go to any length to secure this contract.*

go to bat against so *Fig.* to aid someone against someone else. □ *We refused to go to bat against one of our friends.*

go to bat for so *Fig.* to support or help someone. □ *I heard them gossiping about Sally, so I went to bat for her.*

go to bat for sth *Fig.* to take up the advocacy of something; to support something. □ *Don't worry, I'll go to bat for your plan when you present it to the committee.*

go to bed to go to where one's bed is, get into it, and go to sleep. □ *I want to go to bed, but there is too much work to do.*

go to bed (with so**)** Go to go all the way (with so).

go to bed with the chickens *Fig.* to go to bed at sundown—at the same time that chickens go to sleep. □ *We always go to bed with the chickens and get up early too.*

Go to blazes! *Fig. Inf.* Go to hell. □ *Go to blazes! Stop pestering me!*

go to extremes (to do sth**)** AND **go to any extreme (to** do sth**); stop at nothing (to** do sth**); not stop at anything (to** do sth**)** *Fig.* to be excessive in one's efforts to do something, trying everything. □ *Auntie Jane will go to extremes to make us all comfortable.* □ *Let's not go to extremes! We've already spent enough on gifts for the kids.*

go to great lengths (to do sth**)** AND **go to any lengths (to** do sth**)** *Fig.* to work very hard to accomplish something; to expend great efforts in trying to do something. (See also go to any length.) □ *I went to great lengths to explain to him that he was not in any trouble.*

go to so's **head 1.** *Fig.* [for something, such as fame or success] to make someone conceited. □ *Don't let all this praise go to your head.* **2.** *Fig.* [for alcohol] to affect someone's brain. □ *That last glass of champagne went right to her head.*

go to hell AND **go to (the devil) 1.** *Inf.* to go to hell and suffer the agonies

therein. (Often a command.) □ *Go to hell, you creep!* **2.** *Inf.* to become ruined; to go away and stop bothering someone. □ *This old house is just going to hell. It's falling apart everywhere.*

go to hell in a bucket AND **go to hell in a handbasket** *Fig.* to get rapidly worse and worse. □ *His health is going to hell in a handbasket ever since he started drinking again.*

go to hell in a handbasket Go to previous.

go to it 1. *Fig.* to start something actively; to do something with vigor. □ *Time to play ball. Go to it!* **2.** *Fig.* to fight. □ *Come on, let's go to it! I'm gonna beat the daylights out of you!*

go to one's **(just) reward** *Euph.* to die. □ *Let us pray for our departed sister, who has gone to her just reward.*

go to pieces AND **fall to pieces 1.** [for something] to fall apart into many pieces. □ *The vase—which had been repaired many times—just went to pieces when I put it down.* **2.** *Fig.* [for something] to become nonfunctional. (Fig. on ①.) □ *All her hopes and ideas went to pieces in that one meeting.* **3.** *Fig.* [for someone] to have a mental collapse. (Fig. on ①.) □ *Fred went to pieces during the trial.*

go to pot AND **go to the dogs** *Fig.* to go to ruin; to deteriorate. □ *My whole life seems to be going to pot.*

go to press *Fig.* [for a publication] to be sent to the printing presses. □ *The book went to press last week. We expect finished books by the first of the month.*

go to press with sth *Fig.* [for someone] to cause something to be printed. □ *We are going to press with a series of books on textiles.*

go to rack and ruin AND **go to wrack and ruin** *Fig.* to become ruined. (The words *rack* and *wrack* mean wreckage and are found only in this expression.) □ *That lovely old house on the corner is going to go to rack and ruin.*

go to sea *Fig.* to become a sailor. □ *I went to sea at an early age.*

go to seed AND **run to seed 1.** *Fig.* [for a plant] to grow long enough to produce seed; [for a plant] to spend its energy going to seed. □ *Plants like that ought not to be allowed to go to seed.* **2.** *Fig.* [for a lawn or a plant] to produce seeds because it has not had proper care. □ *You've got to mow the grass. It's going to seed.* **3.** *Fig.* [for something] to decline in looks, status, or utility due to lack of care. □ *This old coat is going to seed. Have to get a new one.*

go to the bathroom 1. *Fig.* to go into and use a restroom, bathroom, or toilet. □ *Bill: Where is Bob? Jane: He went to the bathroom.* **2.** *Euph.* to eliminate bodily wastes. □ *Billy's in there going to the bathroom. Don't disturb him.*

go to the bother (of doing sth**)** Go to go to the trouble (of doing sth).

go to (the devil) Go to go to hell.

go to the dogs Go to go to pot.

go to the expense (of doing sth**)** *Fig.* to pay the (large) cost of doing something. □ *It needs to be done, so you'll have to go to the expense.*

go to the lavatory *Euph.* to go into a restroom and use a toilet. □ *Bob requested to leave the room to go to the lavatory.*

go to the limit *Fig.* to do as much as is possible to do. □ *Okay, we can't afford it, but we'll go to the limit.*

go to the mat (on sth**)** Go to go to the wall (on sth).

go to the polls *Fig.* to go to a place to vote; to vote. □ *Our community goes to the polls in November.*

go to the toilet *Fig.* to use a toilet for defecation or urination. □ *Jimmy washed his hands after he went to the toilet.*

go to the trouble (of doing sth**)** AND **go to the bother (of** doing sth**); take the trouble (to** do sth**)** *Fig.* to make the effort to do something; to take the pains to do something. □ *I'm so pleased you went to the trouble to prepare my favorite dish.*

go to the wall (on sth**)** AND **go to the mat (on** sth**)** to take on great risk or to hold out to the very last on some issue. (See also push so to the wall. *Mat* alludes to wrestling.) □ *This is a very important matter, and I will go to the wall if necessary.*

go to town *Inf.* to work hard or very effectively. □ *Look at all those ants working. They are really going to town.*

go to trial *Fig.* [for a case] to go into court to be tried. □ *When will this case go to trial?*

go to war (over so/sth**)** *Fig.* to wage a war over someone or something. (Often an exaggeration.) □ *We aren't going to go to war over this, are we?*

go to waste *Fig.* [for something] to be wasted; to be unused (and therefore thrown away). □ *We shouldn't let all those nice herbs go to waste. Let's pick some before the first hard frost.*

go to wrack and ruin Go to go to rack and ruin.

go under 1. *Fig.* [for something] to fail. □ *The company went under exactly one year after it opened.* **2.** *Fig.* to become unconscious from anesthesia. □ *Tom went under and the operation began.*

go under the hammer Go to come under the hammer.

go under the knife *Inf.* to submit to surgery; to have surgery done on oneself. □ *Frank lives in constant fear of having to go under the knife.*

go under the name of sth *Fig.* [for someone or something] to be known under a particular name. (Very close to go by the name of sth. This entry head implies that the name is a little more official.) □ *The man you just met goes under the name of Walter Sampson.*

go under the wrecking ball *Fig.* to be wrecked or torn down. □ *That lovely old building finally went under the wrecking ball.*

go up against so *Fig.* to compete with someone; to face someone in competition. □ *The champ went up against the challenger in a match last Friday.*

go up in flames AND **go up in smoke** *Fig.* [for value or investment] to be lost suddenly and totally. □ *Everything we own has gone up in flames with the stock crash.* □ *The entire investment went up in smoke.*

go up in smoke Go to previous.

go whole hog *Inf.* to do everything possible; to be extravagant. □ *Let's go whole hog. Order steak and lobster.*

go wild *Fig.* to get very excited. □ *At the end of the football game, the kick was good, and the crowd went wild.*

go window-shopping *Fig.* to go about looking at goods in store windows without actually buying anything. □ *The office workers go window-shopping on their lunch hour, looking for things to buy when they get paid.*

go with (so/sth) to depart in the company of someone or a group. □ *Jim's not here. He went with the last busload.* □ *I'm leaving now. Do you want to go with?*

go with sth 1. to accompany something agreeably. □ *Milk doesn't go with grapefruit.* **2.** *Fig.* to choose something (over something else). □ *We decided to go with the oak table rather than the walnut one.*

go with one's gut (feeling) *Fig.* to obey or heed one's hunches or inner feelings. □ *When you really don't have the information to choose one or the other, just go with your gut.*

go with it Go to next.

go with the flow AND **go with it; take it as it comes; go with the tide** *Fig. Inf.* to cope with adversity; to accept one's lot; to relax and accept things. □ *No, just relax and go with the flow.*

go with the territory Go to come with the territory.

go with the tide Go to go with the flow.

go without AND **do without** *Fig.* to manage while not having any of something that is needed; to not have any of something. □ *We were a poor family and usually went without.*

go wrong *Fig.* to become bad; to turn bad; to fail. □ *Something has gone wrong with my cell phone.*

*****the **go-ahead** AND *****the **green light;** *****a **green light** *Fig.* a signal to start or continue. (*Typically: **get** ~; **give** so/sth ~.*) □ *We have to wait here until we have the go-ahead.* □ *I hope we get the green light on our project soon.*

(God) bless you! a formulaic expression said when someone sneezes. □ *A: Kerchoo! B: Bless you!*

God forbid! AND **Heaven forbid!** *Fig.* a phrase expressing the desire that God would forbid the situation that the speaker has just mentioned from ever happening. □ *Tom: It looks like taxes are going up again. Bob: God forbid!*

God only knows! *Inf.* Only God knows.; No one knows but God. □ *Tom: How long is all this going to take? Alice: God only knows!*

God rest so's soul. *Fig.* May God bless a previously mentioned person who has died. □ *I remember what my mother, God rest her soul, used to say about that.*

God's gift (to women) *Fig.* a desirable or perfect man. (Usually sarcastic.) □ *Tom thinks he's God's gift to women, but if the truth were known, they laugh at him behind his back.*

God willing. If God wants it to happen. (An expression indicating that there is a high certainty that something will happen, so high that only God could prevent it.) □ *John: Please try to be on time. Alice: I'll be there on time, God willing.*

God willing and the creek don't rise. AND **Lord willing and the creek don't rise.** *Rur.* If all goes well. □ *Tom: Will you be able to get the house painted before the cold weather sets in? Jane: Yes, God willing and the creek don't rise.* □ *We'll be able to visit our daughter for Christmas, Lord willing and the creek don't rise.*

goes for so/sth (too) [something] applies as well to someone or something else. □ *I told Bill to stay at home, and that goes for* *you too.* □ *I can't afford the filet and that goes for the lobster too.*

the **going** the condition of a path of travel or progress. □ *I decided to sell my stock while the going was still good.*

going, going, gone 1. *Fig.* [in an auction] close to being sold, almost sold, sold. □ *Going, going, gone. The new owner is the handsome gentleman in the back row.* **2.** *Fig.* disappearing and finally gone. □ *The little car is going, going, gone.*

going great guns *Fig.* going fast or energetically. □ *I'm over my cold and going great guns.*

Going my way? Go to (Are you) going my way?

the **going rate** *Fig.* the current rate or the current charges for something. □ *Our babysitter charges us the going rate.*

going strong *Fig.* functioning well or energetically. □ *We are still well and going strong.*

going to tattle Go to next.

going to tell AND **going to tattle** *Fig.* a threat that one is going to report someone's misdeed to someone in authority. □ *If you do that again, I'm going to tell!* □ *Sally just went to the teacher. She's going to tattle.*

a **gold mine of information** *Fig.* someone or something that is full of information. □ *Grandfather is a gold mine of information about World War I.*

a **golden opportunity** *Fig.* an excellent opportunity that is not likely to be repeated. □ *When I failed to finish college, I missed my golden opportunity to prepare myself for a good job.*

gone but not forgotten *Cliché* gone or dead and still remembered. □ *Uncle Harry is gone but not forgotten. The stain where he spilled the wine is still visible in the parlor carpet.*

gone goose *Fig.* someone or something that has departed or run away. □ *Surely, the burglar is a gone goose by now.*

gone on *Euph.* died. □ *My husband, Tom—he's gone on, you know—was a great one for golf.*

gone to meet one's **maker** *Euph.* died. □ *After a long illness, Reggie went to meet his maker.*

gone with the wind *Fig.* gone as if taken away by the wind. (A phrase made famous by the Margaret Mitchell novel and subsequent film *Gone with the Wind.* The phrase is used to make *gone* have a stronger force.) □ *Everything we worked for was gone with the wind.*

a **goner** *Fig.* be a dead or dying creature or person. □ *The boy brought the sick fish back to the pet store to get his money back. "This one is a goner," he said.*

a **good** (amount or distance) *Fig.* approximately a relatively large number, amount, or distance. □ *That town is a good 30 miles from here.* □ *Why, a new window will cost me a good $300.*

good and sth *Fig.* very or completely something. (*Something* is a state of being.) □ *Joe never does anything till he's good and ready.* □ *Mary's good and mad, all right.*

*****good as** sth *Fig.* the same as being done; almost done. (*Also:* **as** ~. *Something* can be *done, cooked, dead, finished, painted, typed,* etc.) □ *This job is as good as done. It'll just take another second.* □ *Yes, sir, if you hire me to paint your house, it's as good as painted.* □ *When I hand my secretary a package to be shipped, I know that it's as good as delivered right then and there.*

*****good as gold** *Cliché* very good. (*Also:* **as** ~.) □ *Mother: Thank you for taking care of Gretchen; I hope she hasn't been too much trouble. Grandmother: Not at all; she's been as good as gold.*

*****good as new** *Cliché* as good as when it was new; as well or as healthy as normal. (*Also:* **as** ~.) □ *A little rest and I'll be as good as new.*

a **good bet** *Fig.* a great likelihood. □ *It's a good bet that he will be late because of the rain.*

the **Good Book** the Bible. □ *Sally's always quoting from the Good Book.*

*a **(good) dressing-down** *Fig.* a severe scolding. (*Typically: **get** ~; **have** ~; **give** so ~.) □ *The boss gave Fred a real dressing-down for breaking the machine.*

a **good egg** *Fig.* a good and dependable person. (See also rotten egg; bad egg.) □ *He seems like a good egg. I'll take a chance on him.*

good enough for so/sth *Fig.* adequate for someone or something. □ *This seat is good enough for me. I don't want to move.*

good enough for government work Go to close enough for government work.

good for what ails you *Rur.* [something] able to cure any problem or illness. (Usually used to describe food or liquor.) □ *Sally's beef broth is good for what ails you.*

Good for you! a complimentary expression of encouragement for something that someone has done or received. □ *Jane: I really told him what I thought of his rotten behavior. Sue: Good for you! He needs it.*

Good golly, Miss Molly! *Inf.* Good grief!; Wow! □ *Good golly, Miss Molly! This place is a mess!*

a **(good) grasp of** sth Go to a (solid) grasp of sth.

Good grief! *Inf.* an exclamation of surprise, shock, or amazement. □ *Bill: There are seven newborn kittens under the sofa! Jane: Good grief!*

(Good) heavens! *Inf.* an exclamation of surprise, shock, or amazement. □ *John: Good heavens! Look at that diamond ring she has! Bill: I bet it's not real.*

Good luck! 1. a wish of good luck to someone. □ *Mary: I have my recital tonight. Jane: I know you'll do well. Good luck!* **2.** *Inf.* You will certainly need luck, but it probably will not work. (Sarcastic.) □ *Bill: I'm sure I can get this cheaper at another store. Clerk: Good luck!*

a **good many** *Fig.* quite a few. □ *I have a good many kinfolk in Texas.*

good old boy AND **good ole boy** *Rur.* a good guy; a dependable companion. □ *One of these good ole boys will give you a hand.*

the **good old days** back in an earlier time that everyone remembers as a better time, even if it really wasn't. □ *Back in the good old days, during World War I, they used real cactus needles in record players.*

good riddance (to bad rubbish) *Cliché* [it is] good to be rid of worthless persons or things. (See also good-bye and good riddance.) □ *She slammed the door behind me and said, "Good riddance to bad rubbish!"*

a **good sport** *Fig.* someone who can accept a loss in a competition or can accept being the butt of a joke. □ *Bob is usually a good sport, but this time he didn't seem to appreciate your joke.*

*a **(good) talking to** *Fig.* a scolding; a stern lecture. (*Typically: **get** ~; **have** ~; **give** so ~.) □ *I think I'll have to give Pete a good talking to.*

A good time was had by all. *Cliché* everyone had a good time. □ *After seeing the movie, the ten of us went out for ice cream, and a good time was had by all.*

good to go *Fig.* all ready to go; all checked and pronounced ready to go. □ *Everything's good to go, and we will start immediately.*

*a **(good) working over** *Fig.* a good scolding. (*Typically: **get** ~; **have** ~; **give** so ~.) □ *The boss gave me a good working over before firing me.*

good-bye and good riddance *Cliché* a phrase marking the departure of someone or something unwanted. □ *As the garbage truck drove away, carrying the drab old chair that Mary hated so much, she said, "Good-bye and good riddance."*

Good-bye for now. AND **(Good-bye) until next time.; Till next time.; Bye for now.; Till we meet again.; Until we meet again.** *Fig.* Good-bye, I'll see you soon.; Good-bye, I'll see you next time. (Often said by the host at the end of a radio or television program.) □ *Alice: See* *you later. Good-bye for now.* John: Bye, Alice. □ Mary: *See you later.* Bob: *Good-bye for now.* □ *The host of the talk show always closed by saying, "Good-bye until next time. This is Wally Ott, signing off."*

(Good-bye) till later. Go to (Good-bye) until then.

(Good-bye) until later. Go to (Good-bye) until then.

(Good-bye) until next time. Go to Good-bye for now.

(Good-bye) until then. AND **(Good-bye) till then.; (Good-bye) till later.; (Good-bye) until later.** *Fig.* Good-bye until sometime in the future. □ Sally: *See you tomorrow. Good-bye until then.* Sue: *Sure thing. See you.* □ Mary: *See you later.* Bob: *Until later.* □ *The announcer always ended by saying, "Be with us again next week at this time. Good-bye until then."*

good-for-nothing 1. *Fig.* worthless. □ *Here comes that good-for-nothing boy now.* **2.** *Inf.* a worthless person. □ *Bob can't get a job. He's such a good-for-nothing.*

***the **goods on** so** *Inf.* something potentially damaging or embarrassing about someone. (*Typically: **get** ~; **have** ~; **give** so ~.) □ *John beat me unfairly in tennis, but I'll get even. I'll get the goods on him and his cheating.*

goof around *Inf.* to act silly. □ *The kids were all goofing around, waiting for the bus.*

goof off *Sl.* to waste time. □ *Quit goofing off and get to work!*

goof on so *Inf.* to tease or kid. □ *I don't believe you. I think you're just goofing on me.*

goof so/sth **up**† *Inf.* to mess someone or something up; to ruin someone's plans; to make something nonfunctional. □ *Who goofed this machine up?*

goof up (on sth) *Inf.* to make an error with something; to blunder while doing something. □ *Please don't goof up on this job.*

***goose bumps** AND ***goose pimples** *Fig.* a prickly feeling related to having bumps on one's skin due to fear, excitement, or cold. (*Typically: **get** ~; **have** ~; **give** so ~.) □ *When I hear that old song, I get goose bumps.* □ *I never have goose pimples, but my teeth chatter when it's cold.*

goose egg 1. *Fig.* a raised bump on the skull as when one's head has been struck. □ *I walked into the edge of the door and got a terrible goose egg.* **2.** *Fig.* in a sports score, zero. □ *At the end of the game there was nothing but goose eggs next to our name.*

one's **goose is cooked** *Inf.* one is finished; one has been found out and is in trouble. □ *If I get caught, my goose is cooked.*

goose pimples Go to goose bumps.

the **gospel truth** *Fig.* the undeniable truth. (As true as the gospel [Bible].) □ *The witness swore he was telling the gospel truth.*

got game has spirit, skill, sex appeal, spunk, etc. (Black and pseudo-black in that there is no auxiliary between the subject and *got*, as with "He got game.") □ *Look at her play ball. She got game.*

gotta get up pretty early in the morning to do sth *Rur.* it would be difficult to do something (specified) because of the ability or quality involved. □ *You gotta get up pretty early in the morning to cheat Bill Johnson. He's a sharp businessman for sure.*

grab a bite (to eat) Go to a bite (to eat).

grab a chair AND **grab a seat** *Fig.* to quickly sit down in a seat. □ *Grab a chair and join the group!*

grab a seat Go to previous.

grab so's **attention** AND **get** so's **attention; grip** so's **attention** *Fig.* to draw or attract someone's attention. □ *The bright colors on the poster are there to grab your attention.*

grace sth **with** sth *Fig.* to adorn something or some place with something, especially a person's presence. □ *The lovely lady graced our home with her presence.*

grace so/sth **with** one's **presence** *Fig.* to honor someone or something with one's presence. □ *"How nice of you to grace us with your presence," Mr. Wilson told Mary* sarcastically as she entered the classroom late. □ The banquet was graced with the presence of the governor.

graced with sth made elegant by means of some ornament or decoration. □ The altar was graced with lovely white flowers.

***graceful as a swan** very graceful. (*Also: **as** ~.) □ The boat glided out onto the lake as graceful as a swan.

a **gracious plenty** AND an **elegant sufficiency** Euph. enough (food). □ At Thanksgiving, we always have an elegant sufficiency and are mighty thankful for it.

a **grain of truth** even the smallest amount of truth. □ The attorney was unable to find a grain of truth in the defendant's testimony.

the **granddaddy of them all** Go to the daddy of them all.

a **grandfather clause** Fig. a clause in an agreement that protects certain rights granted in the past even when conditions change in the future. □ The contract contained a grandfather clause that protected my pension payments against claims such as might arise from a future lawsuit.

grandfather so/sth in† Fig. to protect someone or a right through the use of a grandfather clause. □ My payments were grandfathered in years ago.

grant so **no quarter** AND **give** so **no quarter** Fig. not to allow someone any mercy or indulgence. (Originally meant to refuse to imprison and simply to kill one's prisoner.) □ The professor was harsh on lazy students. During class, he granted them no quarter.

grapple with sth Fig. to deal with a problem; to get a "good hold" on a problem. (Fig. on the image of fighting or struggling with a problem as if it were fighting back.) □ I cannot grapple with any additional problems.

grasping at straws AND **clutching at straws** Fig. to depend on something that is useless; to make a futile attempt at something. □ John couldn't answer the teacher's question. He was just grasping at straws.

grass widow Fig. a woman abandoned by her husband. □ Bill ran off and left Mary a grass widow.

grate on so('s **nerves**) Fig. to annoy someone; to bother someone. □ My obnoxious brother is grating on my nerves. □ Your whining really grates on me.

grateful beyond words Go to beyond words.

the **graveyard shift** Fig. the night shift (in employment). □ I worked on the graveyard shift so long that I forgot what the sun looked like.

a **gray area** Fig. an area of a subject or question that is difficult to put into a particular category because it is not clearly defined and may have connections or associations with more than one category. □ The responsibility for social studies in the college is a gray area. Several departments are involved.

***gray hair(s) 1.** a lightening of the hair caused by aging or hereditary factors. (*Typically: **get** ~; **have** ~; **give** so ~.) □ I get more gray hair the older I get. **2.** Fig. a lightening of the hair caused by stress or frustration. (*Typically: **get** ~; **have** ~; **give** so ~.) □ I have gray hair from raising four kids.

gray matter Fig. intelligence; brains; power of thought. □ Use your gray matter and think what will happen if the committee resigns.

grease so's **palm** AND **oil** so's **palm** Fig. to bribe someone. □ If you want to get something done around here, you have to grease someone's palm.

grease the skids Inf. to help prepare for or ease the way for the success or failure of someone or something. □ We need someone to grease the skids for the Wilson contract.

a **greasy spoon** Fig. a cheap diner, where the silverware might not be too clean. □ The corner greasy spoon is always busy at lunchtime.

Great balls of fire! Inf. Good heavens!; Wow! □ Mary got up to play the fiddle, and great balls of fire! That girl can play!

the **great beyond** *Euph.* life after death. □ *The fortune-teller claimed to get messages from the great beyond.*

Great day (in the morning)! *Rur.* My goodness! (An exclamation of surprise.) □ *Great day in the morning! I didn't expect to see you here.*

a **great deal** much; a lot. □ *You can learn a great deal about nature by watching television.*

Great Scott! *Inf.* an exclamation of shock or surprise. □ *"Great Scott! You bought a truck!" shrieked Mary.*

the **great unwashed** *Fig.* the general public; the lower middle class. □ *The Simpsons had a tall iron fence around their mansion—put there to discourage the great unwashed from wandering up to the door by mistake, I suppose.*

the **greatest thing since indoor plumbing** AND the **greatest thing since sliced bread** *Rur.* the most wonderful invention or useful item in a long time. □ *As far as I'm concerned, this new food processor is the greatest thing since indoor plumbing.* □ *Joe thinks Sally is the greatest thing since sliced bread. You can tell just by the way he looks at her.*

the **greatest thing since sliced bread** Go to previous.

Greek to so *Inf.* incomprehensible to someone; as mysterious as Greek writing. □ *I don't understand this. It's all Greek to me.*

green around the gills Go to pale around the gills.

*__green as grass__ very green. (*Also: **as** ~.) □ *His face turned as green as grass just before he vomited.*

green stuff *Fig.* money; U.S. paper money. □ *I've run out of green stuff. Can you loan me a few bucks?*

*__green with envy__ *Fig.* appearing jealous; appearing envious. (*Typically: **be** ~; **become** ~.) □ *Bill was green with envy that I won first place.*

Greetings and felicitations! AND **Greetings and salutations!** *Fig.* Hello and good wishes. (A bit stilted.) □ *"Greetings and felicitations! Welcome to our talent show!" said the master of ceremonies.* □ *Bill: Greetings and salutations, Bob! Bob: Come off it, Bill. Can't you just say "Hi" or something?*

Greetings and salutations! Go to previous.

the **grim reaper** *Fig.* death. □ *I think I have a few years to go yet before the grim reaper pays me a call.*

grin and bear it *Fig.* to endure something unpleasant in good humor. □ *I hate having to work for rude people. I guess I have to grin and bear it.*

grin from ear to ear AND **smile from ear to ear; be all smiles** *Fig.* to smile a very wide, beaming smile. □ *We knew Timmy was happy because he was grinning from ear to ear.*

grind away (at so**)** *Fig.* to needle, criticize, and nag someone continually. □ *Why are you always grinding away at me?*

grind so **down**† *Fig.* to wear someone down by constant requests; to wear someone down by constant nagging. □ *If you think you can grind me down by bothering me all the time, you are wrong.*

grind to a halt *Fig.* to slow down and stop. □ *Every day about noon, traffic in town grinds to a halt.*

grip so's **attention** Go to grab so's attention.

*a **grip on** oneself *Fig.* control of one's emotions. (*Typically: **get** ~; **have** ~.) □ *Calm down, man! Get a grip on yourself!*

*a **grip on** sth **1.** AND *a **hold on** sth a good grasp on something. (*Typically: **get** ~; **have** ~; **give** so ~.) □ *Try to get a grip on the ropes and pull yourself up.* **2.** *Fig.* a thorough knowledge of some topic. (*Typically: **get** ~; **have** ~; **give** so ~.) □ *I need to have a grip on the basics of accounting.*

gripe one's **soul** *Inf.* to annoy someone. □ *That kind of thing really gripes my soul!*

grist for the mill AND **grist for** so's **mill; grist to the mill** *Fig.* something useful or needed. □ *Bob bases the novels he* *writes on his own experience, so everything that happens to him is grist for the mill.*

grist to the mill Go to previous.

grit one's **teeth** *Fig.* to grind or clench one's teeth together in anger or determination. □ *All through the race, Sally was gritting her teeth. She was really determined.*

groan under sth *Fig.* to suffer under a burden. □ *For years, the people had groaned under the cruel ruler.*

gronk (out) *Sl.* to conk out; to crash, as with a car or a computer. □ *My car gronked out on the way to work this morning.*

groove on so/sth *Inf.* to show interest in someone or something; to relate to someone or something. □ *Fred was beginning to groove on new age music when he met Phil.*

gross so **out**† *Inf.* to disgust someone. □ *Those horrible pictures just gross me out.*

ground so *Fig.* to take away someone's privileges. (Usually said of a teenager.) □ *My father said that if I didn't get at least Cs, he'd ground me.*

ground so **in** sth *Fig.* to instruct someone in an area of knowledge. □ *We grounded all our children in the basics of home cooking.*

ground sth **on** sth *Fig.* to build a firm basis for something on something else. □ *His thinking was grounded on years of reading.*

grounded in (actual) fact *Fig.* based on facts. □ *The stories in this book are all grounded in actual fact.*

*grounds for sth the basis or cause for legal action such as a lawsuit. (*Typically: **be** ~; **become** ~.) □ *Your negligence is grounds for a lawsuit.*

grow apart (from so/sth**)** *Fig.* [for people] to separate emotionally from one another gradually. □ *Over the years, they grew apart from each other.*

grow by leaps and bounds Go to by leaps and bounds.

grow in sth *Fig.* [for someone] to increase in some quality, such as wisdom, strength, stature, etc. □ *As I got older, I was supposed to grow in wisdom and other good things.*

grow on so *Fig.* [for something] to become familiar to and desired by someone; [for something] to become habitual for someone. □ *This kind of music grows on you after a while.*

grow out of sth **1.** *Fig.* [for a problem] to develop from something less serious. □ *A big argument has grown out of a tiny disagreement!* **2.** *Fig.* to age out (of sth); to outgrow something; to abandon something as one matures. □ *Haven't you grown out of your fear of the dark yet?* **3.** *Fig.* to grow so much that some article of clothing does not fit. □ *Timmy's getting so tall that he's grown out of all his clothes.*

grow out of (all) proportion Go to out of (all) proportion.

grow to do sth to gradually begin to do certain things, using verbs such as *feel, know, like, need, respect, sense, suspect, think, want, wonder,* etc. □ *I grew to hate Bob over a period of years.*

a **growth experience** AND a **growth opportunity;** a **learning experience** *Euph.* an unpleasant experience. □ *Jim said that his trip to Mexico turned out to be a real learning experience.*

a **growth opportunity** Go to previous.

*gruff as a bear gruff; curt and unsociable. (*Also: **as** ~.) □ *I'm always as gruff as a bear before I've had my first cup of coffee.*

grunt work *Fig.* work that is menial and thankless. □ *I did all of the grunt work on the project, but my boss got all of the credit.*

Guess what! *Inf.* a way of starting a conversation; a way of forcing someone into a conversation. □ *John: Guess what! Jane: What? John: Mary is going to have a baby. Jane: Oh, that's great!*

guest of honor a guest who gets special attention from everyone; the person for whom a party, celebration, or ceremony is given. □ *Bob is the guest of honor, and* *many people will make speeches about him.*

gulp for air *Fig.* to eagerly or desperately try to get air or a breath. □ *Tom gulped for air after trying to hold his breath for three minutes.*

gum the works up† Go to next.

gum sth **up**† AND **gum the works up**† *Fig.* to make something inoperable; to ruin someone's plans. □ *Please, Bill, be careful and don't gum up the works.*

gun so/animal **down**† *Fig.* to shoot someone or an animal. □ *Spike tried to gun a policeman down.*

gun for so **1.** *Inf.* to seek one out to shoot one. □ *They say that Tex is gunning for the sheriff.* **2.** *Inf.* to seek someone out in anger. □ *The boss is gunning for you.*

gung ho (on so/sth**)** *Inf.* enthusiastically in favor of someone or something. □ *Bobby is really gung ho on his plan to start his own company.*

gush over so/sth *Fig.* [for someone] to heap praise, flattery, and compliments on someone or something. □ *Aunt Mattie always gushed over us children so much that we dreaded her coming.*

gussied up *Rur.* dressed up fancy. □ *All the girls got gussied up for the dance, but the guys wore their regular clothes.*

gut feeling AND **gut reaction; gut response** a personal, intuitive feeling or response. □ *I have a gut feeling that something bad is going to happen.*

gut reaction Go to previous.

gut response Go to gut feeling.

hack sth *Inf.* to endure something; to deal with something. (The *something* is usually *it*.) □ *John works very hard, but he can't seem to hack it.*

hack so/sth **apart**† *Fig.* to criticize someone or something severely. □ *The review just hacked him apart for his poor showing in the play.*

hack around *Inf.* to waste time. □ *I'm just hacking around and doing nothing.*

hack so **(off)** *Inf.* to annoy someone; to embarrass someone. □ *It really hacks me when you drum your fingers like that.*

hacked (off) *Inf.* angry; annoyed. □ *Wally was really hacked off about the accident.*

had best do sth Go to next.

had better do sth AND **had best** do sth ought to do something. □ *I had best bring in the potted plants before they freeze.*

had (just) as soon do sth AND **would (just) as soon** do sth *Fig.* prefer to do something else; to be content to do something. (The *would* or *had* is usually expressed as the contraction 'd.) □ *If you're cooking stew tonight, we'd as soon eat somewhere else.* □ *I would just as soon stay home as pay to go to see a bad movie.*

(had) known it was coming Go to knew it was coming.

had rather do sth AND **had sooner** do sth *Fig.* prefer to do something. (The *had* is usually expressed as the contraction 'd.) □ *I'd rather go to town than sit here all evening.* □ *They'd rather not.*

had sooner do sth Go to previous.

hadn't oughta *Inf.* should not have. □ *You hadn't oughta teased me like that.* □ *I know I hadn't oughta stolen that candy.*

hail a cab AND **hail a taxi** *Fig.* to signal to a taxi that you want to be picked up. □ *See if you can hail a cab. I don't want to walk home in the rain.*

hail a taxi Go to previous.

hail so **as** sth *Fig.* to praise someone for being something. □ *The active members hailed him as fraternity brother of the year.*

hail from some place *Fig.* to come from some place as one's hometown or birthplace; to originate in some place. □ *He hails from a small town in the Midwest.*

hail-fellow-well-met *Fig.* friendly to everyone; falsely friendly to everyone. (Usually said of males.) □ *He's not a very sincere person. Hail-fellow-well-met—you know the type.* □ *What a pain he is. Good old Mr. Hail-fellow-well-met. What a phony!*

the **hair of the dog (that bit** one**)** *Fig.* a drink of liquor taken when one has a hangover; a drink of liquor taken when one is recovering from drinking too much liquor. (Often the same type of liquor as one got drunk on.) □ *That's some hangover you've got there, Bob. Here, drink this. It's some of the hair of the dog that bit you.*

hale and hearty *Cliché* healthy. □ *The young infant was hale and hearty.*

half a bubble off plumb *Inf.* giddy; crazy. □ *Tom is just half a bubble off plumb, but he is all heart.*

half a loaf *Fig.* a small or incomplete portion of something. (From the proverb "Half a loaf is better than none.") □ *Why do you think I will be satisfied with half a loaf? I want everything that's due me.*

half the battle *Fig.* a significant part of an effort. □ *Getting through traffic to the airport was half the battle. The flight was nothing at all.*

half the time *Fig.* sometimes; in half or many of the instances. □ *She says she's my friend, but she can't remember my name, half the time.*

half under 1. *Fig.* semiconscious. □ *I was half under and could hear what the doctor was saying.* **2.** *Inf.* to be intoxicated; to be tipsy. □ *He was half under and could barely find the tavern door.*

half-and-half 1. a liquid that is half milk and half cream. □ *Harry would always pour half-and-half on his breakfast cereal in spite of what his doctor told him.* **2.** a substance composed half of one thing and half of another. □ *This coffee is half-and-half, so there isn't quite as much caffeine as in regular coffee.*

halfhearted (about so/sth**)** *Fig.* unenthusiastic about someone or something. □ *Ann was halfhearted about the choice of Sally for president.*

ham sth **up**† *Fig.* to make a performance seem silly by showing off or exaggerating one's part. (A show-off actor is known as a *ham*.) □ *Come on, Bob. Don't ham it up!*

hammer (away) at so AND **plug (away) at** so *Fig.* to interrogate someone; to ask questions endlessly of someone. □ *The cops kept hammering away at the suspect until he told them everything they wanted to know.*

hammer (away) at sth AND **plug (away) at** sth *Fig.* to dwell overly long on a point or a question; to continue doing something, hoping for success. □ *The agents asked question after question. They would not stop hammering at the issue.*

hammer sth **home**† *Fig.* to try extremely hard to make someone understand or realize something. □ *The boss hopes to hammer the firm's poor financial position home to the staff.*

hammer sth **into** sth AND **pound** sth **into** sth; **hammer** sth **in**†; **pound** sth **in**† to teach something to someone intensively, as if one were driving the information in by force. □ *Her parents had hammered good manners into her head since she was a child.*

hammer sth **out**† **1.** *Fig.* to arrive at an agreement through argument and negotiation. □ *The two parties could not hammer a contract out.* **2.** *Fig.* to play something on the piano. □ *She hammered the song out loudly and without feeling.*

hand so sth *Inf.* to tell someone something; to tell someone nonsense. □ *She handed me a line about being a famous author.*

hand sth **down**† **from** so **to** so to pass something down through many generations. □ *I hope we can make it a tradition to hand this down from generation to generation.*

hand sth **down**† **(to** so**) 1.** *Fig.* to give something to a younger person. (Either at death or during life.) □ *John handed his old shirts down to his younger brother.* □ *I hope my uncle will hand down his golf clubs to me when he dies.* **2.** *Fig.* to announce or deliver a (legal) verdict or indictment. □ *The grand jury handed seven indictments down last week.*

*a hand in (doing) sth AND ***a part in (doing)** sth *Fig.* a part in establishing or running something. (*Typically: **get** ~; **have** ~; **give** so ~; **keep** ~.) □ *I would like to have a hand in the planning process.*

*hand in glove (with so**)** *Fig.* very close to someone. (*Typically: **be** ~; **go** ~; **work** ~.) □ *John always works hand in glove with Sally. They are a team.*

*hand in hand 1. holding hands. (*Typically: **do** sth ~; **sit** ~; **walk** ~.) □ *They walked down the street hand in hand.* **2.** *Fig.* [of two things] together, one with the other. (*Typically: **go** ~.) □ *Cookies and milk seem to go hand in hand.*

Hand it over. Give it to me. (Fixed order.) □ *Come on. Give me the box of jewels. Hand it over!*

hand sth **off**† **(to** so**) 1.** to give a football directly to another player. □ *Roger handed the ball off to Jeff.* **2.** to give something to someone else to do or complete. (Fig.

on ①.) □ *I'm going to hand this assignment off to Jeff.*

hand sth **on (to** so/sth**)** *Fig.* to bequeath something to someone or a group. □ *I want to hand this land on to my children.*

hand sth **out to** so *Fig.* to give out information or propaganda to someone. □ *Do they really expect us to believe the stuff they hand out to us?*

hand sth **over**† to give something (to someone); to relinquish something (to someone); to turn something over (to someone). □ *Come on, John! Hand my wallet over.*

hand over fist *Fig.* [for money and merchandise to be exchanged] very rapidly. □ *What a busy day. We took in money hand over fist.*

hand over hand *Fig.* [moving] one hand after the other (again and again). □ *The man climbed up the rope hand over hand.*

Hand to God! Go to (My) hand to God!

*a **hand with** sth *Fig.* assistance with something, especially using the hands. (*Typically: **get** ~; **have** ~; **give** so ~.) □ *Mary would really like to get a hand with that. It's too much for one person.*

*a **handful** *Fig.* someone, often a child, who is difficult to deal with. (*Typically: **be** ~; **become** ~.) □ *Bobby can be a real handful when he needs a nap.*

*a **handle on** sth *Fig.* a means of understanding something; an aid to understanding something. (*Typically: **get** ~; **have** ~; **give** so ~.) □ *Now that I have a handle on the concept, I can begin to understand it.*

handle so **with kid gloves** AND **treat** so **with kid gloves** *Fig.* to be very careful with a touchy person. □ *Bill has become so sensitive. You really have to handle him with kid gloves.*

hand-me-down *Fig.* something, such as an article of used clothing, that has been handed down from someone. (See also hand sth **down (to** so).) □ *Why do I always have to wear my brother's hand-me-downs? I want some new clothes.*

so's **hands are tied** *Fig.* someone is not able to help or intervene. □ *I'm sorry. There's nothing I can do. My hands are tied.*

hands down *Inf.* easily; unquestionably. □ *They declared her the winner hands down.*

do sth **hands down** *Fig.* to do something easily and without opposition. □ *She was chosen hands down.*

Hands off! *Inf.* Do not touch someone or something. □ *Careful! Don't touch that wire. Hands off!*

Hands up! AND **Stick 'em up!; Put 'em up!** *Inf.* Raise your hands in the air; this is a robbery! (Underworld and Old West.) □ *Hands up! Don't anybody move a muscle. This is a heist.* □ *Stick 'em up! Give me all your valuables.*

hands-on 1. *Fig.* concerning a training session where novices learn by actual use of the device—such as a keyboard or control panel—that they are being taught to use. □ *Please plan to attend a hands-on seminar on the new computers next Thursday.* **2.** *Fig.* concerning an executive or manager who participates directly in operations. □ *We expect that he will be the kind of hands-on president we have been looking for.* **3.** *Fig.* concerning an activity or process requiring actual personal use of the keyboard by the operator. (Computer jargon.) □ *This new application requires a hands-on operator at all times.*

hang a few on† *Inf.* to take a few drinks; to have a few beers. □ *They went out to hang a few on.*

hang a huey *Sl.* to make a U-turn. □ *Hang a huey in the middle of the block.*

hang a left AND **hang a louie** *Inf.* to turn left. □ *He hung a left at the wrong corner.*

hang a louie Go to previous.

hang a ralph Go to next.

hang a right AND **hang a ralph** *Inf.* to turn right. □ *I told him to hang a right at the next corner, but he went on.*

hang around (some place**)** AND **stick around (**some place**)** *Fig.* to loiter some place; to be in a place or in an area, doing nothing in particular. □ *It's comfortable here. I think I'll hang around here for a while.*

hang around (with so) AND **go around (with so)** *Fig.* to spend a lot of time with someone; to waste away time with someone. □ *John hangs around with Bill a lot.* □ *They've been going around with the Smiths.*

hang by a hair AND **hang by a thread** **1.** to hang by something very thin, such as a thread or a hair. □ *The tiniest part of the mobile hangs by a thread; the rest are on plastic cords.* **2.** AND **hang on by a hair; hang on by a thread** *Fig.* to depend on something very insubstantial; to hang in the balance. □ *Your whole argument is hanging on by a thread.*

hang by a thread Go to previous.

hang so by the neck to execute someone or kill oneself by tying a noose around the neck and dropping the victim in order to break the neck or strangle the victim. □ *The executioner hanged him by the neck until he died.*

hang fire *Fig.* to delay or wait; to be delayed. □ *I think we should hang fire and wait for other information.*

hang five AND **hang ten** *Sl.* to stand toward the front of a surfboard or diving board and hang the toes of one or both feet over the edge. (Surfing.) □ *Get out there and hang five. You can swim. Nothing can go wrong.*

hang so for sth *Fig.* to extract an overly severe punishment for some deed. (An exaggeration.) □ *They are trying to hang me for a parking ticket!*

hang one's hat (up) some place to take up residence somewhere. □ *Bill moves from place to place and never hangs his hat up anywhere.*

hang one's head *Fig. Lit.* to feel or show sorrow, perhaps by bowing or drooping one's head. □ *He was very sorry, and he hung his head in despair.*

hang so in effigy *Fig.* to hang a dummy or some other figure of a hated person. □

The angry mob hanged the president in effigy.

hang in the balance Go to in the balance.

Hang in there. *Fig.* Be patient, things will work out. □ *Bob: Everything is in such a mess. I can't seem to get things done right. Jane: Hang in there, Bob. Things will work out.*

Hang it all! *Inf.* Damn it all! □ *He's late again! Hang it all!*

hang it up *Sl.* to quit something. (Fixed order.) □ *I've had it with this job. It's time to hang it up.*

hang loose AND **stay loose** *Inf.* to relax and stay calm. □ *Just hang loose, man. Everything'll be all right.* □ *Stay loose, chum. See ya later.*

*the **hang of sth** *Fig.* the knowledge or knack of doing something correctly. (*Typically: **get** ~; **have** ~; **teach** so ~.) □ *As soon as I get the hang of this computer, I'll be able to work faster.*

hang off to wait quietly to one side. □ *The boys hung off a little, waiting to see what would happen next.*

hang on **1.** *Fig.* to wait awhile. □ *Hang on. Let me catch up with you.* **2.** *Fig.* to survive for awhile. □ *I think we can hang on without electricity for a little while longer.* **3.** *Fig.* [for an illness] to linger or persist. □ *This cold has been hanging on for a month.* **4.** *Fig.* be prepared for fast or rough movement. (Usually a command.) □ *Hang on! We're going to crash!* **5.** *Fig.* to pause in a telephone conversation. □ *Please hang on until I get a pen.*

hang sth on so *Sl.* to blame something on someone; to frame someone for something. □ *Don't try to hang the blame on me!* □ *The sheriff tried to hang the bank robbery on Jed.*

hang on by a hair Go to hang by a hair.

hang on so's coattails Go to ride on so's coattails.

hang on (so's) every word *Cliché* to listen closely or with awe to what someone says. □ *The audience hung on her every word throughout the speech.*

hang on for dear life AND **hold on for dear life** *Cliché* to hang on tight. □ *As the little plane bounced around over the mountains, we hung on for dear life.*

hang on (to so/sth**)** AND **hold on (to** so/sth**)** *Fig.* to detain someone or something. □ *Please hang on to Tom if he's still there. I need to talk to him.*

Hang on to your hat! AND **Hold on to your hat!** *Fig.* Get ready for what's coming!; Here comes a big shock! □ *There is a rough road ahead. Hang on to your hat!*

hang one on Go to tie one on.

hang out (some place**) 1.** to spend time in a place habitually. □ *Is this where you guys hang out all the time?* **2.** to spend time aimlessly; to waste time. □ *Bill: What are you doing this afternoon? Tom: Oh, I'll just hang out.*

hang so **out to dry** *Inf.* to defeat or punish someone. □ *The boss was really angry at Billie. He yelled at him and hung him out to dry.*

hang out (with so/sth**)** *Fig.* to associate with someone or a group on a regular basis. □ *I wish you would stop hanging out with that crowd of boys.*

hang over so/sth **1.** to be suspended over someone or something. □ *A fancy crystal chandelier hung over us.* **2.** [for some pervading quality] to seem to hover over someone or something. □ *A dismal pall hung over the gathering.*

hang over so('s **head)** *Fig.* [for something unpleasant] to worry someone. □ *I hate to have medical problems hanging over me.*

hang ten Go to hang five.

hang together 1. *Fig.* [for something or a group of people] to hold together; to remain intact. □ *I don't think that this car will hang together for another minute.* **2.** *Fig.* [for a story] to flow from element to element and make sense. (Fig. on ①.) □ *This story simply does not hang together.* **3.** *Fig.* [for people] to spend time together. (Fig. on ①.) □ *We hung together for a few hours and then went our separate ways.*

hang tough (on sth**)** *Sl.* to stick to one's position (on something). □ *I decided I'd hang tough on it. I tend to give in too easy.*

hang up 1. [for a machine or a computer] to grind to a halt; to stop because of some internal complication. □ *Our computer hung up right in the middle of printing the report.* **2.** to replace the telephone receiver after a call; to terminate a telephone call. □ *Please hang up and place your call again.*

hang up (in so's **ear)** Go to next.

hang up (on so/sth**) 1.** AND **hang up (in** so's **ear)** *Fig.* to end a telephone call by returning the receiver to the cradle while the other party is still talking. □ *I had to hang up on all that rude talk.* **2.** *Inf.* to give up on someone or something; to quit dealing with someone or something. □ *Finally, I had to hang up on Jeff. I can't depend on him for anything.*

hang with so *Sl.* to spend or waste time with someone. □ *Dave spent the afternoon hanging with Don, and neither one got anything done.*

hang-up *Inf.* a problem or concern; a fear; an obsession. □ *She's got some serious hang-ups about cats.*

hanker after so/sth AND **hanker for** so/sth *Rur.* to want someone or something; to long for someone or something. □ *I hanker after a nice big beefsteak for dinner.*

happen before so's **time** Go to before so's time.

happen (up)on so/sth Go to come (up)on so/sth.

*happy as a clam (at high tide) AND ***happy as a clam (in butter sauce); *happy as a lark; *happy as can be** contented; very happy. (*Also: **as** ~.) □ *I've been as happy as a clam since I moved to the country.* □ *I don't need much. Just somewhere to live, some work to do, and a TV to watch, and I'm happy as a clam at high tide.* □ *Matthew was happy as a lark throughout his whole vacation.*

happy as a lark Go to previous.

happy as can be Go to happy as a clam (at high tide).

a **happy camper** *Inf.* a happy person. □ *The boss came in this morning and found his hard disk trashed. He was not a happy camper.*

happy hour *Fig.* a time to drink a cocktail, starting at about 5:00 p.m. (Often bars have lower prices during happy hour.) □ *I think that Mary has been starting happy hour a little early. Before noon I think.*

a **harbinger of things to come** AND a **portent of things to come;** a **sign of things to come** a sample of the events that are to occur in the future. □ *The first cuts in our budget are a harbinger of things to come.*

harbor sth **against** so/sth to have and retain a bad feeling of some kind toward someone or something. □ *Alice does not harbor any bad feeling against the company that let her go.*

a **hard act to follow** Go to a tough act to follow.

*****hard as a rock** AND *****hard as stone** very hard. (*Also: **as** ~.) □ *This cake is as hard as a rock!*

*****hard as nails** AND *****tough as nails** *Cliché* [of someone] stern and unyielding. (*Also: **as** ~.) □ *Don't try to bargain with Liz. She's as hard as nails.*

hard as stone Go to hard as a rock.

hard at sth AND **hard at** doing sth *Fig.* working hard at something. □ *Tom's busy. He's hard at work on the lawn.*

*****hard feelings** *Fig.* feelings of resentment or anger. (*Typically: **cause** ~; **have** ~; **give** so ~.) □ *The argument caused a lot of hard feelings, but finally we got over it.*

a **hard nut to crack** AND a **tough nut to crack** *Fig.* a difficult person or problem to deal with. □ *This problem is getting me down. It's a hard nut to crack.*

hard of hearing *Fig.* [of someone] unable to hear well or partially deaf. □ *Please speak loudly. I am hard of hearing.*

hard on so *Fig.* harming someone's feelings; demanding much from someone. □ *I wish you wouldn't be so hard on me. So I make mistakes. I never said I was perfect.*

hard on so's **heels** Go to on so's heels.

hard on the heels of sth Go to on the heels of sth.

hard put (to do sth) AND **hard-pressed (to** do sth) *Fig.* able to do something only with great difficulty. □ *I get hard put like that about once a month.*

a **hard row to hoe** Go to a tough row to hoe.

hard sale Go to next.

hard sell 1. a person who requires a lot of attention or sales pressure to sell something to. □ *That last customer was a hard sell, but he finally bought the car.* **2.** AND **hard sale** the act of selling something using lots of sales pressure. (In the speech of some, the distinction between *sale* and *sell* is not observed, neutralizing the difference between ① and ②.) □ *That last deal was a hard sale, but it was worth it.*

hard sledding AND **tough sledding** *Fig.* a very difficult time. □ *It was tough sledding for sure when our crops failed that year.*

*a **hard time** AND *a **bad time;** *a **rough time** *Fig.* trouble [over something]; unnecessary difficulty. (*Typically: **have** ~; **give** so ~.) □ *Please don't give me a hard time.*

hard times Go to bad times.

hard to believe AND **hard to swallow** *Fig.* not easily believed; hardly believable. □ *Her story was hard to swallow, and it finally was proven to be a lie.*

hard to come by difficult to find or obtain. □ *There are lots of green ones, but red ones are hard to come by.*

hard to swallow Go to hard to believe.

hard to take *Fig.* difficult or painful to accept. □ *The news was hard to take, but we soon realized that it was all for the best.*

hard up (for sth) *Fig.* greatly in need of something, especially money. □ *I was so hard up, I couldn't afford to buy food.*

hard-and-fast *Fig.* rigid, especially when applied to rules, laws, or regulations. □ *The company has a hard-and-fast rule about the use of radios, even in private offices.*

harden one's **heart (against** so/sth**)** AND **harden** one's **heart (toward** so/sth**)** *Fig.* to become angry at or hostile to someone or something. □ *After many failed attempts to make friends with them, she hardened her heart toward them and actually was rude.*

harden sth **off**[†] *Fig.* to accustom a young plant to normal weather so it can be moved from a protected environment to the out-of-doors. □ *We put the plants by the open window to harden them off.*

harden oneself **to** sth *Fig.* to make oneself capable of bearing something unpleasant. □ *You will have to learn to harden yourself to tragedies like this. They happen every day in a hospital.*

hardly dry behind the ears Go to wet behind the ears.

hardly have time to breathe AND **scarcely have time to breathe** *Fig.* to be very busy. □ *This was such a busy day. I hardly had time to breathe.* □ *They made him work so hard that he scarcely had time to breathe.*

hardly have time to think so busy that one can hardly think properly; very busy. □ *I've been so busy that I hardly have time to think.*

hard-nosed *Fig.* stern and unforgiving. □ *Mr. Howe was known to be very hard-nosed, but he could really be friendly if you got to know him.*

hard-pressed (to do sth**)** Go to hard put (to do sth).

hark(en) back to sth **1.** to have originated as something; to have started out as something. (*Harken* is an older word meaning "pay heed to.") □ *Our modern breakfast cereals hark back to the porridge and gruel of our ancestors.* **2.** to remind one of something. □ *Seeing a horse and buggy in the park harks back to the time when horses drew milk wagons.* □ *Sally says it harkens back to the time when everything was delivered by horse-drawn wagons.*

harp on so/sth *Fig.* to keep talking or complaining about someone or something; to refer to someone or something again and again. □ *Stop harping on my mistakes and correct your own.*

has come and gone has already arrived and has already departed. □ *Sorry, you are too late for your appointment. The doctor has come and gone.*

sth **has legs** *Fig.* something can be stolen or "borrowed" too easily. □ *Mrs. Ferguson always locks up the supply cabinet. All those pens and pencils have legs you know.*

one **has** one's **moments** AND **it has its moments** *Fig.* something or a person has superior moments, often scattered though ordinary performances or activities. □ *She is an average singer, but she has her moments.*

hash sth **over**[†] **(with** so**)** AND **hash** sth **out**[†] **(with** so**)** *Fig.* to discuss something with someone. □ *I need to hash this matter over with you.*

hash sth **up**[†] *Sl. Fig.* to mess something up. □ *Somebody hashed my manuscript up!*

hassle so **about** sth AND **hassle** so **with** sth to harass someone about something. □ *Come on! Don't hassle me about the deadline!*

hat in hand Go to (with) hat in hand.

hatchet man *Fig.* a man who does the cruel or difficult things for someone else; someone who does someone else's dirty work. □ *He served as the president's hatchet man and ended up doing all the dirty work.*

hate so's **guts** *Fig.* to hate someone very much. □ *You may hate my guts for saying so, but I think you're getting gray hair.*

hate so/sth **like sin** *Fig.* to hate someone or something a great deal. □ *I don't want that man anywhere near me. I hate him like sin.*

hats off to so/sth *Fig.* let us salute or honor someone or something. □ *Hats off to*

211

Perry for planning the dinner and finding such a good band.

haul so **in**† *Fig.* to arrest someone; [for a police officer] to take someone to the police station. □ *The cop hauled the drunk driver in.*

haul off and do sth **1.** *Fig. Inf.* to draw back and do something, such as strike a person. □ *Max hauled off and poked Lefty in the nose.* **2.** *Rur.* to do something without a great deal of preparation. □ *The old man hauled off and bought himself a house.*

haul so **on the carpet** Go to call so on the carpet.

haul so **over the coals** Go to rake so over the coals.

haul up (some place) AND **pull up** (some place) *Fig.* to stop somewhere; to come to rest somewhere. □ *My hat blew away just as the bus pulled up to the stop.*

have oneself sth *Fig.* to get, have, or take something. □ *I'll have myself some of that coconut cream pie, if you don't mind.*

have a bad attitude *Fig.* to have a negative outlook on things; to be uncooperative. □ *Perry has a bad attitude and has nothing positive to contribute to the conversation.*

have a bad effect (on so/sth**)** to be bad for someone or something. □ *Aspirin has a bad effect on me.*

have a ball *Inf.* to have an exciting time. □ *Come on, everybody! Let's have a ball!*

have a beef with so/sth *Fig.* to have a complaint to settle with someone. □ *If you have a beef with me, you tell me, not everybody else in town!*

have a bellyful *Inf.* to have as much as one can stand. □ *I've had a bellyful of your whining. Be quiet!*

have a big mouth *Fig.* to be a gossiper; to be a person who tells secrets. □ *Mary has a big mouth. She told Bob what I was getting him for his birthday.*

have a blast *Inf.* to have a great time; to have a lot of fun. □ *The food was good,*

and we had a blast. Thanks for inviting us to the party.

Have a blimp! *Sl.* Have a good year! (A reference to the Goodyear blimp, which is famous for being at notable events.) □ *Good-bye. Have a blimp!*

have a blowout 1. [for one's car tire] to burst. □ *If you have a blowout in one tire, you should check the other tires.* **2.** *Sl.* to have a big, wild party; to enjoy oneself at a big party. □ *Mary and Bill had quite a blowout at their house Friday night.*

have a bone to pick (with so**)** *Fig.* to have a disagreement to discuss with someone; to have something to argue about with someone. □ *Hey, Bill. I've got a bone to pick with you. Where is the money you owe me?*

have a brush with sth *Fig.* to have a brief contact with something; to have an experience with something. (Especially with the law. Sometimes a *close* brush.) □ *Ann had a close brush with the law. She was nearly arrested for speeding.*

have a buzz on *Fig. Inf.* to be intoxicated. (Fixed order.) □ *Both of them had a buzz on by the end of the celebration.*

have a case (against so**)** to have much evidence that can be used against someone in court. □ *Do the police have a case against John?*

have a case of sth Go to a case of sth.

have a change of heart *Fig.* to change one's attitude or decision, usually from a negative to a positive position. □ *I had a change of heart at the last minute and gave the beggar some money.*

have a chip on one's **shoulder** Go to a chip on one's shoulder.

have a close call Go to next.

have a close shave AND **have a close call** *Fig.* to have a narrow escape from something dangerous. □ *What a close shave I had! I nearly fell off the roof when I was working there.*

have a conniption (fit) *Rur.* to get angry or hysterical. (See also have a fit) □ *I got* *so mad I thought I was going to have a conniption.*

have a corner on the market (for sth**)** Go to corner the market (on sth).

have a death wish *Fig.* to seem to be willing to take all sorts of needless risks. □ *Look at the way that guy drives. He must have some sort of a death wish.*

have a drinking problem Go to have an alcohol problem.

have a falling-out with so Go to fall out with so.

have a familiar ring (to it) *Fig.* [for a story or an explanation] to sound familiar. □ *Your excuse has a familiar ring. Have you done this before?*

have a feel for sth Go to a feel for sth.

have a few too many Go to have one too many.

have a field day *Fig.* to experience freedom from one's usual work schedule; to have a very enjoyable time. (As with children who are released from classes to take part in sports and athletic contests.) □ *The air was fresh and clear, and everyone had a field day in the park during the lunch hour.*

have a finger in the pie AND **have** one's **finger in the pie; have** one's **finger in every pie** *Fig.* to have a role in something; to be involved in something. □ *Tess wants to have a finger in the pie. She doesn't think we can do it by ourselves.*

have a fit AND **throw a fit** *Fig.* to be very angry; to show great anger. (See also have a conniption (fit).) □ *The teacher had a fit when the dog ran through the classroom.*

have a flair for sth *Fig.* to have a talent for doing something; to have a special ability in some area. □ *Alice has quite a flair for designing.*

have a foot in both camps Go to a foot in both camps.

have a free rein (with sth**)** Go to have free reign (over sth).

have a frog in one's **throat** Go to a frog in one's throat.

have a gift for (doing) sth *Fig.* to have a natural talent for doing something. □ *Tony has a gift for writing short stories.*

have a glass jaw *Fig.* to be susceptible to a knockout when struck on the head. (Said only of boxers who are frequently knocked down by a blow to the head.) □ *When the prizefighter was knocked out cold by a right to the chin in the first round, the newspapers said he had a glass jaw.*

have a good arm *Fig.* to have a strong and conditioned arm for sports, especially pitching in baseball. □ *Perry had a good arm, but he often pitched wide of the plate.*

have a good command of sth *Fig.* to know something well. □ *Jane has a good command of economic theory.*

Have a good day. Go to Have a nice day.

have a (good) head for sth *Fig.* have the mental capacity for something. □ *Jane has a good head for directions and never gets lost.*

have a good head on one's **shoulders** *Fig.* to have common sense; to be sensible and intelligent. □ *John has a good head on his shoulders and can be depended on to give good advice.*

have a (good) mind to do sth AND **have half a mind to** do sth; **have half a notion to** do sth; **be of a (good) mind to** do sth *Fig.* have an inclination to do something. (Half a mind sounds a bit agitated.) □ *She had a mind to go to college, but her folks talked her out of it.*

Have a good one. Go to Have a nice day.

have a good run AND **have a long run** *Fig.* [for some experience or activity] to last a long time. (Originally referred to a theatrical performance.) □ *We had a good run. Our marriage lasted over 60 years.* □ *The show had a long run and made millions.*

have a good thing going *Fig.* to have something of an ongoing nature arranged for one's own benefit. □ *John inherited a* fortune and doesn't have to work for a living anymore. He's got a good thing going.

have a green thumb *Fig.* to have the ability to grow plants well. □ *Just look at Mr. Simpson's garden. He has a green thumb.*

have a grudge (against so**)** Go to bear a grudge (against so).

have a hand with sth Go to a hand with sth.

have a heart *Fig.* to be compassionate; to be generous and forgiving; to have an especially compassionate heart. □ *Oh, have a heart! Give me some help!*

have a heart of gold *Cliché* to be generous, sincere, and friendly. □ *Mary is such a lovely person. She has a heart of gold.*

have a heart of stone *Fig.* to be cold and unfriendly. □ *The villain in the play had a heart of stone. He was cruel to everyone.*

have a heart-to-heart (talk) *Fig.* to have a sincere and intimate talk. □ *I had a heart-to-heart talk with my father before I went off to college.*

have a hidden talent AND **have hidden talents** *Fig.* to have talents or skills that no one knows about. □ *Wow, Perry! I didn't know you had so many hidden talents.*

have a hitch in one's **gitalong** *Rur.* to have a permanent or temporary limp. □ *Pappy's got quite a hitch in his gitalong since he broke his hip.*

have a hold on so Go to a hold on so.

have a hollow leg *Fig.* to have a great capacity or need for food or drink, usually the latter. □ *Bobby can drink more beer than I can afford. I think he has a hollow leg!*

have a hunch (that sth **is the case)** AND **have a hunch about** sth to have an idea about what did, will, or should happen; to have a feeling that something will or should happen. □ *I had a hunch that you would be here when I arrived.*

have a keen interest in sth to have a strong interest in something; to be very interested in something. □ *Tom had al-*ways had a keen interest in music, so he started a band.

have a kick to it *Fig.* to have a strong or spicy flavor; to have a high alcohol content. □ *I like that salsa. It has a kick to it.*

have a line on so/sth Go to a line on so/sth.

have a long run Go to have a good run.

have a look-see Go to a look-see.

have a lot going (for one**)** *Fig.* to have many things working to one's benefit. □ *Jane is so talented. She has a lot going for her.*

have a lot on one's **mind** *Fig.* to have many things to worry about; to be preoccupied. □ *I'm sorry that I'm so grouchy. I have a lot of troubles on my mind.*

have a lot on one's **plate** Go to have too much on one's plate.

have a low boiling point *Fig.* to anger easily. □ *Mr. Jones sure has a low boiling point. I hardly said anything, and he got angry.*

have a lump in one's **throat** Go to a lump in one's throat.

have a mental block (against sth**)** Go to a mental block (against sth).

have a mind as sharp as a steel trap *Fig.* to be very intelligent. □ *They say the professor has a mind as sharp as a steel trap, but then why can't he figure out which bus to take in the morning?*

have a mind of one's **own** *Fig.* to be very independent. □ *There is no point in telling her what to do. She has a mind of her own.*

have a near miss *Fig.* to nearly crash or collide. □ *The airplanes—flying much too close—had a near miss.*

Have a nice day. AND **Have a good day.; Have a nice one.; Have a good one.** *Cliché* an expression said when parting or saying good-bye. (This is now quite hackneyed, and many people are annoyed by it.) □ *Clerk: Thank you. Tom: Thank you. Clerk: Have a nice day.* □ *Bob: See you, man! John: Bye, Bob. Have a good one!*

Have a nice flight. Please enjoy your flight. (Said when wishing someone well on an airplane trip. Often said by airline personnel to their passengers.) □ *Clerk: Here's your ticket, sir. Have a nice flight. Fred: Thanks.*

Have a nice one. Go to Have a nice day.

have a nose for sth *Fig.* to have the ability to sense or find something, such as news, trouble, gossip, etc. □ *She really has a nose for news. She's a good reporter.*

have a one-track mind *Fig.* to think entirely or almost entirely about one subject. □ *Adolescent boys often have one-track minds. All they're interested in is the opposite sex.*

have a passion for so/sth *Fig.* to have a strong feeling of need or desire for someone, something, or some activity. □ *John has a passion for fishing, so he fishes as often as he can.*

have a penchant for doing sth *Fig.* to have a taste, desire, or inclination for doing something. □ *John has a penchant for eating fattening foods.*

have a place in sth to have a role in some plan or some activity. □ *Do I have a place in the negotiations?*

have a prayer (of doing sth**)** Go to stand a chance (of doing sth).

have a price on one's **head** Go to a price on one's head.

have a quarrel with sth to have a disagreement about something; to have a complaint about something. □ *I have no quarrel with your approach, but I think my way is just as good.*

have a rare old time *Inf.* a fine and enjoyable time at a party or something similar. □ *We had a rare old time at Tom's the other night.*

have a rough time (of it) AND **have a tough time (of it)** *Fig.* to experience a difficult period. □ *Since his wife died, Mr. Brown has been having a rough time of it.*

have a roving eye *Euph.* to be flirtatious; to be interested in having sexual relations outside of marriage. (Usually used to describe men.) □ *When they were first married, he had a roving eye.*

have a run of sth *Fig.* to have a continuous series of events. □ *The company had a run of huge sales increases over the last few years.*

have a run of bad luck *Fig.* to have bad luck repeatedly; to have bad things happen a number of times. (From gambling, but often used in other contexts.) □ *I have had a run of bad luck, and I have no more money to spend.*

have a run-in (with so/sth**)** *Fig.* to have trouble with someone or something. □ *I had a run-in with Mrs. Wilson. She's a hard case.*

Have a safe journey. Go to next.

Have a safe trip. AND **Have a safe journey.** I hope that your journey is safe.; Be careful and ensure that your journey is safe. (Said as someone is about to leave for a trip.) □ *Bill: Well, we're off for London. Sally: Have a safe trip.*

have a score to settle (with so**)** AND **have an old score to settle (with** so**)** *Fig.* to have a problem to clear up with someone; to have to get even with someone about something. □ *I have a score to settle with John since he insulted me at our party.*

have a scrape (with so/sth**)** *Fig.* to come into contact with someone or something; to have a small battle with someone or something. □ *I had a scrape with the county sheriff.*

have a screw loose AND **have a loose screw** *Inf.* to be silly or eccentric. □ *Yes, he has a screw loose somewhere. He wears a heavy jacket in the middle of summer.*

have a seat *Fig.* to sit down. (Often a polite invitation to sit down.) □ *Have a seat. I'll be with you in a minute.*

have a set-to (with so**)** *Fig.* to have an argument or fight with someone. □ *Perry and Elbert had quite a set-to over the choice of music.*

have a sinking feeling Go to a sinking feeling.

have a sinking feeling in the pit of one's **stomach** Go to a sinking feeling in the pit of one's stomach.

have a soft spot (in one's **heart) for** so/sth/animal *Fig.* to have a fondness for someone, something, or an animal. □ *I have a soft spot in my heart for Jeff. I'll always be his friend.*

have a (solid) grasp of sth Go to a (solid) grasp of sth.

have a stake in sth *Fig.* to have something at risk in something; to have a financial or other interest in something. □ *I have a stake in that company. I want it to make a profit.*

have a stroke *Fig.* to experience sudden unconsciousness or paralysis due to an interruption in the blood supply to the brain. (Also used as an exaggeration.) □ *The patient who received an artificial heart had a stroke two days after the operation.*

have a sweet tooth *Fig.* to desire to eat many sweet foods—especially candy and pastries. □ *I have a sweet tooth, and if I don't watch it, I'll really get fat.*

have a thing about so/sth **1.** *Fig.* to have a special fear or dislike of someone or something. □ *Kelly has a thing about Tim. She simply hates him.* **2.** *Fig.* to have a craving for someone or something. □ *I have a thing about Maggie. I guess I'm in love.* □ *Elaine has a thing about strawberry ice cream. She can't get enough of it.*

have a thing going (with so) AND **have something going (with** so) *Fig.* to have a romance or a love affair with someone. □ *John and Mary have a thing going.*

have a thirst for sth *Fig.* to have a craving or desire for something. □ *The tyrant had an intense thirst for power.*

have a tiger by the tail AND **have got a tiger by the tail; have a bear by the tail** *Fig.* to have become associated with something powerful and potentially dangerous; to have a very difficult problem to solve. □ *You have a tiger by the tail. You bit off more than you could chew.*

have a tough time (of it) Go to have a rough time (of it).

have (a) use for so/sth to like someone or something. (Often negative. Note the use of *any* and *no*.) □ *I don't have any use for sweet potatoes.* □ *I have no use for Harry.*

have a voice (in sth) Go to a voice (in sth).

have a way with so/sth *Fig.* to have a special and effective way of dealing with someone or something. □ *She has a way with Jeff. She can get him to do anything.* □ *Sarah has a way with flowers. She can arrange them beautifully.*

have a way with words *Fig.* to have talent in the effective or stylish use of words. (See also have the gift of gab.) □ *Ask Perry to make the announcement. He has a way with words.*

have a weakness for so/sth *Fig.* to be unable to resist someone or something; to be (figuratively) powerless against someone or something. □ *I have a weakness for chocolate.* □ *John has a weakness for Mary. I think he's in love.*

have a weight problem *Euph.* to be fat; to be overweight. □ *He had a weight problem when he was a teenager, but he slimmed down once he started exercising.*

have a whale of a time *Fig.* to have an exciting or fun time; to have a big time. (Whale = big.) □ *We had a whale of a time at Sally's birthday party.*

have a word with so **(about** sth**)** Go to a word with so (about sth).

have a yellow belly AND **have a yellow streak down** one's **back** *Fig.* to be cowardly. □ *Tex has a yellow streak down his back a mile wide. He's afraid to cross the street!*

have a yellow streak down one's **back** Go to previous.

have so/sth **about** AND **have** so/sth **around** to have someone or something nearby habitually. □ *I really don't want to have all those people about all the time.*

have sth **against** so/sth AND **have nothing against** so/sth; **not have anything against** so/sth *Fig.* to have a reason to dislike someone or something; to have no reason to dislike someone or something. □ *Do you have something against me?* □ *I have nothing against chocolate ice cream.*

have all one's **marbles** *Inf.* to have all one's mental faculties; to be mentally sound. (Very often with a negative or said to convey doubt.) □ *I don't think he has all his marbles.*

have all the answers AND **know all the answers** to seem to know everything. (Sarcastic. Used also in irony when someone's answers or suggestions are wrong.) □ *You always have all the answers. Too bad they are usually wrong.*

have (all) the makings of sth *Fig.* to possess the qualities that are needed for something. □ *The young boy had the makings of a fine baseball player.*

have all the time in the world *Fig.* to have a very large amount of time. □ *Don't worry. I can wait. I have all the time in the world.*

have an accident *Fig. Euph.* to lose control of the bowels or the bladder. (Usually said of a young child.) □ *Mother asked Billy to go to the bathroom before they left so that he wouldn't have an accident in the car.*

have an ace up one's **sleeve** Go to have sth up one's sleeve.

have an affair (with so**)** *Fig.* to have a love affair with someone. □ *When I was 20, I had an affair with a rock star and really made a fool of myself.*

have an alcohol problem AND **have a drinking problem** *Euph.* to be a drunkard. □ *He has an alcohol problem. It got so bad that he almost lost his job.*

have an appetite for sth *Fig.* to have a desire to have, see, hear, etc. something. □ *Bobby has a big appetite for sports and activity.*

have an ax(e) to grind (with so**)** *Fig.* to have a problem to discuss or settle with someone; to have a complaint against someone. □ *I need to talk with Chuck. I have an axe to grind with him.*

have an ear for sth *Fig.* to have the ability to learn music or languages. □ *Bill doesn't have an ear for music. He can't carry a tune.*

have an ear to the ground Go to keep an ear to the ground.

have an easy time of it *Fig.* to have an experience with something that is less difficult or severe than others have experienced. □ *We were given a hard assignment, but Fred had an easy time of it.*

have an eye for so/sth *Fig.* to have a taste or an inclination for someone or something. □ *Bob has an eye for beauty.*

have an eye on so/sth Go to keep an eye on so/sth.

have an eye out (for so/sth**)** Go to keep an eye out (for so/sth).

have an impact on so/sth *Fig.* to leave an impression on someone or something. □ *The sharp change in interest rates had an impact on the housing market.*

have an in (with so**)** Go to an in (with so).

have an inkling (about so/sth**)** Go to an inkling (about so/sth).

have an itch for sth Go to an itch for sth.

have an itchy palm Go to an itchy palm.

have so **around (for** sth**)** *Fig.* to have someone come for a visit, tea, dinner, etc. □ *We really should have the Wilsons around for an evening of bridge.*

have arrived *Fig.* to reach a position of power, authority, or prominence. □ *Jane saw her picture on the cover of the magazine and felt that she had finally arrived.*

have at so *Fig.* to go at someone; to attack someone. □ *The boys had at the gang members and gave them a beating.*

have so **at a disadvantage** Go to at a disadvantage.

have sth **at** one's **fingertips** AND **have** sth **at hand** *Fig.* to have something within (one's) easy reach. □ *I have a dictionary at my fingertips.* □ *I try to have everything I need at hand.*

have sth **at hand** Go to previous.

Have at it. *Fig.* Start doing it.; Start eating your food. □ *John: Here's your hamburger. Have at it. Jane: Thanks. Where's the mustard?* □ *John: Did you notice? The driveway needs sweeping. Jane: Here's the broom. Have at it.*

have one's **back against the wall** *Fig.* to be pressed into an (figuratively) awkward position. □ *I need to borrow a few hundred dollars. The loan company has my back against the wall.*

have back (at so**)** Go to back (at so).

have one's **back to the wall** *Fig.* to be in a defensive position. □ *He'll have to give in. He has his back to the wall.*

have bags under one's **eyes** to have puffs of flesh beneath each of one's eyes. □ *I know I'm not getting enough sleep, because I have bags under my eyes.*

have bats in one's **belfry** *Inf.* to be crazy. □ *You must really have bats in your belfry if you think I'll put up with that kind of stuff.*

have (some) bearing on sth *Fig.* to have relevance to something. (*Some* can include *no* and *any* in the negative.) □ *I know something that has some bearing on the issue you are discussing.* □ *What bearing does John's decision have on the situation?*

have been around (the block) *Fig.* to be experienced in life, often sexually experienced. □ *Ask Sally about how the government works. She's been around the state capital for years.*

have been had Go to been had.

have been to hell and back *Fig.* to have survived a great deal of trouble. □ *After a day of shopping, I feel like I have been to hell and back.*

have so's **best interest(s) at heart** *Fig.* to make decisions based on someone's best interests. □ *I know she was only doing what would benefit her, but she said she had my best interests at heart.*

have bigger fish to fry AND **have other fish to fry; have more important fish to fry** *Fig.* to have other things to do; to have more important things to do. □ *I*

won't waste time on your question. I have bigger fish to fry.

have (so's**) blood on** one's **hands** *Fig.* to be responsible for someone's death; to be guilty of causing someone's death. □ *The murderer had the late king's blood on his hands.*

have broad shoulders *Fig.* to have the ability to cope with unpleasant responsibilities; to have the ability to accept criticism or rebuke. □ *No need to apologize to me. I can take it. I have broad shoulders.*

have one's **cake and eat it too** AND **eat** one's **cake and have it too** *Cliché* to have in one's possession something and be able to use or exploit it; to have it both ways. (Usually stated in the negative.) □ *Don't buy a car if you want to walk and stay healthy. You can't eat your cake and have it too.*

have carnal knowledge of so *Euph.* to have had sex with someone. (Formal or jocular.) □ *He had never before had carnal knowledge of a woman.*

have cause to do sth to have a justifiable reason to do something. □ *Do you have cause to think that Mary took your money?*

have sth **cinched** *Fig.* to have something settled; to have the results of some act ensured. □ *Don't worry. I've got it cinched.*

have clean hands *Fig.* to be guiltless. (As if a guilty person would have dirty or bloody hands.) □ *The police took him in, but let him go after questioning because he had clean hands.*

have come a long way *Fig.* to have accomplished much; to have advanced much. □ *Tom has come a long way in his career in a short time.*

have so/sth **cornered 1.** to have someone or something trapped, as in a corner. □ *We had the wild cat cornered, but it jumped over the wall and got away.* **2.** *Fig.* to have someone or something located and under control. (Fig. on ①.) □ *I think I have the part you need cornered in a warehouse in Indiana. We'll order it.*

have so **dead to rights** *Fig.* to have caught someone red-handed; to have irrefutable

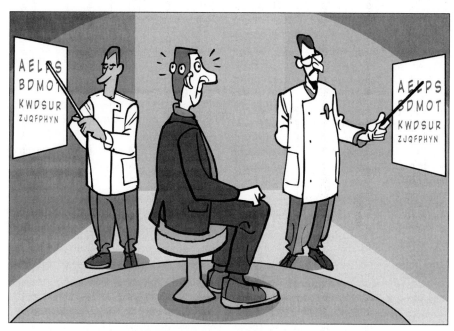

have eyes in the back of one's head

evidence about someone's misdeed. □ *We have you dead to rights on this one.*

have designs on so/sth *Fig.* to have plans to exploit or somehow take advantage of someone or something. □ *Mrs. Brown has designs on my apple tree. I think she's going to cut off the part that hangs over her fence.*

have dibs on sth *Fig.* to reserve something for oneself; to claim something for oneself. (Often said by children.) □ *John has dibs on the last piece again. It isn't fair.*

have sth **doing** AND **have** sth **on** *Fig.* to have plans for a particular period of time. (*Something* includes "anything." Fixed order.) □ *Bob: Are you busy Saturday night? Bill: Yes, I've got something doing.* □ *I don't have anything doing Sunday night.*

have sth **down pat** Go to down pat.

have sth **down to a T** *Fig.* to have something mastered. □ *I can do it. I have it down to a T.*

have one's **druthers** Go to have one's rathers.

have egg on one's **face** *Fig.* to be embarrassed by something one has done. (As if one went out in public with a dirty face.) □ *I was completely wrong, and now I have egg on my face.*

have enough and some to spare *Fig.* plenty. □ *Mary: Can I borrow a cup of milk? Tom: Don't worry about borrowing. Take it. I have enough and some to spare.*

have enough (sth) **to go around** *Fig.* to have enough of something to allow everyone present to have a share. □ *I don't think I have enough mashed potatoes to go around.* □ *Here are the reports. There's just enough to go around, so only take one.*

have so's **eye** *Fig.* [for someone] to establish and hold eye contact with someone. □ *When Tom at last had her eye, he smiled at her.*

have eyes in the back of one's **head** *Fig.* to seem to be able to sense what is going on behind or outside of one's field of vision. □ *My teacher has eyes in the back of her head.*

have faith in so to believe someone; to trust someone to do or be what is claimed. □ *We have faith in you and know you can do the job well.*

have feet of clay *Fig.* [for a strong person] to have a defect of character. □ *Sally was popular and successful. She was nearly 50 before she learned that she, too, had feet of clay.*

have one's **feet on the ground** Go to keep one's feet on the ground.

have one's **fill of** so/sth Go to one's fill of so/sth.

have one's **finger in too many pies** *Fig.* to be involved in too many things; to have too many tasks going to be able to do any of them well. (See also have a finger in the pie.) □ *She never gets anything done because she has her finger in too many pies.*

have one's **finger on the pulse of** sth Go to keep one's finger on the pulse of sth.

have one's **finger(s) in the till** Go to have one's hand in the till.

have sth **for** a meal to serve or eat something at a particular meal (such as breakfast, lunch, dinner, supper, etc.). □ *We had eggs for breakfast.*

have so **for breakfast** Go to eat so for breakfast.

have forty winks Go to catch forty winks.

have free reign (over sth**)** AND **have a free rein (with** sth**)** to have complete control. (This *free reign* was probably originally *free reins* as with a horse's reins, but since *reign* [= rule or control] is possible, both are listed. *Absolute reign* would be unambiguous.) □ *Will you agree to be in charge of the celebration if we let you have free reign?*

have friends in high places *Fig.* to have influential and powerful friends. □ *You can't put me in jail! I have friends in high places! Do you know who you are dealing with?*

have sth **going (for** oneself**)** *Fig.* [for someone] to have a beneficial scheme or op-

eration going. □ *John really has something going for himself. He's a travel agent, and he gets to travel everywhere for free.* □ *I wish I could have something like that going.*

have (got) a glow on *Fig. Inf.* to be intoxicated; to be tipsy. (Fixed order.) □ *Since you already have quite a glow on, I guess you won't want another drink.*

have (got) a load on *Sl.* to be intoxicated. □ *Fred has a load on and is finished drinking for the evening.*

have (got) one's **ass in a sling** *Sl.* to be dejected or hurt; to be pouting. (Caution with *ass.*) □ *So you didn't get a perfect score! Why do you have your ass in a sling?*

have (got) sth **coming (to** one**)** *Fig.* to deserve punishment (for something). □ *That's it, Bill. Now you've got it coming!*

have (got) it made *Fig.* to have succeeded; to be set for life. □ *I have a good job and a nice little family. I have it made.*

have (got) one's **mind in the gutter** *Inf.* tending to think of or say things that are obscene. □ *Why do you tell so many dirty jokes? Do you always have your mind in the gutter?*

have (got) to hand it to so *Fig.* to give someone credit [for something]. (Includes an expression of obligation, such as *must, got to, have to,* etc.) □ *You've really got to hand it to Jane. She has done a fine job.*

have (got) what it takes *Fig.* to have the skills, power, intelligence, etc. to do something. □ *I guess I don't have what it takes to be a composer.*

have growing pains 1. [for a child] to have pains—which are attributed to growth—in the muscles and joints. □ *The old doctor said that all Mary had were growing pains and that nothing was really wrong.* **2.** *Fig.* [for an organization] to have difficulties in its early stages of growth. (Fig. on ①.) □ *The banker apologized for losing my check and said the bank was having growing pains.*

have had it (up to here) AND **have just about had it** *Fig.* to have reached the end of one's endurance or tolerance. (When used with *up to here*, can be accompanied by a gesture, such as the hand held at the neck.) □ *Okay, I've just about had it. You kids go to bed this instant.* □ *We've all had it up to here with you, John. Get out!*

have had its day *Fig.* to be no longer useful or successful. □ *Some people think that the fountain pen has had its day, but others prefer it to other kinds of pens.*

have half a mind to do sth Go to have a (good) mind to do sth.

have half a notion to do sth Go to have a (good) mind to do sth.

have one's **hand in** sth *Fig.* to exercise control over something; to play an identifiable role in doing something. □ *She always has to have her hand in everything.*

have one's **hand in the till** AND **have** one's **finger(s) in the till** *Fig.* to regularly or occasionally steal money from one's employer. □ *Sally was outraged when she found that one of her sales clerks had his fingers in the till.*

have one's **hands full (with** so/sth) *Fig.* to be busy or totally occupied with someone or something. □ *I have my hands full with my three children.*

have one's **hands tied** *Fig.* to be prevented from doing something. (As if one's hands were made immobile.) □ *I can't help you. I was told not to, so I have my hands tied.*

have sth **hanging over** one's **head** *Fig.* to have something bothering or worrying one; to have a deadline worrying one. □ *I have a history paper that is hanging over my head.*

have one's **head in the clouds** *Fig.* to be unaware of what is going on from fantasies or daydreams. □ *She walks around all day with her head in the clouds. She must be in love.*

have one's **head in the sand** Go to bury one's head in the sand.

have so's **head on a platter** *Fig.* have someone punished severely and thoroughly. (This is a reference to Salome's demand that Herod Antipas deliver the head of John the Baptist to her on a platter.) □ *I'm so mad it him! I'll have his head on a platter!*

have one's **head screwed on right** Go to next.

have one's **head screwed on straight** AND **have** one's **head screwed on right;** **have** one's **head screwed on tight** *Fig.* to be alert and thinking clearly. (See also One would forget one's head if it wasn't screwed on.) □ *I just got up. I don't have my head screwed on straight yet.*

have one's **head screwed on tight** Go to previous.

have one's **heart (dead) set against** sth *Fig.* to be totally against something; to be opposed to something. □ *Jane has her heart dead set against going to Australia.*

have one's **heart go out to** so *Fig.* to have compassion for someone. □ *To give generously to charity shows that one's heart goes out to those who are suffering.*

have one's **heart in** one's **mouth** *Fig.* to feel strongly emotional about someone or something. (See also one's heart is in one's mouth.) □ *I had my heart in my mouth when I heard the national anthem.*

have one's **heart in the right place** *Fig.* to have good intentions, even if there are bad results. □ *Good old Tom. His gifts are always tacky, but his heart's in the right place.*

have one's **heart on** one's **sleeve** Go to wear one's heart on one's sleeve.

have one's **heart set on** sth AND **set** one's **heart on** sth *Fig.* to be desiring and expecting something. □ *Bob will be disappointed. He had his heart set on going to college this year.*

have one's **heart stand still** *Fig.* an expression said when one's heart (figuratively) stops beating because one is shocked or feeling strong emotions. □ *I had my heart stand still once when I was overcome with joy.*

have hell to pay Go to have the devil to pay.

have so's hide *Fig.* to punish someone severely. □ *The sheriff swore he'd have the outlaw's hide.*

have (high) hopes of sth *Fig.* to be expecting something. □ *We have high hopes that John and Mary will have a girl.*

Have I got something for you! *Inf.* I have something really exciting for you! (Said earnestly, before saying or showing something surprising or exciting.) □ *Have I got something for you! Wait'll you hear about it!*

Have I made myself clear? Do you understand exactly what I am telling you? (Indicates anger or dominance.) □ *I don't intend to warn you again. Have I made myself clear?*

have so in to call or invite someone into one's home. (Fixed order.) □ *We had friends in for bridge last night.*

have sth **in common (with** so/sth**)** [for groups of people or things] to resemble one another in specific ways. □ *Bill and Bob both have red hair. They have that in common with each other.*

have so in one's **corner** *Fig.* to have someone supporting one's position or goals. (Originally from boxing.) □ *As long as I have Mr. Howe in my corner, I feel confident about what I have to say.*

have sth **in hand** Go to in hand.

have so/sth **in** one's **hands 1.** to hold someone or something in one's hands. (*Have* can be replaced with *leave* or *put*.) □ *I have the tools you need in my hands, ready to give them to you when you need them.* **2.** *Fig.* to have control of or responsibility for someone or something. (Fig. on ①. *Have* can be replaced with *leave* or *put*.) □ *You have the whole project in your hands.*

have so/sth **in mind** *Fig.* to be thinking of someone or something as a candidate for something. □ *I have something in mind for the living-room carpeting.*

have so in one's **pocket** AND **have so in the palm of** one's **hand** *Fig.* to have complete control over someone. □ *John will do just what I tell him. I've got him and his brother in my pocket.*

have so/sth **in** one's **sights 1.** to have one's gun aimed at someone or something. □ *The sniper had the soldier in his sights.* **2.** *Fig.* to consider someone or something one's goal or conquest. (Fig. on ①.) □ *I've had Sally in my sights for years. I intend to marry her.*

have so in one's **spell** AND **have so under** one's **spell** *Fig.* to have enchanted or captivated the attention of someone. □ *Ken has Karen under his spell.*

have sth **in stock** *Fig.* to have merchandise available and ready for sale. □ *Do you have extra large sizes in stock?*

have sth **in store (for** so**)** *Fig.* to have something planned for one's future. □ *Tom has a large inheritance in store for him when his uncle dies.*

have sth **in the bag** Go to in the bag.

have so in the palm of one's **hand** Go to **have so in** one's **pocket**.

have so/sth **in tow** AND **with** so/sth **in tow** *Fig.* to lead, pull, or tow someone or something around. □ *Mrs. Smith has her son in tow, and they both look hungry.*

have intimate relations with so *Euph.* to have sex with someone. □ *I understand that Jim once had intimate relations with Sarah.*

have it (all) over so/sth **(in** sth**)** *Fig.* to be much better than someone or something. □ *This cake has it all over that one.*

have it all together AND **have got it all together** *Inf.* to be mentally and physically organized; to be of sound mind. □ *Try me again later when I have it all together.*

have it bad *Fig.* to have a serious need for something. (The *it* is the need, and the need is often romantic.) □ *He has it bad for that dame. I don't know why. She's a bubble head.*

have it both ways *Fig.* to have both of two incompatible things. □ *John wants the security of marriage and the freedom of being single. He wants to have it both ways.*

have it in for so *Fig.* to be mad at someone; to wish to harm someone. □ *Jane seems to have it in for Jerry. I don't know why.*

have it in one **(to** do sth) *Fig.* to have the motivation or inspiration to do something. □ *She just doesn't have it in her to go back home.*

have it made in the shade AND **have got it made in the shade** *Sl.* to have succeeded; to be set for life. □ *Sarah's got it made in the shade with her huge inheritance.*

Have it your way. It will be done your way.; You will get your way. (Usually shows irritation on the part of the speaker.) □ *Tom: I would like to do this room in blue. Sue: I prefer yellow. I really do. Tom: Okay. Have it your way.*

have just about had it Go to have had it (up to here).

have kittens to get extremely upset. □ *My mother pretty near had kittens when she found out I got fired.*

have one's **luck run out** *Fig.* for one's good luck to stop; for one's good fortune to come to an end. □ *I hate to have my luck run out just when I need it.*

have sth **made** to hire someone to make something. □ *Isn't it a lovely coat? I had to have it made because I couldn't find one I liked in a store.*

have mixed feelings (about so/sth) Go to mixed feelings (about so/sth).

have more important fish to fry Go to have bigger fish to fry.

have more luck than sense *Fig.* to be lucky but not intelligent. □ *Jane went driving out into Death Valley without any water. She survived—she has more luck than sense.*

have no business doing sth *Fig.* to be wrong to do something; to be extremely unwise to do something. □ *You have no business bursting in on me like that!*

have no staying power to lack endurance; not to be able to last. □ *Sally can swim fast for a short distance, but she has no staying power.*

have no stomach for sth Go to not have the stomach for sth.

have no truck with sth *Rur.* to have nothing to do with something. □ *We only show good, wholesome movies at this theater. We have no truck with most of that Hollywood trash.*

have no use for so/sth Go to have (a) use for so/sth.

have none of sth to tolerate or endure no amount of something. □ *I'll have none of your talk about quitting school.*

have one's **nose in a book** *Fig.* to be reading a book; to read books all the time. □ *His nose is always in a book. He never gets any exercise.*

have one's **nose in the air** *Fig.* to be conceited or aloof. □ *Mary always seems to have her nose in the air.*

have one's **nose out of joint** Go to get one's nose out of joint.

have not lived until one **has** done sth *Fig.* [one] has not experienced life at its best until one has done something. (An exaggeration.) □ *You haven't lived until you've tasted Creamy Crisp Chicken!*

have nothing against so/sth Go to have sth against so/sth.

have nothing doing (at some time) AND **have nothing on (**at some time) not to have any appointments or plans for a particular time. □ *Sure, I'll come over and watch the Bears. I have nothing doing now.*

have nothing on so *Fig.* to lack any advantage over someone. □ *Roger has nothing on me when it comes to basketball.*

have nothing on so/sth *Fig.* to have no information about someone or something. (See also have nothing on so.) □ *Fred said that the library has nothing on the topic of my paper.*

have nothing on (at some time) Go to have nothing doing (at some time).

have nothing to do with so/sth AND **not have anything to do with** so/sth to prefer not to associate or be associated with someone or something. □ *I don't like*

Mike, so I won't have anything to do with the books he writes.

have so's **number** AND **(have) got** so's **number** *Fig.* to have knowledge of what appeals to or irritates someone. □ *Of course they know how to push your buttons. They've got your number for sure!*

have sth **on** so/sth Go to on so/sth.

have sth **on file** to have a written record of something in storage. □ *I'm sure I have your letter on file. I'll check again.*

have sth **on good authority** *Fig.* to have heard something from a dependable source. □ *I have it on good authority that Peach Computers is recalling all its operating systems.*

have so/sth **on** one's **hands** to be burdened with someone or something. □ *I run a record store. I sometimes have a large number of unwanted records on my hands.*

have so/sth **on** one's **mind** AND **have** so/sth **on the brain** (More informal with *brain.*) to think often about someone or something; to be obsessed with someone or something. □ *John has Mary on his mind every minute.* □ *Karen has Ken on the brain.*

have sth **on** one('s **person)** to carry something about with one. □ *Do you have any money on your person?*

have sth **on the ball** *Inf.* to have a particular amount of smartness or cleverness. □ *I think I'd do better in school if I had more on the ball. I learn slowly.*

have so/sth **on the brain** Go to have so/sth on one's mind.

have so **on the string** *Fig.* to have someone waiting for a decision. □ *Sally has John on the string. He has asked her to marry him, but she hasn't replied yet.*

have sth **on the tip of** one's **tongue** Go to on the tip of one's tongue.

have one foot in the grave *Fig.* to be almost dead. □ *I was so sick, I felt as if I had one foot in the grave.*

have one in the oven *Fig.* to be pregnant with a child. □ *She's got three kids now and one in the oven.*

have one too many AND **have a few too many** *Euph.* to be drunk. □ *You'd better not drive. I think you've had a few too many.*

have only just done sth to have just now done something. □ *He has just now come out from under the anesthetic.*

have other fish to fry Go to have bigger fish to fry.

have sth **out** to have something, such as a tooth, stone, tumor, removed surgically. (Fixed order.) □ *I don't want to have my tooth out!*

have sth **out (with** so**)** to settle a disagreement or a complaint. (Fixed order.) □ *John has been mad at Mary for a week. He finally had it out with her today.*

have so **over a barrel** Go to over a barrel.

have so **over (for** sth**)** to invite someone to come to one's home, for a meal, party, visit, cards, the evening, etc. (Fixed order.) □ *We will have you over for dinner someday.*

have so **pegged as** sth Go to peg so as sth.

have one's **pick of** so/sth Go to take one's pick (of so/sth).

have pity (on so/animal**)** Go to take pity (on so/animal).

have pull with so *Fig.* to have influence with someone. (Also with *some, much, lots,* etc.) □ *Do you know anyone who has some pull with the bank president? I need a loan.*

have qualms (about so/sth**)** Go to qualms (about so/sth).

have one's **rathers** AND **have** one's **druthers** *Fig.* to have what one prefers; to have one's way. (*Druthers* is informal.) □ *If I had my rathers, we'd go out every Friday night.* □ *I suspect that if Joe had his druthers, he'd be taking Mary to the dance instead of Jill.*

have relations with so *Euph.* to have sexual relations with someone. □ *She was having relations with one of her employees, which was strictly against policy.*

have rocks in one's **head** *Inf.* to be silly or crazy. □ *I don't have rocks in my head—I'm just different.*

have one's **say** Go to one's **say**.

have second thoughts (about so/sth**)** Go to second thoughts (about so/sth).

have seen better days *Euph.* to be in bad condition. □ *My old car has seen better days, but at least it's still running.*

have several irons in the fire Go to have too many irons in the fire.

have one's **shoulder to the wheel** AND **keep** one's **shoulder to the wheel; put** one's **shoulder to the wheel** *Fig.* to do the hard work that needs to be done; to focus on getting a job done. (Fig. on the image of having one's body in a working position.) □ *You won't accomplish anything unless you put your shoulder to the wheel.*

have one's **sights set on** so/sth Go to set one's sights on so/sth.

have one's **sights trained on** sth Go to train one's sights on sth.

have so Go to have too.

have some elbow room Go to some elbow room.

have (some) time to kill *Fig.* to have extra time; to have a period of time with nothing to do. □ *Whenever you have some time to kill, call me up and we'll chat.*

have stars in one's **eyes** Go to stars in one's eyes.

have sth **stick in** one's **craw** *Fig.* to have something irritate or displease someone. □ *I don't like to have someone's words stick in my craw.*

have sticky fingers *Fig.* to have a tendency to steal. □ *The little boy had sticky fingers and was always taking his father's small change.*

have the advantage of so Go to the advantage of so.

have the blues Go to the blues.

have the cards stacked against one AND **have the deck stacked against** one *Fig.* to have one's chance at future success limited by factors over which one has no control; to have luck against one. □ *You can't get very far in life if you have the deck stacked against you.*

have the cart before the horse Go to put the cart before the horse.

have the courage of one's **convictions** *Fig.* to have enough courage and determination to carry out one's goals. □ *It's fine to have noble goals in life and to believe in great things. If you don't have the courage of your convictions, you'll never reach your goals.*

have the deck stacked against one Go to have the cards stacked against one.

have the devil to pay AND **have hell to pay** *Inf.* to have a great deal of trouble. □ *If you cheat on your income taxes, you'll have the devil to pay.* □ *I came home after three in the morning and had hell to pay.*

have the facts straight Go to get the facts straight.

have the floor Go to the floor.

have the gall to do sth *Fig.* to have sufficient arrogance to do something. □ *Only Jane has the gall to ask the boss for a second raise this month.*

have the gift of gab AND **have a gift for gab** *Fig.* to have a great facility with language; to be able to use language very effectively. (See also have **a way with words**.) □ *My brother really has the gift of gab. He can convince anyone of anything.*

have the hots for so *Fig.* to be sexually aroused by someone. □ *Perry has the hots for Julie.*

have the last word Go to the last word.

have the Midas touch *Fig.* to have the ability to be successful, especially the ability to make money easily. (From the name of a legendary king whose touch turned everything to gold.) □ *The poverty-stricken boy turned out to have the Midas touch and was a millionaire by the time he was 25.*

have the patience of a saint AND **have the patience of Job** *Fig.* to have a great deal of patience. □ *Dear Martha has the patience of a saint; she raised six children by herself.*

have the patience of Job Go to previous.

have the presence of mind to do sth *Fig.* to have the calmness and ability to act sensibly in an emergency or difficult situation. □ *The child had the presence of mind to write down the car's license-plate number.*

have the shoe on the other foot *Fig.* to experience the opposite situation (from a previous situation). □ *I used to be a student, and now I'm the teacher. Now I have the shoe on the other foot.*

have the time of one's **life** *Fig.* to have a very good time; to have the most exciting time in one's life. □ *What a great party! I had the time of my life.*

have the wherewithal (to do sth**)** Go to the wherewithal (to do sth).

have the worse of both worlds Go to the worse of both worlds.

have them rolling in the aisles Go to rolling in the aisles.

have sth **to burn** *Fig.* to have lots of something, such as money, power, food, space, cars, etc.; to have more of something than one needs. □ *Look at the way Tom buys things. You'd think he had money to burn.*

have to do with so/sth to be associated with or related to someone or something. □ *Sally's unhappiness has to do with the way you insulted her.*

have to get married *Euph.* [for a couple] to get married because the woman is pregnant. □ *They didn't have a long engagement. They had to get married, you see.*

have to go some (to do sth**)** *Fig.* to need to try very hard to accomplish something. □ *That's really great, Jean! I have to go some to do better than that!*

have to live with sth to have to endure something. □ *We don't like the carpeting*

in the living room, but since money is so tight we'll have to live with it.

have sth **to shout about** Go to sth to shout about.

have sth **to show for** sth to have tangible results from one's efforts. (The *something* is often literally *something* or *nothing.*) □ *I have nothing to show for all my hard work.*

have sth **to spare** *Fig.* to have more than enough of something. □ *Ask John for some firewood. He has firewood to spare.*

have too AND **have so** to have done something (despite anything to the contrary). (This is an emphatic way of affirming that something has happened.) □ *Mother: You haven't made your bed. Bob: I have too!* □ *I have so turned in my paper! If you don't have it, you lost it!*

have too many irons in the fire AND **have several irons in the fire** *Fig.* to be doing too many things at once. □ *Tom had too many irons in the fire and missed some important deadlines.*

have too much on one's **plate** AND **have a lot on** one's **plate** *Fig.* to be too busy; to have many burdens and problems. □ *I'm sorry, I can't help you. I just have too much on my plate right now.*

have (too much) time on one's **hands** *Fig.* to have extra time; to have time to spare. □ *Your problem is that you have too much time on your hands.*

have two left feet *Fig.* to be very awkward with one's feet. (Often refers to awkwardness at dancing.) □ *I'm sorry I can't dance better. I have two left feet.*

have two strikes against one Go to two strikes against one.

have so under a spell Go to under a spell.

have sth **under** one's **belt** Go to under one's belt.

have sth **up** one's **sleeve** AND **have an ace up** one's **sleeve** *Fig.* to have a secret or surprise plan or solution (to a problem). (Refers to cheating at cards by having a card hidden in one's sleeve.) □ *The man-*

ager has an ace up her sleeve. She'll surprise us with it later.

have one's **way with** so *Euph.* to have sexual relations with someone, possibly with that person being reluctant. □ *He invited her up to his apartment, hoping to have his way with her.*

have so/sth **(well) in hand** *Fig.* to have someone or something under control. □ *I have the child well in hand now. She won't cause you any more trouble.*

have one's **wires crossed** *Fig.* to have one's mental processes in disarray; to be confused. □ *You don't know what you are talking about. You've really got your wires crossed!*

have words (with so**) (over** so/sth**)** *Fig.* to quarrel with someone over someone or something. □ *Elaine had words with Tony over his driving habits.*

have one's **work cut out for** one *Fig.* to have a large and difficult task prepared for one. □ *They sure have their work cut out for them, and it's going to be hard.*

(Have you) been keeping busy? AND **(Have you been) keeping busy?; You been keeping busy?** *Inf.* a vague greeting asking about how someone has been occupied. □ *Sue: Hi, Fred. Have you been keeping busy? Fred: Not really. Just doing what I have to.*

(Have you) been keeping cool? AND **(Have you been) keeping cool?; You been keeping cool?** *Inf.* an inquiry about how someone is surviving very hot weather. □ *Tom: What do you think of this hot weather? Been keeping cool? Sue: No, I like this weather just as it is.*

(Have you) been keeping out of trouble? AND **(Have you been) keeping out of trouble?; You been keeping out of trouble?** *Inf.* a vague greeting asking one what one has been doing. □ *Bob: Hi, Mary. Have you been keeping out of trouble? Mary: Yeah. And you? Bob: Oh, I'm getting by.*

Haven't I seen you somewhere before? AND **Haven't we met before?** *Fig.* a polite or coy way of trying to introduce yourself to someone. □ *Bob: Hi. Haven't I seen you somewhere before? Mary: I hardly think so.*

Haven't seen you in a month of Sundays. *Rur.* Haven't seen you in a long time, such as about 30 weeks. □ *Bob: Well, Fred! Come right in! Haven't seen you in a month of Sundays! Fred: Good to see you, Uncle Bob.*

Haven't we met before? Go to Haven't I seen you somewhere before?

Having a wonderful time; wish you were here. Go to (I'm) having a wonderful time; wish you were here.

hazard a guess *Fig.* to guess. □ *If you don't know the answer, hazard a guess.*

hazard an opinion *Fig.* to give an opinion. □ *Don't feel like you have to hazard an opinion on something you know nothing about.*

a **head** AND **per head** [for] a person; [for] an individual. □ *How much do you charge per head for dinner?*

*****head and shoulders above** so/sth *Fig.* clearly superior to someone or something. (*Typically: **be** ~; **stand** ~; **tower** ~.) □ *This wine is head and shoulders above that one.* □ *John stands head and shoulders above Bob.*

head for the hills AND **take to the hills; run for the hills 1.** to flee to higher ground. □ *The river's rising. Head for the hills!* **2.** *Fig.* to depart quickly. □ *Everyone is heading for the hills because that boring Mr. Simpson is coming here again.*

head for the last roundup *Euph.* to reach the end of usefulness or of life. (Originally said of a dying cowboy.) □ *This ballpoint pen is headed for the last roundup. I have to get another one.*

head sth **off**† *Fig.* to prevent something. □ *I think I can head off the disaster if I act quickly.*

head so **off** some place *Fig.* to intercept someone. (Informal. In Old West movies, the place would be "the pass." Fixed order.) □ *I need to talk to John before he gets into the boss's office. I'll head him off at* *the pass.* □ *Wait here. I'll head him off at the corner.*

head over heels in debt *Fig.* deeply in debt. □ *I couldn't stand being head over heels in debt, so I always pay off my bills immediately.*

head South Go to go South.

*a **head start (on** so) *Fig.* an early start [at something], before someone else starts. (*Typically: **get** ~; **have** ~; **give** so ~.) □ *Bill always gets there first because he gets a head start on everybody else.*

*a **head start (on** sth) an early start on something [before someone else starts]. (*Typically: **get** ~; **have** ~; **give** so ~.) □ *I was able to get a head start on my reading during the holidays.*

head to toe Go to (from) head to toe.

head toward so/sth *Fig.* to be developing into something; to be moving toward a specific result. (The object is a thing, goal, etc.) □ *The problem will head toward a solution when you stop making the situation worse than it is.*

head sth **up**† *Fig.* to be in charge of something; to be the head of some organization. □ *I was asked to head the new committee up for the first year.*

headed for sth *Fig.* destined for something. □ *Harry is headed for real trouble.*

heads or tails *Fig.* either the face of a coin or the other side of a coin. (Often used in an act of coin tossing, where one circumstance is valid if the front of a coin appears and another circumstance is valid if the other side appears.) □ *Jim looked at Jane as he flipped the coin into the air. "Heads or tails?" he asked.*

Heads up! Raise your head and look around you carefully for information or something that you need to see or avoid. □ *Heads up! There is a car coming.*

heads will roll *Fig.* people will get into severe trouble. (Fig. on the image of executions involving beheadings.) □ *Heads will roll when the principal sees the damaged classroom.*

a **heap of** sth *Inf.* a great deal of something. □ *A teacher has to have a heap of patience as well as a lot of smarts.*

heap sth **(up)on** so/sth *Fig.* to give someone too much of something, such as homework, praise, criticism, etc. (*Upon* is formal and less commonly used than *on.*) □ *Don't heap too much praise on her. She will get conceited.*

hear a peep out of so AND **hear a peep from** so *Fig.* to get some sort of a response from someone; to hear the smallest word from someone. (Usually in the negative.) □ *I didn't know they were there. I didn't hear a peep out of them.*

hear so **out**† *Fig.* to hear all of what someone has to say. □ *Please hear me out. I have more to say.* □ *Let him talk! Hear him out! Listen to his side!*

hear the last of so/sth Go to see the last of so/sth.

hear sth **through the grapevine** Go to through the grapevine.

hearing impaired *Euph.* deaf or nearly deaf. □ *This program is closed-captioned for our hearing-impaired viewers.*

hearken to so/sth to listen to someone or something; to pay attention to someone or something. (Formal or stilted.) □ *Please hearken to me. I speak the truth.*

heart and soul *Fig.* the central core [of someone or something]. □ *Now we are getting to the heart and soul of the matter.*

one's **heart bleeds for** so *Fig.* a person has great empathy for someone. □ *I'm so sorry to hear of your troubles. My heart bleeds for you and I share your pain.*

one's **heart goes out to** so *Fig.* one feels great sympathy for someone. □ *My heart goes out to the grieving family.*

one's **heart is (dead) set against** sth *Fig.* one is totally against something. □ *Jane's heart is set against going to that restaurant ever again.*

one's **heart is in** one's **mouth** *Fig.* one feels strongly emotional (about someone or something). (See also **have** one's **heart in** one's **mouth**.) □ *"Gosh, Mary," said John, "My heart is in my mouth whenever I see you."*

one's **heart is in the right place** *Fig.* one has good intentions, even if the results are bad. □ *He is awkward, but his heart is in the right place.*

one's **heart is set on** sth *Fig.* one desires and expects something. □ *Jane's heart is set on going to London.*

one's **heart isn't in** sth *Fig.* a person isn't sincerely enthusiastic about (doing) something. □ *I would like to continue helping you with this project, but my heart isn't in it.*

one's **heart misses a beat** AND one's **heart skips a beat** *Fig.* one's heart seems to flutter as with a strong emotional reaction. □ *Whenever I'm near you, my heart skips a beat.*

one's **heart skips a beat** Go to previous.

one's **heart stands still** *Fig.* one's heart (figuratively) stops beating because of strong emotions. □ *When I first saw you, my heart stood still.*

a **heartbeat away from being** sth *Cliché* set to be the next ruler upon the final heartbeat of the current ruler. (The decisive heartbeat would be the current ruler's last heartbeat.) □ *The vice president is just a heartbeat away from being president.*

heat up *Fig.* to grow more animated or combative. (Fig. on making something hot, as with cooking food.) □ *Their argument was heating up, and I was afraid there would be fighting.*

heat sth **up**† *Fig.* to cause something to be more active or contentious. (Fig. on making something hot, as with cooking food.) □ *His comments heated up the discussion, and people began to threaten one another.*

heave in(to) sight *Fig.* to move into sight in the distance. □ *As the fog cleared, a huge ship heaved into sight.*

heave to *Fig.* to stop a sailing ship by facing it directly into the wind. □ *The captain gave the order to heave to.*

heave sth **up**† *Fig.* to vomit something up. □ *The dog heaved most of the cake up on the kitchen floor.*

Heaven forbid! Go to God forbid!

Heaven help us! *Fig.* Good grief!; That's awful. □ *He fell and broke his hip! Heaven help us! What's next?*

heaven on earth AND **paradise on earth** *Fig.* a very pleasant location, dwelling, or situation. □ *The place we went for our vacation was just heaven on earth. We loved it.*

Heavens to Betsy! *Inf.* My goodness! (A mild oath or exclamation.) □ *Heavens to Betsy! What was that noise?*

heavy going *Fig.* difficult to do, understand, or make progress with. □ *Talking to Mary is heavy going. She has nothing interesting to say.*

heavy into so/sth *Inf.* much concerned with someone or something; obsessed with someone or something. □ *Freddie was heavy into auto racing and always went to the races.*

a **heck of a** so/sth Go to a **hell of a** so/sth.

hedge one's **bets** *Fig.* to reduce one's loss on a bet or on an investment by counterbalancing the loss in some way. □ *John bought some stock and then bet Mary that the stock would go down in value in one year. He has hedged his bets perfectly. If the stock goes up, he sells it, pays off Mary, and still makes a profit. If it goes down, he reduces his loss by winning the bet he made with Mary.*

the **height of** sth **1.** *Fig.* at the most intense or forceful aspect of something. □ *At the height of his career, Tom was known around the world.* **2.** *Fig.* the most extreme kind of a rude behavior, usually arrogance. □ *Her remark was the height of arrogance.* □ *His term in office was the height of greed and corruption in this town.*

*hell AND ***the devil 1.** *Inf.* a severe scolding. (*Typically: **get** ~; **catch** ~; **give** so ~.) □ *I'm really going to give Tom hell when he gets home.* **2.** *Inf.* trouble; pain. (*Typically: **give** so ~.) □ *My arthritis is giving me hell in this weather.*

hell around *Sl.* to go around making trouble or noise. □ *Who are those kids who are out there helling around every night?*

a **hell hole** *Fig.* a terrible place. □ *This place is a hell hole! I want out of here now!*

a **hell of a** so/sth AND a **helluva** so/sth; a **heck of a** so/sth; **one heck of a** so/sth; **one hell of a** so/sth **1.** *Inf.* a very bad person or thing. □ *That's a hell of a way to treat someone.* **2.** *Inf.* a very good person or thing. □ *He is one hell of a guy. We really like him.*

a **hell of a mess** *Inf.* a terrible mess or situation. □ *This is really a hell of a mess you've gotten us into.*

a **hell of a note** *Inf.* a surprising or amazing piece of news. □ *So you're just going to leave me like that? Well, that's a hell of a note!*

hell on earth *Fig.* a very unpleasant situation, as if one were in hell. □ *That man made my life hell on earth!*

The **hell you say!** *Fig.* Nonsense!; I don't believe it! □ *A: I won the lottery! B: The hell you say!*

hell-bent for some place or sth *Fig.* riding or driving somewhere very fast or recklessly. □ *Fred sped along, hell-bent for home, barely missing another car.*

hell-bent for leather *Inf.* moving or behaving recklessly; riding a horse fast and recklessly. □ *They took off after the horse thief, riding hell-bent for leather.*

Hellfire and damnation! *Inf.* Damn it! (An oath used to express anger or irritation.) □ *Hellfire and damnation! Turn that radio down!*

Hell's bells (and buckets of blood)! *Inf.* an exclamation of anger or surprise. □ *Bill: Well, Jane, looks like you just flunked calculus. Jane: Hell's bells and buckets of blood! What do I do now?*

a **helluva** so/sth Go to a hell of a so/sth.

help so/animal **(get) over** sth *Fig.* to aid someone or an animal to recover from something. □ *Sharon wanted to help Roger get over his illness.*

help so **through** sth AND **see** so **through** sth *Fig.* to aid someone to endure or survive an ordeal. □ *My brother saw me through the funeral and supported me when I remarried.*

Help yourself. *Fig.* Please take what you want without asking permission. □ *Sally: Can I have one of these doughnuts? Bill: Help yourself.*

*a (helping) hand *Fig.* help; physical help, especially with the hands. (*Typically: **get** ~; **need** ~; **give** so ~; **lend** ~; **lend** so ~; **offer** ~; **offer** so ~.) □ *When you feel like you need a helping hand making dinner, just let me know.*

hem and haw (around) *Inf.* to be uncertain about something; to be evasive; to say "ah" and "eh" when speaking—avoiding saying something meaningful. □ *Stop hemming and hawing around. I want an answer.*

hem so **in** Go to back so into a corner.

*hepped (up) *Sl.* to be intoxicated. (*Typically: **be** ~; **get** ~.) □ *Wally is a little too hepped up to drive home.*

the **here and now** *Fig.* the present, as opposed to the past or the future. □ *I don't care what's happening tomorrow or next week! I care about the here and now.*

here and there *Fig.* at this place and that; from place to place. □ *We find rare books in used bookstores here and there.*

Here goes nothing. *Inf.* I am beginning to do something that will fail or be poorly done. □ *Sally stood on the diving board and said, "Here goes nothing."*

Here (it) goes. *Inf.* Something is going to start.; I will start now.; I will do it now. □ *Okay, it's my turn to kick the ball. Here it goes!*

here, there, and everywhere *Fig.* everywhere; at all points. □ *Fred searched here,*

there, and everywhere, frantically looking for the lost check.

Here we go again. *Inf.* We are going to experience the same thing again.; We are going to hear about or discuss the same thing again. □ *Fred: We must continue our discussion of the Wilson project. Sue: Here we go again. Fred: What's that? Sue: Nothing.*

Here you are. Go to There you go.

Here you go. Go to There you go.

Here's looking at you. Go to Bottoms up!

Here's mud in your eye. Go to Bottoms up!

here's to so/sth an expression used as a toast to someone or something to wish someone or something well. □ *Here's to Jim and Mary! May they be very happy!* □ *Here's to money and the aldermen it can buy!*

Here's to you. Go to Bottoms up!

hew to sth *Fig.* to conform to a rule or principle. □ *Sarah refuses to hew to the company policies.*

a **hidden agenda** *Fig.* a secret plan; a concealed plan; a plan disguised as a plan with another purpose. □ *I am sure that the chairman has a hidden agenda. I never did trust him anyway.*

hide one's **face (in shame)** *Fig.* to cover one's face because of shame or embarrassment. □ *Mary was so embarrassed. She could only hide her face in shame.*

hide one's **head in the sand** Go to bury one's head in the sand.

hide one's **light under a bushel** *Fig.* to conceal one's good ideas or talents. (A biblical theme.) □ *Jane has some good ideas, but she doesn't speak very often. She hides her light under a bushel.*

hide-and-(go-)seek *Fig.* a children's game where all the players except one hide themselves and the remaining person tries to find them. □ *We played hide-and-seek, and we still haven't found Jimmy.*

high and dry *Fig.* safe; unbothered by difficulties; unscathed. (As if someone or something were safe from a flood. See also leave so high and dry.) □ *While the riot was going on down on the streets, I was high and dry in my apartment.*

***high and mighty** *Fig.* arrogant. (*Typically: **act** ~; **be** ~; **seem** ~.) □ *She always acts so high and mighty! Who does she think she is?*

***high as a kite** AND ***high as the sky 1.** very high. (*Also: **as** ~.) □ *Our pet bird got outside and flew up high as the sky.* **2.** drunk or drugged. (*Also: **as** ~.) □ *Bill drank beer until he got as high as a kite.*

high as the sky Go to previous.

high man on the totem pole *Fig.* the person at the top of the hierarchy; the person in charge of an organization. □ *I don't want to talk to a vice president. I demand to talk to the high man on the totem pole.*

high on sth *Sl.* **1.** excited or enthusiastic about something. □ *Tom is really high on the idea of going to Yellowstone this summer.* **2.** intoxicated. □ *John is acting as if he is high on something. Has he been doing drugs again?*

a **high roller** *Fig.* a gambler who bets heavily; a big spender. □ *They welcomed me at the casino because I had the same name as one of their high rollers.*

***the **high sign** *Fig.* a prearranged signal for going ahead with something. (Often refers to a hand signal or some other visual signal. *Typically: **get** ~; **give** so ~.) □ *The train's engineer got the high sign and began to move the train out of the station.*

high-pressure so **into** sth *Fig.* to urge someone forcefully to do something. □ *Here comes Jill. Watch out. She will try to high-pressure you into working on her committee.*

hightail it out of some place *Rur.* to run or ride a horse away from somewhere fast; to leave in a hurry. (Typically heard in western movies.) □ *Here comes the sheriff. We'd better hightail it out of here.*

highway robbery Go to daylight robbery.

highways and byways 1. major and minor roads. □ *The city council voted to plant new trees along all the highways and byways of the town.* **2.** *Cliché* routes and pathways, both major and minor. □ *I hope I meet you again someday on life's highways and byways.*

hind end *Rur.* the rump of someone or some creature. □ *If you say that again, I'll swat you right across the hind end.*

hinge (up)on so/sth *Fig.* to depend on someone or something; to depend on what someone or something does. (*Upon* is formal and less commonly used than *on.*) □ *The success of the project hinges upon you and how well you do your job.*

*hip to so/sth *Inf.* knowing about someone or something; adapting to someone or something. (*Typically: be ~; get ~; become ~.*) □ *The boss began to get hip to Mary and her deviousness.*

hiss at so/sth [for someone] to make a hissing sound at someone to show disapproval. □ *The audience hissed at the performer, who was not all that bad.*

hiss so **off ((of) the stage)** *Fig.* [for the audience] to hiss and drive a performer off the stage. □ *The audience, angry with the quality of the singers, tried to hiss them all off the stage.*

hissy (fit) *Rur.* a tantrum. (Often with *throw.* Probably refers to an angry, hissing cat.) □ *The boss is really mad today. It's just one hissy fit after another.*

history in the making *Fig.* history being made right at this moment. □ *This is a very important conference with an important vote to be taken. We are witnessing history in the making.*

hit so *Fig.* [of a meaning] being understood by someone. □ *I didn't understand what she was getting at until it suddenly hit me. She was asking for a ride home!*

hit a happy medium Go to strike a happy medium.

hit a home run AND **score a home run 1.** to hit a ball in baseball that allows the hitter to complete the circuit of the bases and score. □ *John hit a home run with the*

bases loaded and four points were scored. **2.** *Fig.* to do something very worthwhile; to succeed brilliantly. □ *You really hit a home run when you got the Wonder Widget Company to sign the contract.*

hit a plateau *Fig.* to reach a higher level of activity, sales, production, output, etc. and then stop and remain unchanged for a time. □ *When my sales hit a plateau, my boss gave me a pep talk.*

hit a (raw) nerve AND **touch a (raw) nerve** *Fig.* to mention a subject that will bring on a strong negative reaction. (Fig. on something that might be experienced in a dentist's chair. *Raw* = unprotected. More severe than **touch a sore spot.**) □ *When you mentioned debt, you really hit a raw nerve.*

hit a snag *Fig.* to run into an unexpected problem. □ *We've hit a snag with the building project.*

hit a sore point Go to touch a sore spot.

hit a sour note Go to strike a sour note.

hit and miss AND **hit or miss** carelessly; aimlessly; without plan or direction. □ *We handed out the free tickets hit or miss. Some people got one. Others got five or six.*

hit so **below the belt 1.** [for a boxer] to strike an opponent below the belt. (An unfair blow.) □ *The champ hit the contender below the belt, and the crowd began to boo like fury.* **2.** *Fig.* to deal someone an unfair blow. (Fig. on ①.) □ *That's not fair! You told them I was the one who ordered the wrong-size carpet. That's hitting me below the belt.*

hit bottom *Fig.* to reach the lowest or worst point. □ *Our profits have hit bottom. This is our worst year ever.*

hit one **close to home** Go to hit one where one lives.

hit so **hard** *Fig.* to affect someone's emotions strongly. (Fig. on the image of someone being struck.) □ *The investors were hit hard by the falling stock prices.*

hit home AND **strike home** *Fig.* to really make sense; [for a comment] to make a very good point. □ *The teacher's com-*

ment struck home, and the student vowed to work harder.

hit it off (with so**)** *Fig.* to quickly become good friends with someone. □ *Look how John hit it off with Mary.*

hit sth **off**[†] to begin something; to launch an event. □ *The mayor hit the fair off by giving a brief address.*

hit on so *Inf.* to flirt with someone; to make a pass at someone. □ *The women were all hitting on George, but he didn't complain.*

hit or miss Go to hit and miss.

hit pay dirt AND **strike pay dirt 1.** *Fig.* to discover something of value. (Refers to discovering valuable ore.) □ *I tried to borrow money from a lot of different people. They all said no. Then when I went to the bank, I hit pay dirt.* **2.** *Fig.* to get great riches. □ *Jane's doing well. She really hit pay dirt with her new business.*

hit so **(right) between the eyes 1.** to strike someone between the eyes. □ *The baseball hit her right between the eyes.* **2.** *Fig.* to become completely apparent; to surprise or impress someone. (Fig. on ①.) □ *Suddenly, it hit me right between the eyes. John and Mary were in love.* □ *Then—as he was talking—the exact nature of the evil plan hit me right between the eyes.*

hit (rock) bottom Go to (rock) bottom.

hit one's **stride** Go to reach one's stride.

hit the books AND **pound the books** *Inf.* to study hard. □ *I spent the weekend pounding the books.* □ *I gotta go home and hit the books. I have finals next week.*

hit the booze Go to next.

hit the bottle AND **hit the booze** *Inf.* to go on a drinking bout; to get drunk. □ *Jed's hitting the bottle again.*

hit the brakes 1. *Fig.* to activate a vehicle's brakes hard and fast. □ *I came around the curve too fast and had to hit the brakes immediately.* **2.** *Fig.* to stop [something]. □ *The project seemed to be getting nowhere so we hit the brakes before too much more money was spent.*

hit the bricks AND **hit the pavement 1.** *Inf.* to start walking; to go into the streets. □ *I have a long way to go. I'd better hit the bricks.* **2.** *Inf.* to go out on strike. □ *The workers hit the pavement on Friday and haven't been back on the job since.*

hit the (broad) side of a barn *Fig.* to hit an easy target. (Usually negative.) □ *He can't park that car! He can't hit the broad side of a barn, let alone that parking place.*

hit the bull's-eye 1. to hit the very center of a circular target. □ *The archer hit the bull's-eye three times in a row.* **2.** *Fig.* to achieve the goal perfectly. (Fig. on ①.) □ *Your idea really hit the bull's-eye. Thank you!*

hit the ceiling AND **hit the roof** *Fig.* to get very angry. □ *She really hit the ceiling when she found out what happened.*

hit the deck 1. *Fig.* to fall down; to drop down to the floor, deck, or ground. □ *I hit the deck the minute I heard the shots.* **2.** *Fig.* to get out of bed. □ *Hit the deck! Time to rise and shine!*

hit the fan *Inf.* to become publicly known; to become a scandal. (From the phrase *when the shit hit the fan.*) □ *It hit the fan, and within 10 minutes the press had spread it all over the world.*

hit the ground running *Fig.* to start the day very energetically. □ *A decade ago I had a lot more energy. I would wake up, hit the ground running, and never stop until I went to bed again.*

hit the hay AND **hit the sack** *Fig.* to go to bed. □ *I have to go home and hit the hay pretty soon.*

hit the headlines AND **make the headlines** *Fig.* to be of sufficient interest to be made into a newspaper headline. □ *The story of her discovery hit the headlines in every paper in the country.*

hit the high spots *Fig.* to do only the important, obvious, or good things. □ *I won't discuss the entire report. I'll just hit the high spots.*

hit the jackpot 1. *Fig.* to win a large amount of money gambling or in a lottery. □ *I hit the jackpot in the big contest.* **2.** *Fig.* to be exactly right; to find exactly what was sought. (Fig. on ①.) □ *I hit the jackpot when I found this little cafe on Fourth Street.*

hit the nail (right) on the head *Fig.* to do exactly the right thing; to do something in the most effective and efficient way.

hit the panic button AND **press the panic button; push the panic button** *Fig.* to panic suddenly. □ *Don't press the panic button. Relax and keep your eyes open.*

hit the pavement Go to hit the bricks.

hit the right note Go to strike the right note.

hit the road *Fig.* to depart; to begin one's journey, especially on a road trip; to leave for home. □ *We have to hit the road very early in the morning.*

hit the roof Go to hit the ceiling.

hit the sack Go to hit the hay.

hit the skids *Fig.* to decline; to decrease in value or status. □ *Jed hit the skids when he started drinking.*

hit the spot AND **ring the bell** *Inf.* to be exactly right; to be refreshing. □ *This cool drink really hits the spot.*

hit the trail *Inf.* to leave. (As if one were hiking or riding a horse.) □ *I have to hit the trail before sunset.*

hit town *Fig.* to arrive in town. □ *The minute he hit town, he checked into a hotel and took a long nap.*

hit so up† **(for sth)** *Fig.* to ask someone for a loan of money or for some other favor. □ *The tramp hit up each tourist for a dollar.*

hit (up)on sth *Fig.* to discover something. □ *She hit on a new scheme for removing the impurities from drinking water.*

hit one **where** one **lives** AND **hit** one **close to home** *Fig.* to affect one personally and intimately. □ *Her comments really hit me where I live. Her words seemed to apply directly to me.*

hit so with sth **1.** *Fig.* to give someone notice of a bill or fine. □ *The tax people hit us with a huge tax bill.* **2.** *Fig.* to present someone with shocking or surprising news. □ *He was shocked when she hit him with the news that she was leaving.*

hit-and-run *Fig.* [of] an accident where the driver of a car strikes a person or another vehicle and speeds away without admitting to the deed or stopping to help. □ *The state passed a law making any kind of hit-and-run accident a felony.*

hitch a ride Go to thumb a ride.

hither and thither Go to next.

hither, thither, and yon AND **hither and thither** everywhere; here, there, and everywhere. (Formal and archaic.) □ *The prince looked hither, thither, and yon for the beautiful woman who had lost the glass slipper.*

hitting on all cylinders Go to firing on all cylinders.

a **hive of activity** *Fig.* a location where things are very busy. □ *The hotel lobby was a hive of activity each morning.*

*****hoarse as a crow** very hoarse. (*Also: **as** ~.) □ *After shouting at the team all afternoon, the coach was as hoarse as a crow.*

hobnob with so/sth *Fig.* to associate with someone or a group, especially with those more wealthy, famous, etc. □ *Walter is spending a lot of time hobnobbing with the very rich.*

Hobson's choice *Fig.* the choice between taking what is offered and getting nothing at all. (From the name of a stable owner in the 17th century who always hired out the horse nearest the door.) □ *We didn't really want that particular hotel, but it was a case of Hobson's choice. We booked very late and there was nothing else left.*

hog wild *Inf.* wild; out of control. □ *I went hog wild at the sale and bought six new pairs of shoes.*

hoist with one's **own petard** AND **hoist by** one's **own petard** *Fig.* to be harmed or disadvantaged by an action of one's own that was meant to harm someone else; specifically, for the bomber to be blown up with the bomb. (From a line in Shakespeare's *Hamlet*, Act 3, Scene 4. *With* is original. *By* is a later form. The *petard* is a small bomb but has its origin in a word that meant "burst of intestinal gas." *Hoist* is a past tense of *hoise* = lift.) □ *She intended to murder her brother but was hoist with her own petard when she ate the poisoned food intended for him.*

hold a job down† *Fig.* to manage to retain a job. □ *He's had trouble holding down a job because of his health.*

hold a meeting *Fig.* to meet; to have a meeting (of an organization). □ *We'll have to hold a meeting to make a decision.*

hold so **accountable (for** sth) AND **hold** so **responsible (for** sth) to consider someone responsible for something; to blame something on someone. □ *I hold you accountable for John's well-being.*

hold sth **against** so *Fig.* to blame something on someone; to bear a grudge against someone; to resent someone. □ *You're holding something against me. What is it?*

hold all the aces AND **hold all the cards** *Inf.* to be in a favorable position; to be in a controlling position. (Refers to having possession of all four aces or all the high cards in a card game.) □ *How can I advance in my career when my competitor holds all the aces?* □ *If I held all the aces, I'd be able to do great things.*

hold all the cards Go to previous.

hold so/sth **at arm's length** Go to keep so/sth at arm's length.

hold so/sth **at bay** Go to at bay.

hold so's **attention** *Fig.* to keep someone's attention; to keep someone interested. □ *The mystery novel held my attention and I couldn't put it down.*

hold so **back** Go to keep so back.

hold sth **back**† Go to keep sth back†.

hold sth **back for a rainy day** Go to save (sth) for a rainy day.

hold back (on sth) to withhold something; to give or take only a limited amount. □ *Hold back on the gravy. I'm on a diet.*

hold one's **breath** *Fig.* to wait or delay until something special happens. (Usually in the negative.) □ *I expect the mail to be delivered soon, but I'm not holding my breath. It's often late.* □ *He said he would be here by now, but don't hold your breath.*

hold by sth AND **stick by** sth *Fig.* to maintain or keep a promise. □ *I hope that you will hold by our agreement.*

hold court *Fig.* to manage to make oneself the center of interest in a group of people, all of whom listen respectfully to what one has to say. □ *There is Barton, holding court in the lunchroom. Can't anybody see through this guy?*

hold so **down**† AND **keep** so **down**† *Fig.* to prevent someone from advancing. □ *Too much debt held down my company while others profited.*

hold one's **end of the bargain up**† AND **keep** one's **end of the bargain up**†; **keep** one's **side of the bargain; live up to** one's **side of the bargain; keep** one's **end of the bargain** *Fig.* to do one's part as agreed; to attend to one's responsibilities as agreed. □ *If you don't hold your end up, the whole project will fail.* □ *You can't quit now. You have to live up to your end of the bargain.* □ *Bob isn't keeping his end of the bargain, so I am going to sue him.*

hold one's **end up**† to carry one's share of the burden; to do one's share of the work. □ *You're not holding your end up. We're having to do your share of the work.*

Hold everything! *Inf.* Stop everything!; Everyone, stop! □ *"Hold everything!" cried Mary. "There's a squirrel loose in the kitchen!"*

hold so's **feet to the fire** Go to put the heat on (so).

hold one's **fire 1.** to refrain from shooting (a gun, etc.). □ *Please hold your fire until I get out of the way.* **2.** *Fig.* to postpone one's criticism or commentary. (Fig. on

①.) □ *Now, now, hold your fire until I've had a chance to explain.*

hold sth **for** so **1.** to keep something safe for someone. □ *Do you want me to hold your wallet for you while you swim?* **2.** [for a merchant] to set something aside for a purchaser who will pay for it and take delivery at a later date. □ *I will hold it for you until you can pay for it.*

hold forth (on so/sth**)** *Fig.* to speak at great length about someone or something. □ *Sadie held forth on the virtues of home cooking.*

hold good for so/sth *Fig.* [for an offer] to remain open to someone or a group. □ *Does your offer of help still hold good for us?*

hold one's **ground** Go to stand one's ground.

hold so's **hand** *Fig.* to comfort someone who is anxious or frightened. □ *You'll be all right, won't you? You don't need anyone to hold your hand, do you?*

hold one's **head above water** Go to keep one's head above water.

hold one's **head high** *Fig. Lit.* to act proud and unashamed, which may include actually holding one's head up higher. □ *You needn't be ashamed. You can hold your head high.*

hold one's **head up**† *Fig.* to be confident of the respect of other people; to hold up one's head with pride rather than bowing one's head. (A bowed head would indicate a lack of confidence.) □ *I am so embarrassed. I will never be able to hold my head up again.*

hold sth **in**† AND **keep** sth **in**†; **hold** sth **inside ((of)** one(self)**); keep** sth **inside ((of)** one(self)**)** to keep one's emotions inside oneself. □ *You really shouldn't hold those feelings inside of you.* □ *I have kept all this inside myself too long.* □ *You shouldn't hold in all that anger.*

hold sth **in abeyance** *Fig.* to stall or postpone something. □ *This is a good plan but not at this time. Let's just hold it in abeyance until things get better.*

hold so/sth **in check** Go to keep so/sth in check.

hold so **in good stead** Go to stand so in good stead.

hold so/sth **in high regard** *Fig.* to think well of someone or something. □ *All of us hold the vice president in high regard.*

hold so/sth **in low regard** *Fig.* to think poorly of someone or something. □ *I'm afraid that Hazel holds you in low regard.*

hold so/sth **in reserve** AND **keep** so/sth **in reserve** *Fig.* to hold back someone or something for future needs. □ *I am holding the frozen desserts in reserve, in case we run out of cake.*

hold sth **inside ((of)** one(self)**)** Go to hold sth in†.

Hold it! *Inf.* Stop right there! □ *Tom: Hold it! Mary: What's wrong? Tom: You almost stepped on my contact lens.*

hold one's **liquor** *Fig.* to be able to drink alcohol in quantity without ill effects. □ *I asked him to leave because he can't hold his liquor.*

hold one's **mouth the right way** *Fig.* do something very carefully under optimal conditions. □ *It was a tedious task. If I didn't hold my mouth just the right way, I wouldn't be able to do it.*

hold no brief for so/sth *Fig.* not to tolerate someone or something; to be opposed to someone or something. □ *I hold no brief for Wally and his friends.*

hold one's **nose 1.** *Fig.* to use one's fingers to keep one's nose closed to avoid a bad smell or to keep water out. **2.** *Fig.* to attempt to ignore something unpleasant, illegal, or "rotten." (Fig. on ①.) □ *He hated doing it, but he held his nose and made the announcement everyone dreaded.*

hold on *Fig.* to be patient; wait. □ *Just hold on. Everything will work out in good time.*

*a **hold on** so a strong and secure influence on someone. (*Typically: **get** ~; **have** ~; **give** so ~.) □ *The strange religion seemed to have a strong hold on its followers.*

Hold on (a minute)! AND **Hold on for a minute!; Wait (just) a minute!** *Fig.* Stop right there!; Wait a minute! (*Minute* can be replaced by *moment, second,* or other time periods.) □ *Bob: Hold on, Tom. Tom: What? Bob: I want to talk to you.*

hold on for dear life Go to hang on for dear life.

Hold on to your hat! Go to Hang on to your hat!

hold one's or **its own** *Fig.* to do as well as any other. □ *I can hold my own in a footrace any day.* □ *Our team is holding its own against the other team.*

hold out (against so/sth**)** *Fig.* to continue one's defense against someone or something. □ *We can hold out against them only a little while longer.*

hold out (for so/sth**)** *Fig.* to strive to wait for someone or something. □ *I will hold out for someone who can do the job better than the last person we interviewed.*

hold out on so to keep from telling someone (about) something; □ *Don't hold out on me. Tell me everything you know.*

hold out the olive branch *Fig.* to offer to end a dispute and be friendly; to offer reconciliation. (The olive branch is a symbol of peace and reconciliation. A biblical reference.) □ *Jill was the first to hold out the olive branch after our argument.*

hold sth **over** so('s **head)** *Fig.* to have knowledge of something about a person and to use that knowledge to control the person. (Fig. on the image of holding information like a club over a person's head, threatening to harm the person with it.) □ *So I made a mistake when I was young. Are you going to hold that over my head all my life?*

hold one's **peace** *Fig.* to remain silent. □ *Bill was unable to hold his peace any longer. "Don't do it!" he cried.*

Hold, please. Go to Hold the phone.

hold promise AND **show promise** to appear likely to succeed or do something well. □ *The new design holds promise, and I think we will approve it.* □ *Bob shows promise as a piano tuner.*

hold so **responsible (for** sth**)** Go to hold so accountable (for sth).

hold still for sth AND **stand still for** sth *Fig.* to tolerate or endure something. (Often in the negative.) □ *I won't stand still for that kind of behavior!* □ *She won't hold still for that kind of talk.*

hold sway (among a group**)** AND **hold sway (within** a group**)** [for something] to be the norm within a group. □ *We find that conservative doctrines hold sway among the senior citizens more than any other group.*

hold sway (over so/sth**)** to control someone or something. □ *Off the school grounds, the teacher's influence no longer holds sway over the students.*

hold terror for so *Fig.* [for something] to be frightening to a person. □ *The thought of flying to Rio by myself held great terror for me.*

hold the fort *Fig.* to take care of a place while someone who is usually there is gone, such as a store or one's home. (From western movies.) □ *You should open the store at eight o'clock and hold the fort until I get there at ten.*

hold the line (at so/sth**)** AND **hold the line (on** so/sth**)** *Fig.* not to exceed a certain limit regarding someone or something. □ *Having your wife on the payroll is one thing, but no one else from the family is permitted. I will hold the line at her employment only.*

hold the line (on so/sth**)** Go to previous.

Hold the line(, please). Go to next.

Hold the phone. 1. AND **Hold the wire(, please).; Hold, please.; Hold the line(, please).; Hold the phone(, please).; Please hold.** *Fig.* Please wait on the telephone and do not hang up. (A phrase in use before telephone "hold" circuitry came into wide use. *Wire* is older use.) □ *Bill: Hold the wire, please. (turning to Tom) Tom, the phone's for you. Tom: Be right there.* □ *Rachel: Do you wish to* *speak to Mr. Jones or Mr. Franklin? Henry: Jones. Rachel: Thank you. Hold the line, please.* □ *Sue: Good afternoon, Acme Motors, hold please. Bill (hanging up): That makes me so mad!* **2.** *Fig.* Wait just a minute.; Don't rush into something. (Fig. on ①.) □ *Hold the phone! Let's think about it a little longer.*

Hold the phone(, please). Go to Hold the phone.

hold the purse strings Go to control the purse strings.

Hold the wire(, please). Go to Hold the phone.

hold so **to** sth *Fig.* to make someone adhere to an agreement. □ *You promised me that you would buy six of them, and I'm going to hold you to your promise.*

hold one's **tongue** *Fig.* to refrain from speaking; to refrain from saying something unpleasant. □ *I felt like scolding her, but I held my tongue.*

hold true *Fig.* [for something] to be true; [for something] to remain true. □ *Does this rule hold true all the time?*

hold up 1. *Fig.* to endure; to last a long time. □ *I want my money back for this chair. It isn't holding up well.* **2.** AND **hold up (for** so/sth) *Fig.* to wait; to stop and wait for someone or something. □ *Hold up for Wallace. He's running hard to catch up to us.*

hold so/sth **up**[†] **1.** *Fig.* to rob someone or a group. □ *Some punk tried to hold me up.* **2.** *Fig.* to delay someone or something. □ *An accident on Main Street held up traffic for 30 minutes.*

hold so/sth **up**[†] **as an example** *Fig.* to single out someone or something as a person or thing worthy of imitation. □ *I hate to hold myself up as an example, but if you would do what I do, at least I wouldn't criticize you.*

hold so/sth **up**[†] **to ridicule** *Fig.* to ridicule someone or something. □ *They must stop holding Matt up to ridicule! Who do they think they are?*

hold so/sth **up to scorn**[†] *Fig.* to single out someone or something for repudiation. □ *The entire crowd held Randy up to scorn for his part in the riot.*

Hold your horses! AND **Hold your taters!** *Inf.* Wait! □ *Tom: Let's go! Let's go! Mary: Hold your horses.*

Hold your taters! Go to previous.

holding a gun to so's **head** *Fig.* threatening someone with severe consequences. □ *You didn't* have to *stay out all night drinking. It's not like somebody was holding a gun to your head!*

hole in one 1. an instance of hitting a golf ball from the tee to the hole in only one try. (From the game of golf.) □ *John made a hole in one yesterday.* **2.** *Fig.* an instance of succeeding the first time. □ *It worked the first time I tried it—a hole in one.*

a **hole in the wall** *Fig.* a tiny shop, room, etc. not much wider than its doorway. □ *His office is just a hole in the wall.*

hole up (some place**) 1.** to take shelter somewhere. □ *During the blizzard, we holed up in a lean-to made of branches.* **2.** to hide somewhere. □ *The police are looking for me. I need somewhere to hole up.*

holier-than-thou *Fig.* excessively pious; acting as though one is more virtuous than other people. □ *Jack always adopts a holier-than-thou attitude to other people, but people say he has been in prison.*

holler bloody murder Go to cry bloody murder.

holler uncle AND **cry uncle; say uncle** *Fig.* to admit defeat. □ *Joe kept pounding on Jim, trying to get him to holler uncle.*

Holy cow! *Inf.* Wow! □ *Give me a chance! Holy cow, don't rush me!*

holy Joe 1. *Inf.* a chaplain; a cleric; a clergyman. (Also a term of address.) □ *I went to see the holy Joe, and he was a lot of help.* □ *Old holy Joe wants to see all of us at services.* **2.** *Inf.* a very pious person. □ *Martin looks stuffy, but he's no holy Joe.*

Holy mackerel! *Inf.* Wow! □ *Holy mackerel! What's this? A new car?*

Holy moley! *Inf.* Wow! □ *Holy moley! A whole quarter!*

a **home away from home** Go to next.

one's **home away from home** AND a **home away from home** *Fig.* a place, other than one's home, where one can feel at home. □ *Please make our house your home away from home when you are in town.*

home folks *Rur.* one's family, especially one's parents. □ *It sure is good to see the home folks again.*

*home free *Fig.* safe and without problems. (Not necessarily about home or about money. *Typically: be ~; get ~.)* □ *Everyone else had a lot of trouble with the bureaucrats, but we got home free.*

home in (on so/sth**)** *Fig.* to aim directly at someone or something. □ *She came into the room and homed in on the chocolate cake.*

home on(to sth**)** *Fig.* to aim directly at something; to fix some type of receiver on a signal source. □ *The navigator homed onto the radio beam from the airport.*

honest and aboveboard AND **open and aboveboard** *Fig.* in the open; visible to the public; honest. □ *Don't keep it a secret. Let's make sure that everything is honest and aboveboard.*

Honest to God. Go to next.

Honest to goodness. AND **Honest to God.; Honest to Pete.** *Inf.* I speak the truth. □ *Did he really say that? Honest to goodness?* □ *Honest to Pete, I've been to the South Pole.*

Honest to Pete. Go to previous.

The **honeymoon is over.** The early pleasant beginning (as at the start of a marriage) has ended. □ *Okay, the honeymoon is over. It's time to settle down and do some hard work.* □ *I knew the honeymoon was over at my new job when they started yelling at me to work faster.*

honor bound (to do sth**)** bound or forced to do something in keeping with a pledge or promise. □ *I am honor bound to provide for her support.*

Honor bright. On my honor. (Said when giving a pledge or promise.) □ *Don't worry. I will do just as you ask. Honor bright.*

honor so's **check** *Fig.* to accept someone's personal check in payment of an obligation. □ *The bank didn't honor your check when I tried to deposit it. Please give me cash.*

hoodwink so **into** sth *Fig.* to deceive someone into doing something. □ *She will try to hoodwink you into driving her to the airport. Watch out.*

hoodwink so **out of** sth *Fig.* to get something away from someone by deception. □ *Spike tried to hoodwink the old lady out of all her money.*

hoof it *Inf.* to walk. □ *If nobody gives us a ride, we'll have to hoof it.* □ *She hoofed it home from the dance in her high-heeled shoes.*

hook sth **down**† *Sl.* to eat something quickly; to gobble something up. □ *Wally hooked the first hamburger down and ordered another.*

hook oneself **on** so/sth *Inf.* to become enamored of someone or something. □ *I'm afraid I've hooked myself on Alice.* □ *He hooked himself on Bach organ music.*

hook so **on** sth *Inf.* to addict someone to a drug or alcohol. □ *Careful, or you'll hook yourself on those tranquilizers.*

hook up with so **1.** *Inf.* to meet with someone. □ *Well, hello, Tom. I didn't think I'd hook up with you again so soon.* **2.** *Fig.* to join forces with someone. □ *These two competitors have hooked up together, and we now have a real problem.* **3.** *Fig.* to make a date with someone, especially a date based solely on physical attraction. □ *I hooked up with a neat guy for Saturday night.*

hooked on sth **1.** *Fig.* addicted to a drug or something similar. □ *Jenny is hooked* on cocaine. **2.** *Fig.* enthusiastic about something; supportive of something. (Fig. on ①.) □ *Bob is hooked on football. He never misses a game.*

hoot at so/sth Go to **howl at** so/sth.

hoot so **off the stage** *Fig.* [for an audience] to boo and hiss until a performer leaves the stage. □ *The rude audience hooted Carl off the stage.*

a **hop, skip, and a jump** *Fig.* a short distance. □ *Bill lives just a hop, skip, and a jump from here. We can be there in two minutes.*

Hop to it! *Inf.* Get started right now! □ *Bill: I have to get these things stacked up before I go home. Bob: Then hop to it! You won't get it done standing around here talking.*

hop sth **up**† *Sl.* to make a machine, especially a car, run extra fast or give it extra power. □ *He will take that junk heap home and hop it up.*

hope against (all) hope *Fig.* to have hope even when the situation appears to be hopeless. □ *We hope against all hope that she'll see the right thing to do and do it.*

hope for the best *Fig.* to desire the best to happen. □ *Mary is worried, but she hopes for the best.*

hopped up 1. *Sl.* intoxicated with drugs or alcohol; stimulated by drugs or alcohol. □ *The old man was hopped up again. He was addicted to opium.* **2.** *Fig.* [of an engine] made to run with greater power than it was designed to have. □ *He drives a hopped-up Ford that can beat anything on the road.* **3.** *Inf.* excited; enthusiastic. □ *What are you hopped up about now? You're certainly cheery.*

hopping mad *Fig.* very angry. □ *Joe got hopping mad when the sales clerk was rude to him.*

horn in (on so**)** *Fig.* to attempt to displace someone; to interfere with someone, especially with someone's romantic interests. □ *I'm going to ask Sally to the party. Don't you dare try to horn in on me!*

horn in (on sth**)** *Fig.* to attempt to participate in something without invitation or consent. (*Horn* is probably the nose, such as the one in **poke** one's **nose in(to** sth**)**.) □ *Are you trying to horn in on my conversation with Sally?*

horse around (with so/sth**) 1.** *Fig.* to play around roughly with someone or something, possibly abusing someone or something. □ *Stop horsing around with your little brother. Leave him alone.* **2.** *Fig.* to join someone in boisterous play; to participate in rough play with someone. □ *He's horsing around with his little brother. They are really having a good time.*

a **horse of a different color** Go to next.

a **horse of another color** AND a **horse of a different color** *Fig.* another matter altogether. □ *I was talking about trees, not bushes. Bushes are a horse of another color.*

horse sense *Fig.* common sense; practical thinking. □ *Bob is no scholar, but he has a lot of horse sense.*

hose so **down**† *Sl.* to kill someone. (Underworld. From the image of spraying someone with bullets.) □ *Mr. Big told Sam to hose Wilbur down.*

hot and bothered 1. *Fig.* excited; anxious. □ *Now don't get hot and bothered. Take it easy.* **2.** *Fig.* amorous; interested in romance or sex. □ *John gets hot and bothered whenever Mary comes into the room.*

hot and heavy *Fig.* referring to serious passion or emotions. □ *The movie had one hot and heavy scene after another. Pretty soon it got to be a joke.*

*****hot as fire** AND *****hot as hell** very hot; burning hot. (*Also: **as** ~.) □ *I'm afraid Betsy has a high fever. Her forehead is hot as fire.*

hot as hell Go to previous.

Hot damn! *Inf.* Wow!; Hooray! (Older. An exclamation of surprise and delight.) □ *Hot damn! I just won a vacation trip to Florida!*

Hot diggety (dog)! AND **Hot dog!; Hot ziggety!** *Inf.* an expression of excitement and delight. (These expressions have no meaning and no relationship to dogs or to wieners.) □ *Rachel: I got an A! Hot diggety dog! Henry: Good for you!*

Hot dog! Go to previous.

hot off the press *Fig.* freshly printed; just released by a publisher. □ *Here is a copy of the new Perry Hodder novel. It's hot off the press.*

hot on sth *Fig.* enthusiastic about something; very much interested in something; knowledgeable about something. □ *Meg's hot on animal rights at the moment.*

hot on so's **heels** Go to on so's heels.

hot on the heels of sth Go to on the heels of sth.

hot on the trail (of so/sth/animal) *Fig.* very close to finding or catching up with someone, some creature, or something. □ *I am hot on the trail of the book that I have been seeking for months.*

a **hot ticket** *Fig.* something that is really popular and attractive at the moment. □ *Singers who can dance are a hot ticket right now. Who knows what folks will like next month?*

hot under the collar *Fig.* very angry. □ *The boss was really hot under the collar when you told him you lost the contract.* □ *I get hot under the collar every time I think about it.*

Hot ziggety! Go to Hot diggety (dog)!

a **hotbed of** sth *Fig.* a nest of something; a gathering place of something. □ *This office is a hotbed of lazy people.*

hotfoot it (off to) some place *Inf.* to go somewhere as fast as possible. □ *When they heard the police sirens, the thieves hotfooted it home.*

hotfoot it out of some place *Inf.* to run away from a place. □ *Things are looking bad. I think we had better hotfoot it out of here.*

hound so/animal **down**† to pursue and capture someone or an animal. □ *I will hound the killer down if it takes me the rest of my life.*

hound so **from** some place AND **hound** so **out (of** sth/some place) to chase someone out of some place; to force someone out of something or some place. □ *The sheriff hounded Tex out of town.*

hound sth **out of** so *Fig.* to force someone to give information. □ *We are going to have to hound the information out of her.*

house moss Go to curly dirt.

a **house of cards** *Fig.* a fantasy; an imaginary scenario. (Fig. on the image of a structure built out of playing cards stacked on edge.) □ *That means that all my ideas for the future were nothing more than a house of cards.*

house of correction *Euph.* a prison. □ *He was sentenced to five years in the county's house of correction.*

a **house of ill fame** Go to next.

a **house of ill repute** AND a **house of ill fame** *Euph.* a house of prostitution. □ *The sign says "Health Club," but everyone knows it's a house of ill repute.*

*a **household name** AND *a **household word** *Fig.* well known by everyone; commonly and widely known. (*Typically: **be** ~; **become** ~; **make** sth ~.) □ *I want my invention to become a household word.* □ *Some kid named Perry Hodder has become a household name!*

a **household word** Go to previous.

hover between sth **and** sth else *Fig.* to waver between choosing one thing and another, most often life and death. □ *Uncle Jed hovered between life and death for days.*

hover over so/sth *Fig.* [for someone] to stay close to someone or something, waiting, ready to advise or interfere. □ *Please don't hover over me, watching what I am doing.*

hovering between life and death Go to caught between life and death.

How about doing sth? Would you like to do something? □ *How about going with me to a movie?*

How (a)bout that! *Inf.* Isn't that surprising! □ *A: My husband and I just celebrated our 60th anniversary. B: How about that!*

How about you? What do you think?; What is your choice? □ *Bob: How are you, Bill? Bill: I'm okay. How about you? Bob: Fine, fine. Let's do lunch sometime.* □ *Waiter: Can I take your order? Bill: I'll have the chef's salad and ice tea. Waiter (turning to Sue): How about you? Sue: I'll have the same.*

How (are) you doing? a standard greeting inquiry. (The entry without *are* is informal and usually pronounced "How ya doin'?") □ *Jane: How are you doing? Mary: I'm okay. What about you? Jane: Likewise.* □ *Sally: Sue, this is my little brother, Bill. Sue: How are you, Bill? Bill: Okay. How you doing?*

How are you getting on? *Fig.* How are you managing?; How (are) you doing? □ *Jane: Well, Mary, how are you getting on? Mary: Things are great, Jane!*

How 'bout them apples? AND **How do you like them apples?** *Rur.* What do you think of that? (Often used to express admiration, as in the first example; *'bout* is short for *about*.) □ *Tom: I got first prize! Mary: Well! How 'bout them apples?* □ *Joe got a job as a newspaper reporter. How do you like them apples?*

How come? *Fig.* How did that come about?; Why? □ *Sally: I have to go to the doctor. Mary: How come? Sally: I'm sick, silly.*

How could you (do sth)? *Fig.* How could you bring yourself to do a thing like that? (No answer is expected.) □ *Tom: Then I punched him in the nose. Rachel: Oh, how could you?*

How dare you! *Fig.* That is so rude!; What an affront! □ *A: You are really getting chubby. B: How dare you!*

How do you do. a standard inquiry and response on greeting or meeting someone. (This expression never has rising question intonation, but the first instance of its use calls for a response. Sometimes the response does, in fact, explain how one is.) □ *Sally: Hello. How do you do. Bob: How do you do.*

How do you know? *Inf.* What makes you think you are correct?; Why do you think you have enough information to make this judgment? (Contentious. The heaviest stress is on *you*.) □ *Tom: Having a baby can be quite an ordeal. Mary: How do you know? Tom: I read a lot.*

How do you like that? 1. *Fig.* an expression said when administering punishment. □ *"How do you like that?" growled Tom as he punched John in the stomach.* **2.** *Fig.* an expression said to show surprise at someone's bad or strange behavior or at some surprising event. □ *Tom (shouting at Sue): Shut up! Go away! Sue (looking at Mary, aghast): Well, how do you like that! Mary: Let's get out of here!*

How do you like them apples? Go to How 'bout them apples?

How does that grab you? AND **How's that grab you?** *Inf.* What do you think of that? (Pronounced more like *How ZAT grab ya?*) □ *Looks good, okay? How does that grab you?* □ *How's that grab you? Is it okay?*

How goes it (with you)? AND **How's it going?** *Inf.* Hello, how are you? □ *Hi, Mary. How goes it with you?*

How is so **fixed for** sth? *Fig.* Is there enough of something? □ *How are you fixed for ketchup? Do you have enough for the picnic?*

How is so **making out?** *Fig.* How is someone doing?; How is someone surviving or getting along? □ *How are you making out since your retirement?*

How many times do I have to tell you? *Inf.* a phrase admonishing someone who has forgotten instructions. □ *Mother: How many times do I have to tell you? Do your homework! Bill: Mom! I hate school!*

How should I know? AND **Don't ask me.** *Inf.* I do not know.; Why should I be expected to know? (Shows impatience or rudeness.) □ *Bill: Why is the orca called the killer whale? Mary: How should I* know? □ *Sally: Where did I leave my glasses? Tom: Don't ask me.*

How so? *Fig.* Please explain your remark. □ *A: You have to bring all the lawn furniture in. B: How so?*

how the other half lives *Fig.* how poorer people live; how richer people live. □ *Now that I am bankrupt, I am beginning to understand how the other half lives.*

howl at so/sth **1.** AND **hoot at** so/sth *Fig.* to yell out at someone or something. □ *The audience howled at the actors and upset them greatly.* **2.** *Fig.* to laugh very hard at someone or something. □ *Everyone just howled at Tom's joke.*

How's it going? Go to How goes it (with you)?

How's that (again)? Go to Say what?

How's that for sth? Isn't that a remarkable display of something? □ *Did you see that guy jump? How's that for great jumping?* □ *Did you see what she did? How's that for rudeness?*

How's the world (been) treating you? *Inf.* How are you? □ *Hi, Jane. How's the world treating you?*

How's tricks? *Inf.* a greeting inquiry. □ *Bob: Fred! How's tricks? Fred: How are you doing, Bob? Bob: Doing great!*

*a hue and cry (about sth) *Fig.* a loud public protest of opposition. (*Typically: **be** ~; **raise** ~.) □ *The city council raised a hue and cry about the mayor's proposed budget.* □ *There was a loud hue and cry when the city government tried to build houses on the playing field.*

huff and puff *Fig.* to breathe very hard; to pant as one exerts effort. □ *John came up the stairs huffing and puffing.*

hum with activity *Fig.* [for a place] to be busy with activity. □ *Our main office was humming with activity during the busy season.*

hung up (on so/sth) obsessed with someone or something; devoted to someone or something. □ *John is really hung up on Mary.*

hunger after so/sth AND **hunger for** so/sth *Fig.* to desire someone or something; to yearn for someone or something. □ *I hunger for you. I want you madly!*

*hungry as a bear AND ***hungry as a hunter** *Cliché* very hungry. (*Also: **as** ~.) □ *We'd better have a big meal ready by the time Tommy gets home; he's always hungry as a hunter after soccer practice.*

hungry as a hunter Go to previous.

hungry for sth *Fig.* desiring something other than food. □ *The orphan was hungry for the warmth of a family.*

hunker down and do sth *Fig.* to bend over one's work and get something done; to commit oneself to do work. (Fig. on squatting down.) □ *It's time you hunkered down and got your homework done.*

hunt so/sth **down**† AND **sniff** so/sth **out**† **1.** to chase and catch someone or something. □ *I don't know where Amy is, but I'll hunt her down. I'll find her.* **2.** to locate someone or something. □ *I have to hunt down a good dentist.*

hunt high and low (for so/sth) AND **look high and low (for** so/sth); **search high and low (for** so/sth) *Fig.* to look carefully in every possible place for someone or something. □ *The Smiths are searching high and low for the home of their dreams.*

hunt so/sth **up**† Go to look so/sth up†.

hunt-and-peck *Fig.* a slow "system" of typing where one searches for a certain key and then presses it. (Fig. on the image of the movement used by fowls when feeding.) □ *I can't type. I just hunt-and-peck, but I get the job done—eventually.*

hurry up and wait *Fig.* to do some things in a series fast and then have to wait a long time to do the next things in the series. (Originally military.) □ *Hurry up and wait! That's the army for you.*

hurt for so/sth Go to ache for so/sth.

hurtin' for sth *Rur.* in need of something. □ *Jim was hurtin' for a new set of tools.*

a hush fell over so/sth *Fig.* a sudden silence enveloped something or a group. □ *As the* conductor raised his arms, a hush fell over the audience.

hush money *Fig.* money paid as a bribe to persuade someone to remain silent and not reveal certain information. □ *Bob gave his younger sister hush money so that she wouldn't tell Jane that he had gone to the movies with Sue.*

hush so **up**[†] **1.** to make someone quiet. □ *Please hush the children up. I have a telephone call.* **2.** *Sl.* to kill someone. □ *The*

gang was afraid the witness would testify and wanted to hush him up.

hush sth **up**[†] *Fig.* to keep something a secret; to try to stop a rumor from spreading. □ *We just couldn't hush it up.*

Hush your mouth! *Inf.* Please be quiet. (Not very polite.) □ *I've heard enough of that talk. Hush your mouth!*

hustle and bustle *Fig.* confusion and business. □ *There is a lot of hustle and bustle in this office at the end of the fiscal year.*

I

I could eat a horse! *Fig.* I am very hungry! □ *Where's dinner? I could eat a horse!*

(I) could(n't) care less. *Inf.* It doesn't matter to me. (The *less* bears the heaviest stress in both versions. Despite the apparent contradiction, either reading of this—both the affirmative and negative—usually have the same meaning. The exception would be in a sentence where the *could* bears the heaviest stress: *I could care less, [but I don't.].*) □ *Tom: The rain is coming! The carpet will get wet! Mary: I couldn't care less.* □ *Bill: I'm going to go in there and tell off the boss! John: I could care less.*

I (do) declare! *Inf.* I am surprised to hear that! (Old-fashioned.) □ *A plane had landed right in the middle of the cornfield. The old farmer shook his head in disbelief. "I do declare!" he said over and over as he walked toward the plane.*

I don't want to wear out my welcome. *Fig.* a phrase said by a guest who doesn't want to be a burden to the host or hostess or to visit too often. □ *Bob: We had a fine time. Glad you could come to our little gathering. Hope you can come again next week. Fred: I don't want to wear out my welcome, but I'd like to come again. Bob: Good. See you next week. Bye. Fred: Bye.*

I hate to eat and run. *Cliché* an apology made by someone who must leave a social event soon after eating. □ *Bill: Well, I hate to eat and run, but it's getting late. Sue: Oh, you don't have to leave, do you? Bill: I think I really must.*

I need it yesterday. *Inf.* an answer to the question "When do you need this?" (Indicates that the need is urgent.) □ *Bob: When do you need that urgent survey? Bill: I need it yesterday.* □ *Mary: Where's the Wilson contract? Sue: Do you need it now? Mary: I need it yesterday! Where is it?*

I owe you one. *Inf.* Thank you, now I owe you a favor.; I owe you something similar in return. □ *Bob: I put the extra copy of the book on your desk. Sue: Thanks, I owe you one.*

I promise you! *Inf.* I assure you! (Compare this with Trust me! This usage has nothing to do with a promise that is to be fulfilled.) □ *Sue: I'll be there exactly when I said. Bob: Are you sure? Sue: I promise you, I'm telling the truth!*

I read you loud and clear. 1. *Fig.* a response used by someone communicating by radio stating that the hearer understands the transmission clearly. (See also **Do you read me?**) □ *Controller: This is Aurora Center, do you read me? Pilot: Yes, I read you loud and clear.* **2.** *Fig.* I understand what you are telling me. (Fig. on ①. Used in general conversation, not in radio communication.) □ *Bob: Okay. Now, do you understand exactly what I said? Mary: I read you loud and clear.*

I rest my case. 1. I have completed the presentation of my argument. (Said by a lawyer.) □ *Clearly the defendant is guilty. I rest my case.* **2.** *Fig.* What you just heard sums up my point of view. □ *Your remark just supported my position! I rest my case.*

I spoke out of turn. *Fig.* I said the wrong thing.; I should not have said what I did. (An apology.) □ *Bill: You said I was the one who did it. Mary: I'm sorry. I spoke out of turn. I was mistaken.*

I spoke too soon. *Fig.* What I had said was just now contradicted. □ *Bob: It's begin-*

ning to brighten up. I guess it won't rain after all. John: I'm glad to hear that. Bob: Whoops! I spoke too soon. I just felt a raindrop on my cheek.

(I) would if I could(, but I can't). *Fig.* I simply can't do it. □ *Jane: Can't you fix this yourself? John: I would if I could, but I can't.*

(I) wouldn't bet on it. AND **(I) wouldn't count on it.** *Fig.* I do not believe that something will happen. (Also with *that* or some specific happening.) □ *John: I'll be a vice president in a year or two. Mary: I wouldn't bet on that.*

(I) wouldn't count on it. Go to previous.

I wouldn't touch it with a ten-foot pole. *Cliché* I would not have anything to do with it under any circumstances. (Said about something you think is untrustworthy, as in the example, or in response to a remark that seems to invite a nasty reply. The British version is "I would not touch it with a barge-pole.") □ *Jill: This advertisement says I can buy land in Florida for a small investment. Do you think I should? Jane: I wouldn't touch it with a ten-foot pole.*

the **icing on the cake** *Fig.* an extra enhancement. □ *Oh, wow! A tank full of gas in my new car. That's icing on the cake!*

I'd better get on my horse. *Inf.* an expression indicating that it is time that one departed. □ *John: It's getting late. Better get on my horse. Rachel: Have a safe trip. See you tomorrow.*

I'd (just) as leave do sth I would rather do something. □ *Tom: Do you want to go to Joe's party? Jane: We can if you want to, but I'd as leave not.*

I'd (just) as soon (as) do sth *Fig.* I would prefer to do something. □ *Tom: Why don't you give Joe a call? Jane: I'd as soon as you did it.*

identify with so/animal to feel like one understands and has empathy for someone or some creature in a situation. □ *I can identify with Ginger, since we are both orphans.* □ *I can sure identify with that. I've done that too.*

if one's **a day** *Fig.* a phrase attached to an expression of someone's age. □ *She's 50 if she's a day!*

if all else fails AND **if everything else fails** if every other effort or attempt fails. □ *If all else fails, I will have to fly there and make the presentation myself.*

if everything else fails Go to previous.

if I were you an expression introducing a piece of advice. □ *John: If I were you, I'd get rid of that old car. Alice: Gee, I was just getting to like it.*

if I've told you once, I've told you a thousand times *Fig.* an expression that introduces a scolding, usually to a child. □ *"If I've told you once, I've told you a thousand times, keep out of my study!" yelled Bob.*

if one **knows what's good for** one *Fig.* one had better do what is expected of one. □ *If you know what's good for you, you'll call and apologize.*

if looks could kill a catchphrase said when someone makes a frown at someone or when someone casts a dirty look. □ *Did you see the way she looked at me? If looks could kill . . .*

if my memory serves (me correctly) *Fig.* if I have remembered it correctly . . . □ *If my memory serves me correctly, you are the cousin of my closest friend.*

if need be if necessary; if it is needed. □ *I can be there first thing in the morning if need be.*

if only [regretfully] if. □ *If only it were not so.* □ *If only he would floss, I would marry him in an instant.*

if push comes to shove Go to when push comes to shove.

If that don't beat all! AND **That beats everything!; Don't that (just) beat all!** *Rur.* That surpasses everything!; That is amazing!; That takes the cake! (The grammar error *that don't* is built into this catchphrase.) □ *Tom: The mayor is kicking the baseball team out of the city. Bill: If that don't beat all!*

if the going gets tough Go to when the going gets tough.

If you don't mind! 1. *Fig.* an expression that rebukes someone for some minor social violation. □ *When Bill accidentally sat on Mary's purse, which she had placed in the seat next to her, she said, somewhat angrily, "If you don't mind!"* **2.** a polite way of introducing a request. □ *Bill: If you don't mind, could you move a little to the left? Sally: No problem. (moving) Is that all right? Bill: Yeah. Great! Thanks!* **3.** a vague phrase answering yes to a question that asks whether one should do something. □ *Tom: Do you want me to take these dirty dishes away? Mary: If you don't mind.*

if you get my drift *Fig.* if you understand what I am saying or implying. (Akin to **get so's drift.**) □ *I've heard enough talk and seen enough inaction—if you get my drift.*

if you know what's good for you *Fig.* if you know what will be to your benefit; if you know what will keep you out of trouble. □ *Mary: I see that Jane has put a big dent in her car. Sue: You'll keep quiet about that if you know what's good for you.*

if you will if you will accept my stating it in this manner. (Perhaps a bit aloof. It is a clue to look for a hidden meaning or that a euphemism is being used.) □ *I was obliged to tend to some personal matter, if you will.*

if you'll pardon the expression *Fig.* excuse the expression I am about to say or just said. □ *This thing is—if you'll pardon the expression—loused up.*

Ignorance is bliss. *Fig.* Not knowing is better than knowing and worrying. □ *A: I never knew that the kid who mows our lawn has been in trouble with the police. B: Ignorance is bliss!*

ill at ease *Fig.* uneasy; anxious. □ *You look ill at ease. Please relax.*

I'll be a monkey's uncle! *Fig.* I am amazed! □ *A: I just won $500,000 in the lottery! B: Well, I'll be a monkey's uncle!*

I'll bite. *Inf.* Okay, I will answer your question.; Okay, I will listen to your joke or play your little guessing game. □ *John: Did you hear the joke about the used car salesman? Jane: No, I'll bite.*

I'll drink to that! *Inf.* I agree with that! (Originally used as a reply to a proposed toast.) □ *Great idea! I'll drink to that.*

I'll eat my hat. *Fig.* I will be very surprised. (Used to express strong disbelief in something.) □ *If Joe really joins the Army, I'll eat my hat.*

I'll get right on it. *Fig.* I will begin work on that immediately. □ *Bob: Please do this report immediately. Fred: I'll get right on it.*

ill will hostile feelings or intentions. □ *I hope you do not have any ill will toward me because of our argument.*

ill-disposed to doing sth *Fig.* not friendly; not favorable; opposed. □ *The police chief was ill-disposed to discussing the details of the case to the news reporters.*

ill-gotten gains *Fig.* money or other possessions acquired in a dishonest or illegal fashion. □ *Mary is enjoying her ill-gotten gains. She deceived an old lady into leaving her $5,000 in her will.*

I'm all ears. Go to I'm listening.

I'm damned if I do and damned if I don't. *Fig.* I am wrong no matter which alternative I choose. □ *I can't win. I'm damned if I do and damned if I don't.* □ *No matter whether I go or stay, I am in trouble. I'm damned if I do and damned if I don't.*

I'm gone. *Inf.* an expression said just before leaving. (See also I'm out of here.) □ *Bob: Well, that's all. I'm gone. Bill: See ya!*

I'm good. 1. I have enough, thanks. (Said to a host or server when asked if one has enough food or drink.) □ *Q: Would you like some more cheese? A: I'm good.* **2.** I'm fine.; I'm okay. (Said in response to "How are you?" or equivalent. A few decades ago, the answer would have been "I'm well." *I'm good.* = I'm virtuous.) □ *Q: How're you? A: I'm good.*

(I'm) having a wonderful time; wish you were here. *Cliché* a catchphrase that is

I'll eat my hat.

thought to be written onto postcards by people who are away on vacation. □ *John wrote on all his cards, "Having a wonderful time; wish you were here." And he really meant it too.*

I'm having the time of my life. *Fig.* I am having the best time ever. □ *Bill: Are you having a good time, Mary? Mary: Don't worry about me. I'm having the time of my life.*

I'm here to tell you *Inf.* I am happy to say; I certainly do say. □ *I'm here to tell you that you make the best fried chicken in the county, maybe the whole state!*

I'm history. *Inf.* Good-bye, I am leaving. □ *I'm history. See you tomorrow.*

I'm like you *Fig.* an expression introducing a statement of a similarity that the speaker shares with the person spoken to. □ *Mary: And what do you think about this pair? Jane: I'm like you, I like the ones with lower heels.*

I'm listening. AND **I'm all ears.** *Inf.* You have my attention, so you should talk. □

Bob: Look, old pal. I want to talk to you about something. Tom: I'm listening. □ *Bill: I guess I owe you an apology. Jane: I'm all ears.*

I'm not kidding. *Fig.* I am telling the truth.; I am not trying to fool you. □ *John (gesturing): The fish I caught was this big! Jane: I don't believe it! John: I'm not kidding!*

I'm off. *Fig.* an expression said by someone who is just leaving. □ *Sue: Well, it's been a great party. Good-bye. Got to go. Mary: I'm off too. Bye.*

I'm out of here. AND **I'm outa here.** *Inf.* I am leaving this minute. □ *In three minutes I'm outa here.*

I'm with you. *Fig.* I agree with you.; I will join with you in doing what you suggest. (With a stress on both *I* and *you*.) □ *Sally: I think this old bridge is sort of dangerous. Jane: I'm with you. Let's go back another way.*

Imagine that! Go to Fancy that!

immediate occupancy [of an apartment or house] ready to be moved into at this moment. □ *This house is for immediate occupancy. You can move in today if you want.*

immersed in thought Go to lost in thought.

*__in a bad mood__ sad; depressed; grouchy; with low spirits. (*Typically: **be** ~; **get** ~; **put** so ~.) □ *Please try to cheer me up. I'm in a bad mood.*

in a bad way Go to in bad shape.

in a big way *Inf.* very much; intensely. □ *I'm really interested in her in a big way.*

*__in a bind__ AND *__in a jam__ *Fig.* in a tight or difficult situation; stuck on a problem. (*Typically: **be** ~; **get** [**into**] ~; **find** oneself ~.) □ *I'm in a bind. I owe a lot of money.*

in a (blue) funk *Inf.* sad; depressed. □ *Don't get in a funk about your job. Things'll get better.*

*__in a body__ *Fig.* as a group of people; as a group; in a group. (*Typically: **arrive** some place ~; **go** ~; **leave** ~; **reach** some place ~; **travel** ~.) □ *Members of the audience arrived in a body, and we ended up with a full house after all.*

in a class by oneself or **itself** *Fig.* unique; not categorizable with similar things. □ *This car is in a class by itself. There's nothing else like it out there.*

in a cold sweat *Inf.* in a state of fear. □ *He stood there in a cold sweat, waiting for something bad to happen.*

in a (constant) state of flux Go to in flux.

in a coon's age AND **in a month of Sundays** *Rur.* in a very long time. (The *coon* is a *raccoon*.) □ *I haven't had a piece of apple pie this good in a coon's age.*

in a dead heat *Fig.* [finishing a race] at exactly the same time; tied. □ *The two horses finished the race in a dead heat.*

in a delicate condition *Euph.* pregnant. □ *Are you sure you're up for this hike? I know you're in a delicate condition.*

in a dither confused; nervous; bothered. □ *Don't get yourself in a dither!*

*__in a family way__ AND *__in the family way__ *Fig.* pregnant. (*Typically: **be** ~; **get** so ~.) □ *I've heard that Mrs. Smith is in a family way.*

*__in a fix__ *Fig.* in a bad situation. (*Typically: **be** ~; **get** [**into**] ~.) □ *I really got myself into a fix. I owe a lot of money on my taxes.*

in a flash *Fig.* quickly; immediately. □ *It happened in a flash. Suddenly my wallet was gone.*

in a fog AND **in a haze** *Fig.* dazed; not paying attention to what is going on around one; not alert. □ *When I get up, I'm in a fog for an hour.* □ *After surgery, I was in a haze until the anesthetic wore off.*

in a good light *Fig.* [displayed or presented] in a favorable aspect. □ *I would say the Rev. Smith is seen by most of his flock in a good light. Some don't like him though.*

in a haze Go to in a fog.

do sth **in a heartbeat** *Fig.* to do something almost immediately. □ *Just tell me that you need me, and I'll come there in a heartbeat.*

*__in a huff__ *Fig.* in an angry or offended manner. (*Typically: **be** ~; **get** [**into**] ~.) □ *He heard what we had to say, then left in a huff.* □ *She came in a huff and ordered us to bring her something to eat.*

in a jam Go to in a bind.

in a jiffy *Fig.* very fast; very soon. □ *Just wait a minute. I'll be there in a jiffy.*

*__in a lather__ *Fig.* flustered; excited and agitated. (*Typically: **be** ~; **get** [**into**] ~.) □ *I always get in a lather when I'm late.*

in a little bit *Fig.* in a small amount of time. □ *I will be there in a little bit. Please wait.*

in a mad rush *Fig.* in a hurry. □ *I ran around all day today in a mad rush, looking for a present for Bill.*

in a manner of speaking *Fig.* in some ways; in the best way it can be explained.

□ *He is annoying. He's a real pest, in a manner of speaking.*

in a month of Sundays Go to in a coon's age.

in a New York minute Go to a New York minute.

in a nutshell *Fig.* [of news or information] in a (figurative) capsule. □ *This cable channel provides the latest news in a nutshell.*

In a pig's ass! Go to In a pig's eye!

In a pig's ear! Go to next.

In a pig's eye! AND **In a pig's ass!; In a pig's ear!** *Rur.* Nonsense! □ *Tom: I wasn't going to steal it. I was just looking at it. Jane: In a pig's eye! I saw you put it in your pocket!*

in a pinch as a substitute. □ *In a pinch, you can use folded paper to prop up the table leg so the table won't rock.*

*in a (pretty) pickle *Fig.* in a mess; in trouble. (*Pickle* is used here in the sense of pickling solution or the fluid in which pickles are made. Being in a pickle of this type is viewed as unpleasant if not painful. Shakespeare referred to this kind of pickling [without the *pretty*] in *The Tempest*, Act 5, Scene 1, and *Antony and Cleopatra*, Act 2, Scene 5. The use in *Antony and Cleopatra* is almost literal. Now it is used only figuratively. *Typically: **be** ~; **get [into]** ~.) □ *John has gotten himself into a pickle. He has two dates for the party.*

*in a quandary uncertain about what to do; perplexed. (*Typically: **be** ~; **get [into]** ~.) □ *Mary was in a quandary about what college to go to.* □ *I couldn't decide what to do. I was in such a quandary.*

in a row *Fig.* in a sequence of periods of time. (*Row* rhymes with *know.*) □ *This is the third day in a row that we have not got any mail.*

*in a rut *Fig.* in a type of boring habitual behavior. (As when the wheels of a buggy travel in the ruts worn into the ground by other buggies, making it easiest to go exactly the way all the other buggies have

gone before. *Typically: **be** ~; **be stuck** ~; **get [into]** ~.) □ *My life has gotten in a rut.* □ *I'm really tired of being stuck in a rut!*

in a sense AND **in a way** in one way of looking at it; sort of. □ *In a sense, cars make life better.*

in (a) shambles *Fig.* in a messy state; destroyed. □ *The TV set was in a shambles after John tried to fix it.*

in a short space of time *Fig.* in a brief amount of time. □ *It's hard to believe that it could happen twice in such a short space of time.*

*in (a) single file *Fig.* lined up, one behind the other; in a line, one person or one thing wide. (*Typically: **be** ~; **get [into]** ~; **march** ~; **walk** ~.) □ *Have you ever seen ducks walking in single file?*

in a single stroke Go to at one blow.

in a snit *Inf.* in a fit of anger or irritation. □ *Mary is in a snit because they didn't ask her to come to the shindig.*

in a split second Go to a split second.

in a stage whisper *Fig.* in a loud whisper that everyone can hear. □ *John said in a stage whisper, "This play is boring."*

*in a stew (about so/sth**)** *Fig.* upset or bothered about someone or something. (*Typically: **be** ~; **get [into]** ~.) □ *Now, now. Don't get in a stew. She'll be back when she gets hungry.*

in a stupor in a dazed condition; in a condition in which one cannot concentrate or think. □ *In the morning, Mary remains in a stupor until she drinks coffee.*

*in a (tight) spot *Fig.* caught in a problem; in a bind. (*Typically: **be** ~; **get [into]** ~.) □ *Look, John, I'm in a tight spot. Can you lend me $20?*

*in a tizzy *Fig.* in an excited and confused condition. (*Typically: **be** ~; **get [into]** ~.) □ *Mary was in a tizzy when she couldn't find her keys.*

in a twit *Inf.* upset; frantic. □ *She's all in a twit because she lost her keys.*

in a twitter *Inf.* in a giddy state; silly. □ *We were all in a twitter over the upcoming event.*

in a vacuum *Fig.* isolated from other things or people. □ *Reggie lives in a vacuum. He has no idea about what is important to other people.*

*in a vicious circle *Fig.* in a situation in which the solution of one problem leads to a second problem, and the solution of the second problem brings back the first problem, etc. (*Typically: **be ~; get [into]** ~.) □ *Life is so strange. I seem to be in a vicious circle most of the time.*

in a way Go to in a sense.

in a word *Fig.* said simply; concisely said. □ *Mrs. Smith is—in a word—haughty.*

*in a world of one's **own** *Fig.* aloof; detached; self-centered. (*Typically: **be ~; get [into] ~; live** ~.) □ *John lives in a world of his own. He has very few friends.*

in abeyance *Fig.* set aside for possible use later. □ *Until the judge determined that the evidence could be used in the trial, it was held in abeyance.*

in action working; involved in activity. (Even when not a lot of fast action is involved.) □ *It's wonderful to see him in action. He is a highly skilled glass blower.*

in advance *Fig.* [of something given, paid, or provided] before it is due. □ *The bill isn't due for a month, but I paid it in advance.*

in (all) good conscience *Fig.* having good motives; displaying motives that will not result in a guilty conscience. □ *In all good conscience, I could not recommend that you buy this car.*

in all its glory AND **in all** one's **glory** *Fig.* presented or displayed spectacularly or dramatically. (Often sarcastic or ironic.) □ *Well, here's my new car, just sitting there in all its glory.* □ *He just stood there in all his glory with one brown shoe and one black one.*

in all likelihood Go to in all probability.

in all my born days *Rur.* in my entire life. □ *I've never seen such fireworks in all my born days.*

in all probability AND **in all likelihood** very likely; almost certainly. □ *In all probability, they'll finish the work today.*

*in an interesting condition *Euph.* pregnant. (*Typically: **be ~; get** ~.) □ *Young Mrs. Lucas is in an interesting condition.*

*in an ivory tower *Fig.* in a place, such as a university, where one can be aloof from the realities of living. (*Typically: **be ~; dwell ~; live ~; work** ~.) □ *If you didn't spend so much time in your ivory tower, you'd know what people really think!*

in and of itself *Fig.* considering it alone. □ *The idea in and of itself is not bad, but the side issues introduce many difficulties.*

in any case AND **in any event** no matter what happens. □ *I intend to be home by supper time, but in any case by eight o'clock.*

in any event Go to previous.

in any way, shape, or form *Fig.* in any manner. □ *I refuse to tell a lie in any way, shape, or form!*

*in apple-pie order *Fig.* in very good order; very well organized. (*Typically: **be ~; get** sth **~; put** sth ~.) □ *Please put everything in apple-pie order before you leave.*

*in arrears *Fig.* [of debts; of an account] overdue. (*Typically: **be ~; get** ~.) □ *Jane's student-loan payments are in arrears.*

in at the kill AND **in on the kill 1.** present and participating in the killing of prey. □ *The baby cheetah wanted to be in on the kill.* **2.** *Fig.* involved at the final moment of something in order to share in the spoils. (Fig. on ①.) □ *The press packed the room, wanting to be in on the kill when the governor's resignation was to be announced.*

in awe (of so/sth**)** fearful and respectful of someone or something. □ *Everyone in the country was in awe of the king and queen.*

in bad faith *Fig.* without sincerity; with bad or dishonest intent; with duplicity. □ *It appears that you acted in bad faith and didn't live up to the terms of our agreement.*

in bad shape AND **in a bad way 1.** *Fig.* injured or debilitated in some manner. □ *Fred had a little accident, and he's in bad shape.* **2.** *Inf.* pregnant. □ *Yup, she's in bad shape all right—about three months in bad shape.* **3.** *Inf.* intoxicated. □ *Fred is in bad shape. I think he's going to toss his cookies.*

in bad sorts *Fig.* in a bad humor. □ *Bill is in bad sorts today. He's very grouchy.*

in bad taste AND **in poor taste** *Fig.* rude; vulgar; obscene. □ *We found the play to be in poor taste, so we walked out in the middle of the second act.*

***in bad (with** SO) *Fig.* in trouble with someone. (*Typically: **be** ~; **get** ~.) □ *We got in bad with each other from the start.*

in bed with SO *Fig.* in close association with someone. □ *Now that John's in bed with our competitor, we are losing old clients weekly.*

in behalf of SO AND **in** SO's **behalf; on behalf of** SO; **on** SO's **behalf; on the part of** SO; **in** SO's **name** [doing something] as someone's agent; [doing something] in place of someone; for the benefit of someone. □ *I'm writing in behalf of Mr. Smith, who has applied for a job with your company.* □ *I'm calling on behalf of my client, who wishes to complain about your actions.* □ *I'm acting on your behalf.*

***in** one's **birthday suit** *Fig.* naked; nude. (In the "clothes" in which one was born. *Typically: **be** ~; **get** [into] ~.) □ *We used to go down to the river and swim in our birthday suits.*

***in black and white** *Fig.* [of an agreement, contract, or statement] official, in writing or printing. (*Typically: **be** ~; **get** sth ~.) □ *I have it in black and white that I'm entitled to three weeks of vacation each year.*

in one's **blood** Go to in the blood.

in bloom Go to next.

in blossom AND **in bloom** blooming; covered with blossoms. □ *All the apple trees are in blossom now.*

in one's **book** *Fig.* according to one's own opinion. □ *He's okay in my book.*

in brief *Fig.* briefly; concisely. □ *The whole story, in brief, is that Bob failed algebra because he did not study.*

in broad daylight *Fig.* in the open light of day; clearly visible. □ *The crime was committed in broad daylight.*

in bulk *Fig.* in large quantities or amounts, rather than smaller, more convenient quantities or amounts. □ *Dave purchased cereal in bulk because his family used so much of it.*

in business *Inf.* operating; equipped or ready to operate. □ *We're in business now, and things are running smoothly.*

in cahoots (with SO) *Rur.* in conspiracy with someone; in league with someone. □ *The mayor is in cahoots with the construction company that got the contract for the new building.*

in SO's **care** Go to in the care of SO.

in care of SO [to be delivered to someone] through someone or by way of someone. (Indicates that mail is to be delivered to a person at some other person's address. See also in the care of SO.) □ *Bill Jones is living at his father's house. Address the letter to Bill in care of Mr. John Jones.*

in case (sth happens**)** *Fig.* in the event that something takes place. □ *She carries an umbrella in case it rains.* □ *He keeps a fire extinguisher in his car, just in case.*

in case of sth if a problem occurs; if something happens; in the event that something happens. □ *In case of an accident, call the police.*

in character *Fig.* typical of someone's behavior. □ *For Tom to shout that way wasn't at all in character. He's usually quite pleasant.*

in clover *Fig.* having good fortune; in a very good situation, especially financially. □ *If I get this contract, I'll be in clover for the rest of my life.*

in cold blood *Fig.* without feeling; with cruel intent. (Frequently said of a crime, especially murder.) □ *The killer walked up and shot the woman in cold blood.* □ *How insulting! For a person to say something like that in cold blood is just horrible.*

in cold storage *Inf.* dead; in a state of death. (Refers to the actual storage of certain things, such as fur coats, in cold store rooms.) □ *The assassin gets paid for putting his subjects in cold storage.* □ *Poor old Jed is in cold storage.*

in concert (with so**)** *Fig.* in cooperation with someone; with the aid of someone. □ *Mrs. Smith planned the party in concert with her sister.*

in conclusion . . . concluding my speech or statement, I will say . . . □ *In conclusion let me thank all of you for coming to hear me.*

in condition AND ***in shape*** *Fig.* in good health; strong and healthy; fit. (*Typically: **be** ~; **get [into]** ~.) □ *Bob exercises frequently, so he's in condition.* □ *If I were in shape, I could run faster and farther.*

in consequence (of sth**)** as a result of something; because of something. □ *The wind blew down the wires. In consequence, we had no electricity.*

in consideration of sth in return for something; as a result of something. □ *In consideration of your many years of service, we are pleased to present you with this gold watch.*

in contempt (of court) *Fig.* [a charge of] showing disrespect for a judge or courtroom procedures. □ *The judge found the juror in contempt of court when she screamed at the attorney.*

in one's **crosshairs** *Fig.* on one's agenda for immediate action; being studied for action at this moment. (Refers to the crosshairs of a gun sight.) □ *I recognize that the problem exists, and I have it in my crosshairs as we speak.*

in one's **cups** *Euph.* drunk. □ *The speaker—who was in his cups—could hardly be understood.*

in debt *Fig.* having debts; having much debt; owing money. □ *I am in debt to the bank for my car loan.*

in deep 1. *Fig.* deeply involved (with someone or something). □ *Wilbur got in deep with the mob.* **2.** *Fig.* deeply in debt. (Often with with or to.) □ *Willie is in deep with his bookie.*

in deep water *Fig.* in a dangerous or vulnerable situation; in a serious situation, especially one that is too difficult or is beyond the level of one's abilities; in trouble. (Fig. on the image of someone at risk of drowning in deep water.) □ *Bill got in deep water in algebra class. The class is too difficult for him, and he's almost failing.*

in denial *Fig.* in a state of refusing to believe something that is true. □ *Mary was in denial about her illness and refused treatment.*

in detail *Fig.* with lots of details; giving all the details. (Often used with an adjective showing the level or detail.) □ *I explained the policy to the customer in quite some detail.* □ *We planned the entire project in great detail.*

in dire straits *Fig.* in very serious, bad circumstances. □ *We are nearly broke and need money for medicine. We are in dire straits.*

in disguise *Fig.* hidden behind a disguise; looking like something else. □ *What I thought was terrible turned out to be a blessing in disguise!*

in dispute Go to under dispute.

in drag *Inf.* wearing the clothing of the opposite sex. (Usually refers to a man wearing women's clothing.) □ *Two actors in drag did a skit about life on the farm.*

in dribs and drabs *Inf.* in small portions; bit by bit. □ *The whole story is being revealed in dribs and drabs.*

in droves *Fig.* in large numbers. (See also out in large numbers.) □ *The settlers arrived on the prairie in droves.*

in due course AND **in due time; in good time; in the course of time; in time** in a normal or expected amount of time. □ *The roses will bloom in due course.* □ *The vice president will become president in due course.* □ *Just wait, my dear. All in good time.* □ *In time, things will improve.*

in due time Go to previous.

***in Dutch (with** so**)** *Fig.* in trouble with someone. (*Typically: **be** ~; **get** ~.) □ *I'm in Dutch with my parents for my low grades.*

***in earnest** *Fig.* with sincerity; with purpose. (*Typically: **act** ~; **be** ~; **speak** ~.) □ *I've done all the research I need. I spent the day writing the paper in earnest.*

in effect *Fig.* producing a particular effect; effectively. □ *This policy harms domestic manufacturers. In effect, all our clothing will be made in foreign countries.*

in one's **element** *Fig.* in a natural or comfortable situation or environment. □ *Bob loves to work with color and texture. When he's painting, he's in his element.*

in essence *Fig.* basically; essentially. □ *I have lots of detailed advice for you, but in essence, I want you to do the best you can.*

in evidence Go to (much) in evidence.

in exchange (for so/sth**)** in return for someone or something. □ *They gave us two of our prisoners in exchange for two of theirs.* □ *John gave Mary a book and got a sweater in exchange.*

in existence *Fig.* now existing; currently and actually being. □ *All the oil in existence will not last the world for another century.*

***in** so's **face** *Sl.* in a provocative attitude, as if ready to fight or argue. (*Typically: **be** ~; **get** ~.) □ *Ted's a real pain. He likes to get in your face. He'll argue about anything.*

in fact *Fig.* in reality; really; actually. □ *I'm over 40. In fact, I'm 46.*

in fashion *Fig.* in style; current and socially acceptable. □ *Is that kind of thing still in fashion?*

in so's **favor 1.** to someone's advantage or credit. (Especially in sports scores, as in the example.) □ *The score was 10 to 12 in our favor.* **2.** AND ***in** so's **favor** liked by someone; approved of by someone. (*Typically: **be** ~; **get [into]** ~.) □ *John might be able to help me. I hope I'm currently in his favor.*

in favor of so *Fig.* to someone, as when writing a check. □ *Please make out a check for $300 in Tom's favor.*

in favor (of so/sth**)** approving, supporting, or endorsing someone or something. □ *Are you in favor of lower taxes?*

in fear and trembling *Cliché* with anxiety or fear; with dread. □ *In fear and trembling, I went into the room to take the test.*

in fine feather 1. *Fig.* well dressed; of an excellent appearance. (Fig. on the image of a bird that has clean, bright, and flawless feathers.) □ *Well, you are certainly in fine feather today.* **2.** *Fig.* in good form; in good spirits. (Fig. on ①.) □ *Mary was really in fine feather tonight. Her concert was great!*

in flight *Fig.* while flying. □ *A passenger became ill in flight, and the pilot had to return to the airport.*

in flux AND **in a (constant) state of flux** *Fig.* in constant change; ever-changing. □ *I can't describe my job, because it's in a constant state of flux.*

***in focus 1.** [of an image] seen clearly and sharply. (*Typically: **be** ~; **come [into]** ~; **get [into]** ~; **get** sth **[into]** ~.) □ *I have the slide in focus and can see the bacteria clearly.* **2.** [for optics, such as lenses, or an optical device, such as a microscope] to be aligned to allow something to be seen clearly and sharply. □ *I can't get my binoculars into focus.* **3.** *Fig.* [of problems, solutions, appraisals of people or things] perceived or understood clearly. (Fig. on ①. *Typically: **be** ~; **get [into]** ~; **get** sth **[into]** ~.) □ *Now that things are in focus, I feel better about the world.*

in for sth *Fig.* due to receive a surprise; due to receive punishment. (When the something is *it*, the *it* usually means punishment.) □ *I hope I'm not in for any surprises when I get home.* □ *Tommy, you broke my baseball bat. You're really in for it!*

in some transaction **for** so having value for someone; having a benefit for someone. (Usually a question: *What's in it for me?*) □ *What is in this deal for me?* □ *There is a lot of money in it for you.*

*****in force 1.** *Fig.* [of a rule or law] currently valid or in effect. (*Typically: **be** ~.) □ *Is this rule in force now?* **2.** AND **in full force** *Fig.* in a very large group. (*Typically: **arrive** ~; **attack** ~.) □ *The mosquitoes will attack in full force this evening.*

in full flight *Fig.* fleeing at great speed; escaping rapidly. □ *The robbers were in full flight before the bank manager even called the sheriff.*

in full force Go to in force.

*****in full swing** AND *****in high gear** *Fig.* at the peak of activity; moving fast or efficiently. (*Typically: **be** ~; **get [into]** ~; **move [into]** ~.) □ *In the summer months, things really get into full swing around here.* □ *We go skiing in the mountains each winter. Things are in high gear there in November.*

in general *Fig.* referring to the entire class being discussed; speaking of the entire range of possibilities; in most situations or circumstances. □ *In general, I prefer a hotel room on a lower floor but will take a higher room if it's special.* □ *Do you want to know about today's weather or weather in general?*

in one's **glory** *Fig.* at one's happiest or best. □ *When I go to the beach on vacation, I'm in my glory.*

in glowing terms *Fig.* using words of praise; using complimentary expressions. □ *The college president described his accomplishments in glowing terms and awarded him with an honorary degree.*

*****in good company** with lots of companions; in a group of people with similar experiences. (Expresses the notion that "you are not the only one." *Typically: **be**

~; **find** oneself **in** ~.) □ *So, your taxes went up this year also. Well, you're in good company. Everyone I know has the same problem.*

in good condition Go to in good shape.

in good faith *Fig.* with good and honest intent; with sincerity. □ *We are convinced you were acting in good faith, even though you made a serious error.*

*****in** so's **good graces** *Fig.* in good with someone; in someone's favor. (*Typically: **be** ~; **get** ~.) □ *I'm not in her good graces so I shouldn't be the one to ask her.*

in good hands AND **in safe hands** *Fig.* in the safe, competent care of someone. □ *Don't worry. Your children are in good hands. Sally is an experienced baby-sitter.*

in good repair *Fig.* operating well; well taken care of. (Usually said of a thing rather than a person.) □ *The house is in good repair and ought to attract a number of potential buyers.*

*****in good shape** AND *****in good condition** physically and functionally sound and sturdy. (Used for both people and things. *Typically: **be** ~; **get [into]** ~; **keep** ~.) □ *This car isn't in good shape. I'd like to have one that's in better condition.* □ *Mary is in good condition. She exercises and eats right to stay healthy.* □ *You have to make an effort to get into good shape.*

in good spirits *Fig.* happy and cheerful; positive and looking toward the future, despite unhappy circumstances. □ *The patient is in good spirits and that will speed her recovery.*

in good time Go to in due course.

*****in (good) (with** so) *Fig.* in someone's favor. (*Typically: **be** ~; **get** ~.) □ *I hope I can get in good with the teacher. I need an A in the course.*

in (great) demand *Fig.* wanted by many people. □ *Liz is in great demand as a singer.*

in great haste *Fig.* very fast; in a big hurry. □ *John always did his homework in great haste, and most of it was wrong.*

*in so's **hair 1.** tangled in someone's hair. (*Typically: **be** ~; **get [into]** ~.) □ *My bubble gum got in my hair, and I had to cut it out.* **2.** *Fig.* being an annoyance to someone. (Fig. on ①. *Typically: **be** ~; **get [into]** ~.) □ *I wish you wouldn't get in my hair when I'm trying to do something.*

*in **hand** *Fig.* in one's possession or control. (*Typically: **be** ~; **have** sth ~.) □ *The papers are in hand. Have no fear.*

*in **harmony (with** so/sth**) 1.** in musical concord with someone or something. (*Typically: **be** ~; **get** ~.) □ *The tenor part is not in harmony with the accompaniment.* **2.** *Fig.* agreeable or compatible with someone or something. (Fig. on ①. *Typically: **be** ~; **get** ~.) □ *This is in complete harmony with our earlier discussions.*

*in **harm's way** *Fig.* liable to be harmed; subject to potential causes of harm; in danger. (Particularly in battle. *Typically: **be** ~; **get** ~; **put** so ~.) □ *Soldiers are expected to know what to do when they are in harm's way.*

*in **heat** *Fig.* in a period of sexual excitement; in the period of time in which females are most willing to breed. (This expression is usually used for animals. It has been used for humans in a joking sense. *Typically: **be** ~; **get [into]** ~; **go [into]** ~.) □ *Our dog is in heat again.*

in **heaven** *Fig.* in a state of absolute bliss or happiness. □ *Resting in his hammock, John was simply in heaven.*

in **high dudgeon** *Fig.* feeling or exhibiting great resentment; taking great offense at something. □ *After the rude remarks, the person who was insulted left in high dudgeon.*

in **high gear** Go to in full swing.

in **(high) hopes of** sth *Fig.* expecting something. □ *We are in high hopes that John and Mary will have a girl.*

in **hindsight** Go to in retrospect.

in **hock** *Fig.* in debt. □ *After buying the luxury car, Bob was in hock for years.*

in **hog heaven** *Fig.* very happy; having a wonderful time. □ *Jane loves to quilt, so she was in hog heaven when they opened that new store for quilters.*

in **honor of** so/sth *Fig.* showing respect or admiration for someone or something. □ *Our club gave a party in honor of the club's president.*

in **hopes of** doing sth hoping that one would be able to do something. □ *I was in hopes of going on vacation next spring.*

in **hopes of** so's doing sth AND **in hopes that** one **would** do sth with the hope that someone will accomplish some task. □ *I was in hopes of your going on vacation next spring.* □ *I was in hopes that you would go on vacation next spring.*

in **horror** *Fig.* with intense shock or disgust. □ *Mike stepped back from the rattlesnake in horror.* □ *The jogger recoiled in horror when she came upon a body in the park.*

in **(hot) pursuit of** sth chasing after something. □ *Every year Bob goes into the countryside in pursuit of butterflies.*

*in **hot water** *Fig.* in trouble. (*Typically: **be** ~; **get [into]** ~.) □ *I'm in hot water at home for coming in late last night.*

*in **hot water (with** so**) (about** so/sth**)** *Fig.* in trouble. (*Typically: **be** ~; **get [into]** ~.) □ *You are going to get into hot water with Rebecca about that.*

in so's **infinite wisdom** AND **in its infinite wisdom; in their infinite wisdom** *Fig.* according to some kind of knowledge of which most people are ignorant. (Usually sarcastic, referring to someone's bad or silly decision.) □ *The board, in its infinite wisdom, has decided to give us two fewer holidays this year.*

in **ink** *Fig.* written or signed with a pen that uses ink, not with a pencil. □ *You must sign your checks in ink.*

in **its entirety** AND **in their entirety** *Fig.* completely; until completely done or gone. □ *I watched the basketball game in its entirety.*

in hog heaven

in one's or **its prime** *Fig.* at one's or its peak or best time. □ *Our dog—which is in its prime—is very active.* □ *The building was in its prime back in the '50s, but it has not been well maintained.*

in jeopardy *Fig.* to be at risk; to be at peril. □ *John puts himself in jeopardy every time he goes skydiving.*

in jest for the sake of joking; just joking. (A little formal.) □ *I meant no harm. I only said it in jest.*

in (just) a minute Go to in (just) a second.

in (just) a moment Go to next.

in (just) a second AND **in (just) a minute; in (just) a moment** in a very short period of time. □ *I'll be there in a second.* □ *I'll be with you in just a minute. I'm on the phone.*

in keeping (with sth**)** AND **in line with** sth in accord or harmony with something; following the rules of something. □ *In keeping with your instructions, I've can-*

celed your order. □ *I'm disappointed with your behavior. It really wasn't in line with what it should be.*

in kind 1. *Fig.* in goods rather than in money. □ *The country doctor was usually paid in kind. He accepted two pigs as payment for an operation.* **2.** *Fig.* similarly; [giving] something similar to what was received. □ *John punched Bill, and Bill gave it back in kind.*

in labor *Fig.* [of a woman] experiencing the pains and exertion of childbirth. □ *Susan was in labor for nearly eight hours.*

in large part Go to for the most part.

in league (with so**)** *Fig.* [of people] secretly cooperating, often to do something bad or illegal. □ *The car thieves and some crooked police are in league to make money from stolen cars.*

in less than no time *Fig.* very quickly. (See also in no time (at all).) □ *Don't worry. This won't take long. It'll be over with in less than no time.*

in lieu of sth *Fig.* in place of something; instead of something. (The word *lieu* occurs only in this phrase.) □ *We gave money to charity in lieu of sending flowers to the funeral.*

***in limbo 1.** a region of the afterlife on the border of hell. (In some Christian religions, there is a *limbo* set aside for souls that do not go to either heaven or hell. This sense is used only in this religious context. *Typically: **be** ~; **remain** ~; **stay** ~.) □ *The baby's soul was in limbo because she had not been baptized.* **2.** *Fig.* in a state of neglect; in a state of oblivion; in an indefinite state; on hold. (Fig. on ①. *Typically: **be** ~; **leave** sth ~; **put** sth ~.) □ *After I got hit on the head, I was in limbo for about 10 minutes.*

in line AND **on line** standing and waiting in a line of people. (*On line* is used especially in the New York City area.) □ *I've been in line for an hour.* □ *We waited on line to see the movie.*

in line for sth *Fig.* due for something; expected to receive consideration for something. □ *They say that Wallace is in line for a big promotion, but I don't see why.*

in line with sth Go to in keeping (with sth).

in living memory Go to (with)in living memory.

in luck *Fig.* fortunate; lucky. □ *You want a red one? You're in luck. There is one red one left.*

in many respects Go to in some respects.

in marching order organized and equipped; ready to go. (Originally military.) □ *Is our luggage all packed and in marching order?*

in memory of so *Fig.* to continue the good memories of someone; for the honor of a deceased person. □ *Many streets were renamed in memory of John F. Kennedy.*

in midair in a point high in the air. □ *The planes crashed in midair.* □ *Extra fuel was released from the plane in midair.*

in one's **mind's eye** *Fig.* in one's mind or imagination. (Fig. on visualizing something in one's mind.) □ *In my mind's eye, I can see trouble ahead.*

***in mint condition** *Fig.* in perfect condition. (*Typically: **be** ~; **find** sth ~.) □ *This is a fine car. It runs well and is in mint condition.*

in my humble opinion *Cliché* a phrase introducing the speaker's opinion. □ *"In my humble opinion," began Fred, arrogantly, "I have achieved what no one else ever could."*

in my opinion Go to as I see it.

in so's **name 1.** *Fig.* in someone's ownership; as someone's property. □ *The house is in my name. I own all of it.* □ *The car is in our names.* **2.** Go to in behalf of so.

in name only *Fig.* nominally; not actual, only by terminology. □ *The president is head of the country in name only. Congress makes the laws.*

in some **neck of the woods** *Rur.* in some vicinity or neighborhood; in some remote place. (The *some* is usually *this, that, your, their*, etc.) □ *I think that the Smiths live in your neck of the woods.*

in need (of sth) **1.** [of someone or an animal] requiring something. □ *The company is in need of a larger building to hold all its employees.* **2.** needing one or more of life's basic requirements. □ *The homeless families are really in need and would appreciate your help.*

in no mood to do sth *Fig.* not feeling like doing something; not wishing to do something. □ *Mother is in no mood to put up with our arguing.*

in no time (at all) *Fig.* very quickly. (Similar to in nothing flat; in no time flat.) □ *It won't take long. I'll be finished in no time at all.*

in no time flat Go to in nothing flat.

in no uncertain terms *Cliché* in very specific and direct language. □ *I was so mad. I told her in no uncertain terms to leave and never come back.*

in nothing flat AND **in no time flat** *Fig.* very quickly; in much less time than expected. □ *We covered the distance between New York and Philadelphia in nothing flat.* □ *The waiter brought our food in no time flat.*

*in on sth **1.** *Fig.* involved with something, such as an organization or an idea; informed about special plans. (*Typically: **be** ~; **come** ~; **get** ~; **let** so ~.) □ *There is a party upstairs, and I want to get in on it.* **2.** *Fig.* receiving a share of something. (*Typically: **be** ~; **come** ~; **get** ~; **let** so ~.) □ *I want to get in on the new European business that is supposed to develop.*

*in on the act *Fig.* involved in something with someone else. (Often refers to an unwelcome attempt to join someone's performance. *Typically: **be** ~; **get** ~; **let** so ~.) □ *Everybody wants to get in on the act.*

*in on the ground floor *Fig.* involved at the very beginning of something. (Fig. on the image of people riding in an elevator that got increasingly crowded as it ascended. You will be able to get in most easily at the lowest level. *Typically: **be** ~; **get** ~; **let** so ~.) □ *Invest now so you can get in on the ground floor.*

in on the kill Go to in at the kill.

in one breath Go to (all) in one breath.

in one fell swoop Go to at one fell swoop.

in one piece Go to (all) in one piece.

in one's **opinion** according to one's belief or judgment. □ *In my opinion, that is a very ugly picture.*

*in orbit 1. [of something] circling a heavenly body. (*Typically: **be** ~; **put** sth **[into]** ~.) □ *The moon is in orbit around the earth.* □ *They put the satellite into orbit.* **2.** *Inf.* ecstatic; thrilled; emotionally high. (*Typically: **be** ~.) □ *John went into orbit when he got the check in the mail.* **3.** *Inf.* intoxicated. □ *After having six drinks all to herself, Julie was in orbit.*

in order 1. in the right sequence. □ *As soon as I get all the encyclopedias in order, I will start on the rest of the books.* **2.** correct; properly prepared and executed. □ *Your* papers are in order, and you are free to pass. **3.** suitable; appropriate. □ *It's a little cool out, and jackets are in order.*

in other words AND **that is to say** *Fig.* a phrase introducing a restatement of what has just been said. □ *Henry: Sure I want to do it, but how much do I get paid? Andrew: In other words, you're just doing it for the money.*

*in over one's **head (with** so/sth**) 1.** in water that is deeper than one is tall. (*Typically: **be** ~; **get** ~.) □ *Johnny! Don't go out too far! You are in over your head.* **2.** *Fig.* too deeply involved with someone or something, beyond what one can deal with. (Fig. on ①. *Typically: **be** ~; **get** ~.) □ *They are all in over their heads with this money business.* **3.** *Fig.* having more difficulties than one can manage. □ *Calculus is very hard for me. I'm in over my head.*

in one's **(own) backyard** *Fig.* very close to one, where one lives, or where one is. □ *That kind of thing is quite rare. Imagine it happening right in your backyard.*

in one's **(own) (best) interest(s)** *Fig.* to one's advantage; as a benefit to oneself. □ *It is not in your own interests to share your ideas with Jack. He will say that they are his.*

in one's **own right** owing to one's own talent or ability. □ *Mary can play the piano extremely well, and her husband is quite a pianist in his own right.*

in part *Fig.* partly; to a lesser degree or extent. □ *I was not there, in part because of my disagreement about the purpose of the meeting. I also had a previous appointment.*

in particular *Fig.* specifically; especially. □ *Of the three ideas, there is one I like in particular.*

in passing *Fig.* casually; said or mentioned as an aside. □ *I just heard your name in passing. I didn't hear more than that.*

in pencil *Fig.* written or signed with a pencil. □ *You can't sign a check in pencil!*

in perpetuity *Fig.* for an indefinitely long period of time; eternally. □ *My trust fund generates income in perpetuity.*

in person appearing as oneself, rather than filmed or recorded. □ *Once I met Frank Sinatra in person. I was very excited, but he wasn't.*

*in perspective *Fig.* within a reasonable view or appraisal. (*Typically: **be** ~; **get** sth ~; **have** sth ~; **keep things** ~; **put** sth [**into**] ~.) □ *Let's try to keep everything in perspective.* □ *If we put the matter into perspective, I think we can discuss it reasonably.*

*in one's **place 1.** *Fig.* in the proper rank or station. (Now, usually said with scorn for the concept of "place." *Typically: **keep** one ~; **put** one ~.) □ *I know enough to keep myself in my place.* **2.** AND **in** so's **stead; in place of** so substituting for someone; acting or representing someone. □ *I am busy. My elder brother will attend in my stead.*

in so else's **place** Go to in so else's shoes.

in plain English Go to next.

*in plain language AND ***in plain English** *Fig.* in simple, clear, and straightforward language. (*Typically: **be** ~; **put** sth ~; **say** sth ~; **write** sth ~.) □ *That's too confusing. Please say it again in plain English.* □ *Tell me again in plain language.*

*in play 1. *Fig.* [of a ball, in a game] under the effect of the rules of the game. (*Typically: **be** ~; **get back** ~; **put** sth **back** ~.) □ *The ball is in play again, and the activity is furious.* **2.** *Fig.* [of a company or its stock] in the process of being bought out by another company. (Fig. on ①. *Typically: **be** ~; **put** sth ~.) □ *The company I bought stock in is now in play.*

in point of fact *Fig.* just to point out a fact; in fact. □ *In point of fact, I am not late. You are simply way too early.*

in poor taste Go to in bad taste.

*in so's **possession** held by someone; owned by someone. (*Typically: **be** ~; **come** [**into**] ~.) □ *The book is now in my possession.*

*in power *Fig.* in control; in charge. (*Typically: **be** ~; **come** [**into**] ~; **get** [**into**] ~.) □ *Who is in power now?* □ *No one is in power.*

in practice 1. in the actual doing of something; in reality. □ *The instructions say not to set it too high. In practice I always set it as high as possible.* **2.** *Fig.* well-rehearsed; well-practiced; well-exercised. □ *I play the piano for a living, and I have to keep in practice.*

in so's **prayers** [of someone] remembered and called by name when someone prays. □ *I am sorry to hear of your sickness. You will be in our prayers.*

in press *Fig.* [of a book or other document] in the process of being printed. □ *This book is in press. It won't be available for at least two months.*

in principle generally; basically as described. □ *We can approve your blueprints in principle, but the details will have to be worked out before we sign the contract.*

in print *Fig.* [of a book, magazine, newspaper, or other written material] to be available from the publisher. □ *Ten thousand copies of the first edition remain in print.*

in private *Fig.* privately; without others present. □ *I enjoy spending the evening in private.*

in progress happening now. □ *The play is in progress, so you can't go into the theater now.*

in proportion *Fig.* showing the correct size or proportion relative to something else. □ *That man's large head is not in proportion to his small body.*

in public *Fig.* in a place or way so that other people can see or know about something. □ *John always tries to embarrass me whenever we're in public.*

in quest of so/sth AND **in search of** so/sth seeking or hunting something; trying to find something. □ *They went into town in quest of a reasonably priced restaurant.*

so/sth **in question** the person or thing mentioned. (There is not necessarily any question involved.) □ *The time in question is not the best time for me.* □ *The person in question is no longer employed here.*

in rags *Fig.* in worn-out and torn clothing. □ *Oh, look at my clothing. I can't go to the party in rags!*

in rare form 1. *Fig.* well-tuned for a good performance; at one's best. □ *The goalie is in rare form today; that's his third great save already.* **2.** *Inf.* intoxicated. □ *Gert is in rare form, but she'll have time to sleep it off.*

in reality *Fig.* viewing things realistically; really. □ *John looks happy, but in reality, he is miserable.*

in receipt of sth in a state of having received something. (Used in business correspondence.) □ *When we are in receipt of your check for the full balance, we will mark your bill as paid.*

in recent memory *Fig.* the period of time in which things are still remembered and discussed. □ *Never in recent memory has there been this much snow!*

in reduced circumstances *Euph.* in poverty. □ *After Frederick lost his position, we lived in reduced circumstances while waiting for my inheritance.*

in regard to so/sth Go to with regard to so/sth.

in rehearsal *Fig.* a stage of development in the production of a play, opera, or concert, involving many rehearsals. □ *The play is in rehearsal now and will open next month.*

in remission *Fig.* [of a serious disease] not worsening or progressing. □ *While the disease was in remission, John got to leave the hospital.*

in respect to so/sth AND **with respect to** so/sth; **with reference to** so/sth concerning someone or something; mentioning someone or something. □ *I have nothing else to say in respect to William.*

in retrospect AND **in hindsight** reconsidering the past with the knowledge one now has. □ *David realized, in hindsight, that he should have finished school.*

in one's **right mind** *Fig.* sane; rational and sensible. (Often in the negative.) □ *That was a stupid thing to do. You're not in your right mind.*

in round figures Go to next.

***in round numbers** AND ***in round figures** *Fig.* as an estimated number; a figure that has been rounded off. (*Typically: **be** ~; **express** sth ~; **write** sth ~.) □ *I don't need the exact amount. Just give it to me in round figures.*

***in ruins** *Fig.* in a state of destruction. (*Typically: **be** ~; **lay** ~; **leave** sth ~.) □ *The enemy army left the cities it attacked in ruins.*

in safe hands Go to in good hands.

in one's **salad days** *Fig.* in one's youth. (Usually formal or literary. Comparing the greenness of a salad with the greenness, or freshness and inexperience, of youth.) □ *I recall the joys I experienced on school vacations in my salad days.*

in search of so/sth Go to in quest of so/sth.

in season 1. *Fig.* [of a game animal] subject to legal hunting. □ *You cannot shoot ducks. They are not in season.* **2.** *Fig.* [of a female animal] ready to breed; in estrus; in heat. □ *The cat's in season again.* **3.** *Fig.* to be currently available for selling. (Some foods and other things are available only at certain seasons. *Typically: **be** ~; **come [into]** ~.) □ *Strawberries aren't in season in January.*

in one's **second childhood** *Fig.* [of an adult] interested in things or people that normally interest children. □ *My father bought himself a toy train, and my mother said he was in his second childhood.*

in secret *Fig.* secretly. □ *I will tell her in secret so no one else will hear.*

in service *Fig.* [of something] operating or operable. (See also put sth in(to) service.) □ *Is this elevator in service?*

in session *Fig.* [of a court, congress, or other organization] operating or functioning. □ *The spectators must remain quiet while court is in session.*

in seventh heaven *Fig.* in a very happy state. □ *Ann was really in seventh heaven when she got a car of her own.*

in so's **shadow** Go to in the shadow of so.

in shape Go to in condition.

in so else's **shoes** AND **in** so else's **place** *Fig.* seeing or experiencing something from someone else's point of view. □ *You might feel different if you were in her shoes.*

in short *Fig.* stated briefly. □ *At the end of the financial report, the board president said, "In short, we are okay."*

in short order *Fig.* very quickly. □ *I can straighten out this mess in short order.*

in short supply *Fig.* scarce. □ *Fresh vegetables are in short supply in the winter.*

in sight 1. within the range of vision; visible. □ *The end of the road is in sight.* **2.** *Fig.* known; expected. (Fig. on ①.) □ *The end of the project is finally in sight.*

in so many words *Fig.* exactly; explicitly; in plain, clear language. □ *I told her in so many words to leave me alone.*

in some respects AND **in many respects** *Fig.* with regard to some or many details. □ *The three proposals are quite different in many respects.*

in spades *Fig.* in the best or most extreme way possible; extravagantly. □ *He flunked the test in spades!*

in one's **spare time** *Fig.* in one's extra time; in the time not reserved for work or doing something else. □ *I'll try to paint the house in my spare time.*

in spite of so/sth without regard to someone or something; even though another course had been prescribed; ignoring a warning. □ *In spite of the bad weather, I had fun on vacation.*

in so's **stead** Go to in one's place.

*in step (with so) *Fig.* [marching or dancing] in cadence with another person. (*Typically: **be** ~; **get [into]** ~; **keep** ~; **march** ~.) □ *Please keep in step with*

Jane. □ *You two, back there. You aren't in step.*

in step (with so/sth) *Fig.* as up-to-date as someone or something. (Fig. on in step (with so).) □ *Bob is not in step with the times.*

in step (with sth) AND **in time (with** sth) *Fig.* keeping in cadence with music. □ *John, your violin isn't in step with the beat. Sit up straight and try it again.*

in stitches *Fig.* laughing very hard. □ *Charlie had us in stitches with all his jokes.*

in stock *Fig.* to have merchandise available and ready for sale. □ *Of course, we have all sizes and colors in stock.*

in storage in a place where things are stored or kept. □ *Mary placed her winter clothes in storage during the summer.*

*in store (for so) *Fig.* awaiting someone in the future. (*Typically: **be** ~; **hold** sth ~; **lie** ~.) □ *None of us knows what lies in store for us tomorrow.*

in style 1. in fashion; fashionable. □ *This old coat isn't in style anymore.* **2.** *Fig.* in elegance; in luxury. □ *If I had a million dollars, I could really live in style.*

in summary AND **in sum** summarizing what has been said. □ *In summary, our company is prepared to move onward in spite of the imprisonment of upper management.*

*in one's **Sunday best** *Rur.* in one's best clothes; in the clothes one wears to church. (*Typically: **be** ~; **get [into]** ~.) □ *All the children were dressed up in their Sunday best.*

in surgery *Fig.* to be involved in surgery. (Can refer to a doctor, nurse, or patients.) □ *Dr. Smith is in surgery now.*

in tandem *Fig.* [of two or more things] in single file. □ *We marched to the door in tandem.*

in tatters *Fig.* in torn pieces of cloth. □ *The poor man's clothes hung in tatters.*

in tears crying; sobbing. □ *After the sad movie, many in the audience were in tears.*

in terms of sth *Fig.* regarding something; concerning something. □ *Now, in terms of your proposal, don't you think you're asking for too much?*

in the act (of doing sth**)** while doing something. □ *There he was, in the act of opening the door.* □ *I tripped while in the act of climbing the stairs.*

in the affirmative *Fig.* in the form of an answer that means yes. □ *My manager's response was in the affirmative.*

in the air *Fig.* everywhere; all about. □ *There is such a feeling of joy in the air.*

*in the altogether AND ***in the buff; *in the nude; *in the raw** *Fig.* naked; nude. (*Typically: **be** ~; **get [into]** ~; **sleep** ~.) □ *The museum has a painting of some ladies in the buff.* □ *Mary felt a little shy about getting into the altogether.*

*in the back of so's **mind** *Fig.* remembered by someone, but not very important; vaguely remembered by someone. (*Typically: **have** sth ~; **keep** sth ~; **leave** sth ~; **put** sth ~; **remain** ~; **stay** ~.) □ *You should put this problem in the back of your mind and concentrate on other things.*

*in the bag 1. *Fig.* cinched; achieved. (*Typically: **be** ~; **have** sth ~.) □ *The election is in the bag unless the voters find out about my past.* **2.** *Inf.* intoxicated. (*Typically: **be** ~.) □ *John is in the bag and mean as hell. Don't let him drive.*

*in the balance *Fig.* in an undecided state; at risk. (*Typically: **be** ~; **hang** ~.) □ *With his fortune in the balance, John rolled the dice.*

in the ballpark *Fig.* within prescribed limits; within the anticipated range of possibilities. (Fig. on an enclosed baseball field where a struck ball may remain in the ballpark for further play or be hit out of the park.) □ *Your figures are in the ballpark, so we can continue our negotiations.*

*in the best of health very healthy. (*Typically: **be** ~; **get** oneself ~.) □ *Bill is in the best of health. He eats well and exercises.* □ *I haven't been in the best of health. I think I have the flu.*

in the black *Fig.* not in debt; in a financially profitable condition. (As opposed to in the red.) □ *I wish my accounts were in the black.*

in the blood AND **in** one's **blood; under** one's **skin** *Fig.* built into one's personality or character. (Especially the mid-20th-century Cole Porter song "I've Got You Under My Skin.") □ *John's a great runner. It's in his blood.*

*in the boondocks AND ***in the boonies** *Inf.* in a rural area; far away from a city or population. (*Typically: **be** ~; **camp** ~; **live** ~; **stay** ~.) □ *Perry lives out in the boonies with his parents.*

in the boonies Go to previous.

in the bosom of sth AND **in the heart of** sth *Fig.* in the very central core of someone or something. □ *He was born in the heart of corn country and was destined to become a farmer.* □ *She grew up in the bosom of her little village and spent the rest of her life there.*

in the buff Go to in the altogether.

*in the bullpen 1. *Fig.* [of a baseball pitcher to be] in a special place near the playing field, warming up to pitch. (*Typically: **be** ~; **go [into]** ~.) □ *You can tell who is pitching next by seeing who is in the bullpen.* □ *Our best pitcher just went into the bullpen. He'll be pitching soon.* **2.** in reserve, ready if needed. (Fig. on ①.) □ *I'm willing to be in the bullpen. Just call me if you need me.*

in the can [of a finished film] completely edited and ready to be duplicated for distribution and projection. □ *I won't feel good about this film until it's in the can.*

*in the cards *Fig.* in the future. (*Typically: **be** ~; **see** sth ~.) □ *Well, what do you think is in the cards for tomorrow?* □ *I asked the boss if there was a raise in the cards for me.*

*in the care of so AND ***in the charge of** so; ***in** so's **care; *under** so's **care** in the keeping of someone. (*Typically: **be** ~; **leave** so/sth ~; **place** so/sth **[into]** ~.) □ *I left the baby in the care of my mother.*

□ *I placed the house into the care of my friend.*

in the case of so/sth *Fig.* in the matter of someone or something; in the instance of someone or something. □ *In the case of John, I think we had better allow his request.*

in the catbird seat *Sl.* in a dominant or controlling position. □ *Sally's in the catbird seat—telling everybody where to go.*

in the charge of so Go to in the care of so.

in the chips *Inf.* wealthy; having lots of money. □ *I'm in the chips this month. Let's go squander it.*

*in the clear 1. *Fig.* not obstructed; not enclosed. (*Typically: **be** ~; **get [into]** ~; **get** so/sth **[into]** ~.) □ *You're in the clear. Go ahead and back up.* **2.** *Fig.* to be innocent; not to be guilty. (*Typically: **be** ~; **get [into]** ~; **get** so/sth **[into]** ~.) □ *Don't worry, Tom. I'm sure you're in the clear.*

in the Common Era AND **in the C.E.** [of dates] a year after the year 1 according to the Western calendar. (Offered as a replacement for *anno Domini* and A.D.) □ *The comet was last seen in the year 1986 in the Common Era.* □ *The Huns invaded Gaul in 451* C.E.

in the context of sth in the circumstances under which something happens or has happened. □ *In the context of a funeral, laughing loudly is inappropriate.*

in the course of time Go to in due course.

*in the dark (about so/sth**)** *Fig.* uninformed about someone or something; ignorant about someone or something. (*Typically: **be** ~; **keep** so ~; **leave** so ~; **stay** ~.) □ *I'm in the dark about who is in charge around here.* □ *I can't imagine why they are keeping me in the dark.*

*in the doghouse *Fig.* in trouble; in (someone's) disfavor. (*Typically: **be** ~; **get** ~; **find** oneself ~; **put** so **[into]** ~.) □ *I'm really in the doghouse with my boss. I was late for an appointment.*

*in the doldrums *Fig.* sluggish; inactive; in low spirits. (*Typically: **be** ~; **put** so

[into] ~.) □ *He's usually in the doldrums in the winter.*

*in the drink *Fig.* in the water; in the ocean. (*Typically: **be** ~; **fall** ~; **throw** so ~.) □ *He fell in the drink and had to be rescued.*

in the driver's seat *Fig.* in control; in charge of things. (As if one were driving and controlling the vehicle.) □ *Now that Fred is in the driver's seat, there is a lot less criticism about how things are being done.*

in the end when the episode or series of events is complete. □ *Everything turned out all right in the end.*

in the event of sth if something happens; on the chance that something happens. □ *In the event of rain, the parade will be canceled.*

in the eyes of so/group AND **in** so's/group's **eyes** *Fig.* from the point of view of someone or a group. □ *In the eyes of my friends, I am just your typical middle-aged man.*

in the eyes of the law *Fig.* as far as the law is concerned. □ *You helped the crooks escape. In the eyes of the law, you are just as guilty as if you were there at the scene of the crime.*

in the face of sth *Fig.* in view of the circumstances. □ *In the face of what has happened, you cannot expect me to continue to be your friend.*

in the family Go to (all) in the family.

*in the fast lane *Inf.* in a very active or possible risky manner. (See also life in the fast lane. *Typically: **be** ~; **live** ~; **move** ~; **stay** ~.) □ *Fred lives in the fast lane. It's lucky he's still alive.*

in the final analysis AND **in the last analysis** when all the facts are known; when the truth becomes known. (Usually used when someone is speculating about what the final outcome will be.) □ *In the final analysis, it is usually the children who suffer most in a situation like this.*

in the first instance Go to next.

in the first place AND **in the first instance** *Fig.* initially; to begin with. □ *In* the first place, you don't have enough money to buy one. In the second place, you don't need one.

in the flesh 1. bodily present; in person. □ *I've heard that the queen is coming here in the flesh.* **2.** *Fig.* actually present; physically present. □ *I've wanted a flat-screen TV for years, and now I've got one right here in the flesh.*

in the forefront (of sth) Go to at the forefront (of sth).

in the fullness of time later; at a later time; at a time when things will have had a chance to develop. (Older and formal.) □ *We shall know the answer to that in the fullness of time.*

in the (great) scheme of things *Fig.* fate; the providential plan of everything. □ *I don't know what role I play in the great scheme of things, but I'm sure it's a small one.*

in the grip of sth AND **in** sth's **grip** *Fig.* held under the power of something, such as a disease or a symptom of a disease. □ *She was in the grip of a coughing fit when I came into the room.*

*in the groove *Sl.* attuned to something. (*Typically: **be** ~; **get** ~.) □ *I was uncomfortable at first, but now I'm beginning to get in the groove.*

*in the gutter *Fig.* [of a person] in a low state; poor and homeless. (*Typically: **be** ~; **fall [into]** ~; **put** so **[into]** ~.) □ *You had better straighten out your life, or you'll end in the gutter.*

in the hands of so AND **in** so's **hands** *Fig.* under the control or care of someone. □ *Since I am in the hands of the best doctor in the state, I don't worry at all.*

in the heart of sth Go to in the bosom of sth.

in the hearts and minds of so *Fig.* in the kind memory and regard of someone. □ *He was a hero in the hearts and minds of the citizens.*

in the heat of battle 1. while the battle rages. □ *In the heat of battle, I completely forgot that my leg was bleeding badly.* **2.** AND **in the heat of the moment** in the confusion of argument, negotiation, or fighting. □ *In the heat of battle, my lawyer lost his temper and called the prosecutor a shyster.*

in the heat of the moment Go to previous.

*in the hole *Fig.* in debt. (*Typically: **be** ~; **get** ~; **go** ~; **put** so ~.) □ *I'm $200 in the hole.*

*in the (home)stretch *Fig.* in the last stage of a process. (From horse racing. *Typically: **be** ~; **get** ~.) □ *We're in the homestretch with this project and can't change it now.* □ *We're in the stretch. Only three more days till we graduate.*

in the hopper *Fig.* in process; in line to be processed. (A hopper is a basket for incoming work or material to be processed.) □ *It's in the hopper. I'll get to it.*

in the hot seat Go to on the hot seat.

in the interest of saving time *Fig.* in order to hurry things along; in order to save time. □ *Mary: In the interest of saving time, I'd like to save questions for the end of my talk. Bill: But I have an important question now!*

in the interim in the meantime; temporarily. □ *The organist went on vacation, and three different people played in the interim.*

in the know *Fig.* knowledgeable. □ *I have no knowledge of how to work this machine. I think I can get myself in the know very quickly though.*

in the lap of luxury *Cliché* in luxurious surroundings. □ *John lives in the lap of luxury because his family is very wealthy.*

in the last analysis Go to in the final analysis.

in (the) light of sth *Fig.* because of certain knowledge now in hand; considering something. (As if knowledge or information shed light on something.) □ *In light of what you have told us, I think we must abandon the project.*

in the limelight Go to in the spotlight.

in the line of duty *Fig.* as part of one's expected duties. □ *Police officers have to do things they may not like in the line of duty.*

in the long haul Go to over the long haul.

in the long run Go to over the long haul.

in the loop *Fig.* in the group of persons communicating regularly about a specific plan or project. □ *I'd like to be in the loop so I can hear all the news.*

in the main *Fig.* basically; generally. □ *John: Are you all ready? Sue: I think we're ready, in the main. John: Then, we shall go.*

*in the mainstream (of sth**)** following the current trends or styles that are popular or are considered normal. (*Typically: **be** ~; **get [into]** ~.) □ *Bob is too old-fashioned to be in the mainstream of modern living.*

in the making *Fig.* in development; in the process of developing. □ *This is a real problem in the making. Let's try to keep it from getting any worse.*

*in the market (for sth**)** *Fig.* wanting to buy something. (*Typically: **be** ~; **find** oneself ~.) □ *I'm in the market for a new camera.* □ *If you have a boat for sale, we're in the market.*

in the meantime AND **in the meanwhile** *Fig.* the period of time between two happenings; the period of time between now and when something is supposed to happen. □ *The movie starts at 6:00. In the meantime, let's eat dinner.*

in the meanwhile Go to previous.

*in the middle of nowhere *Fig.* in a very remote place. (*Typically: **be (out)** ~; **drive [into]** ~; **put** so/sth **[into]** ~.) □ *To get to my house, you have to drive into the middle of nowhere.* □ *We found a nice place to eat, but it's out in the middle of nowhere.*

in the money 1. *Fig.* wealthy. □ *John is really in the money. He's worth millions.* **2.** *Fig.* in the winning position in a race or contest. (As if one had won the prize money. In horse racing the top three finishers can pay off on bets.) □ *The horses coming in first, second, and third are said to be in the money.*

in the mood (for sth**)** AND **in the mood (to** do sth**)** having the proper state of mind for a particular situation or for doing something. □ *I'm not in the mood to see a movie tonight.* □ *Are you in the mood for pizza?*

in the mood (to do sth**)** Go to previous.

in the near future *Cliché* in the time immediately ahead. □ *I don't plan to go to Florida in the near future.*

in the neighborhood (of some amount**)** Go to in the vicinity (of some amount).

in the nude Go to in the altogether.

in the offing *Fig.* happening at some time in the future. □ *It's hard to tell what's in the offing if you don't keep track of things.*

*in the open *Fig.* in the outdoors; in an area that is not closed in. (*Typically: **be** ~; **put** sth ~; **leave** sth **out** ~.) □ *John's bike was stolen because he left it out in the open.* □ *Mary loves gardening because she loves to be in the open.*

*in the picture *Fig.* well-informed; aware of what is going on. (*Typically: **be** ~; **keep** so ~; **put** so **[into]** ~.) □ *Please, keep me fully in the picture.* □ *John found out about the plan. He's in the picture now, so take care.*

*in the pink (of condition) AND ***in the pink (of health)** *Fig.* in very good health; in very good condition, physically and emotionally. (*Typically: **be** ~; **get [into]** ~.) □ *He recovered completely from his surgery and has been in the pink ever since.* □ *She was lively and active and in the pink of condition.*

in the pink (of health) Go to previous.

*in the pipeline *Fig.* backed up somewhere in a process; in process; in a queue. (*Typically: **be** ~; **get** sth **[into]** ~.) □ *There's a lot of goods still in the pipeline. That means no more new orders will be shipped for a while.*

*in the poorhouse 1. *Fig.* in a communal dwelling for impoverished persons. (The dwelling is a thing of the past, but the concept survives in the idiom. (*Typically: **live** ~; **end up** ~.) □ *He couldn't pay his debts and had to live in the poorhouse.* **2.** *Fig.* in a state of poverty. (*Typically: **live** ~; **end up** ~.) □ *If I lose my job, we'll end up in the poorhouse.*

in the prime of (one's**) life** *Fig.* in the best and most productive and healthy period of life. □ *He was struck down by a heart attack in the prime of life.*

***in the public eye** *Fig.* publicly; visible to all; conspicuous. (*Typically: **be** ~; **find** oneself ~; **get [into]** ~.) □ *Elected officials find themselves constantly in the public eye.*

in the raw Go to in the altogether.

in the rear located in the space or area behind someone or something; at the back door. □ *All deliveries must be made in the rear.*

***in the red** *Fig.* losing money. (As opposed to in the black. *Typically: **be** ~; **go [into]** ~.) □ *State government has been operating in the red for five straight years.*

in the right *Fig.* correct; morally or legally correct. □ *You are not in the right on this point.*

***in the right direction** *Fig.* toward progress and success. (*Typically: a **step** ~; **go** ~; **make a move** ~; **take a step** ~.) □ *Do you feel that this project is going in the right direction?* □ *You may not get what you want, but you've taken a step in the right direction.*

in the right place at the right time in the location where something good is to happen exactly when it happens. □ *I got a good deal on a car because I was in the right place at the right time.*

in the road AND **in the way** *Inf.* obstructing the way; in the pathway. □ *You are always in the road. Move aside.*

in the running *Fig.* in competition; competing and having a chance to win. □ *Is Tom still in the running? Does he still have a chance to be elected?*

in the same ballpark *Fig.* in the same general area of agreement or discussion.

(Refers to a ballpark figure = a reasonable estimate or guess. When people's estimates are substantially the same, they are in the same ballpark.) □ *I'm glad we're in the same ballpark on this matter. We should be able to strike an agreement in no time.*

***in the same boat (as** so**)** in the same situation; having the same problem. (*Typically: **be** ~; **get [into]** ~.) □ Tom: *I'm broke. Can you lend me $20?* Bill: *Sorry. I'm in the same boat.*

in the same breath *Fig.* [stated or said] almost at the same time. □ *He told me I was lazy, but then in the same breath he said I was doing a good job.*

in the same league as so/sth AND **in the same league with** so/sth *Fig.* in the same [good] class or grouping as someone or something else. □ *You are simply not in the same league with the other players, who practice every day.* □ *This wine isn't in the same league as the domestic equivalent.*

in the second place *Fig.* secondly; in addition. (Usually said after one has said in the first place.) □ *In the first place, you don't have enough money to buy one. In the second place, you don't need one.*

in the shadow of so AND **in** so's **shadow** *Fig.* made to seem lowly by someone with superior characteristics; made to seem less important by someone who is more important. □ *I always lived in the shadow of my father, who was far more successful than I was.*

in the short haul Go to over the short haul.

in the short run Go to over the short haul.

***in the soup** *Fig.* in a bad situation. (*Typically: **be** ~; **get [into]** ~.) □ *Now I'm really in the soup. I broke Mrs. Franklin's window.*

in the spotlight 1. in the beam of a spotlight, as on a stage. □ *The singer was in the spotlight but the band was almost in the dark.* **2.** AND **in the limelight** *Fig.* at the center of attention. (*Limelight* refers to an obsolete type of spotlight, and the word occurs only in this phrase. *Fig.* on

①.) □ *John will do almost anything to get himself into the limelight.* □ *I love being in the spotlight.*

*in the swim of things *Fig.* involved in or participating in events or happenings. (*Typically: **be ~; get [into] ~.**) □ *I've been ill, but soon I'll be back in the swim of things.* □ *I can't wait to settle down and get into the swim of things.*

in the thick of sth *Fig.* in the midst of the greatest activity; deeply involved in argument or negotiation. □ *There was a riot in the streets, and Fred found himself in the thick of it as he tried to get back to his hotel.*

*in the trust of so under the responsibility or in the care of someone. (*Typically: **be ~; leave** so/sth **~; place** so/sth **~.**) □ *The state placed the orphan in the trust of the foster parents.* □ *Our bonds are left in the trust of our broker.*

in the twinkling of an eye AND **in the wink of an eye; in the blink of an eye** *Fig.* very quickly. □ *I gave Bill $10, and in the twinkling of an eye, he spent it.*

in the unlikely event of sth AND **in the unlikely event that** sth happens if something—which probably will not happen—actually happens. □ *In the unlikely event of a fire, please walk quickly to an exit.*

*in the (very) nick of time *Fig.* just in time; at the last possible instant; just before it's too late. (*Typically: **arrive ~; get there (just) ~; happen ~; reach** sth **(just) ~; save** so **(just) ~.**) □ *The doctor arrived in the nick of time. The patient's life was saved.*

*in the vicinity (of some amount**)** AND ***in the neighborhood (of** some amount**)** *Fig.* approximately some amount. (*Typically: **somewhere ~.**) □ *I owe the bank somewhere in the vicinity of $24,000.*

in the wake of sth AND **in** sth's **wake** *Fig.* after something; as a result of some event. (Fig. on the image of a ship's wake.) □ *In the wake of the storm, there were many broken tree limbs.*

in the way Go to in the road.

in the way of sth **1.** as a kind of something; as a style of something. □ *We have nothing in the way of raincoats.* **2.** Go to in so's/sth's way.

in the wind *Fig.* about to happen. □ *There are some major changes in the wind. Expect these changes to happen soon.*

in the wink of an eye Go to in the twinkling of an eye.

in the works *Fig.* being prepared; being planned; being done. □ *There are some new laws in the works that will affect all of us.*

in the worst way 1. *Fig.* very much. □ *Bob wants to retire in the worst way.* **2.** in a manner that is the worst possible. (This is an ambiguity that is exploited in joking.) □ *He wanted to retire in the worst way, so he got himself fired. What could be worse?*

in the wrong *Fig.* wrong; morally or legally incorrect. □ *I am not in the wrong, you are.*

in the wrong place at the wrong time in the location where something bad is to happen exactly when it happens. □ *It isn't my fault. I was just in the wrong place at the wrong time.*

in theory *Fig.* according to a theory; theoretically. □ *In theory, if I take my medicine regularly, I will get well.*

in there *Sl.* sincere; likable. □ *Martha is really in there. Everybody likes her.*

in there pitching *Fig.* trying very hard. □ *Just stay in there pitching. You'll make some progress eventually.*

in these parts *Rur.* around here; in this area. □ *There aren't any big hospitals in these parts.*

the in thing (to do) *Fig.* the fashionable thing to do. □ *Eating low-fat food is the in thing to do.*

in this day and age *Fig.* now; in these modern times. □ *Bill: Taxes keep going up and up. Bob: What do you expect in this day and age?*

in time Go to in due course.

in time (with sth) Go to in step (with sth).

in times past *Fig.* long ago; in previous times. □ *In times past, you would not have been able to wear casual clothing to work.*

in top form 1. [of someone or some creature] in very good physical condition. □ *The runners are in top form, so this should be a good race.* **2.** able to make witty remarks and clever statements quickly and easily. □ *That was really funny, Bob. You are in top form tonight.*

in total Go to all in all.

***in touch (with** so) **1.** *Fig.* in contact with someone by letter or telephone. (*Typically: **be** ~; **get** ~; **keep** ~; **remain** ~; **stay** ~.) □ *I tried to get in touch with her, but she never answered her phone.* **2.** *Fig.* [of oneself] having self-knowledge. (Fig. on ①. *Typically: **be** ~; **get** ~.) □ *I need to get in touch with myself and the way I really feel about things.* **3.** *Fig.* sympathetic or sensitive to someone or something; having good contact or rapport with someone or something. (Fig. on ①. *Typically: **be** ~; **get** ~.) □ *We talk to each other, but we're not really in touch with each other.*

in tow *Fig.* closely following; under someone's control. □ *The nanny walked into the park with three children in tow.*

in transit *Fig.* while in the process of being transported. □ *The new stereo is now in transit from the manufacturer.*

in triplicate *Fig.* [of a document] produced in three copies. □ *Mr. Smith asked me to copy his notes in triplicate.*

***in trouble** *Euph.* pregnant and unmarried. (*Typically: **be** ~; **get [into]** ~.) □ *They had to get married. She was in trouble.*

in tune in a state where musical notes are at their proper intervals so that none are flat or sharp. □ *The choir members all sang in tune.*

***in tune with** so/sth **1.** in musical harmony with someone or something; playing or singing the exact same note as someone

or something. (*Typically: **be** ~; **get** ~.) □ *The violin is in tune with the piano.* **2.** *Fig.* in agreement with someone or something. (Fig. on ①. *Typically: **be** ~; **get** ~.) □ *Bill is just not in tune with the company's policies.*

***in tune with the times** *Fig.* up-to-date; in fashion. (*Typically: **be** ~; **get** ~.) □ *Look at that old jacket, Bill. You're not in tune with the times.*

in turn in the appropriate point in the series or order; when one's turn comes. □ *Someone has to wash the dishes after every meal. All of us will have to do it in turn.*

in two shakes of a lamb's tail *Fig.* in a very short time; very quickly. □ *Jane returned in two shakes of a lamb's tail.*

in unison *Fig.* [of musical notes, instruments, or voices] having the same pitch. □ *The twins sang in unison.*

in use *Fig.* [of some facility or device] occupied or busy. □ *Sorry, this room is in use.*

do sth **in vain** *Fig.* to do something for no purpose; to do something that fails. □ *We tried in vain to get her there on time.*

in view of sth *Fig.* in consideration of something; because of something. □ *In view of the high cost of gasoline, I sold my car.*

***in vogue** *Fig.* fashionable; faddish. (*Typically: **be** ~; **get** ~.) □ *This style of coat is no longer in vogue.*

in so's/sth's **way** AND **in the way of** so/sth **1.** in the pathway of someone. (*Typically: **be** ~; **get [into]** ~; **stand** ~.) □ *Don't get in Bob's way while he is bringing groceries in from the car.* **2.** *Fig.* interfering with a person in the pursuit of plans or intentions; hindering someone's plans. (Fig. on ①. *Typically: **be** ~; **get** ~; **stand** ~.) □ *I am going to leave home. Please don't get in my way.*

***an **in (with** so) *Fig.* a way to request a special favor from someone; an amount of influence with someone. (The *in* is a noun. *Typically: **get** ~; **have** ~; **give** so ~.) □ *Do you have an in with the mayor? I have to ask him a favor.*

*in with so *Fig.* favored by someone; experiencing someone's goodwill. (*Typically: **be** ~; **get** ~.) □ *I'm really in with my Spanish professor.* □ *I am trying to get in with the bank manager so I can get a loan.*

*in writing *Fig.* in written form rather than spoken. (*Typically: **get** sth ~; **have** sth ~; **put** so ~.) □ *Be sure to get their salary offer in writing.*

inch by inch *Fig.* one inch at a time; little by little. □ *Traffic moved along inch by inch.*

include sth **in the bargain** Go to throw sth into the bargain.

incumbent (up)on so **to** do sth serving as an obligation for someone. □ *It is incumbent on you to share some of the costs.*

induce labor in so to cause the onset of childbirth in a mother-to-be through the use of a special drugs. □ *They decided to induce labor in the mother-to-be.*

information superhighway Go to electronic superhighway.

ink sth **in**† **1.** *Fig.* to fill in an outline with ink. □ *Please ink the drawing in with care.* **2.** *Fig.* to write something in ink, especially to sign something. □ *Please ink your name in on the dotted line.*

*an inkling (about so/sth**)** *Fig.* an idea about someone or something; a hint about the nature of someone or something. (*Typically: **get** ~; **have** ~; **give** so ~.) □ *I had an inkling about the problems that you were going to run into.*

*an inkling (of sth**)** *Fig.* a hint about something that is to happen. (*Typically: **get** ~; **have** ~; **give** so ~.) □ *The speeches gave us an inkling of what we could expect from the new president.*

inner city 1. *Fig.* a poor part of a city; a slum. □ *She grew up in a housing project in the inner city.* **2.** *Fig.* having to do with the poor part of a city. □ *The camping program allows inner-city children to enjoy outdoor activities.*

*innocent as a lamb AND ***innocent as a newborn babe 1.** guiltless. (*Also: **as** ~.) □ *"Hey! You can't throw me in jail,"* cried the robber. *"I'm innocent as a lamb."* **2.** naive; inexperienced. (*Also: **as** ~.) □ *She's 18 years old, but innocent as a newborn babe.*

innocent as a newborn babe Go to previous.

the ins and outs (of sth**)** *Fig.* the correct and successful way to do something; the special things that one needs to know to do something. □ *I don't understand the ins and outs of politics.*

inside a week in less than a week. □ *We must get all this sorted out inside a week, all right?*

inside information *Fig.* information known only by those most involved with the issue; secret information relating to an organization. □ *I have some inside information about the Smith Company.*

an inside job a crime committed by someone working or living at the scene of the crime. □ *There was little doubt that it was an inside job, thought the inspector.*

an inside joke *Fig.* a joke that only certain people understand; a joke understood only by people who know certain facts and context. □ *What you said must be an inside joke. It makes no sense to me.*

the inside story *Fig.* an explanation known only by those most involved with the issue. □ *Well, I've heard the inside story, and it isn't what you were told at all!*

inside the box *Fig.* **1.** as if bound by old, nonfunctional, or limiting structures, rules, or practices. (Adverbial. Compare this with outside the box.) □ *If you keep your discussions inside the box, you will be bound by traditional limitations.* **2.** bound by old, nonfunctional, or limiting structures, rules, or practices. (Usually **inside-the-box**; adjectival.) □ *You have some really inside-the-box ideas, Ralph. Why not be more creative?*

*the inside track *Fig.* an advantage (over someone) gained through special connections, special knowledge, or favoritism. (*Typically: **get** ~; **have** ~; **give**

so ~.) □ *The boss likes me. Since I've got the inside track, I'll probably be the new office manager.*

intent on doing sth focused on and determined to do something. □ *He was very intent on sticking the thread through the eye of the needle without sticking the needle in his finger.*

intimate apparel *Euph.* women's underwear. □ *The catalog features intimate apparel for the larger lady.*

***intimate with** so *Euph.* having sexual intercourse with someone. (*Typically: **be** ~; **get** ~.) □ *He had never been intimate with a woman before.*

***into** sth *Fig.* to be interested or involved in something. (*Typically: **be** ~; **get** ~.) □ *I'm into model planes right now.*

in(to) a jam *Fig.* in(to) a difficult situation. □ *Mary cannot keep track of the many times Dave got himself into a jam.*

into being into existence. □ *The new law brought more problems into being.*

in(to) so's clutches *Fig.* in the control of someone who has power or authority over someone else. □ *Snow White fell into the clutches of the evil witch.*

***into overdrive** *Fig.* to pick up speed and energy. (*Typically: **go** ~; **move** ~; **shift** ~.) □ *We go into overdrive around here just before school starts. It's our busiest time.*

invasion of (so's) privacy *Fig.* an intrusion that results in the loss of someone's privacy. □ *The athlete complained about the invasion of his privacy by the press.*

***involved (with so) 1.** *Fig.* associated with someone romantically. (*Typically: **be** ~; **get** ~.) □ *Sally is getting involved with Bill. They've been seeing a lot of each other.* **2.** having established a romantic association with something. (*Typically: **be** ~; **get** ~.) □ *Bill is involved with Jane, and it's looking serious.*

***involved with** sth established in an association with something or some organization. (*Typically: **be** ~; **become** ~;

get ~.) □ *Bill got involved with a volunteer organization.*

iron sth **out**† *Fig.* to ease a problem; to smooth out a problem. (Here *problem* is synonymous with *wrinkle*.) □ *It's only a little problem. I can iron it out very quickly.* □ *We will iron out all these little matters first.*

sth **is (a) no go** *Inf.* something will not take place or be allowed. □ *Sorry, but the picnic is a no go. It has been canceled.*

sth **is killing** so *Fig.* something is causing someone pain. □ *Wow, my feet are killing me!*

One **is known by the company** one **keeps.** one is thought to have the same character and qualities as the people one associates with. (Proverbial or cautionary, warning that someone is associating with bad company.) □ *Bill, who are those people? They don't look at all savory. You are known by the company you keep.*

Is that some quality **or what?** Isn't that something good, such as great, wonderful, yummy, super, jazzy, etc.?; That is really "some quality." □ *Is that delicious or what?* □ *Why does she say "Is that great or what?" when just saying "That is really great!" would sound less flighty?*

(Is) this (seat) taken? an inquiry made by a person in a theater, auditorium, etc. asking someone already seated whether an adjacent seat is available or already taken. □ *Finally, Bill came to a row where there was an empty seat. Bill leaned over to the person sitting beside the empty seat and whispered, "Is this seat taken?"*

It ain't fittin' *Rur.* It is not right. It is inappropriate. □ *It ain't fittin' for the bridegroom to see his bride before the ceremony.*

(It) beats me. AND **(It's) got me beat.; You got me beat.** *Inf.* I do not know the answer.; I cannot figure it out. The question has me stumped. (The stress is on *me*.) □ *Bill: When are we supposed to go over to Tom's? Bill: Beats me.*

it behooves one **to** do sth *Cliché* it is necessary for one to do something; one is obligated to do something. □ *It behooves you to pay for the window that you broke.*

It blows my mind! *Sl.* It really amazes and shocks me. □ *Bill: Did you hear about Tom's winning the lottery? Sue: Yes, it blows my mind!*

It cuts two ways. *Inf.* There are two sides to the situation. □ *It cuts two ways, you know. It can't always all be my fault.*

(It) doesn't hurt to do sth. AND **(It) never hurts to** do sth. *Fig.* a phrase said when one makes an attempt to get approval, as with *try, take a chance, give it a try,* and most usually, *ask.* □ *John: Can I take some of these papers home with me? Jane: No, you can't. You know that. John: Well, it doesn't hurt to ask.*

It figures. *Fig.* It makes sense.; It confirms what one might have guessed.; I'm not surprised. □ *Bob: Tom was the one who broke the window. Bill: It figures. He's very careless.*

It has so's **name on it.** *Fig.* It belongs to someone.; It is meant for someone. □ *A: Is that an extra piece of cake? B: Yes, and it has your name on it.*

It is all over with so. AND **It is all over for** so. *Euph.* Someone is about to die.; Some has just died. □ *The doctor told us that it was all over for Daddy. We sat for a moment in shock.*

(It) just goes to show (you) (sth**).** AND **Just goes to show (you) (**sth**).** *Fig.* That incident or story has an important moral or message. □ *Tom: The tax people finally caught up with Henry. Sally: See! It just goes to show.*

(It) (just) goes without saying AND **That (just) goes without saying** *Cliché* [something] is so obvious that it need not be said. (Each entry head can be followed by a clause or just be used as an adverbial phrase.) □ *It goes without saying that you are to wear formal clothing to the White House dinner.*

It (just) so happens that . . . In fact . . . ; It is the case that . . . (Often said aloofly.)

□ *It just so happens that I am the mayor of this town!*

(It) never hurts to do sth. Go to (It) doesn't hurt to do sth.

It (only) stands to reason. *Fig.* It is only reasonable to hold a certain opinion. □ *It stands to reason that most people will not buy a new car if they don't think they can pay for it.*

It remains to be seen. AND **That remains to be seen.** is yet to be established or revealed; maybe. □ *Q: Will you be giving me a raise next month. A: That remains to be seen.*

It strikes me that . . . *Fig.* It seems to me that. . . . □ *Henry: It strikes me that you are losing a little weight. Mary: Oh, I'm so glad you noticed!*

(It) suits me (fine). *Fig.* It is fine with me. □ *John: I'd like to sit up front where I can hear better. Mary: Suits me fine.*

It takes all kinds (to make a world). *Fig.* There are many different kinds of people, and you should not condemn them for being different. □ *Child: Mommy, I saw a weird man today. He was walking down the street singing real loud. I wish they'd put weird people like that away. Mother: Now, now, honey, it takes all kinds to make a world.*

(It) takes one to know one. *Inf.* You are one also. □ *A: You are a stupid oaf. B: So are you. It takes one to know one.*

It takes (some) getting used to. *Fig.* It is very unpleasant at first, but after a time it will not be so bothersome. (Said in recognition of the unpleasantness of something.) □ *These hot Mexican dishes seem impossible at first. They take some getting used to, I agree. But it's worth it.*

It will be your ass! *Sl.* You will pay dearly!; You will suffer the consequences. □ *If you do that again, it will be your ass!*

It will take some doing. *Fig.* It will require considerable effort and care. □ *It's not impossible. It'll just take some doing.*

It won't wash!

It won't wash! *Fig.* Nobody will believe it! □ *Sorry, it won't wash. Try another approach.*

(It) works for me. *Inf.* It is fine with me. (With stress on *works* and *me*. The answer to a question implying Does it work for you?) □ *Bob: Is it okay if I sign us up for the party? Sally: It works for me.*

it would take an act of Congress to do sth *Fig.* it is almost impossible to do something. □ *It would take an act of Congress to get Bill to wear a necktie.*

*an itch for sth *Inf.* a desire for something. (*Typically: **get** ~; **have** ~; **give** so ~.) □ *I have an itch for some ice cream.*

itch for sth *Fig.* to desire something. □ *I'm just itching for a visit from Amy.*

*an itch to do sth *Fig.* a desire to do something. (*Typically: **get** ~; **have** ~; **give** so ~.) □ *I have an itch to see a movie tonight.*

*itchy feet *Fig.* the need to leave; a feeling of a need to travel; the need to leave or get going. (*Typically: **get** ~; **have** ~; **give** so ~.) □ *Hearing the train whistle at night gives me itchy feet.*

*an itchy palm AND ***an itching palm** *Fig.* [of a hand] in need of a tip. (As if placing money in the palm would stop the itching. *Typically: **get** ~; **have** ~; **give** so ~.) □ *All the waiters at that restaurant have itchy palms.*

It'll all come out in the wash. *Fig.* It does not matter.; No lasting damage has been done. □ *Tom: I feel so bad about what I said to Bill. I don't think he'll ever forgive me. Mary: Oh, don't worry. It'll all come out in the wash.*

It'll be a cold day in hell when sth happens. *Inf.* something will never happen or is highly unlikely. □ *It'll be a cold day in hell when the city council agrees on where to build that bridge.*

It'll never fly. *Fig.* It will never work!; It will never be approved! (Refers originally to an evaluation of an unlikely looking aircraft of some type.) □ *I have read your report and studied your proposal. It'll never fly.*

It's a (dead) cinch. *Fig.* It's a very easy task. (*Dead* = absolutely.) □ *Tom: Did you figure out how to change the tire? Jane: Yep! It was a cinch.*

It's a deal. *Fig.* Okay.; It is agreed. □ *Bill: Let's go to dinner together tonight. Mary: It's a deal.*

It's a funny thing, but . . . AND **Funny thing is that . . . ; Funny thing, . . .** *Inf.* Here's something interesting. (Never laughably funny. A formulaic way of introducing a subject that might be interesting. Note the use of *but*.) □ *It's a funny thing, but I never seem to be able to fill up my iPod.* □ *Funny thing, mine got filled up in a week.*

It's a jungle out there. The real world is severe.; It's hard to get by in everyday life. □ *A: Gee, people are so rude in this town. B: Yup, it's a jungle out there.*

It's a snap. *Inf.* It's really easy to do. □ *Nothing to it. It's a snap. A baby could do it.*

It's a toss-up. *Inf.* It's hard to tell the winner, and it could be won by either player or either team. □ *The game's almost over, and it's a toss-up.*

(It's) about time! *Inf.* It is almost too late!; I've been waiting a long time! (Said with impatience.) □ *So you finally got here! It's about time!*

It's all SO **needs.** Go to That's all SO needs.

It's all over but the shouting. *Fig. Cliché* It is decided and concluded.; It is essentially decided and finished. (Meaning that though there may be more to some process, the outcome is clear. An elaboration of all over = finished.) □ *The last goal was made with only four seconds to go in the game. "Well, it's all over but the shouting," said the coach.*

It's all yours. 1. Take it. I relinquish rights to it. □ *You found the ring on the street.*

It's all yours. **2.** I am letting go of the load, and you have complete control of it. □ *Bob pushed the board through the window into Tom's hands. When it seemed like Tom had it, Bob said, "It's all yours."*

It's anybody's guess. AND **No way to tell. No telling.** *Fig.* There is no way to know.; No one knows, so anyone's guess is as good as anyone else's. □ *A: When will the messenger be here? B: It's anybody's guess.*

It's been. *Inf.* a phrase said on leaving a party or other gathering. (A shortening of "It's been lovely" or some similar expression.) □ *Mary: Well, it's been. We really have to go, though. Andy: So glad you could come over. Bye.*

It's been a slice! *Sl.* It's been good. (Possibly, a "slice of life.") □ *Good-bye and thank you. It's been a slice!*

(It's) better than nothing. *Fig.* Having something that is not satisfactory is better than having nothing at all. □ *John: How do you like your dinner? Jane: It's better than nothing. John: That bad, huh?*

(It's) got me beat. Go to (It) beats me.

it's high time *Inf.* it is about the right time for something. □ *It's high time you started thinking about saving for your old age.*

It's just one of those things. *Fig.* It is something that couldn't have been prevented.; It is an unfortunate thing caused by fate. (In a Cole Porter song title: "Just One of Those Things.") □ *I'm sorry, too. It's not your fault. It's just one of those things.*

It's news to me! No one told me that, and it's contrary to what I already knew. (Said particularly when the news affects the person saying the phrase.) □ *A: You are supposed to clean up the conference room. B: It's news to me! I thought we paid people to come in and do that.*

It's no picnic! *Inf.* There is nothing easy or pleasant about it. □ *I was on welfare for a year, and it's no picnic.*

it's no use (doing sth) AND **there's no use** (doing sth) *Fig.* it is hopeless to do something; it is pointless to do something. □

It's no use trying to call on the telephone. The line is always busy.

It's not cricket. AND **It's not kosher.** *Fig.* It is just not to be done.; It's not acceptable. (The *cricket* is thought to be borrowed from British English, in the sense of "following the laws of cricket in a sportsmanlike manner." *Kosher* is from Hebrew *kasher* meaning fit [for eating] according to Jewish dietary laws.) □ *You can't do that! It's not cricket!*

(It's) not half bad. *Fig.* It's not as bad as one might have thought. □ *Mary: How do you like this play? Jane: Not half bad.*

It's not kosher. Go to It's not cricket.

It's not over till it's over. *Inf.* It is not over yet and will not be until the event has completely played out. □ *It looks like we have won, but it's not over till it's over!*

It's on me. *Fig.* I will pay this bill. (Usually a bill for a meal or drinks. Compare this with This one is on (so).) □ *As the waiter set down the glasses, Fred said, "It's on me," and grabbed the check.*

It's six of one, half a dozen of another. *Cliché* Two options are equivalent. □ *To get downtown, we can either take the highway or the side streets. It's six of one, half a dozen of another, since both routes take the same amount of time.*

It's written all over one's **face.** *Fig.* It is very evident and can easily be detected when looking at someone's face. □ *I know she's guilty. It's written all over her face.*

It's you! *Fig.* It suits you perfectly.; It is just your style. □ *John (trying on a jacket): How does this look? Sally: It's you!*

It's your funeral. *Fig.* If that is what you are going to do, you will have to endure the dire consequences. □ *Tom: I'm going to call in sick and go to the ball game instead of to work today. Mary: Go ahead. It's your funeral.*

It's your move. 1. AND **It's your turn.** *Fig.* [in a game] It's your time to play. □ *It's your move, and I think I have you trapped.* **2.** *Fig.* It is time for you to do something. □ *I've done everything I could do. Now, it's your move.*

It's your turn. Go to previous.

itsy bitsy Go to next.

itty bitty AND **itsy bitsy** very small. (Childish.) □ *I remember when you was just an itty bitty baby.*

(I've) been there(, done that). *Inf.* I know exactly what you are talking about from my own experience.; I know exactly what you are going through. □ *John: Wow! Those sales meetings really wear me out! Jane: I know what you mean. I've been there.*

(I've) (got) better things to do. AND **I have better things to do.** *Fig.* There are better ways to spend my time.; I cannot waste any more time on this matter. □ *Good-bye. I've got better things to do than stand around here listening to you brag.* □ *Mary: How did things go at your meeting with the zoning board? Sally: I gave up. Can't fight city hall. Better things to do.*

(I've) got to go home and get my beauty sleep. *Fig.* a phrase announcing one's need to depart because it is late. □ *Sue: Leaving so early? John: I've got to go home and get my beauty sleep.*

I've had it up to here (with so/sth**).** *Fig.* I will not endure any more of someone or something. □ *Bill: I've had it up to here with your stupidity. Bob: Who's calling who stupid?*

(I've) seen better. *Fig.* a noncommittal and not very positive judgment about something or someone. □ *Alice: How did you like the movie? John: I've seen better.*

(I've) seen worse. *Fig.* a noncommittal and not totally negative judgment about something or someone. □ *Alice: How did you like the movie? John: I've seen worse.*

jack around AND **jerk around** *Sl.* to waste time. □ *Stop jacking around and get some work done!*

jack of all trades someone who can do several different jobs instead of specializing in one. □ *John can do plumbing, carpentry, and roofing—a real jack of all trades.*

jack so **up**† **1.** *Sl.* to excite or stimulate someone, possibly with drugs. □ *Tom jacked up Fred with a bit of meth.* **2.** *Sl.* to motivate someone; to stimulate someone to do something. □ *The mail is late again today. We'll have to jack those people up at the post office.*

jack sth **up**† *Inf.* to raise the price of something. □ *The store keeps jacking prices up.*

a **jam session** *Inf.* an informal session where musicians play together. □ *Andy and Nick had a jam session last night and kept all the neighbors awake.*

jam the brakes on† to press down hard on a vehicle's brakes. □ *Alice jammed the brakes on, and the car skidded all over the place.*

jam sth **up**† **1.** *Fig.* to clog up something; to impede or block the movement of or through something. □ *Rachel jammed traffic up when her car stalled.* **2.** *Fig.* to force something upward in haste or anger. □ *Who jammed the window up?*

jam with so to play music in an improvised band with someone. □ *Andy loves to jam with the other students.*

jazz so/sth **up**† *Inf.* to make someone or something more exciting or sexy; to make someone or something appeal more to contemporary tastes. □ *Let's jazz this room up a little bit.*

jazzed (up) 1. *Inf.* alert; having a positive state of mind. □ *Those guys were jazzed and ready for the game.* **2.** *Inf.* intoxicated. □ *Gert was jazzed out of her mind. Couldn't even stand up.* **3.** *Inf.* enhanced; with something added; made more enticing. □ *The third act was jazzed up with livelier music.* **4.** *Inf.* forged or altered. □ *Better not try to cash a jazzed check at this bank.*

Jekyll and Hyde *Fig.* someone with both an evil and a good personality. (From the novel *The Strange Case of Dr. Jekyll and Mr. Hyde* by Robert Louis Stevenson.) □ *Bill thinks Mary is so soft and gentle, but she can be very cruel—she is a real Jekyll and Hyde.*

jerk around Go to jack around.

jerk so **around**† AND **jerk** so **over**† *Inf.* to hassle someone; to waste someone's time. □ *Stop jerking me around and give me my money back!*

jerk so **over**† Go to previous.

The **jig is up.** Go to The **game is up.**

jim dandy *Inf.* excellent. □ *This is a jim dandy knife. Where'd you get it?*

***the jitters** *Fig.* nervous shaking. (*Typically: **get** ~; **have** ~; **give** so ~.) □ *I was so nervous that I got the jitters and nearly dropped my cup of coffee.*

jockey around to move around as if trying to get into a special position. (Fig. on a jockey trying to move a racehorse into a better position.) □ *She always has to jockey around a bit when she is getting into a parking place.*

jockey for position 1. to work one's horse into a desired position in a horse race. □ *Ken was behind but jockeying for position.*

2. *Inf.* to work oneself into a desired position. (Fig. on ①.) □ *The candidates were jockeying for position, trying to get the best television exposure.*

jog so's **memory** *Fig.* to stimulate someone's memory to recall something. □ *Hearing the first part of the song I'd forgotten really jogged my memory.*

jog to the right or left [for a road, path, etc.] to turn to the right or left. □ *Keep going until the road jogs to the left. Our driveway is on the right side.*

one's **John Henry** AND one's **John Hancock** *Inf.* one's signature. □ *Just put your John Henry on this line, and we'll bring your new car around.*

Johnny-come-lately *Fig.* someone who joins in (something) after it is under way. □ *Don't pay any attention to Sally. She's just a Johnny-come-lately and doesn't know what she's talking about.*

Johnny-on-the-spot *Fig.* someone who is in the right place at the right time. □ *Here I am, Johnny-on-the-spot. I told you I would be here at 12:20.*

join hands [for people] to hold hands so that each person is holding the hands of two other people; [for two people] to hold each other's hands. □ *Let us join hands and pray together.* □ *The dancers joined hands and formed a circle that moved to the left.*

Join the club! *Inf.* an expression indicating that the person spoken to is in the same, or a similar, unfortunate state as the speaker. □ *You don't have any place to stay? Join the club! Neither do we.* □ *Did you get fired too? Join the club!*

join the fray AND **jump into the fray; enter the fray** *Fig.* to join the fight or argument. □ *After listening to the argument, Mary decided to jump into the fray.* □ *Tom joined the fray and immediately got knocked down.*

join the ranks of sth *Fig.* to become part of a group of people. □ *We hope that you too will join the ranks of satisfied customers who enjoy Wonder Widgets each day.*

joined at the hip *Sl.* closely connected; always together. (Fig. on conjoined twins.) □ *Those two are joined at the hip. They are always together.*

The **joke is on** so. **1.** *Fig.* someone is the butt of the joke. □ *The joke is on Bob, so it's good that he is a good sport.* **2.** *Fig.* the joke has backfired on someone. □ *Ha, ha! The joke's on you after all.*

joking aside Go to (all) joking aside.

jot and tittle the smallest detail, especially in reference to correct spelling and punctuation. (A *jot* is an *iota*, the ninth letter of the Greek alphabet or the "i." A *tittle* refers to the dot of the *i* and any other diacritic. Jot and tittle is biblical, Matthew 5:18.) □ *I had to make sure that every jot and tittle was just right; otherwise, my term paper would be rejected.*

jot sth **down**† to make a note of something. □ *This is important. Please jot this down.*

juice and cookies any trivial and uninteresting snacks or refreshments. □ *After juice and cookies, we all went back into the meeting room for another hour of talk, talk, talk.*

jump all over so AND **jump down** so's **throat; jump on** so *Fig.* to scold someone severely. □ *If I don't get home on time, my parents will jump all over me.*

jump at the chance Go to leap at the opportunity (to do sth).

jump at the opportunity Go to leap at the opportunity (to do sth).

jump bail AND **skip bail** *Fig.* to fail to appear in court for trial and forfeit one's bail bond. □ *Not only was Bob arrested for theft, he skipped bail and left town. He's in a lot of trouble.*

jump down so's **throat** Go to jump all over so.

jump for joy Go to leap for joy.

jump in (with both feet) Go to dive in (with both feet).

jump into the fray Go to join the fray.

jump off the deep end Go to go off the deep end.

*the **jump on** so *Inf.* a chance to do something before someone else. (*Typically: **get** ~; **have** ~; **give** so ~.) □ *Each reporter is trying to get the jump on the others with the story about the earthquake.*

jump out of one's **skin** Go to (almost) jump out of one's skin.

jump out of the frying pan (and) into the fire Go to out of the frying pan (and) into the fire.

jump ship 1. *Fig.* to leave one's job on a ship and fail to be aboard it when it sails; [for a sailor] to go AWOL. □ *One of the deck hands jumped ship at the last port.* **2.** *Fig.* to leave any post or position; to quit or resign, especially when there is difficulty with the job. □ *None of the editors liked the new policies, so they all jumped ship as soon as other jobs opened up.*

jump the gun *Fig.* to start before the starting signal. (Originally used in sports contests that are started by firing a gun.) □ *We all had to start the race again because Jane jumped the gun.*

jump the track 1. [for something] to fall or jump off the rails or guides. (Usually said about a train.) □ *The train jumped the track, causing many injuries to the passengers.* **2.** *Fig.* to change suddenly from one thing, thought, plan, or activity to another. □ *The entire project jumped the track, and we finally had to give up.*

jump through a hoop AND **jump through hoops** *Fig.* to do everything possible to obey or please someone. (Trained circus animals jump through hoops.) □ *What do you want me to do—jump through a hoop?*

jump to conclusions AND **leap to conclusions** *Fig.* to judge or decide something without having all the facts; to reach unwarranted conclusions. (See also rush to conclusions.) □ *Now don't jump to conclusions. Wait until you hear what I have to say.* □ *Please find out all the facts so you won't leap to conclusions.*

jump to mind AND **spring to mind** *Fig.* to be remembered suddenly. (More sudden than come to mind.) □ *An idea jumps to mind. What if we simply ignore the deadline?*

jumping-off place Go to next.

jumping-off point AND **jumping-off place** *Fig.* a point or place from which to begin something. □ *The local library is a good jumping-off point for your research.*

jump-start so/sth *Inf.* to get someone or something going or functioning. □ *I need to jump-start Bill early in the morning to get him going in time to get on the road by a decent hour.*

junk mail *Fig.* annoying, unsolicited mail, such as promotional letters, etc. □ *I am so incredibly tired of getting pound after pound of junk mail every day. I could just scream.*

The **jury is still out on (**so/sth**).** *Fig.* A decision has not been reached on someone or something.; The people making the decision on someone or something have not yet decided. □ *The jury is still out on Jane. We don't know what we are going to do about her.*

just a minute AND **just a moment** *Fig.* only a short time; [wait] a short period of time. □ *I'm almost done. I'll be there in just a minute!*

Just a minute(, you)! *Fig.* Stop where you are! (Not very polite.) □ *Just a minute, you! Where are you going with my coat?*

just a moment Go to just a minute.

just as I expected I thought so; I knew it would be this way. □ *Just as I expected. The window was left open and it rained in.*

(just) between you and me Go to between you (and) me and the bedpost.

(just) can't wait (for sth **(to happen))** AND **(just) can't wait (to** do sth**)** to be very eager, as if to be unable to endure the wait for something to happen. (Also with cannot.) □ *Tom can't wait for Mary to return.* □ *I'm glad it's almost summertime—I just can't wait to go swimming!*

just one's **cup of tea** *Fig.* to be something that one prefers or desires. □ *This spy novel is just my cup of tea.*

just fell off the turnip truck *Rur.* ignorant; unsophisticated. □ *He stood there gawking at the buildings in town like he just fell off the turnip truck.*

Just goes to show (you) (sth). Go to (It) just goes to show (you) (sth).

just in case *Fig.* in the event that (something happens). □ *All right. I'll take my umbrella just in case.* □ *I'll take along some aspirin, just in case.*

just in time (to do sth) AND **just in time (for sth)** *Fig.* at the last possible time. □ *He got to the meeting just in time. They had just started the topic he was supposed to talk about.*

just let me say Go to let me (just) say.

just now at this point in time; in the time range that we are speaking about. □ *These square gold earrings are very popular just now.*

just off the boat *Fig.* to be newly immigrated and perhaps gullible and naive. □ *He may act like he's just off the boat, but he's very savvy.*

(just) say the word *Fig.* to give a signal to begin; to say yes or okay. (There is no particular word assumed, but something like *go, okay, start, fire, now, let 'er rip* would be appropriate.) □ *I'm ready to start anytime you say the word.*

just shy of enough just lacking enough of something not to constitute a complete amount. (See also a few bricks shy of a load.) □ *This stack of wood is just shy of a cord.* □ *You are just shy of having enough money to buy this tractor.*

(just) taking care of business *Fig.* doing what I am supposed to do; an answer to the question "What are you doing lately?" (Also abbreviated T.C.B.) □ *Look, officer, I'm just standing here, taking care of business, and this guy comes up and slugs me.*

just the same Go to all the same.

just the same (to so) Go to all the same (to so).

just the ticket *Fig.* to be just the perfect thing. □ *I'm tired! A good, hot cup of coffee will be just the ticket.*

just what the doctor ordered *Fig.* exactly what is required, especially for health or comfort. □ *That meal was delicious, Bob. Just what the doctor ordered.*

K

a **kangaroo court** a bogus or illegal court. □ *I've heard enough accusations! Is this a staff meeting or a kangaroo court?*

Katie bar the door. Prepare immediately for an advancing threat. □ *Katie bar the door, the grandchildren are here and they all look hungry.*

keel over *Fig.* to fall over; to faint. □ *I was so hot in the room that I almost keeled over.*

keen on doing sth willing or eager to do something. (More U.K. than U.S.) □ *The children are keen on swimming this afternoon. Shall I take them?*

keen on so/sth AND **keen about** so/sth to be enthusiastic about someone or something. (More U.K. than U.S.) □ *I'm not too keen on going to Denver.* □ *Sally is fairly keen about getting a new job.*

keep a civil tongue (in one's **head)** *Fig.* to speak decently and politely. □ *Please, John. Don't talk like that. Keep a civil tongue in your head.*

keep a close rein on so/sth Go to keep a tight rein on so/sth.

keep a close watch on so/sth to watch someone or something very carefully. □ *I want to keep a close watch on the house across the street.*

keep a date open (for so/sth**)** Go to leave a date open (for so/sth).

keep a firm grip on so/sth AND **keep a tight grip on** so/sth *Fig.* to keep someone or something under firm control. □ *The manager keeps a firm grip on all the employees.*

keep a low profile Go to a low profile.

keep a promise AND **keep** one's **promise** *Fig.* to make good on a promise; to fulfill one's promise. □ *If you can't keep your promises, you shouldn't make them in the first place.*

keep a secret *Fig.* to know a secret and not tell anyone. □ *Please keep our little secret private.*

keep a straight face Go to a straight face.

keep a tight grip on so/sth Go to keep a firm grip on so/sth.

keep a tight rein on so/sth AND **keep a close rein on** so/sth *Fig.* to watch and control someone or something diligently. (Fig. on the idea of controlling a horse by a tight grip on the reins.) □ *The office manager kept a tight rein on the staff.* □ *Mary keeps a close rein on her children.*

keep abreast of sth AND **stay abreast of** sth *Fig.* to monitor and keep informed about something, usually news. □ *I read the newspaper so I can keep abreast of the news.*

keep after so (**about** sth) AND **keep at** so (**about** sth); **keep on** so (**about** sth); **stay after** so (**about** sth) *Fig.* to remind or nag someone over and over to do something. □ *I'll keep after you until you do it!* □ *Mother stayed after Bill until he did the dishes.* □ *We will have to keep on him about the report until he turns it in.*

keep ahead of the game Go to ahead of the game.

keep an act up[†] AND **keep** one's **act up**[†] *Fig.* to maintain behavior that is a false show; to continue with one's facade. (The *an* can be replaced with *the, this, that,* etc.) □ *How long do I have to keep this* *act up? I am tired of fooling people.* □ *I am weary of keeping up my act.*

keep an ear to the ground AND **have an ear to the ground; keep one's ear to the ground; have one's ear to the ground** *Fig.* to devote attention to watching or listening for clues as to what is going to happen. □ *John had his ear to the ground, hoping to find out about new ideas in computers.*

keep an eye on so/sth AND **have an eye on** so/sth; **keep one's eye(s) on** so/sth; **keep one eye on** so/sth; **have one's eye on** so/sth *Fig.* to watch someone or something; to monitor someone or something closely. □ *I have my eye on the apple tree. When the apples ripen, I'll harvest them.*

keep an eye out (for so/sth**)** AND **have an eye out (for** so/sth**); keep one's eye out (for** so/sth**); have one's eye out (for** so/sth**)** *Fig.* to watch for the arrival or appearance of someone or something. □ *Please try to have an eye out for the bus.* □ *Keep an eye out for rain.* □ *Have your eye out for a raincoat on sale.*

keep an open mind Go to an open mind.

keep at sth *Fig.* to persist at doing something; to continue trying to do something. □ *John kept at his painting until the whole house was done.*

keep so/sth **at a distance** *Fig.* to retain some amount of physical distance from someone or something. □ *Please try to keep Tom at a distance. He just gets in the way.*

keep so/sth **at arm's length** AND **hold** so/sth **at arm's length** *Fig.* to keep someone or something at a distance, either physical or social distance. □ *I can't stand her and tend to keep her at arm's length whenever we meet.*

keep at arm's length from so/sth AND **keep** so/sth **at arm's length** *Fig.* to retain a degree of physical or social remoteness from someone or something. □ *I try to keep at arm's length from Larry since our disagreement.*

keep so/sth **at bay** Go to at bay.

keep so **back** AND **hold** so **back 1.** *Fig.* to keep a child in the same grade for an extra year. □ *We asked them to keep John back a year.* **2.** *Fig.* to keep someone from advancing in life. □ *I think that your limited vocabulary is keeping you back.* **3.** *Fig.* to keep someone, such as a player, in reserve. □ *They keep me back until the third quarter.*

keep sth **back**† AND **hold** sth **back**† **1.** to restrain a dog or other animal. □ *Keep that animal back! I don't wish to be bitten!* **2.** *Fig.* to withhold information. □ *I have the feeling that the witness is holding something back.* **3.** *Fig.* to retain an amount of money owed until a transaction is completed. □ *I'll hold back a thousand until you complete the job. Okay?*

keep banker's hours *Fig.* to work or be open for business for less than eight hours a day. □ *The advertising agency keeps banker's hours. They are open only until 4:00.*

keep body and soul together *Fig.* to manage to keep existing, especially when one has very little money. (Compare this with keep the wolf from the door.) □ *I don't earn enough money to keep body and soul together.*

keep one's cards close to one's **vest** Go to play one's cards close to one's chest.

keep one's chin up *Fig.* to keep one's spirits high; to act brave and confident. □ *Keep your chin up, John. Things will get better.*

keep clear of sth Go to clear of sth.

keep so **company** *Fig.* to sit or stay with someone, especially someone who is lonely. □ *He was very grateful for someone to keep him company. He gets very lonely.*

keep company (with so**) 1.** *Fig.* to spend much time with someone; to associate with or consort with someone. □ *Bill has been keeping company with Ann for three months.* **2.** *Fig.* to be courting someone. □ *I heard that Joe is keeping company with Jim Brown's daughter.*

keep cool *Inf.* to stay calm and undisturbed. □ *If Sally could just keep cool before a race, she could probably win.*

keep one's **cool** *Inf.* to remain calm and in control. □ *It's hard to keep your cool when you've been cheated.*

keep one's **distance from** so/sth Go to stay clear of so/sth.

keep so **down**† Go to hold so down†.

keep sth **down 1.** *Fig.* to retain food in one's stomach rather than throwing it up. □ *I've got the flu, and I can't keep any food down.* **2.** *Fig.* to keep spending under control. □ *I work hard to keep expenses down.*

keep one's **end of the bargain** Go to hold one's end of the bargain up†.

keep one's **end of the bargain up**† Go to hold one's end of the bargain up†.

keep one's **end up**† *Fig.* to carry through on one's part of a bargain. □ *You have to keep your end up like the rest of us.*

keep one's **eye on** so/sth *Fig.* to have one's attention directed to someone or something. □ *Please keep your eye on the children while I go to the store.*

keep one's **eye on the ball 1.** *Fig.* to watch or follow the ball carefully, especially when one is playing a ball game; to follow the details of a ball game very carefully. □ *John, if you can't keep your eye on the ball, I'll have to take you out of the game.* **2.** *Fig.* to remain alert to the events occurring around oneself. (Fig. on ①.) □ *If you want to get along in this office, you're going to have to keep your eye on the ball.*

keep one's **eyes open (for** so/sth**)** AND **keep** one's **eyes peeled (for** so/sth**)** *Fig.* to remain alert and watchful for someone or something. (*Peel* refers to moving the eyelids back.) □ *I'm keeping my eyes open for a sale on winter coats.* □ *Please keep your eyes peeled for Mary. She's due to arrive here any time.*

keep one's **eyes peeled (for** so/sth**)** Go to previous.

keep faith with so/sth *Fig.* to be loyal to someone or something. □ *I intend to keep faith with my people and all they stand for.*

keep one's **feet on the ground** AND **have** one's **feet on the ground; have both feet on the ground** *Fig.* to remain calm and stable. □ *You will do all right if you have your feet on the ground. Don't get carried away.*

keep one's **finger on the pulse of** sth AND **have** one's **finger on the pulse of** sth *Fig.* to monitor the current state of something frequently. (Fig. on the image of someone feeling someone's pulse.) □ *It is hard to keep your finger on the pulse of Washington, D.C., but a good reporter must do it.*

keep one's **fingers crossed (for** so/sth**)** AND **cross** one's **fingers** to wish for luck for someone or something, sometimes by actually crossing one's fingers; to hope for a good outcome for someone or something. □ *I hope you win the race Saturday. I'm keeping my fingers crossed for you.*

keep fit *Fig.* to keep in good physical condition. □ *I do everything I can to keep fit.*

keep sth **for a rainy day** Go to save (sth) for a rainy day.

keep sth **for another occasion** Go to leave sth for another occasion.

keep good time *Fig.* [for a watch or clock] to be accurate. □ *I have to return my watch to the store because it doesn't keep good time.*

keep so **guessing** AND **leave** so **guessing** to keep someone ignorant or confused (about something or oneself). □ *She won't tell men whether she likes them or not. She likes to keep them guessing.*

keep one's **hand in (**sth**)** *Fig.* to remain involved in something, perhaps only a token involvement. □ *I want to keep my hand in things even after I retire.*

keep one's **hands clean** Go to keep one's nose clean.

keep one's **hands off (**sth**)** to refrain from touching or handling something. □ *I'm* *going to put these cookies here. You keep your hands off them.*

keep one's **hands to** oneself *Fig.* to refrain from touching anything or anyone; to refrain from punching or poking someone. □ *Keep your hands to yourself while we are in the toy store.*

keep so/sth **hanging (in midair)** Go to leave so/sth hanging (in midair).

keep harping on sth to continue to talk or complain about something; to keep raising a topic of conversation. (See also harp on so/sth.) □ *Why do you keep harping on the same old complaint?*

keep one's **head** *Fig.* to remain calm and sensible when in an awkward situation that might cause a person to panic or go out of control. □ *She was very angry. We had to calm her down and encourage her to keep her head.*

keep one's **head above water** AND **get** one's **head above water; hold** one's **head above water 1.** to keep from drowning when swimming or floating. □ *I was so tired, cold, and wet I could hardly keep my head above water.* **2.** *Fig.* to manage to survive, especially financially. (Fig. on ①.) □ *We have so little money that we can hardly keep our heads above water.* **3.** *Fig.* to keep up with one's work. (Fig. on ①.) □ *It's all I can do to keep my head above water with the work I have. I can't take on any more.*

keep one's **head down** *Fig. Lit.* to keep oneself safe from harm or criticism by not being an obvious target. (Fixed order. As if one were making one's body more compact to avoid being a good target for gunfire.) □ *Yes, your review is going to be a tough one. Just keep your head down, and try not to draw more criticism.*

keep house *Fig.* to manage a household. □ *I hate to keep house. I'd rather live in a tent than keep house.*

keep so **in (a state of) suspense** to make someone wait anxiously for something. □ *Tell us what happened. Don't keep us in a state of suspense.*

keep so/sth **in check** AND **hold** so/sth **in check** *Fig.* to keep someone or something under control; to restrain someone or something. □ *I was so angry I could hardly hold myself in check.*

keep in good with so *Fig.* to remain in someone's favor. □ *I always try to keep in good with the boss's secretary.*

keep so/animal **in line** *Fig.* to make certain that someone behaves properly. (Fig. on the image of a person trying to keep someone else in a line of people.) □ *It's very hard to keep Bill in line. He's sort of rowdy.*

keep so **in mind** remember that someone is available or eligible to be chosen for something. □ *If you need an experienced floor refinisher, keep me in mind.*

keep sth **in mind** AND **bear** sth **in mind** *Fig.* remember something; be prepared to recall some bit of information. □ *Keep what I told you in mind while you are away at camp.*

keep so/sth **in mind (for** so/sth**)** to remember to mention or think about someone or something in regard to someone or something. □ *I will keep a position in mind for John, since he is graduating soon.*

keep so/sth **in reserve** Go to hold so/sth in reserve.

keep so **in sight** to make sure that a person is visible at all times. □ *He looks suspicious. Keep him in sight at all times.*

keep so **in stitches** *Fig.* to cause someone to laugh loud and hard, for a period of time. □ *The teacher kept the class in stitches, but the students didn't learn anything.*

Keep in there! *Inf.* Keep trying! □ *Andy: Don't give up, Sally. Keep in there! Sally: I'm doing my best!*

Keep in touch. *Inf. Fig.* Good-bye. (Sometimes a sarcastic way of saying good-bye to someone one doesn't care about.) □ *Nice talking to you. Keep in touch.*

keep in touch (with so**)** Go to in touch (with so).

283

keep sth **inside ((of) one(self))** Go to hold sth in†.

keep it down (to a dull roar) *Fig.* to keep quiet or as quiet as possible. □ *Please try to keep it down to a dull roar, could you?*

Keep it up! 1. *Fig.* Keep up the good work.; Keep on doing it.; Keep (on) trying. □ *Jane: I think I'm doing better in calculus. John: Keep it up!* **2.** *Fig.* Just keep acting that way and see what happens to you. (Compare this with **(Go ahead,) make my day!**) □ *John: You're just not doing what is expected of you. Bill: Keep it up! Just keep it up, and I'll quit right when you need me most.* □ *"Your behavior is terrible, young man! You just keep it up and see what happens," warned Alice. "Just keep it up!"*

keep late hours *Fig.* to stay up or stay out until very late at night. (Does not refer to arriving late to work in the morning. It refers to the *cause* of being late in the morning.) □ *I'm always tired because I keep late hours.* □ *If I didn't keep late hours, I wouldn't sleep so late in the morning and I wouldn't be late for work.*

keep one's **mind off (of)** so/sth Go to get one's mind off (of) so/sth.

keep one's **mind on** so/sth *Fig.* to concentrate on someone or something. □ *He is keeping his mind on Jane instead of his work.*

keep one's **mouth shut (about** so/sth**)** *Fig.* to keep quiet about someone or something; to keep a secret about someone or something. □ *They told me to keep my mouth shut about the boss or I'd be in big trouble.*

keep one's **nose clean** AND **keep** one's **hands clean** *Fig.* to keep out of trouble, especially trouble with the law. □ *I'm trying to keep my nose clean by staying away from those rough guys.*

keep one's **nose out of** sth *Fig.* to stay out of something, such as someone else's business. (See also **keep** one's **nose out of** so's **business.**) □ *Try to keep your nose out of stuff that doesn't concern you.* □ *Keep your nose out of my personal affairs.*

keep one's **nose out of** so's **business** *Fig.* to refrain from interfering in someone else's business. (See also **keep** one's **nose out of** sth.) □ *Let John have his privacy, and keep your nose out of my business, too!*

keep one's **nose to the grindstone** *Fig.* to work hard and constantly. □ *Mary kept her nose to the grindstone while her friends were out enjoying themselves.*

keep on (doing sth**)** to continue to do something. □ *Are you going to keep on singing all night?*

keep on sth *Fig.* to pay close attention to something. □ *This is a problem. Keep on it until it's settled.*

keep so **on** Go to next.

keep so **on** sth **1.** *Fig.* to retain someone as an employee. □ *Ken could not be kept on the payroll any longer.* **2.** AND **keep** so **on** *Fig.* to retain someone in employment longer than is required or was planned. □ *She worked out so well that we decided to keep her on.*

keep so **on a short leash** Go to on a short leash.

keep on an even keel *Fig.* to remain cool and calm. (Originally nautical.) □ *If Jane can keep on an even keel and not panic, she will be all right.*

keep sth **on an even keel** *Fig.* to keep something in a steady and untroubled state. □ *The manager cannot keep the firm on an even keel any longer.*

keep on one's **guard** Go to on one's guard.

keep sth **on its feet** *Fig.* to keep something stable and viable. (Fig. on the image of helping something stand up.) □ *It takes a lot of effort to keep this old firm on its feet. We may have to go out of business.*

keep on keeping on *Inf.* keep trying; keep doing what you are doing. □ *I do my best. I just keep on keeping on.*

keep so **on tenterhooks** *Fig.* to keep someone in suspense. □ *Don't keep me on tenterhooks! Tell me your news!*

keep so/sth **on (the) (right) track** *Fig.* to make sure that someone or some process continues to progress properly. □ *You* *have to watch him and keep him on the right track.*

keep on the safe side Go to on the safe side.

keep on top (of so/sth**)** to stay well-informed about the status of someone or something. □ *I need to keep on top of the president, because I am doing a report on him.*

keep on trucking *Inf.* to continue to do well; to continue to try. □ *All I can do is keep on trucking.*

Keep (on) trying. AND **Don't quit trying.** *Fig.* a phrase encouraging continued efforts. □ *Jane: I think I'm doing better in calculus. John: Keep trying! You can get an A.*

keep on with sth *Fig.* to continue with something. □ *Just keep on with your work. Don't pay any attention to me.*

keep one eye on so/sth Go to keep an eye on so/sth.

keep one jump ahead (of so/sth**)** Go to one jump ahead (of so/sth).

keep one step ahead of so/sth Go to one step ahead of so/sth.

keep one's **opinions to** oneself to stop mentioning one's own opinions, especially when they disagree with someone else's. □ *You ought to keep your opinions to yourself rather than upset our guests.*

keep one's **options open** AND **leave** one's **options open** to retain all possibilities and not abandon any of them. □ *I don't think I will be going to Denver, but I am keeping all my options open.*

keep out from under so's **feet** *Fig.* to stay out of someone's way. □ *Please keep out from under my feet. I'm very busy.*

keep out (of sth**)** *Fig.* to remain uninvolved with something. □ *Keep out of this! It's my affair.*

keep so/sth **out (of** sth**)** to keep the subject of someone or something out of a discussion. □ *Keep the kids out of this! I don't want to talk about them.*

Keep out of my way. AND **Stay out of my way.** *Fig.* Don't cause me any trouble. □ *Henry: I'm going to get even no matter what. Keep out of my way. Andy: Keep it up! You'll really get in trouble.*

keep out of the line of fire Go to the line of fire.

keep so/sth **out of the way** to prevent someone or something from getting in the way. □ *Please keep your children out of the way.*

Keep out of this! AND **Stay out of this!** This is not your business, so do not try to get involved. □ *John: Now you listen to me, Fred! Mary: That's no way to talk to Fred! John: Keep out of this, Mary! Mind your own business! Fred: Stay out of this, Mary! Mary: It's just as much my business as it is yours.*

keep one's **own counsel** *Fig.* to keep one's thoughts and plans to oneself; to withhold from other people one's thoughts and plans. □ *Jane is very quiet. She tends to keep her own counsel.*

keep pace (with so/sth**)** *Fig.* to manage to move, learn, change, etc. at the same rate as someone or something. □ *Bill can't keep pace with the geometry class.*

keep so **posted** *Fig.* to keep someone informed (of what is happening); to keep someone up-to-date. □ *If the price of corn goes up, I need to know. Please keep me posted.*

keep one's **powder dry** *Fig.* to save one's most powerful argument, evidence, threat, etc. [for the most opportune time]. □ *It will be a bitter divorce proceeding, and you should let her blow off steam while you keep your powder dry.*

keep sth **quiet** AND **keep** sth **still** *Fig.* to keep something a secret. □ *I'm quitting my job, but my boss doesn't know yet. Please keep it quiet.*

keep one's **seat** *Fig.* to stay seated; to remain in one's chair or place. □ *Please keep your seats until after the question-and-answer period.*

keep one's **shirt on** *Fig.* to be patient. □ *Wait a minute! Keep your shirt on!* □ *Tell him to keep his shirt on.*

keep one's **shoulder to the wheel** Go to have one's shoulder to the wheel.

keep one's **side of the bargain** Go to hold one's end of the bargain up†.

keep sight of so/sth *Fig.* to keep someone or something in view. □ *I want to keep sight of the children at all times.*

Keep smiling. *Fig.* a good-bye phrase encouraging someone to have good spirits. □ *John: Things are really getting tough. Sue: Well, just keep smiling. Things will get better.*

keep sth **still** Go to keep sth quiet.

keep people **straight** *Fig.* to correctly distinguish one person from other people. □ *The twins look exactly alike. Not even their mother can keep them straight.*

keep things **straight** *Fig.* to correctly distinguish one thing from other things. □ *These two bottles look so much alike. It's hard to keep them straight.*

keep tab(s) (on so/sth**)** AND **keep track (of** so/sth**)** *Fig.* to monitor someone or something; to follow the activities of someone or something. □ *I'm supposed to keep track of my books.* □ *Try to keep tabs on everyone who works for you.*

keep one's **temper** AND **hold** one's **temper** *Fig.* to hold back an expression of anger. (The opposite of lose one's temper (at so/sth).) □ *She should have learned to keep her temper when she was a child.* □ *Sally got thrown off the team because she couldn't hold her temper.*

keep the ball rolling Go to the sth rolling.

Keep the home fires burning. *Fig.* to keep things going at one's home or other central location. (From a World War I song.) □ *My uncle kept the home fires burning when my sister and I went to school.*

keep the peace to maintain a truce; to keep things peaceful. □ *We are doing what we can to keep the peace, but the rebels say they will attack again.*

keep the wolf from the door *Fig.* to maintain oneself at a minimal level; to keep from starving, freezing, etc. □ *We have a small amount of money saved, hardly enough to keep the wolf from the door.*

Keep this to yourself. *Fig.* a phrase introducing something that is meant to be a secret. (Notice the unique use of *but*.) □ *Andy: Keep this to yourself, but I'm going to Bora Bora on my vacation. Henry: Sounds great. Can I go too?*

keep time 1. *Fig.* to maintain a musical rhythm. □ *Bob had to drop out of the band because he couldn't keep time.* **2.** *Fig.* to keep watch over the time in a game or an athletic contest. □ *Whoever keeps time has to watch the referee very carefully.* **3.** *Fig.* [for a clock or a watch] to keep track of time accurately. □ *My other watch kept time better.*

keep oneself **to** oneself *Fig.* to remain aloof. □ *He does tend to keep himself to himself.*

keep sth **to** oneself *Fig.* to keep something a secret. □ *I want you to keep this news to yourself.*

keep to oneself *Fig.* to be solitary; to stay away from other people. □ *Ann tends to keep to herself. She doesn't have many friends.*

keep to sth to adhere to an agreement; to follow a plan; to keep a promise. □ *Please keep to the agreed-upon plan.* □ *Can you keep to what we agreed on?*

keep sth **to a minimum** *Fig.* to make something as small, few, or little as possible. □ *Do what you can to keep construction dust to a minimum.*

keep to the straight and narrow (path) *Fig.* to behave properly and correctly; to stay out of trouble. (Fig. on the image of following a pathway. See also the straight and narrow.) □ *If you keep to the straight and narrow, you can't help but win in the end.*

keep track (of so/sth**)** Go to keep tab(s) (on so/sth).

keep sth **under** one's **hat** *Fig.* to keep something a secret; to keep something in one's mind (only). (If the secret stays under your hat, it stays in your mind. Note the unique use of *but* in the examples.) □ *Keep this under your hat, but I'm getting married.* □ *I'm getting married, but keep it under your hat.*

keep sth **under lock and key** Go to under lock and key.

keep so **under** so's **thumb** Go to under so's thumb.

keep sth **under wraps** Go to under wraps.

keep so **up** *Fig.* to prevent someone from going to bed or going to sleep. □ *I'm sorry, was my trumpet playing keeping you up?*

keep sth **up**† **1.** *Fig.* to continue doing something. □ *I love your singing. Don't stop. Keep it up.* **2.** *Fig.* to maintain something in good order. □ *I'm glad you keep the exterior of your house up.*

keep up an act AND **keep up** one's **act** *Fig.* to maintain a false front; to act in a special way that is different from one's natural behavior. □ *Most of the time John kept up an act. He was really not a friendly person.*

keep up appearances *Fig.* to make things look all right whether they are or not. □ *We must keep up appearances even if it means little sacrifices here and there.*

Keep up the good work. *Fig.* Please keep doing the good things that you are doing now. (A general phrase of encouragement.) □ *Father: Your grades are fine, Bill. Keep up the good work. Bill: Thanks, Dad.*

keep up (with so/sth**)** *Fig.* to pay attention to the news about someone or something. □ *I don't see the Smiths a lot since they moved, but I keep up with them by phone.*

keep up with the Joneses *Fig.* to try to match the lifestyle of one's neighbors. □ *I am tired of trying to keep up with the Joneses. Let's just move if we can't afford to live here.*

keep up with the times *Fig.* to try to appear contemporary and fashionable; to learn about contemporary ways of doing things. □ *I am too old-fashioned. I have to keep up with the times better.*

keep watch on so/sth *Fig.* to monitor someone or something. □ *Keep watch on the lady in the big coat. She may be a shoplifter.*

keep watch over so/sth to supervise someone or something; to take care of someone or something. □ *Will you keep watch over Timmy for a minute?*

keep one's **weather eye open** *Fig.* to watch for something (to happen); to be on the alert (for something); to be on guard. □ *Some trouble is brewing. Keep your weather eye open.*

keep (so/sth**) within bounds** *Fig.* to cause someone or something to remain constrained or be reasonable; to cause someone to act or something to be in good taste. □ *Try to keep the children within bounds.*

keep one's **wits about** one Go to one's wits about one.

keep one's **word** *Fig.* to uphold one's promise; to do as one says. (The opposite of **break** one's **word**.) □ *I told her I'd be there to pick her up, and I intend to keep my word.*

Keep your chin up. *Fig.* an expression of encouragement to someone who has to bear some emotional burdens. (Fixed order.) □ *Fred: I really can't take much more of this. Jane: Keep your chin up. Things will get better.*

Keep your head down. *Fig.* Lie low, try not to be noticed. □ *My advice to you is to keep your head down for the moment.*

Keep your nose out of my business. Go to Mind your own business.

Keep your opinions to yourself! *Fig.* I do not want to hear your opinions! □ *Jane: I think this room looks drab. Sue: Keep your opinions to yourself! I like it this way!*

the **key to success** *Fig.* the secret to someone's success. □ *Bob said that the keys to his success are having a good memory, being on time, and being extremely lucky.*

*keyed up (about sth**)** AND ***keyed up (over** sth**)** *Fig.* to be excited or anxious. (*Typically: **be** ~; **get** ~.) □ *Why are you so keyed up about nothing?*

kick a habit AND **kick the habit; shake the habit; shake a habit** *Inf.* to break a habit. □ *It's hard to kick a habit, but it can be done. I stopped biting my nails.*

kick about so/sth *Inf. Fig.* to complain about someone or something. □ *Why are you kicking about your cousin? What has he done now?*

kick around Go to knock around.

kick so/sth/animal **around** *Fig.* to treat someone, something, or an animal badly. □ *I finally quit my job. My boss wouldn't stop kicking me around.*

kick sth **around**[†] *Fig.* to discuss something; to chat about an idea. □ *We got together and kicked her idea around.*

kick so/sth **aside**[†] *Fig.* to get rid of someone or something. □ *He simply kicked aside his wife and took up with some young chick.*

kick ass AND **kick butt** *Sl.* to actively motivate people to do something. (Caution with *ass*.) □ *It looks like I'm going to have to kick ass to get people moving around here.*

kick back 1. *Inf.* to relax; to lean back and relax. □ *It's time to kick back and enjoy life.* **2.** *Inf.* [for an addict] to return to an addiction or a habit, after having "kicked the habit." □ *Lefty kicked back after only a few days of being clean.*

kick butt Go to kick ass.

kick one's **heels up**[†] *Fig.* to act frisky; to be lively and have fun. (Somewhat literal when said of hoofed animals.) □ *For an old man, your uncle is really kicking his heels up.*

kick in (on sth**) (for** so/sth**)** *Inf.* to contribute to something for someone or something. □ *Would you like to kick in on a gift for Joel?*

kick sth **in**[†] **(on** sth**) (for** so/sth**)** *Fig.* to contribute something, such as money, on something for someone or something. □

I will kick a few bucks in on some flowers for the receptionist.

a **kick in the butt** Go to a kick in the (seat of the) pants.

a **kick in the guts** *Fig. Sl.* a severe blow to one's body or spirit. □ *The news was a kick in the guts, and I haven't recovered yet.*

a **kick in the (seat of the) pants** AND a **kick in the ass;** a **kick in the butt;** a **kick in the teeth** *Inf.* a strong message of encouragement or demand. □ *All he needs is a kick in the seat of the pants to get him going.* □ *A kick in the butt will get her moving.*

a **kick in the teeth** Go to previous.

kick like a mule AND **kick like a steer** to kick very hard. □ *They say that ostriches will kick like a mule if you bother them.*

kick like a steer Go to previous.

kick off 1. to start play in a football game by kicking the ball. □ *Tom kicked off in the last game. Now it's my turn.* **2.** AND **kick the bucket** *Inf.* to die. □ *When I kick the bucket, I want a huge funeral with lots of flowers and crying.*

kick sth **off**[†] AND **start** sth **off**[†]; **lead** sth **off**[†] *Fig.* to begin something; to hold a party or ceremony to mark the start of something. (Alludes to starting a football game by *kicking off* the ball for the first play.) □ *The city kicked the centennial celebration off with a parade.*

kick so **off** sth *Fig.* to force someone to leave something. □ *They actually kicked him off the team because he played so badly.* □ *The conductor kicked them off the train because they had no tickets.*

kick so/animal **out**[†] Go to boot so/animal out[†].

kick over Go to turn over.

kick over the traces *Fig.* to do what one is meant not to do; to rebel against authority. (Refers to a horse that steps on the wrong side of the straps that link it to whatever it is pulling.) □ *At the age of 60, Walter kicked over the traces and ran away to Brazil.*

kick some ass (around) *Sl.* to take over and start giving orders; to raise hell (with sth). (Caution with *ass.*) □ *Do I have to come over there and kick some ass around?*

kick the bucket Go to kick off.

kick up a fuss AND **kick up a row; kick up a storm** *Fig.* to become a nuisance; to misbehave and disturb (someone). (*Row* rhymes with *cow.*) □ *The customer kicked up such a fuss about the food that the manager came to apologize.* □ *Oh, what pain! My arthritis is kicking up a storm.*

kick up a row Go to previous.

kick up a stink (about sth**)** Go to create a stink (about sth).

kick up a storm Go to kick up a fuss.

kid around (with so**)** to tease and joke with someone. □ *I like to kid around with John. We are great friends.* □ *Yes, John and I used to kid around a lot.*

kidding aside Go to (all) joking aside.

kid's stuff *Fig.* a very easy task. □ *Driving an automatic car is kid's stuff.*

kill a period of time *Fig.* to use up a period of time, perhaps wasting it. □ *That was a poor way to kill an afternoon.*

kill for sth *Fig. Sl.* to be willing to go to extremes to get something that one really wants or needs. (An exaggeration.) □ *I could kill for a cold beer.*

kill the fatted calf *Fig.* to prepare an elaborate banquet (in someone's honor). (From the biblical story recounting the return of the prodigal son.) □ *Sorry this meal isn't much, John. We didn't have time to kill the fatted calf.*

kill time *Fig.* to use up excess time. (See also kill a period of time.) □ *I killed time by reading a novel.*

kill two birds with one stone *Fig.* to solve two problems at one time with a single action. □ *I have to cash a check and make a payment on my bank loan. I'll kill two birds with one stone by doing them both in one trip to the bank.*

kill so **with kindness** *Fig.* to be enormously kind to someone. □ *You are just killing me with kindness. Why?*

killed outright *Fig.* killed immediately. □ *Twenty people were killed outright in the explosion.*

killer instinct *Cliché* an inborn desire or ability to be ruthless. (Usually figurative. Literal when applied to real killers.) □ *Fred has a real killer instinct. He's a difficult boss to work for.*

so/sth **kills me** *Fig.* something is very funny and making me laugh. □ *That guy's jokes just kill me!*

a **kind of** sth a variety of something that is fairly close to the real thing, even though it is not exactly the real thing. □ *I used a folded newspaper as a kind of hat to keep the rain off.*

kind of sth AND **sort of** sth a type or variety of something. □ *What kind of ice cream do you have?* □ *This is a strange sort of wood paneling on this wall.*

*a **king's ransom** *Fig.* a great deal of money. (To pay an amount as large as one might have to pay to get back a king held for ransom. *Typically: **cost** ~; **pay** ~; **spend** ~.) □ *I would like to buy a nice watch, but I don't want to pay a king's ransom for it.*

kiss and make up 1. [for two people who have been arguing] to kiss each other and apologize. □ *John apologized to his wife for disagreeing with her, and they finally kissed and made up.* **2.** *Fig.* to forgive someone and be friends again. (Fig. on ①. No kissing is involved.) □ *They were very angry, but in the end they kissed and made up.*

kiss and tell *Fig.* to participate in something secret and private, and then tell other people about it. (In actual use, it usually refers to a person of the opposite sex even when it does not refer to actual kissing.) □ *The project was supposed to be a secret between Jane and me, but she spread it all around. I didn't think she was the type to kiss and tell.*

kiss so's **ass** *Fig. Sl.* to fawn over someone; to flatter and curry favor with someone. □ *What does he expect me to do? Kiss his ass?*

kiss sth **good-bye** AND **say good-bye to** sth to anticipate or experience the loss of something. □ *If you leave your camera on a park bench, you can just kiss it good-bye.*

the **kiss of death** *Fig.* an act that puts an end to someone or something. □ *The mayor's veto was the kiss of death for the new law.*

kiss off 1. *Sl.* to die. □ *The cat is going to have to kiss off one of these days soon.* **2.** *Sl.* death. (Usually **kiss-off.**) □ *The kiss-off came wrapped in lead, and it was instant.* **3.** *Sl.* the dismissal of someone or something. (Usually **kiss-off.**) □ *The kiss-off was when I lost the Wilson contract.*

kiss so **off**† *Sl.* to kill someone. □ *Max kissed Lefty off with a small gun he carried in his boot.*

kiss the dust *Sl.* to fall to the earth, because of death or because of being struck. □ *I'll see that you kiss the dust before sunset, cowboy!*

kissing cousins *Fig.* relatives who know one another well enough to kiss when they meet. □ *Technically, we're second cousins once removed, but I just say we're kissing cousins.*

kith and kin *Fig.* friends and relatives; people known to someone. □ *I was delighted to find all my kith and kin waiting for me at the airport to welcome me home.*

klutz around *Sl.* to go about acting stupidly or clumsily. □ *Stop klutzing around and get your act together.*

***knee-deep in** sth **1.** *Fig.* heavily involved in something. (*Typically: **be** ~; **get** ~.) □ *Right now, we are knee-deep in trouble.* **2.** *Fig.* having plenty of something. (*Typically: **be** ~; **stand** ~.) □ *We are knee-deep in orders and loving it.*

***knee-high by the 4th of July** *Fig.* [corn] grown as tall as it should. (Corn seedlings are proverbially supposed to be as high as someone's knee by July 4th. *Typically: **be** ~; **become** ~; **grow** ~.) □ *What with this drought, I don't think the crop will be knee-high by the 4th of July.*

knee-high to a grasshopper Go to next.

***knee-high to a jackrabbit** AND ***knee-high to a grasshopper** *Rur.* very small or short. (Usually used to describe children. *Typically: **be** ~; **since** so **was** ~.) □ *I've known you since you were knee-high to a jackrabbit.* □ *My, how you've grown! The last time I saw you, you were knee-high to a grasshopper!*

a **knee-jerk reaction** *Fig.* an automatic or reflex reaction; an immediate reaction made without examining causes or facts. □ *With one of his typical knee-jerk reactions, he said no immediately, citing some moral argument that no one understood.*

knew it was coming AND **(had) known it was coming** to have expected in advance that something was to happen. □ *I shouldn't act surprised. I knew it was coming.* □ *It's his own fault. He should have known it was coming.*

a **knight in shining armor** *Fig.* a person, usually male, who rescues or assists a person in need of help. □ *I was stalled in the interstate for an hour until a knight in shining armor came along and gave me some help.*

knit one's **brow** to cause one's brow to wrinkle. □ *Bob usually knitted his brow when he was confused.*

knock about (some place) (**with** so) AND **knock around** (some place) (**with** so) *Inf.* to hang around some place with someone; to wander idly about some place with someone. □ *Sally was knocking about France with her friends.*

knock around 1. *Inf.* to waste time. □ *I need a couple of days a week just for knocking around.* **2.** AND **kick around** *Inf.* to wander around; being around. □ *I think I'll knock around a few months before looking for another job.*

knock sth **back**† *Sl.* to drink down a drink of something, especially something alcoholic. (See also knock back a drink.) □

John knocked back two beers in 10 minutes.

knock back a drink AND **knock one back; knock one over** *Sl.* to swallow a drink of an alcoholic beverage. □ *Todd knocked back one drink, and then had another.* □ *She knocked one over and left the bar.*

knock so back (an amount of money) *Fig.* to cost an amount of money. □ *That trip to Spain knocked me back almost $3,500.*

knock so's block off *Sl.* to hit someone hard in the head. □ *He threatened to knock my block off if I didn't do as I was told.*

knock so cold 1. to render someone unconscious by a violent blow. □ *One swipe, and he knocked him cold.* **2.** AND **knock so dead** *Fig.* to put on a stunning performance or display for someone. (*Someone* is often replaced by *'em* from *them.*) □ *This band is going to do great tonight. We're going to knock 'em dead.*

knock so dead Go to previous.

knock sth down† **1.** *Sl.* to drink a portion of liquor. □ *He knocked down a bottle of beer and called for another.* **2.** *Sl.* to earn a certain amount of money. □ *I'm lucky to knock down $20,000.*

knock so down a peg (or two) Go to take so down a peg (or two).

knock so for a loop 1. *Fig.* to strike someone hard. (Often in the passive voice.) □ *I was really knocked for a loop by the falling branch.* **2.** AND **throw so for a loop** *Fig.* to confuse or shock someone. □ *When Bill heard the news, it threw him for a loop.*

knock one's head (up) against a brick wall *Fig.* to be totally frustrated. (Fig. on the image of someone banging his head against a wall in frustration.) □ *Trying to get a raise around here is like knocking your head up against a brick wall.*

knock sth into a cocked hat *Fig.* to demolish a plan, a story, etc. □ *This bad weather has knocked everything into a cocked hat.*

Knock it off! *Inf.* Be quiet!; Stop that noise!; Stop doing that! □ *Sue: All right. Knock it off! Bill: Yeah. Let's get down to business.*

knock one's knees together *Fig.* [for one's knees] to shake together from fright. □ *I stood there freezing for 10 minutes, knocking my knees together in the cold.*

knock off (doing sth) *Inf.* to stop doing something, especially work and especially at the end of the day. □ *Knock off shoveling snow now, and come in for a hot drink.* □ *What time do you knock off work?* □ *I knock off about 5:30.*

knock so off† Go to bump so off†.

knock sth off† **1.** *Inf.* to manufacture or make something, especially in haste. □ *I'll see if I can knock another one off before lunch.* **2.** *Fig.* to knock off some amount from the price of something, lowering its price. □ *The store manager knocked 30 percent off the price of the coat.* **3.** *Inf.* to copy or reproduce a product. □ *They are well-known for knocking off cheap versions of expensive watches.*

knock one off one's feet Go to sweep one off one's feet.

knock on wood to rap on something made of wood. (Said as a wish for good luck. Usually a phrase attached to another statement. Sometimes said while knocking or rapping on real wood.) □ *I think I am well at last—knock on wood.* □ *I knock on wood when I wish something were true.*

knock one back Go to knock back a drink.

knock one over Go to knock back a drink.

knock so out† **1.** to knock someone or oneself unconscious. □ *Fred knocked Mike out and left him there in the gutter.* **2.** *Fig.* [for something] to make someone unconsciousness. (Fig. on (1).) □ *The drug knocked her out quickly.* **3.** *Fig.* to surprise or please someone. (Fig. on (1).) □ *I have some news that will really knock you out.* **4.** *Fig.* to wear someone out; to exhaust someone or oneself. (Fig. on (1).) □ *The day's activities knocked the kids out, and they went right to bed.*

knock sth **out**† Go to take sth out†.

knock oneself **out (to** do sth**) (for** so/sth**)** to make a great effort to do something for someone or some group. (As if one had worked oneself into unconsciousness.) □ *I knocked myself out to plan this party for you!* □ *She knocked herself out for us.*

knock over sth **1.** *Sl.* to steal something. (The *over* is usually before the object in this expression.) □ *The gang knocked over an armored car.* **2.** *Sl.* to rob a place. (The *over* is usually before the object in this expression.) □ *He was the kind of punk who would try to knock over a filling station in broad daylight.*

knock so **over (with a feather)** *Fig.* to leave someone stunned or surprised by something extraordinary. (Fixed order.) □ *I was so surprised that you could have knocked me over with a feather.*

knock so's **socks off** AND **knock the socks off (of)** so *Sl.* to surprise someone thoroughly. (Fixed order. *Of* is usually retained before pronouns.) □ *The news knocked the socks off of everyone in the office.*

knock some heads together *Fig.* to scold some people; to get some people to do what they are supposed to be doing. □ *If you kids don't quiet down and go to sleep, I'm going to come up there and knock some heads together.*

knock some sense into so AND **knock some sense in**†; **shake some sense into** so; **beat some sense into** so to strike one, making one smarter, or at least obedient. □ *I think his father finally knocked some sense into him.*

knock so **some skin** *Sl.* to slap hands with someone, a sign of friendship. □ *Pete knocked Sam some skin, and they left the building together.*

knock the bejeebers out of so/sth *Inf.* to beat someone or something severely. □ *If I catch you doing that again, I'll knock the bejeebers out of you.*

knock the bottom out (of sth**)** *Fig.* [for something] to go down so low as to knock out the bottom. □ *The bad news knocked the bottom out of the stock market.*

knock the habit *Inf.* to stop using drugs; to break a drug addiction. □ *He tried to knock the habit by drinking lots of booze.*

knock the (living) daylights out of so *Inf.* to beat someone severely. □ *If you do that again, I will knock the living daylights out of you.*

knock the props out from under so *Fig.* to destroy someone's emotional, financial, or moral underpinnings; to destroy someone's confidence. □ *When you told Sally that she was due to be fired, you really knocked the props out from under her.*

knock the wind out of so's **sails 1.** *Fig.* to bring someone to an abrupt halt by a heavy blow to the body, presumably knocking the person's wind out. (Fig. on the image of a ship being slowed by positioning another ship to block off the wind from the first ship's sails.) □ *Fred ran into the side of the garage and knocked the wind out of his sails.* **2.** AND **take the wind out of** so's **sails** *Fig.* to humiliate someone. (Fig. on ①.) □ *The sharp rebuke from the boss knocked the wind out of his sails.*

knock sth **together**† *Inf.* to assemble something hastily. □ *I knocked this model together so you could get a general idea of what I had in mind.* □ *This thing has just been knocked together!*

knock so **up**† *Inf.* to make a woman pregnant. □ *They say it was Willie who knocked her up.*

knock-down-drag-out fight a serious fight; a serious argument. □ *Stop calling each other names, or you're going to end up with a real knock-down-drag-out fight.*

knocked out 1. unconscious. □ *The losing boxer lay on the canvas, knocked out.* **2.** *Inf.* exhausted. □ *We were all knocked out at the end of the day.* **3.** *Inf.* overwhelmed. □ *We were just knocked out when we heard your news.* **4.** *Inf.* intoxicated. □ *Gary was completely knocked out when we dropped by, so we tried to sober him up.*

knocked up 1. *Fig.* battered; beaten. □ *This book is a little knocked up, so I'll lower the price.* **2.** *Inf.* pregnant; made pregnant. □ *Sue got knocked up but won't say who the father is.*

know a thing or two (about so/sth**)** Go to a thing or two (about so/sth).

know a trick or two *Fig.* to know some special way of dealing with a problem. □ *I think I can handle all of this with no trouble. I know a trick or two.*

know one's **ABCs** *Fig.* to know the alphabet; to know the most basic things (about something). □ *You can't expect to write a letter when you don't even know your ABCs.*

know all the angles *Inf.* to know all the tricks and artifices of dealing with someone or something. □ *Ask my accountant about taxes. He knows all the angles.*

know all the answers Go to have all the answers.

know so **as** so to know someone by a different name. □ *She has been known as Mary Roger since her marriage.*

know sth **at a glance** AND **know at a glance that . . .** *Fig.* to know (something) without much evidence; to know or understand something without much observation. □ *I knew at a glance that Bobbie was severely injured and had to be gotten to a hospital as soon as possible.*

know sth **backwards and forwards** AND **know** sth **forwards and backwards** *Fig.* to know something very well; to know a passage (of language) so well that one could recite it backwards as well as forwards. □ *Of course I've memorized my speech. I know it backwards and forwards.*

know best to know better than anyone else what is the best choice or procedure. □ *I'll do it your way. You always know best.*

know better (than to do sth**)** to be wise enough, experienced enough, or well trained enough not to have done something wrong. □ *Mary should have known better than to accept a lift from a stranger.*

know so/sth **by** sth to recognize someone or something by a certain characteristic. □ *I know this committee only by its reputation, which is not good, by the way.*

know sth **by heart** Go to by heart.

know so/sth **by name** to recognize the name but not the appearance of someone or something. □ *I know this brand of sausage by name, but I have never tasted it.*

know so **by sight** to recognize a person's face but not know the name. □ *I'm afraid I don't know her by sight.*

know different AND **know otherwise** to have contradictory information [about something]. (*Different* is more informal.) □ *You think nobody knows what you are planning, but I know different. Chuck told me all about it.*

know one **for what** one **is** *Fig.* to recognize someone as some (usually bad) type of person or thing. □ *I know you for what you are, you devil.*

know from sth *Fig.* to know about something. (Used on the eastern seaboard.) □ *Do you know from thermostats?* □ *You don't know from anything!*

know sth **from memory** to have memorized something so that one does not have to consult a written version; to know something well from seeing it very often. (Almost the same as know sth by heart.) □ *Mary didn't need the script, because she knew the play from memory.*

know full well to know [something] very well. □ *I knew full well what I was getting into, and got into it just the same.*

know sth **in** one's **bones** Go to feel sth in one's bones.

know (sth**) in** one's **heart of hearts** Go to feel (sth) in one's heart of hearts.

know so/sth **inside out** *Fig.* to know someone or something very well. □ *I know the history of the company inside out and can tell you some things that would amaze you.*

know so/sth **like a book** Go to know so/sth like the palm of one's hand.

know so/sth **like the back of** one's **hand** Go to next.

know so/sth **like the palm of** one's **hand** AND **know** so/sth **like the back of** one's **hand; know** so/sth **like a book** to know someone or something very well. □ *Of course I know John. I know him like the back of my hand.* □ *I know him like a book.*

know no bounds *Fig.* [for something] to seem to be boundless or endless. □ *His generosity knows no bounds. He donates to every charity.*

know of so/sth to be aware of the existence of someone or something. □ *I think I know of someone who can help you.*

know one's **onions** Go to know one's stuff.

know sth **only too well** to know something very well; to know something from unpleasant experience. □ *I know only too well the kind of problem you must face.*

know otherwise Go to know different.

know one's **place** *Fig.* to know the behavior appropriate to one's position or status in life. □ *I know my place. I won't speak unless spoken to.*

know shit from Shinola AND **tell shit from Shinola** *Fig. Inf.* to know what's what; to be intelligent and aware. (Always in the negative. Shinola is a brand of waxy shoe polish, and a person who cannot tell the two apart is very stupid. Caution with *shit*.) □ *Fred can't tell shit from Shinola, and he's been made my boss.*

know one's **stuff** AND **know** one's **onions; know what** one **is doing; know what** one **is talking about** *Fig.* to know what one is expected to know in order to do something right. (The third and fourth entry heads are also used with their obvious literal meanings.) □ *I know my stuff. I can do my job.* □ *She can't handle the assignment. She doesn't know her onions.*

know the ropes Go to the ropes.

know the score AND **know what's what** *Fig.* to know the facts; to know the facts about life and its difficulties. □ *Bob is so naive. He sure doesn't know the score.*

know the tricks of the trade Go to tricks of the trade.

know one's **way around** *Fig.* to know how to deal with people and situations; to have had much experience at living. (Fig. on knowing distance and direction.) □ *I can get along in the world. I know my way around.*

know what one **is talking about** Go to know one's stuff.

know what's what Go to know the score.

know when one **is not wanted** to sense when one's presence is not welcome; to know when one is not among friends. (Usually said when someone feels hurt by being ignored by people.) □ *I'm leaving this place! I know when I'm not wanted!*

know where all the bodies are buried *Fig.* to know all the secrets and intrigue from the past; to know all the relevant and perhaps hidden details. □ *He is a good choice for president because he knows where all the bodies are buried.*

know where one **is coming from** *Inf.* to understand someone's motivation; to understand and relate to someone's position. □ *I know where you're coming from. I've been there.*

know where it's at *Inf.* to be alert and know how the world—or some part of it—really works. □ *Man, you just don't know where it's at!*

know where so **stands (on** so/sth**)** to know what someone thinks or feels about something. □ *I don't know where John stands on this issue.*

know whereof one **speaks** to know well the subject that one is speaking about; to know something with certainty. □ *You are wrong! You do not know whereof you speak.*

know which is which AND **tell which is which** to be able to distinguish one person or thing from another person or

know where all the bodies are buried

thing. □ *I have an old one and a new one, but I don't know which is which.*

know-how *Fig.* knowledge and skill. □ *Peter doesn't have the know-how to mend that car.*

known fact *Fig.* something that is generally recognized as a fact. □ *It is a known fact that John was in Chicago on the night of the murder.*

known quantity *Fig.* someone whose character, personality, and behavior are recognized and understood. □ *Lisa is a known quantity, and I am sure she will not surprise us by voting with the opposition.*

knuckle down (to sth**)** *Fig.* to get busy doing something. □ *I want you to knuckle down to your work and stop worrying about the past.*

*a **knuckle sandwich** *Inf.* a punch in the face. (*Typically: **ask for** ~; **get** ~; **give** so ~; **want** ~.) □ *A: Ahhh! Your mother smokes cigars! B: You want a knuckle sandwich?*

knuckle under (to so/sth**)** to submit to someone or something; to yield or give in to someone or something. □ *You have to knuckle under to your boss if you expect to keep your job.*

L

a **labor of love** *Fig.* a task that is either unpaid or badly paid and that one does simply for one's own satisfaction or pleasure or to please someone whom one likes or loves. □ *Jane made no money out of the biography she wrote. She was writing about the life of a friend, and the book was a labor of love.*

labor under sth *Fig.* to function believing something; to go about living while assuming something [that may not be so]. □ *I was laboring under the idea that we were going to share the profits equally.*

lack for sth to lack something. □ *We don't lack for new ideas.*

Ladies first. an expression of courtesy indicating that women should go first, as in going through a doorway. □ *Bob stepped back and made a motion with his hand indicating that Mary should go first. "Ladies first," smiled Bob.*

a **ladies' man** *Fig.* a man who likes the company of women and whose company is liked by women, the suggestion being that he likes to flirt with them. □ *John is a real ladies' man. He hates all-male parties.*

lady of the evening *Euph.* a prostitute. □ *I saw several ladies of the evening down on Main Street.*

a **lady-killer** *Fig.* a man who likes to flirt with women and who is popular with them. □ *Fred used to be a real lady-killer, but now women laugh at him.*

laid back 1. *Inf.* calm and relaxed. □ *Willie is not what I would call laid back.* **2.** *Inf.* intoxicated. □ *How can those guys work when they are laid back by noon?*

laid out 1. *Inf.* intoxicated. □ *Man, you got yourself laid out!* **2.** *Sl.* well-dressed. □ *Look at those silks! Man are you laid out!*

laid up *Fig.* [of people or things] immobilized for recuperation or repairs. □ *I was laid up for two weeks after my accident.*

lame duck 1. *Fig.* someone who is in the last period of a term in an elective office and cannot run for reelection. □ *As a lame duck, there's not a lot I can do.* **2.** *Fig.* having to do with someone in the last period of a term in an elective office. (Sometimes **lame-duck.**) □ *Lame-duck Congresses tend to do things they wouldn't dare do otherwise.*

land a blow *Fig.* to make a point. (Fig. on striking someone.) □ *I think I really landed a blow with that remark about extortion.*

land a job *Inf.* to find a job and be hired. □ *As soon as I land a job and start to bring in some money, I'm going to get a stereo.*

land in sth *Fig.* [for someone] to end up in something, such as a mess, jail, trouble, etc. □ *Andy is going to land in hot water if he doesn't start paying his bills.*

Land o' Goshen! *Rur.* My goodness gracious! (A mild oath. Goshen was an agricultural region in Egypt occupied by the Israelites before the Exodus.) □ *Land o' Goshen! Look at that rain come down!*

the **land of Nod** a state of sleep. (Humorous. From the fact that people sometimes nod when they are falling asleep.) □ *Look at the clock! It's time we were all in the land of Nod.*

land (up)on both feet AND **land (up)on one's feet 1.** to end up on both feet after a jump, dive, etc. (*Upon* is formal and less commonly used than *on.*) □ *She jumped over the bicycle and landed upon both feet.* **2.** *Fig.* to come out of something well; to survive something satisfactorily. (Fig. on ①. *Upon* is formal and less commonly used than *on.*) □ *It was a rough period in his life, but when it was over he landed on both feet.*

land-office business *Fig.* a large amount of business done in a short period of time. □ *We keep going. Never do land-office business—just enough to make out.*

Land(s) sakes (alive)! AND **Sakes alive!** *Rur.* My goodness! (A mild oath.) □ *Sakes alive! Can't you even set the table without making a fuss?*

a **landslide victory** a victory by a large margin; a very substantial victory, particularly in an election. □ *The younger candidate won a landslide victory in the presidential election.*

languish in some place to suffer neglect in a place. □ *The bill languished in the Senate for months on end.*

the **lap of luxury** *Fig.* a luxurious situation; in a comfortable, elegant, and expensive place. □ *I rather enjoy living in the lap of luxury.*

lap sth **up**† *Fig.* [for someone] to accept or believe something with enthusiasm. □ *Of course, they believed it. They just lapped it up.*

lapse from grace *Fig.* to fall out of favor. □ *Ted lapsed from grace when he left the lobby door unlocked all weekend.*

lapse into a coma *Fig.* to go into a coma; to fall into unconsciousness. □ *Aunt Mary lapsed into a coma and died.*

*****large as life** *Fig.* in person; actually, and sometimes surprisingly, present at a place. (*Also: **as** ~.) □ *Jean was not expected to appear, but she turned up large as life.*

large as life (and twice as ugly) Go to big as life (and twice as ugly).

larger than life AND **bigger than life** *Fig.* [of someone] having an aura of greatness, perhaps partly illusionary. □ *Perry*

seemed larger than life to those who had only read about him. To the rest of us, he was a boor.

lash out at so **1.** [for something like a whip or strap] to swing out and strike at someone. □ *Something went wrong in the engine while Ted was working on it, and a belt lashed out at him, just missing his head.* **2.** *Fig.* to attack someone verbally, with vehemence and anger. □ *The politician lashed out at her opponent, accusing him of everything evil except cannibalism.*

last but not least *Cliché* last in sequence, but not last in importance. (Often said when introducing people.) □ *The speaker said, "And now, last but not least, I'd like to present Bill Smith, who will give us some final words."*

last call (for sth**)** AND **last chance (for** sth**)** *Fig.* the last opportunity for doing, getting, or having something. □ *This is the last call for ice cream and cake. It's almost all gone.*

last chance (for sth**)** Go to previous.

the **last hurrah** *Fig.* a final appearance, as at the end of one's career; the last time for doing something. □ *Tom is retiring, and we are having a little party as his last hurrah right now. He won't be here the next time you visit our offices.*

*****the **last laugh (on** so**)** *Fig.* laughter or ridicule at someone who has laughed at or ridiculed you. (*Typically: **get** ~; **have** ~; **give** so ~.) □ *Mr. Smith said I was foolish when I bought an old building. I had the last laugh when I sold it a month later for twice what I paid for it.*

the **last person (to single out for** sth**)** the most unlikely person of whom one could think in a particular situation; the most unlikely person to do something. □ *Mary is the last person you should ask to chair the meeting—she's so shy.*

one's **last resting place** *Euph.* one's grave. □ *Daddy has gone to his last resting place.*

the **last roundup** *Inf.* death. (Old West.) □ *To everyone's surprise, he clutched the wound and faced the last roundup with a smile.*

the **last say** Go to the last word.

the **last straw** AND the **straw that broke the camel's back** the final difficulty in a series; the last little burden or problem that causes everything to collapse. (From the image of a camel being loaded down with much weight. Finally, at some point, one more straw will be too much and the camel's back will break.) □ *When she showed up late a third time, that was the straw that broke the camel's back. We had to fire her.*

last will and testament a will; the last edition of someone's will. □ *The lawyer read Uncle Charles's last will and testament to a group of expectant relatives.*

*the **last word** AND *the **final word**; *the **final say**; *the **last say** *Fig.* the final point (in an argument); the final decision (in some matter). (*Typically: **get** ~; **have** ~; **give** so ~.) □ *The boss gets the last word in hiring. Why do you always have to have the final word in an argument?*

the **last word in** sth the most recent style, design, or trend. □ *This leather umbrella is the last word in trendy rain protection.*

*last-ditch effort *Fig.* a final effort; the last possible attempt. (*Typically: **be** ~; **have** ~; **make** ~.) □ *I made one last-ditch effort to get her to stay.*

latch on(to so) to get hold of someone. □ *I don't know where Jane is. Let me try to latch onto her.*

latch onto sth **1.** *Fig.* to obtain something. □ *I have to latch onto a hundred bucks by Friday night.* **2.** *Inf.* to begin to understand something. (Fig. on ①.) □ *When Fred finally latched onto the principles of algebra, he began to get better grades.*

The **latch string is always out.** You are always welcome. □ *Come by anytime. The latch string is always out.*

a **late bloomer 1.** a plant that blooms later than similar plants or that blooms late in the season. □ *There are a few late bloomers in the garden, but by fall, we don't care much anymore about flowers.* **2.** *Fig.* a person who finally develops a use-ful or superior skill or talents later than expected or desired. □ *Joseph was a late bloomer, but turned out to be a formidable scholar in the long run.*

late in life *Fig.* when one is old. □ *Grandma injured her hip running. She's exercising rather late in life.*

late in the day *Fig.* far along in a project or activity; too late in a project or activity for action, decisions, etc. to be taken. (See also at the end of the day.) □ *It was a bit late in the day for him to apologize.*

the **late unpleasantness** *Euph.* the U.S. Civil War. (Old.) □ *The town courthouse was burned in the late unpleasantness.*

the **latest rage** Go to flavor of the month.

lather up 1. [for a horse] to develop a foam of sweat from working very hard. □ *The horses lathered up heavily during the race.* **2.** [for soap] to develop thick suds when rubbed in water. □ *When the soap lathers up, spread the lather on your face and rub.* **3.** AND **lather (oneself) up** [for one] to apply soap lather to one's body. □ *He will spend a few minutes lathering himself up before he rinses.*

a **laugh a minute** Go to a minute.

laugh all the way to the bank *Inf.* to be very happy about money that has been earned by doing something that other people might think is unfair or that they criticized. □ *She makes tons of money doing what no one else will do and laughs all the way to the bank.*

laugh at so/sth **1.** to laugh because someone or something is funny. □ *I love to laugh at your jokes. You really tell jokes well.* □ *Bob laughed when the mugger slipped on a banana peel.* **2.** *Fig.* to ridicule someone or something, possibly with laughter. □ *They laughed at the candidate when he claimed his opponent was a crook.* □ *I wrote a great novel, but the prospective publishers just laughed at it.*

laugh sth **away**† **1.** to spend an amount of time laughing. □ *We laughed the hour away listening to the comedian.* **2.** to get rid of something negative by laughing.

□ *Kelly knows how to laugh her problems away, and it cheers up the rest of us too.*

laugh one's **head off** *Fig.* to laugh very hard and loudly, as if one's head might come off. (Fixed order.) □ *The movie was so funny I almost laughed my head off.*

laugh in so's **face** to laugh in derision directly to someone's face; to show displeasure or ridicule at something one has said by laughing directly into one's face. □ *After I heard what she had to say, I just laughed in her face.*

laugh sth **off**† to treat a serious problem lightly by laughing at it. □ *Although his feelings were hurt, he just laughed the incident off as if nothing had happened.*

laugh so **off the stage** *Fig.* to laugh rudely at a performance, forcing the performer or speaker to leave a stage. □ *The rude audience laughed the politician off the stage.* □ *The children laughed the soprano off the stage. She really wasn't very good, you know.*

laugh sth **out of court** to dismiss something presented in earnest as ridiculous. □ *Bob's request for a large salary increase was laughed out of court.*

laugh out of the other side of one's **face** AND **laugh out of the other side of** one's **mouth; laugh from the other side of** one's **mouth; laugh from the other side of** one's **face** *Fig.* to be forced to take a different or opposite view of something humbly; to sing a different tune. □ *When you get the kind of punishment you deserve, you'll laugh out of the other side of your face.* □ *Phil played a dirty trick on me, but he'll be laughing out of the other side of his mouth when I get through with him.*

laugh out of the other side of one's **mouth** Go to previous.

laugh oneself **silly** *Fig.* to laugh very, very hard. □ *I laughed myself silly when I heard that Steven was really going to give the graduation address.*

laugh up one's **sleeve** to laugh secretly; to laugh quietly to oneself. □ *I told Sally that her dress was darling, but I was laughing up my sleeve because her dress was too small.*

laughingstock (of so/group**)** *Fig.* someone or something that is the target of someone's or some group's ridicule. □ *After he passed out at the president's dinner, he became the laughingstock of all his colleagues.*

launch forth on sth Go to **set forth on** sth.

launch into sth to start doing something, especially saying something or a physical attack. □ *Tim's mother launched into a sermon about how to behave at the dinner table.*

*a **law unto** oneself *Fig.* one who ignores laws or rules; one who sets one's own standards of behavior. (*Typically: **be** ~; **become** ~.) □ *Jane is a law unto herself. She's totally unwilling to cooperate.*

lay a finger on so/sth to touch someone or something, even slightly, as with only a finger. □ *Don't you dare lay a finger on my pencil. Go get your own!*

lay a guilt trip on so Go to next.

lay a (heavy) trip on so **1.** *Inf.* to criticize someone. □ *When he finally does get there, I'm going to lay a heavy trip on him like he'll never forget.* **2.** *Inf.* to confuse or astonish someone. □ *After he laid a heavy trip on me about how the company is almost broke, I cleaned out my desk and left.* **3.** AND **lay a guilt trip on** so *Inf.* to attempt to make someone feel very guilty. □ *Why do you have to lay a guilt trip on me? Why don't you go to a shrink?* □ *Of course, she just had to lay a trip on him about being bossy, self-centered, and aloof.* **4.** *Inf.* to reveal serious or devastating information to someone. □ *That's a powerful story. I didn't know you were going to lay a heavy trip like that on me.*

lay a place (for so**)** to provide a(n additional) table setting for someone. □ *John will be at dinner tonight. Please lay a place for him.*

lay alongside sth [for a ship] to rest afloat next to or in the vicinity of something. □ *The ship lay alongside a lovely island while a shore party searched for fresh water.* □

Our ship lay alongside the narrow wooden pier.

lay an egg *Fig.* [for someone] to do something bad or poorly; to perform poorly on stage. □ *The cast laid an egg in both performances.*

lay sth **at** so's **door** AND **put** sth **at** so's **door**; **lay** sth **on** so **1.** *Fig.* to blame a problem on someone or something; to hold someone responsible for something. (Fig. on the image of someone laying incriminating evidence at the door of a guilty person.) □ *I'm laying responsibility for this mess at your door!* **2.** *Fig.* to give or assign a problem to someone for solving. (Fig. on ①.) □ *I am going to lay this problem right at your door. You are the one who can settle it.*

lay sth **at** so's **doorstep** AND **lay** sth **on** so's **doorstep** *Fig.* in someone's care; as someone's responsibility. □ *Why do you always have to lay your problems at my doorstep?*

lay sth **at** so's **feet** AND **put** sth **at** so's **feet** *Fig.* to hold someone responsible for something. □ *I am going to lay this matter at your feet. You are clearly to blame.*

lay so **away**† *Euph.* to bury someone. □ *Yes, he has passed. We laid him away last week.*

lay sth **away**† **(for** so**)** to put something in storage for someone to receive at a later time. (Often said of a purchase that is held until it is paid for.) □ *Please lay this away for me. I'll pay for it when I have the money.*

lay sth **before** so *Fig.* to present something for someone to judge. □ *All you can do is lay the matter before the teacher and hope for a favorable response.*

lay sth **by** Go to put sth by.

lay one's **cards on the table** AND **put** one's **cards on the table** *Fig.* to be very candid about one's position on some issue. (Fig. on the image of someone laying playing cards on the table, face up.) □ *All right. Let's lay our cards on the table and speak very candidly about this matter.*

lay claim to sth *Fig.* to place a claim on something. □ *Do you really think you can* lay claim to that money after all these years?

lay down *Fig. Inf.* to give up. □ *You really think I should just lay down and let them walk all over me?*

lay down one's **arms 1.** to put one's gun, sword, club, etc. down; to stop fighting; to surrender. □ *The soldiers laid down their arms and surrendered.* **2.** *Fig.* to give up and cease being hostile. □ *I know you're upset, but please lay down your arms and try to be reasonable.*

lay down one's **life (for** so/sth**)** *Fig.* to sacrifice one's life for someone or something. □ *There aren't many things for which I'd lay down my life.*

lay down on the job Go to lie down on the job.

lay down the law (to so**) (about** sth**)** *Fig.* to scold someone; to make something very clear to someone in a very stern manner. □ *Wow, was she mad at Ed. She really laid down the law about drinking to him.* □ *She laid down the law about drinking.*

lay emphasis on sth AND **lay stress on** sth to place emphasis on something; to emphasize something. □ *I'm afraid I laid too much stress on the notion of good attendance. If you are really sick, stay home!*

lay eyes on so/sth Go to set eyes on so/sth.

lay for so/sth to lie in wait for someone or something. □ *The sheriff was laying for the outlaw.*

lay sth **for** so/sth to prepare something (for a meal) for the benefit of someone or a group. □ *She laid a lovely picnic dinner for the two of them.*

lay one's **hands on** so/sth/animal Go to put one's hands on so/sth/animal.

lay sth **in**† to get something and store it for future use. □ *They laid a lot of food in for the holidays.*

lay into so/sth AND **light into** so/sth to attack, consume, or scold someone or something. □ *Bob laid into the big plate of fried chicken.* □ *She lit into him with her usual list of his flaws and failures.*

lay it on the line AND **put it on the line** *Fig.* to make something very clear; to be very definite about something. □ *I am going to lay it on the line and you had better listen to me. If you eat any of these mushrooms you will die.*

lay it on thick AND **lay it on with a trowel; pour it on thick; spread it on thick** *Fig.* to exaggerate or overstate praise, excuses, or blame. □ *Sally was laying it on thick when she said that Tom was the best singer she had ever heard.* □ *Bob always spreads it on thick.*

lay it on with a trowel Go to previous.

lay low Go to lie low.

lay so **low** *Fig.* to defeat, sicken, sadden, demoralize, or depress someone. □ *The sudden loss of his job laid him low for a month or two.* □ *He was laid low by unemployment.*

the **lay of the land 1.** the arrangement of features on an area of land. □ *The geologist studied the lay of the land, trying to determine if there was oil below the surface.* **2.** *Fig.* the arrangement or organization of something other than land. (Fig. on ①.) □ *As soon as I get the lay of the land in my new job, things will go better.*

lay off (so/sth**)** to leave someone or something alone. □ *Lay off the booze for a while, why don't ya?* □ *Lay off me! I didn't do anything!*

lay so **off**† **(from** sth**)** to put an end to someone's employment at something. □ *The automobile factory laid 500 people off from work.*

lay sth **on**† *Fig.* to supply something in abundance. □ *Look at him lay that butter on! What do you suppose the insides of his arteries look like?*

lay sth **on** so Go to lay sth at so's door.

lay one on Go to tie one on.

lay so **out**† **1.** *Sl.* to knock someone down with a punch; to knock someone unconscious. □ *Tom laid out Bill with one punch to the chin.* **2.** to prepare a corpse for burial or for a wake. □ *They laid out their un-*

cle for the wake. **3.** *Sl.* to scold someone severely. □ *She really laid the guy out but good. What did he do, rob a bank?*

lay sth **out**† **1.** *Fig.* to explain a plan of action or a sequence of events. □ *Let me lay it out for you.* **2.** *Fig.* to spend some amount of money. □ *I can't lay that kind of money out every day!* **3.** to spread something out. □ *The nurse laid the instruments out for the operation.*

lay so **out in lavender** *Fig.* to scold someone severely. □ *She was really mad. She laid him out in lavender and really put him in his place.*

lay over (some place**)** to pause some place during one's journey. □ *I had to lay over in San Antonio for a few hours before my plane left.*

lay (some) rubber *Sl.* to spin one's car tires when accelerating, leaving black marks on the street.

lay some sweet lines on so AND **put some sweet lines on** so *Sl.* to speak kindly to someone; to soft soap someone. □ *I just laid some sweet lines on her, and she let me use her car.*

lay stress on sth Go to lay emphasis on sth.

lay the blame (for sth**) on** so *Fig.* to place the blame for something on someone. □ *We could not possibly lay the blame for the accident on you.*

lay the blame on so/sth Go to put the blame on so/sth.

lay the finger on so Go to put the finger on so.

lay to to begin doing something, such as fighting or eating. □ *All right, you guys. Lay to. The stuff will get cold if you don't eat it.*

lay sth **to** sth to attribute something to something. □ *I lay all our problems to the inadequacy of our training.*

lay so **to rest** *Euph.* to bury a dead person. □ *They laid her to rest by her mother and father, out in the old churchyard.*

lay sth **to rest** Go to put sth to rest.

lay sth **to waste** AND **lay waste to** sth *Fig.* to destroy something; to ruin or mess up something. □ *The invaders laid the village to waste.*

lay sth **up**† **1.** to acquire and store something. □ *Try to lay as much of it up as you can.* **2.** [for something] to disable something. □ *The accident laid up the ship for repairs.*

lay waste to sth Go to lay sth to waste.

lay oneself **(wide) open for** sth Go to leave oneself (wide) open for sth.

lead a dog's life AND **live a dog's life** *Fig.* to lead a drab or boring life. □ *Poor Jane really leads a dog's life.*

lead a double life AND **live a double life** *Fig.* to live one life with two identities. □ *Fred was a bigamist, and he led a double life, living in two different cities.*

lead so **astray** to direct or guide someone in the wrong direction. □ *I am afraid that this young man has been leading you astray. I think you had better stop seeing him.*

lead so **by the nose 1.** to force someone to go somewhere (with you); to lead someone by coercion. □ *John had to lead Tom by the nose to get him to the opera.* **2.** *Fig.* to guide someone very carefully and slowly. (Fig. on ①. As if the person were not very smart.) □ *He will never find his way through the tax form unless you lead him by the nose.*

lead so **down the garden path** AND **lead** so **up the garden path** *Fig.* to deceive someone by steering them toward a goal that one has selected for them. (An elaboration of the "lead astray" concept. There is much speculation as to the origin of this phrase. A theme frequently mentioned is that of female to male seduction. Indeed, *garden* has been used as a euphemism for the female genitals. Other questions arise, however. Why would anyone have to be led down a path? Doesn't a path in the garden or yard likely lead to an outhouse and would not the way be known to its users? Unfortunately, the expression has no clear origin backed up by evidence.) □ *I knew the salesman was leading me down the garden path about the flat-screen TV, but I really wanted it anyway, so I bought it.*

lead in(to sth**) 1.** to begin something; to work into something. □ *Let me lead into the first number with a little talk about the composer.* **2.** to make a transition into something; to segue into something. □ *Now, we will lead into the second scene with a little soft orchestral music.*

lead sth **off**† Go to kick sth off†.

lead so **on**† to tease someone; to encourage someone's romantic or sexual interest without sincerity. □ *It's not fair to continue leading him on.*

lead so **on a merry chase** *Fig.* to lead someone in a purposeless pursuit. □ *What a waste of time. You really led me on a merry chase.*

lead the life of Riley AND **live the life of Riley** *Fig.* to live in luxury. (No one knows who *Riley* alludes to.) □ *If I had a million dollars, I could live the life of Riley.*

lead the pack AND **be at the head of the pack** *Fig.* to be the leader in a group of competitors. (See also ahead of the pack.) □ *My goal is to lead the pack and become the boss.*

lead the way *Fig.* to lead (someone) along the proper pathway. □ *I feel better when you're leading the way. I get lost easily.*

lead so **to do** sth *Fig.* to cause someone to do something. □ *This agent led me to purchase a worthless piece of land.*

lead so **to believe** sth *Fig.* to imply something to someone; to cause someone to believe something untrue. □ *But you led me to believe that this watch was guaranteed!*

lead up to sth *Fig.* to prepare to say something; to lay the groundwork for making a point. (Typically with the present participle.) □ *I was just leading up to telling you what happened when you interrupted.*

lead with so/sth to start out with someone or something. □ *The coach led with Walter as pitcher and Sam on first base.*

lead with sth to tend to strike first with a particular fist—the right, the left, one's best, etc. (Boxing.) □ *Watch that guy, Champ, he always leads with his right.* □ *Get in there and lead with your left.*

leading question a question that suggests the kind of answer that the person who asks it wants to hear. □ *The mayor was angered by the reporter's leading questions.*

a **lead-pipe cinch** *Fig.* something very easy to do; something entirely certain to happen. □ *I knew it was a lead-pipe cinch that I would be selected to head the publication committee.*

leaf through sth Go to thumb through sth.

leak out [for information] to become known unofficially. □ *I hope that news of the new building does not leak out before the contract is signed.*

leak sth **(out)** AND **let** sth **(get) out** *Fig.* to disclose special information to the press so that the resulting publicity will accomplish something. (Usually said of government disclosures. Also used for accidental disclosures.) □ *Don't leak that information out.*

leak sth **to** so *Fig.* to tell [otherwise secret] information to someone. □ *The government leaked a phony story to the press just to see how far it would travel.*

lean and mean *Fig.* fit and ready for hard, efficient work. □ *The management is lean and mean and looks to turn a profit next year.*

lean on so *Fig.* to try to make someone do something; to coerce someone to do something. □ *If she refuses to do it, lean on her a bit.*

lean on so/sth *Fig.* to depend on someone or something. □ *You lean on your parents too much. You must be more independent.*

lean over backwards (to do sth**)** Go to fall over backwards (to do sth).

*****lean times (ahead)** *Fig.* a future period of lowered income or revenue; a future period when there will be shortages of goods and suffering. (*Typically: **be** ~; **cause** ~; **have** ~; **be headed for** ~; **mean** ~.) □ *The economy is going sour, which means lean times ahead.*

lean toward doing sth to tend toward doing something; to favor doing something. □ *The union is leaning toward accepting the proposal.*

lean toward so/sth *Fig.* to tend to favor [choosing] someone or something. □ *I am leaning toward Sarah as the new committee head.*

leap at so/sth *Fig.* to accept or choose someone or something eagerly. □ *We leaped at Carl when his department offered him to us.* □ *When we had the chance to hire Carl, we leaped at it.*

leap at the chance (to do sth**)** Go to next.

leap at the opportunity (to do sth**)** AND **leap at the chance (to** do sth**); jump at the chance; jump at something; jump at the opportunity** *Fig.* to accept an opportunity eagerly. □ *Frank leaped at the opportunity to become a commercial artist.* □ *I would leap at the chance to go to Moscow.*

leap for joy AND **jump for joy** *Fig.* to jump up because one is happy; to be very happy. □ *Tommy leaped for joy because he had won the race.*

*****a **leap of faith** *Fig.* acceptance of an idea or conclusion largely on faith. (*Typically: **be** ~; **make** ~; **require** ~.) □ *We had to make quite a leap of faith to accept his promise after the last time he let us down.*

leap to conclusions Go to jump to conclusions.

learn sth **by rote** *Fig.* to learn something by memorizing without giving any thought to what is being learned. □ *I learned history by rote, but I couldn't pass the test that required me to think.*

learn sth **from the bottom up** *Fig.* to learn something thoroughly, from the very basics; to learn all aspects of something, even the least important ones. □ *I started out sweeping the floors and learned everything from the bottom up.*

learn one's **lesson** *Fig.* to receive some kind of punishment [for something]. (See also teach so a lesson.) □ *I guess I learned my lesson. I won't do it again.*

learn (sth) **the hard way** AND **find** (sth) **out the hard way** to learn something by experience, especially by an unpleasant experience. (As opposed to learning in school, from reading, etc.) □ *She learned how to make investments the hard way.* □ *I wish I didn't have to learn things the hard way.*

learn to live with sth *Fig.* to learn to adapt to something unpleasant or painful. □ *The floor plan of the house we bought is not as spacious as we had thought, but we will learn to live with it.*

a **learning experience** Go to a growth experience.

the **least** so **could do** the minimum a person could do and still seem sorry, polite, or friendly. □ *Replacing the window that he broke was the least he could do.*

the **least little thing** the smallest possible thing. □ *He gets upset over the least little thing.*

least of all the thing of smallest importance. □ *There were many things wrong with the new house. Least of all, the water faucets leaked.*

leave a bad taste in so's **mouth** *Fig.* [for something] to leave a bad feeling or memory with someone. □ *The whole business about the missing money left a bad taste in his mouth.*

leave a date open (for so/sth**)** AND **keep a date open (for** so/sth**)** to keep a time available for a future appointment for someone or something. □ *Let's have lunch sometime this month. I'll leave a date open for you.*

leave a lot to be desired AND **leave something to be desired** *Cliché* to be lacking something important; to be inadequate. (A polite way of saying that something is bad.) □ *I'm sorry to have to fire you, Mary, but your work leaves a lot to be desired.*

leave a paper trail Go to a paper trail.

leave a sinking ship Go to desert a sinking ship.

leave ahead of time Go to ahead of time.

leave so/sth/animal **alone** AND **let** so/sth/animal **alone; leave** so/sth/animal **be; let** so/sth/animal **be** to stop bothering someone, something, or some creature. □ *Don't torment the cat. Leave it alone.* □ *Don't argue about it. Let it be!*

leave an impression (on so**)** AND **leave** so **with an impression** *Fig.* to provide a lasting memory for someone after one has left. (Akin to make an impression on so.) □ *Her performance was less than stunning. She didn't leave a very good impression on us.*

leave sth **aside**† AND **put** sth **aside**†; **set** sth **aside**† **1.** to leave something in reserve. □ *Leave some of the sugar aside for use in the icing.* **2.** to ignore something, especially a fact. □ *Let's leave the question of who will pay for it aside for a while.*

leave so/sth **(at)** some place **1.** to abandon someone or something at some place. □ *Betty left her newspaper at the table, hoping someone else would enjoy it.* **2.** to allow someone or something to remain at some place. □ *You leave me here and go on ahead.* **3.** to allow someone or something to stay behind through forgetfulness. □ *I was left at the movie theater by mistake.*

leave so **at loose ends** Go to at loose ends.

leave so/sth/animal **be** Go to leave so/sth/animal alone.

leave so **cold** *Inf.* to leave someone unaffected or bored. □ *The music's good, but the story left the producer cold.*

leave so **flat 1.** *Fig.* to fail to entertain or stimulate someone. □ *We listened carefully to his lecture, but it left us flat.* **2.** *Fig.* to leave someone without any money—flat broke. □ *The robber took all my money and left me flat.* **3.** *Fig.* to leave someone completely and suddenly alone. □ *I was at the dance with Harry, but when he met Alice, he left me flat.*

leave sth **for another occasion** AND **keep** sth **for another occasion** *Fig.* to hold something back for later. (*Occasion* can be replaced with *time, day, person*, etc.) □ *Please leave some cake for another day.* □ *Don't eat all the cheese. Leave some for another occasion.*

leave so **for dead** *Fig.* to abandon someone as being dead. (The abandoned person may actually be alive.) □ *He looked so bad that they almost left him for dead.*

leave so **guessing** Go to keep so guessing.

leave so/sth **hanging (in midair)** AND **keep** so/sth **hanging (in midair)** *Fig.* to suspend dealing with someone or something; to leave someone or something waiting to be finished or continued. □ *Tell me the rest of the story. Don't leave me hanging in midair.*

leave so **high and dry 1.** [for water] to recede and leave someone untouched. □ *The waters receded and left us high and dry.* **2.** *Fig.* to leave someone unsupported and unable to maneuver; to leave someone helpless. (Fig. on ①.) □ *All my workers quit and left me high and dry.* **3.** *Fig.* to leave someone flat broke. (Fig. on ①.) □ *Mrs. Franklin took all the money out of the bank and left Mr. Franklin high and dry.*

leave so **holding the baby** Go to next.

leave so **holding the bag** AND **leave** so **holding the baby** *Fig.* to allow someone to take all the blame; to leave someone appearing to be guilty. □ *They all ran off and left me holding the bag. It wasn't even my fault.*

leave in a body Go to in a body.

leave so/sth **in** one's **hands** *Fig.* to give one control of or responsibility for someone or something. □ *You left the whole project in my hands!*

leave so **in peace** *Fig.* to stop bothering someone; to go away and leave someone alone. (Does not necessarily mean to go away from a person.) □ *Can't you see that you're upsetting her? Leave her in peace.*

leave so **in the lurch** *Fig.* to leave someone waiting for or anticipating your actions. □ *I didn't mean to leave you in the lurch. I thought we had canceled our meeting.*

leave so **in the shade** *Fig.* to outdistance or outperform someone, leaving them behind. □ *We are very productive this quarter and will leave the competition in the shade.*

leave it at that *Fig.* to leave a situation as it is. □ *This is the best we can do. We'll have to leave it at that.*

leave it to so to depend on someone to behave in a certain way. □ *Leave it to Harry to mess things up.*

leave one's **mark on** so AND **leave a mark on** so *Fig.* [for someone like a teacher] to affect the behavior and performance of another person. □ *My father left his mark on me, and I will always remember all his good advice.*

Leave me alone! *Fig.* Stop harassing me!; Don't bother me! □ *John: You did it. You're the one who always does it. Bill: Leave me alone! I never did it.*

leave no stone unturned *Fig.* to search in all possible places. (As if one might search under every rock.) □ *Don't worry. We'll find your stolen car. We'll leave no stone unturned.*

a **leave of absence** *Fig.* a period of time away from one's job, with the employer's permission. □ *Mr. Takaguchi is on leave of absence because he is going back to school.*

leave off (doing sth**)** to stop doing something, perhaps temporarily; to knock off (doing sth). □ *Let's leave off working for a while and take a rest.*

leave sth **on**† **1.** to continue to wear some article of clothing. □ *I think I will leave my coat on. It's chilly in here.* **2.** to allow something [that can be turned off] to remain on. □ *Who left the radio on?*

leave open the possibility (of sth**)** Go to leave the door open (for sth).

leave one's **options open** Go to keep one's options open.

leave so **out in the cold** Go to out in the cold.

305

leave one **scratching** one's **head** AND **send** one **scratching** one's **head** *Fig.* to cause someone to be puzzled. □ *His last remarks left me scratching my head, but I understood the rest.*

leave the door open (for sth) AND **leave open the possibility (of** sth) *Fig.* to provide for the possibility that something might happen. □ *I think that the matter is completely settled, although we have left the door open for one or two last-minute changes.*

leave the nest AND **fly the nest** *Fig.* [for grown children] to leave the parent's home for independent living. (Fig. on birds leaving the nest. *Fly* might imply an eagerness to depart. See also **spread** one's **wings (and fly).**) □ *When the kids left the nest, we were left with a lot of extra space.*

leave the room 1. to go out of the room. □ *I had to leave the room to get drinks for everyone.* **2.** *Euph.* to leave to go to the toilet. □ *I have to leave the room. I'll be back in a minute.*

leave sth **to** so **1.** *Fig.* to will something to someone. □ *My grandfather left his house to my mother.* **2.** to assign work to or reserve a task for someone. □ *I will leave this last little bit of the job to you.*

leave sth **to chance** *Fig.* to allow something to be settled by chance. □ *It is not a good idea to leave any of this to chance.*

leave one **to** one's **fate** *Fig.* to abandon someone to whatever may happen—possibly death or some other unpleasant event. □ *We couldn't rescue the miners and were forced to leave them to their fate.*

leave so **to it** *Fig.* to withdraw and allow someone to finish something alone. □ *I hate to leave before the job is finished, but I'll have to leave you to it.*

leave one **to** one's **own devices** AND **leave** one **to** one's **own resources** *Fig.* to make one rely on oneself. □ *I am sure that she will manage if we leave her to her own devices.*

leave one **to** one's **own resources** Go to previous.

leave so **up in the air** *Fig.* to leave someone waiting for a decision. □ *Please don't leave me up in the air. I want to know what's going to happen to me.*

leave sth **up in the air** *Fig.* to leave a matter undecided. (Fig. on the image of something drifting in the air, moving neither up nor down.) □ *Let's get this settled now. I don't want to leave anything up in the air over the weekend.*

leave sth **up to** so/sth Go to up to so/sth.

leave well enough alone Go to let well enough alone.

leave oneself **(wide) open for** sth AND **leave** oneself **(wide) open to** sth; **lay** oneself **(wide) open for** sth; **lay** oneself **(wide) open to** sth *Fig.* to invite criticism or joking about oneself; to fail to protect oneself from criticism or ridicule. □ *Yes, that was a harsh remark, Jane, but you left yourself wide open to it.*

leave oneself **(wide) open to** sth Go to previous.

leave so **with an impression** Go to leave an impression (on so).

leave word for so **to** do sth *Fig.* to leave a message or a request for someone. (See also leave word (with so).) □ *I left word for you to come to my office.*

leave word (with so) *Fig.* to leave a message with someone (who will pass the message on to someone else). □ *If you decide to go to the convention, please leave word with my secretary.*

lecture at so **(about** sth) to talk to someone about something in the manner of a lecture. □ *There is no need to lecture at me about the problem. I know how serious the matter is.*

left and right Go to right and left.

left-handed compliment Go to backhanded compliment.

*a **leg up** *Fig.* a kind of help where someone provides a knee or crossed hand as a support for someone to place a foot on to get higher, as in mounting a horse or climbing over something. (*Typically:

get ~; **have** ~; **give** so ~.) □ *I gave her a leg up, and soon she was on her horse.*

*a **leg up on** so *Fig.* an advantage that someone else does not have. (*Typically: **get** ~; **have** ~; **give** so ~.) □ *I have a leg up on Walter when it comes to getting around town, since I have a car.*

leg work *Inf.* the physical work accompanying a task. □ *I don't mind making the phone calls if you do the leg work.*

a **legend in** one's **own (life)time** *Fig.* someone who is very famous and widely known for doing something special.

lend so **a hand with** sth AND **give** so **a hand with** sth *Fig.* to help someone with something. (This need not involve hands. See also a (helping) hand.) □ *Could you please lend us a hand with this?*

lend so **a (helping) hand** Go to a (helping) hand.

lend an ear to so/sth AND **lend your ear to** so/sth *Fig.* to listen to someone or what someone has to say. □ *Lend an ear to me, and I will tell you a story.*

lend color to sth *Fig.* to provide an interesting accompaniment for something. □ *Your clever comments lent a great deal of color to the slide show of your vacation.*

lend oneself or **itself to** sth *Fig.* [for someone or something] to be adaptable to something; [for someone or something] to be useful for something. □ *This room doesn't lend itself to bright colors.* □ *John doesn't lend himself to casual conversation.*

lend your ear to so/sth Go to lend an ear to so/sth.

Less is more. *Cliché* Fewer or smaller is better. □ *Simplicity now rules our lives. Less is more. Smaller houses and cars. The world will be a better place!*

less than pleased *Euph.* displeased. □ *We were less than pleased to learn of your comments.*

the **lesser (of the two)** *Fig.* the smaller one (of two); the one having the lesser amount. □ *The last two pieces of pie were not quite the same size, and I chose the lesser of the two.*

the **lesser of two evils** *Fig.* the less bad thing of a pair of bad things. □ *I didn't like either politician, so I voted for the lesser of two evils.*

let so/sth/animal **alone** Go to leave so/sth/animal alone.

let alone do sth [not] to do even something; [not] even do something [which is almost as bad]. □ *I wouldn't consider calling him at this hour, let alone ringing his doorbell!*

let alone so/sth AND **much less** so/sth *Fig.* not to mention or think of someone or something additional; not even to take someone or something into account. □ *Do I have a dollar? I don't even have a dime, let alone a dollar.*

let sth **be known** *Fig.* to announce something openly or permit the information to be passed as gossip. □ *She let it be known that she was divorcing her husband.*

Let bygones be bygones. *Cliché* Forgive someone for something he or she did in the past. □ *Jill: Why don't you want to invite Ellen to your party? Jane: She was rude to me at the office picnic. Jill: But that was six months ago. Let bygones be bygones.*

let so/sth **down**† *Fig.* to fail someone or something; to disappoint someone or a group. □ *I don't want to let you down, but I can't support you in the election.* □ *Please don't let me down. I am depending on you.*

let one's **emotions show** to be emotional, especially where it is not appropriate. □ *I'm sorry for the outburst. I didn't mean to let my emotions show.*

let fly with sth *Fig.* to throw or thrust something, such as a rock, ball, punch, etc. □ *The pitcher wound up and let fly with a strike—right over the plate.*

Let George do it. *Fig.* Let someone else do it; it doesn't matter who. □ *Billie always says, "Let George do it." She is unwilling to help with things that don't interest her.*

let so **get by with** sth to allow someone to do something wrong and not be punished or reprimanded. (An elaboration of get by (with sth).) □ *She lets those kids get by with anything.*

let sth **(get) out** Go to leak sth (out).

let sth **get out** AND **let** sth **slip (out)** *Fig.* to give out a bit of information as if by accident; to leak sth (out). □ *She let it slip out that she would be interested in getting some job offers.*

let oneself **go 1.** *Fig.* to become less constrained; to get excited and have a good time. □ *I love to dance and just let myself go.* **2.** *Fig.* to let one's appearance and health to suffer. □ *When I was depressed, I let myself go and was really a mess.*

let so **go** *Euph.* to fire someone. □ *I'm afraid we're going to have to let you go.*

let go (with sth**)** AND **cut loose (with** sth**); let loose (with** sth**) 1.** *Inf.* to shout something out or expel something; to shout or express something wildly. □ *The whole team let go with a loud shout.* **2.** *Inf.* to deliver a strong verbal reprimand. □ *Dave cut loose with a vengeful retort.*

let grass grow under one's **feet** *Fig.* to do nothing; to stand still. □ *Mary doesn't let the grass grow under her feet. She's always busy.*

let one's **guard down**† AND **lower** one's **guard; drop** one's **guard** *Fig.* to stop guarding oneself against trouble; to relax one's vigilance and become vulnerable. □ *He never let's his guard down because he trusts no one.*

let one's **hair down 1.** to undo one's hair and let it fall freely. □ *When she took off her glasses and let her hair down, she was incredibly beautiful.* **2.** *Fig.* to tell [someone] everything; to tell one's innermost feelings and secrets. (Fig. on ①.) □ *Let your hair down and tell me all about it.*

let so **have it (with both barrels)** *Fig.* to strike someone or attack someone verbally. (*With both barrels* intensifies the phrase; it alludes to firing a double-barreled shotgun.) □ *I really let Tom have it with both barrels. I told him he had better not do that again if he knows what's good for him.*

Let her rip! AND **Let it roll!** *Inf.* Let it go!; Let it start! □ *There's the signal! Let it roll!*

let oneself **in for** sth to make oneself vulnerable to some difficulty. □ *I don't want to let myself in for a lot of extra work.*

let so **in for** sth to cause someone to be involved in something, usually something unpleasant. □ *Fred had no idea what his brother had let him in for when he agreed to take his place in the race.*

let it all hang out *Inf.* to be yourself, assuming that you generally are not; to become totally relaxed and unpretentious. □ *Come on. Relax! Let it all hang out.*

Let it be. *Fig.* Leave the situation alone as it is. □ *Alice: I can't get over the way he just left me there on the street and drove off. What an arrogant pig! Mary: Oh, Alice, let it be. You'll figure out some way to get even.*

Let it go. *Fig.* Forget it.; Stop worrying about it. □ *Don't get so angry about it. Let it go.*

Let it roll! Go to Let her rip!

let loose of so/sth to become independent from someone or something. □ *Dave can't let loose of his childhood.*

let loose (with sth**)** Go to let go (with sth).

Let me have it! AND **Let's have it!** *Inf.* Tell me the news. □ *Bill: I'm afraid there's some bad news. Bob: Okay. Let me have it!*

let me (just) say AND **just let me say** *Fig.* a phrase introducing something that the speaker thinks is important. □ *Rachel: Let me say how pleased we all are with your efforts. Henry: Why, thank you very much.*

let nature take its course *Fig.* to let life progress normally as with the course of a disease, illness leading to death, or the development of sexual interests. □ *The dog was quite old and not suffering, so we decided to let nature takes its course.* □ *Well, a couple together with moonlight and soft music. They let nature take its course and were engaged by dawn.*

let sth **off**† *Fig.* to release something; to give something off. □ *The engine let some evil-smelling smoke off.*

let so **off (easy)** AND **let** so **off**† *Fig.* to release or dismiss someone without punishment. □ *The teacher let me off easy even though I broke a window.*

let off (some) steam AND **blow off (some) steam 1.** [for something] to release steam. □ *The locomotive let off some steam after it came to a halt.* **2.** *Fig.* to work or play off excess energy. (Fig. on ①.) □ *Those boys need to get out and let off some steam.* **3.** *Fig.* to release one's pent-up emotions, such as anger, usually verbally. (Fig. on ①.) □ *I'm sorry I yelled at you. I guess I needed to let off some steam.*

let on (about so/sth**) 1.** *Fig.* to confirm or reveal something about someone or something. □ *I won't let on about Kate.* □ *You promised you wouldn't let on about Sally and her new job!* **2.** AND **let on (about** so/sth**) (to** so**)** to admit someone or something to someone. □ *He was having money troubles, but he never let on about it to us.*

let out [for an event that includes many people] to end. (The people are then permitted to come out.) □ *What time does the movie let out? I have to meet someone in the lobby.* □ *The meeting let out at about seven o'clock.*

let sth **out**† **1.** *Fig.* to reveal something; to tell about a secret or a plan. (See also leak sth (out).) □ *It was supposed to be a secret. Who let it out?* **2.** *Fig.* to enlarge an article of clothing. □ *She had to let her overcoat out because she had gained some weight.*

let out some kind of sound [for a living creature] to make some kind of a noise or sound. □ *Be quiet. Don't let out a sound!*

let out (with) sth **1.** *Fig.* to state or utter something loudly. □ *She let out a torrent of curses.* **2.** *Fig.* to give forth a scream or yell. □ *She let out with a blood-curdling scream when she saw the snake in her chair.*

let sth **ride** *Fig.* to allow something to continue or remain as it is. □ *It isn't the best plan, but we'll let it ride.*

let so **slide by** *Fig.* to permit someone to get past a barrier or a challenge too easily. □ *You let too many students slide by. You need to be more rigorous.*

let sth **slide by** Go to next.

let sth **slip by** AND **let** sth **slide by 1.** *Fig.* to forget or miss an important time or date. □ *I'm sorry I just let your birthday slip by.* **2.** *Fig.* to waste a period of time. □ *You wasted the whole day by letting it slip by.*

let sth **slip (out)** *Fig.* to reveal a secret carelessly or by accident. □ *John let the plans slip when he was talking to Bill.*

let the cat out of the bag *Fig.* to reveal a secret or a surprise by accident. □ *When Bill glanced at the door, he let the cat out of the bag. We knew then that he was expecting someone to arrive.*

let the chips fall (where they may) *Fig.* and do not worry about the results. □ *I have to settle this matter in my own way. I will confront her with the evidence and let the chips fall where they may.*

let things slide AND **let** sth **slide** *Fig.* to ignore the things that one is supposed to do; to fall behind in the doing of one's work. □ *I am afraid that I let the matter slide while I was recovering from my operation.*

let up 1. to diminish. □ *When the snow lets up so I can see, I will drive to the store.* **2.** to stop [doing something] altogether. □ *The rain let up about noon, and the sun came out.*

let up (on so/sth**)** *Fig.* to reduce the pressure or demands on someone or to do something. □ *You had better let up on Tom. He can't handle any more work.*

let well enough alone AND **leave well enough alone** *Fig.* to leave things as they are (and not try to improve them). □ *There isn't much more you can accomplish here. Why don't you just let well enough alone?*

Let's call it a day. *Fig.* Let us end what we are doing for the day. □ *Bob: Let's call it a day. I'm tired. Tom: Me too. Let's get out of here.*

Let's get down to business. *Fig.* a phrase marking a transition to a business discussion or serious talk. □ *"All right, ladies and gentlemen, let's get down to business," said the president of the board.*

Let's have it! Go to Let me have it!

Let's rock and roll! *Inf.* Let's get started!; Let's get moving! □ *A: Everybody ready? B: Yeah. A: Good. Let's rock and roll!*

let's say *Fig.* introduces an estimate, proposal, or speculation. □ *I need about—let's say—20 pounds.* □ *Let's say I go over and talk to him. What do you think?*

(Let's) say that . . . *Fig.* Let's assume [something]; Let's suppose [that something were so]. □ *Say that two trains leave two different cities at the same time.*

Let's see. Let me or us think or check to determine the answer. □ *Q: How many pints in a quart? A: Let's see. Is it about three?*

Let's talk (about it). Let us talk about the problem and try to settle things. □ *Sally: I've got a real problem. Bob: Let's talk about it.*

level a charge against so *Fig.* to place a charge against someone; to accuse someone of something. □ *The cops leveled an assault charge against Spike.*

level sth **at** so/sth **1.** to aim a weapon at someone. □ *The sheriff leveled his rifle at the bandit.* **2.** *Fig.* to direct something at someone or something; to aim a remark at someone. □ *Why did you think you had to level that barrage of words at me? I didn't make the problem.*

so's **level best** *Inf.* one's very best effort. □ *Don't go to a whole lot of trouble. Your level best is good enough!*

level off *Fig.* to become more like normal after a period of greater activity. □ *Business will level off after the year-end buying season.*

a **level playing field** *Fig.* a situation that is fair to all; a situation where everyone has the same opportunity. □ *If we started off with a level playing field, everyone would have an equal chance.*

level the (playing) field *Fig.* to create a state where everyone has the same opportunity. □ *Let's level the playing field and give everyone a chance.*

level sth **to the ground** to crush or demolish something down to the ground. □ *They were forced to level the building to the ground, because they could not afford to maintain it.*

level with so **(about** so/sth**)** *Fig.* to be straightforward with someone about something; to be sincere or truthful about someone or something. □ *The police encouraged the criminal to level with them about the crime.*

license to do sth permission, right, or justification to do something. □ *Who granted you license to enter my house without knocking?*

*a **lick and a promise** *Fig.* a hasty bit of work; a quick once-over. (*Typically: **finish** sth **with** ~; **give** sth ~.) □ *Mary spent so much time on her history paper that she had to finish her math homework with a lick and a promise.*

lick one's **chops 1.** to show one's eagerness to eat something by licking one's lip area. (Said especially about an animal.) □ *The big bad wolf licked his chops when he saw the little pigs.* **2.** *Fig.* to show one's eagerness to do something. □ *Fred started licking his chops when he heard about the high-paying job offered at the factory.*

lick so/sth **into shape** AND **whip** so/sth **into shape** to press or force someone or something into good shape or condition. □ *The drama coach will try to lick her into shape by performance time.* □ *I want to whip this house into shape for Saturday night.*

lick one's **lips 1.** *Fig.* to show eagerness or pleasure about a future event. (Fig. on people licking their lips when they are about to enjoy eating something.) □ *The author's readers were licking their lips in anticipation of her new novel.* **2.** Go to smack one's lips.

a **lick of work** a bit of work. (Used with a negative.) □ *I couldn't get her to do a lick of work all day long!*

lick one's **wounds** *Fig.* to recover from a defeat or a rebuke. (Also literal for an animal.) □ *After the terrible meeting and all the criticism, I went back to my office to lick my wounds.*

*a licking *Fig.* a spanking; a beating in a fight. (*Typically: **get ~; take ~; give so ~.**) □ *Billy, you had better get in here if you don't want to get a licking.*

*the lid on sth **1.** a cover on something, such as a pot, pan, etc. (*Typically: **get ~; keep ~; put ~.**) □ *Keep the lid on the pot until the stew is almost done.* **2.** *Fig.* a scheme to suppress a scandalous or embarrassing situation and keep it secret. (Fig. on ①. *Typically: **get ~; keep ~; put ~.**) □ *We can't keep the lid on this any longer. The press has got wind of it.*

lie at anchor [for a ship] to wait or rest at anchor. □ *The ship lay at anchor throughout the day while a shore party searched for the runaway.*

lie at death's door *Fig.* to be close to dying. □ *I do not want to lie at death's door suffering. I hope to pass on quickly.*

lie behind so/sth [for something] to be in someone's or a group's past. □ *Now that all of our difficulties lie behind us, we can get on with our business.*

lie beyond so/sth to be outside the grasp or the ability of someone or a group. □ *The solution lies beyond the power of the committee.*

lie doggo *Fig.* to remain unrecognized (for a long time). □ *If you don't find the typos now, they will lie doggo until the next edition.*

lie down on the job AND **lay down on the job** *Fig.* to do one's job poorly or not at all. (*Lay* is a common error for *lie*.) □ *Tom was fired because he was laying down on the job.*

lie fallow 1. [for farmland] to exist unplanted for a period of time. □ *The fields lay fallow under the burning sun. It had been too wet to plant last spring.* **2.** *Fig.* [for a skill and talent] to remain unused and neglected. □ *You should not let your*

talent lie fallow. *Practice the piano before you forget how to play it.*

lie in *Fig.* [for a woman] to lie in bed awaiting the birth of her child. □ *She did not lie in at all. She worked right up to the onset of labor pains.*

lie in sth to recline in something, such as a bed, a puddle, etc. □ *I found my wallet lying in a puddle. My money was soaked!*

lie in ruins *Fig.* to exist in a state of ruin, such as a destroyed city, building, scheme, plan, etc. □ *My garden lay in ruins after the cows got in and trampled everything.*

lie in state *Fig.* [for a dead body] to be on display for public mourning. □ *The president will lie in state in the capitol rotunda.*

lie in store (for so**)** Go to in store (for so).

lie in wait (for so/sth**)** *Fig.* to stay still and hidden, waiting for someone or something. □ *Bob was lying in wait for Anne so he could scold her about something.*

lie like a rug *Sl.* to tell lies shamelessly. □ *He says he didn't take the money, but he's lying like a rug.*

lie low AND **lay low** *Fig.* to keep quiet and not be noticed; to avoid being conspicuous. (*Lay* is a common error for *lie.*) □ *The robber said that he would lay low for a short time after the robbery.*

lie through one's **teeth** *Fig.* to lie boldly. □ *I knew she was lying through her teeth, but I didn't want to say so just then.*

life after sth *Fig.* a good quality of living [available] after one has ceased doing or being something. (Patterned and punning on *life after death.*) □ *Jane wants to know if there is life after divorce.*

life and limb [a person's] life and body, with reference to safety and survival. (Always treated as a generic concept and not possessed or counted. *Limb* refers to the arms and legs, and therefore, the body.) □ *Your first thought when motorcycling is the protection of life and limb.*

life in the fast lane *Inf.* a very active or possibly risky way to live. (See also in the fast lane.) □ *Life in the fast lane is too much for me.*

life is too short *Fig.* life is short and there is no point in wasting it on things like worry, hatred, vengeance, etc. □ *I am not going to spend any more time trying to get even with Wally. Life's too short.*

*a **life of its own** *Fig.* [of a thing] having an independent existence that seems to be self-sustaining. (*Typically: **have** ~; **give** sth ~; **take on** ~; **acquire** ~.) □ *After a while, the committee seemed to take on a life of its own. It went on and on with no purpose other than its own continued existence.*

the **life of the party** *Fig.* a person who is lively and helps make a party fun and exciting. □ *Bill is always the life of the party. Be sure to invite him.*

Life's been good (to me). I am grateful that I am doing well in life. □ *I can't complain. Life's been good to me.*

lift a hand (against so/sth**)** AND **raise a hand (against** so/sth**); lift** one's **hand (against** so/sth**); raise** one's **hand (against** so/sth**)** *Fig.* to threaten (to strike) someone or something. (Often in the negative.) □ *She's very peaceful. She wouldn't lift a hand against a fly.* □ *Would you raise your hand against your own brother?*

lift one's **elbow** Go to bend one's elbow.

lift so **from** sth Go to raise so from sth.

light as a feather AND **light as air** *Cliché* light in weight; [of cakes and pastries] delicate and airy. (*Also: **as** ~.) □ *Carrying Esther from the car to the house was no problem. She was as light as a feather.* □ *What a delicious cake, Tom! And light as air, too.*

light as air Go to previous.

light into so/sth Go to lay into so/sth.

light out (for some place**)** Go to cut out (for some place).

light out (of some place**) (for** some place**)** *Fig.* to leave a place in a great hurry for some place. □ *I lit out of there for home as fast as I could.*

light up [for someone] to become interested and responsive in something. □ *We could tell from the way Sally lit up that she recognized the man in the picture.*

light (up)on so/sth *Fig.* to arrive at something by chance; to happen upon something. □ *The committee lit upon a solution that pleased almost everyone.*

lighten so's **load** AND **ease** so's **burden 1.** *Fig.* to make things easier for someone; to relieve someone of some responsibilities; to reduce someone's workload. (As if actual weight were being lifted.) □ *The boss decided to lighten Tom's load.* **2.** *Fig.* to relieve someone of worries or distress. (Fig. on ①.) □ *I meditated for an hour, and that helped relieve my burden.*

lighten up (on so/sth**)** to be less rough and demanding or rude with someone or something. □ *Please lighten up on her. You are being very cruel.*

like a bat out of hell *Inf.* very fast or sudden. □ *The car pulled away from the curb like a bat out of hell.*

like a bolt out of the blue AND **like a bolt from the blue** *Fig.* suddenly and without warning. (Refers to a bolt of lightning coming out of a clear blue sky.) □ *The news came to us like a bolt from the blue.* □ *Like a bolt out of the blue, the boss came and fired us all.*

like a bump on a log *Fig.* completely inert. (Derogatory.) □ *You can never tell what Julia thinks of something; she just stands there like a bump on a log.*

like a fish out of water *Fig.* appearing to be completely out of place; in a very awkward manner. □ *Bob stood there in his rented tuxedo, looking like a fish out of water.*

like a house on fire AND **like a house afire** *Rur.* rapidly and with force. □ *The truck came roaring down the road like a house on fire.*

like a kid with a new toy *Fig.* very pleased; happily playing with something. □ *Every time Bill gets a new gadget for his kitchen, he's like a kid with a new toy.*

like a fish out of water

***like a million (dollars)** *Fig.* very good or well. (*Typically: **feel** ~; **look** ~; **run** ~.) □ *This old buggy runs like a million dollars.*

like a sitting duck Go to a sitting duck.

like a three-ring circus *Fig.* chaotic; exciting and busy. □ *Our household is like a three-ring circus on Monday mornings.*

***like a ton of bricks** *Inf.* like a great weight or burden. (*Typically: **fall** ~; **hit** ~; **hit** so ~.) □ *The sudden tax increase hit like a ton of bricks. Everyone became angry.*

like as not as likely as not; equally likely and not likely. □ *Like as not, John will not be there on time.*

like crazy AND **like mad** *Fig.* furiously; very much, fast, many, or actively. □ *People are coming in here like crazy. There isn't enough room for them all.*

***like death warmed over** *Fig.* very ill; appearing very sickly. (*Typically: **feel** ~; **look** ~.) □ *Oh dear, I feel like death warmed over.*

like fighting snakes AND **like herding frogs; like herding cats** *Rur.* chaotic; challenging. □ *It's like fighting snakes to get anything done at this time of year.* □ *Try to get those people to cooperate is like herding cats.*

like gangbusters *Inf.* with great excitement and speed. (From the phrase "Come on like gangbusters," a radio show that "came on" with lots of noise and excitement.) □ *She works like gangbusters and gets the job done.*

like greased lightning *Rur.* very fast. □ *Once I get her tuned up, this old car will go like greased lightning.*

like hell Go to like the devil.

Like hell (so did)! I don't believe (that someone) did it! □ *A: He ran the stop sign! B: Like hell he did! C: Yeah! Like hell!*

like hell on wheels *Fig. Inf.* very fast. □ *This old wreck of a car, as you call it, is hell on wheels!*

313

Like hell you will! You won't do it if I can stop you! □ *A: I'm going to take the car out tonight, Dad. B: Like hell you will!*

like herding cats Go to like fighting snakes.

like herding frogs Go to like fighting snakes.

like I was saying Go to as I was saying.

like it is going out of style *Fig.* rapidly or frequently. (Often in the past tense without reference to the tense of the main verb.) □ *I'm worried about Sally. She's taking aspirin like it's going out of style.*

Like it or lump it! *Inf.* There is no other choice. Take that or none. (Older.) □ *John: I don't like this room. It's too small. Bill: Like it or lump it. That's all we've got.*

Like it's such a big deal! *Inf.* It really isn't all that important! (Sarcastic.) □ *So I dropped the glass. Like it's such a big deal.*

like lambs to the slaughter AND **like a lamb to the slaughter** *Fig.* quietly and without seeming to realize the likely difficulties or dangers of a situation. □ *Our team went on the football field like lambs to the slaughter to meet the league-leaders.*

like looking for a needle in a haystack AND **like trying to find a needle in a haystack** *Fig.* like being engaged in a hopeless search. (Fig. on an example of a hopeless task.) □ *Trying to find a white glove in the snow is like looking for a needle in a haystack.*

like mad Go to like crazy.

like nobody's business *Inf.* very well; very much. □ *She can sing like nobody's business. What a set of pipes!*

like nothing on earth 1. *Fig.* very untidy or very unattractive. □ *Joan arrived at the office looking like nothing on earth. She had fallen in the mud.* **2.** *Fig.* very unusual; very distinctive. □ *The new car models look like nothing on earth this year.*

like one of the family *Fig.* as if someone (or a pet) were a member of one's family. □ *We treat our dog like one of the family.*

like one owned the place AND **as if one owned the place** *Fig.* [showing ownership of a building by] the way one enters a building. (Meant to be said in irony by the owner of the place.) □ *Let's use the front door like we owned the place.* □ *I'll park in the driveway as if I owned the place.*

like pulling teeth *Fig.* like doing something very difficult. □ *Trying to get him to pay attention is like pulling teeth.*

like shooting fish in a barrel AND **as easy as shooting fish in a barrel** *Rur.* ridiculously easy. □ *That comedian has an easy job. Making fun of politicians is like shooting fish in a barrel.*

*like stink *Inf.* rapidly. (As fast as a smell spreads. *Typically: **go** ~; **move** ~; **run** ~; **swim** ~.) □ *Those kids moved through the whole test like stink. Real eager-beavers.* □ *The wood chipper went through the brush like stink and turned it into a small pile in minutes.*

like taking candy from a baby AND **as easy as taking candy from a baby** *Cliché* very easy. □ *Getting to the airport was easy. It was like taking candy from a baby.*

*like the devil AND ***like the dickens; *like hell** *Fig.* with a fury; in a great hurry; with a lot of activity. (*Typically: **fight** ~; **run** ~; **scream** ~; **thrash around** ~.) □ *We were working like the dickens when the rain started and made us quit for the day.*

like the dickens Go to previous.

*like the wind *Fig.* very fast; as fast and easy as the wind. (*Typically: **go** ~; **move** ~; **run** ~.) □ *The racehorse ran like the wind, beating its nearest opponent by several lengths.*

like there's no tomorrow AND **like there ain't no tomorrow; as if there's no tomorrow** *Rur.* eagerly; rapidly; without stopping. □ *You can't go on eating candy bars like there's no tomorrow.*

like to did sth *Rur.* almost. □ *Mary like to passed out when she saw how bad her house was damaged in the storm.*

like to hear oneself **talk** [for someone] to enjoy one's own talking more than people enjoy listening to it. □ *I guess I don't really have anything to say. I just like to hear myself talk, I guess.*

like trying to find a needle in a haystack Go to like looking for a needle in a haystack.

like (two) peas in a pod *Cliché* very close or intimate. (Compare this with alike as (two) peas in a pod.) □ *Yes, they're close. Like two peas in a pod.*

like water off a duck's back *Fig.* easily; without any apparent effect. □ *Insults rolled off John like water off a duck's back.* □ *The bullets had no effect on the steel door. They fell away like water off a duck's back.*

like, you know *Inf.* a combining of the (almost meaningless) expressions *like* and *you know*. (Never used in formal writing.) □ *She is, well, like, you know, uncool.*

*likely as not *Fig.* probably; with an even chance either way. (*Also: **as** ~.) □ *He will as likely as not arrive without warning.* □ *Likely as not, the game will be canceled.*

liken so/sth **to** so/sth to compare someone or something to someone or something, concentrating on the similarities. □ *He is strange. I can only liken him to an eccentric millionaire.*

the **likes of** so/sth someone or something similar to that person or thing; the equal or equals of someone or something. □ *We admired the splendid old ships, the likes of which will never be built again.*

*the line of fire 1. the pathway of bullets being fired. (*Typically: **in** ~; **get in(to)** ~; **out of** ~; **keep out of** ~; **get out of** ~.) □ *They are having target practice in the field next door. Please don't get into the line of fire.* **2.** *Fig.* the flow of criticism or punishment. (*Typically: **in** ~; **get in(to)** ~; **out of** ~; **keep out of** ~; **get**

out of ~.) □ *The boss is fine unless he is angry. In that case, you had better not get into the line of fire.*

the **line of least resistance** Go to the path of least resistance.

*a line on so/sth *Fig.* an idea on how to locate someone or something; an idea for finding someone who can help with someone or something. (*Typically: **get** ~; **have** ~; **give** so ~.) □ *I got a line on a book that might help explain what you want to know.*

line one's **own pocket(s)** *Fig.* to make money for oneself in a greedy or dishonest fashion. □ *They are interested in lining their pockets first and serving the people second.*

line so/sth **up**† *Fig.* to schedule someone or something [for something]. □ *Please line somebody up for the entertainment.*

line so/sth **up**† **with** so/sth *Fig.* to schedule a meeting date with someone or a group of people. □ *Will you line everyone up with us for a Monday morning meeting?*

linger on (after so/sth**)** AND **stay on (after** so/sth**)** to outlast someone or something; to live longer than someone else or long after an event. □ *Aunt Sarah lingered on only a few months after Uncle Herman died.*

link so/sth **and** so/sth **together** Go to next.

link so/sth **to** so/sth AND **link** so/sth **and** so/sth **together; link** so/sth **together with** so/sth; **link** so/sth **with** so/sth to discover a connection between people and things, in any combination. □ *I would never have thought of linking Fred to Tom. I didn't even know they knew each other.*

the **lion's share (of** sth**)** *Fig.* the largest portion of something. □ *The lion's share of the surplus cheese goes to school cafeterias.*

So's **lips are sealed.** Go to My lips are sealed.

liquor up *Fig.* to drink an alcoholic beverage, especially to excess. □ *They seem to liquor up almost every night of the week.*

liquor so **up**† *Fig.* to get someone tipsy or drunk. □ *He liquored her up and tried to take her home with him.*

listen to reason to yield to a reasonable argument; to take the reasonable course. □ *She got into trouble because she wouldn't listen to reason.*

listen up *Fig. Sl.* to listen carefully. (Usually a command.) □ *Now, listen up! This is important.*

litmus test *Fig.* a question or experiment that seeks to determine the state of one important factor. □ *His performance on the long exam served as a litmus test to determine whether he would go to college.*

A **little bird told me.** *Fig.* a way of indicating that you do not want to reveal who told you something. (Sometimes used playfully, when you think that the person you are addressing knows or can guess who was the source of your information.) □ *Jill: Thank you for the beautiful present! How did you know I wanted a green silk scarf? Jane: A little bird told me.*

a **little bit (of** sth**)** a small amount; some. □ *Can I have a little bit of candy?*

little bitty *Fig.* very little. □ *Can I have just a little bitty piece of that lemon meringue pie?*

little by little *Fig.* gradually, a little bit at a time. □ *I earned enough money, little by little, to buy a car.*

(a **little) new to (all) this** an apologetic way of saying that one is experiencing something new or participating in something new. □ *I'm sorry I'm slow. I'm a little new to all this.*

a **(little) nip in the air** a cold feeling; cold weather. □ *There's more of a nip in the air as winter approaches.*

little old so/sth ordinary; harmless. (Said to downplay or minimize the importance of something. Also cute or jocular.) □ *Aw, honey, I wasn't gambling. I just went to one little old poker game.* □ *Charlie: Did you eat that whole chocolate cake that I was saving for the party? Jane: Little old me?*

a **little pricey** Go to a little steep.

little shaver *Rur.* a child; a baby. □ *Tom thinks his grandson is the cutest little shaver there ever was.*

(a **little) short on one end** *Rur.* short. (Jocular.) □ *You'll recognize Bill right away. He's got red hair, and he's a little short on one end.*

a **little steep** AND a **little pricey** *Fig.* relatively expensive; costing more than one wants to pay. □ *The food here is a little pricey, but you get a lot of it.*

a **little white lie** *Fig.* a small, usually harmless lie; a fib. □ *Every little white lie you tell is still a lie, and it is still meant to mislead people.*

live a dog's life Go to lead a dog's life.

live a double life Go to lead a double life.

live a lie *Fig.* to live a life of deception, where everything about one's public image is false. □ *Since he got out of prison, Jamie has been forced to live a lie. If people knew what he was, he'd be ostracized.*

live a life of sth *Fig.* to have a life of a certain quality or style. □ *The movie star lived a life of luxury.*

live and breathe sth *Fig.* to be completely immersed in the doing of something. □ *My cousin is a musician, and she lives and breathes flute music.*

live and learn *Cliché* to increase one's knowledge by experience. (Usually said when one is surprised to learn something.) □ *I didn't know that snakes could swim. Well, live and learn!*

live and let live *Cliché* not to interfere with other people's business or preferences. □ *I don't care what they do! Live and let live, I always say.*

live beyond one's **means** *Fig.* to spend more money than one can afford. □ *The Browns are deeply in debt because they are living beyond their means.*

live by some kind of effort to survive by doing or using something in particular. (See also live by one's **wits**.) □ *She lives by her* own hard work. □ *We live by the skills that we have—and hard work, of course.*

live by one's **wits** *Fig.* to survive by being clever. □ *When you're in the kind of business I'm in, you have to live by your wits.*

live sth **down**† *Fig.* to overcome the shame or embarrassment of something. □ *Wilbur will never be able to live down what happened at the party last night.*

live for so/sth to exist to enjoy or serve someone or something. □ *She lives for her vacations in Acapulco.*

live for the moment *Fig.* to live only for the pleasures of the present time without planning for the future. □ *You need to make plans for your future. You cannot live just for the moment!*

live from day to day *Fig.* to survive on limited means one day at a time with no plans or possibilities for the future. □ *The Simpsons just live from day to day. They never plan for the future.*

live from hand to mouth *Fig.* to live in poor circumstances. □ *We lived from hand to mouth during the war. Things were very difficult.*

live happily ever after *Cliché* to live in happiness after a specific event. (A formulaic phrase at the end of fairy tales.) □ *They went away from the horrible haunted castle and lived happily ever after.*

live in an ivory tower Go to in an ivory tower.

live in hope(s) of sth *Fig.* to live with the hope that something will happen. □ *Greg lives in hope of winning a million dollars in the lottery.*

live in sin *Fig.* to live with and have sex with someone to whom one is not married. (Sometimes serious and sometimes jocular.) □ *Would you like to get married, or would you prefer that we live in sin for a few more years?*

live in the fast lane Go to in the fast lane.

live in the past *Fig.* to live while dwelling on past memories without participating in the present or planning for the future. □ *You are just living in the past. Join us in the 21st century.*

live in the present *Fig.* to deal with contemporary events and not be dominated by events of the past or planning for the future. □ *It was no longer possible to get Uncle Herman to live in the present.*

live it up *Fig.* to have an exciting time; to do what one pleases—regardless of cost—to please oneself. □ *At the party, John was really living it up.* □ *Come on! Have fun! Live it up!*

live off the fat of the land *Fig.* to live on stored-up resources or abundant resources. (Similar to the following entry.) □ *If I had a million dollars, I'd invest it and live off the fat of the land.*

live off the land *Fig.* to live by eating only the food that one produces from the land; to survive by gathering or stealing food, fruits, berries, eggs, etc. while traveling through the countryside. □ *We lived off the land for a few years when we first started out farming.* □ *The unemployed wandered about, living off the land.*

live on (after so/sth**)** to be remembered long after someone or something might otherwise be forgotten, or dead, in the case of persons. □ *Fears of war will live on after the actual conflict.*

live on borrowed time *Fig.* to exist only because of good fortune; to live on when death was expected. □ *The doctors told him he was living on borrowed time.*

live on the edge Go to on the edge.

live sth **out**† to act out something such as one's fantasies. □ *He has a tendency to try to live out his fantasies.*

live out one's **days** AND **live out** one's **life** *Fig.* to live for the remainder of one's life. (Usually with some reference to a place.) □ *Where do you plan to live out your days?*

live out one's **life** Go to previous.

live out of a suitcase *Fig.* to stay very briefly in several places, never unpacking one's luggage. □ *I hate living out of a suit-*

case. *For my next vacation, I want to go to just one place and stay there the whole time.*

live out of cans *Fig.* to eat only canned food. □ *We lived out of cans for the entire camping trip.*

live (pretty) high off the hog AND **live (pretty) high on the hog; eat (pretty) high off the hog; eat high on the hog** to live well and eat good food. (The accepted story is that the higher up the cut of meat on a [standing up] hog, the better and more choice it is. However, the pork shoulder, hog jowl, and back ribs are from the upper pig and are not really the most choice. The ever-popular hams and bellies [bacon] are lower, in fact. It's also possible that these phrases are simply elaborations of "living high.") □ *After they discovered oil on their land, they lived pretty high on the hog.*

live (pretty) high on the hog Go to previous.

live the life of Riley Go to lead the life of Riley.

live to the (ripe old) age of sth *Fig.* to survive to a specific [advanced] age. □ *Sally's aunt lived to the ripe old age of 100.*

live under the same roof (with so**)** *Fig.* to share a dwelling with someone. (Implies living in a close relationship, as a husband and wife.) □ *I don't think I can go on living under the same roof with her.*

live up to sth *Fig.* to fulfill expectations; to satisfy a goal or set of goals. (Often with *one's reputation, promise, word, standards,* etc.) □ *I hope I can live up to my reputation.*

live up to one's **side of the bargain** Go to hold one's end of the bargain up†.

live with so **1.** to live in the same dwelling with someone. □ *I lived with my grandparents for years.* **2.** *Euph.* to live in a romantic relationship with someone outside of marriage. □ *Sandy is living with her domestic partner.*

live with sth to put up with something; to endure something. (Does not mean "to dwell with.") □ *That is not acceptable. I*

can't live with that. Please change it. □ *Mary refused to live with the proposed changes.*

live within one's **means** *Fig.* to spend no more money than one has. □ *We have to struggle to live within our means, but we manage.*

the **living end** *Fig.* the absolute best [person]. □ *We really like Ralph. He is the living end as far as his girlfriend is concerned.*

a **living hell** *Fig.* as bad as hell would be if experienced by a living person. □ *For the two years that we were married, she made my life a living hell.*

living large living in luxury; spending time in grand style. □ *George loved living large, especially dining at fine French restaurants.*

Lo and behold! *Cliché* Look here!; Thus! (An expression of surprise.) □ *Lo and behold! There is Fred! He beat us here by taking a shortcut.*

*a **load off** one's **feet** *Fig.* the weight of one's body no longer supported by one's feet, as when one sits down. (*Typically: **get** ~; **take** ~.) □ *Come in, John. Sit down and take a load off your feet.*

*a **load off** one's **mind** AND *a **weight off** one's **mind** *Fig.* the relief from a mental burden gained by saying what one is thinking or by speaking one's mind. (*Typically: **get** ~; **take** ~.) □ *I think you'll feel better after you get a load off your mind.*

loaded for bear 1. *Inf.* angry. (*Fig.* on hunting for bear, for which one needs a very powerful weapon.) □ *He left here in a rage. He was really loaded for bear.* **2.** *Sl.* drunk. (An elaboration of *loaded = drunk.*) □ *By the end of the party, Bill was loaded for bear.*

loaded to the barrel Go to next.

loaded to the gills AND **loaded to the barrel** *Sl.* intoxicated. □ *Man, he's loaded to the barrel and fighting mad.*

loads of sth Go to tons of sth.

local yokel *Inf.* a local resident of a rural place. (Mildly derogatory.) □ *One of the local yokels helped me change the tire.*

lock horns (with so) *Fig.* to get into an argument with someone. □ *Let's settle this peacefully. I don't want to lock horns with the boss.*

lock, stock, and barrel *Cliché* everything. (Usually thought to have meant the whole gun, lock, stock, and barrel, being parts of a rifle.) □ *We had to move everything out of the house—lock, stock, and barrel.*

log in Go to log on.

log off AND **log out** to record one's exit from a computer system. (This action may be recorded, or logged, automatically in the computer's memory.) □ *I closed my files and logged off.*

log so **off**† AND **log** so **out**† [for someone] to cause someone to exit from a computer system. (This exit may be recorded, or logged, automatically in the computer's memory.) □ *Mary had to rush off to an appointment, so I logged her off.*

log on AND **log in** to begin to use a computer system, as by entering a password, etc. (This action may be recorded, or logged, automatically in the computer's memory.) □ *What time did you log on to the system this morning?*

log so **on**† **(to** sth) to allow someone to link (electronically) to a computer system. (This action may be recorded, or logged, automatically in the computer's memory.) □ *I will log you on to the system if you forgot how to do it.*

log out Go to log off.

log so **out** Go to log so off†.

the long and (the) short of it AND the **short and (the) long of it** *Fig.* the most important point; the summary of the matter. □ *Jill: Is there some reason that you've spent the last half hour complaining about Fred? Jane: The long and the short of it is, I hate working with him so much that I'm going to resign.*

the **long arm of the law** *Fig.* the police; the law. □ *The long arm of the law is going to tap you on the shoulder some day, Lefty.*

long gone *Fig.* gone a long time ago; used up a long time ago. □ *The ice cream and cake are long gone. You are simply too late for the refreshments.*

long in the tooth *Fig.* old. □ *That actor is getting a little long in the tooth to play the romantic lead.*

long on sth *Fig.* having more than is needed of something. □ *We're long on fish today, so ask all the waiters to tell people it's fresh.*

*a **long shot** *Fig.* a risky bet; an attempt, bet, or proposition that has a low probability of success. (See also not by a long shot. *Typically: **be** ~; **not by** ~; **seem like** ~.) □ *Your solution is a long shot, but we'll try it and hope it works.*

long story short *Sl.* to make a long story short. □ *Then the guy comes over, and says—long story short—"You got a match?"*

Long time no see. *Cliché* I have not seen you in a long time.; We have not seen each other in a long time. □ *Tom: Hi, Fred. Where have you been keeping yourself? Fred: Good to see you, Tom. Long time no see.*

look a gift horse in the mouth *Fig.* to be ungrateful to someone who gives you something; to treat someone who gives you a gift badly. (Usually with a negative.) □ *Never look a gift horse in the mouth.* □ *I advise you not to look a gift horse in the mouth.*

look after so/sth/animal to care for and protect living creatures or things. □ *If I buy you a pet, will you look after it?* □ *I have to look after the children and cook and clean. Can't you do anything but watch television?*

look after number one AND **look out for number one** *Fig. Inf.* to take care of oneself first. □ *It's a good idea to look out for number one. Who else will?*

look one's **age** to look as old as one is. (This in spite of efforts to the contrary.) □ *I am beginning to look my age, alas.*

look ahead *Fig.* to think about what may be in the future. □ *When I look ahead, I realize that we haven't saved enough money for retirement.*

Look alive! *Fig.* Act alert and responsive! □ *"Come on, Fred! Get moving! Look alive!" shouted the coach, who was not happy with Fred's performance.*

look as if butter wouldn't melt in one's **mouth** *Fig.* to appear to be cold and unfeeling (despite any information to the contrary). □ *What a sour face. He looks as if butter wouldn't melt in his mouth.*

look askance at so/sth *Fig.* to regard someone or something negatively; to view someone or something judgmentally. □ *The nice folks down at police headquarters tend to look askance at jerks like you who drive like maniacs!*

look at so **cross-eyed** *Fig.* to merely appear to question, threaten, or mock someone. (Often in the negative.) □ *If you so much as look at me cross-eyed, I will send you to your room.*

Look (at) what the cat dragged in! AND **See what the cat dragged in!** *Inf.* Look who's here! (A good-humored and familiar way of showing surprise at someone's presence in a place, especially if the person looks a little rumpled. Compare this with look like sth the cat dragged in.) □ *Mary: Hello, everybody. I'm here! Jane: Look at what the cat dragged in!*

look back (at so/sth**)** AND **look back (on** so/sth**)** *Fig.* to think about someone or something in the past. □ *When I look back on Frank, I do remember his strange manner, come to think of it.*

look becoming on so Go to becoming on so.

look daggers at so AND **shoot daggers at** so *Fig.* to give someone a dirty look. □ *Tom must have been mad at Ann from the way he was looking daggers at her.*

look down (at so/sth**)** AND **look down** one's **nose at** so/sth; **look down on** so/sth to view someone or something as lowly or unworthy. □ *Don't look down your nose at my car just because it's rusty and noisy.*

look down one's **nose at** so/sth Go to previous.

look fit to kill *Fig.* [dressed up] to look very fancy or sexy. □ *John looked fit to kill in his new tuxedo.*

look for sth **(to happen)** *Fig.* to anticipate that something will happen. □ *We look for things to improve in the third quarter.*

look for trouble Go to ask for trouble.

look forward to sth *Fig.* to anticipate something with pleasure. □ *I'm really looking forward to your visit next week.*

look good on paper to seem fine in theory, but not perhaps in practice; to appear to be a good plan. □ *This looks good on paper. Let's hope it works in the real world.*

Look here! AND **See here!** Give me your attention! □ *Look here! I need help from you, not criticism.*

look high and low (for so/sth**)** Go to hunt high and low (for so/sth).

look in on so AND **check in on** so to visit someone and see how they are. □ *I will stop by the house and look in on her and call you if there are any problems.*

look so **in the eye** Go to next.

look so **in the face** AND **look** so **in the eye; stare** so **in the face** *Fig.* to face someone directly. □ *She looked him in the face and said she never wanted to see him again.*

look into sth AND **check into** sth; **see into** sth *Fig.* to investigate something. □ *Don't worry about your problem. I'll see into it.*

look like a (dead) ringer (for so**)** Go to a (dead) ringer (for so).

look like sth **the cat dragged in** *Fig.* to look very shabby, worn, exhausted, or abused. (Sometimes with *drug*.) □ *Poor Dave looks like something the cat drug in. He must have been out late last night.*

look like the cat that swallowed the canary *Fig.* to appear as if one had just had a great success. □ *Your presentation must* *have gone well. You look like the cat that swallowed the canary.*

Look me up when you're in town. *Fig.* When you next come to my town, try to find me (and we will get together). (A vague and perhaps insincere invitation.) □ *Bob: Nice to see you, Tom. Bye now. Tom: Yes, indeed. Look me up when you're in town. Bye.*

look on the bright side *Fig.* consider the positive aspects of a negative situation. □ *Look on the bright side. Things could have been much worse than they are.*

look on (with so**)** to share and read from someone else's notes, paper, book, music, etc. □ *Carla has a copy of the music. She doesn't mind if I look on.*

Look out! AND **Watch out!** Caution! Be alert to nearby danger! □ *Look out! The rope is coming loose.* □ *Watch out! Here comes the lion!*

look out for so AND **watch out for** so **1.** to protect and care for someone. □ *When I get older, I will need someone to look out for me.* **2.** to beware of someone who may be a threat. □ *You had better watch out for Wallace. He is in a very bad mood.*

look out for number one Go to look after number one.

look so/sth **over**† AND **give** so/sth **the once-over** to examine someone or something. □ *I think you ought to make an appointment to have your doctor look you over. You look sort of pale.*

look right through so *Fig.* to appear to gaze through a person as if no one were there. (A way of ignoring someone.) □ *I tried to catch her attention and say hello, but she looked right through me.*

look the other way *Fig.* to ignore something on purpose. □ *John could have prevented the problem, but he looked the other way.* □ *By looking the other way, he actually made the problem worse.*

look the part to appear to be quite suitable for casting in some role. □ *John was chosen to play the priest because he looks the part.*

look through sth to examine the parts, pages, samples, etc. of something. □ *Look through this report and see what you make of it.*

look to so/sth **for** sth AND **turn to** so/sth **for** sth *Fig.* to request something from someone or something. (The request is for something helpful or something that is required.) □ *I was forced to turn to the county for help with getting food.*

look to one's **laurels** *Fig.* to take care not to lower or diminish one's reputation or position, especially in relation to that of someone else potentially better; to guard one's reputation or rewards for past accomplishments. □ *With the arrival of the new member of the football team, James will have to look to his laurels and strive to remain as the highest scorer.*

look under the hood to examine the engine of a car; to check the oil, water, and other such routine items associated with the engine of a car. □ *I finished putting gas in. I need to look under the hood.*

look so/sth **up**† AND **hunt** so/sth **up**† **1.** to seek someone, a group, or something out. □ *I am going to look up an old friend when I am in Chicago.* **2.** to seek information about someone or something in a book or online. □ *I don't recognize his name. I'll look him up and see what I can find.*

look up to so *Fig.* to view someone with respect and admiration. □ *Everyone in the class looked up to the teacher.*

Look who's talking! *Fig.* You are guilty of doing the same thing that you have criticized someone else for doing or that you accused someone else of doing. □ *Andy: You criticize me for being late! Look who's talking! You just missed your flight!*

looking over one's **shoulder** *Fig.* keeping watch for danger or threats to oneself. □ *Bob's a little paranoid. He's always looking over his shoulder.*

looking up showing promise of improvement. □ *My prospects for a job are looking up.*

*****a **look-see** *Rur.* a look at someone or something; a peek. (*Typically: **get** ~;

have ~; give so ~; take ~.) □ *A: Do you think they have finished painting your office yet? B: Let's go down there and take a look-see.*

loom large (on the horizon) *Cliché* to be of great importance, especially when referring to an upcoming problem, danger, or threat. □ *Eviction was looming large when the tenants could not pay their rent.*

a **loose cannon** *Inf.* a person whose actions are unpredictable and uncontrollable; someone who gives away secrets. □ *Some loose cannon in the State Department has been leaking stories to the press.*

Loose lips sink ships. Don't talk carelessly because you don't know who is listening. (From wartime. Literally, "Don't reveal even the location of a loved one on a ship, because the location could be communicated to the enemy by a spy.") □ *You never know who is going to hear what you say and how they will use what they hear. Remember, loose lips sink ships.*

a **loose translation** Go to a free translation.

loosen so's **tongue** *Fig.* to make someone willing to speak more freely. (The agent is often alcohol.) □ *A little whisky tends to loosen my tongue and make me say things I wished I hadn't said.* □ *We have ways of making spies like you loosen your tongue.*

lord it over so *Fig.* to dominate someone; to direct and control someone. □ *Mr. Smith seems to lord it over his wife.* □ *The boss lords it over everyone in the office.*

Lord knows I've tried. *Fig.* I certainly have tried very hard. □ *Alice: Why don't you get Bill to fix this fence? Mary: Lord knows I've tried. I must have asked him a dozen times—this year alone.*

Lord love a duck! *Fig.* My goodness! (An exclamation of surprise.) □ *Lord love a duck! Did you see that cat chasing that dog?*

(the) **Lord only knows** *Inf.* No one but God knows. □ *How Mary can stay so cheerful through her terrible illness, the Lord only knows.*

Lord willing and the creek don't rise. Go to God willing and the creek don't rise.

the **Lord's Day** *Fig.* Sunday; the Christian day of worship. □ *He believed that all businesses should close on the Lord's Day.*

lose a bundle *Sl.* to lose a lot of money. □ *I know I would lose a bundle if I went to a casino and gambled.*

lose (all) one's marbles AND **lose one's mind** *Fig.* to go crazy; to go out of one's mind. □ *What a silly thing to say! Have you lost your marbles?* □ *I can't seem to remember anything. I think I'm losing my mind.*

lose one's appetite *Fig.* to lose one's desire to eat. □ *After that gory movie, I'm afraid I've lost my appetite.*

lose one's cool AND **blow one's cool** *Inf.* to lose one's temper. □ *Wow, he really lost his cool! What a tantrum!*

lose one's edge *Fig.* to lose any advantage one had over other people; [for one's special skills] to fade and become average. □ *At the age of 28, I began to lose my edge and could no longer compete as a wrestler.*

lose face *Fig.* to lose status; to become less respectable. □ *Things will go better if you can explain to him where he was wrong without making him lose face.*

lose favor (with so**)** Go to fall out of favor (with so).

lose one's grip on so/sth Go to lose one's hold on so/sth.

lose ground (to so/sth**)** *Fig.* to fall behind someone or something; to become less valuable or productive than someone or something. □ *We were losing ground to the opposite team in our quest for the trophy.*

lose one's head (over so/sth**)** *Fig.* to become confused or overly emotional about someone or something. □ *Don't lose your head over John. He isn't worth it.*

lose heart AND **lose one's nerve** *Fig.* to lose one's courage or confidence. □ *What a disappointment! It's enough to make one lose heart.*

lose one's **heart to** so/animal *Fig.* to fall in love with someone or a pet. (Similar to **give** one's **heart to** so.) □ *I lost my heart to the little puppy with the white feet.*

lose one's **hold on** so/sth AND **lose** one's **grip on** so/sth; **lose** one's **hold over** so/sth *Fig.* to give up control over someone or something. □ *The manager lost her hold over her employees and was fired.*

lose it 1. *Sl.* to empty one's stomach; to vomit. □ *Oh, God! I think I'm going to lose it!* **2.** *Sl.* to get angry; to lose one's temper. □ *I sat there calmly, biting my lip to keep from losing it.*

lose one's **lunch** Go to blow (one's) lunch.

lose one's **mind** Go to lose (all) one's marbles.

lose money on sth to have a net loss on something, such as an investment. □ *I don't want to lose money on any investment.*

lose one's **nerve** Go to lose heart.

lose no time AND **waste no time; not lose any time; not waste any time** to do something fast; to avoid not having enough time by hurrying. □ *I wasted no time getting here. I drove over the speed limit.* □ *We lost no time buying a house and settling down.*

lose out on sth *Fig.* not to be involved in something and thereby fail to get its benefits. □ *I hated to lose out on the chance to see the opera, but I was in Boston.*

lose out to so/sth *Fig.* to lose a competition to someone or something. □ *Our team lost out to the other team.*

lose patience (with so/sth**)** *Fig.* to stop being patient with someone or something; to become impatient with someone or something. □ *Please try to be more cooperative. I'm losing patience with you.*

lose one's **reason** *Fig.* to lose one's power of reasoning, possibly in anger. □ *Bob seems to have lost his reason when he struck John.*

lose one's **shirt** *Fig.* to lose a lot of money; to lose all of one's assets (as if one had even lost one's shirt). □ *No, I can't loan you $200. I just lost my shirt at the racetrack.*

lose sight of so/sth *Fig.* to forget to consider someone or something. □ *Don't lose sight of the basic value of the land on which the house sits.*

lose sleep over so/sth AND **lose sleep about** so/sth *Fig.* to worry about someone or something a lot, sometimes when one should be sleeping. (Often used with *any* and the negative.) □ *Yes, Kelly is in a little bit of trouble, but I'm not going to lose any sleep over her.*

lose one's **temper (at** so/sth**)** *Fig.* to become angry at someone or something. □ *I hate to lose my temper at someone. I always end up feeling guilty.*

lose the thread (of sth**)** *Fig.* to fail to follow the details of thinking or reasoning, written or spoken. □ *I'm sorry, but I've lost the thread of the conversation. What are you guys talking about?*

lose the use of sth to be deprived of the use of something. □ *After the accident, I lost the use of my left arm for a few days.*

lose time AND **waste time** *Fig.* to be slowed down or otherwise hampered from using time efficiently. (See also the opposite: lose no time.) □ *I lost time on the freeway because of the traffic.* □ *You wasted a lot of time at lunch and have to stay late to get your work done.*

lose one's **touch (with** so/sth**)** *Fig.* to lose one's ability to handle someone or something. □ *I seem to have lost my touch with my children. They won't listen to me anymore.*

lose touch (with so**)** Go to lose track (of so).

lose touch with reality to begin to think unrealistically; to become unrealistic. □ *I am so overworked that I am losing touch with reality.*

lose track (of so**)** AND **lose touch (with** so**)** to lose contact with someone. □ *I lost track of all my friends from high school.*

lose track (of sth**)** to lose something and how to find it easily again. □ *I've lost* track of my checkbook. I guess I'd better call the bank.

lose one's **train of thought** *Fig.* to forget what one was talking or thinking about. □ *Excuse me, I lost my train of thought. What was I talking about?*

*a **losing streak** *Fig.* a series of losses [in sports, for instance]. (*Typically: **be on** ~; **have** ~; **continue** one's ~.) □ *The team was on a losing streak that started nearly three years ago.*

lost and gone forever *Fig.* lost; permanently lost. □ *My money fell out of my pocket, and I am sure that it is lost and gone forever.*

a **lost cause** a futile attempt; a hopeless matter. □ *Our campaign to have the new party on the ballot was a lost cause.*

lost for words Go to at a loss (for words).

*lost in** sth enveloped in something; engrossed in something. (*Typically: **be** ~; **get** ~.) □ *Ed sat under the tree, lost in reverie.* □ *Excuse me. I didn't hear you. I was lost in my own thoughts.*

lost in the confusion Go to next.

*lost in the shuffle** AND *lost in the confusion** lost, forgotten about, or overlooked because of a chaotic situation. (*Typically: **be** ~; **end up** ~; **get** ~; **find** oneself ~.) □ *I'm afraid that your application got lost in the confusion.* □ *Bob got lost in the shuffle, and we finally found him boarding the wrong plane at the wrong gate.*

lost in thought AND **deep in thought; immersed in thought** thinking and not paying much attention to anything else. □ *She was deep in thought when I came into the room. I gave her a start.*

*lost on** so *Fig.* wasted on someone; not valued or appreciated by someone. (*Typically: **be** ~; **get** ~.) □ *The humor of the situation was lost on Mary. She was too upset to see it.*

lost-and-found *Fig.* an office or department that handles items that someone has lost that have been found by someone else. □ *The lost-and-found office had*

an enormous collection of umbrellas and four sets of false teeth!

a **lot of** so/sth AND **lots of** people/things a large number of people or things; much of something. □ *I got a lot of presents for my birthday.* □ *I ate lots of cookies after dinner.*

(a lot of) credit (for sth**)** Go to (much) credit (for sth).

a **lot of give-and-ake 1.** *Fig.* a lot of two-way discussion. □ *It was a good meeting. There was a lot of give-and-take, and we all learned.* **2.** *Fig.* a lot of negotiating and bargaining. □ *After an afternoon of give-and-take, we were finally able to put all the details into an agreement.*

*a **lot of nerve 1.** *Fig.* great rudeness; a lot of audacity or brashness. (*Typically: **have** ~; **take** ~.) □ *He walked out on her, and that took a lot of nerve!* □ *You have a lot of nerve! You took my parking place!* **2.** *Fig.* courage. (*Typically: **have** ~; **take** ~.) □ *He climbed the mountain with a bruised foot. That took a lot of nerve.* □ *He has a lot of nerve to go into business for himself.*

*a **lot of promise** *Fig.* much promise for the future. (*Typically: **have** ~; **show** ~.) □ *Sally is quite young, but she has a lot of promise.*

Lots of luck! 1. *Fig.* Good luck! □ *I'm glad you're giving it a try. Lots of luck!* **2.** *Fig.* You don't have a chance!; Good luck, you'll need it! (Sarcastic.) □ *Think you stand a chance? Lots of luck!*

loud and clear *Fig.* clear and distinctly. (Originally said of radio reception that is heard clearly and distinctly.) □ *Tom: If I've told you once, I've told you a thousand times: Stop it! Do you hear me? Bill: Yes, loud and clear.*

love at first sight *Fig.* love established when two people first see one another. □ *Bill was standing at the door when Ann opened it. It was love at first sight.*

Love is blind. *Cliché* If you love someone, you cannot see any faults in that person. □ *Jill: I don't understand why Joanna likes*

Tom. He's inconsiderate, he's vain, and he isn't even good-looking. Jane: Love is blind.

love of money is the root of all evil money causes all sorts of problems. (Often abridged to *money is the root of all evil.* This is biblical, 1 Timothy 6:10. The full version tells us that it is greed, not money itself, that causes grief.) □ *Whoever thought that the love of money is the root of all evil hasn't even seen Tiffany in a bikini.*

love so/animal **to death** AND **love** so/animal **to pieces; love** so/animal **to bits** *Fig.* to love someone or some creature a very great amount. □ *Look at Crystal. She just loves that new puppy to bits.*

love so/animal **to pieces** Go to previous.

a **love-hate relationship** *Fig.* a relationship of any kind that involves both devotion and hatred. □ *Tommy has a love-hate relationship with his teacher. Mostly, though, it's hate.*

Lovely weather for ducks. AND **Fine weather for ducks.** *Cliché* a greeting meaning that this unpleasant rainy weather must be good for something. □ *Sally: What a lot of rain! Tom: Yeah. Lovely weather for ducks. Don't care for it much myself.*

low man on the totem pole *Fig.* the least important or lowest-ranking person of a group. □ *I was the last to find out because I'm low man on the totem pole.*

*a **low profile** *Fig.* a persona or character that does not draw attention. (*Typically: **assume** ~; **have** ~; **keep** ~; **give** oneself ~; **maintain** ~.) □ *I try to be quiet and keep a low profile. It's hard because I just love attention.*

*the **lowdown (on** so/sth) *Inf.* the full story about someone or something. (*Typically: **get** ~; **have** ~; **give** so ~.) □ *Sally wants to get the low-down on the new pension plan. Please tell her all about it.*

lower one's **guard** Go to let one's **guard** down†.

lower one's **sights** *Fig.* to set one's goals lower. (Fig. on the image of someone pointing the barrel of a rifle lower to lower the aim of the rifle.) □ *Even though you get frustrated, don't lower your sights.*

lower the boom on so *Fig.* to scold or punish someone severely; to crack down on someone; to throw the book at so. □ *If Bob won't behave better, I'll have to lower the boom on him.*

lower oneself **to** some level AND **lower** oneself **to** (doing) sth; **stoop to** some level; **stoop to** (doing) sth *Fig.* to bring oneself down to some lower level of behavior. □ *I refuse to lower myself to your level! □ Has TV news stooped to the level of the tabloids?*

lower one's **voice** *Fig.* to speak more softly. □ *Please lower your voice or you'll disturb the people who are working.*

low-hanging fruit 1. *Fig.* the easiest thing to get or achieve; an easy profit. □ *All the potential profit is just low-hanging fruit. There's no way to lose.* **2.** *Fig.* the easiest person(s) to sell something to, to convince of something, or to fool. (Akin to easy pickings.) □ *Don't be satisfied with the low-hanging fruit. Go after the hard-sell types.*

luck into sth *Fig.* to find something by luck; to get involved in something by luck. □ *I lucked into this apartment on the very day I started looking.*

the **luck of the draw** *Inf.* the results of chance; the lack of any choice. □ *The team was assembled by chance. It was just the luck of the draw that we could work so well together.*

the **luck of the Irish** *Fig.* luck associated with the Irish people. (Also said as a catchphrase for any kind of luck.) □ *Bill: How did you manage to do it, Jeff? Jeff: It's the luck of the Irish, I guess.*

luck out *Inf.* to be fortunate; to strike it lucky. □ *I really lucked out when I ordered the duck. It's excellent.*

luck out of sth *Inf.* to get out of something by luck alone. □ *I lucked out of taking a driving test. I only had to pass a vision test to get my license.*

one's **luck runs out** *Fig.* one's good luck stops. □ *She will quit gambling when her luck runs out.*

a **lucky break** AND a **nice break; a big break** significant good fortune or opportunity. □ *I need a lucky break about now.* □ *Mary is going to get a big break soon.*

a **lucky dog** *Fig.* a lucky person. (Older.) □ *You won the lottery? You are a lucky dog!*

lucky for you *Fig.* a phrase introducing a description of an event that favors the person being spoken to. □ *Jane: I hope I'm not too late. Sue: Lucky for you, everyone else is late too.*

*a **lucky streak** AND *a **streak of luck** *Fig.* a series of lucky wins in gambling or games. (*Typically: **be on** ~; **have** ~.) □ *Thanks to a lucky streak, I won enough in Las Vegas to pay for the trip.*

the **lull before the storm** AND the **calm before the storm** a quiet period just before a period of great activity or excitement. (Literal in reference to weather.) □ *In the brief calm before the storm, the clerks prepared themselves for the doors to open and bring in thousands of shoppers.*

lull so **into a false sense of security** *Cliché* to lead someone into believing that all is well before attacking or doing someone bad. □ *We lulled the enemy into a false sense of security by pretending to retreat. Then we launched an attack.*

lump so **and** so else **together** AND **lump** sth **and** sth else **together** *Fig.* to classify people or things as members of the same category. □ *You just can't lump Bill and Ted together. They are totally different kinds of people.*

*a **lump in** one's **throat** the feeling of something in one's throat—as if one were going to cry. (*Typically: **get** ~; **have** ~; **give** one ~.) □ *Whenever they play the national anthem, I get a lump in my throat.*

Lump it! *Inf.* Forget it!; Go away! (Older.) □ *Well, you can just lump it!*

the **lunatic fringe** the more extreme members of a group. □ *Most of the members of that religious sect are quite reasonable, but Lisa belongs to the lunatic fringe.*

M

*mad as a hatter AND ***mad as a March hare 1.** crazy. (Refers to the crazy characters in Lewis Carroll's *Alice's Adventures in Wonderland.* *Also: **as** ~.) □ *All these screaming children are driving me mad as a hatter.* **2.** angry. (This is a misunderstanding of *mad* in the first sense. *Also: **as** ~.) □ *You make me so angry! I'm as mad as a hatter.* □ *John can't control his temper. He's always mad as a hatter.*

*mad as a hornet AND ***mad as a wet hen; *mad as hell** very angry. (*Also: **as** ~.) □ *You make me so angry. I'm as mad as a hornet.* □ *What you said made Mary mad as a wet hen.*

mad as a March hare Go to mad as a hatter.

mad as a wet hen Go to mad as a hornet.

mad as hell Go to mad as a hornet.

*mad (at so/sth**)** angry at someone or something. (*Typically: **be** ~; **get** ~; **make** so ~.) □ *I got mad at my car. It won't start.*

mad enough to chew nails (and spit rivets) AND **angry enough to chew nails; mad enough to spit nails** *Inf.* very angry, as if to be able to bite through metal nails. □ *I am mad enough to chew nails! Who took my checkbook?* □ *Her sudden tirade made him angry enough to chew nails.*

mad enough to spit nails Go to previous.

made for so *Fig.* created to please someone or look good on someone in particular. □ *This suit was just made for me!*

made for each other *Fig.* [of two people] very well suited romantically. □ *Mr. and Mrs. Smith were not exactly made for each other. They really don't get along.*

made from the same mold Go to cut from the same cloth.

made to measure *Fig.* [of clothing] made especially to fit the measurements of a particular person. □ *Jack has his suits made to measure because he's rather large.*

made to order *Fig.* made to one's own measurements and on request. □ *This suit fits so well because it's made to order.* □ *His feet are so big that all his shoes have to be made to order.*

maiden voyage *Fig.* the first voyage of a ship or boat. □ *Jim is taking his yacht on its maiden voyage.*

main strength and awkwardness *Fig.* great force; brute force. □ *They finally got the piano moved into the living room by main strength and awkwardness.*

major in sth to specialize in a certain subject in college. □ *I majored in history in college.*

make so *Sl.* to identify someone. (Used especially in the context of law enforcement.) □ *The cop stared at Wilbur and tried to make him but failed to identify him and let him go.*

make sth to attend an event. □ *I am sorry, but I won't be able to make it.*

make a beeline for so/sth *Fig.* to head straight toward someone or something. (Fig. on the straight flight of a bee.) □ *Billy came into the kitchen and made a beeline for the cookies.*

make a believer (out) of so *Fig.* to convince someone decisively about something. □ *The game they played made a be-*

liever out of me; from now on, I'm betting on them.

make a big deal about sth Go to make a federal case out of sth.

make a (big) stink (about so/sth**)** AND **raise a (big) stink (about** so/sth**)** *Inf.* to make trouble about someone or something. □ *Why did you raise a big stink about it?*

make a bolt for so/sth *Fig.* to run quickly to or at someone or something. □ *The dog made a bolt for the door the minute I opened it.*

make (a break) for so/sth *Fig.* to run suddenly toward someone or something; to seize an opportunity to run toward someone or something. □ *The crook made a break for the cop in order to get his gun.* □ *When he made for the door, he tripped on a rug.*

make a bundle AND **make a pile** *Inf.* to make a lot of money. □ *John really made a bundle on that deal.*

make a case for sth to build an argument in favor of something; to establish a plan of advocacy for something. □ *You make a pretty good case for just leaving things as they are.*

make a clean breast of sth **(to** so**)** *Fig.* to admit something to someone. □ *You should make a clean breast of the matter to someone.*

make a clean sweep *Fig.* to do something completely or thoroughly, with no exceptions. □ *They made a clean sweep through the neighborhood, repairing all the sidewalks.*

make a comeback *Fig.* to return to one's former (successful) career. □ *After 10 years in retirement, the singer made a comeback.*

make a day of doing sth AND **make a day of it** *Fig.* to spend the whole day doing something. □ *We went to the museum to see the new exhibit and then decided to make a day of it.*

make a day of it Go to previous.

make a deal with so to strike a bargain with someone. □ *I want to buy your car, and I think I can make a deal with you.*

make a dent in sth AND **put a dent in** sth **1.** to make a depression in something. □ *I kicked the side of the car and made a dent in it.* **2.** *Fig.* to use only a little of something; to make a small amount of progress with something. (Fig. on ①.) □ *Look at what's left on your plate! You hardly made a dent in your dinner.*

make a difference in so/sth to cause a noticeable (usually good) change in someone or something. □ *Getting a job made a big difference in my lifestyle.*

make a difference to so [for one choice or another] to matter to someone. □ *The big one or the little one—does it really make a difference to anyone?*

make a face to attempt to communicate to someone through facial gestures, usually an attempt to say "no" or "stop." □ *I started to tell John where I was last night, but Bill made a face so I didn't.*

make a face (at so**)** AND **make faces (at** so**)** to show a funny or distorted expression to someone in ridicule. □ *Mother, Billy made a face at me!* □ *Billy, are you making faces at Kim?*

make a fast buck AND **make a quick buck** *Inf.* to make money with little effort or in a short time. □ *Tom is always ready to make a fast buck.*

make a federal case out of sth AND **make a big deal about** sth; **make a (whole) production out of** sth *Inf.* to exaggerate the seriousness of something. □ *Come on. It was nothing! Don't make a federal case out of it.*

make a fool of so Go to make an ass of so.

make a go of sth *Fig.* to succeed at something. (Often with *it.*) □ *She just didn't have the energy or inclination to make a go of her marriage.* □ *I did everything I could to make a go of it.*

make a great show of sth *Fig.* to make something obvious; to do something in a showy fashion. □ *Jane displayed her ir-*

ritation at our late arrival by making a great show of serving the cold dinner.

make a hit with so *Fig.* to please someone; to impress someone. □ *The dessert you served really made a hit with the guests.*

make a killing *Fig.* to have a great success, especially in making money. □ *Bill made a killing at the racetrack yesterday.*

Make a lap! *Sl.* to sit down. □ *Pull up a chair and make a lap!*

make oneself or sth **a laughingstock** Go to next.

make a laughingstock (out) of oneself or sth AND **make** oneself or sth **a laughingstock** *Fig.* to make oneself a source of ridicule or laughter; to do something that invites ridicule. □ *Laura made herself a laughingstock by arriving at the fast-food restaurant in full evening dress.*

make a (kind of) life for oneself *Fig.* to develop and live a particular kind of lifestyle for oneself. □ *She made a good life for herself in New York City, working as a freelancer.*

make a living by doing sth Go to next.

make a living from sth AND **make a living by** doing sth to earn a living from something or by doing something. □ *Can you really make a living by selling jewelry?*

make a long story short AND **cut a long story short** *Fig.* to leave out parts of a story to make it shorter; to bring a story to an end. (A formula that introduces a summary of a story or a joke. See also long story short.) □ *And—to make a long story short—I never got back the money that I lent him.*

make a man of so *Fig.* to make a young male into an adult male. □ *The experience will make a man of Ted.* □ *Send Wally into the army. That'll make a man of him.*

make a (mental) note of sth *Fig.* to commit something to memory for future reference. □ *You want to be considered for promotion. I'll make a note of it.*

make a mistake *Fig.* to commit an error; to do something wrong accidentally. □ *I*

made a mistake, and I am really sorry about it.

make a mockery of sth *Fig.* to make a deliberate parody or a poor imitation of something. □ *What a mess. You made a mockery of the task.*

make a mountain out of a molehill *Cliché* to make a major issue out of a minor one; to exaggerate the importance of something. □ *Come on, don't make a mountain out of a molehill. It's not that important.*

make a name (for oneself**)** *Fig.* to become famous. □ *Sally wants to work hard and make a name for herself.*

make a night of it *Fig.* to spend the entire evening or night doing something. (Especially when one had intended to devote only a little time to the outing.) □ *We went out to have a bite to eat and were having such a good time that we decided to make a night of it.*

make a note of sth **1.** to write something down in order to remember it. □ *I'll make a note of it for future reference.* **2.** Go to make a (mental) note of sth.

make a pass at so *Fig.* to flirt with or suggest sexual activity with someone. □ *Can you believe it? Larry made a pass at me!*

make a pig of oneself *Fig.* to eat too much, too fast, or too noisily; to eat more than one's share. □ *Sam is making a pig of himself and taking more than his share.*

make a pile Go to make a bundle.

make a pitch (for so/sth**)** AND **plump for** so/sth *Fig.* to say something in support of someone or something; to attempt to promote, sell, or advance someone or something. □ *The theatrical agent came in and made a pitch for her client.* □ *Every time I turn on the television set, someone is making a pitch.*

make a play (for so**)** *Fig.* to attempt to attract the romantic interest of someone. □ *Ann made a play for Bill, but he wasn't interested in her.*

make a point AND **make (some) points; score a point; score (some) points 1.**

to score a point in a game. □ *Karen made 20 points in the second half.* **2.** *Fig.* to state an item of importance; to say something worthy and convincing. □ *He spoke for an hour without making a point.*

make a point of doing sth AND **make a point of** sth *Fig.* to make an effort to do something. □ *Please make a point of mailing this letter. It's very important.*

make a practice of (doing) sth AND **make** sth **a practice** *Fig.* to turn something into a habitual activity. □ *Jane makes a practice of planting daisies every summer.*

make a quick buck Go to make a fast buck.

make a reservation AND **make reservations** to reserve a seat, as in an airplane, restaurant, or theater, in advance; to reserve a room, as in a hotel, in advance. □ *Did you make a reservation, or are we just going to chance getting a table?*

make a run for it *Fig.* to run fast to get away or get somewhere. □ *When the guard wasn't looking, the prisoner made a run for it.*

make a scene AND **create a scene** *Fig.* to make a public display or disturbance. □ *Oh, John, please don't make a scene. Just forget about it.*

make a secret of sth *Fig.* to act as if something were a secret. □ *I'm not making a secret of it. I am quitting this job.*

make a spectacle of so Go to make an ass of so.

make a stand (against so/sth**)** Go to take a stand (against so/sth).

make a start on sth to set out to do something; to make a beginning on something. □ *I will try to make a start on the cleaning before I leave today.*

make a stink (about sth**)** Go to create a stink (about sth).

make a (whole) production out of sth Go to make a federal case out of sth.

make a world of difference (in so/sth**)** AND **do a world of good (for** so/sth**); do** so/sth **a world of good** *Fig.* to benefit someone or something very much; to cause a basic change in someone or something. □ *The new curtains have made a world of difference in this room.* □ *A little vacation made a world of difference in how I feel.*

make a world of difference (to so/sth**)** AND **make (**so/sth**) a world of difference** *Fig.* to matter very much to someone or something. □ *After our little discussion, I was a little upset. Your thoughtful note has made a world of difference to me, and I feel that we are friends again.*

make advances to so AND **make advances at** so to flirt with someone; to begin to seduce someone. □ *She began making advances to me, and I left the room.*

make allowance(s) (for so/sth**)** to make excuses or explanations for someone or something; to take into consideration the negative effects of someone or something. □ *We have to make allowance for the age of the house when we judge its condition.*

make amends (to so**) (for** sth**)** to make up or apologize to someone for something. □ *Don't worry. I will make amends to her for my sister, who behaved so badly.*

make an all-out effort Go to an all-out effort.

make an ass of so AND **make a fool of** so; **make a spectacle of** so *Fig.* to make someone or oneself look very silly or foolish. (This *ass* can be considered to be a donkey or a short version of *asshole.* Caution with *ass.*) □ *Don't get out onstage and make an ass of yourself. Remember, nobody has a sense of humor like yours.*

make an entrance *Fig.* to enter [a place] in some formal or special way, such as onto the stage in a play or opera. □ *She made her entrance too early and threw everyone into confusion.*

make an example of so *Fig.* to do something to someone that shows the bad results of bad behavior; to point to someone as a bad example. □ *The judge said that he would make an example of Sally and would fine her the maximum amount.*

make an exhibition of oneself

make an exception (for so) *Fig.* to suspend a rule or practice for someone in a single instance. □ *The rule is a good one, and I will not make an exception for anyone.*

make an exhibition of oneself *Fig.* to show off; to try to get a lot of attention for oneself. □ *She is not just dancing, she is making an exhibition of herself.*

make an honest woman of so *Fig.* to marry a woman. (Usually jocular.) □ *So you finally made an honest woman out of Denise.*

make an impression on so *Fig.* to produce a positive memorable effect on someone while one is present. □ *Tom made quite an impression on the banker.*

make an uproar Go to create an uproar.

make as if you* AND **make like you*** *Inf.* to make it seem like you. . . . (*Typically: ~ **are** (doing sth); ~ do (sth); ~ **can;** ~ **will;** ~ **have**.) □ *A: Are you busy? B: Not really. A: Well make like you are. Here comes the boss.*

make away with so/sth Go to make off with so/sth.

make believe (that) . . . to pretend (that). . . . □ *Make believe you live in a big house with two swimming pools, one hot and one cold.*

make so's **blood boil** *Fig.* to make someone very angry. □ *It just makes my blood boil to think of the amount of food that gets wasted around here.*

make so's **blood run cold** *Fig.* to shock or horrify someone. □ *I could tell you things about prisons that would make your blood run cold.*

make book on sth **1.** *Sl.* to make or accept bets on something. □ *Well, she might win the race, but I wouldn't make book on it.* **2.** *Sl.* to feel confident enough about something to accept wagers on it. □ *Of course the delivery date is certain. You can make book on it!*

make (both) ends meet *Fig.* to earn and spend equal amounts of money. (Usually in reference to a meager living with little if any money after basic expenses.) □ *Through better budgeting, I am learning to make both ends meet.*

make change (for so) (for sth) 1. to return change (coins) for someone to use for some purpose. □ *Will you please make change for me for the telephone?* **2.** to return change (coins, bills, or both) to someone for paper money. □ *The clerk refused to make change for her for the dollar bill.*

make chin music *Inf.* to talk or chatter. □ *You were making chin music when you should have been listening.*

make sth **clear to** so to help someone understand something. □ *I want to make it clear to you, so ask questions if you want.*

make oneself **conspicuous** *Fig.* to attract attention to oneself. □ *Ann makes herself conspicuous by wearing brightly colored clothing.*

make cracks about so/sth *Fig.* to make jokes or smart remarks about someone or something. □ *Stop making cracks about my cousin.*

make do (with so/sth**)** *Fig.* to do as well as possible with someone or something. □ *You'll have to make do with less money next year. The economy is very weak.*

make so **eat crow** *Fig.* to cause someone to retract a statement or admit an error. □ *Because Mary was completely wrong, we made her eat crow.*

make (enough) time (for so/sth**)** AND **save (enough) time (for** so/sth**); set (enough) time aside**† **(for** so/sth**)** *Fig.* to make certain that enough time is scheduled for someone or something. □ *Set aside some time for a meeting with Fred.* □ *Please make enough time for Fred.* □ *I'll save time for Fred's conference.*

make every effort to do sth *Fig.* to try very hard to accomplish something. □ *I will make every effort to be there on time.*

make eyes at so *Fig.* to flirt with someone. □ *Mother, he's making eyes at me!*

make fast work of so/sth Go to make short work of so/sth.

make so's **flesh crawl** AND **make** so's **skin crawl** to cause someone's skin to feel funny or get goose pimples through fright. □ *Just to hear the story of the killings made my flesh crawl.*

make free with so/sth Go to take liberties with so/sth.

make friends with so *Fig.* to work to become a friend of someone. □ *I want to make friends with all the people I am going to be working with.*

make fun of so/sth to ridicule someone or something. □ *Are you making fun of me?*

make sth **good** Go to set sth right.

make good as sth to succeed in a particular role. □ *John made good as a football player.*

make good ((at) sth**)** to succeed at something. □ *Bob worked hard to make good at selling.* □ *He made good selling Wonder Widgets.*

make good money *Fig.* to earn a sizable amount of money. □ *I don't know what she does, but she makes good money.*

make good ((on) sth**) 1.** *Fig.* to fulfill a promise. □ *Tom made good on his pledge to donate $1,000.* □ *He made good his pledge.* **2.** *Fig.* to repay a debt. (See also set sth right.) □ *I couldn't make good on my debts, and I got in a lot of trouble.*

make good time *Fig.* to proceed at a fast or reasonable rate. □ *On our trip to Toledo, we made good time all the way.*

make so's **hair curl** Go to curl so's hair.

make so's **hair stand on end** AND **cause** so's **hair to stand on end** *Fig.* to cause someone to be very frightened. (See feel one's hair stand on end.) □ *The horrible scream made my hair stand on end.*

make hamburger (out) of so Go to make mincemeat (out) of so.

make hay (while the sun shines) *Fig.* to get work done while it's easiest to do. (It is difficult or impossible to cut and bale hay in bad weather.) □ *Come on, let's get to work before everyone else gets here and gets in our way. Let's make hay while the sun shines.*

make so's **head spin** Go to next.

make so's **head swim** AND **make** so's **head spin 1.** *Fig.* to make someone dizzy or disoriented. □ *Riding the merry-go-round makes my head spin.* **2.** *Fig.* to confuse or overwhelm someone. □ *All these numbers make my head swim.*

make heads or tails (out) of so/sth *Fig.* [to be] able to understand someone or something. (Usually negative.) □ *John is so strange. I can't make heads or tails of him.* □ *Do this report again. I can't make heads or tails out of it.*

make headway 1. to be moving forward. (Originally nautical.) □ *We tried to move through the crown, but we were unable to make headway.* **2.** AND **make headway on** sth *Fig.* to make progress on a task or project. □ *I'm stuck. I can't make any headway on the report I have to write.*

make oneself **heard** to speak loudly so that one will be heard above background noise. □ *He screamed to make himself heard over the sound of the plane's engines.*

make sth **into a fine art** AND **turn** sth **into a fine art; get** sth **down to a science** *Fig.* to turn a task, procedure, or an assignment into an effort that shows great skills and accomplishment. (Sometimes sarcastic or ironic.) □ *She doesn't just cook pancakes. She has turned their preparation into a fine art!*

make it 1. *Fig.* to achieve one's goals. □ *I can see by looking around this room that you have really made it.* **2.** *Fig.* to copulate (with someone). □ *There was no doubt in his mind that those bedroom eyes were telling him their owner wanted to make it with him.*

make it as far as sth Go to make it (until sth).

make it big *Inf.* to become successful, especially financially. □ *I always knew that someday I would make it big.*

make it one's **business to** do sth AND **take it upon** oneself **to** do sth *Fig.* to do something on one's own even if it means interfering in something that does not directly concern one. (As opposed to minding one's own business.) □ *I know it doesn't concern me, but I made it my business to call city hall because someone had to.*

make it one's **business (to know** sth**)** to consider it one's duty to know or find out about everything. □ *I make it my business to find out what's happening in my neighborhood.*

make it hot for so Go to put the heat on (so).

Make it snappy! *Inf.* Hurry up!; Move quickly and smartly. □ *Andy: Make it snappy! I haven't got all day. Bob: Don't rush me.*

make it (to) some place to reach some place; to be able to attend an event at a place. □ *He didn't think his car could make it to Cleveland, but it did.*

Make it two. *Fig.* I wish to order the thing that someone else just now ordered. (Said to a food or drink server.) □ *Waiter: Would you like something to drink? Tom: Just a coke. Waiter (turning to Mary): And you? Mary: Make it two.*

make it (until sth**)** AND **make it to** sth; **make it as far as** sth *Fig.* to endure until something; to last until some time. □ *I hope my medicine makes it until the end of the month.*

make it worth so's **while** *Euph.* to tip or offer special (usually extra) payment to someone. □ *I made it worth the waiter's while to give us good service.*

make last-ditch effort Go to last-ditch effort.

make life miserable for so *Fig.* to give someone misery; to be a great nuisance to someone. □ *This nagging backache is making life miserable for me.*

make light of sth *Fig.* to treat something as if it were unimportant or humorous. □ *I wish you wouldn't make light of his problems. They're quite serious.*

make like a tree and leave *Sl.* to leave; to depart. (Jocular. A pun on the *leaf* of a tree.) □ *Hey, Jane. Don't you have an* appointment somewhere? Why don't you make like a tree and leave?

make love (to so) 1. *Fig.* to kiss and caress someone. (Early 20th century.) □ *Ernest made love to Linda in the garden in the moonlight.* **2.** *Euph.* to have sex with someone, especially when *someone* is omitted. (Since mid-20th century.) □ *I really think that he wanted to make love to me.*

make one's **mark** *Fig.* to do something that allows one to receive appropriate recognition. □ *Perry made his mark by inventing a special kind of holder for a cell phone.*

make mention of so/sth *Fig.* to mention someone or something. □ *I will have to make mention of your failure to secure additional business.*

make merry *Fig.* to have fun; to have an enjoyable time. □ *The children were making merry in the backyard.*

make mincemeat (out) of so AND **make hamburger (out) of** so *Fig.* to beat or pound someone or something; to treat someone or something roughly. (As if chopping someone up.) □ *If you don't behave, I'll make mincemeat out of you.*

make so's **mind up**† to decide; to do something that decides something for someone. □ *Will you please make your mind up?* □ *I will help make up your mind.*

make one's **mind up**† **(about** so/sth**)** to decide about someone or something. □ *Make up your mind about her!* □ *I just couldn't make my mind up.*

Make mine sth. *Fig.* I wish to have the thing named. (The *something* can be a particular food or drink, a flavor of a food, a size of a garment, or a type of almost anything. Most typically used for food or drink.) □ *Bill: I want some pie. Yes, I'd like apple. Tom: Make mine cherry.*

make mischief *Fig.* to cause trouble. □ *Don't believe what Mary says. She's just trying to make mischief.*

make oneself **miserable** to do things which cause one to be unhappy. □ *You're just*

making yourself miserable by trying to do something you aren't qualified to do.

make one's **money stretch** Go to stretch one's money.

make so's **mouth water** *Fig.* to make someone hungry (for something). (Also literal for causing saliva to flow into someone's mouth. Informal.) □ *That beautiful salad makes my mouth water.*

make one's **move 1.** [when playing a game] to take one's turn; to move one's game piece, such as a checker or Monopoly piece. □ *Are you going to make your move or just sit there?* **2.** *Fig.* to do the thing that one has planned to do as part of one's strategy. (This may or may not involve making some sort of movement.) □ *With Reggie out of the way, Clifford made his move and asked Evelyn to marry him.*

Make my day! Go to (Go ahead,) make my day!

make no apologies not to apologize for something the speaker does not consider to have done wrong. □ *I make no apologies. I did it and I'm glad.*

make no bones about sth *Fig.* not to make a mistake (about something); no need to doubt it; absolutely. □ *Make no bones about it, Mary is a great singer.*

make no difference (to so**)** [for a choice] not to matter to someone. (*Any* is used with negatives.) □ *Pick whom you like. It makes no difference to me.*

Make no mistake (about it)! *Inf.* Do not be mistaken!; You can be certain. □ *I'm very angry with you! Make no mistake about it!*

make no move to do sth Go to not make a move (to do sth).

make noises about sth *Fig. Inf.* to mention or hint about something. □ *The boss has been making noises about letting some people go.*

make nonsense of sth *Fig.* to make something appear to be silly or nonsensical. □ *You are just making nonsense of everything I have tried to do.*

make nothing of sth *Fig.* to ignore something as if it had not happened; to think no more about something. (Often with *it.*) □ *I saw him leave early, but I made nothing of it.*

make sth **of** oneself **1.** to succeed in life. (In this sense *something* is usually the word *something.*) □ *I'm going to college because I plan to make something of myself.* □ *I want to make a success of myself.* **2.** to become a particular unpleasant kind of person. (In this sense *something* can be a pest, bother, nuisance, etc.) □ *Stop making a nuisance of yourself!*

make sth **of** sth **1.** *Fig.* to make an interpretation of something. □ *Look through this and see what sense you can make of it.* **2.** *Fig.* to turn an incident into a dispute. (Usually with *it*. Often as an invitation to fight. See also make sth (out) of sth.) □ *Do you want to make something of it?*

make sth **off (of)** so/sth to make money from someone or something. (*Of* is usually retained before pronouns.) □ *Are you trying to make your fortune off of me?*

make off with so/sth AND **make away with** so/sth to steal something or kidnap someone. □ *The robbers made off with the silverware and iPods.* □ *Nicholas made off with the rich couple's baby.*

make or break so [of a task, job, career choice] to bring success or ruin to someone. □ *It's a tough assignment, and it will either make or break him.*

make sth **out**† to decipher, read, or figure out something written or spoken. □ *Sorry, would you repeat that? I couldn't make out what you said.*

make (out) like sth *Rur.* to pretend something; to pretend that one is something. □ *Joe made out like he had a lot of money, and folks believed him.*

make sth **(out) of** sth **1.** *Fig.* to make an interpretation of something. □ *Can you make anything out of this message? I don't understand it.* **2.** *Fig.* to interpret something negatively. (Fig. on ①. Often with *it*. See also make sth of sth.) □ *The hostess made too much out of my absence.*

make sth **out of nothing 1.** AND **make** sth **from nothing** to create something of value from nearly worthless parts. □ *My uncle—he sells sand—made a fortune out of nothing.* **2.** *Fig.* to make an issue of something of little importance. (Fig. on ①.) □ *Relax, John, you're making a big problem out of nothing.*

make out (with so**)** *Fig.* to kiss and pet with someone. □ *All evening long, he was trying to make out with me.*

make out (with sth**)** to succeed with something. □ *So, it was your first day on the job. How did you make out?*

make so **over**† Go to do so over†.

make one's **(own) bed 1.** to restore order to the bedclothes on one's own bed. □ *Jimmy, you are old enough to make your own bed.* **2.** *Fig.* to be the cause of one's own misery. (Fig. on ①.) □ *Well, I guess I made my own bed. Now I have to lie in it.*

make (one's) peace with so/sth to reconcile oneself with someone or something. □ *After many years, Frank made his peace with the Church and started participating again.*

make points (with so**)** *Fig.* to gain favor with someone; to impress someone. (See also make a point.) □ *Tom is trying to make points with Ann. He wants to ask her out.*

make so's **position clear** to clarify where someone stands on an issue. □ *I can't tell whether you are in favor of or against the proposal. Please make your position clear.*

make one's **presence felt (**some place**)** *Fig.* to do something to make it clear that one is present (somewhere) or at least involved. □ *Ted always makes his presence felt in meetings by speaking well about the things that are important to him.*

make ready (to do sth**)** to get [things] ready to do something. □ *I'm making ready to leave for work.*

make sth **right** Go to set sth right.

make oneself **scarce** *Fig.* [for someone] to become difficult to find; [for someone] to go into hiding. □ *Tom is mad and is looking for you. Better make yourself scarce.*

make sense AND **talk sense** to speak carefully and sensibly. □ *You don't make sense when you are tired.* □ *Talk sense or shut up!*

make short work of so/sth AND **make fast work of** so/sth *Fig.* to finish with someone or something quickly. □ *Billy made fast work of his dinner so he could go out and play.*

make so **sick** *Fig.* to disgust someone. □ *I am really tired of your vile talk. You make me sick!*

make so's **skin crawl** Go to make so's flesh crawl.

make (so) bold (as) to do sth *Fig.* to dare to do something. (Sounds a bit aloof.) □ *Would you care to dance, if I may make so bold as to ask?*

make (some) sense (out) of so/sth to understand someone or something. □ *No one can make sense out of Tom's story.*

make sth **stick** *Fig.* to make certain that a criminal charge [against someone] cannot be gotten out of. (Fig. on sticking to someone like glue.) □ *We charged Lefty with theft again, and this time we'll make it stick.*

make sure all the bases are covered Go to cover all the bases.

make the arrangements *Euph.* to arrange a funeral. □ *A funeral services practitioner will be happy to help you make the arrangements.*

make the bed (up†) AND **make** so's **bed (up†)** *Fig.* to restore a bed to an unslept-in condition. □ *Please make all the beds up early today.*

make the best of sth *Fig.* to do as well as possible with something that is not too promising. □ *I don't like it, but I will try to make the best of my summer landscaping job by getting a good tan.*

make the best of a bad situation to do as well as possible in a bad situation. □ *The room we were given was really bad, but we decided to stay anyway and make the best of a bad situation.*

make the feathers fly Go to next.

make the fur fly AND **make the feathers fly** *Fig.* to cause a fight or an argument; to create an uproar. (Fig. on the image of animals fighting.) □ *When your mother gets home and sees what you've done, she'll really make the fur fly.*

make the grade *Fig.* to be satisfactory; to be what is expected. □ *I'm sorry, but your work doesn't exactly make the grade.*

make the headlines Go to hit the headlines.

make the most of sth *Fig.* to make something appear as good as possible; to exploit something; to get as much out of something as is possible. □ *They designed the advertisements to make the most of the product's features.*

make so **the scapegoat for** sth to make someone take the blame for something. □ *They made Tom the scapegoat for the whole affair. It wasn't all his fault.*

make the scene 1. *Sl.* to attend an event. □ *I hope everybody can make the scene.* **2.** *Sl.* to understand a situation; to appreciate the situation. □ *I can't quite make the scene, but it looks like Willie punched the guy over here. Then he moved to the window over here, and that's when the woman across the street saw him.*

make the team *Fig.* to have been qualified enough to be selected to play on a sports team. □ *I tried out, but I didn't make the team.*

make time (with so**)** *Fig.* to flirt with, date, or hang around with someone. □ *I hear that Tom's been making time with Ann.*

make sth **to order** *Fig.* to custom-make an item; to make an item to fit someone's specifications. □ *The carpenter made the built-in bookcase to order for us.*

make (too) much of so/sth to pay too much attention to someone or something. □ *Don't make too much of it. It was really nothing.*

make tracks (for sth) *Fig.* to move rapidly toward something or some place. □ *The cowboys all made tracks for the chuck wagon.*

make trouble *Fig.* to cause trouble or additional work. □ *I don't want to make trouble, but I have a few suggestions that could make things work more smoothly.*

make sth **up**† **1.** *Fig.* to redo something; to do something that one has failed to do in the past. □ *Can I make the lost time up?* **2.** *Fig.* to assemble something. □ *The railroad will make up the train in Chicago, and it will leave on time.* □ *We made up a team out of the best players.* **3.** *Fig.* to think up something; to make and tell a lie. □ *That's not true! You just made that up!* **4.** *Fig.* to mix something up; to assemble something. □ *John: Is my prescription ready? Druggist: No, I haven't made it up yet.*

make up a foursome *Fig.* to assemble into a team of four people. □ *We have three people now. Who can we get to make up a foursome?*

make up for so/sth to compensate for something or something someone did. □ *We all had to do extra work to make up for Harry, who was very tired from being out late the night before.*

make up for lost time *Fig.* to catch up; to go fast to balance a period of going slow or not moving. □ *We drove as fast as we could, trying to make up for lost time.*

make sth **up**† **out of whole cloth** *Fig.* to fabricate a story or a lie. (Fig. on making clothing from uncut fabric.) □ *That's a lie. You just made that up out of whole cloth.*

make sth **up to** so *Fig.* to make amends to someone. □ *I'm so sorry. I will do what I can to make it up to you.*

make up (to so) **1.** *Fig.* to apologize to someone. □ *It's too late to make up to me.*

2. *Fig.* to try to become friends with someone. □ *Look how the cat is making up to Richard!*

make up (with so) *Fig.* to reconcile with someone; to end a disagreement (with someone). □ *They made up with each other and are now very good friends.*

make war (on so/sth) *Fig.* to actively oppose someone or something. □ *The police made war on violent street crime.*

make water *Euph.* to urinate. □ *She's got some kind of condition where it hurts when she makes water.*

make waves *Sl.* to cause difficulty. (Often in the negative.) □ *If you make waves too much around here, you won't last long.*

make way *Fig.* to make progress; to move ahead. (Originally nautical. See also **make way (for** so/sth).) □ *A sailboat can't make way if there is no wind.*

make way (for so/sth) *Fig.* to clear a path for someone or something. □ *Here comes the doctor—make way!*

make one's **way in the world** *Fig.* to succeed in the world independently. □ *I intend to prepare myself to make my way in the world by getting a college degree.*

make with sth *Sl.* to deliver something. □ *Make with the information, Spike, or you will stay in jail even longer!*

Make yourself at home. *Fig.* Please make yourself comfortable in my home. (Also a signal that a guest can be less formal.) □ *Andy: Please come in and make yourself at home. Sue: Thank you. I'd like to.*

makes one's **heart sink** *Fig.* to cause one to respond to something unpleasant by developing an empty feeling inside. (See also **have a sinking feeling in the pit of** one's **stomach.**) □ *When I heard her say those terrible things, it made my heart sink.*

man about town *Fig.* a fashionable man who leads a sophisticated life. □ *He prefers a nightclub to a quiet night at home—a man about town.*

a **man after my own heart** *Fig.* a man with similar tastes and preferences to mine. (Also with various substitutions for *man*.) □ *You like creamed chip-beef on toast? There's a man after my own heart.*

the **man in the street** *Fig.* the ordinary person; ordinary people. □ *The man in the street has little interest in literature.*

a **man of few words** *Fig.* a man who speaks concisely or not at all. □ *He is a man of few words, but he usually makes a lot of sense.*

a **man of his word** AND a **man of my word** [to be] someone whose word or vow can be trusted. (Other combinations of numbers and genders are also possible.) □ *You can trust him. He's a man of his word.*

a **man of the cloth** *Fig.* a clergyman. □ *Father Brown is a man of the cloth and is welcome at our table for dinner every Sunday.*

man to man AND **woman to woman** *Fig.* speaking frankly and directly, one person to another. □ *Let's discuss this man to man so we know what each other really thinks.*

manna from heaven *Fig.* unexpected help or comfort. (A biblical reference.) □ *The arrival of the rescue team was like manna from heaven to the injured climber.*

man's best friend *Fig.* a dog; dogs in general. □ *Man's best friend just peed all over my shoes!*

man's inhumanity to man *Fig.* human cruelty toward other humans. □ *It doesn't take a war to remind us of man's inhumanity to man.*

many a so/sth many people or things. (A way of expressing a generic in the singular.) □ *Many a young man has started out life with the burden of many responsibilities.* □ *Many an automobile has been damaged by the frequent hailstorms in this part of the country.*

many a time often; many times. □ *Many a time, I have wanted to take a cruise.* □ *Many is the time when I wanted to take a cruise.*

many (and many)'s the time *Fig.* there have been many times. □ *Many and many's the time I warned him not to go to the swimmin' hole by himself.*

many is the person **who** . . . there have been many persons who. . . . □ *Many is the woman who would seek help with this kind of problem.*

map sth **out**† Go to block sth out†.

march on *Fig.* [for time] to continue. □ *Time marches on. We are all getting older.* □ *As the day marches on, try to get everything completed.*

march to (the beat of) a different drummer *Fig.* to believe in a different set of principles. □ *John is marching to a different drummer, and he doesn't associate with us anymore.*

mark sth **down**† **1.** to record a fact by making a mark on paper. □ *He turned in his paper on time, and I marked the time down in my grade book.* **2.** to reduce the price of goods for sale. □ *We marked down all the spring merchandise at the end of the season.*

mark so **for life** *Fig.* to affect someone for life. □ *The tragedy marked her for life, and she was never the same.*

mark my word(s) *Fig.* remember what I'm telling you. □ *This whole project will fail—mark my words.*

mark time *Fig.* to wait; to do nothing but wait. □ *Do you expect me to just stand here and mark time?*

mark sth **up**† **1.** to grade a paper and make lots of informative marks and comments on it. □ *The teacher really marked up my term paper.* **2.** to raise the price of something. □ *The grocery store seems to mark the price of food up every week.*

*a **marked man** *Fig.* to be someone, usually a male, who is in danger from harm by someone else. (*Typically: **be** ~; **live like** ~.) □ *Bob's a marked man. His parents found out that he's skipping school.*

a **marriage made in heaven** AND a **match made in heaven** *Fig.* an ideal pairing of people for matrimony. □ *Theirs was a marriage made in heaven—wall-to-wall bliss.*

marry one's **way out of** sth to get out of something, such as poverty, by marrying someone. □ *She was able to marry her way out of poverty but regretted it in the long run.*

a **marvel to behold** someone or something quite exciting or wonderful to see. □ *Our new high-definition television is a marvel to behold.*

a **match for** so/sth/animal someone, something, or an animal that is the equal of someone, something, or some other animal, especially in a contest. □ *Your horse is no match for mine in a race. Mine will always win.*

a **match made in heaven** Go to a marriage made in heaven.

match wits (with so) *Fig.* to enter into intellectual competition with someone. □ *Whenever I try to match wits with Fred, he always ends up running circles around me with his clever repartee.*

a **matter of** (doing) sth Go to a question of (doing) sth.

a **matter of life and death** *Cliché* an issue of great urgency; an issue that will decide between living and dying. □ *We must find a doctor. It's a matter of life and death.*

a **matter of opinion** the question of how good or bad someone or something is. □ *How strong the company is is a matter of opinion. John thinks it's great, and Fred thinks it's poor.*

a **matter of principle** a question of following the law, guidelines, or rules. □ *I always obey the speed limit whether there's a cop around or not. It's a matter of principle.*

a **matter of time** Go to a question of time.

matter-of-fact businesslike; unfeeling. □ *Don't expect a lot of sympathy from Ann. She's very matter-of-fact.*

max out *Inf.* to reach one's maximum in something, such as weight in weight lifting or credit on a credit card. □ *Randy just knew when he had maxed out. Something in his body told him to stop.*

maxed out 1. *Sl.* exhausted; tired; used up; used to the maximum. □ *I am just maxed out. I haven't been getting enough sleep.* □ *Somebody picked my pocket downtown, and my credit cards are maxed out.* **2.** *Sl.* intoxicated. □ *I hadn't seen Barlowe so maxed out in years. He was nearly paralyzed.*

may as well Go to might as well.

(May I) buy you a drink? Go to (Could I) buy you a drink?

May I come in? Go to Could I come in?

May the best man win. AND **May the best team win.** a proverb hoping that the best or most qualified will win. □ *Before the vote was taken, Bob said to his opponent, "May the best man win."*

May the best team win. Go to previous.

mean business *Inf.* to be very, very serious. □ *Stop laughing! I mean business.*

mean no offense *Fig.* not to intend to offend. (See also take no offense.) □ *It was simply a slip of the tongue. He meant no offense by it.*

a **mean streak** *Fig.* a tendency for a person to do things that are mean. □ *I think that Spike has a mean streak that no one ever saw before this incident.*

mean to (do sth) *Fig.* to intend to do something. □ *No, it was an accident. I didn't mean to.*

mean well *Fig.* to intend to be nice, polite, helpful, etc. but fail in the effort. □ *I know you mean well, but your comments are sort of insulting.*

a **means to an end** just a way of getting something accomplished. (Can refer to a person.) □ *He never loved Tiffany. Sweet*

Tiff and her millions were just a means to an end.

meant to be destined to exist. □ *Our love was meant to be!*

meant to be sth destined or fated to be a particular thing. □ *I was meant to be rich, but something didn't work right!*

measure up to so/sth Go to stack up to so/sth.

meat-and-potatoes *Fig.* basic, sturdy, and hearty. (Often refers to a robust person, usually a man, with simple tastes in food and other things.) □ *There is no point in trying to cook up something special for the Wilsons. They are strictly meat-and-potatoes.*

a **Mecca for** so *Fig.* a place that is frequently visited by a particular group of people because it is important to them for some reason. (From the city of Mecca, the religious center of Islam.) □ *Broadway in New York City is a Mecca for theatergoers.*

*****meek as a lamb** [of someone] shy, quiet, and docile. (*Also: **as** ~.) □ *Only an hour after their argument, Joe went to Elizabeth and, meek as a lamb, asked her to forgive him.*

meet one's **death** AND **meet** one's **end** *Fig.* to die. □ *After 20 years, my dog finally met his death when he got hit by a bus.* □ *The sky diver met his end when his parachute didn't open.*

meet one's **end** Go to previous.

meet so **halfway** *Fig.* to compromise with someone. □ *They settled the argument by agreeing to meet each other halfway.*

meet one's **match** *Fig.* to meet one's equal; to encounter someone who can match or outdo one in some activity, talent, etc. □ *John played tennis with Bill yesterday, and it looks as if John has finally met his match.*

meet one's **Waterloo** *Fig.* to meet one's final and insurmountable challenge. (Refers to the final defeat of Napoleon at Waterloo.) □ *The boss is being very hard*

on Bill. It seems that Bill has finally met his Waterloo.

meet with sth *Fig.* to happen to experience or encounter something. □ *Sam met with an accident on the way to the game. He's okay, though.* □ *I met with some good luck at work today.*

a **meeting of the minds** the establishment of agreement; complete agreement. □ *We struggled to bring about a meeting of the minds on the issues.*

a **mell of a hess** *Inf.* a hell of a mess. (A deliberate spoonerism.) □ *Have you ever seen such a mell of a hess?*

melt down *Fig.* [for a nuclear reactor] to become hot enough to melt through its container. □ *The whole system was on the verge of melting down.*

melt in one's **mouth 1.** to taste very good. (Also can be literal.) □ *This cake is so good it'll melt in your mouth.* **2.** [of meat] to be very, very tender. □ *My steak is so tender it could melt in my mouth.*

mend (one's**) fences** *Fig.* to restore good relations (with someone). □ *Sally called up her uncle to apologize and try to mend fences.*

mend one's **ways** AND **change** one's **ways** *Fig.* to improve one's behavior. □ *You'll have to mend your ways if you go out with Mary. She hates people to be late.*

*****a **mental block (against** sth) *Fig.* to have some psychological barrier that prevents one from doing something. (*Typically: **get** ~; **have** ~; **give** so ~.) □ *Perry has a mental block against speaking in public.*

a **mere trifle** *Fig.* a tiny bit; a small, unimportant matter; a small amount of money. □ *But this isn't expensive! It costs a mere trifle!*

*****merry as a cricket** AND *****merry as the day is long** very happy and carefree. (*Also: **as** ~.) □ *The little children are as merry as the day is long.*

merry as the day is long Go to previous.

mess around AND **mess about 1.** *Inf.* to waste time; to do something ineffectu-

middle-of-the-road

ally. □ *Stop messing around and get busy.* **2.** AND **mess around with** so *Inf.* to play with someone sexually. □ *Those two have been messing around. You can tell.*

mess around (with sth**)** AND **mess about (with** sth**); monkey around (with** sth**) 1.** *Inf.* to play with or fiddle with something idly and with no good purpose. □ *Don't mess around with the ashtray.* **2.** *Inf.* to experiment with something; to use and learn about something. □ *We had been messing about with some new video techniques when we made our discovery.*

mess around with so Go to mess around.

mess so **over**[†] *Sl.* to treat someone badly; to beat or harm someone. □ *Max messed Lefty over and sent him to the hospital.*

mess up (on sth**)** Go to screw up (on sth).

messed up 1. *Inf.* confused. □ *I'm sort of messed up since my divorce.* **2.** *Inf.* intoxicated. □ *Somehow I must have got messed up. What caused it, do you think?*

mete punishment **out**[†] *Fig.* to determine and deliver punishment; to deal out punishment. (Other things can be dealt out with mete, but punishment is the most common.) □ *The principal will decide the kind of punishment she will mete out.*

*method in one's **madness** *Fig.* a purpose in what one is doing, even though it seems to be crazy. (*Typically: **be** ~**; have** ~.) □ *Wait until she finishes; then you'll see that she has method in her madness.*

a **middle ground** *Fig.* a position of compromise; a state of thinking where two opposing parties can discuss an issue politely and productively. □ *If we could only reach a middle ground on this issue, things wouldn't be so confrontational.*

the **middle of nowhere** *Inf.* a very isolated place. □ *I was stranded in the middle of nowhere for an hour with a flat tire.*

middle-of-the-road halfway between two extremes, especially political extremes. □

341

Jane is very left-wing, but her husband is politically middle-of-the-road.

might and main *Cliché* great physical strength; great force. □ *The huge warrior, with all his might and main, could not break his way through the castle gates.*

might as well AND **may as well** *Fig.* a phrase indicating that it is probably better to do something than not to do it. □ *Bill: Should we try to get there for the first showing of the film? Jane: Might as well. Nothing else to do.*

*a **mile a minute** *Fig.* very fast. (*Typically: **go** ~; **move** ~; **talk** ~; **travel** ~.) □ *She talks a mile a minute and is very hard to keep up with.*

a **milestone in** so's **life** AND an **important milestone in** so's **life** a very important event or point in one's life. (From the [former] stone markers at the side of a road showing the distance to or from a place.) □ *Joan's wedding was a milestone in her mother's life.*

milk so **for** sth *Fig.* to pressure someone into giving information or money. □ *The reporter milked the mayor's aide for information.*

the **milk of human kindness** *Fig.* natural kindness and sympathy shown to others. (From Shakespeare's play *Macbeth*, Act 1, Scene 5.) □ *Mary is completely hard and selfish—she doesn't have the milk of human kindness in her.*

*a **million miles away** *Fig.* lost in thought; [of someone] daydreaming and not paying attention. (Only one's mind is far away. *Typically: **be** ~; **look to be** ~.) □ *Look at her. She is a million miles away, not paying any attention to what she is doing.*

a **millstone about** one's **neck** a continual burden or handicap. □ *This huge and expensive house is a millstone about my neck.*

mince (one's**) words** to soften the effect of one's words. (Often negative.) □ *A frank person never minces words.* □ *I won't mince words. You are a jerk!*

the **mind boggles (at** sth**)** *Fig.* one's mind is confused by something. □ *The mind boggles at the thought of having 11 children.*

one's **mind goes blank** *Fig.* someone's mind experiences total forgetfulness. □ *He knew all his lines in rehearsal, but his mind went blank when he went before an audience.*

mind over matter *Fig.* [an instance where there are] intellectual powers overriding threats, difficulties, or problems. □ *You need to concentrate harder. Pay no attention to your surroundings. This is a case of mind over matter.*

mind one's **own business** *Fig.* to attend only to the things that concern oneself. □ *I'd be fine if John would mind his own business.*

mind one's **Ps and Qs** AND **watch** one's **Ps and Qs** *Fig.* pay attention to details. (Older. There are numerous attempts to explain the origin of this phrase, and none is conclusive. The best of a weak set of possibilities is that the letters *p* and *q* held some difficulty for writers or typesetters. It is over 200 years old, and its origins have been a mystery for much of that time.) □ *When you go to the party, mind your Ps and Qs.*

mind the store AND **watch the store** *Fig.* to take care of things while someone else is away. □ *Please stay here in the office and mind the store while I go to the conference.*

mind your own beeswax *Inf.* to mind one's own business. (Juvenile.) □ *You just mind your own beeswax!*

Mind your own business. AND **Get your nose out of my business.; Keep your nose out of my business.** *Fig.* Stop prying into my affairs. (Impolite. The expressions with *get* and *keep* can have the literal meanings of removing and keeping removed.) □ *Andy: This is none of your affair. Mind your own business. Sue: I was only trying to help.* □ *Bob: How much did you pay in federal taxes last year? Jane: Good grief, Bob! Keep your nose out of my business!*

a **mine of information** *Fig.* someone or something that is full of information. □ *Grandfather is a mine of information about World War II.*

*a **minute** *Fig.* [something delivered] regularly and frequently. (*Typically: **a laugh** ~; **a smile** ~; **a joke** ~.) □ *You can depend on Joey for a laugh a minute. He's a real joker.*

the **minute** sth happens the point in time at which an event happens. □ *I'll be inside the minute it rains.*

a **miscarriage of justice** a wrong or mistaken decision, especially one made in a court of law. □ *Sentencing the old man on a charge of murder proved to be a miscarriage of justice.*

miss a trick *Fig.* to miss an opportunity or chance. (Typically with the negative.) □ *She hardly ever misses a trick.*

miss (sth) **by a mile** *Fig.* to fail to hit something by a great distance; to land wide of the mark. □ *Ann shot the arrow and missed the target by a mile.*

miss out (on sth**)** not to be able to attend, participate in, or do something. □ *I don't want to miss out on her wedding.* □ *I missed out on the celebration.*

miss the boat *Fig.* to miss out (on sth); to be ignorant (of something). (Fig. on the notion of someone's failure to get on a boat in time for departure.) □ *Tom really missed the boat when it came to making friends.* □ *If you think you can do that, you have just missed the boat.*

miss the point *Fig.* to fail to understand the important part of something. □ *I'm afraid you missed the point. Let me explain it again.*

mission in life one's purpose in life; the reason for which one lives. □ *My mission in life is to help people live in peace.*

the **mists of time** *Fig.* a long time ago. □ *Those old people have lived in that house since the mists of time.*

mix and match 1. to assemble a limited number of items, usually clothing, in a number of different ways. □ *Gary always bought black, blue, and gray trousers and shirts so he could mix and match without too many bad combinations.* **2.** to select a number of items from an assortment, often in order to get a quantity discount. (As opposed to getting a quantity discount for buying a lot of only one item.) □ *The candles were 25 percent off, and you could mix and match colors and sizes.*

mix business with pleasure to combine business discussions or transactions in a social or holiday setting. (Always spoken of negatively, even though it is widely practiced.) □ *Well, as you know, I hate to mix business with pleasure, but I think we can discuss the matter on my fishing boat in the Gulf. If that's all right with you.*

a **mixed bag** a varied collection of people or things. (Refers originally to a bag of game brought home after a day's hunting.) □ *The furniture I bought is a mixed bag. Some of it is antique and the rest is quite contemporary.*

*mixed feelings (about** so/sth**) *Fig.* uncertainty about someone or something. (*Typically: **get** ~; **have** ~; **give** so ~.) □ *I have mixed feelings about Bob. Sometimes I think he likes me. Other times I don't.*

mixed up 1. *Fig.* confused; mentally troubled. (This is hyphenated before a nominal.) □ *I was a little mixed up after the accident.* □ *She's a crazy mixed-up kid.* **2.** *Inf.* alcohol intoxicated. □ *I'm just a little mixed up, nothing serious. No reason you should be swaying around like that.*

*mixed up in** sth *Fig.* involved in something, especially something wrong or illegal. (*Typically: **be** ~; **get** ~.) □ *The youth has had problems ever since he got mixed up in a group of boys that stole a car.*

*mixed up with** so else *Fig.* involved with another person, possibly romantically. (Suggests a negative judgment about the involvement. *Typically: **be** ~; **get** ~.) □ *I hear that Sam is mixed up with Sally.*

moist around the edges *Inf.* intoxicated. □ *Charlie is more than moist around the edges. He is soused.*

the **moment everyone has been waiting for** Go to the big moment.

the **moment of truth** *Fig.* the point at which someone has to face the reality of a situation. □ *The moment of truth is here. Turn over your exam papers and begin.*

Money burns a hole in so's **pocket.** An expression describing someone who spends money as soon as it is earned. □ *Sally can't seem to save anything. Money burns a hole in her pocket.*

money from home 1. *Inf.* easily gotten money. (Underworld.) □ *This job is like taking candy from a kid. It's money from home.* **2.** *Inf.* something as welcome as long-awaited money from home. □ *This cool drink is money from home right now.*

money is no object AND **expense is no object** *Fig.* it does not matter how much something costs. □ *I want the finest earrings you have. Don't worry about how much they cost because expense is no object.*

money talks *Fig.* money gives one power and influence to help get things done or get one's own way. □ *Don't worry. I have a way of getting things done. Money talks.*

*one's **money's worth** *Fig.* everything that one has paid for; the best quality for the money paid. (*Typically: **get** ~; **have** ~.) □ *Weigh that package of meat before you buy it. Be sure you're getting your money's worth.*

monkey around (with sth) Go to mess around (with sth).

monkey business AND **funny business** silliness; dishonest tricks. □ *That's enough monkey business. Now settle down.*

monkey suit *Inf.* a tuxedo. (Jocular. Possibly in reference to the fancy suit worn by an organ grinder's monkey.) □ *All the men except me wore monkey suits at dinner on the cruise.*

months running Go to days running.

mop the floor up† **with** so Go to clean the floor up† with so.

a **mopping-up operation** a cleanup operation; the final stages in a project where the loose ends are taken care of. □ *It's all over except a small mopping-up operation.*

more and more *Fig.* an increasing amount; additional amounts. □ *As I learn more and more, I see how little I really know.*

more bark than bite *Fig.* more threat than actual harm. (Alludes to the dog whose bark is more threatening than its bite is harmful.) □ *Don't worry about the boss. He's more bark than bite.*

more dead than alive *Fig.* exhausted; in very bad condition; near death. (Almost always an exaggeration.) □ *We arrived at the top of the mountain more dead than alive.*

more fun than a barrel of monkeys Go to as much fun as a barrel of monkeys.

more often than not *Fig.* usually. □ *This kind of dog will grow up to be a good watchdog more often than not.*

more or less *Fig.* somewhat; approximately. (A phrase used to express vagueness or uncertainty.) □ *Henry: I think this one is what I want, more or less. Clerk: A very wise choice, sir.*

More power to so. *Fig.* Good for someone.; Let them act that way, because I don't care. □ *A: The Smiths just bought a new Mercedes. B: More power to them.*

More power to you! *Fig.* Well done!; You really stood up for yourself!; You really did something for your own benefit! (The stress is on *to*, and the *you* is usually "ya.") □ *Bill: I finally told her off, but good. Bob: More power to you!*

more than one **bargained for** *Fig.* more than one thought one would get. (Usually in reference to trouble or difficulty.) □ *When Betsy brought home the sweet little puppy for a companion, she got more than she bargained for. That animal has cost her hundreds of dollars in bills.*

more than one **can bear** AND **more than** one **can take; more than** one **can stand** more of something, such as trouble or something bad, than a person can endure. □ *I've heard enough of this horrid music. It's more than I can stand.*

more so/sth **than** one **can shake a stick at** *Rur.* a lot; too many to count. □ *There were more snakes than you could shake a stick at.*

more than one **can stand** Go to **more than** one **can bear.**

more than one **can take** Go to **more than** one **can bear.**

more sth **than Carter has (liver) pills** *Fig.* a great deal of something. (Older. Refers to a product called Carter's Little Liver Pills.) □ *Why he's got more problems than Carter has pills!*

the **more the merrier** *Cliché* the more people there are, the happier the situation will be. □ *The manager hired a new employee even though there's not enough work for all of us now. Oh, well, the more the merrier.*

more (to sth**) than meets the eye** *Fig.* [there are] hidden values or facts regarding something. □ *There is more to that problem than meets the eye.*

more's the pity *Fig.* it is a great pity or shame; it is sad. (Sometimes with *the.*) □ *Jack can't come and he'll miss out on everything! More's the pity.*

the **morning after (the night before)** *Inf.* a hangover; the feelings associated with having drunk too much alcohol. □ *Do worries about the morning after keep you from having a good time at parties?*

the **mother of all** sth *Fig. Inf.* a large, severe, or dominant thing. □ *Wow, I have the mother of all headaches!*

motherhood and apple pie *Fig.* an often parodied sentiment expressed about allegedly quintessential elements of American home life. □ *Fred is so old-fashioned. Everything about old times is good to him. He's all motherhood and apple pie.*

mount up *Fig.* [for something] to increase in amount or extent. □ *Medical expenses mount up very fast when you're in the hospital.*

a **mouth full of South** *Sl.* a Southern accent. □ *I just love to hear a man with a mouth full of South.*

mouth off *Inf.* to speak out of turn; to talk back. □ *If you mouth off, I will ground you for three weeks.*

a **movable feast 1.** a religious holiday that is on a different date from year to year. □ *Easter is the best-known movable feast.* **2.** *Fig.* a meal that is served in motion or with different portions of the meal served at different locations. (Jocular or a complete misunderstanding of ① but in wide use.) □ *We enjoyed a real movable feast on the train from Washington to Miami.*

move away from sth *Fig.* to change by becoming less like something. □ *We are moving away from building homes with hardwood floors and granite countertops. Wooden counters and tile floors are the coming thing.*

move for sth to make a parliamentary or legal motion in favor of something. □ *I move for dismissal of the case against my client.*

move heaven and earth to do sth *Fig.* to make a major effort to do something. □ *"I'll move heaven and earth to be with you, Mary," said Bill.*

move in for the kill Go to **close in for the kill.**

move on Go to **get on with** one's **life.**

move so **to tears** to bring someone to the point of crying. □ *The story moved me to tears.*

move up in the world AND **come up in the world** *Fig.* to advance (oneself) and become successful. □ *The harder I work, the more I move up in the world.*

movers and shakers *Inf.* people who get things done; organizers and managers. □ *The movers and shakers in this firm haven't exactly been working overtime.*

moving right along moving quickly on to the next item. □ *Moving right along, we will now discuss the purchase of a new car for each member of the board of directors.*

Mr. Nice Guy *Inf.* a friendly, forgiving fellow. □ *You'll find that I am Mr. Nice Guy as long as you play fair with me.*

Mr. Right *Inf.* the one man who is right for a woman to marry. □ *Some day Mr. Right will come along and sweep you off your feet.*

much ado about nothing *Cliché* a furor over something unimportant. (The name of a Shakespeare play.) □ *All this arguing is much ado about nothing.*

*(much) credit (for sth**)** AND ***(a lot of) credit (for** sth**) 1.** *Fig.* praise or recognition for one's role in something. (*Typically: **get** ~; **have** ~; **give** so ~.) □ *Mary should get a lot of credit for the team's success.* □ *Each of the team captains should get credit for this great season.* **2.** *Fig.* praise or recognition of someone for having a particular quality. (*Typically: **get** ~; **have** ~; **give** so ~.) □ *We give her a lot of credit for her ability to get people to work out their differences.* **3.** *Fig.* credit granted to someone's account for some other financial transaction. (*Typically: **get** ~; **have** ~; **give** so ~.) □ *I will give you credit for the merchandise you returned to the store.*

(much) in evidence *Cliché* very visible or evident. □ *Your influence is much in evidence. I appreciate your efforts.*

much less so/sth Go to let alone so/sth.

Much obliged. *Rur.* Thankful and owing a debt of gratitude. □ *A: Sit down and have a drink on me. B: Much obliged.*

*much sought after *Cliché* wanted or desired very much. (*Typically: **be** ~; **become** ~.) □ *This kind of crystal is much sought after. It's very rare.*

muddle through (sth**)** to succeed without making too great an effort. □ *He doesn't work very hard at his assignments. He always seems to muddle through, though.*

muddy the water(s) *Fig.* to make something less clear; to make matters confusing; to create difficulty where there was none before. (Fig. on the notion of stirring up mud from the bottom of a pond or river.) □ *Things were going along quite smoothly until you came along and muddied the water.*

muddy sth **up**† *Fig.* to make something unclear. □ *You have really muddied this issue up. I thought I understood it.*

muff one's **lines** Go to fluff one's lines.

mull sth **over**† Go to chew sth over†.

Mum's the word. *Fig.* Nothing is to be said about this.; Don't say anything about this.; I promise to say nothing. (*Mum-mum-mum* is the sound one would make while attempting to talk with the mouth closed or lips sealed. Based on Shakespeare's *King Henry VI*, Part 2, Act 1, Scene 2: "Seal up your lips, and give no words but mum.") □ *Don't repeat a word of this. Mum's the word.*

muscle in (on so/sth**)** *Inf.* to try forcefully to displace someone or take over someone's property, interests, or relationships. □ *Are you trying to muscle in on my scheme?*

mushroom into sth *Fig.* to grow suddenly into something large or important. □ *The question of pay suddenly mushroomed into a major matter.*

music to so's **ears** *Fig.* a welcome sound to someone; news that someone is pleased to hear. □ *A: Here's your paycheck for this month. B: Ah, that's music to my ears!*

(My) hand to God! I so swear!; I pledge that what I am saying is the truth. □ *I saw her standing right there on the corner! Hand to God!*

My house is your house. AND **Our house is your house.** *Fig.* a polite expression said to make a guest feel at home. (From the Spanish phrase *Mi casa, su casa*.) □ *Bill: Hello, Tom. Tom (entering): So nice you can put me up for the night. Bill: My* *house is your house; make yourself at home.*

(My,) how time flies! AND **Time flies! 1.** Time has gone by quickly, and it is time for me to go. □ *John: My watch says it's nearly midnight. How time flies! Jane: Yes, it's late. We really must go.* **2.** Time passes quickly. (Said especially when talking about how children grow and develop.) □ *Tom: It seems it was just yesterday that I graduated from high school. Now I'm a grandfather. Mary: My, how time flies.*

My lips are sealed. AND So's **lips are sealed.** *Fig.* I will tell no one this secret or this gossip. (The concept appears in a few of the plays of Shakespeare, such as *Henry VI*, Part 2, Act 1, Scene 2: "Seal up your lips, and give no words but mum.") □ *Mary: I hope you don't tell anyone about this. Alice: Don't worry. My lips are sealed.*

my one and only one's spouse or lover. (Informal. See also the one and only.) □ *Look at the time. I've got to get home to my one and only.*

N

nail sth **down**† AND **pin** sth **down**† *Fig.* to negotiate an agreement, contract, or agenda. (As if the agreement cannot be changed easily after it is nailed down.) □ *Let's get this agreement nailed down, and then we'll go out for dinner.*

nail so's **ears back**† AND **pin** so's **ears back**† **1.** *Inf. Fig.* to beat someone, especially about the head. □ *Don't talk to me like that or I will pin your ears back!* **2.** *Inf. Fig.* to give someone a good scolding. □ *Did you hear him? He really pinned Chuck's ears back.*

nail in so's/sth's **coffin** Go to (another) nail in so's/sth's coffin *Fig.* something that will harm or destroy someone or something. (Alludes to the sealing of a coffin with nails.) □ *Every word of criticism that Bob said about the boss was another nail in his coffin.*

nail so('s **hide) to the wall** Go to next.

nail so **to a cross** AND **nail** so('s **hide) to the wall** *Fig.* to punish or scold someone severely. (Literally, to crucify someone or to nail someone's skin to the wall like that of a captured animal.) □ *She must hate your guts. She sure nailed your hide to the wall.*

***naked as a jaybird** Cliché naked; bare. (*Also: **as** ~.) □ *Two-year-old Matilda escaped from her nurse, who was bathing her, and ran out naked as a jaybird into the dining room.*

***the naked eye** the human eye, unassisted by optics, such as a telescope, microscope, or spectacles. (*Typically: **appear to** ~; **look to** ~; **see with** ~; **visible to** ~.) □ *I can't see the bird's markings with the naked eye.* □ *That's how it appears to the naked eye.*

the naked truth *Inf.* the complete, unembellished truth. □ *Sorry to put it to you like this, but it's the naked truth.*

***one's **name in lights** one's name spelled out on a lighted theater marquee. (In the last century this was done with small lightbulbs. *Typically: **have** ~; **see** ~.) □ *I hope someday, I will see my name in lights. I practice every day so I will be famous.*

one's **name is mud *Fig.* one is in trouble or humiliated. □ *If I can't get this contract signed, my name will be mud.*

name names to reveal the names of people who have done something wrong. (The frequently used negative is **not name any names**.) □ *Rollo went to the cops, and he's going to name names.* □ *I don't want to name any names, but somebody we both know broke the window.*

the name of the game *Inf.* the way things are; the way things can be expected to be. □ *The name of the game is money, money, money.*

narrow sth **down**† **(to** people/things**)** to reduce a list of possibilities from many to a selected few. □ *We can narrow the choice down to green or red.*

a nature stop *Fig.* a stop to use the toilet, especially during road travel. □ *I think I need a nature stop when it's convenient.*

near and dear to so close to emotionally and in importance to someone. □ *We all want to protect those who are near and dear to us.*

so's **nearest and dearest someone's family and close family members. □ *I can't wait to get out of this city and back home to my nearest and dearest.*

nearly jump out of one's **skin** Go to (almost) jump out of one's skin.

***neat as a pin** Cliché neat and orderly. (*Also: **as** ~.) □ Joanne certainly is well-organized. Her desk is neat as a pin.

neck and neck Fig. exactly even, especially in a race or a contest. □ Mary and Ann were neck and neck in the spelling contest. Their scores were tied.

need a pick-me-up Go to a pick-me-up.

need a reality check Go to a reality check.

need a smoke Go to a smoke.

Need I say more? Do I have to coax or explain more [than what I have already said]? □ We need your help here. Please come. Need I say more?

need sth **like a hole in the head** Inf. not to need something at all. □ I need a house cat like I need a hole in the head!

need sth **yesterday** Inf. to require something in a very big hurry. □ Yes, I'm in a hurry! I need it yesterday!

needless to say Fig. It is so obvious that it doesn't need to be said, but. . . . □ Needless to say, I should have spent more time on the report, but I just didn't have it.

one **needs to have** one's **head examined** Fig. said to someone who has made a silly choice. (Psychiatrists are said to "examine" heads or brains.) □ You did that! You need to have your head examined!

neither fish nor fowl Cliché not any recognizable thing. □ The car that they drove up in was neither fish nor fowl. It must have been made out of spare parts.

neither here nor there Cliché of no consequence or meaning; irrelevant and immaterial. □ Whether you go to the movie or stay at home is neither here nor there.

***(neither) hide nor hair** Cliché no sign or indication of someone or something. (*Typically: **find** ~; **see** ~.) □ We could find neither hide nor hair of him. I don't know where he is.

***neither rhyme nor reason** Cliché without logic, order, or planning. (Describes something disorganized. *Typically: **be**

~; **have** ~.) □ This silly novel's plot has neither rhyme nor reason.

nerves of steel Fig. very steady nerves; great patience and courage. □ I was scared to death, but Fred, who has nerves of steel, faced the thugs bravely.

a **(nervous) breakdown** Fig. a physical and mental collapse brought on by great anxiety over a period of time. □ After month after month of stress and strain, Sally had a nervous breakdown.

never a dull moment Fig. [it's] always exciting around here. (Describes an exciting or hectic situation.) □ Every time I visit Jean, she has dozens of things planned for us to do: parties and theaters to attend, restaurants to try, scenic places to see. Never a dull moment.

sth **never fails** Fig. a particular thing always works. □ My old folk remedy for hiccups never fails.

never had it so good Fig. never had so much good fortune. □ Mary is pleased with her new job. She's never had it so good.

never hear the end of sth Fig. never to hear the final rebuke or criticism for a misdeed; to continue to be reminded of a misdeed. □ I was late for our anniversary dinner, and I have never heard the end of it.

Never mind (about sth**).** Fig. Forget about something that was done.; Don't worry about something, since little harm was done. □ Q: Sorry. Did I step on your toe? A: Never mind. □ A: I think I broke your glasses. B: Oh, never mind about it. I hated the frames.

never would have guessed 1. never would have thought something to be the case. (Not used in other tenses.) □ I never would have guessed that he wanted the job. He kept it a very good secret. **2.** knew it all the time because it was so obvious. (Sarcastic. Not used in other tenses.) □ Now she wants to go back home? I never would have guessed! She has been homesick for days.

new blood Go to (some) new blood.

the **new kid on the block 1.** a child who has just moved to a certain neighborhood. □ *The new kid on the block turned out to be a really good baseball player.* **2.** *Fig.* the newest person in a group. (Fig. on ①.) □ *I'm just the new kid on the block. I've only been working here for a month.*

a **new lease on life** *Cliché* a renewed and revitalized outlook on life. □ *When I got out of the hospital, I felt as if I had a new lease on life.*

*a **New York minute** *Fig.* a very short period of time. (Probably from the late 1960s. There seems to be no compelling story of origin other than that people seem to be in a hurry in New York City. *Typically: **in ~; quicker than ~.***) □ *Just give me a call and I'll be there in a New York minute.*

next best thing something almost as good as something else. □ *It isn't real peach ice cream, but it's the next best thing.*

one's **next of kin** *Fig.* one's closest living relative or relatives. □ *The police notified the dead man's next of kin.*

next to impossible almost impossible. □ *It's next to impossible to find some kid to shovel snow these days.*

next to nothing almost nothing. □ *They manage to live on next to nothing. They really could use some cash.*

the **next world** *Euph.* life after death. □ *He believed he had made contact with spirits from the next world.*

nice and some quality [being or having] enough of some quality; adequate; sufficient. □ *I think your steak is nice and done now, just the way you like it.*

a **nice break** Go to a lucky break.

nickel and dime so **(to death)** *Inf.* to make numerous small monetary charges that add up to a substantial sum. □ *Just give me the whole bill at one time. Don't nickel and dime me for days on end.*

night and day Go to day and night.

a **night on the town** a night of celebrating (at one or more places in a town). □ *After we got the contract signed, we celebrated with a night on the town.*

night owl *Fig.* someone who stays up at night; someone who works at night. □ *My roommate is a night owl and usually reads until 5:00 A.M.*

a **night person** *Fig.* someone who is more alert and active at night than in the daytime. (Compare this with a day person.) □ *I'm really not efficient until after supper. I am the quintessential night person.*

a **nine days' wonder** *Fig.* something that is of interest to people only for a short time. □ *Don't worry about the story about you in the newspaper. It'll be a nine days' wonder and then people will forget.*

nine times out of ten *Fig.* usually; almost always. □ *Nine times out of ten people will choose coffee rather than tea.*

nine-to-five job a job with normal daytime hours. □ *I used to work nights with lots of overtime, but now I have a nine-to-five job.*

nip and tuck *Fig.* almost even; almost tied. □ *The horses ran nip and tuck for the first half of the race. Then my horse pulled ahead.*

nip sth **in the bud** *Fig.* to put an end to something before it develops into something larger. (Refers to destroying a flower bud before it blooms.) □ *The whole idea was nipped in the bud. It never had a chance.*

no big deal AND **no biggie** *Inf.* [of something] not difficult or troublesome. □ *Don't worry. It's no big deal to wash the car.*

no biggie Go to previous.

no buts about it Go to no ifs, ands, or buts (about it).

no call for sth AND **no call to** do sth *Fig.* no need, motivation, or justification for something. □ *Now, now. There's no call for shouting at us!* □ *Please! There's no call to shout.*

No comment. I have nothing to say on this matter. □ *Q: Georgie, did you chop down the cherry tree? A: No comment.*

no contest 1. *Fig.* [in games] a situation where one team fails to appear for a competition. □ *It was declared no contest because the opposing team was stuck in traffic out on the expressway.* **2.** *Fig.* a situation where the winner-to-be of a contest is obvious even before holding the contest. □ *It was no contest. The wrestler was so big and strong that no one could have defeated him.*

no dice *Inf.* no; not possible. □ *When I asked about a loan, he said, "No dice."*

no earthly reason *Inf.* no conceivable reason. □ *I can think of no earthly reason why the repairs should cost so much.*

no end in sight *Fig.* [with] no end anticipated or predicted. (As if one were waiting at a railroad crossing for a very long train to pass.) □ *We have been having constant troubles with our shipping department, and there's no end in sight.*

no end (of sth**)** *Inf.* an endless supply of something. □ *I've had no end of trouble ever since I bought this car.*

no fewer than (some number**)** Go to no less than (some amount).

no flies on so *Fig.* someone is not slow; someone is not wasting time. (On the image of flies not being able to land on someone moving fast.) □ *There are no flies on Robert. He does his work very fast and very well.*

no great shakes *Inf.* someone or something that is not very good. (There is no affirmative version of this.) □ *Your idea is no great shakes, but we'll try it anyway.*

no hard feelings AND **not any hard feelings** *Fig.* no anger or resentment. □ *I hope you don't have any hard feelings.* □ *No, I have no hard feelings.*

No harm done. *Fig.* It is all right; no one or nothing has been harmed. □ *A: I am sorry I stepped on your toe. B: No harm done.*

no holds barred *Fig.* with no restraints. (Fig. on a wrestling match in which all holds are legal.) □ *When Ann negotiates a contract, she goes in with no holds barred and comes out with a good contract.*

no ifs, ands, or buts (about it) AND **no buts about it** *Fig.* absolutely no discussion, dissension, or doubt about something. □ *I want you there exactly at 8:00, no ifs, ands, or buts about it.*

no joke *Fig.* a serious matter. □ *It's certainly no joke when you have to walk home.*

No kidding! 1. *Inf.* You are not kidding me, are you? (An expression of mild surprise.) □ *Jane: I got elected vice president of the club. Bill: No kidding! That's great!* **2.** *Inf.* Everyone already knows that! Did you just find that out? (Sarcastic.) □ *Alice: I'm afraid I'm putting on a little weight. Jane: No kidding!*

no laughing matter *Fig.* a serious issue or problem. □ *This disease is no laughing matter. It's quite deadly if not treated immediately.*

no less *Fig.* surprisingly; in spite of what you might have thought. □ *I will be there to pick you up in a brand new car, no less!*

no less than so/sth AND **none other than** so/sth *Fig.* not some other less interesting, important, or exciting person or thing. □ *No less than the president of the company showed up at our party.* □ *None other than Tom Williams, the head auditor, stopped by my desk to have a word with me.*

no less than (some amount**)** AND **no fewer than (**some number**)** not a smaller amount or number than what is stated. (The difference between *amount* and *number* is not rigidly observed here.) □ *I got no fewer than four invitations to New Year's Eve parties!*

no matter* . . . regardless of . . . (*Typically: ~ **what;** ~ **when;** ~ **how;** ~ **who.** And each of the foregoing can be followed by a clause, as with "no matter who you are or where you are.") □ *No matter what you have done, I will stand behind you.* □ *Come at whatever time you want. No matter when.*

no matter how you slice it *Fig.* no matter what your perspective is; no matter how you try to portray something. □ *No matter how you slice it, the results of the meeting present all sorts of problems for the office staff.*

No rest for the wicked.

no mean sth not just an average thing or type of person. (*mean = average, typical*.) □ *Jeff is no mean guitarist!*

No need. Go to (There is) no need (to).

No news is good news. *Fig.* Not hearing any news signifies that nothing is wrong. □ *Jane: I'm worried about my sister. She hasn't called me for months. Alan: No news is good news, right?*

no offense meant *Fig.* I did not mean to offend [you]. (See also **no offense taken**.) □ *Mary: Excuse that last remark. No offense meant. Susan: It's okay. I was not offended.*

no offense taken *Fig.* I am not offended [by what you said]. (See also **no offense meant**.) □ *Pete: Excuse that last remark. I did not want to offend you. Tom: It's okay. No offense taken.*

No pain, no gain. *Fig.* If you want to improve, you must work so hard that it hurts. (Associated with sports and physical exercise.) □ *Player: I can't do any more push-ups. My muscles hurt. Coach: No pain, no gain.*

no point in sth no purpose in doing something. □ *There is no point in locking the barn door now that the horse has been stolen.*

no problem Go to **no sweat**; **Think nothing of it**.

no questions asked *Fig.* no inquiries [to be] made to find out who did something. □ *Fines at the library will be suspended, no questions asked, for all late books returned during the first week of July.*

No rest for the wicked. *Fig.* It's because you are wicked that you have to work hard. (Usually jocular.) □ *A: I can't seem to ever get all my work done. B: No rest for the wicked.*

no sale *Inf.* no. □ *I wanted to go to Florida for the holidays, but my father said, "No sale."*

no skin off so's **nose** Go to next.

no skin off so's **teeth** AND **no skin off** so's **nose** *Fig.* no difficulty for someone; no cause for concern to someone. □ *It's no skin off my nose if she wants to act that way.* □ *She said it was no skin off her teeth if we wanted to sell the house.*

no soap *Inf.* no. □ *No soap, I don't lend money to anyone.*

No sooner said than done. *Fig.* an expression indicating that something has been done quickly and obediently. □ *Jill: Can I help you out? Jane: Yes! Put these files in alphabetical order. Jill: No sooner said than done.*

no sooner than some time not earlier than a stated time. □ *It will be ready no sooner than February and probably a lot later.*

no spring chicken *Fig.* a person well past youth; an old person. □ *That actress is no spring chicken, but she does a pretty good job of playing a 20-year-old girl.*

no stranger to sth *Fig.* [of someone] accustomed to or familiar with something. □ *As a child of poverty, she was no stranger to hunger and cold.* □ *Raised in an affluent home, she was no stranger to nice clothes and fine wines.*

no stress *Inf.* no problem; no bother. □ *Relax. No stress. What you said didn't bother me at all.*

No such luck. *Fig.* The luck needed for success simply was not available. □ *I'd hoped to be able to get a job in Boston, but no such luck. No one needs my skills there.*

no sweat AND **no problem** *Inf.* no difficulty; do not worry. □ *Of course I can have your car repaired by noon. No sweat.*

No telling. Go to It's anybody's guess.

no thanks to you *Fig.* I cannot thank you for what happened, because you did not cause it.; I cannot thank you for your help, because you did not give it. □ *Bob: Well, despite our previous disagreement, he seemed to agree to all our demands. Alice: Yes, no thanks to you. I wish you'd learn to keep your big mouth shut!*

no time to lose *Fig.* no extra time; no surplus of time. □ *Hurry. We have no time to lose.*

No way! *Inf.* No! □ *Me join the Army? No way!*

No way, José! *Inf.* No! (An elaboration of *No. José* is pronounced with an initial *H.*) □ *Bob: Can I borrow a hundred bucks? Bill: No way, José!*

No way to tell. Go to It's anybody's guess.

no wonder *Fig.* [something is] not surprising. □ *No wonder the baby is crying. She's wet.* □ *It's no wonder that plant died. You watered it too much.*

nobody's fool *Fig.* a sensible and wise person who is not easily deceived. □ *Anne may seem as though she's not very bright, but she's nobody's fool.*

*the **nod** *Fig.* someone's choice for a position or task. (*Typically: **get** ~; **have** ~; **give** so ~.) □ *The manager is going to pick the new sales manager. I think Ann will get the nod.* □ *I had the nod for captain of the team, but I decided not to do it.*

none of the above none of the things named in the list of possibilities just listed or recited. □ *Q: What's wrong, Sally? Are you sick, tired, frightened, or what? A: None of the above. I have no idea what's wrong.*

None of your beeswax! Go to next.

None of your business! AND **None of your beeswax!** nothing that you need to know about. (*Beeswax* is nothing more than a play on the word *business* and is a little milder.) □ *Just never mind! It's none of your beeswax!*

None of your lip! *Fig.* Shut up!; I don't want to hear anything from you about anything! □ *A: You are being a real nuisance about the broken window. B: None of your lip! Just help me clean it up.*

none other than so/sth Go to no less than so/sth.

none the wiser AND **not any the wiser** *Fig.* not knowing any more in spite of events or exposure to facts. □ *I was none* the wiser about black holes after the lecture. It was a complete waste of time.

*none the worse for wear *Fig.* no worse because of use or effort. (See also the worse for wear. *Typically: **be ~; become ~; look ~.**) □ *I lent my car to John. When I got it back, it was none the worse for wear.*

none too sth *Fig.* not very something; not at all something. □ *The towels in the bathroom were none too clean.*

noodle around *Inf.* to wander around; to fiddle around with something. □ *I couldn't find the instructions so I spent the afternoon noodling around, trying to find out how it worked.*

noodle over *Inf.* to think about. □ *Let's noodle over this problem for a bit and discuss it at our next meeting.*

nose so/group **out**† to defeat someone or something by a narrow margin. (Alludes to a horse winning a race "by a nose.") □ *Karen nosed Bobby out in the election for class president by one vote.*

nose about (for so/sth**)** AND **nose around (for** so/sth**)** to search here and there to find someone or something. □ *We spent an hour nosing about for a newspaper.* □ *I will nose around for someone to help you.*

nose around (sth**)** to pry into something; to snoop around something. □ *I caught her nosing around my desk.*

one's **nose is in the air** *Fig.* one is acting conceited or aloof. □ *Mary's nose is always in the air since she got into that exclusive boarding school.*

nosh on sth *Inf.* to make a snack of something. □ *After Thanksgiving, we noshed on turkey for three days.*

not a bit AND **not in the least** *Fig.* none at all; not at all. □ *Am I unhappy? Not a bit.*

Not a chance. No.; There is no possibility. □ *Q: Can you lend me $100? A: Not a chance.*

not a clue Go to not a glimmer (of an idea).

not a dry eye (in the place**)** *Fig.* no one in a place is free from tears or sobbing. □ *As*

Melinda sang, there wasn't a dry eye in the church.

not a glimmer (of an idea) AND **not a clue** *Fig.* no idea. □ *A: Where's the subway? B: Sorry. Not even a glimmer of an idea.* □ *How long till we're there? Not a clue.*

not a kid anymore *Fig.* no longer in one's youth. □ *You can't keep partying all weekend, every weekend. You're not a kid anymore.*

not a living soul *Fig.* nobody. □ *I won't tell anybody—not a living soul.*

not a moment to spare AND **without a moment to spare** just in time; with no extra time. □ *I arrived without a moment to spare.*

not able to bear so/sth Go to not able to stand so/sth.

not able to call one's **time** one's **own** *Fig.* too busy; so busy as not to be in charge of one's own schedule. □ *It's been so busy around here that I haven't been able to call my time my own.*

not able to get sth **for love (n)or money** *Fig.* not able to get something at any price; completely unable to get something. (See also not for love nor money.) □ *I wanted to go to the concert, but I was not able to get a ticket for love or money.*

not able to make head or tail of sth AND **not able to make heads or tails of** sth *Fig.* not able to understand something at all. (The idioms refer to a lack of ability to tell one end from the other end—the head and the tail—but have been mixed with the notion of heads or tails as in the flipping of coins.) □ *I couldn't make heads or tails of the professor's geology lecture this morning.*

not able to see the forest for the trees *Cliché* allowing many details of a situation to obscure the situation as a whole. (*Not able to* is often *can't*.) □ *The solution is obvious. You missed it because you can't see the forest for the trees.*

not able to stand so/sth AND **not able to bear** so/sth *Fig.* not able to endure or tolerate someone or something. (*Not able to* is often *can't* or *cannot*.) □ *I just can't bear candied sweet potatoes.* □ *I can't stand pain.*

not able to stomach so/sth AND **cannot stomach** so/sth *Fig.* not to be able to put up with someone or something; not to be able to tolerate or endure someone or something. □ *Jane cannot stomach violent movies.*

not about to do sth most unlikely to do a particular thing; absolutely will not do a particular thing. □ *I'm not about to pay for his tickets! He can just come up with the money himself.*

not all sth **is cracked up to be** AND **not what** sth **is cracked up to be** *Fig.* not as good as something is said to be. (Not always in the negative.) □ *This isn't a very good pen. It's not all it's cracked up to be.*

not all there *Fig.* not mentally adequate; crazy or silly. □ *Sometimes I think you're not all there.*

not amount to a hill of beans Go to not worth a hill of beans.

not any hard feelings Go to no hard feelings.

not any the wiser Go to none the wiser.

not as young as one **used to be** *Fig.* getting old. □ *Aunt Lila isn't as young as she used to be. She can't take a lot of trips anymore.*

Not bad (at all). 1. *Fig.* [Someone or something is] quite satisfactory. (Compare this with (It's) not half bad.) □ *Bill: How do you like your new teacher? Jane: Not bad.* □ *Bob: Is this pen okay? Bill: I guess. Yeah. Not bad.* **2.** *Fig.* [Someone or something is] really quite good. (The person or thing can be named, as in the example.) □ *John: How do you like that new car of yours? Mary: Not bad. Not bad at all.*

not bat an eye Go to next.

not bat an eyelid AND **not bat an eye** *Fig.* to show no signs of distress even when something bad happens or something shocking is said. □ *Sam didn't bat an eye-*

lid when the mechanic told him how much the car repairs would cost.

not believe one's **ears** *Fig.* not believe the news that one has heard. □ *I couldn't believe my ears when Mary said I won the first prize.*

not believe one's **eyes** *Fig.* not to believe what one is seeing; to be shocked or dumbfounded at what one is seeing. □ *When Jimmy opened his birthday present, he could hardly believe his eyes. Just what he wanted!*

not born yesterday *Fig.* experienced; knowledgeable in the ways of the world. □ *I know what's going on. I wasn't born yesterday.*

not breathe a word (about so/sth**)** AND **not breathe a word of it** *Fig.* to keep a secret about someone or something. □ *Don't worry. I won't breathe a word about this matter.* □ *I won't breathe a word of it.*

not budge an inch AND **not give an inch** *Fig.* not to yield at all in a dispute. □ *I argued with her for an hour, but she would not give an inch.*

not buy sth *Fig.* not accept something (to be true). □ *The police wouldn't buy his story.*

not by a long shot *Fig.* not by a great amount; not. (See also a long shot.) □ *Did I win the race? Not by a long shot.*

not by any means Go to by no means.

not by any stretch of the imagination AND **by no stretch of the imagination** *Fig.* to the maximum extent of someone's imagination. □ *I don't see how anyone by any stretch of the imagination could fail to understand what my last sentence meant.*

not care a fig AND **not give a fig** *Fig.* not to care at all. □ *I don't care a fig whether you come back at all!*

not care two hoots about so/sth AND **not give two hoots about** so/sth; **not give a hang about** so/sth; **not give a hoot about** so/sth *Inf.* not to care at all about someone or something. □ *I don't care two hoots about whether you go to the picnic or not.* □ *I don't give a hang about it.*

not one's **cup of tea** *Fig.* not one's choice or preference. (Used to describe an activity you do not enjoy.) □ *You three visit the museum without me. Looking at fussy old paintings is not my cup of tea.*

not dry behind the ears Go to wet behind the ears.

not enough room to swing a cat not very much space. (Probably referred to swinging a cat-o-nine-tails, a complex whip of nautical origins.) □ *How can you work in a small room like this? There's not enough room to swing a cat.*

not for a moment *Fig.* not at all; not even for a short amount of time; never. □ *I could not wish such a horrible punishment on anyone. Not for a moment!*

not for all the tea in China *Fig.* not even if you rewarded me with all the tea in China; not for anything at all. □ *No I won't do it—not for all the tea in China.*

not for anything in the world AND **not for love nor money; not on your life** *Fig.* not (in exchange) for anything (no matter what its value). □ *I won't do it for love nor money.* □ *He said he wouldn't do it—not for anything in the world.*

not for hire *Fig.* [of a taxi] not available to take new passengers. □ *The taxi was going to pick someone up at a nearby hotel and was not for hire.*

not for love nor money Go to not for anything in the world.

Not for my money. *Fig.* Not as far as I'm concerned. (Not necessarily associated with money or finance.) □ *John: We think that Fred is the best choice for the job. Do you think he is? Mary: Not for my money, he's not.*

not for publication not to be talked about openly; secret. □ *This report is not for publication, so keep it to yourself.*

not get one's **hopes up** *Fig.* [one] should not expect something to happen; [one] should not start hoping that something will happen. □ *The rain could stop so we can go to the beach, but you should not get your hopes up.*

not give a fig Go to not care a fig.

not give a hang about so/sth Go to not care two hoots about so/sth.

not give a shit *Fig.* not to really care. (Caution with *shit*.) □ *I don't give a shit whether you do it or not!*

not give a (tinker's) damn *Fig.* not to care at all. (A *tinker's damn* or *dam* may be a worthless curse from a tinker or a small dam or barrier used to contain molten metal.) □ *I don't give a tinker's damn whether you go or not!*

not give an inch Go to not budge an inch.

not give it a(nother) thought not to worry about something anymore. (A polite way of accepting someone's apology.) □ *It's okay. Please don't give it another thought.*

not give much for so's **chances** not to consider that someone has much of a chance [with something]. □ *He plans to enter the contest, but I wouldn't give much for his chances.*

not give so **the time of day** *Fig.* to ignore someone (usually out of dislike). (Alludes to refusing a simple request by a stranger for the correct time from someone who has a watch.) □ *I couldn't get an appointment with Mr. Smith. He wouldn't even give me the time of day.*

not give two hoots about so/sth Go to not care two hoots about so/sth.

not grow on trees *Fig.* not to be abundant; not to be expendable. (Usually said about money.) □ *I can't afford that. Money doesn't grow on trees, you know.*

not have a care in the world *Fig.* free and casual; unworried and carefree. □ *I really feel good today—as if I didn't have a care in the world.*

not have a clue (about sth**)** AND **without a clue (about** sth**)** *Fig.* to know anything about something; to have even a hint about something; to be ignorant and unaware about something. □ *I don't have a clue about where to start looking for Jim.*

not have a hope in hell Go to not have a snowball's chance in hell.

not have a leg to stand on *Fig.* [for an argument or a case] to have no support. □ *You may think you're in the right, but you don't have a leg to stand on.*

not have a lot of time for so/sth not to have enough time for something. □ *I just don't have a lot of time for minor problems like yours.*

not have a snowball's chance in hell AND **not have a hope in hell** *Inf.* a very poor chance. (Usually in the negative.) □ *She doesn't have a snowball's chance in hell of getting it done on time.*

not have a specific kind of **bone in** one's **body** *Fig.* to lack absolutely a certain positive characteristic. (The *kind of bone* may be *sympathetic, kind, friendly, apologetic, forgiving*, etc.) □ *Clara can be so unpleasant. She doesn't have a kind bone in her body.*

not have a stitch of clothes (on) *Fig.* naked. □ *He walked through the house and didn't have a stitch of clothes on.*

not have all one's **marbles** *Fig.* not to have all one's mental capacities. □ *John acts as if he doesn't have all his marbles.*

not have anything to do with so/sth Go to have nothing to do with so/sth.

not have the heart to do sth *Fig.* to be too compassionate to do something. □ *I just don't have the heart to tell him the bad news.*

not have the stomach for sth AND **have no stomach for** sth **1.** *Fig.* not to be able to tolerate certain foods. □ *We just don't have the stomach for onions anymore.* **2.** *Fig.* not to have the courage or resolution to do something. □ *I don't have the stomach for watching those horror movies.*

not hold a candle to so/sth Go to next.

not hold a stick to so/sth AND **not hold a candle to** so/sth *Fig.* not to be nearly as good as someone or something. □ *Sally is much faster than Bob. Bob doesn't hold a stick to Sally.*

not hold water *Fig.* not able to be proved; not correct or true. □ *The cop's theory will not hold water. The suspect has an ironclad alibi.*

not hurt a flea AND **not hurt a fly** *Fig.* not to harm anything or anyone, even a tiny insect. (Also with other forms of negation.) □ *Ted would not even hurt a flea. He could not have struck Bill.*

not hurt a fly Go to previous.

Not if one **can help it.** *Fig.* Not if one can avoid doing it. □ *A: I will see you tonight. B: Not if I can help it.*

Not in my book. *Fig.* Not according to my views. (Compare this with Not for my money.) □ *John: Is Fred okay for the job, do you think? Mary: No, not in my book.*

not in the least Go to not a bit.

not in the loop Go to out of the loop.

not just whistling Dixie *Rur.* not talking nonsense. (Refers to a song titled "Dixie." As if the Confederacy were a lost cause.) □ *Man, you are right! You're not just whistling Dixie.*

not know beans (about so/sth**)** *Inf.* to know nothing about someone or something. □ *Bill doesn't know beans about flying an airplane.*

not know enough to come in out of the rain AND **not know enough to come in from the rain** *Fig.* to be very stupid. □ *Bob is so stupid he doesn't know enough to come in out of the rain.*

not know so **from Adam** *Fig.* not to know someone by sight at all. □ *I wouldn't recognize John if I saw him up close. I don't know him from Adam.*

not know if one **is coming or going** Go to not know whether one is coming or going.

not know one's **own strength** not to realize how destructive or harmful one's strength can be. □ *I didn't mean to hurt you. I guess I don't know my own strength.*

not know the first thing about so/sth *Fig.* not to know anything about someone or something. □ *I don't know the first thing about flying an airplane.*

not know what hit one not to realize what has caused physical harm to oneself. (Particularly when someone is knocked out or killed.) □ *Poor guy. Died instantly* when the falling rock struck him. Didn't even know what hit him.

not know what to make of so/sth *Fig.* not to understand someone or something; not to be able to interpret something or the actions of someone. □ *We really don't know what to make of his request.*

not know where to turn AND **not know which way to turn** *Fig.* to have no idea about what to do (about something). □ *I was so confused I didn't know where to turn.* □ *We needed help, but we didn't know which way to turn.*

not know whether one **is coming or going** AND **not know if** one **is coming or going** *Fig.* to be very confused. □ *I'm so busy that I don't know if I'm coming or going.*

not know whether to laugh or cry *Fig.* [when something has both a humorous and a sad aspect] not to know if one should be happy or sad. □ *Just as the mugger was about to grab the lady's purse, he actually slipped on a banana peel and fell and struck his head. We didn't know whether to laugh or cry.*

not know which end is up *Inf.* not to be alert and knowledgeable. □ *Poor Jed doesn't even know which end is up.*

not lay a hand on so/sth AND **not put a hand on** so/sth not to touch or harm someone or something. □ *If you lay a hand on me, I will scream!*

not let so **catch** so doing sth AND **not want to catch** so doing sth *Fig.* an expression that scolds someone who has done something wrong. (The idea is that the person ought not to do the wrong thing again, not that the person simply avoid getting caught.) □ *If I've told you once, I've told you a thousand times: Don't do that! I don't want to catch you doing it again!*

not let the grass grow under one's **feet** *Fig.* not to stay in one place for a long time; to be always on the move. □ *He is always doing something. He never lets the grass grow under his feet.*

not lift a finger (to help so) AND **not lift a hand (to help** so) *Fig.* to do nothing to help someone. (The *someone* is *anyone* with the negative.) □ *They wouldn't lift a finger to help us.* □ *Sally refused to lift a hand to help her own sister.*

not lift a hand (to help so) Go to previous.

not long for this world *Fig.* about to die. □ *Our dog is nearly 12 years old and not long for this world.*

not made of money *Fig.* [of a person] not having a lot of money; not having an unlimited supply of money. □ *I can't afford a car like that. I'm not made of money you know.*

not make a move (to do sth) AND **make no move to** do sth *Fig.* not to start doing something that one is meant to do. □ *She made no move to clean up the kitchen even though she was instructed to do so.*

not miss a beat AND **not skip a beat** *Fig.* [one's heart does] not vary from its normal pattern of beating. (As if the event happened between normal heartbeats or was so inconsequential as not to disturb the normal beating of the heart. Figurative in any case.) □ *I thought I would be afraid to dive in, but my heart didn't miss a beat.*

not miss a thing Go to not miss much.

not miss sth **for love nor money** Go to next.

not miss sth **for the world** AND **not miss** sth **for love nor money** *Fig.* would not miss something for any reason at all. □ *Of course I'll be at your wedding. I wouldn't miss it for the world.*

not miss much 1. AND **not miss a thing** *Inf.* not to miss observing any part of what is going on. (Usually with *do* as in the examples.) □ *Ted doesn't miss much. He is very alert.* □ *The puppy doesn't miss a thing. He sees every move you make.* **2.** *Inf.* not to miss experiencing something that really was not worth experiencing anyway. (Usually with *do* as in the example.) □ *I missed the big sales meeting* *last week, but I understand I didn't miss much.*

not move a muscle *Fig.* to remain perfectly motionless. □ *Be quiet. Sit there and don't move a muscle.*

not much to look at unattractive; ugly. (Often, a redeeming quality will be noted with this phrase.) □ *This old car is not much to look at, but it runs very well.*

not on any account Go to on no account.

not one iota not even a tiny bit. (An *iota* is the ninth letter of the Greek alphabet, an *i*. An *iota* or *jot* refers to a tiny bit of something, like the letter *i*. See also jot and tittle.) □ *I did not get one iota of encouragement from any of those people.*

not open one's **mouth** AND **not utter a word** *Fig.* not to say anything at all; not to tell anything (to anyone). □ *Don't worry, I'll keep your secret. I won't even open my mouth.* □ *Have no fear. I won't utter a word.*

not one's **place to** do sth *Fig.* not one's role to do something. □ *It was not my place to criticize my boss.*

not playing with a full deck Go to a few bricks shy of a load.

not put a hand on so/sth Go to not lay a hand on so/sth.

not put (a lot) of stock in sth Go to take no stock in sth.

not put it past so *Fig.* to think that someone would have the gall or would dare to do something. □ *I wouldn't put it past Roger to arrive unannounced.*

not rocket science *Fig.* not some very complicated scientific endeavor allegedly beyond most people. □ *Come on. Taxes are easy to figure. It's not rocket science, you know!*

not set foot some place not to go somewhere. □ *I wouldn't set foot in John's room. I'm very angry at him.*

not shed a tear *Fig.* not to show any emotion even when something is very sad. □ *At his uncle's funeral, he didn't shed a tear. They never got along.*

not show one's **face** not to appear somewhere; not to go to some place. □ *After what she said, she had better not show her face around here again.*

not sleep a wink not to be able to sleep at all. □ *Ann hasn't been able to sleep a wink for a week.*

not so hot *Inf.* not very good. □ *The service here is not so hot. This restaurant is highly overrated.*

not spare any effort to do sth Go to spare no effort to do sth.

not stop at anything (to do sth**)** Go to go to extremes (to do sth).

not suffer fools gladly AND **not suffer fools lightly** not to easily endure foolish people; not to tolerate stupid or ignorant people. (Sounds a bit aloof. Biblical. From II Corinthians 11:19: "For ye suffer fools gladly, seeing ye yourselves are wise.") □ *I grow increasingly weary of people who lack the ability to reason, floss, or use apostrophes as intended. Basically, I do not suffer fools gladly, and I am weary of suffering through the results of their foolishness.*

not suffer fools lightly Go to previous.

not take no for an answer *Fig.* not to accept someone's refusal. (A polite way of being insistent.) □ *Now, you must drop over and see us tomorrow. We won't take no for an answer.*

not tell a (living) soul not to reveal something to anyone. □ *Your secret is safe with me. I won't tell a living soul.*

not tell which way the wind is blowing Go to see which way the wind is blowing.

not the end of the world *Fig.* not the worst thing that could happen. □ *Don't fret about the scratch on the side of your new car. It's not the end of the world.*

not to judge a book by its cover 1. to not choose to read or not to read a book because of the picture on the cover. □ *The drawings on the cover of the book didn't even match up with the story inside. I guess I will learn to not judge a book by its cover.* **2.** *Fig.* to not make judgments or decisions based on superficial appearances. (Fig. on ①. Often applies to people.) □ *Bob turned out to be a really nice guy in spite of my first impressions. I should not judge a book by its cover.*

not to mention so/sth Go to to say nothing of so/sth.

not to put too fine a point on sth *Fig.* to make too much out of something; to dwell overly long on a small detail of a complaint or argument. (Formal.) □ *Not to put too fine a point on it, but did you really mean to say that Paul was the former secretary of the organization? Wasn't he the corresponding secretary?*

not to put too fine a point on it *Fig.* a phrase introducing a fine or important point, apologetically. □ *John: I think, not to put too fine a point on it, you ought to do exactly as you are told. Andy: And I think you ought to mind your own business.*

not to see the forest for the trees *Fig.* cannot identify what is being sought, because it is so obvious. (The details tend to overshadow the overall organization of a system.) □ *I had trouble with math. It's simple, but I couldn't see the forest for the trees.*

not to speak of so/sth Go to to say nothing of so/sth.

not to touch a drop *Fig.* not to drink any of something, usually alcohol. □ *He pledged not to touch a drop all weekend, but he broke his pledge on Friday night.*

Not to worry. *Inf.* Please do not worry. □ *Sue: I think we're about to run out of money. Bill: Not to worry. I have some more travelers checks.*

not too shabby 1. *Inf.* nice; well done. (With emphasis on *shabby*.) □ *Is that your car? Not too shabby!* **2.** *Inf.* very shabby; very poor indeed. (With emphasis on *too*. Sarcastic.) □ *Did you see that shot she missed? Not too shabby!*

not touch so/sth **with a ten-foot pole** *Cliché* not to have anything to do with someone or something. (Always nega-

tive.) □ *No, I won't hire Fred. I wouldn't touch him with a ten-foot pole.*

not trouble one's **(pretty) (little) head about** sth *Rur.* not to worry about something. (Considered demeaning by many.) □ *You shouldn't trouble your head about it. Everything will turn out fine.*

not utter a word Go to not open one's mouth.

not want to catch so doing sth Go to not let so catch so doing sth.

not with it *Fig.* not able to think clearly; not able to understand things. □ *Lisa's mother is not really with it anymore. She's going senile.* □ *Tom's not with it yet. He's only just come around from the anesthetic.*

not worth a damn *Inf.* worthless. □ *This pen is not worth a damn.*

not worth a dime AND **not worth a red cent** *Fig.* worthless. □ *This land is all swampy. It's not worth a dime.*

not worth a hill of beans AND **not amount to a hill of beans; not worth a plugged nickel; not worth beans** *Fig.* worthless. □ *Your advice isn't worth a hill of beans.* □ *This old cow isn't worth a plugged nickel.*

not worth a plugged nickel Go to previous.

not worth a red cent Go to not worth a dime.

not worth beans Go to not worth a hill of beans.

not worth mentioning 1. not important enough to require a comment. □ *A small number of books hint at the phenomenon, but they probably aren't worth mentioning.* **2.** [of an error or wrong] not worth apologizing for. □ *No need to apologize to me. No harm done. It's not worth mentioning.*

not worth the paper it's printed on Go to next.

not worth the paper it's written on AND **not worth the paper it's printed on** *Fig.* [of a document] meaningless or without authority; of no value. □ *That* *contract isn't worth the paper it's written on. All the signatures are forged.*

not worth one's **while** not worth bothering with; not worth spending time on. □ *Don't bother trying to collect money from them. It isn't worth your while.*

a **notch above** (so/sth) AND a **notch better than** (so/sth) *Fig.* a little higher in quality than someone or something. □ *This latest candidate we interviewed seems a notch above the rest, so let's hire her.*

a **notch below** (so/sth) *Fig.* a little lower in quality than someone or something. □ *I believe that this wine is a notch below the one we had with the fish.*

*noted for sth *Fig.* famed for something; memorable for something. (*Typically: be ~; become ~.) □ *We were all noted for our polite manners.* □ *The restaurant was noted for its traditional fare.*

nothing but only; just. □ *Bob is nothing but annoying. And I mean that in nothing but kindness.*

nothing but skin and bones AND **(all) skin and bones** *Fig.* very thin or emaciated. □ *Bill has lost so much weight. He's nothing but skin and bones.* □ *That old horse is all skin and bones. I won't ride it.*

Nothing doing! *Inf.* I will not permit it!; I will not participate in it! □ *John: Can I put this box in your suitcase? Bill: Nothing doing! It's too heavy now.*

Nothing is certain but death and taxes. There is always a degree of uncertainty. □ *You can't be too sure about this. Nothing is certain but death and taxes.*

nothing less than some quality AND **nothing short of** some quality *Fig.* not any lower in quality than the quality named. □ *This fried chicken is nothing less than marvelous.*

nothing less than sth AND **nothing short of** sth *Fig.* more or less the same as something bad; as bad as something. □ *His behavior was nothing short of criminal.* □ *Climbing those mountains alone is nothing short of suicide.*

Nothing much. *Inf.* not much; hardly anything; nothing of importance. (Often a reply to a greeting asking what one has been doing.) □ *John: Hey, man! How's by you? Bob: Hiya! Nothing much.*

nothing of the kind 1. no; absolutely not. □ *I didn't tear your jacket—nothing of the kind!* **2.** nothing like that. □ *She did nothing of the kind! She wasn't even there!*

nothing short of some quality Go to nothing less than some quality.

nothing short of sth Go to nothing less than sth.

nothing to boast about *Fig.* not worth bragging about; mediocre. □ *In high school, my grades were acceptable, but they were nothing to boast about.*

nothing to choose from no choice; no choice in the selection; not enough of something to make a choice. □ *By the time I got around to selecting a team of helpers, there was nothing to choose from.*

Nothing to it! Go to (There's) nothing to it!

nothing to sneeze at AND **nothing to be sneezed at** *Fig.* nothing small or unimportant. □ *It's not a lot of money, but it's nothing to sneeze at.* □ *Our house isn't a mansion, but it's nothing to sneeze at.*

nothing to speak of *Fig.* not many; not much. □ *John: What's happening around here? Bill: Nothing to speak of.*

nothing to write home about *Fig.* mediocre; not as good as you expected. □ *I went to that new restaurant last night. It's nothing to write home about.*

nothing upstairs *Fig.* no brains; stupid. □ *Tom is sort of stupid. You know—nothing upstairs.*

Nothing ventured, nothing gained. *Fig.* If you do not take risks, you will never accomplish anything. □ *Bill: Should I ask my boss for a promotion? Jane: Nothing ventured, nothing gained.*

now and then Go to (every) now and then.

*now or never *Fig.* at this time and no other. (*Typically: be ~; become ~.) □

This is your only chance, John. It's now or never.

Now you're talking! Go to That's what I'm talking about!

nowhere near sth *Fig.* not yet on the verge of something; not yet completely done. □ *We are nowhere near an agreement.* □ *The arena is nowhere near full.*

nowhere to be found nowhere; not able to be found; lost. □ *Her lost ring is nowhere to be found.*

no-win situation *Fig.* a situation where there is no correct or satisfactory solution. □ *The general was too weak to fight and too proud to surrender. It was a no-win situation.*

null and void *Cliché* without legal force; having no legal effect. □ *The court declared the law to be null and void.* □ *The millionaire's will was null and void because it was unsigned.*

one's **number is up** *Fig.* one's time to die—or to suffer some other unpleasantness—has come. □ *When my number is up, I hope it all goes fast.*

nurse a grudge (against so) *Fig.* to keep resenting and disliking someone over a period of time. (Usually implies that it has been an unreasonably long time.) □ *Sally is still nursing a grudge against Mary.*

a **nut case** *Fig.* a crazy person; an irrational person. □ *Bob is acting stranger and stranger. He is turning into a real nut case.*

nut up *Sl.* to go crazy. (See also crack up.) □ *I almost nutted up at the last place I worked.*

nuts and bolts *Fig.* the mundane workings of something; the basics of something. (See also get down to the nuts and bolts.) □ *She's got a lot of good, general ideas, but when it comes to the nuts and bolts of getting something done, she's no good.*

*nutty as a fruitcake AND **nuttier than a fruitcake** crazy. (*Also: **as** ~.) □ *Don't pay any attention to John; he's nutty as a fruitcake.*

*obsessed with so/sth preoccupied with someone or something. (*Typically: **be** ~; **become** ~.) □ *Kathy was obsessed with the kitten.*

obstinate as a mule Go to stubborn as a mule.

oceans of so/sth AND an **ocean of** so/sth a very large amount of something. □ *After a week of vacation, there was an ocean of work to do.*

the **odd** sth an extra, minor, or spare something; a chance something. □ *When I travel, I might buy the odd trinket or two, but I never spend much money.*

odd man out *Fig.* an unusual or atypical person or thing. □ *You had better learn to use the new system software unless you want to be odd man out.*

odds and ends *Fig.* miscellaneous things. □ *There were lots of odds and ends in the attic, but nothing of real value.*

the **odds are against** one *Fig.* [for fate] to be against one generally. □ *I know the odds are against me, but I wish to run in the race anyway.*

the **odds-on favorite** *Fig.* the most popular choice of a wager. □ *Fred is the odds-on favorite for president of the board of trustees.*

odor of sanctity *Fig.* an atmosphere or aura of excessive holiness or piety. □ *I hate their house. There's such an odor of sanctity with crosses and holy pictures everywhere.*

of a piece Go to (all) of a piece.

of a single mind (about so/sth**)** Go to of one mind (about so/sth).

*of age *Fig.* old enough to marry, buy or drink alcohol, or sign legal agreements. (*Typically: **be** ~; **come** ~.) □ *Now that Mary is of age, she can buy her own car.*

Of all people! AND **Of all places!; Of all things!** What a surprise!; What an unexpected person, place, or thing! □ *Of all people! I'd heard that you were dead!*

Of all places! Go to previous.

of course yes. (Also in the negative often.) □ *Q: Are you coming? A: Of course.* □ *Q: Are you tired? It's nearly midnight. A: Of course not.*

of late recently; lately. (More formal than lately.) □ *We haven't seen you around here of late.*

of no avail Go to to no avail.

so **of note** *Fig.* a person who is famous. □ *We invited a speaker of note to lecture at the next meeting.*

*of old AND ***of yore** long ago. (*Typically: **in days** ~; **in times** ~; so/sth ~.) □ *Knights in days of yore were probably pretty tough guys.*

of one mind (about so/sth**)** AND **of the same mind (about** so/sth**); of a single mind (about** so/sth**)** *Fig.* in agreement about someone or something. (See also of two minds (about so/sth).) □ *You will have to attend one of the less expensive state universities. Your father and I are of a single mind about this.*

of one's **own accord** AND **of** one's **own free will** *Fig.* by one's own choice, without coercion. □ *I'll have to order her to do it because she won't do it of her own free will.*

of one's **own free will** Go to previous.

of one's **own making** [a problem] that one has created for oneself. □ *You realize, of course, that this mess is of your own making.*

of service (to so) *Fig.* helping someone; serving someone. □ *Good morning, madam. May I be of service to you?*

sth **of sorts** *Fig.* an inferior example of a kind of something. □ *Well, it's a solution of sorts, I suppose.*

of the first water 1. *Fig.* [of a gemstone] of the finest quality. (The *water* is probably from the Arabic word for *water* also having the meaning of luster or splendor. Diamonds or pearls of the first water are of the highest quality.) □ *This is a very fine pearl—a pearl of the first water.* **2.** *Fig.* of an excellent person or thing. □ *Tom is of the first water—a true gentleman.*

of the old school Go to from the old school.

of two minds (about so/sth) *Fig.* holding conflicting opinions about someone or something; being undecided about someone or something. (See also of one mind (about so/sth).) □ *I am of two minds about whether I should go to the convention.*

of yore Go to of old.

off again, on again Go to on again, off again.

off and on Go to on and off.

off and running 1. *Fig.* [of horses, dogs, or people] having started racing. □ *It's a beautiful day at the races, and, yes, they're off and running!* **2.** *Fig.* started up and going. (Fig. on ①.) □ *The construction of the building was going to take two years, but we were off and running, and it appeared we would finish on schedule.*

***off base 1.** *Fig.* [of a runner in baseball] not having a foot touching the base. (*Typically: **be** ~; **get** ~.) □ *The runner was off base but the first baseman didn't tag him out.* **2.** *Fig.* unrealistic; inexact; wrong. (Fig. on ①. *Typically: **be** ~; **get** ~.) □ *I'm afraid you're off base when you state that this problem will take care of itself.*

***off campus** not located or present on the grounds of a college or university. (*Typically: **be** ~; **live** ~; **move** ~. Also attributive uses.) □ *The dean is off campus and cannot be reached.*

off chance slight possibility. □ *There's an off chance that we might be hiring next month. Please check back then.*

***off course 1.** not going in the right direction. (*Typically: **be** ~; **drift** ~; **get** ~.) □ *The ship is off course and may strike the reef!* **2.** *Fig.* not following the plan correctly. (Fig. on ①. *Typically: **be** ~; **get** ~.) □ *The project is off course and won't be finished on time.*

off duty not working at one's job. (The opposite of on duty.) □ *I'm sorry, I can't talk to you until I'm off duty.*

***off** one's **game 1.** *Fig.* not able to play a sport as well as normal. (*Typically: **be** ~; **put** one ~; **throw** one ~.) □ *I'm a little tired, and that generally puts me off my game.* **2.** *Fig.* at one's best. (Fig. on ①.) □ *Harry seemed a little off his game in the sales meeting today.*

off key *Fig.* [of music or singing] off pitch; out of tune. □ *She always sings off key and makes the choir sound awful.*

off kilter Go to out of kilter.

off like a shot away [from a place] very quickly. □ *The thief grabbed the lady's purse and was off like a shot.*

off limits Go to out of bounds.

off one's **nut** Go to off one's rocker.

off on so/sth **1.** off the chosen subject and onto a discussion of someone or something else. □ *Is she off on that same old tale of woe again?* **2.** *Fig.* in a rage about someone or something; on a tirade about someone or something. □ *Are you off on Sally again? Why can't you leave her alone?*

***off (on** sth) **1.** *Fig.* incorrect in one's planning or prediction. (*Typically: **be** ~; **get** ~.) □ *I was off on my estimates a little bit.* **2.** *Fig.* to have started on something, such as a task or a journey. (*Typically: **be** ~; **get** ~.) □ *What time should we be off on our trip?* **3.** *Sl.* to get high on some kind of drug. (*Typically: **get** ~.) □ *Spike likes to get off on marijuana.*

*off on a sidetrack *Fig.* on a digression; discussing a topic that is not the main topic. (Fig. on the image of a train waiting on a siding. *Typically: **be** ~; **get** ~; **get** so ~.) □ *The unruly committee got off on one sidetrack after another.*

*off on a tangent *Fig.* to be on a somewhat related or irrelevant course while neglecting the main subject. (*Typically: **be** ~; **go** ~; **send** so ~.) □ *Just as we started talking, Henry went off on a tangent about the high cost of living.*

*off on the right foot (with so/sth**)** AND ***off to a good start (with** so/sth**)** *Fig.* starting out correctly; beginning something carefully and cautiously. (*Typically: **be** ~; **get** ~.) □ *This time, I want to get off on the right foot with him.*

*off on the wrong foot AND ***off to a bad start** *Fig.* starting something (such as a friendship) with negative factors. (*Typically: **be** ~; **get** ~.) □ *Bill and Tom got off on the wrong foot. They had a minor car accident just before they were introduced.*

*off one's **rocker** AND ***off** one's **nut; *off** one's **trolley** *Fig.* crazy; silly. (*Typically: **be** ~; **go** ~.) □ *Sometimes, Bob, I think you're off your rocker.* □ *Good grief, John. You're off your nut.*

off season *Fig.* not in the busy time of the year. □ *We don't have much to do off season.*

off the air *Fig.* not broadcasting (a radio or television program). □ *When the performers were off the air, the director told them how well they had done.*

off the beaten path Go to next.

*off the beaten track AND ***off the beaten path** *Fig.* away from the frequently traveled routes. (*Typically: **be** ~; **go** ~; **travel** ~.) □ *We found a nice little Italian restaurant off the beaten track.*

off the books [of a business transaction made] without a record. □ *Robby got in* trouble with the tax department because a few of his larger sales were off the books.

off the charts *Fig.* record setting; beyond the expected range of measurement. (Refers especially to huge sales of a book or CD.) □ *His book was a tremendous success. It is off the charts and making heaps of money.*

*off the hook *Fig.* freed from an obligation. (Fig. on the image of a fish freeing itself from a fishhook. *Typically: **be** ~; **get** ~; **get** so ~; **let** so ~.) □ *Thanks for getting me off the hook. I didn't want to attend that meeting.*

off the mark *Fig.* not quite exactly right. □ *You were off the mark when you said we would be a little late to the party. It was yesterday, in fact!*

off the rack *Fig.* [selected] from what is readily available rather than having something custom made. (Fig. on the purchase of ready-made clothing.) □ *I never hire people to write my software. I get my stuff off the rack, and it's cheaper in the long run.*

off the record *Fig.* unofficial; informal. (Of comments to the press that one does not want reported.) □ *Although her comments were off the record, the newspaper published them anyway.*

off the shelf *Fig.* ready-made for purchase; not custom made. (Hyphenated when before a nominal.) □ *I generally buy off-the-shelf clothing. I am a perfect size eight.*

off the subject not concerned with the subject being discussed. □ *I got off the subject and forgot what I was supposed to be talking about.*

off the top of one's **head** Go to (right) off the top of one's head.

off the track 1. Go to off the beaten track. **2.** *Fig.* [of comments] irrelevant and immaterial. (Fig. on off the beaten track.) □ *I'm sorry. I was thinking about dinner, and I got off the track.*

*off the wagon 1. *Inf.* drinking liquor after a period of abstinence. (*Typically: **be** ~; **fall** ~; **get** ~.) □ *Poor John fell off the wagon again. Drunk as a skunk.* **2.** *Inf.*

back on drugs after a period of abstinence. (*Typically: **be** ~; **fall** ~; **get** ~.) □ *He can't be off the wagon, because he has never stopped using, even for a day.*

off to a bad start Go to off on the wrong foot.

*off (to a flying start) *Fig.* having a very successful beginning to something. (*Typically: **be** ~; **get** ~.) □ *We shall need a large donation from the local citizens if the charity is to get off to a flying start.*

off to a good start (with so/sth**)** Go to off on the right foot (with so/sth).

off to a running start with a good, fast beginning, possibly a head start. □ *I got off to a running start in math this year.*

off to one side beside something; (moved) slightly away from something. □ *Our garden has roses in the middle and a spruce tree off to one side.*

off to the races *Fig.* an expression characterizing the activity or excitement that is just beginning; [we are] leaving for something interesting or exciting. □ *The tour bus is out in front waiting, and we've said good-bye to everyone. Looks like we're off to the races.*

*off (to the side) with so *Fig.* moving aside with someone to discuss something. (*Typically: **get** ~; **go** ~; **move** ~; **step** ~.) □ *I moved off to the side with the client and explained the offer a little better.*

*off topic not on the topic of discussion; far from the general subject of a discussion; not part of the purpose of a particular communication channel, such as an Internet news group. (*Typically: **be** ~; **get** ~; **get** so ~.) □ *The boys in the back of the room just love to get the teacher off topic.*

off one's **trolley** Go to off one's rocker.

*off (work) AND **off from work; off of work 1.** having left one's work at the end of the day. (*Typically: **be** ~; **get** ~.) □ *What time do you get off from work?* □ *I get off work about five o'clock.* **2.** absent

from one's work with permission. (*Typically: **be** ~; **get** ~.) □ *Sorry, I can't join you. Things are busy at the office, and I can't get off.*

off-color 1. not the exact color (that one wants). □ *The wall was painted off-color. I think it was meant to be orange.* **2.** *Fig.* in bad taste; rude, vulgar, or impolite. □ *That joke you told was off-color and embarrassed me.*

*an offer one **cannot refuse** *Fig.* a very attractive offer. (*Typically: **give** one ~; **make** ~; **make** one ~.) □ *He made me an offer I could not refuse, so I sold him my car.*

off-line *Fig.* not connected to a computer, by direct connection or via the telephone system, etc. (Compare this with on line.) □ *When he's off-line he's sort of lost.*

off-the-cuff *Fig.* spontaneous; without preparation or rehearsal. □ *Her remarks were off-the-cuff, but very sensible.*

off-the-wall *Fig.* odd; silly; unusual. □ *Why are you so off-the-wall today?*

Oh, ye of little faith. *Fig.* You who trust no one. (Jocular; the world *ye* is an old form of *you* used in the Bible, Matthew 8:25.) □ *You thought I wouldn't show up on time? Oh, ye of little faith.*

oil so's **palm** Go to grease so's palm.

oink out Go to blimp out (on sth).

okay by so Go to fine by so.

*old as Methuselah very old. (Of a person; refers to a biblical figure held to have lived to be 969. *Also: **as** ~.) □ *Old Professor Stone is as old as Methuselah but still gets around with a cane.*

*old as the hills very old; ancient. (*Also: **as** ~.) □ *Our family custom of eating black-eyed peas on New Year's Day is old as the hills.*

old battle axe *Fig.* a bossy old woman. □ *She is such an old battle axe. I'll bet she's hell to live with.*

old college try *Fig.* a valiant effort. □ *Walter made the old college try, but that wasn't enough to get the job done.*

old enough to be so's **father** Go to next.

old enough to be so's **mother** AND **old enough to be** so's **father** as old as someone's parents. (Usually a way of saying that a person is too old.) □ *You can't go out with Bill. He's old enough to be your father!*

an **old hand at** doing sth someone who is experienced at doing something. □ *The maid was an old hand at polishing silver.*

old hat *Fig.* old-fashioned; outmoded. □ *Hardly anybody uses typewriters anymore. That's just old hat.*

*the **(old) heave-ho** *Fig.* the act of throwing someone out; the act of firing someone. (From nautical use, where sailors used *heave-ho* to coordinate hard physical labor. One sailor called "Heave," and all the sailors would pull at the same time on the *ho*. *Typically: **get** ~; **give** so ~.) □ *I wanted to complain to the management, but they called a security guard and I got the old heave-ho. That's right. They threw me out!*

the **old one-two** *Fig.* a series of two punches delivered quickly, one after another. □ *Tom gave Bill the old one-two, and the argument was ended right there.*

one's **old stamping ground** *Fig.* the place where one was raised or where one has spent a lot of time. (There are variants with *stomping* and *grounds.*) □ *I can't wait to get back to my old stomping grounds.*

*an **old warhorse** a performance piece that is performed often. (*Typically: **be** ~; **become** ~; **perform** ~; **play** ~.) □ *The symphony orchestra played a few old warhorses and then some ghastly contemporary stuff that will never again see the light of day.*

an **old wives' tale** *Fig.* a myth or superstition. □ *You really don't believe that stuff about starving a cold do you? It's just an old wives' tale.*

the **oldest trick in the book** *Fig.* a well-known and easily discovered deception. □ *He used the oldest trick in the book and disguised his voice in the phone.*

*on so/sth *Fig.* [incriminating or harmful information] about someone or something. (*Typically: **get** sth ~; **find** sth ~; **have** sth ~; **give** so sth ~.) □ *She is trying to get something on her husband so she can divorce him.*

on sth **1.** *Fig.* taking a medication. □ *I am on an antibiotic for my chest cold.* **2.** *Fig.* taking an illegal drug or controlled substance and acting strangely. □ *She acted as if she were on barbiturates or something.*

*on a diet *Fig.* trying to lose weight by eating less food or specific foods. (*Typically: **be** ~; **go** ~; **put** so ~; **stay** ~.) □ *I didn't eat any cake because I'm on a diet.* □ *I have a lot of trouble staying on a diet.*

*on a first-name basis (with so) *Fig.* knowing someone very well; good friends with someone. (*Typically: **be** ~; **get** ~.) □ *I'm on a first-name basis with John.*

*on a fool's errand *Fig.* involved in a useless journey or task. (*Typically: **be** ~; **go** ~.) □ *Bill went for an interview, but he was on a fool's errand. The job had already been filled.*

on a lark Go to for a lark.

on a moment's notice Go to at a moment's notice.

on (a) par (with so/sth**)** *Fig.* equal to someone or something. □ *Your effort is simply not on par with what's expected from you.*

*on a pedestal *Fig.* elevated to a position of honor or reverence. (*Fig.* on the image of honoring someone on display on a pedestal like a statue. *Typically: **be** ~; **place** so ~; **put** so ~.) □ *He puts his wife on a pedestal. She can do no wrong in his opinion.*

*on a power trip *Inf.* exercising power and authority, especially unduly. (*Typically: **be** ~; **be off** ~; **go** ~; **have** ~.) □ *Old Molly is off on a power trip again. She loves ordering everyone about.*

on a roll *Inf.* in the midst of a series of successes. □ *Things are going great for Larry. He's on a roll now.*

on a shoestring *Fig.* with a very small amount of money. □ *We lived on a shoestring for years before I got a good-paying job.*

***on a short leash** *Fig.* under firm control. (Fig. on the image of a dog on a short leash offering its master greater control of the animal and where it wanders.*Typically: **keep** so ~; **have** so ~; **put** so ~.) □ *His wife keeps him on a short leash, so there isn't much opportunity for him to get into trouble.*

***on a silver platter** *Fig.* using a presentation [of something] that is appropriate for a very formal setting. (Usually with a touch of resentment. *Typically: **give** sth **to** so ~; **present** sth ~; **serve** sth ~; **want** sth ~.) □ *Aren't paper plates good enough for you? You want dinner maybe on a silver platter?*

***on a string** *Fig.* under control, as one would control a marionette. (*Typically: **get** so ~; **have** so ~; **keep** so ~.) □ *She keeps him on a string so he won't get involved with other women.*

on a tight leash 1. [of an animal] on a leash, held tightly and close to its owner. □ *I keep my dog on a tight leash so it won't bother people.* **2.** *Fig.* under very careful control. (Fig. on ①.) □ *We can't do much around here. The boss has us all on a tight leash.* **3.** *Sl.* addicted to some drug. □ *Wilbur is on a tight leash. He has to have the stuff regularly.*

***on a wing and a prayer** *Fig.* to arrive or fly in with one's plane in very bad condition. (From a WWII song about an airplane limping home on one engine after a successful bombing run. Sometimes used figuratively of other vehicles. *Typically: **come (in)** ~; **arrive** ~.) □ *Finally we could see the plane through the smoke, coming in on a wing and a prayer.*

on so's **account** *Fig.* because of someone. □ *Don't do it on my account.*

on account of so/sth because of someone or something. □ *I was late on account of my car. It wouldn't start.*

on active duty in battle or ready to go into battle. (Military.) □ *The soldier was on active duty for 10 months.*

on again, off again AND **off again, on again** *Fig.* uncertain; indecisive. □ *Jane doesn't know if she's going to look for a new job. She's off again, on again about it.*

on all fours *Fig.* on one's hands and knees. □ *I dropped a contact lens and spent an hour on all fours looking for it.*

on and off AND **off and on** *Fig.* occasionally; erratically; now and again. □ *I feel better off and on, but I'm not well yet.*

on any account *Fig.* for any purpose; for any reason; no matter what. □ *On any account, I'll be there on time.* □ *This doesn't make sense on any account.*

on approval *Fig.* for examination, with the privilege of return. □ *Sorry, you can't buy this on approval. All sales are final.*

on automatic (pilot) 1. flying on automatic controls. □ *The pilot set the plane on automatic pilot and went to the restroom.* **2.** [of a person] functioning in a semiconscious manner. (Fig. on ①.) □ *I was out late last night, and today I'm on automatic.*

on one's **back** Go to (flat) on one's back.

on so's **back** Go to on so's case.

on bad terms (with so) unfriendly with someone. □ *Those two are on bad terms and won't say a word to each other.*

on balance with all things considered fairly. □ *On balance, we are pleased with the results of our efforts.*

on behalf of so Go to in behalf of so.

on bended knee *Fig.* kneeling, as in supplication. (The verb form is obsolescent and occurs now only in this phrase.) □ *Do you expect me to come to you on bended knee and ask you for forgiveness?*

on one's **best behavior** *Fig.* being as polite as possible. □ *When we went out, the children were on their best behavior.*

on board 1. *Fig.* aboard (on or in) a ship, bus, airplane, etc. □ *Is there a doctor on board? We have a sick passenger.* □ *When everyone is on board, we will leave.* **2.** *Fig.* employed by someone; working with someone. (Fig. on ①.) □ *Our company has a computer specialist on board to advise us about the latest technology.*

on Broadway *Fig.* located in the Broadway theater district in New York City; performed in the Broadway theater district. (Regarded as having the best of American stage productions.) □ *Our musical is the best thing on Broadway!*

on call *Fig.* ready to serve when called. □ *I'm sorry, but I can't go out tonight. I'm on call at the hospital.*

on campus *Fig.* located or being on the grounds of a college or university. □ *Do you live on campus or off campus?*

***on** so's **case** AND ***on** so's **back** *Inf.* harassing someone about a personal problem; annoying someone. (*Typically: **be** ~; **get** ~; **keep** ~.) □ *I'll get on Tom's case about being late so much.* □ *I'm sorry, I won't get on your back anymore.*

on cloud nine *Fig.* very happy. □ *When the check came, I was on cloud nine for days.*

on consignment *Fig.* [of goods] having been placed in a store for sale, with payments made for the goods by the operator of the store only if they are sold. □ *The artist placed his work in a gallery on consignment.*

***on course** *Fig.* following the plan correctly. (Fig. on a ship or plane following the course that was plotted for it. *Typically: **be** ~; **get** ~; **stay** ~.) □ *Is the project on course?*

on credit *Fig.* using credit; buying something using credit. □ *The Smiths buy everything on credit and are very much in debt.*

on cue [performing] exactly when signaled [to do something]. □ *He came on stage on cue.*

on dangerous ground Go to on shaky ground.

on dead center *Fig.* exactly correct. □ *My estimate wasn't on dead center, but it was very close to the final cost.*

on one's **deathbed** *Fig.* while one is in bed and dying. □ *While he lay on his deathbed, he told his lawyer that he wanted to give all his money to charity.*

on deck *Fig.* ready (to do something); ready to be next (at something). (Fig. on sailors being on deck ready for action.) □ *Ann is on deck. She will be the next batter.*

on demand whenever something is wanted. □ *With my new cable television system, I can watch any movie I want on demand.*

on duty *Fig.* at work; currently doing one's work. (The opposite of off duty.) □ *I can't help you now, but I'll be on duty in about an hour.*

***on earth?** AND ***in creation?; *in heaven's name?; *in the world?** *Fig.* really?; indeed? (*Typically: **Who** ~; **What** ~; **When** ~; **Where** ~; **How** ~.) □ *What on earth do you mean?* □ *How in creation do you expect me to do that?* □ *Who in the world do you think you are?*

on easy street *Fig.* in a state of financial independence and comfort. □ *When I get this contract signed, I'll be on easy street.*

on edge 1. on something's own edge. □ *You should store these narrow crates on edge, not lying flat.* **2.** *Fig.* nervous. (As if one were balanced as in ①.) □ *I have really been on edge lately.* □ *Why are you so on edge?*

on everyone's lips Go to next.

on everyone's tongue AND **on everyone's lips** *Fig.* [of something or a name] known to everyone. □ *She is so popular. Her name is on everyone's tongue.*

on one's **feet 1.** *Fig.* standing up. □ *Get on your feet. They are playing the national anthem.* **2.** *Fig.* well and healthy, especially after an illness. (Fig. on ①.) □ *I can help out as soon as I'm back on my feet.*

on fire 1. *Fig.* burning; being burned with flames. □ *Help! My car is on fire!* **2.** *Sl.*

very attractive or sexy. □ *Look at those jet-set people! Each one of them is just on fire.* **3.** *Inf.* doing very well; very enthusiastic. □ *Jill's new book is really on fire. Everyone is buying it.*

on foot *Fig.* [running or walking] using the feet. □ *We go everywhere around the campus on foot.*

***on** so's **good side** Go to on the good side of so.

on good terms (with so**)** friendly with someone; able to interact well and be friends with someone. □ *Bill is on good terms with the people he works with.*

***on** one's **guard** *Fig.* wary or cautious. (*Typically: **be** ~; **keep** ~; **put** one ~; **remain** ~; **stay** ~.) □ *The menacing growl by the watchdog put me on my guard.*

on hand *Fig.* available; in a good supply. □ *I have to get some more eggs. We usually have enough on hand, but we ran out.*

***on** so's **head** *Fig.* [for something negative] belonging only to one person or group. (*Fig.* on the image of guilt or blame "resting" on someone's head. *Typically: **be** ~; **come to rest** ~; **rest** ~.) □ *I don't think that all the criticism should be on my head!*

***on** so's **heels** *Fig.* following someone very closely; following very closely at someone's heels. (*Typically: **hard** ~; **hot** ~; **right** ~.) □ *Here comes Sally, and John is hot on her heels.*

on one's **high horse** *Fig.* in a haughty manner or mood. □ *The boss is on her high horse about the cost of office supplies.*

on hold 1. *Fig.* waiting; temporarily halted. □ *The building project is on hold while we try to find money to complete it.* **2.** *Fig.* left waiting on a telephone line. □ *I waited on hold for 10 minutes when I called city hall.*

on one's **honor** *Fig.* on one's solemn oath; sincerely. □ *He promised on his honor that he'd pay me back next week.*

on horseback *Fig.* on the back of a horse. □ *Because they loved horses, the couple decided to marry on horseback.*

on ice 1. *Fig.* stored or preserved on ice or under refrigeration. □ *I have a lot of root beer on ice for the picnic.* **2.** *Fig.* [action on someone or something] suspended or left hanging. □ *I was on ice for over a month while the matter was being debated.*

on impulse *Fig.* after having had an impulse or sudden thought. □ *I didn't need a cellular telephone. I just bought it on impulse.*

on in years Go to up in years.

***on its feet** *Fig.* organized and functioning; started up and functioning. (*Typically: **get** sth ~; **have** sth ~; **put** sth ~.) □ *Trying to get this company on its feet is harder than I thought.*

on land *Fig.* on the ground; on the land and not at sea or in the air. □ *When I am at sea, I feel more relaxed than when I am on land.*

on so's/sth's **last legs** *Fig.* for someone or something to be almost worn out or finished. □ *This building is on its last legs. It should be torn down.*

on line 1. *Fig.* connected to a computer or network. (Often **online** or **on-line**.) □ *As soon as I get online, I can check the balance of your account.* **2.** Go to in line.

on loan (from so/sth**)** *Fig.* [of possession] temporarily granted by someone or some group. □ *This lovely painting is on loan from the Kimble Museum for the rest of the year.*

on location *Fig.* [of a movie] being filmed in a place distant from the studio. □ *This movie was shot on location in Ontario.*

on medication taking medicine for a current medical problem. □ *I can't drive the car, since I am on medication.*

on one's **mind** *Fig.* occupying one's thoughts; currently being thought about. □ *You've been on my mind all day.* □ *Do you have something on your mind? You look so serious.*

on moral grounds *Fig.* considering reasons of morality. □ *He complained about the television program on moral grounds.*

There was too much ridicule of his religion.

*on so's **nerves** *Fig.* annoying someone. (*Typically: **be** ~; **get** ~.) □ *Our noisy neighbors are beginning to get on my nerves.*

on no account AND **not on any account** *Fig.* for no reason; absolutely not. □ *On no account will I lend you the money.*

on occasion *Fig.* occasionally. □ *On occasion, Mary would walk her dog through the park.*

on order *Fig.* ordered with delivery expected. □ *I don't have the part in stock, but it's on order.*

on one's **own** *Fig.* independently. □ *Our baby can now walk on his own.*

on one's **own hook** *Inf.* all by oneself. □ *I don't need any help. I can do it on my own hook.*

on one's **own time** *Fig.* not while one is at work. □ *The boss made me write the report on my own time. That's not fair.*

on pain of sth *Fig.* on threats of something bad, typically death. □ *They told him on pain of death never to reveal their names.*

on one's **person** *Fig.* [of something] carried with one. □ *Always carry identification on your person.*

on pins and needles *Fig.* anxious; in suspense. □ *I've been on pins and needles all day, waiting for you to call with the news.*

on principle on the basis of rules, laws, or guidelines. □ *The judge is obliged to act on principle. His personal feelings do not matter at all.*

on probation 1. *Fig.* serving a period of probation, typically after conviction for a crime. □ *While Anne was on probation, she reported to the police regularly.* **2.** *Fig.* serving a trial period. (*Fig.* on ①.) □ *All new members are on probation for a year.*

on purpose *Fig.* intentionally; in a way that is meant or intended; not an accident. □ *Jealous, Jimmy destroyed Billy's sand castle on purpose.*

on so's **radar (screen)** *Fig.* being considered and thought about by someone. (*Fig.* on the monitoring done by air traffic controllers.) □ *The whole matter is on my radar screen, and I will have a solution soon.*

on record AND **on the books** *Fig.* recorded for future reference. □ *We had the coldest winter on record last year.*

on sale *Fig.* available for sale at a reduced price. (Always implies a lower than usual sale price.) □ *I bought these pants on sale for half price.*

on so's **say-so** *Fig.* on someone's authority; with someone's permission. □ *I can't do it on your say-so. I'll have to get a written request.*

on schedule *Fig.* at the expected or desired time. □ *The plane came in right on schedule.*

on second thought *Fig.* having given something more thought; having reconsidered something. □ *On second thought, maybe you should sell your house and move into an apartment.*

on shaky ground AND **on dangerous ground** *Fig.* [of an idea or proposal] on an unstable or questionable foundation; [of an idea or proposal] founded on a risky premise. □ *When you suggest that we are to blame, you are on shaky ground. There is no evidence that we are at fault.*

on short notice AND **at short notice** *Fig.* quickly and without a timely notification of other people; with very little lead time. □ *She called the meeting on such short notice that we had no time to prepare.*

*on so's **shoulders** *Fig.* on someone's own self. (*Typically: **be** ~; **carry** sth ~; **fall** ~; **have** sth ~; **leave** sth ~; **put** sth ~.) □ *Why should all the responsibility fall on my shoulders?* □ *She carries a tremendous amount of responsibility on her shoulders.*

on sight whenever seen; at the moment of seeing [someone]. □ *The sheriff ordered that the murderer be shot on sight.*

on speaking terms (with so**)** *Fig.* on friendly terms with someone. (Often with the negative.) □ *I'm not on speak-*

ing terms with Mary. We had a serious disagreement.

on spec 1. using money risked in the hope of profit; on speculation. □ *He lives by buying and selling houses on spec.* **2.** as specified; right on specifications. □ *It's important to make sure the design is on spec, or the customer will not pay.*

on standby *Fig.* waiting for one's turn, especially describing the status of travelers who wait for a soon-to-depart train, plane, or bus, hoping that a seat will become available. □ *The passenger waited on standby for an available seat.*

on so's tail *Inf.* following someone closely. (See also on so's heels.) □ *Keep on her tail and don't let her out of your sight.*

on tap 1. *Fig.* having to do with beer served from a barrel or keg. □ *Do you have any imported beers on tap here?* **2.** *Fig.* immediately available. (Fig. on ①.) □ *I have just the kind of person you're talking about on tap.*

on the air *Fig.* broadcasting (a radio or television program). □ *The radio station came back on the air shortly after the storm.*

on the alert (for so/sth) *Fig.* watchful and attentive for someone or something. □ *You should be on the alert when you cross the street in heavy traffic.*

on the attack *Fig.* in the process of attacking; acting aggressive or malicious. □ *Watch out, Bob's on the attack and in a bad mood.*

on (the) average *Fig.* generally; usually. □ *On the average, you can expect about a 10 percent failure rate.* □ *This report looks okay, on average.*

***on the back burner** *Fig.* [of something] on hold or suspended temporarily. (Fig. on the image of putting a pot that needs less active attention on a back burner of a stove, leaving space for pots that need to be stirred. Compare this with **on the front burner**. *Typically:* **be** ~; **put** sth ~.) □ *The building project is on the back burner for now.*

on the bad side of so Go to on the wrong side of so.

on the ball *Inf.* knowledgeable; competent; attentive. (See also have sth on the ball.) □ *This guy is really on the ball.*

***on the bandwagon** *Fig.* on the popular side (of an issue); taking a popular position. (*Typically:* **be** ~; **climb** ~; **get** ~; **hop** ~; **jump** ~.) □ *Jane has always had her own ideas about things. She's not the kind of person to jump on the bandwagon.*

on the beam *Fig.* exactly right; thinking along the correct lines. (Fig. on the image of a plane following a radio beacon.) □ *That's the right idea. Now you're on the beam!*

on the bench 1. *Fig.* [of a judge] directing a session of court. □ *I have to go to court tomorrow. Who's on the bench?* **2.** *Fig.* sitting, waiting for a chance to play in a game. (In sports, such as basketball, football, soccer, etc.) □ *Bill is on the bench now. I hope he gets to play.*

on the bias *Fig.* on a diagonal line; on a diagonal pathway or direction. □ *The panels of the dress were cut on the bias.*

on the bird *Inf.* available on satellite television. □ *There is a whole lot of good stuff on the bird, but you need a receiving dish to get it.*

on the bleeding edge Go to on the cutting edge.

on the blink Go to on the fritz.

on the block 1. *Fig.* on a city or suburban block. □ *John is the biggest kid on the block.* **2.** *Fig.* on sale at auction; on the auction block. □ *We couldn't afford to keep up the house, so it was put on the block to pay the taxes.*

on the books Go to on record.

on the borderline *Fig.* in an uncertain position between two statuses; undecided. □ *Bill was on the borderline between an A and a B in biology.*

on the bottom rung (of the ladder) Go to at the bottom of the ladder.

on the bright side *Fig.* [ignoring the bad for a moment] considering the positive aspects of a situation. (See also look on the bright side.) □ *On the bright side, the car you wrecked was covered by insurance.*

on the brink (of doing sth**) AND on the threshold (of** doing sth**)** *Fig.* on the verge of doing something; almost to the point of doing something; at the beginning point of doing something. (Being on the threshold is more momentous than being on the brink.) □ *I was on the brink of selling my car to make ends meet when the tax refund came in the mail.*

on the button *Inf.* exactly right; in exactly the right place; at exactly the right time. □ *That's it! You're right on the button.*

on the cheap cheaply. □ *I like to do my vacations on the cheap. Spending too much money doesn't help me relax.*

on the contrary *Fig.* exactly the opposite. (Very close in meaning to to the contrary, but used adverbially.) □ *She's not in a bad mood. On the contrary, she's as happy as a lark.*

on the cusp (of sth**)** *Fig.* at the point in time that marks the beginning of something. □ *The transistor was on the cusp of a new age in electronics.*

on the cutting edge AND on the bleeding edge; on the leading edge *Inf.* [for someone] to be trendy and very up-to-date; [for something] to be of the latest design; having the most advanced technology; knowing about the most advanced technology. (*Bleeding* is a play on *cutting*.) □ *This gadget is brand new. It's really on the bleeding edge.* □ *Tom is on the leading edge when it comes to optical storage technology.*

*on the defensive *Fig.* weary and ready to defend oneself. (*Typically: **be** ~; **find** oneself ~; **go** ~.) □ *John goes on the defensive when his athletic ability is questioned.* □ *The child was on the defensive when questioned about cheating.*

on the dole *Fig.* receiving welfare money. □ *I spent six months on the dole, and believe me, it's no picnic.*

*on the dot *Fig.* at exactly the right time. (*Typically: **be** some place ~; **arrive (**some

place**)** ~; **get** some place ~; **see** so ~; **show up** ~.) □ *I'll be there at noon on the dot.* □ *I expect to see you here at eight o'clock on the dot.*

on the double *Fig.* very fast; twice as fast as normal. (Originally military. Refers to "double time" in marching.) □ *Get over here right now—on the double!*

*on the edge *Fig.* very anxious and about to become distraught; on the verge of becoming irrational. (See also on edge. *Typically: **be** ~; **live** ~.) □ *After the horrible events of the last week, we are all on the edge.*

on the edge of one's **chair** Go to next.

*on the edge of one's **seat AND *on the edge of** one's **chair** *Fig.* [of a member of an audience] closely following the action and excitement of a performance. (*Typically: **be** ~; **sit** ~.) □ *We sat on the edge of our seats during the entire play.*

on the eve of sth *Fig.* just before something, possibly the evening before something. □ *John decided to leave school on the eve of his graduation.*

on the face of it *Fig.* superficially; from the way it looks. □ *This looks like a serious problem on the face of it. It probably is minor, however.*

on the face of the earth Go to on the surface of the earth.

on the fast track *Fig.* following an expedited procedure; being acted upon sooner or more quickly than is typical. □ *Let's put this project on the fast track, and maybe we'll see results sooner.*

*on the fence (about sth**)** *Fig.* undecided about something. (*Typically: **be** ~; **sit** ~.) □ *Ann is on the fence about going to Mexico.*

do sth **on the fly** *Fig.* to do something while one is moving; to do something (to something that is in motion). (This has nothing to do with actual flight.) □ *We can't stop the machine to oil it now. You'll have to do it on the fly.*

on the fence (about something)

on the fly *Inf.* [done] while something or someone is operating or moving. □ *I'll try to capture the data on the fly.*

on the fringe 1. *Fig.* at the outer boundary or edge of something. □ *He doesn't live in the city, just on the fringe.* **2.** *Fig.* at the extremes of something, typically political thought. □ *He is way out. His political ideas are really on the fringe.*

on the fritz AND **on the blink** *Inf.* not operating; not operating correctly. □ *This vacuum cleaner is on the fritz. Let's get it fixed.* □ *How long has it been on the blink?*

*on the front burner *Fig.* receiving particular attention or consideration. (Compare this with on the back burner. *Typically: **be** ~; **leave** sth ~; **put** sth ~.) □ *So, what's on the front burner for us this week?* □ *Move this project to the front burner so it will get some attention.*

on the go *Fig.* busy; moving about busily. □ *I'm usually on the go all day long.*

*on the good side of SO AND ***on SO's good side** *Fig.* in someone's favor. (*Typically: **be** ~; **get** ~.) □ *I tried to get on the good side of the teacher, but that teacher has no good side.*

*on the heels of sth AND ***on sth's heels** *Fig.* soon after something. (*Typically, as is or: **close** ~; **hard** ~; **hot** ~.) □ *There was a rainstorm on the heels of the windstorm.* □ *The team held a victory celebration on the heels of their winning season.*

on the horizon 1. visible where the sky meets the land or sea. □ *There are storm clouds on the horizon.* □ *Is that a ship on the horizon?* **2.** *Fig.* soon to happen. (Fig. on ①. As if what is on the horizon is heading toward one.) □ *There is some excitement on the horizon, but I can't tell you about it.*

on the horns of a dilemma *Fig.* having to decide between two things, people, etc. □ *Mary found herself on the horns of a dilemma. She didn't know which to choose.*

on the hot seat AND **in the hot seat** *Fig.* in a difficult position; subject to much attention or criticism. □ *Now that John is* on the hot seat, no one is paying any attention to what I do.

on the hour *Fig.* at each hour on the hour mark. □ *I have to take this medicine every hour on the hour.*

on the house *Fig.* [of something] given away free by a merchant. □ *I went to a restaurant last night. I was the ten thousandth customer, so my dinner was on the house.*

on the job *Fig.* working; doing what one is expected to do. □ *I can depend on my furnace to be on the job day and night.*

on the lam *Inf.* running from the police. (Underworld.) □ *The gang leader broke out of prison and is still on the lam.*

on the leading edge Go to on the cutting edge.

on the level Go to (strictly) on the level.

on the line Go to on the (tele)phone.

on the lookout (for so/sth**)** *Fig.* watchful for someone or something. □ *I'm on the lookout for John, who is due here any minute.*

on the loose *Fig.* running around free. □ *Look out! There is a bear on the loose from the zoo.*

on the make 1. *Fig.* building or developing; being made. □ *That was a very good sales strategy, John. You're a real-estate agent on the make.* **2.** *Inf.* making sexual advances; seeking sexual activities. □ *It seems like Bill is always on the make.*

on the mark *Fig.* right on the measurement point; showing just the right amount. □ *It's exactly one quart, right on the mark.*

*on the market *Fig.* openly available for sale. (*Typically: **be** ~; **get** sth ~; **put** sth ~.) □ *We put our house on the market last year, and it still hasn't sold.*

on the mend *Fig.* getting better; becoming healthy again. □ *I took a leave of absence from work while I was on the mend.*

on the money AND **on the nose** *Fig.* exactly right; in exactly the right place; in exactly the right amount (of money). □

This project is going to be finished right on the nose.

on the move 1. *Fig.* moving from place to place. □ *Are the cattle on the move now, or are they still grazing?* **2.** progressing; advancing. □ *Finally the market has turned around now and is really on the move.*

on the nose Go to on the money.

on the off-chance *Fig.* because of a slight possibility that something may happen or might be the case; just in case. □ *I went to the theater on the off-chance that there were tickets for the show left.*

on (the) one hand *Fig.* from one point of view; as one side (of an issue). □ *On one hand, I really ought to support my team. On the other hand, I don't have to time to attend all the games.*

on the other hand *Fig.* a phrase introducing an alternate view. □ *Mary: I like this one. On the other hand, this is nice too. Sue: Why not get both?*

on the other side of the coin *Fig.* from the opposite point of view; [looking at an event] from someone else's point of view. □ *I really want that parcel of property, but on the other side of the coin, Sarah Travelian needs the land to farm.*

on the outs (with so**)** *Inf.* in a mild dispute with someone; sharing ill will with someone. □ *Tom has been on the outs with Bill before. They'll work it out.*

on the part of so Go to in behalf of so.

on the pill *Inf.* taking birth control pills. □ *Is it true that Mary is on the pill?*

on the point of doing sth AND **at the point of** doing sth *Fig.* ready to start doing something. □ *I was just on the point of going out the door.* □ *We were almost at the point of buying a new car.*

on the prowl *Inf.* looking for someone for sexual purposes. (*Fig.* on a prowling cat.) □ *Tom looks like he is on the prowl again tonight.*

on the QT *Fig.* quietly; secretly. (An abbreviation of *quiet.*) □ *The company pres-*

ident was making payments to his wife on the QT.

on the rag 1. *Sl.* menstruating. □ *Kim's on the rag and in a bad mood.* **2.** *Sl.* ill-tempered. □ *Bill is on the rag and making trouble for everyone.*

on the receiving end (of sth**)** to receive punishment, criticism, rebuke, abuse, etc., such as one might give out to someone else. □ *So you don't like to be yelled at either? How does it feel to be on the receiving end?*

on the right track 1. *Fig.* following the right track or trail; riding on the correct track, as with a train. □ *The train was on the right track when it left the station. I can't imagine how it got lost.* **2.** *Fig.* following the right set of assumptions. (Fig. on ①.) □ *You are on the right track to find the answer.*

on the rise *Fig.* increasing in frequency or intensity. □ *The number of auto thefts in Cook County is on the rise again.*

on the road *Fig.* traveling from place to place, not necessarily on the highways; working away from one's home or office. □ *I was on the road with the circus for six months.*

on the road to sth *Fig.* in the process of reaching a different state, such as recovery, ruin, good health, bankruptcy, etc. □ *It's been two weeks since her surgery, and she is on the road to recovery.*

on the rocks 1. *Fig.* [of an alcoholic drink] served with ice cubes. □ *I'd like mine on the rocks, please.* **2.** [of a ship] broken and marooned on rocks in the sea. □ *The ship crashed and was on the rocks until the next high tide.* **3.** *Fig.* in a state of ruin or bankruptcy. (Fig. on ②.) □ *That bank is on the rocks. Don't put your money in it.*

on the run 1. *Fig.* while one is moving from place to place. □ *I will try to pick up some aspirin today on the run.* **2.** *Fig.* running from the police. □ *The gang of crooks is on the run.*

*on the safe side *Fig.* taking the risk-free path. (*Typically: **(just) to be** ~; **stay** ~; **keep** ~; **remain** ~.) □ *I think you*

should stay on the safe side and call the doctor about this fever.

on the same wavelength *Fig.* thinking in the same pattern. (Fig. on tuning into a broadcast signal.) □ *We kept talking until we got on the same wavelength.*

on the sauce *Inf.* drinking regularly; intoxicated. □ *Poor old Ron is on the sauce again.*

on the scene *Fig.* available or present where something is happening or where something has happened. □ *The ambulance was on the scene almost immediately.*

on the shelf 1. *Fig.* not active socially; left to oneself in social matters. (Fig. on the image of something being left or stored on a shelf.) □ *I've been on the shelf long enough. I'm going to make some friends.* **2.** *Fig.* postponed. □ *We'll have to put this matter on the shelf for a while.*

on the side 1. *Fig.* extra, such as with a job or an additional order of food. □ *I would like an order of eggs with toast on the side, please.* □ *She is a bank teller and works as a waitress on the side.* **2.** *Inf.* in addition to one's spouse. □ *She has boyfriends on the side, but her husband knows about them.*

on the sidelines *Fig.* waiting inactively to participate; waiting in reserve. (Fig. on reserve beside the game court or field, waiting to play.) □ *I stayed on the sidelines while Sol gave the presentation.*

on the skids *Sl.* on the decline. □ *Her health is really on the skids, but she stays cheery anyway.*

on the sly *Fig.* secretly and deceptively. □ *She was stealing little bits of money on the sly.*

do sth **on the sly** *Fig.* to do something slyly or sneakily. □ *She was supposed to be losing weight, but she was snacking on the sly.*

*on the spot 1. *Fig.* at exactly the right place; at exactly the right time. (*Typically: **be** ~.) □ *It's noon, and I'm glad you're all here on the spot. Now we can begin.* **2.** *Fig.* in trouble; in a difficult situation. (*Typically: **be** ~; **put** so ~.) □

There is a problem in the department I manage, and I'm really on the spot.

on the spur of the moment *Fig.* suddenly; spontaneously. □ *We decided to go on the spur of the moment.*

***on the stick** *Inf.* organized and busy. (*Typically: **be** ~; **get** ~.) □ *Get on the stick and get this job done!*

on the street 1. *Fig.* widely known. □ *Sue put it on the street, and now everyone knows.* **2.** *Fig.* on Wall Street or elsewhere in the New York City financial districts. (Similar to ③, except that it refers to a specific street. Usually with a capital *S.*) □ *I heard on the Street today that bank stocks are headed up.* **3.** *Fig.* at discount prices; as available at its lowest retail price. (As if some item were being sold on the street by a peddler.) □ *It lists at $2,200 and can be got for about $1,650 on the street.*

on the strength of sth *Fig.* because of the support of something, such as a promise or evidence; due to something. □ *On the strength of your comment, I decided to give John another chance.*

on the stump AND **out stumping (**some place**)** *Fig.* [of a politician] traveling around visiting people and giving political speeches. □ *The president is out stumping the country while important matters pile up on his desk.*

on the surface of the earth AND **on the face of the earth** *Fig.* everywhere; anywhere. □ *That is certainly the ugliest dog on the face of the earth!*

on the table *Fig.* subject to discussion by the group; submitted as a point of discussion. □ *The chairman said we could not discuss salaries, since the topic was no longer on the table.*

on the take *Inf.* taking bribes. (Underworld.) □ *They say that everyone in city hall is on the take.*

***on the (tele)phone** AND **on the line** *Fig.* speaking on the telephone. (*Typically: **be** ~; **get** ~.) □ *She's on the phone but won't be long.*

on the threshold (of doing sth**)** Go to on the brink (of doing sth).

on the throne 1. *Fig.* [of royalty] currently reigning. □ *King Samuel was on the throne for two decades.* **2.** *Sl.* seated on the toilet. □ *I can't come to the phone. I'm on the throne.*

***on the tip of** one's **tongue** *Fig.* [of a thought or idea] about to be said or almost remembered. (*Typically: **be** ~; **have** sth ~.) □ *I have his name right on the tip of my tongue. I'll think of it in a second.*

on the track of so/sth Go to next.

***on the trail of** so/sth AND ***on the track of** so/sth seeking someone or something; about to find someone or something. (*Typically: **be** ~; **get** ~.) □ *I'm on the trail of a new can opener that is supposed to be easier to use.*

on the up-and-up Go to (strictly) on the up-and-up.

on the verge of doing sth AND **on the verge of** sth *Fig.* at the very beginning of doing something; just about to do something. □ *Bill was on the verge of leaving town when he found a job.*

on the wagon *Fig.* not drinking alcohol. □ *Bob's old drinking buddies complained that he was no fun when he went on the wagon.*

on the wait list Go to next.

on the waiting list AND **on the wait list** *Fig.* [for someone's name to be] on a list of people waiting for an opportunity to do something. □ *There is no room for you, but we can put your name on the waiting list.*

on the wane *Fig.* becoming less; fading away. □ *Her influence is on the wane, but she is still the boss.*

on the warpath *Inf.* very angry. □ *I am on the warpath about setting goals and standards again.*

on the watch for so/sth *Fig.* alert and watching for someone or something. □ *I'm always on the watch for Ann. I want to know when she's around.*

on the whole *Fig.* generally; considering everything. □ *Your work—on the whole—is quite good.*

on the wing *Fig.* while flying; while in flight. (Usually refers to birds, fowl, etc., not people or planes.) □ *There is nothing as pretty as a bird on the wing.*

on the (witness) stand *Fig.* [of a witness] giving testimony in court, seated in place in view of the court. □ *I was on the witness stand, answering questions, when the judge declared a recess.*

*on the wrong side of so AND ***on the bad side of** so; ***on** so's **wrong side; *on** so's **bad side** *Fig.* out of favor with someone. (*Typically: **be** ~; **get** ~.) □ *I do what I can not to get on the wrong side of people.*

on the wrong side of the law *Fig.* in the criminal culture; not abiding by the law; having to do with breaking the law and being a lawbreaker. □ *Spike has spent most his life on the wrong side of the law.*

on the wrong track *Fig.* going the wrong way; following the wrong set of assumptions. □ *They won't get it figured out, because they are on the wrong track.*

on thin ice *Fig.* in a risky situation. □ *If you don't want to find yourself on thin ice, you must be sure of your facts.*

on time *Fig.* before the deadline; by the stated time. □ *My taxes were not done on time, so I had to pay a penalty.*

on tiptoe *Fig.* standing or walking on the front part of the feet (the balls of the feet) with no weight put on the heels. (This is done to gain height or to walk quietly.) □ *I came in late and walked on tiptoe so I wouldn't wake anybody up.*

*on one's **toes** *Fig.* alert. (*Typically: **be** ~; **keep** ~; **keep** one ~; **stay** ~.) □ *You have to be on your toes if you want to be in this business.*

on top of sth **1.** *Fig.* up-to-date on something; knowing about the current state of something. □ *This issue is constantly changing. She has to pay attention to it to stay on top of things.* **2.** *Fig.* in addition to something. □ *Jane told Bill he was dull.*

On top of that, she said he was unfriendly. □ *On top of the first problem, we learned that our plane was hours late.*

on tour *Fig.* going from place to place, performing. □ *Our play went on tour across the state.* □ *We were on tour all summer.*

*on track *Fig.* on schedule; progressing as planned. (*Typically: **be** ~; **get** so/sth ~; **have** so/sth ~; **keep** so/sth ~; **put** so/sth ~; **set** so/sth ~.) □ *Try to keep these procedures on track this time.* □ *Please get this discussion on track. Time is limited.*

on trial 1. *Fig.* [of someone] in a legal case before a judge. □ *I am not on trial. Don't treat me like that!* **2.** *Fig.* being tested; being examined or experimented with. (Fig. on ①.) □ *The new strain of wheat is on trial in Kansas at the present time.*

on one's **uppers** destitute; very poor. (Usually figurative. The *uppers* mentioned here are the upper parts of a shoe or boot. The idea is that the sole of the shoe or boot is worn through and the destitute person is walking on the inner lining of the footwear. It may also refer to the part of the footwear that covers the foot, but it is hard to see how one could walk on the tops of one's shoes. This *uppers* is definitely not one's upper teeth, however.) □ *Can you loan me a few bucks? I'm really on my uppers.*

on vacation *Fig.* away, taking time off work; on holiday. □ *I'll be away on vacation for three weeks.*

on view *Fig.* visible; on public display. □ *The painting will be on view at the museum.*

on so's **watch** *Inf.* while someone is on duty; while someone is supposed to be in charge of a situation. □ *I am not responsible since it didn't happen on my watch.*

*on one's **way ((to)** some place**)** leaving one place for another; en route to a place. (*Typically: **be** ~; **get** ~.) □ *I will be there soon. I'm on my way there now.*

on your mark, get set, go AND **ready, set, go** *Fig.* [in preparing to start a race involving speed] move to the starting point, get set to move, go. □ *Runners on your mark, get set, go.*

once again AND **once more** again. □ *It is once again time to clean the garage.*

once and for all *Fig.* finally; permanently. □ *Sue: I'm going to get this place organized once and for all! Alice: That'll be the day!*

once in a blue moon *Cliché* very seldom. (There are two alleged origins of the expression. First, and older, it is the third full moon in a season that has four full moons by a quirk of the calendar. A season is three months long and normally contains three full moons. The second definition is that a blue moon is the second moon in a calendar month that has two full moons. These occurrences are rare, every two to three years apart. All of this simply reinvites the basic question: "Why *blue*?" For this there is no ready answer, except that vast amounts of smoke or ash in the air may make the moon to appear blue. Huge forest fires and volcanic eruptions may make this happen. There is no clear origin.) □ *Jill: Does your husband ever bring you flowers? Ellen: Once in a blue moon.*

once more Go to once again.

once upon a time *Cliché* once in the past. (A formula used to begin a fairy tale. Also used informally.) □ *Once upon a time, there were three bears.* □ *Once upon a time, I had a puppy of my own.*

once-in-a-lifetime chance AND **once-in-a-lifetime opportunity** *Fig.* a chance that will never occur again in one's lifetime. □ *She offered me a once-in-a-lifetime opportunity, but I turned it down.*

once-in-a-lifetime opportunity Go to previous.

*the **once-over** *Fig.* a quick, visual examination. (*Typically: **get** ~; **give** so ~.) □ *Every time John walks by I get the once-over. Does he like me?*

once-over-lightly 1. *Fig.* a quick and careless treatment. (A noun. Said of an act of cleaning, studying, examination, or appraisal.) □ *Bill gave his geometry the once-over-lightly and then quit studying.*

2. *Fig.* cursory; in a quick and careless manner. (An adverb.) □ *Ann washed the dishes once-over-lightly.*

one and all *Fig.* everyone. □ *"Good morning to one and all," said Jane as she walked through the outer office.*

the **one and only** the famous and talented (person). (Used in theatrical introductions.) □ *And now—the one and only—Jane Smith!*

one and the same *Cliché* the very same person or thing. (A common misunderstanding of this is *one (i)n the same.*) □ *John Jones and J. Jones are one and the same.* □ *Men's socks and men's stockings are almost one and the same.*

one at a time Go to next.

one by one AND **one at a time** the first one, then the next one, then the next one, etc.; each in turn. □ *I have to deal with problems one by one. I can't handle them all at once.* □ *Okay, just take things one at a time.*

one day at a time treating a day as an isolated unit separated from other days. □ *The illness is quite severe. We will have to watch it one day at a time, hoping each day will lead to another.*

one false move Go to a false move.

one final thing Go to next.

one final word AND **one final thing** *Fig.* a phrase introducing a parting comment or the last item in a list. □ *John: One final word—keep your chin up. Mary: Good advice!* □ *And one final thing, don't haul around a lot of expensive camera stuff. It just tells the thieves who to rob.*

one for the (record) books *Fig.* a record-breaking or very remarkable act. □ *What a dive! That's one for the record books.* □ *I've never heard such a funny joke. That's really one for the books.*

*one for the road** *Inf.* a drink; a drink before a journey or before leaving a bar. (*Typically: **down** ~; **have** ~; **take** ~.) □ *Don't down one for the road if you are going to be the driver.*

one heck of a so/sth Go to a hell of a so/sth.

one hell of a so/sth Go to a hell of a so/sth.

one in a hundred Go to one in a thousand.

one in a million Go to next.

one in a thousand AND **one in a hundred; one in a million** *Fig.* nearly unique; one of a very few. □ *He's a great guy. He's one in million.*

*****one jump ahead (of** so/sth) AND *****one move ahead (of** so/sth) *Fig.* one step in advance of someone or something. (*Typically: **be** ~; **keep** ~; **stay** ~.) □ *Try to stay one jump ahead of the competition.* □ *If you're one move ahead, you're well prepared to deal with problems. Then, nothing is a surprise.*

one little bit *Fig.* any at all; at all. □ *Jean could not be persuaded to change her mind one little bit.*

one move ahead (of so/sth) Go to one jump ahead (of so/sth).

one of a kind a unique thing; the only one there is; in a class with only one member. □ *This vase is one of a kind. There is not another like it in the entire world.*

one of these days *Fig.* someday; in some situation like this one. □ *One of these days, someone is going to steal your purse if you don't take better care of it.*

one sandwich short of a picnic *Inf.* not very smart; lacking intelligence. (Jocular.) □ *Poor Bob just isn't too bright. He's one sandwich short of a picnic.*

*****one step ahead of** so/sth *Fig.* slightly in advance of someone or something. (*Typically: **be** ~; **keep** ~; **stay** ~.) □ *Al kept one step ahead of Detective Rogers.*

one step at a time Go to step by step.

the **one that got away** *Fig.* the big fish that got away, especially as the subject of a fisherman's story. □ *The one that got away is always bigger than the one that got caught.*

one thing after another one event or problem following something similar, multiple times. □ *What a day. Problems right from the minute I walked in the door. It was just one thing after another all day long.*

One thing leads to another. One event sets things up for another event, and so on. (As an explanation of how little things lead to big problems.) □ *I kept spending more and more money until I was broke. You know how one thing leads to another.*

one to a customer *Fig.* each person can have or receive only one. (As in sales restrictions where each customer is permitted to buy only one.) □ *"Only one to a customer!" said the chef as he handed out the hamburgers.*

one too many *Euph.* one drink of liquor too many, implying drunkenness. □ *I think I've had one too many. It's time to stop drinking.*

*****one up (on** so) *Fig.* ahead of someone; having an advantage over someone. (*Typically: **be** ~; **get** ~.) □ *Tom is one up on Sally because he got a job and she didn't.*

one way or another AND **one way or the other** *Fig.* somehow. □ *John: I think we're lost. Alice: Don't worry. We'll get there one way or another.*

one-horse town *Fig.* a very small town; a small and backward town. □ *I refuse to spend a whole week in that one-horse town!*

one-man show 1. *Fig.* a performance put on by one person. □ *It was a one-man show, but it was very entertaining.* □ *For a one-man show, it was very long.* **2.** *Fig.* an exhibition of the artistic works of one person. □ *She is having a one-man show at the Northside Gallery.*

one-night stand 1. *Fig.* a performance lasting only one night. □ *The band did a series of one-night stands down the East Coast.* **2.** *Fig.* a romance or sexual relationship that lasts only one night. (Fig. on ①.) □ *It looked like something that would last longer than a one-night stand.*

one-track mind *Fig.* a mind that thinks entirely or almost entirely about one subject. □ *Bob has a one-track mind. He can only talk about football.*

(only) a matter of time only in a limited amount of time. □ *It's only a matter of time before this old car stops running.*

the **only game in town** *Fig.* the only choice there is. □ *You have to rent a posthole digger from them. They're the only game in town.*

only have eyes for so *Fig.* [to be] loyal to only one person, in the context of romance. (From the title of a still-popular song written in 1933.) □ *Don't waste any time on Tom. He only has eyes for Ann.*

the **only way to go** *Fig.* the best way to do something; the best choice to make. □ *Get a four-wheel-drive car. It's the only way to go.*

*onto so/sth *Fig.* alerted to or aware of a deceitful plan or person. (*Typically: **be** ~; **get** ~; **catch** ~.) □ *Richard thought he was safe, but the fuzz was onto him from the beginning.*

*onto sth *Fig.* having found something useful or promising; on the verge of discovering something. (*Typically: **be** ~; **get** ~.) □ *I think we are really onto something this time.*

*onto a good thing *Fig.* having found something useful, promising, or profitable. (*Typically: **be** ~; **get** ~.) □ *This is a great scheme. I know I'm onto a good thing.*

ooze (out) (from so/sth**)** AND **ooze out (of** so/sth**)** to seep out of someone or something. □ *The heavy oil oozed out from the hole in the barrel.*

ooze with sth *Fig.* [for someone] to exude an ingratiating or insincere manner. □ *The used-car salesman oozed with insincerity.*

open a can of worms Go to a can of worms.

open a conversation to start a conversation. (See also strike up a conversation.) □ *I tried to open a conversation with him, but he had nothing to say.*

open and aboveboard Go to honest and aboveboard.

an **open book** *Fig.* [of someone or something] easy to understand. □ *Jane's an open book. I always know what she is going to do next.*

open so's **eyes to** so/sth *Fig.* to cause someone, including oneself, to become aware of someone or something. □ *We finally opened our eyes to what was going on around us.*

open fire (on so**)** *Fig.* to start (doing something, such as asking questions or criticizing). □ *When the reporters opened fire, the mayor was smiling, but not for long.*

open for business *Fig.* [of a shop, store, restaurant, etc.] operating and ready to do business. □ *The construction will be finished in March, and we will be open for business in April.*

open one's **heart to** so/sth **1.** *Fig.* to tell all of one's private thoughts to someone. □ *She opened her heart to the wrong magazine, and it published a scandalous story.* **2.** *Fig.* to become loving and solicitous toward someone; to donate money generously to someone or some cause. □ *We opened our hearts to Fred, who was soliciting for a good cause.*

*an open mind *Fig.* a mind or attitude that is open to new ideas and opinions. (*Typically: **get** ~; **have** ~; **keep** ~.) □ *Please try to be nice and keep an open mind. It's all not as bad as you think.*

open Pandora's box *Fig.* to uncover a lot of unsuspected problems. □ *When I asked Jane about her problems, I didn't know I had opened Pandora's box.*

open season (on so**)** *Fig.* a period of time when everyone is criticizing someone. (Fig. on open season (on some creature).) □ *At the news conference, it was open season on the mayor.*

open season (on some creature**)** a time of unrestricted hunting of a particular game animal. □ *It's always open season on rabbits around here.*

an **open secret** something that is supposed to be known only by a few people but is known in fact to a great many people. □

It's an open secret that Max is looking for a new job.

open some doors (for so) AND **open a few doors (for so)** *Fig.* to gain access to opportunity or influence (for someone). □ *Morris was able to open a few doors for Mary and get her an interview with the president.*

open the door to so to make a move or change easier for a person. □ *Ann opened the door to Fred, who wanted to start a new career in writing.*

open the door to sth *Fig.* to invite something to happen. □ *The armistice opened the door to peace talks.*

open the floodgates 1. [on a dam] to open special gates to allow water to quickly leave the lake behind a dam in case of a severe storm, thus preventing water from washing over the dam. □ *They decided to open the floodgates as soon as the rains started. A great deal of rainfall had been predicted.* **2.** *Fig.* to allow or cause the flow or movements of something. □ *Your decision to extend the warranties of all the cars that we have already sold will open the floodgates to a lot of claims for normal wear and tear.* **3.** *Fig.* to begin to cry and produce many tears. □ *Oh goodness. She must have a pain in her tummy. She has really opened the floodgates.*

open to sth Go to **(wide) open to sth**.

open to criticism *Fig.* vulnerable to criticism. □ *Anything the president does is open to criticism.*

open oneself to criticism *Fig.* to do something that makes one vulnerable to criticism. □ *By saying something so stupid in public, you really opened yourself to criticism.*

open to dispute disputable; questionable; [of a question] unsettled. □ *Whether the land is yours or mine is open to dispute.*

open to question *Fig.* [an action or opinion] inviting question, examination, or refutation. □ *Everything he told you is open to question, and you should look into it.*

open up 1. open your door; open your mouth. (Usually **Open up!**) □ *Open up! This is the police.* **2.** *Fig.* to become available. □ *Let me know if any other opportunities open up.* **3.** to become clear, uncluttered, or open. □ *As we drove along, the forest opened up, and we entered into a grassy plain.*

open so up† *Fig.* to perform a surgical operation requiring a major incision on someone. □ *The doctor had to open George up to find out what was wrong.*

open sth up† **1.** *Fig.* to begin examining or discussing something. □ *Now is the time to open up the question of taxes.* **2.** *Fig.* to reveal the possibilities of something; to reveal an opportunity. □ *Your letter opened new possibilities up.* **3.** *Fig.* to start the use of something, such as land, a building, a business, etc.; to make something available. □ *They opened the coastal lands up to resort development.* **4.** *Fig.* to make a vehicle go as fast as possible. (As in opening up the throttle.) □ *We took the new car out on the highway and opened it up.* **5.** to make something less congested. □ *They opened the yard up by cutting out a lot of old shrubbery.*

open up (about so/sth) (with so) AND **open up (on so/sth) (with so)** *Fig.* to speak freely about someone or something; to speak a great deal about someone or something. □ *He opened up with us about the accident.*

open (up) one's kimono *Sl.* to reveal what one is planning. (From the computer industry, referring especially to the involvement of the Japanese in this field.) □ *Even if Tom appears to open up his kimono on this deal, don't put much stock in what he says.*

open up (on so/sth/animal) *Fig.* to fire a gun or other weapon at someone, something, or an animal. □ *The sergeant told the soldiers to open up on the enemy position.*

open up (to so) AND **open up (with so)** *Fig.* to tell [everything] to someone; to confess to someone. □ *If she would only open up to me, perhaps I could help her.*

open up to sth *Fig.* to become more accepting of someone or something. □ *Finally, he opened up to the suggestion that he should leave.*

open with so/sth *Fig.* to begin a season, session, series, or performance with someone or something. □ *The conference will open with a series of invited speakers.*

an **open-and-shut case** *Fig.* a simple and straightforward situation without complications. (Often said of criminal cases where the evidence is convincing.) □ *The murder trial was an open-and-shut case. The defendant was caught with the murder weapon.*

opening gambit *Fig.* an opening movement, tactic, or statement that is made to secure a position that is to one's advantage. □ *The prosecution's opening gambit was to call a witness who linked the defendant to the scene of the crime.*

operate on sth **1.** to work on something; to work with the insides of something. (As a surgeon might operate.) □ *He tried to operate on his watch and ruined it.* **2.** to function or conduct business on a certain principle or assumption. □ *This company has always operated on the theory that the customer is always right.*

operating at cross purposes Go to working at cross purposes.

the **opposite sex** the other sex; [from the point of view of a female] males; [from the point of view of a male] females. (Also with *member of,* as in the example.) □ *Bill is very shy when he's introduced to a member of the opposite sex.*

opt for sth *Fig.* to choose a particular option. □ *I opt for not going out at all.*

opt in favor of so/sth *Fig.* to choose a particular person; to choose a particular thing. □ *Do you think she will opt in favor of this one or that?*

opt in(to sth) *Fig.* to choose to join in. □ *She opted in almost immediately.*

opt out (of sth) *Fig.* to choose not to be in something. □ *If you do that, I'm going to have to opt out of the club.*

or else *Fig.* or there will be negative effects; or you will be punished. □ *You had better do what I tell you or else.*

or words to that effect *Fig.* or similar words meaning the same thing. □ *Sally: She said that I wasn't doing my job well, or words to that effect. Jane: Well, you ought to find out exactly what she means. Sally: I'm afraid I know.*

ordain so **(as)** sth *Fig.* to establish someone as something. (Fig. on the image of ordaining a priest or equivalent.) □ *Was he duly ordained as a Mercedes mechanic?*

order some food **to go** Go to to go.

the **order of the day** something necessary or usual at a certain time. □ *Going to bed early was the order of the day when we were young.*

order so **off the field** *Fig.* [for a game official] to command a player to leave the playing area. □ *The referee will order you off the field.*

the **other place** *Euph.* hell. □ *If you're good, you'll go to heaven, and if you're bad, you'll go to the other place.*

the **other side of the tracks** AND the **wrong side of the tracks; the wrong side of town** *Fig.* the poor part of a town or city. □ *You don't want to buy a house in that neighborhood. It's on the wrong side of the tracks.*

other than so/sth not including someone or something; except someone or something. □ *You can have any flavor other than chocolate. We're out of it.* □ *Anyone other than you can sign as a witness.*

other things being equal AND **all things being equal** *Cliché* if things stay the way they are now; if there are no complications from other factors. □ *Other things being equal, we should have no trouble getting your order to you on time.*

the **other way (a)round** the reverse; the opposite. □ *No, it won't fit that way. Try it the other way round.* □ *It doesn't make any sense like that. It belongs the other way around.*

Our house is your house. Go to My house is your house.

*an **out** *Fig.* an excuse; means of avoiding something. (*Typically: **have** ~; **give** so ~.) □ *He's very clever. No matter what happens, he always has an out.*

out sth *Fig.* lacking something; having lost or wasted something. □ *I'm out ten bucks because of your miscalculation!*

*out and about** *Fig.* outside the house; outdoors. (*Typically: **be** ~; **get** ~.) □ *As soon as I feel better, I'll be able to get out and about.*

out cold AND **out like a light 1.** *Fig.* unconscious. □ *I fell and hit my head. I was out cold for about a minute.* □ *Tom fainted! He's out like a light!* **2.** *Inf.* intoxicated. □ *Four beers and he was out cold.*

out for blood *Inf.* aggressively seeking to harm or get revenge; angry and looking for the cause of one's distress. □ *The opposite team is out for blood, but we have a good defense.*

out from under (so/sth**)** no longer under the control of someone or something. □ *Happily, I am out from under the watchful eye of my landlady, and I can do as I wish.*

out front leading, as in a race. □ *My horse was out front by two lengths until the final turn.*

out (in bloom) Go to next.

*out (in blossom)** AND *out (in bloom)** [of a plant or tree] blooming; [of flowers] open in blooms. (*Typically: **be** ~; **come** ~.) □ *All the trees were out.* □ *The daffodils won't be out until next week.*

out in droves Go to out in large numbers.

*out in force** *Fig.* appearing in great numbers. (*Typically: **be** ~; **come** ~; **go** ~.) □ *What a night! The mosquitoes are out in force.* □ *The police went out in force over the holiday weekend.*

*out in large numbers** AND *out in droves** *Fig.* in evidence in some large amount. (*Typically: **be** ~; **come** ~.) □ *The sidewalk salesmen are out in droves today.* □ *The ants were out in large numbers at the picnic.*

out in left field *Fig.* offbeat; unusual and eccentric. □ *What a strange idea. It's really out in left field.*

*out in the cold 1.** outdoors where it is cold. (*Typically: **be** ~; **keep** so/animal ~; **leave** so/animal ~; **put** so/animal ~.) □ *Open the door! Let me in! Don't keep me out in the cold!* **2.** *Fig.* not informed about what is happening or has happened. (Fig. on ①. *Typically: **be** ~; **keep** so ~; **leave** so ~.) □ *Please don't leave me out in the cold. Share the news with me!* **3.** *Fig.* excluded. (Fig. on ①. *Typically: **be** ~; **keep** so ~; **leave** so ~.) □ *There was a party last night, but my friends left me out in the cold.*

*out in the open 1.** visibly and not concealed. (*Typically: **be** ~; **bring** sth ~; **get** ~; **get** sth ~.) □ *We got a glimpse of the tiger when it was out in the open.* **2.** *Fig.* [for something] to be public knowledge. (Fig. on ①. *Typically: **be** ~; **bring** sth ~; **get** ~; **get** sth ~.) □ *Let's get this in the open and discuss it.*

out like a light Go to out cold.

*out (of** sth**) 1.** gone; having left some place; absent from a place; escaped. (*Typically: **be** ~; **get** ~.) □ *Sam is out of the building at present.* **2.** *Fig.* having no more of something. (*Typically: **be** ~; **run** ~.) □ *We ran out of ketchup and mustard halfway through the picnic.* **3.** *Fig.* free of the responsibility of doing something. (Fig. on ①. *Typically: **get** ~.) □ *Are you trying to get out of this job?*

out of action *Fig.* not operating temporarily; not functioning normally. □ *The pitcher was out of action for a month because of an injury.*

*out of (all) proportion** *Fig.* of exaggerated importance; of an unrealistic importance or size compared to something else. (*Typically: **be** ~; **blow** sth ~; **grow** ~.) □ *Yes, this figure is way out of proportion to the others in the painting.*

*out of bounds 1.** outside the boundaries of the playing area. (*Typically: **be** ~; **get** ~; **go** ~.) □ *The ball went out of bounds just at the end of the game.* **2.** AND *off limits** *Fig.* forbidden. (*Typically:

be ~.) □ *That kind of behavior is off limits. Stop it!*

out of breath AND ***out of wind*** *Fig.* breathing fast and hard; gasping for breath. (*Typically: **be** ~; **get** ~.) □ *Mary gets out of wind when she climbs stairs.*

out of character 1. *Fig.* unlike one's usual behavior. □ *Ann's remark was quite out of character.* **2.** *Fig.* inappropriate for the character that an actor is playing. □ *Bill played the part so well that it was hard for him to get out of character after the performance.*

out of circulation 1. *Fig.* no longer available for use or lending. (Usually said of library materials, certain kinds of currency, etc.) □ *I'm sorry, but the book you want is temporarily out of circulation.* **2.** *Fig.* not interacting socially with other people. (Fig. on ①.) □ *I don't know what's happening, because I've been out of circulation for a while.*

out of so's **class** Go to out of so's **league.**

out of commission *Fig.* broken, unserviceable, or inoperable; not currently in use. □ *My watch is out of commission and needs a new battery.*

out of condition Go to out of shape.

out of consideration (for so/sth**)** with consideration for someone or something; with kind regard for someone or something. □ *They let me do it out of consideration. It was very thoughtful of them.*

out of context *Fig.* [of an utterance or the report of an action] removed from the surrounding context of the event, thereby misrepresenting the intent of the utterance or report. (*Typically: **be** ~; **lift** sth ~; **quote** so/sth ~; **take** sth ~.) □ *You deliberately took her remarks out of context! You're the dishonest person, not her!*

out of control AND ***out of hand*** *Fig.* acting wildly or violently. (*Typically: **be** ~; **get** ~.) □ *Watch out, that dog is out of control.*

out of courtesy (to so**)** in order to be polite to someone; out of consideration for someone. □ *We invited Mary's brother out of courtesy to her.*

out of debt *Fig.* no longer owing a debt. (*Typically: **be** ~; **get** ~; **get** oneself ~.) □ *I've taken a second job so I can get myself out of debt.*

out of one's **depth** Go to beyond one's **depth.**

out of earshot *Fig.* too far from the source of a sound to hear the sound. □ *Mary waited until her children were out of earshot before mentioning the presents she got them.*

out of one's ***element*** *Fig.* not in a natural or comfortable situation. (*Typically: **be** ~; **get** ~.) □ *When it comes to computers, I'm out of my element.*

out of fashion Go to out of style.

out of favor (with so**)** *Fig.* no longer desirable or preferred by someone. (*Typically: **be** ~; **go** ~.) □ *I can't ask John to help. I'm out of favor with him.*

out of focus *Fig.* blurred or fuzzy; seen indistinctly. (*Typically: **be** ~; **get** ~; **go** ~.) □ *What I saw through the binoculars was sort of out of focus.*

out of gas 1. *Lit.* without gasoline (in a car, truck, etc.). (*Typically: **be** ~; **run** ~.) □ *We can't go any farther. We're out of gas.* **2.** *Fig.* tired; exhausted; worn out. (Fig. on ①. *Typically: **be** ~; **run** ~.) □ *I think the old washing machine has finally run out of gas. I'll have to get a new one.*

out of hand Go to out of control.

out of so's ***hands 1.*** no longer in someone's grasp. (*Typically: **get** ~; **pull** sth ~; **take** sth ~.) □ *The police officer took the gun out of Fred's hands.* **2.** *Fig.* no longer in someone's control. (Fig. on ①. *Typically: **get** ~; **pull** sth ~; **take** sth ~.) □ *The contract had to be gotten out of Alice's hands because she announced that she was leaving.*

out of harm's way *Fig.* not liable to be harmed; away from any causes of harm. (*Typically: **be** ~; **get** ~; **get** so ~.) □ *We should try to get all the civilians out of harm's way.*

out of one's **head** Go to out of one's mind.

out of hock 1. *Inf.* [of something] bought back from a pawn shop. □ *When I get my watch out of hock, I will always be on time.* **2.** *Inf.* out of debt; having one's debts paid. □ *When I pay off my credit cards, I'll be out of hock for the first time in years.*

out of it 1. Go to out to lunch. **2.** *Inf.* intoxicated. □ *Two drinks and she was totally out of it.*

out of keeping (with sth**)** *Fig.* [of something said or some behavior] failing to fit in with something. □ *This kind of thing is completely out of keeping with our standards of behavior.*

***out of kilter** AND ***off kilter 1.** *Fig.* out of balance; crooked or tilted. (*Typically: **be** ~; **get** ~; **knock** sth ~.) □ *John, your tie is sort of off kilter. Let me fix it.* **2.** *Fig.* malfunctioning; on the fritz. (*Typically: **be** ~; **go** ~.) □ *My furnace is out of kilter. I have to call someone to fix it.*

out of so's **league** AND **out of** so's **class** *Fig.* better than one's own category [of something]. □ *Those guys are out of my league. I'll never be able to sculpt that well.*

out of left field *Inf.* suddenly; from an unexpected source or direction. □ *Most of your ideas are out of left field.*

out of line (with sth**) 1.** *Fig.* beyond certain set or assumed limits. □ *Your bid on this project is completely out of line with our expectations.* □ *The cost of this meal is out of line with what other restaurants charge.* **2.** *Fig.* [of something said or behavior] improper. □ *I'm afraid that your behavior was quite out of line. I do not wish to speak further about this matter.*

out of luck *Fig.* without good luck; having bad fortune. □ *If you wanted some ice cream, you're out of luck.*

***out of** one's **mind** AND ***out of** one's **head;** ***out of** one's **senses** *Fig.* to be silly and senseless; to be crazy and irrational. (*Typically: **be** ~; **go** ~.) □ *Why did you do that? You must be out of your mind!*

out of necessity *Fig.* because of necessity; due to need. □ *I bought this hat out of ne-*

cessity. I needed one, and this was all there was.

***out of nowhere** AND ***from nowhere** *Fig.* appearing suddenly, without warning. (*Typically: **appear** ~; **come** ~; **materialize** ~.) □ *Suddenly, a truck came out of nowhere.*

out of order 1. [of something or things] out of the proper sequence. □ *All these cards were alphabetized, and now they're out of order.* **2.** *Fig.* [of something] incapable of operating; [of something] broken. □ *The elevator is out of order again.* **3.** *Fig.* not following correct parliamentary procedure. □ *Anne inquired, "Isn't a motion to table the question out of order at this time?"*

***out of patience** annoyed and impatient after being patient for a while. (*Typically: **be** ~; **run** ~.) □ *I finally ran out of patience and lost my temper.*

***out of place 1.** *Fig.* inappropriate. (*Typically: **be** ~; **seem** ~.) □ *That kind of behavior is out of place at a party.* **2.** *Fig.* awkward and unwelcome. (*Typically: **be** ~; **feel** ~; **seem** ~.) □ *I feel out of place at formal dances.*

***out of practice** *Fig.* performing poorly due to a lack of practice. (*Typically: **be** ~; **get** ~; **go** ~.) □ *I used to be able to play the piano extremely well, but now I'm out of practice.*

out of print *Fig.* [for a book] to be no longer available from the publisher. □ *The book you want just went out of print, but perhaps I can find a used copy for you.*

out of reach *Fig.* unattainable. □ *I wanted to be president, but I'm afraid that such a goal is out of reach.*

out of season 1. *Fig.* not now available for sale. □ *Sorry, oysters are out of season. We don't have any.* **2.** *Fig.* not now legally able to be hunted or caught. □ *I caught a trout out of season and had to pay a fine.*

out of one's **senses** Go to out of one's mind.

out of service *Fig.* inoperable; not currently operating. □ *Both elevators had been put out of service, so I had to use the stairs.*

out of shape AND **out of condition** *Fig.* not in good physical condition. □ *I get out of breath when I run because I'm out of shape.*

*out of one's **shell** *Fig.* to make a person become more open and friendly. (Fig. on the image of a shy turtle being coaxed to put its head out of its shell. *Typically: **bring** one ~; **come** ~; **get** one ~.) □ *We tried to bring Greg out of his shell, but he is very shy.* □ *He's quiet, and it's hard to get him out of his shell.*

*out of sight 1. not visible; too far away to be seen. (*Typically: **be** ~; **get** ~; **go** ~; **keep** ~; **stay** ~.) □ *The cat kept out of sight until the mouse came out.* **2.** *Inf.* figuratively stunning, unbelievable, or awesome. (Older. *Typically: **be** ~; **get** ~.) □ *Wow, this music is out of sight!* **3.** *Inf.* very expensive; high in price; [of a price] so high that it cannot "be seen" in the distance. (*Typically: **be** ~; **get** ~; **go** ~.) □ *The cost of medical care has gone out of sight.* **4.** *Sl.* heavily intoxicated. (*Typically: **be** ~.) □ *They've been drinking since noon, and they're out of sight.*

*out of one's **skull** *Sl.* intoxicated. (*Typically: **be** ~; **go** ~.) □ *Oh, man, I drank till I was out of my skull.*

*out of sorts *Fig.* not feeling well; grumpy and irritable. (*Typically: **be** ~; **feel** ~; **get** ~.) □ *I've been out of sorts for a day or two. I think I'm coming down with something.*

out of spite *Fig.* with the desire to harm someone or something. □ *Jane told some evil gossip about Bill out of spite.*

*out of step (with so/sth**) 1.** AND ***out of time (with** so/sth**)** *Fig.* out of cadence with someone else. (*Typically: **be** ~; **dance** ~; **get** ~; **march** ~.) □ *You've gotten out of step with the music.* **2.** not as up-to-date as someone or something. (*Typically: **be** ~; **get** ~.) □ *Billy missed three days and now is out of step with the rest of the class.*

out of stock *Fig.* not immediately available in a store; [for goods] to be temporarily unavailable. □ *Those items are out of stock, but a new supply will be delivered on Thursday.*

*out of style AND ***out of fashion** *Fig.* not fashionable; old-fashioned; obsolete. (See also go out. *Typically: **be** ~; **go** ~.) □ *John's clothes are really out of style.* □ *He doesn't care if his clothes go out of fashion.*

*out of sync *Inf.* uncoordinated; unsynchronized. (An abbreviation for *synchronization.* *Typically: **be** ~; **get** ~.) □ *Our efforts are out of sync.*

out of the ballpark *Fig.* greater than the amount of money suggested or available. □ *Your estimate is completely out of the ballpark. Just forget it.*

*out of the closet 1. *Fig.* revealing that one is homosexual. (*Typically: **be** ~; **come** ~; **bring** so ~.) □ *Tom surprised his parents when he came out of the closet.* **2.** *Fig.* revealing one's secret interests. (*Typically: **be** ~; **come** ~; **get** ~.) □ *It's time that all of you lovers of chamber music came out of the closet and attended our concerts.*

out of the corner of one's **eye** *Fig.* [seeing something] at a glance; glimpsing something, as with peripheral vision. □ *I only saw the accident out of the corner of my eye. I don't know who is at fault.*

*out of the frying pan (and) into the fire AND ***from the frying pan (and) into the fire** *Fig.* from a bad situation to a worse situation. (*Typically: **get** ~; **go** ~; **jump** ~.) □ *When I tried to argue about my fine for a traffic violation, the judge charged me with contempt of court. I really went out of the frying pan into the fire.*

*out of the goodness of one's **heart** *Fig.* simply because one is kind. (*Typically: **be** ~; **do** sth ~.) □ *What are you going to pay me? You don't expect me to do this out of the goodness of my heart, do you?*

out of the hole *Fig.* out of debt. □ *I can't seem to get out of the hole. I keep spending more money than I earn.*

out of the loop AND **not in the loop** *Fig.* not in a group of people who communicate regularly about a plan or project. □ *I'm out of the loop, so I never hear what's going on.*

out of the ordinary *Fig.* unusual. □ *It was a good meal, but not out of the ordinary.*

out of the picture *Fig.* no longer relevant to a situation; departed; dead. □ *Now that Tom is out of the picture, we needn't concern ourselves about his objections.*

out of the public eye *Fig.* not visible or conspicuous. □ *The mayor tends to keep out of the public eye unless she's running for office.*

out of the question *Fig.* not allowed; not permitted. □ *You can't go to Florida this spring. We can't afford it. It's out of the question.*

out of the red *Fig.* out of debt; into profitability. □ *If we can cut down on expenses, we can get out of the red fairly soon.*

out of the running *Fig.* no longer being considered; eliminated from a contest. □ *After the first part of the diving meet, three members of our team were out of the running.*

out of the swim of things *Fig.* not in the middle of activity; not involved in things. □ *I've been out of the swim of things for a few weeks. Please bring me up-to-date.*

*out of the way 1. AND ***out of** so's **way; *out of the road** not blocking or impeding the way. (*Typically: **get** ~; **get** so/sth ~; **move** so/sth ~.) □ *Would you please get your foot out of the way?* **2.** AND ***out of** one's **way** *Fig.* not along the way; not included in the proposed route. (*Typically: **be** ~.) □ *I'm sorry, but I can't give you a ride home. It's out of my way.* **3.** *Fig.* completed; finished. (*Typically: **be** ~; **get** sth ~; **have** sth ~.) □ *I'll be happy to have all this medical stuff out of the way.*

out of the woods *Fig.* past a critical phase; out of the unknown. □ *When the patient got out of the woods, everyone relaxed.*

*out of the woodwork *Fig.* out into the open from other places or a place of concealment. (*Typically: **bring** so/sth ~; **come** ~; **creep** ~.) □ *When the cake appeared, all the office people suddenly came out of the woodwork.*

out of thin air *Fig.* out of nowhere; out of nothing. □ *Suddenly—out of thin air—the messenger appeared.*

out of this world *Fig.* wonderful and exciting. □ *This pie is out of this world.*

out of time (with so/sth**)** Go to **out of step (with** so/sth**)**.

out of touch (with so/sth**)** *Fig.* knowing no news of someone or something; not in touch (with so); not keeping informed of the developments relating to someone or something. □ *I've been out of touch with my brother for many years.*

out of town *Fig.* temporarily not in one's own town. □ *I'll go out of town next week. I'm going to be at a conference.*

*out of tune (with so/sth**) 1.** not in musical harmony with someone or something. (*Typically: **be** ~; **get** ~.) □ *The oboe is out of tune with the flute.* **2.** *Fig.* not in agreement with someone or something. (Fig. on ①. *Typically: **be** ~.) □ *Your proposal is out of tune with my ideas of what we should be doing.*

out of turn *Fig.* not at the proper time; not in the proper or expected order. □ *We were permitted to be served out of turn because we had to leave early.*

*out of w(h)ack 1. *Inf.* crazy, silly, or irrational. (*Typically: **be** ~.) □ *Why do you always act as if you're out of whack?* **2.** *Fig.* out of adjustment; to be out of order. (*Typically: **be** ~; **get** ~.) □ *I'm afraid that my watch is out of whack.*

out of wind Go to **out of breath**.

out of work *Fig.* unemployed; having lost one's job. □ *Todd was out of work for almost a year.*

*out on a limb *Fig.* in a dangerous position to do something; at risk. (*Typically: **be** ~; **go** ~; **put** so ~.) □ *I don't want to go out on a limb, but I think we can afford to do it.*

out on bail *Fig.* out of jail after a court appearance and pending trial because bail bond money has been paid. (The money will be forfeited if the person who is out on bail does not appear for trial at the proper time.) □ *The robber committed another crime while out on bail.*

(out) on parole *Fig.* out of prison, conditionally, before one's total sentence is served. □ *Bob was caught using drugs while out on parole and was sent back to prison.*

(out) on patrol *Fig.* away from a central location, watching over a distant or assigned area. (Said especially of police and soldiers.) □ *The soldiers who are on patrol on this snowy night must be very cold.*

out on strike *Fig.* to be away from one's job in a strike or protest. □ *The workers went out on strike.*

out on the town *Fig.* celebrating at one or more places in a town. □ *We went out on the town to celebrate our wedding anniversary.*

out stumping (some place**)** Go to on the stump.

out the window *Inf.* gone; wasted. □ *All that work gone out the window because my computer crashed.*

out to (a meal**)** to be away, eating a meal. □ *Fred went out to dinner for the evening.*

out to get so *Fig.* intending to harm someone in particular. □ *I know they are out to get me! They hate me!*

out to lunch AND **out of it** *Inf.* not alert; giddy; uninformed. □ *Bill is really out of it. Why can't he pay attention?*

out West *Fig.* in the western part of the United States. □ *We lived out West for nearly 10 years.*

out-and-out sth *Fig.* a complete or absolute something; an indisputable something. (The *something* must always be a specific thing.) □ *If he really said that, he told you an out-and-out lie!*

outguess so *Fig.* to guess what someone else might do; to predict what someone might do. □ *I can't outguess Bill. I just have to wait and see what happens.*

out-of-date old-fashioned; out of style; obsolete. □ *Isn't that suit sort of out-of-date?*

out-of-pocket expenses *Fig.* the actual amount of money spent. (Refers to the money one person pays while doing something on someone else's behalf. One is usually paid back this money.) □ *My employer usually reimburses all out-of-pocket expenses for a business trip.*

outside of so/sth *Fig.* except for someone or something; besides someone or something. □ *Outside of some new shoes, I don't need any new clothing.*

outside the box 1. *Fig.* as if not bound by old, nonfunctional, or limiting structures, rules, or practices. (An adverb. Compare this with inside the box.) □ *Nothing can be done outside the box in such a rigid intellectual environment.* **2.** not bound by old, nonfunctional, or limiting structures, rules, or practices. (Usually **outside-the-box**. An adjective.) □ *You have some really outside-the-box ideas, Ralph.*

***over a barrel** *Fig.* out of one's control; in a dilemma. (*Typically: **get** so ~; **have** so ~; **put** so ~.) □ *He got me over a barrel, and I had to do what he said.*

over and above sth *Fig.* more than something; in addition to something. □ *I'll need another $20 over and above the amount you have already given me.*

***over (and done) with** *Fig.* finished. (*Typically: **be** ~; **get** sth ~; **have** sth ~.) □ *Now that I have college over and done with, I can get a job.*

Over and out. *Fig.* I am finished talking. (From two-way radio communications.) □ *That's all. Good day. Over and out.*

over and over (again) repeatedly. □ *He kept saying "I'm sorry," over and over again.*

over easy *Fig.* [of eggs] turned carefully during cooking. □ *I want mine cooked over easy.*

***over** so's **head 1.** *Fig.* [of the intellectual content of something] too difficult for someone to understand. (*Typically: **be** ~; **go** ~; **pass** ~.) □ *I hope my lecture*

outside the box

didn't go over the students' heads. **2.** AND ***over** SO; ***above** SO *Fig.* to an authority higher than someone. (*Typically: **be** ~; **go** ~.) □ *I don't want to have to go over your head, but I will if necessary.*

Over my dead body! *Inf.* a defiant phrase indicating the strength of one's opposition to something. (A joking response is "That can be arranged.") □ *Bill: I think I'll rent out our spare bedroom. Sue: Over my dead body! Bill (smiling): That can be arranged.*

over the counter *Fig.* [of medication bought or sold] without a prescription. (Hyphenated when prenominal. See also under the counter.) □ *I don't put much trust in over-the-counter medications.*

over the edge *Fig.* excessive; out of control. □ *His performance was over the edge. Too long, too dirty, and too loud!*

*over the hill 1. *Inf.* escaped from prison or the military. (*Typically: **be** ~; **go** ~.) □ *They broke out of jail and went over the hill.* **2.** *Fig.* too old (for something).

(*Typically: **be** ~; **go** ~.) □ *You're only 50! You're not over the hill yet.*

over the hump *Fig.* over the hard part; past the midpoint. □ *Things should be easy from now on. We finally got over the hump.*

over the long haul AND **in the long haul; for the long haul; for the long term; over the long term; in the long run** *Fig.* over a long period of time. □ *Over the long haul, this model will prove best.*

over the moon *Fig.* delighted; amazingly happy. □ *When I got the news, I was just over the moon!*

over the short haul AND **in the short haul; for the short haul; for the short term; in the short run** *Fig.* for the immediate future. □ *Over the short haul, you may wish you had done something different. But things will work out all right.*

over the top 1. *Fig.* having gained more than one's goal. □ *Our fund-raising campaign went over the top by $3,000.* **2.** *Inf.* outrageously overdone. □ *The comedy* *sketch was so over the top that most of the audience was embarrassed.*

*over the wall *Fig. Inf.* reaching freedom from a prison. (*Typically: **be** ~; **go** ~.) □ *Spike tried to go over the wall, but they caught him.*

over with Go to all over.

overplay one's **hand** *Fig.* to risk more than one can afford to risk; to be extravagant in making promises or claims. □ *I'm not surprised that he demanded such a high raise and got fired. He always tends to overplay his hand.*

overstep one's **bounds** AND **overstep the bounds of good taste** *Fig.* to behave as one should not; to fail to observe some kinds of social constraint. □ *I think he was overstepping his bounds a bit when he inquired as to the state of Bob's health.*

overstep the bounds of good taste Go to previous.

owe so **a debt of gratitude** *Fig.* a large amount of thanks owed to someone who deserves gratitude. (Actually payment of the debt is owed.) □ *We owe you a debt of gratitude for all you have done for us.*

owe it to oneself **(to** do sth) to have an obligation to do something to benefit only oneself. □ *I owe it to myself to go back and get my masters degree.*

owe it to so **(to** do sth) are obliged to someone to do something. □ *I feel obliged to Mary to drive her around, since I dented her car and sent it to the shop.*

owe sth **(to** so) **(for** sth) to be under obligation to pay or repay someone for something. □ *I owe $40 to Ann for the dinner.*

own flesh and blood Go to flesh and blood.

own up (to sth) to admit something; to confess to something. □ *I know you broke the window. Come on and own up to it.*

*one's own worst enemy *Fig.* consistently causing oneself to fail; more harmful to oneself than other people are. (*Typically: **be** ~; **become** ~.) □ *Ellen: My boss is my enemy. He never says anything good about me. Jane: Ellen, you're your own worst enemy. If you did your job responsibly, your boss would be nicer.*

P

pace back and forth AND **pace up and down** to walk over and over the same short route nervously or anxiously. □ *The leopard paced back and forth in its cage.* □ *I paced up and down, worrying about a variety of things.*

pace sth **off**† to mark off a distance by counting the number of even strides taken while walking. □ *The farmer paced a few yards off and pounded a stake into the soil.*

pace sth **out**† to measure a distance by counting the number of even strides taken while walking. □ *He paced the distance out and wrote it down.*

pace up and down Go to pace back and forth.

pack a group *Fig.* to fill a group, such as a jury, an appeals court, a committee, etc. with dependable supporters. □ *The defense counsel attempted to pack the jury with people who were sympathetic to the plaintiff.*

pack a punch Go to next.

pack a wallop AND **pack a punch** *Fig.* to provide a burst of energy, power, or excitement. □ *Wow, this spicy food really packs a wallop.*

pack so/sth **(in**†**) like sardines** *Fig.* to squeeze in as many people or things as possible. (From the way that many sardines are packed into a can.) □ *The bus was full. The passengers were packed like sardines.*

pack it in 1. *Fig.* to quit trying to do something; to give up trying something and quit. (More U.K. than U.S.) □ *I was so distressed that I almost packed it in.* **2.** *Fig.*

to go to bed. (More U.K. than U.S.) □ *Good night. It's time for me to pack it in.*

a **pack of lies** a series of lies. □ *The thief told a pack of lies to cover up the crime.* □ *John listened to Bill's pack of lies about the fight and became very angry.*

pack them in AND **reel them in** *Fig.* to draw a lot of people. □ *The circus manager knew he could pack them in if he advertised the lion tamer.*

a **package deal** *Fig.* a collection or group of related goods or services sold as a unit. □ *I got all these tools in a package deal for only $39.95.*

pad the bill *Fig.* to put unnecessary or additional items on a bill to make the total cost higher. □ *The plumber had padded the bill with things we didn't need.*

paddle one's **own canoe** *Fig.* to do something by oneself; to be alone. □ *Sally isn't with us. She's off paddling her own canoe.*

a **pain in the ass** AND a **pain in the butt;** a **pain in the rear** *Inf.* a very annoying thing or person. (An elaboration of *pain*. *Rear* is euphemistic.) □ *That guy is a real pain in the ass.* □ *Things like that give me a pain in the butt.*

a **pain in the butt** Go to previous.

a **pain in the neck** *Inf.* a bother; an annoyance. □ *This assignment is a pain in the neck.*

a **pain in the rear** Go to a pain in the ass.

paint so **into a corner** Go to back so into a corner.

paint the town (red) *Sl.* to go out and celebrate; to go on a drinking bout; to get drunk. □ *I feel like celebrating my promotion. Let's go out and paint the town.*

paint so **with the same brush** AND **tar** so **with the same brush** *Fig.* to "smear" the same blame onto someone [as was smeared onto some other person]. □ *The principal blamed my friends for the broken window and then tarred me with the same brush, and I wasn't even at school that day!*

pal around (with so**)** to associate with someone as a good friend. □ *I like to pal around with my friends on the weekends.*

pal up (with so**)** to join with someone as a friend. □ *I palled up with Henry, and we had a fine time together during the entire week of summer camp.*

pale around the gills AND **blue around the gills; green around the gills** *Fig.* looking sick. (The *around* can be replaced with *about*.) □ *John is looking a little pale around the gills. What's wrong?*

*****pale as a ghost** AND *****pale as death** very pale. (*Also: **as** ~.) □ *Laura came into the room, as pale as a ghost. "What happened?" her friends gasped.*

pale as death Go to previous.

pale at sth to become weak, frightened, or pale from fear of something or the thought of something. □ *Bob paled at the thought of having to drive all the way back to get the forgotten suitcase.*

pale beside so/sth *Fig.* to appear to be weak or unimportant when compared to someone or something. □ *My meager effort at sketching pales beside your masterpiece.*

pale by comparison AND **pale in comparison** *Fig.* to appear to be deficient in comparison to something else. □ *My work pales by comparison with yours. You are a real pro.*

palm so/sth **off**† **(on** so**) (as** so/sth**)** AND **pass** so/sth **off**† **(on** so**) (as** so/sth**); pawn** so/sth **off**† **(on** so**) (as** so/sth**)** *Fig.* to give someone or something undesirable to a person as a gift that appears to be desirable. (As if the gift had been concealed in one's palm until it was gotten rid of.) □ *Are you trying to palm that annoying client off on me as a hot prospect?* □ *Please don't pass*

that problem off on me as a challenge. □ *Don't pass it off on me!* □ *Don't pawn it off on me as something of value.*

pan out Go to work out.

pant for sth **1.** to breathe fast and hard in need of something, such as oxygen, fresh air, etc. □ *The dog was panting for air.* **2.** AND **pant for** so/sth *Fig.* to desire or long for someone or something. (Fig. on ①.) □ *My heart is panting for you!*

paper over sth *Fig.* to conceal something; to cover something up. □ *Don't try to paper over the mess you have made.*

*****a **paper trail** *Fig.* a series of records that is possible to examine to find out the sequence of things that happen. (*Typically: **have** ~; **leave** ~; **make** ~.) □ *The legal department requires all these forms so that there is a paper trail of all activity.*

par for the course *Fig.* typical; about what one could expect. (This refers to golf courses, not school courses.) □ *So he went off and left you? Well that's about par for the course. He's no friend.*

a **paradise (on earth)** *Fig.* a place on earth that is as lovely as paradise. □ *The retirement home was simply a paradise on earth.*

paradise on earth Go to heaven on earth.

parcel sth **out**† Go to deal sth out†.

Pardon me for living! *Inf.* a very indignant response to a criticism or rebuke. □ *Fred: Oh, I thought you had already taken yourself out of here! Sue: Well, pardon me for living!*

Pardon my French. AND **Excuse my French.** *Inf.* Excuse my use of swear words or taboo words. (Does not refer to real French.) □ *Pardon my French, but this is a hell of a day.* □ *What he needs is a kick in the ass, if you'll excuse my French.*

park it (some place**)** *Inf.* sit down somewhere; sit down and get out of the way. □ *Richard, park it over there in the corner. Stop pacing around. You make me nervous.*

parlay sth **into** sth *Fig.* to exploit an asset in such a way as to increase its value to some higher amount. □ *Alice parlayed her inheritance into a small fortune by investing in the stock market.*

part and parcel Go to bag and baggage.

part company (with so) *Fig.* to leave someone; to depart from someone. □ *They parted company, and Tom got in his car and drove away.*

part so's **hair** *Fig.* to come very close to someone. (Usually an exaggeration.) □ *That plane flew so low that it nearly parted my hair.*

***partial to** so/sth favoring or preferring someone or something. (*Typically: **be** ~; **get** ~.) □ *The boys think their teacher is partial to female students.*

partially sighted *Euph.* not able to see well. □ *Carrie is partially sighted, but she is not able to see well enough to read.*

the **particulars of** sth specific details about something. □ *My boss stressed the important particulars of the project.*

a **parting of the ways** AND the **parting of the ways** a point at which people separate and go their own ways. (Often with *come to a, arrive at a, reach a,* etc.) □ *Jane and Bob finally came to a parting of the ways.*

partners in crime persons who cooperate in some legal task. □ *The legal department and payroll are partners in crime as far as the average worker is concerned.*

the **party line** *Fig.* the official ideas and attitudes that are adopted by the leaders of a particular group and that the other members are expected to accept. □ *Tom has left the club. He refused to follow the party line.*

The **party's over.** *Fig.* A happy or fortunate time has come to an end. □ *The staff hardly worked at all under the old management, but they'll find the party's over now.*

a **party to** sth a participant in something; someone who is involved in something. □ *I refuse to be a party to your dishonest plan!*

pass sth **along**† **(to** so) to relay some information to someone. □ *I hope you don't pass this along to anyone, but I am taking a new job next month.*

pass away AND **pass on** *Euph.* to die. □ *My aunt passed away last month.* □ *When I pass on, I won't care about how nice the funeral is.*

pass sth **down**† **(to** so) AND **pass** sth **on**† **(to** so) to will something to someone. □ *My grandfather passed this watch down to me.*

pass for so/sth to be accepted as someone, some type of person, or something. □ *You could pass for your twin brother.* □ *This painting could almost pass for the original.*

pass gas *Euph.* to release intestinal gas through the anus. (The topic is not always welcomed.) □ *Something I ate at lunch made me pass gas all afternoon.*

pass in review *Fig.* [for marchers] to move past an important person for a visual examination. □ *All the soldiers passed in review on the Fourth of July.*

pass judgment (on so/sth) *Fig.* to make a judgment about someone or something. □ *I should not pass judgment on you, but I certainly could give you some good advice about how to be more pleasant.*

pass muster *Fig.* to measure up to the required standards. □ *If you don't wear a jacket and tie, you won't pass muster at that fancy restaurant. They won't let you in.*

pass sth **off**† **(as** sth) Go to shrug sth off† (as sth).

pass so/sth **off**† **(on** so) **(as** so/sth) Go to palm so/sth off† (on so) (as so/sth).

pass sth **off**† **(on** so) **(as** sth) AND **pass** sth **off**† *Fig.* to get rid of something deceptively by giving or selling it to someone as something else. □ *I passed the rhinestone off on John as a diamond.*

pass on Go to pass away.

pass sth **on**[†] **1.** to continue handing something to the next person. □ *Please look at this list and pass it on.* **2.** *Fig.* to tell someone something; to spread news or gossip. □ *Don't pass this on, but Bill isn't living at home any more.*

pass on so/sth to accept or approve someone or something. □ *The committee passed on the proposal, so work can now begin.*

pass on sth AND **take a pass (on** sth**)** not to accept something that is offered. □ *Thanks for the offer of the opera tickets, but I'm afraid I have to pass on them.* □ *I'll have to take a pass on those tickets.*

pass out to faint; to lose consciousness. □ *When he got the news, he passed out.*

pass sentence on so **1.** [for a judge] to read out the sentence of punishment for a convicted criminal. □ *The judge was about to pass sentence on Spike—ten years in prison.* **2.** *Fig.* [for someone] to render a judgment on another person in the manner of a judge. □ *You have no right to pass judgment on me!*

pass the buck *Fig.* to pass the blame (to someone else); to give the responsibility (to someone else). □ *Don't try to pass the buck! It's your fault, and everybody knows it.*

pass the hat (around[†]**) (to** so**)** *Fig.* to collect donations of money from people. □ *Jerry passed the hat around to all the other workers.*

pass the time (of day) to spend time doing something; to consume or use spare time by doing something. (See also the following entry.) □ *I read to pass the time while waiting in the doctor's office.*

pass the time of day *Fig.* to chat with someone casually. □ *Fred likes to stop and pass the time of day with old Walter.*

pass the torch (on) to so *Fig.* to give control and responsibility to someone else. □ *I look forward to when I can pass the torch to my son and leave him to run the company.*

pass through so's **mind** AND **cross** so's **mind** *Fig.* [for a thought] to come into someone's mind briefly; [for an idea] to occur to someone. □ *Let me tell you what just crossed my mind.* □ *As you were speaking, something passed through my mind, and I'd like to discuss it.*

pass so/sth **up**[†] **1.** to fail to select someone or something. □ *The committee passed Jill up and chose Kelly.* **2.** to travel past someone or something. □ *We had to pass the museum up, thinking we could visit there the next time we were in town.*

passport to sth *Fig.* something that allows something good to happen. □ *Anne's new job is a passport to financial security.*

past caring Go to beyond caring.

*a **past master at** sth *Fig.* someone proven extremely good or skillful at an activity. (*Typically: **be** ~; **become** ~.) □ *Pam is a past master at the art of complaining.*

past so's/sth's **prime** *Fig.* beyond the most useful or productive period. □ *This old car's past its prime. I'll need to get a new one.*

paste sth **on** so **1.** *Sl.* to charge someone with a crime. □ *You can't paste that charge on me! Spike did it!* **2.** *Sl.* to land a blow on someone. □ *Max pasted a nasty blow on Lefty's chin.*

paste so **one** *Sl.* to land a blow on someone. □ *I pasted him one right on the nose.*

paste sth **up**[†] to assemble a complicated page of material by pasting the parts together. □ *There is no way a typesetter can get this page just the way you want it. You'll have to paste it up yourself.*

a **pat answer** *Fig.* a quick, easy answer; a simplified or evasive answer. □ *Don't just give them a pat answer. Give some more explanation and justification. Otherwise you will just end up answering a lot more questions.*

pat so **on the back** AND **give** so **a pat on the back 1.** to pat someone's back to show praise. □ *The coach patted each player on the back after the game.* **2.** *Fig.* to praise someone for something. (*Fig.* on ①.) □ *They were patting themselves on the back for winning when the final whistle blew.*

patch a quarrel up† *Fig.* to put an end to a quarrel; to reconcile quarreling parties. □ *Tom and Fred were able to patch their quarrel up.*

patch things up *Fig.* to "repair" the damage done by an argument or disagreement. □ *Mr. and Mrs. Smith are trying to patch things up.*

patch so **up**† *Inf.* to give medical care to someone. □ *That cut looks bad, but the doc over there can patch you up.*

*the **path of least resistance** AND *the **line of least resistance** *Fig.* the easiest course to follow; the easiest route. (*Typically: **follow** ~; **take** ~.) □ *John will follow the path of least resistance.*

*patient as Job** very patient. (Refers to the biblical figure Job. *Also: **as** ~.) □ *If you want to teach young children, you must be as patient as Job.*

the **patter of tiny feet** *Inf.* the sound of young children; having children in the household. □ *I really liked having the patter of tiny feet in the house.*

pave the way (for so/sth**) (with** sth**)** *Fig.* to prepare the way with something for someone to come or something to happen. (Fig. on the image of paving a road.) □ *I will pave the way with an introduction.*

pawn so/sth **off**† **(on** so**) (as** so/sth**)** Go to palm so/sth off† (on so) (as so/sth).

pay so **a back-handed compliment** AND **pay** so **a left-handed compliment** *Fig.* to give someone a false compliment that is really an insult or criticism. □ *John said that he had never seen me looking better. I think he was paying me a left-handed compliment.*

pay a call *Euph.* to go to the toilet; to leave to go to the toilet. □ *Tom left to pay a call. He should be back soon.*

pay a call on so to visit someone. □ *I think I will pay a call on old Mrs. Smith today.*

pay so **a compliment** *Fig.* to give someone a compliment. □ *Tom paid Bill a compliment when he told him he was intelligent.*

pay so **a left-handed compliment** Go to pay so a back-handed compliment.

pay (so/sth**) a visit** AND **pay a visit to** so/sth *Fig.* to visit someone or something. □ *Bill paid a visit to his aunt in Seattle.*

pay a visit to so/sth Go to previous.

pay as you go *Fig.* to pay costs as they occur; to pay for goods as they are bought (rather than charging them). □ *You ought to pay as you go. Then you won't be in debt.*

pay attention (to so/sth**)** *Fig.* to give attention (to someone or something). □ *Please pay attention to the teacher.*

pay so **back**† **1.** to repay someone for a loan. □ *Thanks for the loan. I'll pay you back tomorrow.* **2.** *Fig.* to return a kindness to someone who has been kind. □ *Sally was so nice. I'll pay her back by having her to dinner.* **3.** *Fig.* to get even with someone for harm done. □ *Fred eventually will pay Mike back. He bears grudges for a long time.*

pay court to so *Fig.* to solicit someone's attention; to woo someone. □ *The lobbyist paid court to all the influential members of Congress.*

pay one's **debt (to society)** *Cliché* to serve a sentence for a crime, usually in prison. □ *The judge said that Mr. Simpson had to pay his debt to society.*

pay dividends *Fig.* to give someone an added bonus of some type. (Fig. on the dividends paid by stocks and some other financial assets.) □ *I think that your investment in time at the boys club will pay dividends for you for a long time.*

pay one's **dues** *Fig.* to have earned one's right to something through hard work or suffering. □ *He worked hard to get to where he is today. He paid his dues and did what he was told.*

pay one's **final respects (to** so**)** *Fig.* to attend someone's wake, funeral visitation, or funeral. □ *We went to the funeral home to pay our final respects to Jethro Travelian.*

pay for sth *Fig.* to suffer punishment for something. □ *The criminal will pay for his crimes.*

pay heed to so/sth *Fig.* to listen and obey a person('s commands). □ *You had better pay heed to your father!*

pay homage to so/sth *Fig.* to openly honor or worship someone or something. □ *I refuse to pay homage to your principles.*

pay in advance *Fig.* to pay (for something) before it is received or delivered. □ *I want to make a special order. Will I have to pay in advance?*

pay one's **last respects (to** so) *Fig.* to go to someone's funeral. □ *Scores of people came to pay their last respects.*

pay lip service (to sth) *Fig.* to express loyalty, respect, or support for something insincerely. □ *You don't really care about politics. You're just paying lip service to the candidate.*

pay off to provide benefits. □ *How long do I have to wait for this investment to pay off?*

pay so **off**† **1.** *Fig.* to pay what is owed to a person. □ *I can't pay you off until Wednesday when I get my paycheck.* **2.** *Fig.* to bribe someone. □ *Max asked Lefty if he had paid the cops off yet.*

pay sth **out**† *Fig.* to unravel or unwind wire or rope as it is needed. □ *One worker paid the cable out, and another worker guided it into the conduit.*

pay one's **own way** to pay for one's own transportation, entrance fees, tickets, room, board, etc. □ *I wanted to go to Florida this spring, but my parents say I have to pay my own way.*

pay so **respect** *Fig.* to honor someone; to have and show respect for someone. □ *You really should pay your boss more respect.*

pay one's **respects (to** so) *Fig.* to visit politely with someone. □ *I stopped by Mrs. Smith's house to pay my respects.*

pay the penalty 1. *Fig.* to pay a fine for doing something wrong. □ *You ran the red light, and now you will have to pay the penalty.* **2.** *Fig.* to suffer the consequences for doing something wrong. (Fig. on ①.) □ *My head really hurts. I am paying the penalty for getting drunk last night.*

pay the piper *Fig.* to face the results of one's actions; to receive punishment for something. □ *You can put off paying your debts only so long. Eventually you'll have to pay the piper.*

pay the price AND **pay a price 1.** *Fig.* to pay the price that is asked for goods or services. (Usually implying that the price is high.) □ *If this is the quality of goods that you require, you will have to pay the price.* **2.** *Fig.* to suffer the consequences for doing something or risking something. □ *Oh, my head! I am paying the price for drinking too much last night.*

pay through the nose (for sth) *Fig.* to pay too much [money] for something. □ *Why should you pay through the nose?*

pay tribute to so/sth *Fig.* to salute someone or something; to give public recognition to someone or something. □ *We will have a reception to pay tribute to the work of the committee.*

pay so's **way** to pay the costs (of something) for a person. □ *My aunt is going to pay my way to Florida—only if I take her with me!*

peace of mind *Fig.* a tranquility that results from not having worries, guilt, or problems. □ *If peace of mind is more important to you than earning a lot of money, maybe you should consider teaching.*

peck at sth [for someone] to eat just a little bit of something, being as picky as a bird. □ *Are you well, Betty? You are just pecking at your food.*

*a **peep** a quick look at someone or something. (*Typically: **have** ~; **take** ~.) □ *Have a peep into the refrigerator and see if we need any milk.* □ *I took a peep at the comet through the telescope.*

peg so **as** sth AND **have** so **pegged as** sth *Fig.* to think of someone in a certain way. □ *I had you pegged as an angry rebel before I got to know you.*

peg out *Sl.* to die. □ *I was so scared, I thought I would peg out for sure.*

pencil so/sth **in**† to write something down with a pencil. (Implies that the writing is not final.) □ *This isn't a firm appointment yet, so I will just pencil it in.*

a **penny-pincher** *Fig.* someone who objects to the spending of every single penny. □ *If you weren't such a penny-pincher, you'd have some decent clothes.*

pension so **off**† to retire someone with a pension. □ *The company tried to pension me off before I was ready to retire.*

pepper so/sth **with** sth *Fig.* to shower someone or something with something, such as stones, bullets, etc. □ *The angry crowd peppered the police with stones.*

per head Go to a head.

a **perfect stranger** AND a **total stranger** *Fig.* a person who is completely unknown [to oneself]. □ *I was stopped on the street by a perfect stranger who wanted to know my name.* □ *If a total stranger asked me such a personal question, I am sure I would not answer!*

perish from sth to die from a particular cause, such as a disease. □ *I was afraid that I would perish from hunger.*

Perish the thought. *Fig.* Do not even consider thinking of such a (negative) thing. □ *If you should become ill—perish the thought—I'd take care of you.*

perish with sth to feel bad enough to die because of something, such as heat, hunger, etc. (Often an exaggeration.) □ *Mary felt as if she would perish with the intense heat of the stuffy little room.*

Permit me. Go to Allow me.

*a **perspective on** sth a way of looking at a situation and determining what is important. (*Typically: **get** ~; **have** ~; **give** so ~.) □ *The jury did not have a good perspective on the crime since some of the evidence had to be ignored.*

pester the life out of so *Fig.* to annoy someone excessively. □ *Leave me alone. You are pestering the life out of me.*

pet hate *Fig.* something that is disliked intensely and is a constant or repeated annoyance. □ *Another pet hate of mine is having to stand in line.*

pet peeve *Fig.* a frequent annoyance; one's "favorite" or most often encountered annoyance. □ *My pet peeve is someone who always comes into the theater after the show has started.*

peter out *Inf.* [for something] to die or dwindle away; [for something] to become exhausted gradually. □ *My money finally petered out, and I had to come home.*

*** phony as a three-dollar bill** AND *** queer as a three-dollar bill** phony; bogus. (*Also: **as** ~.) □ *This guy's phony as a three-dollar bill.* □ *The whole deal stinks. It's as queer as a three-dollar bill.*

a **photo op(portunity)** *Fig.* a time or event designed for taking pictures of a celebrity. □ *All the photographers raced toward a photo op with the president.*

*** physical (with** so) **1.** *Fig.* physical in the use of force against someone. (*Typically: **be** ~; **get** ~.) □ *The coach got in trouble for getting physical with some members of the team.* **2.** *Fig.* physical in touching someone in lovemaking. (*Typically: **be** ~; **get** ~.) □ *I've heard that Bill tends to get physical with his dates.*

pick a fight (with so) AND **pick a quarrel (with** so) *Fig.* to start a fight with someone on purpose. □ *Are you trying to pick a fight with me?*

pick a lock *Fig.* to open a lock without using a key. □ *The thief picked the lock on the safe and stole the money.*

pick a quarrel (with so) Go to pick a fight (with so).

pick and choose *Fig.* to choose very carefully from a number of possibilities; to be selective. □ *You must take what you are given. You cannot pick and choose.*

pick so/sth **apart**† *Fig.* to analyze and criticize someone or something negatively. □ *You didn't review her performance; you just picked her apart.*

pick at sth **1.** to scratch or dig at a blemish, sore, or scab. □ *Don't pick at it. You'll get it infected.* **2.** to eat only tiny bits of one's food. □ *He's not well. He's just picking at his dinner.* **3.** to be very critical of something, concentrating on minor matters. □ *The critics picked at the little things, missing the serious problems.*

pick so's **brain(s)** *Fig.* to talk with someone to find out information about something. □ *I spent the afternoon with Donna, picking her brain for ideas to use in our celebration.*

pick holes in sth **1.** *Lit.* to pick at something until holes are made. □ *She just sat there and picked holes in her sweater!* **2.** *Fig.* to point out the flaws or fallacies in an argument. (Fig. on ①.) □ *The lawyer picked holes in the witness's story.*

the **pick of** sth the best of the group. □ *This playful puppy is the pick of the whole lot.*

pick so/sth **off** *Fig.* to aim at and shoot someone or something. □ *Jed picked off a pesky squirrel with his .22.*

pick on so/sth to harass or bother someone or something, usually unfairly. □ *Please stop picking on me! I'm tired of it.*

pick on so **your own size** AND **pick on somebody your own size** *Fig.* to abuse someone who is big enough to fight back. □ *Wilbur should leave his little brother alone and pick on someone his own size.*

pick so's **pocket 1.** to secretly steal something from someone's pocket. □ *Somebody picked my pocket downtown, and now my credit cards are maxed out.* **2.** *Fig.* to take someone's assets legally, as through taxation. (Jocular or cynical.) □ *The governor's been picking our pockets for every little project his friends can dream up!*

pick the slack up† Go to take the slack up†.

pick sth **to pieces 1.** to pick at something until it falls apart. □ *Eat your sandwich, child! Don't just pick it to pieces.* **2.** *Fig.* to destroy an argument or performance by attacking and criticizing every detail.

pick up 1. to tidy up. □ *When you finish playing, you have to pick up.* **2.** *Fig.* to get busy; to go faster. □ *Things usually pick up around here about 8:00.*

pick so **up**† **1.** *Fig.* to attempt to become acquainted with someone for romantic or sexual purposes. □ *Who are you anyway? Are you trying to pick me up?* **2.** *Fig.* [for the police] to find and bring someone to the police station for questioning or arrest. □ *The cop tried to pick her up, but she heard him coming and got away.* **3.** *Fig.* to stop one's car, bus, etc. and offer someone a ride. □ *I picked up a hitchhiker today, and we had a nice chat.*

pick sth **up**† **1.** *Fig.* to tidy up or clean up a room or some other place. (All senses fig. on raising something.) □ *Let's pick this room up in a hurry.* **2.** *Fig.* to find, purchase, or acquire something. □ *Where did you pick that up?* □ *The team picked up its second win of the season last night.* **3.** *Fig.* to learn something; to notice something. □ *I picked up a lot of knowledge about music from my brother.* **4.** *Fig.* to cause something to go faster, especially music. □ *All right, let's pick up the tempo and get it moving faster.* □ *Okay, get moving. Pick it up!* **5.** *Fig.* to resume something. □ *Pick it up right where you stopped.* **6.** *Fig.* to receive radio signals; to bring something into view. □ *I can just pick it up with a powerful telescope.* **7.** *Fig.* to find a trail or route. □ *The dogs finally picked the scent up.*

pick up on sth to become alert to something; to take notice of something; to learn or catch on to something. □ *She's real sharp. She picks up on everything.*

pick up speed AND **pick up steam** to increase speed. (The second entry head is fig. on a steam-powered engine, but not uncommon.) □ *The train began to pick up speed as it went downhill.*

pick up steam Go to previous.

pick up the bill (for sth**)** AND **pick up the tab (for** sth**); pick up the check (for** sth**)** *Fig. Lit.* to pay for something such as a dinner for everyone at the table; to finance a project; to pay for something. □ *We hope that the city will pick up the bill for the new sidewalks.*

pick up the check (for sth**)** Go to previous.

pick up the pace (of sth**)** AND **quicken the pace (of** sth**); quicken the pulse (of** sth**); step** sth **up**† *Fig.* to speed up the tempo; to increase the rate that something is being done. □ *We are going to have to pick up the pace of activity around here if we are to get the job done.*

pick up the pieces (of sth**)** *Fig.* to try to repair emotional, financial, or other damage done to one's life. □ *I need some time to pick up the pieces of my life after the accident.*

pick up the tab (for sth**)** Go to pick up the bill (for sth).

pick one's **way along (**sth**)** *Fig.* to move along carefully and slowly, through a treacherous pathway. □ *I picked my way along the wet and slippery trail, grabbing saplings to steady myself.*

pick one's **way through** sth **1.** *Fig. Lit.* to examine or study the details of objects or documents. □ *It took me hours to pick my way through the contracts.* **2.** *Fig.* to progress through a place that is cluttered and confusing; to work one's way through clutter. □ *She picked her way through the junk piled in the attic, over to the attic window.*

picked over rejected; worn, dirty, or undesirable. □ *This merchandise looks worn and picked over. I don't want any of it.*

*a **pick-me-up** *Fig.* something stimulating or energizing to eat or drink. (*Typically: **get** ~; **have** ~; **give** so ~; **need** ~; **want** ~.) □ *I'd like to have a pick-me-up. I think I'll have a bottle of pop.* □ *You look tired. You need a pick-me-up.*

the **picture of (good) health** in a very healthy condition. □ *The doctor says I am the picture of good health.*

picture perfect *Fig.* looking exactly correct or right. (Hyphenated as a modifier.) □ *Nothing less than a picture-perfect party table will do.*

piddle around *Fig.* to waste time doing little or nothing. □ *Stop piddling around and get busy.*

pie in the sky 1. *Fig.* a future reward after death, considered as a replacement for a reward not received on earth. (From a song [parodying the hymn "In the Sweet, Bye and Bye"] found in a 1911 Wobblies [Industrial Workers of the World] songbook. The words of the chorus: "You will eat, bye and bye,/ In that glorious land above the sky;/ Work and pray, live on hay,/ You'll get pie in the sky when you die." A longer but seldom heard version is **pie in the sky by and by when you die**.) □ *Don't hold out for pie in the sky. Get realistic.* **2.** *Fig.* having to do with a hope for a special reward. (This is hyphenated before a nominal.) □ *Get rid of your pie-in-the-sky ideas!* □ *What these pie-in-the-sky people really want is money.*

piece of cake *Fig.* something easy to do. □ *No problem. When you know what you're doing, it's a piece of cake.*

a **piece (of the action)** AND a **bit of the action**; a **slice of the action**; a **piece of the pie** *Sl.* a share in the activity or the profits. (Especially of a business scheme or gambling activity.) □ *If you get in on that real estate deal, I want a piece, too.*

a **piece of the pie** Go to previous.

piece sth **together**† *Fig.* to put some complicated thing, plan, or analysis together as if assembling something. □ *This is a complicated crime. First we have to piece together exactly what happened.*

a **piercing scream** *Fig.* a very loud and shrill scream. □ *Suddenly, there was a piercing scream from the next room.*

pig out Go to blimp out (on sth).

pile the work on so AND **pile the work on**† *Fig.* to give someone a lot of work to do. □ *The boss really piled the work on me this week.*

pile up 1. [for things] to gather or accumulate. □ *The newspapers began to pile up after a few days.* □ *Evidence is beginning to pile up that Reggie is the murderer.* **2.** *Fig.* [for a number of vehicles] to crash together. (Fig. on ①.) □ *Nearly 20 cars piled up on the bridge this morning.*

pie in the sky

pile sth **up**† *Fig.* to crash or wreck something. □ *Drive carefully if you don't want to pile the car up.*

pillar of strength AND **pillar of support** someone or something that consistently provides moral, emotional, or financial support as does a pillar. □ *My parents are my pillars of support.* □ *John looked to God as his pillar of strength.*

pillar of support Go to previous.

pin sth **down**† Go to nail sth down†.

pin so **down**† **(on** sth**)** *Fig.* to pressure someone to deal with or settle something. (See also nail sth down.) □ *It was very hard to pin her down on the date, but we finally came to an agreement.*

pin so's **ears back**† Go to nail so's ears back†.

pin one's **faith on** so/sth AND **pin** one's **hopes on** so/sth *Fig.* to "fasten" or "attach" one's faith or hope to someone or something. □ *Don't pin your faith on Tom. He can't always do exactly what you want.* □ *He pinned his hopes on being rescued soon.*

pin one's **hopes on** so/sth Go to previous.

pin sth **on** so *Inf.* to blame something on someone; to frame someone for a crime; to make it appear that an innocent person has actually committed a crime. □ *Don't try to pin that crime on me! I didn't do it.*

pinch and scrape Go to scrimp and save.

pinch so **for** sth *Sl.* to arrest someone for something. □ *The cops pinched Spike for driving without a license.*

pinch sth **from** so/sth *Sl.* to steal something from someone or something. □ *Sam pinched an apple from the produce stand.*

pinch-hit for so **1.** *Fig.* to bat for someone else in a baseball game. □ *Rodney Jones is pinch-hitting for Babe DiMaggio.* **2.** AND **fill in for** so *Fig.* to substitute for someone in any situation. (Fig. on ①.) □ *Bart will pinch-hit for Fred, who is at another meeting today.*

pine away (after so/sth**)** to waste away in melancholy and longing for someone or something. □ *A year later, he was still pining away after Claire.*

pipe down *Inf.* to become quiet; to cease making noise; to shut up. (Especially as a rude command.) □ *Come on! Pipe down and get back to work!*

a **pipe dream** *Fig.* a wish or an idea that is impossible to achieve or carry out. (From the dreams or visions induced by the smoking of an opium pipe.) □ *Going to the West Indies is a pipe dream. We'll never have enough money.*

pipe sth **into** some place AND **pipe** sth **in**† *Fig.* to bring music or other sound into a place over wires. □ *They piped music into the stairways and elevators.*

pipe up (with sth**)** *Fig.* to interject a comment; to interrupt with a comment. □ *Nick piped up with an interesting thought.*

pique so's **curiosity** AND **pique** so's **interest** *Fig.* to arouse interest; to arouse curiosity. □ *The advertisement piqued my curiosity about the product.*

pique so's **interest** Go to previous.

Piss off! *Fig.* Go away!; Stop bothering me. (Caution with *piss*.) □ *Shut up, Charlie. Piss off!*

piss so **off**† *Inf.* to make someone angry. (Caution with *piss*, even though it is commonly heard.) □ *She really pissed me off!*

pissed (off) *Inf.* angry. (Caution with *piss*, even though it is commonly heard.) □ *I was so pissed off I could have screamed.*

the **pit of** one's **stomach** *Fig.* the middle of one's stomach; the location of a "visceral response." □ *I got a strange feeling in the pit of my stomach when they told me the bad news.*

pitch so **a curve (ball)** *Fig.* to surprise someone with an unexpected act or event. (Alludes to a curve ball in baseball. It is the route of the ball that is curved, not the ball itself. See also throw so a curve (ball).) □ *You really pitched me a curve ball when you said I had done a poor job. I did my best.*

pitch a tent to erect a tent at a campsite. □ *The campers pitched their tent in a clearing in the woods.*

pitch sth **at** so/sth *Fig.* to aim advertising at a particular group. □ *These comedy programs are pitched at the lowest level of mentality.*

pitch camp to set up or arrange a campsite. □ *Two campers went ahead of us to pitch camp while it was still light.*

pitch in (and help) (with sth**)** *Fig.* to join in and help someone with something. □ *Would you please pitch in and help with the party?*

pitch (the) woo *Inf.* to kiss and caress; to woo someone. (Old but still heard.) □ *Old Ted can hardly see anymore, but he can still pitch the woo.*

place so *Fig.* to recall someone's name; to recall the details about a person that would help you identify the person. □ *I am sorry, I can't seem to place you. Could you tell me your name again?*

place a premium on sth Go to put a premium on sth.

place a strain on so/sth *Fig.* to tax the resources or strength of someone, a group, or something to the utmost. □ *All of the trouble at work placed quite a strain on Kelly.*

place so/sth **above** so/sth *Fig.* to hold someone or something in higher regard than someone or something else. □ *She seems to place money above her family.*

place an order to submit an order. □ *My secretary placed an order for a new computer.*

place so/sth **at** sth to figure that someone or something was in a certain place. □ *The detective placed Randy at the scene of the crime about midnight.*

place one's **hopes on** so/sth Go to build one's hopes on so/sth.

place so **in an awkward position** *Fig.* to put someone in an embarrassing or delicate situation. □ *Your decision places me in an awkward position.*

place so/sth **in jeopardy** to put someone or something at risk. □ *Do you realize that what you just said places all of us in jeopardy?*

place so/sth **in the trust of** so Go to in the trust of so.

place of business *Fig.* a place where business is done; a factory or office. □ *You will have to come to our place of business to make a purchase.*

a **place of concealment** *Fig.* a hiding place. □ *She brought her little safe out of a place of concealment where it had been for decades.*

a **place to call** one's **own** *Fig.* a home of one's very own. □ *I am tired of living with my parents. I want a place to call my own.*

place one's **trust in** so/sth *Fig.* to trust someone or something. □ *If you place your trust in me, everything will work out all right.*

plain and simple Go to pure and simple.

plain as a pikestaff Go to next.

***plain as day** AND ***plain as a pikestaff** **1.** *Cliché* very plain and simple. (*Also: **as** ~.) □ *Fred: I have a suspicion that Marcia is upset with me. Alan: A suspicion? Come on, Fred, that's been plain as a pikestaff for quite some time!* **2.** *Cliché* [of someone's face] plain and unattractive. □ *Although his face was as plain as day, his smile made him look interesting and friendly.* **3.** AND ***plain as the nose on** one's **face** *Cliché* clear and understandable. (*Also: **as** ~.) □ *Jane: I don't understand why Professor Potter has been so friendly this week. Alan: It's plain as the nose on your face. He wants to be nominated for Professor of the Year.*

plain as the nose on one's **face** Go to previous.

plan of action a plan of doing something. (A bit redundant, but in wide use.) □ *I am planning a new plan of action for next year's fundraiser.*

plant sth **in** sth **1.** *Fig.* to put an idea in someone's brain or thinking. □ *Who planted that silly idea in your head?* **2.** *Inf.*

to conceal something in something. □ *The crook planted the money in the back of his refrigerator.*

plant sth **on** so *Inf.* to hide incriminating evidence on a person for later discovery and use in prosecution or for the purpose of smuggling. (Drugs. Allegedly a police practice used to entrap drug offenders.) □ *The cops planted crack on Rudy and then arrested him for carrying it.* □ *The crooks planted the stuff on a passenger but couldn't find him when the plane landed.*

plaster one's **hair down**† *Fig.* to use water, oil, or cream to dress the hair for combing. (The result looks plastered to the head.) □ *Tony used some strange substance to plaster his hair down.*

play a big part (in sth**)** AND **play a large part (in** sth**)** *Fig.* to serve as a major part of some situation or event. □ *The incredible amount of duplicative paperwork played a large part in my decision to find employment elsewhere.*

play a bit part *Fig.* to perform a small part in a play or a movie. □ *She played a few bit parts in minor Broadway plays, and then got the lead in an exciting new musical.*

play a joke on so to make a joke that tricks someone. □ *I don't like it when you play jokes on me.*

play a large part (in sth**)** Go to play a big part (in sth).

play a part in sth AND **play a role in** sth **1.** to participate in something in a specific way. □ *I hope to play a part in the development of the new product.* **2.** *Fig.* to portray a character in a performance. □ *He played a part in* The Mikado, *but it was not a major role.*

play a prank on so Go to play a trick on so.

play a role in sth Go to play a part in sth.

play a trick on so AND **play a prank on** so to do a trick that affects someone. □ *The little boys planned to play a trick on their teacher by turning up the heat in the classroom.*

play along (with so/sth) 1. to play a musical instrument with someone or a group. □ *The trombonist sat down and began to play along with the others.* **2.** *Fig.* to pretend to cooperate with someone or something in a joke, scam, etc. (Fig. on ①.) □ *I decided that I would play along with Larry for a while and see what would happen.*

play around (with so/sth) 1. AND **play about (with so/sth)** to play and frolic with someone or something. □ *Kelly likes to play around with the other kids.* **2.** *Euph.* to have a romantic or sexual affair with someone or persons in general. □ *Kelly found out that her husband had been playing around with Susan.*

play sth at full blast Go to at full blast.

play ball (with so) *Fig.* to cooperate with someone. □ *Why can't you guys play ball with us?*

play both ends (against the middle) *Fig.* [for one] to scheme in a way that pits two sides against each other (for one's own gain). □ *If you try to play both ends, you're likely to get in trouble with both sides.*

play by ear Go to next.

play sth by ear 1. *Fig.* to be able to play a piece of music after just listening to it a few times, without looking at the notes. □ *I can play "Stardust" by ear, but not very well.* **2.** AND **play by ear** *Fig.* to play a musical instrument well, usually the piano, without formal training. □ *John can play the piano by ear.* □ *If I could play by ear, I wouldn't have to take lessons—or practice!* **3.** *Fig.* to improvise; to decide one's next steps after one is already involved in a situation. □ *If we go into the meeting unprepared, we'll have to play everything by ear.* □ *He never prepared his presentations. He always played things by ear.*

play one's cards close to one's chest AND **play one's cards close to one's vest; keep one's cards close to one's chest; keep one's cards close to one's vest** *Fig.* to keep to oneself or be very cautious in one's dealing with people. (Informal. As if one were playing cards and not per-

mitting anyone to see any of the cards.) □ *He is very cautious. He plays his cards close to his chest.*

play one's cards close to one's vest Go to previous.

play one's cards right AND **play one's cards well** *Fig.* to work or negotiate correctly and skillfully. □ *If you play your cards right, you can get whatever you want.*

play one's cards well Go to previous.

play cat and mouse with so *Fig.* to be coy and evasive with someone. □ *I know what you are up to. Don't play cat and mouse with me!*

play dead *Fig.* to pretend to be dead. □ *When the bear attacked me, I just dropped down and played dead.*

play sth down† Go to soft pedal sth.

play down to so to condescend to one's audience. □ *Don't play down to the people who have paid their money to see you. They may be smarter than you think.*

play fast and loose (with so/sth) *Fig.* to act carelessly, thoughtlessly, and irresponsibly. □ *Bob got fired for playing fast and loose with the company's money.*

play first chair 1. *Fig.* to be the leader of a section of instruments in an orchestra or a band. □ *Sally learned to play the violin so well that she now plays first chair in the orchestra.* **2.** *Fig.* to act as a leader. (Fig. on ①.) □ *I need someone to make sure this job gets done. Who plays first chair around here?*

play footsie with so 1. *Inf.* to get romantically or sexually involved with someone. (Refers literally to secretly pushing or rubbing feet with someone under the table.) □ *Someone said that Ruth is playing footsie with Henry even though they are both married to someone else.* **2.** *Inf.* to get involved in a scheme with someone; to cooperate with someone. (Fig. on ①.) □ *The guy who runs the butcher shop was playing footsie with the city meat inspector.*

play so for a fool *Fig.* to treat someone like a fool; to assume someone is naive or stupid. □ *Don't play me for a fool. I won't have it.*

play for keeps *Fig.* to do things with permanent effect; to be serious in one's actions. (From the game of marbles, where the winner actually keeps all the marbles won.) □ *Are we playing for keeps, or can we give everything back at the end of the game?*

play for time *Fig.* to stall; to act in such a way as to gain time. □ *The lawyers for the defense were playing for time while they looked for a witness.*

play freeze-out *Inf.* to open windows and doors or turn down a thermostat, making someone cold. □ *Wow, it's cold in here! Who's playing freeze-out?*

play games (with so**)** *Fig.* to use clever strategies against someone. □ *Come on! Stop playing games with me. Let's talk this over.*

play hard to get *Fig.* to be coy, intentionally shy, and fickle. (Usually refers to someone of the opposite sex.) □ *Why can't we go out? Why do you play so hard to get?*

play hardball (with so**)** *Inf.* to act strong and aggressive about an issue with someone. □ *Things are getting a little tough. The president has decided to play hardball on this issue.*

play havoc with so/sth Go to raise havoc with so/sth.

play one's **heart out** Go to cry one's heart out.

play hell with so/sth *Fig.* to cause enormous disruptions with someone or something. □ *Your proposal would play hell with Gerry and his plans.*

play hob with so/sth Go to raise hob with so/sth.

play hooky *Fig.* to fail to attend school or some other event. □ *Why aren't you in school? Are you playing hooky?* □ *I don't have time for the sales meeting today, so I think I'll just play hooky.*

play in the big leagues *Fig.* to be involved in something of large or important proportions. (Refers originally to playing a professional sport at the highest level.) □ *The conductor shouted at the oboist, "You're playing in the big leagues now! Tune up or ship out!"*

play innocent *Fig.* to pretend to be innocent and not concerned. □ *John is playing innocent, and he knows more than he is telling us.*

play into so's **hands** *Fig.* [for a person one is scheming against] to assist one in one's scheming without realizing it. □ *John is doing exactly what I hoped he would. He's playing into my hands.*

play it cool 1. *Inf.* to do something while not revealing insecurities or incompetence; to act blasé. □ *Play it cool, man. Look like you belong there.* **2.** *Inf.* to hold one's temper. □ *Don't let them get you mad. Play it cool.*

play it for all it's worth *Fig.* to exploit a problem, disability, or injury to get as much sympathy or compensation as possible. □ *He injured his hand before the examination, and he played it for all it was worth in order to get the exam delayed.*

play it safe *Fig.* to be or act safe; to avoid taking a risk. □ *If you have a cold or the flu, play it safe and go to bed.*

play itself out *Fig.* to run its course; to work through all its processes until it is finished. (Fixed order.) □ *We shouldn't interfere. This little drama of life will just have to play itself out.*

play on so's **heartstrings** AND **tug at** so's **heartstrings; pull on** so's **heartstrings; pull at** so's **heartstrings** *Fig.* to attempt to get sympathy from someone. □ *She is crying so she can play on your heartstrings and try to get you to take her home.*

play politics 1. *Fig.* to negotiate politically. □ *Everybody at city hall is playing politics as usual.* **2.** to allow politics to dominate in matters where principle should prevail. □ *They're not making reasonable decisions. They're just playing politics.*

play possum *Fig.* to pretend to be inactive, unobservant, asleep, or dead. (The *possum* refers to an opossum.) □ *I knew that Bob wasn't asleep. He was just playing pos-*

sum. □ *I can't tell if this animal is dead or just playing possum.*

play second fiddle (to so) *Fig.* to be in a subordinate position to someone. □ *I'm better trained than he, and I have more experience. I shouldn't always play second fiddle.*

play (the) devil's advocate *Fig.* to put forward arguments against or objections to a proposition—which one may actually agree with—purely to test the validity of the proposition. (The devil's advocate challenges the evidence presented for the canonization of a saint to make sure that the grounds for canonization are sound.) □ *Mary offered to play devil's advocate and argue against our case so that we would find out any flaws in it.*

play the devil with sth *Fig.* to cause disruption with something; to foul something up. □ *Your being late really played the devil with my plans for the day.*

play the field *Fig.* to date many different people rather than just one. □ *When Tom told Ann good-bye, he said he wanted to play the field.*

play the fool to act in a silly manner in order to amuse other people. □ *The teacher told Tom to stop playing the fool and sit down.*

play the heavy *Fig.* to act the part of a mean person; to do the unpleasant tasks that no one else wants to do. (Refers originally to playing the role of someone evil in a movie, etc.) □ *I'm a nice guy, but at work, I am required to play the heavy. The boss makes me do all the cruel things like firing people.*

play the horses Go to next.

play the ponies AND **play the horses** *Inf.* to wager on horse races. □ *I used to play the ponies every afternoon during the summer. Then I ran out of money.*

play the race card Go to the race card.

play the (stock) market *Fig.* to invest in the stock market. (As if it were a game or as if it were gambling.) □ *I've learned my lesson playing the market. I lost a fortune.*

play through [for golfers] to pass someone on the golf course. □ *Do you mind if we play through? We have to get back to the courtroom by two o'clock.*

play to the crowd Go to next.

play to the gallery AND **play to the crowd** *Fig.* to perform in a manner that will get the strong approval of the audience; to perform in a manner that will get the approval of the lower elements in the audience. □ *John is a competent actor, but he has a tendency to play to the crowd.* □ *When he made the rude remark, he was just playing to the gallery.*

play tricks on so *Fig.* [for something, such as the eyes] to deceive someone. □ *Did I see him fall down, or are my eyes playing tricks on me?* □ *My brain is playing tricks on me. I can't remember a word you said.*

play one's **trump card 1.** [in certain card games] to play a card that, according to the rules of the game, outranks certain other cards and is thus able to take any card of another suit. □ *Bob played his trump card and ended the game as the winner.* **2.** *Fig.* to use a special trick; to use one's most powerful or effective strategy or device. (Fig. on ①.) □ *I thought that the whole situation was hopeless until Mary played her trump card and solved the whole problem.*

play sth **up**† *Fig.* to emphasize something; to be a booster of something. □ *The press played the scandal up so much that everyone became bored with it.*

play up to so *Fig.* to flatter someone; to try to gain influence with someone. □ *It won't do any good to play up to me. I refuse to agree to your proposal.*

play (up)on sth **1.** *Fig.* to exploit something—including a word—for some purpose; to develop something for some purpose. (Upon is formal and less commonly used than on.) □ *You are playing on a misunderstanding.* **2.** to play a game on a field or court. □ *Shall we play on the floor or on the table?* **3.** *Fig.* [for light] to sparkle on something. □ *The reflections of the candles played on the surface of the wall.*

play with so/sth to toy with someone or something. □ *You are just playing with me. Can't you take me seriously?* □ *Please don't play with that crystal vase.*

play with a full deck *Fig.* to operate as if one were mentally sound. (Usually in the negative. One cannot play cards properly with a partial deck.) □ *Look sharp, you dummies! Pretend you are playing with a full deck.*

play with fire *Fig.* to do something dangerous or risky. (Usually *playing with fire.*) □ *Be careful with that knife! You are playing with fire!*

a **play-by-play description 1.** *Lit.* a detailed description of a sporting event while it is being played. □ *And now here is Bill Jones with a play-by-play description of the baseball game.* **2** *Fig.* a detailed description of a (nonsporting) event given as the event is taking place. □ *John was giving me a play-by-play description of the argument going on next door.*

played out *Fig.* too exhausted to continue. □ *After the race, we were played out for the rest of the day.*

please oneself *Fig.* to do what one wishes. □ *We don't mind whether you stay or not. Please yourself!*

*****pleased as Punch** delighted; very pleased. (This refers to Punch from the "Punch and Judy" shows. *Also: **as** ~.) □ *Fred was pleased as Punch to discover that Ellen was making lemon pie, his favorite, for dessert.*

plight one's **troth to** so *Fig.* to become engaged to be married to someone. (Literary or jocular.) □ *I chose not to plight my troth to anyone who acts so unpleasant to my dear aunt.*

The **plot thickens.** Things are becoming more complicated or interesting. □ *John is supposed to be going out with Mary, but I saw him last night with Sally. The plot thickens.*

plow through sth *Fig.* to work through something with determination. □ *She plowed through the book to learn everything she could.*

plug (away) at so Go to hammer (away) at so.

plug (away) at sth Go to hammer (away) at sth.

plumb loco *Rur.* completely crazy. (*Loco* is from a Spanish word meaning "mad.") □ *You're plumb loco if you think I'll go along with that.*

plumb the depths of sth *Fig.* to test, determine, or prove the depth of something such as despair, someone's intellect, one's soul, someone's insight, vileness, etc. and state the results; to study in detail the extent of something. (Fig. on the use of a plumb bob [a lead weight] in a cord used to sound [determine] a depth.) □ *The poet wasted about 30 sheets of printer paper plumbing the depths of his own shallow self-absorption.*

plummet to earth to fall rapidly to earth from a great height. □ *The rocket plummeted to earth and exploded as it struck.*

plump for so/sth Go to make a pitch (for so/sth).

a **pocket of resistance** *Fig.* a small group of people who resist change or domination. □ *The accounting department seems to be a pocket of resistance when it comes to automating.*

poetic justice *Fig.* appropriate, ideal, or ironic punishment. □ *The car thieves tried to steal a car with no gas. That's poetic justice.*

poetic license *Fig.* liberties or license of the type taken by artists, especially poets, to violate patterns of rhyme, harmony, structure, etc. □ *I couldn't tell whether he kept making spelling mistakes or if it was just poetic license.*

so's **point is well taken** *Fig.* someone's idea or opinion is accepted and appreciated. □ *Your point is well taken, and I will see that it is not forgotten.*

*****the **point of (**doing**)** sth *Fig.* to the extreme of doing something; so much as to cause someone to do something. (*Typically: **be at** ~; **drive** so **to** ~; **push** so **to** ~.) □ *You are going to drive me to the point* *of screaming!* □ *I'm at the point of leaving just now.*

*the **point of no return** *Fig.* the halfway point; the point at which it is too late to turn back. (*Typically: **cross** ~; **past** ~; **reach** ~.) □ *The flight was past the point of no return, so we had to continue to our destination.* □ *The entire project has reached the point of no return, so we will have to continue with it.*

point of view *Fig.* a way of thinking about something; [someone's] viewpoint; an attitude or expression of self-interest. □ *From my point of view, all this talk is a waste of time.*

point the finger at so *Fig.* to blame someone; to identify someone as the guilty person. □ *Don't point the finger at me! I didn't take the money.*

poised to do sth *Fig.* ready to do something; in the right position to do something. □ *The army is poised to attack at dawn.*

poison so **against** so/sth *Fig.* to cause someone to have negative or hateful thoughts about someone, a group, or something. □ *Your negative comments poisoned everyone against the proposal.*

poke fun at so/sth to make fun of someone or something. □ *You shouldn't poke fun at me for my mistakes.*

poke sth **into** sth AND **poke** sth **in**† to stick or cram something into something. □ *He poked his finger into the jam, pulled it out again, and licked it.*

poke one's **nose in(to** sth) AND **stick** one's **nose in(to** sth) *Fig.* to interfere with something; to be nosy about something. □ *I wish you'd stop poking your nose into my business.* □ *She was too upset for me to stick my nose in and ask what was wrong.*

***poles apart** *Fig.* very different; far from coming to an agreement. (Refers to the distance between the north and south poles. *Typically: **be** ~; **become** ~; **grow** ~.) □ *They'll never sign the contract because they are poles apart.*

polish sth **off**† *Fig.* to eat, consume, exhaust, or complete all of something. □ *Who polished the cake off?*

polish sth **up**† to rub something until it shines. □ *Polish the silver up, and make it look nice and shiny.*

a **political football** *Fig.* an issue that becomes politically divisive; a problem that doesn't get solved because the politics of the issue get in the way. □ *The question of campaign contributions has become a political football. All the politicians who accept questionable money are pointing fingers at each other.*

pony an amount **up**† to produce an amount of money. □ *You'd better pony up $20 now!*

pony up pay what is owed. □ *You owe me! Pony up!*

pooch out *Inf.* to stick or bulge out, as with a belly. □ *His chubby tummy pooched out when he relaxed.*

poop out *Inf.* to quit; to wear out and stop. □ *He pooped out after about an hour of hard work.*

pooped (out) *Inf.* [of a person or an animal] exhausted; worn out. □ *I'm really pooped out.* □ *The horse looked sort of pooped in the final stretch.*

*poor as a church mouse** AND *poor as church mice** very poor. (*Also: **as** ~.) □ *My aunt is as poor as a church mouse.*

poor but clean *Cliché* having little money but clean and of good habits, nonetheless. (Either extremely condescending or jocular.) □ *My salary isn't very high, and I only have one old car. Anyway, I'm poor but clean.*

pop around (for a visit) AND **pop by (for a visit); pop in (for a visit); pop over (for a visit)** *Inf.* to come by [someone's residence] for a visit. □ *You simply must pop around for a visit sometime.*

pop back (for sth) *Inf.* to come back to a place for just a moment. □ *I have to pop back for something I forgot.*

pop by (for a visit) Go to pop around (for a visit).

pop one's **cork 1.** *Inf.* to suddenly become mentally disturbed; to go crazy. □ *I was so upset that I nearly popped my cork.*

2. *Inf.* to become very angry. □ *My mother popped her cork when she heard about my low grades.*

pop for sth *Inf.* to pay for a treat (for someone). □ *Let's have some ice cream. I'll pop for it.*

pop in (for a visit) Go to pop around (for a visit).

pop off 1. *Sl.* to make an unnecessary remark; to interrupt with a remark; to sound off. □ *Bob keeps popping off when he should be listening.* **2.** *Sl.* to lose one's temper. □ *I don't know why she popped off at me. All I did was say hello.* **3.** *Sl.* to die. □ *I hope I'm asleep when I pop off.* **4.** *Sl.* to leave; to depart in haste. □ *Got to pop off. I'm late.*

pop so **off**† *Inf.* to kill someone. □ *Max was told to pop Lefty off because he was trying to muscle in on the gang's turf.*

pop sth **out of** sth AND **pop** sth **out**† to release something from something so that it jumps or bursts out, possibly with a popping sound. □ *Sue popped the cork out of the champagne bottle.*

pop (some) tops *Sl.* to drink beer. □ *We are going to pop tops and watch the B-ball game.*

pop the question *Inf.* [for a man] to ask a woman to marry him. (Could also be used by a woman asking a man.) □ *She waited for years for him to pop the question.*

pop up 1. *Fig.* [for a baseball batter] to hit a baseball that goes high upward rather than outward. □ *The catcher came to bat and popped up.* **2.** *Fig.* [for a baseball] to fly high upward rather than outward. □ *The ball will always pop up if you hit it in a certain way.* **3.** *Fig.* to arise suddenly; to appear without warning. □ *Billy popped up out of nowhere and scared his mother.*

pork out (on sth**)** Go to blimp out (on sth).

pose a challenge to represent a challenge; to be a challenge [for someone]. □ *Finding places to seat all the guests in this small room really poses a challenge.*

pose a question *Fig.* to ask a question; to imply the need for asking a question. □ *Genetic research poses many ethical questions.*

***possessed by** sth *Fig.* obsessed or driven by something. (*Typically: be ~; become ~.) □ *Ned was possessed by a desire to become the best at everything he did.*

***possessed of** sth *Fig.* having something; possessing something. (*Typically: be ~; become ~.) □ *She is possessed of a large amount of money.* □ *Todd wishes he were possessed of a large car and a fine house.*

post so some place to place someone, as if on guard, near something or at some place. □ *The boss posted himself at the water cooler to catch up on the gossip.*

postage and handling charges for shipping [something] and for wrapping and handling the item. □ *The cost of the book was quite reasonable, but the postage and handling was outrageous.*

a **poster child (for** sth**)** *Fig.* someone who is a classic example of a state or type of person. (From mid-20th-century *poster boy*, the term for a specific child stricken with polio who appeared on posters encouraging contributions to The March of Dimes. Later *poster girls* brought on the *child*.) □ *She is a poster child for soccer moms.*

a **pot of gold 1.** a container filled with gold, as in the myth where it is guarded by a leprechaun. □ *I was hoping to find a pot of gold in the cellar, but there were only cobwebs.* **2.** *Fig.* an imaginary reward. □ *Whoever gets to the porch first wins a pot of gold.*

pound a beat *Fig.* to walk a regular route. □ *The old cop pounded the same beat for years and years.*

pound one's **ear** *Sl.* to sleep. □ *She went home to pound her ear an hour or two before work.*

pound for pound *Fig.* [usually of value, quality, strength, etc.] considering the amount of weight involved. □ *Pound for pound, a dog fed properly is much stronger than a dog that has to fend for itself.*

pound so's **head in**† *Inf.* to beat someone, especially about the head. □ *Fred looked like he wanted to pound Mike's head in; he was so mad!*

pound sth **into** sth Go to hammer sth into sth.

*a **pound of flesh** *Fig.* a payment or punishment that involves suffering and sacrifice on the part of the person being punished. (*Typically: **give** so ~; **owe** so ~; **pay** so ~; **take** ~.) □ *He wants revenge. He won't be satisfied until he takes his pound of flesh.*

pound sth **out**† **1.** *Fig.* to play something loudly on the piano, perhaps with difficulty or clumsily. □ *Here, pound this one out. A little softer, please.* **2.** *Fig.* to type something on a keyboard. □ *He pounded out a quick note and sent it off to the office.*

pound the books Go to hit the books.

pound the pavement *Inf.* to walk through the streets looking for a job. □ *I spent two months pounding the pavement after the factory I worked for closed.*

pour cold water on sth AND **dash cold water on** sth; **throw cold water on** sth *Fig.* to discourage doing something; to reduce enthusiasm for something. (Fig. on the notion of cooling passion with cold water.) □ *When my father said I couldn't have the car, he poured cold water on my plans.*

pour down (on so/sth**)** *Fig.* [for blessings, criticism, praise, kudos, etc.] to flow down on someone or something. □ *Blessings poured down on the early settlers in the form of good harvests and plentiful game.*

pour good money after bad Go to throw good money after bad.

pour one's **heart (and soul) into** sth Go to put one's heart (and soul) into sth.

pour one's **heart out to** so AND **pour** one's **heart out**† *Fig.* to tell one's personal feelings to someone else. □ *I didn't mean to pour my heart out to you, but I guess I just had to talk to someone.*

pour in(to sth**)** *Fig.* [for people or things] to continue to arrive in great numbers. □ *Complaints poured into the television station after the scandalous broadcast.*

pour oneself **into** sth **1.** *Fig.* to get deeply involved with something. □ *He distracted himself from his grief by pouring himself into his work.* **2.** *Fig.* to fit oneself into clothing that is very tight. (Usually jocular.) □ *Marilyn didn't put that dress on, she poured herself in!*

pour money down the drain AND **throw money down the drain** *Fig.* to waste money; to throw money away. □ *Don't buy any more of that low-quality merchandise. That's just throwing money down the drain.*

pour oil on troubled water(s) *Fig.* to calm someone or something down. (A thin layer of oil will actually calm a small area of a rough sea.) □ *Don can calm things down. He's good at pouring oil on troubled waters.*

pour out (of sth**)** *Fig.* [for people] to come out of a place in great numbers. □ *At the end of the game, people poured out of the stadium for an hour.*

pour out one's **soul** *Fig.* to confess something [to someone]; to reveal one's deepest concerns. □ *Every time she calls me up, she takes an hour or more to pour out her soul.*

powder one's **face** Go to next.

powder one's **nose** AND **powder** one's **face** to depart to the bathroom. (Usually said by women, or jocularly by men.) □ *Excuse me, I have to powder my nose.*

powder up *Sl.* to drink heavily; to get drunk. □ *Let's go out and powder up.*

the **power behind the throne** *Fig.* the person who actually controls the person who is apparently in charge. □ *Mr. Smith appears to run the shop, but his brother is the power behind the throne.*

a **power play** *Fig.* a strategy using one's power or authority to carry out a plan or to get one's way. □ *In a blatant power play, the manager claimed he had initiated the sales campaign.*

power sth **with** sth to provide something as the source of energy for something to operate. □ *The government decided to power its vans with natural gas engines.*

the **powers that be** *Fig.* the people who are in authority. □ *I have applied for a license, and the powers that be are considering my application.*

A **pox on** so/sth! *Fig.* A curse on someone or something! (Old. Now usually jocular.) □ *I've been trying to make this computer work all day. A pox on it!*

Practice what you preach! *Fig.* Behave the way you tell others to behave. □ *You just slammed the door like you always tell us not to. Practice what you preach!*

praise so/sth **to the skies** *Fig.* to give someone or something much praise. □ *He wasn't very good, but his friends praised him to the skies.*

pray to the porcelain god *Sl.* to kneel at the toilet bowl and vomit from drunkenness. □ *Wally spent a while praying to the porcelain god last night.*

preach to the choir AND **preach to the converted** *Fig.* to make one's case primarily to one's supporters; to make one's case only to those people who are present or who are already friendly to the issues. □ *There is no need to convince us of the value of hard work. We already know that. You are just preaching to the choir.* □ *Bob found himself preaching to the converted when he was telling Jane the advantages of living in the suburbs. She already hates city life.*

preach to the converted Go to previous.

*****precedence over** so/sth the right to come before someone or something else; greater importance than someone or something else. (*Typically: **take** ~; **have** ~; **be given** ~.) □ *My manager's concerns take precedence over mine.*

precious few AND **precious little** very few; very little. (*Few* for people or things that can be counted, and *little* for amounts.) □ *We get precious few tourists here in the winter.* □ *There's precious little food in the house, and there is no money.*

precious little Go to previous.

precipitate into sth *Fig.* [for something] to become a more serious matter. □ *By then, the street fight had precipitated into a riot.*

preclude so/sth **from** sth to prevent someone or something from being included in something; to eliminate someone from something in advance. □ *Your remarks do not preclude me from trying again, do they?*

predicate sth **(up)on** sth to base something on something. □ *There is no need to predicate my promotion upon the effectiveness of my secretary!*

a **prelude to** sth an act or event that comes before and signals another act or event. □ *Her rudeness to her boss was a prelude to her resignation.*

prepare so **for** sth to build someone up for shocking news. □ *I went in and had a talk with her to prepare her for the report.*

press ahead Go to press on.

press for sth to urge for something to be done; to request something. □ *The mayor is pressing for an early settlement to the strike.*

press forward to move forward; to struggle forward; to continue. □ *We must press forward and complete this work on time.*

press so/sth **into service** to force someone or something to serve or function. □ *I don't think you can press him into service just yet. He isn't trained.* □ *I think that in an emergency, we could press this machine into service.*

press one's **luck** Go to push one's luck.

press on AND **press ahead; forge ahead** **1.** *Fig.* to move onward physically. □ *It was late, but we had to reach Skagway before sunset, so we pressed on, moving as fast as we could.* **2.** *Fig.* to make progress on a project; to work hard to complete something. □ *Even though we really didn't understand what we were doing, we forged ahead.*

press (the) flesh *Sl.* to shake hands, especially in the context of one person shaking many hands. (Older.) □ *You have to* get out there, meet the people, and press flesh if you want to get elected.

press the panic button Go to hit the panic button.

press so **to the wall** Go to push so to the wall.

***pressed for cash** Go to next.

***pressed for money** AND ***pressed for cash; *pushed for cash; *pushed for money** *Fig.* needful of money; short of money. (*Typically: **be** ~; **become** ~; **get** ~.) □ *We are usually pushed for money at this time of year.* □ *I'm a little pressed for money just now.*

***pressed for time** AND ***pushed for time** *Fig.* needing time; in a hurry. (*Typically: **be** ~; **become** ~; **get** ~; **seem** ~.) □ *If I weren't so pressed for time, I could help you.* □ *I can't talk to you. I'm too pushed for time.*

pretend to sth to claim to have a skill or quality. □ *I can hardly pretend to the artistry that Wally has, but I can play the piano a bit.*

***pretty as a picture** very pretty. (*Also: **as** ~.) □ *Sweet little Mary is as pretty as a picture.*

pretty nearly *Inf.* almost. □ *We pretty nearly got lost trying to find Skagway.*

a **pretty pickle** *Fig.* a difficult situation. (Ironic. *Pickle* = a bad situation.) □ *Well, this is a pretty pickle you've gotten us into.*

pretty soon *Fig.* fairly soon; soon. □ *I'll be there pretty soon.*

a **pretty state of affairs** AND a **fine state of affairs**; a **sorry state of affairs**; a **sad state of affairs** an unpleasant state of affairs. (The first two are ironic.) □ *This is a pretty state of affairs, and it's all your fault.* □ *What a fine state of affairs you've got us into.*

prey (up)on so/sth *Fig.* to take advantage of someone or something. □ *The people of that island prey on tourists and do not give them polite treatment.*

the **price** one **has to pay** *Fig.* the sacrifice that one has to make; the unpleasantness that one has to suffer. □ *Being away from*

home a lot is the price one has to pay for success.

***a **price on** one's **head** *Fig.* a reward for one's capture. (*Typically: **get** ~; **have** ~; **put** ~; **place** ~.) □ *We captured a thief who had a price on his head, and the sheriff gave us the reward.*

prick up its ears† AND **prick up** one's **ears**† *Fig.* [for an animal or a person] to become attentive. (The animal will adjust its ears toward the sound.) □ *The sound made the dog prick its ears up.* □ *When Fred heard his name, he pricked up his ears.*

pride and joy *Fig.* something or someone that one is very proud of. (Often in reference to a baby, a car, a house, etc. Fixed order.) □ *And this is Roger, our little pride and joy.*

pride oneself **on** sth to take pride in the way one does something or on one's quality, product, or ability. □ *She prides herself on her chocolate cakes.* □ *Bob prides himself on his window cleaning.*

prime mover *Fig.* the force that sets something going; someone or something that starts something off. □ *The assistant manager was the prime mover in getting the manager sacked.* □ *Discontent with his job was the prime mover in John's deciding to retire early.*

prime sth **with** sth to enable something to start working or functioning with something. □ *Larry primed the pump with a little water, and it began to do its work.*

the **primrose path** *Fig.* invitingly appealing prospects that soon evaporate. □ *She led him down the primrose path until she got tired of him.*

privy to sth *Fig.* knowledgeable about something secret or private. □ *The reporter became privy to the senator's evil plan.*

proceed against so/sth to start legal action against someone or something. □ *The district attorney will proceed against the suspect next week.*

profit by sth AND **profit from** sth *Fig.* to learn from something. □ *I am sure you will profit by your unpleasant experience.*

promise the moon (to so**)** AND **promise** so **the moon** to make extravagant promises to someone. □ *Bill will promise you the moon, but he won't live up to his promises.*

propose a toast to make a toast before a celebratory drink. □ *At the wedding reception, the bride's father proposed a toast to the new couple.*

*proud as a peacock AND ***vain as a peacock** overly proud; vain. (*Also: **as** ~.) □ *Mike's been strutting around proud as a peacock since he won that award.*

prove one's **mettle** Go to show one's mettle.

prove sth **to** oneself AND **prove to** oneself **that** one **could** do sth to demonstrate that one is capable of doing something well. □ *He went on a yearlong trip around the world just to prove to himself that he could do it.*

provide for so to support someone with clothes, food, and housing. □ *I know I have to provide for my children, but I really love to go to the racetrack.*

provide for sth AND **allow for** sth to foresee the possibility of something happening and plan for it. □ *We provided for a future bathroom in the large closet.* □ *Allow for traffic when you plan your drive to the airport.*

pry into sth to snoop into something; to get into someone else's business. □ *Why are you prying into my affairs all the time?*

psyched up (for sth**)** Inf. excited and enthusiastic. □ *I can play a great tennis game if I'm psyched up.*

publish or perish Fig. [for a professor] to try to publish scholarly books or articles to prevent getting released from a university or falling into disfavor in a university. (Also occurs as other parts of speech. See the example.) □ *This is a major research university, and publish or perish is the order of the day.*

pull a boner Inf. to do something stupid or silly. (Some people will recognize boner as a slang term for the erect penis.) □ *If you pull a boner like that again, you're fired!*

pull a fast one (on so**)** Inf. to succeed in an act of deception. □ *Don't try to pull a fast one with me! I know what you're doing.*

pull a gun (on so**)** AND **pull a knife (on** so**)** Inf. to bring out a gun or knife suddenly so that it is ready for use against someone.

pull a job Sl. to carry out a crime, especially a robbery. (Police and underworld.) □ *Willie and Richard left town after they pulled the bank job.*

pull a knife (on so**)** Go to pull a gun (on so).

pull a muscle Fig. to strain a muscle and suffer the attendant pain. □ *I pulled a muscle in my back and can't play golf today.*

pull a stunt (on so**)** AND **pull a trick (on** so**)** Fig. to deceive someone; to play a trick on someone. □ *Don't you dare pull a stunt like that!*

pull a trick (on so**)** Go to previous.

pull all the stops out† Fig. to use everything available; to not hold back. (Fig. on the image of pulling out all of the stops on an organ so that it will sound as loud and full as possible.) □ *Todd pulled all the stops out for his exhibition and impressed everyone with his painting artistry.*

pull one's **belt in**† **(a notch)** Go to take one's belt in† (a notch).

pull (an amount of money**) down**† Fig. Inf. to earn a stated amount of money. (*An amount of money* = a figure or other indication of an actual amount.) □ *They pull down pretty good salaries.*

pull one's **hair (out)** Go to tear one's hair (out).

pull in one's **ears** Fig. to stop listening in on someone or something. □ *Now, pull in your ears. This is none of your business.*

pull in one's **horns** Go to draw in one's horns.

pull so's **leg** Fig. to kid, fool, or trick someone. □ *You don't mean that. You're just pulling my leg.*

pull sth **on** so Fig. to play a trick on someone; to deceive someone with a trick.

(The word *something* is often used.) □ *You wouldn't pull a trick on me, would you?* □ *Who would pull something like that on an old lady?*

pull on so's **heartstrings** Go to play on so's heartstrings.

pull out (of sth**)** Go to bail out (of sth).

pull sth **out of** so *Fig.* to draw or force information out of someone. □ *The cops finally pulled a confession out of Spike.*

pull sth **out of a hat** AND **pull** sth **out of thin air; pull** sth **from a hat; pull** sth **from thin air 1.** [for a magician] to make something, such as a live rabbit, seem to appear by pulling it out of a top hat or out of the air. □ *He pulled a rabbit out of a hat and then pulled a chicken out of thin air.* **2.** *Fig.* to produce something seemingly out of nowhere. (Fig. on ①.) □ *I don't know where she found the book. She pulled it out of thin air, I guess.*

pull sth **out of the fire** AND **pull** sth **from the fire** *Fig.* to rescue something; to save something just before it's too late. □ *Can we rescue this project? Is there time to pull it out of the fire?*

pull sth **out of thin air** Go to pull sth out of a hat.

pull one's **(own) weight** Go to carry one's (own) weight.

pull one's **punches 1.** *Fig.* [for a boxer] to strike with light blows to enable the other boxer to win. □ *Bill has been barred from the boxing ring for pulling his punches.* **2.** *Fig.* to hold back in one's criticism. (Fig. on ①. Usually in the negative. The *one's* can be replaced with *any* in the negative.) □ *I didn't pull any punches. I told her exactly what I thought of her.*

pull rank on so *Fig.* to use one's higher position, office, or rank to pressure someone into doing something. (Fig. on military usage.) □ *I hate to pull rank on you, but I'll take the lower bunk.*

pull (some) strings AND **pull a few strings** to use influence (with someone to get something done). □ *Is it possible to get anything done around here without pulling some strings?*

pull so's/sth's **teeth** *Fig.* to reduce the power or efficacy of someone or something. (Fig. on the notion of taking the "bite" out of something.) □ *The mayor tried to pull the teeth of the new law.*

pull the plug (on so**) 1.** *Fig.* to turn off someone's life support system in a hospital. (Fig. on pull the plug (on sth). This results in the death of a person whose life support has been terminated.) □ *Fred signed a living will, making it possible to pull the plug on him without a court order.* **2.** *Fig.* to put an end to someone's activities or plans. □ *David pulled the plug on Fred, who was taking too long with the project.*

pull the plug (on sth**)** *Fig.* to reduce the power or effectiveness of something; to disable something. □ *Jane pulled the plug on the whole project.*

pull the rug out† **(from under** so**)** *Fig.* to make someone or someone's plans fall through; to upset someone's plans. (Fig. on the image of upsetting someone by jerking the rug that they are standing on.) □ *Don pulled the rug out from under me in my deal with Bill Franklin.*

pull the wool over so's **eyes** *Fig.* to deceive someone. □ *Don't try to pull the wool over her eyes. She's too smart.*

pull through (sth**)** to survive something. □ *I am sure that your uncle will pull through the illness.*

pull sth **to** to close something, usually a door of some type. □ *The door is open a little. Pull it to so no one will hear us.*

pull oneself **together** to become more calm and controlled after an emotional upset. □ *I cried for an hour and then pulled myself together so I could go to the funeral home.*

pull sth **together** AND **scrape** sth **together; get** sth **together 1.** *Fig.* to assemble something, such as a meal. □ *I will hardly have time to pull a snack together.* **2.** *Fig.* to organize something; to arrange something. □ *How about a party? I'll see if I can pull something together for Friday night.*

pull so/sth **under** *Fig.* to cause someone or something to fail. □ *The heavy debt load pulled Don under. He went out of business.*

pull up (some place**)** Go to haul up (some place).

Pull up a chair. *Fig.* Please get a chair and sit down and join us. (Assumes that there is seating available. The speaker does not necessarily mean that the person spoken to actually has to move a chair.) □ *Tom: Well, hello, Bob! Bob: Hi, Tom. Pull up a chair.*

pull oneself **up by** one's **(own) bootstraps** *Fig.* to improve or become a success by one's own efforts. □ *If Sam had a little encouragement, he could pull himself up by his bootstraps.*

pull up one's **roots** Go to pull up stakes.

pull so **up short** to cause someone to stop short. □ *The sudden thought that everything might not be all right pulled Tom up short.*

pull up stakes AND **pull up** one's **roots; pull** one's **roots up** *Fig.* to end one's ties to a particular place; to get ready to move away from a place where one has lived or worked for a long time. □ *Even after all these years, pulling up stakes is easier than you think.*

pump so **for** sth *Inf.* to try to get information about something out of someone. □ *The representative of the other company pumped Harry for information, but he refused to say anything.*

pump (some) iron *Sl.* to lift weights for exercise. □ *Andy went down to the gym to pump some iron.*

pump sth **up**† *Sl.* to exercise to make muscles get bigger and stronger.

pumped (up) *Sl.* excited; physically and mentally ready. □ *The team is really pumped up for Friday's game.*

punch a clock *Fig.* to punch or register one's arrival or departure on a workplace time clock or other similar record-keeping device on a daily basis. □ *Now that I am my own boss, I don't have to punch a clock every day.*

punch in to record one's arrival at one's workplace at a certain time. □ *What time did you punch in?*

punch so's **lights out** *Sl.* to knock someone out with a fist. □ *You had better stop that, or I will punch your lights out!*

punch out to record that one has left one's workplace at a certain time. □ *Why didn't you punch out when you left last night?*

punctuate sth **with** sth to add emphasis to one's speaking by adding phrases, exclamations, or other devices. □ *Her comments were punctuated with a few choice swear words.*

puppy love *Fig.* mild infatuation; infatuation as in a crush. (Used especially of adolescent relationships.) □ *Look at them together. It may be puppy love, but it looks wonderful.*

pure and simple AND **plain and simple** *Fig.* absolutely; without further complication or elaboration. □ *I told you what you must do, and you must do it, pure and simple.* □ *Will you kindly explain to me what it is, pure and simple, that I am expected to do?*

*pure as the driven snow pure and chaste. (Often used ironically. *Also: **as** ~.) □ *Jill: Sue must have gone to bed with every man in town. Jane: And I always thought she was as pure as the driven snow.*

pure luck AND **blind luck** *Fig.* complete luck; nothing but plain luck. □ *I have no skill. I won by pure luck.*

purr like a cat AND **purr like a kitten** **1.** *Fig.* [for an engine] to run well and smoothly. (Fig. on the soft steady noise cats make when content.) □ *New spark plugs and this old heap will really purr like a cat.* **2.** *Fig.* [for a person] to be very pleased, and perhaps moan or purr with pleasure. (Fig. on ①.) □ *She was so pleased that she purred like a cat.*

purr like a kitten Go to previous.

push so's **buttons** *Fig.* to arouse or anger a person by bringing up things that are sure to draw a lively response or to use a manner that will draw a lively response. (The response is usually negative.) □ *You always know how to get me mad! Why do you always punch my buttons when you know it makes me so upset?*

push for sth to request or demand something. □ *The citizens are pushing for an investigation of the police department.*

push one's **luck** AND **press** one's **luck** to expect continued good fortune; to expect to continue to escape bad luck. (Often implies unreasonable expectation.) □ *Bob pressed his luck too much and got into a lot of trouble.*

push off AND **shove off** *Fig.* to leave. (As if one were pushing a boat away from a dock.) □ *Well, it looks like it's time to push off.*

push on (to sth**) 1.** *Fig.* to move on to another topic; to stop doing one thing and move on to another. □ *Okay. Let's push on to the next topic.* **2.** *Fig.* to travel onward to something or some place. □ *We left Denver and pushed on to Omaha.*

push the panic button Go to hit the panic button.

push sth **through (**sth**)** *Fig.* to force passage of a motion or law. □ *The committee chairman managed to push the bill through the committee.*

push sth **to** to close or nearly close something, such as a door. □ *The door is open a little. Please push it to.*

push so **to the wall** AND **press** so **to the wall** to force someone into a position where there is only one choice to make; to put someone in a defensive position. □ *There was little else I could do. They pushed me to the wall.*

push so **too far** *Fig.* to antagonize someone too much; to be too confrontational with someone. □ *I guess I pushed him too far, because he began shouting at me and threatening to hit me.*

*pushed for cash Go to pressed for money.

pushed for time Go to pressed for time.

pushing the envelope *Fig.* attempting to expand the definition, categorization, dimensions, or perimeters of something farther than is usual. □ *The engineers wanted to completely redesign the product but were pushing the envelope when it came to public acceptance.*

pushing up (the) daisies *Fig.* dead and buried. (Usually in the future tense.) □ *If you talk to me like that again, you'll be pushing up the daisies!*

pussyfoot around *Fig.* to go about timidly and cautiously. (Alludes to a cat walking carefully.) □ *Stop pussyfooting around! Get on with it!* □ *I wish that they would not pussyfoot around when there are tough decisions to be made.*

put a bee in one's **bonnet** Go to a bee in one's bonnet.

put a cap on sth *Fig.* to put a limit on something. □ *The city put a cap on the amount each landlord could charge.*

put a contract out on so *Fig.* [for an underworld character] to order someone to kill someone else. □ *The mob put out a contract on some small-time crook from Detroit.*

put a damper on sth *Fig.* to have a dulling or numbing influence on something. □ *The bad news really put a damper on everything.*

put a dent in sth Go to make a dent in sth.

put a dog off the scent to distract a dog from trailing the scent of someone or an animal. □ *The odor of a skunk put the dogs off the scent.*

put a figure on sth Go to put a price (tag) on sth.

put a hold on sth to place restriction on something so that it is reserved, delayed, or inactivated. □ *The bank put a hold on my credit card until I paid my bill.*

put a horse out to pasture *Fig.* to retire a horse by allowing it to live out its days in a pasture with no work. □ *The horse could no longer work, so we put it out to pasture.*

put a plug in† **(for** so/sth**)** *Fig.* to say something favoring someone or something; to advertise someone or something. □ *I hope that when you are in talking to the manager, you put a plug in for me.*

put a premium on sth AND **place a premium on** sth *Fig.* to make something harder or more expensive to obtain or do. □ *The recent action of the bank directors put a premium on new home loans.*

put a price (tag) on sth AND **put a figure on** sth to establish and state the cost of something. □ *It is very valuable. I couldn't possibly put a price on it.*

put a smile on so's **face** *Fig.* to please someone; to make someone happy. □ *We are going to give Andy a pretty good raise, and I know that'll put a smile on his face.*

Put a sock in it! Go to Stuff a sock in it!

put a spin on sth *Fig.* to twist a report or story to one's advantage; to interpret an event to make it seem favorable or beneficial to oneself or one's cause. □ *The mayor tried to put a positive spin on the damaging polls.*

put a stop to sth to end something. □ *Don't worry. I'll put a stop to all this nonsense.*

put a strain on so/sth to burden or overload someone or something. □ *All this bad economic news puts a strain on everyone's nerves.*

put oneself **across** *Fig.* to make oneself convincing and acceptable, especially when attempting to advance oneself. □ *You should work harder at putting yourself across at meetings with clients.*

put so **across (in** a good way**)** AND **get** so **across (in** a good way**)** *Fig.* to present someone in a good way or a good light. □ *I don't want Tom to make the speech. He doesn't put himself across well.*

put sth **across (to** so**)** AND **get** sth **across (to** so**)** *Fig.* to make something clear to someone; to convince someone of something; to get a plan accepted. □ *I don't know how to put this point across to my class. Can you help?*

put so/sth **ahead (of** so/sth**)** to think of someone or something as more important than someone or something. □ *She put herself ahead of everyone else and expected special treatment.*

put all one's **eggs in one basket** *Fig.* to make everything dependent on only one thing; to place all one's resources in one place, account, etc. (If the basket is dropped, all is lost.) □ *Don't invest all your money in one company. Never put all your eggs in one basket.*

put an end to sth to terminate or end something. □ *The police are finally putting an end to all the speeding and reckless driving in our small town.*

put another way Go to to put it another way.

put sth **aside**† Go to leave sth aside†.

put sth **aside for a rainy day** Go to save (sth) for a rainy day.

put one's **ass on the line** Go to put one's neck on the line.

put sth **at** an amount to price something at a certain amount of money; to estimate something at a certain figure. □ *I would put the charges at about $200.*

put sth **at a premium** *Fig.* to make something available only at an extra cost or through extra effort. □ *The scarcity of fresh vegetables at this time of year puts broccoli at a premium.*

put so/sth **at** so's **disposal** Go to at so's disposal.

put sth **at** so's **door** Go to lay sth at so's door.

put one **at (**one's**) ease** *Fig.* to cause someone to relax or feel welcome. □ *She usually tells a little joke to put you at your ease.*

put so/sth **at risk** Go to at risk.

put so/sth **at stake** Go to at stake.

put so **away**† **1.** *Sl.* to kill someone. (Underworld.) □ *The gangster threatened to put me away if I told the police.* **2.** *Euph.* to bury someone. □ *My uncle died last week. They put him away on Saturday.* **3.** AND **send** so **away** *Euph.* to have

put one's best foot forward

someone put into a mental institution. □ *My uncle became irrational, and they put him away.* □ *They sent away my aunt the year before.* **4.** AND **send** so **away** *Euph.* to sentence someone to prison for a length of time. (Underworld.) □ *They sent Rocky away for 15 years.* □ *The judge put away the whole gang.*

put sth **away**† *Fig.* to eat something. □ *Are you going to put this last piece of cake away?*

put one's **back (in)to** sth **1.** to apply great physical effort to lift or move something. □ *You can lift it if you put your back to it!* **2.** *Fig.* to apply a lot of mental or creative effort to doing something. (Fig. on ①.) □ *If we put our backs to it, we can bake 12 dozen cookies today.*

put so's **back up** Go to get so's dander up.

put balls on sth *Sl.* to make something more masculine or powerful; to give something authority and strength. (*Balls* = testicles. Use with discretion.) □ *This*

story is too namby-pamby. Put some balls on it.

put sth **behind** one *Fig.* to try to forget about something. □ *I look forward to putting all my problems behind me.*

put so **behind bars** Go to behind bars.

put one's **best foot forward** *Fig.* to act or appear at one's best; to try to make a good impression. □ *When you apply for a job, you should always put your best foot forward.*

put sth **by** AND **lay** sth **by** *Fig.* to reserve a portion of something; to preserve and store something, such as food. □ *I put some money by for a rainy day.*

put one's **cards on the table** Go to lay one's cards on the table.

put one's **dibs on** sth *Fig.* to lay a claim to something; to announce one's claim to something. □ *She put her dibs on the last piece of cake.*

put an animal **down**† *Euph.* to take the life of an animal mercifully. □ *We put down our old dog last year.*

put so/sth **down**† *Fig.* to belittle or degrade someone or something. □ *It's an old car, but that's no reason to put it down.* □ *Why are you always putting me down?*

put sth **down**† Go to set sth down†.

put so **down as** sth bad *Fig.* to judge that someone is bad or undesirable in some way. □ *He was so rude that I put him down as someone to be avoided.* □ *If you act silly all the time, people will put you down as a fool.*

put so **down (for** sth**)** to put someone's name on a list of people who volunteer to do something or give an amount of money. □ *Can I put you down for $10?* □ *We're having a picnic, and you're invited. Everyone is bringing something. Can I put you down for potato salad?*

put sth **down**† **in black and white** AND **set** sth **down**† **in black and white** *Fig.* to write down the terms of an agreement; to draw up a written contract; to put the details of something down on paper. (Refers to black ink and white paper.) □ *I think I understand what you are talking about, but we need to put down the details in black and white.*

put sth **down to** sth AND **set** sth **down to** sth to explain something as being caused by something else. □ *We set your failure down to your emotional upset.*

put sth **down to experience** *Fig.* to consider a failure to be a valuable learning experience. □ *I wasted a lot of money on a used car and couldn't get my money back. I just put it all down to experience.*

Put 'em up! Go to Hands up!

put so's **eye out**† to puncture or harm someone's eye and destroy its ability to see. □ *Careful with that stick or you'll put your eye out.*

put one's **face on** *Fig.* [for a woman] to apply cosmetics. □ *We'll be on our way once my wife has put her face on.*

put one's **feet up**† to sit down, lean back, and rest; to lie down. □ *He was really exhausted and had to go put his feet up.*

put one's **finger on** sth *Fig.* to identify and state the essence of something. □ *That is correct! You have certainly put your finger on the problem.*

put one's **foot down (about** so/sth**)** AND **put** one's **foot down (on** so/sth**)** *Fig.* to assert one's authority to put an end to something. □ *The boss put her foot down and refused to accept any more changes to the plan.*

put one's **foot in** one's **mouth** AND **put** one's **foot in it; stick** one's **foot in** one's **mouth** *Fig.* to say something that you regret; to say something stupid, insulting, or hurtful. □ *When I told Ann that her hair was more beautiful than I had ever seen it, I really put my foot in my mouth. It was a wig.*

put (sth**) forth** to exert effort. (See also put sth forward.) □ *You are going to have to put more effort forth if you want to succeed.*

put sth **forth**† Go to next.

put sth **forward**† AND **put** sth **forth**† to state an idea; to advance an idea. □ *Toward the end of the meeting, Sally put a new idea forward.*

put hair on so's **chest** *Fig.* to do or take something to invigorate or virilize someone, always a male, except in jest. □ *Here, have a drink of this stuff! It'll put hair on your chest.*

put one's **hand to the plow** *Fig.* to get busy; to help out; to start working. (Fig. on the image of grasping a plow, ready to work the fields.) □ *You should start work now. It's time to put your hand to the plow.*

put one's **hands on** so/sth/animal AND **lay** one's **hands on** so/sth/animal; **get** one's **hands on** so/sth/animal **1.** *Fig.* to locate and get hold of someone, something, or some creature. □ *As soon as I can lay my hands on him, I'll get him right over here.* **2.** *Fig.* to get hold of someone or some creature with punishment or harm as a goal. □ *I* *can't wait to get my hands on that cat! Will I ever teach it a lesson!*

put one's **head on the block (for** so/sth) *Fig.* to take great risks for someone or something; to go to a lot of trouble or difficulty for someone or something; to attempt to gain favor for someone or something. (Fig. on the notion of sacrificing one's life by decapitation for the sake of someone else.) □ *I don't know why I should put my head on the block for Joan. What has she ever done for me?*

put people's **heads together** *Fig.* to join together with someone to confer. □ *Let's put our heads together and come up with a solution to this problem.*

put one's **heart (and soul) into** sth AND **pour** one's **heart (and soul) into** sth *Fig.* to put all of one's sincere efforts into something. □ *She put her heart and soul into the singing of the national anthem.*

put one's **house in order** AND **set** one's **house in order; get** one's **house in order** *Fig.* to put one's business or personal affairs into good order. (As if one were cleaning one's house. Very close to **put** one's **own house in order.**) □ *There was some trouble in the department office, and the manager was told to put his house in order.*

put ideas into so's **head** *Fig.* to suggest something—usually something bad—to someone (who would not have thought of it otherwise). □ *Bill keeps getting into trouble. Please don't put ideas into his head.*

put sth **in**[†] *Fig.* to submit something, such as an order, request, or demand. □ *In fact, I put the order in some time ago.*

put in some place *Fig.* [for a vessel] to dock temporarily some place. □ *The ship put in at Bridgetown, Barbados, for repairs.*

put in a good word (for so) *Fig.* to say something (to someone) in support of someone else. □ *Yes, I want the job. If you see the boss, please put in a good word.*

put in a hard day at work AND **put in a hard day's work** *Fig.* to work very hard at one's job. □ *I put in a hard day at work*

at the office, and now I want to be left alone to rest.

put sth **in a nutshell** *Fig.* to state something very concisely. (Fig. on the small size of a nutshell and the amount that it would hold.) □ *The entire explanation is long and involved, but let me put it in a nutshell for you.*

put in an appearance (at sth) *Fig.* to appear briefly at some place or at some event. □ *I only wanted to put in an appearance at the reception, but I ended up staying for two hours.*

put in for sth *Fig.* to apply for something; to make a request for something. □ *I put in for a transfer, but I bet I don't get it.* □ *She put in for a new file cabinet, but she never got one.*

put sth **in layaway** AND **put** sth **in will-call** *Fig.* to purchase something by paying part of the price initially and not receiving the goods until all the money has been paid. □ *I couldn't afford a winter coat right now, so I picked one out and put it in layaway.*

put so **in mind of** so/sth to remind someone of someone or something. □ *Mary puts me in mind of her mother when she was that age.*

put sth **in mothballs** *Fig.* to put something into storage or reserve. (Often said of warships.) □ *The navy put the old cruiser in mothballs, and no one ever expected to see it again.*

put sth **in motion** Go to set sth in motion.

put sth **in perspective** Go to in perspective.

put one in one's **place** Go to in one's place.

put oneself in so else's **place** AND **put** oneself **in** so else's **shoes** to allow oneself to see or experience something from someone else's point of view. □ *Put yourself in someone else's place, and see how it feels.* □ *I put myself in Tom's shoes and realized that I would have made exactly the same choice.*

put oneself **in** so else's **shoes** Go to previous.

put so **in touch with** so/sth to cause or help someone to communicate with someone or something. □ *Would you please put me in touch with the main office?*

put sth **in will-call** Go to put sth in layaway.

put sth **into effect** AND **put** sth **into force** to make something take effect; to begin using or enforcing a policy or procedure. □ *When will the city council put this law into effect?*

put sth **into force** Go to previous.

put sth **in(to)** so's **head** *Fig.* to give ideas to someone who might not have thought of them without help. □ *No one put it in my head. I thought of it all by myself.*

put so/sth **in(to) jeopardy** *Fig.* to put someone or something into danger. □ *The information you gave out puts Bill into jeopardy.*

put so/sth **into order** to put people or things into a proper sequence. □ *Would you please put these people into order by height so we can march into the auditorium?*

put sth **into practice** *Fig.* to make a suggested procedure the actual procedure. □ *That is a good policy. I suggest you put it into practice immediately.*

put sth **in(to) print** AND **get** sth **in(to) print** to publish something; to record something spoken in printed letters. (*Get* can imply more speed and effort.) □ *The article looks good. We will put it into print as soon as possible.* □ *We'll get it into print as soon as we can.*

put sth **in(to) service** AND **put** sth **into use; bring** sth **into service** *Fig.* to start to use a thing; to make a device operate and function. □ *I hope that they are able to put the elevator into service again soon. I am tired of climbing stairs.* □ *When can we put the new copier into use?*

put sth **into use** Go to previous.

put sth **into words** *Fig.* to form an idea into sentences that can be spoken or written. □ *I find it hard to put my thoughts into words.*

put it on the line Go to lay it on the line.

put one's life on the line Go to put one's neck on the line.

put so's **mind at ease (about** so/sth**)** Go to set so's mind at ease (about so/sth).

put one's mind to sth AND **set one's mind to** sth *Fig.* to concentrate on doing something; to give the doing of something one's full attention. □ *I know I can do it if I put my mind to it.*

put one's money on so/sth **(to** do sth**) 1.** *Fig.* to bet money that someone or something will accomplish something. □ *I put my money on the favorite to win the race.* **2.** *Fig.* to predict the outcome of an event involving someone or something, and as a consequence, announce support for someone or something. (This is not a wager.) □ *Alice put her money on the most popular candidate.*

put money up[†] **(for** sth**)** *Fig.* to provide the funding for something. □ *The government put the money up for the cost of construction.*

put one's neck on the line AND **put one's life on the line; put one's ass on the line** *Fig.* to put oneself at great risk. (*Ass* = one's body. Caution with *ass.*) □ *I put my neck on the line and recommended you for the job, and now look what you've done! I'm ruined!*

put no stock in sth AND **not put any stock in** sth *Fig.* not to believe in something. □ *I put no stock in anything he says. He's just a liar.*

put one's nose in (where it's not wanted) AND **stick one's nose in (where it's not wanted)** *Inf.* to interfere in someone else's business. □ *Please don't put your nose in where it's not wanted!*

put one's nose out of joint Go to get one's nose out of joint.

put one's nose to the grindstone *Fig.* to get busy doing one's work. □ *The boss told me to put my nose to the grindstone.*

put one's oar in[†] AND **stick one's oar in**[†]; **put one's two cents(' worth) in**[†] *Fig.* to add one's comments or opinion, even if unwanted or unasked for. □ *I'm sorry. I shouldn't have stuck my oar in when you* *were arguing with your wife.* □ *Do you mind if I put in my oar? I have a suggestion.*

put so **off**† **1.** *Fig.* to delay dealing with someone until a later time. □ *I hate to keep putting you off, but we are not ready to deal with you yet.* **2.** *Fig.* to repel someone; to distress someone. □ *You really put people off with your scowling face.* **3.** *Fig.* to avoid or evade someone. □ *I won't talk to reporters. Tell them something that will put them off.*

put sth **off**† to postpone something; to schedule something for a later time. □ *I have to put off our meeting until a later time.*

put off by so/sth distressed or repelled by someone or something. □ *I was really put off by your behavior.*

put one **off** one's **stride 1.** *Fig.* to cause one to deviate from a rhythmic stride while walking, running, or marching. □ *A rabbit ran across the path and put me off my stride.* **2.** *Fig.* to interfere with one's normal and natural progress or rate of progress. (Fig. on ①.) □ *Your startling comments put Larry off his stride for a moment.*

put so **off the scent** AND **throw** so **off the scent** *Fig.* to distract someone or a group from following a scent or trail. (Fig. on put a dog off the scent. See also put so off the track.) □ *The clever maneuvers of the bandits put the sheriff's posse off the scent.*

put so **off the track** AND **put** so **off the trail** *Fig.* to cause someone to lose a trail that is being followed. (See also put so off the scent.) □ *I was following an escaped convict and something put me off the trail.*

put so **off the trail** Go to previous.

put so **on** *Fig.* to tease or deceive someone innocently and in fun. □ *He got real mad even though they were only putting him on.*

put on airs AND **give** oneself **airs** *Fig.* to act better than one really is; to pretend to be good or to be superior. □ *Pay no attention to her. She is just putting on airs.*

put on an act *Fig.* to pretend that one is something other than what one is. □ *You don't have to put on an act. We accept you the way you are.*

put one **on** one's **feet** Go to get one on one's feet.

put so **on hold** *Fig.* to stop all activity or communication with someone. (Fig. on put so/sth on hold.) □ *John put Ann on hold and started dating Mary.*

put so/sth **on hold** to put someone or someone's telephone call on an electronic hold. □ *Please don't put me on hold! I'm in a hurry!*

put sth **on hold** to postpone something; to stop the progress of something. (Fig. on put so/sth on hold.) □ *They put the project on hold until they got enough money to finish it.*

put one **on** one's **honor** *Fig.* to inform one that one is trusted to act honorably, legally, and fairly without supervision. □ *I'll put you on your honor when I have to leave the room during the test.*

put so/sth **on ice** *Fig.* to postpone acting on someone or something. □ *I know he keeps pestering you for an answer, but we'll just have to put him on ice until we have more facts to go on.*

put sth **on paper** *Fig.* to write something down. □ *I'm sorry, I can't discuss your offer until I see something in writing. Put it on paper, and then we'll talk.*

put sth **on the cuff** *Fig.* to buy something on credit; to add to one's credit balance. (As if a rough accounting were scribbled on someone's shirt cuff.) □ *I'll take two of those, and please put them on the cuff.*

put on the dog AND **put on the ritz** *Inf.* to make things extra special or dress formally for a special event. □ *Frank's really putting on the dog for the big party Friday night.*

put sth **on the front burner** Go to on the front burner.

put sth **on the map** *Fig.* to make some place famous or popular. □ *Nothing like* a little scandal to put an otherwise sleepy town on the map.

put on the ritz Go to put on the dog.

put sth **on the street** *Sl.* to tell something openly; to spread news. □ *There is no need to put all this gossip on the street. Keep it to yourself.*

put on weight *Fig.* to gain weight; to get fat. □ *I think I am putting on a little weight. I had better go on a diet.*

put one foot in front of the other 1. *Fig.* to walk deliberately. □ *I was so tired that I could hardly even put one foot in front of the other.* **2.** *Fig.* to do things carefully and in their proper order. (Fig. on ①.) □ *Let's do it right now. Just put one foot in front of the other. One thing at a time.*

put oneself **out** *Fig.* to inconvenience oneself. □ *No, I did not put myself out at all. It was no trouble, in fact.*

put so **out**† *Fig.* to distress or anger someone. (Often passive.) □ *She really put him out by her remarks.*

put out a warrant (on so**)** AND **send out a warrant (on** so**)** *Fig.* to issue a warrant for the arrest of someone. □ *The police put out a warrant on Spike.*

put out (about so/sth**)** *Fig.* irritated; bothered. □ *John behaved rudely at the party, and the hostess was quite put out.*

put some creature **out of its misery** *Fig.* to kill an animal in a humane manner. □ *The vet put that dog with cancer out of its misery.*

put so/sth **out of** one's **mind** AND **get** so/sth **out of** one's **mind** *Fig.* to forget someone or something; to make an effort to stop thinking about someone or something. □ *Try to get it out of your mind.*

put one **out of (**one's**) misery 1.** *Fig.* to kill someone as an act of mercy. (See also put some creature **out of its misery.**) □ *He took pills to put himself out of his misery.* **2.** *Fig.* to end a suspenseful situation for someone. □ *Please, put me out of misery; what happened?*

put so **out of the way** *Euph.* to kill someone. □ *The police suspected that she had*

put her uncle out of the way in order to inherit his property.

put out (some) feelers (on so/sth**)** to arrange to find out about something in an indirect manner. □ *I put out some feelers on Betty to try to find out what is going on.*

put so **out to pasture** *Fig.* to retire someone. (Fig. on put a horse out to pasture.) □ *This vice president has reached retirement age. It's time to put him out to pasture.*

put (out) to sea to begin on a sea voyage or perhaps on a career as a sailor. □ *We will put out to sea at dawn and be gone for a month.*

put so/sth **over** *Fig.* to succeed in making someone or something be accepted. □ *Do you think we can put this new product over?*

put sth **over**† *Fig.* to accomplish something; to put something across. (See also put so/sth **over.**) □ *This is a very hard thing to explain to a large audience. I hope I can put over the main points.*

put sth **over on** so AND **put one over on** so *Fig.* to play a trick on someone; to deceive someone with something. □ *I'm too observant. You can't put anything over on me.*

put one's **own house in order** AND **set** one's **own house in order; get** one's **own house in order** to make one's own affairs right, before or instead of criticizing someone else. □ *You should put your own house in order before criticizing someone else.*

put paid to sth *Fig.* to consider something closed or completed; to mark or indicate that something is no longer important or pending. (As if one were stamping a bill "paid.") □ *At last, we were able to put paid to the matter of who is to manage the accounts.*

put pen to paper Go to set pen to paper.

put sth **plainly** *Fig.* to state something firmly and explicitly. □ *To put it plainly, I want you out of this house immediately.*

put sth **right** Go to set sth right.

put roots down† (some place) AND **send roots down**† (some place) *Fig.* to settle down somewhere; to make some place one's permanent home. □ *I'm not ready to put roots down anywhere yet.*

put one's **shoulder to the wheel** Go to have one's shoulder to the wheel.

put some distance between so **and** one-self or sth *Fig.* to move or travel away from someone or something. □ *Jill and I aren't getting along. I need to put some distance between her and me.*

put some sweet lines on so Go to lay some sweet lines on so.

put some teeth into sth *Fig.* to increase the power or efficacy of something. □ *The mayor tried to put some teeth into the new law.*

put (some) years on so/sth *Fig.* to cause someone or something to age prematurely; to cause deterioration in the state of someone or something. (The *some* may be replaced with a specific number or period of time.) □ *The events of the last week have really put a lot of years on Gerald.*

put sth **straight** Go to set sth straight.

Put that in your pipe and smoke it! *Inf.* See how you like that!; It is final, and you have to live with it. □ *Well, I'm not going to do what you want, so put that in your pipe and smoke it!*

put the arm on so *Fig.* to apply pressure to someone. □ *John's been putting the arm on Mary to get her to go out with him.*

put the bite on so **(for** sth**)** AND **put the touch on** so **(for** sth**)** *Sl.* to try to get money from someone. □ *Tom put the bite on me for $10.*

put the blame on so/sth AND **lay the blame on** so/sth; **place the blame on** so/sth *Fig.* to blame someone or something; to assign a bad outcome to someone or something. □ *Don't put the blame on me. I didn't do it.*

put the brakes on so/sth Go to put the clamps on so/sth.

put the cart before the horse AND **have the cart before the horse** *Fig.* to have things in the wrong order; to have things confused and mixed up. □ *You're eating your dessert first! You've put the cart before the horse.* □ *John has the cart before the horse in most of his projects.*

put the chill on so AND **put the freeze on** so *Sl.* to ignore someone; to end social contact with someone. □ *Spike put the chill on the guys who threatened him.*

put the clamps on so/sth AND **put the clamps on**†; **put the brakes on** so/sth *Sl.* to impede or block someone or something; to restrain or restrict someone. □ *Fred had to put the clamps on Tony, who was rushing his work too much.* □ *The boss put the brakes on Gerald, who was trying too aggressively to get promoted.*

put the fear of God in(to) so *Fig.* to frighten someone severely; [for something] to shock someone into contrite behavior. □ *A near miss like that really puts the fear of God into you.*

put the feed bag on† AND **put the nose-bag on**† *Fig.* to eat a meal. (Both refer to a method of feeding a horse by attaching a bag of food at its nose and mouth.) □ *It's time to put the feed bag on! I'm starved!*

put the finger on so AND **lay the finger on** so *Sl.* to accuse someone; to identify someone as the one who did something. □ *Tom put the finger on John, and John is really mad.*

put the freeze on so Go to put the chill on so.

put the heat on (so**)** AND **put the screws on (**so**)**; **tighten the screws on (**so**)**; **make it hot for** so; **turn up the heat (on** so**)**; **hold** so's **feet to the fire**; **put the squeeze on (**so**)** *Sl.* to put pressure on someone (to do something); to coerce someone; to pressure someone to pay money. □ *John wouldn't talk, so the police were putting the heat on him to confess.* □ *When my boss puts the screws on, he can be very unpleasant.*

put the kibosh on so/sth *Fig.* to squelch someone or something; to veto someone or someone's plans. □ *I hate to put the ki-bosh on Randy, but he isn't doing what he is supposed to.*

put the lid on sth Go to the lid on sth.

put the lie to sth Go to give the lie to sth.

put the make on so AND **put the moves on** so; **put the hard word on** so *Sl.* to attempt to seduce or proposition someone. □ *I think he was beginning to put the make on me. I'm glad I left.* □ *James tried to put the hard word on Martha.*

put the moves on so Go to previous.

put the nose-bag on† Go to put the feed bag on†.

put the pedal to the metal *Sl.* to press a car's accelerator to the floor; to drive very fast. □ *Put the pedal to the metal, and we'll make up some lost time.*

put (the) pressure on so **(to** do sth**)** to make demands on someone; to try to get someone to do something. □ *We put the pressure on him to get him to come, but he refused.*

put the roses back into so's **cheeks** *Fig.* [for something] to cause a person to look well and healthy again. □ *A little fresh air will put the roses back into your cheeks.*

put the screws on (so**)** Go to put the heat on (so).

put the skids on (sth**)** AND **put the skids under** so/sth *Sl.* to cause something to fail; to cause someone or something to fail. □ *They put the skids on the project when they refused to give us any more money.* □ *That's the end of our great idea! Somebody put the skids on.*

put the squeeze on (so**)** Go to put the heat on (so).

put the touch on so **(for** sth**)** Go to put the bite on so (for sth).

put one's **thinking cap on**† *Fig.* to start thinking in a serious manner. (Usually used with children.) □ *All right now, let's put on our thinking caps and do some arithmetic.*

put so **through** sth *Fig.* to cause someone to have to endure something. □ *I'm sorry* I put you through all that questioning. It's just routine, you know.

put one **through** one's **paces** AND **put** sth **through its paces** *Fig.* to give someone or something a thorough test; to show what someone or something can do. (Fig. on the image of making a trained animal do a sequence of rehearsed tricks.) □ *I brought the young gymnast out and put her through her paces.*

put so **through the wringer** *Fig.* to give someone a difficult time; to interrogate someone thoroughly. (Fig. on putting something through an old-fashioned clothes wringer.) □ *The lawyer really put the witness through the wringer!*

put so/sth **through (to** so**)** *Fig.* to put someone's telephone call through to someone. □ *Will you please put me through to the international operator?*

put sth **to bed** *Fig.* to complete work on something and send it on to the next step in production, especially in publishing. □ *This week's edition is finished. Let's put it to bed.*

put to bed with a shovel *Sl.* dead and buried. (Fig. on the image of digging a grave.) □ *You wanna be put to bed with a shovel? Just keep talking that way.*

put so **to bed with a shovel** *Sl.* to bury someone; to kill and bury someone. □ *The leader of the gang was getting sort of tired and old, so one of the younger thugs put him to bed with a shovel.*

put so **to death** to kill or execute someone. □ *The executioner put the murderer to death at midnight.*

put sth **to (good) use** *Fig.* to apply a skill or ability; to use a skill or ability. □ *The pianist put his talents to use at the party.*

put to it *Fig.* strained or exhausted. □ *John was put to it to get there on time.*

put sth **to rest** AND **lay** sth **to rest** *Fig.* to put an end to a rumor; to finish dealing with something and forget about it. □ *I've heard enough about Ann and her illness. I'd like to put the whole matter to rest.*

put so **to shame 1.** to embarrass someone; to make someone ashamed. □ *I put him to shame by telling everyone about his bad behavior.* **2.** *Fig.* to show someone up by doing better than they do. □ *Your excellent efforts put us all to shame.*

put so/animal **to sleep** *Euph. Fig.* to kill someone or an animal, usually mercifully. □ *We had to put our dog to sleep.* □ *The robber said he'd put us to sleep forever if we didn't cooperate.*

put so **to sleep 1.** to bore someone. □ *Her long story just put me to sleep.* **2.** Go to put so/animal **to sleep.**

put so/sth **to the test** *Fig.* to see what someone or something can achieve. □ *I'm going to put my car to the test right now, and see how fast it will go.*

put sth **together** *Fig.* to consider some facts and arrive at a conclusion. □ *When I put together all the facts, I found the answer.*

put one's **trust in** so/sth *Fig.* to trust someone or something. □ *You can put your trust in the bank. Its deposits are insured.*

put two and two together *Fig.* to figure something out from the information available. □ *Don't worry. John won't figure it out. He can't put two and two together.*

put two and two together and come up with five *Fig.* to study a matter and still not have it make sense. (This is a roundabout way of saying that the facts don't add up (to sth).) □ *As we study this case and hear all the testimony, there is something missing and we still can't make sense of it. It's like putting two and two together and coming up with five.*

put one's **two cents(' worth) in**† Go to put one's **oar in**†.

put so **under** *Fig.* to anesthetize someone. □ *After you put her under, we will begin the operation.*

put sth **under the microscope** AND **put** sth **under a microscope** *Fig.* to examine, analyze, or study something in great detail. (Can also be used literally, of course.) □ *I'll have to study your proposition. Let me put it under the microscope*

for a while and see what it will cost us in time and money, and I'll get back to you.

put so **up**† to provide lodging for someone. □ *I hope I can find someone to put me up.*

put sth **up**† *Fig.* to store and preserve food by canning or freezing. □ *This year we'll put some strawberries up.*

put up a (brave) front AND **put on a (brave) front; put on a (brave) face** *Fig.* to appear to be brave (even if one is not). □ *Mary is frightened, but she's putting up a brave front.*

put up a fight AND **put up a struggle** *Fig.* to make a struggle, a fight, etc. (Fixed order.) □ *Did he put up a fight?* □ *No, he only put up a bit of a struggle.*

put up a struggle Go to previous.

put so **up against** so to place someone into competition with someone else. □ *The coach put his best wrestler up against the champ from the other team.*

put up one's **dukes** *Fig.* to be prepared to fight. (Older.) □ *He's telling you to put up your dukes.*

put sth **up for sale** Go to up for sale.

Put up or shut up! 1. *Inf.* Do something or stop promising to do it! □ *I'm tired of your telling everyone how fast you can run. Now, do it! Put up or shut up!* **2.** *Inf.* a command that a person bet money in support of what the person advocates. □ *You think you can beat me at cards? Twenty bucks says you're wrong. Put up or shut up!*

put sth **(up) to a vote** *Fig.* to arrange to have a matter voted upon. □ *We could argue all day about this. Let's put it up to a vote.*

put so **up with** so *Fig.* to house someone with someone. □ *I will put her up with my cousin, who has an extra bedroom.*

put up with so/sth AND **stand** so/sth; **bear** so/sth *Fig.* to tolerate or endure someone or something; to be able to stand someone or something. □ *We can put up with John's living here until he finds a place of his own.* □ *She can't stand the sight of* *him!* □ *I can't bear another moment of this pain.*

put upon by so *Fig.* [for a person] to be taken advantage of to an unreasonable degree by someone else. (Typically passive.) □ *My mother was always put upon by her neighbors. She was too nice to refuse their requests for help.*

put wear (and tear) on sth *Fig.* to cause deterioration in the state of something. □ *This road salt puts a lot of wear on cars.*

put weight on† *Fig.* to gain weight; to grow fat. □ *The doctor says I need to put on some weight.*

put words in(to) so's **mouth** *Fig.* to interpret what someone said so that the words mean what you want and not what the speaker wanted. □ *I didn't say that! You are putting words into my mouth.*

Put your money where your mouth is! *Inf.* Stop just talking and stake your own money! (From gambling. Can also be said to someone giving investment advice.) □ *You want me to bet on that horse? Did you? Why don't you put your money where your mouth is?* □ *If this is such a good stock, you buy it. Put your money where your mouth is!*

*****putty in** so's **hands** *Fig.* [of someone] easily influenced by someone else; excessively willing to do what someone else wishes. (Putty is soft and malleable. *Typically: **be** ~; **become** ~; **seem like** ~.) □ *Bob's wife is putty in his hands. She never thinks for herself.* □ *Jane is putty in her mother's hands. She always does exactly what her mother says.*

a **put-up job** *Inf.* a deception; a deceptive event. □ *That's really phony. A put-up job if I ever saw one.* □ *No put-up job is clever enough to fool me.*

puzzle sth **out**† Go to dope sth out†.

Q

quake in one's **boots** Go to shake in one's boots.

quality time *Fig.* time spent with someone allowing interaction and closeness. □ *He was able to spend a few minutes of quality time with his son, Buxton, at least once every two weeks.*

*qualms (about so/sth**)** *Fig.* an uneasy feeling of one's conscience about someone or something. (*Typically: **cause ~; have ~; have no ~; give** so **~.**) □ *Do you have any qualms about telling a little white lie to Mary about her not getting an invitation to the party?*

The **Queen's English** *Fig.* "Official" British English. □ *He can't even speak The Queen's English! Despicable!*

queer as a three-dollar bill Go to phony as a three-dollar bill.

queer for sth *Inf.* in the mood for something; desiring something. (Older.) □ *I'm queer for a beer right now.*

a **question of** (doing) sth AND a **matter of** (doing) sth *Fig.* a subject of (doing) something; a problem of (doing) something. □ *It's not a matter of not wanting to go to the opera. It's a question of money.*

*a question of time AND ***a matter of time** *Fig.* only a certain amount of time will elapse before something happens. (*Typically: **just ~; only ~.**) □ *It's only a matter of time until that tree dies.* □ *He is near death. It's just a question of time.*

queue up (for sth**)** to line up for something. (More U.K. than U.S.) □ *We had to queue up for tickets to the play.*

quick and dirty *Fig.* [done] fast and carelessly; [done] fast and cheaply. □ *The contractor made a lot of money on quick and dirty projects that would never last very long.*

quick as a flash Go to next.

*quick as a wink AND ***quick as a flash; *quick as (greased) lightning; *swift as lightning** very quickly. (*Also: **as ~.**) □ *As quick as a wink, the thief took the lady's purse.* □ *Quick as greased lightning, the thief stole my wallet.*

quick as (greased) lightning Go to previous.

a **quick bite** a snack or a quick meal. □ *Let's stop here for a quick bite. We've got 20 minutes before the plane leaves.*

quick like a bunny *Inf.* really quick. □ *Now's your chance. Do it! Quick like a bunny!*

quick off the mark *Fig.* quick starting or reacting. (Compare this with slow off the mark.) □ *Boy, you were quick off the mark there!*

quick on the draw Go to next.

quick on the trigger AND **quick on the draw 1.** *Fig.* quick to draw a gun and shoot. □ *Some of the old cowboys were known to be quick on the trigger.* **2.** *Fig.* quick to respond to anything. (Fig. on ①.) □ *John gets the right answer before anyone else. He's really quick on the trigger.*

quick on the uptake *Fig.* quick to understand or learn something. □ *Mary understands jokes before anyone else because she's so quick on the uptake.*

a **quick study** *Fig.* a person who is quick to learn things. (Compare this to a slow study.) □ *Jane, who is a quick study,* *caught the joke immediately and laughed before everyone else.*

a **quick temper** AND a **short temper;** a **short fuse** *Fig.* a bad temper that can be easily aroused. □ *Tyler has a quick temper and doesn't mind letting everyone see it.*

quicken the pace (of sth**)** Go to pick up the pace (of sth).

quicken the pulse (of sth**)** Go to pick up the pace (of sth).

quicker than a New York minute Go to a New York minute.

quicker than hell *Inf.* very fast. □ *Be careful in the stock market. You can lose all your money quicker than hell.*

quicker than you can say Jack Robinson Go to before you can say Jack Robinson.

***quiet as a (church) mouse** AND ***quiet as the grave** very quiet. (*Also: as ~.) □ *You'd better be as quiet as a mouse while Grandma takes her nap, so you won't wake her up.*

quiet as the grave Go to previous.

quit while one **is ahead** *Fig.* to stop doing something while one is still successful.

□ *Get into the market. Make some money and get out. Quit while you're ahead.*

quite (a) sth AND **quite the** sth *Fig.* something very good or remarkable. □ *Meg's mother has brought a new hat for the wedding, and it's quite something.*

quite a few AND **quite a lot; quite a bit; quite a number** much or many. □ *Do you need one? I have quite a few.* □ *I have quite a bit—enough to spare some.*

quite a number Go to previous.

quiver with sth **1.** to shake or shiver from something, such as cold, fear, anticipation, etc. □ *On seeing the bear, the dogs quivered with fear.* **2.** *Fig.* to experience eagerness or joy, possibly with actual quivering. (Fig. on ①.) □ *I quivered with delight when I saw the dessert.*

quiz out (of sth**)** *Fig.* to earn permission to waive a college course by successful completion of a quiz or exam. □ *Andrew was able to quiz out of calculus.*

quote, unquote *Fig.* a parenthetical expression said before a word or short phrase indicating that the word or phrase would be in quotation marks if used in writing. □ *So I said to her, quote, unquote, it's time we had a little talk.*

R

race against the clock AND **race against time 1.** *Fig.* a race with time; a great hurry to get something done before a particular time. □ *In a race against the clock, they rushed the accident victim to the hospital.* □ *We were in a race against time to beat the deadline.* **2.** *Fig.* to hurry to beat a deadline. □ *We had to race against time to finish before the deadline.*

race against time Go to prevous.

the **race card** *Cliché* the issue of race magnified and injected into a situation that might otherwise be nonracial. (*Typically: **deal** ~; **play** ~; **use** ~.) □ *At the last minute, the opposition candidate played the race card and lost the election for himself.*

rack one's **brain(s)** *Fig.* to try very hard to think of something. □ *Don't waste any more time racking your brain for the answer. Just go look it up online.*

rack out *Sl.* to go to bed and to sleep. □ *I'm really tired. I've got to go rack out for a while.*

rack sth **up**† **1.** *Inf.* to accumulate something; to collect or acquire something. □ *They all racked a lot of profits up.* **2.** *Sl.* to wreck or damage something. □ *Fred racked up his new car.*

racked with pain *Fig.* suffering from severe pain. □ *My body was racked with pain, and I nearly passed out.*

rag so **about** so/sth *Fig.* to tease someone about someone or something. □ *I wish you would stop ragging me about my hat!*

rag on so AND **rake on** so *Sl.* to bother someone; to irritate someone; to criticize and humiliate someone. □ *I wish you* would stop ragging on me. I don't know why you are so annoyed at me.

rag out *Sl.* to dress up. □ *I like to rag out and go to parties.*

rage out of control to become uncontrollable. (Said of fires, crowds, gangs, and the like.) □ *The fire raged out of control and threatened the residential area.* □ *If we didn't do something quickly, the crowd would be raging out of control.*

rage through sth **1.** *Fig.* [for a fire] to burn rapidly through an area or a building. □ *The fire raged through the unoccupied building.* **2.** *Fig.* [for someone] to move rapidly through some sequence or process, as if in a rage. □ *She raged through the book, angry with everything she read.*

railroad so **into** sth *Fig.* to force someone into doing something in great haste. □ *The salesman tried to railroad me into signing the contract.*

railroad sth **through** (sth) *Fig.* to force something through some legislative body without due consideration. □ *The committee railroaded the new constitution through the ratification process.*

rain cats and dogs *Fig.* to rain very hard. □ *I'm not going out in that storm. It's raining cats and dogs.*

*a **rain check (on** sth) **1.** *Fig.* a piece of paper allowing one to see an event—which has been canceled—at a later time. (Originally said of sporting events that had to be canceled because of rain. *Typically: **get** ~; **have** ~; **take** ~; **give** so ~.) □ *The game was canceled because of the storm, but we all got rain checks on it.* **2.** *Fig.* a reissuing of an invitation at a later date. (Said to someone who has invited you to something that you cannot attend now but would like to attend at a later time. (*Typically: **get** ~; **have** ~; **take** ~; **give** so ~.) □ *We would love to come to your house, but we are busy next Saturday. Could we take a rain check on your kind invitation?* **3.** *Fig.* a piece of paper that allows one to purchase an item on sale at a later date. (Stores issue these pieces of paper when they run out of specially priced sale merchandise. *Typically: **get** ~; **have** ~; **take** ~; **give** so ~.) □ *The store was all out of the shampoo they advertised, but I got a rain check.* □ *Yes, you should always take a rain check so you can get it at the sale price later when they have more.*

rain down on so/sth *Fig.* to fall or drop down on someone or something like rain. □ *The ashes from the incinerator rained down on us, getting our clothes dirty.*

rain sth **down**† **(on** so/sth) *Fig.* to pour something, such as criticism or praise, onto someone or something. (Fig. on rain down on so/sth.) □ *The employees rained criticism down on the personnel manager for the new policy on sick leave.*

rain on so's **parade** AND **rain on** so/sth *Fig.* to spoil something for someone; to cause someone distress in the same way that unwelcome rain would cause distress. □ *I hate to rain on your parade, but your plans are all wrong.* □ *She really rained on our plans.*

rain sth **out**† *Fig.* [for the weather] to spoil something by raining. □ *Oh, the weather looks awful. I hope it doesn't rain the picnic out.*

raise a (big) stink (about so/sth**)** Go to make a (big) stink (about so/sth).

raise a few eyebrows Go to cause (some) eyebrows to raise.

raise a hand (against so/sth**)** Go to lift a hand (against so/sth).

raise a stink (about sth**)** Go to create a stink (about sth).

raise Cain *Fig.* to make a lot of trouble; to raise hell. (A biblical reference, from Genesis 4. Probably a punning mincing

of *raise hell.*) □ *Fred was really raising Cain about the whole matter.*

raise so **from** sth AND **lift** so **from** sth to help someone up from a lowly state. □ *They hoped for some windfall to raise them from their poverty.*

raise so **from the dead** *Fig. Lit.* to bring a dead person back to life. □ *How great are your magic powers? Do you claim to raise people from the dead?* □ *They say her singing could raise people from the dead.*

raise one's **glass to** so/sth *Fig.* a formulaic expression used in proposing a drinking toast in salute to someone or something. □ *Let us all raise our glasses to George Wilson!* □ *They raised their glasses to the successful campaign.*

raise so's **hackles** Go to get so's dander up.

raise havoc with so/sth AND **play havoc with** so/sth; **wreak havoc with** so/sth *Fig.* to create confusion or disruption for or among someone or something. □ *Your announcement raised havoc with the students.* □ *I didn't mean to play havoc with them.*

raise hell (with sth**)** Go to raise the devil (with sth).

raise hob with so/sth AND **play hob with** so/sth *Fig.* to do something devilish to someone or something; to cause trouble for someone or something. (A *hob* is akin to *hobgoblin* = a wicked little elf.) □ *Your sudden arrival is going to play hob with my dinner plans.* □ *Sorry, I didn't mean to raise hob with you.*

raise money for so/sth AND **raise money to** do sth *Fig.* to work to earn money or encourage donations for the benefit of someone, something, or doing something. □ *I worked hard to raise money for college, and then decided not to go.*

raise one's **sights** *Fig.* to set higher goals for oneself. (Fig. on the image of someone lifting the sights of a gun in order to fire farther.) □ *When you're young, you tend to raise your sights too high.* □ *On the other hand, some people need to raise their sights.*

raise the ante Go to up the ante.

raise the bar *Fig.* to make a task a little more difficult. (As with raising the bar in high jumping or pole vaulting.) □ *Just as I was getting accustomed to my job, the manager raised the bar and I had to perform even better.*

raise the devil (with so**)** *Fig.* to severely chastise someone or a group. □ *The coach came in and raised hell with Sally for her error in the first quarter of the game.*

raise the devil (with sth**)** AND **raise hell (with** sth**)** *Fig.* to cause trouble with something. □ *Those caramelized onions raised the devil with my stomach.*

raise the dickens (with so/sth**)** *Fig.* to act in some extreme manner; to make trouble; to behave wildly; to be very angry. □ *John was out all night raising the dickens.* □ *That cheap gas I bought really raised the dickens with my car's engine.*

raise the stakes Go to up the ante.

raise so/sth **to** sth to elevate someone or something to something at a higher level. □ *I helped raise the ladder to the top of the roof.*

raise one's **voice against** so/sth *Fig.* to speak out loudly or angrily against someone or something; to complain about someone or something. □ *I was too timid to raise my voice against the injustices of the day.*

raise one's **voice (to** so**)** *Fig.* to speak loudly or shout at someone in anger. □ *Don't you dare raise your voice to me!* □ *I'm sorry. I didn't mean to raise my voice.*

raised in a barn *Inf.* brought up to behave like a barnyard animal; having crude behavior. □ *Close the door behind you! Were you raised in a barn?*

rake sth **in**† *Inf.* to take in a lot of something, especially money. □ *Our candidate will rake votes in by the thousand.* □ *The shop was raking in tons of cash by selling books at a deep discount.*

rake sth **off**† *Fig.* to steal or embezzle a portion of a payment or an account. □ *They claimed that no one was raking anything off and that the money was only mislaid.*

rake on so Go to rag on so.

rake so **over the coals** AND **haul** so **over the coals** *Fig.* to give someone a severe scolding. □ *My mother hauled me over the coals for coming in late last night.*

rake sth **up**† *Fig.* to find some unpleasant information. □ *His opposition raked an old scandal up and made it public.*

rally to so/sth to unite in support of someone or something. □ *The students rallied to Betty, their elected president.*

ram so/sth **down** so's **throat** Go to shove so/sth **down** so's **throat.**

ramble on 1. to wander about aimlessly. (As with a traveler or a winding path.) □ *The road rambled on through mile after mile of wilderness.* **2.** [for a structure] to spread out over a large area, perhaps randomly. □ *This old house rambles on, way back into the woods.*

ramble on (about so/sth**)** *Fig.* [for someone] to talk endlessly and aimlessly about someone or something. □ *I wish you wouldn't ramble on about your first husband all the time.*

rank and file 1. *Fig.* the regular soldiers, not the officers. □ *I think there is low morale among the rank and file, sir.* **2.** *Fig.* the ordinary members of a group, not the leaders. (Fig. on ①.) □ *The last contract was turned down by the rank and file last year.*

rank so **with** so to judge someone to be equal with someone. □ *Fred ranked himself with Tom when it came to diving.*

rant and rave (about so/sth**)** to shout angrily and wildly about someone or something. □ *Barbara rants and raves when her children don't obey her.*

rap so **across the knuckles** AND **rap** so **on the knuckles; rap** so's **knuckles** to strike someone on the knuckles. □ *As punishment, she rapped him across the knuckles.*

rap with so *Sl.* to have a chat with someone or a group of people. (Older.) □ *Come in, sit down, and rap with me for a while.*

raring to go *Fig. Inf.* extremely keen to act or do something. (Usually **rarin'**. From an older form of *rearing*, as with a horse that rises up on its rear legs in eagerness to get going.) □ *Mary is rarin' to go and can't wait for her university term to start.*

rat on so *Inf.* to report someone's bad behavior to someone in authority; to tattle on someone. □ *John ratted on me, and I got in trouble.*

the **rat race** *Fig.* a fierce struggle for success, especially in one's career or business. □ *Bob got tired of the rat race. He's retired and moved to the country.*

rattle around in sth **1.** *Fig.* to ride about in a vehicle with a rattle. □ *I am perfectly happy to rattle around in my 10-year-old car.* **2.** *Fig.* to live in a place that is much too big. □ *We have been rattling around in this big old house for long enough. Let's move to a smaller place.*

rattle so's **cage** *Fig.* to alert or annoy someone in a way that sets him or her into action. (As if one were trying to excite or stimulate an animal by rattling its cage.) □ *The plumber didn't show up again. I guess I'll have to call and rattle his cage.*

rattle sth **off**† AND **reel** sth **off**† *Fig.* to recite something quickly and accurately. □ *She can really reel song lyrics off.* □ *Listen to Mary rattle off those numbers.*

rattle on (about so/sth**)** *Fig.* to talk endlessly about someone or something. □ *Martin talked incessantly. He would rattle on about any topic whenever he could trap an unfortunate listener.*

rattle one's **saber** AND **rattle its saber** *Fig.* to make threatening statements or actions. (*Sabre* in the U.K. and the rest of the English-speaking world.) □ *The president is just rattling his saber. He would never attack such a small country!*

raunch so **out**† *Sl.* to disgust someone. □ *These dirty socks absolutely raunch me out!*

rave about so/sth **1.** to rage in anger about someone or something. □ *Sarah raved and raved about Gail's insufferable rudeness.* **2.** to sing the praises of someone or something. □ *Even the harshest critic raved about Larry's stage success.*

ravished with delight *Fig.* happy or delighted; overcome with happiness or delight. □ *My parents were ravished with delight when I finally graduated from college.*

***a **raw deal** *Fig.* an instance of unfair or bad treatment. (*Typically: **get** ~; **have** ~; **give** so ~.) □ *I bought a used TV that worked for two days and then quit. I sure got a raw deal.*

raw recruit *Fig.* a new, inexperienced, or fresh recruit, such as someone just entering the army, navy, police, etc. □ *These boys are nothing but raw recruits. They've never seen a gun up close!*

a **ray of sunshine** *Fig.* a bit of good or happy news in an unhappy situation; a person or thing whose presence makes an unhappy situation a little happier. □ *When you came in, you were a ray of sunshine for our little group of homeless children.*

reach so *Fig.* to manage to be understood by someone; to have one's message appreciated by someone. □ *If we could only reach these boys with our message, we might be able to convince them to stay in school.*

reach a compromise to achieve a compromise; to negotiate an agreement. □ *After many hours of discussion, we finally reached a compromise.*

reach a conclusion to complete discussion and decide an issue. □ *It took three days of talks to reach a conclusion.*

reach a decision Go to arrive at a decision.

reach an impasse *Fig.* to progress to the point that a barrier stops further progress. □ *When negotiations with management reached an impasse, the union went on strike.*

reach first base (with so/sth**)** Go to get to first base (with so/sth).

reach for the sky 1. AND **aim for the sky; reach for the stars; shoot for the sky** *Fig.* to set one's sights high. □ *Reach for the sky! Go for it!* **2.** *Inf.* to put one's hands up, as in a burglary. □ *The gunman told the bank teller to reach for the sky.*

reach out 1. to extend one's grasp outward. □ *He reached out, but there was no one to take hold of.* **2.** *Fig.* to enlarge one's circle of friends and experiences. (Fig. on ①.) □ *If you are that lonely, you ought to reach out. Get to know some new friends.*

reach out to so **1.** to offer someone a helping hand. □ *You reached out to me just when I needed help the most.* **2.** *Fig.* to seek someone's help and support. □ *Jane reached out to her friends for the help and support that she needed.*

reach speeds of some number Go to speeds of some number.

reach one's **stride** AND **hit** one's **stride; attain** one's **stride** *Fig.* to do something at one's best level of ability. □ *When I reach my stride, things will go faster, and I'll be more efficient.*

read between the lines *Fig.* to infer something (from something else); to try to understand what is meant by something that is not written explicitly or openly. □ *After listening to what she said, if you read between the lines, you can begin to see what she really means.*

read from the same page AND **sing from the same hymn book; be on the same page; be on the same screen** *Cliché* share the same understanding of something. (*Same screen* refers to a computer screen.) □ *Okay, I think we are reading from the same page now. We can discuss the future of this project more productively.*

read sth **into** sth to find a meaning in something that really may not be there. □ *You are reading too much into John's decision to retire. It is not a criticism of the company. He's just old.*

read it and weep *Inf. Fig.* read the bad news; hear the bad news. □ *I'm sorry to bring you the bad news, but read it and weep.*

read so **like a book** *Fig.* to understand someone very well. □ *I've got John figured out. I can read him like a book.*

read so's **lips** *Fig.* to manage to understand speech by watching and interpreting the movements of the speaker's lips. □ *I couldn't hear her but I could read her lips.*

read so's **mind** *Fig.* to guess what someone is thinking. □ *You'll have to tell me what you want. I can't read your mind, you know.* □ *If I could read your mind, I'd know what you expect of me.*

Read my lips! Go to Watch my lips!

read so **out**[†] **(for** sth**)** AND **dress** so **down**[†] **(for** sth**)** to chastise someone verbally for doing something wrong. □ *The coach read the player out for making a silly error.*

read so **out of** sth *Fig.* to expel someone from an organization, such as a political party. □ *After my simple error they almost read me out of the organization!*

read one one's **rights** *Fig.* to make the required statement of legal rights to a person who has been arrested. □ *All right, read this guy his rights and book him on a charge of theft.*

read the handwriting on the wall Go to see the (hand)writing on the wall.

read so **the riot act** *Fig.* to give someone a severe scolding. □ *The manager read me the riot act for coming in late.*

read oneself **to sleep** to read something in preparation for falling asleep. □ *I need a really dull book so I can read myself to sleep.*

ready, set, go Go to on your mark, get set, go.

ready to roll *Fig. Lit.* ready to start something. (Specifically, of a journey where wheels will be rolling or of filming where film spools or videotape will be rolling—even when digital storage is used.) □ *Everything is set up and we're ready to roll.*

ready, willing, and able *Cliché* eager or at least willing [to do something]. □ *If you need someone to help you move furniture, I'm ready, willing, and able.*

a **(real) go-getter** *Fig.* an active, energetic, and aggressive person. □ *Martin is very aggressive in business. A real go-getter.*

the **real McCoy** *Fig.* an authentic thing or person. (There are many clever tales devised as origins for this expression. There is absolutely no evidence for any of them, however. There is evidence in the U.K. for metaphoric uses of "the Real MacKay" [referring to authentic MacKay Whiskey], but no evidence of how Mac-Kay became McCoy in the U.S.) □ *Of course it's authentic! It's the real McCoy!*

the **real thing** something that is genuine and not an imitation. □ *I don't want frozen yogurt; I want the real thing! Yes, fatty old hand-churned ice cream!*

*a **reality check** AND *a **sanity check** *Inf.* a realistic appraisal of one's situation. (*Typically: **have** ~; **get** ~; **need** ~. *Sanity* is probably used when sanity is in doubt, but these are both used casually.) □ *Wow, dude! You are talking strange. You need a reality check!*

realize sth **from** sth to reap a profit by selling an asset that has increased in value. □ *He realized a large profit from the sale of the house.*

rear its ugly head *Fig.* [for something unpleasant] to appear or become obvious after lying hidden. □ *The question of money always rears its ugly head in matters of business.*

rear up *Fig.* [for something, especially a problem] to raise up suddenly. (See also raring to go.) □ *A new problem reared up and cost us a lot of time.*

rebound from sth *Fig.* to recover quickly from something, such as an illness or mental distress. □ *Barbara rebounded from her illness in less than a week.*

receive so **with open arms** AND **welcome** so **with open arms** *Fig.* to greet someone eagerly. □ *I'm sure they wanted us to stay for dinner, because they welcomed us with open arms.*

recharge one's **batteries** *Fig.* to get some refreshing rest. (Alludes to recharging electrical storage batteries.) □ *I need to get home and recharge my batteries. I'll be back on the job early tomorrow morning.*

reckon with so/sth AND **cope with** so/sth to deal with someone or something; to anticipate having to deal with problematic people or things. □ *I wasn't prepared to reckon with all the problems the new job held for me.*

recognize so/sth **for** sth *Fig.* to show appreciation to someone or something for something. □ *The organization recognized Laura for her excellent contributions to the philanthropy committee.*

recognize sth **for what it is** AND **recognize** one **for what** one **is** *Fig.* to see and understand exactly what someone or something is or represents. □ *The disease represented a serious threat to all peoples, and Dr. Smith recognized it for what it was.*

*red as a cherry** AND *red as a poppy; *red as a rose; *red as a ruby; *red as blood** bright red or some shade of red. (*Also: **as** ~.) □ *When the children came in from ice-skating, Clara's nose was as red as a cherry.* □ *I would like to make a dress out of that beautiful velvet that is red as a rose.* □ *Jane painted her fingernails with polish as red as a ruby.*

red as a poppy Go to previous.

red as a rose Go to red as a cherry.

red as a ruby Go to red as a cherry.

red as blood Go to red as a cherry.

a **red herring** a piece of information or suggestion introduced to draw attention away from the real facts of a situation. (A smoked [and therefore red] herring is a strong-smelling fish that could be drawn across a trail of scent to mislead hunting dogs and put them off the scent. It is extracted from an earlier U.K. expression: *Draw a red herring across the trail.*) □ *The detectives were following a red herring, but they're on the right track now.* □ *The mystery novel has a couple of red herrings that keep readers off-guard.*

red in the face *Fig.* embarrassed. □ *The speaker kept making errors and became red in the face.*

red ink *Fig.* debt; indebtedness as shown in red ink on a financial statement. □ *There* is too much red ink in my financial statement.

red tape *Fig.* over-strict attention to the wording and details of rules and regulations, especially by government workers. (From the color of the tape used by government departments in England to tie up bundles of documents.) □ *Because of red tape, Frank took weeks to get a visa.*

*the **red-carpet treatment** *Fig.* very special treatment; royal treatment. (*Typically: **get** ~; **have** ~; **give** so ~.) □ *I love to go to fancy stores where I get the red-carpet treatment.*

a **red-letter day** *Fig.* an important or significant day. (From the practice of printing holidays in red on the calendar.) □ *Today was a red-letter day in our history.*

reduce so **to** sth to cause someone to feel or display something unpleasant. □ *The bad news reduced them to tears.* □ *Bad economic conditions reduced me to poverty.*

reek of sth *Fig.* to give a strong impression of something. □ *The deal reeked of dishonesty.*

reel sth **off**† Go to rattle sth off†.

reel them in Go to pack them in.

reel under sth **1.** to stagger under the weight of something. □ *Tony reeled under the weight of the books.* **2.** *Fig.* to stagger because of a blow. (Fig. on ①.) □ *Fred reeled under the beating that Mike gave him.* **3.** *Fig.* to suffer because of a burden. (Fig. on ①.) □ *Gary reeled under the responsibilities he had been given.*

refill a prescription to provide or obtain a second or subsequent set of doses of a medicine upon a doctor's orders. (A pharmacist actually does the refilling, but the expression is also used to mean [for the patient] to have a prescription refilled.) □ *The pharmacist refused to refill my prescription because it had expired.* □ *The doctor told me just to refill the prescription he had given me last month.*

reflected in sth **1.** [of something] mirrored in something, such as a mirror, water, ice, etc. □ *His image was reflected in the mirror,* giving him a good view of his sunburn. **2.** *Fig.* [of something] shown in a result. (Fig. on ①.) □ *The extra charges will be reflected in next month's bill.*

refresh so's **memory (about** so/sth) *Fig.* tell someone again because they have forgotten. □ *I've forgotten what she said. Please refresh my memory.*

regain one's **composure** *Cliché* to become calm and composed after being angry or agitated. □ *I found it difficult to regain my composure after the argument.*

regain one's **feet 1.** *Fig.* to stand up again after falling or stumbling. □ *I helped my uncle regain his feet as he tried to get up from the floor.* **2.** *Fig.* to become independent after financial difficulties. (Fig. on ①. See also back on one's **feet**.) □ *I'll be able to pay my bills when I regain my feet.*

regarded as armed and dangerous Go to armed and dangerous.

*regular as clockwork** *Cliché* very regular; completely predictable. (*Also: **as** ~.) □ *George goes down to the bus stop at 7:45 every morning, as regular as clockwork.*

a **regular fixture** *Fig.* someone who is found so frequently in a place as to be considered a fixture of, or part of, the place. □ *The manager attached himself to the luncheon club and became a regular fixture there.*

a **regular guy** *Fig.* a normal and dependable guy. □ *Don't worry about Tom. He's a regular guy. He won't give you any trouble.*

reinvent the wheel *Fig.* to make unnecessary or redundant preparations. □ *You don't need to reinvent the wheel. Read up on what others have done.*

*related to** so connected through blood kinship or through marriage to someone. (*Typically: **be** ~; **become** ~.) □ *I wonder if he is related to you, because he looks a little like you.*

relative to so/sth **1.** concerning someone or something; relating to someone or something. □ *I have something to say relative* to Bill. □ *Do you have any information relative to the situation in South America?* **2.** in proportion to someone or something. □ *I can spend an amount of money relative to the amount of money I earn.*

relieve oneself *Euph.* to urinate or defecate. □ *She needed badly to relieve herself, but there was no bathroom in sight.*

relieve so of sth **1.** to unburden someone of something. □ *At last, he could relieve himself of the problem.* **2.** *Fig.* to lessen someone's responsibilities. (Fig. on ①.) □ *I will relieve you of some of the responsibility you have carried for so long.*

relieve one of one's **duties** *Euph.* to fire someone; to dismiss someone from employment. □ *I am afraid I must relieve you of your duties.* □ *After the scandal, she was relieved of her duties at the embassy.*

*__religion__ *Fig.* [being] serious (about something), usually after a powerful experience. (Sometimes literal. *Typically: **get** ~; **have** ~; **give** so ~.) □ *I've always had religion. I don't need a crisis to make me get it.* □ *When I had an automobile accident, I really got religion. Now I'm a very safe driver.*

religious about doing sth *Fig.* strict about something; conscientious about something. □ *Bob is religious about paying his bills on time.*

remain in touch (with so**)** Go to in touch (with so).

remain in touch (with so/sth**)** Go to keep in touch (with so/sth).

remember so **to** so to carry the greetings of someone to someone else. □ *I will remember you to my brother, who asks of you often.*

render sth **down**† **1.** to cook the fat out of something. □ *Polly rendered the chicken skin down to some flavorful grease that she would use in cooking a special dish.* **2.** *Fig.* to reduce or simplify something to its essentials. (Fig. on ①.) □ *Let's render this problem down to the considerations that are important to us.*

repair to some place *Fig.* to move oneself to some place. □ *I will repair to my room until the crisis is over.*

report in sick *Fig.* to call one's office to say that one will not come to work because one is sick. (See also call in sick.) □ *I don't feel well today. I will report in sick.*

*a **reputation (as a** sth**)** a state of having a particular kind of reputation for being something. (Can be a good or a bad reputation. *Typically: **get** ~; **have** ~; **give** so ~.) □ *Unfortunately, Tom's got a reputation as a cheat.*

*a **reputation (for** doing sth**)** a state of having a particular kind of reputation for doing something. (Often a bad reputation, as in the example. *Typically: **get** ~; **have** ~; **give** so ~.) □ *I don't want to get a reputation for being late, so I always arrive early.*

resonate with so *Fig.* [for an idea, issue, or concept] to appeal to someone or cause someone to relate to it. (Very close to a cliché.) □ *The concept of wearing worn-looking clothing seems to resonate with young people.* □ *Your notion just doesn't resonate with the public in general.*

the **responsible party** the person or organization responsible or liable for something. □ *I intend to find the responsible party and get some answers to my questions.*

rest assured to be assured; to be certain. □ *Rest assured that you'll receive the best of care.* □ *Please rest assured that we will do everything possible to help.*

rest in sth *Fig.* [for something] to have its source in something. □ *The source of her magnetism rests in the way she uses her eyes.*

rest in peace *Fig.* to lie dead peacefully for eternity. (A solemn entreaty used in funeral prayers, eulogies, etc.) □ *We prayed that the deceased would rest in peace.*

The **rest is gravy.** *Fig.* Any additional money received is just an easily acquired bonus. □ *There is some cost involved in buying the raw materials, but the cost of*

rest on one's laurels

manufacturing is negligible. When we pay off the costs, the rest is gravy.

The **rest is history.** *Fig.* Everyone knows the rest of the story that I am referring to. □ *Bill: Then they arrested all the officers of the corporation, and the rest is history.* □ *Bob: Hey, what happened between you and Sue? Bill: Finally we realized that we could never get along, and the rest is history.*

rest on one's **laurels** *Fig.* to stop trying because one is satisfied with one's past achievements. □ *We rested on our laurels too long. Our competitors took away a lot of our business.*

retool for sth *Fig.* to prepare oneself for a different kind of work. □ *He decided to retool for a new job in the computer industry.*

return the compliment AND **return** so's **compliment** to pay a compliment to someone who has paid you a compliment. □ *When someone says something nice, it is polite to return the compliment.*

return the favor *Fig.* to do a good deed for someone who has done a good deed for you. (Sometimes used ironically for the return of a bad deed.) □ *You helped me last week, so I'll return the favor and help you this week.*

return to haunt one Go to come back to haunt one.

rev up to increase in amount or activity. □ *We're hoping business will rev up soon.*

rev sth **up**[†] to make an idling engine run very fast, in short bursts of power. □ *Hey! Stop revving it up!*

revolve around so/sth AND **revolve about** so/sth *Fig.* [for people or things] to center upon someone or something or to be primarily concerned with someone or something. □ *The way all of this is going to turn out revolves around Bob.*

*rhyme or reason *Cliché* without purpose, order, or reason. (Fixed order. *Typically: **with neither ~; without ~; have no ~.**) □ *The teacher said my report was dis-*

organized. My paragraphs were ordered without rhyme or reason.

*rid of so/sth *Fig.* free of someone or something. (*Typically: **be** ~**; get** ~.) □ *I'm trying to get rid of Mr. Smith. He's bothering me.*

ride so **about** sth *Fig.* to continue to bother someone about something. □ *Stop riding me about my weight! This is how I'm supposed to be!*

ride off in all directions *Fig.* to behave in a totally confused manner; to try to do everything at once. □ *Bill has a tendency to ride off in all directions. He's not organized enough.*

ride on sth *Fig.* to be borne on something and carried along. □ *She rode on a wave of popularity to reelection.*

ride on so's **coattails** AND **hang on** so's **coattails** *Fig.* to make one's good fortune or success on the strength of someone else's. (Also with *else*.) □ *Bill isn't very creative, so he rides on John's coattails.*

ride out the storm Go to weather the storm.

ride roughshod over so/sth AND **run roughshod over** so/sth *Fig.* to treat someone or something with disdain or scorn. □ *You shouldn't have come into our town to ride roughshod over our laws and our traditions!*

ride the gravy train *Fig.* to live in ease or luxury. □ *I wouldn't like loafing if I were rich. I don't want to ride the gravy train.*

ride up (on so**)** *Fig.* [for clothing, especially underpants] to keep moving higher on one's body. □ *I don't like it when my pants ride up on me.*

riding for a fall *Fig.* risking failure or an accident, usually due to overconfidence. □ *Tom drives too fast, and he seems too sure of himself. He's riding for a fall.*

rig so/sth **out**† **(in** sth**)** AND **rig** so/sth **out**† **(with** sth**)** to outfit someone or something in something; to decorate or dress someone or something in something. (*Fig.* on rigging on a sailing ship.) □ *Joan rigged her daughter out in a witch's cos-*

tume for the Halloween party. □ *He rigged out his car with lights for the parade.*

rig sth **up**† *Fig.* to prepare something, perhaps on short notice or without the proper materials. □ *We don't have what's needed to make the kind of circuit you have described, but I think we can rig something up anyway.* □ *We will rig up whatever you need.*

right and left AND **left and right** to both sides; on all sides; everywhere. □ *There were children everywhere—running right and left.*

*right as rain *Cliché* perfectly fine; all right. (Based on the alliteration with *r*. *Also: **as** ~.) □ *Lily has sprained her ankle, but after a few weeks of rest she should be as right as rain.*

right down so's **alley** AND **right up** so's **alley** *Fig.* ideally suited to one's interests or abilities. □ *Skiing is right down my alley. I love it.*

right here and now at this time and in this place; immediately. □ *I insist that you tell me the whole story right here and now!*

right in the kisser *Inf.* right in the mouth or face. □ *Wilbur poked the cop right in the kisser.*

right off the bat AND **straight off the bat** *Fig.* immediately; first thing. (*Fig.* on the notion of something happening at the instant that a ball leaves a bat.) □ *When he was learning to ride a bicycle, he fell on his head right off the bat.*

(right) off the top of one's **head** *Fig.* without giving it too much thought or without precise knowledge. □ *Mary: How much do you think this car would be worth on a trade? Fred: Well, right off the top of my head, I'd say about a thousand.*

Right on! *Sl.* Exactly!; That is exactly right! □ *After the speaker finished, many people in the audience shouted, "Right on!"*

(right) on target *Fig.* on schedule; exactly as predicted. □ *Your estimate of the cost was right on target.*

right on time *Fig.* at the correct time; no later than the specified time. □ *If you get* *there right on time, you'll get one of the free tickets.*

(right) out of the (starting) blocks AND **(right) out of the (starting) gate** *Fig.* just started; just having started. (As if one had just started a race.) ☐ *He got into trouble right out of the blocks. He was doomed to failure from the start.*

(right) out of the (starting) gate Go to previous.

right side up *Fig.* with the correct (top) side upwards, as with a box or some other container. ☐ *Please set your coffee cup right side up so I can fill it.*

the **right stuff** *Fig.* the right or correct character or set of skills to do something well. ☐ *She's got the right stuff to be a winner.*

*a **right to** do sth AND *the **right to** do sth the freedom to do something; the legal or moral permission or license to do something. (*Typically: **get** ~; **have** ~; **give** so ~.) ☐ *You don't have the right to enter my home without my permission.*

*a **right to** sth AND *the **right to** sth a privilege or license to have something. (*Typically: **get** ~; **have** ~; **give** so ~.) ☐ *I have the right to have the kind of house I want.* ☐ *You have a right to any house you can afford.*

(right) under so's **(very) nose 1.** *Fig.* right in front of someone. ☐ *I thought I'd lost my purse, but it was sitting on the table under my very nose.* **2.** *Fig.* in someone's presence. (Fig. on ①. Note the variation in the example.) ☐ *The jewels were stolen from under the very noses of the security guards.*

right up so's **alley** Go to right down so's alley.

*the **right-of-way** the legal right to occupy a particular space on a public roadway. (*Typically: **get** ~; **have** ~; **give** so ~; **yield** ~.) ☐ *Don't pull out onto a highway if you haven't yielded to the right-of-way.*

ring a bell *Fig.* [for something] to cause someone to remember something or for it to seem familiar. (Fig. on a bell serving as a reminder or alarm.) ☐ *I've never met John Franklin, but his name rings a bell.*

ring false AND **ring hollow** to seem false; not to ring true. ☐ *Everything you have said so far rings hollow. Tell us the truth!*

ring hollow Go to previous.

ring in so's **ears** AND **ring in** so's **mind** *Fig.* [for words or a sound] to linger in one's consciousness. ☐ *Her words rang in my ears for days.* ☐ *The sound of the choir rang in their minds long after they had finished their anthem.*

ring in so's **mind** Go to previous.

ring in the new year *Fig.* to celebrate the beginning of the new year at midnight on December 31. ☐ *We are planning a big party to ring in the new year.*

ring off the hook *Fig.* [for a telephone] to ring incessantly and repeatedly. ☐ *What a busy day! The telephone has been ringing off the hook all day long.*

ring out the old (year) *Fig.* to celebrate the end of a year while celebrating the beginning of a new one. ☐ *I don't plan to ring out the old this year. I'm just going to go to bed.*

ring the bell Go to hit the spot.

ring the curtain down† **(on** sth**)** AND **bring the curtain down**† **(on** sth**) 1.** *Fig.* to lower a theater curtain, usually at the end of an act or a play. ☐ *After 100 performances, it's time to ring the curtain down on our show for the last time.* **2.** *Fig.* to bring something to an end; to declare something to be at an end. (Fig. on ①.) ☐ *It's time to ring the curtain down on our relationship. We have nothing in common anymore.*

ring the curtain up† **1.** *Fig.* to raise the curtain in a theater. (Refers to sending the signal to raise the curtain.) ☐ *The stagehand rang the curtain up precisely on time.* **2.** *Fig.* to start a series of activities or events. (Fig. on ①.) ☐ *I am set to ring up the curtain on a new lifestyle.*

ring true *Fig.* to sound or seem true or likely; not to ring false. (From testing the quality of metal or glass by striking it and evaluating the sound made.) □ *The student's excuse for being late doesn't ring true.*

ring sth **up** *Fig.* to enter a sale into a cash register or equivalent, whether it is a cash or credit card sale. (From the days when mechanical cash registers had bells that sounded when a sale was totaled.) □ *I'm in a hurry. Please ring up these two items. I have exact change.*

a **riot of color** *Cliché* a selection of many bright colors. □ *The landscape was a riot of color each autumn.*

rip into so/sth *Fig.* to criticize or censure someone or something severely. □ *The critics really ripped into Larry's poor performance.*

rip so **off**† *Inf.* to steal [something] from someone; to cheat someone. □ *That merchant ripped me off!*

rip sth **off**† *Inf.* to steal something [from someone]. □ *Jane ripped off a lot of money.*

rip on so *Sl.* to give someone a hard time; to hassle someone. □ *Stop ripping on me! What did I do to you?* □ *Tim is ripping on Mary again, and she is getting really mad.*

rip snorter *Rur.* a remarkable person or thing; a hilarious joke. □ *Let me tell you a rip snorter about a farmer and his cow.*

rip so/sth **to** sth *Fig.* to criticize someone or something mercilessly. □ *The critics ripped Gerald to pieces even though the audience just loved his show.*

a **ripe old age** *Fig.* a very old age. □ *Mr. Smith died last night, but he lived to the ripe old age of 99.* □ *All the Smiths seem to reach a ripe old age.*

ripen into sth *Fig.* to mature into something. □ *This problem is going to ripen into a real crisis if we don't do something about it right now.*

(rip-)off artist *Inf.* a con artist. □ *Beware of the rip-off artist who runs that shop.*

a **ripple of** sth the sound or excitement of quiet but widespread laughter, protest, expectation, etc. □ *A ripple of excitement spread through the crowd.*

ripple through sth *Fig.* to move through something or a group of people in a ripple or wave motion. □ *A murmur of excitement rippled through the crowd.*

rise above sth *Fig.* [for one] to ignore petty matters and do what one is meant to do in spite of them. □ *He was able to rise above the squabbling and bring some sense to the proceedings.*

Rise and shine! *Fig.* Get out of bed and be lively and energetic! (Often a command.) □ *Father always calls "Rise and shine!" in the morning when we want to go on sleeping.*

rise from the ashes *Fig.* [for a structure] to be rebuilt after destruction. □ *The entire west section of the city was destroyed, and a group of new buildings rose from the ashes in only a few months.*

rise from the dead AND **rise from the grave** *Fig.* to come back to life after being dead. □ *Albert didn't rise from the dead. He wasn't dead in the first place.* □ *The movie was about a teenager who rose from the grave and haunted his high school friends.*

rise from the grave Go to previous.

rise from the ranks Go to come up through the ranks.

rise to one's **feet** *Fig.* to stand up. □ *The entire audience rose to its feet, applauding wildly.*

rise to the bait Go to the bait.

rise to the challenge *Fig.* to accept a challenge. (Usually in reference to success with the challenge.) □ *You can depend on Kelly to rise to the challenge.*

rise to the occasion *Fig.* to meet the challenge of an event; to try extra hard to do a task. □ *John was able to rise to the occasion and make the conference a success.*

risk one's **neck (to** do sth**)** *Fig.* to accept the risk of physical harm in order to accomplish something. □ *Look at that traffic! I refuse to risk my neck just to cross the street to buy a paper.*

risk of rain AND **risk of showers; risk of thunder(storms)** *Fig.* a chance of precipitation. (Used only in weather forecasting. There is no "risk" of hazard or injury involved.) □ *And for tomorrow, there is a slight risk of showers in the morning.*

risk of showers Go to previous.

risk of thunder(storms) Go to risk of rain.

rivet so's **attention** *Fig.* to keep someone's attention fixed [on something]. □ *The movie riveted the audience's attention for three hours straight.*

riveted to the ground *Fig.* [of someone or someone's feet] unable to move. □ *My feet were riveted to the ground, and I could not move an inch.*

road hog *Fig.* someone who drives carelessly and selfishly. □ *Look at that road hog driving in the middle of the road and stopping other drivers from passing him.*

roar at so/sth *Fig.* to bellow with laughter at someone or something. □ *The audience roared at the clown.*

rob so **blind 1.** *Inf.* to steal freely from someone. □ *Her maid was robbing her blind.* **2.** *Inf.* to overcharge someone. □ *Those auto repair shops can rob you blind if you don't watch out.*

rob Peter to pay Paul *Fig.* to take or borrow from one in order to give or pay something owed to another. □ *Why borrow money to pay your bills? That's just robbing Peter to pay Paul.*

rob the cradle *Fig.* to marry or date someone who is much younger than oneself. □ *Uncle Bill—who is nearly 80—married a 30-year-old woman. That is really robbing the cradle.*

*(rock) bottom *Inf.* the lowest point or level. (*Typically: **be at** ~; **hit** ~; **reach** ~.) □ *Prices have reached rock bottom.* □ *After my life finally hit bottom, I gradually began to feel much better.*

rock the boat *Fig.* to cause trouble where none is welcome; to disturb a situation that is otherwise stable and satisfactory. (Often negative.) □ *Look, Tom, everything is going fine here. Don't rock the*

boat! □ *You can depend on Tom to mess things up by rocking the boat.*

rocket (in)to sth *Fig.* [for someone] to ascend rapidly into something, such as fame or prominence. □ *Jill rocketed into prominence after her spectacular performance on the guitar.*

a **rocky road** *Fig.* a difficult period of time. □ *Bob's been going down quite a rocky road since his divorce.* □ *Life is a rocky road.*

Roger (wilco). *Fig.* Yes. (From aircraft radio communication. Wilco = will comply.) □ *Mary: I want you to take this over to the mayor's office. Bill: Roger wilco.*

roll along *Fig.* [for something] to progress smoothly. □ *The project is rolling along nicely.*

roll around (again) AND **come around (again)** *Fig.* to be at a season or date again. □ *Well, summer has rolled around again, and the days are getting longer.*

roll sth **back** Go to cut sth down†.

roll by *Fig.* to move (past), as if rolling. □ *The clouds were rolling by, spreading patterns of light and dark across the land.*

roll in *Fig.* to come in large numbers or amounts, easily, as if rolling. (Fig. on the image of the arrival of many wheeled conveyances.) □ *We didn't expect many people at the party, but they just kept rolling in.*

roll on *Fig.* [for something, such as time] to move on slowly and evenly, as if rolling. □ *As the hours rolled on, I learned just how bored I could get without going to sleep.*

roll out the red carpet (for so) **1.** to unwind a roll of red carpet for someone important to walk on. □ *The city council decided to roll out the red carpet for the visit of the foreign prince.* **2.** *Fig.* to give someone treatment befitting royalty. (Fig. on ①.) □ *The citizens of the small community enjoyed rolling out the red carpet for important visitors.*

roll sth **over**† *Fig.* to renew a financial instrument as it expires. □ *Do you plan to roll this certificate of deposit over?*

roll over and play dead *Fig.* to just give up and be unable to cope with life or a problem. □ *Why can't I complain about this? Am I supposed to roll over and play dead?*

roll (over) in one's **grave** Go to turn (over) in one's grave.

roll one's **sleeves up**† *Fig.* to prepare to get to work. □ *Let's roll our sleeves up and get this job done!*

roll with the punches *Fig.* to absorb the force of a blow, as in boxing. □ *You have to learn to roll with the punches. Accept what is dealt to you.*

rolled into one Go to (all) rolled into one.

*the sth **rolling** *Fig.* a continuing process; the movement and perpetuation of a process. (Usually the *something* is *ball*, but also: *party, meeting, conversation*, etc. *Always: **get** ~; **keep** ~; **set** ~; **start** ~.) □ *If I could just get the ball rolling, then other people would help.* □ *I had to start the party rolling.*

rolling in sth AND **rolling in it** *Fig.* having large amounts of something, usually money. □ *Bob doesn't need to earn money. He's rolling in it.*

*rolling in the aisles** *Fig.* [of an audience] wild with laughter. (*Typically: **get them** ~; **have them** ~; **leave them** ~.) □ *I have the best jokes you've ever heard. I'll have them rolling in the aisles.*

romp on so AND **romp all over** so *Inf. Fig.* to scold someone. □ *The teacher romped on the students for their behavior.*

romp through sth *Fig.* to perform something fast and playfully. □ *The conductor romped through the slow movement of the symphony as if it were a march.*

room and board *Fig.* food to eat and a place to live; the cost of food and lodging. □ *That college charges too much for room and board.*

root for so/sth to cheer and encourage someone or something. □ *Are you root-*ing for anyone in particular, or are you just shouting because you're excited?*

*the **root of the problem** *Fig.* the cause or basis of a problem. (*Typically: **determine** ~; **figure out** ~; **find** ~; **get to** ~; **get at** ~.) □ *It will take a little more study to get to the root of the problem.*

root sth **out**† *Fig.* to get rid of something completely; to destroy something to its roots or core. □ *No government will ever root out crime completely.*

rooted in sth *Fig.* based on something; connected to a source or cause. □ *This fictional book was rooted in actual events.*

*rooted to** sth *Fig.* [of someone] firmly attached to something. (Usually refers to something such as land, soil, country, home, etc. *Typically: **be** ~; **become** ~.) □ *The farmer is rooted to the land and will not leave.*

*rooted to the spot** *Fig.* unable to move because of fear or surprise. (Fig. on the image of an animate creature made inanimate because roots extend from the feet into the ground. *Typically: **appear to be** ~; **be** ~; **become** ~.) □ *Jane stood rooted to the spot when she saw the ghostly figure.*

rope so **into (doing)** sth AND **rope** so **in**† *Fig.* to cause someone to get involved in some project. □ *She's always trying to rope me into her club.*

*the **ropes** *Fig.* knowledge of how to do something; how to work something. (*Typically: **know** ~; **learn** ~; **show** so ~; **teach** so ~.) □ *I'll be able to do my job very well when I know the ropes.*

rot in hell (before one **would** do sth**)** Go to see so in hell first.

a **rotten apple** *Inf.* a single bad person or thing. (Sometimes there is the implication that the "rot" will spread to others, as with the one rotten apple that spoils the rest in the barrel.) □ *There always is a rotten apple to spoil it for the rest of us.* □ *Leave it to one rotten apple to bring down the conversation to the basest level.*

a **rotten egg** AND a **bad egg** *Inf.* a bad or despised person; an evil influence. □ *She sure has turned out to be a rotten egg.*

rotten luck *Fig.* bad luck. □ *Of all the rotten luck!* □ *I've had nothing but rotten luck all day.*

rotten to the core *Fig.* really bad; corrupt. □ *That lousy punk is rotten to the core.*

rough and ready Go to next.

rough and tumble AND **rough and ready** *Fig.* disorderly; aggressive. □ *George is too rough and ready for me. He doesn't know how to act around civilized people.*

*a **rough idea (about** sth) AND *a **rough idea (of** sth) *Fig.* a general idea; an estimate. (*Typically: **get** ~; **have** ~; **give** so ~.) □ *I need to get a rough idea of how many people will be there.*

rough it *Fig.* to live without luxury; to live simply; to camp out in primitive conditions. □ *During the blackout, we roughed it without electricity.* □ *The campers roughed it in the remote cabin for a week.*

rough stuff *Fig.* unnecessary roughness; physical violence or threats of violence. □ *Okay, let's cut out the rough stuff!*

a **rough time** Go to a hard time.

rough so **up**† *Fig.* to beat someone up; to maltreat someone. □ *Am I going to have to rough you up, or will you cooperate?*

round sth **down**† to reduce a fractional part of a number to the next lowest whole number. (See also round off to sth.) □ *You can round this figure down if you want. It won't affect the total all that much.*

round down to sth Go to round off to sth.

round sth **off**† to change a number to the next higher or lower whole number. (See also round off to sth.) □ *You should round 8.122 off.*

round off to sth AND **round up to** sth; **round down to** sth to express a number in the nearest whole amount or nearest group of 1, 10, 100, 1,000, 1/10, 1/100, 1/1,000, etc. □ *When doing taxes, Anne rounded her figures off to the nearest dol-*

lar. □ *These census population figures are rounded up to the nearest million.*

round sth **off**† **(with** sth) *Fig.* to finish something with something; to complement something with something. (See also round sth off.) □ *We rounded off the meal with a sinful dessert.*

round sth **out**† *Fig.* to complete or enhance something. □ *We will round the evening out with dessert at a nice restaurant.*

round so/sth **up**† *Fig.* to locate and gather someone or something. (Not necessarily plural.) □ *Please round the suspects up for questioning.*

a **rounding error** *Fig.* a large amount of money that is relatively small in comparison to a much larger sum. □ *To a large company like Smith & Co., a few thousand dollars is just a rounding error. It's not a lot at all.*

round-trip ticket a ticket (for a plane, train, bus, etc.) that allows one to go to a destination and return. □ *A round-trip ticket is usually cheaper than two one-way tickets.*

a **royal pain** *Fig.* a great annoyance. □ *This guy's a royal pain, but we have to put up with him because he's the boss.*

the **royal treatment** very good treatment; very good and thoughtful care of a person. □ *I really got the royal treatment when I stayed at that expensive hotel.*

rub elbows (with so) AND **rub shoulders with** so *Fig.* to associate with someone; to work closely with someone. (No physical contact is involved.) □ *I don't care to rub elbows with someone who acts like that!*

rub so's **fur the wrong way** AND **rub** so **the wrong way** *Fig.* to irritate someone. (Fig. on the rubbing of a cat's or dog's fur the wrong way.) □ *I'm sorry I rubbed your fur the wrong way. I didn't mean to upset you.*

rub sth **in**† *Fig.* to keep reminding one of one's failures; to nag someone about something. □ *I like to rub it in. You deserve it!*

rub so's **nose in it** *Fig.* to remind one of something one has done wrong; to remind one of something bad or unfortunate that has happened. (Fig. on a method of housebreaking pets.) □ *Mary knows she shouldn't have broken off her engagement. Don't rub her nose in it.*

rub off (on so**)** *Fig.* [for a characteristic of one person] to seem to transfer to someone else. □ *I'll sit by Ann. She has been lucky all evening. Maybe it'll rub off on me.*

rub so **out**† *Sl.* to kill someone. (Underworld.) □ *The gunman was eager to rub somebody out.*

rub salt in a wound *Fig.* to deliberately make someone's unhappiness, shame, or misfortune worse. □ *Don't rub salt in the wound by telling me how enjoyable the party was.*

rub shoulders with so Go to rub elbows (with so).

rub so **the wrong way** Go to rub so's fur the wrong way.

ruffle so's **feathers** *Fig.* to irritate or annoy someone. (As a bird might expand its feathers out.) □ *I didn't mean to ruffle his feathers. I just thought that I would remind him of what he promised us.*

rug rat *Sl.* a small child, especially an infant or toddler. (Also a term of address.) □ *You got any rug rats at your house?* □ *Hey, you cute little rug rat, come over here.*

the **ruin of** so/sth *Fig.* the cause of destruction; a failure. □ *Your bad judgment will be the ruin of this company!*

a **rule of thumb** *Fig.* a general principle developed through experiential rather than scientific means. □ *As a rule of thumb, I move my houseplants outside in May.*

rule so/sth **out**† to eliminate or preclude someone or something. □ *I would like to join the team. I hope you don't rule me out just because I am small.*

rule the roost *Fig.* to be the boss or manager, especially at home. □ *Who rules the roost at your house?*

rule with a velvet glove *Fig.* to rule in a very gentle way. □ *She rules with a velvet glove, but she gets things done, nonetheless.*

rule with an iron fist *Fig.* to rule in a very stern manner. □ *The dictator ruled with an iron fist and terrified the citizens.*

ruminate about sth *Fig.* to ponder and think about something. (Fig. on the image of a cow, relaxing and chewing its cud, as if it were thinking.) □ *He sat, ruminating about the events of the day, humming and eating peanuts.*

rumor has it that . . . *Fig.* there is a rumor that. . . . □ *Rumor has it that Fred is seeing Mary and that they are engaged.*

rump session *Fig.* a meeting held after a larger meeting. □ *A rump session continued after the meeting was adjourned.*

run a comb through sth to comb one's hair quickly. □ *Mom ran a comb through Timmy's hair and tried to make him look presentable.*

run a fever AND **run a temperature** *Fig.* to have a body temperature higher than normal; to have a fever. □ *The baby is running a temperature and is grouchy.*

run a make on so *Inf.* to perform an identity check on someone. □ *The cops ran a make on Lefty and learned about his prison record.*

run a red light *Fig.* to pass through an intersection having a red traffic light without stopping. □ *Sam got a ticket for running a red light.*

run a risk (of sth**)** AND **run the risk (of** sth**)** *Fig.* to take a chance that something (bad) will happen. □ *I don't want to run the risk of losing my job.*

run a tab *Fig.* to accumulate charges on a bill at a bar or tavern. □ *They won't let me run a tab here. I have to pay for each drink as I order it.*

run a taut ship Go to run a tight ship.

run a temperature Go to run a fever.

run a tight ship AND **run a taut ship** *Fig.* to run a ship or an organization in an orderly and disciplined manner. (*Taut* and *tight* mean the same thing. *Taut* is correct nautical use. Whereas *taut* may well refer to a sailing ship's rigging being pulled tightly, it usually characterizes the discipline and cooperation among the crew.) □ *The new office manager really runs a tight ship.* □ *Captain Jones is known for running a taut ship.*

run afoul of so/sth *Fig.* to get into conflict with someone or something. (*Afoul* = entangled and is nautical in origin.) □ *I ran afoul of the head of the department and had quite an argument.*

run against the grain Go to against the grain.

run aground (on sth**)** [for a ship] to ram its hull into something beneath the water and get stuck. □ *The ship ran aground on a reef and had to wait for high tide to get free.*

run along to leave. □ *Please run along and leave me alone.*

run amuck AND **run amok** *Fig.* to go awry; to go bad; to turn bad; to go into a frenzy. (From the Malay word *amok* = fighting in a violent frenzy.) □ *Our plan ran amok.* □ *He ran amuck early in the school year and never quite got back on track.*

run an errand AND **do an errand; go on an errand** to take a short trip to do a specific thing; to complete an errand. □ *I've got to run an errand. I'll be back in a minute.*

run (around) in circles Go to next.

run around like a chicken with its head cut off AND **run (around) in circles** *Fig.* to run around frantically and aimlessly; to be in a state of chaos. (Fig. on a chicken that continues to run around aimlessly after its head has been chopped off.) □ *I spent all afternoon running around like a chicken with its head cut off.*

run around with so *Fig.* to be friends with someone; to go places with regular friends. □ *John and I were great friends. We used to run around with each other all the time.*

a **run at** sth Go to a try at sth.

run away with so *Fig.* [for two people] to elope. □ *Jill ran away with Jack, much to her father's relief.*

run away with sth *Fig.* to capture or steal a performance by being the best performer. □ *Henry ran away with the show, and everyone loved him.*

run behind to be late; to run late. □ *We are running behind. You had better hurry.*

run sth **by** (so**) (again)** *Fig.* to explain something to someone again; to say something to someone again. □ *I didn't hear you. Please run that by me again.*

run circles around so AND **run rings around** so *Fig.* to outdo (including outrunning) someone. (Fig. on the image of someone who runs fast enough to run in circles around a competitor and yet still win the race.) □ *John is a much better speaker than Mary. He can run circles around her.*

run counter to sth *Fig.* to be in opposition to something; to run against something. (This has nothing to do with running.) □ *Your proposal runs counter to what is required by the manager.*

run down 1. *Fig.* [for something] to lose power and stop working. □ *The toy ran down and wouldn't go again until it had been wound.* **2.** *Fig.* to become worn or dilapidated. □ *The property was allowed to run down, and it took a lot of money to fix it up.*

run so/sth **down**† **1.** *Fig.* to criticize or deride someone or something. □ *Please stop running me down all the time. I can't be that bad!* **2.** Go to track so/sth **down**†.

run down to some place *Fig.* to travel to a place. (By running or any other means.) □ *I have to run down to the store and get some bread.*

run one's **eye over** sth *Fig.* to gaze at the whole of something; to glance at all of something. □ *She ran her eyes over the lines of the automobile and nodded her approval.*

run one's feet off *Fig.* to run very hard and fast. □ *I ran my feet off, and I'm really tired now that the race is over.*

run one's fingers through one's **hair** AND **run** one's **hand through** one's **hair** to comb one's hair with one's fingers. □ *I came in out of the wind and ran my fingers through my hair to straighten it out a bit.*

run for it *Fig.* to escape by running. □ *The dogs were coming after me fast. There was nothing I could do but run for it.*

run for one's **life** *Fig.* to run away to save one's life. □ *The captain told us all to run for our lives.*

*a run for one's **money 1.** *Fig.* the results or rewards one deserves, expects, or wants. (*Typically: **get** ~; **have** ~; **give** so ~.) □ *I get a run for my money at the club tennis tournament.* **2.** *Fig.* a challenge. (*Typically: **get** ~; **have** ~; **give** so ~.) □ *Bob got a run for his money when he tried to beat Mary at pool.*

run for the hills Go to head for the hills.

run one's hand through one's **hair** Go to run one's fingers through one's hair.

run one's head against a brick wall *Fig.* to be frustrated by coming up against an insurmountable obstacle. □ *There is no point in running your head against a brick wall. If you can't succeed in this case, don't even try.*

run so in† *Fig.* to arrest and transport a person to the police station. □ *The cops ran George in so they could question him extensively.*

run in the family *Fig.* [for a characteristic] to appear in many (or all) members of a family. □ *My grandparents lived well into their 90s, and it runs in the family.*

run into so Go to bump into so.

run (in)to sth *Fig.* to amount to a certain amount of money. □ *In the end, the bill ran to thousands of dollars.*

run into a stone wall *Fig.* to come to a barrier against further progress. □ *Algebra was hard for Tom, but he really ran into a stone wall with geometry.*

run sth into the ground AND **drive sth into the ground** *Fig.* to carry something too far. □ *It was a good joke at first, Tom, but you've run it into the ground.*

run it down *Sl.* to tell the whole story; to tell the truth. □ *I don't care what happened. Run it down. I can take it.*

run its course *Fig.* [for something] to continue through its cycle of existence, especially a disease. □ *Sorry. There is no medicine for it. It will just have to run its course.*

run like clockwork *Fig.* to run very well; to progress very well. □ *I want this office to run like clockwork—with everything on time and everything done right.*

run like stink Go to like stink.

run like the wind Go to like the wind.

run low (on sth**)** to near the end of a supply of something. □ *We are running low on salt. It's time to buy more.*

run off 1. *Fig.* to have diarrhea. □ *One of the children was running off and had to stay home from school.* **2.** to run away. □ *The rabbit ran off before we could get near it.*

run sth off† *Fig.* to duplicate something, using a mechanical duplicating machine. □ *If the master copy is ready, I will run some other copies off.*

run off at the mouth *Sl.* to talk too much. □ *Tom runs off at the mouth too much. I wish he would temper his remarks.*

run off in all directions *Fig.* [for people] to set out to do something or go somewhere in an aimless and disorganized fashion. (Can also apply to one person. See also ride off in all directions.) □ *Stop running off in all directions, and focus your energy.*

run off (with so**)** *Fig.* to run away with someone, as in an elopement. □ *Tom and Ann ran off and got married.*

run on all cylinders 1. *Fig.* [for an engine] to run well and smoothly. □ *This car is* *now running on all cylinders, thanks to the tune-up.* **2.** *Fig.* to function well or energetically. (Fig. on ①.) □ *Our department seems to be running on all cylinders. Congratulations.*

run out of gas Go to out of gas.

run out of patience Go to out of patience.

run out of steam *Fig.* to lose momentum and fail. □ *Toward the end of the lecture, he seemed to run out of steam, leaving us with no summary or conclusion.*

run out of time to have used up most of the allotted time; to have no time left. □ *I ran out of time before I could finish the test.*

run over sth **with** so *Fig.* to review something with someone. □ *I would like to run over this with you one more time.*

run so **ragged** *Fig.* to keep someone or something very busy. □ *This busy season is running us all ragged at the store.*

run rampant *Fig.* to run, develop, or grow out of control. □ *Weeds have run rampant around the abandoned house.*

run one's **rhymes** *Sl.* to say what you have to say; to give one's speech or make one's plea. □ *Go run your rhymes with somebody else!*

run rings around so Go to run circles around so.

run riot AND **run wild** *Fig.* to get out of control. □ *The children ran wild at the birthday party and had to be taken home.*

run roughshod over so/sth Go to ride roughshod over so/sth.

run scared *Fig.* to behave as if one were going to fail. □ *When we lost that big contract, everyone in the office was running scared. We thought we'd be fired.*

run short (of sth**)** *Fig.* to begin to run out of something. □ *We are running short of eggs. We've got to buy some more.*

Run that by (me) again. AND **Run it by (me) again.** *Inf.* Please repeat what you just said.; Please go over that one more time. □ *Alice: Do you understand? Sue:*

No. I really didn't understand what you said. Run that by me again, if you don't mind.

run the gamut to cover a wide range [from one thing to another]. □ *She wants to buy the house, but her requests run the gamut from expensive new carpeting to completely new landscaping.* □ *His hobbies run the gamut from piano repair to portrait painting.*

run the gauntlet 1. to race, as a punishment, between parallel lines of men who thrash one as one runs. (Also spelled gantlet.) □ *The knight was forced to doff his clothes and run the gauntlet.* **2.** AND **run the gauntlet of** sth *Fig.* to endure a series of problems, threats, or criticism. (Fig. on ①.) □ *After the play, the director found himself running the gauntlet of questions and doubts about his ability.*

run the good race *Fig.* to do the best that one could; to live life as well and as fully as possible. □ *He didn't get what he wanted, but he ran the good race.*

run the show *Fig.* to be in charge; to be in command. □ *Who's running this show?*

run through sth **1.** *Fig.* to go through a procedure or sequence; to rehearse a procedure or sequence. □ *I want to run through Act Two again before we end this rehearsal.* **2.** *Fig.* to read or examine something quickly. □ *Sally ran through the list, checking off the names of the people who had already paid for tickets.* **3.** *Fig.* to spend or use a supply of something wastefully and rapidly. □ *Have we run through all the peanut butter already?*

run so **through** sth **1.** *Fig.* to guide a person through a process. □ *Let me run you through the process so you will know what is happening to you.* **2.** *Fig.* to rehearse someone. □ *The director ran the cast through the last act three times.*

run sth **through** sth *Fig.* to process something by going through a procedure, a deliberative body, or a department. □ *I will have to run this through the board of directors.*

run to seed Go to go to seed.

run sth **up**† **1.** *Fig.* to cause something to go higher, such as the price of stocks or commodities. □ *A rumor about higher earnings ran the price of the computer stocks up early in the afternoon.* **2.** *Fig.* to accumulate indebtedness. □ *I ran up a huge phone bill last month.* **3.** *Fig.* to stitch something together quickly. □ *She's very clever. I'm sure she can run up a costume for you.*

run wild Go to run riot.

run with so/sth *Fig.* to stay in the company of someone or some group. □ *Fred was out running with Larry when they met Vernon.*

run with sth *Fig.* to take over something and handle it aggressively and independently. (Fig. on the image of someone seizing something and carrying it while running.) □ *I know that Alice can handle the job. She will take it on and run with it.*

run with the hare and hunt with the hounds *Fig.* to support both sides of a dispute. □ *In our office politics, Sally always tries to run with the hare and hunt with the hounds, telling both the clerical workers and the management that she thinks they should prevail.*

*the **runaround** a series of excuses, delays, and referrals. (*Typically: **get** ~; **have** ~; **give** so ~.) □ *You'll get the runaround if you ask to see the manager.*

a **running battle** *Fig.* a continuing battle; a constant and repeated argument. □ *I have been involved in a running battle about money with my wife for years.*

running high *Fig.* [for feelings] to be in a state of excitement or anger. □ *Feelings were running high as the general election approached.*

running on empty *Fig.* [of a person] with hardly any energy left. (Fig. on the state of a car with almost no fuel left.) □ *I haven't been getting enough sleep, and I'm just running on empty.*

running on fumes AND **running on vapor** **1.** *Fig.* [of a car engine] running with an (almost) empty gas tank and using just the gasoline vapor from the gas tank. (An exaggeration.) □ *I'm almost out of gas, and I think the old buggy is just running on fumes.* **2.** *Fig.* just managing to run, operate, play, survive, etc. (Fig. on ①.) □ *Our town's baseball team is just running on vapor. They just haven't got what it takes.*

running on vapor Go to previous.

run-of-the-mill *Fig.* common or average; typical. □ *The restaurant we went to was nothing special—just run-of-the-mill.*

the **runt of the family** Go to next.

the **runt of the litter** **1.** *Fig.* the smallest animal born in a litter; the animal in a litter least likely to survive. □ *No one wanted to buy the runt of the litter, so we kept it.* **2.** AND the **runt of the family** *Fig.* the smallest child in the family. □ *I was the runt of the litter and the butt of all the jokes.*

rush hour *Fig.* the period of time when heavy traffic is moving into or out of a city. □ *This is the slowest rush hour I have ever been in. Traffic is almost in gridlock.*

rush in(to sth**)** to begin doing something without the proper preparation. □ *Don't rush into this job without thinking it through.*

rush sth **into print** to print up something hastily. □ *The story was so timely that the newspaper editor rushed it into print without checking all the details.*

a **rush on** sth AND a **run on** sth a large demand for something. □ *There was a rush on bottled water during the drought.*

rush sth **through (**sth**)** *Fig.* to move something through some process or office in a hurry. □ *He was in a hurry, so we rushed his order through the shipping department.*

rush to conclusions *Fig.* to try to reach a conclusion too fast, probably with insufficient evidence; to jump to conclusions. □ *I'm afraid you are rushing to conclusions when you speak of canceling the performance.*

rush so to the hospital to take someone to the hospital very quickly. □ *They had to rush her to the hospital because she had stopped breathing.*

the **rust belt** *Fig.* the industrial north of the U.S. (Patterned on the sun belt. Also capitalized.) □ *The salt they put on the roads in the winter made my car all rusty. I guess that's why they call this area the rust belt.*

rustle sth **up**† *Rur.* to manage to prepare a meal, perhaps on short notice. □ *I think I can rustle something up for dinner.*

S

*the sack AND ***the ax** *Inf.* dismissal from one's employment. (*Typically: **get** ~; **give** so ~.) □ *Poor Tom got the sack today. He's always late.* □ *I was afraid that Sally was going to get the ax.*

sack out *Inf.* to go to bed or go to sleep. □ *Let's sack out early tonight.*

sacked out *Inf.* asleep. □ *Here it is ten o'clock, and you are still sacked out!*

a **sacred cow** *Fig.* something that is regarded by some people with such respect and veneration that they do not like it being criticized by anyone in any way. (From the fact that the cow is regarded as sacred in India and is not eaten or mistreated.) □ *A university education is a sacred cow in the Smith family. Fred is regarded as a failure because he quit school at 16.*

sacrifice so/sth **on the altar of** sth *Fig.* to abandon someone or something in the cause of something else. □ *I was young and I sacrificed my career on the altar of love. I dropped out of school and got married.*

a **sad sight** Go to a sorry sight.

a **sad state of affairs** Go to a pretty state of affairs.

sadder but wiser *Cliché* unhappy but knowledgeable [about someone or something—after an unpleasant event]. □ *After the accident, I was sadder but wiser and would never make the same mistake again.*

saddle so **with** so/sth AND **stick** so **with** so/sth *Fig.* to burden someone with someone or something undesirable, annoying, or difficult to deal with. (*Stick* is more informal than *saddle*.) □ *I apologize for saddling you with my young cousin all day.*

saddled with so/sth *Fig.* burdened with someone or something. □ *I've been saddled with the children all day. Let's go out tonight.*

safe and sound *Fig.* unharmed and whole or healthy. □ *It was a rough trip, but we got there safe and sound.*

safety in numbers safety achieved by being concealed in or united with large numbers of people or other creatures. □ *We stayed close together, thinking that there was safety in numbers.*

sage advice *Fig.* very good and wise advice. □ *My parents gave me some sage advice when I turned 18.*

sail into so/sth *Fig.* to crash into someone or something. □ *The missile sailed into the soldiers, injuring a few.*

sail (right) through sth **1.** *Fig.* to go through something very quickly and easily. □ *The kids just sailed right through the ice cream and cake. There was not a bit left.* **2.** *Fig.* to get through a procedure, evaluation, or vote quickly and easily. □ *The proposal sailed through the committee with no debate.*

sail under false colors 1. to sail with false identification. (Pirates often sailed under the national flag of the ship they planned on attacking.) □ *The ship, sailing under false colors, suddenly started to pursue our ship.* **2.** *Fig.* to function deceptively. (Fig. on ①.) □ *You are not who you seem to be. You are sailing under false colors.*

Sakes alive! Go to Land(s) sakes (alive)!

sally forth *Fig.* to go forth; to leave and go out. □ *The soldiers sallied forth from behind the stone wall.*

salt sth **away**† **1.** *Lit.* to store and preserve a foodstuff by salting it. □ *The farmer's wife salted a lot of fish and hams away for the winter.* **2.** *Fig.* to store something; to place something in reserve. (Fig. on ①.) □ *I need to salt some money away for my retirement.*

the **salt of the earth** *Fig.* the most worthy of people; a very good or worthy person. (A biblical reference, Matthew 5:13.) □ *Mrs. Jones is the salt of the earth. She is the first to help anyone in trouble.*

salt sth **with** sth *Fig.* to put something into something as a lure. (Fig. on the image of putting a bit of gold dust into a mine in order to deceive someone into buying the mine.) □ *The land agent salted the bank of the stream with a little gold dust hoping for a land rush to start.*

same difference *Inf.* the same; no difference at all. □ *Pink, fuchsia, what does it matter? Same difference.*

Same here. *Fig.* Me too!; I agree! □ *Bob: I'll have chocolate ice cream! Bill: Same here.*

same o(l)′ same o(l)′ AND the **same old thing** *Sl.* the same thing that one has had before or is used to. □ *I'm getting tired of the same ol' same ol'.*

the **same old story** something that occurs or has occurred in the same way often. □ *The company is getting rid of workers. It's the same old story—a shortage of orders.*

the **same old thing** Go to same o(l)′ same o(l)′.

the **same to you** *Fig.* the same comment applies to you. (This can be a polite or a rude comment.) □ *Bill: Have a pleasant evening. Bob: Thank you. The same to you.*

the **sands of time** *Fig.* the accumulated tiny amounts of time; time represented by the sand in an hourglass. □ *The sands of time will make you grow old like everyone else.*

a **sanity check** Go to a reality check.

Saturday night special *Fig.* a small, easily obtainable pistol. □ *There was another*

killing last night with a Saturday night special.

saunter along to walk along slowly; to ramble along. □ *Bob sauntered along, looking as if he didn't have a care in the world.*

save a bundle (on sth**)** *Fig.* to save a lot of money on the purchase of something. □ *I managed to save a bundle on a car by buying a used one.*

save one's **ass** Go to save so's skin.

save one's **bacon** Go to save so's skin.

save one's **breath** *Fig.* to refrain from talking, explaining, or arguing. □ *There is no sense in trying to convince her. Save your breath.*

save (enough) time (for so/sth**)** Go to make (enough) time (for so/sth).

save (one's) face *Fig.* to preserve one's good standing, pride, or high position (after a failure). □ *The ambassador was more interested in saving his face than winning the argument.*

save (sth) for a rainy day AND **put** sth **aside for a rainy day; hold** sth **back for a rainy day; keep** sth **for a rainy day.** *Fig.* to reserve something—usually money—for some future need. □ *Keep some extra allowance for a rainy day.*

save oneself **(for marriage)** *Euph.* to remain a virgin until marriage. □ *No, I can't. I love you, but I'm saving myself for marriage.*

Save it! *Inf.* Stop talking.; Shut up!; Tell it to me later. □ *I've heard enough. Save it!*

save so's **neck** Go to next.

save so's **skin** AND **save** so's **neck; save** one's **bacon; save** one's **ass** *Fig.* to save someone from injury, embarrassment, or punishment. □ *I saved my skin by getting the job done on time.*

save the day *Fig.* to produce a good result when a bad result was expected. □ *The team was expected to lose, but Sally made three points and saved the day.*

saved by the bell *Cliché* saved by the timely intervention of someone or something. (Fig. on a boxer who is saved from being counted out by the bell that ends a round.) □ *I was going to have to do my part, but someone knocked on the door and I didn't have to do it. I was saved by the bell.*

saving grace *Cliché* the one thing that saves or redeems someone or something that would otherwise be a total disaster. □ *The saving grace for the whole evening was the good music played by the band.*

saw against the grain Go to against the grain.

***one's say** *Fig.* one's stance or position; what one thinks. (*Typically: **get** ~; **have** ~.) □ *I want to have my say on this matter.*

say a mouthful *Fig.* to say a lot; to say something very important or meaningful. □ *When you said things were busy around here, you said a mouthful. It is terribly busy.*

Say cheese! *Inf.* an expression used by photographers to get people to smile, which they must do while saying the word *cheese*. (Sometimes used jocularly as a way of asking people to smile.) □ *"All of you please stand still and say cheese!" said the photographer.*

say sth **for** sth *Fig.* [for something] to imply something good about something. □ *The speed with which we were able to sell the house says something for the state of the real estate market.*

say good-bye to sth Go to kiss sth good-bye.

say grace to say a prayer of gratitude before or after a meal. □ *Grandfather always says grace at Thanksgiving.*

a **say (in** sth) Go to a voice (in sth).

Say no more. *Inf.* I agree.; I will do it.; I concede, no need to continue talking. □ *John: Someone ought to take this stuff outside. Bill: Say no more. Consider it done.*

say one's **piece** AND **speak** one's **piece** *Fig.* to say what one must say; to recite what one has planned to say. □ *Look, just say your piece and get out of here.*

say sth **(right) to** so's **face** to say something (unpleasant) directly to someone. □ *I*

thought she felt that way about me, but I never thought she'd say it to my face.

Say that . . . Go to (Let's) say that. . . .

say sth **to** oneself *Fig.* to think something to oneself. □ *When I thought of him as a basketball player, I said to myself that he really isn't tall enough.*

say uncle Go to holler uncle.

Say what? AND **What say?; How's that (again)?; Come again.** *Inf. Rur.* What did you say?; Please repeat what you said.; Please repeat because I did not hear or understand you. □ *Sally: Would you like some more salad? Fred: Say what? Sally: Salad? Would you like some more salad?* □ *John: Put this one over there. Sue: How's that? John: Never mind, I'll do it.* □ *Tom: The car door is frozen closed. Bob: Come again? Tom: The car door is frozen closed.*

Say when. *Inf.* Tell me when I have given you enough of something, usually a liquid. (Sometimes answered simply with *When*.) □ *Tom (pouring milk into Fred's glass): Say when, Fred. Fred: When.*

Says me! AND **Sez me!** *Inf.* a formulaic answer to *Says who?* □ *Tom: Says who? Fred: Says me, that's who!*

Says who? AND **Sez who?** *Inf.* a formulaic challenge indicating disagreement with someone who has said something. □ *She drew herself up to her full height, looked him straight in the eye, and said, "Says who?"*

Says you! *Inf.* That's just what you say!; You don't know what you are talking about! □ *Mary: People who go around correcting other people were found to be very annoying in a recent survey. Bill: Says you!*

***scarce as hen's teeth** AND **scarcer than hen's teeth** *Cliché* scarce; seldom found. (*Also: **as** ~.) □ *I do declare, decent people are as scarce as hen's teeth in these chaotic times.*

scarcely have time to breathe Go to hardly have time to breathe.

scarcer than hen's teeth Go to scarce as hen's teeth.

scare sth **out of** so to frighten someone very badly. (The *something* can be *the living daylights, the wits, the hell, the shit,* etc.) □ *Gee, you scared the living daylights out of me!* □ *The police tried to scare the truth out of her.* □ *The door blew shut and scared the hell out of me.*

scare so **out of a year's growth** Go to frighten one out of one's wits.

scare one **out of** one's **mind** Go to frighten one out of one's wits.

scare one **out of** one's **wits** Go to frighten one out of one's wits.

scare so **stiff** *Fig.* to frighten someone severely. (*Stiff* = dead.) □ *That loud noise scared me stiff.*

scare the living daylights out of so Go to frighten the hell out of so.

scare the pants off (of) so *Inf.* to frighten someone very badly. (*Of* is usually retained before pronouns.) □ *Wow! You nearly scared the pants off me!*

scare the shit out of so Go to frighten the hell out of so.

scare the wits out of so Go to frighten the hell out of so.

scare so **to death** Go to frighten so to death.

scare so/sth **up**† Go to dig so/sth up†.

scared silly frightened very much. □ *I was scared silly by the loud explosion.*

scared stiff *Fig.* badly frightened. □ *I was scared stiff when the dog growled at me.*

scared to death Go to frightened to death.

scarf sth **down**† *Sl.* to eat something, perhaps in a hurry; to swallow something, perhaps in a hurry. □ *Are you going to scarf this whole thing down?*

scarf out Go to blimp out (on sth).

scattered far and wide Go to far and wide.

schiz(z) out *Sl.* to freak out; to lose mental control. □ *I schizzed out during the test. Got an F.*

school so **in** sth *Fig.* to train, discipline, or coach someone in something. □ *The voice coach schooled the singer in excellent breathing techniques.*

the **school of hard knocks** *Fig.* the school of life's experiences, as opposed to a formal, classroom education. □ *I didn't go to college, but I went to the school of hard knocks. I learned everything by experience.*

school of thought *Fig.* a particular philosophy or way of thinking about something. □ *One school of thought holds that cats cause allergic reactions.*

scoot down (to some place) *Inf.* to go (down) somewhere in a hurry. □ *I want you to scoot down to the store and get me a dozen eggs. Okay?* □ *I'll scoot down as soon as I finish reading the newspaper.*

scoot over to slide sideways while seated. □ *If you scoot over, we can get another person in this row.*

scoot over to so/sth *Inf.* to travel or move over to someone or something or some place in a hurry. □ *Scoot over to Don and ask him to come here for a minute.*

scope (on) so *Sl.* to evaluate a member of the opposite sex visually. □ *He wouldn't like it if somebody scoped on him. Or would he?*

scope so/sth **out**† Go to case so/sth out†.

score a home run Go to hit a home run.

score a point Go to make a point.

score sth **for** sth **1.** to arrange music for one or more musical instruments; to arrange music for a particular type of voice or voices. □ *The arranger scored the song for a four-part chorus.* **2.** to scratch something, such as glass, for breaking. □ *Valerie scored the piece of glass for breaking, and then snapped it off.*

score with so/group *Inf.* to please someone or a group. □ *Her rendition of "Old Kentucky Home" really scored with the audience.*

scour sth **for** so/sth *Fig.* to look carefully and thoroughly in something for someone or something. □ *I scoured the entire roster of members for a person who would agree to run for president.*

scout around (for so/sth) *Fig.* to look around for someone or something. □ *I don't know who would do a good job for* *you, but I'll scout around for a likely candidate.*

scrape along (on sth**)** AND **scrape along (with** sth**); scrape by (on** sth**); scrape by (with** sth**)** *Fig.* to manage just to get along with a minimum amount of something. □ *We can just scrape along on the money I earn from my sewing.*

scrape the bottom of the barrel to select from among the worst; to choose from what is left over. □ *The worker you sent over was the worst I've ever seen. Send me another—and don't scrape the bottom of the barrel.*

scrape through (sth**)** *Fig.* to get by something just barely; to pass a test just barely. □ *Alice passed the test, but she just scraped through it.* □ *I just scraped through my calculus test.*

scrape sth **together** Go to pull sth together.

scratch about (for sth**)** AND **scratch around (for** sth**)** *Fig.* to look very hard for something. □ *The children were scratching about the kitchen for something to eat.*

scratch so's **back** *Fig.* to do a favor for someone in return for a favor done for you. □ *You scratch my back, and I'll scratch yours.*

scratch the surface *Fig.* to just begin to find out about something; to examine only the superficial aspects of something. □ *We don't know how bad the problem is. We've only scratched the surface.*

scream bloody murder Go to cry bloody murder.

scream down (on so/sth**)** *Fig.* [for something, such as birds or bombs] to dive down on someone or something with a loud noise or very swiftly. □ *As the bombs screamed down, some people ran and some prayed.*

scream (sth**) from the rooftops** Go to shout (sth) from the rooftops.

screeching (drunk) *Sl.* intoxicated; very drunk. □ *How can anybody be so screeching drunk on four beers?*

screw around 1. *Inf.* to mess around; to waste time. □ *Stop screwing around and*

get to work! **2.** *Inf.* to play sexually; to indulge in sexual intercourse. □ *A few couples were screwing around at the party.*

screw so **around** *Inf.* to harass or bother someone. □ *Don't screw me around, man! I bite back!*

screw around with so/sth *Inf.* to fiddle with or mess around with someone or something. □ *Andy screwed around with his clock until he broke it.*

screw off *Inf.* to waste time. □ *Stop screwing off and get busy!* □ *I'm not screwing off. This is my lunch hour.*

screw so **out of** sth *Inf.* to cheat someone out of something. □ *I think you screwed me out of 10 bucks on that deal.*

screw so **over**† *Sl.* to give someone a very bad time; to scold someone severely. □ *Those guys really screwed you over. What started it?*

screw so **up**† *Inf.* to confuse someone mentally. □ *Please don't screw me up again!*

screw sth **up**† Go to futz sth up†.

screw up one's **courage** *Fig.* to build up one's courage. □ *I spent all morning screwing up my courage to take my driver's test.*

screw up (on sth**)** AND **mess up (on** sth**)** *Inf.* to blunder (on something). □ *I hope I don't screw up this time.*

screwed, blued, and tattooed 1. *Sl.* taken advantage of. □ *When John bought his wreck of a car, he got screwed, blued, and tattooed.* **2.** *Sl.* intoxicated. □ *All four of them went down to the tavern and got screwed, blued, and tattooed.*

screwed up *Inf.* ruined; messed up. □ *Your schedule is completely screwed up. Let's try to fix it.*

scrimp and save AND **pinch and scrape** *Fig.* to be very thrifty; to live on very little money, often in order to save up for something. □ *We had to scrimp and save in order to send the children to college.*

scrub up good Go to clean up well.

scrunch down to squeeze or huddle down into a smaller shape. □ *Mary scrunched down, trying to hide behind the chair.*

scuzz so **out**† *Sl.* to nauseate someone. □ *It's not nice to scuzz out people like that, especially when you hardly know them.*

a **sea change** *Fig.* a major change or transformation. □ *This is not the time for a sea change in our manufacturing division. There are too many orders at the moment.*

*one's **sea legs** *Fig.* one's ability to tolerate the movement of a ship at sea. (*Typically: **get** ~; **have** ~.) □ *Jean was a little awkward on the cruise at first, but in a few days she got her sea legs and was fine.*

seal a bargain AND **seal the bargain** *Fig.* to signify or celebrate the reaching of an agreement or bargain. □ *They signed the papers and sealed the bargain by drinking champagne.*

seal so's **fate** AND **seal the fate of** so *Fig.* to determine finally the fate of someone. □ *His lying and cheating sealed his fate. He was convicted and sent to prison.*

seal the bargain Go to seal a bargain.

sealed with a kiss AND **SWAK** *Inf.* written and sent with love and care. (The initialism is sometimes written on love letters. Also an acronym.) □ *All her letters come SWAK.*

the **seamy side of life** *Fig.* the most unpleasant or roughest aspect of life. (A reference to the inside of a garment where the seams show.) □ *Mary saw the seamy side of life when she worked as a volunteer in the homeless shelter.*

search high and low (for so/sth**)** Go to hunt high and low (for so/sth).

Search me. *Inf.* I do not know.; You can search my clothing and my person, but you won't find the answer to your question anywhere near me. (The two words have equal stress.) □ *Jane: What time does Mary's flight get in? Sally: Search me.*

search sth **with a fine-tooth(ed) comb** Go to go over sth with a fine-tooth(ed) comb.

*second nature to so *Fig.* easy and natural for someone. (*Typically: **be** ~; **become** ~.) □ *Flying a helicopter is no problem for Bob. It's become second nature to him.*

*second thoughts (about so/sth) *Fig.* new doubts about someone or something. (*Typically: **get** ~; **have** ~; **give** so ~.) □ *I'm beginning to get second thoughts about Tom.* □ *You're giving me second thoughts about going there.*

second to none *Fig.* better than everything else. □ *Her suggestion was second to none, and the manager accepted it eagerly.*

*one's **second wind 1.** *Fig.* one's stabilized breathing after exerting oneself for a short time. (*Typically: **get** ~; **have** ~.) □ *John was having a hard time running until he got his second wind.* **2.** *Fig.* one's greater or renewed energy and productivity, gained at some time after starting. (*Typically: **get** ~; **have** ~.) □ *I usually get my second wind early in the afternoon.*

second-guess so *Fig.* to try to predict what some person will do before it is known to anyone, including the person. □ *There is no point in trying to second-guess Bob. He is completely unpredictable.*

secondhand *Fig.* from another person or source, not directly from personal experience or observation. (Fig. on a term describing used goods.) □ *Frank tells stories about the Gulf War, but he got them secondhand. He wasn't actually in the desert with the troops.*

second-rate *Fig.* not of the best quality; inferior. □ *Bill's a second-rate tennis player compared with Bob.*

seduce so **from** sth *Fig.* to lure someone away from something. □ *Frank was seduced from his honest ways by the offer of money.*

see a man about a dog *Fig.* to leave for some unmentioned purpose. (Often refers to going to the restroom.) □ *When John said he was going to see a man about a dog, I thought he would be gone for only a minute.*

see beyond sth *Fig.* to be able to imagine the future beyond a certain time or event. □ *He can't see beyond the next day—no sense of the future.*

see sth **coming** *Fig.* to anticipate that something will happen. □ *Yes, I got laid off. I should have seen it coming.*

see double *Fig.* to see two of everything instead of one, owing to a medical disorder. □ *When I was driving, I saw two people on the road instead of one. I'm seeing double. There's something wrong with my eyes.*

see eye to eye (about so/sth**) (with** so**)** AND **see eye to eye (on** so/sth**) (with** so**)** *Fig.* [for someone] to agree about someone or something with someone else. □ *Will labor and management ever see eye to eye on the new contract?*

see fit (to do sth**)** *Fig.* to decide to do something. □ *If I see fit to return, I'll bring Bill with me.* □ *She'll do it if she sees fit.*

see so **in hell first** AND **see** so **in hell (before** one **would** do sth**); rot in hell (before** one **would** do sth**)** *Fig.* would just as likely die as to do something. □ *I will never sell you my land. I'll see you in hell first!*

see into sth Go to look into sth.

see one's **name in lights** Go to one's name in lights.

see no further than the end of one's **nose** AND **cannot see (any) further than the end of** one's **nose; can't see beyond the end of** one's **nose 1.** *Fig.* to lack any ability to plan or project into the future or to foresee consequences. □ *All he thinks about is now. He can't see further than the end of his nose.* **2.** *Fig.* to be narrow-minded; to lack understanding and perception. □ *She is so preoccupied she can see no further than the end of her nose.*

see red to be angry. □ *Whenever I think of the needless destruction of trees, I see red.*

see (right) through so/sth *Fig.* to understand or detect the true nature of someone or something. □ *You can't fool me*

anymore. *I can see through you and all your tricks.*

see stars *Fig.* to seem to see flashing lights after receiving a blow to the head. □ *I saw stars when I bumped my head on the attic ceiling.*

see the color of so's **money** *Fig.* to verify that someone has money or has enough money. □ *So, you want to make a bet? Not until I see the color of your money.*

see the error of one's **ways** *Fig.* to understand that one has done something wrong. □ *I thought you would see the error of your ways if I kept pointing it out to you.* □ *I saw the error of my ways and reformed my behavior.*

see the (hand)writing on the wall AND **read the handwriting on the wall** *Fig.* to interpret the details and clues about future events; to know that something is about to happen. (Biblical, Daniel 5:25. At Belshazaar's feast a prediction of the death of the king is written on the wall by a disembodied hand. The prediction comes true.) □ *If you don't improve your performance, they'll fire you. Can't you see the writing on the wall?*

see the last of so/sth AND **hear the last of** so/sth *Fig.* to have experienced the last visit, episode, adventure, etc. with someone or something. □ *I hope I have seen the last of Robert Ellis!* □ *We have seen the last of Grandma's homemade strawberry jam.*

see the light 1. *Fig.* to understand something clearly at last. □ *After a lot of studying and asking many questions, I finally saw the light.* □ *I know that geometry is difficult. Keep working at it. You'll see the light pretty soon.* **2.** AND **(begin to) see the light (at the end of the tunnel)** *Fig.* to foresee an end to one's problems after a long period of time. □ *I had been horribly ill for two months before I began to see the light at the end of the tunnel.*

see the light (at the end of the tunnel) Go to previous.

see the light (of day) *Fig.* to come to the end of a very busy time. □ *Finally, when the holiday season was over, we could see the light of day. We had been so busy!*

see the sights *Fig.* to see the important things in a place; to see what tourists usually see. □ *Everyone left the hotel early in the morning to see the sights.*

see sth **through** *Fig.* to follow through on something until it is completed. □ *It's going to be an unpleasant experience, but I hope you'll see it through.*

see so **through** sth Go to help so through sth.

see to so/sth *Fig.* to take care of someone or something. □ *Tom will see to the horses. Come to the house and freshen up.*

see (to it) that sth **is done** *Fig.* to make sure of something; to make certain of something; to be certain to do something. □ *The manager saw to it that everyone began working on time.*

see so **to the door** Go to show so (to) the door.

see one's **way (clear) (to** do sth**)** *Fig.* to find it possible to do something. □ *I'd be happy if you could see your way clear to attend our meeting.*

See what the cat dragged in! Go to Look (at) what the cat dragged in!

see which way the wind is blowing *Fig.* to determine what is the most expedient thing to do under the conditions at hand. (Also with *tell* in the negative.) □ *We studied the whole situation to see which way the wind was blowing and decided to avoid any conflict at that time.* □ *Sam failed to see which way the wind was blowing and got himself caught up in an argument.*

See you in church. AND **See you in the funny papers.** *Fig.* I will see you somewhere later. (*Funny papers* = comic section of a newspaper. The first entry head can be used literally.) □ *Bye, Bill. See you in church.*

See you in the funny papers. Go to previous.

See you later, alligator. AND **Later, (alli)gator.** *Inf.* Good-bye. (The formulaic reply is After while(, crocodile).) □ *Bob: See you later, alligator. Jane: After while, crocodile.*

seeing as how . . . Go to next.

seeing that . . . AND **seeing as how . . . ; in view of the fact that . . .** because; since we can observe that. . . . □ *Seeing that everyone is here, we can begin.* □ *In view of the fact that the property is worthless, there is no point in fighting over who inherits it!*

seek professional help *Euph.* to get psychiatric or psychological treatment. □ *If you are seriously thinking of suicide, now is the time to seek professional help.*

seize the day Go to strike while the iron is hot.

seize the opportunity to take advantage of an opportunity when offered. □ *My uncle offered me a trip to Europe, so I seized the opportunity.*

seize up to freeze or halt; to grind suddenly to a stop. □ *My knee seized up in the middle of a football game. Yeouch!*

seize (up)on sth *Fig.* to accept or adopt something, such as a plan, idea, etc. □ *We all heard her great new ideas and seized upon them immediately.*

seized with sth *Fig.* affected suddenly by something, such as laughter, coughing, sneezing, fits of rage, etc. □ *Mary was seized with laughter at the sight of Ted in a clown suit.*

sell so **a bill of goods** *Fig.* to get someone to believe something that isn't true; to deceive someone. □ *Don't pay any attention to what John says. He's just trying to sell you a bill of goods.*

sell so **down the river** Go to sell so out†.

sell sth **for a song** *Fig.* to sell something for very little money. (As in trading something of value for the singing of a song.) □ *I had to sell my car for a song because I needed the money in a hurry.*

sell like hotcakes *Fig.* [for something] to be sold very fast. □ *The new gas and electric hybrid cars are selling like hotcakes.*

sell so **on** sth *Fig.* to convince someone to do something; to convince someone to accept an idea. □ *John sold Anne on switching cell phone companies.*

sell so out† AND **sell so down the river** *Inf.* to betray someone; to reveal damaging information about someone. □ *Bill told about Bob's past, and that sold Bob down the river.*

sell out (to so) *Fig.* to betray someone or something to someone. □ *I think that you have sold out to the enemy!*

sell so/sth short *Fig.* to underestimate someone or something; to fail to see the good qualities of someone or something. □ *When you say that John isn't interested in music, you're selling him short. Did you know he plays the violin quite well?*

sell one's soul (to the devil) *Fig.* to do something very extreme [in order to obtain or accomplish something]. □ *I would sell my soul for a good steak about now.* □ *Tom would sell his soul to the devil to go out with Tiffany.*

sell the farm AND **bet the farm (on sth); bet the ranch (on sth)** *Fig.* to liquidate all one's assets on order to raise money to invest in something. (Both entry heads are elliptical: sell the farm = sell one's only asset, the farm, and invest the proceeds; bet the farm (on sth) = mortgage the farm and invest the proceeds of the loan. Both usually appear in the negative.) □ *It sounds promising, but I wouldn't sell the farm.* □ *It's a risky proposition. I wouldn't bet the farm on it.*

a **selling point** *Fig.* a feature of a product or idea that is worth mentioning when trying to sell the product or idea. □ *The fact that the book had large type is an important selling point.*

send so a message *Fig.* to give someone a hint, leaving the person to figure out what is really meant. (A way of giving one bad news about one's future.) □ *He suggested that Tom would be happier in a smaller firm. He was definitely sending Tom a message.*

send one about one's business *Fig.* to send someone away, usually in an unfriendly way. □ *Is that annoying man on the telephone again? Please send him about his business.*

send so away Go to put so away†.

send so flying Go to send so packing.

send so from pillar to post *Fig.* to send someone to many different places, none of which is the correct place. (Similar to send so on a wild-goose chase.) □ *Jill sent Roger from pillar to post to look for a special kind of paper.*

send so in for so to send someone into a game as a replacement for someone else. □ *The coach sent Jill in for Alice, who was beginning to tire.*

Send so my love. Go to Give so my love.

send so on a wild-goose chase *Fig.* to send someone on a pointless or futile search. □ *Fred was sent on a wild-goose chase while his friends prepared a surprise party for him.*

send out a warrant (on so) Go to put out a warrant (on so).

send so (out) on an errand to dispatch someone to perform an errand. □ *Jerry will be back in a minute. I sent him out on an errand.*

send out the wrong signals AND **send so the wrong signals** *Fig.* to signify something that is not true; to imply something that is not true. □ *I hope I haven't been sending out the wrong signals, but I do not really care to extend this relationship.*

send so packing AND **send so flying** *Fig.* to send someone away; to dismiss someone, possibly rudely. □ *I couldn't stand him anymore, so I sent him packing.*

send one scratching one's head Go to leave one scratching one's head.

send one to one's death *Fig.* to order one to go on a mission or journey that will result in one's death. □ *The general sent many fine young men to their deaths that day.*

send so to glory 1. *Fig.* to kill someone. □ *One shot sent him to glory.* **2.** *Inf. Fig.* to officiate at the burial services for someone. □ *The preacher sent him to glory amidst the sobs of his relatives.*

send so to the locker room Go to next.

send so to the showers AND **send so to the locker room** *Fig.* to order a player from the playing field, thus ending the player's participation for the day. □ *The coach had sent four players to the showers before the end of the game.*

send so/sth **up**[†] *Fig.* to parody or ridicule someone or something. □ *Comedians love to send the president or some other famous person up.*

send up a trial balloon *Inf.* to suggest something and see how people respond to it; to test public opinion. □ *Mary had an excellent idea, but when we sent up a trial balloon, the response was very negative.*

send so **up (the river)** *Inf.* to send someone to prison. (Underworld. As done by a judge or indirectly by the police.) □ *I'm gonna send you up the river if it's the last thing I do.*

send word to so *Fig.* to get a message to someone by any means. □ *I will send word to her as soon as I have something to report.*

a **sense of humor** *Fig.* the ability to appreciate good humor and jokes; the ability to create jokes and say funny things. □ *Does he have a sense of humor? He looks like he has never laughed in his life.*

separate the men from the boys AND **separate the sheep from the goats** *Fig.* to separate the competent from those who are less competent. (Both entry heads are metaphorical. Not necessarily about males and rarely about sheep and goats.) □ *This is the kind of task that separates the men from the boys.* □ *Working in a challenging place like this really separates the sheep from the goats.*

separate the sheep from the goats Go to previous.

separate the wheat from the chaff *Fig.* to separate the good sense from the less sensible; to separate good things and people from the less good. (Fig. on wheat kernels and hulls. Probably biblical in origin.) □ *You will hear a lot of things when you go away to college. You will have to learn to separate the wheat from the chaff.*

the **separation of church and state** the constitutional barrier in the U.S. that prevents government from establishing a state religion. (This refers to eliminating evidence of religion in connection with government as well as assuring that the U.S. government does not establish a state religion.) □ *The city council stopped beginning each meeting with a prayer because someone suggested that it violated the principle of the separation of church and state.*

serve as a guinea pig *Fig.* [for someone] to be experimented on; to allow some sort of test to be performed on one. (Fig. on the use of guinea pigs for biological experiments.) □ *Jane agreed to serve as a guinea pig. She'll be the one to try out the new flavor of ice cream.*

serve notice (on so**)** *Fig.* to formally or clearly state or announce something to someone. □ *John served notice that he wouldn't prepare the coffee anymore.* □ *I'm serving notice that I'll resign as secretary next month.*

serve so's **purpose** Go to answer so's purpose.

serve so **right** *Fig.* [for an act or event] to punish someone fairly (for doing something). □ *John copied off my test paper. It would serve him right if he fails the test.*

serve time AND **do time** *Fig.* to spend a certain amount of time in jail. □ *After the felon served his time, he was released from prison.*

serve sth **to** so to deliver something officially, such as a subpoena, to someone. □ *The sheriff at the door was there to serve a subpoena to Fred.*

serve sth **up**[†] to distribute or deliver food for people to eat. □ *The cook served the stew up and then passed around the bread.*

set a precedent *Fig.* to establish a pattern; to set a policy that must be followed in future cases. □ *We've already set a precedent in matters such as these.*

set a trap 1. to adjust and prepare a trap to catch an animal. □ *The old man set a trap to catch an annoying squirrel.* **2.** to arrange to entrap a person in a way that exposes the person's errors or wrongdoings. □ *In lying to Spike that they had an eyewitness who saw him rob the bank, the police set a trap that caused Spike to admit the crime.*

set about doing sth AND **set about to** do sth to begin to do something. □ *We will set about painting the house when the weather gets a little cooler.*

set so/sth **above** so/sth *Fig.* to regard someone or something as better than someone or something else. □ *Fred set his wife and children above everyone else.*

set sth **against** so/sth *Fig.* to make someone hate or oppose someone or something. □ *His second wife set him against his former in-laws.*

set sth **aside**† Go to leave sth aside†.

set so **back** (some amount of money) *Fig.* to cost someone (an amount of money). □ *That fancy dinner at the restaurant last night really set us back.*

set one **(back) on** one's **feet** AND **set** one **on** one's **feet again** *Fig.* to reestablish someone; to help someone become active and productive again. □ *Gary's uncle helped set him back on his feet.* □ *We will all help set you on your feet again.*

set one **back on** one's **heels** *Fig.* to surprise or shock someone. □ *I'll bet that news really set her back on her heels!* □ *The bill for the repairs set me back on my heels.*

set sth **down**† AND **put** sth **down**† **1.** *Fig.* to write something on paper. □ *Let me put this down on paper so we will have a record of what was said.* **2.** *Fig.* to land an aircraft. □ *The pilot put the plane down exactly on time.*

set sth **down**† **in black and white** Go to put sth down† in black and white.

set so **down (on(to)** sth) to place a person one is carrying or lifting onto something. □ *I set the small boy down onto the desk and gave him a piece of candy.*

set sth **down to** sth Go to put sth down to sth.

set (enough) time aside† **(for** so/sth) Go to make (enough) time (for so/sth).

set eyes on so/sth AND **lay eyes on** so/sth *Fig.* to see someone or something for the first time. □ *I knew when I set eyes on that car that it was the car for me.*

set fire to so/sth AND **set** so/sth **on fire** to ignite someone or something; to put someone or something to flames. □ *The poor man accidentally set himself on fire.*

set foot in some place *Fig.* to enter into some place; to begin to enter some place. □ *The judge ordered him never to set foot in her house again.*

set for life *Fig.* prepared to exist for the rest of one's life; having adequate supplies for the rest of one's life. □ *As soon as I win the lottery, I will be set for life. I'll never have to work again!*

set forth on sth AND **launch forth on** sth **1.** *Fig.* to start out on something, such as a journey. □ *We intend to set forth on our journey very early in the morning.* **2.** *Fig.* to begin presenting a speech or an explanation. (Fig. on ①.) □ *Every time he launches forth on a presentation, it's a half hour before he shuts up.*

set a timepiece **forward** to reset a timepiece to a later time. □ *You are supposed to set your clock forward at this time of year.*

set great store by so/sth *Fig.* to have positive expectations for someone or something; to have high hopes for someone or something. □ *I set great store by my computer and its ability to help me in my work.*

set one's **heart against** sth *Fig.* to turn against something; to become totally against something. □ *Jane set her heart against going to Australia.*

set one's **heart on** so/sth *Fig.* to be determined to get or do someone or something. (See also have one's heart set on sth.) □ *Jane set her heart on going to London.*

set one's **hopes on** so/sth *Fig.* to have one's hopes or expectations dependent on someone or something. □ *Please don't set your hopes on me in the race. I can't run as fast as I used to.*

set one's **house in order** Go to put one's house in order.

set in *Fig.* to begin; [for a process] to start. □ *Rigor mortis is just beginning to set in.* □ *Winter is setting in, and it's going to be a bad one.*

set sth **in** some place to locate the action of a play or movie in a place. □ *The author set the second act in a wooded glade.*

set sth **in** a typeface to set something in type, a particular style of type, or a particular font. □ *Why not set this section in italics to make it stand out from the rest?*

set in cement Go to carved in stone.

set in concrete Go to carved in stone.

set sth **in motion** AND **put** sth **in motion** *Fig.* to start something moving. □ *The mayor set the project in motion by digging the first shovelful of soil.*

set in one's **ways** *Fig.* leading a fixed lifestyle; living according to one's own established patterns. □ *If you weren't so set in your ways, you'd be able to understand young people better.*

set so's **mind at ease (about** so/sth**)** AND **put** so's **mind at ease (about** so/sth**)** to make someone feel mentally comfortable about someone or something. □ *Alice is upset. I will have to do something to set her mind at ease about the accident.*

set one's **mind to** sth Go to put one's mind to sth.

a **set of pipes** *Fig.* a very loud voice; a good singing voice. □ *With a set of pipes like that, she's a winner.*

a **set of wheels** *Fig.* a car. □ *Man, look at that set of wheels that chick has!*

set so **off**† *Fig.* to cause someone to become very angry; to ignite someone's anger. □ *That kind of thing really sets me off!*

set sth **off**† **1.** *Fig.* to ignite something, such as fireworks. □ *The boys were setting firecrackers off all afternoon.* **2.** *Fig.* to cause something to begin. □ *The coach set the race off with a shot from the starting pistol.* **3.** *Fig.* to make something distinct or outstanding. □ *The lovely stonework sets the fireplace off quite nicely.*

set so **on fire** *Fig.* to excite someone; to make someone passionate. (*Fig.* on set fire to so/sth.) □ *Ted's presentation didn't exactly set me on fire, but it was a good summary of the project.*

set some place **on its ear** AND **turn** sth **on its ear** *Fig.* to excite, impress, or scandalize the people living in a place. (Typical places are: the world, the whole town, the campus, the office, etc.) □ *Her rowdy behavior set the whole town on its ear.*

set out (on sth**)** *Fig.* to begin a journey; to begin a project. □ *We set out on our trip exactly as planned.*

set out on one's **own** Go to strike out on one's own.

set out to do sth *Fig.* to begin to do something; to intend to do something. □ *Jill set out to weed the garden, but pulled up a few valuable plants in the process.*

set out to be sth to start on the process of becoming something. □ *I set out to be a doctor, but ended up being a lawyer.*

set one's **own house in order** Go to put one's own house in order.

set one's **own pace** *Fig.* to determine how rapidly one works or moves. □ *I do better when I set my own pace.*

set pen to paper AND **put pen to paper** *Fig. Lit.* to write something down. □ *As soon as I have enough time to set pen to paper, I'll write a letter to you.*

set sth **right** AND **make** sth **right; make** sth **good; put** sth **right** *Fig.* to correct something; to alter a situation to make it more fair. □ *This is a very unfortunate situation. I'll ask the people responsible to set this matter right.* □ *I'm sorry that we overcharged you. We'll try to put it right.*

set sail (for some place**)** *Fig.* to leave in a ship or boat for some place. (Not limited to ships having sails.) □ *We set sail for Grenada at noon.*

set one's **sights on** so/sth AND **have** one's **sights set on** so/sth *Fig.* to regard having someone or something as one's goal. □ *He wanted a wife, and he had set his sights on Alice.*

set so **straight** to make certain that someone understands something exactly. (Often said in anger or domination.) □ *Please set me straight on this matter. Do you or do you not accept the responsibility for the accident?*

set sth **straight** AND **put** sth **straight** *Fig.* to figure out and correct something; to straighten out a mess. □ *I am sorry for the error. I am sure we can set it straight.*

set so's **teeth on edge 1.** *Fig.* [for a scraping sound] to irritate someone's nerves. (Fig. on the facial expression someone might assume when enduring such a sound.) □ *That noise sets my teeth on edge!* □ *Tom's teeth were set on edge by the incessant screaming of the children.* **2.** *Fig.* [for a person or an idea] to upset someone very much. (Fig. as in ①.) □ *Her overbearing manner usually sets my teeth on edge.*

set the pace *Fig.* to determine the rate at which something is done. (Fig. on establishing a moving speed.) □ *I like to be able to set the pace that I work at.*

set the record straight AND **put the record straight** *Fig.* to put right a mistake or misunderstanding; to make sure that an account, etc. is correct. □ *The manager thought Jean was to blame, but she soon set the record straight.*

set the scene for sth Go to next.

set the stage for sth AND **set the scene for** sth **1.** to arrange a stage for an act or scene of a production. □ *They set the stage for the second scene while the orchestra played.* **2.** *Fig.* to prepare something for some activity. (Fig. on ①.) □ *The initial meeting set the scene for further negotiations.*

set the table *Fig.* to place plates, glasses, napkins, etc. on the table before a meal. (The opposite of clear the table.) □ *Jane, would you please set the table? Be sure to use the salad forks tonight.*

set the tone *Fig.* to establish the manner, type, or level of behavior, ranging from casual to serious. □ *John's positive speech set the tone for a conference where positive goals were the rule, rather than negative criticism.*

set the world on fire *Fig.* to do exciting things that bring fame and glory. (Frequently with the negative.) □ *You don't have to set the world on fire. Just do a good job.*

set to *Fig.* to begin to fight; to attack or commence someone or something. □ *They set to and fought for about 10 minutes, cursing and screaming.*

***set to** do sth ready to do something. (*Typically: **be** ~; **get** ~.) □ *We are set to leave at a moment's notice.*

set sth **to music** *Fig.* to write a piece of music to accompany a set of words. □ *The clever musician set my complicated lyrics to music.*

set so/sth **to work** to start someone or something working; to cause someone or something to begin functioning. □ *The captain set everyone to work repairing the tears in the fabric of the sails.*

set to work (on so/sth**)** to begin working on someone or something. □ *We have finished questioning Tom, so we will set to work on Fred.*

set tongues (a)wagging *Fig.* to cause people to start gossiping. □ *If you don't get the lawn mowed soon, you will set tongues wagging in the neighborhood.*

set type *Fig.* to arrange type for printing; to prepare finished pages for printing. (Originally for setting lead type by hand, and then by using machines such as the Linotype. Now also for computerized work as with a word processor.) □ *Have you finished setting the type for page one yet?*

set so **up**† *Fig.* to lead—by deception—a person to play a particular role in an event; to arrange an event—usually by deception—so that a specific person suffers the consequences for the event; to frame someone. □ *I had nothing to do with the robbery! I was just standing there. Somebody must have set me up!*

set sth **up**† *Fig.* to establish or found something. □ *We set up a fund to buy food for the needy.*

set up housekeeping to furnish a house and provide kitchen equipment to make a house livable; to settle down and prepare to live in a house, perhaps with someone else. □ *My brother and I bought a house and set up housekeeping. Then he got married and left me with the mess.*

set so **up (in business)** *Fig.* to help establish someone in business; to provide the money someone needs to start a business. □ *He helped set them up so he could keep the business in the family.*

set up shop some place *Fig.* to establish one's place of work somewhere. □ *The police officer said, "You can't set up shop right here on the sidewalk!"*

set sth **up**† **(with** so**)** *Fig.* to make plans for something. □ *John is hard at work setting something up with Bill and Mary.* □ *Sally and Tom set up a party for Saturday night.*

set upon so/sth *Fig.* to attack someone or something violently. □ *Bill set upon Tom and struck him hard in the face.*

settle a score with so AND **settle the score (with** so**)** *Fig.* to clear up a problem with someone; to get even with someone. □ *John wants to settle a score with his neighbor.*

settle so's **affairs** *Fig.* to deal with one's business matters; to manage the business affairs of someone who can't. □ *When my uncle died, I had to settle his affairs.* □ *I have to settle my affairs before going to Mexico for a year.*

settle down 1. *Fig.* to calm down. □ *Now, children, it's time to settle down and start class.* **2.** *Fig.* to settle into a stable way of life; to get married and settle into a stable way of life. □ *Tom, don't you think it's about time you settled down and stopped all of this running around?*

settle for sth *Fig.* to agree to accept something (even though something else would be better). □ *Ask your grocer for Wilson's canned corn—the best corn in cans. Don't settle for less.*

settle so's **hash** *Sl.* to calm someone down, perhaps by threats or by violence. □ *If he comes in here, I'll settle his hash.*

settle in(to sth**)** *Fig.* to become accustomed to one's new surroundings; to get used to living in a place or a new dwelling. □ *I need a little time to settle in; then I can think about buying a car.*

settle (sth**) (out of court)** *Fig.* to end a disagreement and reach an agreement without having to go through trial in a court of justice. □ *The plaintiff and defendant decided to settle before the trial.* □ *Mary and Sue settled out of court before the trial.*

settle up with so *Fig.* to figure out the amount that is owed and pay it; to compute and pay one one's share of something. □ *I must settle up with Jim for the bike I bought for him.* □ *Bob paid the whole restaurant bill, and we all settled up with him later.*

settle (up)on sth to decide on something. □ *We've discussed the merits of all of them, and we've settled on this one.*

a **seven-day wonder** *Fig.* a person or a process supposedly perfected in only seven days. (Sarcastic.) □ *Tommy is no seven-day wonder. It took him six years to get through high school!*

the **seven-year itch** *Inf.* a real or imagined longing for other women in a man's seventh year of marriage. □ *Looks like Jack has the seven-year itch.*

sever ties with so *Fig.* to end a relationship or agreement suddenly or completely. □ *The company severed its ties with the dishonest employee.*

sew so/sth **up**† *Fig.* to complete one's dealings with or discussion of someone or something. □ *It's time to sew this up and go home.*

*****sewed up 1.** [the sewing of a gap in cloth] completed. (*Typically: **get** sth ~; **have** sth ~.) □ *Have you got that tear sewed up yet?* **2.** AND *****wrapped up** *Fig.* settled or finished. (Fig. on ①. *Typically: **get** sth ~; **have** sth ~.) □ *I'll take the contract to the mayor tomorrow morning. I'll get the whole deal sewed up by noon.*

sever ties with someone

shack up (with so**)** *Sl.* to sleep or live with someone temporarily in a sexual relationship. □ *They shacked up for over a year until her parents found out and stopped sending her money.*

shades of so/sth *Fig.* reminders of someone or something; a thing that is reminiscent of someone or something. □ *When I met Jim's mother, I thought "shades of Aunt Mary."*

*a **shadow of** oneself AND *a **shadow of it-self;** *a **shadow of** one's **former self** *Fig.* someone or something that is not as strong, healthy, full, or lively as before. (*Typically: **be** ~; **become** ~.) □ *The sick man was a shadow of his former self.* □ *The abandoned mansion was merely a shadow of itself.*

a **shady character** AND a **suspicious character** *Fig.* an untrustworthy person; a person who makes people suspicious. □ *There is a suspicious character lurking about in the hallway. Please call the police.*

a **shady deal** *Fig.* a questionable and possibly dishonest deal or transaction. □ *The lawyer got caught making a shady deal with a convicted felon.*

*the **shaft** *Sl.* maltreatment; deception; betrayal; chastisement. (Typically: **get** ~; **give** so ~.) □ *Why do I get the shaft when I did nothing wrong?* □ *The boss really gave Wally the shaft.*

shagged out *Sl.* exhausted. □ *What a day! I'm shagged out!* □ *You guys look sort of shagged out.*

a **shaggy-dog story** a kind of funny story that relies for its humor on its length and its sudden ridiculous ending. □ *Don't let John tell his favorite shaggy-dog story. It'll go on for hours.*

shake a leg 1. *Inf.* to hurry; to move faster. (Often as a command. Older.) □ *Let's shake a leg, you guys. We gotta be there in 20 minutes.* **2.** *Inf.* to dance. (Older.) □ *Hey, Jill! You wanna shake a leg with me?*

shake so **down**† **1.** *Inf.* to blackmail someone. (Underworld.) □ *Fred was trying to* shake Jane down, but she got the cops in on it. **2.** *Inf.* to put pressure on someone to lend one money. □ *We tried to shake down Spike for a few hundred, but no deal.*

shake sth **down**† Go to shake sth out†.

shake (hands) on sth AND **shake** so's **hand (on** sth**)** *Fig.* to clasp and shake the hand of someone as a sign of agreement about something. □ *I think it would be better to sign an agreement than just shake on it.*

shake in one's **boots** AND **quake in** one's **boots** *Fig.* to be afraid; to shake from fear. □ *I was shaking in my boots because I had to go see the manager for being late.*

Shake it (up)! *Inf.* Hurry!; Move faster! □ *Get going, chum! Shake it up!*

shake a disease or illness **off**† *Fig.* [for the body] to fight off a disease or illness. □ *I thought I was catching a cold, but I guess I shook it off.*

shake so/sth **off**† *Fig.* to get rid of someone; to get free of someone who is bothering you. □ *Stop bothering me! What do I have to do to shake you off?*

shake sth **out**† AND **shake** sth **down**† *Fig.* to test something to find out how it works or what the problems are. □ *I need to spend some time driving my new car to shake it out.*

shake some sense into so Go to knock some sense into so.

shake the foundations of sth *Fig.* to disturb or question the essence or underlying principles of something. □ *The death of his father shook the very foundations of his religious beliefs.*

shake the habit Go to kick a habit.

shake the lead out Go to get the lead out.

shake so **up**† *Inf.* to shock or upset someone. □ *The sight of the injured man shook me up.*

shake sth **up**† *Fig.* to reorganize a group or organization, not always in a gentle way. □ *The new manager shook the office up and made things run a lot better.*

shaken up AND **shook up** *Inf.* upset; shocked. (See also (all) shook up. *Shaken* is standard English past participle of *shake. Shook* is the past tense.) □ *Relax, man! Don't get shook up!* □ *I always get shook up when I see a bad accident.*

The **shame of it (all)!** *Fig.* That is so shameful!; I am so embarrassed.; I am shocked. (Considerable use jocularly or as a parody. Compare this with For shame!) □ *John: Good grief! I have a pimple! Always, just before a date. Andy: The shame of it all!*

shank it *Sl.* to use one's legs to get somewhere; to walk. □ *My car needs fixing, so I had to shank it to work today.*

shank's mare *Fig.* travel on foot. □ *You'll find that shank's mare is the quickest way to get across town.*

shape up 1. *Fig.* to improve; to reform. □ *I guess I'd better shape up if I want to stay in school.* **2.** *Fig.* to assume a final form or structure. □ *Her objectives began to shape up in her senior year.*

shape so **up**† *Fig.* to get someone into good physical shape; to make someone behave or perform better. □ *I've got to shape myself up to improve my health.*

Shape up or ship out. *Fig.* Either improve one's performance or behavior or leave. (Used as a command.) □ *John was late again, so I told him to shape up or ship out.*

share and share alike *Cliché* having or taking equal shares. (*Share* may be interpreted as either a noun or a verb.) □ *The two roommates agreed that they would divide expenses—share and share alike.*

share so's **pain** *Fig.* to understand and sympathize with someone's pain or emotional discomfort. (Said in order to sound sympathetic.) □ *I am sorry about the loss of your home. I share your pain.*

share so's **sorrow** to grieve as someone else grieves. □ *I am sorry to hear about the death in your family. I share your sorrow.*

***sharp as a razor 1.** very sharp. (*Also: as ~.*) □ *The carving knife will have to be as sharp as a razor to cut through this gristle.* **2.** AND ***sharp as a tack** very sharp-witted or intelligent. (*Also: **as** ~.) □ *Sue can figure things out from even the slightest hint. She's as sharp as a tack.*

*sharp as a tack Go to previous.

a **sharp tongue** *Fig.* an outspoken or harsh manner; a critical manner of speaking. □ *He has quite a sharp tongue. Don't be totally unnerved by what he says or the way he says it.*

a **sharp wit** *Fig.* a good and fast ability to make jokes and funny comments. □ *Terry has a sharp wit and often makes cracks that force people to laugh aloud at inappropriate times.*

shed crocodile tears AND **cry crocodile tears** *Fig.* to shed false tears; to pretend that one is weeping. □ *The child wasn't really hurt, but she shed some crocodile tears anyway.*

shed (some) light on sth AND **throw (some) light on** sth; **throw (any) light on** sth *Fig.* to reveal something about something; to clarify something. □ *This discussion has shed some light on the problem.* □ *Let's see if Ann can throw any light on this question.*

shell out (an amount of money**)** *Inf.* to spend a certain amount of money. □ *I'm not going to shell out $400 for that!*

*a shellacking 1. *Fig.* a physical beating. (*Typically: **get** ~; **take** ~; **give** so ~.) □ *The boxer took a shellacking and lost the fight.* **2.** *Fig.* a beating—as in overcoming the opposite team in sports. (*Typically: **get** ~; **take** ~; **give** so ~.) □ *Our team played well but got a shellacking anyway.*

shift for oneself AND **fend for** oneself *Fig.* to get along by oneself; to support oneself. □ *When I became 20 years old, I left home and began to fend for myself.*

shift gears AND **switch gears** *Fig.* to change the topic of conversation; to change to another kind of task. □ *When I'm concentrating on one thing and the telephone rings, it's hard to shift gears and deal with the caller's questions.*

shift into overdrive Go to into overdrive.

shine up to so *Fig.* to try to gain someone's favor by being extra nice. □ *John is a nice guy, except that he's always trying to shine up to the professor.*

shipping and handling the costs of handling a product and transporting it to a customer. □ *The cost of the goods was low and shipping and handling added only a few dollars.*

ships that pass in the night *Cliché* people who meet each other briefly by chance, sometimes having a sexual liaison, and who are unlikely to meet again or have an ongoing relationship. □ *Mary wanted to see Jim again, but to him, they were ships that passed in the night.* □ *We will never be friends. We are just ships that passed in the night.*

shirk one's **duty** *Fig.* to neglect one's job or task. □ *The guard was fired for shirking his duty.*

*the shock of one's **life** *Fig.* a serious (emotional) shock. (*Typically: **get** ~; **have** ~; **give** one ~.) □ *I opened the telegram and got the shock of my life.*

shook up Go to shaken up.

shoot so/sth **(all) to hell** *Fig.* to destroy, exhaust, or damage someone or something. □ *The hard work in the morning shot me all to hell for the rest of the day.*

shoot one's **breakfast** Go to next.

shoot one's **cookies** AND **shoot** one's **breakfast; shoot** one's **supper** *Sl.* to empty one's stomach; to vomit. □ *I shot my supper, and I was glad to get rid of it.*

shoot daggers at so Go to look daggers at so.

shoot sth **down**† *Fig.* to foil a plan through criticism; to counter an idea with devastating criticism. □ *He raised a good point, but the others shot him down almost immediately.* □ *Liz shot down Jeff's best idea.*

shoot so **down in flames** *Inf.* to ruin someone; to bring about someone's downfall. (See also go down in flames.) □ *It was a bad idea, okay, but you didn't have to shoot me down in flames at the meeting.*

shoot for sth *Fig.* to aim for something; to set something as one's goal. □ *You have to shoot for the very best. Don't be satisfied with less.*

shoot for the sky Go to reach for the sky.

shoot from the hip *Fig.* to speak directly and frankly. (Alluding to the rapidness of firing a gun from the hip.) □ *John has a tendency to shoot from the hip, but he generally speaks the truth.*

shoot oneself **in the foot** *Fig.* to cause oneself difficulty; to be the cause of one's own misfortune. □ *Again, he shot himself in the foot by saying too much to the press.*

shoot one's **mouth off**† *Inf.* to boast or talk too much; to tell secrets. □ *Don't pay any attention to Bob. He's always shooting his mouth off.*

shoot (some) hoops *Fig.* to attempt to score baskets (in basketball) as entertainment. □ *Hey, Wilbur! Let's go shoot some hoops.*

shoot one's **supper** Go to shoot one's cookies.

shoot the breeze *Inf.* to chat casually and without purpose. □ *We spent the entire afternoon just shooting the breeze.*

shoot the bull AND **shoot the crap; shoot the shit** *Inf.* to chat and gossip. (The same as throw the bull. Caution with *crap, shit.*) □ *Let's get together sometime and shoot the bull.*

shoot the cat *Sl.* to empty one's stomach; to vomit. □ *I must have shot the cat a dozen times during the night.*

shoot the crap Go to shoot the bull.

shoot the shit Go to shoot the bull.

shoot the works 1. *Inf.* to do everything; to use everything; to bet all one's money. □ *Okay, let's go out to dinner and shoot the works.* **2.** *Sl.* to empty one's stomach; to vomit. □ *Suddenly she turned sort of green, and I knew she was going to shoot the works.*

shoot one's **wad** *Inf.* to spend all or nearly all one's cash on hand. (Some people will recognize this as a slang term referring to seminal ejaculation.) □ *I can't afford a cab. I shot my wad at the restaurant.*

shop around (for sth**)** to shop at different stores to find what you want at the best price. □ *I've been shopping around for a new car, but they are all priced too high.*

shopping list *Fig.* a list of things, especially questions or things one wants. □ *He showed up for the interview with a shopping list so long that it took two pages.*

short and sweet *Cliché* brief (and pleasant because of briefness). □ *That was a good sermon—short and sweet.* □ *I don't care what you say, as long as you make it short and sweet.*

the **short and (the) long of it** Go to the long and (the) short of it.

*the **short end (of the stick)** *Fig.* the smaller or less desirable part, rank, task, or amount. (*Typically: **get** ~; **have** ~; **give** so ~; **end up with** ~.) □ *Why do I always get the short end of the stick? I want my fair share!* □ *She's unhappy because she has the short end of the stick again.*

short for sth *Fig.* [of a form] being a shortened form of a word or phrase. □ *Photo is short for* photograph. □ *Dave is short for* David.

a **short fuse** Go to a quick temper.

short of sth *Fig.* not having enough of something. □ *Usually at the end of the month, I'm short of money.*

short on sth *Fig.* having less than is needed of something. □ *We're short of fish today, so ask all the waiters to tell people loudly that the roast chicken is an excellent choice.*

(a) **short shrift** *Fig.* a brief period of consideration of a person's ideas or explanations. □ *My plan got short shrift from the board—a 10-minute presentation; they then voted it down.*

a **short temper** Go to a quick temper.

*short with so *Fig.* abrupt and a little bit rude in speaking to a person. (*Typically: **be** ~; **become** ~; **get** ~.) □ *Please don't be short with me. I am doing the best that I can.*

a **shot at** so Go to a try at so.

a **shot at** sth Go to a try at sth.

shot full of holes AND **shot to ribbons; shot to hell; shot to pieces 1.** *Fig.* [of an argument that is] demolished or comprehensively destroyed. □ *Come on, that theory was shot full of holes ages ago.* □ *Your argument is all shot to hell.* **2.** *Inf.* totally ruined. □ *My car is all shot to hell and can't be depended on.*

a **shot in the arm 1.** an injection of medicine. □ *The doctor administered the antidote to the poison by a shot in the arm.* **2.** *Inf.* a boost or act of encouragement. (Fig. on ①.) □ *The pep talk was a real shot in the arm for all the guys.* **3.** *Inf.* a drink of liquor. □ *How about a little shot in the arm, bartender?*

a **shot in the dark** *Inf.* a very general attempt; a wild guess. □ *It was just a shot in the dark. I had no idea I was exactly correct.*

shot through with sth *Fig.* containing something; interwoven, intermixed, or filled with something. □ *The rose was a lovely pink shot through with streaks of white.*

shot to hell Go to shot full of holes.

shot to pieces Go to shot full of holes.

shot to ribbons Go to shot full of holes.

a **shotgun wedding** *Fig.* a forced wedding. (From imagery of the bride's father having threatened the bridegroom with a shotgun to force him to marry the bride because he made her pregnant.) □ *Mary was six months pregnant when she married Bill. It was a real shotgun wedding.*

should have stood in bed *Fig.* an expression used on a bad day, when one should have stayed in one's bed. □ *The minute I got up and heard the news this morning, I knew I should have stood in bed.*

*****shoulder to shoulder** *Fig.* side by side; with a shared purpose. (*Typically: **stand** ~; **work** ~.) □ *The strikers said they would stand shoulder to shoulder against the management.*

shouldn't happen to a dog *Fig.* an expression of something that is so bad that no creature deserves it. □ *This cold I got shouldn't happen to a dog.*

shout (sth) **from the rooftops** AND **scream** (sth) **from the rooftops; yell** (sth) **from the rooftops** *Fig.* to announce something enthusiastically. □ *I wanted to shout it from the rooftops that Tiffany agreed to marry me!*

shove so **around**† *Fig.* to harass someone. □ *Stop shoving me around! Who do you think you are?*

shove so/sth **down** so's **throat** AND **ram** so/sth **down** so's **throat; force** so/sth **down** so's **throat** *Fig.* to force someone to accept something. □ *Don't try to force that stupid idea down my throat! I don't want it!* □ *You can't force that child down my throat! Find someone else to babysit.*

shove off Go to push off.

show a lot of promise Go to a lot of promise.

show and tell *Inf.* a session where objects are presented and described. (Essentially a kindergarten or grade school activity, but often used figuratively.) □ *It was a short lecture with lots of show and tell.*

show good faith *Fig.* to demonstrate good intentions or good will. □ *I'm certain that you showed good faith when you signed the contract.*

show one's **hand** AND **tip** one's **hand** *Fig.* to reveal one's intentions to someone. (From card games.) □ *I don't know whether Jim is intending to marry Jane or not. He's not one to show his hand.* □ *If you want to get a raise, don't show the boss your hand too soon.*

show one's **mettle** AND **prove** one's **mettle** to demonstrate one's skill, courage, and ability. □ *The contest will be an opportunity for you to prove your mettle.*

a **show of hands** *Fig.* a display of raised hands [in a group of people] that can be counted for the purpose of votes or surveys. □ *Jack wanted us to vote on paper, not by a show of hands, so that we could have a secret ballot.*

show promise Go to hold promise.

show so one's **stuff** *Fig.* to show someone how well one can do something. □ *We'll audition Kate now. Okay, Kate, show us your stuff.*

show one's **teeth** AND **bare** one's **teeth** *Fig.* to act in an angry or threatening manner. (Fig. on what an angry wolf or dog does.) □ *The enemy forces didn't expect the country they invaded to bare its teeth.*

show so **to a seat** AND **show** one **to** one's **seat** *Fig.* to lead or direct someone to a place to sit. □ *May I show you to your seat, sir?*

show sth **to good advantage** *Fig.* to display the best features of something; to display something so that its best features are apparent. □ *Put the vase in the center of the table and show it to good advantage.*

show so **(to) the door** AND **see** so **to the door** *Fig.* to lead or take someone to the door or exit. □ *After we finished our talk, she showed me to the door.*

show one's **(true) colors** *Fig.* to show what one is really like or what one is really thinking. □ *Whose side are you on, John? Come on. Show your colors.*

show up *Inf.* to appear; to arrive. □ *Where is John? I hope he shows up soon.* □ *Weeds began to show up in the garden.*

show up ahead of time Go to ahead of time.

show up on the dot Go to on the dot.

show so **who's boss** *Fig.* to demonstrate that one is completely in charge. □ *So, he thinks he can push me around and give me orders. I'll show him who's boss!*

shower so/sth **with** sth to cover someone or something with cascades of something. □ *Mary's friends showered her with gifts on her 21st birthday.*

a **shrinking violet** *Fig.* someone who is very shy and not assertive. □ *I am not exactly a shrinking violet, but I don't have the guts to say what you said to her.*

shrug sth **off**† **(as** sth**)** AND **pass** sth **off**† **(as** sth**)** to ignore something unpleasant or offensive as if it meant something else. □ *She shrugged off the criticism as harmless.* □ *I passed off the remark as misinformed.*

shuck sth **off**† *Fig.* to get rid of someone or something. □ *Tom shucked off one girlfriend after another.*

shuffle off this mortal coil *Euph.* to die. (Often jocular or formal euphemism. Not often used in consoling someone.) □ *When I shuffle off this mortal coil, I want to go out in style—bells, flowers, and a long, boring funeral.*

shut down Go to close down.

shut one's **eyes to** sth Go to close one's **eyes to** sth.

shut the door (up)on so/sth AND **close the door on** so/sth; **close the door to** so/sth *Fig.* to eliminate an opportunity for someone or something. □ *They closed the door on further discussions.*

Shut up! *Inf.* Be quiet! (Impolite.) □ *Bob: And another thing. Bill: Oh, shut up, Bob!*

Shut your cake hole! AND **Shut your pie hole!; Shut your face!** *Inf.* Shut up!; Shut your mouth! □ *I've heard enough! Shut your cake hole!*

Shut your pie hole! Go to previous.

shy away from so/sth *Fig.* to avoid or evade someone or something, owing to apprehension. □ *I shy away from crowds during the flu season.* □ *Bob shies away from John since their argument.*

sick abed sick and in bed. □ *He was sick abed for over a week with the flu.*

*__sick (and tired) of__ so/sth *Fig.* tired of someone or something, especially something that one must do again and again or someone or something that one must deal with repeatedly. (*Typically: **be** ~; **become** ~; **get** ~; **grow** ~.) □ *I am sick and tired of cleaning up after you.* □ *Mary was sick of being stuck in traffic.*

*__sick as a dog__ *Cliché* very sick; sick and vomiting. (*Also: **as** ~.) □ *We've never been so ill. The whole family was sick as dogs.*

*__sick at heart__ *Fig.* distressed and depressed. (*Typically: **be** ~; **become** ~;

make so ~.) □ *I became sick at heart just looking at all the homeless children.*

sick in bed remaining in bed while (one is) ill. □ *Tom is sick in bed with the flu.*

sick to death (of so/sth**)** *Inf.* totally disgusted with someone or something. □ *This reporting about the scandals in the government just has me sick to death.*

side against so/sth Go to take sides (against so/sth).

side with so *Fig.* to join with someone; to take someone else's part; to be on someone's side. □ *Why is it that you always side with him when he and I argue?*

*****sidetracked** diverted from one's task. (*Typically: **be** ~; **get** ~.) □ *I'm sorry the work is not completed. I got sidetracked.*

a **sight for sore eyes** *Fig.* a welcome sight. □ *Oh, am I glad to see you here! You're a sight for sore eyes.*

sign in to indicate that one has arrived somewhere and at what time by signing a piece of paper or a list. □ *Please sign in so we will know you are here.*

sign one's **life away** *Fig.* to sign a document, usually a mortgage loan, that requires many years of payments and obligations. □ *Well, I signed my life away, but at least we have a house with wood floors and granite counters!*

a **sign of the times** *Fig.* something that signifies the situation evident in the current times. □ *Your neighbor's unmowed grass is just a sign of the times. Nobody really cares any longer.*

sign off 1. *Fig.* [for a broadcaster] to announce the end of programming for the day; [for an amateur radio operator] to announce the end of a transmission. □ *Wally signed off and turned the transmitter off.* **2.** *Fig.* to quit doing what one has been doing and leave, go to bed, quit trying to do something, etc. (Fig. on ①.) □ *When you finally sign off tonight, please turn out all the lights.*

sign off on sth *Fig.* to sign a paper, indicating that one has finished with some-

thing or agrees with the state of something. □ *The publisher signed off on the book and sent it to be printed.* □ *I refuse to sign off on this project until it is done correctly.*

sign on *Fig.* to announce the beginning of a broadcast transmission. □ *The announcer signed on and then played "The Star-Spangled Banner."*

sign on the dotted line *Fig.* to indicate one's agreement to something. □ *He is thinking favorably about going with us to Canada, but he hasn't signed on the dotted line.*

sign on (with so/sth**) (as** sth**)** to join with someone or something in a particular capacity by signing a contract or agreement. □ *I signed on with the captain of the Felicity Anne as first mate.*

sign out *Fig.* to indicate that one is leaving a place or going out temporarily by signing a piece of paper or a list. □ *I forgot to sign out when I left.*

sign one's **own death warrant** *Fig.* to do something (knowingly) that will most likely result in severe trouble. (As if one were ordering one's own execution.) □ *The killer signed his own death warrant when he walked into the police station and gave himself up.*

signed, sealed, and delivered *Fig.* formally and officially signed; [for a formal document to be] executed. (*Sealed* refers to the use of a special seal that indicates the official nature of the document.) □ *I can't begin work on this project until I have the contract signed, sealed, and delivered.*

*****silent as the dead** AND *****silent as the grave** completely silent. (Has ominous connotations because of the reference to death. Usually used to promise someone that you will be silent and therefore not betray a secret. *Also: **as** ~.) □ *I knew something was wrong as soon as I entered the classroom; everyone was silent as the dead.* □ *Jessica is as silent as the grave on the subject of her first marriage.*

silent as the grave Go to previous.

*silly as a goose very foolish. (*Also: **as ~.**) □ *Edith is as silly as a goose. She thinks that reading aloud to her houseplants will help them grow.*

simmer down *Fig.* [for someone] to become calm or less agitated. □ *Please simmer down, you guys!*

simply not done not proper to do; improper and embarrassing to do. (A bit aloof sounding.) □ *You what? Sorry, but that kind of thing is simply not done!*

since day one Go to day one.

since time immemorial *Fig.* since a very long time ago. (Literally, since time before recorded history.) □ *My hometown has had a big parade on the Fourth of July since time immemorial.*

sing a different tune AND **sing another tune; change** one's **tune** *Fig.* to change one's manner, usually from bad to good. (Almost the same as dance to another tune.) □ *When she learned that I was a bank director, she began to sing a different tune.*

sing another tune Go to previous.

sing from the same hymn book Go to read from the same page.

sing one's **heart out** Go to cry one's heart out.

sing so's/sth's **praises** AND **sing the praises of** so/sth *Fig.* to praise someone highly and enthusiastically. □ *The theater critics are singing the praises of the young actor.*

singing the blues *Fig.* expressing one's sadness or regret. (Fig. on how one feels when singing a style of balladry associated with lost love and unfaithful lovers.) □ *I failed to get the contract from the client, and that left me singing the blues.*

sink in *Fig.* [for knowledge] to be understood. □ *I pay careful attention to everything I hear in calculus class, but it usually doesn't sink in.*

sink sth **in(to)** so/sth AND **sink** sth **in**† *Fig.* to invest time or money in someone or something. (Sometimes implying that the money or time was wasted.) □ *You would not believe how much money I've sunk into that company!*

sink into despair *Fig.* to become depressed; to become completely discouraged. □ *After facing the hopelessness of the future, Jean Paul sank into despair.*

sink into oblivion *Fig.* to fade into obscurity. □ *In his final years, Wally Wilson sank into oblivion and just faded away.*

sink or swim *Fig.* to fail or succeed. (Fig. on the choices available to someone who has fallen into the water.) □ *After I've studied and learned all I can, I have to take the test and sink or swim.*

sink one's **teeth into** sth Go to get one's teeth into sth.

sink to (doing) sth *Fig.* to lower oneself to doing something bad or mean. □ *I never thought he would sink to doing that.*

*a sinking feeling *Fig.* the feeling that everything is going wrong. (*Typically: **get ~; have ~; give** so **~.**) □ *I get a sinking feeling whenever I think of the night of the accident.*

*a sinking feeling in the pit of one's **stomach** a strange, empty feeling in one's stomach owing to anxiety. (Sometimes heard as *have a pit in the stomach.* Typically: **have ~; get ~; give** so **~.**) □ *When I'm worried, I wake up with a sinking feeling in the pit of my stomach.*

siphon sth **off**† **(from** sth**)** *Fig.* to embezzle or steal something a little at a time. □ *She siphoned off a few dollars from the collection every week or so.*

sit at the feet of so *Fig.* to pay homage to someone; to pay worshipful attention to someone. □ *The graduate student sat at the feet of the famous professor for years.*

sit back and let sth happen *Fig.* to relax and not interfere with something; to let something happen without playing a part in it. □ *I can't just sit back and let you waste all our money!*

sit bolt upright *Fig.* to sit up straight. □ *After sitting bolt upright for almost an hour in that crowded airplane, I swore I would never fly again.*

sit for so **1.** *Fig.* to care for someone in the role of babysitter. □ *I sit for Timmy some-*

times. I like him. He's a good little kid. **2.** *Fig.* to serve as a babysitter in someone's employ. □ *I sit for Mrs. Franklin every now and then.* **3.** *Fig.* to serve as a model or subject for someone, such as an artist. □ *She sat for the portrait painter every day for a week.*

sit for an exam *Fig.* to take an exam to qualify for a license, such as a bar exam. □ *When do you sit for the bar exam?*

sit for one's **portrait** *Fig.* to serve as the subject of a portrait being done by a painter or photographer. □ *I sat for my portrait for weeks, and even then, it didn't look like me.*

sit idly by AND **stand idly by** *Fig.* to remain close, doing nothing to help. □ *I do not intend to stand idly by while my children need my help.*

sit in (for so**)** *Fig.* to act as a substitute for someone. (Usually involves actual sitting, such as at a meeting.) □ *I am not a regular member of this committee. I am sitting in for Larry Smith.*

sit in judgment (up)on so/sth to make a judgment about someone or something. (*Upon* is formal and less commonly used than *on*.) □ *I don't want to sit in judgment upon you or anyone else, but I do have some suggestions.*

sit in (on sth**)** *Fig.* to attend something as a visitor; to act as a temporary participant in something. □ *Do you mind if I sit in on your discussion?*

sit on so/sth *Fig.* to hold someone or something back; to delay someone or something. □ *The project cannot be finished, because the city council is sitting on the final approval.*

sit on one's **ass** *Inf.* to sit idle; to sit around doing nothing. (Caution with *ass.*) □ *Don't just sit on your ass! Get busy!*

sit on one's **hands** *Fig.* to do nothing; to fail to help. (See also **sit on its hands.**) □ *We need the cooperation of everyone. You can't sit on your hands!*

sit on its hands AND **sit on their hands** *Fig.* [for an audience] to refuse to applaud. (See also **sit on** one's **hands.**) □ *The*

performance was really quite good, but the audience sat on its hands.

sit on the edge of one's **seat** Go to **on the edge of** one's **seat.**

sit on the fence *Fig.* not to take sides in a dispute; not to make a clear choice between two possibilities. (Fig. on the image of someone straddling a fence, representing indecision.) □ *When Jane and Tom argue, it is best to sit on the fence and not make either of them angry.*

sit right with so AND **sit well with** so *Fig.* to be acceptable to someone. □ *Your explanation of your absence doesn't sit well with the president.* □ *What you just said doesn't really sit right with me. Let's talk about it.*

sit still for sth *Fig.* to remain passive rather than act to prevent something; to endure or tolerate something. □ *I won't sit still for that kind of treatment.*

sit tight *Fig.* to wait; to wait patiently. (This does not necessarily refer to sitting.) □ *We were waiting in line for the gates to open when someone came out and told us to sit tight because it wouldn't be much longer before we could go in.*

sit up and take notice *Fig.* to become alert and pay attention. □ *A loud noise from the front of the room caused everyone to sit up and take notice.*

sit well with so Go to **sit right with** so.

***a **sitting duck** *Fig.* someone or something vulnerable to attack, physical or verbal. (Fig. on the image of a duck floating on the water, not suspecting that it is the object of a hunter or predator. *Typically: **be ~; like ~; looking like ~.**) □ *You look like a sitting duck out there. Get in here where the enemy cannot fire at you.*

sitting on a gold mine *Fig.* in control of something very valuable; in control of something potentially very valuable. □ *When I found out how much the old book was worth, I realized that I was sitting on a gold mine.*

sitting on a powder keg *Fig.* in a risky or explosive situation; in a situation where something serious or dangerous may

sitting on top of the world

happen at any time. (A powder keg is a keg of gunpowder.) □ *Things are very tense at work. The whole office is sitting on a powder keg.*

sitting on top of the world *Fig.* being successful and feeling pleased about it. □ *Wow, I'm sitting on top of the world.*

***sitting pretty** *Fig.* living in comfort or luxury; living in a good situation. (*Typically: **be** ~; **leave** so ~.) □ *My uncle died and left enough money for me to be sitting pretty for the rest of my life.*

six feet under *Fig.* dead and buried. □ *They put him six feet under two days after he died.*

a **sixth sense** *Fig.* a supposed power to know or feel things that are not perceptible by the five senses of sight, hearing, smell, taste, and touch. □ *My sixth sense told me to avoid going home by my usual route. Later I discovered there had been a fatal accident on it.*

the **sixty-four-dollar question** *Fig.* the most important question; the question that everyone wants to know the answer to. □ *Now for the sixty-four-dollar question. What's the stock market going to do this year?*

size so/sth **up**† *Fig.* to observe someone or something to get information. □ *The comedian sized the audience up and decided not to use his new material.*

skate on thin ice *Fig.* to be in a risky situation. (Fig. on the image of someone taking the risk of ice skating on thin ice.) □ *I try to stay well informed so I don't end up skating on thin ice when the teacher asks me a question.*

skeleton(s) in the closet a hidden and shocking secret. □ *You can ask anyone about how reliable I am. I don't mind. I don't have any skeletons in the closet.*

sketch sth **out**† Go to block sth out†.

skim sth **off (of)** sth AND **skim** sth **off**† *Fig.* to remove a portion of something of value, such as money, from an account. (*Of* is usually retained before pronouns.)

□ *The auditor was skimming a few dollars a day off the bank's cash flow.*

skim over sth *Fig.* to go over or review something hastily. □ *I just skimmed over the material and still got an A on the test!*

skim through sth *Fig.* to go through something hastily; to read through something hastily. □ *She skimmed through the catalogs, looking for a nice gift for Gary.*

skin so **alive** *Fig.* to be very angry with someone; to scold someone severely. (Fig. on being angry enough to do this kind of bodily harm to someone.) □ *If I don't get home on time, my parents will skin me alive.*

skin and bones Go to (all) skin and bones.

Skin me! Go to Give me five!

***skinny as a beanpole** very thin; very skinny. (*Also: **as** ~.) □ *I exercised and dieted until I was skinny as a beanpole.*

skinny dip *Fig.* to swim naked. □ *The boys were skinny dipping in the creek when Bob's mother drove up.*

skip bail Go to jump bail.

skip off (with sth**)** *Fig.* to leave and take something with one. □ *The little kid with the freckles skipped off with a candy bar.*

skip out (on so/sth**)** *Fig.* to sneak away from someone or some event; to leave someone or an event suddenly or in secret. □ *I'm not surprised. I thought he should have skipped out long ago.*

The **sky's the limit.** *Inf.* there is no upper limit. □ *You can do anything you set your mind to, Billy. The sky's the limit.*

slack off *Fig.* [for someone] to become lazy or inefficient. □ *Near the end of the school year, Sally began to slack off, and her grades showed it.*

slam dunk 1. [in basketball] a goal scored by shooting the ball down from above the rim. □ *He was wide open and scored on an easy slam dunk.* **2.** *Fig.* an action or accomplishment that is easily done. (Fig. on ①.) □ *Finishing that project with all his experience should be a slam dunk for George.*

slam the brakes on† *Fig.* to push on a vehicle's brakes suddenly and hard. (Informal. *The* can be replaced by a possessive pronoun.) □ *The driver in front of me slammed her brakes on, and I nearly ran into her.*

slam the door in so's **face** *Fig.* suddenly to withdraw an opportunity from someone. □ *The events of the last week effectively slammed the door in my face for future employment.*

slap so **down**† *Fig.* to squelch someone; to rebuke or rebuff someone. □ *I had a great idea, but the boss slapped me down.*

a **slap in the face** *Fig.* an insult; an act that causes disappointment or discouragement. □ *Failing to get into a good college was a slap in the face to Tim after his years of study.*

slap sth **on**† *Inf. Fig.* to dress in something hastily. □ *Henry slapped a shirt on and went out to say something to the garbage hauler.*

*a **slap on the wrist 1.** a hit on the wrist as a mild punishment for putting one's hands where they shouldn't be or taking something. (*Typically: **get** ~; **give** so ~.) □ *When Billy tried to grab another cookie, he got a slap on the wrist.* **2.** *Fig.* to get a light punishment (for doing something wrong). (Fig. on ①. *Typically: **get** ~; **give** so ~.) □ *He created quite a disturbance, but he only got a slap on the wrist from the judge.*

slap so **on the wrist** AND **slap** so's **wrist** *Fig.* to administer only the mildest of punishments to someone. □ *The judge did nothing but slap the mugger on the wrist.*

slash and burn 1. of a farming technique where vegetation is cut down and burned before crops are planted. (Hyphenated before nominals.) □ *The small farmers' slash-and-burn technique destroyed thousands of acres of forest.* **2.** *Fig.* of a crude and brash way of doing something. (Hyphenated before nominals.) □ *The new manager's method was strictly slash and burn. He looks decisive to his boss and merciless to the people he fires.*

*slated for sth *Fig.* scheduled for something. (As if a schedule had been written on a slate. *Typically: **be** ~; **have** so ~.) □ *John was slated for Friday's game, but he couldn't play with the team.*

*slated to do sth *Fig.* scheduled to do something. (*Typically: **be** ~; **have** so ~.) □ *Mary is slated to go to Washington in the fall.*

*a slave to sth *Fig.* someone who is under the control of something; someone whose time or attention is controlled or "owned" by something. (*Fig.* on being a slave to a person. *Typically: **be** ~; **become** ~.) □ *Mary is a slave to her job.*

sleep around the clock *Fig.* to sleep for a full 24 hours; to sleep for a very long time. □ *I was so tired I could have slept around the clock.*

sleep around (with so) *Inf.* to have sex with several partners over time; to be promiscuous. □ *They say she sleeps around with just anybody all the time.*

sleep in *Fig.* to oversleep; to sleep late in the morning. □ *I really felt like sleeping in this morning, but I dragged myself out of bed.*

sleep like a baby Go to next.

sleep like a log AND **sleep like a baby** to sleep very soundly. □ *Everyone in our family sleeps like a log, so no one heard the thunderstorm in the middle of the night.*

sleep sth **off**† *Fig.* to sleep while the effects of anesthesia, liquor, or drugs pass away. □ *John drank too much and went home to sleep it off.*

sleep on sth *Fig.* to postpone a decision until one has slept through the night. (As if one were going to think through the decision while sleeping.) □ *It sounds like a good idea, but I'd like to sleep on it before giving you my response.*

sleep tight *Fig.* to sleep warm and safe; to sleep snugly. (Usually said with *Good night* to someone going to bed. When a door fits its opening well, it is snug or tight. This is the sense of *tight* used here. There have been tales made up that relate this phrase to the crisscross ropes strung to support a mattress on a bed frame. The story, which is told by tour guides throughout the English-speaking world, states that the ropes would often break, startling the sleeper. Thus people warned the sleeper [not the bed] to have tight ropes, lest they be startled. There is no evidence for this expression being used in this fashion. The phrase was part of one of the lines of a nursery rhyme having versions that include a few of the following lines: Good night, sleep tight/ Through the night/Don't let the bedbugs bite/Wake up bright/In the morning light/To do what is right/With all your might.) □ *Sleep tight, Bobby. See you in the morning.*

sleep together *Euph.* [for two people] to copulate. (Actual sleep may occur before and/or after.) □ *Ted and Alice slept together a lot when they were in college.*

sleep with so *Euph.* to copulate with someone. □ *I hear Sam's sleeping with Sally now.*

a sleeping giant *Fig.* a great power that is still and waiting. □ *The huge country to the south is a sleeping giant, waiting for its chance to become sufficiently industrialized to have real prosperity.*

a slice of the action Go to a piece (of the action).

a slice of the cake a share of something. □ *There's not much work around, and so everyone must be content with a slice of the cake.*

*slick as a whistle quickly and cleanly; quickly and skillfully. (*Also: **as** ~.) □ *Tom took a broom and a mop and cleaned the place up as slick as a whistle.*

a slim chance *Fig.* a slight chance; a small chance. □ *There is a slim chance that I will arrive on Monday, but Tuesday is more likely.*

slip so **a Mickey** *Inf.* to secretly put a *Mickey Finn* in someone's alcoholic drink. (Older. This drug either made the victim pass out or caused immediate diarrhea. It was usually chloral hydrate. Sometimes used as a way of getting rid of troublesome drunks.) □ *Somebody* slipped Barlowe a Mickey and sent him into action. □ For a 10-spot, the bartender slipped Slim a Mickey.

slip away 1. AND **slip off** to go away or escape quietly or in secret; to slip out. □ *I slipped away when no one was looking.* □ *Let's slip off somewhere and have a little talk.* **2.** *Euph.* to die. □ *Uncle Charles slipped away in his sleep last night.*

slip between the cracks *Fig.* [for someone or something] to be forgotten or neglected. (*Fig.* on something being lost by falling between floorboards.) □ *This issue seems to have slipped between the cracks and become forgotten.*

slip by *Fig.* [for time] to pass quickly or unnoticed. □ *Goodness, almost an hour has slipped by! How time flies.*

slip so **five** *Sl.* to shake someone's hand. □ *Billy slipped me five, and we sat down to discuss old times.*

Slip me five! Go to Give me five!

Slip me some skin! Go to Give me five!

slip one's **mind** *Fig.* [for something that was to be remembered] to be forgotten. □ *I meant to go to the grocery store on the way home, but it slipped my mind.*

a **slip of the tongue** *Fig.* an error in speaking in which a word is pronounced incorrectly, or in which the speaker says something unintentionally. □ *I failed to understand the instructions because the speaker made a slip of the tongue at an important point.*

slip out 1. [for information] to be spoken without realizing that it is secret or privileged. □ *The secret about her divorce slipped out when we were discussing old friends.* **2.** to leave [a place] quietly and unobserved. □ *I have to slip out early to get home and fix dinner.*

slip sth **over (on** so/sth) AND **slip one over (on** so/sth) *Fig.* to deceive someone. □ *Are you trying to slip something over on me?* □ *I think he tried to slip one over on me.*

slip sth **through (**sth**)** *Fig.* to get something approved without much fuss by a group of people, perhaps by deception. □ *I will try to slip this through the committee.*

slip through so's **fingers** *Fig.* to escape from someone; to elude someone's capture or control. □ *The prisoner slipped through the sheriff's fingers.*

slip through the cracks Go to through the cracks.

slip one's **trolley** *Sl.* to become a little crazy; to lose one's composure. (*Fig.* on the old-fashioned U.S. streetcar, which got its electric power via spring-loaded poles that pushed upward into contact with overhead electric wires. If the wheels that rode on the wires slipped off, the streetcar came to a stop.) □ *He slipped his trolley and went totally bonkers.*

slip up (on sth**)** to make an error in something. □ *I guess I slipped up on that last job.* □ *Fred slipped up on compiling that list—there are a lot of names missing.*

*slippery as an eel devious and untrustworthy, but impossible to catch. (*Also: as ~.) □ *The crook was as slippery as an eel. Although he defrauded many people, he never went to prison.*

a **slippery customer 1.** a slimy or slippery creature. □ *This little fish is a slippery customer. Get me something to scoop it back into its bowl.* **2.** *Fig.* a clever and deceitful customer. (*Fig.* on ①.) □ *Watch out for that guy with the big padded coat. He may snatch something. He's a real slippery customer.*

a **slippery slope** *Fig.* a dangerous pathway or route to follow; a route that leads to trouble. □ *The matter of euthanasia is a slippery slope with both legal and moral considerations.*

slob up *Sl.* to eat. □ *Fred stopped slobbing up long enough to change the channel on the TV set.*

slobber over so/sth *Fig.* to drool with delight or eagerness at the thought of someone or something. □ *Jamie was slobbering over Mary's new car.*

slough (off) Go to sluff (off).

slough sth **off**† AND **sluff** sth **off**† *Fig.* to ignore or disregard a negative remark or incident. (*Sluff* is considered slang or an error by some. It is used widely in this idiom, however.) □ *I could see that the remark had hurt her feelings, but she just pretended to slough it off.*

*slow as molasses in January AND **slower than molasses in January** very slow-moving. (*Also: as ~.) □ *Can't you get dressed any faster? I declare, you're as slow as molasses in January.*

slow but sure AND **slowly but surely** slow but unstoppable. □ *Nancy is finishing the paint job on her house, slowly but surely.*

slow going *Fig.* the rate of speed when one is making slow progress. □ *It was slow going at first, but I was able to finish the project by the weekend.*

slow off the mark 1. *Fig.* slow in starting or reacting. □ *If you are always that slow off the mark, you will never win the race.* **2.** *Fig.* slow-witted. □ *Yes, I'm afraid Tony is a bit slow off the mark when it comes to trigonometry.*

slow on the draw 1. slow in drawing a gun. (Cowboy and gangster talk.) □ *The gunslinger said, "I have to be fast. If I'm slow on the draw, I'm dead."* **2.** AND **slow on the uptake** *Fig.* slow to figure something out; slow-thinking. (Fig. on ①.) □ *Sally didn't get the joke because she's sort of slow on the draw.* □ *Bill—who's slow on the uptake—didn't get the joke until it was explained to him.*

slow on the uptake Go to previous.

a **slow study** *Fig.* a person who is slow to learn things. (Compare this to a quick study.) □ *Fred, who is a slow study, never caught on to the joke.*

slower than molasses in January Go to slow as molasses in January.

slowly but surely Go to slow but sure.

sluff (off) AND **slough (off)** *Sl.* to waste time; to goof off. (See comment at slough sth off.) □ *Watch him. He will sluff off if you don't keep after him.* □ *He won't sluff. I know I can trust him.*

sluff sth **off**† Go to slough sth off†.

slug it out AND **fight** sth **out 1.** *Inf.* to fight something out. □ *They finally went outside to slug it out.* **2.** *Fig.* to argue intensely about something. □ *We'll just have to sit down in the conference room and slug it out.*

slur over sth *Fig.* to avoid talking about or mentioning an issue. (As if one were actually distorting one's speech.) □ *The mayor slurred over the major issue of the day.*

*sly as a fox AND ***cunning as a fox** *Cliché* smart and clever. (*Also: as ~.) □ *You have to be cunning as a fox to outwit me.*

smack (dab) in the middle *Fig.* exactly in the middle. □ *I want a piece that is not too big and not too small—just smack in the middle.*

smack so **down**† *Fig.* to rebuke someone. □ *He has an unpleasant way of smacking down people who ask stupid questions.*

a **smack in the face** *Inf.* something that will humiliate someone, often when it is considered deserved; an insult. □ *Being rejected by Jane was a real smack in the face for Tom, who thought she was fond of him.*

smack one's **lips** AND **lick** one's **lips** to lick and move one's lips in anticipation of eating something. □ *The children smacked their lips when they saw the huge pink cake.*

smack of sth to be reminiscent of something; to imply something. □ *The whole scheme smacked of dishonesty and deception.*

smack the road *Sl.* to leave; to hit the road. □ *Let's smack the road. I have to get up early.*

small change *Fig.* an insignificant person. (Also a rude term of address.) □ *Don't worry about him. He's just small change.* □ *Look, small change, why don't you just move along?*

a **small fortune** *Inf.* a rather sizable amount of money. □ *I've got a small fortune tied up in home theater equipment.*

small fry 1. newly hatched fish; small, juvenile fish. □ *The catch was bad today. Nothing but small fry.* **2.** *Fig.* unimportant people. (Fig. on ①.) □ *The police have only caught the small fry. The leader of the gang is still free.* **3.** *Fig.* children. (Fig. on ①.) □ *Wallace is taking the small fry to the zoo for the afternoon.*

the **small hours (of the night)** AND the **wee hours (of the night)** *Fig.* the hours immediately after midnight. □ *The dance went on into the small hours of the night.*

small potatoes *Fig.* something or someone insignificant; small fry. □ *This contract is small potatoes, but it keeps us in business till we get into the real money.*

small print AND **fine print** *Fig.* an important part of a document that is not easily noticed because of the smallness of the printing. □ *You should always read the fine print in an insurance policy.*

small-time *Fig.* small; on a small scale. □ *Our business is small-time just now, but it's growing.* □ *He's a small-time crook.*

smart ass *Inf.* someone who makes wisecracks and acts cocky. (Caution with *ass*.) □ *Some smart ass came in here and asked for a sky hook.*

smart at sth AND **smart from** sth to suffer the pains of something. □ *He smarted for hours after the blow to his heel.* **2.** *Fig.* to suffer mental distress from something. □ *He smarted for hours from the rude rebuff.*

smart money *Inf.* money belonging to smart or clever people. □ *Most of the smart money is going into utility stocks right now.*

smart mouth *Inf.* someone who makes wisecracks; a cocky person who speaks out of turn. □ *Don't be a smart mouth with me!*

a **smash hit** *Fig.* a play, movie, musical, etc. that is a big success. □ *Her first book was a smash hit. The second was a disaster.*

a **smear campaign (against** so**)** a campaign aimed at damaging someone's reputation by making accusations and spreading rumors. □ *The politician's opponents are engaging in a smear campaign against him.*

smear so/sth **with** sth *Fig.* to damage the reputation of someone or something by spreading serious charges or rumors. □ *He smeared his opponent with all sorts of charges.*

smell a rat *Fig. Inf.* to suspect that something is wrong; to sense that someone has caused something wrong. □ *I don't think this was an accident. I smell a rat. Bob had something to do with this.*

smell blood *Fig. Inf.* to be ready for a fight; to be ready to attack; to be ready to act. (Fig. on the behavior of sharks, which are sent into a frenzy by the smell of blood.) □ *Lefty was surrounded, and you could tell that the guys from the other gang smelled blood.*

smell fishy *Fig. Inf.* to seem suspicious. □ *Barlowe squinted a bit. Something smells fishy here, he thought.*

smell like a rose *Inf.* to seem innocent. □ *I came out of the whole mess smelling like a rose, even though I caused all the trouble.*

smell to (high) heaven *Fig.* to give signals that cause suspicion. □ *This deal is messed up. It smells to high heaven.*

smell to high heaven Go to stink to high heaven.

smell sth **up**† AND **stink** sth **up**† *Fig.* to cause a bad or strong odor in a place or on something. □ *Your cooking sure smelled this place up!*

smile from ear to ear Go to grin from ear to ear.

Smile when you say that. *Inf.* I will interpret that remark as a joke or as kidding. □ *John: You're a real pain in the neck. Bob: Smile when you say that.*

smiling like a Cheshire cat *Fig.* smiling very broadly. (Refers to the grinning cat in *Alice's Adventures in Wonderland*.) □

There he stood, smiling like a Cheshire cat, waiting for his weekly pay.

*a smoke *Fig.* the act of smoking a cigarette, cigar, or pipe. (*Typically: **get** ~; **have** ~; **give** so ~; **need** ~; **want** ~.) □ *Can I have a smoke? I'm very nervous.*

smoke and mirrors *Fig.* deception and confusion. (Said of statements or more complicated rhetoric used to mislead people rather than inform them. Refers to the way a magician uses optical illusion to create believability while performing a trick. Fixed order.) □ *Most people know that the politician was just using smoke and mirrors to make things look better than they really were.*

smoke like a chimney *Inf.* to smoke a great deal of tobacco or other smokable substances. □ *Anyone who smokes like a chimney in a restaurant ought to be thrown out.*

smoke so/sth/animal **out of** sth AND **smoke** so/sth/animal **out**† *Fig.* to drive someone or something out into public view, as if using smoke or something similar. □ *What will it take to smoke these crooks out of government?*

smoke-filled room *Fig.* a room where a small group of people make important decisions. (Usually used in reference to political parties.) □ *The smoke-filled rooms are still producing the candidates for most offices, despite all the political reforms.*

the **smoking gun** *Inf.* the indisputable sign of guilt. (Fig. on a murderer being caught just after shooting the victim.) □ *The chief of staff decided that the aide should be found with the smoking gun.*

*smooth as glass AND ***smooth as silk** *Cliché* smooth and shiny. (Often used to describe calm bodies of water. *Also: **as** ~.) □ *The bay is as smooth as glass, so we should have a pleasant boat trip.*

smooth as silk Go to previous.

smooth sth **out**† **1.** *Fig.* to polish and refine something. □ *The editor smoothed out John's awkward writing style.* **2.** AND **smooth** sth **over**† *Fig.* to reduce the in-tensity of an argument or a misunderstanding; to try to make people feel better about something disagreeable that has happened. □ *Mary and John had a terrible argument, and they are both trying to smooth it over.*

smooth (so's) **ruffled feathers** *Fig.* to attempt to calm or placate someone who is upset. (As a bird tries to align and neaten ruffled feathers.) □ *Crystal looks a little upset. Do you think I should try to smooth her ruffled feathers?*

smooth sailing Go to clear sailing.

smother so/sth **with** sth AND **smother** so/sth **in** sth *Fig.* to cover someone or something with something. (An exaggeration.) □ *She smothered him with kisses.* □ *I always smother my steak with mushrooms.*

snake in the grass *Fig.* a sneaky and despised person. □ *How could I ever have trusted that snake in the grass?*

snakebite medicine *Inf.* inferior whiskey; strong whiskey; homemade whiskey. □ *Snakebite medicine is a tremendous protection against snakebites if you can get the snake to drink the stuff before it bites you.*

snap at so *Fig.* to speak sharply or angrily to someone. (Refers to speaking sharply, perhaps alluding to the snapping of the jaws of an angry, barking dog.) □ *Why did you snap at me? I did nothing wrong.*

snap at sth *Fig.* to seize an opportunity. (Referring to reaching out and grabbing something.) □ *It is such a good deal, I knew you would snap at it.* □ *Just as I thought, Ted snapped at my final offer.*

snap back (at so) to give a sharp or angry response to someone. □ *The telephone operator, unlike in the good old days, snapped back at the caller.*

snap one's **cookies** *Sl.* to vomit; to regurgitate. □ *I think I'm gonna snap my cookies.*

snap so's **head off** *Fig.* to speak very sharply to someone. □ *How rude! Don't snap my head off!*

Snap it up! *Inf.* Hurry up! □ *John: Come on, Fred. Snap it up! Fred: I'm hurrying! I'm hurrying!*

snap out of sth *Fig.* to become suddenly freed from a condition. (The condition can be a depression, an illness, unconsciousness, etc.) □ *It isn't often that a cold gets me down. Usually I can snap out of it quickly.*

snap to (attention) *Fig.* to move quickly to military attention. □ *The troops snapped to attention when they saw the general appear.*

Snap to it! *Inf.* Move faster!; Look alert! □ *Get in line there. Snap to it!*

snap sth **up**† **1.** *Fig.* to grasp something quickly. □ *Karen snapped her pencil up and strode out of the room.* **2.** *Fig.* to purchase something quickly, because the price is low or because the item is so hard to find. (Fig. on ①.) □ *We put the cheap shirts out for sale this morning, and people snapped them up in only a few minutes.* **3.** *Fig.* to believe something eagerly; to believe a lie readily. (Fig. on ①.) □ *They are so gullible that you can say anything and they'll snap it up.*

snatch sth **up**† *Inf.* to collect or acquire as many of something as possible. □ *The shoppers snatched the sale merchandise up very quickly.*

snatch victory from the jaws of defeat *Cliché* to win at the last moment. □ *At the last moment, the team snatched victory from the jaws of defeat with a last-second full-court basket.*

snazz sth **up**† *Sl.* to make something classy or exciting. □ *Come on, let's try to snazz this up.*

sneak around so/sth *Fig.* to circumvent the control or censorship of someone or some group. □ *I think we can sneak around the board of directors and authorize this project ourselves.*

sniff at so/sth *Fig.* to show one's disapproval of someone or something by sniffing audibly. (Sometimes this is figurative, with the "sniffing" being expressed by tone of voice or gesture.) □ *I made one suggestion, but Claire just sniffed at me.*

sniff so/sth **out**† Go to hunt so/sth down†.

snipe at so/sth *Fig.* to make petty complaints attacking someone or something. □ *Stop sniping at me and everything I do.*

a **snow job** *Inf.* a systematic deception; a deceptive story that tries to hide the truth. □ *You can generally tell when a student is trying to do a snow job.*

snow so/sth **under with** sth AND **snow** so/sth **under**† *Fig.* to burden someone or something with something, usually with too much work. □ *The busy season snowed us all under with too much work.*

snowball into sth *Fig.* [for something] to become larger or more serious by growing like a snowball being rolled. □ *This whole problem is snowballing into a crisis very rapidly.*

snowed under *Fig.* overworked; exceptionally busy. □ *Look, I'm really snowed under at the moment. Can this wait?*

snuff so **out**† *Sl.* to kill someone. □ *Spike really wanted to snuff the eyewitness out, once and for all.*

*****snug as a bug in a rug** *Cliché* wrapped up tight, warm, and comfortable. (Playful; often used when addressing a child. *Also: **as** ~.) □ *The bedroom in Aunt Jane's house was cold, but after she wrapped me up in four or five quilts and put a stocking cap on my head, I was snug as a bug in a rug and ready to go to sleep.*

snuggle up (with a (good) book) Go to cuddle up with a (good) book.

*****so bad** one **can taste it** *Inf.* very much, indeed. (*Typically: **need** sth ~; **want** sth ~; **have to** do sth ~; **want to** do sth ~; **need to** do sth ~.) □ *He wanted to get to Philadelphia so bad he could taste it.*

so be it *Fig.* this is the way it will be. □ *If you insist on running off and marrying her, so be it. Only don't say I didn't warn you!*

so clean you could eat off the floor [of a room or a house] very clean. □ *Her* *kitchen is so clean you could eat off the floor!*

so far as anyone **knows** Go to as far as anyone knows.

so far as I can see Go to as far as I can see.

so far as so **is concerned** Go to as far as so is concerned.

so far as sth **is concerned** Go to as far as sth is concerned.

so far as possible Go to as far as possible.

so far, so good all is well at this point in time. □ *Q: How is school going? A: So far, so good.*

So help me(, God)! *Fig.* I so pledge and vow in God's name. □ *I will do it. I really will, so help me, God!*

So it goes. AND **That's life.; That's life in the big city.** *Inf.* That is the kind of thing that happens.; That is the way life is. □ *I just lost a 20-dollar bill, and I can't find it anywhere. So it goes.*

So long. *Inf.* Good-bye. □ *It's been good talking to you. So long.*

so long as Go to as long as.

so mad I could scream *Fig.* very mad. □ *I am just so mad I could scream! Why is he such a jerk?* □ *She makes me so mad I could scream.*

so much as sth with as little or as much as something. □ *If you so much as blink an eye, I will send you home!*

so much for so/sth *Fig.* that is the last of someone or something; there is no need to consider someone or something anymore. □ *So much for Gloria. I hope she never comes back!*

So much for that. *Inf.* That is the end of that.; We will not be dealing with that anymore. □ *John tossed the stub of a pencil into the trash. "So much for that," he muttered, fishing through his drawer for another.*

so much so that . . . to such a great degree that. . . . □ *We are very tired. So much so that we have decided to retire for the night.*

so much the better *Fig.* even better; all to the better. □ *Please come to the picnic. If you can bring a salad, so much the better.*

so quiet you could hear a pin drop Go to next.

so still you could hear a pin drop AND **so quiet you could hear a pin drop; so still you can hear a pin drop; so quiet you can hear a pin drop** *Fig.* very quiet. □ *When I came into the room, it was so still you could hear a pin drop. Then everyone shouted, "Happy birthday!"*

So, sue me! *Fig.* If you are so angry, why don't you go ahead and sue me! (A rude way of brushing off an angry person.) □ *A: You ran into my car! You didn't even look where you were going! B: So, sue me!*

so to speak *Fig.* as one might say; said a certain way, even though the words are not exactly accurate. □ *I just love my little poodle. She's my baby, so to speak.*

So (what)? *Inf.* Why does that matter? (Can be considered rude. The main entry head has a heavy stress on *so* and falling intonation on *what. So* by itself has rising intonation.) □ *Bob: Your attitude always seems to lack sincerity. Mary: So what?* □ *John: Your car sure is dusty. Sue: So?*

(So) what else is new? *Inf.* This isn't new. It has happened before.; Not this again. □ *Mary: Taxes are going up again. Bob: So what else is new?*

soak one's **face** *Sl.* to drink heavily. □ *Well, I guess I'll go soak my face in a few beers.*

soak sth **up**[†] *Fig.* to learn or absorb some information; to learn much information. □ *I can't soak information up as fast as I used to be able to.*

soaked to the skin wet clear through one's clothing to the skin. □ *Oh, come in and dry off! You must be soaked to the skin.*

so-and-so *Fig.* a despised person. (This expression is used in place of other very insulting terms. Often modified, as in the example.) □ *You dirty so-and-so! I can't stand you!*

sob one's **heart out** Go to cry one's heart out.

sob story *Fig.* a sad story that is likely to draw tears. □ *I've heard nothing but sob stories today. Isn't anybody happy?*

*sober as a judge 1. *Cliché* very formal, somber, or stuffy. (*Also: **as ~**.) □ *You certainly look gloomy, Bill. You're sober as a judge.* **2.** *Cliché* not drunk; alert and completely sober. (*Also: **as ~**.) □ *You should be sober as a judge when you drive a car.*

sober so **up**† **1.** to take actions that will cause a drunken person to become sober. □ *He tried to sober himself up because he had to drive home.* **2.** *Fig.* to cause someone to face reality. (Fig. on ①.) □ *The arrival of the police sobered up all the revelers.*

sock sth **away**† *Fig.* to place something, such as money, into reserve; to store something in a secure place. □ *I try to sock a little money away each month for my vacation.*

sock so/sth **in**† *Fig.* [for fog] to cause someone or something to remain in place. □ *The heavy fog socked us in for six hours.*

sock it to so **1.** *Inf.* to punch someone; to punch one's fist at someone. □ *Lefty socked it to Roger and knocked him down.* **2.** *Inf.* to tell bad news to someone in a straightforward manner. □ *I don't care how bad it seems. Sock it to me!*

soft as a baby's backside Go to next.

*soft as a baby's bottom AND ***soft as a baby's backside; *soft as down; *soft as silk; *soft as velvet** *Cliché* very soft and smooth to the touch. (*Also: **as ~**.) □ *This cloth is as soft as a baby's bottom.* □ *The kitten's fur was as soft as down.* □ *Your touch is soft as silk.* □ *This lotion will make your skin soft as velvet.*

*soft as down Go to previous.

*soft as silk Go to soft as a baby's bottom.

*soft as velvet Go to soft as a baby's bottom.

soft in the head *Inf.* stupid; witless. □ *George is just soft in the head. He'll never get away with his little plan.*

soft money AND **easy money** *Inf.* money obtained without much effort. □ *In college he got spoiled by soft money—a check from his parents every week.*

*soft on so **1.** *Fig.* romantically attracted to someone. (*Typically: **be ~; get ~**.) □ *He looked like he was getting a little soft on Sally.* **2.** *Fig.* not severe enough on someone; too easy on someone or a class of people. (*Typically: **be ~; get ~; grow ~**.) □ *The judge was viewed as being too soft on drug pushers.*

soft on sth too easy when judging something; prone to agreeing with something. □ *In his youth, he had been accused of being soft on communism.*

soft pedal sth AND **play** sth **down**† *Inf.* to de-emphasize something. (Refers to the soft pedal on the piano, which reduces the volume.) □ *Try to soft pedal the problems we have with the cooling system.* □ *Please play down the problems with the air-conditioning.*

soft sell *Inf.* a polite attempt to sell something; a very gentle sales pitch. □ *Some people won't bother listening to a soft sell. You gotta let them know you believe in what you are selling.*

soft soap 1. *Inf.* flattering but insincere talk; sweet talk. □ *Don't waste my time with soft soap. I know you don't mean it.* **2.** *Inf.* to attempt to convince someone (of something) by gentle persuasion. (Usually **soft-soap**.) □ *Don't try to soft-soap her. She's an old battle-ax.*

soft touch 1. *Fig.* a gentle way of handling someone or something. □ *Kelly lacks the kind of soft touch needed for this kind of negotiation.* **2.** *Inf.* a gullible person; a likely victim of a scheme. □ *Here comes the perfect soft touch—a nerd with a gleam in his eye.*

soften one's **stance (on** so/sth**)** *Fig.* to reduce the severity of one's position regarding someone or something. □ *If he would soften his stance on the matter, I could easily become more cooperative.*

soften the blow AND **cushion the blow 1.** to lessen the force of a blow as with something positioned between the blow and its target. □ *I raised my arm in front of my face to cushion the blow against the windshield.* **2.** to lessen the emotional shock of very bad news by presenting it carefully, politely, and thoughtfully. □ *The detective tried to soften the blow by leading the mother to realize that her son had been shot in the robbery, without actually telling her straightaway.*

soften up *Fig.* [for someone] to adopt a more gentle manner. □ *After a while, she softened up and was more friendly.*

soften so **up**† *Fig.* to prepare to persuade someone of something. □ *I will talk to Fred and soften him up for your request.*

soil one's **diaper(s)** [for a baby] to excrete waste into its diaper. □ *The baby soiled his diapers. Yeek!*

soil one's **hands** Go to get one's **hands** dirty.

sold on so/sth *Fig.* convinced of the value of someone or something. □ *The crowd was sold on Gary. Nothing he had done or could do would cool their enthusiasm.*

sold out [of a product] completely sold with no more items remaining; [of a store] having no more of a particular product. □ *I wanted new shoes like yours, but they were sold out.*

*solid as a rock *Cliché* very solid; dependable. (*Also: **as** ~.) □ *Jean has been lifting weights every day, and her arm muscles are solid as a rock.*

*a (solid) grasp of sth AND ***a (sound) grasp of** sth; ***a (good) grasp of** sth *Fig.* a firm understanding of something. (*Typically: **get** ~; **have** ~; **give** so ~.) □ *John was unable to get a solid grasp of the methods used in his work, and we had to let him go.*

*some elbow room *Fig.* room to move about in; extra space to move about in. (*Typically: **allow** ~; **get** ~; **have** ~; **give** so ~; **need** ~.) □ *This table is too crowded. We all need some elbow room.*

*some loose ends *Fig.* some things that are not yet finished; some problems not yet solved. (*Typically: **have** ~; **leave** ~; **tie** ~ **up**†; **take care of** ~.) □ *I have to stay in town this weekend and tie up some loose ends.*

(some) new blood AND **fresh blood** *Fig.* new personnel; new members brought into a group to revive it. □ *We're trying to get some new blood in the club. Our membership is falling.*

some pumpkins AND **some punkins** *Inf.* someone or something great or special. (Older.) □ *Isn't this little gadget really some pumpkins?*

*some shut-eye *Fig.* some sleep. (*Typically: **get** ~; **have** ~; **use** ~; **need** ~.) □ *I need to get home and get some shut-eye before I do anything else.*

something of the sort *Fig.* something similar to the kind just mentioned. □ *Jane has a cold or something of the sort.*

something or other *Fig.* something unspecified; one thing or another. □ *A messenger came by and dropped off something or other at the front desk.*

something to that effect *Fig.* something like that just mentioned. □ *She said she wouldn't be available until after three, or something to that effect.*

Something's got to give. *Fig.* Emotions or tempers are strained, and there is going to be an outburst. □ *Alice: There are serious problems with Mary and Tom. They fight and fight. Sue: Yes, something's got to give. It can't go on like this.*

something's up *Fig.* something is going to happen; something is going on. □ *From the looks of all the activity around here, I think something's up.*

somewhere along the line AND **at some point (in the past)** *Fig.* at sometime in the past chain of events that lead up to this point in time. □ *Somewhere along the line, Charlie got the idea that other people were there to serve him.*

somewhere down the line AND **at some point (in the future)** *Fig.* a point in the future. □ *Somewhere down the line, you will wish you had done things as I instructed you.*

son of a bachelor Go to son of a gun.

son of a bitch 1. *Inf.* a very horrible person. (Usually intended as a strong insult. Never used casually.) □ *Bill called Bob a son of a bitch, and Bob punched Bill in the face.* **2.** *Inf.* a useless thing. □ *This bumpy old road needs paving. It's a real son of a bitch.* **3.** *Inf.* a difficult task. □ *I can't do this kind of thing. It's too hard—a real son of a bitch.*

son of a gun AND **son of a bachelor** *Fig.* a worthless person. (A substitute for son of a bitch.) □ *That tightfisted son of a gun won't buy me a beer.*

son of a sea biscuit *Inf.* a person, usually a male. (Often jocular. Sometimes a substitute for son of a bitch.) □ *Why, good to see you, you old son of a sea biscuit.*

*soon as possible *Fig.* at the earliest time. (*Also: **as** ~.) □ *I'm leaving now. I'll be there as soon as possible.*

sooner or later *Fig.* at some point in time; now or later. □ *Sooner or later you will have to face the consequences.*

The **sooner the better.** *Fig.* The sooner something [referred to] gets done, the better things will be. □ *Bob: When do you need this? Mary: The sooner the better.*

sorry (a)bout that *Inf.* sorry; whoops. (A gross understatement, said more as a self-deprecating joke than as an apology. *Bout is often 'bout.*) □ *You spill hot cocoa on my coat, and all you can say is "Sorry 'bout that"?*

a **sorry sight** AND a **sad sight** *Fig.* a sight that one regrets seeing; someone or something that is unpleasant to look at.

a **sorry state of affairs** Go to a pretty state of affairs.

Sorry you asked? Go to (Are you) sorry you asked?

sort of sth Go to kind of sth.

sort oneself **out** to figure out what to do about one's problems. □ *I had a terrible week so I am taking Monday off. I need some time to sort myself out.*

sort sth **out**† *Fig.* to study a problem and figure it out. □ *I can't sort this out without some more time.*

so-so *Inf.* not good and not bad; mediocre. □ *I didn't have a bad day. It was just so-so.*

*sound as a bell in perfect condition or health; undamaged. (*Also: **as** ~.) □ *I thought the vase was broken when it fell, but it was as sound as a bell.*

*sound as a dollar 1. *Cliché* very secure and dependable. (*Also: **as** ~.) □ *I wouldn't put my money in a bank that isn't sound as a dollar.* **2.** *Cliché* sturdy and well-constructed. (*Also: **as** ~.) □ *The garage is still sound as a dollar. Why tear it down?*

sound asleep *Fig.* completely asleep; in a deep sleep. □ *I was sound asleep when the fire broke out.*

a **(sound) grasp of** sth Go to a (solid) grasp of sth.

sound like a broken record to say the same thing over and over again. (Fig. on a scratch in a phonograph record causing the stylus or "needle" to stay in the same groove and play it over and over.) □ *He's always complaining about the way she treats him. He sounds like a broken record!*

sound off (about sth**) 1.** *Fig.* to complain about something; to gripe about something. □ *You are always sounding off about something that gripes your soul.* **2.** *Fig.* to speak out of turn about something; to speak when you should not. □ *Who asked you to sound off about this?* □ *Don't just sound off without raising your hand.*

sound so **out**† AND **feel** so **out**† *Fig.* to try to find out what someone thinks (about something). □ *I don't know what Jane thinks about your suggestion, but I'll sound her out.*

sound sth **out**† *Fig.* to pronounce the letters or syllables of a word as a means of figuring out what the word is. (Usually said to a child.) □ *This word is easy, Bobby. Try to sound it out.*

sound the death knell 1. [for a bell] to ring slowly signaling a funeral or a death. □ *The old bell sounded the death knell many times during the plague.* **2.** *Fig.* to signal the end of something. □ *The elimination of the funding for the project sounded the death knell for Paul's pet project.*

soup sth **up**† *Inf.* to increase the power of something. □ *If only I could soup up this computer to run just a little faster.*

Soup's on! *Rur.* The meal is ready to eat. (Said for any food, not just soup.) □ *Tom: Soup's on! Bill: The camp chef has dished up yet another disaster.*

***sour as vinegar 1.** [of something] very sour. (*Also: **as** ~.) □ *The juice they gave us is sour as vinegar.* **2.** [of someone] ill-natured and disagreeable. (Fig. on ①. *Also: **as** ~.) □ *Jill: Is Mary in a bad mood today? Jane: Yes, sour as vinegar.*

sour grapes *Fig.* something that one cannot have and so disparages as if it were never desirable. □ *Of course you want to buy this expensive jacket. Criticizing it is just sour grapes, but you still really want it.*

sow one's **wild oats** to do wild and foolish things in one's youth. (Extended from a sexual meaning originally having to do with early male copulatory experiences.) □ *Jack was out sowing his wild oats last night, and he's in jail this morning.* □ *Mrs. Smith told Mr. Smith that he was too old to be sowing his wild oats and that he would hear from her lawyer.*

space out *Inf.* to become giddy or disoriented. □ *Judy spaced out during the meeting, and I didn't understand a word she said.*

spaced (out) AND **spacey** *Inf.* silly; giddy. □ *I have such spaced-out parents!* □ *I love my spacey old dad.*

spade sth **up**† to turn over the soil in a garden plot with a spade. □ *Please go out and spade the garden up so I can plant the potatoes and onions.*

spar with so *Fig.* to argue or quibble with someone. □ *I think you really enjoy sparring with people just to irritate them.*

spare no effort to do sth AND **not spare any effort to** do sth to try hard to do something; to use all one's resources to do something. □ *I know it's important that I be there on time, so I will spare no effort to get there at the time you specified.*

spare no expense to spend liberally or as much as needed. □ *Please go out and buy the biggest turkey you can find, and spare no expense.*

spare tire 1. *Inf.* a thickness in the waist; a roll of fat around one's waist. □ *I've got to get rid of this spare tire.* **2.** *Inf.* an unneeded person; an unproductive person. □ *You spare tires over there! Get to work.*

spark sth **off**† **1.** to ignite something flammable or explosive. □ *The lightning sparked a fire off.* **2.** *Fig.* to cause or start some violent or energetic activity. (Fig. on ①.) □ *We were afraid there would be a riot, and the speaker nearly sparked one off.*

speak as one Go to as one.

speak at great length Go to at great length.

speak down to so to address someone in simpler terms than necessary; to speak condescendingly to someone. □ *There is no need to speak down to me. I can understand anything you are likely to say.*

speak for oneself *Fig.* to speak on one's own behalf. □ *Speak for yourself. What you say does not represent my thinking.*

speak for so/sth *Fig.* to lay claim to someone or something. □ *I want to speak for the red one.*

speak for itself AND **speak for themselves** *Fig.* [for something] not to need explaining; to have an obvious meaning. □ *The facts speak for themselves. Tom is guilty.*

speak highly of so/sth **1.** *Fig.* [for someone] to say good things about someone or something. □ *Everyone spoke highly of this movie, but it is not good.* **2.** *Fig.* [for a fact] to reflect well on someone or something. (Fig. on ①.) □ *The success of your project speaks highly of you.*

speak ill of so *Fig.* to say something bad about someone. □ *I refuse to speak ill of any of my friends.*

speak so's **language** *Fig.* to say something that one agrees with or understands. □ *I gotcha. Now you're speaking my language.*

speak one's **mind** *Fig.* to say frankly what one thinks (about something). □ *You can always depend on John to speak his mind. He'll let you know what he really thinks.*

speak of so/sth *Fig.* [for a type of behavior or action] to reflect a particular quality. □ *Jeff's behavior spoke of a good upbringing.*

speak of the devil (and he appears) AND **speak of the devil (and in he comes)** *Fig.* someone (male or female) who was just mentioned comes in or appears. (Also with additional number and gender variants.) □ *Speak of the devil. Hi, Jane. We were just talking about you.*

speak of the devil (and in he comes) Go to previous.

speak off the cuff *Fig.* to speak without preparing a speech; to speak extemporaneously; to render a spoken opinion or estimate. (As if one's notes had been written hastily on one's cuff. □ *She is capable of making sense and being convincing even when she speaks off the cuff.*

speak out of turn AND **talk out of turn** *Fig.* to say something unwise or imprudent; to say something at the wrong time. □ *Excuse me if I'm speaking out of turn, but what you are proposing is quite wrong.*

speak out (on sth**)** *Fig.* to say something frankly and directly; to speak one's mind. □ *This law is wrong, and I intend to speak out on it until it is repealed.*

speak one's **piece** Go to say one's piece.

speak the same language *Fig.* [for people] to have similar ideas, tastes, etc. □ *Jane and Jack get along very well. They really speak the same language about almost everything.*

speak to sth *Fig.* [for something] to address, indicate, or signal something. □ *This event speaks to the value of good communication.* □ *Your present state of employment speaks to your need for a better education.*

speak too soon to declare something settled before it is settled. □ *You spoke too soon when you said there was no chance of storms tonight.*

speak up 1. to speak more loudly. □ *They can't hear you in the back of the room. Please speak up.* □ *What? Speak up, please. I'm hard of hearing.* **2.** *Fig.* to speak out (on sth). □ *If you think that this is wrong, you must speak up and say so.*

speak volumes *Fig.* [for something that is seen] to reveal a great deal of information. □ *The unsightly yard and unpainted house speaks volumes about what kind of people live there.*

speak with a forked tongue AND **to speak out of both sides of** one's **mouth** *Fig.* to tell lies; to try to deceive someone; to speak ambiguously. (The presumed immediate source of the first entry head is an image, usually in old movies or on radio, of an American Indian accusing a white man of saying one thing but meaning another, that is, lying. Of course, there is also the forked-tongue serpent in Genesis, which allegedly put Eve up to tasting of the fruit of the tree of knowledge—and we think that means sex.) □ *Jean's mother sounds very charming, but she speaks with a forked tongue.*

speak with so **(about** so/sth**)** *Fig.* to reprimand one about one's dealing with someone or something. □ *He should not have insulted Kelly. I will speak with him about her.*

speak with one voice *Fig.* [for members of a group] to think and mean the same thing; [for a group of people] to advocate a single position. □ *I'm sure we all speak with one voice in this matter. There will be no tree harvest in the forest!*

***speeds of** some number *Fig.* a variety of speeds (of movement) of a certain level. (*Typically: **clock** so **at** ~; **have** ~; **hit**

~; **reach** ~.) □ *The cops clocked him at speeds of up to 100 miles per hour.*

spell so **(at** sth**)** *Fig.* to take a turn at doing something while the person who was doing it can take a rest.

spell disaster *Fig.* to indicate or predict disaster. □ *What a horrible plan! It would spell disaster for all of us!*

spell sth **out**† *Fig.* to give all the details of something. □ *I want you to understand this completely, so I'm going to spell it out very carefully.*

spell trouble *Fig.* to signify future trouble; to mean trouble. □ *The sky looks angry and dark. That spells trouble.*

spend money like it's going out of style AND **spend money like there's no tomorrow** *Fig.* to spend money recklessly; to spend money as if it were worthless or will soon be worthless. □ *Extravagant? She spends money like it's going out of style!*

spend money like there's no tomorrow Go to previous.

spending money *Inf.* cash, as opposed to money in the bank. □ *I'm a little short of spending money at the present. Could I borrow 10 dollars?*

spew one's **guts (out)** **1.** *Sl.* to empty one's stomach; to vomit. □ *Fred is spewing his guts out because of that lousy fish you served.* **2.** *Sl.* to tell everything that one knows; to confess everything. (Underworld.) □ *Lefty was sitting there in the police station spewing his guts out about the bank job.*

spice sth **up**† *Fig.* to make something more interesting, lively, or sexy. □ *Judy liked to spice her lectures up by telling jokes.*

spick-and-span *Fig.* very clean. □ *I have to clean up the house and get it spick-and-span for the party Friday night.*

spiff sth **up**† *Fig.* to polish and groom something very well; to make something clean and tidy. □ *See if you can spiff this place up a little.*

spiffed out *Sl.* to be dressed in one's finest clothes and well-groomed. □ *He got him-*

self all spiffed out for the wedding reception.

spill one's **guts** *Inf.* to tell all; to confess. □ *I had to spill my guts about the broken window. I didn't want you to take the blame.*

spill (out) into sth AND **spill (over) into** sth to be so great in number or volume as to expand into another area. □ *The well-wishers spilled over into the neighbor's yard.*

spill the beans AND **spill the works** *Fig.* to give away a secret or a surprise. □ *There is a surprise party for Heidi on Wednesday. Please don't spill the beans.*

spill the works Go to previous.

spin a yarn *Fig.* to tell a tale. □ *My uncle is always spinning yarns about his childhood.*

spin doctor *Fig.* someone who gives a twisted or deviously deceptive version of an event. (Usually in the context of manipulating the news for political reasons.) □ *Things were going bad for the candidate, so he got himself a new spin doctor.*

spin in one's **grave** Go to turn (over) in one's grave.

spin sth **off**† **1.** *Fig.* [for a business] to divest itself of one of its subparts. □ *The large company spun one of its smaller divisions off.* **2.** *Fig.* [for an enterprise] to produce useful or profitable side effects or products. □ *We will be able to spin off a number of additional products.*

spin one's **wheels** *Inf.* to waste time; to remain in a neutral position, neither advancing nor falling back. (Fig. on a car that is running but is not moving because its wheels are spinning in mud, etc.) □ *I'm just spinning my wheels in this job. I need more training to get ahead.*

spirit so/sth **away**† **(some place)** *Fig.* to sneak someone or something away to another place. □ *The police spirited the prisoner away before the crowd assembled in front of the jail.*

*****the **spit and image of** so AND *****the **spitting image of** so *Fig.* the very likeness of someone, especially the likeness of a father and son; a very close resemblance to someone. (Probably from the older form *spitten image*, as in *spit, spat, spitten*. The allusion is not clear or even suggested by the component words. *Typically: **be** ~; **look like** ~.) □ *John is the spit and image of his father.*

spit and polish *Fig.* orderliness; ceremonial precision and orderliness. □ *I like spit and polish. It comes from being in the military.*

spit sth **out**† **1.** *Fig.* to manage to say something. □ *Come on! Say it! Spit it out!* **2.** *Fig.* to say something scornfully. (Refers to the manner of speaking.) □ *He spit out his words in utter derision.*

spit up *Euph.* to vomit. □ *The food was so bad, she was afraid she would spit up.*

spit sth **up**† *Euph.* to vomit something. □ *She almost spit her dinner up.*

the **spitting image of** so Go to the spit and image of so.

splash down *Fig.* [for a space capsule] to land in the water. □ *The capsule splashed down very close to the pickup ship.*

split a gut AND **bust a gut** **1.** *Fig. Inf.* to laugh very hard. □ *He laughed until he nearly split a gut.* **2.** *Fig. Inf.* to work very hard to get something done. □ *I split a gut to get this place fixed up in a week.* □ *Don't bust a gut cleaning up for me. I love things that are a bit messy.*

split hairs *Fig.* to quibble; to try to make petty distinctions. □ *They don't have any serious differences. They are just splitting hairs.*

split people up† *Fig.* to separate two or more people (from one another). □ *If you two don't stop chattering, I'll have to split you up.*

*a **split second** *Fig.* an instant; a tiny period of time. (*Typically: **for** ~; **in** ~.) □ *The lightning struck, and in a split second the house burst into flames.*

split one's **sides (with laughter)** *Fig.* to laugh so hard that one's sides almost split. (Always an exaggeration.) □ *The members of the audience almost split their sides with laughter.*

split the difference *Fig.* to divide the difference evenly (with someone else). □ *You want to sell for $120, and I want to buy for $100. Let's split the difference and close the deal at $110.*

split up (with so**)** *Fig.* [for someone] to separate from someone; to break up a marriage or love affair. □ *I had heard that they had split up with each other.*

a **splitting headache** *Fig.* a severe headache, as if one's head were splitting open. □ *I'm sorry, I can't. I have a splitting headache. Maybe Fred will play bridge with you.*

spoiled rotten *Fig.* indulged in; greatly spoiled. □ *I was spoiled rotten when I was a child, so I'm used to this kind of wasteful luxury.*

spoiling for a fight *Fig.* argumentative; asking for a fight. □ *They were just spoiling for a fight, and they went outside to settle the matter.*

spoken for *Fig.* taken; reserved (for someone). □ *I'm sorry, but this piece of cake is already spoken for.*

sponge sth **off of** so/sth AND **sponge** sth **off**† *Fig.* to beg or borrow money or food from someone or a group. □ *Please stop sponging food and money off your relatives!*

spook so/sth *Fig.* to startle or disorient someone or something. □ *A snake spooked my horse, and I nearly fell off.*

spoon-feed so *Fig.* to treat someone with too much care or help; to teach someone with methods that are too easy and do not stimulate the learner to independent thinking. □ *You mustn't spoon-feed the new recruits by telling them what to do all the time. They must learn to use their initiative.*

the **sport of kings** *Fig.* horse racing. □ *The sport of kings has sure impoverished a lot of commoners.*

sport with so/sth *Fig.* to tease or play with someone or something. □ *What a tease you are! You are just sporting with me!*

a **sporting chance** *Fig.* a reasonably good chance. □ *If you hurry, you have a sporting chance of catching the bus.*

spot so (sth) **1.** *Sl.* to give an advantage of game points to someone. □ *I'll spot you 20 points.* **2.** *Sl.* to lend someone something. □ *Can you spot me a few bucks?*

spout off (about so/sth) **1.** *Inf.* to brag or boast about someone or something. □ *Stop spouting off about Tom. Nobody could be that good!* **2.** *Inf.* to speak out publicly about someone or something; to reveal information publicly about someone or something. □ *I wish you wouldn't spout off about my family affairs in public.*

spout sth **out**† *Fig.* to blurt something out; to speak out suddenly, revealing some important piece of information. □ *She spouted the name of the secret agent out under the effects of the drug.*

sprain one's **ankle** *Inf.* to become pregnant. □ *From the looks of her, she must have sprained her ankle some months ago.*

spread like wildfire *Fig.* [for something] to spread rapidly. □ *Rumors spread like wildfire when people are angry.*

spread the word *Fig.* to tell many people some kind of information. □ *I need to spread the word that the meeting is canceled for this afternoon.*

spread oneself **too thin** *Fig.* to do so many things at one time that you can do none of them well. □ *It's a good idea to get involved in a lot of activities, but don't spread yourself too thin.*

spread one's **wings (and fly)** *Fig.* to begin something new; to start a new career; to become independent. (Especially after a period of being restrained or inactive.) □ *After she finished her graduate degree, she really spread her wings.*

spring for sth AND **bounce for** sth *Sl.* to treat someone by buying something. □ *Ralph sprang for drinks, and we all had a great time.*

spring into action *Fig.* to suddenly begin moving or doing something. □ *As soon as the boss came in the door, everyone sprang into action.*

spring sth **on** so **1.** *Fig.* to surprise someone with something. □ *I hate to spring this on you at the last moment, but I will need some money to travel on.* **2.** *Fig.* to pull a trick on someone. □ *Let me tell you about the trick I sprang on Sally.*

spring to attention *Fig.* to move quickly to assume the military posture of attention. □ *The recruit sprang to attention.*

spring to so's **defense** *Fig.* to go quickly to defend someone. (Can be against physical or verbal attack.) □ *We sprang to Mary's defense when she was accused of doing wrong.*

spring to one's **feet** *Fig.* to stand up quickly. □ *The audience sprang to its feet and cheered madly when the soprano finished.*

spring to life *Fig.* to become suddenly alive or more alive. □ *The entire city sprang to life at dawn.*

spring to mind Go to jump to mind.

sprout wings *Fig.* to behave so well as to resemble an angel. □ *The kid is not about to sprout wings, but he probably won't get into jail again.*

spruce so/sth **up**† **1.** AND **tidy** so/sth **up**† *Fig.* to clean up and groom someone or something. □ *Laura's mother took a few minutes to spruce her daughter up for the party.* **2.** *Fig.* to refurbish or renew someone or something. □ *Do you think we should spruce this room up a little?*

spur so **on**† *Fig.* to urge someone onward; to egg someone on. (Fig. on applying spurs to a horse.) □ *The crowd spurred the runners on throughout the race.*

square accounts (with so) **1.** *Fig.* to settle one's financial accounts with someone. □ *I have to square accounts with the bank this week, or it'll take back my car.* **2.** *Fig.* to get even with someone; to straighten out a misunderstanding with someone. (Fig. on ①.) □ *I'm going to square accounts with Tom. He insulted me in public, and he owes me an apology.*

a **square deal** *Fig.* a fair and honest transaction; fair treatment. □ *All the workers want is a square deal, but their boss underpays them.*

square off (for sth) *Fig.* to get ready for an argument or a fight. □ *When those two square off, everyone gets out of the way.*

a **square peg (in a round hole)** *Fig.* someone who is uncomfortable or who does not belong in a particular situation. (Also the cliché: *trying to fit a square peg into a round hole* = trying to combine two things that do not belong or fit together.) □ *I feel like a square peg in a round hole at my office. Everyone else there seems so ambitious, competitive, and dedicated to the work, but I just want to make a living.*

square up to so/sth *Fig.* to face someone or something bravely; to tackle someone or something. □ *You'll have to square up to the bully or he'll make your life miserable.*

square up with so *Fig.* to pay someone what one owes; to pay one's share of something to someone. □ *Bob said he would square up with Tom for his share of the gas.*

square with so **1.** *Fig.* to settle a disagreement with someone. □ *I will try to square with Fred before the end of the school year.* **2.** *Fig.* to apologize to someone. □ *I will try to square with Harold. I really am sorry, you know.*

square with sth *Fig.* [for a statement] to agree, match, or correspond to something. □ *The figures I have don't square with those the government has.*

squared away *Fig.* arranged or properly taken care of. □ *Is Ann squared away in her dorm room yet?*

squawk about sth *Fig.* to complain about something. □ *Stop squawking about how much money you lost. I lost twice as much.*

squeak by (so/sth**) 1.** *Fig.* to manage just to squeeze past someone or something. □ *I squeaked by the fat man in the hallway only to find myself blocked by another.* **2.** *Fig.* to manage just to get past a barrier represented by a person or thing, such as a difficult teacher or an examination. □ *Judy just squeaked by Professor Smith, who has a reputation for flunking students.*

squeak through (sth) *Fig.* to manage just to get past a barrier, such as an examination or interview. □ *Sally just barely squeaked through the interview, but she got the job.*

squeak sth **through** *Fig.* to manage just to get something accepted or approved. □ *Tom squeaked the application through at the last minute.*

squeal (on so**) (to** so) *Inf.* to report someone to someone. □ *Sally threatened to squeal to the boss.*

squeeze sth **from** sth *Fig.* to get a little more of something from something. □ *Let's see if we can squeeze a few more miles from this tank of gas before we fill up again.*

squeeze so **out**† Go to freeze so out†.

squeeze (themselves) up [for people] to press themselves closely together. □ *Everyone squeezed themselves up in the tiny car so there would be room for one more.* □ *Let's squeeze up so Jamie can sit down.*

squirm out (of sth) *Fig.* to escape doing something; to escape the responsibility for having done something. □ *He agreed to go but squirmed out at the last minute.*

squirrel sth **away**† *Fig.* to hide something or store something in the way that a squirrel stores nuts for use in the winter. □ *I squirreled a little money away for an occasion such as this.*

a **stab at** so Go to a try at so.

a **stab at** sth Go to a try at sth.

stab so **in the back** *Fig.* to betray someone. □ *I wish you would not gossip about me. There is no need to stab me in the back.*

stack the cards (against so/sth) Go to next.

stack the deck (against so/sth) AND **stack the cards (against** so/sth) *Fig.* to arrange things against someone or something. (Originally from card playing. *Stacking the deck* = cheating by arranging the cards to be dealt out to one's advantage.) □ *I* *can't get ahead at my office. Someone has stacked the cards against me.*

stack up to so/sth AND **measure up to** so/sth; **stack up against** so/sth; **measure up against** so/sth *Fig.* [for someone or something] to be appraised as good when compared to someone or something. □ *How do you think I stack up to Liz?*

stain sth **with** sth *Fig.* to injure or blemish someone's reputation. □ *They stained his reputation with their charges.*

stake so/sth **out**[†] **1.** *Fig.* to position a person so that someone else or something can be observed or followed. □ *The cops staked the car out and made the arrest.* □ *Barlowe staked out the apartment building and watched patiently for an hour.* **2.** *Fig.* to position a person to observe someone else or something. □ *He staked his best operative out in front of the building.*

stake (out) a claim to sth AND **stake (out) a claim on** sth *Fig.* to claim or obtain something. □ *We staked out a claim on two seats at the side of the auditorium.*

stake one's **reputation on** so/sth *Fig.* to risk harming one's reputation on someone or something. □ *Of course Denise is great. I will stake my reputation on her!*

stake so **to** sth to make a loan of something to someone. □ *I will stake you to a hundred bucks if that will help.*

stall so/sth **off**[†] *Fig.* to put off or delay someone or something. □ *The sheriff is at the door. I'll stall him off while you get out the back door.*

stamp so **out**[†] *Sl.* to get rid of or kill someone. (Fig. on **stamp** sth **out.**) □ *You just can't stamp somebody out on your own!*

stamp sth **out**[†] *Fig.* to eliminate something. □ *The doctors hope they can stamp cancer out.*

stand so/sth Go to put up with so/sth.

stand a chance (of doing sth**)** AND **have a prayer (of** doing sth**)** to have a chance of doing something. (Often negative.) □ *Do you think I stand a chance of winning first place?* □ *No. You don't have a prayer.*

stand and deliver *Fig.* to give up something to someone who demands it. (Originally used by highway robbers asking for passengers' valuables.) □ *And when the tax agent says, "Stand and deliver" you have to be prepared to pay what is demanded.*

stand apart (from so/sth**)** *Fig.* to appear clearly different from other things or people. □ *Alice really stands apart from her peers.*

stand aside *Fig.* to withdraw and ignore something; to remain passive while something happens. □ *He just stood aside and let his kids behave as they pleased.*

stand behind so/sth Go to stand (in) back of so/sth.

stand by *Fig.* to wait and remain ready. (Generally heard in communication, such as broadcasting, telephones, etc.) □ *Your transatlantic telephone call is almost ready. Please stand by.*

stand by so AND **stick by** so *Fig.* to support someone; to continue supporting someone even when things are bad. □ *I feel as though I have to stand by my brother even if he goes to jail.*

stand corrected *Fig.* to admit that one has been wrong. □ *We appreciate now that our conclusions were wrong. We stand corrected.*

stand down 1. *Fig.* to step down, particularly from the witness stand in a courtroom. □ *The bailiff told the witness to stand down.* **2.** *Fig.* [for military forces] to move away from readiness for war. □ *After the peace treaty was signed, troops on both sides stood down.*

stand for sth **1.** *Fig.* to permit something; to endure something. □ *The teacher won't stand for any whispering in class.* **2.** to signify something. □ *In a traffic signal, the red light stands for "stop."* □ *The abbreviation Dr. stands for "doctor."* **3.** *Fig.* to endorse or support an ideal. □ *Every candidate for public office stands for all the good things in life.*

stand one's **ground** AND **hold** one's **ground** *Fig.* to stand up for one's rights; to resist an attack. □ *The lawyer tried to confuse me when I was giving testimony, but I managed to stand my ground.*

stand head and shoulders above so/sth *Fig.* [for someone or something] to be considerably superior to someone or something. □ *Alice stands head and shoulders above all the rest of the people we interviewed.*

stand idly by Go to sit idly by.

stand in awe (of so/sth**)** *Fig.* to be overwhelmed with respect for someone or something. □ *Bob says he stands in awe of a big, juicy steak. I think he's exaggerating.*

stand (in) back of so/sth AND **stand behind** so/sth *Fig.* to guarantee someone or something; to guarantee the performance or worth of someone or something. (See also behind (so/sth).) □ *I will stand back of Elaine. I trust her totally.*

stand in (for so**)** *Fig.* to substitute for someone; to serve in someone's place. □ *The famous opera singer was ill, and an inexperienced singer had to stand in for her.*

stand so **in good stead** AND **hold** so **in good stead** *Fig.* [for something] to be of great use and benefit to someone. □ *Any experience you can get in dealing with the public will stand you in good stead no matter what line of work you go into.*

stand so/sth **off**† AND **fight** so/sth **off**† *Fig.* to repel the attack of someone or something; to defend against someone or something; to stave someone or something off. □ *The soldiers stood off the attackers as long as they could.*

stand on ceremony *Fig.* to hold rigidly to protocol or formal manners. (Often in the negative.) □ *We are very informal around here. Hardly anyone stands on ceremony.*

stand on one's **dignity** *Fig.* to remain dignified in spite of difficulties. □ *She stood on her dignity and ignored all the nonsense going on around her.*

stand on one's **head** *Fig.* to attempt to impress someone by hard work or difficult feats. □ *You don't have to stand on your head to succeed in this office. Just do your assigned work on time.*

stand sth **on its head** AND **turn** sth **on its head** *Fig.* to stir up, baffle, or surprise a group or organization. □ *The new owners came into the company and stood it on its head. Nothing will ever be the same.*

stand on one's **(own) two feet** *Fig.* to act in an independent and forthright manner. □ *Dave will be better off when he gets a job and can stand on his own feet.*

stand out from the crowd AND **stand out from the rest** *Fig.* to appear different from the rest of them. □ *You will recognize her. She is over six feet tall and tends to stand out from the crowd.*

stand out from the rest Go to previous.

stand out like a sore thumb Go to stick out like a sore thumb.

stand pat (on sth**)** *Fig.* to stick firmly to one's position or opinions. □ *I thought you would stand pat in the absence of new information.*

stand still for sth Go to hold still for sth.

stand tall *Inf.* to be brave and proud. □ *Our athletes stand tall in the knowledge that they did their best.*

stand the test of time Go to (with)stand the test of time.

stand there with one's **bare face hanging out** *Rur.* to stand some place looking helpless and stupid. □ *She just stood there with her bare face hanging out while they took away everything she owned.*

stand so **to a treat** *Fig.* to pay for a treat for someone. □ *It seems as if I am always standing someone to a treat.*

stand to lose sth *Fig.* to be likely to lose something or have it taken away. □ *I stand to lose hundreds of dollars if I am not there on time.*

stand to reason *Fig.* to seem reasonable. □ *It stands to reason that it'll be colder in January than it is in November.*

stand together *Fig.* to remain united. □ *We must stand together if we want to defeat this enemy.*

stand trial *Fig.* to be the accused person in a trial before a judge; to be on trial. □ *He had to stand trial for perjury and obstruction of justice.*

stand up 1. *Fig.* to wear well; to remain sound and intact. □ *This material just doesn't stand up well when it's washed.* **2.** *Fig.* [for an assertion] to remain believable. □ *When the police checked the story, it did not stand up.*

stand so **up**† *Fig.* to fail to show up for a meeting or a date. □ *He stood her up once too often, so she broke up with him.*

stand up against so/sth *Fig.* to withstand or hold one's own against someone or something. □ *He's good, but he can't stand up against Jill.*

stand up and be counted *Fig.* to state one's support (for someone or something). □ *If you believe in more government help for farmers, write your representative—stand up and be counted.*

stand up before so Go to up before so.

stand up for so/sth *Fig.* to take the side of someone or something; to defend someone or something. □ *I hope you will stand up for me if the going gets rough.*

stand up in court *Fig.* [for a case] to survive a test in a court of law. □ *These charges will never stand up in court. They are too vague.*

stand up to so/sth Go to take a stand (against so/sth).

stand up (under sth**)** Go to bear up (under sth).

stand well with so *Fig.* to be acceptable or agreeable to someone. □ *That idea doesn't stand well with the management.*

stand with so *Fig. Lit.* to unite with someone, as in defense. □ *Don't worry. I'll stand with you to the end.* □ *He stood with her, and they faced the threat together.*

a **standing joke** *Fig.* a subject that regularly and over a period of time causes amusement whenever it is mentioned. □ *Their mother's inability to make a decision was a standing joke in the Smith family all their lives.*

star as so/sth *Fig.* [for someone] to be a featured performer, representing a particular person, or play in a particular role. □ *Judy starred as Evita in the Broadway production of the same name.*

star in sth *Fig.* to be a featured actor in a play, movie, opera, etc. □ *Mary always wanted to star in her own movie, but it was not to be.*

star-crossed lovers *Fig.* ill-fated lovers. □ *I suppose that Romeo and Juliet are star-crossed lovers.*

stare so **in the face** Go to look so in the face.

stare sth **in the face** *Fig.* to face a problem directly and prepare to deal with it. □ *We had to stare the results of our greed in the face and see just what our indulgence had done.*

stark raving mad *Cliché* totally insane; completely crazy; out of control. (Often an exaggeration.) □ *When she heard about what happened at the office, she went stark raving mad.*

*****stars in** one's **eyes** *Fig.* an obsession with celebrities, movies, and the theater. (Refers to movie stars. *Typically: **get** ~; **have** ~; **give** one ~.) □ *Many young people have stars in their eyes at this age.*

*****one's **start** *Fig.* one's first career opportunity. (*Typically: **get** ~; **have** ~; **give** one ~.) □ *I had my start in painting when I was 30.* □ *She helped me get my start by recommending me to the manager.*

start sth *Fig.* to start a fight or an argument. (*Something* can be replaced by *anything* or *nothing* with the negative.) □ *Hey, you! Better be careful unless you want to start something.*

start a fire under so Go to a fire under so.

start from scratch *Fig.* to start from the very beginning; to start from nothing. □ *Whenever I bake a cake, I start from scratch. I never use a cake mix in a box.*

start sth **off**† Go to kick sth off†.

start off on the wrong foot AND **step off on the wrong foot** *Fig.* to begin things incorrectly. (As if one were beginning to march and began on the right rather than the left foot.) □ *Give me some advice. I don't want to start off on the wrong foot.*

start (off) with a bang *Fig.* to begin with considerable excitement. □ *The program started off with a bang, and the whole show was great.*

start (off) with a clean slate AND **start (over) with a clean slate** *Fig.* to start out again afresh; to ignore the past and start over again. □ *I plowed under all last year's flowers so I could start with a clean slate next spring.*

start on so/sth to begin to castigate someone or something. □ *The politician started on the opposing party, and everyone in the audience cheered.*

start (over) with a clean slate Go to start (off) with a clean slate.

start the ball rolling Go to the sth rolling.

state of mind *Fig.* basic attitude or outlook at a point in time. □ *She was in a terrible state of mind when she was interviewed for a job.*

state of the art *Fig.* using the most recent technology. (Hyphenated before nouns.) □ *This state-of-the-art radio is capable of filling the whole room with sound.*

station so **at** sth to position or place someone near something. □ *Would you station a guard at the back door to keep people out?*

stave so/sth **off**† to hold someone or something off; to defend against the attack of someone or something. (See also stave sth off.) □ *The citizen was not able to stave the mugger off.*

stave sth **off**† to delay or postpone something unwanted, such as hunger, foreclosure, death, etc. □ *He could stave his thirst off no longer. Despite the enemy sentries, he made a dash for the stream.*

stay abreast of sth Go to keep abreast of sth.

stay after so **(about** sth) Go to keep after so (about sth).

stay ahead of the game Go to ahead of the game.

stay clear of so/sth AND **keep** one's **distance from** so/sth to establish and maintain a physical distance from something, usually something dangerous. □ *Please stay clear of me. I have the flu.*

stay in touch (with so/sth) Go to keep in touch (with so/sth).

stay loose Go to hang loose.

stay on sth *Fig.* to continue to pursue something. □ *She stayed on the matter for weeks until it had been dealt with.*

stay on (after so/sth) Go to linger on (after so/sth).

stay on top of so/sth *Fig.* to keep well-informed about someone or something; to keep watch over someone or something. □ *You have to stay on top of her if you want her to do it right.*

stay out (of sth) *Fig.* to remain uninvolved in some piece of business. □ *I decided to stay out of it and let someone else handle it.*

Stay out of my way. Go to Keep out of my way.

Stay out of this! Go to Keep out of this!

stay the course *Fig.* to keep going the way things are even though things are difficult. (This is the current usage, but *stay* can also mean stop. Both nautical and equestrian origins have been proposed. Currently, it seems to be used a lot by politicians.) □ *Don't be panicked by the market into selling your assets. Stay the course and you will be better off.*

*steady as a rock *Cliché* very steady and unmovable; very stable. (*Also: **as** ~.) □ *His hand was steady as a rock as he made each incision.*

steal a base *Fig.* to sneak from one base to another in baseball. □ *The runner stole second base, but he nearly got put out on the way.*

steal a march on so/sth to precede someone who has the same goal; to accomplish something before someone else does. □ *Our competitor stole a march on us and got the big contract.*

steal so's **heart** *Fig.* to capture someone's affections; to cause a person to fall in love with oneself. □ *When I first met him, I knew he would steal my heart away. And he did.*

steal over so/sth **1.** *Fig.* [for a covering of some sort] to move slowly over someone or something. (As with the sun or the shade of a cloud.) □ *The shade stole over the sunbathers and ended their day.* **2.** *Fig.* [for a feeling] to spread through someone gradually. (Fig. on ①.) □ *A feeling of gloom stole over the crowd.*

steal the show Go to next.

steal the spotlight AND **steal the show** *Fig.* to give the best performance in a show, play, or some other event; to get attention for oneself. □ *The lead in the play was very good, but the butler stole the show.*

steal so's **thunder** *Fig.* to lessen someone's force or authority. □ *What do you mean by coming in here and stealing my thunder? I'm in charge here!*

steam across sth *Fig.* [for a ship] to cross a body of water under power. (Originally referred to steam engines but now can be any sort of engine or propulsion.) □ *How long does it take to steam across the Atlantic these days?*

steam so's **beam** *Sl.* to make someone angry. □ *Being stood up really steams my beam!*

steam up *Inf.* to drink heavily; to get drunk. □ *Fred and Mike were steaming up in the back room.*

steam so **up**† **1.** *Sl.* to get someone excited. □ *Steam yourselves up and get in there and win this game!* **2.** *Sl.* to get someone angry. □ *This whole mess steamed me up but good.*

steamed (up) 1. *Inf.* angry. □ *Now, now, don't get so steamed up!* **2.** *Sl.* intoxicated and fighting. □ *By midnight, Larry was too steamed to drive home, and he had to spend the night right here on the couch.*

steaming (mad) *Fig.* very angry; very mad; very upset. □ *The principal was steaming mad when he found that his office had been vandalized.*

steel so **against** so/sth *Fig.* to fortify someone against someone or something; to prepare someone to endure someone or something. □ *I tried to steel Liz against Carl, who was bringing her some very bad news.*

steel oneself **for** sth *Fig.* to prepare oneself for something difficult or unpleasant; to get ready to face someone or something. □ *I think something is going wrong. We had better steel ourselves for a shock.*

a **steely gaze** *Cliché* an intense, staring gaze. □ *The principal turned a steely gaze toward the frightened student and suddenly smiled.*

steep so **in** sth *Fig.* to immerse someone in some kind of knowledge or other experience; to saturate someone with some kind of experience or training. □ *Her parents steeped her in good literature and music.*

steer clear of so/sth Go to give so/sth a wide berth.

stem from sth *Fig.* [for an event] to result from something. □ *These problems all stem from your mismanagement.*

stem the flow (of so/sth**)** Go to next.

stem the tide (of so/sth**)** AND **stem the flow (of** so/sth**); halt the flow (of** so/sth**)** *Fig.* to stop an increasing "flow" of bad or unwanted things or people. □ *They seem not to be able to stem the flow of illegal immigrants.*

step aside (for so**)** *Fig.* to retire from an office so someone else can take over. □ *The president retired and stepped aside for someone else.*

step away from one's **desk** Go to away from one's desk.

step back in time Go to back in time.

step by step AND **one step at a time;** a **step at a time** little by little; a little distance at a time. (Refers both to walking and following instructions.) □ *Just follow* *the instructions step by step, and everything will be fine.*

step down (from sth**)** *Fig.* to resign a job or a responsibility. □ *The mayor stepped down from office last week.*

step forward *Fig.* to volunteer to present important information. □ *If you have information to present, you should step forward and seek recognition to do so.*

step into so's **shoes** Go to fill so's shoes.

step in(to the breach) *Fig.* [for someone] to assume a position or take on a responsibility when there is a need or an opportunity to do so. □ *The person who was supposed to help didn't show up, so I stepped into the breach.*

step off on the wrong foot Go to start off on the wrong foot.

step off (to the side) with so Go to off (to the side) with so.

step on it Go to next.

step on the gas AND **step on it** *Inf.* to hurry up; to make a vehicle go faster. (As if stepping on an automobile's accelerator.) □ *Step on the gas. We are going to be late!*

step on so's **toes** AND **tread on** so's **toes** *Fig.* to offend or insult someone, as if causing physical pain. (*Tread* is more U.K. than U.S.) □ *You're sure I won't be stepping on her toes if I talk directly to her supervisor?*

step out of line *Fig.* to misbehave; to deviate from normal, expected, or demanded behavior. □ *Tom stepped out of line once too often and got yelled at.*

step out (on so**)** *Fig.* to be unfaithful to a spouse or lover. □ *Jeff has been stepping out on Judy.*

step outside *Fig.* to go outside to fight or settle an argument. □ *I find that insulting. Would you care to step outside?*

step right up *Fig.* to come right to where the speaker is; to come forward to the person speaking. (Used by people selling things, as at carnival sideshows.) □ *Don't be shy! Step right up and buy one of these.*

step sth **up**† Go to pick up the pace (of sth).

step up to the plate 1. *Fig.* [for a batter in baseball] to move near home plate in preparation for striking the ball when it is pitched. □ *The batter stepped up to the plate and glared at the pitcher.* **2.** *Fig.* to move into a position where one is ready to do a task. □ *It's time for Tom to step up to the plate and take on his share of work.*

stew in one's **own juice** *Fig.* to be left alone to suffer one's anger or disappointment. □ *John has such a terrible temper. When he got mad at us, we just let him go away and stew in his own juice.*

stick around (some place**)** Go to hang around (some place).

stick by so Go to stand by so.

stick by sth Go to hold by sth.

Stick 'em up! Go to Hands up!

stick one's **foot in** one's **mouth** Go to put one's foot in one's mouth.

stick one's **head in the sand** Go to bury one's head in the sand.

stick in so's **mind** *Fig.* to remain in someone's thinking. □ *The image of her smiling face stuck in Henry's mind for a long time.*

stick in the mud *Fig.* a dull and old-fashioned person. □ *Some stick in the mud objected to the kind of music we wanted to play in church.*

stick it to so *Inf.* to give someone a problem; to confront someone. □ *He was late, and the boss really stuck it to him.*

stick man *Sl.* a police patrol officer (who carries a stick). □ *The stick man is due here in about three minutes. Hurry.*

stick one's **neck out**† **(for** so/sth**)** *Fig.* to take a risk. □ *He made a risky investment. He stuck his neck out for the deal because he thought he could make some big money.*

stick one's **nose in (where it's not wanted)** Go to put one's nose in (where it's not wanted).

stick one's **nose in(to** sth**)** Go to poke one's nose in(to sth).

stick one's **nose up in the air** *Fig.* to behave in a haughty manner. □ *Don't stick your nose up in the air. Come down to earth with the rest of us.*

stick one's **oar in**† Go to put one's oar in†.

stick sth **out**† *Fig.* to endure something; to stay with something. (The *something* can be vaguely expressed using *it*.) □ *I will stick it out as long as I can.*

stick out a mile *Fig.* to project outward very obviously. □ *His stomach sticks out a mile. What do you suppose is in there?*

stick out like a sore thumb AND **stand out like a sore thumb** *Fig.* to be very obvious. □ *Do you think I would stick out like a sore thumb at the party if I wear this dress?*

stick to so/sth *Fig.* to continue to accompany someone or something. □ *Stick to the group of us, and you'll be okay.*

stick to so's **fingers** *Fig.* to remain in someone's possession; to be stolen by someone. □ *Watch that clerk. Your change tends to stick to his fingers.*

stick to one's **guns** *Fig.* to remain firm in one's convictions; to stand up for one's rights. (Fig. on a soldier remaining in place to fire a gun even when the battle appears to be lost.) □ *Bob can be persuaded to do it our way. He probably won't stick to his guns on this point.*

stick to one's **ribs** *Fig.* [for food] to last long and fortify one well; [for food] to sustain one even in the coldest weather. □ *This oatmeal ought to stick to your ribs. You need something hearty on a cold day like this.*

stick together *Inf.* to remain in one another's company. □ *Let us stick together so we don't get lost.*

stick so/sth **up**† *Fig.* to rob someone or a business establishment. (Presumably with the aid of a gun. The phrase refers to the demand that those being robbed should stick their hands up into the air so that they cannot draw guns or otherwise defend themselves against the robbers.) □ *Spike tried to stick the drugstore up.* □ *Spike stuck up the messenger.*

stick up for so/sth *Fig.* to support someone or something; to speak in favor of someone or something. □ *Everyone was making unpleasant remarks about John, but I stuck up for him.*

stick so **with** so/sth Go to saddle so with so/sth.

Stick with it. *Fig.* Do not give up. Stay with your task. □ *Bill: I'm really tired of calculus. Father: Stick with it. You'll be a better person for it.*

*****stiff as a poker** rigid and inflexible; stiff and awkward. (Usually used to describe people. *Also: as ∼.) □ *This guy's dead. He's cold and as stiff as a poker.*

*****still as death** *Cliché* immobile; completely still. (The reference to death gives this expression ominous connotations. *Also: as ∼.) □ *George sat as still as death all afternoon.* □ *When the storm was over, everything was suddenly still as death.*

stink on ice *Sl.* to be really rotten. (So rotten as to reek even when frozen.) □ *This show stinks on ice.*

stink to high heaven AND **smell to high heaven** *Fig.* to smell very bad. □ *What happened? This place stinks to high heaven.*

stink sth **up**† Go to smell sth up†.

stinking rich *Inf.* very rich. □ *I'd like to be stinking rich for the rest of my life.*

stinking with sth *Inf.* having lots of something. □ *Mr. Wilson is just stinking with cash.*

*****stir crazy** *Fig.* crazy from being confined. (*Stir* is a slang word for prison. *Typically: be ∼; become ∼; go ∼; get ∼; make* so ∼.) □ *I am going to go stir crazy if I don't get out of this office.*

stir so **up**† *Fig.* to get someone excited; to get someone angry. (Fig. on **stir** sth **up**.) □ *The march music really stirred us up.*

stir sth **up**† *Fig.* to cause trouble. □ *Why are you always trying to stir trouble up?*

stir up a hornet's nest *Fig.* to create a lot of trouble. □ *If you say that to her, you will be stirring up a hornet's nest.*

stock in trade 1. goods in inventory awaiting sale; salable assets. (Sometimes misstated as *stock and trade*.) □ *His stock in trade consisted of both cut and uncut diamonds.* **2.** *Fig.* a person's special skill or forte; a talent awaiting use. (Fig. on ①.) □ *Of course I am glad to help. Packing household goods is my stock in trade.*

stock up on sth to build up a supply of something. □ *We should stock up on bottled water and canned food before the storm.*

stoke sth **up**† **1.** to poke or add fuel to a fire to make it burn hotter. □ *Grandpa had to go down each winter morning to stoke the fire up.* **2.** *Sl.* to start something, such as an engine. (Fig. on ①.) □ *Stoke this old car up so we can leave.*

***stoked on** so/sth *Sl.* excited by someone or something. (*Typically: **be** ~; **get** ~.) □ *I am so stoked on that movie.*

stoked out *Sl.* exhausted. □ *Alex is totally stoked out from working in the hot sun.*

stomp on so *Fig.* to repress someone. □ *Every time I get a good idea, the boss stomps on me.*

stone (cold) sober AND **cold sober** *Inf.* absolutely sober. □ *I found the secret to waking up cold sober. Don't drink.*

stone dead *Rur.* dead; unquestionably dead; long dead. □ *The cat was stone dead and stiff as a board by the time we got to him.*

a **stone's throw away** *Fig.* a short distance; a relatively short distance. □ *John saw Mary across the street, just a stone's throw away.*

stool (on so) *Sl.* to inform (on someone). □ *Jane would stool on anybody, even her own mother.*

stoop to some level Go to lower oneself to some level.

stop at nothing (to do sth) Go to go to extremes (to do sth).

stop so **cold** *Fig.* to halt someone immediately. □ *When you told us the bad news, it stopped me cold.*

stop (dead) in one's **tracks** *Fig.* to stop completely still suddenly because of fear, a noise, etc. □ *The deer stopped dead in its tracks when it heard the hunter step on a fallen branch.*

stop so/sth **dead in** so's/sth's **tracks** *Fig.* exactly where someone or something is at the moment; at this instant. (Akin to **stop (dead) in** one's **tracks.**) □ *Her unkind words stopped me dead in my tracks.* □ *When I heard the rattlesnake, I stopped dead in my tracks.*

stop, look, and listen *Fig.* to exercise caution, especially at street corners and railroad crossings, by stopping, looking to the left and to the right, and listening for approaching vehicles or a train. □ *Sally's mother trained her to stop, look, and listen at every street corner.*

stop on a dime *Inf.* to come to a stop in a very short distance. □ *This thing will stop on a dime.*

stop short of some place not to go as far as something. □ *The speeding car stopped short of the sidewalk where children were playing.*

stop short (of doing sth) not to go as far as doing something. □ *The boss criticized Jane's work but stopped short of firing her.* □ *Jack was furious but stopped short of hitting Tom.*

stop-and-go halting repeatedly; stopping and continuing repeatedly. □ *This project has been stop-and-go since we began. Problems keep appearing.*

storm at so/sth *Fig.* to direct one's anger at someone or something. □ *She stormed at him because he was late again.*

storm in(to some place) *Fig.* to burst into something or some place angrily. □ *The army stormed into the town and took many of the citizens as prisoners.*

A **storm is brewing. 1.** There is going to be a storm. □ *Look at the clouds. A storm is brewing.* **2.** *Fig.* There is going to be trouble or emotional upset. (Fig. on ①.) □ *He looks angry. A storm is brewing.*

storm out (of some place**)** *Fig.* to burst out of some place angrily. □ *Carol stormed out of the office in a rage.*

straddle the fence *Fig.* to support both sides of an issue. (As if one were partly on either side of a fence.) □ *The mayor is straddling the fence on this issue, hoping the public will forget it.*

the **straight and narrow** *Fig.* a straight and law-abiding route through life. (Referring to a morally rigid and correct course or pathway of behavior. Fixed order. Probably extracted from Matthew 7:14, "Because strait is the gate, and narrow is the way, which leadeth unto life, and few there be that find it.") □ *You should have no trouble with the police if you stick to the straight and narrow.*

*straight as an arrow 1. *Cliché* [of something] very straight. (*Also: **as** ~.) □ *The road to my house is as straight as an arrow, so it should be very easy to follow.* **2.** *Cliché* [of someone] honest or forthright. (*Straight* here means honest. *Also: **as** ~.) □ *Tom is straight as an arrow. I'd trust him with anything.*

the **straight dope** *Inf.* the true information; the full story. □ *I want the straight dope. I can take it.*

*a straight face *Fig.* a face free from smiles or laughter. (*Typically: **have** ~; **keep** ~.) □ *It's hard to keep a straight face when someone tells a funny joke.*

*(straight) from the horse's mouth *Fig.* from an authoritative or dependable source. (Alludes to the authenticity of a tip about the winner of a horse race. A tip that came straight from the horse could be assumed to be true. An exaggeration in any case. *Typically: **be** ~; **come** ~; **get** sth ~; **hear** sth ~.) □ *I know it's true! I heard it straight from the horse's mouth!* □ *This comes straight from the horse's mouth, so it has to be believed.*

straight from the shoulder *Fig.* very direct, without attenuation or embellishment. (The allusion is not clear, but it could refer to a straight shot from a rifle.) □ *Okay, I'll give it to you straight from the shoulder. You're broke.*

straight low *Sl.* the absolute truth. (From *lowdown* = the story; the truth.) □ *Can you give me the straight low on this mess?* □ *Nobody ain't gonna tell no warden the straight low! You can be sure of that.*

straight man *Fig.* someone who sets up jokes or gags so that someone else can say the punch line. □ *I'm tired of being a straight man for a has-been comic.*

straight off the bat Go to right off the bat.

straight out *Fig.* frankly; directly. □ *Bob told Pam straight out that he didn't want to marry her.*

straight shooter *Fig.* an honest person. □ *We need a straight shooter in office who will work for the people rather than some lobbyists.*

straight talk *Fig.* direct and honest talk. □ *If they want straight talk and can handle straight talk, give 'em straight talk.*

straight up 1. *Sl.* upright. □ *She is one of the most straight-up brokers in town.* **2.** *Sl.* [of a drink] served without ice; neat. □ *I'll have a bourbon, straight up, please.* **3.** *Sl.* [of eggs] cooked sunny-side up; having to do with eggs cooked with the yolks facing up. □ *I like my eggs straight up, but the white part has to be cooked solid.*

straighten out *Fig.* to improve one's behavior or attitude. □ *I hope he straightens out before he gets himself into real trouble.*

straighten so **out**† **1.** *Fig.* to cause someone to behave better or to have a better attitude; to reform someone. □ *You are terrible. Someone is going to have to straighten you out!* **2.** *Fig.* to help someone become less confused about something. □ *Can you straighten me out on this matter?*

straighten sth **out**† **1.** *Fig.* to clean up a mess; to arrange something or things into the proper order; to tidy so/sth up. □ *Will you please straighten out this mess!* **2.** *Fig.* to put an end to confusion by explaining something; to undo an error of understanding. □ *The members of the committee were confused about the date until I straightened it out.*

straighten up *Fig.* to behave better. □ *Bill was acting badly for a while; then he straightened up.*

straighten so/sth **up**† to tidy up someone or something. □ *John straightened himself up a little before going out for dinner.*

straighten up and fly right *Fig.* to improve one's behavior or attitude and perform better. (Originally referred to an airplane.) □ *If you want to keep out of trouble, you had better straighten up and fly right.*

strain at the leash *Fig.* [for a person] to want to move ahead with things, aggressively and independently. (Fig. on the image of an eager or poorly disciplined dog pulling on its leash, trying to hurry its owner along.) □ *She wants to fix things right away. She is straining at the leash to get started.*

*strapped for sth *Fig.* needing something, usually money. (*Typically: **be** ~; **get** ~.) □ *I am really strapped for cash. Can you lend me some?*

a **straw man** *Fig.* a weak proposition posited only to be demolished by a simple countering argument. □ *So you can knock down your own straw man! Big deal. The question is how can you deal with real problems.*

the **straw that broke the camel's back** Go to the last straw.

a **streak of bad luck** AND a **string of bad luck** *Fig.* a series of events that are only bad luck. □ *After a long string of bad luck, we finally got a lucky break.*

a **streak of good luck** AND a **string of good luck** *Fig.* a series of fortunate events. □ *After a series of failures, we started out on a streak of good luck.*

a **streak of luck** Go to a lucky streak.

stretch a point AND **stretch the point** *Fig.* to interpret a point flexibly and with great latitude. □ *Would it be stretching a point to suggest that everyone is invited to your picnic?*

stretch one's **legs** *Fig. Lit.* to walk around, stretch, and loosen one's leg muscles af-

ter sitting down or lying down for a time. (This means, of course, to stretch or exercise only the muscles of the legs.) □ *After sitting in the car all day, the travelers decided to stretch their legs.*

stretch one's **money** AND **make** one's **money stretch** *Fig.* to economize so that one's money lasts longer. □ *We have to stretch our money in order to be able to buy groceries at the end of the month.*

stretch the point Go to stretch a point; next.

stretch the truth AND **stretch the point; stretch it** *Fig.* to exaggerate. □ *Sally tends to stretch the truth when telling tales about her wild teenage years.*

*stricken with sth afflicted or overwhelmed with something. (*Typically: **be** ~; **become** ~; **get** ~.) □ *Fred was stricken with remorse because of his rude remarks.* □ *Tom was stricken with the flu after his trip to Russia.*

strictly business 1. *Fig.* a matter or issue that is all business and no pleasure. □ *This meeting is strictly business. We don't have time for any leisure activity.* **2.** *Fig.* a person who is very businesslike and does not waste time with nonbusiness matters. □ *Joe is strictly business. I don't think he has a sense of humor. At least I have never seen it.*

strictly from hunger *Sl.* very mediocre; acceptable only when nothing else is available. □ *This kind of entertainment is strictly from hunger.*

(strictly) on the level *Fig.* honest; dependably open and fair. □ *How can I be sure you're on the level?* □ *You can trust Sally. She's strictly on the level.*

(strictly) on the up-and-up *Fig.* honest; fair and straight. □ *Do you think that the mayor is on the up-and-up?*

strictly speaking *Fig.* being very exact; technically or following rules or the law strictly. □ *Strictly speaking, you can't stop on a two-lane street where you might stop traffic.*

strike a balance (between two things**)** *Fig.* to find a satisfactory compromise between two extremes. □ *Jane is overdressed for the party and Sally is underdressed. What a pity they didn't strike a balance between them.*

strike a bargain AND **strike a deal** *Fig.* to reach an agreement on a price or negotiation (for something). □ *They argued for a while and finally struck a bargain.*

strike a blow against so/sth **1.** to physically strike someone, some creature, some part of a person, or something. □ *I struck a blow against his jaw, and he fell to the ground.* **2.** *Fig.* to take aggressive action against someone or something; to perform an act of opposition against someone or something. (Fig. on ①.) □ *Congratulations! Your speech really struck a blow against oppression and corruption!*

strike a blow for so/sth *Fig.* to perform an act in support of someone or something. □ *Congratulations! Your speech really struck a blow for freedom and free trade.*

strike a chord (with so**)** *Fig.* to cause someone to remember something; to remind someone of something; to be familiar. (Possibly alluding to a harmonic musical chord heard in the midst of otherwise chaotic sounds. Perhaps as one "strikes" a chord on a harp.) □ *The woman in the portrait struck a chord with me, and I realized that it was my grandmother.*

strike a deal Go to strike a bargain.

strike a happy medium AND **hit a happy medium; find a happy medium** *Fig.* to find a compromise position; to arrive at a position halfway between two unacceptable extremes. □ *Ann likes very spicy food, but Bob doesn't care for spicy food at all. We are trying to find a restaurant that strikes a happy medium.* □ *Tom is either very happy or very sad. He can't seem to hit a happy medium.*

strike a match *Fig.* to light a match by rubbing it on a rough surface. □ *When Sally struck a match to light a cigarette, Jane said quickly, "No smoking, please."*

strike a pose *Fig.* to position oneself in a certain posture. □ *Lisa walked into the room and struck a pose, hoping she would be noticed.*

strike a sour note AND **hit a sour note** *Fig.* to signify something unpleasant. □ *Jane's sad announcement struck a sour note at the annual banquet.* □ *News of the accident hit a sour note in our holiday celebration.*

strike so **as** sth **1.** *Fig.* [for a thought or behavior] to affect someone a certain way. □ *Mary's attitude struck me as childish.* **2.** *Fig.* [for a person] to impress someone as something or a particular type of person. □ *You don't strike me as the type of person to do something like that.*

strike sth **down**† *Fig.* [for a court] to invalidate a ruling or law. □ *The higher court struck the ruling of the lower court down.*

strike so's **fancy** AND **catch** so's **fancy; tickle** so's **fancy** *Fig.* to appeal to someone. □ *I'll have some ice cream, please. Chocolate strikes my fancy right now.*

strike so **funny** *Fig.* to seem funny to someone. □ *Sally has a great sense of humor. Everything she says strikes me funny.*

strike home with so [for something] to awaken recognition and acceptance in a person. (See also hit home.) □ *What you said really strikes home with me.*

strike it rich *Fig.* to acquire wealth suddenly. □ *Sally ordered a dozen oysters and found a huge pearl in one of them. She struck it rich!*

strike out 1. *Fig.* [for a baseball batter] to be declared out after making three strikes. □ *He struck out in the second inning, and the manager took him out then.* **2.** *Fig.* to fail. (Fig. on ①.) □ *I hear you struck out on that Acme proposal. Better luck next time.*

strike sth **out**† *Fig.* to cross something out of a section of printing or writing. □ *This is wrong. Please strike it out.*

strike out on one's **own** AND **set out on** one's **own** *Fig.* to start out to live, work, or travel by oneself. □ *I couldn't get along with my business partner, so I decided to strike out on my own.*

strike pay dirt Go to hit pay dirt.

strike the right note AND **hit the right note** *Fig.* to achieve the desired effect; to do something suitable or pleasing. (Alludes to singing or playing the correct musical note.) □ *Meg struck the right note when she wore a dark suit to the interview.* □ *The politician's speech failed to hit the right note with the crowd.*

strike up a conversation (with so**)** to begin a conversation with someone. (Fixed order.) □ *We tried to strike up a conversation—to no avail.*

strike up a friendship (with so**)** to establish a friendship with someone. (Fixed order.) □ *They struck up a friendship with each other quite easily.*

strike up the band 1. *Fig.* to cause a (dance) band to start playing. □ *Strike up the band, maestro, so we all can dance the night away.* **2.** *Fig.* to cause something to start.* □ *Strike up the band! Let's get moving or we'll be late.*

strike while the iron is hot AND **seize the day** *Fig.* to do something at the most opportune time; to do something when one has a good chance to do it. (The first entry head alludes to the best time for a blacksmith to hammer iron.) □ *She was in a good mood, so I asked her if I could have the day off. It's best to strike while the iron is hot.*

string so **along** *Fig.* to maintain someone's attention or interest, probably insincerely. □ *You are just stringing me along because you like to borrow my car. You are not a real friend.*

string along (with so**) 1.** *Fig.* to follow with someone. □ *Do you mind if I string along with you?* **2.** *Fig.* to agree with someone's policies and actions. □ *Okay. I will string along with you this time, but I don't know about the future.*

a **string of bad luck** Go to a streak of bad luck.

a **string of good luck** Go to a streak of good luck.

string sth **out**[†] *Fig.* to cause something to take more time than it ought to. □ *Is there*

any good reason to string this meeting out any longer?

string so **up**[†] *Fig.* to hang someone. □ *The sheriff swore he would string Tex up whenever he caught him.*

*****strings attached** *Fig.* having conditions or obligations associated. (*Typically: **with some** ~; **without any** ~; **with no** ~; **with a few** ~.) □ *My parents gave me use of their car without any strings attached.*

strip to sth *Fig.* to take off one's clothing down to a particular level, usually to one's skin, the waist, or some euphemistic way of expressing nudity or near nudity. □ *Tom stripped to the waist and continued to labor in the hot sun.*

stroke so's **ego** *Fig.* to flatter and praise someone. □ *If you have trouble with him, just take a few minutes and stroke his ego. You'll soon have him eating out of your hand.*

a **stroke of genius** *Fig.* an act of genius; a very clever and innovative idea or task. □ *Your idea of painting the rock wall red was a stroke of genius.*

a **stroke of good fortune** Go to next.

a **stroke of luck** AND a **stroke of good fortune** *Fig.* a bit of luck; a lucky happening. □ *I had a stroke of luck and found Tom at home when I called. He's not usually there.* □ *Unless I have a stroke of good fortune, I'm not going to finish this report by tomorrow.*

strong as a bull Go to next.

*****strong as a horse** AND *****strong as an ox; *****strong as a bull; *****strong as a lion** *Cliché* [of a living creature] very strong. (*Also: **as** ~.) □ *Jill: My car broke down; it's sitting out on the street. Jane: Get Linda to help you push it; she's as strong as a horse.* □ *The athlete was strong as an ox; he could lift his own weight with just one hand.*

strong as a lion Go to previous.

strong as an ox Go to strong as a horse.

the **strong, silent type** *Fig.* a strong, quiet man. □ *Clark looks like the strong, silent* *type. Actually he is slightly deaf and that's fat, not muscle.*

strong-arm tactics *Fig.* the use of force. □ *Strong-arm tactics are out. The boss says be gentle and don't hurt anybody.*

struggle to the death *Fig.* a serious problem with someone or something; a difficult challenge. □ *I had a terrible time getting my car started. It was a struggle to the death, but it finally started.*

strung out 1. extended in time; overly long. (See also **string** sth **out.**) □ *Why was that lecture so strung out? She talked and talked.* **2.** *Sl.* doped or drugged. □ *Bob acted very strangely—as if he were strung out or something.*

strut one's **stuff** *Sl.* to walk proudly and show off one's best features or talents. □ *Get out there on that stage and strut your stuff!*

stub sth **out**[†] *Fig.* to put out something, such as a cigarette or cigar, by crushing the burning end against a hard object. □ *Spike stubbed his cigar out and tossed it into the street.*

*stubborn as a mule AND ***obstinate as a mule** *Cliché* very stubborn. (*Also: **as** ~.) □ *I tried to convince Jake to go to the doctor, but he's as stubborn as a mule.*

*stuck on so/sth **1.** *Fig.* in love with someone or something; entranced with someone or something. (*Typically: **be** ~; **become** ~; **get** ~.) □ *Judy is really stuck on Jeff.* **2.** *Fig.* to be confused by something, such as a puzzle or a task. (Typically: **be** ~; **become** ~; **get** ~.) □ *I'm stuck on this question about the tax rates.*

stuck with so/sth burdened with someone or something; left having to care for or deal with someone or something. □ *Please don't leave me stuck with your aunt. She talks too much.*

Stuff a sock in it! AND **Put a sock in it!** *Inf.* Shut up! □ *I've heard enough. Stuff a sock in it!*

stuff and nonsense *Fig.* foolishness; foolish talk. □ *I don't understand this book. It's all stuff and nonsense as far as I am concerned.*

stuff sth **down** so's **throat** *Inf. Fig.* to force someone to hear, learn, endure, etc. some kind of information. □ *I don't like the nonsense they are stuffing down our throats.*

stuff one's **face** Go to **fill** one's **face.**

stuff so's **head with** sth *Fig.* to fill someone's brain with certain kinds of thoughts. □ *Tex thought that the government was stuffing peoples' heads with all sorts of propaganda.*

stuff the ballot box *Fig.* to fill a ballot box with illegal votes or with more votes than the number of actual voters. □ *The politician was charged with stuffing the ballot box.*

stumble across so/sth AND **stumble (up)on** so/sth; **stumble into** so/sth *Fig.* to find someone or something, usually by accident. □ *I stumbled across an interesting book yesterday when I was shopping.* □ *Guess who I stumbled into at the library yesterday?*

a **stumbling block** *Fig.* something that prevents or obstructs progress. □ *We'd like to buy that house, but the high price is a stumbling block.*

stump so *Fig.* to confuse or puzzle someone. □ *I have a question that will really stump you. When was the Achaean League established?*

stump for so to go about making political speeches in support of someone. □ *The vice president was out stumping for members of Congress who were running this term.*

sub for so/sth *Fig.* to substitute for someone or something. □ *I have to sub for Roger at work this weekend.*

subject to sth likely to have something, such as a physical disorder. □ *The sick man was subject to dizzy spells.*

subscribe to sth **1.** to agree with a policy. □ *I don't subscribe to the scheme you have just described.* **2.** to hold a standing order for a magazine or other periodical, or for a computer service. □ *I subscribe to three magazines, and I enjoy them all.*

succeed so **as** sth to take the place of someone as something; to supplant someone in something. □ *Jeff will succeed Claude as president of the organization.*

such as it is *Cliché* in the imperfect state that one sees it; in the less-than-perfect condition in which one sees it. □ *This is where I live. This is my glorious home—such as it is.*

suck so's **hind tit** *Sl.* to be forced to do someone's bidding no matter how unpleasant or impossible. (Fig. on the idea of the last of a litter of animals to get its mother's milk.) □ *She acts like everybody has to suck her hind tit to keep their jobs.*

suck so **in**† AND **take** so **in**† *Fig.* to deceive someone. □ *I think that someone sucked in both of them. I don't know why they bought this car.*

suck sth **in**† *Fig.* to draw in one's belly, gut, or stomach. □ *Suck that belly in!*

suck up to so *Sl.* to attempt to gain influence with or favor from someone. □ *Don't suck up to me. It won't do any good.*

a **sucker for** so/sth *Inf.* someone who is prejudiced in favor of someone or something. □ *I'm a sucker for a pretty face.*

a **sucker for punishment** *Fig.* someone who seems to do things frequently that result in punishment or being put at a disadvantage. □ *I don't know why I volunteered for this job. I'm a sucker for punishment I guess.*

sucker so **into** sth AND **sucker** so **in**† *Sl.* to deceive someone into some sort of scam or confidence game; to play someone for a fool. □ *Surely you don't think you can sucker me into doing something as stupid as that, do you?*

sucker list *Fig.* a list of potential dupes; a list of people who might be taken in by deception. □ *I'm sure on their sucker list. They are trying to get me to come to a seminar and receive a free clock or something.*

sue the pants off (of) so *Sl.* to sue someone for a lot of money. (*Of* is usually retained before pronouns.) □ *If they harm me in any way, I'll sue the pants off of them.*

suffer a setback *Fig.* to have a minor or temporary failure. □ *We suffered a setback when much of our vineyard was damaged by a fungus.*

suffer an attack (of an illness**)** Go to an attack (of an illness).

suffer the consequences AND **take the consequences; face the consequences** *Fig.* to experience and endure the (negative) consequences for one's acts. □ *You can do it if you want, but you'll have to suffer the consequences.*

*****suggestive of** sth reminiscent of something; suggesting something. (*Typically: **be** ~; **become** ~; **seem** ~.) □ *The new movie was suggestive of an old one I had seen on TV.*

suit one's **actions to** one's **words** *Fig.* to behave in accordance with what one has said; to do what one has promised or threatened to do. □ *Mr. Smith suited his actions to his words and punished the children.*

suit so's **fancy** *Fig.* to appeal to someone's imagination, fantasy, or preferences. □ *Does this handbag suit your fancy, or would you prefer something larger?*

suit so **to a T** AND **fit** so **to a T** *Fig.* to be very appropriate for someone. □ *This kind of job suits me to a T. □ This is Sally's kind of house. It fits her to a T.*

Suit yourself. *Inf.* You decide the way you want it.; Have it your way. □ *John (reading the menu): The steak sounds good, but it's hard to pass up the fried chicken. Sally: Suit yourself. I'll have the steak.*

*****suited for** sth appropriate for something. (*Typically: **be** ~; **become** ~.) □ *Do you think I am suited for this kind of work?*

Suits me (fine). Go to (It) suits me (fine).

sum and substance *Fig.* a summary; the gist. □ *In trying to explain the sum and substance of the essay, Thomas failed to mention the middle name of the hero.*

the **sun belt** *Fig.* the southern U.S. states, where it is generally warm and sunny. (Also capitalized.) □ *I want to retire to the sun belt.*

505

Sunday best AND **Sunday-go-to-meeting clothes** *Fig.* one's best clothing, which one would wear to church. □ *We are in our Sunday best, ready to go.* □ *John was all dressed up in his Sunday-go-to-meeting clothes.*

Sunday driver *Fig.* a slow and leisurely driver who appears to be sightseeing and enjoying the view, holding up traffic in the process. (Also a term of address.) □ *I'm a Sunday driver, and I'm sorry. I just can't bear to go faster.*

Sunday-go-to-meeting clothes Go to Sunday best.

sunny-side up *Fig.* [of eggs] with yolks facing up and not turned over or cooked through; straight up. □ *I'll have my eggs sunny-side up, with toast and coffee.*

one's **sunset years** *Euph.* one's old age. □ *Now is the time to think about financial planning for your sunset years.*

supposed to do sth expected or intended to do something; obliged or allowed to do something. (Has nothing to do with supposition, as one might otherwise suspect.) □ *Mom says you're supposed to come inside for dinner now.*

sure as eggs is eggs Go to sure as God made little green apples.

sure as fate Go to next.

*****sure as God made little green apples** AND *****sure as eggs is eggs**; *****sure as fate**; *****sure as I'm standing here**; *****sure as you live** *Fig.* absolutely certain. (*Also: **as** ~.) □ *I'm as sure as God made little green apples that he's the one.* □ *I'm right, as sure as you live!*

*****sure as hell** *Inf.* very sure. (*Also: **as** ~.) □ *As sure as hell, I'll be there on time.*

sure as I'm standing here Go to sure as God made little green apples.

Sure as shooting! *Inf.* Absolutely yes! (An elaboration of *Sure.*) □ *Bill: Are you going to be there Monday night? Bob: Sure as shooting!*

sure as you live Go to sure as God made little green apples.

a **sure bet** AND a **sure thing** *Fig.* a certainty; something that is sure to take place. □ *Of course, this land will become valuable in a few years. It's a sure thing!*

a **sure thing** Go to previous.

surf and turf *Fig.* fish and beef; lobster and beef. (A meal incorporating both expensive seafood and an expensive cut of beef. Refers to the sea and to the pasture. Fixed order.) □ *Walter ordered the surf and turf, but Alice ordered only a tiny salad.*

surf the Net *Fig.* to browse around in the contents of the Internet. □ *I spend an hour a day or more surfing the Net.*

the **survival of the fittest** *Fig.* the idea that the most able or fit will survive (while the less able and less fit will perish). (This is used literally as a principle of the process of evolution.) □ *In college, it's the survival of the fittest. You have to keep working in order to survive and graduate.*

susceptible to sth **1.** easily persuaded; easily influenced. □ *The students were susceptible to the allure of drugs.* **2.** likely to contract a sickness; likely to become sick. □ *Infants and the elderly are more susceptible to illness than other people.*

a **suspicious character** Go to a shady character.

swallow sth **hook, line, and sinker** AND **fall for** sth **hook, line, and sinker** *Fig.* to believe something completely. (These terms refer to fishing and fooling a fish into being caught.) □ *I made up a story about why I was so late. The boss swallowed it hook, line, and sinker.*

swallow one's **pride** *Fig.* to forget one's pride and accept something humiliating. □ *When you're trying to master a new skill, you find yourself swallowing your pride quite often.*

swallow so/sth **up**[†] *Fig.* to engulf or contain someone or something. □ *The huge sweater swallowed up the tiny child.*

swan song *Fig.* the last work or performance of a playwright, musician, actor, etc. before death or retirement. □ *We*

surf the Net

didn't know that her performance last night was the singer's swan song.

swap notes (on so/sth**)** *Fig.* to share information on someone or something. □ *The two girls sat around swapping notes on guys they knew.*

sway so **to** sth to convince someone to do something. □ *I think I can sway her to join our side.*

swear by so/sth *Fig.* to announce one's full faith and trust in someone or something. □ *I would swear by Roger anytime. He is a great guy, and he tells the truth.*

swear like a trooper *Inf.* to curse and swear with great facility. (The *trooper* here refers to a soldier.) □ *The clerk started swearing like a trooper, and the customer started crying.*

swear (sth**) off**† *Fig.* to pledge to avoid or abstain from something. □ *No dessert for me. I've sworn off.*

swear on a stack of Bibles AND **swear on** one's **mother's grave; swear up and**

down to state something very earnestly, pledging to tell the truth. (The *stack of Bibles* refers in an exaggerated way to swearing to tell the truth in court by placing one's hand on a Bible. Multiple Bibles implies the truest of truth.) □ *I swear on a stack of Bibles that I am telling the truth.* □ *Of course, I'm telling the truth. I swear on my mother's grave!*

swear on one's **mother's grave** Go to previous.

sweat blood AND **sweat bullets** *Inf.* to be very anxious and tense. □ *What a terrible test! I was really sweating blood at the last.* □ *Bob is such a bad driver. I sweat bullets every time I ride with him.*

sweat bullets Go to previous.

sweat for sth *Fig.* to work very hard for something. □ *I sweat for every dollar I bring in.*

sweat weight **off**† *Fig.* to get rid of excess fat or weight by exercising or taking a steam bath to produce sweat. □ *I think I can sweat a lot of this fat off.*

sweat sth **out**† **1.** *Fig.* to endure something unpleasant. □ *It was an ordeal, but I sweated it out.* **2.** *Fig.* to endure suspense about something. □ *She sweated the two-hour wait out until she heard the results of her bar exams.* **3.** Go to **sweat** sth **out of** so.

sweat sth **out of** so AND **sweat** sth **out**† *Fig.* to force someone to reveal information under pressure. (The stress associated with extreme and intense questioning leads to anxiety that produces sweating.) □ *The cops couldn't sweat the information out of Spike.*

sweep so **away** Go to **sweep** one **off** one's feet.

sweep so **into** sth AND **sweep** so **in**† to place someone into an elective position decisively. □ *The decisive victory swept all the candidates of the reform party into office.*

sweep one **off** one's **feet** AND **knock** one **off** one's **feet; sweep** so **away** *Fig.* to overwhelm someone, particularly in matters of romance. (See also **whirlwind courtship.**) □ *Mary is madly in love with Bill. He swept her off her feet.* □ *The news was so exciting that it knocked me off my feet.*

sweep out of some place to exit from some place quickly with style or grace. □ *She swept out of her dressing room and walked on stage just as her cue was uttered.*

sweep sth **under the carpet** AND **sweep** sth **under the rug** *Fig.* to hide or ignore something. □ *You made a mistake that you can't sweep under the carpet.*

sweep sth **under the rug** Go to previous.

sweet and sour *Fig.* a combination of fruity sweet and sour, but not necessarily salty, flavors. (Typically referring to certain Chinese-American foods.) □ *Alice does not care for sweet and sour dishes, but she will usually eat whatever we serve her.*

*sweet as honey AND **sweeter than honey; *sweet as sugar** very sweet; charming. (*Also: **as** ~.) □ *Larry's words were sweeter than honey as he tried to convince Alice to forgive him.* □ *Jill: Is Mary*

Ann nice? Jane: Yes, indeed. She's as sweet as honey.

*sweet as sugar Go to previous.

sweet nothings *Fig.* affectionate but unimportant or meaningless words spoken to a loved one. □ *Jack was whispering sweet nothings in Joan's ear when they were dancing.*

*sweet on so fond of someone. (*Typically: **be** ~; **become** ~.) □ *Tom is sweet on Mary. He may ask her to marry him.*

sweeten the pot *Fig.* to increase the amount of money bet in a card game with hopes of encouraging other players to bet more enthusiastically. □ *John sweetened the pot hoping others would follow.*

sweeten (up) the deal *Fig.* to make a bargain or a business transaction more appealing by adding value to the transaction. □ *The dealer sweetened the deal by throwing in free car washes.* □ *He wasn't willing to do anything to sweeten the deal, so I left.*

sweeter than honey Go to **sweet as honey.**

sweetheart agreement AND **sweetheart deal** *Fig.* a private agreement reached between a public agency or government official and a private company that includes illicit payments or special favors. □ *They found that the mayor was involved in a number of sweetheart agreements.*

sweetheart deal Go to previous.

sweet-talk so *Rur.* to talk convincingly to someone with much flattery. □ *He sweet-talked her for a while, and she finally agreed to go to the dance with him.*

swell with sth *Fig.* to seem to swell with a feeling such as pride. □ *His chest swelled with pride at the thought of his good performance.*

*a swelled head AND ***a big head** *Fig.* a state of being conceited. (*Typically: **get** ~; **have** ~; **give** so ~.) □ *John got a swelled head after he won the prize.* □ *Don't get a big head from all this success.*

swift and sure *Fig.* fast and certain. (As with the flight of a well-aimed arrow.)

□ *The response of the governor to the criticism by the opposing party was swift and sure.*

*swift as an arrow AND ***swift as the wind; *swift as thought** very fast. (*Also: **as** ~.) □ *The new intercity train is swift as an arrow.*

swift as lightning Go to quick as a wink.

swift as the wind Go to swift as an arrow.

swift as thought Go to swift as an arrow.

swim against the current Go to next.

swim against the tide AND **swim against the current** *Fig.* to do something that is in opposition to the general movement of things. □ *Why can't you cooperate? Do you always have to swim against the tide?*

swimming in sth *Fig.* to experience an overabundance of something. □ *We are just swimming in orders right now. Business is good.*

swing sth *Fig.* to make something happen. □ *I hope I can swing a deal that will make us all a lot of money.*

swing by Go to drop over.

swing into high gear *Inf.* to begin operating at a fast pace; to increase the rate of activity. □ *The chef swings into high gear around six o'clock in preparation for the theater crowd.*

switch gears Go to shift gears.

switch off *Fig.* [for someone] to stop paying attention; to become oblivious to everything. □ *I got tired of listening and switched off.*

switch on *Sl.* [for someone] to become alert or excited. □ *The wild music made all the kids switch on and start to dance.*

switched on 1. *Sl.* alert and up-to-date; with it. □ *My brother is switched on and has lots of friends.* **2.** *Sl.* excited. □ *I get switched on by that kind of music.*

T

tab so **for** sth *Inf.* to choose someone for something. □ *The director tabbed Sam for a walk-on part.*

table a motion *Fig.* to postpone the discussion of something during a meeting. □ *The motion for a new policy was tabled until the next meeting.*

tack sth **onto** sth AND **tack** sth **on**† to add something onto something. □ *The waiter kept tacking charges onto my bill.*

tag so **out**† *Fig.* [in baseball] to touch with the ball and thereby put someone out. □ *The shortstop tagged the runner out and retired the side.*

tail off to dwindle to nothing. □ *The number of people filing for unemployment insurance is beginning to tail off.* □ *As the storms tailed off, we began to realize how much damage had been done.*

the **tail wagging the dog** a situation where a small part is controlling the whole of something. □ *John was just hired yesterday, and today he's bossing everyone around. It's a case of the tail wagging the dog.*

take sth *Fig.* to endure something; to survive something. □ *I don't think I can take any more scolding today. I've been in trouble since I got up this morning.*

take a backseat (to so/sth**)** *Fig.* to become less important than someone or something else. □ *My homework had to take a backseat to football during the play-offs.*

take a bath (on sth**)** *Sl.* to accumulate large losses on a business transaction or an investment. (Refers to *getting soaked* = being heavily charged for something.) □ *Sally took a bath on that stock that she bought. Its price went down to nothing.*

take a beating *Fig.* to be defeated. □ *Our team really took a beating in the game last weekend.*

take a bite out of sth *Fig.* to take or use a part of something. □ *Taxes take quite a bite out of my paycheck.*

take a bow *Fig.* to bow and acknowledge credit for a good performance. □ *The audience applauded wildly and demanded that the conductor come out and take a bow again.*

take a break AND **take** one's **break** *Fig.* to have a short rest period in one's work. □ *It's ten o'clock—time to take a break.*

take a chance on so/sth to gamble that something good might happen or that someone might do well; to take a risk that something would go wrong or that someone would do badly. □ *I just couldn't take a chance on Walter, so I picked David.*

Take a deep breath. *Fig. Lit.* Take a breath and relax instead of getting stressed or angry. □ *A: I am so mad, I could scream. B: Now, take a deep breath and just relax.*

take a dig at so AND **take a jab at** so; **take digs at** so *Fig.* to insult or pester someone. □ *You're always taking digs at people who think they're your friends.* □ *Jane is always taking digs at Bob, but she never really means any harm.*

take a dim view of so/sth *Fig.* to disapprove of someone or something. □ *Of all the boys, the teacher likes Dave the least. She takes a dim view of him.*

take a dive Go to take a fall.

take a drag (on sth**)** Go to a drag (on sth).

take a fall AND **take a dive** to fake being knocked out in a boxing match. (See also take the fall.) □ *The boxer took a dive in the second round and made everyone suspicious.*

take a fancy to so/sth AND **take a liking to** so/sth; **take a shine to** so/sth *Fig.* to develop a fondness or a preference for someone or something. □ *John began to take a fancy to Sally late last August at the picnic.* □ *I've never taken a liking to cooked carrots.*

take a firm grip on so/sth *Fig.* to gain control of someone or something. □ *You will have to take a firm grip on Andrew. He has a mind of his own.*

take a (firm) stand on sth *Fig.* to express and maintain a strong opinion of something. □ *I hope you take a firm stand on the need for more office security.*

take a gander (at so/sth) *Fig.* to look at someone or something. □ *I wanted to take a gander at the new computer before they started using it.*

take a hand in sth *Fig.* to help with something; to participate in something. □ *Ted refused to take a hand in the preparations for the evening meal.*

take a hard line (with so) *Fig.* to be firm with someone; to have a firm policy for dealing with someone. □ *The manager takes a hard line with people who show up late.*

take a hike AND **take a walk** *Inf.* to leave; to beat it. □ *I had enough of the boss and the whole place, so I cleaned out my desk and took a walk.*

take a hint AND **take the hint** *Fig.* to understand a hint and behave accordingly. □ *I said I didn't want to see you anymore. Can't you take a hint? I don't like you.*

take a jab at so Go to take a dig at so.

take a leaf out of so's **book** AND **take a page out of** so's **book; take a leaf from** so's **book; take a page from** so's **book** *Fig.* to behave or to do something in the way that someone else would. □ *You had better do it your way. Don't take a leaf out of my book. I don't do it well.*

take a leak *Inf.* to urinate. (Usually in reference to a male.) □ *I gotta go take a leak. Back in a minute.*

take a liking to so/sth Go to take a fancy to so/sth.

take a load off one's **feet** Go to a load off one's feet.

take a load off (of) so's **mind** AND **take a lot off (of)** so's **mind** *Fig.* to relieve one's mind of a problem or a worry. (*Of* is usually retained before pronouns.) □ *I'm glad to hear that. It sure takes a load off of my mind.*

take a long hard look at so/sth **1.** *Fig.* to look at someone or something very carefully. □ *I took a long hard look at the kitchen and decided we needed to redo it.* **2.** *Fig.* to think about and study someone or something very thoroughly. □ *I took a long hard look at my life and decided that I was really a fine person.*

Take a long walk off a short pier. AND **Go play in the traffic.** *Inf.* Get out of here!; Go do something that will get you permanently out of here! □ *Get out of here! Take a long walk off a short pier!*

take a lot off (of) so's **mind** Go to take a load off (of) so's mind.

take a lot out of so AND **take a lot from** so *Fig.* to drain a lot of energy from someone. □ *This kind of workout takes a lot out of the team.*

take a nosedive Go to go into a nosedive.

take a page from so's **book** Go to take a leaf out of so's book.

take a pass (on sth) Go to pass on sth.

take a poke at so Go to next.

take a pop at so AND **take a poke at** so *Inf.* to punch at someone. □ *The drunk took a poke at the cop—which was the wrong thing to do.*

take a potshot at so/sth **1.** *Fig.* to shoot at someone or something, as with a shotgun. (A *potshot* refers to the type of shooting done to provide meat for the cooking pot.) □ *The hunters were taking potshots at each other in the woods.* **2.** *Fig.* to criticize or censure someone or something, often just to be mean. (Fig. on ①.) □ *Everyone in the audience was taking potshots at the comedian's toupee.*

take a powder *Sl.* to leave; to leave town. (Underworld.) □ *Willie took a powder and will lie low for a while.*

Take a running jump (in the lake)! *Sl.* Go away!; Get away from me! □ *You can just take a running jump in the lake, you creep!*

take a shine to so/sth Go to take a fancy to so/sth.

take a spill *Fig.* to have a fall; to tip over. (Also with *bad, nasty, quite,* etc. Also with *have.*) □ *John had quite a spill when he fell off his bicycle.*

take a stand (against so/sth) AND **make a stand (against so/sth); stand up to** so/sth *Fig.* to take a position in opposition to someone or something; to oppose or resist someone or something. □ *The treasurer was forced to take a stand against the board because of its wasteful spending.*

take a step in the right direction Go to in the right direction.

take a turn for the better *Fig.* to start to improve; to start to get well. □ *Things are taking a turn for the better at my store. I may make a profit this year.*

take a turn for the worse *Fig.* to start to get worse. □ *It appeared that she was going to get well; then, unfortunately, she took a turn for the worse.*

take a walk Go to take a hike.

take a whiff of sth Go to a whiff of sth.

take account of sth to consider something; to include something in one's thinking. □ *Please do not fail to take account of the amount of time you will have to spend repainting the room.*

take action (against so/sth) to act against someone or something; to bring someone or something to the attention of the authorities. □ *The police took action against the ring of thieves.*

take advantage of so **1.** *Fig.* to deceive someone. □ *Please don't take advantage of me the way you took advantage of Carl.* **2.** *Fig.* to impose on someone. □ *I am*

glad to have your help. I hope I am not taking advantage of you.

take advantage of so/sth to utilize someone or something to the fullest extent. □ *Please take advantage of the consultant while she is here in the office.*

take after so *Fig.* to resemble a close, older relative. □ *Don't you think that Sally takes after her mother?*

take aim at so/sth *Fig.* to prepare to deal with someone or something; to focus on someone or something. □ *The critics took aim at the star of the musical and tore her to pieces.*

take sth **amiss** AND **take** sth **the wrong way** *Fig.* to understand something as wrong or insulting. □ *Would you take it amiss if I told you I thought you look lovely?*

take an interest in so/sth *Fig.* to become concerned or interested in someone or something. □ *You should take an interest in everything your child does.*

take an oath *Fig.* to make an oath; to swear to something. □ *You must take an oath that you will never tell anyone about this.*

take so **apart**† **1.** *Inf.* to beat someone up. □ *Don't talk to me that way, or I'll take you apart.* **2.** *Inf.* to criticize or defame someone or something. □ *They really took me apart, but I just ignore bad reviews.*

take sth **apart**† **1.** *Fig.* to damage or ruin something. □ *The wreck took both cars apart.* **2.** *Fig.* to criticize something severely. □ *The critic took the play apart and caused it to close.*

take sth **as Gospel** Go to as Gospel.

take so **aside** Go to take so to one side.

take so/sth **at face value** *Fig.* to accept someone or something just as it appears; to believe that the way things appear is the way they really are. □ *He means what he says. You have to take him at face value.* □ *I don't know whether I can take her story at face value, but I will assume that she is not lying.*

take one **at** one's **word** *Fig.* to believe what someone says and act accordingly. □ *She told me to go jump in the lake, and I took her at her word.* □ *You shouldn't take her at her word. She frequently says things she doesn't really mean.*

take attendance *Fig.* to make a record of persons attending something. □ *The teacher took attendance before starting the class.*

take away from so/sth to lessen the value or esteem of someone or something; to detract from someone or something. □ *The huge orange spot in the center of the painting takes away from the intense green of the rest of the work.*

take sth **away**† **(from** so/sth**)** to detract from someone or something. □ *The bright costume on the soprano takes a lot away from the tenor, who is just as important.*

take sth **back**† to retract a statement; to rescind one's remark. □ *You had better take back what you said about my sister.*

take one **back ((to)** some time**)** *Fig.* to cause one to think of a time in the past. □ *Your pictures take me back a few years.* □ *This takes me back to the time I spent the summer in Paris.*

take one's **belt in**† **(a notch)** AND **pull** one's **belt in**† **(a notch)** *Fig.* to reduce expenditures; to live or operate a business more economically. (As if one were going to have to eat less.) □ *They had to take their belts in a notch budgetwise.*

take so's **blood pressure** *Fig.* to measure a person's blood pressure. □ *The doctor takes my blood pressure every time I am in the office.*

take so's **breath away** *Fig.* to overwhelm someone with beauty or grandeur; to surprise or astound someone. □ *The magnificent painting took my breath away.*

take so/sth **by storm 1.** *Fig.* to conquer someone or something in a fury. □ *The army took city after city by storm.* **2.** *Fig.* to succeed overwhelmingly with someone, some place, or a group. □ *The singing star took the audience in each town by storm.*

take so **by surprise** AND **catch** so **by surprise** *Fig.* to startle someone; to surprise someone with something unexpected. □ *Oh! You took me by surprise because I didn't hear you come in.*

take so/sth **by surprise** *Fig.* to startle or surprise someone or something. □ *She bolted into the room and took them by surprise.*

take care of so **1.** *Fig.* to tip someone. □ *Did you remember to take care of the waiter?* **2.** *Inf.* to kill or dispose of someone. □ *Spike said he was going to take care of Lefty once and for all.*

take care of number one AND **take care of numero uno** *Inf.* to take care of oneself. □ *Mike, like everybody else, is most concerned with taking care of number one.*

take care of some loose ends Go to some loose ends.

Take care (of yourself). Good-bye. □ *See you next week. Take care.*

take center stage *Fig.* [for someone or something] to manage to become the central attraction. □ *The new arthritis drug took center stage at the medical convention.*

take charge (of so/sth**)** Go to charge (of so/sth).

take cold Go to catch cold.

take cover *Fig.* to seek shelter from gunfire or other projectiles. □ *As soon as the firing started, we took cover behind a huge boulder.*

take one's **cue from** so to use someone else's behavior or reactions as a guide to one's own. (From the theatrical cue = a signal to speak, enter, exit, etc.) □ *If you don't know which spoons to use at the dinner, just take your cue from John.*

take sth **down**† **1.** to take some large or complicated things apart. □ *They plan to take all these buildings down and turn the land into a park.* **2.** to write something down in something. □ *Please take these figures down in your notebook.*

take so **down a notch (or two)** Go to next.

take care of number one

take so **down a peg (or two)** AND **take** so **down a notch (or two); knock** so **down a peg (or two); bring** so **down a peg (or two); knock** so **down a notch (or two)** *Fig.* to reprimand someone who is acting too arrogant. □ *He was so rude that someone was bound to knock him down a peg or two.*

take effect Go to go into effect.

take exception (to sth**) 1.** *Fig.* to take offense at something. □ *Sue took exception to Fred's characterization of Bill as a cheapskate.* **2.** *Fig.* to disagree with something. □ *The manager took exception to the statement about having only three employees.*

take five *Sl.* to take a five-minute rest period; to take a short break. □ *Hey, Bob. I'm tired. Can we take five?*

take an amount of money **for** sth *Fig.* to charge a certain amount for something. □ *How much will you take for a big bag of flour?*

take so **for** sth *Inf.* to cheat someone by a certain amount of money. □ *That crook took me for a hundred bucks.*

take so **for a fool** Go to take so for an idiot.

take so **for a ride 1.** *Fig.* to deceive someone. □ *You really took those people for a ride. They really believed you.* **2.** *Fig.* to take away and murder a person. (Underworld.) □ *Mr. Big told Mike to take Fred for a ride.*

take so **for an idiot** AND **take** so **for a fool** *Fig.* to assume that someone is stupid. □ *I wouldn't do anything like that! Do you take me for an idiot?*

take so **for dead** *Fig.* to assume that someone who is still alive is dead. □ *When we found her, we took her for dead, but the paramedics were able to revive her.*

take so/sth **for granted** *Fig.* to expect someone or something to be always available to serve in some way without thanks or recognition; to value someone or something too lightly. □ *I guess that I take a lot of things for granted.*

take forty winks Go to catch forty winks.

take sth **from** so *Fig.* to endure abuse from someone. (Often in the negative.) □ *Stop! I cannot take any more from you!*

take one's **gloves off**† AND **take the gloves off**† *Fig.* to stop being calm or civil and show an intention of winning a dispute by any means. (As if boxers were to remove their gloves in order to inflict more damage.) □ *Both of them took their gloves off and really began arguing.*

take (great) pains (to do sth**)** AND **be at (great) pains (to** do sth**); go to (great) pains (to** do sth**)** *Fig.* to make a great effort to do something. □ *Tom took pains to decorate the room exactly right.*

take one's **hat off**† **to** so *Fig.* to salute or pay an honor to someone. □ *Good work. I take my hat off to you.*

take so's **head off** *Inf.* to scold or berate someone severely. □ *There is no need to take his head off about such a simple matter.*

take heart (from sth**)** *Fig.* to receive courage or comfort from some fact. □ *Even though you did not win the race, take heart from the fact that you did your best.*

take heed (of so/sth**)** *Fig.* to be cautious with someone or something; to pay attention to someone or something. □ *We will have to take heed of Wendy and see what she will do next.*

take hold Go to take root.

take sth **home (with** oneself**)** *Fig.* to take a thought, idea, or concept away [to one's home] from a meeting or conference. □ *Take this idea home with you—diversify your investments.*

take so **hostage** *Fig.* to kidnap or seize someone to be a hostage. □ *The terrorists planned to take the ambassador hostage.*

take ill Go to take sick.

take so **in**† Go to suck so in†.

take sth **in**† **1.** *Fig.* to reduce the size of a garment. □ *This is too big. I'll have to take it in around the waist.* **2.** *Fig.* to view and study something; to attend something involving viewing. □ *Would you like to take in a movie?* **3.** *Fig.* to receive money as payment or proceeds. □ *How much did we take in today?* **4.** *Fig.* to receive something into the mind, usually visually. □ *Could you take those explanations in? I couldn't.* **5.** *Fig.* to inhale, drink, or eat something. □ *I think I'll go for a walk and take some fresh air in.*

take so **in hand** *Fig.* to take control of someone; to assume the responsibility of guiding someone. □ *Someone is going to have to take Tim in hand and help him out.*

take sth **in (**one's**) stride** *Fig.* to accept advances or setbacks as the normal course of events. □ *She faced a serious problem, but she was able to take it in her stride.*

take so/sth **into account** AND **take into account** so/sth *Fig.* to remember to consider someone or something. □ *I hope you'll take Bill and Bob into account when you plan the party.*

take sth **into account** AND **take** sth **into consideration** *Fig.* to consider something to be an important factor in some decision. □ *We will take your long years of service into account when we make our final decision.*

take so **into** one's **confidence** *Fig.* to trust someone with confidential information; to tell a secret to someone and trust the person to keep the secret. □ *We are good friends, but I didn't feel I could take her into my confidence.*

take sth **into consideration** Go to take sth into account.

take a task **into** one's **hands** *Fig.* to assume the completion of a task. □ *You have so messed this up! I'm going to have to take this into my own hands and do it right!*

take sth **into** one's **head** *Fig.* to get an obsession or overpowering idea into one's thinking. □ *George took this strange idea into his head about fixing the car himself.*

take so/animal **into** one's **heart** *Fig.* to grow to love and trust someone or an animal; to receive a newcomer graciously and lovingly. □ *He was such a cute little boy. We took him into our hearts immediately.*

take inventory *Fig.* to make an inventory list of goods for sale. □ *They are taking inventory in the warehouse, counting each item and writing the number on a list.*

take issue with so *Fig.* to argue with someone. □ *I heard your last statement, and I have to take issue with you.*

take issue with sth *Fig.* to disagree with or argue about something. □ *I want to take issue with the last statement you made.*

take it *Fig.* to endure something, physically or mentally. (Often negative.) □ *I just can't take it anymore.*

take it as it comes Go to go with the flow.

Take it away! *Inf.* Start up the performance!; Let the show begin! (Typically a public announcement of the beginning of a musical performance.) □ *And now, here is the band playing "Song of Songs." Take it away!*

Take it easy. 1. *Inf.* Good-bye and be careful. □ *Mary: Bye-bye. Bill: See you, Mary. Take it easy.* **2.** *Inf.* Be gentle.; Treat someone carefully. □ *Sue: Then I want you to move the piano and turn all the mattresses. Andy: Come on. Take it easy! I'm not made of steel, you know.* **3.** *Inf.* Calm down.; Relax.; Do not get excited. □ *Mary could see that Sally was very upset at the news. "Now, just take it easy," said Mary. "It can't be all that bad."*

take it easy on so/sth/animal *Fig.* to be gentle on someone, something, or an animal. (See also Take it easy.) □ *Please take it easy on the furniture. It has to last us many years.*

take it easy on sth *Fig.* to use less of something (rather than more). □ *Take it easy on the soup. There's just enough for one serving for each person.*

take it from me *Inf.* believe me. □ *Take it from me, this is a very good day for this part of the country.*

take it from the top *Fig.* to begin [again] at the beginning, especially the beginning of a piece of music. (Originally in reference to the top of a sheet of music.) □ *The conductor stopped the band and had the players take it from the top again.*

take it into one's **head to** do sth *Fig.* to decide to do something. □ *For some reason, she took it into her head to go into the city for the day. She told no one she was going there.*

take it like a man *Fig.* [for a male] to suffer misfortune stoically. □ *She said some really cutting things to him, but he took it like a man.*

take it on the chin AND **take it on the nose 1.** *Inf.* to stand up to something adverse, such as criticism. (Fig. on taking a direct punch to the head in boxing.) □ *They laid some blunt criticism on him, but he took it on the chin.* **2.** *Inf.* to receive the full brunt of something. □ *Why do I have to take it on the chin for something I didn't do?*

take it on the lam *Sl.* to get out of town; to run away. (Underworld.) □ *Both crooks took it on the lam when things got hot.*

take it on the nose Go to take it on the chin.

Take it or leave it. *Inf.* Take this one or none; you have no choice. □ *That's my final offer. Take it or leave it.* □ *Bill: Aw, I want eggs for breakfast, Mom. Mother: There's only cornflakes left. Take it or leave it.*

take it out on so/sth *Fig.* to punish or harm someone or something because one is angry or disturbed about something. □ *I'm sorry about your difficulty, but don't take it out on me.*

take it slow *Fig.* to go slowly and carefully. □ *Just relax and take it slow. You've got a good chance.*

take it that . . . *Fig.* to understand it to be thus. . . . □ *Am I to take it that you think this is the end of our relationship?*

take it to one's **grave** to carry a secret with one until one dies. □ *I will never tell anyone. I'll take your secret to my grave.*

take it to the street *Sl.* to tell everyone about your problems. □ *If there's something bothering her, she's gonna take it to the street, first thing.*

take it upon oneself **to** do sth Go to make it one's business to do sth.

take it with one *Fig.* to take possessions with you when you die. (Usually negative.) □ *Spend a little on yourself. You can't take it with you, you know.*

take its course *Fig.* to continue along its way; [for a disease] to progress the way it normally progresses until it is cured naturally. □ *There is really no good medicine for this. This disease simply has to take its course.*

take kindly to sth AND **take well to** sth *Fig.* to be agreeable to something. (Often negative.) □ *My father doesn't take kindly to anyone using his tools.*

take (one's) leave (of so) *Fig.* to say goodbye to someone and leave. □ *I took leave of the hostess at an early hour.*

take leave of so/sth *Fig.* to go away from someone or something. □ *It saddened me to take leave of the city I grew up in.*

take leave of one's **senses** *Fig.* to become irrational. (Often verbatim with *one's.*) □ *What are you doing? Have you taken leave of your senses?* □ *What a terrible situation! It's enough to make one take leave of one's senses.*

take liberties with so/sth AND **make free with** so/sth *Fig.* to freely use or abuse someone or something. (The first entry head is used euphemistically for sexual imposition, and that sense often comes to mind first.) □ *You are overly familiar with me, Mr. Jones. One might think you were taking liberties with me.* □ *I don't like it when you make free with my lawn mower. You should at least ask when you want to borrow it.*

take so's **life** *Fig.* to kill someone. (Can include oneself.) □ *It's the executioner's job to take people's lives.*

take one's **life into** one's **(own) hands** *Fig.* to risk one's life; to do something that puts one's life at risk. □ *If you choose to swim in that rushing river, you are taking your life into your hands.*

take one's **lumps** *Inf.* to accept the result or punishment one deserves. (See also get one's lumps.) □ *You've got to learn to take your lumps if you're going to be in politics.*

take sth **lying down** *Fig.* to endure something unpleasant without fighting back. □ *He insulted me publicly. You don't expect me to take that lying down, do you?*

take one's **medicine** *Fig.* to accept the consequences or the bad fortune that one deserves. (Fig. on the image of having to take unpleasant-tasting medicine.) □ *Billy knew he was going to get spanked, and he didn't want to take his medicine.*

Take my word for it. *Fig.* Believe me.; Trust me! I am telling you the truth. □ *Take my word for it. These are the best power tools you can buy.*

take no offense *Fig.* not to be or act offended at a deed or something that was said. □ *I am glad that you took no offense at my little error.*

take no prisoners *Fig.* to be extremely ruthless with the opposition. □ *The new manager takes no prisoners. He is ruthless and stern.*

take no stock in sth AND **not take stock in** sth; **not put (a lot) of stock in** sth *Fig.* to pay no attention to someone; not to believe or accept something. □ *He doesn't take stock in your opinions either.*

take note of so/sth *Fig.* to notice someone or something; to commit something about someone or something to one's memory, possibly by making a note on paper. □ *I took note of her when she came in. I thought she had left the company.*

take notice of so/sth *Fig.* to notice the presence or existence of someone or something. □ *I took notice of the amount of the bill.*

take off 1. *Inf.* [for someone] to leave in a hurry. □ *She really took off from there quickly.* **2.** *Inf.* [for something] to start selling well. □ *Ticket sales really took off after the first performance.* **3.** *Inf.* to become active and exciting. □ *Did the party ever take off, or was it dull all night?*

take so/sth **off**† *Sl.* to rob someone or something. (Underworld.) □ *Weren't you in that bunch that took the bank off in Philly?*

take oneself **off** some place to go away to some place more private. □ *She kept her sanity by taking herself off to her bedroom for a few hours each day.*

take off (after so/sth**)** AND **take out (after** so/sth**)** *Fig.* to begin to chase someone or something. □ *The bank guard took off after the robber.* □ *It took out after the bank robber's car.*

take off (for some place**)** *Fig.* to leave for some place. □ *The girls took off for home when they heard the dinner bell.*

take off from work AND **take ((some) time) off from work; take off (from work)** *Fig.* not to appear at one's place of work for a period of time, hours or days. (Often used of an excused or planned absence.) □ *I will have to take off from work to go to the doctor.* □ *I want to take some time off from work and paint the house.*

take so/sth **off** so's **hands** *Fig.* to relieve someone of the burden or bother of someone or something. □ *I would be happy to take your uncle off your hands for a few hours.*

take off (on sth**)** *Fig.* to start out speaking on something; to begin a discussion of something. □ *My father took off on the subject of taxes and talked for an hour.*

take offense at sth *Fig.* to be or act offended at a deed or something that was said. □ *I'm sorry you took offense at what I said. I meant no harm.*

take office *Fig.* to begin serving as an elected or appointed official. □ *All the elected officials took office just after the election.*

take so **on**† **1.** *Fig.* to enter into a fight or argument with someone. □ *I pretended to agree because I really didn't want to take him on.* **2.** *Fig.* to employ someone. □ *I*

think we could take you on as an assistant editor, but it doesn't pay very well.*

take so/sth **on**† *Fig.* to accept the task of handling a difficult person or thing. □ *I'll take it on if nobody else will do it.*

take on a life of its own Go to a life of its own.

take on a new meaning Go to next.

take on a new significance AND **take on a new meaning** *Fig.* [for an event] to acquire a new interpretation; [for something] to become more meaningful or more significant. □ *All these monuments take on a new meaning when you realize the amount of human artistry and skill it took to design and build them.*

take sth **on faith** *Fig.* to accept or believe something on the basis of little or no evidence. □ *Please try to believe what I'm telling you. Just take it on faith.*

take on (so) *Fig.* to behave very emotionally. (Usually negative.) □ *Stop crying. Please don't take on so.*

take sth **on the chin 1.** *Fig.* to absorb a blow on the chin. □ *The boxer tried to duck, but took the blow on the chin.* **2.** *Fig.* to experience and endure bad news or other trouble. (Fig. on ①.) □ *The worst luck comes my way, and I always end up taking it on the chin.*

take sth **on trust** *Fig.* to accept that something is true through trust. □ *You will have to take it on trust because I can't prove it.*

take so **out**† **1.** *Fig.* to date someone. □ *I hope he'll take me out soon.* **2.** AND **take** so **down**† *Sl.* to destroy someone; to kill someone. (Underworld.) □ *Mr. Gutman told Lefty to take Spike out.*

take sth **out**† AND **knock** sth **out**† *Inf.* to bomb or destroy something. □ *The enemy took out one of the trucks, but not the one carrying the medicine.*

take out a loan *Fig.* to get a loan of money, especially from a bank. □ *Mary took out a loan to buy a car.*

take sth **out in trade** *Fig.* to accept someone's goods or services in payment of a bill. □ *The grocer told the plumber that he would pay the plumber by allowing him to take his bill out in trade.*

take sth **out of context** Go to out of context.

take sth **out of** so's **hands** Go to out of so's hands.

take sth **out**† **on** so/sth *Fig.* to punish someone or something because of something, such as anger, hurt feelings, frustration, etc. □ *I know you're angry, but don't take it out on me!*

take sth **over**† **1.** to assume responsibility for a task. □ *It looks as if I'm going to have to take the project over.* **2.** to acquire all of an asset; [for a company] to acquire another company. □ *Carl set out to take the failing airline over with the help of a number of investment bankers.* **3.** to take control of something. □ *The dictator hoped to take over the world little by little.*

take over (from so**)** to assume the role or job of someone. □ *Liz takes over and will be in charge.*

take over the reins (of sth**)** *Fig.* to take control. □ *I'm ready to retire and will do so when they find someone else to take over the reins of the company.*

take one's **own life** Go to die by one's own hand.

take pains with so/sth *Fig.* to deal with someone or something with great care. □ *He really took pains with me to make sure I understood it all.*

take so's **part** AND **take** so's **side** *Fig.* to take a side in an argument; to support someone in an argument. □ *My sister took my mother's part in the family argument.*

take part (in sth**)** *Fig.* to participate in something. □ *Everyone is asked to take part in the celebration.*

take sth **personally** *Fig.* to interpret a remark as if it were mean or critical about oneself. □ *Don't take it personally, but you really need a haircut.*

take one's **pick (of** so/sth**)** AND **have** one's **pick of** so/sth to be able to have one's choice of someone or something. □ *Can I take my pick of anyone in the group?*

take pity (on so/animal**)** AND **have pity (on** so/animal**)** *Fig.* to feel sorry for someone or an animal. □ *She took pity on the little dog and brought it in to get warm.*

take place to happen. □ *When will this party take place?*

take possession (of sth**)** *Fig.* to assume ownership of something. □ *I am to take possession of the house as soon as we sign the papers.*

take precedence over so/sth Go to precedence over so/sth.

take pride in so/sth *Fig.* to be proud of someone or something. □ *She takes pride in her work, and it shows in her products.*

take sth **public 1.** *Fig.* to make something known to the public. □ *Don't take it public. You'll just get talked about.* **2.** *Fig.* to sell shares in a company to the general public. (Securities markets.) □ *The board decided not to take the company public.*

take so's **pulse** *Fig.* to measure the frequency of the beats of a person's pulse. □ *The nurse took my pulse and said I was fine.*

take (quite a) toll (on so/sth**)** AND **take its toll (on** so/sth**)** *Fig.* [for something] to cause damage or wear by using something or by hard living. □ *Drug abuse takes a heavy toll on the lives of people.*

take root AND **take hold** *Fig.* to begin to have effect; to begin to control a process. □ *Things will begin to change when my new policies take root.*

take shape *Fig.* [for something, such as plans, writing, ideas, arguments, etc.] to begin to be organized and specific. □ *As my manuscript took shape, I started showing it to publishers.*

take sick AND **take ill** *Fig.* to become ill. □ *I hope I don't take ill before final exams.*

take so's side Go to take so's part.

take sides (against so/sth) AND side against so/sth *Fig.* to join a faction opposing someone or something; to establish a faction against someone or something. □ *Both of them took sides against me. It wasn't fair.*

take solace (in sth) *Fig.* to console oneself with some fact. □ *I am inordinately impoverished, but I take solace in the fact that I have a splendiferous vocabulary.*

take (some) names *Sl.* to make a list of wrongdoers. (Often figuratively, referring to a schoolteacher making a list of the names of misbehaving students to be sent to the principal.) □ *Gary is coming by to talk about the little riot last night, and I think he's taking names.*

take steps (to prevent sth) *Fig.* to do what is necessary to prevent something. □ *I took steps to prevent John from learning what we were talking about.*

take stock (of sth) *Fig.* to make an appraisal of resources and potentialities. □ *I spent some time yesterday taking stock of my good and bad qualities.*

take so's temperature *Fig.* to measure a person's body temperature with a thermometer. □ *The nurse took my temperature and said I was okay.*

take the bait Go to the bait.

take the bit in one's teeth AND take the bit between the teeth to put oneself in charge; to take charge. □ *Someone needed to direct the project, so I took the bit in my teeth.*

take the bull by the horns *Fig.* to confront a problem head-on and deal with it openly. □ *It's time to take the bull by the horns and get this job done.*

take the chill off ((of) some place) *Fig.* to do something that warms a place up slightly. □ *Let's build a fire and take the chill off this place.*

take the consequences Go to suffer the consequences.

take the coward's way out *Euph.* to kill oneself. □ *I can't believe that Bill would take the coward's way out. His death must have been an accident.*

take the cure *Inf.* to enter into any treatment program or treatment center. (Especially those dealing with drugs and alcohol.) □ *I wanted to take the cure, but I just couldn't bring myself to do it.*

take the day off Go to the day off.

take the easy way out *Fig.* to get free of something by taking the path of least resistance. □ *You can depend on Kelly to take the easy way out of a tough situation.*

take the edge off ((of) sth) *Fig.* to decrease the effect of something; to make something less blunt, critical, etc. (*Of* is usually retained before pronouns.) □ *He did not mean to insult the guest, and he quickly thought of something to say that would take the edge off his remark.*

take the fall *Sl.* to get arrested for a particular crime. (Especially when others are going unpunished for the same crime.) □ *Walt and Tony pulled the job off together, but Tony took the fall.*

take the Fifth (Amendment) *Fig.* to claim that telling someone something would get the teller in trouble. (Fig. on the use of the Fifth Amendment to the U.S. Constitution. This amendment is sometimes cited by persons testifying to Congress because it allows a person to decline to answer a question that will result in self-incrimination or the admission of guilt.) □ *She asked me where I'd been last night, but I took the Fifth.*

take the floor *Fig.* to stand up and address the audience. □ *When I take the floor, I'll make a short speech.* □ *The last time you had the floor, you talked for an hour.*

take the heat AND take some heat *Sl.* to receive or put up with criticism (for something). □ *The cops have been taking a lot of heat about the Quincy killing.* □ *If you can't take the heat, stay out of the kitchen.*

take the coward's way out

take the heat off (of) so/sth *Fig.* to relieve the pressure on someone or something. (*Of* is usually retained before pronouns.) □ *The change in the deadline takes the heat off the office staff.*

take the initiative (to do sth**)** to activate oneself to do something even if one has not been asked to do it. □ *The door hinges squeak because no one will take the initiative to oil them.*

take the law into one's **own hands** *Fig.* to attempt to administer the law; to pass judgment on someone who has done something wrong. □ *The shopkeeper took the law into his own hands when he tried to arrest the thief.*

take the liberty of doing sth *Fig.* to do something for someone voluntarily; to do something slightly personal for someone that would be more appropriate if one knew the person better. (Often used as an overly polite exaggeration in a request.) □ *I took the liberty of ordering an entree for you. I hope you don't mind.*

take the lid off (of) sth AND **take the lid off**† *Fig.* to reveal a set of previously concealed problems. (*Of* is usually retained before pronouns.) □ *You took the lid off this mess. You straighten it out!*

take the (long) count *Sl.* to die. (Fig. on a boxer being counted out and losing a fight.) □ *The poor cat took the long count at last.*

take the pledge *Fig.* to promise to abstain from drinking alcohol. (Refers to the temperance pledge of T-Totalism [teetotalism] = total abstinence.) □ *I'm not ready to take the pledge yet, but I will cut down.*

take the plunge *Inf.* to marry someone. □ *I'm not ready to take the plunge yet.*

take the pulse of sth *Inf.* to sample or survey something to learn about its progress or state. □ *Two executives came in to take the pulse of the local business unit.*

take the rap (for so**)** *Inf.* to take the blame [for doing something] for someone else.

□ *John robbed the bank, but Tom took the rap for him.*

take the rap (for sth**)** *Inf.* to take the blame for (doing) something; to receive the criminal charge for committing a crime. □ *I won't take the rap for the crime. I wasn't even in town.* □ *Who'll take the rap for it? Who did it?*

take (the) roll Go to call (the) roll.

take the slack up† AND **pick the slack up**† *Fig.* to do what needs to be done; to do what has been left undone. □ *Jill did her job poorly, and I have to take up the slack.*

take the spear (in one's **chest)** *Sl.* to accept full blame for something; to accept the full brunt of the punishment for something. (Alludes to being out in front of everyone else in battle.) □ *The CFO got the short straw and had to take the spear in his chest.*

take the stage *Fig.* to become the center of attention; to become the focus of everyone's attention. □ *Later in the day, the problems in the warehouse took the stage, and we discussed them until dinner time.*

take the stand *Fig.* to go to and sit in the witness chair in a courtroom. □ *I was in court all day, waiting to take the stand.*

take the starch out of so **1.** *Fig.* to make someone less arrogant or stiff. □ *I told a joke that made Mr. Jones laugh very hard. It really took the starch out of him.* **2.** *Fig.* to make someone tired and weak. □ *This hot weather really takes the starch out of me.*

take the time to do sth *Fig.* to be careful and go slowly so as not to make mistakes. □ *You should always take the time to do it right.*

take the wind out of so's **sails** Go to knock the wind out of so's sails.

take the words out of so's **mouth** *Fig.* to say something just before someone else was going to say the same thing; to say something that someone who agrees with you might have said. □ *When you said*

"expensive," you took the words right out of my mouth!

take sth **the wrong way** Go to take sth amiss.

take things easy 1. *Fig.* to live well and comfortably. □ *I'll be glad when I can make enough money to take things easy.* **2.** *Fig.* to relax temporarily and recuperate. □ *The doctor says I'm supposed to take things easy for a while.*

take one's **time** to go as slow as one wants or needs to; to use as much time as is required. □ *There is no hurry. Please take your time.*

take time out *Fig.* to spend time away from studying or working. □ *He's taking time out between high school and starting at the university.*

take to so/sth *Fig.* to become fond of or attracted to someone or something. □ *Mary didn't take to her new job, and she quit after two weeks.* □ *The puppy seems to take to this new food just fine.*

take to one's **bed** *Fig.* to go to bed, as with an illness. □ *I feel a little ill, so I'll take to my bed for a day or so.*

take so **to court** *Fig.* to sue someone; to force someone to appear in court. □ *I will take you to court if you persist in pestering my client.*

take sth **to heart** *Fig.* to consider that some comment is significant to oneself. □ *Mary listened to Bob's advice and took it all to heart.*

take to one's **heels** AND **turn on** one's **heel** *Fig.* to run away. □ *The little boy said hello and then took to his heels.* □ *He turned on his heel and ran.*

take so **to one side** AND **take** so **aside** *Fig.* *Lit.* to lead someone to a relatively private place, to say something private or give private instructions. □ *Gary took Fran to one side to talk to her.* □ *I will take Sue aside and have a word with her about this matter.*

take so **to task** *Fig.* to scold or reprimand someone. □ *I lost a big contract, and the boss took me to task in front of everyone.*

take so **to the cleaners 1.** *Sl.* to take a lot of someone's money; to swindle someone. □ *The lawyers took the insurance company to the cleaners, but I still didn't get enough to pay for my losses.* **2.** *Sl.* to defeat or best someone. □ *Look at the height they've got! They'll take us to the cleaners!*

take to the hills Go to head for the hills.

take too much on† *Fig.* to undertake to do too much work or too many tasks at one time. □ *Don't take too much on, or you won't be able to do any of it well.*

take one's **turn** *Fig.* [when playing a game] to make one's move or play one's cards; [when alternating with someone, waiting for one's opportunity or place in a sequence] to perform one's task. □ *Somebody please wake Spike up so he can take his turn.*

take turns (doing sth**)** [for two or more people] to alternate doing something. □ *We can't both do it at once. Let's take turns.* □ *The girls took turns rolling the ball.*

take umbrage at sth *Fig.* to feel that one has been insulted by something. □ *Mary took umbrage at the suggestion that she was being unreasonable.*

take sth **under advisement** *Fig.* to hear an idea and think about it carefully. □ *The suggestion was taken under advisement, and a reply was not expected for at least a month.*

take so **under** so's **wing(s)** Go to under so's wing(s).

take so **up**† *Fig.* to discuss or deal with someone. (See also take sth up.) □ *What are we going to do about Bill? Are we going to take Bill up today at the board meeting?*

take sth **up**† **1.** *Fig.* [for someone or a group] to deliberate something. □ *When will the board of directors take this up?* **2.** to raise something, such as the height of a hem. □ *The skirt is too long. I'll have*
to take it up. **3.** *Fig.* to continue with something after an interruption. □ *They took it up where they left off.* **4.** *Fig.* to begin something; to start to acquire a skill in something. □ *I took up skiing last fall.* **5.** to absorb something. □ *This old sponge doesn't take much water up.* **6.** *Fig.* to adopt something new. □ *Toby took up the life of a farmer.*

take up one's **abode** some place *Fig.* to make some place one's home. □ *I will take up my abode in this place and hope to find a job close by.*

take up arms (against so/sth**)** *Fig.* to prepare to fight against someone or something. □ *They were all so angry that the leader convinced them to take up arms.*

take so **up on** sth *Fig.* to accept an offer that someone has made. □ *That's a good offer. I'll take you up on it.*

take up residence some place *Fig.* to make a residence of a place. □ *It looks as if a family of mice has taken up residence in the cupboard.*

take up room Go to next.

take up space AND **take up room** *Fig.* to fill or occupy space. □ *John, you're not being any help at all. You're just taking up space.*

take up the challenge *Fig.* to respond to a challenge and do what the challenge asks. □ *I am not prepared to take the challenge up.*

take up (so's**) time** *Fig.* to require too much of someone else's time; to waste someone's time. (Also with so much of or too much of.) □ *You're taking up my time. Please go away.* □ *This problem is taking up too much of my time.*

take up where one/sth **left off** *Fig.* to start up again in the very place that one has stopped. □ *It's time to stop for lunch. After lunch, we will take up where we left off.*

take sth **up**† **(with** so**)** *Fig.* to raise and discuss a matter with someone. □ *This is a very complicated problem. I'll have to take it up with the office manager.*

take up with so *Fig.* to become close with someone; to become friends with someone. □ *I did not want Lefty to take up with Spike, but he did, and look where it's gotten him.*

take sth **(up)on** oneself *Fig.* to accept the entire burden of something on oneself. (*Upon* is formal and less commonly used than *on*.) □ *You didn't need to take it all upon yourself. There are others here who can help, you know.*

take well to sth Go to take kindly to sth.

take sth **with a grain of salt** Go to next.

take sth **with a pinch of salt** AND **take** sth **with a grain of salt** *Fig.* to listen to a story or an explanation with considerable doubt. □ *You must take anything she says with a grain of salt. She doesn't always tell the truth.*

take so's **word for** sth AND **take** so's **word on** sth *Fig.* to believe what someone says about something without seeking further information or proof. □ *I can't prove it. You will have to take my word on it.*

take so **wrong** AND **get** so **wrong** to misunderstand someone. □ *Please don't take me wrong, but I believe that your socks don't match.*

take years off (of) so/sth *Fig.* to make someone seem or look younger. (*Of* is usually retained before pronouns.) □ *Your shorter haircut has taken years off of your face.*

take your chances just try it and hope for the best; take whatever risks are involved; take a chance. □ *I think there may be room for you in our car. Just show up at my house and take your chances.*

taken aback *Cliché* surprised and confused. □ *When I told my parents I was married, they were completely taken aback.*

taken for dead *Fig.* appearing to be dead; assumed to be dead. □ *The accident victims were so seriously injured that they were taken for dead at first.*

taken with so/sth *Fig.* highly attracted to someone or something. □ *She was really quite taken with the young man who escorted her to the ball.*

take-off artist *Sl.* a thief. (Underworld.) □ *A take-off artist known as the Cat is cleaning out closets and jewelry boxes all over town.*

tale of woe *Fig.* a sad story; a list of personal problems; an excuse for failing to do something. □ *This tale of woe that we have all been getting from Kelly is just too much.*

talk a blue streak *Fig.* to talk very much and very rapidly. □ *Billy didn't talk until he was two, and then he started talking a blue streak.*

talk a mile a minute Go to a mile a minute.

talk about so/sth to discuss someone or something. □ *I don't want to talk about Jerry anymore.*

Talk about so/sth . . . ! *Fig.* If you think that thing or person is remarkable, then. . . . □ *Talk about ugly buildings! This one is horrendous.*

talk around sth *Fig.* to talk but avoid talking directly about the subject. □ *You are just talking around the matter! I want a straight answer!*

talk back (to so**)** *Fig.* to challenge verbally a parent, an older person, or one's superior. □ *Please don't talk back to me!*

talk big *Inf.* to brag; to make grandiose statements. □ *He has some deep need to talk big, but it's just talk—no action.*

talk down to so *Fig.* to speak to someone in a patronizing manner; to speak to someone in the simplest way. □ *The manager insulted everyone in the office by talking down to them.*

talk so's **ear off** Go to talk so's head off.

talk one's head off AND **yack** one's **head off** *Fig.* to talk a great deal. (*Yack* is informal.) □ *Jane talked her head off and ended up with a sore throat.*

talk so's **head off 1.** *Inf.* [for someone] to speak too much. □ *Why does John always talk his head off? Doesn't he know he bores people?* **2.** AND **talk** so's **ear off** *Inf.* to talk to and bore someone. □ *John is very friendly, but watch out or he'll talk your head off.* □ *My uncle always talked my ear off whenever I went to visit him.*

talk in circles *Fig.* to talk in a confusing or roundabout manner. □ *I couldn't understand a thing he said. All he did was talk in circles.*

the **talk of** some place *Fig.* someone or something who is the subject of a conversation somewhere, such as the town, the office, the community, etc. (See also the **toast of** some place.) □ *The handsome new teacher was the talk of the town.*

talk oneself **out** *Fig.* to talk until one can talk no more. □ *She talked herself out and was silent for the rest of the day.*

talk out of turn Go to speak out of turn.

talk over so's **head** *Fig.* to say things that someone cannot understand; to speak on too high a level for one's audience. □ *The speaker talked over our heads, and we learned nothing.*

talk sense Go to make sense.

talk shop *Fig.* to talk about business or work matters at a social event where such talk is out of place. □ *All right, everyone, we're not here to talk shop. Let's have a good time.*

talk the talk and walk the walk AND **talk the talk; walk the walk** *Cliché* to behave as one is expected to behave in looks and manner of speech. □ *Listen to him wow the boss. He can sure talk the talk, but can he walk the walk?*

talk sth **through**† **1.** to discuss something in detail. □ *Let's talk the issue through and get it decided.* **2.** to get something approved by talking convincingly. □ *The board was reluctant to approve it, but I talked it through.*

talk through one's **hat** *Inf.* to brag or exaggerate; to talk nonsense. □ *Pay no attention to Mary. She is just talking through her hat.*

talk to so *Fig.* to lecture to someone; to reprimand someone. □ *I wish you would talk to your son. He is creating havoc in the classroom.*

talk to hear one's **own voice** *Fig.* to talk far more than is necessary; to talk much, in an egotistical manner. □ *Am I just talking to hear my own voice, or are you listening to me?*

talk turkey *Fig.* to talk business; to talk frankly. □ *John wanted to talk turkey, but Jane just wanted to joke around.*

talk until one **is blue in the face** *Inf.* to talk until one is exhausted. □ *I talked until I was blue in the face, but I couldn't change her mind.*

talk so/sth **up**† *Fig.* to promote or speak in support of someone or something. □ *I've been talking up the party all day, trying to get people to come.*

talk up a storm Go to up a storm.

talk one's **way out of** sth *Fig.* to get out of something by verbal persuasion. □ *If I get into some sort of problem, I will try to talk my way out of it.*

talked out tired of talking; having said everything that could be said. □ *I'm talked out now. It's time for some more convincing persuasion.*

***a tall order** *Fig.* a request that is difficult to fulfill. (*Typically: **be** ~; **give** so ~.) □ *Well, it's a tall order, but I'll do it.*

tall timber(s) *Fig.* some remote place in the country or the woods. □ *Oh, Chuck lives out in the tall timbers somewhere. He only has a post office box number.*

tally with sth *Fig.* [for one thing] to agree or correlate with another. □ *What you just said doesn't tally with what you told me before.*

tan so's **hide** *Fig. Rur.* to spank someone. □ *Billy's mother said she'd tan Billy's hide if he ever did that again.*

tangle with so/sth **(over** so/sth**)** *Fig.* to battle against someone or something about someone or something. □ *Tim tangled with Karen over the children.* □ *I hope I don't have to tangle with the bank over this loan.*

tank up (on sth**)** AND **tank up with** sth *Sl.* to drink some kind of alcoholic beverage. □ *Toby spent the evening tanking up on bourbon.*

tap dance like mad *Sl.* to appear busy continuously; to have to move fast or talk cleverly to distract someone. □ *Any public official knows how to tap dance like mad when the press gets too nosy.*

tap so **(for** sth**)** AND **tap** so **(to** do sth**)** *Fig.* to select someone for some purpose or position. □ *The committee tapped John to run for Congress.* □ *I had thought they were going to tap Sally.*

tap out 1. *Sl.* to lose one's money in gambling or in the securities markets. □ *I really tapped out on that gold-mining stock.* **2.** *Sl.* to die; to expire. □ *Mary was so tired that she thought she was going to tap out.*

tap sth **out**† **1.** *Fig.* to send a message in Morse code, as on a telegraph. □ *The telegraph operator tapped a message out and waited for a reply.* **2.** *Fig.* to thump the rhythm of a piece of music [on something]. □ *Tap the rhythm out until you get it right.*

tar and feather so to punish or humiliate someone by coating them with tar and feathers. □ *The people of the village tarred and feathered the bank robber and chased him out of town.*

tar so **with the same brush** Go to paint so with the same brush.

tarred with the same brush *Fig.* sharing the same characteristic(s); having the same good or bad points as someone else. (This, in its history and origins, has no racial connotations but has recently been misinterpreted as linking skin color and tar. This expression has probably been confused with the pejorative phrase *a touch of the tar brush* referring to mixed racial ancestry.) □ *Jack and his brother*

are tarred with the same brush. They're both crooks.

taste blood *Fig.* to experience something exciting, and perhaps dangerous, for the first time. □ *She had tasted blood once, and she knew that the life of a race-car driver was for her.*

*****a **taste for** sth *Fig.* a desire for a particular food, drink, or experience. (*Typically: **get** ~; **have** ~; **give** so ~; **acquire** ~.) □ *The Smiths have a taste for adventure and take exotic vacations.*

taste like more *Fig.* to taste very good; to taste so good as to make one want to eat more. □ *Mom's cooking always tastes like more.*

a **taste of** sth an experience; an example. □ *My friend used a parachute and got a taste of what it's like to be a bird.*

*****a **taste of** one's **own medicine** AND *****a **dose of** one's **own medicine** *Fig.* a sample of the unpleasantness that one has been giving other people. (*Typically: **get** ~; **have** ~; **give** so ~.) □ *Now you see how it feels to have someone call you names! You are getting a taste of your own medicine!*

tax so/sth **with** sth *Fig.* to burden or tire someone or something with something. □ *Please don't tax me with any more requests for my immediate attention.*

tax-and-spend *Fig.* spending freely and taxing heavily. (Referring to a legislative body that repeatedly passes expensive new laws and keeps raising taxes to pay for the cost. Fixed order.) □ *The only thing worse than a tax-and-spend legislature is one that spends and runs up a worsening deficit.*

teach so **a lesson** *Fig.* to get even with someone for bad behavior. (See also learn one's lesson.) □ *John tripped me, so I punched him. That ought to teach him a lesson.*

teach one's **grandmother to suck eggs** *Fig.* to try to tell or show someone more knowledgeable or experienced than oneself how to do something. □ *Don't sug-*

gest showing Mary how to knit. It will be like teaching your grandmother to suck eggs.

teach school to serve as a teacher. (Obviously, it is the students, not the school, that is being taught.) □ *My sister teaches school, but I have no desire to be a schoolteacher.*

*the **teacher's pet** *Fig.* the teacher's favorite student. (*Typically: **be** ~; **become** ~.) □ *Sally is the teacher's pet. She always gets special treatment.*

a **team player** *Fig.* someone who works well with the group; someone who is loyal to the group. □ *Ted is a team player. I am sure that he will cooperate with us.*

tear some place **apart**† *Fig.* to search somewhere to the point of destruction. □ *The cops came with a search warrant and tore your room apart.*

tear so **apart**† **1.** *Fig.* to cause two people, presumably lovers, to separate unwillingly. □ *The enormous disruption of the accident tore them apart and they separated.* **2.** *Fig.* to cause someone enormous grief or emotional pain. □ *The death of her dog tore her apart.* **3.** *Fig.* to criticize someone mercilessly. □ *Why do you have to tear yourself apart for making a little error?*

tear sth **apart**† **1.** *Fig.* to criticize something mercilessly. □ *The critic tore apart the entire cast of the play.* **2.** to divide something or the members of a group, citizens of a country, etc. □ *The financial crisis tore the club apart.*

tear one's **hair (out)** AND **pull** one's **hair (out)** *Fig.* to be anxious, frustrated, or angry. □ *I had better get home. My parents will be tearing their hair out.*

tear one's **heart out** *Fig.* to cause someone great emotional pain. □ *The story of her childhood just tore my heart out.*

tear into so **1.** to attack someone physically. □ *The thug tore into the old man and threw him to the ground.* **2.** *Fig.* to scold someone severely; to attack someone

with criticism. □ *I was late, and the boss tore into me like a mad dog.*

tear so/animal **limb from limb** to rip someone or an animal to bits. □ *The crocodiles attacked the wading zebras and tore them limb from limb.*

tear so **up**† *Fig.* to cause someone much grief. □ *The news of Tom's death really tore Bill up.*

tee off 1. *Fig.* to start the first hole in a game of golf. □ *It's time to tee off. Let's get on the course.* **2.** *Fig.* to begin [doing anything]; to be the first one to start something. (Fig. on ①.) □ *The master of ceremonies teed off with a few jokes and then introduced the first act.*

tee so **off**† *Sl.* to make someone angry. □ *That really teed me off!*

teething troubles 1. pain and crying on the part of a baby whose teeth are growing in. □ *Billy has been whining because of teething troubles.* **2.** *Fig.* difficulties and problems experienced in the early stages of a project, activity, etc. (Fig. on ①.) □ *There have been a lot of teething troubles with the new computer system.*

telegraph one's **punches 1.** *Fig.* to signal, unintentionally, what blows one is about to strike. (Boxing.) □ *Don't telegraph your punches, kid! You'll be flat on your back in three seconds.* **2.** *Fig.* to signal, unintentionally, one's intentions. (Fig. on ①.) □ *When you go in there to negotiate, don't telegraph your punches. Don't let them see that we're in need of this contract.*

tell all *Fig.* to tell everything, even the secrets. □ *Some reporter got hold of the actress's maid, who offered to tell all for a fee.*

tell so/sth **by** sth to identify someone or something by something. □ *You can tell Jim by the old-fashioned shoes he wears.*

Tell it like it is. *Inf.* Speak frankly.; Tell the truth no matter who is criticized or how much it hurts. □ *Come on man, tell it like it is!*

Tell it to the marines! *Inf.* I do not believe you (maybe the marines will)!; Muster up the courage to tell it to someone who can respond appropriately. □ *Your excuse is preposterous. Tell it to the marines.*

tell its own story AND **tell its own tale** *Fig.* [for the state of something] to indicate clearly what has happened. □ *The upturned boat told its own tale. The fisherman had drowned.*

tell its own tale Go to previous.

Tell me about it! *Fig.* I agree. □ *A: It's sure windy today! B: Tell me about it!*

Tell me another (one)! *Inf.* What you just told me was a lie, so go ahead and tell me another lie! (Indicates incredulity.) □ *Bill: Did you know that the football coach was once a dancer in a movie? Tom: Go on! Tell me another one!*

tell so **off**† *Fig.* to scold someone; to attack someone verbally. (This has a sense of finality about it.) □ *I was so mad at Bob that I told him off.*

tell on so *Fig.* to report someone's bad behavior; to tattle on someone. (Fixed order.) □ *If you do that again, I'll tell on you!* □ *Please don't tell on me. I'm in enough trouble as it is.*

tell so **on** so to tattle to someone about someone. □ *I'm going to tell your mother on you!*

tell shit from Shinola Go to know shit from Shinola.

tell tales out of school *Fig.* to tell secrets or spread rumors. □ *I wish that John would keep quiet. He's telling tales out of school again.*

tell the (whole) world *Fig.* to spread around someone's private business. □ *Well, you don't have to tell the whole world.*

tell time 1. *Fig.* [for a watch or clock] to keep or report the correct time. □ *This clock doesn't tell time very accurately.* **2.** *Fig.* [for a person] to be able to read time from a clock or watch. □ *Billy is only four. He can't tell time yet.*

tell one **to** one's **face** *Fig.* to tell [something] to someone directly. □ *I'm sorry that Sally* feels that way about me. I wish she had told me to my face.

tell so **what to do with** sth *Inf.* to reject someone's idea by suggesting that someone do something rude with something. (With the unspoken notion that one should stick it up one's ass.) □ *If that's the way he wants to be, you can just tell him what to do with it.*

tell so **where to get off** *Fig.* to scold someone; to express one's anger to someone; to tell so off. □ *She told me where to get off and then started in scolding Tom.*

tell which is which Go to know which is which.

temper sth **with** sth **1.** *Fig.* to harden something, such as metal, with something. □ *You have to temper the metal pieces with very high heat.* **2.** *Fig.* to soften the impact of something, such as news, with something. □ *We can temper this disaster story a bit with a picture of the happy survivors.*

a **tempest in a teacup** AND a **tempest in a teapot** an argument or disagreement over a very minor matter. □ *The entire issue of who was to present the report was just a tempest in a teapot.*

a **tempest in a teapot** Go to previous.

tempt fate *Fig.* to do something that results in something bad happening. (Bad results are somewhat less certain than with flirt with disaster.) □ *I know I am tempting fate by taking my computer on vacation with me, but I want to be able to send some e-mails.*

tender age young age. □ *When he was at the tender age of three, his hair reached down to his shoulders.*

the **tender age of** a number of years *Fig.* the young age of. . . . □ *She left home at the tender age of 17 and got married to a rock singer.*

tender sth **for** sth to offer something (of value) for something. □ *The shareholders were asked to tender one of their shares for two of the offering company's.*

terminate so **1.** *Euph.* to fire someone. □ *If your work habits do not improve, we may be forced to terminate you.* **2.** *Sl.* to kill someone. □ *If any one should see you, terminate him at once.*

test out (of sth**)** to score high enough on a placement test that one does not need to take a particular course. □ *I tested out of calculus.*

test the water(s) *Fig.* to try something; to see what something is like before getting involved too deeply with it. (Fig. on finding out the temperature of water before swimming or bathing in it.) □ *I attended a meeting of the club once just to test the water before I joined as a dues-paying member.*

Thank God for small favors. Be thankful that something good has happened in a bad situation. □ *He had a heart attack, but it was right there in the doctor's office, so they could take care of him right away. Thank God for small favors.*

Thank goodness! AND **Thank heavens!; Thank God!** *Fig.* Oh, I am so thankful! □ *John: Well, we finally got here. Sorry we're so late. Mother: Thank goodness! We were all so worried.*

Thank heavens! Go to previous.

thank one's **lucky stars** *Fig.* to be thankful for one's luck. □ *I thank my lucky stars that I studied the right things for the test.*

Thank you. I am grateful to you and offer you my thanks. □ *Bill: Here, have some more cake. Bob: Thank you.*

Thank you a lot. Go to Thanks (a lot).

Thank you for sharing. *Inf.* a sarcastic remark made when someone tells something that is unpleasant, overly personal, disgusting, or otherwise annoying. □ *Thank you for sharing. I really needed to hear about your operation.*

*thankful for small blessings *Fig.* grateful for any small benefits or advantages one has, especially in a generally difficult situation. (*Typically: **be** ~; **become** ~.) □ *We have very little money, but we must be thankful for small blessings. At least we have enough food.*

thanks a bunch *Inf.* thanks. □ *Thanks a bunch for your help.* □ *He said, "Thanks a bunch," and walked out.*

Thanks (a lot). AND **Thank you a lot. 1.** Thank you very much.; I am very grateful. □ *Thank you a lot. Your advice was very helpful.* **2.** That is not worth much.; That is nothing to be grateful for. (Sarcasm is indicated by the tone of voice used with this expression.) □ *John: I'm afraid that you're going to have to work the night shift. Bob: Thanks a lot.*

Thanks a million. *Inf.* Thanks (a lot). □ *Bill: Oh, thanks a million. You were very helpful. Bob: Just glad I could help.*

Thanks awfully. *Fig.* Thank you very much. □ *John: Here's one for you. Jane: Thanks awfully.* □ *Mary: Here, let me help you with all that stuff. Sue: Thanks awfully.*

Thanks, but no thanks. *Inf.* Thank you, but I am not interested. (A way of turning down something that is not very desirable.) □ *Alice: How would you like to buy my old car? Jane: Thanks, but no thanks.* □ *John: What do you think about a trip over to see the Wilsons? Sally: Thanks, but no thanks. We don't get along.*

Thanks loads. *Inf.* Thanks (a lot). □ *Mary: Here, you can have these. And take these too. Sally: Thanks loads.* □ *John: Wow! You look great! Sally: Thanks loads. I try.*

thanks to so/sth due to someone or something; because of someone or something. (This does not necessarily suggest gratitude.) □ *Thanks to the storm, we have no electricity.* □ *Thanks to Mary, we have tickets to the game. She bought them early before they were sold out.*

That ain't hay. *Inf.* That is not a small amount of money. (The highly informal word *ain't* is built into the expression.) □ *I paid $40 for it, and that ain't hay!*

That ain't the way I heard it. That is not the way I heard the story told. (The highly informal word *ain't* is built into the expression. Made popular by a character called "The Old Timer" on the *Fibber McGee and Molly* radio program, running from the mid-1930s until the mid-1950s.) □ *John: It seemed like a real riot, then Sally called the police and things calmed down. Sue: That ain't the way I heard it. John: What? Sue: Somebody said the neighbors called the police.*

That (all) depends. *Fig.* My answer depends on factors that have yet to be discussed. □ *Tom: Will you be able to come to the meeting on Thursday night? Mary: That all depends.*

That beats everything! Go to If that don't beat all!

That does it! AND **That tears it!** *Inf.* That's the last straw!; Enough is enough! □ *Bill: We're still not totally pleased with your work. Bob: That does it! I quit!*

that is to say Go to in other words.

That makes two of us. *Inf.* The same is true for me. □ *Bill: I just passed my biology test. Bob: That makes two of us!*

That (really) burns me (up)! *Inf.* That makes me very angry! □ *Sue: Fred is telling everyone that you are the one who lost the party money. Mary: That burns me! It was John who had the money in the first place.*

That remains to be seen. Go to It remains to be seen.

That sucks. AND **It sucks.** *Sl.* That is worthless. □ *Yuck! That sucks!* □ *This meat loaf is terrible. It sucks.*

That takes care of that. *Inf.* That is settled. □ *I spent all morning dealing with this matter, and that takes care of that.*

That takes the cake! 1. *Inf.* That is good, and it wins the prize! (Assuming that the prize is a cake.) □ *"What a performance!" cheered John. "That takes the cake!"* □ *Sue: Wow! That takes the cake! What a dive! Rachel: She sure can dive!* **2.** *Inf.* That is too much; That does it! □ *Bob: Wow! That takes the cake! Bill: What is it? Bob: That stupid driver in front of me just*

hit the car on the left and then swung over and hit the car on the right.

That tears it! Go to That does it!

That will do. *Fig.* That is enough.; Do no more. □ *"That will do," said Mr. Jones when he had heard enough of our arguing.*

That'll be the day! *Inf.* It will be an unusually amazing day when that happens! □ *Sue: I'm going to get this place organized once and for all! Alice: That'll be the day!*

That'll teach so! *Inf.* What happened to someone is a suitable punishment! (The someone is usually a pronoun.) □ *Bill: Tom, who has cheated on his taxes for years, finally got caught. Sue: That'll teach him.*

That's a fine how-do-you-do. *Inf.* That is a terrible situation. □ *That's a fine how-do-you-do. I come home and find the kids are playing catch with my best crystal bowl.*

That's a new one on me! *Inf.* I had not heard that before. □ *Bob: Did you hear? They're building a new highway that will bypass the town. Fred: That's a new one on me! That's terrible!*

That's about the size of it. *Inf.* That is the way it is. (Often a response to someone who has acknowledged bad news.) □ *Bob: We only have a few hundred dollars left in the bank. Sally: That means that there isn't enough money for us to go on vacation? Bob: That's about the size of it.*

That's all folks! That is everything.; It's over. (The formulaic announcement of the end of a Warner Brothers color cartoon in movie theaters. Usually stuttered by Porky Pig.) □ *We're finished playing for the evening. That's all folks!*

That's all for so. *Inf.* Someone will get no more chances to do things correctly. □ *You've gone too far, Mary. That's all for you. Good-bye!*

That's all so needs. AND **It's all so needs.; (It's) just what you need.; That's just what you need.** *Inf.* Someone does not need that at all.; That's the last straw! (Always sarcastic. The someone can be a person's name or a pronoun.) □ *Jane: The dog died and the basement is just starting to flood. Fred: That's all we need.* □ *Bob: On top of having too many bills to pay, now I have car trouble! Mary: That's just what you need!*

That's all she wrote. AND **That's what she wrote.** *Inf.* That is all of it.; That is the last of it. (This may have derived from the finality of a "Dear John letter" wherein a serviceman is told that his wife or sweetheart has replaced him with another man.) □ *Here's the last one we have to fix. There, that's all she wrote.*

That's easy for you to say. *Inf.* You can say that easily because it really does not affect you the way it affects others. □ *Waiter: Here's your check. Mary: Thanks. (turning to others) I'm willing to just split the check evenly. Bob: That's easy for you to say. You had lobster!*

That's funny. That is strange or peculiar. □ *Bill: Tom just called from Detroit and says he's coming back tomorrow. Mary: That's funny. He's not supposed to.* □ *Sue: The sky is turning very gray. Mary: That's funny. There's no bad weather forecast.*

That's (just) the nature of the beast. *Fig.* That's just the way it is.; That's the way things are. (Sometimes the beast is a machine, such as an automobile.) □ *She won't start up on cold mornings. That's just the nature of the beast.*

That's just what you need. Go to That's all so needs.

That's life. Go to So it goes.

That's life in the big city. Go to So it goes.

That's more like it. *Fig.* That is better.; That is a better response this time. □ *Waiter: Here is your order, sir. Roast chicken as you requested. Sorry about the mix-up. John: That's more like it.*

That's my boy. AND **That's my girl.** *Inf.* That is my child of whom I am proud.; I'm proud of this young person. □ *After the game, Tom's dad said, "That's my boy!"*

That's my girl. Go to previous.

That's not the half of it! *Fig.* It is much worse than you think!; There is much more to this than you think! □ *Yes, the window broke, but that's not the half of it. The rain came in and ruined the carpet!*

That's show business (for you). *Inf.* That is the way that life really is. (Also with *biz* and *show biz*.) □ *And now the car won't start. That's show business for you.*

That's that! *Inf.* That is the end of that! Nothing more can be done. □ *Tom: Well, that's that! I can do no more. Sally: That's the way it goes.*

That's the spirit! *Fig.* That is the right attitude and preferred evidence of high motivation. □ *A: I am sure I can do it! B: That's the spirit!*

That's the story of my life. *Fig.* This recent failure is just typical of the way everything in my life has been. □ *A: Sorry, but it looks like another year for you in the eighth grade. B: That's the story of my life.*

That's the ticket! *Inf.* That is what is required! □ *Mary: I'll just get ready and drive the package directly to the airport! Sue: That's the ticket. Take it right to the airport post office.*

(That's the) way to go! *Inf.* a phrase encouraging someone to continue the good work. □ *As John ran over the finish line, everyone cried, "That's the way to go!"*

That's what I'm talking about! AND **That's it!; Now you're talking!** *Inf.* Yes, that's the stuff!; Now you see what I mean!; That's what I've been trying to get you to do! (Usually *talkin'*.) □ *Now, you're playin' the kind a' shit I wanna hear. That's what I'm talkin' about!*

Them as has, gits. *Rur.* Those who have assets acquire more assets.; Rich people can always get more. □ *The millionaire keeps making more and more money, because he has lots of money to invest. Them as has, gits.* □ *Tom: Bill already owns half the property in town, and here the court went and awarded him that vacant lot. Jane: You know how it is—them as has, gits.*

Them's fighting words! *Rur.* What you just said will lead to a fight. (Said as a threat.) □ *I heard what you said about my brother, and them's fighting words.*

then and there *Cliché* right at that time and place. □ *I decided to settle the matter then and there and not wait until Monday.*

There are plenty of (other) fish in the sea. *Fig.* There are other choices. (Used to refer to persons.) □ *When John broke up with Ann, I told her not to worry. There are plenty of other fish in the sea.* □ *It's too bad that your secretary quit, but there are plenty of other fish in the sea.*

There aren't enough hours in the day. There are too many things to do and not enough time. □ *I am behind in all my work. There aren't enough hours in the day!*

There is a fine line between sth **and** sth else. AND **There is a thin line between** sth **and** sth else. *Fig.* There is little difference between something and something else. □ *There is a fine line between a frown and a grimace.*

There is a thin line between sth **and** sth else. Go to previous.

there is no doing sth *Fig.* it is not possible to do something (as specified). □ *There is no arguing with Bill.*

There is no love lost (between so **and** so else**).** *Fig.* There is no friendship wasted between someone and someone else (because they are enemies). □ *Ever since their big argument, there has been no love lost between Tom and Bill.*

(There is) no need (to). You do not have to.; It is not necessary. □ *Mary: Shall I try to save all this wrapping paper? Sue: No need. It's all torn.*

There is something to be said for sth. *Fig.* There is (also) something good about something. □ *Chocolate chip is good, but there is something to be said for plain old vanilla.*

There will be hell to pay. AND **There will be the devil to pay.** *Inf.* There will be a lot of trouble if something is done or if something is not done. (See also have the devil to pay.) □ *Fred: If you break another window, Andy, there will be hell to pay. Andy: I didn't do it! I didn't.*

There will be the devil to pay. Go to previous.

There you are. Go to next.

There you go. 1. *Inf.* Hooray! You did it right! □ *There you go! That's the way!* **2.** *Inf.* That is the way things are, just like I told you.; Isn't this just what you would expect? □ *There you go, acting rude and ugly!* **3.** *Inf.* You are doing it again. □ *I just told you not to put that junk on the table, and there you go.* **4.** AND **There you are.; Here you go.; Here you are.** *Inf.* Here is what you wanted. (As might be said by a food server in a restaurant when placing your food in front of you.) □ *"There you go," said the waiter.* □ *Who ordered the fried shrimp? . . . Here you go.*

thereby hangs a tale *Fig.* there is an interesting story connected with this matter. □ *Yes, she comes in late most mornings, and thereby hangs a tale. She has a drinking problem.*

There's a time and place for everything. This is not the appropriate time or place [for doing what you are doing or going to do]. □ *Stop that Jimmy! There's a time and place for everything.*

There's more than one way to skin a cat. *Fig.* There is more than one way to do something. (Some suggest that this refers to skinning a catfish, but there are not really many ways to skin a catfish.) □ *I think I know a better way to do this. There's more than one way to skin a cat.*

There's no flies on so. *Rur.* someone is full of energy and drive. □ *There's no flies on Jane. She's up at five every morning, training for the big race.*

There's no such thing as a free lunch. Nothing is really free because there is always some obligation. (Perhaps from a time when you could get enough free food at a bar with the purchase of a beer or two.) □ *I ended up paying even more* when they added on tax and carrying charges. *There's no such thing as a free lunch.*

There's no time like the present. Do it now. □ *Ask her to marry you before another day goes by. There's no time like the present.*

There's no two ways about it. *Fig.* no choice about it; no other interpretation of it. (Note the form *there's* rather than *there are*.) □ *You have to go to the doctor whether you like it or not. There's no two ways about it.*

there's no use (doing sth) Go to it's no use (doing sth).

There's nobody home. *Inf.* There are no brains in someone's head. □ *There's lots of goodwill in that head, but there's nobody home.*

(There's) nothing to it! **1.** *Inf.* It is easy! □ *Bill: Me? I can't dive off a board that high! I can hardly dive off the side of the pool! Bob: Aw, come on! Nothing to it!* **2.** *Inf.* The rumor you heard is not true. □ *Pay no attention to all that talk. There's nothing to it.*

There's the rub. *Fig.* That's the problem. (From Shakespeare's *Hamlet*, Act 3, Scene 1, in the famous line "To sleep: perchance to dream: ay, there's the rub . . . ".) □ *It's available online, but they require a credit card and I don't have one. There's the rub.*

They don't make them like they used to. *Cliché* Goods are not as well made now as they were in the past. (Often used as a catchphrase. Them is often 'em.) □ *Why don't cars last longer? They just don't make 'em like they used to.*

They must have seen you coming. *Inf.* You were really cheated. They saw you coming and decided they could cheat you easily. □ *Andy: It cost $200 dollars. Rachel: You paid $200 for that thing? Boy, they must have seen you coming.*

They went that a'way. *Cliché* The villains went in that direction. (From Western movies.) □ *Those guys aren't here. They went that a'way.*

thick and fast *Fig.* in large numbers or amounts and at a rapid rate. □ *New problems seem to come thick and fast.*

*****thick as a short plank** AND *****thick as two short planks** exceptionally dimwitted. (*Also: **as** ~.) □ *Dumb? He's as thick as a short plank, more like.*

*****thick as pea soup** [of fog] very thick. (*Also: **as** ~.) □ *This fog is as thick as pea soup. You can't see 10 feet in front of you.*

*****thick as thieves** *Cliché* very close-knit; friendly; allied. (Thick = close and loyal. *Also: **as** ~.) □ *Mary, Tom, and Sally are as thick as thieves. They go everywhere together.*

thick as two short planks Go to thick as a short plank.

*****thick-skinned** *Fig.* not easily upset or hurt; insensitive. (The opposite of thin-skinned. *Typically: **be** ~; **become** ~; **grow** ~.) □ *Jane's so thick-skinned she didn't realize Fred was being rude to her.*

a **thing of the past** something that is old-fashioned or obsolete. □ *Taking off hats in elevators is a thing of the past.*

*a **thing or two (about** so/sth) **1.** *Fig.* bits of information or criticism about someone or something; a few facts about someone or something. (*Typically: **find out** ~; **know** ~; **learn** ~; **tell** so ~.) □ *I know a thing or two about Mary that would really shock you.* **2.** *Fig.* a few points of criticism about someone or something. (*Typically: **tell** so ~.) □ *I told her a thing or two about her precious little boy!*

Things are looking up. *Fig.* Conditions are looking better. □ *Things are looking up at school. I'm doing better in all my classes.*

Things getting you down? Go to (Are) things getting you down?

think a great deal of so/sth Go to next.

think a lot of so/sth AND **think a great deal of** so/sth; **think highly of** so/sth; **think much of** so/sth *Fig.* to think well of someone or something. □ *The teacher thinks a lot of Mary and her talents.*

think ahead of one's **time** Go to ahead of one's time.

think better of so/sth to raise one's opinion of someone or something. □ *I think better of him since I saw how well he does in the sales meetings.*

think better of sth *Fig.* to reconsider doing something and end up not doing it. □ *I hope that you will think better of what you are doing and how many people you are hurting.*

Think big. *Fig.* Think and plan ambitiously. □ *Don't just wait for things to come your way! Go after what you want. Think big.*

think for oneself to do one's own thinking; to think independently. □ *Sam has to learn to think for himself. He can't let other people make his decisions for him all his life.*

think so **hung the moon (and stars)** AND **think** so **is God's own cousin** *Rur.* to think someone is perfect. □ *Joe won't listen to any complaints about Mary. He thinks she hung the moon and stars.*

think inside the box *Fig.* to think in traditional fashion, bound by old, nonfunctional, or limiting structures, rules, or practices. (As if thinking or creativity were confined or limited by a figurative box. See also **inside the box.** Compare this with **think outside the box.**) □ *You guys only think inside the box and will never find a better solution.*

think so **is God's own cousin** Go to **think** so hung the moon (and stars).

think little of so/sth AND **think nothing of** so/sth *Fig.* to have a low opinion of someone or something. □ *People may think nothing of it now, but in a few years everyone will praise it.*

think nothing of doing sth *Fig.* to give no thought or hesitation to doing something. □ *She thinks nothing of helping other people at any time of day or night.*

think nothing of so/sth Go to **think little of** so/sth.

Think nothing of it. AND **Don't mention it.; No prob(lem).** *Fig.* You are welcome (in response to thanks). (Formulaic responses to an expression of gratitude. In descending order of politeness.) □ *A: We are very grateful for your kindness. B: Think nothing of it.* □ *A: Thanks, dude! B: No prob, dude.*

think on one's **feet** *Fig.* to be able to speak and reason well while (standing and talking) in front of an audience, especially extemporaneously. □ *I am not able to think on my feet too well before a bunch of people.*

think out loud *Fig.* to say one's thoughts aloud. □ *Excuse me. I didn't really mean to say that. I was just thinking out loud.*

think outside the box *Fig.* to think freely, not bound by old, nonfunctional, or limiting structures, rules, or practices. (As if thinking or creativity were confined in or limited by a figurative box. See also **outside the box.** Compare this with **think inside the box.**) □ *Let's think outside the box for a minute and try to find a better solution.*

think straight *Fig.* to think clearly. (Often negative.) □ *I'm so tired I can't think straight.*

think the sun rises and sets on so *Fig.* to think someone is the most important person in the world. □ *She worships that boyfriend of hers. She thinks the sun rises and sets on him.*

think the world of so/sth *Fig.* to be very fond of someone or something. □ *The old lady thinks the world of her cats.*

think twice about so/sth *Fig.* to give careful consideration to someone or something. □ *Ed may be a good choice, but I suggest that you think twice about him.*

think twice (before doing sth**)** *Fig.* to consider carefully whether one should do something; to be cautious about doing something. (Often negative, showing a lack of caution.) □ *You should think twice before quitting your job.* □ *I don't think twice about driving through Chicago at rush hour.*

think under fire Go to under fire.

*thin-skinned *Fig.* easily upset or hurt; sensitive. (The opposite of thick-skinned. *Typically: **be** ~; **become** ~; **grow** ~.) ☐ *You'll have to handle Mary's mother carefully. She's very thin-skinned.*

*the third degree *Fig.* a long and detailed period of questioning. (*Typically: **get** ~; **give** so ~.) ☐ *Why is it I get the third degree from you every time I come home late?*

thirst for sth *Fig.* to have a strong desire for something. ☐ *In the old days, students were said to thirst for knowledge.*

thirsty for sth *Fig.* craving or desiring something. ☐ *That evil tyrant is thirsty for power.*

This is where I came in. *Fig.* I have heard all this before. (Said when a situation begins to seem repetitive, as when a film one has seen part of before reaches familiar scenes.) ☐ *John sat through a few minutes of the argument, and when Tom and Alice kept saying the same thing over and over, John said, "This is where I came in," and left the room.*

This one is on so. *Fig.* The cost of this drink or meal will be paid by the person named or designated. ☐ *A: Should we ask for separate checks or what? B: No, no, this one's on the boss!*

This (seat) taken? Go to (Is) this (seat) taken?

thither and yon *Fig.* there and everywhere. (Stilted or jocular.) ☐ *I sent my résumé thither and yon, but no one responded.*

a **thorn in** so's **flesh** Go to next.

*a thorn in so's **side** AND ***a thorn in** so's **flesh; *a thorn in the side of** so *Fig.* a constant bother or annoyance to someone. (*Typically: **be** ~; **become** ~.) ☐ *John was a thorn in my flesh for years before I finally got rid of him.*

Those were the days. *Cliché* The days we have been referring to were the greatest of times. ☐ *Those were the days. Back when people knew right from wrong.*

thoughts to live by Go to words to live by.

thrash sth **out**† *Fig.* to discuss something thoroughly and solve any problems. ☐ *The committee took hours to thrash the whole matter out.*

three sheets in the wind AND **three sheets (to the wind); two sheets to the wind** *Inf.* intoxicated and unsteady. (Sheets are the ropes used to manage a ship's sails. It is assumed that if these ropes were blowing in the wind, the ship would be out of control.) ☐ *He had gotten three sheets to the wind and didn't pay attention to my warning.*

three squares (a day) *Inf.* three nourishing meals a day. (With breakfast, lunch, and dinner considered the usual three meals. *Square* is clearly from *square meal*, which means, strangely, well-rounded meal. The *square* is the same as that found in *square deal*. Tales about sailors eating off of square plates or military academy cadets eating while sitting squarely in their chairs, while enticing, are not linked by any evidence to this term.) ☐ *If I could limit myself to three squares, I could lose some weight.*

thrill so **to death** Go to next.

thrill so **to pieces** AND **thrill** so **to death; thrill** so **to bits** *Fig.* to please or excite someone very much. (Not only figurative, but exaggerated.) ☐ *John sent flowers to Ann and thrilled her to pieces.* ☐ *Your wonderful comments thrilled me to death.*

thrilled to death AND **thrilled to pieces** *Fig.* very excited; to be very pleased. ☐ *She was thrilled to death to get the flowers.*

thrilled to pieces Go to previous.

through and through *Fig.* thoroughly; completely. ☐ *I've studied this report through and through trying to find the facts you've mentioned.*

through hell Go to through the mill.

through hell and high water *Fig.* through all sorts of severe difficulties. ☐ *I came through hell and high water to get to this* *meeting on time. Why don't you start on time?*

*through the cracks *Fig.* [moving] past the elements that are intended to catch or detect such things. (*Typically: **fall** ~; **go** ~; **slip** ~.) □ *I am afraid that some of these issues will slip through the cracks unless we make a note about each one.*

*through the grapevine AND ***by the grapevine** *Fig.* by way of rumor. (From prisons and the military. Fig. on the mental picture of a grapevine growing rapidly from cell to cell in a prison. *Typically: **hear** sth ~; **heard it** ~; **spread** sth ~.) □ *How do I know? I heard it through the grapevine. I can't tell you any more than that.*

*through the mill AND ***through hell** *Fig.* badly treated; abused and exhausted. (Fig. on a grain mill. *Typically: **been** ~; **go** ~; **put** so ~; **send** so ~.) □ *This has been a rough day. I've really been through the mill.* □ *This old car is banged up, and it hardly runs. We really put it through the mill.*

through thick and thin *Cliché* through good times and bad times. □ *We've been together through thick and thin, and we won't desert each other now.*

throw so *Fig.* to confuse someone. □ *The question the teacher asked was so hard that it threw me, and I became very nervous.*

throw so **a curve (ball) 1.** to pitch a curve ball to someone in baseball. □ *The pitcher threw John a curve, and John swung wildly against thin air.* **2.** *Fig.* to confuse someone by doing something tricky or unexpected. (Fig. on ①.) □ *When you said "house" you threw me a curve. The password was supposed to be "home."*

throw a fight *Fig.* to lose a boxing match on purpose. (Other words can replace *a*.) □ *I just know that Wilbur didn't throw that fight.*

throw a fit Go to **have a fit**.

throw a game *Fig.* to lose a game on purpose. □ *There's a couple of those guys who*

would throw a game if they got enough money to do it.

throw a (monkey) wrench in the works *Inf.* to cause problems for someone's plans. (*Monkey wrench* = a type of flat jawed adjustable wrench. *Monkey wrench* is alleged to be named for Charles Moncky, who is credited with its invention. The idiom alludes to the image of sabotage committed by tossing a wrench into the gear works of a large machine.) □ *I don't want to throw a wrench in the works, but have you checked your plans with a lawyer?*

throw a party (for so**)** *Fig.* to have a party; to hold a party; to arrange a party. □ *Bill threw a party for his sister before she went away to college.*

throw a punch *Inf.* to jab; to punch. □ *She tried to throw a punch at me, but I blocked it.*

throw a (temper) tantrum *Fig.* to have a temper tantrum; to put on an active display of childish temper. □ *I never dreamed that Bob would throw a tantrum right there in the department store. You must be so embarrassed!*

throw oneself **at** so AND **fling** oneself **at** so *Fig.* to give oneself willingly to someone else for romance. □ *I guess that Mary really likes John. She practically threw herself at him when he came into the room.*

throw oneself **at** so's **feet 1.** *Fig.* to bow down humbly at someone's feet; to prostrate oneself before someone. □ *In his guilt and horror, he threw himself at the feet of his master and begged forgiveness.* **2.** *Fig.* to beg someone's mercy, forgiveness, blessing, etc. (Fig. on ①.) □ *I throw myself at your feet and beg for your blessing.*

throw oneself **at the mercy of** some authority AND **throw** oneself **on the mercy of** some authority; **throw** oneself **(up)on** so's **mercy** *Fig.* to seek mercy from a court of law, especially at one's sentencing for a crime; to seek help from an official or institution. □ *He pleaded guilty and threw himself at the mercy of the court.*

throw caution to the wind *Cliché* to become very careless. □ *Jane, who is usually cautious, threw caution to the wind and went swimming in the ocean.*

throw cold water on sth Go to pour cold water on sth.

throw doubt on so/sth Go to cast doubt on so/sth.

throw down the gauntlet *Fig.* to challenge someone to an argument or to (figurative) combat. (This *gauntlet* was a glove.) □ *When Bob challenged my conclusions, he threw down the gauntlet. I was ready for an argument.*

throw so **for a loop** Go to knock so for a loop.

throw so **for a loss** *Fig.* to cause someone to be uncertain or confused. (Often passive.) □ *The stress of being in front of so many people threw Ann for a loss. She forgot her speech.*

throw good money after bad AND **pour good money after bad** *Fig.* to waste additional money after wasting money once. □ *The Browns are always throwing good money after bad. They bought an acre of land that turned out to be swamp and then paid to have it filled in, but nothing will grow there.*

throw one's **hands up**† **(in despair) 1.** to make a gesture of throwing up one's hands indicating futility, despair, finality, etc. □ *He threw his hands up in despair and walked away.* **2.** *Fig.* to give up in despair. (Fig. on ①.) □ *John threw his hands up in despair because they wouldn't let him see his brother in the hospital.*

throw one's **hat in the ring** Go to toss one's hat into the ring.

throw in one's **lot with** so/sth Go to cast one's lot with so/sth.

throw in the sponge Go to next.

throw in the towel AND **throw in the sponge; toss in the sponge** *Fig.* to signal that one is going to quit; to quit. (From boxing, where this is done by a boxer's trainer to stop the fight.) □ *When*

John could stand no more of Mary's bad temper, he threw in the towel and left.

throw in with so *Fig.* to join with someone; to join someone's enterprise. □ *I will throw in with you, and we can all go hunting together.*

throw oneself **into** sth **1.** *Fig.* to jump into something, such as a body of water. □ *He stood on the bridge and threw himself into the river because he was unhappy with life.* **2.** *Fig.* to enter into or join something eagerly and wholeheartedly. (Fig. on ①.) □ *Todd always threw himself into a project from start to finish.*

throw sth **in(to)** so's **face** *Fig.* to confront someone with a problem or criticism. □ *Jerry caused this mess. I'll just throw the whole problem into his face and tell him to fix it.*

throw sth **into the bargain** AND **include** sth **in the bargain; throw** sth **in**† *Fig.* to include something extra in a deal. □ *To encourage me to buy a new car, the car dealer threw a satellite radio into the bargain.*

throw sth **in(to) the pot** *Fig.* to add an idea or suggestion to the discussion. (Fig. on making a pot of soup or stew.) □ *Let me throw something in the pot. Let's think about selling stock in the company.*

throw an amount of **light on** so/sth to present some revealing information about someone or something. □ *What you have just told me throws a lot of light on George and his motivation.*

throw money at sth *Fig.* to try to solve a problem by indiscriminately spending money on it. □ *This agency has thrown money at the housing problem, but it has been nothing but a long-term disaster.*

throw money down the drain Go to pour money down the drain.

throw so's **name around** *Fig.* to impress people by saying you know a famous or influential person. □ *You won't get anywhere around here by throwing the mayor's name around.*

throw sth **off**† **1.** *Fig.* to resist or recover from a disease. □ *It was a bad cold, but I managed to throw it off in a few days.* **2.** *Fig.* to emit or give off an odor. □ *The small animal threw a strong odor off.*

throw so **off balance 1.** to cause someone to falter (and probably fall). □ *The cyclist bumped into me and threw me off balance.* **2.** *Fig.* to confuse or disorient one. (Fig. on ①.) □ *The teacher was thrown off balance by the students' difficult questions.*

throw so **off the scent** Go to put so off the scent.

throw so **off the track 1.** AND **throw** so **off the trail** to cause someone to lose the trail (when following someone or something). □ *The raccoon threw us off the track by running through the creek.* **2.** *Fig.* to cause one to lose one's place in the sequence of things. (Fig. on ①.) □ *The interruption threw me off the track for a moment, but I soon got started again with my presentation.*

throw so **off the trail** Go to previous.

throw one **out on** one's **ear** *Inf.* to remove someone from a place forcibly. □ *Straighten up, or I'll throw you out on your ear.*

throw sth **out**† **(to** so/sth**)** Go to toss sth out† (to so/sth).

throw (some) light on sth Go to shed (some) light on sth.

throw the baby out† **with the bath(water)** *Fig.* to dispose of the good while eagerly trying to get rid of the bad. (Fig. on the image of carelessly emptying a tub of both the water inside as well as the baby that was being washed.) □ *In her haste to talk down a project that had only a few disagreeable points, she has thrown the baby out with the bathwater.*

throw the book at so *Fig.* to charge or convict someone with as many crimes as is possible. □ *I made the police officer angry, so he took me to the station and threw the book at me.*

throw the bull AND **throw the crap** *Inf.* to chat; to boast. (*Bull* = bullshit. Caution with *crap*.) □ *Tom could really throw the bull and sound right as rain.*

throw the crap Go to previous.

throw so **to the dogs** *Fig.* to abandon someone to enemies or evil. □ *The spy served the evil empire well, but in the end, they threw him to the dogs.*

throw so **to the wolves** *Fig.* to sacrifice someone to save the rest; to abandon someone to harm. (Fig. on the image of giving one person to the wolves to eat so the rest can get away.) □ *The investigation was going to be rigorous and unpleasant, and I could see they were going to throw someone to the wolves.*

throw up *Fig.* to vomit. □ *I was afraid I would throw up, the food was so horrible.*

throw sth **up**† **1.** *Fig.* to build or erect something in a hurry. □ *They threw up the building in only a few weeks.* **2.** *Fig.* to vomit something. □ *Poor Wally threw his dinner up.*

throw sth **up to** so *Fig.* to confront someone with something. □ *I threw the whole matter up to her, but she had nothing to say about it.*

throw one's **voice** *Fig.* to project one's voice so that it seems to be coming from some other place. □ *Jane can throw her voice, so I thought she was standing behind me.*

throw one's **weight around** *Fig.* to attempt to boss people around; to give orders. □ *The district manager came to our office and tried to throw his weight around, but no one paid any attention to him.*

throw one's **weight behind** so/sth *Fig.* to use one's influence to advocate for someone or something. □ *The mayor threw her weight behind her own candidate for water commissioner.*

thrust and parry *Fig.* to enter into verbal combat [with someone]; to compete actively [with someone]. (Fig. on the sport of fencing.) □ *I spent the entire afternoon thrusting and parrying with a committee* *of so-called experts in the field of insurance.*

thumb a ride AND **hitch a ride** *Fig.* to get a ride from a passing motorist; to make a sign with one's thumb that indicates to passing drivers that one is asking for a ride. □ *My car broke down on the highway, and I had to thumb a ride to get back to town.*

thumb one's **nose at** so/sth **1.** *Fig.* to show a sign of derision at someone or something by placing the thumb to the side of the nose. (Often while wiggling the other fingers of the hand.) □ *Don't thumb your nose at me unless you want a fight.* **2.** *Fig.* to dismiss someone or something as worthless, verbally. (Fig. on ①.) □ *Walter thumbed his nose at Fred and asked the gang to send someone else to do the job.*

thumb through sth AND **leaf through** sth *Fig.* to look through a book, magazine, or newspaper, without reading it carefully. □ *I've only thumbed through this book, but it looks very interesting.* □ *I leafed through a magazine while waiting to see the doctor.*

a **thumbnail sketch** *Fig.* a brief or small picture or description. □ *The manager gave a thumbnail sketch of her plans.*

thumbs-down 1. *Fig.* a sign of disapproval. □ *The administration's tax bill got a thumbs-down in Congress.* **2.** *Fig.* disapproving; negative. □ *It was thumbs-down, and I was disappointed.*

thumbs-up 1. *Fig.* a sign of approval. □ *It was a thumbs-up on the new filtration plant at Thursday's village board meeting.* **2.** *Fig.* approving; positive. □ *The new filtration plant got a thumbs-up decision at the board meeting.*

thump sth **out**[†] **(on the piano)** *Inf.* to pound out music on a piano. □ *Joel thumped a happy tune out on the piano.*

thunder across sth *Fig.* to move across something, making a rumbling sound. □ *As the race car thundered across the track, people strained to get a better view.*

thunder sth **out**[†] *Fig.* to respond with words spoken in a voice like thunder. □ *He thundered the words out so everyone could hear them.*

thunder past so/sth *Fig.* to move past someone or something, rumbling. □ *As the traffic thundered past, I wondered why there was so much of it.*

tick so **off**[†] *Inf.* to make someone angry. □ *That really ticks me off!*

tick sth **off**[†] to recite items from a list. (As if one were making a check mark while reciting.) □ *Fred quickly ticked off the list of things he needed from the store.*

ticked (off) *Inf.* angry. □ *Wow, was she ticked off!*

tickle so's **fancy** Go to strike so's **fancy**.

tickle so **pink** *Fig.* to please or entertain someone very much. □ *Bill told a joke that really tickled us all pink.*

tickle the ivories *Inf.* to play the piano. □ *I used to be able to tickle the ivories real nice.*

tickle so **to death** AND **tickle** so **to pieces** *Fig.* to please someone a great deal. □ *What you told her just tickled her to death!*

tickle so **to pieces** Go to previous.

tickled pink *Fig.* very much pleased or entertained. □ *We were tickled pink when your flowers arrived.*

tide so **over**[†] **(until** sth**)** *Fig.* to supply someone until a certain time or until something happens. □ *There is enough food here to tide over the entire camp until next month.*

the **tide turned 1.** *Fig.* the tide changed from high tide to low tide or vice versa. □ *The tide turned before the ship had sailed out of the harbor.* **2.** *Fig.* the trend changed from one thing to another. □ *We planned our investments to take advantage of the growth of the stock market. Then the tide turned, and we lost buckets of money.*

tidy so/sth **up**[†] Go to spruce so/sth **up**[†].

tie so **down**[†] *Fig.* [for responsibilities] to limit a person; to keep a person in an association or relationship. □ *I was afraid that getting married would tie me down, but it's been great.*

tie so's **hands** *Fig.* to prevent someone from doing something. □ *I'd like to help you, but my boss has tied my hands.*

tie one on AND **hang one on; lay one on; tie it on** *Sl.* to get drunk. □ *The boys went out to tie one on.* □ *They laid one on, but good.*

tie the knot 1. *Fig.* to marry a mate. □ *We tied the knot in a little chapel on the Arkansas border.* **2.** *Fig.* [for a cleric or other authorized person] to unite a couple in marriage. □ *It only took a few minutes for the ship's captain to tie the knot.*

tie so **to** sth *Fig.* to associate someone with something; to make a connection between someone and something. □ *The police are trying to tie Lefty to the burglary.*

tie so/sth **up**† *Fig.* to keep someone or something busy or occupied. □ *The meeting tied me up all afternoon.*

tie sth **up**† **1.** *Fig.* to conclude and finalize something. □ *Let's try to tie up this deal by Thursday.* **2.** *Fig.* to block or impede something, such as traffic or progress. □ *The stalled bus tied traffic up for over an hour.*

tie so **(up) in knots** *Fig.* to become anxious or upset. □ *John tied himself in knots worrying about his wife during her operation.*

tied down *Fig.* restricted by responsibilities. □ *I don't feel tied down, even though I have a lot of responsibility.*

tied to one's **mother's apron strings** *Fig.* dominated by one's mother; dependent on one's mother. □ *Isn't he a little old to be tied to his mother's apron strings?*

tied up *Fig.* busy. □ *I will be tied up in a meeting for an hour.*

*tight as a drum 1. stretched tight. (*Also: **as** ~.) □ *Julia stretched the upholstery fabric over the seat of the chair until it was as tight as a drum.* **2.** sealed tight. (*Also: **as** ~.) □ *Now that I've caulked all the*

windows, the house should be tight as a drum. **3.** AND ***tight as Midas's fist** very stingy. (*Also: **as** ~.) □ *Old Mr. Robinson is tight as Midas's fist. Won't spend money on anything.*

*tight as a tick 1. very tight. (Fig. on the image of a tick swollen tight with blood or of a tick stuck tightly in someone's skin. *Also: **as** ~.) □ *The windows were closed—tight as a tick—to keep the cold out.* **2.** intoxicated. (Fig. on full as a tick. *Also: **as** ~.) □ *The old man was tight as a tick, but still lucid.* **3.** [of a race] close, as if the racers are moving very closely together. (*Also: **as** ~.) □ *This election is as tight as a tick.* **4.** very friendly and close; thick as thieves. (*Also: **as** ~.) □ *Those two are tight as a tick. They are always together.*

tight as Midas's fist Go to tight as a drum.

a **tight race** *Fig.* a close race. □ *It was a tight race right up to the final turn when my horse pulled ahead and won easily.*

tighten one's **belt** *Fig.* to manage to spend less money; to use less of something. (See also take one's belt in (a notch).) □ *Things are beginning to cost more and more. It looks like we'll all have to tighten our belts.*

tighten the screws on (so**)** Go to put the heat on (so).

tighten up 1. *Fig.* [for someone or a group] to become miserly. □ *We almost went out of business when we couldn't get credit because the bank tightened up.* **2.** *Fig.* [for someone or something] to become more restrictive. (Fig. on ①.) □ *There are more rules, and the people who enforce them are tightening up.*

tightfisted (with money) AND **close-fisted (with money)** *Fig.* very stingy with money. □ *The manager is very close-fisted with expenditures.*

till kingdom come *Fig.* until the end of the world; forever. □ *Do I have to keep assembling these units till kingdom come?*

Till next time. Go to Good-bye for now.

till the bitter end Go to to the bitter end.

till the cows come home Go to (un)til the cows come home.

till the fat lady sings AND **when the fat lady sings** *Fig.* at the end; a long time from now. (Supposedly from a tale about a child—sitting through an opera—who asks a parent when it will be over. "Not until the fat lady sings" is the answer, referring to the archetypal bulky opera singer. Of course, it means not until *after* the fat lady sings.) □ *We can leave with everybody else when the fat lady sings.*

Till we meet again. Go to Good-bye for now.

tilt at windmills *Fig.* to fight battles with imaginary enemies; to fight against unimportant enemies or issues. (As with the fictional character Don Quixote, who attacked windmills. *Tilt* = joust with.) □ *I'm not going to fight this issue. I've wasted too much of my life tilting at windmills.*

tilt toward so/sth *Fig.* to favor choosing someone or something; to lean toward doing sth. □ *I am tilting toward Roger for my assistant.*

time after time AND **time and (time) again** *Fig.* repeatedly; over and over (again). □ *You've made the same error time after time! Please try to be more careful!* □ *I've told you time and again not to do that.*

Time flies! Go to (My,) how time flies!

time flies (when you're having fun) *Fig.* time passes very quickly. (From the Latin *tempus fugit.*) □ *I didn't really think it was so late when the party ended. Doesn't time fly?*

time hangs heavy (on so's **hands)** *Fig.* there is too much time and not enough to do. □ *I'm bored and nervous. Time hangs heavy on my hands.*

so's **time has come** AND some creature's **time has come** *Euph.* someone or some creature is about to die. □ *The poor old dog's time has come.*

time in *Fig.* to record one's arrival time. □ *Did you remember to time in this morning?*

time so **in**† *Fig.* to record someone's arrival time. □ *I timed you in at noon. Where were you?*

Time is money. *Fig.* (My) time is valuable, so don't waste it. □ *I can't afford to spend a lot of time standing here talking. Time is money, you know!*

Time is of the essence. *Fig.* Timing and meeting all the deadlines are essential and required. (Often seen in contractual agreements. It means that if the stated deadlines are not met exactly, the agreement is terminated and there is no recourse.) □ *The final payment is due on the first day of December, by midnight. Time is of the essence.*

time is on so's **side** *Fig.* the more time that elapses before something happens, the better. □ *Time is on your side. The money she demands is earning interest for you until the matter gets to court.*

the **time is ripe (for** sth) *Fig.* now is the right time for something. □ *When the time is ripe, I'll bring up the subject again.*

time is running out *Fig.* the allotted time is about to expire. (Possibly alluding to the running out of the sand in an hourglass.) □ *Hurry up. Time is running out.*

*****time is up 1.** [one's] lifetime has reached the end. (*Always: one's ~; so's or some creature's ~.) □ *The old dog knew when her time was up. She just lay down and died.* **2.** the allowed time period has expired. (*Typically: **its** ~; the ~.) □ *The time is up for this warranty.* □ *A bell rings when your time is up.*

one's **time of life** *Fig.* at one's age or state of life. □ *Why are you planning to start a new career at your time of life?*

*****time off** *Fig.* a period of time that is free from employment. (*Typically: **get** ~; **have** ~; **give** so ~; **take (some)** ~.) □ *I'll have to get time off for jury duty.*

*****time off for good behavior 1.** *Fig.* a reduction in one's prison sentence because of good behavior. (*Typically: **get** ~; **have** ~; **give** so ~.) □ *Bob will get out of jail tomorrow rather than next week. He* got *time off for good behavior.* **2.** *Fig.* a shortened time period—such as a meeting, period of punishment, school class, etc. (Fig. on ①. Jocular. *Typically: **get** ~; **have** ~; **give** so ~.) □ *They let me out of the meeting early. They said I got time off for good behavior.*

Time (out)! *Fig.* Stop everything for just a minute! □ *"Hey, stop a minute! Time out!" yelled Mary as the argument grew in intensity.*

time out *Fig.* to record one's departure time. □ *Did you remember to time out when you left work?*

time so **out**† *Fig.* to record someone's departure time. □ *Harry had to time everyone out because the time clock was broken.*

time period **after** time period AND time period **by** time period extending over a series of similar time periods, usually implying that the overall time period is long and boring. (Includes: **second after second; minute after minute; hour after hour; day after day; night after night; week after week; month after month; year after year;** and similarly with *by*.) □ *Week after week, we sat and waited to be rescued.*

time stands still *Fig.* time seems not to progress at all. □ *Time stood still while I gazed at her beauty.*

time was (that) . . . it was the custom at a previous time that. . . . □ *Time was a child didn't speak to his elders that way.*

Time will tell. *Fig.* Something will become known in the course of time. □ *Who knows what the future will bring? Only time will tell.*

a **tin ear** *Fig.* a poor ear for music; a poor hearing ability when it comes to music and distinguishing pitches. □ *I think I had better not try to sing along with you. I have a tin ear and would ruin your performance.*

tip one's **hand** Go to **show** one's **hand.**

the **tip of the iceberg** *Fig.* only the part of something that can be easily observed, but not the rest of it, which is hidden.

(Referring to the fact that the major bulk of an iceberg is below the surface of the water.) □ *The problems that you see here now are just the tip of the iceberg. There are numerous disasters waiting to happen.*

tip the balance AND **tip the scales** *Fig.* to be the bit of information needed to reach a conclusion or decision. (This may refer to the "scales of justice," but the metaphor is used more widely than in law alone.) □ *This piece of new evidence is just enough to tip the scales in favor of the defendant.*

tip the scales at sth to weigh a particular weight. (See also **tip the scales at tip the balance.**) □ *The champ weighed in and tipped the scales at 180.*

tits and ass *Fig.* a public display of [the human female] breasts and buttocks. (Referring to television, film, and stage performances in which breasts and buttocks are emphasized or displayed prominently. Fixed order. Caution with *ass*.) □ *We have a really fine choice on television tonight. There is a live autopsy on channel 2, vampire horror on channel 5, and tits and ass on channel 10.*

to a great extent *Cliché* mainly; largely. □ *I've finished my work to a great extent. There is nothing important left to do.*

to a man including each person; without exception. □ *The club voted to a man to remain independent.*

to advantage to good effect; for an advantage; to one's or its benefit. □ *She used bright colors to advantage, catching the eye with reds and yellows.*

to and fro *Fig.* [of movement] toward and away from something. □ *The lion in the cage moved to and fro, watching the people in front of the cage.*

to beat the band *Inf.* very briskly; very fast; in an extreme way. (Possibly originally meaning to make more noise than the band or to march faster than a marching band.) □ *He's selling computers to beat the band since he started advertising.*

to boot *Inf.* in addition; to complement or complete. □ *She got an F on her term paper and flunked the final to boot.*

so/sth **to call** one's **own** one's own thing or kind of person. □ *I'll be so glad when I have a wife to call my own.*

to date up to the present time. □ *I've done everything I'm supposed to have done to date.*

to die for *Sl.* important or desirable enough to die for; worth dying for. □ *We had a beautiful room at the hotel and the service was to die for.*

To each his own. AND **To each their own.; To each his or her own.; To each her own.** One makes one's own choices.; People have different tastes. (The first entry head is the original. The others assume that the original one referred exclusively to males and seek to remedy that situation.) □ *So she likes peanut butter and banana sandwiches. To each his own.*

To each their own. Go to previous.

*****to go 1.** *Fig.* [of a purchase of cooked food] to be taken elsewhere to be eaten. (*Typically: **buy** some food ~; **get** some food ~; **have** some food ~; **order** some food ~.) □ *I didn't thaw anything for dinner. Let's stop off on the way home and get something to go.* **2.** *Fig.* [of a number or an amount] remaining; yet to be dealt with. □ *I finished with two of them and have four to go.*

sth **to hang** one's **hat on** *Fig.* an idea or plan that one can accept and work with. □ *These vague ideas of yours are not getting us anywhere. I need something to hang my hat on, something solid and well planned.*

some place **to hang (up)** one's **hat** *Fig.* a place to live; a place to call one's home. □ *What I need is somewhere to hang up my hat. I just can't stand all this traveling.*

to one's **heart's content** *Fig.* as much as one wants. □ *John wanted a week's vacation so he could go to the lake and fish to his heart's content.*

to hell and gone Go to all over creation.

To hell with so/sth! *Inf.* I reject someone or something. (Very stern or angry.) □ *Mary: I think we ought to go to the dance Friday night. Tom: To hell with that! Mary: To hell with you!*

to so's **liking** *Fig.* fitting someone's personal preferences. □ *I had my house painted, but the job was not to my liking.*

to little avail Go to to no avail.

to my mind Go to next.

to my way of thinking AND **to my mind** *Fig.* in my opinion. □ *To my way of thinking, this is the perfect kind of vacation.*

to no avail AND **of no avail; to little avail** *Cliché* with no effect; unsuccessful. □ *Everything I did to help was of no avail. Nothing worked.*

to put it another way AND **put another way** *Fig.* a phrase introducing a restatement of what someone, usually the speaker, has just said. □ *Father: You're still very young, Tom. To put it another way, you don't have any idea about what you're getting into.*

to put it mildly *Fig.* to understate something; to say something politely. □ *She was angry at almost everyone—to put it mildly.*

to say nothing of so/sth AND **not to mention** so/sth; **not to speak of** so/sth *Fig.* ignoring the mention of someone or something in addition. (Very close to let alone so/sth.) □ *What a day! We had lots of troublesome callers this morning, not to mention the leak in the roof.*

to say the least *Fig.* at the very least; without overemphasizing the subject; **to put it mildly.** □ *We were not at all pleased with her work—to say the least.*

*****sth **to shout about** *Fig.* something that causes one to show pride or enthusiasm about someone or something. (*Typically: **be** ~; **have** ~.) □ *Getting into med school is really something to shout about.*

to some extent *Fig.* to some degree; in some amount; partly. □ *I've solved this problem to some extent.*

to speak out of both sides of one's **mouth** Go to speak with a forked tongue.

to the best of one's **ability** as well as one is able. □ *I did the work to the best of my ability.*

to the bitter end AND **till the bitter end** *Fig.* to the very end. (Originally nautical. This originally had nothing to do with bitterness.) □ *It took me a long time to get through school, but I worked hard at it all the way to the bitter end.*

to the contrary *Fig.* as the opposite of what has been stated; contrary to what has been stated. (As with **evidence** ~; **proof** ~. Very close in meaning to on the contrary but always used to modify one of a small set of nouns.) □ *We thought the whole house needed a new roof, but evidence to the contrary indicated it would last a few more years.*

to the core *Fig.* all the way through; basically and essentially. (Usually with some negative sense, such as *evil, rotten,* etc.) □ *Bill said that John is evil to the core.*

to the ends of the earth *Fig.* to the remotest and most inaccessible points on the earth. □ *I'll pursue him to the ends of the earth.*

to the hilt *Fig.* [in] as far as possible. (Fig. on the hilt of a sword being stabbed all the way in.) □ *We enjoyed it to the hilt.* □ *Fill it all the way to the hilt.*

to the last *Fig.* to the very end; to the conclusion. □ *It was a very boring play, but I sat through it to the last.*

to the letter *Fig.* exactly as instructed; exactly as written. □ *We didn't prepare the recipe to the letter, but the cake still turned out very well.*

to the manner born AND **to the manor born 1.** *Fig.* expected to behave in a particular manner that comes naturally. (This sense is close to Shakespeare's original in *Hamlet* and is meant to be the *manner* version and should be spelled that way.) □ *Everyone in the valley is in the habit of drinking heavily, and since I was born here, I am legitimately to the manner born.* **2.** *Fig.* privileged; acting as if one had been born in a manor house and were used to the privileges and pleasures thereof. (This originated as a misunderstanding or mishearing of the *Hamlet* line and has then acquired a meaning more appropriate to the spelling *manor.* The punning potential was further developed in the BBC television series *To the Manor Born* starring Penelope Keith, whose manner was definitely appropriate to the manor house she was forced to sell.) □ *I'm not exactly to the manor born, but I can hold my own among those with wealth and station.*

to the max *Sl.* as much as possible, maximally. □ *They worked to the max their whole shift.*

to the nth degree *Fig.* to the maximum amount. □ *Jane is a perfectionist and tries to be careful to the nth degree.*

to the point *Fig.* relevant; associated with the topic of discussion. (See also get to the point.) □ *I wish your comments were more to the point.*

to the tune of some amount of money *Fig.* to a certain amount of money. □ *My checking account is overdrawn to the tune of $340.*

to whom it may concern *Cliché* to the person to whom this applies. (A form of address used when you do not know the name of the person who handles the kind of business you are writing about.) □ *When you don't know who to write to, just say, "To whom it may concern."*

to wit *Fig.* namely; that is; that is to say. □ *Many students, to wit Mary, Bill, Sue, and Anne, complained about their teacher.*

the **toast of** some place *Fig.* a notably famous and sought-after person in a particular place. (This suggests that this person would frequently be the subject of toasts. One of the most popular places is *the town.*) □ *Since she became the American Idol, she is the toast of every town in the U.S.* □ *Tony, the city's favorite weather man, is the toast of St. Louis.*

toe the line Go to next.

toe the mark AND **toe the line** *Fig.* to do what one is expected to do; to follow the rules. (Sometimes spelled incorrectly as *tow the line. The mark* and *line* refer to a line on the ground that must act either as a barrier or a line that one must stand behind to show readiness. The link between the alleged origins and the current use is not comfortably clear.) □ *You'll get ahead, Sally. Don't worry. Just toe the mark, and everything will be okay.*

toing and froing (on sth**)** *Fig.* moving back and forth on an issue, first deciding one way and then changing to another. □ *The boss spent most of the afternoon toing and froing on the question of who was to handle the Wilson account.*

a **token gesture** *Fig.* an action or a decision that is so small or inconsequential as to be only symbolic. □ *Offering to pay for my dinner was only a token gesture. That does little to make up for my inconvenience.*

Tom, Dick, and Harry Go to (every) Tom, Dick, and Harry.

tongue-in-cheek *Fig.* insincere; joking. □ *The play seemed very serious at first, but then everyone saw that it was tongue-in-cheek, and they began laughing.*

*a **tongue-lashing** *Fig.* a severe scolding. (*Typically: **get** ~; **have** ~; **give** so ~.) □ *I really got a tongue-lashing when I got home.*

tons of sth AND **loads of** sth; **heaps of** sth *Inf.* lots of something. □ *We got tons of fried chicken, so help yourself.*

too big for one's **britches** *Rur.* too haughty for one's status or age. □ *Bill's getting a little too big for his britches, and somebody's going to straighten him out.*

too close for comfort *Cliché* [for a misfortune or a threat] to be dangerously close or threatening. (Usually in the past tense.) □ *When I was in the hospital, I nearly died from pneumonia. Believe me, that was too close for comfort.*

too close to call [of a game or contest] too nearly equal in score to allow anyone to predict the final outcome. □ *As of this moment, the election is too close to call.*

(too) close to the bone *Fig.* [of a remark] revealing or unpleasantly perceptive in that it is deep and penetrating; very close to an unpleasant truth. (Fig. on an accidental slice of a knife. See also too close for comfort.) □ *I appreciate your speaking frankly, but some of your remarks hurt. They cut a little close to the bone.*

*too funny for words** *Fig.* extremely funny. (*Typically: **be** ~; **get** ~.) □ *Tom is usually too funny for words at parties.*

*too good to be true** *Fig.* almost unbelievable; so good as to be unbelievable. (*Typically: **be** ~; **become** ~; **get** ~.) □ *When I finally got a big raise, it was too good to be true.*

too hot to handle 1. too hot to touch without getting burned. □ *My coffee is too hot to handle.* **2.** *Inf. Fig.* too exciting or risky to deal with; very "hot" or exciting. (Fig. on ①.) □ *This new singer is great. He's almost too hot to handle.*

too little too late too little help after the help was needed; too little money after there was a need for it. □ *Your thoughtfulness is appreciated, but your gift was too little too late, and we lost the house.*

*too much** *Fig.* overwhelming; excellent. (*Typically: **be** ~; **get to be** ~.) □ *It's wonderful. It's just too much!*

too much of a good thing *Fig.* more of a thing than is good or useful. □ *Too much of a good thing can make you sick, especially if the good thing is chocolate.*

too much too soon too much responsibility too early; too much money too soon in one's career. □ *Sarah got too much too soon and became lazy because there was no longer any motivation for her to work.*

too rich for so's **blood 1.** *Fig.* too expensive for one's budget. □ *This hotel is too rich for my blood.* **2.** *Fig.* too high in fat content for one's diet. □ *This dessert is too rich for my blood.*

tool around (in sth**)** *Inf.* to go around in a car; to speed around in a car. □ *Who is that kid tooling around in that souped-up car?*

tools of the trade 1. the special hand tools one needs to do one's physical labor. □ *Chisels and knives are the tools of the trade for a woodcarver.* **2.** *Fig.* the equipment, supplies, books, computers, telephones, etc. people need to work in the professions and allied support groups. □ *We have to have computers! Computers are the tools of the trade for writers!*

toot one's **own horn** Go to blow one's own horn.

top brass *Fig.* the highest leader(s); the boss(es). (Originally military.) □ *You'll have to check it out with the top brass. She'll be home around five.*

top notch *Fig.* the absolute best. (Hyphenated before a nominal.) □ *He prepared a top-notch meal before the movie, and dessert for afterwards.*

the **top of the heap** AND the **top of the ladder** *Fig.* a position superior to everyone else. □ *She fought her way to the top of the heap and means to stay there.*

the **top of the ladder** Go to previous.

top sth **off**† **1.** to add fluid to a container to bring the level of fluid closer to the top. □ *Sir, may I top off your drink?* □ *The sign says you are not supposed to top off your gas tank.* **2.** to serve as the final thing. □ *To top it all off, the cat died under the china cabinet.* □ *She topped off the evening by singing a song she had composed herself.*

top story AND **upper story** *Sl.* the brain; one's mind and intellect. □ *A little weak in the upper story, but other than that, a great guy.*

tore (up) AND **torn (up) 1.** *Sl.* distraught; emotionally upset. □ *Fred's really torn up about the accident.* **2.** *Sl.* intoxicated. □ *He wasn't just drunk—he was massively tore up.*

torn (up) Go to previous.

toss a salad *Fig.* to mix the various ingredients of a salad together. (The components of the salad are lifted and dropped in the bowl repeatedly in order to coat everything with dressing.) □ *I tossed the salad just before my guests arrived.*

toss and turn to sleep fitfully, turning and moving about during the night. (Fixed order.) □ *I tossed and turned all night long. Never got a wink of sleep.*

toss one's **cookies** *Sl.* to vomit. □ *Don't run too fast after you eat or you'll toss your cookies.*

toss (so) for sth *Fig.* to decide with someone, by tossing a coin, who will get or do something. □ *Let's see who gets to go first. I'll toss you for it.*

toss one's **hat into the ring** AND **throw** one's **hat in the ring** *Fig.* to announce that one is running for an elective office. □ *Jane wanted to run for treasurer, so she tossed her hat into the ring.*

toss in the sponge Go to throw in the towel.

toss sth **off**† **1.** *Fig.* to ignore or resist the bad effects of something. □ *John insulted Bob, but Bob just tossed it off.* **2.** *Fig.* to produce something easily or quickly. □ *I tossed that article off in only an hour.* **3.** *Fig.* to drink a drink very quickly. □ *He tossed a few beers off and left.*

toss sth **out**† **(to** so/sth**)** AND **throw** sth **out**† **(to** so/sth**)** *Fig.* to submit something, such as an idea to someone or something. □ *Let me toss out an idea that might help us all.* □ *Bob threw out an idea to the committee.*

a **total stranger** Go to a perfect stranger.

touch a (raw) nerve Go to hit a (raw) nerve.

touch a sore point Go to next.

touch a sore spot AND **touch a sore point; hit a sore point; hit on a sore point** *Fig.* to refer to a sensitive matter that will upset someone. (Fig. on the notion of touching an injury and causing pain.) □ *I seem to have touched a sore spot. I'm sorry. I didn't mean to upset you.*

touch and go *Fig.* very uncertain or critical. □ *Jane had a serious operation, and everything was touch and go for two days after her surgery.*

touch base (with so**)** *Inf.* to talk to someone; to confer with someone briefly. □ *John and I touched base on this question yesterday, and we are in agreement.*

a **touch of** sth **1.** *Fig.* a mild case of some illness. □ *I have a touch of the flu and need some more bed rest.* **2.** *Inf.* a little bit of something, particularly a small helping of food or drink. □ *A: How about some more? What do you need? B: I'll have just a touch of that meat loaf if there's enough to go around.*

touch so **(up) for** sth *Fig.* to approach someone and ask for something; to beg or borrow something from someone. □ *Jerry tried to touch me for 20 bucks, but I didn't have it.*

touch (up)on sth *Fig.* to mention something; to talk about something briefly. □ *In tomorrow's lecture I'd like to touch on the matter of taxation.*

touched by so/sth *Fig.* emotionally affected or moved by someone or something. □ *Sally was very nice to me. I was very touched by her.*

touched (in the head) crazy. □ *Sometimes Bob acts like he's touched in the head.*

a **tough act to follow** AND a **hard act to follow** *Fig.* a difficult presentation or performance to follow or improve upon with one's own performance. □ *Bill's speech was excellent. It was a tough act to follow, but my speech was good also.*

*****tough as an old boot** AND *****tough as (old) (shoe) leather 1.** [of meat] very tough. (*Also: **as** ~.) □ *Bob couldn't eat the steak. It was as tough as an old boot.* **2.** [of someone] very strong willed. (*Also: **as** ~.) □ *When Brian was lost in the mountains, his friends did not fear for him; they knew he was tough as leather.* **3.** [of someone] not easily moved by feel-

ings such as pity. (*Also: **as** ~.) □ *He was born tough as an old boot and has only grown more rigid.*

tough as nails Go to hard as nails.

tough as (old) (shoe) leather Go to tough as an old boot.

a **tough break** *Fig.* a bit of bad fortune. □ *John had a lot of tough breaks when he was a kid, but he's doing okay now.*

a **tough call** *Fig.* a difficult judgment to make. □ *We're still undecided on whether to buy a place or rent—it's a tough call.*

a **tough cookie** *Fig.* a person who is difficult to deal with. □ *There was a tough cookie in here this morning who demanded to see the manager.*

tough cookies Go to tough luck.

a **tough customer** *Fig.* someone who is difficult to deal with. □ *Some of those bikers are really tough customers.*

tough going *Fig.* progress that is difficult. □ *It was tough going for the first few miles, but the trail became much easier as we got farther into the forest.*

tough guy *Fig.* a strong and severe man; a man who might be part of the underworld. □ *He was your typical tough guy—jutting chin, gruff voice—but he was just our decorator checking up on the drapes.*

tough luck AND **tough cookies** *Fig.* That is too bad. (Said as a reply to someone relating an unfortunate situation.) □ *Tough luck, but that's the way the cookie crumbles.*

a **tough nut to crack** Go to a hard nut to crack.

*****tough on** so *Fig.* severe and demanding in dealing with someone. (*Typically: **act** ~; **be** ~; **become** ~; **get** ~.) □ *My boss is very tough on me, but I need the structure and discipline.*

tough sth **out** *Fig.* to carry on with something despite difficulties or setbacks. □ *I think I can tough this job out for another month.*

a tough row to hoe AND a **hard row to hoe** *Fig.* a difficult task to carry out; a heavy set of burdens. □ *This is not an easy task. This is a hard row to hoe.*

tough sledding Go to hard sledding.

tough times Go to bad times.

Tout suite! *Fig.* right away; with all haste. (Older. Pronounced "toot sweet." From French *toute de suite*.) □ *"I want this mess cleaned up, tout suite!" shouted Sally, hands on her hips and steaming with rage.*

tower head and shoulders above so/sth *Fig.* to be far superior to someone or a group. □ *The new vice president towers head and shoulders above the old one.*

a tower of strength *Fig.* a person who can always be depended on to provide support and encouragement, especially in times of trouble. □ *Jack was a tower of strength during the time that his father was unemployed.*

town-and-gown *Fig.* the relations between a town and the university located within the town; the relations between university students and the nonstudents who live in a university town. (Usually in reference to a disagreement. Fixed order.) □ *There is another town-and-gown dispute in Adamsville over the amount the university costs the city for police services.*

toy with so *Fig.* to tease someone; to deal lightly with someone's emotions. □ *Ann broke up with Tom because he was just toying with her. He was not serious at all.*

toy with sth *Fig.* to play with something; to fiddle with something. □ *Please don't toy with the stereo controls.*

track so/sth **down**† AND **run** so/sth **down**†; **chase** so/sth **down**† *Fig.* to locate someone or something; to search for and find someone or something. □ *I spent half the day tracking down someone who knew what was wrong with my DVD player.*

trade places (with so**)** AND **change places (with** so**)**; **exchange places (with** so**)** to experience what it feels like to be in someone else's situation; to exchange situations or lifestyles (usually hypothetically) with someone else. □ *How would you like to trade places with him for a while and have to support all those relatives?*

a trade secret 1. a secret way of making or selling a product; a business secret. □ *The exact formula of the soft drink is a trade secret.* **2.** *Fig.* any secret method. (Fig. on ①. Jocular.) □ *A: How do you manage to sell so many of these each month? B: It's a trade secret.*

trade (up)on sth *Fig.* to use a fact or a situation to one's advantage. □ *Tom was able to trade on the fact that he had once been in the Army.*

traffic in sth *Fig.* to deal in something; to trade in something, usually something illegal. □ *Spike had been trafficking in guns for years before they caught him.*

a traffic jam *Fig.* vehicle traffic that is so heavy and slow that it can no longer move. □ *Going to the airport, we got stuck in a traffic jam for nearly an hour and missed our plane.*

trail away Go to next.

trail off AND **trail away** *Fig.* to fade away, as with speech, words, singing, etc. □ *Her voice trailed off as she saw who was waiting at the door.*

so's train of thought *Fig.* someone's pattern of thinking or sequence of ideas; what a person was just thinking about. (See also **lose** one's **train of thought**.) □ *I cannot seem to follow your train of thought on this matter. Will you explain it a little more carefully, please?*

train one's **sights on** sth AND **have** one's **sights trained on** sth *Fig.* to have something as a goal; to direct something or oneself toward a goal. (Fig. on the image of someone using gun sights to aim a gun.) □ *You should train your sights on getting a promotion in the next year.*

trap so **in** sth to catch someone in an inconsistency or contradiction. □ *The lawyer trapped the witness in his inconsistencies.*

travel at a good clip Go to at a good clip.

trial balloon

a **travesty of justice** *Fig.* a miscarriage of justice; an act of the legal system that is an insult to the system of justice. □ *The lawyer complained that the judge's ruling was a travesty of justice.*

tread lightly (with so/sth**)** AND **tread lightly (around** so/sth**)** *Fig.* to be cautious and careful around someone or something. (Meaning not to **step on** so's **toes**.) □ *Tread lightly around the boss. He had a bad meeting with the president this morning.* □ *Tread lightly with the board. They are watching you carefully.*

tread on so's **toes** Go to **step on** so's **toes.**

tread water *Fig.* to make no progress. (Fig. on the idea of just staying afloat.) □ *I'm not getting anywhere in my career. I'm just treading water, hoping something good will happen.*

treat so **like dirt** AND **treat** so **like shit; treat** so **like the scum of the earth** *Fig.* to treat someone as something totally worthless. (Caution with *shit.*) □ *I knew I had upset the salesman, but he treated me like shit until I left the store.*

treat so **like shit** Go to previous.

treat so **like the scum of the earth** Go to **treat** so **like dirt.**

treat so **with kid gloves** Go to **handle** so **with kid gloves.**

tree so/animal *Fig.* to trap or corner someone or some animal. □ *The lawyer's shrewd questions treed the witness.*

trial and error *Fig.* trying repeatedly for success. □ *Sometimes trial and error is the only way to get something done.*

trial balloon *Inf.* a test of someone's or the public's reaction. □ *It was just a trial balloon, and it didn't work.*

trials and tribulations *Cliché* problems and tests of one's courage or perseverance. □ *I promise not to tell you of the trials and tribulations of my day if you promise not to tell me yours!*

Trick or treat! *Fig.* Give me a treat of some kind or I will play a trick on you! (The formulaic expression said by children after they ring someone's doorbell and the door is answered on Halloween. It is now understood to mean simply that the child is requesting a treat of some kind—candy, fruit, popcorn, etc.) □ *"Trick or treat!" cried Jimmy when the door opened.*

trick sth **out**† *Fig.* to overdecorate something; to equip something with lots of extras. □ *I want my next car to be fully tricked out.*

trickle down (to so/sth**)** *Fig.* [for something] to be distributed to someone or something in little bits at a time. □ *The results of the improved economy trickled down to people at lower-income levels.*

trickle in(to sth**)** *Fig.* [for someone or something] to come into something or a place, a few at a time. □ *The audience trickled into the hall little by little.*

trickle out (of sth**)** *Fig.* [for someone or something] to go out of something or a place, a few at a time. □ *The dissatisfied members of the audience trickled out of the theater three and four at a time.*

*tricks of the trade *Fig.* special skills and knowledge associated with any trade or profession. (*Typically: **know the** ~; **learn the** ~; **know a few** ~; **show** so **the** ~; **teach** so **a few** ~.) □ *I know a few tricks of the trade that make things easier.*

tried and true *Cliché* trustworthy; dependable. (Hyphenated before nominals.) □ *Finally, her old tried-and-true methods failed because she hadn't fine-tuned them to the times.*

(a trip down) memory lane *Fig.* recollections of past memories. (Often with *have* or *take*.) □ *We had coffee and took a little trip down memory lane.*

trip the light fantastic *Fig.* to dance. (Jocular.) □ *Shall we go trip the light fantastic?*

trip so **up**† *Fig.* to cause someone to falter. □ *Mary came in while the speaker was talking, and the distraction tripped him up.*

trot sth **out**† *Fig.* to mention something regularly or habitually, without giving it much thought. (Fig. on the image of trotting out a pony for display.) □ *Bob always trots out the same excuses for being late.*

trouble so **for** sth *Fig.* to ask someone to pass something or give something. (Usually a question.) □ *Could I trouble you for some advice?*

trouble one's **head about** so/sth to worry about someone or something. □ *I wish you wouldn't trouble your head about the problem. We can solve it.*

trouble oneself **(to** do sth**)** to bother oneself to do something. □ *No, thank you. I don't need any help. Please don't trouble yourself.*

trudge through sth *Fig.* to work one's way through something difficult. □ *I have to trudge through a lot of work before I can go home.*

*true as steel very loyal and dependable. (*Also: **as** ~.) □ *Through all my troubles, my husband has been as true as steel.*

so's **true colors** *Fig.* a person's true attitude, opinions, and biases. □ *When he lost his temper at his wife, I began to see his true colors.*

true to form *Fig.* exactly as expected; following the usual pattern. □ *And true to form, Mary left before the meeting was adjourned.*

true to one's **word** *Fig.* keeping one's promise. □ *We'll soon know if Jane is true to her word. We'll see if she does what she promised.*

trump sth **up**† *Fig.* to think something up; to contrive something. □ *Do you just sit around trumping charges up against innocent people?*

trumped up 1. *Fig.* heavily promoted; overly praised. (Hyphenated before nominals.) □ *That movie was so trumped up. I expected to see something much better than it turned out to be.* **2.** *Fig.* made up;

contrived. □ *They put Larry in the slammer on some trumped-up charge.*

Trust me! *Fig.* I am telling you the truth. Please believe me. □ *Tom said with great conviction, "Trust me! I know exactly what to do!"*

try as I may AND **try as I might** *Cliché* a phrase that introduces an expression of regret or failure. □ *Bill: Try as I may, I cannot get this thing put together right. Andy: Did you read the instructions?*

try as I might Go to previous.

*a try at SO AND ***a shot at** SO; ***a crack at** SO; ***a go at** SO; ***a stab at** SO *Fig.* an attempt to convince someone of something; an attempt to try to get information out of someone; an attempt to try to train someone to do something. (The expressions with *shot* and *crack* are more informal than the main entry phrase. *Typically: **take** ~; **have** ~; **make** ~; **give** so ~.) □ *Let me have a crack at him. I can make him talk.* □ *Let the new teacher have a try at Billy. She can do marvels with unwilling learners.*

*a try at sth AND ***a shot at** sth; ***a crack at** sth; ***a go at** sth; ***a run at** sth; ***a stab at** sth; ***a whack at** sth *Fig.* to take a turn at trying to do something. (*Typically: **take** ~; **have** ~; **make** ~; **give** so ~.) □ *Let Sally have a shot at it.* □ *If you let me have a crack at it, maybe I can be successful.*

try so **back (again)** *Fig.* to try to return someone's telephone call again. □ *She's not in, so I'll try her back later.*

try so **for** sth *Fig.* to put someone through a court trial for some crime or wrongdoing. □ *The prosecutor wanted to try Harry for fraud.*

try one's **hand (at** sth**)** *Fig.* to take a try at something. □ *Someday I'd like to try my hand at flying a plane.*

try one's **luck (at** sth**)** *Fig.* to attempt to do something (where success requires luck). □ *My great-grandfather came to California to try his luck at finding gold.*

Try me. *Fig.* Ask me.; Give me a chance. □ *A: I don't suppose you know what the Achaean League is. B: Try me.*

try sth **(on**†**) (for size)** *Fig.* to evaluate an idea or proposition. (Fig. on trying on clothing.) □ *Try this plan for size. I think you'll like it.*

try out (for sth**)** *Fig.* to audition for a part in some performance or other activity requiring skill. □ *I intend to try out for the play.*

try so's **patience** *Fig.* to strain someone's patience; to bother someone as if testing the person's patience. (*Try* means *test* here.) □ *You really try my patience with all your questions!*

try one's **wings (out**†**)** *Fig.* to try to do something one has recently become qualified to do. (Fig. on the image of a young bird trying to fly.) □ *I recently learned to snorkel, and I want to go to the seaside to try my wings.*

trying times Go to bad times.

tub of lard *Inf.* a fat person. (Insulting.) □ *That tub of lard can hardly get through the door.*

tuck sth **away**† *Fig.* to eat something. □ *The boys tucked away three pizzas and an apple pie.*

tuck into sth *Fig.* to begin eating something vigorously. □ *I could see from the way that they tucked into their meal that they were really hungry.*

tucker so **out** *Fig.* to tire someone out. □ *All this work has tuckered me out.*

tug at so's **heartstrings** Go to play on so's heartstrings.

tune sth **in**† *Fig.* to adjust a radio or television set so that something can be received. □ *Could you tune the newscast in?*

tune in (on so/sth**)** AND **tune in (to** so/sth**)** **1.** *Fig.* to adjust a radio or television set to receive a broadcast of someone or something. □ *Let's tune in on the late news.* **2.** *Fig.* to pay attention to someone or something. (Fig. on ①.) □ *I listen and I try, but I just can't tune in.*

tune out *Inf.* to cease paying attention to anything at all. □ *I think that most of the audience tuned out during the last part of the lecture.*

tune so/sth **out**† *Inf.* to put someone or something out of one's consciousness; to cease paying attention to someone or something. □ *I tuned out what the speaker was saying and daydreamed for a while.*

tune up [for one or more musicians] to bring their instruments into tune. □ *You could hear the orchestra behind the curtain, tuning up.*

tune sth **up**† *Fig.* to adjust an engine to run the best and most efficiently. □ *Please tune up this engine so it will run more economically.*

tuned in *Inf.* aware; up-to-date. □ *Jan is tuned in and alert to what is going on around her.*

tunnel vision 1. *Fig.* a visual impairment wherein one can only see what is directly ahead of oneself. □ *I have tunnel vision, so I have to keep looking from side to side.* **2.** *Fig.* an inability to recognize other ways of doing things or thinking about things. □ *The boss really has tunnel vision about sales and marketing. He sees no reason to change anything.*

a **turkey's nest** Go to a dust bunny.

turn a blind eye (to so/sth**)** *Fig.* to ignore something and pretend you do not see it. □ *The usher turned a blind eye to the little boy who sneaked into the theater.*

turn a deaf ear (to so/sth**)** to ignore what someone says; to ignore a cry for help. □ *How can you just turn a deaf ear to their cries for food and shelter?*

turn a profit *Fig.* to earn a profit. □ *The company plans to turn a profit two years from now.*

turn a trick *Sl.* to perform an act of prostitution. □ *She can turn a trick and be on the streets again in six minutes flat.*

turn sth **around**† *Fig.* to produce a great change or reversal in something. □ *The new manager really turned around the de-partment. Now we are winning praise rather than criticism.*

turn one's **back (on** so/sth**)** *Fig.* to abandon or ignore someone or something. □ *Don't turn your back on your old friends.*

turn back the clock *Fig.* to try to make things the way they were before; to reverse some change. □ *Jill: I wish I was back in college. I had so much fun then. Jane: You can't turn back the clock. Even if you went back to school, it wouldn't be the same.*

turn belly up AND **go belly up 1.** *Sl.* to fail. (See also turn turtle.) □ *The computer—on its last legs anyway—turned belly up right in the middle of an important job.* **2.** *Sl.* to die. (As a fish does when it dies.) □ *The cat was acting strangely for a while before she turned belly up.*

turn sth **down**† **1.** *Fig.* to decrease the volume of something. □ *Please turn the radio down.* **2.** *Fig.* to reject something; to deny someone's request. □ *The board turned our request down.*

turn one's **hand to** sth *Fig.* to begin to or to be able to do something. □ *He gave up accounting and turned his hand to writing poetry.*

turn so's **head** *Fig.* [for flattery or success] to distract someone; to cause someone not to be sensible. □ *Her successes had turned her head. She was now quite arrogant.*

turn in *Fig.* [for someone] to go to bed. □ *It's time to turn in. Good night.*

turn some place **inside out** *Fig.* to search some place thoroughly. □ *I will find that book if I have to turn this place inside out!*

turn sth **into a career** AND **turn** sth **into a full-time job** *Fig.* to take a very long time to do a simple task. □ *Yes, be careful and do it right, but don't turn it into a career.*

turn sth **into a fine art** Go to make sth into a fine art.

turn sth **into a full-time job** Go to turn sth into a career.

turn one's **nose up**[†] **at** so/sth *Fig.* to sneer at someone or something; to reject someone or something. □ *John turned his nose up at Ann, and that hurt her feelings.*

a **turn of fate** Go to a twist of fate.

the **turn of the century** the time when the year changes to one with two final zeros, such as from 1899 to 1900. (Although technically incorrect—a new century begins with the year ending in 01—most people ignore this.) □ *My family moved to America at the turn of the century.*

turn so **off**[†] *Inf.* to dull someone's interest in someone or something. □ *The boring prof turned me off to the subject.*

turn on *Inf.* to become interested or excited. □ *He turns on when he sees the mountains.*

turn so **on**[†] *Inf.* to excite or interest someone. □ *Fast music with a good beat turns me on.*

turn on a dime *Fig.* [for a vehicle] to turn in a very tight turn. □ *I need a vehicle that can turn on a dime.*

turn on one's **heel** Go to take to one's heels.

turn sth **on its ear** Go to set some place on its ear.

turn sth **on its head** Go to stand sth on its head.

turn on the waterworks *Fig.* to begin to cry. □ *Every time Billy got homesick, he turned on the waterworks.*

turn on, tune in, drop out *Inf.* a slogan (popularized by Dr. Timothy Leary) promoting the use of LSD among young people. □ *The key phrase in the heyday of acid was "turn on, tune in, drop out."*

turn one hundred and eighty degrees Go to do a one-eighty.

turn onto so/sth *Inf.* to become interested in someone or something. □ *Jeff turned onto electronics at the age of 14.*

turn sth **out**[†] *Fig.* to manufacture or produce something in numbers. □ *The factory turns out about 75 cars a day.*

turn out (for sth) *Fig.* [for people, especially an audience] to [leave home to] attend some event. □ *Almost all the residents turned out for the meeting.*

turn out somehow *Fig.* to end in a particular way, such as well, badly, all right, etc. □ *I hope everything turns out all right.*

turn over 1. AND **kick over** *Fig.* [for an engine] to start or to rotate. □ *My car engine was so cold that it wouldn't even turn over.* **2.** *Fig.* to undergo exchange; to be replaced. □ *The employees turn over pretty regularly in this department.*

turn over a new leaf *Fig.* to begin again, fresh; to reform and begin again. (Fig. on turning to a fresh page. The leaf is a page—a fresh, clean page.) □ *I have made a mess of my life. I'll turn over a new leaf and hope to do better.*

turn (over) in one's **grave** AND **roll (over) in** one's **grave; spin in** one's **grave** *Fig.* to show enormous disfavor for something that has happened after one's death. □ *Please don't change the place around too much when I'm dead. I do not wish to be rolling in my grave all the time.*

turn sth **over**[†] **in** one's **mind** *Fig.* to think about something. □ *After Alice had turned the matter over in her mind, she gave us her verdict.*

turn some heads *Fig.* to cause people to look (at someone or something); to get attention (from people). □ *That new bikini of yours is sure to turn some heads.*

turn so's **stomach** *Fig.* to upset one's stomach. □ *The rich, creamy food turned John's stomach.*

turn tail (and run) *Inf.* to flee; to run away in fright. □ *I couldn't just turn tail and run, but I wasn't going to fight that monster, either.*

turn the clock back[†] *Fig.* to try to return to the past. □ *You are not facing up to the future. You are trying to turn the clock back to a time when you were more comfortable.*

turn the corner *Fig.* to pass a critical point in a process. □ *The patient turned the cor-*

ner last night. She should begin to show improvement now.

turn the heat up[†] **(on so)** *Fig.* to use force to persuade someone to do something; to increase the pressure on someone to do something. □ *Management is turning the heat up to increase production.*

turn the other cheek *Fig.* to ignore abuse or an insult. □ *When Bob got mad at Mary and yelled at her, she just turned the other cheek.*

turn the other way *Fig.* to look away and ignore someone or something. □ *When I tried to talk to her, she turned the other way and made it clear that she was angry.*

turn the tables (on so) *Fig.* to cause a reversal in someone's plans; to make one's plans turn back on one. □ *I went to Jane's house to help get ready for a surprise party for Bob. It turned out that the surprise party was for me! Jane really turned the tables on me!*

turn the tide *Fig.* to cause a reversal in the direction of events; to cause a reversal in public opinion. □ *It looked as if the team was going to lose, but near the end of the game, our star player turned the tide.*

turn three hundred and sixty degrees Go to do a three-sixty.

turn thumbs-down (on so/sth) *Fig.* to reject someone or something; to grow to reject someone or something. □ *The boss turned thumbs-down on Tom. They would have to find someone else.*

turn thumbs-up (on so/sth) *Fig.* to accept someone or something; to approve someone or something. □ *The board of directors turned thumbs-up on my proposal and voted to fund the project.*

turn to *Fig.* to begin to get busy. □ *If you people will turn to, we can finish this work in no time at all.*

turn sth to one's **advantage** *Fig.* to make an advantage for oneself out of something (which might otherwise be a disadvantage). □ *The ice-cream store manager was able to turn the hot weather to her advantage.*

turn to so/sth for sth Go to look to so/sth for sth.

turn sth to good account *Fig.* to use something in such a way that it is to one's advantage; to make good use of a situation, experience, etc. □ *Many people turn their retirement time to good account and take up interesting hobbies.*

turn turtle *Fig.* to turn upside down. (See also turn belly up.) □ *The sailboat turned turtle, but the sailors only got wet.*

turn up 1. *Fig.* to happen. □ *I am sorry I was late. Something turned up at the last minute.* **2.** *Fig.* to appear; to arrive and attend. □ *Guess who turned up at my door last night?*

turn so/sth up[†] **1.** *Fig.* to increase the volume of a device emitting the sound of someone or something. □ *I can't hear the lecturer. Turn her up.* **2.** *Fig.* to discover or locate someone or something. □ *See if you can turn up any evidence for his presence on the night of January 16.*

turn up the heat (on so) Go to put the heat on (so).

turn up one's **toes** *Sl.* to die. □ *When I turn up my toes, I want a big funeral with lots of flowers.*

turn (up)on so/sth to attack or oppose someone or something, especially the person or group in charge. (*Upon* is formal and less commonly used than *on*.) □ *I never thought that my own dog would turn on me!*

turn some place **upside down** *Fig.* to search a place thoroughly. □ *The cops turned the whole house upside down but never found the gun.*

turn so/sth upside down *Fig.* to upset someone or something; to thoroughly confuse someone or something. □ *The whole business turned me upside down. It'll take days to recover.*

turn so's **water off**[†] *Sl.* to deflate someone; to silence someone. □ *He said you were stupid, huh? Well, I guess that turns your water off!*

turned off *Inf.* uninterested. □ *I'm sort of turned off to stuff like that these days. Part of getting older, I guess.* □ *I can't pay attention if I'm turned off, now can I?*

*a **turning point** *Fig.* a time when things may change; a point at which a change of course is possible or desirable. (Originally nautical. Fig. on the image of a ship approaching a point where a change of course has been planned. *Typically: **be at** ~; **come to** ~; **reach** ~.*) □ *Things are at a turning point. Bob can no longer afford the payments on his car.*

twelve good men and true *Fig.* a jury composed of trustworthy men. □ *He was convicted by a jury of twelve good men and true. Not a wino in the lot.*

twiddle one's **thumbs** *Fig.* to pass the time by twirling one's thumbs. □ *What am I supposed to do while waiting for you? Sit here and twiddle my thumbs?*

twilight years *Fig.* the last years before death. □ *In his twilight years, he became more mellow and stopped yelling at people.*

twist so's **arm** *Fig.* to pressure someone. (Fig. on the image of hurting someone until they agree to cooperate.) □ *Do I have to twist your arm, or will you cooperate?*

a **twist of fate** AND a **turn of fate** *Fig.* a fateful event; an unanticipated change in a sequence of events. □ *A strange turn of fate brought Fred and his ex-wife together at a New Year's Eve party in Queens.*

twist (slowly) in the wind *Inf.* to suffer the agony of some humiliation or punishment. (Refers originally to an execution by hanging.) □ *The prosecutor was determined that Richard would twist slowly in the wind for the crime.*

twist the knife (in so's **back)** *Fig.* to do or say something that makes a bad situation worse. (As if someone had been stabbed and the assailant caused even more pain by twisting the knife in the wound.) □ *Your remarks were cruel enough as it was. There was no need to twist the knife by repeating them to everyone.*

twist so's **words (around)** to restate someone's words inaccurately; to misrepresent what someone has said. □ *Stop twisting my words around! Listen to what I am telling you!* □ *You are twisting my words again. That is not what I said!*

Two can play (at) this game (as well as one). *Fig.* Both competitors—not just one—can compete in this manner or with this strategy. (See also a **game that two can play**.) □ *You are not the only one who knows how to cheat and lie. Two can play this game.*

two jumps ahead of so *Fig.* a good way ahead of someone. □ *I was just starting to think of vacation plans, not realizing that my wife was two jumps ahead of me. She had already made hotel reservations.*

two of a kind *Fig.* people or things of the same type or that are similar in character, attitude, etc. □ *Jack and Tom are two of a kind. They're both ambitious.*

two shakes of a lamb's tail *Inf.* quickly; rapidly. □ *I'll be there in two shakes of a lamb's tail.*

two sheets to the wind Go to three sheets in the wind.

two sides of the same coin *Fig.* two sides of the same underlying thing; two facades of the same interior. □ *Fear and an overactive ego are often two sides of the same coin.*

*two strikes against one *Fig.* a critical number of things against one; a position wherein success is unlikely or where the success of the next move is crucial. (*Typically: **get** ~; **have** ~.*) □ *Poor Bob had two strikes against him when he tried to explain where he was last night.*

a **two-edged sword** AND a **double-edged sword** *Fig.* something that offers both a good and bad consequence. (While the fore edge of the sword can cut the enemy, the rear edge can harm its wielder.) □ *Her authority in the company is a two-edged sword. She makes more enemies than allies.*

two-fisted *Fig.* [of a male] aggressive and feisty. □ *Perry is a real, two-fisted cowboy, always ready for a fight or a drunken brawl.*

two-time SO AND **cheat on** SO *Sl.* to cheat on or betray one's spouse or lover by dating or seeing someone else. □ *When Mrs. Franklin learned that Mr. Franklin was two-timing her, she left him.*

a **two-time loser** *Inf.* a confirmed loser; a person who has already failed at a previous attempt at some task. □ *Martin is a two-time loser, or at least he looks like one.*

a **two-way street** *Inf.* a reciprocal situation. □ *This is a two-way street, you know. You will have to help me someday in return.*

U

*ugly as a toad [of a living creature] very ugly. (*Also: **as** ∼.) □ *The shopkeeper was ugly as a toad, but he was kind and generous, and everyone loved him.*

*ugly as sin *Cliché* extremely ugly. (*Also: **as** ∼.) □ *Why would anyone want to buy that dress? It's as ugly as sin!*

under a cloud (of suspicion) *Fig.* suspected of something. □ *Someone stole some money at work, and now everyone is under a cloud of suspicion.*

under a deadline Go to under pressure.

*under a spell *Fig.* enchanted; under the control of magic. (*Typically: **be** ∼; **have** so ∼; **put** so ∼.) □ *Her soft voice and faint perfume put Buxton under a spell. Then the enchantment was broken when he found his wallet missing.*

*under arrest arrested and in the custody of the police in preparation for the filing of a charge. (*Typically: **be** ∼; **put** so ∼.) □ *Am I under arrest, officer? What did I do?*

under attack *Fig.* being attacked. □ *Close the doors of the fort! We are under attack.*

*under one's **belt 1.** *Fig.* eaten or drunk and in one's stomach. (Fig. on the image of swallowed food ending up under one's belt. *Typically: **get** sth ∼; **have** sth ∼.) □ *I want to get a nice juicy steak under my belt.* **2.** *Fig.* achieved; counted or scored. (Fig. on ①. *Typically: **have** sth ∼.) □ *This fighter pilot has over 20 kills under his belt.* **3.** *Fig.* learned; mastered. (Fig. on ①. *Typically: **get** sth ∼.) □ *When I get the right procedures under my belt, I will be more efficient.*

*under one's **breath** *Fig.* [spoken] so softly that almost no one can hear it. (*Typically: **curse** ∼; **curse** so/sth ∼; **mutter** ∼; **mutter** sth ∼; **say** sth ∼.) □ *I'm glad he said it under his breath. If he had said it out loud, it would have caused an argument.*

under so's **care** Go to in the care of so.

under certain circumstances only when there are specific conditions or circumstances. □ *I am permitted to drive the car, but only under certain circumstances. For instance, only with a parent in the front seat.*

*under (close) scrutiny *Fig.* being watched or examined closely. (*Typically: **be** ∼; **have** so/sth ∼; **keep** so/sth ∼.) □ *The suspect was kept under scrutiny throughout the investigation.*

under construction *Fig.* being built or repaired. □ *Our new home has been under construction all summer. We hope to move in next month.*

*under control *Fig.* manageable; restrained and controlled; not out of control. (*Typically: **be** ∼; **bring** so/sth ∼; **get** so/sth ∼; **have** so/sth ∼; **keep** so/sth ∼.) □ *We finally got things under control and functioning smoothly.* □ *The doctor felt she had the disease under control and that I would get well soon.*

under dispute AND **in dispute** [of matters] being argued or negotiated. □ *The question of who owns that little strip of land is under dispute.*

*under fire *Fig.* during an attack; being attacked. (*Typically: **be** ∼; **resign** ∼; **think** ∼.) □ *There was a scandal in city hall, and the mayor was forced to resign under fire.*

*under lock and key *Fig.* safely locked up. (*Typically: **have** sth ~; **keep** sth ~; **put** sth ~; **store** sth ~.) □ *You should keep your passport and money under lock and key when you are traveling.*

under no circumstances never; not at all. □ *Under no circumstances are you permitted to drive the car ever again!*

under oath *Fig.* bound by an oath; having taken an oath. □ *I was placed under oath before I could testify in the trial.*

under one's **own steam** *Fig.* by one's own power or effort. □ *I missed my ride to class, so I had to get there under my own steam.*

*under pressure 1. AND ***under a deadline**; ***under the gun (about** sth**)** *Fig.* facing or enduring something such as pressure or a deadline. (*Typically: **be** ~; **get** ~.) □ *I am under a lot of pressure lately.* □ *The management is under the gun for the mistakes made last year.* **2.** [of a gas or liquid] being forced, squeezed, or compressed. (*Typically: **be** ~; **deliver** sth ~; **put** sth ~.) □ *The gas in the pipes leading to the oven are under pressure.*

under one's **skin** Go to in the blood.

under the aegis of so AND **under the auspices of** so *Fig.* under the sponsorship or protection of someone or some group; under the control or monitoring of someone or some group. □ *The entire project fell under the aegis of Thomas.* □ *The entire program is under the auspices of Acme-Global Paper Co., Inc.*

under the auspices of so Go to previous.

under the banner of sth *Fig.* under the identity of something; bearing a label representing a particular organization or advocacy. □ *We rallied under the banner of a clean environment, and took great pains to not leave a mess where we met.*

under the circumstances *Fig.* in a particular situation; because of the circumstances. □ *I'm sorry to hear that you're ill. Under the circumstances, you may take the day off.* □ *We won't expect you to come to work for a few days, under the circumstances.*

under the counter *Fig.* [bought or sold] in secret or illegally. (Compare this to over the counter.) □ *The drugstore owner was arrested for selling liquor under the counter.*

under the influence (of alcohol) *Euph.* drunk; nearly drunk; affected by alcohol. □ *Ed was stopped by a police officer for driving while under the influence.*

under the sun *Fig.* anywhere on earth at all. □ *Isn't there anyone under the sun who can help me with this problem?*

under the table 1. *Sl.* intoxicated. □ *Jed was under the table by midnight.* **2.** *Fig.* secret; clandestine. (Hyphenated before a nominal.) □ *It was strictly an under-the-table deal.*

under the weather 1. *Inf.* ill. □ *I feel sort of under the weather today.* □ *Whatever I ate for lunch is making me feel a bit under the weather.* **2.** *Inf.* intoxicated. □ *Daddy's had a few beers and is under the weather again.*

under the wire *Fig.* just barely in time or on time. □ *Bill was the last person to get in the door. He got in under the wire.*

*under so's **thumb** *Fig.* under someone's control and management. (*Typically: **get** so ~; **have** so ~; **hold** so ~; **keep** so ~.) □ *You can't keep your kids under your thumb all their lives.* □ *I don't want to have these people under my thumb. I'm not the manager type.*

under so's **(very) nose** Go to (right) under so's (very) nose.

*under way *Fig.* moving; running; started. (*Typically: **be** ~; **get** sth ~; **have** sth ~.) □ *Now that the president has the meeting under way, I can relax.*

*under so's **wing(s)** *Fig.* receiving someone's care and nurturing. (*Typically: **get** so ~; **have** so ~; **take** so ~.) □ *John wasn't doing well in geometry until the teacher took him under her wing.*

*under wraps *Fig.* concealed; suppressed; covered or wrapped up. (*Typically: **be** ~; **have** sth ~; **hold** sth ~; **keep** sth ~.) □ *We kept the candidate's conviction under wraps until after the election.* □ *The*

(un)til the cows come home

plan we had under wraps had to be scrapped anyway.

unfamiliar territory an area of knowledge unknown to the speaker. □ *Astronomy is unfamiliar territory for me, and I cannot answer any questions about the stars.*

unfold into sth *Fig.* [for a story] to develop into something interesting. □ *The story unfolded into a real mystery.*

*an **unknown quantity** *Fig.* a person or thing about which no one is certain. (*Typically: **be** ~; **become** ~.) □ *The new clerk is an unknown quantity. Things may not turn out all right.*

unsung hero *Fig.* a hero who has gotten no praise or recognition. □ *The time has come to recognize all the unsung heroes of the battle for low-cost housing.*

until all hours *Fig.* until very late. □ *If I'm up until all hours two nights in a row, I'm just exhausted.*

(un)til hell freezes over *Inf.* forever. □ *That's all right, boss; I can wait till hell freezes over for your answer.*

(un)til the cows come home *Rur.* until the last; until very late. (Referring to the end of the day, when the cows come home to be fed and milked.) □ *Where've you been? Who said you could stay out till the cows come home?*

Until we meet again. Go to Good-bye for now.

*up a blind alley** *Fig.* at a dead end; on a route that leads nowhere. (*Typically: **be** ~; **go** ~.) □ *I have been trying to find out something about my ancestors, but I'm up a blind alley. I can't find anything.*

*up a storm** *Fig.* [doing or making] a great amount. (*Typically: **cook** ~; **gab** ~; **sing** ~; **talk** ~.) □ *Everyone was gabbing up a storm and didn't hear the chairman come in.*

up a tree 1. *Inf.* confused; without an answer to a problem; in difficulty. □ *This whole business has me up a tree.* **2.** *Inf.* intoxicated. □ *My buddy here is up a tree and needs a place to crash for the night.*

*up against so/sth in opposition to someone or something, as in a contest. (*Typically: **be** ~; **come** ~; **go** ~; **run** ~; **team** ~.) □ *Let's team up against Paul and Tony in the footrace.*

*up against sth **1.** resting firmly against something. (*Typically: **be** ~; **place** sth ~.) □ *The car is up against the back of the garage! Back out a little!* **2.** *Fig.* in conflict with something; facing something as a barrier. (Fig. on ①. *Typically: **be** ~; **run** ~; **go** ~.) □ *I am up against some serious problems.*

*up against the wall *Fig.* in serious difficulties. (*Typically: **be** ~; **get** ~; **push** so ~.) □ *Let's face it, we're up against the wall this time.* □ *It's when you're up against the wall that your true character shows.*

*(up and) about AND ***up and around** out of bed and moving about. (*Typically: **be** ~; **get** ~.) □ *The flu put Alice into bed for three days, but she was up and around on the fourth.*

up and around Go to previous.

up and at 'em *Fig.* up and taking action. □ *Dad woke me at seven, saying, "Up and at 'em!"*

up and running *Fig.* [of a machine] functioning. □ *As soon as we can get the tractor up and running, we will plant the corn crop.*

*up before so *Fig.* standing in front of someone to receive something. (Especially in front of a judge. *Typically: **be** ~; **stand** ~.) □ *Have you been up before me before?*

*up for sth **1.** *Fig.* [of someone] mentally ready for something. (*Typically: **be** ~; **get** ~; **get** oneself ~.) □ *The team is up for the game tonight.* **2.** *Sl.* agreeable to something. (*Typically: **be** ~.) □ *I'm up for a pizza. Anybody want to chip in?*

*up for auction *Fig.* to be sold at an auction. (*Typically: **be** ~; **come** ~; **go** ~; **put** sth ~.) □ *The old farm where I lived as a child is up for auction.*

up for grabs 1. *Fig.* available for anyone; not yet claimed. (As if something, such as a handful of money, had been thrown up into the air, and people were to grab at as many bills as they could get.) □ *The election is up for grabs. Everything is still very chancy.* **2.** *Fig.* in total chaos. □ *This is a madhouse. The whole place is up for grabs.*

*up for reelection *Fig.* to be running for reelection to an office or position. (*Typically: **be** ~; **come** ~.) □ *The governor is up for reelection in the fall.* □ *Lily is up for reelection this fall.*

*up for sale *Fig.* available for purchase. (*Typically: **be** ~; **come** ~; **put** sth ~.) □ *When this lot comes up for sale, let me know.*

up front 1. *Fig.* at the beginning; in advance. □ *The more you pay up front, the less you'll have to finance.* **2.** *Fig.* open; honest; forthcoming. □ *She is a very upfront gal—trust her.*

*up in arms 1. *Fig.* in armed rebellion. (*Typically: **be** ~; **get** ~.) □ *The entire population is up in arms.* **2.** *Fig.* very angry. (Fig. on ①, but without weapons. *Typically: **be** ~; **get** ~.) □ *Wally was up in arms about the bill for the broken window.*

up in the air (about so/sth**)** *Fig.* undecided about someone or something; uncertain about someone or something. □ *I don't know what Sally plans to do. Things were sort of up in the air the last time we talked.*

up in years AND **advanced in years; along in years; on in years** *Fig.* old; elderly. □ *Many people lose their hearing somewhat when they are along in years.*

up North to or at the northern part of the country or the world. □ *When you say "up North," do you mean where the polar bears live, or just in the northern states?*

up on so/sth *Fig.* knowledgeable about someone or something. □ *Ask Tom about the author of this book. He's up on stuff like that.*

up shit creek Go to up the creek (without a paddle).

up stakes *Inf.* to prepare for leaving and then leave. (*Up* has the force of a verb here. The phrase suggests pulling up tent stakes in preparation for departure.) □ *It's that time of the year when I feel like upping stakes and moving to the country.*

up the ante AND **raise the ante 1.** *Fig.* to raise the opening stakes in a betting game. □ *Don't up the ante any more. You're betting far too much money already.* **2.** AND **raise the stakes** *Fig.* to increase a price. (Fig. on ①.) □ *Sensing how keen the people looking at the house were, Jerry upped the ante another $5,000.*

up the creek (without a paddle) AND **up a creek; up shit creek** *Inf.* in an awkward position with no easy way out. (Caution with *shit*.) □ *You are up a creek! You got yourself into it, so get yourself out.*

up the pole *Inf.* intoxicated. □ *You sound a little up the pole. Why don't you call back when you're sober?*

up the river *Sl.* in prison. (Underworld.) □ *Gary was up the river for a couple of years, but that doesn't make him an outcast, does it?*

*up the wall *Fig.* in a very bad situation; very upset or anxious. (*Typically: **be** ~; **go** ~; **drive** so ~; **send** so ~.) □ *We were all up the wall until the matter was resolved.*

up to doing sth *Fig.* [feeling] able to do something. □ *Do you feel up to going back to work today?*

*up to so/sth *Fig.* decided by someone. (*Typically: **be** ~; **become** ~; **leave** sth ~.) □ *It is up to the decision of the judges!*

up to sth **1.** *Fig.* [of someone] plotting something. □ *I think they are up to something.* **2.** *Fig.* [of someone] well enough or rested enough to do something. □ *Are you up to a game of volleyball?* **3.** to be as good as something; to be good enough for something. □ *Your last essay was not up to your best.*

up to one's **ears (in** sth) Go to up to one's neck (in sth).

up to one's **eyeballs (in** sth) Go to up to one's neck (in sth).

*up to here (with sth) *Inf.* having had as much as one can bear. (*Typically: **be** ~; **get** ~.) □ *We are all up to here with this mystery.*

*up to one's **knees** *Inf.* deep in something, such as paperwork or water. (The idea is that it is hard to move or make progress. *Typically: **be** ~; **get** ~.) □ *We're up to our knees with orders and getting more all the time.*

*up to one's **neck (in** sth) AND ***up to** one's **ears (in** sth); ***up to** one's **eyeballs (in** sth) *Fig.* having a lot of something; very much involved in something; immersed in something. (*Typically: **be** ~; **get** ~.) □ *I can't come to the meeting. I'm up to my neck in these reports.* □ *I am up to my eyeballs in things to do! I can't do any more!*

up to no good *Fig.* doing something bad. □ *There are three boys in the front yard. I don't know what they are doing, but I think they are up to no good.*

up to par *Fig.* as good as the standard or average; up to standard. □ *I'm just not feeling up to par today. I must be coming down with something.*

up to scratch Go to next.

up to snuff AND **up to scratch** *Fig.* as good as is required; meeting the minimum requirements. (*Snuff* almost certainly refers to powdered tobacco, and *scratch* most likely refers to a line drawn [scratched] on the floor of a boxing ring, but the connections to the specific meanings here are not clear or comfortable. Often negative.) □ *Sorry, Tom. Your performance isn't up to snuff. You'll have to improve or find another job.*

*up to speed 1. *Fig.* moving, operating, or functioning at a normal or desired rate. (*Typically: **be** ~; **bring** sth ~; **get** ~; **get** sth ~.) □ *Terri did everything she could to bring her workers up to speed, but couldn't.* **2.** AND ***up to speed on** so/sth *Fig.* fully apprised about someone or something; up-to-date on the state of someone or something. (*Typically: **be** ~; **bring** so ~; **get** ~; **get** so ~.) □ *I'll*

561

feel better about it when I get up to speed on what's going on.

*up to the minute *Fig.* current. (*Typically: **be** ~; **bring** sth ~.) □ *This report is up to the minute and fresh from the wire services.*

up-and-coming *Fig.* enterprising and alert. □ *Jane is a hard worker—really up-and-coming.* □ *Bob is also an up-and-coming youngster who is going to become well-known.*

an **uphill battle** AND an **uphill struggle** *Fig.* a hard struggle. (Battling an opponent who holds ground on a higher level is very difficult.) □ *Convincing the senator to see our point of view was an uphill battle, but we finally succeeded.*

an **uphill struggle** Go to previous.

*(up)on so *Fig.* being someone's obligation or responsibility. (*Typically: **be** ~; **lie** ~.) □ *The obligation is upon you to settle this.* □ *The major part of the responsibility is on you.*

upon impact *Fig.* at the place or time of an impact. □ *The car crumpled upon impact with the brick wall.*

upper crust *Fig.* the higher levels of society; the upper class. (From the top, as opposed to the bottom, crust of a pie.) □ *Jane speaks like that because she pretends to be part of the upper crust, but her father was a miner.*

*the upper hand (on so**)** *Fig.* a position superior to someone; the advantage of someone. (*Typically: **get** ~; **have** ~; **give** so ~.) □ *John is always trying to get the upper hand on someone.*

upper story Go to top story.

so's **ups and downs** *Fig.* a person's good fortune and bad fortune. □ *I've had my ups and downs, but in general life has been good to me.*

upset the apple cart *Fig.* to mess up or ruin something. □ *Tom really upset the apple cart by telling Mary the truth about Jane.*

the **upshot of** sth *Fig.* the result or outcome of something. □ *The upshot of the argu-*

ment was an agreement to hire a new secretary.

*upside down *Fig.* in a financial state such that one owes more money on a car, truck, house, etc. than its resale value. (*Typically: **be** ~; **get** ~.) □ *When I tried to trade in the car, I found that I was upside down and couldn't close the deal without more money.*

up-to-date modern; up to the current standards of fashion; having the most current information. (Always hyphenated before nominals. Also seen unhyphenated after nominals.) □ *I'd like to see a more up-to-date report on Mr. Smith.*

up-to-the-minute *Fig.* the very latest or most recent. □ *I want to hear some up-to-the-minute news on the hostage situation.*

use one's **head** AND **use** one's **noggin; use** one's **noodle** *Fig.* to use one's own intelligence. (The words *noggin* and *noodle* are slang terms for "head.") □ *You can do better in math if you'll just use your head.* □ *Jane uses her noggin and gets things done correctly and on time.*

use one's **noggin** Go to previous.

use one's **noodle** Go to use one's **head.**

use some elbow grease *Fig.* use some effort, as in scrubbing something. (As if lubricating one's elbow would make one more efficient. Note the variation in the example.) □ *I tried elbow grease, but it doesn't help get the job done.*

use so **up** *Fig.* to use all the effort or talent a person has. □ *I used myself up. I'm done. I can't function anymore.*

Use your head! AND **Use your noggin!; Use your noodle!** *Fig.* Start thinking!, Use your brain! □ *Andy: Come on, John, you can figure it out. A kindergartner could do it. Use your noggin! John: I'm doing my best.*

Use your noggin! Go to previous.

Use your noodle! Go to Use your head!

used to do sth to have done something [customarily] in the past. □ *We used to go swimming in the lake before it became polluted.*

*used to so/sth *Fig.* accustomed to someone or something; familiar and comfortable with someone or something. (*Typically: **be** ~; **become** ~; **get** ~.) □ *I am used to eating better food than this.*

user friendly *Fig.* easy to use. (Hyphenated before nominals.) □ *The setup instructions for the printer were not user friendly.* □ *I have a user-friendly computer that listens to my voice and does what I tell it.*

usher so **in**† to lead or guide someone into a place. □ *Four policemen ushered a sad-faced Wallace Travelian into the station house.*

usher sth **in**† *Fig.* to introduce or welcome something; to signal the beginning of something, such as spring, colder weather, the New Year, the shopping season, etc. □ *Warm temperatures ushered spring in early this year.*

V

vain as a peacock Go to proud as a peacock.

vale of tears *Fig.* the earth; mortal life on earth. (*Vale* is a literary word for *valley*.) □ *When it comes time for me to leave this vale of tears, I hope I can leave some worthwhile memories behind.*

vanish into thin air AND **disappear into thin air** *Cliché* to disappear without leaving a trace. □ *When I came back, my car was gone. I had locked it, and it couldn't have vanished into thin air!*

veg out *Inf.* to cease working and take it easy; to vegetate. □ *Someday, I just want to veg out and enjoy life.*

vegged out *Inf.* debilitated by drugs or alcohol. □ *Ernie is vegged out and has quit his job and everything.*

vent one's **spleen** *Fig.* to get rid of one's feelings of anger caused by someone or something by attacking someone or something else. □ *Jack vented his spleen at his wife whenever things went badly at work.*

vent sth **(up)on** so/sth to release one's emotional tension on someone or something. (*Upon* is formal and less commonly used than *on*.) □ *Henry vented his anger on Carl.* □ *It's no use to vent your hatred on a door. Kicking it won't help.*

venture forth 1. to set out; to go forward; to go out cautiously. □ *George ventured forth into the night.* **2.** *Fig.* to go forth bravely. □ *We will arm ourselves and venture forth against our foe.*

the **(very) picture of** sth *Fig.* the perfect example of something; an exact image of something. □ *The young newlyweds were the picture of happiness.* □ *My doctor told me that I was the very picture of good health.*

the **very thing** *Fig.* the exact thing that is required. □ *The vacuum cleaner is the very thing for cleaning the stairs.*

*a **vested interest in** sth *Fig.* a personal or biased interest, often financial, in something. (*Typically: **have** ~; **give** so ~.) □ *Margaret has a vested interest in wanting her father to sell the family firm. She has shares in it and would make a large profit.*

the **villain of the piece** *Fig.* someone or something that is responsible for something bad or wrong. (*Fig.* on the role of the villain in a drama or other literary work.) □ *We couldn't think who had stolen the meat. The dog next door turned out to be the villain of the piece.*

vim and vigor *Cliché* energy; enthusiasm. □ *Show more vim and vigor! Let us know you're alive.*

virtual reality *Fig.* computer imaging that attempts to mimic real scenes or places. □ *The movie had so much virtual reality that the regular photographic scenes began to look funny.*

a **visit from the stork** *Fig.* a birth. (According to legend, babies are brought to their parents by a stork.) □ *I hear that Maria is expecting a visit from the stork.*

visit the plumbing Go to check out the plumbing.

visit sth **(up)on** so *Fig.* to inflict something upon someone. (Stilted. *Upon* is formal and less commonly used than *on*.) □ *The FBI visited a plague of investigations on the mayor's staff.*

visually impaired *Euph.* blind or partly blind. □ *I am visually impaired, but I like TV just as much as the next person.*

a **voice crying in the wilderness** *Fig.* a voice unheard; a messenger to whom no one pays any attention. (The biblical basis for this is Isaiah 40:3. This passage is quoted or referred to in all four Christian Gospels. In some translations of Isaiah, the voice is "in the wilderness," and in others the voice is requesting that a highway be prepared "in the wilderness." This is the difference between "a voice crying: 'In the wilderness prepare . . .'" and "a voice crying in the wilderness: 'Prepare . . .'." Neither of these readings actually gives rise to the meaning of this entry head, but the second reading at least puts the voice into the wilderness. The source of the entry head is biblical, nonetheless. In any case, there is no weeping involved.) □ *Didn't you hear what I said? Am I just a voice crying in the wilderness?* □ *He's like a voice crying in the wilderness. He says the same thing over and over, and no one pays any attention any longer.*

*a **voice (in** sth**)** AND *a **say (in** sth**)** *Fig.* a part in making a decision. (*Typically: **get** ~; **have** ~; **give** so ~.) □ *I'd like to have a voice in choosing the carpet.* □ *John wanted to have a say in the issue also.*

vomit sth **out**† *Fig.* [for something] to spill forth a great deal of something. □ *The volcano vomited the lava out for days.*

vote a split ticket *Fig.* to cast a ballot on which one's votes are divided between two or more parties. □ *I always vote a spilt ticket since I detest both parties.*

vote a straight ticket *Fig.* to cast a ballot on which all one's votes are for members of the same political party. □ *I'm not a member of any political party, so I never vote a straight ticket.*

vote sth **into law** AND **vote** sth **in**† to take a vote on a proposal and make it a law. □ *They voted the proposal into law.*

a **vote of confidence 1.** a specific act of voting that signifies whether a governing body still has the majority's support. □ *The government easily won the vote of confidence called for by the opposition.* **2.** *Fig.* a statement of confidence in a person or a group. □ *The little talk that his father gave him before the game served as a great vote of confidence for Billy.*

a **vote of thanks** *Fig.* a speech expressing appreciation and thanks to a speaker, lecturer, organizer, etc. and inviting the audience to applaud. □ *Mary was given a vote of thanks for organizing the dance.*

vote with one's **feet** *Fig.* to express one's dissatisfaction with something by leaving, especially by walking away. □ *I think that the play is a total flop. Most of the audience voted with its feet during the second act.*

vote with one's **wallet** *Fig.* to show one's displeasure at a business establishment's goods or pricing by spending one's money elsewhere. (Probably derived from **vote with** one's **feet.**) □ *If you didn't like it, you should have complained to the manager and voted with your wallet.*

vouch for so/sth to declare that someone or something is as represented. □ *I can vouch for Bob's honesty.* □ *Who will vouch for the accuracy of this report?*

wade in(to sth) *Fig.* to get quickly and directly involved in something. (Fig. on the image of someone wading into water.) □ *Don't just wade into things. Stop and think about what you are doing.*

wade through sth *Fig.* to struggle through something with difficulty. (Fig. on the image of slogging through something such as water or mud.) □ *I have to wade through 40 term papers in the next two days.*

wag one's **chin** *Rur.* to talk. □ *She loves to visit. She'll wag her chin for hours.*

wait for the next wave Go to catch the next wave.

wait for the other shoe to drop *Fig.* to wait for the inevitable next step or the final conclusion. □ *He just opened his mail and moaned. Now, I'm waiting for the other shoe to drop when he finds the subpoena.*

Wait (just) a minute! Go to Hold on (a minute)!

wait on so **hand and foot** *Fig.* to serve someone very well, attending to all personal needs. □ *I don't mind bringing you your coffee, but I don't intend to wait on you hand and foot.*

wait (on) tables *Fig.* to serve food and tend diners, as at a restaurant. □ *I waited on tables for years to pay my college tuition.*

wait one's **turn** *Fig.* to keep from doing something until everyone ahead of you has done it. □ *You can't cross the intersection yet. You must wait your turn.*

wait (up)on so *Fig.* to pay homage to someone. (Stilted.) □ *Do you expect me to wait upon you like a member of some medieval court?*

wait-and-see attitude *Fig.* a skeptical attitude; an uncertain attitude in which someone will just wait to see what happens before reacting. □ *His wait-and-see attitude seemed to indicate that he didn't really care what happened.*

waiting in the wings *Fig.* ready or prepared to do something, especially to take over someone else's job or position. (*Wings* refers to the sides of the stage, out of view of the audience, where actors enter or exit. Actors wait in the wings to go on stage.) □ *Mr. Smith retires as manager next year, and Mr. Jones is just waiting in the wings.*

wake the dead *Fig.* to be so loud as to wake those who are "sleeping" the most soundly: the dead. □ *You are making enough noise to wake the dead.*

wake up and smell the coffee *Fig.* to become aware and sense what is going on around oneself. □ *You are so without a clue. Wake up and smell the coffee! Life is passing you by.*

wake up on the wrong side of bed Go to get up on the wrong side of bed.

wake up to sth *Fig.* to become aware of something. □ *When I finally woke up to the damage I was doing to myself by overeating, I went on a diet.*

walk a tightrope *Fig.* to be in a situation where one must be very cautious. □ *Our business is about to fail. We've been walking a tightrope for three months.*

walk all over so/sth *Fig.* to treat someone or something very badly; to beat someone or something soundly in a competition.

□ *The prosecution walked all over the witness.*

walk arm in arm Go to arm in arm.

walk away from so/sth *Fig.* to abandon someone or something; to go away and leave someone or something. □ *I walked away from him and never saw him again.*

walk away with sth AND **walk off with** sth **1.** *Fig.* to win something easily. (With little more effort than is required to carry off the winning trophy.) □ *John won the tennis match with no difficulty. He walked away with it.* **2.** *Fig.* to take or steal something. □ *I think somebody just walked off with my purse!*

walk so's **feet off** *Fig.* to walk too much and tire out someone's feet, including one's own. □ *I've gone all over town today. I walked my feet off, looking for just the right present for Jill.*

walk off the job 1. *Fig.* to abandon a job abruptly. □ *Fred almost walked off the job when he saw how bad things were.* **2.** *Fig.* to go on strike at a workplace. □ *The workers walked off the job and refused to negotiate.*

walk off with sth Go to walk away with sth.

walk on air *Fig.* to be very happy; to be euphoric. □ *On the last day of school, all the children are walking on air.*

walk on eggshells 1. *Fig.* to walk very carefully; to take steps gingerly. □ *Since he stumbled and fell against the china cabinet, Bill has been walking on eggshells.* **2.** *Fig.* to be very diplomatic and inoffensive. □ *I was walking on eggshells trying to explain the remark to her without offending her further.*

walk on thin ice *Fig.* to be in a very precarious position. □ *Careful with radical ideas like that. You're walking on thin ice.*

walk out (on so**)** *Fig.* to abandon someone; to leave one's spouse. □ *Mr. Franklin walked out on Mrs. Franklin last week.*

walk out (on sth**)** *Fig.* to leave a performance (of something by someone). □ *John was giving a very dull speech, and a few people even walked out on him.*

walk (right) into sth *Fig.* to fall right into a trap or deception. □ *You walked right into my trap. Now I have you right where I want you.*

walk soft *Inf.* to be unobtrusive; to be gentle and humble. □ *The guy's a tyrant. He walks soft just to mislead people.*

walk tall *Fig.* to be brave and self-assured. □ *You go out on that stage and walk tall. There is no reason to be afraid.*

walk the extra mile Go to go the extra mile.

walk the floor *Fig.* to pace nervously while waiting. □ *Walking the floor won't help. You might as well sit down and relax.*

walk the plank *Fig.* to suffer punishment at the hand of someone. (Fig. on the image of pirates making their blindfolded captives die by walking off the end of a plank jutting out over the open sea.) □ *Fred may think he can make the members of my department walk the plank, but we will fight back.*

walk through sth *Fig.* to rehearse something in a casual way; to go through a play or other performed piece, showing where each person is to be located during each speech or musical number. □ *Let's walk through this scene one more time.*

walk so **through** sth AND **talk** so **through** sth *Fig.* to lead someone through a complex problem or thought process. □ *Mary walked Jane through the complex solution to the calculus problem.*

***one's walking papers** *Fig.* a notice that one is fired from one's job. (*Typically: **get** ~; **have** ~; **give** one ~.) □ *They are closing down my department. I guess I'll get my walking papers soon.*

wall-to-wall sth *Fig.* covered with something in all places. (From *wall-to-wall carpeting*.) □ *The beach was wall-to-wall tourists.*

waltz around sth *Fig.* to move around or through a place happily or proudly. □ *Who is that person waltzing around, trying to look important?*

waltz in(to some place) *Fig.* to step or walk into a place briskly and easily. ☐ *She waltzed into the room and showed off her ring.*

waltz off *Fig.* to depart briskly and easily. ☐ *They said good-bye and waltzed off.*

waltz off (with sth**)** *Fig.* to take something away easily. ☐ *They just picked the thing up and waltzed off. Nobody asked them any questions.*

waltz through sth *Fig.* to get through something easily. ☐ *I waltzed through my comps and started on my research in my second year of grad school.*

waltz up (to so**)** *Fig.* to approach someone boldly. ☐ *He just waltzed up to her and introduced himself.*

Want a piece of me? Go to (You) want a piece of me?

want for sth *Fig.* to lack something; to need something. ☐ *I certainly don't want for advice. In fact, I have had too much.*

want for nothing *Fig.* not to lack anything; to have everything one needs or desires. ☐ *The Smiths don't have much money, but their children seem to want for nothing.*

want sth **so bad** one **can taste it** Go to so bad one can taste it.

Want to know something? Go to Do you want to know something?

*warm as toast very warm and cozy. (*Also: **as** ~.) ☐ *We were as warm as toast by the side of the fire.*

warm body *Inf.* a person; just any person (who can be counted on to be present). ☐ *See if you can get a couple of warm bodies to stand at the door and hand out programs.*

warm the bench *Fig.* [for a player] to remain out of play during a game—seated on a bench. ☐ *Mary never warms the bench. She plays from the beginning to the end.*

warm the cockles of so's **heart** *Fig.* to make someone feel warm and happy. ☐ *Hearing that old song again warmed the cockles of her heart.*

warm up to so/sth *Fig.* to become more fervent and earnest toward someone, something, or a group; to become more responsive and receptive to someone, a group, or something. ☐ *I warmed up to the committee as the interview went on.*

warmed over *Inf.* not very original; rehashed. ☐ *I am not interested in reading warmed-over news on a computer screen.*

warts and all *Cliché* in spite of the flaws. ☐ *It's a great performance—warts and all.*

was had Go to been had.

wash one's **dirty linen in public** Go to air one's dirty linen in public.

wash sth **down**† **(with** sth**)** *Fig.* to use fluid to aid the swallowing of food or medicine. ☐ *Molly washed the pills down with a gulp of coffee.*

wash one's **hands of** so/sth *Fig.* to end one's association with someone or something. (Fig. on the notion of getting rid of a problem by removing it as if it were dirt on the hands.) ☐ *I washed my hands of Tom. I wanted no more to do with him.*

wash out 1. *Inf.* to fail and be removed from something, such as school. ☐ *I studied all I could, but I still washed out.* **2.** *Inf.* to have a serious wreck; to wipe out. ☐ *The little car washed out on the curve.* **3.** *Inf.* to lose a large amount of money. ☐ *Fred washed out on that stock deal.* **4.** *Inf.* to break down or collapse from exhaustion. ☐ *Finally, after a long day, I just washed out. They had to call the paramedics.*

wash so **out of** sth AND **wash** so **out**† *Fig.* to make it necessary for a person to leave a place or program; to wash someone up. ☐ *That professor just loves to wash students out of the course.*

wash over so *Fig.* [for a powerful feeling] to flood over a person. ☐ *A feeling of nausea washed over me.*

washed out *Inf.* exhausted; tired. ☐ *I feel too washed out to go to work today.*

washed up *Fig.* finished. ☐ *Wilbur is washed up as a bank teller.*

waste so *Sl.* to kill someone. □ *The thief tried to waste the bank guard after the bank robbery.*

waste one's **breath** *Fig.* to waste one's time talking; to talk in vain. □ *Don't waste your breath talking to her. She won't listen.*

waste no time Go to lose no time.

a **waste of space** something that is completely without value. □ *The wrecked furniture in here is just a waste of space.*

waste time Go to lose time.

watch one's **back** *Fig.* to guard against treachery and betrayal. □ *Until you have testified and the trial is over, I suggest that you watch your back.*

watch so/sth **like a hawk** *Fig.* to watch someone or something very closely. (Hawks have very good eyesight and watch carefully for prey.) □ *The teacher didn't trust me. During tests, she used to watch me like a hawk.*

Watch my lips! AND **Read my lips!** *Inf.* I am going to say something rude to you that I will not say out loud! □ *You jerk! Watch my lips!*

Watch out! Go to Look out!

watch one's **Ps and Qs** Go to mind one's Ps and Qs.

watch one's **step** *Fig.* to act with care and caution so as not to make a mistake or offend someone. □ *John had better watch his step with the new boss. He won't put up with his lateness.*

watch the store Go to mind the store.

water sth **down**† *Fig.* to reduce the effectiveness or force of something. □ *Please don't water my declaration down.*

water over the dam AND **water under the bridge** *Fig.* past and unchangeable events. □ *Your quarrel with Lena is water over the dam, so you ought to concentrate on getting along with her.* □ *George and I were friends once, but that's all water under the bridge now.*

water under the bridge Go to previous.

watering hole 1. *Lit.* a place where there is water for animals (and people) to drink. □ *The elephants came down to the watering hole and chased away the lions so they could drink in peace.* **2.** *Inf.* a bar or tavern. □ *Fred is down at the local watering hole boozing it up.*

wax and wane *Fig.* to increase and then decrease, as the phases of the moon. □ *Voter sentiment about the tax proposal waxes and wanes with each passing day.*

wax angry AND **wax wroth** *Fig.* to speak in anger and with indignity. □ *Seeing the damage done by the careless children caused the preacher to wax wroth at their parents.*

wax eloquent *Fig.* to speak with eloquence. □ *Perry never passed up a chance to wax eloquent at a banquet.*

wax poetic *Fig.* to speak poetically. □ *I hope you will pardon me if I wax poetic for a moment when I say that your lovely hands drift across the piano keys like swans on the lake.*

wax wroth Go to wax angry.

the **way I see it** Go to from my perspective.

the **way it plays** *Sl.* the way it is; the way things are. □ *The world is a rough place, and that's the way it plays.*

way off (base) *Inf.* on the wrong track; completely wrong. □ *Sorry. You are way off. You should just give up.*

way out 1. *Inf.* extreme; arcane. □ *Some of your ideas are really way out.* **2.** *Inf.* heavily intoxicated. □ *That guy is way out—can't even walk.*

the **way things stand** Go to as it is.

Way to go! Go to (That's the) way to go!

We all gotta go sometime. *Inf.* We all must die sometime. (As jocular as possible.) □ *Sorry to hear about old Bubba, but we all gotta go sometime.*

*****weak as a baby** AND *****weak as a kitten** *Cliché* [of someone] physically very weak. (*Also: **as** ~.) □ *Six weeks of illness left the athlete as weak as a baby.*

weak as a kitten Go to previous.

the **weak link (in the chain)** *Fig.* the weak point or person in a system or organization. □ *Joan's hasty generalizations about the economy were definitely the weak link in her argument.*

weak sister *Inf.* a timid person, usually a male. □ *We've got to pull together and stop playing like a bunch of weak sisters.*

weak stomach *Fig.* a stomach not able to tolerate bad food or gory sights. □ *Because he had a weak stomach, he turned his head away when the doctor cleaned the wound.*

a **wealth of** sth *Fig.* a large amount of something. □ *There's a wealth of information on parrots at the library.*

wear and tear *Fig.* damage to something through use. □ *This old couch shows some wear and tear, but generally, it's in good shape.*

wear and tear (on sth) *Fig.* the process of wearing down or breaking down something by regular use. □ *I drive carefully and have my car serviced regularly to avoid wear and tear.*

wear one's **heart on** one's **sleeve** AND **have** one's **heart on** one's **sleeve** *Fig.* to display one's feelings openly and habitually, rather than keep them private. □ *John always has his heart on his sleeve so that everyone knows how he feels.*

wear more than one hat AND **wear two hats** *Fig.* to have more than one set of responsibilities; to hold more than one office. □ *The mayor is also the police chief. She wears more than one hat.*

wear on so *Fig.* to bother or annoy someone. □ *We stayed with them only a short time because my children seemed to wear on them.*

wear out one's **welcome** *Fig.* to stay too long (at an event to which one has been invited); to visit somewhere too often. □ *At about midnight, I decided that I had worn out my welcome, so I went home.*

wear the britches (in the family) AND **wear the pants (in the family)** *Rur.* to be in charge in the family. □ *Mary's a strong-minded woman, but her husband still wears the britches.*

wear the pants (in the family) Go to previous.

wear thin *Fig.* to become tiresome, weak, tedious, dulled, ineffective, etc. □ *Stop that noise! My patience is wearing thin.* □ *Your constant apologies are wearing thin. I don't believe you anymore.*

wear so **to a frazzle** *Fig.* to exhaust someone. □ *Taking care of all those kids must wear you to a frazzle.*

weasel out (of sth) *Fig.* to sneak out of something; to avoid doing something. □ *Don't try to weasel out of your responsibility!*

weather permitting *Fig.* if the weather allows it. □ *The plane lands at midnight, weather permitting.*

weather the storm AND **ride out the storm 1.** *Fig.* to experience and survive a storm. □ *We decided to stay in the building and weather the storm there with the other visitors.* **2.** *Fig.* to experience something and survive it. (Fig. on ①.) □ *The manager went on another shouting rampage and frightened his assistants. The rest of us stayed in our offices to weather the storm.*

weave sth **from** sth *Fig.* to make a story or explanation out of a small amount of information. □ *You have woven the entire tale from something you heard me say to Ruth.*

weave sth **into** sth *Fig.* to turn separate episodes into a story. □ *Skillfully, the writer wove the elements into a clever story.*

wedded to sth *Fig.* mentally attached to something; firmly committed to something. □ *The manager was wedded to the idea of getting new computers.*

the **wee hours (of the night)** Go to the small hours (of the night).

week in, week out *Fig.* every week, week after week. □ *We have the same old food, week in, week out.*

weeks running Go to days running.

weep for joy *Fig.* to cry out of happiness. □ *We all wept for joy at the safe return of the child.*

weigh (up)on SO *Fig.* to burden or worry someone. (*Upon* is formal and less commonly used than *on.*) □ *The problems at the office were beginning to weigh upon Mr. Franklin.*

weigh SO's **words 1.** *Fig.* to consider carefully what someone says. □ *I listened to what he said, and I weighed his words very carefully.* **2.** *Fig.* to consider one's own words carefully when speaking. □ *I always weigh my words when I speak in public.*

a **weight off** one's **mind** Go to a load off one's mind.

welcome SO **with open arms** Go to receive SO with open arms.

well and good Go to (all) well and good.

***well disposed to(ward)** SO/sth *Fig.* friendly with someone or something; having a positive or favorable attitude toward someone or something. (*Typically: **be** ~; **become** ~.) □ *We are well disposed to all of them despite their attitudes.*

well done done nicely; done politely and efficiently. □ *Good job, Tom! Well done!*

well in hand *Fig.* under control. □ *We have everything well in hand. Don't worry.*

***well into** sth *Fig.* far into something or far along in something. (*Typically: **be** ~; **get** ~.) □ *The car was well into the tunnel when it broke down.*

well up in years *Euph.* aged; old. □ *Jane's husband is well up in years. He is nearly 75.*

well up (inside SO**)** *Fig.* [for a feeling] to seem to swell and move inside one's body. □ *Burning resentment welled up, and George knew he was going to lose his temper.*

well-fixed Go to next.

well-heeled AND **well-fixed; well-off** *Fig.* wealthy; with sufficient money. □ *My uncle can afford a new car. He's well-heeled.*

well-off Go to previous.

well-to-do *Fig.* wealthy and of good social position. (Often with *quite,* as in the example.) □ *There is a gentleman waiting for you at the door. He appears quite well-to-do.*

went out with the buggy whip Go to next.

went out with the horse and buggy AND **went out with the horse and carriage; went out with the buggy whip** *Fig.* went out of style when horse traffic went out of fashion. (A symbol of old-fashionedness or out-of-dateness.) □ *I thought suspenders went out with the horse and carriage, but I see them everywhere now.*

went out with the horse and carriage Go to previous.

Were you born in a barn? *Rur.* an expression chiding someone who has left a door open or who is ill-mannered or messy. □ *Fred: Can't you clean this place up a little? Were you born in a barn? Bob: I call it the messy look.*

wet behind the ears AND **not dry behind the ears; hardly dry behind the ears** *Fig.* young and inexperienced. □ *John's too young to take on a job like this! He's still wet behind the ears!* □ *Tom is going into business by himself? Why, he's hardly dry behind the ears.*

a **wet blanket** *Fig.* a dull or depressing person who spoils other people's enjoyment. □ *Jack's fun at parties, but his brother's a wet blanket.*

wet one's **whistle** *Rur.* to take a drink. □ *I don't need a big glass of water. Just enough to wet my whistle.*

a **whack at** sth Go to a try at sth.

whacked (out) *Sl.* intoxicated. □ *Dave was so whacked out he couldn't stand up.*

whale the tar out of SO *Inf.* to spank or beat someone. (See also **beat the living daylights out of someone.**) □ *I'll whale the tar out of you when we get home if you don't settle down.*

What are you driving at? *Fig.* What are you trying to say?; What are you implying? □ *I don't understand your line of questioning. What are you driving at?*

What can I say? *Inf.* I have no explanation or excuse. What do you expect me to say? (See also **What do you want me to say?**) □ *Bob: You're going to have to act more aggressive if you want to make sales. You're just too timid. Tom: What can I say? I am what I am.*

What can I tell you? *Inf.* I haven't any idea of what to say. (Compare this with **What can I say?**) □ *John: Why on earth did you do a dumb thing like that? Bill: What can I tell you? I just did it, that's all.*

What do you know? 1. *Inf.* Hello, how are you? (A detailed answer is not expected.) □ *A: Hi, Chuck. What do you know? B: Tsup, dog?* **2.** *Inf.* I'm mildly surprised.; Isn't that interesting. (Often with *well*.) □ *Jethro: Hi, Chuck. Chuck: Well, what do you know? It's old Jethro. What are you doing here?*

What do you want me to say? *Inf.* You caught me and I'm sorry, and I don't know what more to say. □ *What do you want me to say? I apologized. There is nothing more I can do.*

What one doesn't know won't hurt one. *Cliché* Unknown facts cannot worry or upset a person. □ *Don't tell me that I have made a mistake. What I don't know won't hurt me.*

*what for 1. *Fig.* a scolding; a stern lecture. (*Typically: **get** ~; **give** so ~.) □ *Billy's mother gave him what for because he didn't get home on time.* **2.** Why?; For what reason? □ *Father: "I want you to clean your room." Child: "What for? It's clean enough."*

What I wouldn't give for a sth! I would give anything for something. □ *What I wouldn't give for a cold drink about now.*

what so/sth **is cracked up to be** *Fig.* what someone or something is supposed to be. □ *This pizza isn't what it's cracked up to be.*

what makes so **tick** *Fig.* something that motivates someone; something that makes someone behave in a certain way. (Fig. on **what makes** sth **tick**.) □ *When you get to know people, you find out what makes them tick.*

what makes sth **tick** *Fig.* the sense or mechanism that makes something run or function. (With reference to the ticking of a clock representing the functioning of the clock.) □ *I took apart the radio to find out what made it tick.*

What on earth? Go to **on earth?**

What price sth? *Fig.* What is the value of something?; What good is something? (Said when the value of the thing referred to is being diminished or ignored.) □ *Jane's best friend told us all about Jane's personal problems. What price friendship?*

What so **said.** *Sl.* I agree with what someone just said, although I might not have been able to say it as well or so elegantly. □ *What John said. And I agree 100 percent.*

What say? Go to **Say what?**

What the devil? AND **What the fuck?; What the hell?; What the shit?** *Fig.* What has happened?; What? (Often with the force of an exclamation. Caution with **shit, fuck**.) □ *What the devil? Who put sugar in the salt shaker?* □ *What the fuck? Who are you? What are you doing in my room?* □ *What the shit are you doing here? You're supposed to be at work.*

What the fuck? Go to previous.

What the heck! *Inf.* It doesn't matter! (Often with the force of an exclamation.) □ *Oh, what the heck! I'll have another beer. Nobody's counting.*

What the hell? Go to **What the devil?**

What the shit? Go to **What the devil?**

what with sth because of something. □ *What with the children being at home and my parents coming to stay, I have too much to do.*

What you see is what you get. *Fig.* The product you are looking at is exactly what you get if you buy it. □ *It comes just like this. What you see is what you get.*

whatever comes down the pike Go to comes down the pike.

whatever comes into one's **head (first)** Go to the first thing that comes into one's head.

Whatever floats your boat. *Cliché* Whatever interests, stimulates, excites, or satisfies you. □ *Go there if you want. It makes no difference to me. Whatever floats your boat.*

Whatever turns you on. 1. *Inf.* Whatever pleases or excites you is okay. □ *Mary: Do you mind if I buy some of these flowers? Bill: Whatever turns you on.* **2.** *Inf.* a comment implying that it is strange to get so excited about something. (Essentially sarcastic.) □ *Bob: I just go wild whenever I see pink gloves on a woman. I don't understand it. Bill: Whatever turns you on.*

What's coming off? AND **What's going down?** *Inf.* What is happening here?; What is going to happen? (Also a greeting inquiry.) □ *Bill: Hey, man! What's coming off? Tom: Oh, nothing, just takin' it easy.*

***what's coming to** one *Fig.* what one deserves. (*Typically: **get** ~; **have** ~; **give** one ~.) □ *If you cheat, you'll get in trouble. You'll get what's coming to you.*

What's cooking? *Inf.* What is happening?; How are you? □ *Bob: Hi, Fred! What's cooking? Fred: How are you doing, Bob?*

What's eating so? *Inf.* What is bothering someone? □ *Tom: Go away! Bob: Gee, Tom, what's eating you?*

What's going down? Go to What's coming off?

What's got(ten) into so? *Fig.* What is bothering someone?; What caused someone to act that way? (Past or perfect only. The *has* is contracted except for emphasis.) □ *I just don't know what's gotten into her.*

what's more Go to furthermore.

What's the (big) idea? *Inf.* Why did you do that? (Usually said in anger.) □ *Please don't do that! What's the idea?*

What's the catch? *Sl.* What is the drawback?; It sounds good, but are there any hidden problems? □ *Sounds too good to be true. What's the catch?*

What's the damage? *Sl.* What are the charges?; How much is the bill? □ *Bill: That was delicious. Waiter, what's the damage? Waiter: I'll get the check, sir.*

What's the drill? 1. *Inf.* What is going on here? □ *Bill: I just came in. What's the drill? Tom: We have to carry all this stuff out to the truck.* **2.** *Inf.* What are the rules and procedures for doing this? □ *Bill: I have to get my computer repaired. Who do I talk to? What's the drill? Bob: You have to get a purchase order from Fred.*

What's the world coming to? There are too many changes, and they are all bad. □ *Look at how people speed down this street now. What's the world coming to?*

wheel and deal *Fig.* to take part in clever (but sometimes dishonest or immoral) business deals. □ *Jack got tired of all the wheeling and dealing of big business and retired to a farm out west.*

when all is said and done Go to after all is said and done.

when so's **back is turned** Go to while so's back is turned.

when one **is good and ready** *Fig.* when one is completely ready. □ *Ann will finish the job when she's good and ready and not a minute sooner.*

when it comes right down to it AND **all things considered** *Cliché* when one really thinks about something. □ *When it comes right down to it, he can't really afford a new car.* □ *All things considered, I deserve a new car anyway.*

when it comes to sth *Fig.* as for something; speaking about something. □ *When it comes to trouble, Mary really knows how to cause it.*

when it comes to the crunch AND **when it gets down to the crunch** when events become critical and challenging. □ *When it comes down to the crunch, Sally is strong and capable. She will do the job.*

when it gets down to the crunch Go to previous.

when least expected when one does not expect something. □ *An old car is likely to give you trouble when least expected.*

when push comes to shove AND **if push comes to shove** *Fig.* when things get a little pressed; when the situation gets more active or intense. □ *When push comes to shove, you know I'll be on your side.*

when one's **ship comes in** *Fig.* when one becomes rich and successful. □ *When your ship comes in, Otto, I'll probably die of amazement!*

when the chips are down *Fig.* at the final, critical moment; when things really get difficult. □ *When the chips are down, I know that I can depend on Jean to help out.*

when the dust settles 1. *Fig.* when the dust falls out of the air onto the ground or floor. □ *When the dust settles, we will have to begin sweeping it up.* **2.** *Fig.* when things have calmed down. (Fig. on ①.) □ *When the dust settles, we can start patching up all the hurt feelings.*

when the fat lady sings Go to till the fat lady sings.

when the going gets tough AND **if the going gets tough; when the going gets rough; if the going gets rough** *Fig.* as things get extremely difficult; when it becomes difficult to proceed. (There is a slogan based on this: *When the going gets tough, the tough get going.*) □ *When the going gets tough, I will be there to help you.*

when the shit hits the fan *Sl.* when all the expected trouble materializes. (Caution with *shit.*) □ *When the shit hits the fan, you had better be prepared to support those of us who are involved in this mess.*

When they made so/sth, **they broke the mold.** *Fig.* Someone or something is unique in some way (not always a positive way). (Alludes to casting something and then destroying the mold so that no more items can be cast.) □ *He's sort of ec-*

centric. *When they made him, they broke the mold.*

when you get a chance Go to next.

when you get a minute AND **when you get a chance** *Fig.* a phrase introducing a request, especially to talk to someone. □ *Bill: Tom? Tom: Yes. Bill: When you get a minute, I'd like to have a word with you.*

Where do (you think) you get off? *Inf.* What do you think you are doing?; Who do you think you are? (A sharp reply to something offensive or impolite.) □ *Where do you get off, talking to me like that?*

where so's **head is at** *Inf.* the state of one's mental well-being. □ *As soon as I figure where my head is at, I'll be okay.*

where one **is coming from** *Fig.* one's point of view. □ *I think I know what you mean. I know where you're coming from.*

Where on (God's green) earth? *Inf.* (Exactly) where? (An intensive form of *where*. See examples for variations.) □ *Where on God's green earth did you get that ridiculous hat?* □ *Where on earth is my book?* □ *Where on God's green earth were you?*

where the action is *Inf.* where important things are happening. □ *Right there in city hall. That's where the action is.*

where the rubber meets the road *Fig.* at the point in a process where there are challenges, issues, or problems. □ *Now we have spelled out the main area of dissent. This is where the rubber meets the road.*

where the sun don't shine *Sl.* in a dark place, namely the anus. □ *I don't care what you do with it. Just put it where the sun don't shine.*

Where there's smoke, there's fire. *Fig.* Where there is evidence of an event, the event must have happened. □ *She found lipstick on his collar. Knowing that where there's smoke, there's fire, she confronted him.*

Where's the beef? *Inf.* Where is the substance?; Where is the important content?

□ *Where's the beef? There's no substance in this proposal.*

Where's the fire? *Inf.* Where are you going in such a hurry? (Typically said by a police officer after stopping a speeding driver.) □ *Officer: Okay, where's the fire? Mary: Was I going a little fast?*

*the **wherewithal (to** do sth) *Fig.* the means to do something, especially energy or money. (*Typically: **get** ~; **have** ~; **give** so ~.) □ *He has good ideas, but he doesn't have the wherewithal to carry them out.*

whet so's **appetite** *Fig.* to cause someone to be interested in something and to be eager to have, know, learn, etc. more about it. □ *Seeing that film really whetted my sister's appetite for horror films. She now sees as many as possible.*

*a **whiff of** sth **1.** the smell or odor of something. (*Typically: **get** ~; **catch** ~; **have** ~; **take** ~; **give** so ~.) □ *I caught a whiff of something rather unpleasant in the attic. I think there is a dead mouse up there.* **2.** *Fig.* a bit of knowledge of something. (Fig. on ①. *Typically: **get** ~; **catch** ~; **give** so ~.) □ *No one will get a whiff of your trouble with the police. I'll see to that.*

while some time **away**† to find a way to spend a period of time. □ *I while away the hours knitting.* □ *We whiled half the day away waiting for the janitor to show up and unlock the door.*

while so's **back is turned** AND **when** so's **back is turned** *Fig.* while someone's guard is down; while someone is not paying close attention. (Fig. on the idea of something happening behind one's back.) □ *I hope no one manages to change the board's mind while my back is turned.*

while one **is at it** while already in the process of doing something. □ *If you are going to the kitchen, please take these books to the den while you're at it.*

whip so/sth **into shape** Go to lick so/sth into shape.

whip sth **off**† **1.** *Fig.* to do or create something quickly. □ *If you need another receipt, I can whip one off in a jiffy.* **2.** to remove something, such as an item of clothing, quickly. □ *He whipped the coat off and dived into the water.*

whip sth **up**† *Fig.* to prepare, create, or put something together. □ *I haven't written my report yet, but I'll whip one up before the deadline.*

a **whipping boy** *Fig.* someone who is punished for someone else's misdeeds. □ *The president has turned out to be the whipping boy for his party.*

whirlwind courtship *Fig.* a very fast courtship or relationship such as before marriage. (See also sweep one off one's feet.) □ *After a whirlwind courtship, they were married at midnight by a justice of the peace.*

whistle in the dark *Inf.* to guess aimlessly; to speculate as to a fact. □ *She was just whistling in the dark. She has no idea of what's going on.*

white as a ghost Go to next.

white as a sheet AND ***white as a ghost; *white as snow; *white as the driven snow** [of someone] extremely pale, as if frightened. (*Also: **as** ~.) □ *Marilyn turned as white as a sheet when the policeman told her that her son had been in a car wreck.* □ *Did something scare you? You're white as a sheet!* □ *Jane made up the bed with her best linen sheets, which are always as white as snow.*

white as snow Go to previous.

white as the driven snow Go to white as a sheet.

a **white elephant** something that is large and unwieldy and is either a nuisance or expensive to maintain. (*White elephant* is a term for a revered elephant in Southeast Asia that typically has white or pink features, namely toenails, roof of the mouth, genitals, and parts of the cornea. Further, it has white or light brown hairs and white, light gray, light brown, or pink areas of skin as well as a long tail. Albinism is not typical or required. A royal white elephant was kept in the palace, where the most lavish of care and reverence was applied to the upkeep of such an animal. The well-being of the elephant signaled the well-being of the ruler who owned it and his kingdom. If such an animal were given as a gift, the new owner would be expected to accept the burden of maintaining the animal with lavish care. The cost of such care could be devastating. The term has dwindled down to refer to an unwelcome gift or unwanted possession that takes up space.) □ *Those antique vases Aunt Mary gave me are white elephants. They're ugly and I have no place to put them.*

white knuckle sth *Fig.* to survive something threatening through strained endurance, that is to say, holding on tight. □ *The flight from New York was terrible. We had to white knuckle the entire flight.*

white-collar *Fig.* of the class of salaried office workers or lower-level managers. (Compare this with blue-collar.) □ *His parents were both white-collar employees and had good-paying jobs.*

whittle so **down to size** AND **cut** so **down to size** *Fig.* to reduce someone's ego; to cause someone to have better, more respectful behavior. □ *After a few days at camp, the counselors had whittled young Walter down to size.*

whiz (right) through sth *Fig.* to work one's way through something quickly. □ *She whizzed right through the test with no trouble.*

Who could have thought? Go to next.

Who would have thought? AND **Who could have thought?; Who would'a thunk (it)?** *Fig.* I would never have guessed that something so surprising could happen. (A question phrase indicating surprise or amazement. No answer is expected. The *thunk* version is very informal and jocular.) □ *Tom: Fred just quit his job and went to Africa. Bill: Who would have thought he could do such a thing?* □ *Andy: They say Bill is training for the Olympics in his spare time. Rachel: Who would'a thunk?*

Who would'a thunk (it)? Go to previous.

whole bag of tricks *Fig.* everything; every possibility. □ *Well now. I've used my whole bag of tricks, and we still haven't solved this.*

the **whole ball of wax** AND the **whole shooting match** *Inf.* the whole thing; the whole matter or affair; the entire affair or organization. (As if it were composed of little bits of wax rolled together into one big ball. There are a number of fanciful stories as to the origin of this, but they lack convincing evidence.) □ *John is not a good manager. Instead of delegating jobs to others, he runs the whole shooting match himself.* □ *I am tired of this job. I am fed up with the whole ball of wax.*

the **whole enchilada** *Inf.* the whole thing; everything. (From Spanish.) □ *Nobody, but nobody, ever gets the whole enchilada.*

a **(whole) hell of a lot** AND a **(whole) heck of a lot** *Inf.* a lot; much. □ *A whole hell of a lot you care about my problems!*

the **whole kit and caboodle** *Inf.* a group of pieces of equipment or belongings. (The word *caboodle* is used only in this expression.) □ *When I bought Bob's motor home, I got furniture, refrigerator, and linen—the whole kit and caboodle.*

a **(whole) new ball game** *Inf.* a completely different situation; something completely different. □ *With a faster computer, it's a whole new ball game.*

the **whole nine yards** *Sl.* the entire amount; everything, as far as possible. (Especially with *go*. While there are quite a few made-up origins of this expression, there is absolutely no evidence that any one of them gave rise to *whole nine yards*. Whatever it may be referring to, if in fact it even has a tale worth telling, it means all or everything. The mystery number *nine* also occurs in nine times out of ten; dressed to the nines; and on cloud nine where it has drawn less attention.) □ *For you I'll go the whole nine yards.* □ *I didn't want the whole nine yards.*

a **whole nother story** Go to next.

a **whole nother thing** AND a **whole nother story; another thing; another story** *Rur.* a completely different matter. (Often "corrected" to *a whole other thing.* This is *another thing* with the word *whole* infixed between *a* and *nother*. It might better be written as *a-whole-nother*, parallel to *abso-bloody-lutely*.) □ *Ah, underlying causes! That's a whole nother thing!* □ *Yes, he did it, but how he did it is another story.*

the **whole shebang** *Inf.* everything; the whole thing. □ *Mary's all set to give a fancy dinner party. She's got a fine tablecloth, good crystal, and silverware, the whole shebang.*

the **whole shooting match** Go to the whole ball of wax.

the **whole wide world** *Fig.* everywhere; everywhere and everything. □ *I've searched the whole wide world for just the right hat.*

the **whole works** *Fig.* everything; the complete amount. □ *I cashed my paycheck and lost the whole works playing the ponies.*

whoop it up *Fig.* to celebrate, especially with cheers and whoops. □ *It was a very noisy party. Everyone was whooping it up well past midnight.*

the **whys and wherefores of** sth *Fig.* the reasons or causes relating to something. □ *I refuse to discuss the whys and wherefores of my decision. It's final.*

wide awake *Fig.* completely awake. □ *After two cups of coffee, I'm wide awake.*

***wide of the mark 1.** Fig.* far from the target; [falling] short of or to the side of the goal. (*Typically: **be** ~; **fall** ~.) □ *Tom's shot was wide of the mark.* □ *The arrow fell wide of the mark.* **2.** *Fig.* inadequate; far from what is required or expected. (*Typically: **be** ~; **fall** ~.) □ *Jane's efforts were sincere, but wide of the mark.*

wide open 1. *Fig.* as fast as possible; at full throttle. □ *I was driving along wide open when I became aware of a flashing red light.* **2.** *Fig.* [of a town or place] full of crime or corruption; vice-ridden. □ *This town is wide open! Hardly any law enforcement at all.* **3.** *Fig.* [of a choice] undecided; open to all possibilities. □ *The matter is still wide open. The board meets next week to decide.*

(wide) open to sth **1.** *Fig.* unprotected against something. □ *If you do that, you're just leaving yourself open to a lawsuit.* **2.** *Fig.* willing to consider suggestions, ideas, solutions, further discussions, etc. □ *Any other thoughts? I'm wide open to any suggestions.*

a **wide place in the road** *Inf.* a very small town. □ *The town is little more than a wide place in the road.*

wiggle out of sth *Fig.* to manage to get out of a job, the blame for something, or a responsibility. □ *He always tries to wiggle out of the difficult assignments.*

wild and wooly *Fig.* wild and exciting. (*Wooly* may allude to *hairy* = risky and dangerous.) □ *This is a great roller coaster. You are in for a wild and wooly ride.*

a **wild-goose chase** a worthless hunt or chase; a futile pursuit. □ *I wasted all afternoon on a wild-goose chase.*

will be the death of so/sth **(yet)** *Fig.* [the thing named] will be the end or ruin of someone or something. □ *This job will be the death of me!* □ *These rough roads will be the death of these tires.*

will not hear of sth AND **won't hear of** sth will refuse to tolerate or permit something. □ *You mustn't drive home alone. I will not hear of it.* □ *My parents won't hear of my staying out that late.*

Win a few, lose a few. *Fig.* Sometimes one succeeds, and sometimes one fails. □ *Tom: Well, I lost out on that Wilson contract, but I got the Jones job. Sally: That's life. Win a few, lose a few.*

win all the marbles Go to all the marbles.

win by a nose *Fig.* to win by the slightest amount of difference. □ *I ran the fastest race I could, but I only won by a nose.*

win so's **heart** AND **win the heart of** so *Fig.* to gain the affection of someone; to win the love of someone exclusively. □ *I hope to win her heart and make her my bride.*

win the day Go to carry the day.

win the heart of so Go to win so's heart.

wind so **up 1.** *Inf.* to get someone excited. □ *That kind of music really winds me up!*

2. *Inf.* to get someone set to do a lot of talking. (*Fig.* on winding up a clock.) □ *The excitement of the day wound Kelly up, and she talked almost all night.*

wind sth **up**[†] *Fig.* to conclude something. □ *Today we'll wind that deal up with the bank.*

wind up some place AND **end up** some place; **land up** some place to finish a journey at a place that one did not anticipate being at. □ *We drove around for a while trying to get to Cape Cod and wound up in Boston.*

wind up somehow AND **end up** somehow to reach the end [of some process] in a specific state that one did not anticipate being in. □ *We drove around for a long time and ended up tired and angry.*

wind up (by) doing sth AND **end up (by)** doing sth to finish a process by doing something that was not anticipated. □ *We drove around for a while completely lost and ended up asking for directions.*

a **window of opportunity** *Fig.* a brief time period in which an opportunity exists. □ *This afternoon, I had a brief window of opportunity when I could discuss this with the boss, but she wasn't receptive.*

window-shopping *Fig.* the habit or practice of looking at goods in shop windows or stores without actually buying anything. □ *Mary and Jane do a lot of window-shopping in their lunch hour, looking for things to buy when they get paid.*

wine and dine so *Fig.* to treat someone to an expensive meal of the type that includes fine wines; to entertain someone lavishly. □ *The lobbyists wined and dined the senators one by one in order to influence them.*

wing it *Inf.* to improvise; to do something extemporaneously. □ *I lost my lecture notes, so I had to wing it.*

wink at sth *Fig.* to pretend not to see something; to condone something wrong. □ *The police officer winked at my failure to make a complete stop.*

winner take all *Fig.* a situation where the one who defeats others takes all the spoils of the conflict. □ *The contest was a case of winner take all. There was no second place or runner-up.*

winter over (some place) *Fig.* to spend the winter at some place. □ *The bears all winter over in their dens.* □ *All the animals are getting ready either to migrate or to winter over.* □ *My parents winter over in Florida.*

wipe so/sth **from the face of the earth** Go to wipe so/sth off the face of the earth.

wipe sth **off (one's face)** *Fig.* to remove a smile, grin, silly look, etc. from one's face. □ *Wipe that silly grin off your face, private!* □ *Wipe that smile off!*

wipe so/sth **off the face of the earth** AND **wipe** so/sth **from the face of the earth**; **wipe** so/sth **from the map**; **wipe** so/sth **off the map** *Fig.* to demolish every trace of someone or something. □ *A great storm will come and wipe all the people off the face of the earth.*

wipe out 1. *Inf.* to crash. □ *The car wiped out on the curve.* **2.** *Inf.* to fall off or away from something, such as a bicycle, skates, a surfboard, a skateboard, etc. □ *I wiped out and skinned my knee.* **3.** *Inf.* to fail badly. □ *The test was terrible! I'm sure I wiped out.*

wipe so **out**[†] **1.** *Sl.* to kill someone. □ *Spike intended to wipe Lefty's gang out.* **2.** *Sl.* to exhaust or debilitate someone. □ *The long walk wiped me out.* **3.** *Inf.* to ruin someone financially. □ *The loss of my job wiped us out.*

wipe sth **out**[†] *Sl.* to use up all of something. □ *I wiped the cookies out—not all at once, of course.*

wipe so's **slate clean** AND **wipe the slate clean** *Fig.* to get rid of or erase someone's (bad) record. (As if erasing information recorded on a slate.) □ *I'd like to wipe my slate clean and start all over again.*

wipe the floor up[†] **with** so *Fig. Inf.* to beat or physically abuse someone. (Usually said as a threat.) □ *You say that to me one* *more time, and I'll wipe the floor up with you.*

wired into so/sth *Sl.* closely concerned with someone or something; really involved with someone or something. □ *Mary is really wired into classical music.*

wise as an owl Go to next.

*wise as Solomon AND ***wise as an owl** very wise. (*Also: **as** ~.) □ *If you are in trouble, get Chris to advise you. He's as wise as Solomon.*

*wise to so/sth *Inf.* fully aware of someone or something. (*Typically: **be** ~; **get** ~; **put** so ~.) □ *The cops are wise to the plan.*

wise so **up (about** so/sth**)** *Inf.* to instruct someone about something; to give someone important information. □ *Let me wise you up about the way we do things around here.*

wise up (to so/sth**)** Go to catch on (to so/sth).

wish list *Fig.* a list of things one wishes to have. □ *I put a new car at the top of my wish list.*

wish so **the best of luck** to wish someone good luck. □ *Good-bye, and we wish you the best of luck.*

wishful thinking *Fig.* believing that something is true or that something will happen just because one wishes that it were true or would happen. □ *Hoping for a car as a birthday present is just wishful thinking.*

with a capital letter name spelled with a capital letter for emphasis. □ *Didn't you hear me? I said no, with a capital N.*

with a heavy heart *Cliché* sadly. □ *With a heavy heart, she said good-bye.*

with a vengeance *Cliché* with determination and eagerness. □ *Bill ate all his dinner and gobbled up his dessert with a vengeance.*

with a view to doing sth AND **with an eye to** doing sth *Fig.* with the intention of doing something. □ *I came to this school with a view to getting a degree.* □ *The mayor took office with an eye to improving the town.*

with a will *Fig.* with determination and enthusiasm. □ *The workers set about manufacturing the new products with a will.*

with all due respect not meaning to be disrespectful. □ *With all due respect, your honor, I think you are making a mistake.*

with all one's **heart (and soul)** *Cliché* very sincerely. □ *Oh, Bill, I love you with all my heart and soul, and I always will!*

with all the fixin(g)s *Rur.* with all the condiments or other dishes that accompany a certain kind of food. □ *Dario likes his hamburgers with all the fixings.*

with all the trimmings *Fig.* with all the extra things, especially with food. □ *We had a lovely Thanksgiving dinner with all the trimmings.*

with bated breath *Fig.* while holding one's breath; with one's breathing suspended or abated. (Often spelled incorrectly as *baited. Bated* is from *abated* and only appears in this phrase, which appeared first in Shakespeare's *The Merchant of Venice.* It means holding one's breath.) □ *We stood there with bated breath while the man hung onto the side of the bridge.*

with bells on (one's **toes)** *Fig.* eagerly, willingly, and on time. □ *Oh, yes! I'll meet you at the restaurant. I'll be there with bells on.* □ *All the smiling children were there waiting for me with bells on their toes.*

with child pregnant. (Old-fashioned and euphemistic. Now somewhat jocular.) □ *Well, I see you are with child. Isn't this your third?*

with every (other) breath *Fig.* [saying something] repeatedly or continually. □ *Bob was out in the yard, raking leaves and cursing with every other breath.*

with everything (on it) [of a sandwich] ordered with everything available on it, such as ketchup, mustard, onions, cheese, peppers, chili, lettuce, tomato, etc., as appropriate. □ *Give me a cheeseburger with everything on it.*

with (one's) eyes (wide) open *Fig.* totally aware of what is going on. □ *We all*

with bells on (one's toes)

started with eyes open but didn't realize what could happen to us.

with flying colors *Cliché* easily and excellently. (A ship displaying flags and pennants presents itself with flying colors.) □ *John passed his geometry test with flying colors.*

with gay abandon with complete and oblivious abandon or innocent carelessness. (This has nothing to do with *gay* = homosexual.) □ *She ran through her homework with gay abandon and still got an A in every subject.*

with (great) relish *Fig.* with pleasure or enjoyment. (Often seen as a pun as if this were pickle relish.) □ *John put on his new coat with great relish.* □ *We accepted the offer to use their beach house with relish.*

(with) hat in hand *Fig.* with humility. (Fig. on the image of someone standing, respectfully, in front of a powerful person, asking for a favor.) □ *We had to go hat in hand to the committee to get a grant for our proposal.*

with impunity *Fig.* without risk of punishment; with immunity from the negative consequences of an act; while being exempt from punishment. □ *The diplomat parked in illegal parking spaces with impunity.*

with so/sth **in tow** Go to have so/sth in tow.

with it 1. *Inf.* alert and knowledgeable. □ *Jane isn't making any sense. She's not really with it tonight.* □ *Jean's mother is not really with it anymore. She's going senile.* **2.** *Inf.* up-to-date. □ *My parents are so old-fashioned. I'm sure they were never with it.*

with my blessing *Fig.* a phrase expressing consent or agreement; yes. □ *Mary: Shall I drive Uncle Tom to the airport a few hours early? Sue: Oh, yes! With my blessing!*

with one hand tied behind one's **back** AND **with both hands tied behind** one's **back; with one arm tied behind** one's **back** *Fig.* (even if) under a handicap; easily. □ *I could put an end to this argu-*

ment with one hand tied behind my back. □ *John could do this job with both hands tied behind his back.*

with regard to so/sth AND **in regard to** so/sth**; as regards** so/sth as for someone or something; about someone or something. □ *With regard to transportation, you ought to take the bus.*

with respect to so/sth Go to in respect to so/sth.

with one's **tail between** one's **legs** *Fig.* appearing frightened or cowardly. (Fig. on the image of a frightened or defeated dog going off threatened or humiliated.) □ *John seems to lack courage. When people criticize him unjustly, he just goes away with his tail between his legs and doesn't tell them that they're wrong.*

with the best of them with all the other good ones; as well as the best of them. □ *After I took diving lessons, I could go out and compete and hold my own with the best of them.*

with the best will in the world *Fig.* however much one wishes to do something or however hard one tries to do something. □ *With the best will in the world, Jack won't be able to help Mary get the job.*

with the naked eye *Fig.* with eyes that are not aided by telescopes, microscopes, or binoculars. □ *Bacteria are too small to be seen with the naked eye.*

with sth **to spare** Go to and sth to spare.

wither on the vine AND **die on the vine** *Fig.* [for someone or something] to be ignored or neglected and thereby be wasted. □ *I hope I get a part in the play. I don't want to just wither on the vine.*

within a stone's throw (of sth**)** AND **(just) a stone's throw away (from** sth**); (just) a stone's throw (from** sth**)** *Fig.* very close (to something). (Possibly as close as the distance one could throw a stone. It usually refers to a distance that is really much greater than most people could throw a stone.) □ *The police department was located within a stone's throw of our house.*

within an ace of (doing**)** sth AND **within a hair('s-breadth) of (**doing**)** sth *Fig.* very close to doing something. □ *We were within an ace of beating the all-time record.* □ *We were within a hair's-breadth of beating the all-time record.*

within an inch of one's **life** *Fig.* very close to losing one's life; almost to death. □ *When Mary was seriously ill in the hospital, she came within an inch of her life.*

within bounds Go to within limits.

within calling distance Go to within hailing distance.

***within earshot (of** sth**)** close enough to something to hear it. (*Typically: **be** ~; **come** ~; **get** ~; **move** ~.) □ *As soon as I got within earshot of the music, I decided that I really didn't belong there.*

***within** one's **grasp** AND ***within** one's **reach 1.** where one can grasp something with one's hand. (*Typically: **be** ~; **get** ~; **get** sth ~.) □ *The rope was within his grasp, but he was too weak to reach for it.* **2.** *Fig.* [for something] to be obtainable; [for a goal] to be almost won. (Fig. on ①. Does not involve grabbing or grasping with the hands. *Typically: **be** ~; **get** ~; **get** sth ~.) □ *Victory is within our grasp, so we must keep playing the game to win.* □ *Her goal is within her grasp at last.*

within hailing distance AND **within calling distance; within shouting distance** *Fig.* close enough to hear someone call out. □ *When the boat came within hailing distance, I asked if I could borrow some gasoline.*

within limits AND **within bounds** *Fig.* up to a certain point; with certain restrictions. □ *You're free to do what you want— within limits, of course.*

(with)in living memory *Fig.* in the past but within the memory of anyone still alive at this time. (Perhaps within the last 90 years.) □ *This is the worst flood in living memory.*

within one's **means** *Fig.* affordable. □ *I think that a TV set with a smaller screen would be more within our means.*

within one's **reach** Go to within one's grasp.

within reason *Fig.* reasonable; reasonably. □ *You can do anything you want within reason.* □ *I'll pay any sum you ask—within reason.*

*within one's rights *Fig.* acting legally in one's own interest. (*Typically: **be ~; act ~**.) □ *I know I am within my rights when I make this request.*

within spitting distance Go to next.

within striking distance AND **within spitting distance** *Fig. Lit.* within a fairly small distance of about an arm's length. □ *He was within striking distance, but he still could not hear me.*

without a clue (about sth**)** Go to not have a clue (about sth).

without a hitch *Inf.* with no problem(s). □ *Everything went off without a hitch.*

without a moment to spare Go to not a moment to spare.

without a shadow of a doubt AND **beyond the shadow of a doubt** *Fig.* without the smallest amount of doubt. □ *I felt the man was guilty beyond the shadow of a doubt.*

without any strings attached Go to strings attached.

without batting an eye *Fig.* without showing alarm or response; without blinking an eye. □ *Right in the middle of the speech—without batting an eye—the speaker walked off the stage.*

without fail *Fig.* for certain; absolutely. □ *The plane leaves on time every day without fail.*

without further ado without any more being said or done; without any additional introductory comments. (Sometimes in fun or ignorance *without further adieu* = without any more good-byes.) □ *Without further ado, here is the next president of the club!*

without half trying *Rur.* effortlessly. □ *He was so strong, he could bend an iron bar without half trying.*

without missing a beat *Fig.* without pausing for any potential interruption. □ *He*

kept right on giving his speech without missing a beat, despite the interruptions.

without question *Fig.* absolutely; certainly. □ *She agreed to help without question.*

without rhyme or reason Go to rhyme or reason.

without (so much as) a (for or) by your leave *Fig.* without (the least hint of) asking for permission. □ *Without so much as a for or by your leave, they just walked into our house.*

(with)stand the test of time *Fig.* to pass an imaginary "test" wherein something is of sufficient significance to remain viable throughout a long period of time. □ *I don't think this theory of yours will stand the test of time.*

*one's wits about one *Fig.* [keeping] calm making one's mind work smoothly, especially in a time of stress. (*Get* = to acquire and *have, keep* = retain. *Typically: **get ~; have ~; keep (all) ~**.) □ *Let me get my wits about me so I can figure this out.* □ *If Jane hadn't kept her wits about her during the fire, things would have been much worse.*

Woe is me! *Fig.* I am unfortunate.; I am unhappy. (Usually humorous.) □ *Woe is me! I have to work when the rest of the office staff is off.*

wolf sth **down**† *Inf.* to eat something very rapidly and in very large pieces. (As a wolf might eat.) □ *Don't wolf your food down!*

a **wolf in sheep's clothing** *Fig.* a dangerous person pretending to be harmless. □ *Carla thought the handsome stranger was gentle and kind, but Susan suspected he was a wolf in sheep's clothing.*

The **wolf is at the door.** *Fig.* The threat of poverty is upon someone. □ *I lost my job, my savings are gone, and now the wolf is at the door.*

woman to woman Go to man to man.

wonder at so/sth to be amazed at or in awe of someone or something. (Stilted.) □

The people wondered at the bright light that lit up the sky.

won't hold water *Fig.* to be inadequate, insubstantial, or ill-conceived. □ *Sorry, your ideas won't hold water. Nice try, though.*

the **woods are full of** so/sth *Fig.* there are lots and lots of people or things. □ *The woods are full of nice-looking guys who'll scam you if you aren't careful.*

wool-gathering daydreaming. (From the practice of wandering along collecting tufts of sheep's wool from hedges.) □ *I wish my new secretary would get on with the work and stop wool-gathering.*

word by word *Fig.* one word at a time. □ *We examined the contract word by word to make sure everything was the way we wanted.*

word for word *Fig.* in the exact words; verbatim. □ *I can't recall word for word what she told us.*

*word (from so/sth) *Fig.* messages or communication from someone or something. (*Typically: **get** ~; **have** ~; **hear** ~; **receive** ~.) □ *We have just received word from Perry that the contract has been signed.*

one's **word is** one's **bond** *Fig.* one's statement of agreement is as sound as a posting of a performance bond. □ *Of course, you can trust anything I agree to verbally. My word is my bond. There's no need to get it in writing.*

so's **word is final** Go to so's **word is law.**

so's **word is good** *Fig.* someone can be believed and trusted. □ *You can believe her. Her word is good.*

so's **word is law** AND so's **word is final** *Fig.* a person's word is completely authoritative. □ *You had better listen to her. Her word is law.*

so's **word of honor** *Fig.* someone's trustworthy pledge or promise. □ *He gave me his word of honor that he would bring the car back by noon today.*

a **word to the wise** *Fig.* a good piece of advice; a word of wisdom. □ *If I can give you a word to the wise, I would suggest going to the courthouse about an hour before your trial.*

*a word with so **(about** sth) *Fig.* a chance to talk to someone about something, usually briefly. (*Typically: **get** ~; **get in** ~; **have** ~.) □ *Can I have a word with you about your report?*

one's **words stick in** one's **throat** *Fig.* one is so overcome by emotion that one can hardly speak. □ *I was so irritated that my words stuck in my throat.*

words to live by AND **thoughts to live by** *Fig.* useful philosophical or spiritual expressions. □ *Thank you for your expression of gratitude. You gave us words to live by.*

work one's **ass off** Go to work one's **tail off.**

work one's **buns off** Go to work one's **tail off.**

work one's **butt off** Go to work one's **tail off.**

work some **fat off**† AND **work** some **weight off**† to get rid of body fat by doing strenuous work. □ *I was able to work a lot of weight off by jogging.*

work one's **fingers to the bone** *Cliché* to work very hard. □ *I worked my fingers to the bone so you children could have everything you needed. Now look at the way you treat me!*

work hand in glove (with so) Go to hand in glove (with so).

work so/sth **into** sth AND **work** so/sth **in**† *Fig.* to fit someone or something into a sequence or series. □ *I don't have an appointment open this afternoon, but I'll see if I can work you into the sequence.*

one's **work is cut out for** one *Fig.* one's task is prepared for one; one has a lot of work to do. □ *This is a big job. My work is cut out for me.* □ *The new president's work is cut out for him.*

work its magic on so/sth *Fig.* [for something] to charm, influence, or transform someone or something, usually in some trivial way. □ *You will be pleased at how Jimson's Wax works its magic on your floors and woodwork.* □ *The beautician* *worked her magic on Mrs. Uppington, and she looked two years younger.*

work itself out [for a problem] to solve itself. □ *Eventually, all the problems worked themselves out without any help from us.*

work like a beaver AND **work like a mule; work like a horse; work like a slave** *Fig.* to work very hard. □ *She has an important deadline coming up, so she's been working like a beaver.* □ *You need a vacation. You work like a slave in that kitchen.* □ *I'm too old to work like a horse. I'd prefer to relax more.*

work like a charm to succeed very easily. (Refers to a magic charm or spell.) □ *Try this specially designed potato peeler. It works like a charm.*

work like a horse Go to work like a beaver.

work like a mule Go to work like a beaver.

work like a slave Go to work like a beaver.

work of art 1. *Fig.* a piece of artwork, such as a painting or statue. □ *She purchased a lovely work of art for her living room.* **2.** *Fig.* a good result of one's efforts. □ *Your report was a real work of art. Very well done.*

work sth off† **1.** *Fig.* to get rid of anger, anxiety, or energy by doing physical activity. □ *I was so mad! I went out and played basketball to work my anger off.* **2.** *Fig.* to pay off a debt through work rather than by money. □ *I had no money so I had to work the bill off by washing dishes.*

work on so **1.** [for a physician] to treat someone; [for a surgeon] to operate on someone. □ *The doctor is still working on your uncle. There is no news yet.* **2.** *Fig.* [for someone] to try to convince someone of something. □ *I'll work on her, and I am sure she will agree.*

work out 1. AND **pan out** *Fig.* [for something] to turn out all right in the end. □ *Don't worry. Everything will work out.* **2.** *Fig.* [for someone] to do a program of exercise. □ *I work out at least twice a week.*

work out for the best *Fig.* [for a bad situation] to turn out all right in the end. □ *Don't worry. Everything will work out for the best.*

work so **over**† **1.** *Inf.* to threaten, intimidate, or beat someone. □ *Walt threatened to work Sam over.* **2.** *Fig.* to give someone's body a thorough examination or treatment. (Fig. on ①.) □ *The doctors worked her over to the tune of $1,500 but couldn't find anything wrong with her.*

work one's **tail off** AND **work** one's **buns off; work** one's **ass off; work** one's **butt off** *Inf.* to work very hard. (Caution with ass.) □ *I worked my tail off to get done on time.* □ *You spend half your life working your butt off—and for what?*

work through channels AND **go through (the proper) channels** *Fig.* to try to get something done by going through the proper procedures and persons. □ *I tried going through channels, but it takes too long. This is an emergency.*

work oneself **up** *Fig.* to allow oneself to become emotionally upset. □ *Todd worked himself up, and I thought he would scream.*

work up a sweat Go to work oneself (up) into a lather.

work up a thirst Go to get up a thirst.

work oneself **(up) into a lather** AND **work** oneself **(up) into a sweat 1.** AND **work up a sweat** *Fig.* to work very hard and sweat very much. (In the way that a horse works up a lather of sweat.) □ *Don't work yourself up into a lather. We don't need to finish this today.* **2.** *Fig.* to get excited or angry. (An elaboration of work oneself up (to sth).) □ *He had worked himself into such a sweat, I was afraid he would have a stroke.*

work oneself **(up) into a sweat** Go to previous.

work oneself **up (to sth) 1.** *Fig.* to prepare oneself with sufficient energy or courage to do something. □ *I can't just walk in there and ask for a raise. I have to work myself up to it.* **2.** AND **work** one's **way up (to sth)** *Fig.* to progress in one's work to a particular rank or status. □ *I worked myself up to sergeant in no time at all.*

work up to sth **1.** *Fig.* [for something] to build or progress to something. (Usually concerning the weather.) □ *The sky is working up to some kind of storm.* **2.** *Fig.* [for someone] to lead up to something. □ *You are working up to telling me something unpleasant, aren't you?*

work (one's **way) into** sth *Fig.* to get more deeply involved in something gradually. □ *I don't quite understand my job. I'll work my way into it gradually.*

work (one's **way) through** sth **1.** to work to earn money to pay the bills while one is in college, medical school, law school, etc. □ *I worked my way through college as a waiter.* **2.** *Fig.* to progress through something complicated. □ *I spent hours working my way through the tax forms.* **3.** *Fig.* to struggle through an emotional trauma. (Fig. on ②.) □ *When she had finally worked through her grief, she was able to function normally again.*

work some **weight off**† Go to **work** some **fat off**†.

work wonders (with so/sth**)** *Fig.* to be surprisingly beneficial to someone or something; to be very helpful with someone or something. □ *This new medicine works wonders with my headaches.*

*worked up (over sth**)** AND ***worked up (about** sth**)** *Fig.* excited and agitated about something. (*Typically: **be** ~; **get** ~; **get** oneself ~.) □ *Don't get so worked up about something that you can't do anything about.*

working at cross purposes AND **operating at cross purposes** doing things that oppose or counteract each other. □ *Tom, we are working at cross purposes. Why don't we cooperate?*

a **working stiff** *Fig.* someone who works, especially in a nonmanagement position. (Originally and typically referring to males.) □ *But does the working stiff really care about all this economic stuff?*

*the works *Fig.* a lot of something; everything possible. (*The works* can be a lot of food, good treatment, bad treatment, etc. *Typically: **get** ~; **have** ~; **give** so ~.) □ *Bill: Shall we order a snack or a big meal? Jane: I'm hungry. Let's get the works.*

works both ways Go to cut both ways.

Works for me. Go to (It) works for me.

The **world is** one's **oyster.** *Fig.* One rules the world.; One is in charge of everything. □ *The world is my oyster! I'm in love!*

*worlds apart *Fig.* greatly separated by differing attitudes, needs, opinions, or temperaments. (*Typically: **be** ~; **grow** ~; **live** ~; **think** ~.) □ *They are worlds apart. I can't imagine how they ever decided to get married.*

worm sth **out of** so to draw or manipulate information out of someone. □ *I managed to worm the name of the doctor out of her before she ran off.*

the **worm turns** *Fig.* someone who is lowly or meek attempts self-defense or assertiveness. (Probably from Shakespeare, *King Henry IV*, Part 3, Act 2, Scene 2: "The smallest worm will turn being trodden on, . . ." Also used punningly to mean that a wretched person or "worm" changes and becomes less of a worm.) □ *So, the worm turns! Now you're acting like a man.*

worm (one's **way) in(to** sth**)** *Fig.* to manipulate one's way into participation in something. □ *You can't have a part, so don't try to worm in.*

worm (one's **way) out (of** sth**)** *Fig.* to manipulate oneself out of a job or responsibility. □ *Don't try to worm yourself out of this affair. It is your fault!*

worried sick (about so/sth**)** *Fig.* very worried or anxious about someone or something. □ *Oh, thank heavens you are all right. We were worried sick about you!*

worry through sth to think and fret through a problem. □ *I can't talk to you now. I have to worry through this tax problem.* □ *We worried through the financial problem over a three-day period.*

the **worse for wear 1.** damaged or worn through use. □ *The truth is it's the worse for wear; you will just have to get a new one.* **2.** *Fig.* injured. □ *Tom fell into the street and he's much the worse for wear.*

*the **worse of both worlds** AND *the **worst of all worlds** *Fig.* the worst possible choice of those available. (*Typically: **suffer** ~; **have** ~; **live in** ~.) □ *I live by the train tracks, work at the end of a runway, and drive back and forth on a broken-up road. I suffer the worst of all worlds.*

worship the ground so **walks on** *Fig.* to honor someone to a great extent. □ *She always admired the professor. In fact, she worshiped the ground he walked on.*

*the **worst of** sth the smallest share of something; the worst part of something. (*Typically: **get** ~; **have** ~; **give** so ~.) □ *I knew I would get the worst of the deal because I was absent when the goods were divided up.*

the **worst-case scenario** *Cliché* the worst possible future outcome. □ *Now, let's look at the worst-case scenario.*

worth its weight in gold AND **worth** one's **weight in gold** *Fig.* to be valuable and worth the equivalent weight in gold; to be as valuable as gold. (Also for abstract things.) □ *Your ideas are always worth their weight in gold.* □ *Oh, Bill. You're wonderful. You're worth your weight in gold.*

worth one's **salt** *Fig.* worth (in productivity) what it costs to keep or support one. □ *We decided that you are worth your salt, and you can stay on as office clerk.*

worth so's **while** *Fig.* worth one's time and trouble. □ *The job pays so badly it's not worth your while even going for an interview.*

worthy of the name *Fig.* deserving to be so called; good enough to enjoy a specific designation. □ *Any art critic worthy of the name would know that painting to be a fake.*

One **would forget** one's **head if it wasn't screwed on.** *Fig.* That person is very absent-minded and forgetful. (*Wasn't* is sometimes *weren't*.) □ *She doesn't remember things. She'd forget her head if it wasn't screwed on.*

would give anything for sth to be willing to exchange anything to get something or to cause something to happen. (Usually an exaggeration.) □ *I would give anything for a cold beer about now.*

would (just) as soon do sth Go to had (just) as soon do sth.

would not be caught dead (doing sth) Go to next.

would not be seen dead (doing sth) AND **would not be caught dead** (doing sth) *Inf.* would not do something under any circumstances. □ *Martha would not be caught dead going into a place like that.*

wouldn't dream of doing sth *Fig.* would not even consider doing something. □ *I wouldn't dream of taking your money!*

wouldn't touch so/sth **with a ten-foot pole** *Cliché* would not be involved with something under any circumstances. □ *I know about the piece of vacant land for sale on Maple Street. I wouldn't touch it with a ten-foot pole, because there used to be a gas station there and the soil is polluted.*

wouldn't want to be in so's **shoes** *Fig.* would not trade places with someone who is in a bad situation. □ *Now Jim has to explain to his wife how he wrecked their car. I wouldn't want to be in his shoes.*

wrack and ruin *Cliché* complete destruction or ruin. □ *They went back after the fire and saw the wrack and ruin that used to be their house.*

wrap one's **car around** sth *Inf.* to drive one's car into something at fairly high speed. □ *If he hadn't wrapped his car around a tree, he'd be here with us tonight.*

wrap sth **up**† to complete work on something; to bring something to an end. □ *I will wrap the job up this morning. I'll call you when I finish.*

***wrapped up** Go to sewed up.

*wrapped up (with so/sth**)** *Fig.* involved with someone or something. (*Typically: **be** ~**; get** ~.) □ *She is all wrapped up with her husband and his problems.*

wreak havoc with so/sth Go to raise havoc with so/sth.

wreak vengeance (up)on so/sth *Cliché* to seek and get revenge on someone by harming someone or something. □ *The general wanted to wreak vengeance on the opposing army for their recent successful attack.*

wrestle with sth *Fig.* to struggle with a difficult problem; to struggle with a moral decision. □ *We wrestled with the problem and finally decided to go ahead.*

wriggle out (of sth**)** *Fig.* to get out of having to do something; to evade a responsibility. □ *Don't try to wriggle out of this.*

wring one's **hands 1.** to nervously rub one's hands as if one were washing them. □ *He was so upset that he was actually wringing his hands.* **2.** *Fig.* to do something ineffective while one is very upset. (Fig. on ①.) □ *Don't just stand there weeping and wringing your hands! Call the police!*

writ large *Fig.* magnified; done on a larger scale; made more prominent. (Formal or learned.) □ *As the child grew bigger, his behavior grew worse, and too soon the man was but the flawed boy writ large.*

write sth **off**† **(on** one's **taxes)** to deduct something from one's income taxes. □ *Can I write this off on my income taxes?*

writer's block *Fig.* the temporary inability for a writer to think of what to write. □ *I have writer's block at the moment and can't seem to get a sensible sentence on paper.*

writhe under sth *Fig.* to suffer under a mental burden. □ *I writhed under her constant verbal assault and finally left the room.*

written in stone Go to carved in stone.

*the wrong number 1. an incorrect telephone number. (*Typically: **get** ~**; have** ~**; dial** ~**; give** so ~.) □ *When a young child answered, I knew I had the wrong number.* **2.** *Fig.* [a state of being] incorrect, late, inaccurate, etc. (*Typically: **get** ~**; have** ~**; give** so ~.) □ *Boy, do you have the wrong number! Get with it!*

the **wrong side of the tracks** Go to the other side of the tracks.

wrote the book on sth *Fig.* to be very authoritative about something; to know enough about something to write the definitive book on it. (Always in past tense.) □ *Ted wrote the book on unemployment. He's been looking for work in three states for two years.* □ *Do I know about misery? I wrote the book on misery!*

*wrought up *Fig.* disturbed or excited. (*Wrought* is an old past tense and past participle meaning "worker." *Typically: **be** ~**; get** ~.) □ *She is so wrought up, she can't think.*

X, Y, Z

X marks the spot *Fig.* this is the exact spot. (Sometimes the speaker will draw an X in the spot while saying this.) □ *This is where the rock struck my car—X marks the spot.*

yack one's **head off** Go to talk one's head off.

Ye gods (and little fishes)! *Inf.* What a surprising thing! □ *Ye gods and little fishes! Someone covered my car with broken eggs!*

year in, year out *Fig.* year after year; for years. □ *I seem to have hay fever year in, year out. I never get over it.* □ *John wears the same old suit, year in, year out.*

year round Go to (all) year round.

years running Go to days running.

yell bloody murder Go to cry bloody murder.

yell (sth) from the rooftops Go to shout (sth) from the rooftops.

yell one's **guts out** Go to next.

yell one's **head off** AND **yell** one's **guts out 1.** *Inf.* to yell loud and long. □ *I was yelling my head off at the football game.* □ *Stop yelling your guts out and listen to me.* **2.** *Inf.* to complain bitterly and loudly. □ *Some lady is yelling her head off about shoddy workmanship out in the lobby.*

a **yellow streak (down** so's **back)** *Inf.* a tendency toward cowardice. □ *Tim's got a yellow streak down his back a mile wide.*

yield the right-of-way Go to the right-of-way.

a **yoke around** so's **neck** *Fig.* something that oppresses people; a burden. □ *John's greedy children are a yoke around his neck.*

you ain't (just) whistlin' Dixie *Rur.* you are right. □ *Tom: Sure is hot today. Bill: Yeah, you ain't just whistlin' Dixie. It's a scorcher.*

You (always) think you have all the answers! AND **You (always) think you know all the answers!; You think you're so smart!** You are annoying because you act like you know everything! □ *Don't you tell me how to lead my life! You always think you have all the answers!*

You and what army? Go to next.

You and who else? AND **You and what army?** *Inf.* a phrase that responds to a threat by implying that the threat is a weak one. □ *Bill: I'm going to punch you in the nose! Bob: Yeah? You and who else?*

You are only young once. You might as well do a thing, since you may never have the chance again. (Typically said to a younger person and jocular when said to an older person.) □ *Of course, you should go backpacking to Europe. You're only young once.*

You are what you eat. You are made up of the nutritional content of the food you eat. □ *You shouldn't eat pizza and hamburgers every day. After all, you are what you eat!*

You asked for it! 1. *Fig.* You are getting what you requested. □ *The waiter set a huge bowl of ice cream, strawberries, and whipped cream in front of Mary, saying apologetically, "You asked for it!"* **2.** *Inf.* You are getting the punishment you deserve! □ *Bill: The tax people just ordered me to pay a big fine. Bob: The careless way you do your tax forms caused it. You asked for it!*

You been keeping busy? Go to (Have you) been keeping busy?

You been keeping cool? Go to (Have you) been keeping cool?

You been keeping out of trouble? Go to (Have you) been keeping out of trouble?

You bet your boots! Go to next.

You bet your (sweet) life! AND **You bet your boots!; You bet your life!; You bet!; You bet your (sweet) bippy.** *Inf.* You can be absolutely certain of something! (*Bippy* dates to the mid-1960s in the TV program "Laugh In." No one ever knew what a bippy was.) □ *Mary: Will I need a coat today? Bill: You bet your sweet life! It's colder than an iceberg out there.* □ *Bill: Will you be at the game Saturday? Tom: You bet your boots!*

You can (just) think again. Go to You've got another think coming.

You can't fight city hall. Go to fight city hall.

(You) can't get there from here. *Inf.* a catchphrase said jokingly when someone asks directions to get to a place that can be reached only by a circuitous route. □ *"Galesburg? Galesburg, you say?" said the farmer. "By golly, you can't get there from here!"*

(You) can't win them all. AND **(You) can't win 'em all.** *Inf.* a catchphrase said when someone, including the speaker, has lost in a contest or failed at something. (The *you* is impersonal, meaning *one, anyone.* The apostrophe on *'em* is not always used.) □ *"Can't win 'em all," muttered Alice as she left the boss's office with nothing accomplished.*

You could have knocked me over with a feather. *Inf.* I was extremely surprised.; I was so surprised that it was as if I was disoriented and could have been knocked over easily. □ *When she told me she was going to get married, you could have knocked me over with a feather.*

You doing okay? Go to (Are you) doing okay?

You go to your church, and I'll go to mine. You do it your way, and I'll do it mine. □ *Yes, you are faster, but I am more exact. You go to your church, and I'll go to mine.*

You got it! 1. *Inf.* I agree to what you asked!; You will get what you want! □ *You want a green one? You got it!* **2.** *Inf.* You are right! □ *That's exactly right! You got it!*

You got me beat. Go to (It) beats me.

You have me at a disadvantage. *Fig.* I am sorry, but you know my name and I do not know yours, leaving me at a disadvantage as far as social protocol is concerned.; We haven't been formally introduced. (More U.K. than U.S.) □ *A: Good evening, Sir John. I hope you are comfortable here. B: I'm sorry, but you have me at a disadvantage, Sir. Have we met?*

you name it you just name anything that you want. □ *A: I have to ask you a favor. B: Sure. You name it.*

(You) want a piece of me? *Sl.* Do you want to fight with me? □ *Come on, Wussy. You want a piece of me?*

You want to make something of it? Go to (Do you) want to make something of it?

You'll get the hang of it. *Fig.* Don't worry. You will learn soon how it is done. □ *Mary: It's harder than I thought to glue these things together. Tom: You'll get the hang of it.*

*young at heart *Fig.* having a youthful spirit no matter what one's age. (*Typically: **act** ~; **be** ~; **keep** so ~; **stay** ~.) □ *I am over 70, but I still feel young at heart.*

Your guess is as good as mine. AND **Anybody's guess is as good as mine.** You or anybody is as likely to know the answer as I am. □ *Q: What time will we arrive? A: Your guess is as good as mine.*

You're on! *Fig. Inf.* The bet, challenge, or invitation is accepted! □ *Q: What about a few beers at the club? A: You're on!*

You're the doctor. *Inf.* You are in a position to tell me what to do.; I yield to you and your knowledge of this matter. (Usually jocular; the person being addressed is most likely not a physician.) □ *Bill: Eat your dinner, then you'll feel more like playing ball. Get some energy! Tom: Okay, you're the doctor.*

You've got another think coming. AND **You can (just) think again.** *Inf.* You will have to rethink your position. (Both of the entry heads are usually found with a conditional phrase, such as "If you think so-and-so, then you've got another think coming." The first entry head is also heard as *thing* rather than *think*.) □ *Rachel: If you think I'm going to stand here and listen to your complaining all day, you've got another think coming!*

You've got me stumped. *Inf.* I can't possibly figure out the answer to your question. □ *Bill: How long is the Amazon River? Jane: You've got me stumped.* □

Bob: Do you know of a book that would interest a retired sea captain? Sally: You've got me stumped.

zero in (on so/sth**)** *Fig.* to aim directly at someone or something. □ *The television camera zeroed in on the little boy scratching his head.* □ *Mary is very good about zeroing in on the most important and helpful ideas.*

zero tolerance *Fig.* absolutely no toleration of even the smallest infraction of a rule. □ *Because of the zero-tolerance rule, the kindergartner was expelled from school because his mother accidentally left a table knife in his lunch box.*

Zip (up) your lip! AND **Zip it up!** *Inf.* Be quiet!; Close your mouth and be quiet! □ *"I've heard enough. Zip your lip!" hollered the coach.* □ *Andy: All right, you guys. Shut up! Zip it up! Bob: Sorry. Andy: That's better.*

Key Word Index

When seeking a particular expression, always look it up first in the body of the dictionary. Consult this index for key words that are not the first word in an entry but are contained within the entry and are therefore not available through a normal alphabetical search. This allows you to find a phrasal entry by looking up any noninitial key word in the phrase. Index entries containing a key word will include all instances of that key word, even if it is the first word in an entry. Words in **boldface type** are Index entries, and words in sans serif type are entries in the body of the dictionary. Always consult the dictionary first, and then this index.

A

aback taken aback

abandon abandon ship ♦ abandon oneself to sth ♦ with gay abandon

ABC the ABCs of sth ♦ know one's ABCs

abed sick abed

abet aid and abet so

abeyance hold sth in abeyance ♦ in abeyance

abide abide by sth ♦ abide with so

ability to the best of one's ability

aboard get aboard sth

abode take up one's abode some place

aboveboard aboveboard ♦ honest and aboveboard ♦ open and aboveboard

abreast keep abreast of sth ♦ stay abreast of sth

absence be conspicuous by one's absence ♦ conspicuous by one's absence ♦ a leave of absence

absent an absent-minded professor

acceptable acceptable damage ♦ acceptable losses

accident have an accident

accidentally accidentally-on-purpose

accord of one's own accord

account balance the accounts ♦ a blow-by-blow account ♦ bring so to account ♦ call so to account ♦ cook the accounts ♦ give a good account of oneself ♦ give an account of so/sth (to so) ♦ not on any account ♦ on so's account ♦ on account of so/sth ♦ on any account ♦ on no account ♦ square accounts (with so) ♦ take account of sth ♦ take so/sth into account ♦ take sth into account ♦ turn sth to good account

accountable hold so accountable (for sth)

ace ace in the hole ♦ ace in(to sth) ♦ ace so out ♦ ace out ♦ ace out (of sth) ♦ black as the ace of spades ♦ come within an ace of sth ♦ have an ace up one's sleeve ♦ hold all the aces ♦ within an ace of (doing) sth

ache ache for so/sth ♦ aching heart ♦ a splitting headache

Achilles' Achilles' heel

acid the acid test

acquire acquire a taste for sth

act an act of faith ♦ an act of God ♦ an act of war ♦ act out ♦ Act your age! ♦ caught in the act ♦ clean one's act up ♦ get one's act together ♦ get in(to) the act ♦ go into one's act ♦ a hard act to follow ♦ in on the act ♦ in the act (of doing sth) ♦ it would take an act of Congress to do sth ♦ keep an act up ♦ keep up an act ♦ put on an act ♦ read so the riot act ♦ a tough act to follow

action all talk (and no action) ♦ a bit of the action ♦ course of action ♦ galvanize so into action ♦ in action ♦ out of action ♦ a piece (of the action) ♦ plan of action ♦ a slice of the action ♦ spring into action ♦ suit one's actions to one's words ♦ take action (against so/sth) ♦ where the action is

active on active duty

activity a hive of activity ♦ hum with activity

actual grounded in (actual) fact

Adam not know so from Adam

add add fuel to the fire ♦ add fuel to the flame ♦ add insult to injury ♦ add sth up ♦ add up (to sth) ♦ add up to the same thing

adieu bid adieu to so/sth

ado much ado about nothing ♦ without further ado

advance advanced in years ♦ in advance ♦ make advances to so ♦ pay in advance

advantage the advantage of so ♦ get the advantage of so ♦ have the advantage of so ♦ show sth to good advantage ♦ take advantage of so ♦ take advantage of so/sth ♦ to advantage ♦ turn sth to one's advantage

advice sage advice

advisement take sth under advisement

advocate play (the) devil's advocate

aegis under the aegis of so

affair a fine state of affairs ♦ have an affair (with so) ♦ a pretty state of affairs ♦ a sad state of affairs ♦ settle so's affairs ♦ a sorry state of affairs

affirmative in the affirmative

afoul run afoul of so/sth

afraid afraid of one's own shadow

aft fore and aft

again oneself again ♦ able to breathe (easily) again ♦ able to breathe (freely) again ♦ again and again ♦ Again(, please). ♦ all over again ♦ at it again ♦ back at it (again) ♦ back in the saddle (again) ♦ Call again. ♦ Come again. ♦ come around (again) ♦ (every) now and again ♦ feel like oneself again ♦ Here we go again. ♦

How's that (again)? ♦ off again, on again ♦ on again, off again ♦ once again ♦ over and over (again) ♦ roll around (again) ♦ run sth by (so) (again) ♦ Run that by (me) again. ♦ Till we meet again. ♦ try so back (again) ♦ Until we meet again. ♦ You can (just) think again.

age Act your age! ♦ Age before beauty. ♦ age out (of sth) ♦ come of age ♦ feel one's age ♦ go on for an age ♦ in a coon's age ♦ in this day and age ♦ live to the (ripe old) age of sth ♦ look one's age ♦ of age ♦ a ripe old age ♦ tender age ♦ the tender age of a number of years

agenda a hidden agenda

agog all agog

agree agree to disagree

agreement sweetheart agreement

aground run aground (on sth)

ahead ahead of schedule ♦ ahead of the game ♦ ahead of the pack ♦ ahead of time ♦ ahead of one's time ♦ dead ahead ♦ full steam ahead ♦ get ahead (in sth) ♦ get ahead of the game ♦ the go-ahead ♦ (Go ahead,) make my day! ♦ keep ahead of the game ♦ keep one jump ahead (of so/sth) ♦ keep one step ahead of so/sth ♦ lean times (ahead) ♦ leave ahead of time ♦ look ahead ♦ one jump ahead (of so/sth) ♦ one move ahead (of so/sth) ♦ one step ahead of so/sth ♦ press ahead ♦ put so/sth ahead (of so/sth) ♦ quit while one is ahead ♦ show up ahead of time ♦ stay ahead of the game ♦ think ahead of one's time ♦ two jumps ahead of so

ahold catch (a)hold of so/sth ♦ get (a)hold of so

aid aid and abet so ♦ be in aid of

ails good for what ails you

aim aim for the sky ♦ aim to do sth ♦ take aim at so/sth

air the air ♦ air one's belly ♦ air one's dirty linen in public ♦ air one's grievances ♦ air one's pores ♦ a breath of fresh air ♦ build castles in the air ♦ clear the air ♦ come up for air ♦ dance on air ♦ disappear into thin air ♦ float on air ♦ free as (the) air ♦ full of hot air ♦ give oneself airs ♦ give so the air ♦ gulp for air ♦ have one's nose in the air ♦ in the air ♦ leave so up in the air ♦

leave sth up in the air ♦ light as air ♦ a
(little) nip in the air ♦ one's nose is in the
air ♦ off the air ♦ on the air ♦ out of thin
air ♦ pull sth out of thin air ♦ put on airs ♦
stick one's nose up in the air ♦ up in the
air (about so/sth) ♦ vanish into thin air ♦
walk on air

aisle have them rolling in the aisles ♦
rolling in the aisles

alcohol have an alcohol problem ♦ under
the influence (of alcohol)

alert on the alert (for so/sth)

alike alike as (two) peas in a pod ♦ share
and share alike

alive alive and kicking ♦ alive and well ♦
alive with people/things ♦ eat so alive ♦
Land(s) sakes (alive)! ♦ Look alive! ♦ more
dead than alive ♦ Sakes alive! ♦ skin so
alive

all the be all (and) (the) end all

alley right down so's alley ♦ right up so's
alley ♦ up a blind alley

alligator See you later, alligator.

allow allow for sth ♦ Allow me.

allowance make allowance(s) (for so/sth)

almighty the almighty dollar

almost (almost) jump out of one's skin ♦
almost lost it

alone go it alone ♦ leave so/sth/animal alone
♦ Leave me alone! ♦ leave well enough
alone ♦ let so/sth/animal alone ♦ let alone do
sth ♦ let alone so/sth ♦ let well enough
alone

along all along ♦ along in years ♦ along the
line(s) of sth ♦ along those lines ♦ barrel
along ♦ breeze along ♦ buzz along ♦ get
along ♦ get along on sth ♦ get along (on a
shoestring) ♦ get along (with so) ♦ get
along without (so/sth) ♦ go along with
so/sth ♦ go along (with so) for the ride ♦
moving right along ♦ pass sth along (to so)
♦ pick one's way along (sth) ♦ play along
(with so/sth) ♦ roll along ♦ run along ♦
saunter along ♦ scrape along (on sth) ♦
somewhere along the line ♦ string so
along ♦ string along (with so)

alongside lay alongside sth

alpha alpha and omega

alphabet alphabet soup

already All right(y) already!

also also-ran

altar sacrifice so/sth on the altar of sth

altogether in the altogether

always (always) chasing rainbows ♦ The
latch string is always out. ♦ You (always)
think you have all the answers!

ambulance ambulance chaser

amendment take the Fifth (Amendment)

amends make amends (to so) (for sth)

American American as apple pie ♦ the
American dream

amiss take sth amiss

amount amount to sth ♦ amount to much
♦ amount to the same thing ♦ not amount
to a hill of beans

amuck run amuck

analysis in the final analysis ♦ in the last
analysis

anchor lie at anchor

ancient ancient history

anger bristle with anger

angle angle for sth ♦ know all the angles

angry angry enough to chew nails ♦ wax
angry

ankle by ankle express ♦ sprain one's ankle

annals go down in the annals of history

anon ever and anon

another another country heard from ♦
another pair of eyes ♦ at one time or
another ♦ at some time or another ♦ one
can (just) get oneself another boy ♦ dance
to another tune ♦ go at one another tooth
and nail ♦ a horse of another color ♦ It's
six of one, half a dozen of another. ♦
keep sth for another occasion ♦ leave sth
for another occasion ♦ not give it
a(nother) thought ♦ one thing after
another ♦ One thing leads to another. ♦
one way or another ♦ put another way ♦
sing another tune ♦ Tell me another
(one)! ♦ to put it another way ♦ a whole
nother story ♦ a whole nother thing ♦
You've got another think coming.

answer answer back (to so) ♦ answer for
so ♦ answer for so/sth ♦ answer so's purpose
♦ answer the call ♦ answer the door ♦ so's
answer to so/sth ♦ answer to so ♦ the
answer to so's prayer(s) ♦ answer to the
description of so ♦ answer to the name
(of) sth ♦ have all the answers ♦ know all

the answers ♦ not take no for an answer
♦ a pat answer ♦ You (always) think you
have all the answers!

ant ants in one's pants ♦ get ants in one's
pants

ante raise the ante ♦ up the ante

anybody Anybody's guess is as good as
mine. ♦ It's anybody's guess.

anymore not a kid anymore

anyone Anyone I know? ♦ Don't breathe a
word of this to anyone.

anything anything but ♦ Anything you say.
♦ can't do anything with so/sth ♦ Don't do
anything I wouldn't do. ♦ not for anything
in the world ♦ not have anything to do
with so/sth ♦ not stop at anything (to do
sth) ♦ would give anything for sth

anytime Anytime you are ready. ♦ Come
back anytime.

apart come apart (at the seams) ♦ fall
apart (at the seams) ♦ grow apart (from
so/sth) ♦ hack so/sth apart ♦ pick so/sth apart
♦ poles apart ♦ stand apart (from so/sth) ♦
take so apart ♦ take sth apart ♦ tear so
apart ♦ tear some place apart ♦ tear sth apart
♦ worlds apart

ape go ape (over so/sth)

apology make no apologies

apparel intimate apparel

appear appear as sth ♦ appear in court ♦
appear under the name of some name ♦
speak of the devil (and he appears)

appearance by all appearances ♦ keep up
appearances ♦ put in an appearance
(at sth)

appetite get up an appetite ♦ have an
appetite for sth ♦ lose one's appetite ♦ whet
so's appetite

apple American as apple pie ♦ the apple of
so's eye ♦ apple-polisher ♦ the Big Apple ♦
compare apples and oranges ♦ easy as
(apple) pie ♦ How 'bout them apples? ♦
How do you like them apples? ♦ in apple-
pie order ♦ motherhood and apple pie ♦ a
rotten apple ♦ sure as God made little
green apples ♦ upset the apple cart

apply apply within

appoint at the appointed time

approval on approval

apron tied to one's mother's apron strings

area a gray area

argue arguing for the sake of arguing

arm an arm and a leg ♦ arm in arm ♦
armed and dangerous ♦ armed to the
teeth ♦ a babe in arms ♦ bear arms ♦ busy
as a one-armed paperhanger ♦ cost an
arm and a leg ♦ give one's right arm (for
so/sth) ♦ have a good arm ♦ hold so/sth at
arm's length ♦ keep so/sth at arm's length ♦
keep at arm's length from so/sth ♦ lay
down one's arms ♦ the long arm of the law
♦ put the arm on so ♦ receive so with
open arms ♦ regarded as armed and
dangerous ♦ a shot in the arm ♦ strong-
arm tactics ♦ take up arms (against so/sth)
♦ twist so's arm ♦ up in arms ♦ walk arm
in arm ♦ welcome so with open arms

armor a chink in one's armor ♦ a knight in
shining armor

army You and what army?

arrangement make the arrangements

arrears in arrears

arrest under arrest

arrival dead on arrival

arrive arrive at a decision ♦ arrive on the
scene ♦ have arrived

arrow straight as an arrow ♦ swift as an
arrow

art make sth into a fine art ♦ state of the
art ♦ turn sth into a fine art ♦ work of art

article article of faith ♦ the genuine article

artist flimflam artist ♦ (rip-)off artist ♦
take-off artist

ash rise from the ashes

aside (all) joking aside ♦ (all) kidding
aside ♦ as an aside ♦ aside from sth ♦
brush so/sth aside ♦ joking aside ♦ kick
so/sth aside ♦ kidding aside ♦ leave sth
aside ♦ put sth aside ♦ put sth aside for a
rainy day ♦ set sth aside ♦ set (enough)
time aside (for so/sth) ♦ stand aside ♦ step
aside (for so) ♦ take so aside

ask (Are you) sorry you asked? ♦ ask after
so ♦ ask so back ♦ ask so (for) a favor ♦ ask
for it ♦ ask for the moon ♦ ask for trouble
♦ ask for sth bad ♦ Ask no questions and
hear no lies. ♦ ask so out (to sth) ♦ ask so
over ♦ asking price ♦ Couldn't ask for
more. ♦ Don't ask. ♦ Don't ask me. ♦ one's
for the asking ♦ for the asking ♦ (free) for

the asking ♦ no questions asked ♦ Sorry you asked? ♦ You asked for it!

askance look askance at so/sth

asleep asleep at the switch ♦ asleep at the wheel ♦ fall asleep at the switch ♦ sound asleep

aspersions cast aspersions on so

ass bust ass out of some place ♦ bust (one's) ass (to do sth) ♦ cold as a well digger's ass (in January) ♦ cover one's ass ♦ don't know one's ass from a hole in the ground ♦ don't know one's ass from one's elbow ♦ flat on one's ass ♦ get one's ass in gear ♦ get off one's ass ♦ Get your ass over here! ♦ have (got) one's ass in a sling ♦ In a pig's ass! ♦ It will be your ass! ♦ kick ass ♦ kick some ass (around) ♦ kiss so's ass ♦ make an ass of so ♦ a pain in the ass ♦ put one's ass on the line ♦ save one's ass ♦ sit on one's ass ♦ smart ass ♦ tits and ass ♦ work one's ass off

assassination character assassination

assault assault and battery ♦ assault the ear

assure rest assured

astray go astray ♦ lead so astray

ate The dog ate my homework.

attach attach importance to sth ♦ strings attached ♦ without any strings attached

attack an attack (of an illness) ♦ on the attack ♦ suffer an attack (of an illness) ♦ under attack

attain attain one's stride

attendance take attendance

attention bring so/sth to so's attention ♦ call so's attention to sth ♦ call attention to so/sth ♦ call so to attention ♦ the center of attention ♦ come to so's attention ♦ come to attention ♦ get so's attention ♦ grab so's attention ♦ grip so's attention ♦ hold so's attention ♦ pay attention (to so/sth) ♦ rivet so's attention ♦ snap to (attention) ♦ spring to attention

attitude cop an attitude ♦ devil-may-care attitude ♦ have a bad attitude ♦ wait-and-see attitude

auction Dutch auction ♦ up for auction

audience bring an audience to its feet

auspices under the auspices of so

author the author of one's own problem

authority have sth on good authority

automatic on automatic (pilot)

avail avail oneself of sth ♦ of no avail ♦ to little avail ♦ to no avail

avenue avenue of escape

average average out to a figure ♦ a cut above average ♦ on (the) average

avoid avoid so/sth like the plague

awagging set tongues (a)wagging

awake wide awake

away away from one's desk ♦ away from it all ♦ back away (from so/sth) ♦ blow so away ♦ break away (from so/sth) ♦ breeze away ♦ come away empty-handed ♦ dash away ♦ die away ♦ do away with oneself ♦ do away with so/animal ♦ do away with sth ♦ eat (away) at so ♦ explain sth away ♦ faint dead away ♦ far and away the best ♦ far and away the greatest ♦ far and away the worst ♦ far-away look ♦ fritter sth away ♦ gamble sth away ♦ get away from it all ♦ get away with sth ♦ get away with murder ♦ get carried away ♦ give so/sth away ♦ give so away (to so) ♦ give sth away (to so) ♦ give the game away ♦ gnaw (away) at so ♦ Go away! ♦ go away empty-handed ♦ grind away (at so) ♦ hammer (away) at so ♦ hammer (away) at sth ♦ a heartbeat away from being sth ♦ a home away from home ♦ one's home away from home ♦ laugh sth away ♦ lay so away ♦ lay sth away (for so) ♦ make away with so/sth ♦ a million miles away ♦ move away from sth ♦ the one that got away ♦ pass away ♦ pine away (after so/sth) ♦ plug (away) at so ♦ plug (away) at sth ♦ put so away ♦ put sth away ♦ put sth in layaway ♦ run away with so ♦ run away with sth ♦ salt sth away ♦ send so away ♦ shy away from so/sth ♦ sign one's life away ♦ slip away ♦ sock sth away ♦ spirit so/sth away (some place) ♦ squared away ♦ squirrel sth away ♦ step away from one's desk ♦ a stone's throw away ♦ sweep so away ♦ take sth away (from so/sth) ♦ take away from so/sth ♦ take so's breath away ♦ Take it away! ♦ trail away ♦ tuck sth away ♦ walk away from so/sth ♦ walk away with sth ♦ while some time away

awe in awe (of so/sth) ♦ stand in awe (of so/sth)

awfully Thanks awfully.

awkward awkward as a cow on a crutch ♦ awkward as a cow on roller skates ♦ by main strength and awkwardness ♦ main strength and awkwardness ♦ place so in an awkward position

AWOL go AWOL

axe the ax ♦ get axed ♦ have an ax(e) to grind (with so) ♦ old battle axe

B

babe a babe in arms ♦ a babe in the woods ♦ innocent as a newborn babe

baby as easy as taking candy from a baby ♦ bald as a baby's backside ♦ leave so holding the baby ♦ like taking candy from a baby ♦ sleep like a baby ♦ soft as a baby's backside ♦ soft as a baby's bottom ♦ throw the baby out with the bath(water) ♦ weak as a baby

bachelor son of a bachelor

back answer back (to so) ♦ ask so back ♦ back and fill ♦ back and forth ♦ back (at so) ♦ back at it (again) ♦ back away (from so/sth) ♦ back down (from so/sth) ♦ back down (on sth) ♦ back East ♦ back so for sth ♦ back in business ♦ back in the game ♦ back in (the) harness ♦ back in the saddle (again) ♦ back in time ♦ back so into a corner ♦ back in(to) circulation ♦ the back of the beyond ♦ back off (from so/sth) ♦ back on one's feet ♦ back on track ♦ back out (of sth) ♦ back the wrong horse ♦ back to basics ♦ back to square one ♦ back to the drawing board ♦ back to the salt mines ♦ back so up ♦ back up ♦ back up (to sth) ♦ back-order sth ♦ back-to-back ♦ behind so's back ♦ bite back (at so/sth) ♦ bounce back (from sth) ♦ break one's back (to do sth) ♦ break the back of sth ♦ bring sth back ♦ bring so back out ♦ bring sth back (to so) ♦ bring sth back to life ♦ call back ♦ Come back and see us. ♦ Come back anytime. ♦ come back (to so/sth) ♦ come back to haunt one ♦ Come back when you can stay longer. ♦ a crick in one's back ♦ feel the hair on the back of

one's neck stand on end ♦ (flat) on one's back ♦ from way back ♦ get back (at so) ♦ get back in (the) harness ♦ get back in(to) circulation ♦ get back on one's feet ♦ get sth back on track ♦ get so's back up ♦ get one's ears pinned back ♦ get so off so's back ♦ Get off so's back! ♦ Get off my back! ♦ give so a pat on the back ♦ give so the shirt off one's back ♦ go back a long way ♦ go back on one's pledge ♦ go back on one's promise ♦ go back on one's word ♦ go back quite a way(s) ♦ go back to square one ♦ go back to the drawing board ♦ go back to the salt mines ♦ go behind so's back ♦ hark(en) back to sth ♦ have a yellow streak down one's back ♦ have one's back against the wall ♦ have back (at so) ♦ have one's back to the wall ♦ have been to hell and back ♦ have eyes in the back of one's head ♦ hold so back ♦ hold sth back ♦ hold sth back for a rainy day ♦ hold back (on sth) ♦ in the back of so's mind ♦ keep so back ♦ keep sth back ♦ kick back ♦ knock sth back ♦ knock back a drink ♦ knock so back (an amount of money) ♦ knock one back ♦ know so/sth like the back of one's hand ♦ laid back ♦ like water off a duck's back ♦ look back (at so/sth) ♦ nail so's ears back ♦ on one's back ♦ on so's back ♦ on horseback ♦ on the back burner ♦ pace back and forth ♦ pat so on the back ♦ pay so a backhanded compliment ♦ pay so back ♦ pin so's ears back ♦ pop back (for sth) ♦ put one's back (in)to sth ♦ put so's back up ♦ put the roses back into so's cheeks ♦ roll sth back ♦ scratch so's back ♦ set so back (some amount of money) ♦ set one (back) on one's feet ♦ set one back on one's heels ♦ sit back and let sth happen ♦ snap back (at so) ♦ stab so in the back ♦ stand (in) back of so/sth ♦ step back in time ♦ the straw that broke the camel's back ♦ take a backseat (to so/sth) ♦ take sth back ♦ take one back ((to) some time) ♦ talk back (to so) ♦ try so back (again) ♦ turn one's back (on so/sth) ♦ turn back the clock ♦ turn the clock back ♦ twist the knife (in so's back) ♦ watch one's back ♦ when so's back is turned ♦ while so's back is turned ♦ with one hand tied behind one's back ✦ a yellow streak (down so's back)

backfire backfire on so

backhanded backhanded compliment ✦ pay so a backhanded compliment

backroom the backroom boys ✦ the boys in the backroom

backseat backseat driver ✦ take a backseat (to so/sth)

backside bald as a baby's backside ✦ soft as a baby's backside

backwards bend over backwards (to do sth) ✦ fall over backwards (to do sth) ✦ know sth backwards and forwards ✦ lean over backwards (to do sth)

backyard in one's (own) backyard

bacon bring home the bacon ✦ save one's bacon

bad as bad as all that ✦ bad blood (between people) ✦ a bad egg ✦ a bad hair day ✦ a bad penny ✦ a bad time ✦ bad times ✦ come to a bad end ✦ go bad ✦ go from bad to worse ✦ have a bad attitude ✦ have a bad effect (on so/sth) ✦ have a run of bad luck ✦ have it bad ✦ in a bad mood ✦ in a bad way ✦ in bad faith ✦ in bad shape ✦ in bad sorts ✦ in bad taste ✦ in bad (with so) ✦ (It's) not half bad. ✦ leave a bad taste in so's mouth ✦ make the best of a bad situation ✦ Not bad (at all). ✦ off to a bad start ✦ on bad terms (with so) ✦ on the bad side of so ✦ pour good money after bad ✦ so bad one can taste it ✦ a streak of bad luck ✦ a string of bad luck ✦ throw good money after bad ✦ want sth so bad one can taste it

bag bag and baggage ✦ bag of bones ✦ bag of tricks ✦ bag on so ✦ bag some rays ✦ Bag that! ✦ the cat is out of the bag ✦ check so's bags through (to some place) ✦ a doggy bag ✦ have bags under one's eyes ✦ have sth in the bag ✦ in the bag ✦ leave so holding the bag ✦ let the cat out of the bag ✦ a mixed bag ✦ put the feed bag on ✦ put the nose-bag on ✦ whole bag of tricks

baggage bag and baggage

bail bail so out ✦ bail so/sth out ✦ bail sth out ✦ bail out (of sth) ✦ jump bail ✦ out on bail ✦ skip bail

bait the bait ✦ bait and switch ✦ crow bait ✦ Fish or cut bait. ✦ rise to the bait ✦ take the bait

baker a baker's dozen

balance the balance of power ✦ balance out ✦ balance the accounts ✦ balance the books ✦ catch so off balance ✦ checks and balances ✦ hang in the balance ✦ in the balance ✦ on balance ✦ strike a balance (between two things) ✦ throw so off balance ✦ tip the balance

bald bald as a baby's backside ✦ bald as a coot

baleful baleful as death

balk balk at sth

ball (all) balled up ✦ ball and chain ✦ the ball in so's court ✦ the ball is in so's court ✦ ball of fire ✦ ball so/sth up ✦ ball sth up ✦ the balls of one's feet ✦ behind the eight ball ✦ break (so's) balls ✦ break one's balls to do sth ✦ bring sth out of mothballs ✦ bust (so's) balls ✦ carry the ball ✦ drop the ball ✦ the end of the ball game ✦ go under the wrecking ball ✦ Great balls of fire! ✦ have a ball ✦ have sth on the ball ✦ keep one's eye on the ball ✦ keep the ball rolling ✦ not have a snowball's chance in hell ✦ on the ball ✦ pitch so a curve (ball) ✦ play ball (with so) ✦ play hardball (with so) ✦ put balls on sth ✦ put sth in mothballs ✦ snowball into sth ✦ start the ball rolling ✦ throw so a curve (ball) ✦ the whole ball of wax ✦ a (whole) new ball game

ballistic go ballistic

balloon go over like a lead balloon ✦ send up a trial balloon ✦ trial balloon

ballot stuff the ballot box

ballpark a ballpark figure ✦ in the ballpark ✦ in the same ballpark ✦ out of the ballpark

banana go bananas

band strike up the band ✦ to beat the band

bandwagon climb on the bandwagon ✦ on the bandwagon

bandy bandy sth about

bang (bang) dead to rights ✦ bang for the buck ✦ bang one's head against a brick wall ✦ bang sth out ✦ bang the drum for so/sth ♦ give so a bang ♦ go over with a bang ♦ start (off) with a bang

bank bank on sth ♦ break the bank ♦ can take it to the bank ♦ cry all the way to the bank ♦ laugh all the way to the bank

banker banker's hours ♦ keep banker's hours

banner under the banner of sth

baptism baptism of fire

bar bar none ♦ behind bars ♦ Katie bar the door. ♦ no holds barred ♦ put so behind bars ♦ raise the bar

bare the bare sth ♦ bare-bones ♦ bare one's soul (to so) ♦ bare one's teeth ♦ bare sth to so ♦ stand there with one's bare face hanging out

bargain bargaining chip ♦ drive a hard bargain ♦ hold one's end of the bargain up ♦ include sth in the bargain ♦ keep one's end of the bargain ♦ keep one's end of the bargain up ♦ keep one's side of the bargain ♦ live up to one's side of the bargain ♦ more than one bargained for ♦ seal a bargain ♦ seal the bargain ♦ strike a bargain ♦ throw sth into the bargain

barge barge in (on so/sth) ♦ barge in(to some place)

bark bark at so ♦ One's bark is worse than one's bite. ♦ bark sth out at so ♦ bark up the wrong tree ♦ more bark than bite

barn all around Robin Hood's barn ♦ broad as a barn door ♦ can't hit the (broad) side of a barn ♦ hit the (broad) side of a barn ♦ raised in a barn ♦ Were you born in a barn?

barrel as easy as shooting fish in a barrel ♦ as much fun as a barrel of monkeys ♦ barrel along ♦ a barrel of fun ♦ the bottom of the barrel ♦ crooked as a barrel of fish hooks ♦ have so over a barrel ♦ let so have it (with both barrels) ♦ like shooting fish in a barrel ♦ loaded to the barrel ♦ lock, stock, and barrel ♦ more fun than a barrel of monkeys ♦ over a barrel ♦ scrape the bottom of the barrel

barrelhead cash on the barrelhead

base cover all the bases ♦ get to first base (with so/sth) ♦ make sure all the bases are covered ♦ off base ♦ reach first base

(with so/sth) ♦ steal a base ♦ touch base (with so) ♦ way off (base)

basic back to basics

basis on a first-name basis (with so)

bask bask in sth

basket a basket case ♦ can't carry a tune (in a bushel basket) ♦ go to hell in a handbasket ♦ put all one's eggs in one basket

bastard Don't let the bastards wear you down.

bat bat sth around ♦ blind as a bat ♦ go to bat against so ♦ go to bat for so ♦ go to bat for sth ♦ have bats in one's belfry ♦ like a bat out of hell ♦ not bat an eye ♦ not bat an eyelid ♦ right off the bat ♦ straight off the bat ♦ without batting an eye

batch batch (it)

bated with bated breath

bath take a bath (on sth)

bathroom go to the bathroom

bathwater throw the baby out with the bath(water)

batten batten down the hatches

battery assault and battery ♦ recharge one's batteries

battle battle of the bulge ♦ a battle royal ♦ do battle with so/sth ♦ fight a losing battle ♦ half the battle ♦ in the heat of battle ♦ old battle axe ♦ a running battle ♦ an uphill battle

batty drive so batty

bawl give so a (good) bawling out

bay at bay ♦ hold so/sth at bay ♦ keep so/sth at bay

beam Beam me up, Scotty! ♦ beam up ♦ broad in the beam ♦ on the beam ♦ steam so's beam

bean don't know beans (about sth) ♦ full of beans ♦ not amount to a hill of beans ♦ not know beans (about so/sth) ♦ not worth a hill of beans ♦ not worth beans ♦ skinny as a beanpole ♦ spill the beans

bear bear so/sth ♦ bear a grudge (against so) ♦ bear arms ♦ bear one's cross ♦ bear fruit ♦ bear sth in mind ♦ bear in mind that . . . ♦ bear sth out ♦ bear the brunt (of sth) ♦ bear up (under sth) ♦ bear watching ♦ bear with so/sth ♦ bear witness to sth ♦ bring sth to bear on sth ♦ busy as a hibernating bear ♦ grin and bear it ♦ gruff as a bear ♦ hungry as a bear ♦ loaded for bear ♦ more than one can bear ♦ not able to bear so/sth

bearing one's bearings ♦ get one's bearings ♦ have (some) bearing on sth

beast That's (just) the nature of the beast.

beat beat a dead horse ♦ beat a (hasty) retreat ♦ beat a path to so's door ♦ beat around the bush ♦ beat one at one's own game ♦ beat so's brains out ♦ beat one's brains out (to do sth) ♦ beat city hall ♦ beat so down ♦ beat one's gums ♦ beat one's head against the wall ♦ Beat it! ♦ beat the bushes for so/sth ♦ beat the clock ♦ beat the drum for so/sth ♦ beat the gun ♦ beat the hell out of so ♦ beat the living daylights out of so ♦ beat the pants off (of) so ♦ beat the rap ♦ beat the shit out of so ♦ beat the socks off (of) so ♦ beat the stuffing out of so ♦ beat the system ♦ beat the tar out of so ♦ beat so to a pulp ♦ beat so to the draw ♦ beat so to the punch ♦ beat oneself up ♦ Don't that (just) beat all! ♦ one's heart misses a beat ♦ one's heart skips a beat ♦ a heartbeat away from being sth ♦ If that don't beat all! ♦ do sth in a heartbeat ♦ (It) beats me. ♦ (It's) got me beat. ♦ march to (the beat of) a different drummer ♦ not miss a beat ♦ off the beaten path ♦ off the beaten track ♦ pound a beat ♦ take a beating ♦ That beats everything! ♦ to beat the band ♦ without missing a beat ♦ You got me beat.

beauty Age before beauty. ♦ the beauty of sth ♦ a bevy of beauties ♦ (I've) got to go home and get my beauty sleep.

beaver busy as a beaver (building a new dam) ♦ eager beaver ♦ work like a beaver

beck at so's beck and call

become become of so/sth ♦ become rooted to sth ♦ becoming on so ♦ look becoming on so

bed bed-and-breakfast ♦ bed down some place ♦ bed down (for sth) ♦ a bed of roses ♦ between you (and) me and the bedpost ♦ fall out of bed ♦ get into bed with so ♦ get out of the wrong side of bed ♦ get up on the wrong side of bed ♦ go to bed ♦

go to bed (with so) ♦ go to bed with the chickens ♦ a hotbed of sth ♦ in bed with so ♦ make one's (own) bed ♦ make the bed (up) ♦ on one's deathbed ♦ put sth to bed ♦ put so to bed with a shovel ♦ put to bed with a shovel ♦ should have stood in bed ♦ sick abed ♦ sick in bed ♦ take to one's bed ♦ wake up on the wrong side of bed

bedpost between you (and) me and the bedpost

bee a bee in one's bonnet ♦ the birds and the bees ♦ busy as a bee ♦ get a bee in one's bonnet ♦ put a bee in one's bonnet

beef beef about so/sth ♦ beef sth up ♦ have a beef with so/sth ♦ Where's the beef?

beeline make a beeline for so/sth

beer (all) beer and skittles ♦ beer and skittles ♦ cry in one's beer

beeswax mind your own beeswax ♦ None of your beeswax!

beg beg off (on sth) ♦ beg so's pardon ♦ beg the question ♦ beg to differ (with so) ♦ go begging

begin begin by doing sth ♦ begin to see daylight ♦ (begin to) see the light (at the end of the tunnel) ♦ the beginning of the end

beginner beginner's luck

behalf in behalf of so ♦ on behalf of so

behavior on one's best behavior ♦ time off for good behavior

behold Lo and behold! ♦ a marvel to behold

behoove it behooves one to do sth

bejeebers knock the bejeebers out of so/sth

belabor belabor the point

belch belch out

belfry have bats in one's belfry

believe believe it or not ♦ Believe you me! ♦ hard to believe ♦ lead so to believe sth ♦ make a believer (out) of so ♦ make believe (that) . . . ♦ not believe one's ears ♦ not believe one's eyes

bell bell, book, and candle ♦ bells and whistles ♦ can't unring the bell ♦ clear as a bell ♦ Hell's bells (and buckets of blood)! ♦ ring a bell ♦ ring the bell ♦ saved by the bell ♦ sound as a bell ♦ with bells on (one's toes)

belly air one's belly ♦ belly up ♦ belly up (to sth) ♦ go belly up ♦ have a bellyful ♦ have a yellow belly ♦ turn belly up

belt belt a drink down ♦ belt sth out ♦ belt the grape ♦ have sth under one's belt ♦ hit so below the belt ♦ pull one's belt in (a notch) ♦ the rust belt ♦ the sun belt ♦ take one's belt in (a notch) ♦ tighten one's belt ♦ under one's belt

bench on the bench ♦ warm the bench

bend (a)round the bend ♦ bend so's ear ♦ bend one's elbow ♦ bend so out of shape ♦ bend over backwards (to do sth) ♦ bend the law ♦ bend the rules ♦ drive so around the bend ♦ go (a)round the bend ♦ on bended knee

bender fender bender

benefit the benefit of the doubt ♦ give so the benefit of the doubt

bent bent on doing sth ♦ bent out of shape ♦ hell-bent for leather ♦ hell-bent for some place or sth

berry brown as a berry ♦ give so the raspberry

berth give so/sth a wide berth

best (all) for the best ♦ All the best to so. ♦ as one think(s) best ♦ at one's best ♦ at best ♦ at its best ♦ best as one can ♦ best bet ♦ one's best bib and tucker ♦ the best-case scenario ♦ the best of both worlds ♦ the best of the best ♦ the best of the lot ♦ the best of times ♦ the best part of sth ♦ one's best shot ♦ bring out the best in so ♦ come off second best ♦ do one's (level) best ♦ far and away the best ♦ for the best ♦ get the best of so ♦ Give my best to so. ♦ had best do sth ♦ have so's best interest(s) at heart ♦ hope for the best ♦ in one's (own) (best) interest(s) ♦ in one's Sunday best ♦ in the best of health ♦ know best ♦ so's level best ♦ make the best of sth ♦ make the best of a bad situation ♦ man's best friend ♦ May the best man win. ♦ May the best team win. ♦ next best thing ♦ on one's best behavior ♦ put one's best foot forward ♦ Sunday best ♦ to the best of one's ability ♦ wish so the best of luck ♦ with the best of them ♦ with the best will in the world ♦ work out for the best

bet best bet ♦ bet one's bottom dollar ♦ bet so dollars to doughnuts ♦ bet one's life ♦ bet on the wrong horse ♦ bet the farm (on sth) ♦ bet the ranch (on sth) ♦ Don't bet on it! ♦ a good bet ♦ hedge one's bets ♦ (I) wouldn't bet on it. ♦ a sure bet ♦ You bet your boots! ♦ You bet your (sweet) life!

betsy crazy as a betsy bug ♦ Heavens to Betsy!

better against one's better judgment ♦ all better (now) ♦ one's better half ♦ Better late than never. ♦ better left unsaid ♦ Better luck next time. ♦ better off (doing sth) ♦ better off (some place) ♦ the better part of sth ♦ better safe than sorry ♦ build a better mousetrap ♦ change for the better ♦ a (damn) sight better ♦ do so one better ♦ do one one better (than that) ♦ for better or (for) worse ♦ for the better ♦ get the better of so ♦ go on to a better land ♦ go (so) one better ♦ go one one better (than that) ♦ had better do sth ♦ have seen better days ♦ I'd better get on my horse. ♦ (It's) better than nothing. ♦ (I've) (got) better things to do. ♦ (I've) seen better. ♦ know better (than to do sth) ♦ so much the better ♦ The sooner the better. ♦ take a turn for the better ♦ think better of so/sth ♦ think better of sth

betwixt betwixt and between

bevy a bevy of beauties

beyond above and beyond (the call of duty)

bias on the bias

bib one's best bib and tucker

Bible swear on a stack of Bibles

bid bid adieu to so/sth ♦ do so's bidding

bide bide one's time

big be big on sth ♦ big and bold ♦ the Big Apple ♦ big as all outdoors ♦ big as life (and twice as ugly) ♦ a big break ♦ big bucks ♦ a big drink of water ♦ the big eye ♦ a big frog in a small pond ♦ a big hand for sth ♦ a (big) head ♦ big man on campus ♦ the big moment ♦ big of so ♦ the big picture ♦ a big send-off ♦ big with so ♦ bigger than life ♦ bigger than life (and twice as ugly) ♦ bite the big one ♦ buy the big one ♦ cut a big swath ♦ one's eyes are bigger than one's stomach ♦ get the big picture ♦ give so a big hand for sth ♦ give so a (big) head ♦ give so a big send-off ♦ give so the big eye ♦ go over big (with so) ♦ have a big mouth ♦ have bigger fish to fry ♦ in a big way ♦ Like it's such a big deal! ♦ make a big deal about sth ♦ make a (big) stink (about so/sth) ♦ make it big ♦ no big deal ♦ no biggie ♦ play a big part (in sth) ♦ play in the big leagues ♦ raise a (big) stink (about so/sth) ♦ talk big ♦ That's life in the big city. ♦ Think big. ♦ too big for one's britches ♦ What's the (big) idea?

bill a clean bill of health ♦ Could I have the bill? ♦ fill the bill ♦ fit the bill ♦ foot the bill (for sth) ♦ give so a clean bill of health ♦ pad the bill ♦ phony as a three-dollar bill ♦ pick up the bill (for sth) ♦ queer as a three-dollar bill ♦ sell so a bill of goods

bind in a bind

binge binge and purge ♦ go on a binge

bird A bird in the hand (is worth two in the bush). ♦ a bird's-eye view ♦ the birds and the bees ♦ early bird ♦ eat like a bird ♦ flip so the bird ♦ for the birds ♦ free as a bird ♦ in the catbird seat ♦ kill two birds with one stone ♦ A little bird told me. ♦ naked as a jaybird ♦ on the bird

birth give birth to sth

birthday in one's birthday suit

biscuit son of a sea biscuit

bit a bit much ♦ a bit of the action ♦ a bit off ♦ champ at the bit ♦ chomp at the bit ♦ do one's bit ♦ the hair of the dog (that bit one) ♦ in a little bit ♦ a little bit (of sth) ♦ not a bit ♦ one little bit ♦ play a bit part ♦ take the bit in one's teeth

bitch bitch about so/sth ♦ a bitch of a so/sth ♦ bitch so off ♦ bitch so/sth up ♦ son of a bitch

bite One's bark is worse than one's bite. ♦ bite back (at so/sth) ♦ bite so's head off ♦ bite one's nails ♦ bite off more than one can chew ♦ bite on so ♦ bite the big one ♦ bite the bullet ♦ bite the dust ♦ bite the hand that feeds one ♦ Bite the ice! ♦ a bite (to eat) ♦ bite one's tongue ♦ bitten by the same bug ♦ grab a bite (to eat) ♦ I'll bite. ♦ more bark than bite ♦ put the bite on so

(for sth) ♦ a quick bite ♦ snakebite medicine ♦ take a bite out of sth

bits blow so/sth to bits

bitsy itsy bitsy

bitter a bitter pill (to swallow) ♦ till the bitter end ♦ to the bitter end

bitty itty bitty ♦ little bitty

blab blab sth around

black black and blue ♦ black and white ♦ black as a skillet ♦ black as a stack of black cats ♦ black as coal ♦ black as one is painted ♦ black as night ♦ black as pitch ♦ black as the ace of spades ♦ a black eye ♦ a black mark beside one's name ♦ black sth out ♦ black out ♦ the black sheep of the family ♦ get sth down (in black and white) ♦ get sth in black and white ♦ in black and white ♦ in the black ♦ put sth down in black and white ♦ set sth down in black and white

blame lay the blame (for sth) on so ♦ lay the blame on so/sth ♦ put the blame on so/sth

blanche carte blanche ♦ give so carte blanche

blank a blank check ♦ draw a blank ♦ Fill in the blanks. ♦ give so a blank check ♦ give so a blank look ♦ give so a blank stare ♦ go blank ♦ one's mind goes blank

blanket a wet blanket

blast at full blast ♦ a blast from the past ♦ have a blast ♦ play sth at full blast

blaze blaze a trail ♦ Go to blazes!

bleed bleed so dry ♦ bleed for so ♦ bleed to death ♦ bleed so white ♦ bleeding heart ♦ one's heart bleeds for so ♦ on the bleeding edge

bleep bleep sth out

bless Bless so's heart! ♦ blessed event ♦ blessed with sth ♦ a blessing in disguise ♦ count one's blessings ♦ (God) bless you! ♦ thankful for small blessings ♦ with my blessing

blimp blimp out (on sth) ♦ Have a blimp!

blind blind as a bat ♦ blind luck ♦ a case of the blind leading the blind ♦ Love is blind. ♦ rob so blind ♦ turn a blind eye (to so/sth) ♦ up a blind alley

blindfolded able to do sth blindfolded

blink on the blink

bliss bliss so out ♦ bliss out ♦ Ignorance is bliss.

blitz blitz so out ♦ blitzed out

block block sth out ♦ block so up ♦ a chip off the old block ♦ have a mental block (against sth) ♦ have been around (the block) ♦ knock so's block off ♦ a mental block (against sth) ♦ the new kid on the block ♦ on the block ♦ put one's head on the block (for so/sth) ♦ (right) out of the (starting) blocks ♦ a stumbling block ♦ writer's block

blood bad blood (between people) ♦ blood and guts ♦ blood, sweat, and tears ♦ bloody but unbowed ♦ blue blood ♦ cry bloody murder ♦ curdle so's blood ♦ draw blood ♦ flesh and blood ♦ fresh blood ♦ get so's blood up ♦ have (so's) blood on one's hands ♦ Hell's bells (and buckets of blood)! ♦ holler bloody murder ♦ in one's blood ♦ in cold blood ♦ in the blood ♦ make so's blood boil ♦ make so's blood run cold ♦ new blood ♦ out for blood ♦ own flesh and blood ♦ red as blood ♦ scream bloody murder ♦ smell blood ♦ (some) new blood ♦ sweat blood ♦ take so's blood pressure ♦ taste blood ♦ too rich for so's blood ♦ yell bloody murder

bloom come into bloom ♦ in bloom ♦ a late bloomer ♦ out (in bloom)

blossom blossom (forth) ♦ blossom (out) into sth ♦ bring sth into blossom ♦ come into blossom ♦ in blossom ♦ out (in blossom)

blot a blot on the landscape ♦ blot sth out

blow at one blow ♦ blow sth ♦ blow a bundle (on so) ♦ blow a fuse ♦ blow a gasket ♦ blow so a kiss ♦ blow so away ♦ blow so's brains out ♦ a blow-by-blow account ♦ a blow-by-blow description ♦ blow one's cookies ♦ blow one's cool ♦ blow one's cork ♦ blow so's cover ♦ blow so's doors off ♦ blow one's groceries ♦ blow hot and cold ♦ blow in(to some place) (from some place) ♦ Blow it out your ear! ♦ blow itself out ♦ blow one's lid ♦ blow one's lines ♦ blow (one's) lunch ♦ blow so's mind ♦ blow one's nose ♦ blow so/sth off ♦ blow off ♦ blow off (some) steam ♦ Blow on it! ♦ blow so out ♦ blow so/sth out of the water

♦ blow so over ♦ blow over ♦ blow one's own horn ♦ blow one's stack ♦ blow the joint ♦ blow the lid off (sth) ♦ blow the whistle (on so/sth) ♦ blow so to sth ♦ blow so/sth to bits ♦ blow so/sth to kingdom come ♦ blow so/sth to pieces ♦ blow so/sth to smithereens ♦ blow one's top ♦ blow so/sth up ♦ blow sth up ♦ blow up ♦ blow up in so's face ♦ blow sth wide open ♦ blown (up) ♦ come to blows (over so/sth) ♦ cushion the blow ♦ deal so/sth a death blow ♦ deal so/sth a fatal blow ♦ a full-blown sth ♦ It blows my mind! ♦ land a blow ♦ not tell which way the wind is blowing ♦ see which way the wind is blowing ♦ soften the blow ♦ strike a blow against so/sth ♦ strike a blow for so/sth

blowout have a blowout

blue between the devil and the deep blue sea ♦ black and blue ♦ blue around the gills ♦ blue blood ♦ blue-collar ♦ the blues ♦ a bolt from the blue ♦ burn with a low blue flame ♦ come out of a clear blue sky ♦ feel blue ♦ have the blues ♦ in a (blue) funk ♦ like a bolt out of the blue ♦ once in a blue moon ♦ screwed, blued, and tattooed ♦ singing the blues ♦ talk a blue streak ♦ talk until one is blue in the face

bluff bluff one's way in(to sth) ♦ bluff one's way out (of sth) ♦ call so's bluff

blush at first blush

boar crazy as a peach-orchard boar

board across the board ♦ back to the drawing board ♦ fall overboard ♦ flat as a board ♦ go back to the drawing board ♦ go by the board ♦ go overboard ♦ on board ♦ room and board

boast nothing to boast about

boat in the same boat (as so) ♦ just off the boat ♦ miss the boat ♦ rock the boat ♦ Whatever floats your boat.

bodily bodily functions

body bodily functions ♦ the body politic ♦ enough to keep body and soul together ♦ in a body ♦ keep body and soul together ♦ know where all the bodies are buried ♦ leave in a body ♦ not have a specific kind of bone in one's body ♦ Over my dead body! ♦ warm body

bog bog so/sth down ♦ bogged down

boggle boggle so's mind ♦ the mind boggles (at sth)

boil boil sth down ♦ boil down to sth ♦ bring so to a boil ♦ come to a boil ♦ have a low boiling point ♦ make so's blood boil

bold big and bold ♦ bold as brass ♦ make (so) bold (as) to do sth

bolster bolster so up

bolt bolt sth down ♦ a bolt from the blue ♦ get down to the nuts and bolts ♦ like a bolt out of the blue ♦ make a bolt for so/sth ♦ nuts and bolts ♦ sit bolt upright

bomb bomb out (of sth)

bombshell drop a bomb(shell) ♦ explode a bombshell

bond one's word is one's bond

bone (all) skin and bones ♦ bag of bones ♦ bare-bones ♦ bone of contention ♦ bone up (on sth) ♦ chilled to the bone ♦ close to the bone ♦ crazy bone ♦ cut so to the bone ♦ cut sth to the bone ♦ dry as a bone ♦ feel sth in one's bones ♦ funny bone ♦ have a bone to pick (with so) ♦ know sth in one's bones ♦ make no bones about sth ♦ not have a specific kind of bone in one's body ♦ nothing but skin and bones ♦ pull a boner ♦ skin and bones ♦ (too) close to the bone ♦ work one's fingers to the bone

bonkers drive so bonkers

bonnet a bee in one's bonnet ♦ get a bee in one's bonnet ♦ put a bee in one's bonnet

boo boo so off the stage

booby booby prize

boogie boogie down (to some place)

book balance the books ♦ bell, book, and candle ♦ book (on) out ♦ by the book ♦ close the books on so/sth ♦ coffee-table book ♦ cook the books ♦ crack a book ♦ cuddle up with a (good) book ♦ curl up (with a (good) book) ♦ every trick in the book ♦ go by the book ♦ go down in the history books ♦ the Good Book ♦ have one's nose in a book ♦ hit the books ♦ in one's book ♦ know so/sth like a book ♦ make book on sth ♦ Not in my book. ♦ not to judge a book by its cover ♦ off the books ♦ the oldest trick in the book ♦ on the books ♦ one for the (record) books ♦ an open book ♦ pound the books ♦ read so like a book ♦ sing from the same hymn book ♦ snuggle up (with a (good) book) ♦ take a leaf out of so's book ♦ take a page from so's book ♦ throw the book at so ♦ wrote the book on sth

boom boom sth out ♦ lower the boom on so

boondocks in the boondocks

boonies in the boonies

boot the boot ♦ boot so/animal out ♦ boot up ♦ boot sth up ♦ die in one's boots ♦ die with one's boots on ♦ give so the boot ♦ quake in one's boots ♦ shake in one's boots ♦ to boot ♦ tough as an old boot ♦ You bet your boots!

bootstraps pull oneself up by one's (own) bootstraps

booze booze it up ♦ booze up ♦ hit the booze

border border on sth ♦ border (up)on sth

borderline on the borderline

bore bore one out of one's mind ♦ bore so stiff ♦ bore the pants off of so ♦ bore through so ♦ bore so to death ♦ bore so to tears ♦ bored out of one's mind ♦ bored silly ♦ bored stiff ♦ bored to distraction ♦ bored to tears ♦ die of boredom

boredom die of boredom

born born and bred some place ♦ born and raised some place ♦ born lazy ♦ born out of wedlock ♦ born to do sth ♦ born to be so/sth ♦ born with a silver spoon in one's mouth ♦ in all my born days ♦ innocent as a newborn babe ♦ not born yesterday ♦ to the manner born ♦ Were you born in a barn?

borrow borrow trouble ♦ live on borrowed time

bosom bosom buddy ♦ bosom pal ♦ in the bosom of sth

boss be one's own boss ♦ boss so around ♦ show so who's boss

both the best of both worlds ♦ both sheets in the wind ♦ burn the candle at both ends ♦ can't find one's butt with both hands (in broad daylight) ♦ cut both ways ♦ dive in (with both feet) ♦ a foot in both camps ♦ have a foot in both camps ♦ have it both ways ♦ have the worse of both worlds ♦ jump in (with both feet) ♦ land (up)on both feet ♦ let so have it (with both barrels) ♦ make (both) ends meet ♦ play both ends (against the middle) ♦ to speak out of both sides of one's mouth ♦ works both ways ♦ the worse of both worlds

bother bother one's (pretty little) head about so/sth ♦ can't be bothered to do sth ♦ Don't bother. ♦ Don't bother me! ♦ go to the bother (of doing sth) ♦ hot and bothered

bottle the bottle ♦ bottle sth up ♦ chief cook and bottle washer ♦ crack a bottle open ♦ hit the bottle

bottom at the bottom of the hour ♦ at the bottom of the ladder ♦ bet one's bottom dollar ♦ the bottom fell out (of sth) ♦ the bottom line ♦ the bottom of the barrel ♦ the bottom of the heap ♦ the bottom of the pile ♦ bottom out ♦ Bottoms up! ♦ from the (bottom of one's) heart ♦ from top to bottom ♦ get to the bottom of sth ♦ hit bottom ♦ hit (rock) bottom ♦ knock the bottom out (of sth) ♦ learn sth from the bottom up ♦ on the bottom rung (of the ladder) ♦ (rock) bottom ♦ scrape the bottom of the barrel ♦ soft as a baby's bottom

bounce bounce sth around (with so) ♦ bounce back (from sth) ♦ bounce for sth ♦ bounce sth off (of) so/sth

bound bound and determined ♦ bound for some place ♦ bound hand and foot ♦ bound to do sth ♦ bound up in sth ♦ bound up with sth ♦ by leaps and bounds ♦ duty bound to do sth ♦ grow by leaps and bounds ♦ honor bound (to do sth) ♦ keep (so/sth) within bounds ♦ know no bounds ♦ out of bounds ♦ overstep one's bounds ♦ overstep the bounds of good taste ♦ within bounds

bow bow and scrape ♦ bow before so/sth ♦ bow down to so/sth ♦ bow out (of some place) ♦ bow out (of sth) ♦ bow to sth ♦ fire a shot across the bow ♦ take a bow

bowel Don't get your bowels in an uproar! ♦ evacuate one's bowels

bowl bowl so over

box box so's ears ♦ box so/sth in ♦ boxed in ♦ boxed (up) ♦ go home in a box ♦ inside the box ♦ open Pandora's box ♦ outside the box ♦ stuff the ballot box ♦ think inside the box ♦ think outside the box

boy the backroom boys ♦ the boys in the backroom ♦ one can (just) get oneself another boy ♦ fair-haired boy ♦ good old boy ♦ separate the men from the boys ♦ That's my boy. ♦ a whipping boy

brace brace oneself for sth ♦ brace up

brain beat so's brains out ♦ beat one's brains out (to do sth) ♦ blow so's brains out ♦ brain so ♦ the brains behind sth ♦ have so/sth on the brain ♦ pick so's brain(s) ♦ rack one's brain(s)

brake hit the brakes ♦ jam the brakes on ♦ put the brakes on so/sth ♦ slam the brakes on

branch branch out (from sth) ♦ branch out (into sth) ♦ hold out the olive branch

brand brand spanking new

brass bold as brass ♦ brass so off ♦ double in brass (as sth) ♦ get down to brass tacks ♦ top brass

brave brave sth out ♦ put up a (brave) front

breach step in(to the breach)

bread so's bread and butter ♦ bread-and-butter letter ♦ bread and water ♦ break bread with so ♦ the greatest thing since sliced bread

breadth by a hair('s breadth)

break all hell broke loose ♦ at the break of dawn ♦ a big break ♦ a break ♦ break a code ♦ break a habit ♦ break a law ♦ Break a leg! ♦ break a record ♦ break a story ♦ break away (from so/sth) ♦ break one's back (to do sth) ♦ break (so's) balls ♦ break one's balls to do sth ♦ break bread with so ♦ break camp ♦ break so down ♦ break sth down ♦ break down ♦ break sth down (for so) ♦ break sth down (into sth) ♦ break even ♦ break so's fall ♦ break for sth ♦ break free (from so/sth) ♦ break ground (for sth) ♦ break so's heart ♦ break so in ♦ break sth in ♦ break in (on so) ♦ break in (on sth) ♦ break into sth ♦ break into a gallop ♦ Break it up! ♦ break loose (from so/sth) ♦ break one's neck (to do sth) ♦ break new ground ♦ break so/sth of sth ♦ break off (with so/group) ♦ break out ♦ break out in a cold sweat ♦ break out in a rash ♦

break out (in pimples) ✦ break out in(to) tears ✦ break out (of sth) ✦ break out with sth ✦ break out (with a rash) ✦ break ranks with so/sth ✦ break silence ✦ break one's stride ✦ break the back of sth ✦ break the bank ✦ break the habit ✦ break the ice ✦ break the law ✦ break the news (to so) ✦ break the silence ✦ break the spell ✦ break through (sth) ✦ break sth to so ✦ break up ✦ break so up ✦ break sth up ✦ break up (with so) ✦ break wind ✦ break with so/group ✦ break with tradition ✦ break one's word ✦ break sth off ✦ break sth out ✦ breaking and entering ✦ the breaking point ✦ broken dreams ✦ a broken reed ✦ cut so a break ✦ dead broke ✦ die of a broken heart ✦ an even break ✦ flat broke ✦ Gimme a break! ✦ give so a break ✦ give so an even break ✦ Give me a break! ✦ go broke ✦ go for broke ✦ a lucky break ✦ make (a break) for so/sth ✦ make or break so ✦ a nice break ✦ sound like a broken record ✦ the straw that broke the camel's back ✦ take a break ✦ a tough break ✦ When they made so/sth, they broke the mold.

breakdown a (nervous) breakdown

breakfast bed-and-breakfast ✦ eat so for breakfast ✦ have so for breakfast ✦ shoot one's breakfast

breast make a clean breast of sth (to so)

breath (all) in one breath ✦ a breath of fresh air ✦ catch one's breath ✦ Don't hold your breath. ✦ Don't waste your breath. ✦ hold one's breath ✦ in one breath ✦ in the same breath ✦ out of breath ✦ save one's breath ✦ Take a deep breath. ✦ take so's breath away ✦ under one's breath ✦ waste one's breath ✦ with bated breath ✦ with every (other) breath

breathe able to breathe (easily) again ✦ able to breathe (freely) again ✦ As I live and breathe! ✦ breathe a sigh of relief ✦ breathe down so's neck ✦ breathe easy ✦ breathe one's last ✦ breathe new life into sth ✦ breathe sth (of sth) (to so) ✦ Don't breathe a word of this to anyone. ✦ hardly have time to breathe ✦ live and breathe sth ✦ not breathe a word (about so/sth) ✦ scarcely have time to breathe

bred born and bred some place

breeze breeze along ✦ breeze away ✦ breeze in(to some place) ✦ breeze off ✦ breeze out (of some place) ✦ breeze through (sth) ✦ bright and breezy ✦ fan the breeze ✦ shoot the breeze

breezy bright and breezy

brew brew a plot ✦ brew up ✦ brew sth up ✦ A storm is brewing.

brick bang one's head against a brick wall ✦ bricks and mortar ✦ brick(s)-and-mortar ✦ built like a brick outhouse ✦ built like a brick shithouse ✦ drop a brick ✦ a few bricks short of a load ✦ a few bricks shy of a load ✦ hit the bricks ✦ knock one's head (up) against a brick wall ✦ like a ton of bricks ✦ run one's head against a brick wall

bridge bridge the gap ✦ burn one's bridges (behind one) ✦ burn one's bridges in front of one ✦ cross bridges before one comes to them ✦ cross that bridge before one comes to it ✦ cross that bridge when one comes to it ✦ water under the bridge

bridle bridle at so/sth

brief hold no brief for so/sth ✦ in brief

bright bright and breezy ✦ bright and early ✦ bright as a button ✦ bright as a new pin ✦ bright-eyed and bushy-tailed ✦ a bright idea ✦ One's future looks bright. ✦ get a bright idea ✦ Honor bright. ✦ look on the bright side ✦ on the bright side

brim brim with sth ✦ brimming over (with sth) ✦ filled to the brim

bring bring a dog to heel ✦ bring a verdict in ✦ bring sth about ✦ bring an audience to its feet ✦ bring so around ✦ bring so around (to consciousness) ✦ bring so around (to one's way of thinking) ✦ bring sth back ✦ bring so back out ✦ bring sth back (to so) ✦ bring sth back to life ✦ bring sth crashing down (around one) ✦ bring so down ✦ bring sth down ✦ bring so down a peg (or two) ✦ bring sth down on one('s head) ✦ bring so down (to earth) ✦ bring home the bacon ✦ bring sth home to so ✦ bring so in (on sth) ✦ bring sth into being ✦ bring sth into blossom ✦ bring sth into focus ✦ bring sth into line (with sth) ✦ bring sth into play ✦ bring sth into question ✦

bring so into the world ♦ bring money in ♦ bring sth off ♦ bring so on ♦ bring sth on ♦ bring sth on so ♦ bring sth out ♦ bring sth out (in so) ♦ bring people/animals out in droves ♦ bring sth out of mothballs ♦ bring out the best in so ♦ bring the curtain down (on sth) ♦ bring the house down ♦ bring so to ♦ bring one to oneself ♦ bring so to do sth ♦ bring so to a boil ♦ bring sth to a climax ♦ bring sth to a close ♦ bring sth to a dead end ♦ bring sth to a head ♦ bring sth to a standstill ♦ bring so to account ♦ bring so/sth to so's attention ♦ bring sth to bear on sth ♦ bring one to one's feet ♦ bring sth to fruition ♦ bring so to heel ♦ bring one to one's knees ♦ bring so/sth to life ♦ bring so/sth to light ♦ bring sth to light ♦ bring sth to mind ♦ bring sth to rest ♦ bring one to one's senses ♦ bring sth to the fore ♦ bring sth to the party ♦ bring sth to the table ♦ bring so/sth to trial ♦ bring so together ♦ bring so/sth up ♦ bring sth up ♦ bring so up for sth ♦ bring so up on sth ♦ bring so up sharply ♦ bring so up short ♦ bring up the rear ♦ bring so/sth up-to-date ♦ bring so up-to-date (on so/sth) ♦ bring sth (up)on oneself ♦ bring sth with

brink on the brink (of doing sth)

bristle bristle at sth ♦ bristle with anger ♦ bristle with indignation ♦ bristle with rage

britches too big for one's britches ♦ wear the britches (in the family)

broad broad as a barn door ♦ broad in the beam ♦ can't find one's butt with both hands (in broad daylight) ♦ can't hit the (broad) side of a barn ♦ have broad shoulders ♦ hit the (broad) side of a barn ♦ in broad daylight

Broadway on Broadway

bronco bust a bronco

brother be one's brother's keeper ♦ everybody and his brother

brow by the sweat of one's brow ♦ knit one's brow

brown brown as a berry ♦ brown so off ♦ brown out ♦ browned (off) ♦ do sth up brown

bruise cruisin(g) for a bruisin(g)

brunt bear the brunt (of sth)

brush brush so/sth aside ♦ brush so off ♦ the brush-off ♦ brush over so/sth ♦ brush sth up ♦ brush up (on sth) ♦ a brush with death ♦ give so the brush-off ♦ have a brush with sth ♦ paint so with the same brush ♦ tar so with the same brush ♦ tarred with the same brush

brute by brute strength

buck bang for the buck ♦ big bucks ♦ buck for sth ♦ The buck stops here. ♦ buck the system ♦ buck up ♦ make a fast buck ♦ make a quick buck ♦ pass the buck

bucket can't carry a tune in a bucket ♦ a drop in the bucket ♦ For crying in a bucket! ♦ go to hell in a bucket ♦ Hell's bells (and buckets of blood)! ♦ kick the bucket

buckle buckle down (to sth) ♦ buckle under (sth)

bud a budding genius ♦ nip sth in the bud

buddy bosom buddy ♦ buddy up (to so) ♦ buddy up (with so)

budge not budge an inch

buff in the buff

bug bitten by the same bug ♦ bug so ♦ bug out ♦ crazy as a betsy bug ♦ cute as a bug's ear ♦ snug as a bug in a rug

buggy go the way of the horse and buggy ♦ went out with the buggy whip ♦ went out with the horse and buggy

build build a better mousetrap ♦ build castles in Spain ♦ build castles in the air ♦ build one's hopes on so/sth ♦ build sth into sth ♦ build sth to order ♦ build so/sth up ♦ build sth up ♦ build so up (for sth) ♦ build so/sth up (from sth) ♦ build up to sth ♦ build (up)on sth ♦ build sth (up)on sth ♦ built like a brick outhouse ♦ built like a brick shithouse ♦ busy as a beaver (building a new dam)

bulge battle of the bulge

bulk bulk so up ♦ in bulk

bull cock-and-bull story ♦ full of bull ♦ hit the bull's-eye ♦ shoot the bull ♦ strong as a bull ♦ take the bull by the horns ♦ throw the bull

bulldoze bulldoze into sth ♦ bulldoze through sth

bullet bite the bullet ♦ sweat bullets

bullpen in the bullpen

bully Bully for you!

bum bum around (with so) ♦ bum sth off so ♦ bum so out ♦ bum out ♦ the bum's rush ♦ a bum steer ♦ bummed (out) ♦ give so a bum steer ♦ give so the bum's rush

bump bump into so ♦ bump so off ♦ Bump that! ♦ bump so/sth up ♦ goose bumps ♦ like a bump on a log

bumper bumper to bumper

bun Get your buns over here! ♦ work one's buns off

bunch a bunch of fives ♦ bunch up ♦ bunch so/sth up ♦ thanks a bunch

bundle blow a bundle (on so) ♦ bundle from heaven ♦ bundle of joy ♦ a bundle of nerves ♦ drop a bundle (on so) ♦ drop a bundle (on sth) ♦ lose a bundle ♦ make a bundle ♦ save a bundle (on sth)

bung bung sth in ♦ bung sth up ♦ bunged up

bunk bunk down (for the night) ♦ bunk (up) with so

bunny a dust bunny ♦ quick like a bunny

buoy buoy so up

burden burden so with so/sth ♦ ease so's burden

burger flip burgers

burn burn so at the stake ♦ burn one's bridges (behind one) ♦ burn one's bridges in front of one ♦ burn so down ♦ burn one's fingers ♦ burn sth in ♦ burn so in effigy ♦ burn sth into sth♦ burn out ♦ burn so out ♦ burn the candle at both ends ♦ burn the midnight oil ♦ burn sth to a crisp ♦ burn so up ♦ burn sth up ♦ burn with a low blue flame ♦ burned to a cinder ♦ burned up ♦ a burning question ♦ crash and burn ♦ do a slow burn ♦ fiddle while Rome burns ♦ get one's fingers burned ♦ have sth to burn ♦ Keep the home fires burning. ♦ Money burns a hole in so's pocket. ♦ on the back burner ♦ on the front burner ♦ put sth on the front burner ♦ slash and burn ♦ That (really) burns me (up)!

burst burst ♦ burst at the seams ♦ burst forth ♦ burst in (on so/sth) ♦ burst into sth ♦ burst into flame(s) ♦ burst into sight ♦ burst into tears ♦ burst onto the scene ♦ burst out doing sth ♦ burst out crying ♦ burst out with sth ♦ burst with sth

bury bury one's head in the sand ♦ bury oneself in sth ♦ bury the hatchet ♦ dead and buried ♦ know where all the bodies are buried

bush beat around the bush ♦ beat the bushes for so/sth ♦ A bird in the hand (is worth two in the bush). ♦ bright-eyed and bushy-tailed

bushel can't carry a tune (in a bushel basket) ♦ hide one's light under a bushel

business about one's business ♦ back in business ♦ the business ♦ business as usual ♦ the business end of sth ♦ do a land-office business ♦ do one's business ♦ funny business ♦ get down to business ♦ get one's nose out of so's business ♦ Get your nose out of my business. ♦ give so the business ♦ go about one's business ♦ go out of business ♦ have no business doing sth ♦ in business ♦ (just) taking care of business ♦ keep one's nose out of so's business ♦ Keep your nose out of my business. ♦ land-office business ♦ Let's get down to business. ♦ like nobody's business ♦ make it one's business to do sth ♦ make it one's business (to know sth) ♦ mean business ♦ mind one's own business ♦ Mind your own business. ♦ mix business with pleasure ♦ monkey business ♦ None of your business! ♦ open for business ♦ place of business ♦ send one about one's business ♦ set so up (in business) ♦ strictly business ♦ That's show business (for you).

busman a busman's holiday

bust bust a bronco ♦ bust a gut ♦ bust a move ♦ bust ass out of some place ♦ bust (one's) ass (to do sth) ♦ bust (so's) balls ♦ bust one's butt to do sth ♦ bust one's nuts to do sth ♦ bust so one ♦ bust out laughing ♦ bust out (of some place) ♦ bust so out of some place ♦ bust (some) suds ♦ bust (so's) stones ♦ bust up ♦ bust so up ♦ bust sth up ♦ bust sth wide open ♦ flat busted

bustle hustle and bustle

busy busy as a beaver (building a new dam) ♦ busy as a bee ♦ busy as a cat on a hot tin roof ♦ busy as a cranberry merchant (at Thanksgiving) ♦ busy as a fish peddler in Lent ♦ busy as a hibernating bear ♦ busy as a one-armed paperhanger ♦ busy as Grand Central Station ♦ busy as popcorn on a skillet ♦ get busy ♦ (Have you) been keeping busy? ♦ You been keeping busy?

butt bust one's butt to do sth ♦ butt in (on so/sth) ♦ the butt of a joke ♦ butt out ♦ can't find one's butt with both hands (in broad daylight) ♦ get off one's butt ♦ Get your butt over here! ♦ kick butt ♦ a kick in the butt ♦ a pain in the butt ♦ work one's butt off

butter so's bread and butter ♦ bread-and-butter letter ♦ one's (butter and) egg money ♦ butter so up ♦ look as if butter wouldn't melt in one's mouth

butterfly butterflies in one's stomach ♦ gaudy as a butterfly ♦ get butterflies in one's stomach

button bright as a button ♦ button up ♦ button (up) one's lip ♦ hit the panic button ♦ on the button ♦ press the panic button ♦ push so's buttons ♦ push the panic button

buttress buttress sth up

buy buy sth ♦ buy a pig in a poke ♦ buy a round (of drinks) ♦ buy sth for a song ♦ buy in(to sth) ♦ buy it ♦ buy so off ♦ buy sth on time ♦ buy sth sight unseen ♦ buy the big one ♦ buy the farm ♦ buy the next round (of drinks) ♦ buy time ♦ buy trouble ♦ buy one's way in(to sth) ♦ buy one's way out (of sth) ♦ buy so's wolf ticket ♦ Buy you a drink? ♦ (Can I) buy you a drink? ♦ (Could I) buy you a drink? ♦ (May I) buy you a drink? ♦ not buy sth

buzz buzz along ♦ buzz for so ♦ buzz in(to some place) ♦ buzz so into some place ♦ buzz off ♦ buzz with sth ♦ give so a buzz ♦ have a buzz on

bye Bye for now. ♦ good-bye and good riddance ♦ Good-bye for now. ♦ (Good-bye) till later. ♦ (Good-bye) until later. ♦ (Good-bye) until next time. ♦ (Good-bye) until then. ♦ kiss sth good-bye ♦ say good-bye to sth

bygone Let bygones be bygones.

byways highways and byways

C

cab hail a cab

caboodle the whole kit and caboodle

cadge cadge sth from so

cage cage so/sth in ♦ rattle so's cage

cahoots in cahoots (with so)

Cain raise Cain

cake eat one's cake and have it too ♦ flat as a pancake ♦ have one's cake and eat it too ♦ the icing on the cake ♦ nutty as a fruitcake ♦ piece of cake ♦ sell like hotcakes ♦ Shut your cake hole! ♦ a slice of the cake ♦ That takes the cake!

calf kill the fatted calf

call above and beyond (the call of duty) ♦ answer the call ♦ at so's beck and call ♦ call a halt (to sth) ♦ call a meeting ♦ call a meeting to order ♦ call a spade a spade ♦ Call again. ♦ call (all) the shots ♦ call at some place ♦ call so's attention to sth ♦ call attention to so/sth ♦ call back ♦ call so's bluff ♦ call so by a name ♦ call so down ♦ call sth down (on so) ♦ call for so/sth ♦ call hogs ♦ call so in (on sth) ♦ call in sick ♦ call sth into question ♦ call it a day ♦ call it a night ♦ call it quits ♦ Call my service. ♦ call so names ♦ the call of nature ♦ call sth off ♦ call the dogs off ♦ call on so ♦ call on sth ♦ call so on the carpet ♦ call so out ♦ call sth square ♦ call (the) roll ♦ call the tune ♦ call so to account ♦ call so to attention ♦ call sth to mind ♦ Can I call you? ♦ can't call one's soul one's own ♦ a close call ♦ Could I call you? ♦ Don't call us, we'll call you. ♦ give so a call ♦ Give me a call. ♦ have a close call ♦ last call (for sth) ♦ Let's call it a day. ♦ no call for sth ♦ not able to call one's time one's own ♦ on call ♦ pay a call ♦ pay a call on so ♦ a place to call one's own ♦ put sth in will-call ♦ so/sth to call one's own ♦ too close to call ♦ a tough call ♦ within calling distance

calm the calm before the storm ♦ cool, calm, and collected

camel the straw that broke the camel's back

camp break camp ♦ camp it up ♦ camp out (some place) ♦ a foot in both camps ♦ a happy camper ◆ have a foot in both camps ◆ pitch camp

campaign a smear campaign (against so)

campus big man on campus ◆ off campus ◆ on campus

can live out of cans

canary look like the cat that swallowed the canary

cancel cancel so's Christmas ◆ cancel each other out ◆ cancel out (of sth) ◆ cancel so out of sth

candidate a candidate for a pair of wings

candle bell, book, and candle ◆ burn the candle at both ends ◆ not hold a candle to so/sth

candy as easy as taking candy from a baby ◆ like taking candy from a baby

cannon a loose cannon

canoe paddle one's own canoe

cap cap and gown ◆ a feather in one's cap ◆ put a cap on sth ◆ put one's thinking cap on

capital with a capital letter name

capitalize capitalize on sth

captain captain of industry

capture capture so's imagination

car wrap one's car around sth

card a card ◆ card-carrying member ◆ the cards are stacked against so ◆ a drawing card ◆ a few cards short of a deck ◆ have the cards stacked against one ◆ hold all the cards ◆ a house of cards ◆ in the cards ◆ keep one's cards close to one's vest ◆ lay one's cards on the table ◆ play one's cards close to one's chest ◆ play one's cards close to one's vest ◆ play one's cards right ◆ play one's cards well ◆ play the race card ◆ play one's trump card ◆ put one's cards on the table ◆ stack the cards (against so/sth) ◆ the race card

care beyond caring ◆ care for sth ◆ could(n't) care less ◆ devil-may-care attitude ◆ devil-may-care manner ◆ didn't care a whit ◆ don't care who knows it ◆ for all I care ◆ (I) could(n't) care less. ◆ in so's care ◆ in care of so ◆ in the care of so ◆ (just) taking care of business ◆ not care a fig ◆ not care two hoots about so/sth ◆ not have a care in the world ◆ past caring ◆ take care of so ◆ take care of number one

◆ take care of some loose ends ◆ Take care (of yourself). ◆ That takes care of that. ◆ under so's care

career turn sth into a career

caress cold as a witch's caress

carnal have carnal knowledge of so

carpet call so on the carpet ◆ haul so on the carpet ◆ the red-carpet treatment ◆ roll out the red carpet (for so) ◆ sweep sth under the carpet

carriage went out with the horse and carriage

carry can't carry a tune in a bucket ◆ can't carry a tune (in a bushel basket) ◆ can't carry a tune in a paper sack ◆ card-carrying member ◆ carry (a lot of) weight (with so/sth) ◆ carry a secret to the grave ◆ carry a torch (for so) ◆ carry one's cross ◆ carry on ◆ carry on (about so/sth) ◆ carry sth out ◆ carry one's (own) weight ◆ carry the ball ◆ carry the day ◆ carry the torch ◆ carry the weight of the world on one's shoulders ◆ carry so through sth ◆ carry weight (with so) ◆ cash-and-carry ◆ get carried away

cart have the cart before the horse ◆ put the cart before the horse ◆ upset the apple cart

carte carte blanche ◆ give so carte blanche

Carter more sth than Carter has (liver) pills

carve carve sth in stone ◆ carve out a niche ◆ carve out a reputation ◆ carved in stone

case a basket case ◆ the best-case scenario ◆ a case in point ◆ a case of sth ◆ a case of mistaken identity ◆ a case of the blind leading the blind ◆ case so/sth out ◆ case the joint ◆ a feeling (that sth is the case) ◆ get down to cases ◆ Get off so's case! ◆ get on so's case ◆ have a case (against so) ◆ have a case of sth ◆ have a hunch (that sth is the case) ◆ I rest my case. ◆ in any case ◆ in case (sth happens) ◆ in case of sth ◆ in the case of so/sth ◆ just in case ◆ live out of a suitcase ◆ make a case for sth ◆ make a federal case out of sth ◆ a nut case ◆ on so's case ◆ an open-and-shut case ◆ the worst-case scenario

cash cash-and-carry ◆ cash one's checks in ◆ cash (one's chips) in ◆ cash flow problem

chance ◆ a slim chance ◆ a sporting chance ◆ stand a chance (of doing sth) ◆ take a chance on so/sth ◆ take your chances ◆ when you get a chance

change and change ◆ change for the better ◆ change hands ◆ change horses in midstream ◆ change horses in the middle of the stream ◆ change so's mind ◆ the change (of life) ◆ a change of pace ◆ a change of scenery ◆ change off ◆ change out of sth ◆ change places (with so) ◆ change the channel ◆ change the subject ◆ change one's tune ◆ change so's tune ◆ change one's ways ◆ change with the times ◆ a chunk of change ◆ for a change ◆ go through the changes ◆ have a change of heart ◆ make change (for so) (for sth) ◆ a sea change ◆ small change

channel change the channel ◆ go through (the proper) channels ◆ work through channels

chapter chapter and verse

character character assassination ◆ in character ◆ out of character ◆ a shady character ◆ a suspicious character

charge charge (of so/sth) ◆ get a charge out of so/sth ◆ give so a charge ◆ in the charge of so ◆ level a charge against so ◆ take charge (of so/sth)

charley a charley horse

charm charm the pants off so ◆ work like a charm

chart off the charts

chase (always) chasing rainbows ◆ ambulance chaser ◆ chase so/sth down ◆ chasing rainbows ◆ cut to the chase ◆ give chase (to so/sth) ◆ Go chase yourself! ◆ lead so on a merry chase ◆ send so on a wild-goose chase ◆ a wild-goose chase

cheap cheap at half the price ◆ dirt cheap ◆ on the cheap

cheat cheat on so

check a blank check ◆ cash one's checks in ◆ check sth at the door ◆ check so's bags through (to some place) ◆ check sth in ◆ check into sth ◆ check so's luggage through (to some place) ◆ check so/sth out ◆ check out the plumbing ◆ Check, please. ◆ check that ◆ check so/sth through (sth) ◆ checks and balances ◆ Could I have the check? ◆

cut (so) a check ◆ double-check ◆ give so a blank check ◆ hold so/sth in check ◆ honor so's check ◆ keep so/sth in check ◆ need a reality check ◆ pick up the check (for sth) ◆ a rain check (on sth) ◆ a reality check ◆ a sanity check

checkup a checkup

cheek cheek by jowl ◆ put the roses back into so's cheeks ◆ tongue-in-cheek ◆ turn the other cheek

cheese cheese so off ◆ cheesed off ◆ Say cheese!

cherry cherry pick sth ◆ red as a cherry

Cheshire smiling like a Cheshire cat

chest get sth off one's chest ◆ play one's cards close to one's chest ◆ put hair on so's chest ◆ take the spear (in one's chest)

chew angry enough to chew nails ◆ bite off more than one can chew ◆ chew on sth ◆ chew so out ◆ chew sth over ◆ chew the fat ◆ chew the rag ◆ chew so/sth up ◆ chew one's cud ◆ mad enough to chew nails (and spit rivets)

chicken chicken feed ◆ chicken-hearted ◆ chicken out (of sth) ◆ count one's chickens before they hatch ◆ for chicken feed ◆ go to bed with the chickens ◆ no spring chicken ◆ run around like a chicken with its head cut off

chief chief cook and bottle washer

child child's play ◆ expecting (a child) ◆ a poster child (for sth) ◆ with child

childhood in one's second childhood

chill chill out ◆ chilled to the bone ◆ put the chill on so ◆ take the chill off ((of) some place)

chime chime in (with sth)

chimney smoke like a chimney

chin chin music ◆ chuck so under the chin ◆ keep one's chin up ◆ Keep your chin up. ◆ make chin music ◆ take it on the chin ◆ take sth on the chin ◆ wag one's chin

China not for all the tea in China

chink a chink in one's armor

chip bargaining chip ◆ cash (one's chips) in ◆ chip in (on sth) ◆ chip in (with sth) (on sth) (for so) ◆ a chip off the old block ◆ a chip on one's shoulder ◆ have a chip on one's shoulder ◆ in the chips ◆ let the chips fall (where they may) ♦ when the chips are down

chisel chisel in (on so/sth) ♦ chisel so out of sth

chock chock full of sth

choice Hobson's choice

choir preach to the choir

choke choke up

chomp chomp at the bit

choose choose (up) sides ♦ nothing to choose from ♦ pick and choose

chops lick one's chops

chord strike a chord (with so)

chow chow (sth) down

Christmas cancel so's Christmas

chuck chuck it in ♦ chuck so under the chin

chunk a chunk of change

church church key ♦ poor as a church mouse ♦ quiet as a (church) mouse ♦ See you in church. ♦ the separation of church and state ♦ You go to your church, and I'll go to mine.

churn churn sth out

chute down the chute ♦ go down the chute

cigar Close, but no cigar.

cinch have sth cinched ♦ It's a (dead) cinch. ♦ a lead-pipe cinch

cinder burned to a cinder

circle come full circle ♦ go (a)round in circles ♦ in a vicious circle ♦ run (around) in circles ♦ run circles around so ♦ talk in circles

circulation back in(to) circulation ♦ get back in(to) circulation ♦ out of circulation

circumstance extenuating circumstances ♦ in reduced circumstances ♦ under certain circumstances ♦ under no circumstances ♦ under the circumstances

circus like a three-ring circus

city beat city hall ♦ city slicker ♦ fight city hall ♦ inner city ♦ That's life in the big city. ♦ You can't fight city hall.

civil keep a civil tongue (in one's head)

claim claim a life ♦ so's claim to fame ♦ lay claim to sth ♦ stake (out) a claim to sth

clam clam up ♦ happy as a clam (at high tide)

clamp clamp down on so ♦ clamp down on sth ♦ put the clamps on so/sth

clap clap so in(to) some place

class cut class ♦ in a class by oneself or itself ♦ out of so's class

clause a grandfather clause

claw claw one's way to the top ♦ one's claws are showing

clay have feet of clay

clean clean one's act up ♦ clean as a hound's tooth ♦ clean as a whistle ♦ a clean bill of health ♦ clean so out ♦ clean one's plate (up) ♦ a clean sweep ♦ clean the floor up with so ♦ clean up good ♦ clean up (on sth) ♦ clean up well ♦ clean-cut ♦ cleaned out ♦ come clean (with so) (about sth) ♦ give so a clean bill of health ♦ have clean hands ♦ keep one's hands clean ♦ keep one's nose clean ♦ make a clean breast of sth (to so) ♦ make a clean sweep ♦ poor but clean ♦ so clean you could eat off the floor ♦ start (off) with a clean slate ♦ start (over) with a clean slate ♦ take so to the cleaners ♦ wipe so's slate clean

cleaners take so to the cleaners

clear clear as a bell ♦ clear as crystal ♦ clear as mud ♦ a clear conscience (about so/sth) ♦ clear so's name ♦ clear of sth ♦ clear off ((of) some place) ♦ clear out (of some place) ♦ clear sailing ♦ clear the air ♦ clear the decks ♦ clear the table ♦ Clear the way! ♦ clear one's throat ♦ The coast is clear. ♦ come out of a clear blue sky ♦ Do I make myself (perfectly) clear? ♦ free and clear ♦ Have I made myself clear? ♦ I read you loud and clear. ♦ in the clear ♦ keep clear of sth ♦ loud and clear ♦ make sth clear to so ♦ make so's position clear ♦ see one's way (clear) (to do sth) ♦ stay clear of so/sth ♦ steer clear of so/sth

click click with so

climax bring sth to a climax

climb climb on the bandwagon ♦ climb the wall(s) ♦ Go climb a tree!

clip at a good clip ♦ clip so's wings ♦ travel at a good clip

cloak cloak-and-dagger ♦ cloak so/sth in secrecy

collar blue-collar ◆ hot under the collar ◆ white-collar

collect collect one's thoughts ◆ cool, calm, and collected

college old college try

color come through sth (with flying colors) ◆ a horse of a different color ◆ a horse of another color ◆ lend color to sth ◆ off-color ◆ a riot of color ◆ sail under false colors ◆ see the color of so's money ◆ show one's (true) colors ◆ so's true colors ◆ with flying colors

Columbia give so Hail Columbia

coma lapse into a coma

comb go over sth with a fine-tooth(ed) comb ◆ go through sth with a fine-tooth(ed) comb ◆ run a comb through sth ◆ search sth with a fine-tooth(ed) comb

come as some quality as they come ◆ blow so/sth to kingdom come ◆ come a cropper ◆ come about ◆ come across ◆ come across so/sth ◆ come across like so/sth (to so) ◆ come across (to sth) ◆ come across (with sth) ◆ Come again. ◆ Come an(d) get it! ◆ come apart (at the seams) ◆ come (a)round ◆ come around (again) ◆ come around (to doing sth) ◆ come as no surprise ◆ come at a price ◆ come away empty-handed ◆ Come back and see us. ◆ Come back anytime. ◆ come back (to so/sth) ◆ come back to haunt one ◆ Come back when you can stay longer. ◆ come before so/sth ◆ come by sth ◆ come by sth honestly ◆ come clean (with so) (about sth) ◆ come close (to so/sth) ◆ come down ◆ come down (from sth) ◆ come down (hard) on so ◆ come down (hard) on sth ◆ come down in the world ◆ come down on the side of so/sth ◆ come down to sth ◆ come down to earth ◆ come forward with sth ◆ come from behind ◆ come from far and wide ◆ come from nowhere ◆ come full circle ◆ come hell or high water ◆ come home (to so) ◆ come home (to roost) ◆ come in ◆ Come in and get some weight off your feet. ◆ Come in and make yourself at home. ◆ Come in and sit a spell. ◆ Come in and sit down. ◆ Come in and take a load off your feet. ◆ come in for sth ◆ come in handy ◆ come in on a

wing and a prayer ◆ come in out of the cold ◆ come in out of the rain ◆ come in useful ◆ come into (some) money ◆ come into a fortune ◆ come into being ◆ come into bloom ◆ come into blossom ◆ come into so's hands ◆ come in(to) heat ◆ come into one's or its own ◆ come into play ◆ come into season ◆ come into service ◆ come into the world ◆ come Monday ◆ come naturally (to so) ◆ come of age ◆ come off ◆ come off as so/sth ◆ Come off it! ◆ come off second best ◆ come on ◆ come on as sth ◆ come on (duty) ◆ Come on in. ◆ Come on in, the water's fine! ◆ come on like gangbusters ◆ come on strong ◆ come on the scene ◆ come on (to so) ◆ come on(to) so/sth ◆ come out ◆ come out against so/sth ◆ come out at an amount ◆ come out fighting ◆ come out for so/sth ◆ come out in favor of so/sth ◆ come out in the wash ◆ come out in(to) the open ◆ come out in(to) the open with sth ◆ come out (of sth) ◆ come out of a clear blue sky ◆ come out of left field ◆ come out of nowhere ◆ come out of one's shell ◆ come out of the closet ◆ come out on sth ◆ come out on top ◆ come out smelling like a rose ◆ come out swinging ◆ come out with sth ◆ come over so ◆ come rain or (come) shine ◆ Come right in. ◆ come (right) on top of sth ◆ come short of sth ◆ come through ◆ come through sth (with flying colors) ◆ come to ◆ come to oneself ◆ come to sth ◆ come to a bad end ◆ come to a boil ◆ come to a conclusion ◆ come to a dead end ◆ come to a head ◆ come to a pretty pass ◆ come to an untimely end ◆ come to so's attention ◆ come to attention ◆ come to blows (over so/sth) ◆ come to one's feet ◆ come to grief ◆ come to grips with so/sth ◆ come to life ◆ come to light ◆ come to mind ◆ come to much ◆ come to naught ◆ come to no good ◆ come to nothing ◆ come to so's notice ◆ come to pass ◆ come to one's senses ◆ come to terms (with so/sth) ◆ come to the same thing ◆ come to think of it ◆ come to this ◆ come true ◆ come under sth ◆ come under the hammer ◆ come unglued ◆ come up ◆ come up for sth ◆ come up for air ♦ come (up) from behind ♦ come up heads ♦ come up in the world ♦ come up smelling like a rose ♦ come up tails ♦ come up through the ranks ♦ come up to so's expectations ♦ come up to so's standards ♦ come up with so/sth ♦ come (up)on so/sth ♦ come what may ♦ come with the territory ♦ come within an ace of sth ♦ come within an inch of doing sth ♦ come-hither look ♦ comes down the pike ♦ coming out of one's ears ♦ Could I come in? ♦ cross bridges before one comes to them ♦ cross that bridge before one comes to it ♦ cross that bridge when one comes to it ♦ a dream come true ♦ easy come, easy go ♦ easy to come by ♦ Everything's coming up roses. ♦ the first thing that comes into one's head ♦ get what's coming to one ♦ (had) known it was coming ♦ a harbinger of things to come ♦ hard to come by ♦ has come and gone ♦ have come a long way ♦ have (got) sth coming (to one) ♦ How come? ♦ if push comes to shove ♦ It'll all come out in the wash. ♦ Johnny-come-lately ♦ knew it was coming ♦ know where one is coming from ♦ May I come in? ♦ not know enough to come in out of the rain ♦ not know if one is coming or going ♦ not know whether one is coming or going ♦ put two and two together and come up with five ♦ see sth coming ♦ speak of the devil (and in he comes) ♦ take it as it comes ♦ They must have seen you coming. ♦ This is where I came in. ♦ till kingdom come ♦ till the cows come home ♦ so's time has come ♦ (un)til the cows come home ♦ up-and-coming ♦ What's coming off? ♦ what's coming to one ♦ What's the world coming to? ♦ whatever comes down the pike ♦ whatever comes into one's head (first) ♦ when it comes right down to it ♦ when it comes to sth ♦ when it comes to the crunch ♦ when push comes to shove ♦ when one's ship comes in ♦ where one is coming from ♦ You've got another think coming.

comeback make a comeback

comedy Cut the comedy!

comeuppance get one's comeuppance

comfort cold comfort ♦ creature comforts ♦ too close for comfort

comfortable comfortable as an old shoe

command the chain of command ♦ have a good command of sth

comment No comment.

commission out of commission

commit commit to so ♦ commit to sth ♦ commit sth to memory

commode commode-hugging drunk

common common as an old shoe ♦ common as dirt ♦ a common thread (to all this) ♦ have sth in common (with so/sth) ♦ in the Common Era

commotion cause a commotion ♦ create a commotion

company in good company ♦ One is known by the company one keeps. ♦ keep so company ♦ keep company (with so) ♦ part company (with so)

compare compare apples and oranges

comparison pale by comparison

compliment backhanded compliment ♦ fish for a compliment ♦ left-handed compliment ♦ pay so a backhanded compliment ♦ pay so a compliment ♦ pay so a left-handed compliment ♦ return the compliment

composure regain one's composure

comprise comprised of so/sth

compromise reach a compromise

concealment a place of concealment

concern as far as so is concerned ♦ as far as sth is concerned ♦ so far as so is concerned ♦ so far as sth is concerned ♦ to whom it may concern

concert in concert (with so)

conclusion come to a conclusion ♦ a foregone conclusion ♦ in conclusion . . . ♦ jump to conclusions ♦ leap to conclusions ♦ reach a conclusion ♦ rush to conclusions

concrete set in concrete

condition in a delicate condition ♦ in an interesting condition ♦ in condition ♦ in good condition ♦ in mint condition ♦ in the pink (of condition) ♦ out of condition

confidence take so into one's confidence ♦ a vote of confidence

confusion lost in the confusion

Congress it would take an act of Congress to do sth

conk conk out

connect connect (with so)

conniption have a conniption (fit)

conquer divide and conquer

conscience a clear conscience (about so/sth) ♦ in (all) good conscience

consciousness bring so around (to consciousness)

consequence face the consequences ♦ in consequence (of sth) ♦ suffer the consequences ♦ take the consequences

consider all things considered

consideration in consideration of sth ♦ out of consideration (for so/sth) ♦ take sth into consideration

consignment on consignment

conspicuous be conspicuous by one's absence ♦ conspicuous by one's absence ♦ make oneself conspicuous

constant in a (constant) state of flux

construction under construction

contempt beneath contempt ♦ in contempt (of court)

content to one's heart's content

contention bone of contention

contest no contest

context in the context of sth ♦ out of context ♦ take sth out of context

contract put a contract out on so

contradiction a contradiction in terms

contrary on the contrary ♦ to the contrary

control control the purse strings ♦ out of control ♦ rage out of control ♦ under control

convenience at so's earliest convenience

conversation open a conversation ♦ strike up a conversation (with so)

converted preach to the converted

conviction have the courage of one's convictions

cook chief cook and bottle washer ♦ cook so's goose ♦ cook the accounts ♦ cook the books ♦ cook sth up (with so) ♦ cooking with gas ♦ one's goose is cooked ♦ What's cooking?

cookie blow one's cookies ♦ juice and cookies ♦ shoot one's cookies ♦ snap one's cookies ♦ toss one's cookies ♦ a tough cookie ♦ tough cookies

cool blow one's cool ♦ cool as a cucumber ♦ cool, calm, and collected ♦ cool so down ♦ cool down ♦ cool one's heels ♦ Cool it! ♦ cool so off ♦ cool off ♦ cool out ♦ (Have you) been keeping cool? ♦ keep one's cool ♦ keep cool ♦ lose one's cool ♦ play it cool ♦ You been keeping cool?

cooler cooler heads prevail

coon in a coon's age

coop fly the coop

coot bald as a coot

cop cop a packet ♦ cop a plea ♦ cop a squat ♦ cop an attitude ♦ cop onto sth ♦ cop out ♦ cop out (of sth) ♦ cop some Zs

cope cope with so/sth

cord cut the (umbilical) cord

core rotten to the core ♦ to the core

cork blow one's cork ♦ pop one's cork

corn busy as popcorn on a skillet

corner around the corner ♦ back so into a corner ♦ corner the market (on sth) ♦ cut corners ♦ from all corners of the world ♦ from the four corners of the earth ♦ have a corner on the market (for sth) ♦ have so/sth cornered ♦ have so in one's corner ♦ out of the corner of one's eye ♦ paint so into a corner ♦ turn the corner

correct if my memory serves (me correctly) ♦ stand corrected

correction house of correction

cost at a cost ♦ at all costs ♦ at any cost ♦ cost a pretty penny ♦ cost an arm and a leg ♦ cost sth out ♦ cost the earth

couch couch sth in sth ♦ a couch potato

cough cough one's head off ♦ cough sth up

counsel keep one's own counsel

count count so among sth ♦ count one's blessings ♦ count one's chickens before they hatch ♦ count for naught ♦ count heads ♦ count so in ♦ count noses ♦ count on so/sth ♦ count so out ♦ down for the count ♦ every minute counts ♦ every moment counts ♦ (I) wouldn't count on it. ♦ take the (long) count

counted stand up and be counted

counter over the counter ♦ run counter to sth ♦ under the counter

country another country heard from ♦ a country mile

couple a couple of ♦ a couple three

courage Dutch courage ♦ get enough courage up (to do sth) ♦ have the courage of one's convictions ♦ screw up one's courage

course as a matter of course ♦ course of action ♦ a crash course in sth ♦ in due course ♦ in the course of time ♦ let nature take its course ♦ of course ♦ off course ♦ on course ♦ par for the course ♦ run its course ♦ stay the course ♦ take its course

court appear in court ♦ the ball in so's court ♦ the ball is in so's court ♦ hold court ♦ in contempt (of court) ♦ a kangaroo court ♦ laugh sth out of court ♦ pay court to so ♦ settle (sth) (out of court) ♦ stand up in court ♦ take so to court

courtesy out of courtesy (to so)

courtship whirlwind courtship

cousin kissing cousins ♦ think so is God's own cousin

cover blow so's cover ♦ cover a lot of ground ♦ cover a multitude of sins ♦ cover all the bases ♦ cover one's ass ♦ cover for so ♦ cover the territory ♦ cover the waterfront ♦ cover so's tracks (up) ♦ cover sth up ♦ cover (up) for so ♦ duck and cover ♦ from cover to cover ♦ make sure all the bases are covered ♦ not to judge a book by its cover ♦ take cover

cow awkward as a cow on a crutch ♦ awkward as a cow on roller skates ♦ cow juice ♦ Don't have a cow! ♦ Holy cow! ♦ a sacred cow ♦ till the cows come home ♦ (un)til the cows come home

coward take the coward's way out

crack at the crack of dawn ♦ crack a book ♦ crack a bottle open ♦ crack a joke ♦ crack a smile ♦ a crack at so ♦ a crack at sth ♦ crack down (on so/sth) ♦ crack some suds ♦ crack the door (open) ♦ crack the window (open) ♦ crack under the strain ♦ crack up ♦ crack so up ♦ crack sth (wide) open ♦ cracked ♦ cracked up to be sth ♦ dirty crack ♦ fall through the cracks ♦ first crack at sth ♦ a hard nut to crack ♦ make cracks about so/sth ♦ not all sth is cracked up to be ♦ slip between the cracks ♦ slip

through the cracks ♦ through the cracks ♦ a tough nut to crack ♦ what so/sth is cracked up to be

cradle from the cradle to the grave ♦ rob the cradle

cram cram for an exam(ination)

cramp cramp so's style

cranberry busy as a cranberry merchant (at Thanksgiving)

crank crank sth out ♦ crank so up ♦ crank sth up

cranny every nook and cranny

crap crap out ♦ crap out (of sth) ♦ crap out (of sth) (on so) ♦ full of crap ♦ shoot the crap ♦ throw the crap

crash bring sth crashing down (around one) ♦ crash and burn ♦ a crash course in sth ♦ crash down (around so/sth) ♦ crash with so

craw have sth stick in one's craw

crawl crawl out of the woodwork ♦ crawling with so ♦ crawling with some kind of creature ♦ make so's flesh crawl ♦ make so's skin crawl

crazy be crazy about so/sth ♦ crazy as a betsy bug ♦ crazy as a loon ♦ crazy as a peach-orchard boar ♦ crazy bone ♦ crazy in the head ♦ drive so crazy ♦ go crazy ♦ go stir crazy ♦ like crazy ♦ stir crazy

cream the cream of the crop

create create a commotion ♦ create a scene ♦ create a stink (about sth) ♦ create an uproar

creation all over creation

creature creature comforts

credence give credence to so/sth

credit cash or credit ♦ a credit to so/sth ♦ credit so with sth ♦ do so credit ♦ do credit to so ♦ (a lot of) credit (for sth) ♦ (much) credit (for sth) ♦ on credit

creek God willing and the creek don't rise. ♦ Lord willing and the creek don't rise. ♦ up shit creek ♦ up the creek (without a paddle)

creep creep across sth ♦ the creeps

crib crib sth from so/sth

crick a crick in one's back ♦ a crick in one's neck

cricket It's not cricket. ♦ merry as a cricket

crime partners in crime

crisp burn sth to a crisp

criticism open to criticism ◆ open oneself to criticism

crocodile After while(, crocodile). ◆ cry crocodile tears ◆ shed crocodile tears

crook by hook or (by) crook

crooked crooked as a barrel of fish hooks ◆ crooked as a dog's hind leg ◆ crooked as a fish hook

crop the cream of the crop ◆ crop up

cropper come a cropper

cross at cross-purposes ◆ bear one's cross ◆ carry one's cross ◆ cross so ◆ cross bridges before one comes to them ◆ cross one's fingers ◆ cross one's heart (and hope to die) ◆ cross so's mind ◆ cross so/sth off (of) sth ◆ cross so/sth out ◆ cross over ◆ cross (over) the line ◆ cross so's palm with silver ◆ cross paths (with so) ◆ cross swords (with so) ◆ cross that bridge before one comes to it ◆ cross that bridge when one comes to it ◆ cross the Rubicon ◆ cross so up ◆ cross-examine so ◆ have one's wires crossed ◆ keep one's fingers crossed (for so/sth) ◆ look at so cross-eyed ◆ nail so to a cross ◆ operating at cross purposes ◆ star-crossed lovers ◆ working at cross purposes

crossfire caught in the crossfire

crosshairs in one's crosshairs

crossroad at a crossroad(s)

crow as the crow flies ◆ crow about sth ◆ crow bait ◆ crow over sth ◆ eat crow ◆ hoarse as a crow ◆ make so eat crow

crowd far from the madding crowd ◆ follow the crowd ◆ play to the crowd ◆ stand out from the crowd

crown crown so with sth

cruise cruisin(g) for a bruisin(g)

crumb crum(b) sth up

crunch when it comes to the crunch ◆ when it gets down to the crunch

crush a crush on so ◆ crushed by sth

crust upper crust

crutch awkward as a cow on a crutch ◆ funny as a crutch

crux the crux of the matter

cry burst out crying ◆ cry all the way to the bank ◆ cry before one is hurt ◆ cry bloody murder ◆ cry crocodile tears ◆ cry one's eyes out ◆ cry one's heart out ◆ cry in one's beer ◆ cry out for sth ◆ cry over spilled milk ◆ cry oneself to sleep ◆ cry uncle ◆ cry wolf ◆ a crying need (for so/sth) ◆ a crying shame ◆ a far cry from sth ◆ For crying in a bucket! ◆ For crying out loud! ◆ a hue and cry (about sth) ◆ not know whether to laugh or cry ◆ a voice crying in the wilderness

crystal clear as crystal

cucumber cool as a cucumber

cud chew one's cud

cuddle cuddle up with a (good) book

cue cue so in ◆ on cue ◆ take one's cue from so

cuff off-the-cuff ◆ put sth on the cuff ◆ speak off the cuff

cunning cunning as a fox

cup cup one's hands together ◆ in one's cups ◆ just one's cup of tea ◆ not one's cup of tea ◆ a tempest in a teacup

curdle curdle so's blood

cure take the cure

curiosity die from curiosity ◆ die of curiosity ◆ pique so's curiosity

curl curl so's hair ◆ curl up and die ◆ curl up (with a (good) book) ◆ curly dirt ◆ make so's hair curl

currency give currency to sth

current swim against the current

curry curry favor with so

curtain bring the curtain down (on sth) ◆ curtain falls on sth ◆ ring the curtain down (on sth) ◆ ring the curtain up

curve pitch so a curve (ball) ◆ throw so a curve (ball)

cushion cushion the blow

cusp on the cusp (of sth)

cuss cuss so out

customer one to a customer ◆ a slippery customer ◆ a tough customer

cut able to cut sth ◆ clean-cut ◆ cut a big swath ◆ cut so a break ◆ cut (so) a check ◆ cut a dashing figure ◆ cut a deal ◆ cut a fine figure ◆ cut a long story short ◆ cut a rug ◆ cut a wide swath ◆ a cut above sth ◆ a cut above average ◆ cut across sth ◆ cut against the grain ◆ cut and dried ◆ cut and paste ◆ cut and run ◆ cut both ways ◆ cut class ◆ cut corners ◆ cut sth down ◆ cut down (on sth) ◆ cut so down to size ◆

619 Key Word Index

cut one's (eye)teeth on sth ♦ cut from the same cloth ♦ cut in ♦ Cut it out! ♦ cut loose (with sth) ♦ cut one's losses ♦ cut no ice (with so) ♦ cut so off at the pass ♦ cut off one's nose to spite one's face ♦ cut so off without a penny ♦ cut out (for some place) ♦ cut out to be sth ♦ cut one's (own) throat ♦ cut school ♦ cut so some slack ♦ cut some Zs ♦ cut teeth ♦ Cut the comedy! ♦ cut the deadwood out ♦ cut the dust ♦ Cut the funny stuff! ♦ cut the ground out from under so ♦ cut the pie up ♦ cut the (umbilical) cord ♦ cut through red tape ♦ cut to so/sth ♦ cut so/sth to ribbons ♦ cut so to the bone ♦ cut sth to the bone ♦ cut to the chase ♦ cut so to the quick ♦ cut up ♦ cut up (about so/sth) ♦ cut so's water off ♦ cut one's wolf loose ♦ end up on the cutting room floor ♦ Fish or cut bait. ♦ have one's work cut out for one ♦ It cuts two ways. ♦ on the cutting edge ♦ run around like a chicken with its head cut off ♦ one's work is cut out for one

cute cute as a bug's ear

cylinder firing on all cylinders ♦ hitting on all cylinders ♦ run on all cylinders

D

dab smack (dab) in the middle

daddy the daddy of them all

dagger cloak-and-dagger ♦ look daggers at so ♦ shoot daggers at so

daily daily dozen ♦ the daily grind

daisy fresh as a daisy ♦ pushing up (the) daisies

dam busy as a beaver (building a new dam) ♦ water over the dam

damage acceptable damage ♦ do so damage ♦ What's the damage?

damn a (damn) sight better ♦ damn so/sth with faint praise ♦ do one's damnedest ♦ Hellfire and damnation! ♦ Hot damn! ♦ I'm damned if I do and damned if I don't. ♦ not give a (tinker's) damn ♦ not worth a damn

damnation Hellfire and damnation!

damper put a damper on sth

dance dance at so's wedding ♦ dance on air ♦ dance to a different tune ♦ dance to another tune ♦ dance with death ♦ go into a song and dance (about sth) ♦ go into one's song and dance ♦ go into the same old song and dance (about sth) ♦ tap dance like mad

dander get so's dander up

dandy fine and dandy ♦ jim dandy

danger fly into the face of danger ♦ fraught with danger

dangerous armed and dangerous ♦ on dangerous ground ♦ regarded as armed and dangerous

Danish coffee and Danish

dare How dare you!

dark a dark cloud (looming) on the horizon ♦ dark horse ♦ the dark side of so/sth ♦ darken so's door ♦ in the dark (about so/sth) ♦ a shot in the dark ♦ whistle in the dark

darn darn tootin(g)

dart dart a glance at so/sth

dash cut a dashing figure ♦ dash a letter off ♦ dash a note off ♦ dash away ♦ dash cold water on sth ♦ dash so's hopes ♦ dash off ♦ dash sth to pieces

dashing cut a dashing figure

date at an early date ♦ bring so/sth up-to-date ♦ bring so up-to-date (on so/sth) ♦ drop dead date ♦ keep a date open (for so/sth) ♦ leave a date open (for so/sth) ♦ out-of-date ♦ to date ♦ up-to-date

Davy Davy Jones's locker

dawn at the break of dawn ♦ at the crack of dawn ♦ dawn (up)on so ♦ from dawn to dusk

day all day long ♦ all hours (of the day and night) ♦ all in a day's work ♦ all the livelong day ♦ at the end of the day ♦ a bad hair day ♦ by day ♦ by the day ♦ by the end of the day ♦ call it a day ♦ carry the day ♦ day after day ♦ day and night ♦ day by day ♦ day in and day out ♦ a day late and a dollar short ♦ the day off ♦ day one ♦ a day person ♦ day-to-day ♦ day-tripper ♦ one's days are numbered ♦ days running ♦ different as night and day ♦ dog days ♦ Don't give up your day job. ♦ Don't quit your day job. ♦ sth du jour ♦ first see the light of day ♦ for days on end ♦ for (some) days running ♦ forever and a day ♦ from day to day ♦ from this day forward ♦ from this day on ♦ (Go ahead,) make my day! ♦ Great day (in the morning)! ♦ have a field day ♦ Have a good day. ♦ Have a nice day. ♦ have had its day ♦ have seen better days ♦ hold sth back for a rainy day ♦ if one's a day ♦ in all my born days ♦ in one's salad days ♦ in this day and age ♦ It'll be a cold day in hell when sth happens. ♦ keep sth for a rainy day ♦ late in the day ♦ Let's call it a day. ♦ live from day to day ♦ live out one's days ♦ the Lord's Day ♦ make a day of doing sth ♦ make a day of it ♦ Make my day! ♦ merry as the day is long ♦ night and day ♦ a nine days' wonder ♦ not give so the time of day ♦ one day at a time ♦ one of these days ♦ the order of the day ♦ pass the time (of day) ♦ pass the time of day ♦ plain as day ♦ put sth aside for a rainy day ♦ put in a hard day at work ♦ a red-letter day ♦ save (sth) for a rainy day ♦ save the day ♦ see the light (of day) ♦ seize the day ♦ a seven-day wonder ♦ since day one ♦ take the day off ♦ That'll be the day! ♦ There aren't enough hours in the day. ♦ Those were the days. ♦ three squares (a day) ♦ win the day

daylight beat the living daylights out of so ♦ begin to see daylight ♦ can't find one's butt with both hands (in broad daylight) ♦ frighten the living daylights out of so ♦ in broad daylight ♦ knock the (living) daylights out of so ♦ scare the living daylights out of so

days the good old days

dead at a dead end ♦ (bang) dead to rights ♦ beat a dead horse ♦ bring sth to a dead end ♦ come to a dead end ♦ dead ahead ♦ dead and buried ♦ dead and gone ♦ dead as a dodo ♦ dead as a doornail ♦ dead broke ♦ dead center ♦ dead certain ♦ dead drunk ♦ a dead duck ♦ dead easy ♦ dead from the neck up ♦ a dead giveaway ♦ dead in the water ♦ dead letter ♦ a dead loss ♦ dead meat ♦ dead on ♦ dead on arrival ♦ dead on one's feet ♦ a (dead) ringer (for so) ♦ dead

serious ♦ dead set against so/sth ♦ dead to rights ♦ dead to the world ♦ dead wrong ♦ dead-end kid ♦ deader than a doornail ♦ deadly dull ♦ drop dead ♦ drop-dead date ♦ drop-dead gorgeous ♦ faint dead away ♦ flog a dead horse ♦ give so up for dead ♦ have so dead to rights ♦ have one's heart (dead) set against sth ♦ one's heart is (dead) set against sth ♦ in a dead heat ♦ It's a (dead) cinch. ♦ knock so dead ♦ leave so for dead ♦ look like a (dead) ringer (for so) ♦ more dead than alive ♦ on dead center ♦ Over my dead body! ♦ play dead ♦ raise so from the dead ♦ rise from the dead ♦ roll over and play dead ♦ silent as the dead ♦ stone dead ♦ stop (dead) in one's tracks ♦ stop so/sth dead in so's/sth's tracks ♦ take so for dead ♦ taken for dead ♦ wake the dead ♦ would not be caught dead (doing sth) ♦ would not be seen dead (doing sth)

deadline under a deadline

deadwood cut the deadwood out

deaf deaf and dumb ♦ deaf as a post ♦ fall on deaf ears ♦ turn a deaf ear (to so/sth)

deal close a deal ♦ cut a deal ♦ deal so/sth a death blow ♦ deal so/sth a fatal blow ♦ deal so in ♦ deal sth out ♦ deal so out of sth ♦ deal with so ♦ dirty deal ♦ a done deal ♦ a great deal ♦ It's a deal. ♦ Like it's such a big deal! ♦ make a big deal about sth ♦ make a deal with so ♦ no big deal ♦ a package deal ♦ a raw deal ♦ a shady deal ♦ a square deal ♦ strike a deal ♦ sweeten (up) the deal ♦ sweetheart deal ♦ think a great deal of so/sth ♦ wheel and deal

dear dear departed ♦ a Dear John letter ♦ Dear me! ♦ dear to one's heart ♦ hang on for dear life ♦ hold on for dear life ♦ near and dear to so ♦ so's nearest and dearest

death at death's door ♦ baleful as death ♦ bleed to death ♦ bore so to death ♦ a brush with death ♦ catch one's death (of cold) ♦ caught between life and death ♦ dance with death ♦ deal so/sth a death blow ♦ death on sth ♦ die a natural death ♦ a fate worse than death ♦ fight to the death ♦ flog sth to death ♦ freeze so/sth to death ♦ frighten so to death ♦ frightened to death ♦ have a death wish ♦ hovering between life and death ♦ the kiss of death ♦ lie at death's door ♦ like death warmed over ♦ love so/animal to death ♦ a matter of life and death ♦ meet one's death ♦ nickel and dime so (to death) ♦ Nothing is certain but death and taxes. ♦ pale as death ♦ put so to death ♦ scare so to death ♦ scared to death ♦ send one to one's death ♦ sick to death (of so/sth) ♦ sign one's own death warrant ♦ sound the death knell ♦ still as death ♦ struggle to the death ♦ thrill so to death ♦ thrilled to death ♦ tickle so to death ♦ will be the death of so/sth (yet)

deathbed on one's deathbed

debt head over heels in debt ♦ in debt ♦ out of debt ♦ owe so a debt of gratitude ♦ pay one's debt (to society)

decay fall into decay

decision arrive at a decision ♦ eleventh-hour decision ♦ reach a decision

deck clear the decks ♦ decked out (in sth) ♦ a few cards short of a deck ♦ have the deck stacked against one ♦ hit the deck ♦ not playing with a full deck ♦ on deck ♦ play with a full deck ♦ stack the deck (against so/sth)

declare I (do) declare!

deep between the devil and the deep blue sea ♦ deep in thought ♦ deep-six so/sth ♦ dig deep ♦ get in deeper ♦ go off the deep end ♦ in deep ♦ in deep water ♦ jump off the deep end ♦ knee-deep in sth ♦ Take a deep breath.

defeat go down in defeat ♦ snatch victory from the jaws of defeat

defense spring to so's defense

defensive on the defensive

definitely Definitely not!

degree by degrees ♦ get the third degree ♦ the third degree ♦ to the nth degree ♦ turn one hundred and eighty degrees ♦ turn three hundred and sixty degrees

delicate in a delicate condition

delight ravished with delight

deliver deliver the goods ♦ signed, sealed, and delivered ♦ stand and deliver

demand in (great) demand ♦ on demand

den a den of iniquity

denial in denial

dent make a dent in sth ♦ put a dent in sth

depart dear departed ♦ depart this life

depend That (all) depends.

depth beyond one's depth ♦ out of one's depth ♦ plumb the depths of sth

description answer to the description of so ♦ a blow-by-blow description ♦ a play-by-play description

desert desert a sinking ship ♦ get one's just deserts

design have designs on so/sth

desire leave a lot to be desired

desist cease and desist

desk away from one's desk ♦ step away from one's desk

despair sink into despair ♦ throw one's hands up (in despair)

detail down to the last detail ♦ go into detail(s) ♦ in detail

determine bound and determined

device leave one to one's own devices

devil between the devil and the deep blue sea ♦ the devil ♦ devil-may-care attitude ♦ devil-may-care manner ♦ a devil of a job ♦ a devil of a time ♦ the devil's own job ♦ for the devil of it ♦ full of the devil ♦ give so the devil ♦ give the devil his due ♦ go to (the devil) ♦ have the devil to pay ♦ like the devil ♦ play (the) devil's advocate ♦ play the devil with sth ♦ raise the devil (with so) ♦ raise the devil (with sth) ♦ sell one's soul (to the devil) ♦ speak of the devil (and he appears) ♦ speak of the devil (and in he comes) ♦ There will be the devil to pay. ♦ What the devil?

dialogue dialogue with so

diamond a diamond in the rough

diaper soil one's diaper(s)

diarrhea diarrhea of the jawbone ♦ diarrhea of the mouth

dibs dibs on sth ♦ have dibs on sth ♦ put one's dibs on sth

dice no dice

Dick any Tom, Dick, and Harry ♦ (every) Tom, Dick, and Harry ♦ Tom, Dick, and Harry

dickens like the dickens ♦ raise the dickens (with so/sth)

die cross one's heart (and hope to die) ♦ curl up and die ♦ die a natural death ♦ die away ♦ die behind the wheel ♦ die by one's own hand ♦ die for so/sth ♦ die from curiosity ♦ die in one's boots ♦ The die is cast. ♦ die laughing ♦ die of a broken heart ♦ die of boredom ♦ die of curiosity ♦ die on so ♦ die with one's boots on ♦ do or die ♦ dying to do sth ♦ to die for

diet on a diet

differ beg to differ (with so)

difference a difference of opinion ♦ make a difference in so/sth ♦ make a difference to so ♦ make a world of difference (in so/sth) ♦ make a world of difference (to so/sth) ♦ make no difference (to so) ♦ same difference ♦ split the difference

different dance to a different tune ♦ different as night and day ♦ a horse of a different color ♦ know different ♦ march to (the beat of) a different drummer ♦ sing a different tune

difficult difficult times

dig dig at so/sth ♦ dig deep ♦ dig ditches ♦ dig down ♦ dig for sth ♦ dig one's heels in ♦ dig in one's heels ♦ dig in(to sth) ♦ dig sth out ♦ dig one's own grave ♦ dig some dirt up (on so) ♦ dig so/sth up ♦ Dig up! ♦ give so a dig ♦ take a dig at so

digger cold as a well digger's ass (in January) ♦ cold as a well digger's ears (in January) ♦ cold as a well digger's feet (in January)

diggety Hot diggety (dog)!

dignity beneath one's dignity ♦ stand on one's dignity

dilemma on the horns of a dilemma

dim take a dim view of so/sth

dime a dime a dozen ♦ get off the dime ♦ nickel and dime so (to death) ♦ not worth a dime ♦ stop on a dime ♦ turn on a dime

dine dine out ♦ wine and dine so

ding dinged out

dinner Dinner is served.

dint by dint of sth

dip dip into one's savings ♦ skinny dip

dire in dire straits

direction in the right direction ♦ ride off in all directions ♦ run off in all directions ♦ take a step in the right direction

dirt common as dirt ♦ curly dirt ♦ dig some dirt up (on so) ♦ dirt cheap ♦ dish the dirt ♦ hit pay dirt ♦ strike pay dirt ♦ treat so like dirt

dirty air one's dirty linen in public ♦ dirty crack ♦ dirty deal ♦ dirty dog ♦ dirty one's hands ♦ so's dirty laundry ♦ a dirty look ♦ dirty old man ♦ a dirty word ♦ dirty work ♦ do so dirt(y) ♦ down and dirty ♦ get one's hands dirty ♦ give so a dirty look ♦ quick and dirty ♦ wash one's dirty linen in public

dis dis(s) (on) so

disadvantage at a disadvantage ♦ have so at a disadvantage ♦ You have me at a disadvantage.

disagree agree to disagree ♦ disagree with so

disappear disappear into thin air

disappoint disappointed at so/sth

disaster a disaster of epic proportions ♦ flirt with disaster ♦ spell disaster

discount five-finger discount

disease the disease to please ♦ foot-in-mouth disease

disfavor fall into disfavor

disgrace fall into disgrace

disguise a blessing in disguise ♦ in disguise

dish dish on so ♦ dish sth out ♦ dish the dirt

dishes do the dishes

dishwater dull as dishwater

disorder drunk and disorderly

dispense dispense with so/sth

disposal at so's disposal ♦ put so/sth at so's disposal

dispose dispose of so

disposed ill-disposed to doing sth ♦ well disposed to(ward) so/sth

dispute in dispute ♦ open to dispute ♦ under dispute

diss dis(s) (on) so

dissolve dissolve into sth

distance distance oneself from so/sth ♦ go the distance ♦ a good (amount or distance) ♦ keep so/sth at a distance ♦ keep one's distance from so/sth ♦ put some distance between so and oneself or sth ♦ within calling distance ♦ within hailing distance ♦ within spitting distance ♦ within striking distance

distraction bored to distraction ♦ drive so to distraction

disuse fall into disuse

ditch dig ditches ♦ last-ditch effort ♦ make last-ditch effort

ditchwater dull as ditchwater

dither in a dither

dive dive in (with both feet) ♦ dive in(to sth) ♦ go into a nosedive ♦ take a dive ♦ take a nosedive

divide divide and conquer

dividend pay dividends

divorce divorce oneself from sth

Dixie not just whistling Dixie

doctor Doctor Livingstone, I presume? ♦ doctor's orders ♦ just what the doctor ordered ♦ spin doctor ♦ You're the doctor.

dodo dead as a dodo ♦ go the way of the dodo

dog bring a dog to heel ♦ call the dogs off ♦ crooked as a dog's hind leg ♦ dirty dog ♦ dog and pony show ♦ The dog ate my homework. ♦ dog days ♦ dog in the manger ♦ dog-eat-dog ♦ a doggy bag ♦ go to the dogs ♦ the hair of the dog (that bit one) ♦ Hot diggety (dog)! ♦ Hot dog! ♦ lead a dog's life ♦ live a dog's life ♦ a lucky dog ♦ put a dog off the scent ♦ put on the dog ♦ rain cats and dogs ♦ see a man about a dog ♦ a shaggy-dog story ♦ shouldn't happen to a dog ♦ sick as a dog ♦ the tail wagging the dog ♦ throw so to the dogs

doggo lie doggo

doggy a doggy bag

doghouse in the doghouse

doldrums in the doldrums

dole on the dole

doll (all) dolled up

dollar the almighty dollar ♦ bet one's bottom dollar ♦ bet so dollars to doughnuts ♦ a day late and a dollar short ♦ dollar for dollar ♦ feel like a million (dollars) ♦ like a million (dollars) ♦ phony as a three-dollar bill ♦ queer as a three-dollar bill ♦ the sixty-four-dollar question ♦ sound as a dollar

domestic domestic partner ♦ domestic worker

doom gloom and doom

door answer the door ♦ at death's door ♦ beat a path to so's door ♦ behind closed doors ♦ blow so's doors off ♦ broad as a barn door ♦ check sth at the door ♦ close the door on so/sth ♦ crack the door (open) ♦ darken so's door ♦ door-to-door ♦ from door to door ♦ get one's foot in the door ♦ Katie bar the door. ♦ keep the wolf from the door ♦ lay sth at so's door ♦ leave the door open (for sth) ♦ lie at death's door ♦ open some doors (for so) ♦ open the door to so ♦ open the door to sth ♦ put sth at so's door ♦ see so to the door ♦ show so (to) the door ♦ shut the door (up)on so/sth ♦ slam the door in so's face ♦ The wolf is at the door.

doornail dead as a doornail ♦ deader than a doornail

doorstep lay sth at so's doorstep

dope do dope ♦ dope sth out ♦ the straight dope

dose a dose of one's own medicine ♦ go through so like a dose of the salts

dot on the dot ♦ show up on the dot ♦ sign on the dotted line

dote dote on so/sth

double do a double take ♦ double-check ♦ a double-edged sword ♦ double in brass (as sth) ♦ a double whammy ♦ lead a double life ♦ live a double life ♦ on the double ♦ see double

doubt the benefit of the doubt ♦ beyond a reasonable doubt ♦ beyond the shadow of a doubt ♦ cast doubt on so/sth ♦ doubting Thomas ♦ give so the benefit of the doubt ♦ throw doubt on so/sth ♦ without a shadow of a doubt

doughnut bet so dollars to doughnuts

down (Are) things getting you down? ♦ back down (from so/sth) ♦ back down (on sth) ♦ batten down the hatches ♦ beat so down ♦ bed down some place ♦ bed down (for sth) ♦ belt a drink down ♦ bog so/sth down ♦ bogged down ♦ boil sth down ♦ boil down to sth ♦ bolt sth down ♦ boogie down (to some place) ♦ bow down to so/sth ♦ break down ♦ break so down ♦ break sth down ♦ break sth down (for so) ♦ break sth down (into sth) ♦ breathe down so's neck ♦ bring sth crashing down (around one) ♦

◆ rain sth down (on so/sth) ◆ rain down on so/sth ◆ ram so/sth down so's throat ◆ render sth down ◆ right down so's alley ◆ ring the curtain down (on sth) ◆ round sth down ◆ round down to sth ◆ run down ◆ run so/sth down ◆ run down to some place ◆ run it down ◆ scarf sth down ◆ scoot down (to some place) ◆ scream down (on so/sth) ◆ scrunch down ◆ sell so down the river ◆ set sth down ◆ set sth down in black and white ◆ set so down (on(to) sth) ◆ set sth down to sth ◆ settle down ◆ shake so down ◆ shake sth down ◆ shoot sth down ◆ shoot so down in flames ◆ shove so/sth down so's throat ◆ shut down ◆ simmer down ◆ slap so down ◆ smack so down ◆ soft as down ◆ somewhere down the line ◆ speak down to so ◆ splash down ◆ stand down ◆ step down (from sth) ◆ strike sth down ◆ stuff sth down so's throat ◆ take sth down ◆ take so down a notch (or two) ◆ take so down a peg (or two) ◆ take sth lying down ◆ talk down to so ◆ Things getting you down? ◆ throw down the gauntlet ◆ throw money down the drain ◆ thumbs down ◆ tie so down ◆ tied down ◆ track so/sth down ◆ trickle down (to so/sth) ◆ (a trip down) memory lane ◆ turn sth down ◆ turn thumbs down (on so/sth) ◆ turn so/sth upside down ◆ turn some place upside down ◆ upside down ◆ wash sth down (with sth) ◆ water sth down ◆ What's going down? ◆ whatever comes down the pike ◆ when it comes right down to it ◆ when it gets down to the crunch ◆ when the chips are down ◆ whittle so down to size ◆ wolf sth down ◆ a yellow streak (down so's back)

downhill downhill all the way ◆ downhill from here on ◆ go downhill

downs so's ups and downs

dozen a baker's dozen ◆ by the dozen ◆ by the dozens ◆ daily dozen ◆ a dime a dozen ◆ It's six of one, half a dozen of another.

drabs in dribs and drabs

draft feel a draft

drag drag one's feet (on or over sth) ◆ drag one's heels (on or over sth) ◆ drag on ◆ a drag (on so) ◆ a drag (on sth) ◆ drag on sth

◆ drag out ◆ drag so through the mud ◆ dragged out ◆ in drag ◆ knock-down-drag-out fight ◆ Look (at) what the cat dragged in! ◆ look like sth the cat dragged in ◆ See what the cat dragged in! ◆ take a drag (on sth)

drain down the drain ◆ go down the drain ◆ pour money down the drain ◆ throw money down the drain

draw back to the drawing board ◆ beat so to the draw ◆ draw a blank ◆ draw a line in the sand ◆ draw blood ◆ draw so's fire ◆ draw in one's horns ◆ draw on sth ◆ draw so out ◆ draw sth out ◆ draw one out (of oneself) ◆ draw straws for sth ◆ draw the line (at sth) ◆ draw the line between sth and sth (else) ◆ a drawing card ◆ get the draw on so ◆ go back to the drawing board ◆ the luck of the draw ◆ quick on the draw ◆ slow on the draw

drawers drop one's drawers

drawn drawn and quartered ◆ drawn like a moth to a flame

dream the American dream ◆ broken dreams ◆ a dream come true ◆ Dream on. ◆ a pipe dream ◆ wouldn't dream of doing sth

dredge dredge so/sth up

dress (all) dressed up ◆ all dressed up and nowhere to go ◆ dress so down (for sth) ◆ dressed to kill ◆ dressed to the nines ◆ dressed to the teeth ◆ dressed (up) fit to kill ◆ a dressing down ◆ give so a (good) dressing-down ◆ a (good) dressing-down

dribs in dribs and drabs

drift (Do you) get my drift? ◆ drift off to sleep ◆ get so's drift ◆ Get my drift? ◆ get the drift of sth ◆ if you get my drift

drill drill sth into so ◆ What's the drill?

drink belt a drink down ◆ a big drink of water ◆ buy a round (of drinks) ◆ buy the next round (of drinks) ◆ Buy you a drink? ◆ (Can I) buy you a drink? ◆ (Could I) buy you a drink? ◆ drink like a fish ◆ drink to excess ◆ drink so under the table ◆ Drink up! ◆ drive so to drink ◆ have a drinking problem ◆ I'll drink to that! ◆ in the drink ◆ knock back a drink ◆ (May I) buy you a drink?

drive drive a coach and horses through sth
♦ drive a hard bargain ♦ drive so around
the bend ♦ drive so batty ♦ drive so
bonkers ♦ drive so crazy ♦ drive sth home
(to so) ♦ drive so insane ♦ drive so mad ♦
drive so nuts ♦ drive one out of one's mind
♦ drive so to distraction ♦ drive so to drink
♦ drive so to the wall ♦ drive so up the
wall ♦ the driving force (behind so/sth) ♦
into overdrive ♦ pure as the driven snow
♦ shift into overdrive ♦ What are you
driving at? ♦ white as the driven snow

driver backseat driver ♦ in the driver's seat
♦ Sunday driver

drop at the drop of a hat ♦ drop so ♦ drop
a bomb(shell) ♦ drop a brick ♦ drop a
bundle (on so) ♦ drop a bundle (on sth) ♦
drop a hint ♦ drop so a line ♦ drop so a
note ♦ drop by ♦ drop by the wayside ♦
drop dead ♦ drop-dead date ♦ drop-dead
gorgeous ♦ drop one's drawers ♦ drop
everything ♦ drop so/sth from sth ♦ drop
one's guard ♦ Drop in sometime. ♦ a drop
in the bucket ♦ a drop in the ocean ♦ drop
in one's tracks ♦ drop into one's lap ♦ Drop
it! ♦ drop so/sth like a hot potato ♦ drop
like flies ♦ drop so's name ♦ drop names ♦
drop off ♦ drop so/sth off (some place) ♦ drop
off the face of the earth ♦ drop off the
map ♦ drop off (to sleep) ♦ drop sth on so
♦ drop out (of sth) ♦ drop out of sight ♦
drop over ♦ drop one's teeth ♦ drop the
ball ♦ drop the other shoe ♦ Drop the
subject! ♦ get the drop on so ♦ not to
touch a drop ♦ so quiet you could hear a
pin drop ♦ so still you could hear a pin
drop ♦ turn on, tune in, drop out ♦ wait
for the other shoe to drop

droves bring people/animals out in droves ♦
in droves ♦ out in droves

drown drown so in sth ♦ drown in sth ♦
drown sth out ♦ drown one's sorrows ♦
drown one's troubles

drug do drugs ♦ a drug on the market

drum bang the drum for so/sth ♦ beat the
drum for so/sth ♦ drum sth into so ♦ drum
sth into so's head ♦ drum so out of sth ♦
tight as a drum

drummer march to (the beat of) a
different drummer

drunk commode-hugging drunk ♦ dead
drunk ♦ drunk and disorderly ♦ drunk as a
lord ♦ drunk as a skunk ♦ screeching
(drunk)

druthers have one's druthers

dry bleed so dry ♦ cut and dried ♦ dry as a
bone ♦ dry as dust ♦ dry out ♦ dry so out ♦
dry run ♦ dry spell ♦ dry-gulch so ♦
exciting as watching (the) paint dry ♦
hang so out to dry ♦ hardly dry behind the
ears ♦ high and dry ♦ keep one's powder
dry ♦ leave so high and dry ♦ not a dry
eye (in the place) ♦ not dry behind the
ears

duck as a duck takes to water ♦ a dead
duck ♦ duck and cover ♦ duck soup ♦ easy
as duck soup ♦ Fine weather for ducks. ♦
get one's ducks in a row ♦ lame duck ♦ like
a sitting duck ♦ like water off a duck's
back ♦ Lord love a duck! ♦ Lovely weather
for ducks. ♦ a sitting duck

dude duded up

dudgeon in high dudgeon

due give the devil his due ♦ in due course
♦ in due time ♦ pay one's dues ♦ with all
due respect

duke duke it out ♦ put up one's dukes

dull deadly dull ♦ dull as dishwater ♦ dull
as ditchwater ♦ keep it down (to a dull
roar) ♦ never a dull moment

dumb deaf and dumb

dummy dummy up

dump do a dump on so/sth ♦ down in the
dumps ♦ dump a load ♦ dump all over
so/sth ♦ dump one's load ♦ dump sth on so ♦
dump on so/sth ♦ dumped on

dunk slam dunk

duration for the duration

dusk from dawn to dusk

dust bite the dust ♦ cut the dust ♦ dry as
dust ♦ a dust bunny ♦ a dust kitten ♦ dust
so's pants ♦ gather dust ♦ kiss the dust ♦
when the dust settles

Dutch Dutch auction ♦ Dutch courage ♦
Dutch treat ♦ Dutch uncle ♦ go Dutch ♦ in
Dutch (with so)

duty above and beyond (the call of duty)
♦ come on (duty) ♦ duty bound to do sth ♦
go above and beyond one's duty ♦ in the
line of duty ♦ off duty ♦ on active duty ♦

on duty ♦ relieve one of one's duties ♦ shirk one's duty

dwell dwell on so/sth

dye dyed-in-the-wool

E

each at each other's throats ♦ cancel each other out ♦ made for each other ♦ To each his own. ♦ To each their own.

eager eager beaver

eagle eagle eye

ear all ears ♦ all eyes and ears ♦ assault the ear ♦ bend so's ear ♦ Blow it out your ear! ♦ box so's ears ♦ cold as a well digger's ears (in January) ♦ coming out of one's ears ♦ cute as a bug's ear ♦ one's ears are red ♦ one's ears are ringing ♦ fall on deaf ears ♦ get one's ears lowered ♦ get one's ears pinned back ♦ get one's ears set out ♦ give (an) ear to so/sth ♦ go in one ear and out the other ♦ grin from ear to ear ♦ hang up (in so's ear) ♦ hardly dry behind the ears ♦ have an ear for sth ♦ have an ear to the ground ♦ I'm all ears. ♦ In a pig's ear! ♦ keep an ear to the ground ♦ lend an ear to so/sth ♦ lend your ear to so/sth ♦ music to so's ears ♦ nail so's ears back ♦ not believe one's ears ♦ not dry behind the ears ♦ pin so's ears back ♦ play by ear ♦ play sth by ear ♦ pound one's ear ♦ prick up its ears ♦ pull in one's ears ♦ ring in so's ears ♦ set some place on its ear ♦ smile from ear to ear ♦ talk so's ear off ♦ throw one out on one's ear ♦ a tin ear ♦ turn a deaf ear (to so/sth) ♦ turn sth on its ear ♦ up to one's ears (in sth) ♦ wet behind the ears

earful an earful ♦ give so an earful

early at an early date ♦ at so's earliest convenience ♦ bright and early ♦ early bird ♦ early on ♦ gotta get up pretty early in the morning to do sth

earn earn one's keep

earnest in earnest

earshot out of earshot ♦ within earshot (of sth)

earth all over the earth ♦ bring so down (to earth) ♦ come down to earth ♦ cost the earth ♦ down to earth ♦ drop off the face of the earth ♦ fall off the face of the earth ♦ from the four corners of the earth ♦ heaven on earth ♦ hell on earth ♦ like nothing on earth ♦ move heaven and earth to do sth ♦ no earthly reason ♦ on earth? ♦ on the face of the earth ♦ on the surface of the earth ♦ a paradise (on earth) ♦ paradise on earth ♦ plummet to earth ♦ the salt of the earth ♦ to the ends of the earth ♦ treat so like the scum of the earth ♦ What on earth? ♦ Where on (God's green) earth? ♦ wipe so/sth from the face of the earth ♦ wipe so/sth off the face of the earth

ease at ease ♦ ease so's burden ♦ ill at ease ♦ put one at (one's) ease ♦ put so's mind at ease (about so/sth) ♦ set so's mind at ease (about so/sth)

East back East

easy able to breathe (easily) again ♦ as easy as shooting fish in a barrel ♦ as easy as taking candy from a baby ♦ breathe easy ♦ dead easy ♦ easier said than done ♦ easy as A, B, C ♦ easy as (apple) pie ♦ easy as duck soup ♦ easy as falling off a log ♦ easy come, easy go ♦ Easy does it. ♦ easy money ♦ easy pickings ♦ easy to come by ♦ free and easy ♦ get off (easy) ♦ go easy on so/sth ♦ go easy on sth ♦ have an easy time of it ♦ let so off (easy) ♦ on easy street ♦ over easy ♦ Take it easy. ♦ take it easy on so/sth/animal ♦ take it easy on sth ♦ take the easy way out ♦ take things easy ♦ That's easy for you to say.

eat a bite (to eat) ♦ did everything he could 'cept eat us ♦ (Do) you eat with that mouth? ♦ The dog ate my homework. ♦ dog-eat-dog ♦ eat (a meal) out ♦ eat so alive ♦ eat and run ♦ eat (away) at so ♦ eat one's cake and have it too ♦ eat crow ♦ eat one's fill ♦ eat so for breakfast ♦ eat one's hat ♦ eat one's heart out ♦ eat humble pie ♦ eat like a bird ♦ eat like a horse ♦ eat so's lunch ♦ eat so out ♦ eat out of so's hand ♦ eat so out of house and home ♦ eat (pretty) high off the hog ♦ eat so up ♦ eat sth up ♦ eat one's words ♦ eat(en) up

stars in one's eyes ♦ turn a blind eye (to so/sth) ♦ with (one's) eyes (wide) open ♦ with the naked eye ♦ without batting an eye

eyeball eyeball to eyeball ♦ up to one's eyeballs (in sth)

eyebrow cause (some) eyebrows to raise ♦ down to a gnat's eyebrow ♦ raise a few eyebrows

eyeful an eyeful (of so/sth) ♦ give so an eyeful

eyelid not bat an eyelid

eyes a feast for the eyes

eyeteeth cut one's (eye)teeth on sth

F

face blow up in so's face ♦ can't see one's hand in front of one's face ♦ cut off one's nose to spite one's face ♦ do an about-face ♦ drop off the face of the earth ♦ explode in so's face ♦ face off ♦ a face (that) only a mother could love ♦ face the consequences ♦ face (the) facts ♦ face the music ♦ face-to-face ♦ fall (flat) on one's face ♦ fall off the face of the earth ♦ feed one's face ♦ fill one's face ♦ fly in the face of sth ♦ fly into the face of danger ♦ get out of one's face ♦ give so a red face ♦ have egg on one's face ♦ hide one's face (in shame) ♦ in so's face ♦ in the face of sth ♦ It's written all over one's face. ♦ keep a straight face ♦ laugh in so's face ♦ laugh out of the other side of one's face ♦ look so in the face ♦ lose face ♦ make a face ♦ make a face (at so) ♦ not show one's face ♦ on the face of it ♦ on the face of the earth ♦ plain as the nose on one's face ♦ powder one's face ♦ put a smile on so's face ♦ put one's face on ♦ red in the face ♦ save (one's) face ♦ say sth (right) to so's face ♦ set sth in a typeface ♦ slam the door in so's face ♦ a slap in the face ♦ a smack in the face ♦ soak one's face ♦ stand there with one's bare face hanging out ♦ stare so in the face ♦ stare sth in the face ♦ a straight face ♦ stuff one's face ♦ take so/sth at face value ♦ talk until one is blue in the

face ♦ tell one to one's face ♦ throw sth in(to) so's face ♦ wipe so/sth from the face of the earth ♦ wipe sth off (one's face) ♦ wipe so/sth off the face of the earth

fact after the fact ♦ and that's a fact ♦ as a matter of fact ♦ face (the) facts ♦ the facts of life ♦ get down to the facts ♦ get the facts straight ♦ grounded in (actual) fact ♦ have the facts straight ♦ in fact ♦ in point of fact ♦ known fact ♦ matter-of-fact

factor fudge factor

fade do a fade

fag fagged out

fail if all else fails ♦ if everything else fails ♦ sth never fails ♦ without fail

faint damn so/sth with faint praise ♦ faint dead away ♦ the faint of heart

fair fair and impartial ♦ fair and square ♦ do sth fair and square ♦ fair enough ♦ fair-haired boy ♦ a fair shake ♦ fair to middlin' ♦ fair-weather friend ♦ give so a fair shake

faith an act of faith ♦ article of faith ♦ have faith in so ♦ in bad faith ♦ in good faith ♦ keep faith with so/sth ♦ a leap of faith ♦ Oh, ye of little faith. ♦ pin one's faith on so/sth ♦ show good faith ♦ take sth on faith

fake fake it

fall at one fell swoop ♦ the bottom fell out (of sth) ♦ break so's fall ♦ curtain falls on sth ♦ easy as falling off a log ♦ fall (all) over oneself (to do sth) ♦ fall apart (at the seams) ♦ fall asleep at the switch ♦ fall behind schedule ♦ fall between two stools ♦ fall by the wayside ♦ fall down on the job ♦ fall (flat) on one's face ♦ fall for so ♦ fall for sth ♦ fall for sth hook, line, and sinker ♦ fall from grace ♦ fall from power ♦ fall head over heels ♦ fall head over heels in love (with so) ♦ fall heir to sth ♦ fall ill ♦ fall in love (with so) ♦ fall in love (with sth) ♦ fall into a trap ♦ fall into decay ♦ fall into disfavor ♦ fall into disgrace ♦ fall into disuse ♦ fall into so's hands ♦ fall into one's lap ♦ fall in(to) line ♦ fall in(to) place ♦ fall in(to step) ♦ fall into the habit of doing sth ♦ fall into the rut of doing sth ♦ fall into the trap of doing sth ♦ fall into the wrong hands ♦ fall off the face of the earth ♦ fall off the wagon ♦ fall on deaf ears ♦ fall on hard times ♦ fall on one's knees ♦ fall on one's sword ♦ fall out ♦ fall out of bed ♦ fall out of favor (with so) ♦ fall out of love (with so) ♦ fall out with so ♦ fall over backwards (to do sth) ♦ fall overboard ♦ fall prey to so/sth ♦ fall short ♦ fall short of one's goal(s) ♦ fall short of the goal(s) ♦ fall short of the record ♦ fall through ♦ fall through the cracks ♦ fall to ♦ fall to so ♦ fall to one's knees ♦ fall to pieces ♦ fall victim to so/sth ♦ a falling-out ♦ have a falling-out with so ♦ a hush fell over so/sth ♦ in one fell swoop ♦ just fell off the turnip truck ♦ let the chips fall (where they may) ♦ riding for a fall ♦ take a fall ♦ take the fall

fallow lie fallow

false a false move ♦ lull so into a false sense of security ♦ one false move ♦ ring false ♦ sail under false colors

fame so's claim to fame ♦ a house of ill fame

familiar have a familiar ring (to it) ♦ unfamiliar territory

family (all) in the family ♦ the black sheep of the family ♦ in a family way ♦ in the family ♦ like one of the family ♦ run in the family ♦ the runt of the family ♦ wear the britches (in the family) ♦ wear the pants (in the family)

famine (either) feast or famine

famous famous last words

fan a fan of so ♦ fan the breeze ♦ fan the flames (of sth) ♦ hit the fan ♦ when the shit hits the fan

fancy catch so's fancy ♦ fancy so's chances ♦ fancy footwork ♦ Fancy meeting you here! ♦ Fancy that! ♦ flight of fancy ♦ footloose and fancy-free ♦ strike so's fancy ♦ suit so's fancy ♦ take a fancy to so/sth ♦ tickle so's fancy

fantastic trip the light fantastic

far as far as anyone knows ♦ as far as sth goes ♦ as far as I can see ♦ as far as so is concerned ♦ as far as sth is concerned ♦ as far as possible ♦ come from far and wide ♦ far and away the best ♦ far and away the greatest ♦ far and away the worst ♦ far and wide ♦ far be it from me (to do sth) ♦ a far cry from sth ♦ far from doing sth ♦ far from it ♦ far from the madding crowd

♦ far gone ♦ far into the night ♦ far-away look ♦ far-off look ♦ far-out ♦ few and far between ♦ from far and near ♦ from near and far ♦ go so far as doing sth ♦ make it as far as sth ♦ push so too far ♦ scattered far and wide ♦ so far as anyone knows ♦ so far as I can see ♦ so far as so is concerned ♦ so far as sth is concerned ♦ so far as possible ♦ so far, so good

farm bet the farm (on sth) ♦ buy the farm ♦ sell the farm

fart fart around

fashion after a fashion ♦ after the fashion of so/sth ♦ in fashion ♦ out of fashion

fast fast and furious ♦ fast friends ♦ a fast one ♦ faster and faster ♦ fast-talk so into sth ♦ fast-talk so out of sth ♦ get nowhere fast ♦ go nowhere fast ♦ hard-and-fast ♦ in the fast lane ♦ life in the fast lane ♦ live in the fast lane ♦ make a fast buck ♦ make fast work of so/sth ♦ on the fast track ♦ play fast and loose (with so/sth) ♦ pull a fast one (on so) ♦ thick and fast

fat chew the fat ♦ fat and happy ♦ fat and sassy ♦ fat as a pig ♦ fat cat ♦ fat chance ♦ the fat hit the fire ♦ give so a fat lip ♦ kill the fatted calf ♦ live off the fat of the land ♦ till the fat lady sings ♦ when the fat lady sings ♦ work some fat off

fatal deal so/sth a fatal blow

fate so's fate is sealed ♦ a fate worse than death ♦ leave one to one's fate ♦ seal so's fate ♦ sure as fate ♦ tempt fate ♦ a turn of fate ♦ a twist of fate

father father sth on so ♦ old enough to be so's father

fault at fault ♦ generous to a fault

fauna flora and fauna

favor ask so (for) a favor ♦ come out in favor of so/sth ♦ curry favor with so ♦ do oneself a favor ♦ Don't do me any favors! ♦ fall out of favor (with so) ♦ go in so's favor ♦ in so's favor ♦ in favor (of so/sth) ♦ in favor of so ♦ lose favor (with so) ♦ opt in favor of so/sth ♦ out of favor (with so) ♦ return the favor ♦ Thank God for small favors.

favorite the odds-on favorite

fear in fear and trembling ♦ put the fear of God in(to) so

feast (either) feast or famine ♦ feast one's eyes ((up)on so/sth) ♦ a feast for the eyes ♦ a movable feast

feather a feather in one's cap ♦ feather one's (own) nest ♦ in fine feather ♦ knock so over (with a feather) ♦ light as a feather ♦ make the feathers fly ♦ ruffle so's feathers ♦ smooth (so's) ruffled feathers ♦ tar and feather so ♦ You could have knocked me over with a feather.

fed fed up (with so/sth)

federal make a federal case out of sth

feed bite the hand that feeds one ♦ chicken feed ♦ fed up (with so/sth) ♦ feed so a line ♦ feed one's face ♦ feed the kitty ♦ a feeding frenzy ♦ for chicken feed ♦ put the feed bag on ♦ spoon-feed so

feel feel a draft ♦ feel one's age ♦ feel at home ♦ feel blue ♦ a feel for sth ♦ feel for so ♦ feel free (to do sth) ♦ feel one's hair stand on end ♦ feel sth in one's bones ♦ feel (sth) in one's heart of hearts ♦ feel (kind of) puny ♦ feel like a million (dollars) ♦ feel like a new person ♦ feel like oneself again ♦ feel like (having) sth ♦ feel one's oats ♦ the feel of sth ♦ feel on top of the world ♦ feel so out ♦ feel out of place ♦ feel the hair on the back of one's neck stand on end ♦ feel the pinch ♦ feel one's way ♦ get the feel of sth ♦ have a feel for sth

feelers put out (some) feelers (on so/sth)

feeling beyond feeling ♦ feeling no pain ♦ a feeling (that sth is the case) ♦ go with one's gut (feeling) ♦ gut feeling ♦ hard feelings ♦ have a sinking feeling ♦ have a sinking feeling in the pit of one's stomach ♦ have mixed feelings (about so/sth) ♦ mixed feelings (about so/sth) ♦ no hard feelings ♦ not any hard feelings ♦ a sinking feeling ♦ a sinking feeling in the pit of one's stomach

felicitations Greetings and felicitations!

fellow hail-fellow-well-met

fence fence an animal in ♦ mend (one's) fences ♦ on the fence (about sth) ♦ sit on the fence ♦ straddle the fence

fend fend for oneself

fender fender bender

ferret ferret sth out

fetch fetch up at some place

fever run a fever

few few and far between ♦ a few bricks short of a load ♦ a few bricks shy of a load ♦ a few cards short of a deck ♦ get off a few good ones ♦ hang a few on ♦ have a few too many ♦ a man of few words ♦ precious few ♦ quite a few ♦ raise a few eyebrows ♦ Win a few, lose a few.

fewer no fewer than (some number)

fiddle fiddle about (with so) ♦ fiddle around (with so) ♦ fiddle around (with sth) ♦ fiddle while Rome burns ♦ fit as a fiddle ♦ play second fiddle (to so)

field come out of left field ♦ field questions ♦ have a field day ♦ a level playing field ♦ level the (playing) field ♦ order so off the field ♦ out in left field ♦ out of left field ♦ play the field

fifth a fifth wheel ♦ take the Fifth (Amendment)

fifty fifty-fifty ♦ go fifty-fifty (on sth)

fig not care a fig ♦ not give a fig

fight come out fighting ♦ Don't give up without a fight! ♦ fight a losing battle ♦ fight against time ♦ fight city hall ♦ fight sth down ♦ fight fire with fire ♦ fight so/sth hammer and tongs ♦ fight so/sth off ♦ fight sth out ♦ fight the good fight ♦ fight to the death ♦ fight so/sth tooth and nail ♦ a fighting chance ♦ give up the fight ♦ go down fighting ♦ knock-down-drag-out fight ♦ like fighting snakes ♦ pick a fight (with so) ♦ put up a fight ♦ spoiling for a fight ♦ Them's fighting words! ♦ throw a fight ♦ You can't fight city hall.

figment a figment of one's imagination

figure a ballpark figure ♦ cut a dashing figure ♦ cut a fine figure ♦ figure in sth ♦ flatter one's figure ♦ Go figure. ♦ in round figures ♦ It figures. ♦ put a figure on sth

file have sth on file ♦ in (a) single file ♦ rank and file

fill back and fill ♦ eat one's fill ♦ fill a void ♦ fill one's face ♦ fill so full of lead ♦ fill in for so ♦ fill so in on sth ♦ Fill in the blanks. ♦ one's fill of so/sth ♦ fill so's shoes ♦ fill the bill ♦ fill the gap ♦ filled to the brim ♦ have one's fill of so/sth ♦ smoke-filled room

filthy filthy lucre ♦ filthy rich

final a final fling ♦ final touch(es) ♦ the final word ♦ in the final analysis ♦ one final thing ♦ one final word ♦ pay one's final respects (to so) ♦ so's word is final

financially financially embarrassed

find can't find one's butt with both hands (in broad daylight) ♦ find oneself ♦ find a happy medium ♦ find enough time to do sth ♦ find one's feet ♦ find for so/sth ♦ find it in one's heart (to do sth) ♦ find (sth) out the hard way ♦ find one's own level ♦ find the time to do sth ♦ find one's tongue ♦ like trying to find a needle in a haystack

fine Come on in, the water's fine! ♦ cut a fine figure ♦ fine and dandy ♦ fine by so ♦ a fine how-do-you-do ♦ a fine kettle of fish ♦ fine print ♦ a fine state of affairs ♦ Fine weather for ducks. ♦ fine-tune sth ♦ go over sth with a fine-tooth(ed) comb ♦ go through sth with a fine-tooth(ed) comb ♦ in fine feather ♦ (It) suits me (fine). ♦ make sth into a fine art ♦ not to put too fine a point on sth ♦ not to put too fine a point on it ♦ search sth with a fine-tooth(ed) comb ♦ Suits me (fine). ♦ That's a fine how-do-you-do. ♦ There is a fine line between sth and sth else. ♦ turn sth into a fine art

finger burn one's fingers ♦ cross one's fingers ♦ finger so as so ♦ five-finger discount ♦ get one's fingers burned ♦ give so the finger ♦ have a finger in the pie ♦ have one's finger in too many pies ♦ have one's finger on the pulse of sth ♦ have one's finger(s) in the till ♦ have sticky fingers ♦ keep one's finger on the pulse of sth ♦ keep one's fingers crossed (for so/sth) ♦ lay a finger on so/sth ♦ lay the finger on so ♦ not lift a finger (to help so) ♦ point the finger at so ♦ put one's finger on sth ♦ put the finger on so ♦ run one's fingers through one's hair ♦ slip through so's fingers ♦ stick to so's fingers ♦ work one's fingers to the bone

fingertip at one's fingertips ♦ have sth at one's fingertips

finish finishing touch(es) ♦ from start to finish

fire add fuel to the fire ♦ ball of fire ♦ baptism of fire ♦ caught in the crossfire ♦ draw so's fire ♦ the fat hit the fire ♦ fight fire with fire ♦ fire a shot across the bow ♦ fire sth off ♦ a fire under so ♦ fired up ♦ firing on all cylinders ♦ Great balls of fire! ♦ hang fire ♦ have several irons in the fire ♦ have too many irons in the fire ♦ Hellfire and damnation! ♦ hold so's feet to the fire ♦ hold one's fire ♦ hot as fire ♦ jump out of the frying pan (and) into the fire ♦ keep out of the line of fire ♦ Keep the home fires burning. ♦ like a house on fire ♦ the line of fire ♦ on fire ♦ open fire (on so) ♦ out of the frying pan (and) into the fire ♦ play with fire ♦ pull sth out of the fire ♦ set fire to so/sth ♦ set so on fire ♦ set the world on fire ♦ spread like wildfire ♦ start a fire under so ♦ think under fire ♦ under fire ♦ Where's the fire? ♦ Where there's smoke, there's fire.

firm exercise a firm hand ♦ a firm hand ♦ keep a firm grip on so/sth ♦ take a firm grip on so/sth ♦ take a (firm) stand on sth

first at first ♦ at first blush ♦ at first glance ♦ at first hand ♦ at first light ♦ at first sight ♦ cast the first stone ♦ first and foremost ♦ first and ten ♦ first crack at sth ♦ the first leg (of a journey) ♦ first of all ♦ first off ♦ first see the light of day ♦ first thing (in the morning) ♦ the first thing that comes into one's head ♦ First things first. ♦ the firstest with the mostest ♦ get to first base (with so/sth) ♦ in the first instance ♦ in the first place ♦ Ladies first. ♦ love at first sight ♦ not know the first thing about so/sth ♦ of the first water ♦ on a first-name basis (with so) ♦ play first chair ♦ reach first base (with so/sth) ♦ see so in hell first ♦ whatever comes into one's head (first)

fish as easy as shooting fish in a barrel ♦ busy as a fish peddler in Lent ♦ a cold fish ♦ crooked as a barrel of fish hooks ♦ crooked as a fish hook ♦ drink like a fish ♦ a fine kettle of fish ♦ fish for sth ♦ fish for a compliment ♦ fish in troubled waters ♦ Fish or cut bait. ♦ fish story ♦ fish tale ♦ a fishing expedition ♦ have bigger fish to fry ♦ have more important fish to fry ♦ have other fish to fry ♦ like a fish out of water ♦ like shooting fish in a barrel ♦ neither fish nor fowl ♦ smell fishy ♦ There are plenty of (other) fish in the sea. ♦ Ye gods (and little fishes)!

fishy smell fishy

fist closefisted (with money) ♦ hand over fist ♦ rule with an iron fist ♦ tight as Midas's fist ♦ tightfisted (with money) ♦ two-fisted

fit by fits and starts ♦ dressed (up) fit to kill ♦ fit and trim ♦ fit as a fiddle ♦ fit for a king ♦ fit for the gods ♦ fit like a glove ♦ fit the bill ♦ fit so to a T ♦ fit to be tied ♦ fit to kill ♦ fits and starts ♦ have a conniption (fit) ♦ have a fit ♦ hissy (fit) ♦ It ain't fittin' ♦ keep fit ♦ look fit to kill ♦ see fit (to do sth) ♦ the survival of the fittest ♦ throw a fit

five a bunch of fives ♦ five-finger discount ♦ Give me five! ♦ hang five ♦ nine-to-five job ♦ put two and two together and come up with five ♦ slip so five ♦ Slip me five! ♦ take five

fix a fix ♦ fix an animal ♦ fix sth ♦ a fix on sth ♦ fix so's wagon ♦ fix sth with so ♦ fixed up ♦ fixin(g) to do sth ♦ How is so fixed for sth? ♦ in a fix ♦ well-fixed ♦ with all the fixin(g)s

fixture a regular fixture

flair have a flair for sth

flake flake down

flame add fuel to the flame ♦ burn with a low blue flame ♦ burst into flame(s) ♦ drawn like a moth to a flame ♦ fan the flames (of sth) ♦ flame with sth ♦ go down in flames ♦ go up in flames ♦ shoot so down in flames

flare flare up ♦ flare up at so/sth

flash flash sth around ♦ flash sth at so/sth ♦ a flash in the pan ♦ flash through one's mind ♦ flash with sth ♦ in a flash ♦ quick as a flash

flat catch so flat-footed ♦ fall (flat) on one's face ♦ flat as a board ♦ flat as a pancake ♦ flat broke ♦ flat busted ♦ flat on one's ass ♦ (flat) on one's back ♦ flat out ♦ in no time flat ♦ in nothing flat ♦ leave so flat

flatter flatter one's figure ♦ Flattery will get you nowhere.

flavor flavor of the month

flea not hurt a flea

fleet fleet of foot ♦ a fleeting glance

flesh flesh and blood ♦ flesh sth out ♦ in the flesh ♦ make so's flesh crawl ♦ own flesh and blood ♦ a pound of flesh ♦ press (the) flesh ♦ a thorn in so's flesh

flex flex so's/sth's muscles ♦ flexed out of shape

flight flight of fancy ♦ Have a nice flight. ♦ in flight ♦ in full flight

flimflam flimflam artist

fling a final fling ♦ fling oneself at so

flip do a flip-flop (on sth) ♦ flip burgers ♦ flip one's lid ♦ flip so off ♦ the flip side ♦ flip so the bird ♦ flip one's wig

flirt flirt with disaster ♦ flirt with the idea of doing sth

float float a loan ♦ float on air ♦ Whatever floats your boat.

flog flog a dead horse ♦ flog sth to death

flood flood in(to sth) ♦ flood out (of sth)

floodgates open the floodgates

floor clean the floor up with so ♦ end up on the cutting room floor ♦ the floor ♦ floor so ♦ floor it ♦ have the floor ♦ in on the ground floor ♦ mop the floor up with so ♦ so clean you could eat off the floor ♦ take the floor ♦ walk the floor ♦ wipe the floor up with so

flop do a flip-flop (on sth)

flora flora and fauna

floral floral tribute

flotsam flotsam and jetsam

flow cash flow problem ♦ go with the flow ♦ stem the flow (of so/sth)

fluff fluff one's lines

flux in a (constant) state of flux ♦ in flux

fly as the crow flies ♦ come through sth (with flying colors) ♦ drop like flies ♦ fly by ♦ fly-by-night ♦ fly by the seat of one's pants ♦ fly in the face of sth ♦ a fly in the ointment ♦ fly into a rage ♦ fly into the face of danger ♦ fly off ♦ fly off the handle ♦ fly off with so/sth ♦ fly out (of some place) ♦ fly the coop ♦ fly the nest ♦ flying high ♦ Go fly a kite! ♦ It'll never fly. ♦ let fly with sth ♦ make the feathers fly ♦ make the fur fly ♦ (My,) how time flies! ♦ no flies on so ♦ not hurt a fly ♦ off (to a flying start) ♦ do sth on the fly ♦ on the fly ♦ send so flying ♦

spread one's wings (and fly) ♦ straighten up and fly right ♦ There's no flies on so. ♦ Time flies! ♦ time flies (when you're having fun) ♦ with flying colors

foam foam at the mouth

focus bring sth into focus ♦ in focus ♦ out of focus

foe friend or foe

fog able to fog a mirror ♦ in a fog

foggy the foggiest (idea)

fold fold one's hands ♦ fold, spindle, or mutilate ♦ fold sth up ♦ fold up ♦ folding money

folks home folks ♦ That's all folks!

follow Do you follow? ♦ follow one's heart ♦ follow in so's footsteps ♦ follow in so's tracks ♦ follow so's lead ♦ follow one's nose ♦ follow on (after so/sth) ♦ follow orders ♦ follow suit ♦ follow the crowd ♦ follow the line of least resistance ♦ a hard act to follow ♦ a tough act to follow

foment foment trouble

fond fond of so/sth

food food for thought ♦ order some food to go

fool any fool thing ♦ every fool thing ♦ fool around ♦ fool (around) with so/sth ♦ a fool's paradise ♦ go on a fool's errand ♦ make a fool of so ♦ nobody's fool ♦ not suffer fools gladly ♦ not suffer fools lightly ♦ on a fool's errand ♦ play so for a fool ♦ play the fool ♦ take so for a fool

foot back on one's feet ♦ the balls of one's feet ♦ bound hand and foot ♦ bring an audience to its feet ♦ bring one to one's feet ♦ catch so flat-footed ♦ cold as a well digger's feet (in January) ♦ cold feet ♦ Come in and get some weight off your feet. ♦ Come in and take a load off your feet. ♦ come to one's feet ♦ dead on one's feet ♦ dive in (with both feet) ♦ drag one's feet (on or over sth) ♦ find one's feet ♦ fleet of foot ♦ a foot in both camps ♦ foot-in-mouth disease ♦ foot the bill (for sth) ♦ get back on one's feet ♦ get cold feet ♦ get one's feet wet ♦ get one's foot in the door ♦ get off on the wrong foot ♦ get one on one's feet ♦ get sth on its feet ♦ get to one's feet ♦ have a foot in both camps ♦ have

feet of clay ♦ have one's feet on the ground ♦ have one foot in the grave ♦ have the shoe on the other foot ♦ have two left feet ♦ hold so's feet to the fire ♦ hotfoot it (off to) some place ♦ hotfoot it out of some place ♦ I wouldn't touch it with a ten-foot pole. ♦ itchy feet ♦ jump in (with both feet) ♦ keep one's feet on the ground ♦ keep sth on its feet ♦ keep out from under so's feet ♦ knock one off one's feet ♦ land (up)on both feet ♦ lay sth at so's feet ♦ let grass grow under one's feet ♦ a load off one's feet ♦ not let the grass grow under one's feet ♦ not set foot some place ♦ not touch so/sth with a ten-foot pole ♦ off on the right foot (with so/sth) ♦ off on the wrong foot ♦ on one's feet ♦ on foot ♦ on its feet ♦ the patter of tiny feet ♦ pussyfoot around ♦ put one's best foot forward ♦ put one's feet up ♦ put one's foot down (about so/sth) ♦ put one's foot in one's mouth ♦ put one on one's feet ♦ put one foot in front of the other ♦ regain one's feet ♦ rise to one's feet ♦ run one's feet off ♦ set one (back) on one's feet ♦ set foot in some place ♦ shoot oneself in the foot ♦ sit at the feet of so ♦ six feet under ♦ spring to one's feet ♦ stand on one's (own) two feet ♦ start off on the wrong foot ♦ step off on the wrong foot ♦ stick one's foot in one's mouth ♦ sweep one off one's feet ♦ take a load off one's feet ♦ think on one's feet ♦ throw oneself at so's feet ♦ vote with one's feet ♦ wait on so hand and foot ♦ walk so's feet off ♦ wouldn't touch so/sth with a ten-foot pole

football a political football

foothold a foothold (some place) ♦ get a foothold (some place)

footloose footloose and fancy-free

footsie play footsie with so

footsteps follow in so's footsteps

footwork fancy footwork

forbid forbidden fruit ♦ God forbid! ♦ Heaven forbid!

force by force of habit ♦ the driving force (behind so/sth) ♦ force so's hand ♦ a force to be reckoned with ♦ force so to the wall

♦ in force ♦ in full force ♦ out in force ♦ put sth into force

fore bring sth to the fore ♦ fore and aft

foreclose foreclose on sth

forefront at the forefront (of sth) ♦ in the forefront (of sth)

foregone a foregone conclusion

foremost first and foremost

forest not able to see the forest for the trees ♦ not to see the forest for the trees

forever forever and a day ♦ forever and ever ♦ lost and gone forever

forget forget oneself ♦ Forget (about) it! ♦ forget one's manners ♦ forgive and forget ♦ gone but not forgotten ♦ One would forget one's head if it wasn't screwed on.

forgive forgive and forget

fork fork some money out (for sth) ♦ fork sth out (to so) ♦ fork sth over (to so) ♦ speak with a forked tongue

form form an opinion ♦ form and substance ♦ in any way, shape, or form ♦ in rare form ♦ in top form ♦ true to form

fort hold the fort

forth and so forth ♦ and so on and so forth ♦ back and forth ♦ blossom (forth) ♦ burst forth ♦ give forth with sth ♦ hold forth (on so/sth) ♦ launch forth on sth ♦ pace back and forth ♦ put (sth) forth ♦ put sth forth ♦ sally forth ♦ set forth on sth ♦ venture forth

fortune come into a fortune ♦ a small fortune ♦ a stroke of good fortune

forty catch forty winks ♦ forty winks ♦ have forty winks ♦ take forty winks

forward come forward with sth ♦ from this day forward ♦ know sth backwards and forwards ♦ look forward to sth ♦ press forward ♦ put one's best foot forward ♦ put sth forward ♦ set a timepiece forward ♦ step forward

foul foul out (of sth) ♦ foul one's own nest ♦ foul play ♦ foul up ♦ foul so/sth up ♦ fouled up

found found money ♦ found sth (up)on sth ♦ lost-and-found ♦ nowhere to be found

foundation shake the foundations of sth

four between you and me and these four walls ♦ four sheets in the wind ♦ from the four corners of the earth ♦ get down (on all fours) ♦ on all fours ♦ the sixty-four-dollar question

foursome make up a foursome

fourth knee-high by the 4th of July

fowl neither fish nor fowl

fox cunning as a fox ♦ sly as a fox

frame frame sth in sth ♦ one's frame of mind

fraught fraught with danger

fray above the fray ♦ enter the fray ♦ join the fray ♦ jump into the fray

frazzle wear so to a frazzle

freak freak so out ♦ freak out (on sth) ♦ freak out (over so/sth)

free able to breathe (freely) again ♦ break free (from so/sth) ♦ feel free (to do sth) ♦ footloose and fancy-free ♦ for free ♦ free and clear ♦ free and easy ♦ free as a bird ♦ free as (the) air ♦ free for all ♦ (free) for the asking ♦ (free) for the taking ♦ free gift ♦ a free hand (with so/sth) ♦ a free ride ♦ a free translation ♦ get home free ♦ get off scot-free ♦ give so a free hand ♦ give free rein to so ♦ go scot-free ♦ have a free rein (with sth) ♦ have free reign (over sth) ♦ home free ♦ make free with so/sth ♦ of one's own free will ♦ There's no such thing as a free lunch.

freedom give one one's freedom

freeze freeze so/sth in one's memory ♦ a freeze on doing sth ♦ freeze so out ♦ freeze one's tail off ♦ freeze so/sth to death ♦ freeze up ♦ freeze so's wages ♦ play freeze-out ♦ put the freeze on so ♦ (un)til hell freezes over

French Excuse my French. ♦ Pardon my French.

frenzy a feeding frenzy

fresh a breath of fresh air ♦ fresh and sweet ♦ fresh as a daisy ♦ fresh blood ♦ fresh from some place ♦ fresh out of sth ♦ a fresh pair of eyes ♦ a fresh start ♦ fresh (with so)

fret Fret not!

friend Any friend of so('s) (is a friend of mine). ♦ fair-weather friend ♦ fast friends ♦ A friend in need is a friend indeed. ♦ friend or foe ♦ friends with so ♦ have friends in high places ♦ make friends with so ♦ man's best friend ♦ user friendly

friendship strike up a friendship (with so)

frighten frighten so out of a year's growth ♦ frighten one out of one's mind ♦ frighten one out of one's wits ♦ frighten the hell out of so ♦ frighten the living daylights out of so ♦ frighten the pants off so ♦ frighten so to death ♦ frightened to death

fringe the lunatic fringe ♦ on the fringe

fritter fritter sth away

fritz on the fritz

fro to and fro ♦ toing and froing (on sth)

frog a big frog in a small pond ♦ a frog in one's throat ♦ have a frog in one's throat ♦ like herding frogs

front burn one's bridges in front of one ♦ can't see one's hand in front of one's face ♦ cover the waterfront ♦ front so some amount of money ♦ front for so/sth ♦ front off (about sth) ♦ front on sth ♦ the front runner ♦ on the front burner ♦ out front ♦ put sth on the front burner ♦ put one foot in front of the other ♦ put up a (brave) front ♦ up front

frost frosted (over)

fruit bear fruit ♦ forbidden fruit ♦ the fruits of one's labor(s) ♦ low-hanging fruit

fruitcake nutty as a fruitcake

fruition bring sth to fruition

fry Go fry an egg! ♦ have bigger fish to fry ♦ have more important fish to fry ♦ have other fish to fry ♦ jump out of the frying pan (and) into the fire ♦ out of the frying pan (and) into the fire ♦ small fry

fuck Fuck you! ♦ What the fuck?

fudge fudge factor

fuel add fuel to the fire ♦ add fuel to the flame

full at full blast ♦ at full speed ♦ at full strength ♦ at full tilt ♦ chock full of sth ♦ come full circle ♦ fill so full of lead ♦ full as a tick ♦ a full-blown sth ♦ full of oneself ♦ full of beans ♦ full of bull ♦ full of crap ♦ full of holes ♦ full of hot air ♦ full of it ♦ full of Old Nick ♦ full of prunes ♦ full of shit ♦ full of the devil ♦ full steam ahead ♦ full up ♦ get up a (full) head of steam ♦ have one's hands full (with so/sth) ♦ in full flight ♦ in full force ♦ in full swing ♦ in the

fullness of time ♦ know full well ♦ a mouth full of South ♦ not playing with a full deck ♦ play sth at full blast ♦ play with a full deck ♦ shot full of holes ♦ turn sth into a full-time job ♦ the woods are full of so/sth

fullness in the fullness of time

fume running on fumes

fun all in fun ♦ as much fun as a barrel of monkeys ♦ a barrel of fun ♦ for the fun of it ♦ fun and games ♦ Getting there is half the fun. ♦ make fun of so/sth ♦ more fun than a barrel of monkeys ♦ poke fun at so/sth ♦ time flies (when you're having fun)

function bodily functions

funeral It's your funeral.

funk in a (blue) funk

funny Cut the funny stuff! ♦ funny as a crutch ♦ funny bone ♦ funny business ♦ funny ha-ha ♦ funny money ♦ funny peculiar ♦ Funny thing is that . . . ♦ It's a funny thing, but . . . ♦ See you in the funny papers. ♦ strike so funny ♦ That's funny. ♦ too funny for words

fur make the fur fly ♦ rub so's fur the wrong way

furious fast and furious

further cannot see (any) further than the end of one's nose ♦ Don't let it go any further. ♦ see no further than the end of one's nose ♦ without further ado

furthermore furthermore

furtive a furtive glance

fuse blow a fuse ♦ a short fuse

fuss kick up a fuss

future at some point (in the future) ♦ One's future looks bright. ♦ in the near future

futz futz around ♦ futz sth up

gab have the gift of gab

gad gad around

gag gag on sth

gain gain from sth ♦ gain ground (on so/sth) ♦ ill-gotten gains ♦ No pain, no gain. ♦ Nothing ventured, nothing gained.

gale gales of laughter

gall have the gall to do sth

gallery play to the gallery

gallivant gallivant around

gallop break into a gallop ◆ gallop through sth

galumph galumph around

galvanize galvanize so into action

gambit opening gambit

gamble gamble sth away ◆ gamble on so/sth

game ahead of the game ◆ at the top of one's game ◆ at this stage (of the game) ◆ back in the game ◆ be game (for sth) ◆ beat one at one's own game ◆ the end of the ball game ◆ fun and games ◆ The game is up. ◆ a game that two can play ◆ get ahead of the game ◆ give the game away ◆ got game ◆ keep ahead of the game ◆ the name of the game ◆ off one's game ◆ the only game in town ◆ play games (with so) ◆ stay ahead of the game ◆ throw a game ◆ Two can play (at) this game (as well as one). ◆ a (whole) new ball game

gamut run the gamut

gander take a gander (at so/sth)

gang gang up (on so)

gangbusters come on like gangbusters ◆ like gangbusters

gap bridge the gap ◆ fill the gap

garbage garbage sth down

garden lead so down the garden path

gas cooking with gas ◆ out of gas ◆ pass gas ◆ run out of gas ◆ step on the gas

gasket blow a gasket

gasp at the last gasp

gate get the gate ◆ give so the gate ◆ (right) out of the (starting) gate

gather gather dust ◆ wool-gathering

gaudy gaudy as a butterfly

gauntlet run the gauntlet ◆ throw down the gauntlet

gay with gay abandon

gaze a steely gaze

gear get one's ass in gear ◆ get one's tail in gear ◆ in high gear ◆ shift gears ◆ swing into high gear ◆ switch gears

general as a (general) rule ◆ in general

generation Generation X(er)

generous generous to a fault

genius a budding genius ◆ a stroke of genius

gentle gentle as a lamb

genuine the genuine article

George Let George do it.

Georgia all over hell and half of Georgia

gesture a token gesture

get (Are) things getting you down? ◆ as all get out ◆ one can (just) get oneself another boy ◆ Cat got your tongue? ◆ Come an(d) get it! ◆ Come in and get some weight off your feet. ◆ (Do you) get my drift? ◆ Don't get your bowels in an uproar! ◆ Don't let so/sth get you down. ◆ Flattery will get you nowhere. ◆ get sth ◆ get a bee in one's bonnet ◆ get a bright idea ◆ get a charge out of so/sth ◆ get a foothold (some place) ◆ get a grip on oneself ◆ get a handle on sth ◆ get a head start (on so) ◆ get a kick out of so/sth ◆ get a licking ◆ Get a life! ◆ get a load of so/sth ◆ get a lot of mileage out of sth ◆ Get a move on. ◆ get a reputation (as a sth) ◆ get a reputation (for doing sth) ◆ get a rise from so ◆ get a ticket ◆ get a word in edgewise ◆ get aboard sth ◆ get so across (in a good way) ◆ get sth across (to so) ◆ get one's act together ◆ get after so ◆ get ahead (in sth) ◆ get ahead of the game ◆ get (a)hold of so ◆ get (all) spruced up ◆ get so (all) wrong ◆ get along ◆ get along on sth ◆ get along (on a shoestring) ◆ get along (with so) ◆ get along without (so/sth) ◆ get ants in one's pants ◆ get around so/sth ◆ get so around the table ◆ get one's ass in gear ◆ get at so ◆ get at sth ◆ get so's attention ◆ get away from it all ◆ get away with sth ◆ get away with murder ◆ get axed ◆ get back (at so) ◆ get back in (the) harness ◆ get back in(to) circulation ◆ get back on one's feet ◆ get sth back on track ◆ get so's back up ◆ get one's bearings ◆ get behind schedule ◆ get so's blood up ◆ get busy ◆ get butterflies in one's stomach ◆ get by (on a small amount of money) ◆ get by (with sth) ◆ get carried away ◆ get close to so ◆ get cold feet ◆ get one's comeuppance ◆ get so's dander up ◆ get down ◆ get so down ◆ get sth down ◆ get sth down (in black and white) ◆ get (down) off one's high horse ◆ get down

get the runaround ♦ get the shock of one's life ♦ get the short end (of the stick) ♦ get the show on the road ♦ get the third degree ♦ get the word ♦ get the worst of sth ♦ get the wrinkles out (of sth) ♦ get through (sth) ♦ get sth through so's thick skull ♦ get through (to so) ♦ get through (to sth) ♦ get one's ticket punched ♦ get to so ♦ get to sth ♦ get to one's feet ♦ get to first base (with so/sth) ♦ get to the bottom of sth ♦ get to the point (of sth) ♦ get to the root of the problem ♦ get to the top (of sth) ♦ get sth together ♦ get sth together (for a particular time) ♦ get together (with so) (on so/sth) ♦ get tough (with so) ♦ get under so's skin ♦ get sth under way ♦ get up ♦ get sth up ♦ get up a (full) head of steam ♦ get up a thirst ♦ get up an appetite ♦ get so up (for sth) ♦ get up on one's hind legs ♦ get up on the wrong side of bed ♦ get up to sth ♦ get up to speed on so/sth ♦ get upside down ♦ get one's walking papers ♦ get what's coming to one ♦ get wind of sth ♦ get wise to so/sth ♦ get with it ♦ get with the program ♦ get word (from so/sth) ♦ get worked up (over sth) ♦ get so wrong ♦ Get your ass over here! ♦ Get your buns over here! ♦ Get your butt over here! ♦ Get your head out of the clouds! ♦ Get your nose out of my business. ♦ Getting there is half the fun. ♦ get-up-and-go ♦ give as good as one gets ♦ Give it all you've got! ♦ got game ♦ gotta get up pretty early in the morning to do sth ♦ have (got) a glow on ♦ have (got) a load on ♦ have (got) one's ass in a sling ♦ have (got) sth coming (to one) ♦ have (got) it made ♦ have (got) one's mind in the gutter ♦ have (got) to hand it to so ♦ have (got) what it takes ♦ Have I got something for you! ♦ have to get married ♦ help so/animal (get) over sth ♦ How are you getting on? ♦ I'd better get on my horse. ♦ if the going gets tough ♦ if you get my drift ♦ I'll get right on it. ♦ ill-gotten gains ♦ (It's) got me beat. ♦ It takes (some) getting used to. ♦ (I've) (got) better things to do. ♦ (I've) got to go home and get my beauty sleep. ♦ let so get by with sth ♦ let sth (get) out ♦ let sth

get out ♦ Let's get down to business. ♦ not able to get sth for love (n)or money ♦ not get one's hopes up ♦ on your mark, get set, go ♦ the one that got away ♦ out to get so ♦ play hard to get ♦ a (real) go-getter ♦ Something's got to give. ♦ tell so where to get off ♦ Things getting you down? ♦ We all gotta go sometime. ♦ What's got(ten) into so? ♦ What you see is what you get. ♦ when it gets down to the crunch ♦ when the going gets tough ♦ when you get a chance ♦ when you get a minute ♦ Where do (you think) you get off? ♦ (You) can't get there from here. ♦ You got it! ♦ You got me beat. ♦ You'll get the hang of it. ♦ You've got another think coming. ♦ You've got me stumped.

getter a (real) go-getter

ghost a ghost of a chance ♦ give up the ghost ♦ pale as a ghost ♦ white as a ghost

giant a sleeping giant

gift free gift ♦ God's gift (to women) ♦ have a gift for (doing) sth ♦ have the gift of gab ♦ look a gift horse in the mouth

giggle for giggles

gild gild the lily

gill blue around the gills ♦ green around the gills ♦ loaded to the gills ♦ pale around the gills

gimme Gimme a break!

gird gird up one's loins

girl That's my girl.

git from the git-go ♦ Them as has, gits.

gitalong have a hitch in one's gitalong

give Don't give me any of your lip! ♦ Don't give me that (line)! ♦ Don't give up! ♦ Don't give up the ship! ♦ Don't give up without a fight! ♦ Don't give up your day job. ♦ Gimme a break! ♦ give so a bang ♦ give so a big hand for sth ♦ give so a (big) head ♦ give so a big send-off ♦ give so a blank check ♦ give so a blank look ♦ give so a blank stare ♦ give so a break ♦ give so a bum steer ♦ give so a buzz ♦ give so a call ♦ give so a charge ♦ give so a clean bill of health ♦ give so a dig ♦ give so a dirty look ♦ give so a fair shake ♦ give so a fat lip ♦ give so a free hand ♦ give sth a go ♦ give a good account of oneself ♦ give so a (good) bawling out ♦ give so a (good) dressing-down ♦ give so a (good) talking to ♦ give so a (good) working over ♦ give so a hand with sth ♦ give so a heads up ♦ give so a kick ♦ give so a leg up ♦ give so a lift ♦ give so a line ♦ give a little ♦ give so a pain ♦ give so a pat on the back ♦ give so a perspective on sth ♦ give so a piece of one's mind ♦ give so a red face ♦ give sth a rest ♦ give so a ride ♦ give so a ring ♦ give sth a shot ♦ give so a start ♦ give sth a try ♦ give sth a whirl ♦ give so/sth a wide berth ♦ give oneself airs ♦ give so an A for effort ♦ give an account of so/sth (to so) ♦ give (an) ear to so/sth ♦ give so an earful ♦ give so an even break ♦ give so an eyeful ♦ Give one an inch and one will take a mile. ♦ give so an out ♦ give as good as one gets ♦ give so/sth away ♦ give so away (to so) ♦ give sth away (to so) ♦ give birth to sth ♦ give so carte blanche ♦ give cause for sth ♦ give chase (to so/sth) ♦ give credence to so/sth ♦ give currency to sth ♦ give evidence of sth ♦ give one's eyeteeth (for so/sth) ♦ give forth with sth ♦ give free rein to so ♦ give one one's freedom ♦ give so gray hair(s) ♦ give so grief (over so/sth) ♦ give ground ♦ give so Hail Columbia ♦ give so/sth half a chance ♦ give one's heart to so ♦ give her the gun ♦ give in (to so/sth) ♦ Give it a rest! ♦ Give it all you've got! ♦ give it the gun ♦ Give it time. ♦ give it to so (straight) ♦ Give it up! ♦ Give me a break! ♦ Give me a call. ♦ Give me a chance! ♦ Give me a rest! ♦ Give me a ring. ♦ Give me five! ♦ Give me (some) skin! ♦ Give my best to so. ♦ Give so my love. ♦ give so no quarter ♦ give (one's) notice ♦ give notice that . . . ♦ give notice to so ♦ give so odds that . . . ♦ give of oneself ♦ give or take an amount ♦ give out ♦ give sth out ♦ give out with sth ♦ give oneself over to so/sth ♦ give so pause (for thought) ♦ give one's right arm (for so/sth) ♦ give rise to sth ♦ give so some lip ♦ give some thought to sth ♦ give so static ♦ give so the air ♦ give so the benefit of the doubt ♦ give so the big eye ♦ give so the boot ♦ give so the brush-off ♦ give so the bum's rush ♦ give so the business ♦ give so

the cold shoulder ♦ give so the devil ♦ give the devil his due ♦ give so the edge on so ♦ give so the eye ♦ give so the finger ♦ give the game away ♦ give so the gate ♦ give so the glad hand ♦ give so the go-by ♦ give so the high sign ♦ give the lie to sth ♦ give so the (old) heave-ho ♦ give so/sth the once-over ♦ give so the once-over ♦ give so the raspberry ♦ give so the sack ♦ give so the shaft ♦ give so the shirt off one's back ♦ give so the slip ♦ give so the works ♦ give so tit for tat ♦ give so sth to talk about ♦ give so to understand sth ♦ give so up for dead ♦ give so/sth up (for lost) ♦ give up the fight ♦ give up the ghost ♦ give up the struggle ♦ give vent to sth ♦ give voice to sth ♦ give weight to sth ♦ give so what for ♦ give with sth ♦ give-and-take ♦ a given ♦ given half a chance ♦ given to doing sth ♦ given to understand ♦ a lot of give-and-take ♦ not give a fig ♦ not give a hang about so/sth ♦ not give a shit ♦ not give a (tinker's) damn ♦ not give an inch ♦ not give it a(nother) thought ♦ not give much for so's chances ♦ not give so the time of day ♦ not give two hoots about so/sth ♦ Something's got to give. ♦ What I wouldn't give for a sth! ♦ would give anything for sth

giveaway a dead giveaway

glad Am I glad to see you! ♦ give so the glad hand ♦ the glad hand ♦ not suffer fools gladly

glance at first glance ♦ dart a glance at so/sth ♦ a fleeting glance ♦ a furtive glance ♦ know sth at a glance

glass have a glass jaw ♦ raise one's glass to so/sth ♦ smooth as glass

glaze glaze over

glean glean sth from so/sth

glimmer not a glimmer (of an idea)

gloom gloom and doom

glory Glory be! ♦ glory in sth ♦ in all its glory ♦ in one's glory ♦ send so to glory

gloss gloss over sth

glove fit like a glove ♦ The gloves are off. ♦ hand in glove (with so) ♦ handle so with kid gloves ♦ rule with a velvet glove ♦ take one's gloves off ♦ treat so with kid gloves ♦ work hand in glove (with so)

glow glow with sth ♦ have (got) a glow on ♦ in glowing terms

glue come unglued ♦ glued to so ♦ glued to sth

glut a glut on the market

glutton a glutton for punishment

gnash gnash one's teeth ♦ a gnashing of teeth

gnat down to a gnat's eyebrow

gnaw gnaw (away) at so

go all dressed up and nowhere to go ♦ all over hell and gone ♦ all show and no go ♦ All systems (are) go. ♦ (Are you) going my way? ♦ as far as sth goes ♦ dead and gone ♦ Don't let it go any further. ♦ easy come, easy go ♦ far gone ♦ from the git-go ♦ from the word go ♦ get going ♦ get so going ♦ get sth going with so ♦ get the go-by ♦ get-up-and-go ♦ give sth a go ♦ give so the go-by ♦ go a long way toward doing sth ♦ go about ♦ go about one's business ♦ go above and beyond one's duty ♦ go above and beyond (what is expected) ♦ go after so ♦ go after so/sth/animal ♦ go against the grain ♦ the go-ahead ♦ (Go ahead,) make my day! ♦ go all out ♦ go all out (for so/sth) ♦ go all the way (with so) ♦ go along with so/sth ♦ go along (with so) for the ride ♦ go ape (over so/sth) ♦ go around ♦ go around so ♦ go around and around (about so/sth) ♦ go (a)round in circles ♦ go (a)round the bend ♦ go around (with so) ♦ go astray ♦ go at it hammer and tongs ♦ go at it tooth and nail ♦ go at one another tooth and nail ♦ Go away! ♦ go away empty-handed ♦ go AWOL ♦ go back a long way ♦ go back on one's pledge ♦ go back on one's promise ♦ go back on one's word ♦ go back quite a way(s) ♦ go back to square one ♦ go back to the drawing board ♦ go back to the salt mines ♦ go bad ♦ go ballistic ♦ go bananas ♦ go begging ♦ go behind so's back ♦ go belly up ♦ go beyond sth ♦ go blank ♦ go broke ♦ go by sth ♦ go by the board ♦ go by the book ♦ go by the name of sth ♦ Go chase yourself! ♦ Go climb a tree! ♦ go cold turkey ♦ go crazy ♦ go down ♦ go down fighting ♦ go down for the third time ♦ go down in defeat ♦ go down in flames ♦ go down (in history) (as so/sth) ♦ go down in the annals of history ♦ go down in the history books ♦ go down on one's knees ♦ go down that road ♦ go down the chute ♦ go down the drain ♦ go down the line ♦ go down the tube(s) ♦ go downhill ♦ go Dutch ♦ go easy on so/sth ♦ go easy on sth ♦ go fifty-fifty (on sth) ♦ Go figure. ♦ Go fly a kite! ♦ go for so/sth ♦ go for a spin ♦ go for broke ♦ Go for it! ♦ go for nothing ♦ go for the jugular (vein) ♦ go for the throat ♦ go from bad to worse ♦ go from one extreme to the other ♦ go from strength to strength ♦ Go fry an egg! ♦ go haywire ♦ go head to head with so ♦ go hog wild ♦ go home in a box ♦ go home to mama ♦ go hungry ♦ go in so's favor ♦ go in for sth ♦ go in one ear and out the other ♦ go in with so (on sth) ♦ go into sth ♦ go into a huddle ♦ go into a nosedive ♦ go into a song and dance (about sth) ♦ go into a tailspin ♦ go into one's act ♦ go into detail(s) ♦ go into effect ♦ go into hiding ♦ go into hock ♦ go into orbit ♦ go into service ♦ go into one's song and dance ♦ go into the same old song and dance (about sth) ♦ go into the service ♦ go it alone ♦ Go jump in the lake! ♦ go like clockwork ♦ go native ♦ go near (to) so/sth ♦ go nowhere fast ♦ go nuts ♦ go off ♦ go off half-cocked ♦ go off on so ♦ go off the deep end ♦ Go on. ♦ go on sth ♦ go on a binge ♦ go on a fool's errand ♦ go on a rampage ♦ go on and on ♦ go on (and on) (about so/sth) ♦ go on before so ♦ go on for an age ♦ go on to a better land ♦ Go on (with you)! ♦ go (so) one better ♦ go one one better (than that) ♦ go one on one with so ♦ go out ♦ go out (for sth) ♦ go out for a spin ♦ go out in search of so/sth ♦ go out like a light ♦ go out of business ♦ go out of one's mind ♦ go out of play ♦ go out of one's skull ♦ go out of one's way (to do sth) ♦ go (out) on strike ♦ go out to so ♦ go out (with so) ♦ go over sth ♦ go over big (with so) ♦ go over like a lead balloon ♦ go over (well) ♦ go over sth (with so) ♦ go over with a bang ♦ go over sth with a fine-tooth(ed) comb ♦ go overboard ♦ go places ♦ Go play in the traffic. ♦ go postal ♦ go public (with sth) ♦ go (right) through so ♦ go scot-free ♦ go sky-high ♦ go so far as doing sth ♦ go sour ♦ go South ♦ go stag ♦ go (steady) with so ♦ go stir crazy ♦ go straight ♦ go (straight) to the top ♦ go that route ♦ go the distance ♦ go the extra mile ♦ go the limit ♦ go the way of the dodo ♦ go the way of the horse and buggy ♦ go their separate ways ♦ go there ♦ go through ♦ go through so/sth ♦ go through sth ♦ go through so like a dose of the salts ♦ go through the changes ♦ go through the mill ♦ go through the motions ♦ go through (the proper) channels ♦ go through the roof ♦ go through with sth ♦ go through sth with a fine-tooth(ed) comb ♦ Go to! ♦ go to any length ♦ go to bat against so ♦ go to bat for so ♦ go to bat for sth ♦ go to bed ♦ go to bed (with so) ♦ go to bed with the chickens ♦ Go to blazes! ♦ go to extremes (to do sth) ♦ go to great lengths (to do sth) ♦ go to so's head ♦ go to hell ♦ go to hell in a bucket ♦ go to hell in a handbasket ♦ go to it ♦ go to one's (just) reward ♦ go to pieces ♦ go to pot ♦ go to press ♦ go to press with sth ♦ go to rack and ruin ♦ go to sea ♦ go to seed ♦ go to the bathroom ♦ go to the bother (of doing sth) ♦ go to (the devil) ♦ go to the dogs ♦ go to the expense (of doing sth) ♦ go to the lavatory ♦ go to the limit ♦ go to the mat (on sth) ♦ go to the polls ♦ go to the toilet ♦ go to the trouble (of doing sth) ♦ go to the wall (on sth) ♦ go to town ♦ go to trial ♦ go to war (over so/sth) ♦ go to waste ♦ go to wrack and ruin ♦ go under ♦ go under the hammer ♦ go under the knife ♦ go under the name of sth ♦ go under the wrecking ball ♦ go up against so ♦ go up in flames ♦ go up in smoke ♦ go whole hog ♦ go wild ♦ go window-shopping ♦ go with (so/sth) ♦ go with sth ♦ go with one's gut (feeling) ♦ go with it ♦ go with the flow ♦ go with the territory ♦ go with the tide ♦ go without ♦ go wrong ♦ goes for so/sth (too) ♦ the going ♦ the going rate ♦ going great guns ♦ Going my way? ♦ going strong ♦ going to tattle ♦ going to tell ♦ gone but not forgotten ♦ gone goose ♦ gone on ♦ gone to meet one's maker ♦ gone with the wind ♦ good to go ♦ has come and gone ♦ have a good thing going ♦ have a lot going (for one) ♦ have a thing going (with so) ♦ have sth going (for oneself) ♦ have enough (sth) to go around ♦ have one's heart go out to so ♦ have to go some (to do sth) ♦ heavy going ♦ one's heart goes out to so ♦ Here goes nothing. ♦ Here (it) goes. ♦ Here we go again. ♦ Here you go. ♦ hide-and-(go-)seek ♦ How goes it (with you)? ♦ How's it going? ♦ if the going gets tough ♦ I'm gone. ♦ sth is (a) no go ♦ (It) just goes to show (you) (sth). ♦ (It) (just) goes without saying ♦ (I've) got to go home and get my beauty sleep. ♦ Just goes to show (you) (sth). ♦ (It) (just) goes without saying ♦ let oneself go ♦ let so go ♦ let go (with sth) ♦ Let it go. ♦ like it is going out of style ♦ long gone ♦ lost and gone forever ♦ make a go of sth ♦ not know if one is coming or going ♦ not know whether one is coming or going ♦ one's mind goes blank ♦ on the go ♦ on your mark, get set, go ♦ the only way to go ♦ order some food to go ♦ pay as you go ♦ raring to go ♦ ready, set, go ♦ a (real) go-getter ♦ slow going ♦ So it goes. ♦ spend money like it's going out of style ♦ stop-and-go ♦ Sunday-go-to-meeting clothes ♦ (That's the) way to go! ♦ There you go. ♦ They went that a'way. ♦ to go ♦ to hell and gone ♦ touch and go ♦ tough going ♦ Way to go! ♦ We all gotta go sometime. ♦ went out with the buggy whip ♦ went out with the horse and buggy ♦ went out with the horse and carriage ♦ What's going down? ♦ when the going gets tough ♦ You go to your church, and I'll go to mine.

goal fall short of one's goal(s) ♦ fall short of the goal(s)

goat get so's goat ♦ separate the sheep from the goats

god an act of God ♦ fit for the gods ♦ (God) bless you! ♦ God forbid! ♦ God only knows! ♦ God rest so's soul. ♦ God's gift (to women) ♦ God willing. ♦ God willing

and the creek don't rise. ♦ Hand to God! ♦
Honest to God. ♦ (My) hand to God! ♦
pray to the porcelain god ♦ put the fear
of God in(to) so ♦ So help me(, God)! ♦
sure as God made little green apples ♦
Thank God for small favors. ♦ think so is
God's own cousin ♦ Where on (God's
green) earth? ♦ Ye gods (and little fishes)!

Godfrey By Godfrey!

gold a gold mine of information ♦ a golden
opportunity ♦ good as gold ♦ have a heart
of gold ♦ a pot of gold ♦ sitting on a gold
mine ♦ worth its weight in gold

golly by guess and by golly ♦ Good golly,
Miss Molly!

goner a goner

good (all) in good time ♦ all to the good ♦
(all) well and good ♦ Anybody's guess is
as good as mine. ♦ as good as done ♦ as
good as one's word ♦ at a good clip ♦ be
of a (good) mind to do sth ♦ but good ♦
clean up good ♦ come to no good ♦
cuddle up with a (good) book ♦ curl up
(with a (good) book) ♦ deliver the goods
♦ do a world of good (for so/sth) ♦ do so's
heart good ♦ do more harm than good ♦
err on the side of sth good ♦ fight the good
fight ♦ for good ♦ for good measure ♦ For
goodness sake(s)! ♦ for the good of so/sth
♦ get so across (in a good way) ♦ get off a
few good ones ♦ get (out) while the
gettin(g)'s good ♦ get the goods on so ♦
give a good account of oneself ♦ give so a
(good) bawling out ♦ give so a (good)
talking to ♦ give so a (good) working over
♦ give as good as one gets ♦ give so a
(good) dressing-down ♦ a good (amount or
distance) ♦ good and sth ♦ good as sth ♦
good as gold ♦ good as new ♦ a good bet
♦ the Good Book ♦ a (good) dressing-down
♦ a good egg ♦ good enough for so/sth ♦
good enough for government work ♦
good for what ails you ♦ Good for you! ♦
Good golly, Miss Molly! ♦ a (good) grasp
of sth ♦ Good grief! ♦ (Good) heavens! ♦
Good luck! ♦ a good many ♦ good old boy
♦ the good old days ♦ a good sport ♦ a
(good) talking to ♦ A good time was had
by all. ♦ good to go ♦ a (good) working
over ♦ good-bye and good riddance ♦

Good-bye for now. ♦ (Good-bye) till later.
♦ (Good-bye) until later. ♦ (Good-bye)
until next time. ♦ (Good-bye) until then. ♦
good-for-nothing ♦ the goods on so ♦ have
a good arm ♦ have a good command of
sth ♦ Have a good day. ♦ have a (good)
head for sth ♦ have a good head on one's
shoulders ♦ have a (good) mind to do sth ♦
Have a good one. ♦ have a good run ♦
have a good thing going ♦ have sth on
good authority ♦ hold good for so/sth ♦
hold so in good stead ♦ Honest to
goodness. ♦ if one knows what's good for
one ♦ if you know what's good for you ♦
I'm good. ♦ in a good light ♦ in (all) good
conscience ♦ in good company ♦ in good
condition ♦ in good faith ♦ in so's good
graces ♦ in good hands ♦ in good repair ♦
in good shape ♦ in good spirits ♦ in good
time ♦ in (good) (with so) ♦ keep good
time ♦ keep in good with so ♦ Keep up
the good work. ♦ kiss sth good-bye ♦ Life's
been good (to me). ♦ look good on paper
♦ make sth good ♦ make good as sth ♦
make good ((at) sth) ♦ make good money
♦ make good ((on) sth) ♦ make good time
♦ never had it so good ♦ No news is good
news. ♦ off to a good start (with so/sth) ♦
on so's good side ♦ on good terms (with
so) ♦ on the good side of so ♦ onto a good
thing ♦ do sth out of the goodness of one's
heart ♦ out of the goodness of one's heart
♦ overstep the bounds of good taste ♦ the
picture of (good) health ♦ pour good
money after bad ♦ put so across (in a good
way) ♦ put in a good word (for so) ♦ put
sth to (good) use ♦ run the good race ♦
say good-bye to sth ♦ scrub up good ♦ sell
so a bill of goods ♦ show good faith ♦
show sth to good advantage ♦ snuggle up
(with a (good) book) ♦ so far, so good ♦
stand so in good stead ♦ a streak of good
luck ♦ a string of good luck ♦ a stroke of
good fortune ♦ Thank goodness! ♦ throw
good money after bad ♦ time off for good
behavior ♦ too good to be true ♦ too
much of a good thing ♦ travel at a good
clip ♦ turn sth to good account ♦ twelve
good men and true ♦ up to no good ♦
well and good ♦ when one is good and

ready ♦ so's word is good ♦ Your guess is as good as mine

goof goof around ♦ goof off ♦ goof on so ♦ goof so/sth up ♦ goof up (on sth)

goose cook so's goose ♦ gone goose ♦ goose bumps ♦ goose egg ♦ one's goose is cooked ♦ goose pimples ♦ send so on a wild-goose chase ♦ silly as a goose ♦ a wild-goose chase

gorgeous drop-dead gorgeous

gosh by guess and by gosh

Goshen Land o' Goshen!

gospel as Gospel ♦ the gospel truth ♦ take sth as Gospel

gotta gotta get up pretty early in the morning to do sth ♦ We all gotta go sometime.

government close enough for government work ♦ good enough for government work

gown cap and gown ♦ town-and-gown

grab grab a bite (to eat) ♦ grab a chair ♦ grab a seat ♦ grab so's attention ♦ How does that grab you? ♦ up for grabs

grace fall from grace ♦ grace sth with sth ♦ grace so/sth with one's presence ♦ graced with sth ♦ in so's good graces ♦ lapse from grace ♦ saving grace ♦ say grace

graceful graceful as a swan

gracious a gracious plenty

grade make the grade

grain against the grain ♦ cut against the grain ♦ go against the grain ♦ a grain of truth ♦ run against the grain ♦ saw against the grain ♦ take sth with a grain of salt

grand busy as Grand Central Station

granddaddy the granddaddy of them all

grandfather a grandfather clause ♦ grandfather so/sth in

grandmother teach one's grandmother to suck eggs

grant grant so no quarter ♦ take so/sth for granted

grape belt the grape ♦ sour grapes

grapevine by the grapevine ♦ hear sth through the grapevine ♦ through the grapevine

grapple grapple with sth

grasp a (good) grasp of sth ♦ grasping at straws ♦ have a (solid) grasp of sth ♦ a (solid) grasp of sth ♦ a (sound) grasp of sth ♦ within one's grasp

grass grass widow ♦ green as grass ♦ let grass grow under one's feet ♦ not let the grass grow under one's feet ♦ snake in the grass

grasshopper knee-high to a grasshopper

grate grate on so('s nerves)

grateful grateful beyond words

gratitude owe so a debt of gratitude

grave carry a secret to the grave ♦ dig one's own grave ♦ from the cradle to the grave ♦ have one foot in the grave ♦ quiet as the grave ♦ rise from the grave ♦ roll (over) in one's grave ♦ silent as the grave ♦ spin in one's grave ♦ swear on one's mother's grave ♦ take it to one's grave ♦ turn (over) in one's grave

graveyard the graveyard shift

gravy The rest is gravy. ♦ ride the gravy train

gray give so gray hair(s) ♦ a gray area ♦ gray hair(s) ♦ gray matter

grease elbow grease ♦ grease so's palm ♦ grease the skids ♦ like greased lightning ♦ quick as (greased) lightning ♦ use some elbow grease

greasy a greasy spoon

great at great length ♦ far and away the greatest ♦ go to great lengths (to do sth) ♦ going great guns ♦ Great balls of fire! ♦ the great beyond ♦ Great day (in the morning)! ♦ a great deal ♦ Great Scott! ♦ the great unwashed ♦ the greatest thing since indoor plumbing ♦ the greatest thing since sliced bread ♦ in (great) demand ♦ in great haste ♦ in the (great) scheme of things ♦ make a great show of sth ♦ no great shakes ♦ set great store by so/sth ♦ speak at great length ♦ take (great) pains (to do sth) ♦ think a great deal of so/sth ♦ to a great extent ♦ with (great) relish

Greek Greek to so

green green around the gills ♦ green as grass ♦ green stuff ♦ green with envy ♦ have a green thumb ♦ sure as God made little green apples ♦ Where on (God's green) earth?

greet Greetings and felicitations! ♦ Greetings and salutations!

grief come to grief ♦ give so grief (over so/sth) ♦ Good grief!

grievance air one's grievances

grim the grim reaper

grin grin and bear it ♦ grin from ear to ear

grind the daily grind ♦ grind away (at so) ♦ grind so down ♦ grind to a halt ♦ have an ax(e) to grind (with so)

grindstone keep one's nose to the grindstone ♦ put one's nose to the grindstone

grip come to grips with so/sth ♦ get a grip on oneself ♦ grip so's attention ♦ a grip on oneself ♦ a grip on sth ♦ in the grip of sth ♦ keep a firm grip on so/sth ♦ keep a tight grip on so/sth ♦ lose one's grip on so/sth ♦ take a firm grip on so/sth

gripe gripe one's soul

grist grist for the mill ♦ grist to the mill

grit get down to the nitty-gritty ♦ grit one's teeth

groan groan under sth

grocery blow one's groceries

gronk gronk (out)

groove groove on so/sth ♦ in the groove

gross gross so out

ground break ground (for sth) ♦ break new ground ♦ cover a lot of ground ♦ cut the ground out from under so ♦ don't know one's ass from a hole in the ground ♦ from the ground up ♦ gain ground (on so/sth) ♦ get sth off the ground ♦ give ground ♦ ground so ♦ ground so in sth ♦ ground sth on sth ♦ grounded in (actual) fact ♦ grounds for sth ♦ have an ear to the ground ♦ have one's feet on the ground ♦ hit the ground running ♦ hold one's ground ♦ in on the ground floor ♦ keep an ear to the ground ♦ keep one's feet on the ground ♦ level sth to the ground ♦ lose ground (to so/sth) ♦ a middle ground ♦ one's old stamping ground ♦ on dangerous ground ♦ on moral grounds ♦ on shaky ground ♦ riveted to the ground ♦ run sth

into the ground ♦ stand one's ground ♦ worship the ground so walks on

group hold sway (among a group) ♦ pack a group

grow grow apart (from so/sth) ♦ grow by leaps and bounds ♦ grow in sth ♦ grow on so ♦ grow out of sth ♦ grow out of (all) proportion ♦ grow to do sth ♦ have growing pains ♦ let grass grow under one's feet ♦ not grow on trees ♦ not let the grass grow under one's feet

growth frighten so out of a year's growth ♦ a growth experience ♦ a growth opportunity ♦ scare so out of a year's growth

grudge bear a grudge (against so) ♦ have a grudge (against so) ♦ nurse a grudge (against so)

gruff gruff as a bear

grunt grunt work

guard catch so off guard ♦ drop one's guard ♦ keep on one's guard ♦ let one's guard down ♦ lower one's guard ♦ on one's guard

guess Anybody's guess is as good as mine. ♦ by guess and by golly ♦ by guess and by gosh ♦ Guess what! ♦ hazard a guess ♦ It's anybody's guess. ♦ keep so guessing ♦ leave so guessing ♦ never would have guessed ♦ outguess so ♦ second-guess so ♦ Your guess is as good as mine.

guest Be my guest. ♦ guest of honor

guilt lay a guilt trip on so

guinea serve as a guinea pig

gulch dry-gulch so

gulp gulp for air

gum beat one's gums ♦ gum the works up ♦ gum sth up

gun beat the gun ♦ give her the gun ♦ give it the gun ♦ going great guns ♦ gun so/animal down ♦ gun for so ♦ holding a gun to so's head ♦ jump the gun ♦ pull a gun (on so) ♦ the smoking gun ♦ son of a gun ♦ stick to one's guns

gung gung ho (on so/sth)

gush gush over so/sth

gussy gussied up

gut blood and guts ♦ bust a gut ♦ get enough guts up (to do sth) ♦ go with one's gut (feeling) ✦ gut feeling ✦ gut reaction ✦ gut response ✦ hate so's guts ✦ a kick in the guts ✦ spew one's guts (out) ✦ spill one's guts ✦ split a gut ✦ yell one's guts out

gutter have (got) one's mind in the gutter ✦ in the gutter

guy Mr. Nice Guy ✦ a regular guy ✦ tough guy

H

ha funny ha-ha

habit break a habit ✦ break the habit ✦ by force of habit ✦ fall into the habit of doing sth ✦ kick a habit ✦ knock the habit ✦ shake the habit

hack cannot hack it ✦ hack sth ✦ hack so/sth apart ✦ hack around ✦ hack so (off) ✦ hacked (off)

hackles get so's hackles up ✦ raise so's hackles

hail give so Hail Columbia ✦ hail a cab ✦ hail a taxi ✦ hail so as sth ✦ hail from some place ✦ hail-fellow-well-met ✦ within hailing distance

hair a bad hair day ✦ by a hair('s breadth) ✦ cause so's hair to stand on end ✦ curl so's hair ✦ fair-haired boy ✦ feel one's hair stand on end ✦ feel the hair on the back of one's neck stand on end ✦ get so out of one's hair ✦ get out of so's hair ✦ give so gray hair(s) ✦ gray hair(s) ✦ the hair of the dog (that bit one) ✦ hang by a hair ✦ hang on by a hair ✦ in so's hair ✦ let one's hair down ✦ make so's hair curl ✦ make so's hair stand on end ✦ (neither) hide nor hair ✦ part so's hair ✦ plaster one's hair down ✦ pull one's hair (out) ✦ put hair on so's chest ✦ run one's fingers through one's hair ✦ run one's hand through one's hair ✦ split hairs ✦ tear one's hair (out)

hale hale and hearty

half all over hell and half of Georgia ✦ sth and a half ✦ at half-mast ✦ one's better half ✦ by halves ✦ cheap at half the price ✦ Getting there is half the fun. ✦ give so/sth half a chance ✦ given half a chance ✦ go off half-cocked ✦ half a loaf ✦ half-and-

half ✦ half the battle ✦ half the time ✦ half under ✦ have half a mind to do sth ✦ have half a notion to do sth ✦ how the other half lives ✦ (It's) not half bad. ✦ It's six of one, half a dozen of another. ✦ That's not the half of it! ✦ without half trying

halfhearted halfhearted (about so/sth)

halfway meet so halfway

hall beat city hall ✦ fight city hall ✦ You can't fight city hall.

halt call a halt (to sth) ✦ grind to a halt

halves by halves

ham ham sth up

hamburger make hamburger (out) of so

hammer come under the hammer ✦ fight so/sth hammer and tongs ✦ go at it hammer and tongs ✦ go under the hammer ✦ hammer (away) at so ✦ hammer (away) at sth ✦ hammer sth home ✦ hammer sth into sth ✦ hammer sth out

hand at first hand ✦ at hand ✦ at the hand(s) of so ✦ a big hand for sth ✦ A bird in the hand (is worth two in the bush). ✦ bite the hand that feeds one ✦ bound hand and foot ✦ by a show of hands ✦ by hand ✦ by the handful ✦ can't find one's butt with both hands (in broad daylight) ✦ can't see one's hand in front of one's face ✦ catch so red-handed ✦ caught red-handed ✦ change hands ✦ close at hand ✦ come away empty-handed ✦ come in handy ✦ come into so's hands ✦ cup one's hands together ✦ die by one's own hand ✦ dirty one's hands ✦ do sth by hand ✦ Don't hand me that (line)! ✦ eat out of so's hand ✦ exercise a firm hand ✦ fall into so's hands ✦ fall into the wrong hands ✦ a firm hand ✦ fold one's hands ✦ force so's hand ✦ a free hand (with so/sth) ✦ from hand to hand ✦ get one's hands dirty ✦ get one's hands on so/sth/animal ✦ give so a big hand for sth ✦ give so a free hand ✦ give so a hand with sth ✦ give so the glad hand ✦ the glad hand ✦ go away empty-handed ✦ go to hell in a handbasket ✦ hand so sth ✦ hand sth down from so to so ✦ hand sth down (to so) ✦ a hand in (doing) sth ✦ hand in glove (with so) ✦ hand in hand ✦ Hand it over. ✦ hand-me-down ✦ hand sth off (to so) ✦ hand sth on (to so/sth) ✦ hand sth out

so/sth ♦ have a bellyful ♦ have a big mouth ♦ have a blast ♦ Have a blimp! ♦ have a blowout ♦ have a bone to pick (with so) ♦ have a brush with sth ♦ have a buzz on ♦ have a case (against so) ♦ have a case of sth ♦ have a change of heart ♦ have a chip on one's shoulder ♦ have a close call ♦ have a close shave ♦ have a conniption (fit) ♦ have a corner on the market (for sth) ♦ have a death wish ♦ have a drinking problem ♦ have a falling-out with so ♦ have a familiar ring (to it) ♦ have a feel for sth ♦ have a few too many ♦ have a field day ♦ have a finger in the pie ♦ have a fit ♦ have a flair for sth ♦ have a foot in both camps ♦ have a free rein (with sth) ♦ have a frog in one's throat ♦ have a gift for (doing) sth ♦ have a glass jaw ♦ have a good arm ♦ have a good command of sth ♦ Have a good day. ♦ have a (good) head for sth ♦ have a good head on one's shoulders ♦ have a (good) mind to do sth ♦ Have a good one. ♦ have a good run ♦ have a good thing going ♦ have a green thumb ♦ have a grudge (against so) ♦ have a hand with sth ♦ have a heart ♦ have a heart of gold ♦ have a heart of stone ♦ have a heart-to-heart (talk) ♦ have a hidden talent ♦ have a hitch in one's gitalong ♦ have a hold on so ♦ have a hollow leg ♦ have a hunch (that sth is the case) ♦ have a keen interest in sth ♦ have a kick to it ♦ have a line on so/sth ♦ have a long run ♦ have a look-see ♦ have a lot going (for one) ♦ have a lot on one's mind ♦ have a lot on one's plate ♦ have a low boiling point ♦ have a lump in one's throat ♦ have a mental block (against sth) ♦ have a mind as sharp as a steel trap ♦ have a mind of one's own ♦ have a near miss ♦ Have a nice day. ♦ Have a nice flight. ♦ Have a nice one. ♦ have a nose for sth ♦ have a one-track mind ♦ have a passion for so/sth ♦ have a penchant for doing sth ♦ have a place in sth ♦ have a prayer (of doing sth) ♦ have a price on one's head ♦ have a quarrel with sth ♦ have a rare old time ♦ have a rough time (of it) ♦ have a roving eye ♦ have a run of sth ♦ have a run of bad luck ♦ have a run-in (with so/sth) ♦

Have a safe journey. ♦ Have a safe trip. ♦ have a score to settle (with so) ♦ have a scrape (with so/sth) ♦ have a screw loose ♦ have a seat ♦ have a set-to (with so) ♦ have a sinking feeling ♦ have a sinking feeling in the pit of one's stomach ♦ have a soft spot (in one's heart) for so/sth/animal ♦ have a (solid) grasp of sth ♦ have a stake in sth ♦ have a stroke ♦ have a sweet tooth ♦ have a thing about so/sth ♦ have a thing going (with so) ♦ have a thirst for sth ♦ have a tiger by the tail ♦ have a tough time (of it) ♦ have (a) use for so/sth ♦ have a voice (in sth) ♦ have a way with so/sth ♦ have a way with words ♦ have a weakness for so/sth ♦ have a weight problem ♦ have a whale of a time ♦ have a word with so (about sth) ♦ have a yellow belly ♦ have a yellow streak down one's back ♦ have so/sth about ♦ have sth against so/sth ♦ have all one's marbles ♦ have all the answers ♦ have (all) the makings of sth ♦ have all the time in the world ♦ have an accident ♦ have an ace up one's sleeve ♦ have an affair (with so) ♦ have an alcohol problem ♦ have an appetite for sth ♦ have an ax(e) to grind (with so) ♦ have an ear for sth ♦ have an ear to the ground ♦ have an easy time of it ♦ have an eye for so/sth ♦ have an eye on so/sth ♦ have an eye out (for so/sth) ♦ have an impact on so/sth ♦ have an in (with so) ♦ have an inkling (about so/sth) ♦ have an itch for sth ♦ have an itchy palm ♦ have so around (for sth) ♦ have arrived ♦ have at so ♦ have so at a disadvantage ♦ have sth at one's fingertips ♦ have sth at hand ♦ Have at it. ♦ have one's back against the wall ♦ have back (at so) ♦ have one's back to the wall ♦ have bags under one's eyes ♦ have bats in one's belfry ♦ have (some) bearing on sth ♦ have been around (the block) ♦ have been had ♦ have been to hell and back ♦ have so's best interest(s) at heart ♦ have bigger fish to fry ♦ have (so's) blood on one's hands ♦ have broad shoulders ♦ have one's cake and eat it too ♦ have carnal knowledge of so ♦ have cause to do sth ♦ have sth cinched ♦ have clean hands ♦ have come a long way ♦ have so/sth cornered ♦ have so dead to rights ♦ have designs on so/sth ♦ have dibs on sth ♦ have sth doing ♦ have sth down pat ♦ have sth down to a T ♦ have one's druthers ♦ have egg on one's face ♦ have enough and some to spare ♦ have enough (sth) to go around ♦ have so's eye ♦ have eyes in the back of one's head ♦ have faith in so ♦ have feet of clay ♦ have one's feet on the ground ♦ have one's fill of so/sth ♦ have one's finger in too many pies ♦ have one's finger on the pulse of sth ♦ have one's finger(s) in the till ♦ have sth for a meal ♦ have so for breakfast ♦ have forty winks ♦ have free reign (over sth) ♦ have friends in high places ♦ have sth going (for oneself) ♦ have (got) a glow on ♦ have (got) a load on ♦ have (got) one's ass in a sling ♦ have (got) sth coming (to one) ♦ have (got) it made ♦ have (got) one's mind in the gutter ♦ have (got) to hand it to so ♦ have (got) what it takes ♦ have growing pains ♦ have had it (up to here) ♦ have had its day ♦ have half a mind to do sth ♦ have half a notion to do sth ♦ have one's hand in sth ♦ have one's hand in the till ♦ have one's hands full (with so/sth) ♦ have one's hands tied ♦ have sth hanging over one's head ♦ have one's head in the clouds ♦ have one's head in the sand ♦ have so's head on a platter ♦ have one's head screwed on right ♦ have one's head screwed on straight ♦ have one's head screwed on tight ♦ have one's heart (dead) set against sth ♦ have one's heart go out to so ♦ have one's heart in one's mouth ♦ have one's heart in the right place ♦ have one's heart on one's sleeve ♦ have one's heart set on sth ♦ have one's heart stand still ♦ have hell to pay ♦ have so's hide ♦ have (high) hopes of sth ♦ Have I got something for you! ♦ Have I made myself clear? ♦ have so in ♦ have sth in common (with so/sth) ♦ have so in one's corner ♦ have sth in hand ♦ have so/sth in one's hands ♦ have so/sth in mind ♦ have so in one's pocket ♦ have so/sth in one's sights ♦ have so in one's spell ♦ have sth in stock ♦ have sth in store (for so) ♦ have sth in the bag ♦ have so in the palm of one's hand ♦ have so/sth in tow ♦ have intimate relations with so ♦ have it

(all) over so/sth (in sth) ♦ have it all together ♦ have it bad ♦ have it both ways ♦ have it in for so ♦ have it in one (to do sth) ♦ have it made in the shade ♦ Have it your way. ♦ have just about had it ♦ have kittens ♦ have one's luck run out ♦ have sth made ♦ have mixed feelings (about so/sth) ♦ have more important fish to fry ♦ have more luck than sense ♦ have no business doing sth ♦ have no staying power ♦ have no stomach for sth ♦ have no truck with sth ♦ have no use for so/sth ♦ have none of sth ♦ have one's nose in a book ♦ have one's nose in the air ♦ have one's nose out of joint ♦ have not lived until one has done sth ♦ have nothing against so/sth ♦ have nothing doing (at some time) ♦ have nothing on so ♦ have nothing on so/sth ♦ have nothing on (at some time) ♦ have nothing to do with so/sth ♦ have so's number ♦ have sth on so/sth ♦ have sth on file ♦ have sth on good authority ♦ have so/sth on one's hands ♦ have so/sth on one's mind ♦ have sth on one('s person) ♦ have sth on the ball ♦ have so/sth on the brain ♦ have so on the string ♦ have sth on the tip of one's tongue ♦ have one foot in the grave ♦ have one in the oven ♦ have one too many ♦ have only just done sth ♦ have other fish to fry ♦ have sth out ♦ have sth out (with so) ♦ have so over a barrel ♦ have so over (for sth) ♦ have so pegged as sth ♦ have one's pick of so/sth ♦ have pity (on so/animal) ♦ have pull with so ♦ have qualms (about so/sth) ♦ have one's rathers ♦ have relations with so ♦ have rocks in one's head ♦ have one's say ♦ have second thoughts (about so/sth) ♦ have seen better days ♦ have several irons in the fire ♦ have one's shoulder to the wheel ♦ have one's sights set on so/sth ♦ have one's sights trained on sth ♦ have so ♦ have some elbow room ♦ have (some) time to kill ♦ have stars in one's eyes ♦ have sth stick in one's craw ♦ have sticky fingers ♦ have the advantage of so ♦ have the blues ♦ have the cards stacked against one ♦ have the cart before the horse ♦ have the courage of one's convictions ♦ have the deck stacked against one ♦ have the devil to pay ♦ have the facts straight ♦ have the floor ♦ have the gall to do sth ♦ have the gift of gab ♦ have the hots for so ♦ have the last word ♦ have the Midas touch ♦ have the patience of a saint ♦ have the patience of Job ♦ have the presence of mind to do sth ♦ have the shoe on the other foot ♦ have the time of one's life ♦ have the wherewithal (to do sth) ♦ have the worse of both worlds ♦ have them rolling in the aisles ♦ have sth to burn ♦ have to do with so/sth ♦ have to get married ♦ have to go some (to do sth) ♦ have to live with sth ♦ have sth to shout about ♦ have sth to show for sth ♦ have sth to spare ♦ have too ♦ have too many irons in the fire ♦ have too much on one's plate ♦ have (too much) time on one's hands ♦ have two left feet ♦ have two strikes against one ♦ have so under a spell ♦ have sth under one's belt ♦ have sth up one's sleeve ♦ have one's way with so ♦ have so/sth (well) in hand ♦ have one's wires crossed ♦ have words (with so) (over so/sth) ♦ have one's work cut out for one ♦ (Have you) been keeping busy? ♦ (Have you) been keeping cool? ♦ (Have you) been keeping out of trouble? ♦ Haven't I seen you somewhere before? ♦ Haven't seen you in a month of Sundays. ♦ Haven't we met before? ♦ Having a wonderful time; wish you were here. ♦ How many times do I have to tell you? ♦ (I'm) having a wonderful time; wish you were here. ♦ I'm having the time of my life. ♦ It has so's name on it. ♦ I've had it up to here (with so/sth). ♦ let so have it (with both barrels) ♦ Let me have it! ♦ Let's have it! ♦ the moment everyone has been waiting for ♦ more sth than Carter has (liver) pills ♦ one needs to have one's head examined ♦ never had it so good ♦ never would have guessed ♦ not have a care in the world ♦ not have a clue (about sth) ♦ not have a hope in hell ♦ not have a leg to stand on ♦ not have a lot of time for so/sth ♦ not have a snowball's chance in hell ♦ not have a specific kind of bone in one's body ♦ not have a stitch of clothes (on) ♦ not have all one's marbles ♦

not have anything to do with so/sth ♦ not have the heart to do sth ♦ not have the stomach for sth ♦ only have eyes for so ♦ the price one has to pay ♦ rumor has it that . . . ♦ scarcely have time to breathe ♦ should have stood in bed ♦ Them as has, gits. ♦ They must have seen you coming. ♦ time flies (when you're having fun) ♦ so's time has come ♦ was had ♦ Who could have thought? ♦ Who would have thought? ♦ You (always) think you have all the answers! ♦ You could have knocked me over with a feather. ♦ You have me at a disadvantage.

havoc play havoc with so/sth ♦ raise havoc with so/sth ♦ wreak havoc with so/sth

haw hem and haw (around)

hawk watch so/sth like a hawk

hay hit the hay ♦ make hay (while the sun shines) ♦ That ain't hay.

haystack like looking for a needle in a haystack ♦ like trying to find a needle in a haystack

haywire go haywire

hazard at hazard ♦ hazard a guess ♦ hazard an opinion

haze in a haze

head able to do sth standing on one's head ♦ bang one's head against a brick wall ♦ be at the head of the pack ♦ beat one's head against the wall ♦ a (big) head ♦ bite so's head off ♦ bother one's (pretty little) head about so/sth ♦ bring sth down on one('s head) ♦ bring sth to a head ♦ bury one's head in the sand ♦ come to a head ♦ come up heads ♦ cooler heads prevail ♦ cough one's head off ♦ count heads ♦ crazy in the head ♦ drum sth into so's head ♦ one's eyes pop out of one's head ♦ fall head over heels ♦ fall head over heels in love (with so) ♦ the first thing that comes into one's head ♦ (from) head to toe ♦ get a head start (on so) ♦ get one's head above water ♦ get one's head together ♦ get sth into so's (thick) head ♦ get up a (full) head of steam ♦ Get your head out of the clouds! ♦ give so a (big) head ♦ give so a heads up ♦ go head to head with so ♦ go to so's head ♦ hang one's head ♦ hang over so('s head) ♦ have a (good) head for sth ♦ have a good head on one's shoulders ♦ have a price on one's head ♦ have eyes in the back of one's head ♦ have sth hanging over one's head ♦ have one's head in the clouds ♦ have one's head in the sand ♦ have so's head on a platter ♦ have one's head screwed on right ♦ have one's head screwed on straight ♦ have one's head screwed on tight ♦ have rocks in one's head ♦ a head ♦ head and shoulders above so/sth ♦ head for the hills ♦ head for the last roundup ♦ head so/sth off ♦ head so off some place ♦ head over heels in debt ♦ head South ♦ a head start (on so) ♦ a head start (on sth) ♦ head to toe ♦ head toward so/sth ♦ head sth up ♦ headed for sth ♦ heads or tails ♦ Heads up! ♦ heads will roll ♦ hide one's head in the sand ♦ hit the nail (right) on the head ♦ hold one's head above water ♦ hold one's head high ♦ hold one's head up ♦ hold sth over so('s head) ♦ holding a gun to so's head ♦ in over one's head (with so/sth) ♦ keep a civil tongue (in one's head) ♦ keep one's head ♦ keep one's head above water ♦ keep one's head down ♦ Keep your head down. ♦ knock one's head (up) against a brick wall ♦ knock some heads together ♦ laugh one's head off ♦ leave one scratching one's head ♦ lose one's head (over so/sth) ♦ make so's head spin ♦ make so's head swim ♦ make heads or tails (out) of so/sth ♦ need sth like a hole in the head ♦ one needs to have one's head examined ♦ not able to make head or tail of sth ♦ not trouble one's (pretty) (little) head about sth ♦ off the top of one's head ♦ on so's head ♦ out of one's head ♦ over so's head ♦ per head ♦ pound so's head in ♦ a price on one's head ♦ put one's head on the block (for so/sth) ♦ put people's heads together ♦ put ideas into so's head ♦ put sth in(to) so's head ♦ rear its ugly head ♦ (right) off the top of one's head ♦ run around like a chicken with its head cut off ♦ run one's head against a brick wall ♦ send one scratching one's head ♦ snap so's head off ♦ soft in the head ♦ stand head and shoulders above so/sth ♦ stand on one's head ♦ stand sth on its head ♦ stick one's head in the sand ♦ stuff

so's head with sth ♦ a swelled head ♦ take so's head off ♦ take sth into one's head ♦ take it into one's head to do sth ♦ talk one's head off ♦ talk so's head off ♦ talk over so's head ♦ touched (in the head) ♦ tower head and shoulders above so/sth ♦ trouble one's head about so/sth ♦ turn so's head ♦ turn sth on its head ♦ turn some heads ♦ use one's head ♦ Use your head! ♦ whatever comes into one's head (first) ♦ where so's head is at ♦ One would forget one's head if it wasn't screwed on. ♦ yack one's head off ♦ yell one's head off

headache a splitting headache

headline hit the headlines ♦ make the headlines

headway make headway

health a clean bill of health ♦ give so a clean bill of health ♦ in the best of health ♦ in the pink (of health) ♦ the picture of (good) health

heap the bottom of the heap ♦ a heap of sth ♦ heap sth (up)on so/sth ♦ the top of the heap

hear another country heard from ♦ Ask no questions and hear no lies. ♦ cannot hear oneself think ♦ (Do) you hear? ♦ hard of hearing ♦ hear a peep out of so ♦ hear so out ♦ hear the last of so/sth ♦ hear sth through the grapevine ♦ hearing impaired ♦ like to hear oneself talk ♦ make oneself heard ♦ never hear the end of sth ♦ so quiet you could hear a pin drop ♦ so still you could hear a pin drop ♦ talk to hear one's own voice ♦ That ain't the way I heard it. ♦ will not hear of sth

hearken hearken to so/sth

heart aching heart ♦ bleeding heart ♦ Bless so's heart! ♦ break so's heart ♦ by heart ♦ chicken-hearted ♦ close to one's heart ♦ cross one's heart (and hope to die) ♦ cry one's heart out ♦ dear to one's heart ♦ die of a broken heart ♦ do so's heart good ♦ eat one's heart out ♦ the faint of heart ♦ feel (sth) in one's heart of hearts ♦ find it in one's heart (to do sth) ♦ follow one's heart ♦ from the (bottom of one's) heart ♦ give one's heart to so ♦ hale and hearty ♦ halfhearted (about so/sth) ♦ harden one's heart (against so/sth) ♦ have a change of heart ♦ have a heart ♦ have a heart of gold ♦ have a heart of stone ♦ have a heart-to-heart (talk) ♦ have a soft spot (in one's heart) for so/sth/animal ♦ have so's best interest(s) at heart ♦ have one's heart (dead) set against sth ♦ have one's heart go out to so ♦ have one's heart in one's mouth ♦ have one's heart in the right place ♦ have one's heart on one's sleeve ♦ have one's heart set on sth ♦ have one's heart stand still ♦ heart and soul ♦ one's heart bleeds for so ♦ one's heart goes out to so ♦ one's heart is (dead) set against sth ♦ one's heart is in one's mouth ♦ one's heart is in the right place ♦ one's heart is set on sth ♦ one's heart isn't in sth ♦ one's heart misses a beat ♦ one's heart skips a beat ♦ one's heart stands still ♦ in the heart of sth ♦ in the hearts and minds of so ♦ know sth by heart ♦ know (sth) in one's heart of hearts ♦ lose heart ♦ lose one's heart to so/animal ♦ makes one's heart sink ♦ a man after my own heart ♦ not have the heart to do sth ♦ open one's heart to so/sth ♦ do sth out of the goodness of one's heart ♦ out of the goodness of one's heart ♦ play one's heart out ♦ play on so's heartstrings ♦ pour one's heart (and soul) into sth ♦ pour one's heart out to so ♦ pull on so's heartstrings ♦ put one's heart (and soul) into sth ♦ set one's heart against sth ♦ set one's heart on so/sth ♦ sick at heart ♦ sing one's heart out ♦ sob one's heart out ♦ steal so's heart ♦ sweetheart agreement ♦ sweetheart deal ♦ take heart (from sth) ♦ take so/animal into one's heart ♦ take sth to heart ♦ tear one's heart out ♦ to one's heart's content ♦ tug at so's heartstrings ♦ warm the cockles of so's heart ♦ wear one's heart on one's sleeve ♦ win so's heart ♦ win the heart of so ♦ with a heavy heart ♦ with all one's heart (and soul) ♦ young at heart

heartbeat a heartbeat away from being sth ♦ do sth in a heartbeat

heat come in(to) heat ♦ heat up ♦ heat sth up ♦ in a dead heat ♦ in heat ♦ in the heat of battle ♦ in the heat of the moment ♦ put the heat on (so) ♦ take the heat ♦ take the heat off (of) so/sth ♦ turn the heat up (on so) ♦ turn up the heat (on so)

heave give so the (old) heave-ho ♦ heave in(to) sight ♦ heave to ♦ heave sth up ♦ the (old) heave-ho

heaven bundle from heaven ♦ For heaven('s) sake(s)! ♦ (Good) heavens! ♦ Heaven forbid! ♦ Heaven help us! ♦ heaven on earth ♦ Heavens to Betsy! ♦ in heaven ♦ in hog heaven ♦ in seventh heaven ♦ manna from heaven ♦ a marriage made in heaven ♦ a match made in heaven ♦ move heaven and earth to do sth ♦ smell to (high) heaven ♦ smell to high heaven ♦ stink to high heaven ♦ Thank heavens!

heavy heavy going ♦ heavy into so/sth ♦ hot and heavy ♦ lay a (heavy) trip on so ♦ play the heavy ♦ time hangs heavy (on so's hands) ♦ with a heavy heart

heck for the heck of it ♦ a heck of a so/sth ♦ one heck of a so/sth ♦ What the heck!

hedge hedge one's bets

heed pay heed to so/sth ♦ take heed (of so/sth)

heel Achilles' heel ♦ bring a dog to heel ♦ bring so to heel ♦ cool one's heels ♦ dig one's heels in ♦ dig in one's heels ♦ down at the heels ♦ drag one's heels (on or over sth) ♦ fall head over heels ♦ fall head over heels in love (with so) ♦ hard on so's heels ♦ hard on the heels of sth ♦ head over heels in debt ♦ hot on so's heels ♦ hot on the heels of sth ♦ kick one's heels up ♦ on so's heels ♦ on the heels of sth ♦ set one back on one's heels ♦ take to one's heels ♦ turn on one's heel ♦ well-heeled

height the height of sth

heir fall heir to sth

hell all hell broke loose ♦ all over hell and gone ♦ all over hell and half of Georgia ♦ beat the hell out of so ♦ catch hell ♦ come hell or high water ♦ for the hell of it ♦ frighten the hell out of so ♦ so/sth from hell ♦ get the hell out (of some place) ♦ go to hell ♦ go to hell in a bucket ♦ go to hell in a handbasket ♦ have been to hell and back ♦ have hell to pay ♦ hell ♦ hell around ♦ a hell hole ♦ a hell of a so/sth ♦ a hell of a mess ♦ a hell of a note ♦ hell on earth ♦ The hell you say! ♦ hell-bent for some place or sth ♦ hell-bent for leather ♦ Hell's bells (and buckets of blood)! ♦ hot as hell ♦ It'll be a cold day in hell when sth happens. ♦ like a bat out of hell ♦ like hell ♦ Like hell (so did)! ♦ like hell on wheels ♦ Like hell you will! ♦ a living hell ♦ mad as hell ♦ not have a hope in hell ♦ not have a snowball's chance in hell ♦ one hell of a so/sth ♦ play hell with so/sth ♦ quicker than hell ♦ raise hell (with sth) ♦ rot in hell (before one would do sth) ♦ see so in hell first ♦ shoot so/sth (all) to hell ♦ shot to hell ♦ sure as hell ♦ There will be hell to pay. ♦ through hell ♦ through hell and high water ♦ to hell and gone ♦ To hell with so/sth! ♦ (un)til hell freezes over ♦ What the hell? ♦ a (whole) hell of a lot

hellfire Hellfire and damnation!

helluva a helluva so/sth

helm at the helm (of sth)

help beyond help ♦ can't help doing sth ♦ can't help but do sth ♦ Heaven help us! ♦ help so/animal (get) over sth ♦ help so through sth ♦ Help yourself. ♦ a (helping) hand ♦ lend so a (helping) hand ♦ Not if one can help it. ♦ not lift a finger (to help so) ♦ not lift a hand (to help so) ♦ pitch in (and help) (with sth) ♦ seek professional help ♦ So help me(, God)!

hem hem and haw (around) ♦ hem so in

hen mad as a wet hen ♦ scarce as hen's teeth ♦ scarcer than hen's teeth

Henry one's John Henry

hepped hepped (up)

herd like herding cats ♦ like herding frogs

here The buck stops here. ♦ downhill from here on ♦ Fancy meeting you here! ♦ from here on (in) ♦ Get out (of here)! ♦ get one right here ♦ Get your ass over here! ♦ Get your buns over here! ♦ Get your butt over here! ♦ have had it (up to here) ♦ Having a wonderful time; wish you were here. ♦ the here and now ♦ here and there ♦ Here goes nothing. ♦ Here (it) goes. ♦ here, there, and everywhere ♦ Here we go again. ♦ Here you are. ♦ Here you go. ♦ (I'm) having a wonderful time; wish you were here. ♦ I'm here to tell you ♦ I'm out

of here. ♦ I've had it up to here (with so/sth). ♦ Look here! ♦ neither here nor there ♦ right here and now ♦ Same here. ♦ sure as I'm standing here ♦ up to here (with sth) ♦ (You) can't get there from here.

here's Here's looking at you. ♦ Here's mud in your eye. ♦ here's to so/sth ♦ Here's to you.

hero unsung hero

herring a red herring

hess a mell of a hess

hew hew to sth

hibernate busy as a hibernating bear

hide go into hiding ♦ have a hidden talent ♦ have so's hide ♦ a hidden agenda ♦ hide one's face (in shame) ♦ hide one's head in the sand ♦ hide one's light under a bushel ♦ hide-and-(go-)seek ♦ nail so('s hide) to the wall ♦ (neither) hide nor hair ♦ tan so's hide

high come hell or high water ♦ eat (pretty) high off the hog ♦ flying high ♦ from on high ♦ get (down) off one's high horse ♦ give so the high sign ♦ go sky-high ♦ happy as a clam (at high tide) ♦ have friends in high places ♦ have (high) hopes of sth ♦ high and dry ♦ high and mighty ♦ high as a kite ♦ high as the sky ♦ high man on the totem pole ♦ high on sth ♦ a high roller ♦ the high sign ♦ high-pressure so into sth ♦ hit the high spots ♦ hold one's head high ♦ hold so/sth in high regard ♦ hunt high and low (for so/sth) ♦ in high dudgeon ♦ in high gear ♦ in (high) hopes of sth ♦ it's high time ♦ knee-high by the 4th of July ♦ knee-high to a grasshopper ♦ leave so high and dry ♦ live (pretty) high off the hog ♦ live (pretty) high on the hog ♦ look high and low (for so/sth) ♦ on one's high horse ♦ running high ♦ search high and low (for so/sth) ♦ smell to (high) heaven ♦ smell to high heaven ♦ speak highly of so/sth ♦ stink to high heaven ♦ swing into high gear ♦ through hell and high water

hightail hightail it out of some place

highway electronic superhighway ♦ highways and byways ♦ information superhighway

hike take a hike

hill head for the hills ♦ make a mountain out of a molehill ♦ not amount to a hill of beans ♦ not worth a hill of beans ♦ old as the hills ♦ over the hill ♦ run for the hills ♦ take to the hills

hilt to the hilt

himself Every man for himself!

hind crooked as a dog's hind leg ♦ get up on one's hind legs ♦ hind end ♦ suck so's hind tit

hindsight in hindsight

hinge hinge (up)on so/sth

hint drop a hint ♦ take a hint

hip hip to so/sth ♦ joined at the hip ♦ shoot from the hip

hire not for hire

hiss hiss at so/sth ♦ hiss so off ((of) the stage)

hissy hissy (fit)

history ancient history ♦ go down (in history) (as so/sth) ♦ go down in the annals of history ♦ go down in the history books ♦ history in the making ♦ I'm history. ♦ The rest is history.

hit can't hit the (broad) side of a barn ♦ the fat hit the fire ♦ hit so ♦ hit a happy medium ♦ hit a home run ♦ hit a plateau ♦ hit a (raw) nerve ♦ hit a snag ♦ hit a sore point ♦ hit a sour note ♦ hit and miss ♦ hit so below the belt ♦ hit bottom ♦ hit one close to home ♦ hit so hard ♦ hit home ♦ hit it off (with so) ♦ hit sth off ♦ hit on so ♦ hit or miss ♦ hit pay dirt ♦ hit so (right) between the eyes ♦ hit (rock) bottom ♦ hit one's stride ♦ hit the books ♦ hit the booze ♦ hit the bottle ♦ hit the brakes ♦ hit the bricks ♦ hit the (broad) side of a barn ♦ hit the bull's-eye ♦ hit the ceiling ♦ hit the deck ♦ hit the fan ♦ hit the ground running ♦ hit the hay ♦ hit the headlines ♦ hit the high spots ♦ hit the jackpot ♦ hit the nail (right) on the head ♦ hit the panic button ♦ hit the pavement ♦ hit the right note ♦ hit the road ♦ hit the roof ♦ hit the sack ♦ hit the skids ♦ hit the

spot ♦ hit the trail ♦ hit town ♦ hit so up (for sth) ♦ hit (up)on sth ♦ hit one where one lives ♦ hit so with sth ♦ hit-and-run ♦ hitting on all cylinders ♦ make a hit with so ♦ not know what hit one ♦ pinch-hit for so ♦ a smash hit ♦ when the shit hits the fan

hitch have a hitch in one's gitalong ♦ hitch a ride ♦ without a hitch

hither come-hither look ♦ hither and thither ♦ hither, thither, and yon

hive a hive of activity

ho give so the (old) heave-ho ♦ gung ho (on so/sth) ♦ the (old) heave-ho

hoarse hoarse as a crow

hob play hob with so/sth ♦ raise hob with so/sth

hobnob hobnob with so/sth

Hobson Hobson's choice

hock go into hock ♦ in hock ♦ out of hock

hoe a hard row to hoe ♦ a tough row to hoe

hog call hogs ♦ eat (pretty) high off the hog ♦ go hog wild ♦ go whole hog ♦ hog wild ♦ in hog heaven ♦ live (pretty) high off the hog ♦ live (pretty) high on the hog ♦ road hog

hoist hoist with one's own petard

hold catch (a)hold of so/sth ♦ Don't hold your breath. ♦ get (a)hold of so ♦ have a hold on so ♦ hold a job down ♦ hold a meeting ♦ hold so accountable (for sth) ♦ hold sth against so ♦ hold all the aces ♦ hold all the cards ♦ hold so/sth at arm's length ♦ hold so/sth at bay ♦ hold so's attention ♦ hold so back ♦ hold sth back ♦ hold sth back for a rainy day ♦ hold back (on sth) ♦ hold one's breath ♦ hold by sth ♦ hold court ♦ hold so down ♦ hold one's end of the bargain up ♦ hold one's end up ♦ Hold everything! ♦ hold so's feet to the fire ♦ hold one's fire ♦ hold sth for so ♦ hold forth (on so/sth) ♦ hold good for so/sth ♦ hold one's ground ♦ hold so's hand ♦ hold one's head above water ♦ hold one's head high ♦ hold one's head up ♦ hold sth in abeyance ♦ hold so/sth in check ♦ hold so in good stead ♦ hold so/sth in high regard ♦ hold so/sth in low regard ♦ hold so/sth in reserve ♦ hold sth inside ((of) one(self)) ♦ Hold it! ♦ hold one's liquor ♦ hold one's mouth the right way ♦ hold no brief for so/sth ♦ hold one's nose ♦ hold on ♦ a hold on so ♦ Hold on (a minute)! ♦ hold on for dear life ♦ Hold on to your hat! ♦ hold one's or its own ♦ hold out (against so/sth) ♦ hold out (for so/sth) ♦ hold out on so ♦ hold out the olive branch ♦ hold sth over so('s head) ♦ hold one's peace ♦ Hold, please. ♦ hold promise ♦ hold so responsible (for sth) ♦ hold still for sth ♦ hold sway (among a group) ♦ hold sway (over so/sth) ♦ hold terror for so ♦ hold the fort ♦ hold the line (at so/sth) ♦ hold the line (on so/sth) ♦ Hold the line(, please). ♦ Hold the phone. ♦ Hold the phone(, please). ♦ hold the purse strings ♦ Hold the wire(, please). ♦ hold so to sth ♦ hold one's tongue ♦ hold true ♦ hold up ♦ hold so/sth up ♦ hold so/sth up as an example ♦ hold so/sth up to ridicule ♦ hold so/sth up to scorn ♦ Hold your horses! ♦ Hold your taters! ♦ holding a gun to so's head ♦ a household name ♦ a household word ♦ leave so holding the baby ♦ leave so holding the bag ♦ lose one's hold on so/sth ♦ no holds barred ♦ not hold a candle to so/sth ♦ not hold a stick to so/sth ♦ not hold water ♦ on hold ♦ put a hold on sth ♦ put so on hold ♦ put so/sth on hold ♦ put sth on hold ♦ take hold ♦ won't hold water

hole ace in the hole ♦ can't see a hole in a ladder ♦ don't know one's ass from a hole in the ground ♦ full of holes ♦ a hell hole ♦ hole in one ♦ a hole in the wall ♦ hole up (some place) ♦ in the hole ♦ Money burns a hole in so's pocket. ♦ need sth like a hole in the head ♦ out of the hole ♦ pick holes in sth ♦ shot full of holes ♦ Shut your cake hole! ♦ Shut your pie hole! ♦ a square peg (in a round hole) ♦ watering hole

holiday a busman's holiday

holler holler bloody murder ♦ holler uncle

hollow have a hollow leg ♦ ring hollow

holy holier-than-thou ♦ Holy cow! ♦ holy Joe ♦ Holy mackerel! ♦ Holy moley!

homage pay homage to so/sth

home at home (with so/sth) ♦ bring home the bacon ♦ bring sth home to so ♦ close to home ♦ come home (to so) ♦ come home (to roost) ♦ Come in and make yourself at home. ♦ drive sth home (to so) ♦ eat so out of house and home ♦ feel at home ♦ get home free ♦ get sth home to so/sth ♦ go home in a box ♦ go home to mama ♦ hammer sth home ♦ hit a home run ♦ hit one close to home ♦ hit home ♦ a home away from home ♦ one's home away from home ♦ home folks ♦ home free ♦ home in (on so/sth) ♦ home on(to sth) ♦ (I've) got to go home and get my beauty sleep. ♦ Keep the home fires burning. ♦ Make yourself at home. ♦ money from home ♦ nothing to write home about ♦ score a home run ♦ strike home with so ♦ take sth home (with oneself) ♦ There's nobody home. ♦ till the cows come home ♦ (un)til the cows come home

homestretch in the (home)stretch

homework do one's homework ♦ The dog ate my homework.

honest come by sth honestly ♦ honest and aboveboard ♦ Honest to God. ♦ Honest to goodness. ♦ Honest to Pete. ♦ make an honest woman of so

honey sweet as honey ♦ sweeter than honey

honeymoon The honeymoon is over.

honor do the honors ♦ guest of honor ♦ honor bound (to do sth) ♦ Honor bright. ♦ honor so's check ♦ in honor of so/sth ♦ on one's honor ♦ put one on one's honor ♦ so's word of honor

hood all around Robin Hood's barn ♦ look under the hood

hoodwink hoodwink so into sth ♦ hoodwink so out of sth

hoof hoof it

hook by hook or (by) crook ♦ crooked as a barrel of fish hooks ♦ crooked as a fish hook ♦ fall for sth hook, line, and sinker ♦ get one's hooks in(to) so/sth ♦ hook sth down ♦ hook oneself on so/sth ♦ hook so on sth ♦ hook up with so ♦ hooked on sth ♦ keep so on tenterhooks ♦ off the hook ♦ on one's own hook ♦ ring off the hook ♦ swallow sth hook, line, and sinker

hooky play hooky

hoop jump through a hoop ♦ shoot (some) hoops

hoot hoot at so/sth ♦ hoot so off the stage ♦ not care two hoots about so/sth ♦ not give two hoots about so/sth

hop a hop, skip, and a jump ♦ Hop to it! ♦ hop sth up ♦ hopped up ♦ hopping mad

hope build one's hopes on so/sth ♦ cross one's heart (and hope to die) ♦ dash so's hopes ♦ have (high) hopes of sth ♦ hope against (all) hope ♦ hope for the best ♦ in (high) hopes of sth ♦ in hopes of doing sth ♦ in hopes of so's doing something ♦ live in hope(s) of sth ♦ not get one's hopes up ♦ not have a hope in hell ♦ pin one's hopes on so/sth ♦ place one's hopes on so/sth ♦ set one's hopes on so/sth

hopper in the hopper ♦ knee-high to a grasshopper

horizon a dark cloud (looming) on the horizon ♦ expand one's horizons ♦ loom large (on the horizon) ♦ on the horizon

horn blow one's own horn ♦ draw in one's horns ♦ horn in (on so) ♦ horn in (on sth) ♦ lock horns (with so) ♦ on the horns of a dilemma ♦ pull in one's horns ♦ take the bull by the horns ♦ toot one's own horn

hornet mad as a hornet ♦ stir up a hornet's nest

horror in horror

horse back the wrong horse ♦ beat a dead horse ♦ bet on the wrong horse ♦ change horses in midstream ♦ change horses in the middle of the stream ♦ a charley horse ♦ dark horse ♦ drive a coach and horses through sth ♦ eat like a horse ♦ flog a dead horse ♦ get (down) off one's high horse ♦ get on one's horse ♦ go the way of the horse and buggy ♦ have the cart before the horse ♦ Hold your horses! ♦ horse around (with so/sth) ♦ a horse of a different color ♦ a horse of another color ♦ horse sense ♦ I could eat a horse! ♦ I'd better get on my horse. ♦ look a gift horse in the mouth ♦ an old warhorse ♦ on one's high horse ♦ one-horse town ♦ play the horses ♦ put a horse out to pasture ♦ put the cart before the horse ♦ (straight) from the horse's mouth ♦ strong

as a horse ♦ went out with the horse and buggy ♦ went out with the horse and carriage ♦ work like a horse

horseback on horseback

hose hose so down

hospital rush so to the hospital

hostage take so hostage

hot blow hot and cold ♦ busy as a cat on a hot tin roof ♦ drop so/sth like a hot potato ♦ full of hot air ♦ have the hots for so ♦ hot and bothered ♦ hot and heavy ♦ hot as fire ♦ hot as hell ♦ Hot damn! ♦ Hot diggety (dog)! ♦ Hot dog! ♦ hot off the press ♦ hot on sth ♦ hot on so's heels ♦ hot on the heels of sth ♦ hot on the trail (of so/sth/animal) ♦ a hot ticket ♦ hot under the collar ♦ Hot ziggety! ♦ in (hot) pursuit of sth ♦ in hot water ♦ in hot water (with so) (about so/sth) ♦ in the hot seat ♦ make it hot for so ♦ not so hot ♦ on the hot seat ♦ strike while the iron is hot ♦ too hot to handle

hotbed a hotbed of sth

hotcake sell like hotcakes

hotfoot hotfoot it (off to) some place ♦ hotfoot it out of some place

hound clean as a hound's tooth ♦ hound so/animal down ♦ hound so from some place ♦ hound sth out of so ♦ run with the hare and hunt with the hounds

hour after hours ♦ all hours (of the day and night) ♦ at the bottom of the hour ♦ at the eleventh hour ♦ at the top of the hour ♦ banker's hours ♦ by the hour ♦ eleventh-hour decision ♦ for hours on end ♦ happy hour ♦ keep banker's hours ♦ keep late hours ♦ on the hour ♦ rush hour ♦ the small hours (of the night) ♦ There aren't enough hours in the day. ♦ until all hours ♦ the wee hours (of the night)

house bring the house down ♦ built like a brick outhouse ♦ built like a brick shithouse ♦ eat so out of house and home ♦ get one's house in order ♦ get one's own house in order ♦ house moss ♦ a house of cards ♦ house of correction ♦ a house of ill fame ♦ a house of ill repute ♦ in the doghouse ♦ in the poorhouse ♦ keep house ♦ like a house on fire ♦ My house is your house. ♦ on the house ♦ Our house is your house. ♦ put one's house in order ♦ put one's own house in order ♦ set one's house in order ♦ set one's own house in order

household a household name ♦ a household word

housekeeping set up housekeeping

hover hover between sth and sth else ♦ hover over so/sth ♦ hovering between life and death

how And how! ♦ a fine how-do-you-do ♦ How about doing sth? ♦ How (a)bout that! ♦ How about you? ♦ How (are) you doing? ♦ How are you getting on? ♦ How 'bout them apples? ♦ How come? ♦ How could you (do sth)? ♦ How dare you! ♦ How do you do. ♦ How do you know? ♦ How do you like that? ♦ How do you like them apples? ♦ How does that grab you? ♦ How goes it (with you)? ♦ How is so fixed for sth? ♦ How is so making out? ♦ How many times do I have to tell you? ♦ How should I know? ♦ How so? ♦ how the other half lives ♦ How's it going? ♦ How's that (again)? ♦ How's that for sth? ♦ How's the world (been) treating you? ♦ How's tricks? ♦ know-how ♦ (My,) how time flies! ♦ no matter how you slice it ♦ seeing as how . . . ♦ That's a fine how-do-you-do.

howl howl at so/sth

Hoyle according to Hoyle

huddle go into a huddle

hue a hue and cry (about sth)

huey hang a huey

huff huff and puff ♦ in a huff

hug commode-hugging drunk

hum hum with activity

human everything humanly possible ♦ the milk of human kindness

humble eat humble pie ♦ in my humble opinion

humor a sense of humor

hump over the hump

hunch have a hunch (that sth is the case)

hundred one in a hundred ♦ turn one hundred and eighty degrees ♦ turn three hundred and sixty degrees

hung hung up (on so/sth) ♦ think so hung the moon (and stars)

hunger hunger after so/sth ♦ strictly from hunger

hungry go hungry ♦ hungry as a bear ♦ hungry as a hunter ♦ hungry for sth

hunker hunker down and do sth

hunt hungry as a hunter ♦ hunt-and-peck ♦ hunt so/sth down ♦ hunt high and low (for so/sth) ♦ hunt so/sth up ♦ run with the hare and hunt with the hounds

hunter hungry as a hunter

hurrah the last hurrah

hurricane the eye of the hurricane

hurry hurry up and wait

hurt cry before one is hurt ♦ hurt for so/sth ♦ hurtin' for sth ♦ (It) doesn't hurt to do sth. ♦ (It) never hurts to do sth. ♦ not hurt a flea ♦ not hurt a fly ♦ What one doesn't know won't hurt one.

hush a hush fell over so/sth ♦ hush money ♦ hush so up ♦ hush sth up ♦ Hush your mouth!

hustle hustle and bustle

Hyde Jekyll and Hyde

hymn sing from the same hymn book

I

ice Bite the ice! ♦ break the ice ♦ cut no ice (with so) ♦ on ice ♦ on thin ice ♦ put so/sth on ice ♦ skate on thin ice ♦ stink on ice ♦ walk on thin ice

iceberg the tip of the iceberg

icing the icing on the cake

idea a bright idea ♦ flirt with the idea of doing sth ♦ the foggiest (idea) ♦ get a bright idea ♦ not a glimmer (of an idea) ♦ put ideas into so's head ♦ a rough idea (about sth) ♦ What's the (big) idea?

identify identify with so/animal

identity a case of mistaken identity

idiot take so for an idiot

idly sit idly by ♦ stand idly by

ignorance Ignorance is bliss.

ill fall ill ♦ a house of ill fame ♦ a house of ill repute ♦ ill at ease ♦ ill-disposed to doing sth ♦ ill-gotten gains ♦ ill will ♦ speak ill of so ♦ take ill

image the spit and image of so ♦ the spitting image of so

imagination capture so's imagination ♦ a figment of one's imagination ♦ not by any stretch of the imagination

imagine Can you imagine? ♦ Imagine that!

immediate immediate occupancy

immemorial since time immemorial

immerse immersed in thought

impact have an impact on so/sth ♦ upon impact

impair hearing impaired ♦ visually impaired

impartial fair and impartial

impasse reach an impasse

importance attach importance to sth

important have more important fish to fry

impossible next to impossible

impression leave an impression (on so) ♦ leave so with an impression ♦ make an impression on so

impulse on impulse

impunity with impunity

inch come within an inch of doing sth ♦ every inch a sth ♦ Give one an inch and one will take a mile. ♦ inch by inch ♦ not budge an inch ♦ not give an inch ♦ within an inch of one's life

include include sth in the bargain

incumbent incumbent (up)on so to do sth

indeed A friend in need is a friend indeed.

indignation bristle with indignation

indoor the greatest thing since indoor plumbing

induce induce labor in so

industry captain of industry

infinite in so's infinite wisdom

influence under the influence (of alcohol)

information for your information ♦ a gold mine of information ♦ information superhighway ♦ inside information ♦ a mine of information

inhumanity man's inhumanity to man

iniquity a den of iniquity

initiative take the initiative (to do sth)

injury add insult to injury

ink in ink ♦ ink sth in ♦ red ink

inkling have an inkling (about so/sth) ♦ an inkling (about so/sth) ♦ an inkling (of sth)

inner inner city

innocent innocent as a lamb ♦ innocent as a newborn babe ♦ play innocent

ins the ins and outs (of sth)

insane drive so insane

instance for instance ♦ in the first instance

instinct killer instinct

insult add insult to injury

intent for all intents and purposes ♦ intent on doing sth

interest have a keen interest in sth ♦ have so's best interest(s) at heart ♦ in an interesting condition ♦ in one's (own) (best) interest(s) ♦ in the interest of saving time ♦ pique so's interest ♦ take an interest in so/sth ♦ a vested interest in sth

interim in the interim

interval at regular intervals

intimate have intimate relations with so ♦ intimate apparel ♦ intimate with so

invasion invasion of (so's) privacy

inventory take inventory

involve involved (with so) ♦ involved with sth

iota not one iota

Irish get so's Irish up ♦ the luck of the Irish

iron cast-iron stomach ♦ get the kinks (ironed) out ♦ have several irons in the fire ♦ have too many irons in the fire ♦ iron sth out ♦ pump (some) iron ♦ rule with an iron fist ♦ strike while the iron is hot

issue take issue with so ♦ take issue with sth

itch have an itch for sth ♦ have an itchy palm ♦ an itch for sth ♦ itch for sth ♦ an itch to do sth ♦ itchy feet ♦ an itchy palm ♦ the seven-year itch

itsy itsy bitsy

itty itty bitty

ivory in an ivory tower ♦ live in an ivory tower ♦ tickle the ivories

J

jab take a jab at so

jack before you can say Jack Robinson ♦ jack around ♦ jack of all trades ♦ jack so up ◆ jack sth up ◆ quicker than you can say Jack Robinson

jackpot hit the jackpot

jam get into a jam ◆ get so out of a jam ◆ get out of a jam ◆ in a jam ◆ in(to) a jam ◆ a jam session ◆ jam the brakes on ◆ jam sth up ◆ jam with so ◆ a traffic jam

January cold as a well digger's ass (in January) ◆ cold as a well digger's ears (in January) ◆ cold as a well digger's feet (in January) ◆ slow as molasses in January ◆ slower than molasses in January

jaw have a glass jaw ◆ snatch victory from the jaws of defeat

jawbone diarrhea of the jawbone

jaybird naked as a jaybird

jazz and all that jazz ◆ jazz so/sth up ◆ jazzed (up)

Jekyll Jekyll and Hyde

jeopardy in jeopardy ◆ place so/sth in jeopardy ◆ put so/sth in(to) jeopardy

jerk jerk around ◆ jerk so around ◆ jerk so over ◆ a knee-jerk reaction

jest in jest

jetsam flotsam and jetsam

jiffy in a jiffy

jig The jig is up.

jim jim dandy

jitters get the jitters ◆ the jitters

job between jobs ◆ a devil of a job ◆ the devil's own job ◆ do a job on so/sth ◆ do a snow job on so ◆ Don't give up your day job. ◆ Don't quit your day job. ◆ fall down on the job ◆ have the patience of Job ◆ hold a job down ◆ an inside job ◆ land a job ◆ lay down on the job ◆ lie down on the job ◆ nine-to-five job ◆ on the job ◆ patient as Job ◆ pull a job ◆ a put-up job ◆ a snow job ◆ turn sth into a full-time job ◆ walk off the job

jockey jockey around ◆ jockey for position

Joe holy Joe

jog jog so's memory ◆ jog to the right or left

John a Dear John letter ◆ one's John Henry

Johnny Johnny-come-lately ◆ Johnny-on-the-spot

join join hands ◆ Join the club! ◆ join the fray ◆ join the ranks of sth ◆ joined at the hip

joint blow the joint ◆ case the joint ◆ get one's nose out of joint ◆ have one's nose out of joint ◆ put one's nose out of joint

joke able to take a joke ◆ (all) joking aside ◆ the butt of a joke ◆ crack a joke ◆ an inside joke ◆ The joke is on so. ◆ joking aside ◆ no joke ◆ play a joke on so ◆ a standing joke

Jones Davy Jones's locker ◆ keep up with the Joneses

José No way, José!

jot jot and tittle ◆ jot sth down

jour sth du jour

journey Have a safe journey.

jowl cheek by jowl

joy bundle of joy ◆ jump for joy ◆ leap for joy ◆ pride and joy ◆ weep for joy

judge not to judge a book by its cover ◆ sober as a judge

judgment against one's better judgment ◆ pass judgment (on so/sth) ◆ sit in judgment (up)on so/sth

jugular go for the jugular (vein)

juice cow juice ◆ juice and cookies ◆ stew in one's own juice

July knee-high by the 4th of July

jump (almost) jump out of one's skin ◆ get the jump on so ◆ Go jump in the lake! ◆ a hop, skip, and a jump ◆ jump all over so ◆ jump at the chance ◆ jump at the opportunity ◆ jump bail ◆ jump down so's throat ◆ jump for joy ◆ jump in (with both feet) ◆ jump into the fray ◆ jump off the deep end ◆ the jump on so ◆ jump out of one's skin ◆ jump out of the frying pan (and) into the fire ◆ jump ship ◆ jump the gun ◆ jump the track ◆ jump through a hoop ◆ jump to conclusions ◆ jump to mind ◆ jumping-off place ◆ jumping-off point ◆ jump-start so/sth ◆ keep one jump ahead (of so/sth) ◆ nearly jump out of one's skin ◆ one jump ahead (of so/sth) ◆ Take a running jump (in the lake)! ◆ two jumps ahead of so

juncture at this juncture

jungle It's a jungle out there.

junk junk mail

jury The jury is still out (on so/sth).

just able to take just so much ◆ one can (just) get oneself another boy ◆ can (just) see the wheels turning ♦ can (just) whistle for sth ♦ one could (just) kick oneself ♦ Don't that (just) beat all! ♦ get one's just deserts ♦ get one's just reward(s) ♦ go to one's (just) reward ♦ had (just) as soon do sth ♦ have just about had it ♦ have only just done sth ♦ I'd (just) as leave do sth ♦ I'd (just) as soon (as) do sth ♦ in (just) a minute ♦ in (just) a moment ♦ in (just) a second ♦ (It) just goes to show (you) (sth). ♦ (It) (just) goes without saying ♦ It (just) so happens that . . . ♦ It's just one of those things. ♦ just a minute ♦ Just a minute(, you)! ♦ just a moment ♦ just as I expected ♦ (just) between you and me ♦ (just) can't wait (for sth (to happen)) ♦ just one's cup of tea ♦ just fell off the turnip truck ♦ Just goes to show (you) (sth). ♦ just in case ♦ just in time (to do sth) ♦ just let me say ♦ just now ♦ just off the boat ♦ (just) say the word ♦ just shy of enough ♦ (just) taking care of business ♦ just the same ♦ just the same (to so) ♦ just the ticket ♦ just what the doctor ordered ♦ let me (just) say ♦ not just whistling Dixie ♦ That's (just) the nature of the beast. ♦ That's just what you need. ♦ Wait (just) a minute! ♦ would (just) as soon do sth ♦ you ain't (just) whistlin' Dixie ♦ You can (just) think again.

justice do justice to sth ♦ a miscarriage of justice ♦ poetic justice ♦ a travesty of justice

K

kangaroo a kangaroo court
Katie Katie bar the door
keel keel over ♦ keep on an even keel ♦ keep sth on an even keel
keen have a keen interest in sth ♦ keen on doing sth ♦ keen on so/sth
keep be one's brother's keeper ♦ earn one's keep ♦ enough to keep body and soul together ♦ for keeps ♦ for safekeeping ♦ (Have you) been keeping busy? ♦ (Have you) been keeping cool? ♦ (Have you) been keeping out of trouble? ♦ in keeping (with sth) ♦ One is known by the company one keeps. ♦ keep a civil tongue (in one's head) ♦ keep a close rein on so/sth ♦ keep a close watch on so/sth ♦ keep a date open (for so/sth) ♦ keep a firm grip on so/sth ♦ keep a low profile ♦ keep a promise ♦ keep a secret ♦ keep a straight face ♦ keep a tight grip on so/sth ♦ keep a tight rein on so/sth ♦ keep abreast of sth ♦ keep after so (about sth) ♦ keep ahead of the game ♦ keep an act up ♦ keep an ear to the ground ♦ keep an eye on so/sth ♦ keep an eye out (for so/sth) ♦ keep an open mind ♦ keep at sth ♦ keep so/sth at a distance ♦ keep so/sth at arm's length ♦ keep at arm's length from so/sth ♦ keep so/sth at bay ♦ keep so back ♦ keep sth back ♦ keep banker's hours ♦ keep body and soul together ♦ keep one's cards close to one's vest ♦ keep one's chin up ♦ keep clear of sth ♦ keep so company ♦ keep company (with so) ♦ keep cool ♦ keep one's cool ♦ keep one's distance from so/sth ♦ keep so down ♦ keep sth down ♦ keep one's end of the bargain ♦ keep one's end of the bargain up ♦ keep one's end up ♦ keep one's eye on so/sth ♦ keep one's eye on the ball ♦ keep one's eyes open (for so/sth) ♦ keep one's eyes peeled (for so/sth) ♦ keep faith with so/sth ♦ keep one's feet on the ground ♦ keep one's finger on the pulse of sth ♦ keep one's fingers crossed (for so/sth) ♦ keep fit ♦ keep sth for a rainy day ♦ keep sth for another occasion ♦ keep good time ♦ keep so guessing ♦ keep one's hand in (sth) ♦ keep one's hands clean ♦ keep one's hands off (sth) ♦ keep one's hands to oneself ♦ keep so/sth hanging (in midair) ♦ keep harping on sth ♦ keep one's head ♦ keep one's head above water ♦ keep one's head down ♦ keep house ♦ keep so in (a state of) suspense ♦ keep so/sth in check ♦ keep in good with so ♦ keep so/animal in line ♦ keep so in mind ♦ keep sth in mind ♦ keep so/sth in mind (for so/sth) ♦ keep so/sth in reserve ♦ keep so in sight ♦ keep so in stitches ♦ Keep in there! ♦ Keep in touch. ♦ keep in touch (with so) ♦ keep sth inside ((of) one(self)) ♦ keep it down (to a dull roar) ♦ Keep it up! ♦ keep late hours ♦

kin kith and kin ✦ one's next of kin

kind feel (kind of) puny ✦ in kind ✦ It takes all kinds (to make a world). ✦ a kind of sth ✦ kind of sth ✦ nothing of the kind ✦ one of a kind ✦ take kindly to sth ✦ two of a kind

kindness kill so with kindness ✦ the milk of human kindness

king cocky as the king of spades ✦ fit for a king ✦ a king's ransom ✦ the sport of kings

kingdom blow so/sth to kingdom come ✦ till kingdom come

kink get the kinks (ironed) out

kiss blow so a kiss ✦ (Do) you kiss your momma with that mouth? ✦ kiss and make up ✦ kiss and tell ✦ kiss so's ass ✦ kiss sth good-bye ✦ the kiss of death ✦ kiss off ✦ kiss so off ✦ kiss the dust ✦ kissing cousins ✦ right in the kisser ✦ sealed with a kiss

kit the whole kit and caboodle

kitchen everything but the kitchen sink

kite Go fly a kite! ✦ high as a kite

kith kith and kin

kitten a dust kitten ✦ feed the kitty ✦ have kittens ✦ purr like a kitten ✦ weak as a kitten

kitty feed the kitty

klutz klutz around

knee at one's mother's knee ✦ bring one to one's knees ✦ fall on one's knees ✦ fall to one's knees ✦ go down on one's knees ✦ knee-deep in sth ✦ knee-high by the 4th of July ✦ knee-high to a grasshopper ✦ a knee-jerk reaction ✦ knock one's knees together ✦ on bended knee ✦ up to one's knees

knell sound the death knell

knew knew it was coming

knife go under the knife ✦ pull a knife (on so) ✦ twist the knife (in so's back)

knight a knight in shining armor

knit knit one's brow

knock Don't knock it. ✦ knock about (some place) (with so) ✦ knock around ✦ knock sth back ✦ knock back a drink ✦ knock so back (an amount of money) ✦ knock so's block off ✦ knock so cold ✦ knock so dead ✦ knock sth down ✦ knock so down a peg (or two) ✦ knock so for a loop ✦ knock one's head (up) against a brick wall ✦ knock sth into a

cocked hat ✦ Knock it off! ✦ knock one's knees together ✦ knock so off ✦ knock sth off ✦ knock off (doing sth) ✦ knock one off one's feet ✦ knock on wood ✦ knock one back ✦ knock one over ✦ knock so out ✦ knock sth out ✦ knock oneself out (to do sth) (for so/sth) ✦ knock over sth ✦ knock so over (with a feather) ✦ knock so's socks off ✦ knock some heads together ✦ knock some sense into so ✦ knock so some skin ✦ knock the bejeebers out of so/sth ✦ knock the bottom out (of sth) ✦ knock the habit ✦ knock the (living) daylights out of so ✦ knock the props out from under so ✦ knock the wind out of so's sails ✦ knock sth together ✦ knock so up ✦ knock-down-drag-out fight ✦ knocked out ✦ knocked up ✦ the school of hard knocks ✦ You could have knocked me over with a feather.

knot tie the knot ✦ tie so (up) in knots

know Anyone I know? ✦ as far as anyone knows ✦ before you know it ✦ Do you want to know something? ✦ don't care who knows it ✦ Don't I know it! ✦ don't know one's ass from a hole in the ground ✦ don't know one's ass from one's elbow ✦ don't know beans (about sth) ✦ for all I know ✦ God only knows! ✦ (had) known it was coming ✦ How do you know? ✦ How should I know? ✦ if one knows what's good for one ✦ if you know what's good for you ✦ in the know ✦ One is known by the company one keeps. ✦ (It) takes one to know one. ✦ know a thing or two (about so/sth) ✦ know a trick or two ✦ know one's ABCs ✦ know all the angles ✦ know all the answers ✦ know so as so ✦ know sth at a glance ✦ know sth backwards and forwards ✦ know best ✦ know better (than to do sth) ✦ know so/sth by sth ✦ know sth by heart ✦ know so/sth by name ✦ know so by sight ✦ know different ✦ know one for what one is ✦ know from sth ✦ know sth from memory ✦ know full well ✦ know sth in one's bones ✦ know (sth) in one's heart of hearts ✦ know so/sth inside out ✦ know so/sth like a book ✦ know so/sth like the back of one's hand ✦ know so/sth like the palm of one's hand ✦ know no bounds ✦

know of so/sth ♦ know one's onions ♦ know sth only too well ♦ know otherwise ♦ know one's place ♦ know shit from Shinola ♦ know one's stuff ♦ know the ropes ♦ know the score ♦ know the tricks of the trade ♦ know one's way around ♦ know what one is talking about ♦ know what's what ♦ know when one is not wanted ♦ know where all the bodies are buried ♦ know where one is coming from ♦ know where it's at ♦ know where so stands (on so/sth) ♦ know whereof one speaks ♦ know which is which ♦ know-how ♦ known fact ♦ known quantity ♦ let sth be known ♦ like, you know ♦ Lord knows I've tried. ♦ make it one's business (to know sth) ♦ not know beans (about so/sth) ♦ not know enough to come in out of the rain ♦ not know so from Adam ♦ not know if one is coming or going ♦ not know one's own strength ♦ not know the first thing about so/sth ♦ not know what hit one ♦ not know what to make of so/sth ♦ not know where to turn ♦ not know whether one is coming or going ♦ not know whether to laugh or cry ♦ not know which end is up ♦ so far as anyone knows ♦ the Lord only knows ♦ an unknown quantity ♦ Want to know something? ♦ What do you know? ♦ What one doesn't know won't hurt one.

knowledge have carnal knowledge of so

knuckle get one's knuckles rapped ♦ knuckle down (to sth) ♦ a knuckle sandwich ♦ knuckle under (to so/sth) ♦ rap so across the knuckles ♦ white knuckle sth

kosher It's not kosher.

L

labor the fruits of one's labor(s) ♦ in labor ♦ induce labor in so ♦ a labor of love ♦ labor under sth

lack lack for sth

ladder at the bottom of the ladder ♦ can't see a hole in a ladder ♦ on the bottom rung (of the ladder) ♦ the top of the ladder

lady Ladies first. ♦ a ladies' man ♦ a lady-killer ♦ lady of the evening ♦ till the fat lady sings ♦ when the fat lady sings

lake Go jump in the lake! ♦ Take a running jump (in the lake)!

lam on the lam ♦ take it on the lam

lamb gentle as a lamb ♦ in two shakes of a lamb's tail ♦ innocent as a lamb ♦ like lambs to the slaughter ♦ meek as a lamb ♦ two shakes of a lamb's tail

lame lame duck

land do a land-office business ♦ go on to a better land ♦ land a blow ♦ land a job ♦ land in sth ♦ Land o' Goshen! ♦ the land of Nod ♦ land (up)on both feet ♦ land-office business ♦ Land(s) sakes (alive)! ♦ the lay of the land ♦ live off the fat of the land ♦ live off the land ♦ on land

landscape a blot on the landscape

landslide a landslide victory

lane down the little red lane ♦ in the fast lane ♦ life in the fast lane ♦ live in the fast lane ♦ (a trip down) memory lane

language in plain language ♦ speak so's language ♦ speak the same language

languish languish in some place

lap drop into one's lap ♦ fall into one's lap ♦ in the lap of luxury ♦ the lap of luxury ♦ lap sth up ♦ Make a lap!

lapse lapse from grace ♦ lapse into a coma

lard tub of lard

large at large ♦ by and large ♦ in large part ♦ large as life ♦ large as life (and twice as ugly) ♦ larger than life ♦ living large ♦ loom large (on the horizon) ♦ out in large numbers ♦ play a large part (in sth) ♦ writ large

lark for a lark ♦ happy as a lark ♦ on a lark

lash lash out at so ♦ a tongue-lashing

last as a last resort ♦ at (long) last ♦ at the last gasp ♦ at the last minute ♦ some time before last ♦ breathe one's last ♦ down to the last bit of money ♦ down to the last detail ♦ every last one ♦ famous last words ♦ get the last laugh (on so) ♦ have the last word ♦ head for the last roundup ♦ hear the last of so/sth ♦ in the last analysis ♦ last but not least ♦ last call (for sth) ♦ last chance (for sth) ♦ the last hurrah

♦ the last laugh (on so) ♦ one's last resting place ♦ the last roundup ♦ the last say ♦ the last straw ♦ last will and testament ♦ the last word ♦ the last word in sth ♦ last-ditch effort ♦ make last-ditch effort ♦ on so's/sth's last legs ♦ pay one's last respects (to so) ♦ see the last of so/sth ♦ the last person (to single out for sth) ♦ to the last

latch latch on(to so) ♦ latch onto sth ♦ The latch string is always out.

late at the latest ♦ Better late than never. ♦ a day late and a dollar short ♦ Johnny-come-lately ♦ keep late hours ♦ a late bloomer ♦ late in life ♦ late in the day ♦ the late unpleasantness ♦ the latest rage ♦ of late ♦ too little too late

later Catch me later. ♦ (Good-bye) till later. ♦ (Good-bye) until later. ♦ See you later, alligator. ♦ sooner or later

lather in a lather ♦ lather up ♦ work oneself (up) into a lather

laugh bust out laughing ♦ die laughing ♦ Don't make me laugh! ♦ for laughs ♦ get the last laugh (on so) ♦ the last laugh (on so) ♦ a laugh a minute ♦ laugh all the way to the bank ♦ laugh at so/sth ♦ laugh sth away ♦ laugh one's head off ♦ laugh in so's face ♦ laugh sth off ♦ laugh so off the stage ♦ laugh sth out of court ♦ laugh out of the other side of one's face ♦ laugh out of the other side of one's mouth ♦ laugh oneself silly ♦ laugh up one's sleeve ♦ no laughing matter ♦ not know whether to laugh or cry

laughingstock laughingstock (of so/group) ♦ make a laughingstock (out) of oneself or sth ♦ make oneself or sth a laughingstock

laughter gales of laughter ♦ split one's sides (with laughter)

launch launch forth on sth ♦ launch into sth

laundry so's dirty laundry

laurel look to one's laurels ♦ rest on one's laurels

lavatory go to the lavatory

lavender lay so out in lavender

law above the law ♦ bend the law ♦ break a law ♦ break the law ♦ in the eyes of the law ♦ a law unto oneself ♦ lay down the law (to so) (about sth) ♦ the long arm of the law ♦ on the wrong side of the law ♦ take the law into one's own hands ♦ vote sth into law ♦ so's word is law

lay get laid ♦ laid back ♦ laid out ♦ laid up ♦ lay a finger on so/sth ♦ lay a guilt trip on so ♦ lay a (heavy) trip on so ♦ lay a place (for so) ♦ lay alongside sth ♦ lay an egg ♦ lay sth at so's door ♦ lay sth at so's doorstep ♦ lay sth at so's feet ♦ lay so away ♦ lay sth away (for so) ♦ lay sth before so ♦ lay sth by ♦ lay one's cards on the table ♦ lay claim to sth ♦ lay down ♦ lay down one's arms ♦ lay down one's life (for so/sth) ♦ lay down on the job ♦ lay down the law (to so) (about sth) ♦ lay emphasis on sth ♦ lay eyes on so/sth ♦ lay for so/sth ♦ lay sth for so/sth ♦ lay one's hands on so/sth/animal ♦ lay sth in ♦ lay into so/sth ♦ lay it on the line ♦ lay it on thick ♦ lay it on with a trowel ♦ lay low ♦ lay so low ♦ the lay of the land ♦ lay off (so/sth) ♦ lay so off (from sth) ♦ lay sth on ♦ lay sth on so ♦ lay one on ♦ lay so out ♦ lay sth out ♦ lay so out in lavender ♦ lay over (some place) ♦ lay some sweet lines on so ♦ lay stress on sth ♦ lay the blame (for sth) on so ♦ lay the blame on so/sth ♦ lay the finger on so ♦ lay to ♦ lay sth to sth ♦ lay so to rest ♦ lay sth to rest ♦ lay sth to waste ♦ lay sth up ♦ lay waste to sth ♦ lay oneself (wide) open for sth ♦ not lay a hand on so/sth

layaway put sth in layaway

lazy born lazy

lead a case of the blind leading the blind ♦ fill so full of lead ♦ follow so's lead ♦ get the lead out ♦ go over like a lead balloon ♦ lead a dog's life ♦ lead a double life ♦ lead so astray ♦ lead so by the nose ♦ lead so down the garden path ♦ lead in(to sth) ♦ lead sth off ♦ lead so on ♦ lead so on a merry chase ♦ lead the life of Riley ♦ lead the pack ♦ lead the way ♦ lead so to do sth ♦ lead so to believe sth ♦ lead up to sth ♦ lead with so/sth ♦ lead with sth ♦ leading question ♦ a lead-pipe cinch ♦ on the leading edge ♦ One thing leads to another. ♦ shake the lead out

leaf leaf through sth ♦ take a leaf out of so's book ♦ turn over a new leaf

league in league (with so) ♦ in the same league as so/sth ♦ out of so's league ♦ play in the big leagues

leak leak out ♦ leak sth (out) ♦ leak sth to so ♦ take a leak

lean lean and mean ♦ lean on so ♦ lean on so/sth ♦ lean over backwards (to do sth) ♦ lean times (ahead) ♦ lean toward doing sth ♦ lean toward so/sth

leap by leaps and bounds ♦ grow by leaps and bounds ♦ leap at so/sth ♦ leap at the chance (to do sth) ♦ leap at the opportunity (to do sth) ♦ leap for joy ♦ a leap of faith ♦ leap to conclusions

learn learn sth by rote ♦ learn sth from the bottom up ♦ learn one's lesson ♦ learn (sth) the hard way ♦ learn to live with sth ♦ a learning experience ♦ live and learn

lease a new lease on life

leash keep so on a short leash ♦ on a short leash ♦ on a tight leash ♦ strain at the leash

least at least ♦ at least so many ♦ at the very least ♦ follow the line of least resistance ♦ last but not least ♦ the least so could do ♦ the least little thing ♦ least of all ♦ the line of least resistance ♦ not in the least ♦ the path of least resistance ♦ to say the least ♦ when least expected

leather hell-bent for leather ♦ tough as (old) (shoe) leather

leave I'd (just) as leave do sth ♦ leave a bad taste in so's mouth ♦ leave a date open (for so/sth) ♦ leave a lot to be desired ♦ leave a paper trail ♦ leave a sinking ship ♦ leave ahead of time ♦ leave so/sth/animal alone ♦ leave an impression (on so) ♦ leave sth aside ♦ leave so/sth (at) some place ♦ leave so at loose ends ♦ leave so/sth/animal be ♦ leave so cold ♦ leave so flat ♦ leave sth for another occasion ♦ leave so for dead ♦ leave so guessing ♦ leave so/sth hanging (in midair) ♦ leave so high and dry ♦ leave so holding the baby ♦ leave so holding the bag ♦ leave in a body ♦ leave so/sth in one's hands ♦ leave so in peace ♦ leave so in the lurch ♦ leave so in the shade ♦ leave it at that ♦ leave it to so ♦ leave one's mark on so ♦ Leave me alone! ♦ leave no stone unturned ♦ a leave of absence ♦ leave off

(doing sth) ♦ leave sth on ♦ leave open the possibility (of sth) ♦ leave one's options open ♦ leave so out in the cold ♦ leave one scratching one's head ♦ leave the door open (for sth) ♦ leave the nest ♦ leave the room ♦ leave sth to so ♦ leave sth to chance ♦ leave one to one's fate ♦ leave so to it ♦ leave one to one's own devices ♦ leave one to one's own resources ♦ leave so up in the air ♦ leave sth up in the air ♦ leave sth up to so/sth ♦ leave well enough alone ♦ leave oneself (wide) open for sth ♦ leave oneself (wide) open to sth ♦ leave so with an impression ♦ leave word for so to do sth ♦ leave word (with so) ♦ make like a tree and leave ♦ Take it or leave it. ♦ take (one's) leave (of so) ♦ take leave of so/sth ♦ take leave of one's senses ♦ without (so much as) a (for or) by your leave

lecture lecture at so (about sth)

left better left unsaid ♦ come out of left field ♦ hang a left ♦ have two left feet ♦ jog to the right or left ♦ left and right ♦ left-handed compliment ♦ out in left field ♦ out of left field ♦ pay so a left-handed compliment ♦ right and left ♦ take up where one/sth left off

leg an arm and a leg ♦ Break a leg! ♦ cost an arm and a leg ♦ crooked as a dog's hind leg ♦ the first leg (of a journey) ♦ get one's sea legs ♦ get up on one's hind legs ♦ give so a leg up ♦ sth has legs ♦ have a hollow leg ♦ a leg up ♦ a leg up on so ♦ leg work ♦ not have a leg to stand on ♦ on so's/sth's last legs ♦ pull so's leg ♦ one's sea legs ♦ shake a leg ♦ stretch one's legs ♦ with one's tail between one's legs

legend a legend in one's own (life)time

leisure at (one's) leisure

lend lend so a hand with sth ♦ lend so a (helping) hand ♦ lend an ear to so/sth ♦ lend color to sth ♦ lend oneself or itself to sth ♦ lend your ear to so/sth

length at great length ♦ at length ♦ at some length ♦ go to any length ♦ hold so/sth at arm's length ♦ keep so/sth at arm's length ♦ keep at arm's length from so/sth ♦ on the same wavelength ♦ speak at great length

lengths go to great lengths (to do sth)

Lent busy as a fish peddler in Lent

less could(n't) care less ♦ (I) could(n't) care less. ♦ in less than no time ♦ Less is more. ♦ less than pleased ♦ the lesser (of the two) ♦ the lesser of two evils ♦ more or less ♦ much less so/sth ♦ no less ♦ no less than so/sth ♦ no less than (some amount) ♦ nothing less than some quality

lesson learn one's lesson ♦ teach so a lesson

let Don't let so/sth get you down. ♦ Don't let it go any further. ♦ Don't let it out of this room. ♦ Don't let the bastards wear you down. ♦ just let me say ♦ let so/sth/animal alone ♦ let alone do sth ♦ let alone so/sth ♦ let sth be known ♦ Let bygones be bygones. ♦ let so/sth down ♦ let one's emotions show ♦ let fly with sth ♦ Let George do it. ♦ let so get by with sth ♦ let sth (get) out ♦ let sth get out ♦ let oneself go ♦ let so go ♦ let go (with sth) ♦ let grass grow under one's feet ♦ let one's guard down ♦ let one's hair down ♦ let so have it (with both barrels) ♦ Let her rip! ♦ let oneself in for sth ♦ let so in for sth ♦ let it all hang out ♦ Let it be. ♦ Let it go. ♦ Let it roll! ♦ let loose of so/sth ♦ let loose (with sth) ♦ Let me have it! ♦ let me (just) say ♦ let nature take its course ♦ let sth off ♦ let so off (easy) ♦ let off (some) steam ♦ let on (about so/sth) ♦ let out ♦ let sth out ♦ let out some kind of sound ♦ let out (with) sth ♦ let sth ride ♦ let so slide by ♦ let sth slide by ♦ let sth slip by ♦ let sth slip (out) ♦ let the cat out of the bag ♦ let the chips fall (where they may) ♦ let things slide ♦ let up ♦ let up (on so/sth) ♦ let well enough alone ♦ Let's call it a day. ♦ Let's get down to business. ♦ Let's have it! ♦ Let's rock and roll! ♦ let's say ♦ (Let's) say that . . . ♦ Let's see. ♦ Let's talk (about it). ♦ live and let live ♦ not let so catch so doing sth ♦ not let the grass grow under one's feet ♦ sit back and let sth happen

letter bread-and-butter letter ♦ dash a letter off ♦ dead letter ♦ a Dear John letter ♦ a red-letter day ♦ to the letter

level at sea level ♦ do one's (level) best ♦ find one's own level ♦ level a charge against so ♦ level sth at so/sth ♦ so's level best ♦ level off ♦ a level playing field ♦ level the (playing) field ♦ level sth to the ground ♦ level with so (about so/sth) ♦ on the level ♦ (strictly) on the level

liberty at liberty ♦ take liberties with so/sth ♦ take the liberty of doing sth

license license to do sth ♦ poetic license

lick get a licking ♦ a lick and a promise ♦ lick one's chops ♦ lick so/sth into shape ♦ lick one's lips ♦ a lick of work ♦ lick one's wounds ♦ a licking

lid blow one's lid ♦ blow the lid off (sth) ♦ flip one's lid ♦ the lid on sth ♦ put the lid on sth ♦ take the lid off (of) sth

lie Ask no questions and hear no lies. ♦ give the lie to sth ♦ lie at anchor ♦ lie at death's door ♦ lie behind so/sth ♦ lie beyond so/sth ♦ lie doggo ♦ lie down on the job ♦ lie fallow ♦ lie in ♦ lie in sth ♦ lie in ruins ♦ lie in state ♦ lie in store (for so) ♦ lie in wait (for so/sth) ♦ lie like a rug ♦ lie low ♦ lie through one's teeth ♦ a little white lie ♦ live a lie ♦ a pack of lies ♦ put the lie to sth ♦ take sth lying down

lieu in lieu of sth

life all walks of life ♦ bet one's life ♦ big as life (and twice as ugly) ♦ bigger than life ♦ bigger than life (and twice as ugly) ♦ breathe new life into sth ♦ bring sth back to life ♦ bring so/sth to life ♦ caught between life and death ♦ the change (of life) ♦ claim a life ♦ come to life ♦ depart this life ♦ the evening of life ♦ every walk of life ♦ the facts of life ♦ for life ♦ for the life of me ♦ Get a life! ♦ get on with one's life ♦ get out with one's life ♦ get the shock of one's life ♦ hang on for dear life ♦ have the time of one's life ♦ hold on for dear life ♦ hovering between life and death ♦ I'm having the time of my life. ♦ in the prime of (one's) life ♦ large as life ♦ large as life (and twice as ugly) ♦ larger than life ♦ late in life ♦ lay down one's life (for so/sth) ♦ lead a dog's life ♦ lead a double life ♦ lead the life of Riley ♦ life after sth ♦ life and limb ♦ life in the fast lane ♦ life is too short ♦ a life of its own ♦ the life of the party ♦ Life's been good (to me). ♦ live a dog's life ♦ live a double life ♦ live a life of sth ♦ live out one's life ♦ live the life of Riley ♦ make a (kind of) life for oneself ♦ make life miserable for so ♦ mark so for life ♦ a matter of life and death ♦ a milestone in so's life ♦ mission in life ♦ a new lease on life ♦ pester the life out of so ♦ put one's life on the line ♦ run for one's life ♦ the seamy side of life ♦ set for life ♦ the shock of one's life ♦ sign one's life away ♦ spring to life ♦ take so's life ♦ take one's life into one's (own) hands ♦ take on a life of its own ♦ take one's own life ♦ That's life. ♦ That's life in the big city. ♦ That's the story of my life. ♦ one's time of life ♦ within an inch of one's life ♦ You bet your (sweet) life!

lifetime a legend in one's own (life)time ♦ once-in-a-lifetime chance ♦ once-in-a-lifetime opportunity

lift give so a lift ♦ lift a hand (against so/sth) ♦ lift one's elbow ♦ lift so from sth ♦ not lift a finger (to help so) ♦ not lift a hand (to help so)

light according to one's own lights ♦ all sweetness and light ♦ at first light ♦ (begin to) see the light (at the end of the tunnel) ♦ bring so/sth to light ♦ bring sth to light ♦ come to light ♦ first see the light of day ♦ get off (lightly) ♦ go out like a light ♦ hide one's light under a bushel ♦ in a good light ♦ in (the) light of sth ♦ in the limelight ♦ in the spotlight ♦ light as a feather ♦ light as air ♦ light into so/sth ♦ light out (for some place) ♦ light out (of some place) (for some place) ♦ light up ♦ light (up)on so/sth ♦ lighten so's load ♦ lighten up (on so/sth) ♦ make light of sth ♦ one's name in lights ♦ not suffer fools lightly ♦ once-over-lightly ♦ out like a light ♦ punch so's lights out ♦ run a red light ♦ see one's name in lights ♦ see the light ♦ see the light (at the end of the tunnel) ♦ see the light (of day) ♦ shed (some) light on sth ♦ steal the spotlight ♦ throw an amount of light on so/sth ♦ throw (some) light on sth ♦ tread lightly (with so/sth) ♦ trip the light fantastic

lightning like greased lightning ♦ quick as (greased) lightning ♦ swift as lightning

like and the like ♦ avoid so/sth like the plague ♦ built like a brick outhouse ♦ built like a brick shithouse ♦ come across like so/sth (to so) ♦ come on like gangbusters ♦ come out smelling like a rose ♦ come up smelling like a rose ♦ Don't even look like sth! ♦ drawn like a moth to a flame ♦ drink like a fish ♦ drop so/sth like a hot potato ♦ drop like flies ♦ eat like a bird ♦ eat like a horse ♦ eyes like saucers ♦ feel like a million (dollars) ♦ feel like a new person ♦ feel like oneself again ♦ feel like (having) sth ♦ fit like a glove ♦ go like clockwork ♦ go out like a light ♦ go over like a lead balloon ♦ go through so like a dose of the salts ♦ hate so/sth like sin ♦ How do you like that? ♦ How do you like them apples? ♦ I'm like you ♦ kick like a mule ♦ kick like a steer ♦ know so/sth like a book ♦ know so/sth like the back of one's hand ♦ know so/sth like the palm of one's hand ♦ lie like a rug ♦ like a bat out of hell ♦ like a bolt out of the blue ♦ like a bump on a log ♦ like a fish out of water ♦ like a house on fire ♦ like a kid with a new toy ♦ like a million (dollars) ♦ like a sitting duck ♦ like a three-ring circus ♦ like a ton of bricks ♦ like as not ♦ like crazy ♦ like death warmed over ♦ like fighting snakes ♦ like gangbusters ♦ like greased lightning ♦ like hell ♦ Like hell (so did)! ♦ like hell on wheels ♦ Like hell you will! ♦ like herding cats ♦ like herding frogs ♦ like I was saying ♦ like it is going out of style ♦ Like it or lump it! ♦ Like it's such a big deal! ♦ like lambs to the slaughter ♦ like looking for a needle in a haystack ♦ like mad ♦ like nobody's business ♦ like nothing on earth ♦ like one of the family ♦ like one owned the place ♦ like pulling teeth ♦ like shooting fish in a barrel ♦ like stink ♦ like taking candy from a baby ♦ like the devil ♦ like the dickens ♦ like the wind ♦ like there's no tomorrow ♦ like to did sth ♦ like to hear oneself talk ♦ like trying to find a needle in a haystack ♦ like (two) peas in a pod ♦ like water off a duck's back ♦ like, you know ♦ likely as not ♦ liken so/sth to so/sth ♦ the likes of so/sth ♦ look like a (dead) ringer (for so) ♦ look like sth the cat dragged in ♦ look like the cat that swallowed the canary ♦ make like a tree

and leave ♦ make (out) like sth ♦ need sth
like a hole in the head ♦ off like a shot ♦
out like a light ♦ pack so/sth (in) like
sardines ♦ purr like a cat ♦ purr like a
kitten ♦ quick like a bunny ♦ read so like a
book ♦ run around like a chicken with its
head cut off ♦ run like clockwork ♦ run
like stink ♦ run like the wind ♦ sell like
hotcakes ♦ sleep like a baby ♦ sleep like a
log ♦ smell like a rose ♦ smiling like a
Cheshire cat ♦ smoke like a chimney ♦
sound like a broken record ♦ spend
money like it's going out of style ♦ spend
money like there's no tomorrow ♦ spread
like wildfire ♦ stand out like a sore thumb
♦ stick out like a sore thumb ♦ swear like
a trooper ♦ take a liking to so/sth ♦ take it
like a man ♦ tap dance like mad ♦ taste
like more ♦ Tell it like it is. ♦ That's more
like it. ♦ There's no time like the present.
♦ They don't make them like they used
to. ♦ to so's liking ♦ treat so like dirt ♦ treat
so like shit ♦ treat so like the scum of the
earth ♦ watch so/sth like a hawk ♦ work
like a beaver ♦ work like a charm ♦ work
like a horse ♦ work like a mule ♦ work
like a slave
likelihood in all likelihood
likely likely as not
liken liken so/sth to so/sth
lily gild the lily
limb life and limb ♦ out on a limb ♦ tear
so/animal limb from limb
limbo in limbo
limelight in the limelight
limit go the limit ♦ go to the limit ♦ off
limits ♦ The sky's the limit. ♦ within limits
line along the line(s) of sth ♦ along those
lines ♦ blow one's lines ♦ the bottom line ♦
bring sth into line (with sth) ♦ cash on the
line ♦ cross (over) the line ♦ Don't give
me that (line)! ♦ Don't hand me that
(line)! ♦ draw a line in the sand ♦ draw
the line (at sth) ♦ draw the line between
sth and sth (else) ♦ drop so a line ♦ the end
of the line ♦ fall for sth hook, line, and
sinker ♦ fall in(to) line ♦ feed so a line ♦
fluff one's lines ♦ follow the line of least
resistance ♦ give so a line ♦ go down the
line ♦ have a line on so/sth ♦ hold the line

(at so/sth) ♦ hold the line (on so/sth) ♦ Hold
the line(, please). ♦ in line ♦ in line for sth
♦ in line with sth ♦ in the line of duty ♦ in
the pipeline ♦ keep so/animal in line ♦ keep
out of the line of fire ♦ lay it on the line ♦
lay some sweet lines on so ♦ the line of
fire ♦ the line of least resistance ♦ a line on
so/sth ♦ line one's own pocket(s) ♦ line so/sth
up ♦ line so/sth up with so/sth ♦ muff one's
lines ♦ off-line ♦ on line ♦ on the
borderline ♦ on the line ♦ on the sidelines
♦ out of line (with sth) ♦ the party line ♦
put one's ass on the line ♦ put it on the
line ♦ put one's life on the line ♦ put one's
neck on the line ♦ put some sweet lines
on so ♦ read between the lines ♦ sign on
the dotted line ♦ somewhere along the
line ♦ somewhere down the line ♦ step
out of line ♦ swallow sth hook, line, and
sinker ♦ take a hard line (with so) ♦ There
is a fine line between sth and sth else. ♦
There is a thin line between sth and sth
else. ♦ toe the line
linen air one's dirty linen in public ♦ wash
one's dirty linen in public
linger linger on (after so/sth)
link link so/sth and so/sth together ♦ link
so/sth to so/sth ♦ the weak link (in the chain)
lion the lion's share (of sth) ♦ strong as a
lion
lip button (up) one's lip ♦ Don't give me
any of your lip! ♦ give so a fat lip ♦ give so
some lip ♦ lick one's lips ♦ So's lips are
sealed. ♦ Loose lips sink ships. ♦ My lips
are sealed. ♦ None of your lip! ♦ on
everyone's lips ♦ pay lip service (to sth) ♦
read so's lips ♦ Read my lips! ♦ smack one's
lips ♦ Watch my lips! ♦ Zip (up) your lip!
liquor hold one's liquor ♦ liquor up ♦ liquor
so up
list enter the lists ♦ on the wait list ♦ on
the waiting list ♦ shopping list ♦ sucker
list ♦ wish list
listen I'm listening. ♦ listen to reason ♦
listen up ♦ stop, look, and listen
litmus litmus test
litter the runt of the litter
little able to sit up and take (a little)
nourishment ♦ bother one's (pretty little)
head about so/sth ♦ down the little red

lane ♦ give a little ♦ in a little bit ♦ the least little thing ♦ A little bird told me. ♦ a little bit (of sth) ♦ little bitty ♦ little by little ♦ (a little) new to (all) this ♦ a (little) nip in the air ♦ little old so/sth ♦ a little pricey ♦ little shaver ♦ (a little) short on one end ♦ a little steep ♦ a little white lie ♦ not trouble one's (pretty) (little) head about sth ♦ Oh, ye of little faith. ♦ one little bit ♦ precious little ♦ sure as God made little green apples ♦ think little of so/sth ♦ to little avail ♦ too little too late ♦ Ye gods (and little fishes)!

live all the way live ♦ As I live and breathe! ♦ beat the living daylights out of so ♦ every living soul ♦ do sth for a living ♦ frighten the living daylights out of so ♦ have not lived until one has done sth ♦ have to live with sth ♦ hit one where one lives ♦ how the other half lives ♦ in living memory ♦ knock the (living) daylights out of so ♦ learn to live with sth ♦ live a dog's life ♦ live a double life ♦ live a lie ♦ live a life of sth ♦ live and breathe sth ♦ live and learn ♦ live and let live ♦ live beyond one's means ♦ live by some kind of effort ♦ live by one's wits ♦ live sth down ♦ live for so/sth ♦ live for the moment ♦ live from day to day ♦ live from hand to mouth ♦ live happily ever after ♦ live in an ivory tower ♦ live in hope(s) of sth ♦ live in sin ♦ live in the fast lane ♦ live in the past ♦ live in the present ♦ live it up ♦ live off the fat of the land ♦ live off the land ♦ live on (after so/sth) ♦ live on borrowed time ♦ live on the edge ♦ live sth out ♦ live out one's days ♦ live out one's life ♦ live out of a suitcase ♦ live out of cans ♦ live (pretty) high off the hog ♦ live (pretty) high on the hog ♦ live the life of Riley ♦ live to the (ripe old) age of sth ♦ live under the same roof (with so) ♦ live up to sth ♦ live up to one's side of the bargain ♦ live with so ♦ live with sth ♦ live within one's means ♦ the living end ♦ a living hell ♦ living large ♦ make a living by doing sth ♦ make a living from sth ♦ not a living soul ♦ not tell a (living) soul ♦ Pardon me for living! ♦ scare the living daylights out of so ♦ sure

as you live ♦ thoughts to live by ♦ (with)in living memory ♦ words to live by

livelong all the livelong day

liver more sth than Carter has (liver) pills

Livingstone Doctor Livingstone, I presume?

lo Lo and behold!

load Come in and take a load off your feet. ♦ dump a load ♦ dump one's load ♦ a few bricks short of a load ♦ a few bricks shy of a load ♦ get a load of so/sth ♦ have (got) a load on ♦ lighten so's load ♦ a load off one's feet ♦ a load off one's mind ♦ loaded for bear ♦ loaded to the barrel ♦ loaded to the gills ♦ loads of sth ♦ take a load off one's feet ♦ take a load off (of) so's mind ♦ Thanks loads.

loaf half a loaf

loan float a loan ♦ on loan (from so/sth) ♦ take out a loan

local local yokel

location on location

lock keep sth under lock and key ♦ lock horns (with so) ♦ lock, stock, and barrel ♦ pick a lock ♦ send so to the locker room ♦ under lock and key

locker Davy Jones's locker ♦ send so to the locker room

loco plumb loco

log easy as falling off a log ♦ like a bump on a log ♦ log in ♦ log off ♦ log so off ♦ log on ♦ log so on (to sth) ♦ log out ♦ log so out ♦ sleep like a log

loggerheads at loggerheads (with so) (over sth)

loin gird up one's loins

lonesome all by one's lonesome

long all day long ♦ all night long ♦ as long as ♦ at (long) last ♦ before long ♦ Come back when you can stay longer. ♦ cut a long story short ♦ for the long haul ♦ for the long term ♦ go a long way toward doing sth ♦ go back a long way ♦ have a long run ♦ have come a long way ♦ in the long haul ♦ in the long run ♦ the long and (the) short of it ♦ the long arm of the law ♦ long gone ♦ long in the tooth ♦ long on sth ♦ a long shot ♦ long story short ♦ Long time no see. ♦ make a long story short ♦

merry as the day is long ♦ not by a long shot ♦ not long for this world ♦ over the long haul ♦ the short and (the) long of it ♦ So long. ♦ so long as ♦ take a long hard look at so/sth ♦ Take a long walk off a short pier. ♦ take the (long) count

longer Come back when you can stay longer.

look come-hither look ♦ a dirty look ♦ Don't even look like sth! ♦ far-away look ♦ far-off look ♦ One's future looks bright. ♦ give so a blank look ♦ give so a dirty look ♦ have a look-see ♦ Here's looking at you. ♦ if looks could kill ♦ like looking for a needle in a haystack ♦ look a gift horse in the mouth ♦ look after so/sth/animal ♦ look after number one ♦ look one's age ♦ look ahead ♦ Look alive! ♦ look as if butter wouldn't melt in one's mouth ♦ look askance at so/sth ♦ look at so cross-eyed ♦ Look (at) what the cat dragged in! ♦ look back (at so/sth) ♦ look becoming on so ♦ look daggers at so ♦ look down (at so/sth) ♦ look down one's nose at so/sth ♦ look fit to kill ♦ look for sth (to happen) ♦ look for trouble ♦ look forward to sth ♦ look good on paper ♦ Look here! ♦ look high and low (for so/sth) ♦ look in on so ♦ look so in the eye ♦ look so in the face ♦ look into sth ♦ look like a (dead) ringer (for so) ♦ look like sth the cat dragged in ♦ look like the cat that swallowed the canary ♦ Look me up when you're in town. ♦ look on the bright side ♦ look on (with so) ♦ Look out! ♦ look out for so ♦ look out for number one ♦ look so/sth over ♦ look right through so ♦ look the other way ♦ look the part ♦ look through sth ♦ look to so/sth for sth ♦ look to one's laurels ♦ look under the hood ♦ look so/sth up ♦ look up to so ♦ Look who's talking! ♦ looking over one's shoulder ♦ looking up ♦ a look-see ♦ not much to look at ♦ stop, look, and listen ♦ take a long hard look at so/sth ♦ Things are looking up.

lookout on the lookout (for so/sth)

loom a dark cloud (looming) on the horizon ♦ loom large (on the horizon)

loon crazy as a loon

loop in the loop ♦ knock so for a loop ♦ not in the loop ♦ out of the loop ♦ throw so for a loop

loose all hell broke loose ♦ at loose ends ♦ break loose (from so/sth) ♦ cut loose (with sth) ♦ cut one's wolf loose ♦ hang loose ♦ have a screw loose ♦ leave so at loose ends ♦ let loose of so/sth ♦ let loose (with sth) ♦ a loose cannon ♦ Loose lips sink ships. ♦ a loose translation ♦ loosen so's tongue ♦ on the loose ♦ play fast and loose (with so/sth) ♦ some loose ends ♦ stay loose ♦ take care of some loose ends

lord drunk as a lord ♦ lord it over so ♦ Lord knows I've tried. ♦ Lord love a duck! ♦ (the) Lord only knows ♦ Lord willing and the creek don't rise. ♦ the Lord's Day

lose be on a losing streak ♦ fight a losing battle ♦ lose a bundle ♦ lose (all) one's marbles ♦ lose one's appetite ♦ lose one's cool ♦ lose one's edge ♦ lose face ♦ lose favor (with so) ♦ lose one's grip on so/sth ♦ lose ground (to so/sth) ♦ lose one's head (over so/sth) ♦ lose heart ♦ lose one's heart to so/animal ♦ lose one's hold on so/sth ♦ lose it ♦ lose one's lunch ♦ lose one's mind ♦ lose money on sth ♦ lose one's nerve ♦ lose no time ♦ lose out on sth ♦ lose out to so/sth ♦ lose patience (with so/sth) ♦ lose one's reason ♦ lose one's shirt ♦ lose sight of so/sth ♦ lose sleep over so/sth ♦ lose one's temper (at so/sth) ♦ lose the thread (of sth) ♦ lose the use of sth ♦ lose time ♦ lose one's touch (with so/sth) ♦ lose touch (with so) ♦ lose touch with reality ♦ lose track (of so) ♦ lose track (of sth) ♦ lose one's train of thought ♦ a losing streak ♦ no time to lose ♦ stand to lose sth ♦ a two-time loser ♦ Win a few, lose a few.

loss acceptable losses ♦ at a loss (for words) ♦ cut one's losses ♦ a dead loss ♦ throw so for a loss

lost almost lost it ♦ Get lost! ♦ give so/sth up (for lost) ♦ lost and gone forever ♦ a lost cause ♦ lost for words ♦ lost in sth ♦ lost in the confusion ♦ lost in the shuffle ♦ lost in thought ♦ lost on so ♦ lost-and-found ♦ make up for lost time ♦ There is no love lost (between so and so else).

lot the best of the lot ◆ carry (a lot of) weight (with so/sth) ◆ cast one's lot with so/sth ◆ cover a lot of ground ◆ get a lot of mileage out of sth ◆ have a lot going (for one) ◆ have a lot on one's mind ◆ have a lot on one's plate ◆ leave a lot to be desired ◆ a lot of so/sth ◆ (a lot of) credit (for sth) ◆ a lot of give-and-take ◆ a lot of nerve ◆ a lot of promise ◆ Lots of luck! ◆ not have a lot of time for so/sth ◆ not put (a lot) of stock in sth ◆ show a lot of promise ◆ take a lot off (of) so's mind ◆ take a lot out of so ◆ Thank you a lot. ◆ Thanks (a lot). ◆ think a lot of so/sth ◆ throw in one's lot with so/sth ◆ a (whole) hell of a lot

loud For crying out loud! ◆ I read you loud and clear. ◆ loud and clear ◆ think out loud

louie hang a louie

love a face (that) only a mother could love ◆ fall head over heels in love (with so) ◆ fall in love (with so) ◆ fall in love (with sth) ◆ fall out of love (with so) ◆ For the love of Mike! ◆ Give so my love. ◆ a labor of love ◆ Lord love a duck! ◆ love at first sight ◆ a love-hate relationship ◆ Love is blind. ◆ love of money is the root of all evil ◆ love so/animal to death ◆ love so/animal to pieces ◆ Lovely weather for ducks. ◆ make love (to so) ◆ not able to get sth for love (n)or money ◆ not for love nor money ◆ not miss sth for love nor money ◆ puppy love ◆ Send so my love. ◆ star-crossed lovers ◆ There is no love lost (between so and so else).

lover star-crossed lovers

low burn with a low blue flame ◆ get one's ears lowered ◆ get the lowdown (on so/sth) ◆ have a low boiling point ◆ hold so/sth in low regard ◆ hunt high and low (for so/sth) ◆ keep a low profile ◆ lay low ◆ lay so low ◆ lie low ◆ look high and low (for so/sth) ◆ low man on the totem pole ◆ a low profile ◆ the lowdown (on so/sth) ◆ lower one's guard ◆ lower one's sights ◆ lower the boom on so ◆ lower oneself to some level ◆ lower one's voice ◆ low-hanging fruit ◆ run low (on sth) ◆ search high and low (for so/sth) ◆ straight low

lower get one's ears lowered ◆ lower one's guard ◆ lower one's sights ◆ lower the boom on so ◆ lower oneself to some level ◆ lower one's voice

luck as luck would have it ◆ beginner's luck ◆ Better luck next time. ◆ blind luck ◆ down on one's luck ◆ Good luck! ◆ have a run of bad luck ◆ have one's luck run out ◆ have more luck than sense ◆ in luck ◆ Lots of luck! ◆ luck into sth ◆ the luck of the draw ◆ luck out ◆ luck out of sth ◆ one's luck runs out ◆ a lucky break ◆ a lucky dog ◆ lucky for you ◆ a lucky streak ◆ No such luck. ◆ out of luck ◆ press one's luck ◆ pure luck ◆ push one's luck ◆ rotten luck ◆ a streak of bad luck ◆ a streak of good luck ◆ a streak of luck ◆ a string of bad luck ◆ a string of good luck ◆ a stroke of luck ◆ thank one's lucky stars ◆ the luck of the Irish ◆ tough luck ◆ try one's luck (at sth) ◆ wish so the best of luck

lucre filthy lucre

luggage check so's luggage through (to some place)

lull the lull before the storm ◆ lull so into a false sense of security

lump get one's lumps ◆ have a lump in one's throat ◆ Like it or lump it! ◆ lump so and so else together ◆ a lump in one's throat ◆ Lump it! ◆ take one's lumps

lunatic the lunatic fringe

lunch blow (one's) lunch ◆ eat so's lunch ◆ lose one's lunch ◆ out to lunch ◆ There's no such thing as a free lunch.

lurch leave so in the lurch

luxury in the lap of luxury ◆ the lap of luxury

lying take sth lying down

mackerel Holy mackerel!

mad be mad about so/sth ◆ drive so mad ◆ far from the madding crowd ◆ get mad (at sth) ◆ hopping mad ◆ in a mad rush ◆ like mad ◆ mad as a hatter ◆ mad as a hornet ◆ mad as a March hare ◆ mad as a wet hen ◆ mad as hell ◆ mad (at so/sth) ◆

mad enough to chew nails (and spit rivets) ♦ mad enough to spit nails ♦ method in one's madness ♦ so mad I could scream ♦ stark raving mad ♦ steaming (mad) ♦ tap dance like mad

madding far from the madding crowd

madness method in one's madness

magic work its magic on so/sth

maiden maiden voyage

mail by return mail ♦ junk mail

main by main strength and awkwardness ♦ in the main ♦ main strength and awkwardness ♦ might and main

mainstream in the mainstream (of sth)

major major in sth

make able to make an event ♦ Come in and make yourself at home. ♦ Do I make myself (perfectly) clear? ♦ (Do you) want to make something of it? ♦ Don't make me laugh! ♦ (Go ahead,) make my day! ♦ gone to meet one's maker ♦ have (all) the makings of sth ♦ have (got) it made ♦ Have I made myself clear? ♦ have it made in the shade ♦ have sth made ♦ history in the making ♦ How is so making out? ♦ in the making ♦ It takes all kinds (to make a world). ♦ kiss and make up ♦ made for so ♦ made for each other ♦ made from the same mold ♦ made to measure ♦ made to order ♦ make so ♦ make sth ♦ make a beeline for so/sth ♦ make a believer (out) of so ♦ make a big deal about sth ♦ make a (big) stink (about so/sth) ♦ make a bolt for so/sth ♦ make (a break) for so/sth ♦ make a bundle ♦ make a case for sth ♦ make a clean breast of sth (to so) ♦ make a clean sweep ♦ make a comeback ♦ make a day of doing sth ♦ make a day of it ♦ make a deal with so ♦ make a dent in sth ♦ make a difference in so/sth ♦ make a difference to so ♦ make a face ♦ make a face (at so) ♦ make a fast buck ♦ make a federal case out of sth ♦ make a fool of so ♦ make a go of sth ♦ make a great show of sth ♦ make a hit with so ♦ make a killing ♦ Make a lap! ♦ make oneself or sth a laughingstock ♦ make a laughingstock (out) of oneself or sth ♦ make a (kind of) life for oneself ♦ make a living by doing sth ♦ make a living from sth ♦ make a long story short ♦ make a man of

so ♦ make a (mental) note of sth ♦ make a mistake ♦ make a mockery of sth ♦ make a mountain out of a molehill ♦ make a name (for oneself) ♦ make a night of it ♦ make a note of sth ♦ make a pass at so ♦ make a pig of oneself ♦ make a pile ♦ make a pitch (for so/sth) ♦ make a play (for so) ♦ make a point ♦ make a point of doing sth ♦ make a practice of (doing) sth ♦ make a quick buck ♦ make a reservation ♦ make a run for it ♦ make a scene ♦ make a secret of sth ♦ make a spectacle of so ♦ make a stand (against so/sth) ♦ make a start on sth ♦ make a stink (about sth) ♦ make a (whole) production out of sth ♦ make a world of difference (in so/sth) ♦ make a world of difference (to so/sth) ♦ make advances to so ♦ make allowance(s) (for so/sth) ♦ make amends (to so) (for sth) ♦ make an all-out effort ♦ make an ass of so ♦ make an entrance ♦ make an example of so ♦ make an exception (for so) ♦ make an exhibition of oneself ♦ make an honest woman of so ♦ make an impression on so ♦ make an uproar ♦ make as if you ♦ make away with so/sth ♦ make believe (that) . . . ♦ make so's blood boil ♦ make so's blood run cold ♦ make book on sth ♦ make (both) ends meet ♦ make change (for so) (for sth) ♦ make chin music ♦ make sth clear to so ♦ make oneself conspicuous ♦ make cracks about so/sth ♦ make do (with so/sth) ♦ make so eat crow ♦ make (enough) time (for so/sth) ♦ make every effort to do sth ♦ make eyes at so ♦ make fast work of so/sth ♦ make so's flesh crawl ♦ make free with so/sth ♦ make friends with so ♦ make fun of so/sth ♦ make sth good ♦ make good as sth ♦ make good ((at) sth) ♦ make good money ♦ make good ((on) sth) ♦ make good time ♦ make so's hair curl ♦ make so's hair stand on end ♦ make hamburger (out) of so ♦ make hay (while the sun shines) ♦ make so's head spin ♦ make so's head swim ♦ make heads or tails (out) of so/sth ♦ make headway ♦ make oneself heard ♦ make sth into a fine art ♦ make it ♦ make it as far as sth ♦ make it big ♦ make it one's business to do sth ♦ make it one's business (to know sth) ♦

make it hot for so ♦ Make it snappy! ♦ make it (to) some place ♦ Make it two. ♦ make it (until sth) ♦ make it worth so's while ♦ make last-ditch effort ♦ make life miserable for so ♦ make light of sth ♦ make like a tree and leave ♦ make love (to so) ♦ make one's mark ♦ make mention of so/sth ♦ make merry ♦ make mincemeat (out) of so ♦ make so's mind up ♦ make one's mind up (about so/sth) ♦ Make mine sth. ♦ make mischief ♦ make oneself miserable ♦ make one's money stretch ♦ make so's mouth water ♦ make one's move ♦ Make my day! ♦ make no apologies ♦ make no bones about sth ♦ make no difference (to so) ♦ Make no mistake (about it)! ♦ make no move to do sth ♦ make noises about sth ♦ make nonsense of sth ♦ make nothing of sth ♦ make sth of oneself ♦ make sth of sth ♦ make sth off (of) so/sth ♦ make off with so/sth ♦ make or break so ♦ make sth out ♦ make (out) like sth ♦ make sth (out) of sth ♦ make sth out of nothing ♦ make out (with so) ♦ make out (with sth) ♦ make so over ♦ make one's (own) bed ♦ make (one's) peace with so/sth ♦ make points (with so) ♦ make so's position clear ♦ make one's presence felt (some place) ♦ make ready (to do sth) ♦ make sth right ♦ make oneself scarce ♦ make sense ♦ make short work of so/sth ♦ make so sick ♦ make so's skin crawl ♦ make (so) bold (as) to do sth ♦ make (some) sense (out) of so/sth ♦ make sth stick ♦ make sure all the bases are covered ♦ make the arrangements ♦ make the bed (up) ♦ make the best of sth ♦ make the best of a bad situation ♦ make the feathers fly ♦ make the fur fly ♦ make the grade ♦ make the headlines ♦ make the most of sth ♦ make so the scapegoat for sth ♦ make the scene ♦ make the team ♦ make time (with so) ♦ make sth to order ♦ make (too) much of so/sth ♦ make tracks (for sth) ♦ make trouble ♦ make sth up ♦ make up a foursome ♦ make up for so/sth ♦ make up for lost time ♦ make sth up out of whole cloth ♦ make up (to so) ♦ make sth up to so ♦ make up (with so) ♦ make war (on so/sth) ♦ make water ♦ make waves ♦

make way ♦ make way (for so/sth) ♦ make one's way in the world ♦ make with sth ♦ Make yourself at home. ♦ makes one's heart sink ♦ a marriage made in heaven ♦ a match made in heaven ♦ not able to make head or tail of sth ♦ not know what to make of so/sth ♦ not made of money ♦ not make a move (to do sth) ♦ of one's own making ♦ on the make ♦ put the make on so ♦ run a make on so ♦ sure as God made little green apples ♦ That makes two of us. ♦ They don't make them like they used to. ♦ what makes so tick ♦ what makes sth tick ♦ When they made so/sth, they broke the mold. ♦ You want to make something of it?

makings have (all) the makings of sth

mama go home to mama

man all things to all men ♦ be one's own man ♦ big man on campus ♦ dirty old man ♦ Every man for himself! ♦ hatchet man ♦ high man on the totem pole ♦ a ladies' man ♦ low man on the totem pole ♦ make a man of so ♦ man about town ♦ a man after my own heart ♦ the man in the street ♦ a man of few words ♦ a man of his word ♦ a man of the cloth ♦ man to man ♦ man's best friend ♦ man's inhumanity to man ♦ a marked man ♦ May the best man win. ♦ odd man out ♦ one-man show ♦ see a man about a dog ♦ separate the men from the boys ♦ stick man ♦ straight man ♦ a straw man ♦ take it like a man ♦ to a man ♦ twelve good men and true

manger dog in the manger

manna manna from heaven

manner all manner of so/sth ♦ devil-may-care manner ♦ forget one's manners ♦ in a manner of speaking ♦ to the manner born

many a good many ♦ have a few too many ♦ have one's finger in too many pies ♦ have one too many ♦ have too many irons in the fire ♦ How many times do I have to tell you? ♦ in many respects ♦ in so many words ♦ many a so/sth ♦ many a time ♦ many (and many)'s the time ♦ many is the person who . . . ♦ one too many

map all over the map ♦ drop off the map ♦ map sth out ♦ put sth on the map

marble all the marbles ♦ cold as marble ♦ end up with all the marbles ♦ have all one's marbles ♦ lose (all) one's marbles ♦ not have all one's marbles ♦ win all the marbles

march in marching order ♦ mad as a March hare ♦ march on ♦ march to (the beat of) a different drummer ♦ steal a march on so/sth

mare by shank's mare ♦ shank's mare

marines Tell it to the marines!

mark a black mark beside one's name ♦ leave one's mark on so ♦ make one's mark ♦ mark sth down ♦ mark so for life ♦ mark my word(s) ♦ mark time ♦ mark sth up ♦ a marked man ♦ off the mark ♦ on the mark ♦ on your mark, get set, go ♦ quick off the mark ♦ slow off the mark ♦ toe the mark ♦ wide of the mark ♦ X marks the spot

market corner the market (on sth) ♦ a drug on the market ♦ a glut on the market ♦ have a corner on the market (for sth) ♦ in the market (for sth) ♦ on the market ♦ play the (stock) market

marriage a marriage made in heaven ♦ save oneself (for marriage)

marry have to get married ♦ marry one's way out of sth

marvel a marvel to behold

mast at half-mast

master a past master at sth

mat go to the mat (on sth)

match a match for so/sth/animal ♦ a match made in heaven ♦ match wits (with so) ♦ meet one's match ♦ mix and match ♦ strike a match ♦ the whole shooting match

matter as a matter of course ♦ as a matter of fact ♦ the crux of the matter ♦ for that matter ♦ gray matter ♦ a matter of (doing) sth ♦ a matter of life and death ♦ a matter of opinion ♦ a matter of principle ♦ a matter of time ♦ matter-of-fact ♦ mind over matter ♦ no laughing matter ♦ no matter . . . ♦ no matter how you slice it ♦ (only) a matter of time

max max out ♦ maxed out ♦ to the max

may be that as it may ♦ come what may ♦ devil-may-care attitude ♦ devil-may-care manner ♦ let the chips fall (where they may) ♦ may as well ♦ (May I) buy you a drink? ♦ May I come in? ♦ May the best man win. ♦ May the best team win. ♦ to whom it may concern ♦ try as I may

McCoy the real McCoy

meal eat (a meal) out

mean lean and mean ♦ mean business ♦ mean no offense ♦ a mean streak ♦ mean to (do sth) ♦ mean well ♦ meant to be ♦ meant to be sth ♦ no mean sth ♦ no offense meant ♦ take on a new meaning

meaning take on a new meaning

means beyond one's means ♦ by all means ♦ by all means of sth ♦ by any means ♦ by no means ♦ live beyond one's means ♦ live within one's means ♦ a means to an end ♦ not by any means ♦ within one's means

meantime in the meantime

meanwhile in the meanwhile

measure beyond measure ♦ for good measure ♦ made to measure ♦ measure up to so/sth

meat dead meat ♦ meat-and-potatoes

Mecca a Mecca for so

medication on medication

medicine a dose of one's own medicine ♦ snakebite medicine ♦ take one's medicine ♦ a taste of one's own medicine

medium find a happy medium ♦ hit a happy medium ♦ strike a happy medium

meek meek as a lamb

meet call a meeting ♦ call a meeting to order ♦ Fancy meeting you here! ♦ gone to meet one's maker ♦ hold a meeting ♦ make (both) ends meet ♦ meet one's death ♦ meet one's end ♦ meet so halfway ♦ meet one's match ♦ meet one's Waterloo ♦ meet with sth ♦ a meeting of the minds ♦ more (to sth) than meets the eye ♦ Sunday-go-to-meeting clothes ♦ Till we meet again. ♦ Until we meet again.

meeting call a meeting ♦ call a meeting to order ♦ Fancy meeting you here! ♦ hold a meeting ♦ a meeting of the minds ♦ Sunday-go-to-meeting clothes

mell a mell of a hess

melt look as if butter wouldn't melt in one's mouth ♦ melt down ♦ melt in one's mouth

member card-carrying member

memory commit sth to memory ♦ freeze so/sth in one's memory ♦ if my memory serves (me correctly) ♦ in living memory ♦ in memory of so ♦ in recent memory ♦ jog so's memory ♦ know sth from memory ♦ refresh so's memory (about so/sth) ♦ (a trip down) memory lane ♦ (with)in living memory

mend mend (one's) fences ♦ mend one's ways ♦ on the mend

mental have a mental block (against sth) ♦ make a (mental) note of sth ♦ a mental block (against sth)

mention Don't mention it. ♦ make mention of so/sth ♦ not to mention so/sth ♦ not worth mentioning

merchant busy as a cranberry merchant (at Thanksgiving)

mercy at so's mercy ♦ at the mercy of so ♦ throw oneself at the mercy of some authority

mere a mere trifle

merry lead so on a merry chase ♦ make merry ♦ merry as a cricket ♦ merry as the day is long ♦ the more the merrier

mess get into a mess ♦ get out of a mess ♦ a hell of a mess ♦ mess around ♦ mess around (with sth) ♦ mess around with so ♦ mess so over ♦ mess up (on sth) ♦ messed up

message Get the message? ♦ send so a message

met hail-fellow-well-met ♦ Haven't we met before?

metal put the pedal to the metal

mete mete punishment out

method method in one's madness

Methuselah old as Methuselah

mettle prove one's mettle ♦ show one's mettle

Mickey slip so a Mickey

microscope put sth under the microscope

midair in midair ♦ keep so/sth hanging (in midair) ♦ leave so/sth hanging (in midair)

Midas have the Midas touch ♦ tight as Midas's fist

middle caught in the middle ♦ change horses in the middle of the stream ♦ in the middle of nowhere ♦ a middle ground ♦ the middle of nowhere ♦ middle-of-the-

road ♦ play both ends (against the middle) ♦ smack (dab) in the middle

middling fair to middlin'

midnight burn the midnight oil

midstream change horses in midstream

might high and mighty ♦ might and main ♦ might as well ♦ try as I might

Mike For the love of Mike!

mild to put it mildly

mile by a mile ♦ a country mile ♦ for miles on end ♦ Give one an inch and one will take a mile. ♦ go the extra mile ♦ a mile a minute ♦ a million miles away ♦ miss (sth) by a mile ♦ stick out a mile ♦ talk a mile a minute ♦ walk the extra mile

mileage get a lot of mileage out of sth ♦ get some kind of mileage out of sth

milestone a milestone in so's life

milk coffee, tea, or milk ♦ cry over spilled milk ♦ milk so for sth ♦ the milk of human kindness

mill go through the mill ♦ grist for the mill ♦ grist to the mill ♦ a millstone about one's neck ♦ run-of-the-mill ♦ through the mill ♦ tilt at windmills

million feel like a million (dollars) ♦ like a million (dollars) ♦ a million miles away ♦ one in a million ♦ Thanks a million.

millstone a millstone about one's neck

mince make mincemeat (out) of so ♦ mince (one's) words

mincemeat make mincemeat (out) of so

mind an absent-minded professor ♦ be of a (good) mind to do sth ♦ bear sth in mind ♦ bear in mind that . . . ♦ blow so's mind ♦ boggle so's mind ♦ bore one out of one's mind ♦ bored out of one's mind ♦ bring sth to mind ♦ call sth to mind ♦ change so's mind ♦ come to mind ♦ cross so's mind ♦ Do you mind? ♦ Don't mind me. ♦ drive one out of one's mind ♦ flash through one's mind ♦ one's frame of mind ♦ frighten one out of one's mind ♦ get one's mind off (of) so/sth ♦ give so a piece of one's mind ♦ go out of one's mind ♦ have a (good) mind to do sth ♦ have a lot on one's mind ♦ have a mind as sharp as a steel trap ♦ have a mind of one's own ♦ have a one-track mind ♦ have (got) one's mind in the gutter ♦ have half a mind to do sth ♦ have so/sth in mind ♦ have so/sth on one's mind ♦ have the presence of mind to do sth ♦ If you don't mind! ♦ in one's mind's eye ♦ in one's right mind ♦ in the back of so's mind ♦ in the hearts and minds of so ♦ It blows my mind! ♦ jump to mind ♦ keep an open mind ♦ keep so in mind ♦ keep sth in mind ♦ keep so/sth in mind (for so/sth) ♦ keep one's mind off (of) so/sth ♦ keep one's mind on so/sth ♦ a load off one's mind ♦ lose one's mind ♦ make so's mind up ♦ make one's mind up (about so/sth) ♦ a meeting of the minds ♦ the mind boggles (at sth) ♦ one's mind goes blank ♦ mind over matter ♦ mind one's own business ♦ mind one's Ps and Qs ♦ mind the store ♦ mind your own beeswax ♦ Mind your own business. ♦ Never mind (about sth). ♦ of a single mind (about so/sth) ♦ of one mind (about so/sth) ♦ of two minds (about so/sth) ♦ on one's mind ♦ one-track mind ♦ an open mind ♦ out of one's mind ♦ pass through so's mind ♦ peace of mind ♦ put so in mind of so/sth ♦ put so's mind at ease (about so/sth) ♦ put one's mind to sth ♦ put so/sth out of one's mind ♦ read so's mind ♦ ring in so's mind ♦ scare one out of one's mind ♦ set so's mind at ease (about so/sth) ♦ set one's mind to sth ♦ slip one's mind ♦ speak one's mind ♦ spring to mind ♦ state of mind ♦ stick in so's mind ♦ take a load off (of) so's mind ♦ take a lot off (of) so's mind ♦ to my mind ♦ turn sth over in one's mind ♦ a weight off one's mind

mine back to the salt mines ♦ go back to the salt mines ♦ a gold mine of information ♦ a mine of information ♦ sitting on a gold mine

minimum keep sth to a minimum

mint in mint condition

minute at the last minute ♦ every minute counts ♦ Hold on (a minute)! ♦ in a New York minute ♦ in (just) a minute ♦ just a minute ♦ Just a minute(, you)! ♦ a laugh a minute ♦ a mile a minute ♦ a minute ♦ the minute sth happens ♦ a New York minute ♦ quicker than a New York minute ♦ talk a mile a minute ♦ up to the minute ♦ up-to-the-minute ♦ Wait (just) a minute! ♦ when you get a minute

mirror able to fog a mirror ♦ done by mirrors ♦ done with mirrors ♦ smoke and mirrors

miscarriage a miscarriage of justice

mischief make mischief

miserable make life miserable for so ♦ make oneself miserable

misery put some creature out of its misery ♦ put one out of (one's) misery

miss Good golly, Miss Molly! ♦ have a near miss ♦ one's heart misses a beat ♦ hit and miss ♦ miss a trick ♦ miss (sth) by a mile ♦ miss out (on sth) ♦ miss the boat ♦ miss the point ♦ not miss a beat ♦ not miss a thing ♦ not miss sth for love nor money ♦ not miss sth for the world ♦ not miss much ♦ without missing a beat

mission mission in life

Missouri from Missouri

mist the mists of time

mistake by mistake ♦ a case of mistaken identity ♦ make a mistake ♦ Make no mistake (about it)!

mix get mixed up in sth ♦ have mixed feelings (about so/sth) ♦ mix and match ♦ mix business with pleasure ♦ a mixed bag ♦ mixed feelings (about so/sth) ♦ mixed up ♦ mixed up in sth ♦ mixed up with so else

mockery make a mockery of sth

moist moist around the edges

molasses slow as molasses in January ♦ slower than molasses in January

mold cast in the same mold ♦ made from the same mold ♦ When they made so/sth, they broke the mold.

molehill make a mountain out of a molehill

moley Holy moley!

Molly Good golly, Miss Molly!

moment at a moment's notice ♦ at the moment ♦ the big moment ♦ every moment counts ♦ for the moment ♦ one has one's moments ♦ in (just) a moment ♦ in the heat of the moment ♦ just a moment ♦ live for the moment ♦ the moment everyone has been waiting for ♦ the moment of truth ♦ never a dull moment ♦ not a moment to spare ♦ not for a moment ♦ on a moment's notice ♦

on the spur of the moment ♦ without a moment to spare

momma (Do) you kiss your momma with that mouth?

Monday come Monday

money one's (butter and) egg money ♦ closefisted (with money) ♦ easy money ♦ folding money ♦ for my money ♦ found money ♦ funny money ♦ get one's money's worth ♦ hush money ♦ in the money ♦ lose money on sth ♦ love of money is the root of all evil ♦ make good money ♦ make one's money stretch ♦ Money burns a hole in so's pocket. ♦ money from home ♦ money is no object ♦ money talks ♦ one's money's worth ♦ not able to get sth for love (n)or money ♦ not for love nor money ♦ Not for my money. ♦ not made of money ♦ not miss sth for love nor money ♦ on the money ♦ pour good money after bad ♦ pour money down the drain ♦ pressed for money ♦ put one's money on so/sth (to do sth) ♦ put money up (for sth) ♦ Put your money where your mouth is! ♦ raise money for so/sth ♦ a run for one's money ♦ see the color of so's money ♦ smart money ♦ soft money ♦ spend money like it's going out of style ♦ spend money like there's no tomorrow ♦ spending money ♦ stretch one's money ♦ throw good money after bad ♦ throw money at sth ♦ throw money down the drain ♦ tightfisted (with money) ♦ Time is money.

monkey as much fun as a barrel of monkeys ♦ I'll be a monkey's uncle! ♦ monkey around (with sth) ♦ monkey business ♦ monkey suit ♦ more fun than a barrel of monkeys ♦ throw a (monkey) wrench in the works

month by the month ♦ flavor of the month ♦ for (some) months running ♦ Haven't seen you in a month of Sundays. ♦ in a month of Sundays ♦ months running

mood in a bad mood ♦ in no mood to do sth ♦ in the mood (for sth) ♦ in the mood (to do sth)

moon ask for the moon ♦ The honeymoon is over. ♦ once in a blue moon ♦ over the moon ♦ promise the moon (to so) ♦ think so hung the moon (and stars)

mop mop the floor up with so ♦ a mopping-up operation

moral on moral grounds

more all the more reason for doing sth ♦ bite off more than one can chew ♦ Couldn't ask for more. ♦ didn't exchange more than three words with so ♦ do more harm than good ♦ furthermore ♦ have more important fish to fry ♦ have more luck than sense ♦ Less is more. ♦ more and more ♦ more bark than bite ♦ more dead than alive ♦ more fun than a barrel of monkeys ♦ more often than not ♦ more or less ♦ More power to so. ♦ More power to you! ♦ more than one bargained for ♦ more than one can bear ♦ more so/sth than one can shake a stick at ♦ more than one can stand ♦ more than one can take ♦ more sth than Carter has (liver) pills ♦ the more the merrier ♦ more (to sth) than meets the eye ♦ more's the pity ♦ Need I say more? ♦ once more ♦ Say no more. ♦ taste like more ♦ That's more like it. ♦ There's more than one way to skin a cat. ♦ wear more than one hat ♦ what's more

morning first thing (in the morning) ♦ gotta get up pretty early in the morning to do sth ♦ Great day (in the morning)! ♦ the morning after (the night before)

mortal shuffle off this mortal coil

mortar bricks and mortar ♦ brick(s)-and-mortar

moss house moss

most at most ♦ at (the) most ♦ the firstest with the mostest ♦ for the most part ♦ get the most out of so/sth ♦ make the most of sth

moth drawn like a moth to a flame

mothball bring sth out of mothballs ♦ put sth in mothballs

mother at one's mother's knee ♦ every mother's son (of them) ♦ expectant mother ♦ a face (that) only a mother could love ♦ the mother of all sth ♦ old enough to be so's mother ♦ swear on one's mother's grave ♦ tied to one's mother's apron strings

motherhood motherhood and apple pie

motion go through the motions ♦ put sth in motion ♦ set sth in motion ♦ table a motion

mount mount up

mountain make a mountain out of a molehill

mouse play cat and mouse with so ♦ poor as a church mouse ♦ quiet as a (church) mouse

mousetrap build a better mousetrap

mouth born with a silver spoon in one's mouth ♦ by word of mouth ♦ diarrhea of the mouth ♦ (Do) you eat with that mouth? ♦ (Do) you kiss your momma with that mouth? ♦ down in the mouth ♦ foam at the mouth ♦ foot-in-mouth disease ♦ have a big mouth ♦ have one's heart in one's mouth ♦ one's heart is in one's mouth ♦ hold one's mouth the right way ♦ Hush your mouth! ♦ keep one's mouth shut (about so/sth) ♦ laugh out of the other side of one's mouth ♦ leave a bad taste in so's mouth ♦ live from hand to mouth ♦ look a gift horse in the mouth ♦ look as if butter wouldn't melt in one's mouth ♦ make so's mouth water ♦ melt in one's mouth ♦ a mouth full of South ♦ mouth off ♦ not open one's mouth ♦ put one's foot in one's mouth ♦ put words in(to) so's mouth ♦ Put your money where your mouth is! ♦ run off at the mouth ♦ say a mouthful ♦ shoot one's mouth off ♦ smart mouth ♦ stick one's foot in one's mouth ♦ (straight) from the horse's mouth ♦ take the words out of so's mouth ♦ to speak out of both sides of one's mouth

mouthful say a mouthful

movable a movable feast

move bust a move ♦ a false move ♦ Get a move on. ♦ get moving ♦ It's your move. ♦ make one's move ♦ make no move to do sth ♦ a movable feast ♦ move away from sth ♦ move for sth ♦ move heaven and earth to do sth ♦ move in for the kill ♦ move on ♦ move so to tears ♦ move up in the world ♦ movers and shakers ♦ moving right along ♦ not make a move (to do sth) ♦ not move a muscle ♦ on the move ♦ one false move ♦ one move ahead (of so/sth) ♦ prime mover ♦ put the moves on so

Mr. Mr. Nice Guy ♦ Mr. Right

much able to take just so much ♦ able to take only so much ♦ amount to much ♦ as much fun as a barrel of monkeys ♦ a bit much ♦ come to much ♦ have too much on one's plate ♦ have (too much) time on one's hands ♦ make (too) much of so/sth ♦ much ado about nothing ♦ (much) credit (for sth) ♦ (much) in evidence ♦ much less so/sth ♦ Much obliged. ♦ much sought after ♦ not give much for so's chances ♦ not miss much ♦ not much to look at ♦ Nothing much. ♦ so much as sth ♦ so much for so/sth ♦ So much for that. ♦ so much so that . . . ♦ so much the better ♦ take too much on ♦ too much ♦ too much of a good thing ♦ too much too soon ♦ without (so much as) a (for or) by your leave

mud clear as mud ♦ drag so through the mud ♦ Here's mud in your eye. ♦ muddy the water(s) ♦ muddy sth up ♦ one's name is mud ♦ stick in the mud

muddle muddle through (sth)

muddy muddy the water(s) ♦ muddy sth up

muff muff one's lines

mule kick like a mule ♦ obstinate as a mule ♦ work like a mule

mull mull sth over

multitude cover a multitude of sins

mum Mum's the word.

murder cry bloody murder ♦ get away with murder ♦ holler bloody murder ♦ scream bloody murder ♦ yell bloody murder

muscle flex so's/sth's muscles ♦ muscle in (on so/sth) ♦ not move a muscle ♦ pull a muscle

mushroom mushroom into sth

music chin music ♦ face the music ♦ make chin music ♦ music to so's ears ♦ set sth to music

must all things must pass ♦ They must have seen you coming.

muster pass muster

mutilate fold, spindle, or mutilate

N

nail angry enough to chew nails ♦ bite one's nails ♦ dead as a doornail ♦ deader than a doornail ♦ fight so/sth tooth and nail ♦ go at it tooth and nail ♦ go at one another tooth and nail ♦ hard as nails ♦ hit the nail (right) on the head ♦ mad enough to chew nails (and spit rivets) ♦ mad enough to spit nails ♦ nail sth down ♦ nail so's ears back ♦ nail in so's/sth's coffin ♦ nail so('s hide) to the wall ♦ nail so to a cross ♦ a thumbnail sketch ♦ tough as nails

naked naked as a jaybird ♦ the naked eye ♦ the naked truth ♦ with the naked eye

name answer to the name (of) sth ♦ appear under the name of some name ♦ a black mark beside one's name ♦ call so names ♦ clear so's name ♦ drop so's name ♦ drop names ♦ go by the name of sth ♦ go under the name of sth ♦ a household name ♦ in so's name ♦ in name only ♦ It has so's name on it. ♦ know so/sth by name ♦ make a name (for oneself) ♦ one's name in lights ♦ one's name is mud ♦ name names ♦ the name of the game ♦ on a first-name basis (with so) ♦ see one's name in lights ♦ take (some) names ♦ throw so's name around ♦ worthy of the name ♦ you name it

nap catch so napping

nape by the nape of the neck

narrow keep to the straight and narrow (path) ♦ narrow sth down (to people/things) ♦ the straight and narrow

native go native

natural come naturally (to so) ♦ die a natural death

nature the call of nature ♦ let nature take its course ♦ a nature stop ♦ second nature to so ♦ That's (just) the nature of the beast.

naught come to naught ♦ count for naught

near from far and near ♦ from near and far ♦ go near (to) so/sth ♦ have a near miss ♦ in the near future ♦ near and dear to so ♦ nearly jump out of one's skin ♦ nowhere near sth ♦ pretty nearly

nearest so's nearest and dearest

nearly nearly jump out of one's skin ♦ pretty nearly

neat neat as a pin

necessity out of necessity

neck break one's neck (to do sth) ♦ breathe down so's neck ♦ by the nape of the neck ♦ a crick in one's neck ♦ dead from the neck up ♦ feel the hair on the back of one's neck stand on end ♦ get it in the neck ♦ hang so by the neck ♦ in some neck of the woods ♦ a millstone about one's neck ♦ neck and neck ♦ a pain in the neck ♦ put one's neck on the line ♦ risk one's neck (to do sth) ♦ save so's neck ♦ stick one's neck out (for so/sth) ♦ up to one's neck (in sth) ♦ a yoke around so's neck

need all so needs ♦ a crying need (for so/sth) ♦ A friend in need is a friend indeed. ♦ I need it yesterday. ♦ if need be ♦ in need (of sth) ♦ It's all so needs. ♦ need a pick-me-up ♦ need a reality check ♦ need a smoke ♦ Need I say more? ♦ need sth like a hole in the head ♦ need sth yesterday ♦ needless to say ♦ one needs to have one's head examined ♦ No need. ♦ That's all so needs. ♦ That's just what you need. ♦ (There is) no need (to).

needle like looking for a needle in a haystack ♦ like trying to find a needle in a haystack ♦ on pins and needles

needless needless to say

neighborhood in the neighborhood (of some amount)

neither neither fish nor fowl ♦ neither here nor there ♦ (neither) hide nor hair ♦ neither rhyme nor reason

nerve a bundle of nerves ♦ get enough nerve up (to do sth) ♦ get on so's nerves ♦ grate on so('s nerves) ♦ hit a (raw) nerve ♦ lose one's nerve ♦ a lot of nerve ♦ nerves of steel ♦ on so's nerves ♦ touch a (raw) nerve

nervous a (nervous) breakdown

nest feather one's (own) nest ♦ fly the nest ♦ foul one's own nest ♦ leave the nest ♦ stir up a hornet's nest ♦ a turkey's nest

Net surf the Net

never Better late than never. ♦ (It) never hurts to do sth. ♦ It'll never fly. ♦ never a dull moment ♦ sth never fails ♦ never had it so good ♦ never hear the end of sth ♦ Never mind (about sth). ♦ never would have guessed ♦ now or never

new brand spanking new ♦ break new ground ♦ breathe new life into sth ♦ bright as a new pin ♦ busy as a beaver (building a new dam) ♦ feel like a new person ♦ good as new ♦ in a New York minute ♦ like a kid with a new toy ♦ (a little) new to (all) this ♦ new blood ♦ the new kid on the block ♦ a new lease on life ♦ a New York minute ♦ quicker than a New York minute ♦ ring in the new year ♦ (So) what else is new? ♦ (some) new blood ♦ take on a new meaning ♦ take on a new significance ♦ That's a new one on me! ♦ turn over a new leaf ♦ a (whole) new ball game

newborn innocent as a newborn babe

news break the news (to so) ♦ It's news to me! ♦ No news is good news.

next Better luck next time. ♦ buy the next round (of drinks) ♦ catch the next wave ♦ (Good-bye) until next time. ♦ next best thing ♦ one's next of kin ♦ next to impossible ♦ next to nothing ♦ the next world ♦ Till next time. ♦ wait for the next wave

nice Have a nice day. ♦ Have a nice flight. ♦ Have a nice one. ♦ Mr. Nice Guy ♦ nice and some quality ♦ a nice break

niche carve out a niche

nick full of Old Nick ♦ in the (very) nick of time

nickel nickel and dime so (to death) ♦ not worth a plugged nickel

night all hours (of the day and night) ♦ all night long ♦ black as night ♦ bunk down (for the night) ♦ burn the midnight oil ♦ by night ♦ call it a night ♦ day and night ♦ different as night and day ♦ far into the night ♦ fly-by-night ♦ make a night of it ♦ the morning after (the night before) ♦ night and day ♦ a night on the town ♦ night owl ♦ a night person ♦ one-night stand ♦ Saturday night special ♦ ships that pass in the night ♦ the small hours (of the night) ♦ the wee hours (of the night)

nine dressed to the nines ♦ a nine days' wonder ♦ nine times out of ten ♦ nine-to-five job ♦ on cloud nine ♦ the whole nine yards

nip a (little) nip in the air ♦ nip and tuck ♦ nip sth in the bud

nitty get down to the nitty-gritty

nobody like nobody's business ♦ nobody's fool ♦ There's nobody home.

nod get the nod ♦ the land of Nod ♦ the nod

noggin use one's noggin ♦ Use your noggin!

noise make noises about sth

none bar none ♦ have none of sth ♦ none of the above ♦ None of your beeswax! ♦ None of your business! ♦ None of your lip! ♦ none other than so/sth ♦ none the wiser ♦ none the worse for wear ♦ none too sth ♦ second to none

nonsense make nonsense of sth ♦ stuff and nonsense

noodle noodle around ♦ noodle over ♦ use one's noodle ♦ Use your noodle!

nook every nook and cranny

north up North

nose blow one's nose ♦ cannot see (any) further than the end of one's nose ♦ can't see beyond the end of one's nose ♦ count noses ♦ cut off one's nose to spite one's face ♦ follow one's nose ♦ get one's nose out of so's business ♦ get one's nose out of joint ♦ Get your nose out of my business. ♦ hard-nosed ♦ have a nose for sth ♦ have one's nose in a book ♦ have one's nose in the air ♦ have one's nose out of joint ♦ hold one's nose ♦ keep one's nose clean ♦ keep one's nose out of sth ♦ keep one's nose out of so's business ♦ keep one's nose to the grindstone ♦ Keep your nose out of my business. ♦ lead so by the nose ♦ look down one's nose at so/sth ♦ no skin off so's nose ♦ nose so/group out ♦ nose about (for so/sth) ♦ nose around (sth) ♦ one's nose is in the air ♦ on the nose ♦ pay through the nose (for sth) ♦ plain as the nose on one's face ♦ poke one's nose in(to sth) ♦ powder one's nose ♦ put one's nose in (where it's not wanted) ♦ put one's nose out of joint ♦ put one's nose to the grindstone ♦ put the nose-bag on ♦ (right) under so's (very)

683

nose ♦ rub so's nose in it ♦ see no further than the end of one's nose ♦ stick one's nose in (where it's not wanted) ♦ stick one's nose in(to sth) ♦ stick one's nose up in the air ♦ take it on the nose ♦ thumb one's nose at so/sth ♦ turn one's nose up at so/sth ♦ under so's (very) nose ♦ win by a nose

nosedive go into a nosedive ♦ take a nosedive

nosh nosh on sth

notch a notch above (so/sth) ♦ a notch below (so/sth) ♦ pull one's belt in (a notch) ♦ take one's belt in (a notch) ♦ take so down a notch (or two) ♦ top notch

note dash a note off ♦ drop so a note ♦ a hell of a note ♦ hit a sour note ♦ hit the right note ♦ make a (mental) note of sth ♦ make a note of sth ♦ noted for sth ♦ so of note ♦ strike a sour note ♦ strike the right note ♦ swap notes (on so/sth) ♦ take note of so/sth

nother a whole nother story ♦ a whole nother thing

nothing all for nothing ♦ all or nothing ♦ come to nothing ♦ go for nothing ♦ good-for-nothing ♦ have nothing against so/sth ♦ have nothing doing (at some time) ♦ have nothing on so ♦ have nothing on so/sth ♦ have nothing on (at some time) ♦ have nothing to do with so/sth ♦ Here goes nothing. ♦ in nothing flat ♦ (It's) better than nothing. ♦ like nothing on earth ♦ make nothing of sth ♦ make sth out of nothing ♦ much ado about nothing ♦ next to nothing ♦ nothing but ♦ nothing but skin and bones ♦ Nothing doing! ♦ Nothing is certain but death and taxes. ♦ nothing less than some quality ♦ Nothing much. ♦ nothing of the kind ♦ nothing short of sth ♦ nothing short of some quality ♦ nothing to boast about ♦ nothing to choose from ♦ Nothing to it! ♦ nothing to sneeze at ♦ nothing to speak of ♦ nothing to write home about ♦ nothing upstairs ♦ Nothing ventured, nothing gained. ♦ stop at nothing (to do sth) ♦ (There's) nothing to it! ♦ think nothing of doing sth ♦ think nothing of so/sth ♦ Think nothing of it. ♦ to say nothing of so/sth ♦ want for nothing

nothings sweet nothings

notice at a moment's notice ♦ at short notice ♦ come to so's notice ♦ give (one's) notice ♦ give notice that . . . ♦ give notice to so ♦ on a moment's notice ♦ on short notice ♦ serve notice (on so) ♦ sit up and take notice ♦ take notice of so/sth

notion have half a notion to do sth

nourishment able to sit up and take (a little) nourishment

now all better (now) ♦ Bye for now. ♦ (every) now and again ♦ (every) now and then ♦ from now on ♦ Good-bye for now. ♦ the here and now ♦ just now ♦ now and then ♦ now or never ♦ Now you're talking! ♦ right here and now

nowhere all dressed up and nowhere to go ♦ come from nowhere ♦ come out of nowhere ♦ Flattery will get you nowhere. ♦ get nowhere fast ♦ go nowhere fast ♦ in the middle of nowhere ♦ the middle of nowhere ♦ nowhere near sth ♦ nowhere to be found ♦ out of nowhere

nth to the nth degree

nude in the nude

null null and void

number any number of so/sth ♦ one's days are numbered ♦ do a number on so/sth ♦ have so's number ♦ in round numbers ♦ look after number one ♦ look out for number one ♦ one's number is up ♦ out in large numbers ♦ play by the numbers ♦ quite a number ♦ safety in numbers ♦ take care of number one ♦ the wrong number

nurse nurse a grudge (against so)

nut bust one's nuts to do sth ♦ drive so nuts ♦ everything from soup to nuts ♦ get down to the nuts and bolts ♦ go nuts ♦ a hard nut to crack ♦ a nut case ♦ nut up ♦ nuts and bolts ♦ nutty as a fruitcake ♦ off one's nut ♦ a tough nut to crack

nutshell in a nutshell ♦ put sth in a nutshell

nutty nutty as a fruitcake

o

oar put one's oar in ♦ stick one's oar in
oat feel one's oats ♦ sow one's wild oats
oath take an oath ♦ under oath
object expense is no object ♦ money is no object
oblige Much obliged.
oblivion sink into oblivion
obsess obsessed with so/sth
obstinate obstinate as a mule
occasion keep sth for another occasion ♦ leave sth for another occasion ♦ on occasion ♦ rise to the occasion
occupancy immediate occupancy
ocean a drop in the ocean ♦ oceans of so/sth
odd against all odds ♦ at odds (with so) ♦ give so odds that . . . ♦ the odd sth ♦ odd man out ♦ odds and ends ♦ the odds are against one ♦ the odds-on favorite
offense mean no offense ♦ no offense meant ♦ no offense taken ♦ take no offense ♦ take offense at sth
offer an offer one cannot refuse
office do a land-office business ♦ land-office business ♦ take office
offing in the offing
often every so often ♦ more often than not
oh Oh, ye of little faith.
oil burn the midnight oil ♦ oil so's palm ♦ pour oil on troubled water(s)
oink oink out
ointment a fly in the ointment
okay (Are you) doing okay? ♦ okay by so ♦ You doing okay?
old any old thing ♦ a chip off the old block ♦ comfortable as an old shoe ♦ common as an old shoe ♦ dirty old man ♦ for old time's sake ♦ from the old school ♦ full of Old Nick ♦ give so the (old) heave-ho ♦ go into the same old song and dance (about sth) ♦ good old boy ♦ the good old days ♦ have a rare old time ♦ little old so/sth ♦ live to the (ripe old) age of sth ♦ of old ♦ of the old school ♦ old as Methuselah ♦ old as the hills ♦ old battle axe ♦ old college try ♦ old enough to be so's father ♦ old enough to be so's mother ♦ an old hand at doing sth ♦ old hat ♦ the (old) heave-ho ♦ the old one-two ♦ one's old stamping ground ♦ an old warhorse ♦ an old wives' tale ♦ the oldest trick in the book ♦ ring out the old (year) ♦ a ripe old age ♦ same o(l)' same o(l)' ♦ the same old story ♦ the same old thing ♦ tough as an old boot ♦ tough as (old) (shoe) leather

olive hold out the olive branch

once all at once ♦ at once ♦ (every) once in a while ♦ give so the once-over ♦ give so/sth the once-over ♦ if I've told you once, I've told you a thousand times ♦ once again ♦ once and for all ♦ once in a blue moon ♦ once more ♦ once upon a time ♦ once-in-a-lifetime chance ♦ once-in-a-lifetime opportunity ♦ the once-over ♦ once-over-lightly ♦ You are only young once.

one (all) in one breath ♦ (all) in one piece ♦ (all) rolled into one ♦ as one ♦ at any one time ♦ at one blow ♦ at one fell swoop ♦ at one stroke ♦ at one time ♦ at one time or another ♦ back to square one ♦ bite the big one ♦ bust so one ♦ busy as a one-armed paperhanger ♦ buy the big one ♦ day one ♦ do a one-eighty ♦ do so one better ♦ do one one better (than that) ♦ every last one ♦ a fast one ♦ get off a few good ones ♦ go at one another tooth and nail ♦ go back to square one ♦ go from one extreme to the other ♦ go in one ear and out the other ♦ go (so) one better ♦ go one one better (than that) ♦ go one on one with so ♦ hang one on ♦ Have a good one. ♦ Have a nice one. ♦ have a one-track mind ♦ have one foot in the grave ♦ have one in the oven ♦ have one too many ♦ hole in one ♦ I owe you one. ♦ in one breath ♦ in one fell swoop ♦ in one piece ♦ It's just one of those things. ♦ It's six of one, half a dozen of another. ♦ (It) takes one to know one. ♦ keep one eye on so/sth ♦ keep one jump ahead (of so/sth) ♦ keep one step ahead of so/sth ♦ kill two birds with one stone ♦ knock one back ♦ knock one over ♦ lay one on ♦ like one of the family ♦ (a little) short on one end ♦ look after number one ♦ look out for number one ♦ my one and only ♦ not one iota ♦ of one mind (about so/sth) ♦ off to one side ♦ the old one-two ♦ on (the) one hand ♦ one and all ♦ the one and only ♦ one and the same ♦ one at a time ♦ one by one ♦ one day at a time ♦ one false move ♦ one final thing ♦ one final word ♦ one for the (record) books ♦ one for the road ♦ one heck of a so/sth ♦ one hell of a so/sth ♦ one in a hundred ♦ one in a million ♦ one in a thousand ♦ one jump ahead (of so/sth) ♦ one little bit ♦ one move ahead (of so/sth) ♦ one of a kind ♦ one of these days ♦ one sandwich short of a picnic ♦ one step ahead of so/sth ♦ one step at a time ♦ the one that got away ♦ one thing after another ♦ One thing leads to another. ♦ one to a customer ♦ one too many ♦ one up (on so) ♦ one way or another ♦ one-horse town ♦ one-man show ♦ one-night stand ♦ one-track mind ♦ paste so one ♦ pull a fast one (on so) ♦ put all one's eggs in one basket ♦ put one foot in front of the other ♦ rolled into one ♦ since day one ♦ speak as one ♦ speak with one voice ♦ take care of number one ♦ take so to one side ♦ Tell me another (one)! ♦ That's a new one on me! ♦ There's more than one way to skin a cat. ♦ This one is on so. ♦ tie one on ♦ turn one hundred and eighty degrees ♦ Two can play (at) this game (as well as one). ♦ wear more than one hat ♦ with one hand tied behind one's back

onion know one's onions

only able to take only so much ♦ a face (that) only a mother could love ♦ God only knows! ♦ have only just done sth ♦ if only ♦ in name only ♦ It (only) stands to reason. ♦ know sth only too well ♦ my one and only ♦ the one and only ♦ (only) a matter of time ♦ the only game in town ♦ only have eyes for so ♦ the only way to go ♦ (the) Lord only knows ♦ You are only young once.

ooze ooze (out) (from so/sth) ♦ ooze with sth

open blow sth wide open ♦ bust sth wide open ♦ catch so out in the open ♦ come out in(to) the open ♦ come out in(to) the open with sth ♦ crack a bottle open ♦ crack the door (open) ♦ crack the window (open) ♦ crack sth (wide) open ♦ in the open ♦ keep a date open (for so/sth) ♦ keep an open mind ♦ keep one's eyes open (for so/sth) ♦ keep one's options open ♦ keep one's weather eye open ♦ lay oneself (wide) open for sth ♦ leave a date open (for so/sth) ♦ leave open the possibility (of sth) ♦ leave one's options open ♦ leave the door open (for sth) ♦ leave oneself (wide) open for sth ♦ leave oneself (wide) open to sth ♦ not open one's mouth ♦ open a can of worms ♦ open a conversation ♦ open and aboveboard ♦ an open book ♦ open so's eyes to so/sth ♦ open fire (on so) ♦ open for business ♦ open one's heart to so/sth ♦ an open mind ♦ open Pandora's box ♦ open season (on so) ♦ open season (on some creature) ♦ an open secret ♦ open some doors (for so) ♦ open the door to so ♦ open the door to sth ♦ open the floodgates ♦ open to sth ♦ open to criticism ♦ open oneself to criticism ♦ open to dispute ♦ open to question ♦ open up ♦ open so up ♦ open sth up ♦ open up (about so/sth) (with so) ♦ open (up) one's kimono ♦ open up (on so/sth/animal) ♦ open up (to so) ♦ open up to sth ♦ open with so/sth ♦ an open-and-shut case ♦ opening gambit ♦ out in the open ♦ receive so with open arms ♦ welcome so with open arms ♦ wide open ♦ (wide) open to sth ♦ with (one's) eyes (wide) open

opener for openers

operate operate on sth ♦ operating at cross purposes

operation a mopping-up operation

opinion a difference of opinion ♦ form an opinion ♦ hazard an opinion ♦ in my humble opinion ♦ in my opinion ♦ in one's opinion ♦ keep one's opinions to oneself ♦ Keep your opinions to yourself! ♦ a matter of opinion

opportunity a golden opportunity ♦ a growth opportunity ♦ jump at the opportunity ♦ leap at the opportunity (to do sth) ♦ once-in-a-lifetime opportunity ♦ a photo op(portunity) ♦ seize the opportunity ♦ a window of opportunity

oppose as opposed to sth

opposite the opposite sex

opt opt for sth ♦ opt in favor of so/sth ♦ opt in(to sth) ♦ opt out (of sth)

option keep one's options open ♦ leave one's options open

orange compare apples and oranges

orbit go into orbit ♦ in orbit

orchard crazy as a peach-orchard boar

ordain ordain so (as) sth

order (Are you) ready to order? ♦ back-order sth ♦ build sth to order ♦ call a meeting to order ♦ doctor's orders ♦ follow orders ♦ get one's house in order ♦ get one's own house in order ♦ in apple-pie order ♦ in marching order ♦ in order ♦ in short order ♦ just what the doctor ordered ♦ made to order ♦ make sth to order ♦ on order ♦ order some food to go ♦ the order of the day ♦ order so off the field ♦ out of order ♦ place an order ♦ put one's house in order ♦ put so/sth into order ♦ put one's own house in order ♦ set one's house in order ♦ set one's own house in order ♦ a tall order

ordinary out of the ordinary

other at each other's throats ♦ cancel each other out ♦ Catch me some other time. ♦ drop the other shoe ♦ every other person or thing ♦ go from one extreme to the other ♦ go in one ear and out the other ♦ have other fish to fry ♦ have the shoe on the other foot ♦ how the other half lives ♦ in other words ♦ laugh out of the other side of one's face ♦ laugh out of the other side of one's mouth ♦ look the other way ♦ made for each other ♦ none other than so/sth ♦ on the other hand ♦ on the other side of the coin ♦ the other place ♦ the other side of the tracks ♦ other than so/sth ♦ other things being equal ♦ the other way (a)round ♦ put one foot in front of the other ♦ something or other ♦ There are plenty of (other) fish in the sea. ♦ turn the other cheek ♦ turn the other way ♦ wait for the other shoe to drop ♦ with every (other) breath

otherwise know otherwise

ought hadn't oughta

outdoor big as all outdoors

outguess outguess so

outhouse built like a brick outhouse

outright killed outright

outs the ins and outs (of sth) ♦ on the outs (with so)

outset at the outset ♦ from the outset

outside at the outside ♦ at the (very) outside ♦ (Do) you want to step outside? ♦ outside of so/sth ♦ outside the box ♦ step outside ♦ think outside the box ♦ thinking outside the box

oven have one in the oven

overboard fall overboard ♦ go overboard

overdrive into overdrive ♦ shift into overdrive

overplay overplay one's hand

overstep overstep one's bounds ♦ overstep the bounds of good taste

owe I owe you one. ♦ owe so a debt of gratitude ♦ owe it to oneself (to do sth) ♦ owe it to so (to do sth) ♦ owe sth (to so) (for sth)

owl night owl ♦ wise as an owl

own according to one's own lights ♦ afraid of one's own shadow ♦ as if one owned the place ♦ the author of one's own problem ♦ be one's own boss ♦ be one's own man ♦ be one's own worst enemy ♦ beat one at one's own game ♦ blow one's own horn ♦ can't call one's soul one's own ♦ carry one's (own) weight ♦ come into one's or its own ♦ cut one's (own) throat ♦ the devil's own job ♦ die by one's own hand ♦ dig one's own grave ♦ do one's (own) thing ♦ a dose of one's own medicine ♦ feather one's (own) nest ♦ find one's own level ♦ for one's (own) part ♦ for one's (own) sake ♦ foul one's own nest ♦ get one's own house in order ♦ have a mind of one's own ♦ hoist with one's own petard ♦ hold one's or its own ♦ in a world of one's own ♦ in one's (own) backyard ♦ in one's (own) (best) interest(s) ♦ in one's own right ♦ keep one's own counsel ♦ leave one to one's own devices ♦ leave one to one's own resources ♦ a legend in one's own (life)time ♦ a life of its own ♦ like one owned the place ♦ line one's own pocket(s) ♦ make one's (own) bed ♦ a man after my own heart ♦ mind one's own business ♦ mind your own beeswax ♦ Mind your own business. ♦ not able to call one's time one's own ♦ not know one's own strength ♦ of one's own accord ♦ of one's own free will ♦ of one's own making ♦ on one's own ♦ on one's own hook ♦ on one's own time ♦ own flesh and blood ♦ own up (to sth) ♦ one's own worst enemy ♦ paddle one's own canoe ♦ pay one's own way ♦ pick on so your own size ♦ a place to call one's own ♦ pull one's (own) weight ♦ pull oneself up by one's (own) bootstraps ♦ put one's own house in order ♦ set out on one's own ♦ set one's own house in order ♦ set one's own pace ♦ sign one's own death warrant ♦ stand on one's (own) two feet ♦ stew in one's own juice ♦ strike out on one's own ♦ take one's life into one's (own) hands ♦ take on a life of its own ♦ take one's own life ♦ take the law into one's own hands ♦ talk to hear one's own voice ♦ a taste of one's own medicine ♦ tell its own story ♦ tell its own tale ♦ think so is God's own cousin ♦ so/sth to call one's own ♦ To each his own. ♦ To each their own. ♦ toot one's own horn ♦ under one's own steam

ox strong as an ox

oyster The world is one's oyster.

P

pace at a snail's pace ♦ a change of pace ♦ keep pace (with so/sth) ♦ pace back and forth ♦ pace sth off ♦ pace sth out ♦ pace up and down ♦ pick up the pace (of sth) ♦ put one through one's paces ♦ quicken the pace (of sth) ♦ set one's own pace ♦ set the pace

pack ahead of the pack ♦ be at the head of the pack ♦ lead the pack ♦ pack a group ♦ pack a punch ♦ pack a wallop ♦ pack so/sth (in) like sardines ♦ pack it in ♦ a pack of lies ♦ pack them in ♦ send so packing

package a package deal

packet cop a packet

pad pad the bill

paddle paddle one's own canoe ♦ up the creek (without a paddle)

page be on the same page ♦ read from the same page ♦ take a page from so's book

pain feeling no pain ♦ give so a pain ♦ have growing pains ♦ No pain, no gain. ♦ on pain of sth ♦ a pain in the ass ♦ a pain in the butt ♦ a pain in the neck ♦ a pain in the rear ♦ racked with pain ♦ a royal pain ♦ share so's pain ♦ take (great) pains (to do sth) ♦ take pains with so/sth

paint black as one is painted ♦ close as two coats of paint ♦ Do I have to paint (you) a picture? ♦ exciting as watching (the) paint dry ♦ paint so into a corner ♦ paint the town (red) ♦ paint so with the same brush

pair another pair of eyes ♦ a candidate for a pair of wings ♦ a fresh pair of eyes

pal bosom pal ♦ pal around (with so) ♦ pal up (with so)

pale beyond the pale ♦ pale around the gills ♦ pale as a ghost ♦ pale as death ♦ pale at sth ♦ pale beside so/sth ♦ pale by comparison

pall cast a pall on sth

palm cross so's palm with silver ♦ grease so's palm ♦ have an itchy palm ♦ have so in the palm of one's hand ♦ an itchy palm ♦ know so/sth like the palm of one's hand ♦ oil so's palm ♦ palm so/sth off (on so) (as so/sth)

pan a flash in the pan ♦ jump out of the frying pan (and) into the fire ♦ out of the frying pan (and) into the fire ♦ pan out

pancake flat as a pancake

Pandora open Pandora's box

panic hit the panic button ♦ press the panic button ♦ push the panic button

pant ants in one's pants ♦ beat the pants off (of) so ♦ bore the pants off of so ♦ by the seat of one's pants ♦ catch one with one's pants down ♦ charm the pants off so ♦ dust so's pants ♦ fly by the seat of one's pants ♦ frighten the pants off so ♦ get ants in one's pants ♦ a kick in the (seat of the) pants ♦ pant for sth ♦ scare the pants off (of) so ♦ sue the pants off (of) so ♦ wear the pants (in the family)

paper can't carry a tune in a paper sack ♦ get sth down (on paper) ♦ get one's walking papers ♦ leave a paper trail ♦ look good on paper ♦ not worth the paper it's printed on ♦ not worth the paper it's written on ♦ paper over sth ♦ a paper trail ♦ put sth on paper ♦ put pen to paper ♦ See you in the funny papers. ♦ set pen to paper ♦ one's walking papers

paperhanger busy as a one-armed paperhanger

par above par ♦ below par ♦ on (a) par (with so/sth) ♦ par for the course ♦ up to par

parade rain on so's parade

paradise a fool's paradise ♦ a paradise (on earth) ♦ paradise on earth

parcel parcel sth out ♦ part and parcel

pardon beg so's pardon ♦ if you'll pardon the expression ♦ Pardon me for living! ♦ Pardon my French.

park park it (some place)

parlay parlay sth into sth

parole (out) on parole

parry thrust and parry

part the best part of sth ♦ the better part of sth ♦ for one's (own) part ♦ for so's part ♦ for the most part ♦ in large part ♦ in part ♦ in these parts ♦ look the part ♦ on the part of so ♦ part and parcel ♦ part company (with so) ♦ part so's hair ♦ a parting of the ways ♦ play a big part (in sth) ♦ play a bit part ♦ play a large part (in sth) ♦ play a part in sth ♦ take so's part ♦ take part (in sth)

partial partial to so/sth

partially partially sighted

particular in particular ♦ the particulars of sth

partner domestic partner ♦ partners in crime

party bring sth to the party ♦ a certain party ♦ the life of the party ♦ the party line ♦ The party's over. ♦ a party to sth ♦ the responsible party ♦ throw a party (for so)

pass all things must pass ♦ come to a pretty pass ♦ come to pass ♦ cut so off at the pass ♦ in passing ♦ make a pass at so ♦ pass sth along (to so) ♦ pass away ♦ pass sth down (to so) ♦ pass for so/sth ♦ pass gas ♦ pass in review ♦ pass judgment (on so/sth) ♦ pass muster ♦ pass sth off (as sth) ♦ pass so/sth off (on so) (as so/sth) ♦ pass sth off (on so) (as sth) ♦ pass on ♦ pass sth on ♦ pass on so/sth ♦ pass on sth ♦ pass out ♦ pass sentence on so ♦ pass the buck ♦ pass the hat (around) (to so) ♦ pass the time (of day) ♦ pass the time of day ♦ pass the torch (on) to so ♦ pass through so's mind ♦ pass so/sth up ♦ ships that pass in the night ♦ take a pass (on sth)

passion have a passion for so/sth

passport passport to sth

past at some point (in the past) ♦ a blast from the past ♦ get sth past so/sth ♦ in times past ♦ live in the past ♦ not put it past so ♦ past caring ♦ a past master at sth ♦ past so's/sth's prime ♦ a thing of the past ♦ thunder past so/sth

paste cut and paste ♦ paste sth on so ♦ paste so one ♦ paste sth up

pasture put a horse out to pasture ♦ put so out to pasture

pat down pat ♦ give so a pat on the back ♦ have sth down pat ♦ a pat answer ♦ pat so on the back ♦ stand pat (on sth)

patch patch a quarrel up ♦ patch things up ♦ patch so up

path beat a path to so's door ♦ cross paths (with so) ♦ keep to the straight and narrow (path) ♦ lead so down the garden path ♦ off the beaten path ♦ on the warpath ♦ the path of least resistance ♦ the primrose path

patience have the patience of a saint ♦ have the patience of Job ♦ lose patience (with so/sth) ♦ out of patience ♦ run out of patience ♦ try so's patience

patient patient as Job

patrol (out) on patrol

patter the patter of tiny feet

Paul rob Peter to pay Paul

pause give so pause (for thought)

pave pave the way (for so/sth) (with sth)

pavement hit the pavement ♦ pound the pavement

pawn pawn so/sth off (on so) (as so/sth)

pay have hell to pay ♦ have the devil to pay ♦ hit pay dirt ♦ pay so a backhanded compliment ♦ pay a call ♦ pay a call on so ♦ pay so a compliment ♦ pay so a left-handed compliment ♦ pay (so/sth) a visit ♦ pay a visit to so/sth ♦ pay as you go ♦ pay attention (to so/sth) ♦ pay so back ♦ pay court to so ♦ pay one's debt (to society) ♦ pay dividends ♦ pay one's dues ♦ pay one's final respects (to so) ♦ pay for sth ♦ pay heed to so/sth ♦ pay homage to so/sth ♦ pay in advance ♦ pay one's last respects (to so) ♦ pay lip service (to sth) ♦ pay off ♦ pay so off ♦ pay sth out ♦ pay one's own way ♦ pay so respect ♦ pay one's respects (to so) ♦ pay the penalty ♦ pay the piper ♦ pay the price ♦ pay through the nose (for sth) ♦ pay tribute to so/sth ♦ pay so's way ♦ the price one has to pay ♦ put paid to sth ♦ rob Peter to pay Paul ♦ strike pay dirt ♦ There will be hell to pay. ♦ There will be the devil to pay.

pea alike as (two) peas in a pod ♦ like (two) peas in a pod ♦ thick as pea soup

peace at peace ♦ hold one's peace ♦ keep the peace ♦ leave so in peace ♦ make (one's) peace with so/sth ♦ peace of mind ♦ rest in peace

peach crazy as a peach-orchard boar

peacock proud as a peacock ♦ vain as a peacock

peanut for peanuts

pearl cast (one's) pearls before swine

peck hunt-and-peck ♦ peck at sth

peculiar funny peculiar

pedal put the pedal to the metal ♦ soft pedal sth

peddler busy as a fish peddler in Lent

pedestal on a pedestal

peel keep one's eyes peeled (for so/sth)

peep hear a peep out of so ♦ a peep

peeve pet peeve

peg bring so down a peg (or two) ♦ have so pegged as sth ♦ knock so down a peg (or two) ♦ peg so as sth ♦ peg out ♦ a square peg (in a round hole) ♦ take so down a peg (or two)

pen put pen to paper ♦ set pen to paper

penalty pay the penalty

penchant have a penchant for doing sth

pencil in pencil ♦ pencil so/sth in

penny a bad penny ♦ cost a pretty penny ♦ cut so off without a penny ♦ a penny-pincher

pension pension so off

people Of all people! ♦ split people up

pepper pepper so/sth with sth

per per head

perfect Do I make myself (perfectly) clear? ♦ a perfect stranger ♦ picture perfect

perish perish from sth ♦ Perish the thought. ♦ perish with sth ♦ publish or perish

permit Permit me. ♦ weather permitting

perpetuity in perpetuity

person a day person ♦ feel like a new person ♦ have sth on one('s person) ♦ in person ♦ the last person (to single out for sth) ♦ a night person ♦ on one's person

personal take sth personally

perspective from my perspective ♦ give so a perspective on sth ♦ in perspective ♦ a perspective on sth ♦ put sth in perspective

pester pester the life out of so

pet pet hate ♦ pet peeve ♦ the teacher's pet

petard hoist with one's own petard

Pete For Pete's sake! ♦ Honest to Pete.

peter peter out ♦ rob Peter to pay Paul

phone Hold the phone. ♦ Hold the phone(, please).

phony phony as a three-dollar bill

photo a photo op(portunity)

phrase coin a phrase

physical get physical (with so) ♦ physical (with so)

piano thump sth out (on the piano)

pick cherry pick sth ♦ easy pickings ♦ have a bone to pick (with so) ♦ have one's pick of so/sth ♦ need a pick-me-up ♦ pick a fight (with so) ♦ pick a lock ♦ pick a quarrel (with so) ♦ pick and choose ♦ pick so/sth apart ♦ pick at sth ♦ pick so's brain(s) ♦ pick holes in sth ♦ the pick of sth ♦ pick so/sth off ♦ pick on so/sth ♦ pick on so your own size ♦ pick so's pocket ♦ pick the slack up ♦ pick sth to pieces ♦ pick up ♦ pick so up ♦ pick sth up ♦ pick up on sth ♦ pick up speed ♦ pick up steam ♦ pick up the bill (for sth) ♦ pick up the check (for sth) ♦

pick up the pace (of sth) ♦ pick up the pieces (of sth) ♦ pick up the tab (for sth) ♦ pick one's way along (sth) ♦ pick one's way through sth ♦ picked over ♦ a pick-me-up ♦ take one's pick (of so/sth)

pickings easy pickings

pickle in a (pretty) pickle ♦ a pretty pickle

picnic It's no picnic! ♦ one sandwich short of a picnic

picture the big picture ♦ Do I have to paint (you) a picture? ♦ get the big picture ♦ Get the picture? ♦ in the picture ♦ out of the picture ♦ the picture of (good) health ♦ picture perfect ♦ pretty as a picture ♦ the (very) picture of sth

piddle piddle around

pie American as apple pie ♦ cut the pie up ♦ easy as (apple) pie ♦ eat humble pie ♦ have a finger in the pie ♦ have one's finger in too many pies ♦ in apple-pie order ♦ motherhood and apple pie ♦ pie in the sky ♦ a piece of the pie ♦ Shut your pie hole!

piece (all) in one piece ♦ (all) of a piece ♦ blow so/sth to pieces ♦ dash sth to pieces ♦ down the road a piece ♦ fall to pieces ♦ give so a piece of one's mind ♦ go to pieces ♦ in one piece ♦ love so/animal to pieces ♦ of a piece ♦ pick sth to pieces ♦ pick up the pieces (of sth) ♦ piece of cake ♦ a piece (of the action) ♦ a piece of the pie ♦ piece sth together ♦ say one's piece ♦ shot to pieces ♦ speak one's piece ♦ thrill so to pieces ♦ thrilled to pieces ♦ tickle so to pieces ♦ the villain of the piece ♦ Want a piece of me? ♦ (You) want a piece of me?

pier Take a long walk off a short pier.

pierce a piercing scream

pig buy a pig in a poke ♦ fat as a pig ♦ In a pig's ass! ♦ In a pig's ear! ♦ In a pig's eye! ♦ make a pig of oneself ♦ pig out ♦ serve as a guinea pig

pike comes down the pike ♦ whatever comes down the pike

pikestaff plain as a pikestaff

pile the bottom of the pile ♦ make a pile ♦ pile the work on so ♦ pile up ♦ pile sth up

pill a bitter pill (to swallow) ♦ more sth than Carter has (liver) pills ♦ on the pill

pillar from pillar to post ♦ pillar of strength ♦ pillar of support ♦ send so from pillar to post

pilot on automatic (pilot)

pimple break out (in pimples) ♦ goose pimples

pin bright as a new pin ♦ get one's ears pinned back ♦ neat as a pin ♦ on pins and needles ♦ pin sth down ♦ pin so down (on sth) ♦ pin so's ears back ♦ pin one's faith on so/sth ♦ pin one's hopes on so/sth ♦ pin sth on so ♦ so quiet you could hear a pin drop ♦ so still you could hear a pin drop

pinch feel the pinch ♦ in a pinch ♦ a penny-pincher ♦ pinch and scrape ♦ pinch so for sth ♦ pinch sth from so/sth ♦ pinch-hit for so ♦ take sth with a pinch of salt

pine pine away (after so/sth)

pink in the pink (of condition) ♦ in the pink (of health) ♦ tickle so pink ♦ tickled pink

pipe a lead-pipe cinch ♦ pipe down ♦ a pipe dream ♦ pipe sth into some place ♦ pipe up (with sth) ♦ Put that in your pipe and smoke it! ♦ a set of pipes

pipeline in the pipeline

piper pay the piper

pique pique so's curiosity ♦ pique so's interest

piss don't have a pot to piss in (or a window to throw it out of) ♦ Piss off! ♦ piss so off ♦ pissed (off)

pit have a sinking feeling in the pit of one's stomach ♦ the pit of one's stomach ♦ a sinking feeling in the pit of one's stomach

pitch black as pitch ♦ in there pitching ♦ make a pitch (for so/sth) ♦ pitch so a curve (ball) ♦ pitch a tent ♦ pitch sth at so/sth ♦ pitch camp ♦ pitch in (and help) (with sth) ♦ pitch (the) woo

pity For pity's sake! ♦ have pity (on so/animal) ♦ more's the pity ♦ take pity (on so/animal)

place all over the place ♦ as if one owned the place ♦ between a rock and a hard place ♦ change places (with so) ♦ exchange places (with so) ♦ fall in(to) place ♦ feel out of place ♦ go places ♦ have a place in sth ♦ have friends in high places ♦ have one's heart in the right place

♦ one's heart is in the right place ♦ in one's place ♦ in so else's place ♦ in the first place ♦ in the right place at the right time ♦ in the second place ♦ in the wrong place at the wrong time ♦ jumping-off place ♦ know one's place ♦ one's last resting place ♦ lay a place (for so) ♦ like one owned the place ♦ not one's place to do sth ♦ Of all places! ♦ the other place ♦ out of place ♦ place so ♦ place a premium on sth ♦ place a strain on so/sth ♦ place so/sth above so/sth ♦ place an order ♦ place so/sth at sth ♦ place one's hopes on so/sth ♦ place so in an awkward position ♦ place so/sth in jeopardy ♦ place so/sth in the trust of so ♦ place of business ♦ a place of concealment ♦ a place to call one's own ♦ place one's trust in so/sth ♦ put one in one's place ♦ put oneself in so else's place ♦ take place ♦ There's a time and place for everything. ♦ trade places (with so) ♦ a wide place in the road

plague avoid so/sth like the plague

plain in plain English ♦ in plain language ♦ plain and simple ♦ plain as a pikestaff ♦ plain as day ♦ plain as the nose on one's face ♦ put sth plainly

plan plan of action

plank thick as a short plank ♦ thick as two short planks ♦ walk the plank

plant plant sth in sth ♦ plant sth on so

plaster plaster one's hair down

plate clean one's plate (up) ♦ have a lot on one's plate ♦ have too much on one's plate ♦ step up to the plate

plateau hit a plateau

platter have so's head on a platter ♦ on a silver platter

play at play ♦ bring sth into play ♦ child's play ♦ come into play ♦ foul play ♦ a game that two can play ♦ go out of play ♦ Go play in the traffic. ♦ in play ♦ a level playing field ♦ level the (playing) field ♦ make a play (for so) ♦ not playing with a full deck ♦ overplay one's hand ♦ play a big part (in sth) ♦ play a bit part ♦ play a joke on so ♦ play a large part (in sth) ♦ play a part in sth ♦ play a prank on so ♦ play a role in sth ♦ play a trick on so ♦ play along (with so/sth) ♦ play around (with so/sth) ♦

play sth at full blast ♦ play ball (with so) ♦ play both ends (against the middle) ♦ play sth by ear ♦ play by ear ♦ play by the numbers ♦ play one's cards close to one's chest ♦ play one's cards close to one's vest ♦ play one's cards right ♦ play one's cards well ♦ play cat and mouse with so ♦ play dead ♦ play sth down ♦ play down to so ♦ play fast and loose (with so/sth) ♦ play first chair ♦ play footsie with so ♦ play so for a fool ♦ play for keeps ♦ play for time ♦ play freeze-out ♦ play games (with so) ♦ play hard to get ♦ play hardball (with so) ♦ play havoc with so/sth ♦ play one's heart out ♦ play hell with so/sth ♦ play hob with so/sth ♦ play hooky ♦ play in the big leagues ♦ play innocent ♦ play into so's hands ♦ play it cool ♦ play it for all it's worth ♦ play it safe ♦ play itself out ♦ play on so's heartstrings ♦ play politics ♦ play possum ♦ play second fiddle (to so) ♦ play (the) devil's advocate ♦ play the devil with sth ♦ play the field ♦ play the fool ♦ play the heavy ♦ play the horses ♦ play the ponies ♦ play the race card ♦ play the (stock) market ♦ play through ♦ play to the crowd ♦ play to the gallery ♦ play tricks on so ♦ play one's trump card ♦ play sth up ♦ play up to so ♦ play (up)on sth ♦ play with so/sth ♦ play with a full deck ♦ play with fire ♦ a play-by-play description ♦ played out ♦ a power play ♦ roll over and play dead ♦ a team player ♦ Two can play (at) this game (as well as one). ♦ the way it plays

plea cop a plea

pleasant the late unpleasantness

please Again(, please). ♦ Check, please. ♦ the disease to please ♦ Hold, please. ♦ Hold the line(, please). ♦ Hold the phone(, please). ♦ Hold the wire(, please). ♦ less than pleased ♦ please oneself ♦ pleased as Punch

pleasure mix business with pleasure

pledge go back on one's pledge ♦ take the pledge

plenty a gracious plenty ♦ There are plenty of (other) fish in the sea.

plight plight one's troth to so

plot brew a plot ♦ The plot thickens.

plow plow through sth ♦ put one's hand to the plow

pluck get enough pluck up (to do sth)

plug not worth a plugged nickel ♦ plug (away) at so ♦ plug (away) at sth ♦ pull the plug (on so) ♦ pull the plug (on sth) ♦ put a plug in (for so/sth)

plumb check out the plumbing ♦ the greatest thing since indoor plumbing ♦ plumb loco ♦ plumb the depths of sth ♦ visit the plumbing

plummet plummet to earth

plump plump for so/sth

plunge take the plunge

pocket have so in one's pocket ♦ line one's own pocket(s) ♦ Money burns a hole in so's pocket. ♦ out-of-pocket expenses ♦ pick so's pocket ♦ a pocket of resistance

pod alike as (two) peas in a pod ♦ like (two) peas in a pod

poetic poetic justice ♦ poetic license ♦ wax poetic

point at some point (in the future) ♦ at some point (in the past) ♦ at the point of doing sth ♦ at this point (in time) ♦ be at the point of (doing) sth ♦ belabor the point ♦ beside the point ♦ the breaking point ♦ a case in point ♦ from my point of view ♦ get the point (of sth) ♦ get to the point (of sth) ♦ have a low boiling point ♦ hit a sore point ♦ in point of fact ♦ jumping-off point ♦ make a point ♦ make a point of doing sth ♦ make points (with so) ♦ miss the point ♦ no point in sth ♦ not to put too fine a point on sth ♦ not to put too fine a point on it ♦ on the point of doing sth ♦ so's point is well taken♦ the point of (doing) sth ♦ the point of no return ♦ point of view ♦ point the finger at so ♦ score a point ♦ a selling point ♦ stretch a point ♦ stretch the point ♦ to the point ♦ touch a sore point ♦ a turning point

poise poised to do sth

poison poison so against so/sth

poke buy a pig in a poke ♦ poke fun at so/sth ♦ poke sth into sth ♦ poke one's nose in(to sth) ♦ take a poke at so

poker stiff as a poker

pole high man on the totem pole ♦ I wouldn't touch it with a ten-foot pole. ♦

low man on the totem pole ♦ not touch so/sth with a ten-foot pole ♦ poles apart ♦ skinny as a beanpole ♦ up the pole ♦ wouldn't touch so/sth with a ten-foot pole

polish apple-polisher ♦ polish sth off ♦ polish sth up ♦ spit and polish

politic the body politic ♦ play politics

political a political football

poll go to the polls

pond a big frog in a small pond

pony dog and pony show ♦ play the ponies ♦ pony an amount up ♦ pony up

pooch pooch out

poop poop out ♦ pooped (out)

poor in poor taste ♦ poor as a church mouse ♦ poor but clean

poorhouse in the poorhouse

pop one's eyes pop out of one's head ♦ pop around (for a visit) ♦ pop back (for sth) ♦ pop by (for a visit) ♦ pop one's cork ♦ pop for sth ♦ pop in (for a visit) ♦ pop off ♦ pop so off ♦ pop sth out of sth ♦ pop (some) tops ♦ pop the question ♦ pop up ♦ take a pop at so

popcorn busy as popcorn on a skillet

poppy red as a poppy

porcelain pray to the porcelain god

pore air one's pores

pork pork out (on sth)

port any port in a storm

portrait sit for one's portrait

pose pose a challenge ♦ pose a question ♦ strike a pose

position jockey for position ♦ make so's position clear ♦ place so in an awkward position

possess possessed by sth ♦ possessed of sth

possession in so's possession ♦ take possession (of sth)

possibility leave open the possibility (of sth)

possible as far as possible ♦ everything humanly possible ♦ so far as possible ♦ soon as possible

possum play possum

post between you (and) me and the bedpost ♦ by return post ♦ deaf as a post ♦ from pillar to post ♦ keep so posted ♦

post so some place ♦ send so from pillar to post

postage postage and handling

postal go postal

posted keep so posted

poster a poster child (for sth)

pot don't have a pot to piss in (or a window to throw it out of) ♦ go to pot ♦ hit the jackpot ♦ a pot of gold ♦ sweeten the pot ♦ a tempest in a teapot ♦ throw sth in(to) the pot

potato a couch potato ♦ drop so/sth like a hot potato ♦ meat-and-potatoes ♦ small potatoes

potshot take a potshot at so/sth

pound pound a beat ♦ pound one's ear ♦ pound for pound ♦ pound so's head in ♦ pound sth into sth ♦ a pound of flesh ♦ pound sth out ♦ pound the books ♦ pound the pavement

pour pour cold water on sth ♦ pour down (on so/sth) ♦ pour good money after bad ♦ pour one's heart (and soul) into sth ♦ pour one's heart out to so ♦ pour in(to sth) ♦ pour oneself into sth ♦ pour one's money down the drain ♦ pour oil on troubled water(s) ♦ pour out (of sth) ♦ pour out one's soul

powder keep one's powder dry ♦ powder one's face ♦ powder one's nose ♦ powder up ♦ sitting on a powder keg ♦ take a powder

power the balance of power ♦ fall from power ♦ have no staying power ♦ in power ♦ More power to so. ♦ More power to you! ♦ on a power trip ♦ the power behind the throne ♦ a power play ♦ power sth with sth ♦ the powers that be

pox A pox on so/sth!

practical for all practical purposes

practice in practice ♦ make a practice of (doing) sth ♦ out of practice ♦ Practice what you preach! ♦ put sth into practice

praise damn so/sth with faint praise ♦ praise so/sth to the skies ♦ sing so's/sth's praises

prank play a prank on so

pray pray to the porcelain god

prayer the answer to so's prayer(s) ♦ come in on a wing and a prayer ♦ have a prayer

(of doing sth) ♦ in so's prayers ♦ on a wing and a prayer

preach Practice what you preach! ♦ preach to the choir ♦ preach to the converted

precedence precedence over so/sth ♦ take precedence over so/sth

precedent set a precedent

precious precious few ♦ precious little

precipitate precipitate into sth

preclude preclude so/sth from sth

predicate predicate sth (up)on sth

prelude a prelude to sth

premium at a premium ♦ place a premium on sth ♦ put a premium on sth ♦ put sth at a premium

prepare prepare so for sth

prescription refill a prescription

presence grace so/sth with one's presence ♦ have the presence of mind to do sth ♦ make one's presence felt (some place)

present at present ♦ at the present time ♦ live in the present ♦ There's no time like the present.

press go to press ♦ go to press with sth ♦ hard-pressed (to do sth) ♦ hot off the press ♦ in press ♦ press ahead ♦ press for sth ♦ press forward ♦ press so/sth into service ♦ press one's luck ♦ press on ♦ press (the) flesh ♦ press the panic button ♦ press so to the wall ♦ pressed for cash ♦ pressed for money ♦ pressed for time

pressure high-pressure so into sth ♦ put (the) pressure on so (to do sth) ♦ take so's blood pressure ♦ under pressure

presume Doctor Livingstone, I presume?

pretend pretend to sth

pretty bother one's (pretty little) head about so/sth ♦ come to a pretty pass ♦ cost a pretty penny ♦ eat (pretty) high off the hog ♦ gotta get up pretty early in the morning to do sth ♦ in a (pretty) pickle ♦ live (pretty) high off the hog ♦ live (pretty) high on the hog ♦ not trouble one's (pretty) (little) head about sth ♦ pretty as a picture ♦ pretty nearly ♦ a pretty pickle ♦ pretty soon ♦ a pretty state of affairs ♦ sitting pretty

prevail cooler heads prevail

prevent take steps (to prevent sth)

prey fall prey to so/sth ♦ prey (up)on so/sth

price asking price ♦ at a price ♦ cheap at half the price ♦ come at a price ♦ for a price ♦ have a price on one's head ♦ a little pricey ♦ pay the price ♦ the price one has to pay ♦ a price on one's head ♦ put a price (tag) on sth ♦ What price sth?

prick prick up its ears

pride pride and joy ♦ pride oneself on sth ♦ swallow one's pride ♦ take pride in so/sth

prime in one's or its prime ♦ in the prime of (one's) life ♦ past so's/sth's prime ♦ prime mover ♦ prime sth with sth

primrose the primrose path

principle in principle ♦ a matter of principle ♦ on principle

print fine print ♦ get sth in(to) print ♦ in print ♦ not worth the paper it's printed on ♦ out of print ♦ put sth in(to) print ♦ rush sth into print ♦ small print

prisoner take no prisoners

privacy invasion of (so's) privacy

private in private

privy privy to sth

prize booby prize

probability in all probability

probation on probation

problem cash flow problem ♦ get to the root of the problem ♦ have a drinking problem ♦ have a weight problem ♦ have an alcohol problem ♦ no problem ♦ the root of the problem

proceed proceed against so/sth

production make a (whole) production out of sth

professional seek professional help

professor an absent-minded professor

profile keep a low profile ♦ a low profile

profit profit by sth ♦ turn a profit

program get with the program

progress in progress

project between projects

promise go back on one's promise ♦ hold promise ♦ I promise you! ♦ keep a promise ♦ a lick and a promise ♦ a lot of promise ♦ promise the moon (to so) ♦ show a lot of promise ♦ show promise

prop knock the props out from under so

proper go through (the proper) channels

proportion a disaster of epic proportions ♦ grow out of (all) proportion ♦ in proportion ♦ out of (all) proportion

propose propose a toast

proud do oneself proud ♦ do so proud ♦ proud as a peacock

prove prove one's mettle ♦ prove sth to oneself

provide provide for so ♦ provide for sth

prowl on the prowl

prune full of prunes

pry pry into sth

psych psyched up (for sth)

public air one's dirty linen in public ♦ go public (with sth) ♦ in public ♦ in the public eye ♦ out of the public eye ♦ take sth public ♦ wash one's dirty linen in public

publication not for publication

publish publish or perish

puff huff and puff

pull have pull with so ♦ like pulling teeth ♦ pull a boner ♦ pull a fast one (on so) ♦ pull a gun (on so) ♦ pull a job ♦ pull a knife (on so) ♦ pull a muscle ♦ pull a stunt (on so) ♦ pull a trick (on so) ♦ pull all the stops out ♦ pull one's belt in (a notch) ♦ pull (an amount of money) down ♦ pull one's hair (out) ♦ pull in one's ears ♦ pull in one's horns ♦ pull so's leg ♦ pull sth on so ♦ pull on so's heartstrings ♦ pull out (of sth) ♦ pull sth out of so ♦ pull sth out of a hat ♦ pull sth out of the fire ♦ pull sth out of thin air ♦ pull one's (own) weight ♦ pull one's punches ♦ pull rank on so ♦ pull (some) strings ♦ pull so's/sth's teeth ♦ pull the plug (on so) ♦ pull the plug (on sth) ♦ pull the rug out (from under so) ♦ pull the wool over so's eyes ♦ pull through (sth) ♦ pull sth to ♦ pull oneself together ♦ pull sth together ♦ pull so/sth under ♦ pull up (some place) ♦ Pull up a chair. ♦ pull oneself up by one's (own) bootstraps ♦ pull up one's roots ♦ pull so up short ♦ pull up stakes

pulp beat so to a pulp

pulse have one's finger on the pulse of sth ♦ keep one's finger on the pulse of sth ♦ quicken the pulse (of sth) ♦ take so's pulse ♦ take the pulse of sth

pump pump so for sth ♦ pump (some) iron ♦ pump sth up ♦ pumped (up)

in (where it's not wanted) ♦ put one's nose out of joint ♦ put one's nose to the grindstone ♦ put one's oar in ♦ put so off ♦ put sth off ♦ put off by so/sth ♦ put one off one's stride ♦ put so off the scent ♦ put so off the track ♦ put so off the trail ♦ put so on ♦ put on airs ♦ put on an act ♦ put one on one's feet ♦ put so on hold ♦ put so/sth on hold ♦ put sth on hold ♦ put one on one's honor ♦ put so/sth on ice ♦ put sth on paper ♦ put sth on the cuff ♦ put on the dog ♦ put sth on the front burner ♦ put sth on the map ♦ put on the ritz ♦ put sth on the street ♦ put on weight ♦ put one foot in front of the other ♦ put oneself out ♦ put so out ♦ put out a warrant (on so) ♦ put out (about so/sth) ♦ put some creature out of its misery ♦ put so/sth out of one's mind ♦ put one out of (one's) misery ♦ put so out of the way ♦ put out (some) feelers (on so/sth) ♦ put so out to pasture ♦ put (out) to sea ♦ put so/sth over ♦ put sth over ♦ put sth over on so ♦ put one's own house in order ♦ put paid to sth ♦ put pen to paper ♦ put sth plainly ♦ put sth right ♦ put roots down (some place) ♦ put one's shoulder to the wheel ♦ put some distance between so and oneself or sth ♦ put some sweet lines on so ♦ put some teeth into sth ♦ put (some) years on so/sth ♦ put sth straight ♦ Put that in your pipe and smoke it! ♦ put the arm on so ♦ put the bite on so (for sth) ♦ put the blame on so/sth ♦ put the brakes on so/sth ♦ put the cart before the horse ♦ put the chill on so ♦ put the clamps on so/sth ♦ put the fear of God in(to) so ♦ put the feed bag on ♦ put the finger on so ♦ put the freeze on so ♦ put the heat on (so) ♦ put the kibosh on so/sth ♦ put the lid on sth ♦ put the lie to sth ♦ put the make on so ♦ put the moves on so ♦ put the nose-bag on ♦ put the pedal to the metal ♦ put (the) pressure on so (to do sth) ♦ put the roses back into so's cheeks ♦ put the screws on (so) ♦ put the skids on (sth) ♦ put the squeeze on (so) ♦ put the touch on so (for sth) ♦ put one's thinking cap on ♦ put so through sth ♦ put one through one's paces ♦ put so through the wringer ♦ put so/sth through (to so) ♦ put sth to bed ♦ put to bed with a shovel ♦ put so to bed with a shovel ♦ put so to death ♦ put sth to (good) use ♦ put to it ♦ put sth to rest ♦ put so to shame ♦ put so/animal to sleep ♦ put so to sleep ♦ put so/sth to the test ♦ put sth together ♦ put one's trust in so/sth ♦ put two and two together ♦ put two and two together and come up with five ♦ put one's two cents(' worth) in ♦ put so under ♦ put sth under the microscope ♦ put so up ♦ put sth up ♦ put up a (brave) front ♦ put up a fight ♦ put up a struggle ♦ put so up against so ♦ put up one's dukes ♦ put sth up for sale ♦ Put up or shut up! ♦ put sth (up) to a vote ♦ put so up with so ♦ put up with so/sth ♦ put upon by so ♦ put wear (and tear) on sth ♦ put weight on ♦ put words in(to) so's mouth ♦ Put your money where your mouth is! ♦ a put-up job ♦ to put it another way ♦ to put it mildly

putty putty in so's hands

puzzle puzzle sth out

QT on the QT

quake quake in one's boots

quality quality time

qualm have qualms (about so/sth) ♦ qualms (about so/sth)

quandary in a quandary

quantity known quantity ♦ an unknown quantity

quarrel have a quarrel with sth ♦ patch a quarrel up ♦ pick a quarrel (with so)

quarter drawn and quartered ♦ give so no quarter ♦ grant so no quarter

queen The Queen's English

queer queer as a three-dollar bill ♦ queer for sth

quest in quest of so/sth

question Ask no questions and hear no lies. ♦ beg the question ♦ beside the question ♦ beyond question ♦ bring sth into question ♦ a burning question ♦ call sth into question ♦ field questions ♦ so/sth in question ♦ leading question ♦ no questions asked ♦ open to question ♦ out of the question ♦ pop the question ♦ pose a question ♦ a question of (doing) sth ♦ a question of time ♦ the sixty-four-dollar question ♦ without question

queue queue up (for sth)

quick cut so to the quick ♦ make a quick buck ♦ quick and dirty ♦ quick as a flash ♦ quick as a wink ♦ quick as (greased) lightning ♦ a quick bite ♦ quick like a bunny ♦ quick off the mark ♦ quick on the draw ♦ quick on the trigger ♦ quick on the uptake ♦ a quick study ♦ a quick temper ♦ quicken the pace (of sth) ♦ quicken the pulse (of sth) ♦ quicker than a New York minute ♦ quicker than hell ♦ quicker than you can say Jack Robinson

quiet keep sth quiet ♦ quiet as a (church) mouse ♦ quiet as the grave ♦ so quiet you could hear a pin drop

quit call it quits ♦ Don't quit trying. ♦ Don't quit your day job. ♦ quit while one is ahead

quite cause (quite a) stir ♦ go back quite a way(s) ♦ quite (a) sth ♦ quite a few ♦ quite a number ♦ take (quite a) toll (on so/sth)

quiver quiver with sth

quiz quiz out (of sth)

quote quote, unquote

R

race off to the races ♦ play the race card ♦ race against the clock ♦ race against time ♦ the rat race ♦ run the good race ♦ the race card ♦ a tight race

rack go to rack and ruin ♦ off the rack ♦ rack one's brain(s) ♦ rack out ♦ rack sth up ♦ racked with pain

radar below so's radar (screen) ♦ on so's radar (screen)

rag chew the rag ♦ from rags to riches ♦ in rags ♦ on the rag ♦ rag so about so/sth ♦ rag on so ♦ rag out

rage all the rage ♦ bristle with rage ♦ fly into a rage ♦ the latest rage ♦ rage out of control ♦ rage through sth ♦ run so ragged

railroad railroad so into sth ♦ railroad sth through (sth)

rain come in out of the rain ♦ come rain or (come) shine ♦ hold sth back for a rainy day ♦ keep sth for a rainy day ♦ not know enough to come in out of the rain ♦ put sth aside for a rainy day ♦ rain cats and dogs ♦ a rain check (on sth) ♦ rain sth down (on so/sth) ♦ rain down on so/sth ♦ rain on so's parade ♦ rain sth out ♦ right as rain ♦ risk of rain ♦ save (sth) for a rainy day

rainbow (always) chasing rainbows ♦ chasing rainbows

raise born and raised some place ♦ cause (some) eyebrows to raise ♦ raise a (big) stink (about so/sth) ♦ raise a few eyebrows ♦ raise a hand (against so/sth) ♦ raise a stink (about sth) ♦ raise Cain ♦ raise so from sth ♦ raise so from the dead ♦ raise one's glass to so/sth ♦ raise so's hackles ♦ raise havoc with so/sth ♦ raise hell (with sth) ♦ raise hob with so/sth ♦ raise money for so/sth ♦ raise one's sights ♦ raise the ante ♦ raise the bar ♦ raise the devil (with so) ♦ raise the devil (with sth) ♦ raise the dickens (with so/sth) ♦ raise the stakes ♦ raise so/sth to sth ♦ raise one's voice against so/sth ♦ raise one's voice (to so) ♦ raised in a barn

rake rake sth in ♦ rake sth off ♦ rake on so ♦ rake so over the coals ♦ rake sth up

rally rally to so/sth

ralph hang a ralph

ram ram so/sth down so's throat

ramble ramble on ♦ ramble on (about so/sth)

rampage go on a rampage

rampant run rampant

ran also-ran

ranch bet the ranch (on sth)

random at random

range at close range

rank break ranks with so/sth ♦ close ranks ♦ close ranks (behind so/sth) ♦ come up through the ranks ♦ join the ranks of sth ♦ pull rank on so ♦ rank and file ♦ rank so with so ♦ rise from the ranks

ransom a king's ransom

rant rant and rave (about so/sth)

rap beat the rap ◆ get one's knuckles rapped ◆ rap so across the knuckles ◆ rap with so ◆ take the rap (for so) ◆ take the rap (for sth)

rare have a rare old time ◆ in rare form ◆ raring to go

rash break out in a rash

raspberry give so the raspberry

rat rat on so ◆ the rat race ◆ rug rat ◆ smell a rat

rate at any rate ◆ at that rate ◆ at this rate ◆ the going rate ◆ second-rate

rather had rather do sth ◆ have one's rathers

rattle rattle around in sth ◆ rattle so's cage ◆ rattle sth off ◆ rattle on (about so/sth) ◆ rattle one's saber

raunch raunch so out

rave rant and rave (about so/sth) ◆ rave about so/sth ◆ stark raving mad

ravish ravished with delight

raw hit a (raw) nerve ◆ in the raw ◆ a raw deal ◆ raw recruit ◆ touch a (raw) nerve

ray bag some rays ◆ catch some rays ◆ a ray of sunshine

razor sharp as a razor

reach out of reach ◆ reach so ◆ reach a compromise ◆ reach a conclusion ◆ reach a decision ◆ reach an impasse ◆ reach first base (with so/sth) ◆ reach for the sky ◆ reach out ◆ reach out to so ◆ reach speeds of some number ◆ reach one's stride ◆ within one's reach

reaction gut reaction ◆ a knee-jerk reaction

read Do you read me? ◆ I read you loud and clear. ◆ read between the lines ◆ read from the same page ◆ read sth into sth ◆ read it and weep ◆ read so like a book ◆ read so's lips ◆ read so's mind ◆ Read my lips! ◆ read so out (for sth) ◆ read so out of sth ◆ read one one's rights ◆ read the handwriting on the wall ◆ read so the riot act ◆ read oneself to sleep

ready Anytime you are ready. ◆ (Are you) ready for this? ◆ (Are you) ready to order? ◆ at the ready ◆ make ready (to do sth) ◆ ready, set, go ◆ ready to roll ◆ ready, willing, and able ◆ rough and ready ◆ when one is good and ready

real for real ◆ Get real! ◆ a (real) go-getter ◆ the real McCoy ◆ the real thing

reality in reality ◆ lose touch with reality ◆ need a reality check ◆ a reality check ◆ virtual reality

realize realize sth from sth

really That (really) burns me (up)!

reap the grim reaper

rear bring up the rear ◆ get off one's rear ◆ in the rear ◆ a pain in the rear ◆ rear its ugly head ◆ rear up

reason all the more reason for doing sth ◆ It (only) stands to reason. ◆ listen to reason ◆ lose one's reason ◆ neither rhyme nor reason ◆ no earthly reason ◆ rhyme or reason ◆ stand to reason ◆ within reason ◆ without rhyme or reason

reasonable beyond a reasonable doubt

rebound rebound from sth

receipt in receipt of sth

receive on the receiving end (of sth) ◆ receive so with open arms

recent in recent memory

recharge recharge one's batteries

reckon a force to be reckoned with ◆ reckon with so/sth

recognize recognize so/sth for sth ◆ recognize sth for what it is

record break a record ◆ fall short of the record ◆ for the record ◆ off the record ◆ on record ◆ one for the (record) books ◆ set the record straight ◆ sound like a broken record

recruit raw recruit

red catch so red-handed ◆ caught red-handed ◆ cut through red tape ◆ down the little red lane ◆ one's ears are red ◆ give so a red face ◆ in the red ◆ not worth a red cent ◆ out of the red ◆ paint the town (red) ◆ red as a cherry ◆ red as a poppy ◆ red as a rose ◆ red as a ruby ◆ red as blood ◆ a red herring ◆ red in the face ◆ red ink ◆ red tape ◆ the red-carpet treatment ◆ a red-letter day ◆ roll out the red carpet (for so) ◆ run a red light ◆ see red

reduce in reduced circumstances ◆ reduce so to sth

reed a broken reed

reek reek of sth

reel reel sth off ♦ reel them in ♦ reel under sth

reelection up for reelection

refill refill a prescription

reflect reflected in sth

refresh refresh so's memory (about so/sth)

refuse an offer one cannot refuse

regain regain one's composure ♦ regain one's feet

regard as regards so/sth ♦ hold so/sth in high regard ♦ hold so/sth in low regard ♦ in regard to so/sth ♦ regarded as armed and dangerous ♦ with regard to so/sth

regular at regular intervals ♦ regular as clockwork ♦ a regular fixture ♦ a regular guy

rehearsal in rehearsal

reign have free reign (over sth)

rein give free rein to so ♦ have a free rein (with sth) ♦ keep a close rein on so/sth ♦ keep a tight rein on so/sth ♦ take over the reins (of sth)

reinvent reinvent the wheel

related related to so

relation have intimate relations with so ♦ have relations with so

relationship a love-hate relationship

relative relative to so/sth

relief breathe a sigh of relief

relieve relieve oneself ♦ relieve so of sth ♦ relieve one of one's duties

religion get religion ♦ religion

religious religious about doing sth

relish with (great) relish

remain It remains to be seen. ♦ remain in touch (with so) ♦ remain in touch (with so/sth) ♦ That remains to be seen.

remember remember so to so

remission in remission

render render sth down

repair beyond repair ♦ in good repair ♦ repair to some place

report report in sick

reproach above reproach ♦ beyond reproach

reputation carve out a reputation ♦ get a reputation (as a sth) ♦ get a reputation (for doing sth) ♦ a reputation (as a sth) ♦ a reputation (for doing sth) ♦ stake one's reputation on so/sth

repute a house of ill repute

request at so's request

reservation make a reservation

reserve hold so/sth in reserve ♦ keep so/sth in reserve

residence take up residence some place

resistance follow the line of least resistance ♦ the line of least resistance ♦ the path of least resistance ♦ a pocket of resistance

resonate resonate with so

resort as a last resort

resource leave one to one's own resources

respect in many respects ♦ in respect to so/sth ♦ in some respects ♦ pay one's final respects (to so) ♦ pay one's last respects (to so) ♦ pay so respect ♦ pay one's respects (to so) ♦ with all due respect ♦ with respect to so/sth

response gut response

responsible hold so responsible (for sth) ♦ the responsible party

rest at rest ♦ bring sth to rest ♦ give sth a rest ♦ Give it a rest! ♦ Give me a rest! ♦ God rest so's soul. ♦ I rest my case. ♦ one's last resting place ♦ lay so to rest ♦ lay sth to rest ♦ No rest for the wicked. ♦ put sth to rest ♦ rest assured ♦ rest in sth ♦ rest in peace ♦ The rest is gravy. ♦ The rest is history. ♦ rest on one's laurels ♦ stand out from the rest

retool retool for sth

retreat beat a (hasty) retreat

retrospect in retrospect

return by return mail ♦ by return post ♦ the point of no return ♦ return the compliment ♦ return the favor ♦ return to haunt one

rev rev up ♦ rev sth up

review pass in review

revolve revolve around so/sth

reward get one's just reward(s) ♦ go to one's (just) reward

rhyme neither rhyme nor reason ♦ rhyme or reason ♦ run one's rhymes ♦ without rhyme or reason

rib stick to one's ribs

ribbons cut so/sth to ribbons

rich filthy rich ♦ from rags to riches ♦ stinking rich ♦ strike it rich ♦ too rich for so's blood

riches from rags to riches

rid get rid of so/sth ♦ rid of so/sth

riddance good-bye and good riddance

ride a free ride ♦ give so a ride ♦ go along (with so) for the ride ♦ hitch a ride ♦ let sth ride ♦ ride so about sth ♦ ride off in all directions ♦ ride on sth ♦ ride on so's coattails ♦ ride out the storm ♦ ride roughshod over so/sth ♦ ride the gravy train ♦ ride up (on so) ♦ riding for a fall ♦ take so for a ride ♦ thumb a ride

ridicule hold so/sth up to ridicule

ridiculous from the sublime to the ridiculous

rig rig so/sth out (in sth) ♦ rig sth up

right all right ♦ all right by so ♦ All right for you! ♦ All righty. ♦ All right(y) already! ♦ Am I right? ♦ (bang) dead to rights ♦ be within one's rights ♦ Come right in. ♦ come (right) on top of sth ♦ dead to rights ♦ get one right here ♦ get right on sth ♦ give one's right arm (for so/sth) ♦ go (right) through so ♦ hang a right ♦ have so dead to rights ♦ have one's head screwed on right ♦ have one's heart in the right place ♦ one's heart is in the right place ♦ hit so (right) between the eyes ♦ hit the nail (right) on the head ♦ hit the right note ♦ hold one's mouth the right way ♦ I'll get right on it. ♦ in one's own right ♦ in one's right mind ♦ in the right ♦ in the right direction ♦ in the right place at the right time ♦ jog to the right or left ♦ keep so/sth on (the) (right) track ♦ killed outright ♦ left and right ♦ look right through so ♦ make sth right ♦ moving right along ♦ Mr. Right ♦ off on the right foot (with so/sth) ♦ on the right track ♦ play one's cards right ♦ put sth right ♦ read one one's rights ♦ right and left ♦ right as rain ♦ right down so's alley ♦ right here and now ♦ right in the kisser ♦ right off the bat ♦ (right) off the top of one's head ♦ Right on! ♦ (right) on target ♦ right on time ♦ (right) out of the (starting) blocks ♦ (right) out of the (starting) gate ♦ right side up ♦ the right stuff ♦ a right to do sth ♦ a right to sth ♦ (right) under so's

(very) nose ♦ right up so's alley ♦ the right-of-way ♦ sail (right) through sth ♦ say sth (right) to so's face ♦ see (right) through so/sth ♦ serve so right ♦ set sth right ♦ sit right with so ♦ step right up ♦ straighten up and fly right ♦ strike the right note ♦ take a step in the right direction ♦ walk (right) into sth ♦ when it comes right down to it ♦ whiz (right) through sth ♦ within one's rights ♦ yield the right-of-way

Riley lead the life of Riley ♦ live the life of Riley

ring a (dead) ringer (for so) ♦ one's ears are ringing ♦ give so a ring ♦ Give me a ring. ♦ have a familiar ring (to it) ♦ like a three-ring circus ♦ look like a (dead) ringer (for so) ♦ ring a bell ♦ ring false ♦ ring hollow ♦ ring in so's ears ♦ ring in so's mind ♦ ring in the new year ♦ ring off the hook ♦ ring out the old (year) ♦ ring the bell ♦ ring the curtain down (on sth) ♦ ring the curtain up ♦ ring true ♦ ring sth up ♦ run rings around so ♦ throw one's hat in the ring ♦ toss one's hat into the ring

ringer a (dead) ringer (for so) ♦ look like a (dead) ringer (for so)

riot read so the riot act ♦ a riot of color ♦ run riot

rip Let her rip! ♦ rip into so/sth ♦ rip so off ♦ rip sth off ♦ rip on so ♦ rip snorter ♦ rip so/sth to sth ♦ (rip-)off artist

ripe live to the (ripe old) age of sth ♦ a ripe old age ♦ ripen into sth ♦ the time is ripe (for sth)

ripple a ripple of sth ♦ ripple through sth

rise get a rise from so ♦ give rise to sth ♦ God willing and the creek don't rise. ♦ Lord willing and the creek don't rise. ♦ on the rise ♦ rise above sth ♦ Rise and shine! ♦ rise from the ashes ♦ rise from the dead ♦ rise from the grave ♦ rise from the ranks ♦ rise to one's feet ♦ rise to the bait ♦ rise to the challenge ♦ rise to the occasion ♦ think the sun rises and sets on so

risk at risk ♦ put so/sth at risk ♦ risk one's neck (to do sth) ♦ risk of rain ♦ risk of showers ♦ risk of thunder(storms) ♦ run a risk (of sth)

ritz put on the ritz

river sell so down the river ♦ send so up (the river) ♦ up the river

rivet mad enough to chew nails (and spit rivets) ♦ rivet so's attention ♦ riveted to the ground

road down the road ♦ down the road a piece ♦ down the road a stretch ♦ the end of the road ♦ get the show on the road ♦ go down that road ♦ hit the road ♦ in the road ♦ middle-of-the-road ♦ on the road ♦ on the road to sth ♦ one for the road ♦ road hog ♦ a rocky road ♦ smack the road ♦ a wide place in the road

roar keep it down (to a dull roar) ♦ roar at so/sth

rob rob so blind ♦ rob Peter to pay Paul ♦ rob the cradle

Robin all around Robin Hood's barn

Robinson before you can say Jack Robinson ♦ quicker than you can say Jack Robinson

rock between a rock and a hard place ♦ get one's rocks off (on sth) ♦ hard as a rock ♦ have rocks in one's head ♦ hit (rock) bottom ♦ Let's rock and roll! ♦ on the rocks ♦ (rock) bottom ♦ rock the boat ♦ a rocky road ♦ solid as a rock ♦ steady as a rock

rocker off one's rocker

rocket not rocket science ♦ rocket (in)to sth

Roger Roger (wilco).

role play a role in sth

roll (all) rolled into one ♦ awkward as a cow on roller skates ♦ call (the) roll ♦ get rolling ♦ have them rolling in the aisles ♦ heads will roll ♦ a high roller ♦ keep the ball rolling ♦ Let it roll! ♦ Let's rock and roll! ♦ on a roll ♦ ready to roll ♦ roll along ♦ roll around (again) ♦ roll sth back ♦ roll by ♦ roll in ♦ roll on ♦ roll out the red carpet (for so) ♦ roll sth over ♦ roll over and play dead ♦ roll (over) in one's grave ♦ roll one's sleeves up ♦ roll with the punches ♦ rolled into one ♦ the sth rolling ♦ rolling in sth ♦ rolling in the aisles ♦ start the ball rolling ♦ take (the) roll

Rome fiddle while Rome burns

romp romp on so ♦ romp through sth

roof busy as a cat on a hot tin roof ♦ go through the roof ♦ hit the roof ♦ live under the same roof (with so)

rooftop scream (sth) from the rooftops ♦ shout (sth) from the rooftops ♦ yell (sth) from the rooftops

room Don't let it out of this room. ♦ end up on the cutting room floor ♦ have some elbow room ♦ leave the room ♦ not enough room to swing a cat ♦ room and board ♦ send so to the locker room ♦ smoke-filled room ♦ some elbow room ♦ take up room

roost come home (to roost) ♦ rule the roost

root become rooted to sth ♦ get to the root of the problem ♦ love of money is the root of all evil ♦ pull up one's roots ♦ put roots down (some place) ♦ root for so/sth ♦ the root of the problem ♦ root sth out ♦ rooted in sth ♦ rooted to sth ♦ rooted to the spot ♦ take root

rope at the end of one's rope ♦ know the ropes ♦ rope so into (doing) sth ♦ the ropes ♦ walk a tightrope

rose a bed of roses ♦ come out smelling like a rose ♦ come up smelling like a rose ♦ Everything's coming up roses. ♦ put the roses back into so's cheeks ♦ red as a rose ♦ smell like a rose

rot rot in hell (before one would do sth) ♦ a rotten apple ♦ a rotten egg ♦ rotten luck ♦ rotten to the core ♦ spoiled rotten

rote by rote ♦ learn sth by rote

rough a diamond in the rough ♦ have a rough time (of it) ♦ rough and ready ♦ rough and tumble ♦ a rough idea (about sth) ♦ rough it ♦ rough stuff ♦ a rough time ♦ rough so up

roughshod ride roughshod over so/sth ♦ run roughshod over so/sth

round (all) year round ♦ buy a round (of drinks) ♦ buy the next round (of drinks) ♦ in round figures ♦ in round numbers ♦ round sth down ♦ round down to sth ♦ round sth off ♦ round off to sth ♦ round sth off (with sth) ♦ round sth out ♦ round so/sth up ♦ a rounding error ♦ round-trip ticket ♦

_a square peg (in a round hole) ♦ year round

roundup head for the last roundup ♦ the last roundup

route go that route

rove have a roving eye

row get one's ducks in a row ♦ a hard row to hoe ♦ in a row ♦ kick up a row ♦ a tough row to hoe

royal a battle royal ♦ a royal pain ♦ the royal treatment

rub rub elbows (with so) ♦ rub so's fur the wrong way ♦ rub sth in ♦ rub so's nose in it ♦ rub off (on so) ♦ rub so out ♦ rub salt in a wound ♦ rub shoulders with so ♦ rub so the wrong way ♦ There's the rub.

Rubicon cross the Rubicon

ruby red as a ruby

ruffle ruffle so's feathers ♦ smooth (so's) ruffled feathers

rug cut a rug ♦ lie like a rug ♦ pull the rug out (from under so) ♦ rug rat ♦ snug as a bug in a rug ♦ sweep sth under the rug

ruin go to rack and ruin ♦ go to wrack and ruin ♦ in ruins ♦ lie in ruins ♦ the ruin of so/sth ♦ wrack and ruin

rule as a (general) rule ♦ as a rule ♦ bend the rules ♦ a rule of thumb ♦ rule so/sth out ♦ rule the roost ♦ rule with a velvet glove ♦ rule with an iron fist

ruminate ruminate about sth

rumor rumor has it that . . .

rump rump session

run cut and run ♦ days running ♦ dry run ♦ eat and run ♦ for (some) days running ♦ for (some) months running ♦ for (some) weeks running ♦ for (some) years running ♦ the front runner ♦ have a good run ♦ have a long run ♦ have a run of sth ♦ have a run of bad luck ♦ have a run-in (with so/sth) ♦ have one's luck run out ♦ hit a home run ♦ hit the ground running ♦ hit-and-run ♦ I hate to eat and run. ♦ in the long run ♦ in the running ♦ in the short run ♦ one's luck runs out ♦ make a run for it ♦ make so's blood run cold ♦ months running ♦ off and running ♦ off to a running start ♦ on the run ♦ out of the running ♦ run a comb through sth ♦ run a fever ♦ run a make on

so ♦ run a red light ♦ run a risk (of sth) ♦ run a tab ♦ run a taut ship ♦ run a temperature ♦ run a tight ship ♦ run afoul of so/sth ♦ run against the grain ♦ run aground (on sth) ♦ run along ♦ run amuck ♦ run an errand ♦ run (around) in circles ♦ run around like a chicken with its head cut off ♦ run around with so ♦ a run at sth ♦ run away with so ♦ run away with sth ♦ run behind ♦ run sth by (so) (again) ♦ run circles around so ♦ run counter to sth ♦ run down ♦ run so/sth down ♦ run down to some place ♦ run one's eye over sth ♦ run one's feet off ♦ run one's fingers through one's hair ♦ run for it ♦ run for one's life ♦ a run for one's money ♦ run for the hills ♦ run one's hand through one's hair ♦ run one's head against a brick wall ♦ run so in ♦ run in the family ♦ run into so ♦ run (in)to sth ♦ run into a stone wall ♦ run sth into the ground ♦ run it down ♦ run its course ♦ run like clockwork ♦ run like stink ♦ run like the wind ♦ run low (on sth) ♦ run off ♦ run sth off ♦ run off at the mouth ♦ run off in all directions ♦ run off (with so) ♦ run on all cylinders ♦ run out of gas ♦ run out of patience ♦ run out of steam ♦ run out of time ♦ run over sth with so ♦ run so ragged ♦ run rampant ♦ run one's rhymes ♦ run rings around so ♦ run riot ♦ run roughshod over so/sth ♦ run scared ♦ run short (of sth) ♦ Run that by (me) again. ♦ run the gamut ♦ run the gauntlet ♦ run the good race ♦ run the show ♦ run through sth ♦ run so through sth ♦ run sth through sth ♦ run to seed ♦ run sth up ♦ run wild ♦ run with so/sth ♦ run with sth ♦ run with the hare and hunt with the hounds ♦ a running battle ♦ running high ♦ running on empty ♦ running on fumes ♦ running on vapor ♦ run-of-the-mill ♦ score a home run ♦ Take a running jump (in the lake)! ♦ time is running out ♦ turn tail (and run) ♦ up and running ♦ weeks running ♦ years running

runaround get the runaround ♦ the runaround

rung on the bottom rung (of the ladder)

703

runt the runt of the family ♦ the runt of the litter

rush the bum's rush ♦ give so the bum's rush ♦ in a mad rush ♦ rush hour ♦ rush in(to sth) ♦ rush sth into print ♦ a rush on sth ♦ rush sth through (sth) ♦ rush to conclusions ♦ rush so to the hospital

rust the rust belt

rustle rustle sth up

rut fall into the rut of doing sth ♦ in a rut

S

saber rattle one's saber

sack can't carry a tune in a paper sack ♦ give so the sack ♦ hit the sack ♦ the sack ♦ sack out ♦ sacked out

sacred a sacred cow

sacrifice sacrifice so/sth on the altar of sth

sad a sad sight ♦ a sad state of affairs ♦ sadder but wiser

saddle back in the saddle (again) ♦ saddle so with so/sth ♦ saddled with so/sth

safe better safe than sorry ♦ Have a safe journey. ♦ Have a safe trip. ♦ in safe hands ♦ keep on the safe side ♦ on the safe side ♦ play it safe ♦ safe and sound ♦ safety in numbers

safekeeping for safekeeping

safety safety in numbers

sage sage advice

sail clear sailing ♦ knock the wind out of so's sails ♦ sail into so/sth ♦ sail (right) through sth ♦ sail under false colors ♦ set sail (for some place) ♦ smooth sailing ♦ take the wind out of so's sails

saint have the patience of a saint

sake arguing for the sake of arguing ♦ For goodness sake(s)! ♦ For heaven('s) sake(s)! ♦ for old time's sake ♦ for one's (own) sake ♦ For Pete's sake! ♦ For pity's sake! ♦ for so's/sth's sake ♦ Land(s) sakes (alive)! ♦ Sakes alive!

salad in one's salad days ♦ toss a salad

sale close a sale ♦ for sale ♦ hard sale ♦ no sale ♦ on sale ♦ put sth up for sale ♦ up for sale

sally sally forth

salt back to the salt mines ♦ go back to the salt mines ♦ go through so like a dose of the salts ♦ rub salt in a wound ♦ salt sth away ♦ the salt of the earth ♦ salt sth with sth ♦ take sth with a grain of salt ♦ take sth with a pinch of salt ♦ worth one's salt

salutation Greetings and salutations!

same add up to the same thing ♦ all the same ♦ all the same (to so) ♦ amount to the same thing ♦ at the same time ♦ be on the same page ♦ be on the same screen ♦ bitten by the same bug ♦ by the same token ♦ cast in the same mold ♦ come to the same thing ♦ cut from the same cloth ♦ go into the same old song and dance (about sth) ♦ in the same ballpark ♦ in the same boat (as so) ♦ in the same breath ♦ in the same league as so/sth ♦ just the same ♦ just the same (to so) ♦ live under the same roof (with so) ♦ made from the same mold ♦ on the same wavelength ♦ one and the same ♦ paint so with the same brush ♦ read from the same page ♦ same difference ♦ Same here. ♦ same o(l)' same o(l)' ♦ the same old story ♦ the same old thing ♦ the same to you ♦ sing from the same hymn book ♦ speak the same language ♦ tar so with the same brush ♦ tarred with the same brush ♦ two sides of the same coin

sanctity odor of sanctity

sand bury one's head in the sand ♦ draw a line in the sand ♦ have one's head in the sand ♦ hide one's head in the sand ♦ the sands of time ♦ stick one's head in the sand

sandwich a knuckle sandwich ♦ one sandwich short of a picnic

sanity a sanity check

sardine pack so/sth (in) like sardines

sassy fat and sassy

Saturday Saturday night special

sauce on the sauce

saucer eyes like saucers

saunter saunter along

save dip into one's savings ♦ in the interest of saving time ♦ save a bundle (on sth) ♦ save one's ass ♦ save one's bacon ♦ save one's breath ♦ save (enough) time (for so/sth) ♦ save (one's) face ♦ save (sth) for a rainy day ♦ save oneself (for marriage) ♦ Save it! ♦ save so's neck ♦ save so's skin ♦ save the day ♦ saved by the bell ♦ saving grace ♦ scrimp and save

saw saw against the grain

say after all is said and done ♦ Anything you say. ♦ as I was saying ♦ before you can say Jack Robinson ♦ can't say (a)s I do, (can't say (a)s I don't) ♦ easier said than done ♦ have one's say ♦ The hell you say! ♦ (It) (just) goes without saying ♦ just let me say ♦ (just) say the word ♦ the last say ♦ let me (just) say ♦ let's say ♦ (Let's) say that . . . ♦ like I was saying ♦ Need I say more? ♦ needless to say ♦ No sooner said than done. ♦ on so's say-so ♦ quicker than you can say Jack Robinson ♦ one's say ♦ say a mouthful ♦ Say cheese! ♦ say sth for sth ♦ say good-bye to sth ♦ say grace ♦ a say (in sth) ♦ Say no more. ♦ say one's piece ♦ say sth (right) to so's face ♦ Say that . . . ♦ say sth to oneself ♦ say uncle ♦ Say what? ♦ Say when. ♦ Says me! ♦ Says who? ♦ Says you! ♦ Smile when you say that. ♦ that is to say ♦ That's easy for you to say. ♦ There is something to be said for sth. ♦ to say nothing of so/sth ♦ to say the least ♦ What can I say? ♦ What do you want me to say? ♦ What so said. ♦ What say? ♦ when all is said and done

scale tip the scales ♦ tip the scales at sth

scapegoat make so the scapegoat for sth

scarce make oneself scarce ♦ scarce as hen's teeth ♦ scarcely have time to breathe ♦ scarcer than hen's teeth

scare run scared ♦ scare sth out of so ♦ scare so out of a year's growth ♦ scare one out of one's mind ♦ scare one out of one's wits ♦ scare so stiff ♦ scare the living daylights out of so ♦ scare the pants off (of) so ♦ scare the shit out of so ♦ scare the wits out of so ♦ scare so to death ♦ scare so/sth up ♦ scared silly ♦ scared stiff ♦ scared to death

scarf scarf sth down ♦ scarf out

scatter scattered far and wide

scenario the best-case scenario ♦ the worst-case scenario

scene arrive on the scene ♦ behind the scenes ♦ burst onto the scene ♦ come on the scene ♦ create a scene ♦ make a scene ♦ make the scene ♦ on the scene ♦ set the scene for sth

scenery a change of scenery

scent put a dog off the scent ♦ put so off the scent ♦ throw so off the scent

schedule ahead of schedule ♦ behind schedule ♦ fall behind schedule ♦ get behind schedule ♦ on schedule

scheme in the (great) scheme of things

schizz schiz(z) out

school cut school ♦ from the old school ♦ of the old school ♦ school so in sth ♦ the school of hard knocks ♦ school of thought ♦ teach school ♦ tell tales out of school

science get sth down to a science ♦ not rocket science

scoot scoot down (to some place) ♦ scoot over ♦ scoot over to so/sth

scope scope (on) so ♦ scope so/sth out

score have a score to settle (with so) ♦ know the score ♦ score a home run ♦ score a point ♦ score sth for sth ♦ score with so/group ♦ settle a score with so

scorn hold so/sth up to scorn

scot get off scot-free ♦ go scot-free

Scott Great Scott!

Scotty Beam me up, Scotty!

scour scour sth for so/sth

scout scout around (for so/sth)

scrape bow and scrape ♦ have a scrape (with so/sth) ♦ pinch and scrape ♦ scrape along (on sth) ♦ scrape the bottom of the barrel ♦ scrape through (sth) ♦ scrape sth together

scratch from scratch ♦ leave one scratching one's head ♦ scratch about (for sth) ♦ scratch so's back ♦ scratch the surface ♦ send one scratching one's head ♦ start from scratch ♦ up to scratch

scream a piercing scream ♦ scream bloody murder ♦ scream down (on so/sth) ♦ scream (sth) from the rooftops ♦ so mad I could scream

screech screeching (drunk)

screen be on the same screen ♦ below so's radar (screen) ♦ on so's radar (screen)

screw get screwed ♦ have a screw loose ♦ have one's head screwed on right ♦ have one's head screwed on straight ♦ have one's head screwed on tight ♦ put the screws on (so) ♦ screw around ♦ screw so around ♦ screw around with so/sth ♦ screw off ♦ screw so out of sth ♦ screw so over ♦ screw so up ♦ screw sth up ♦ screw up one's courage ♦ screw up (on sth) ♦ screwed, blued, and tattooed ♦ screwed up ♦ tighten the screws on (so) ♦ One would forget one's head if it wasn't screwed on.

scrimp scrimp and save

scrub scrub up good

scrunch scrunch down

scrutiny under (close) scrutiny

scum treat so like the scum of the earth

scuzz scuzz so out

sea (all) at sea (about sth) ♦ at sea ♦ at sea level ♦ between the devil and the deep blue sea ♦ from sea to shining sea ♦ get one's sea legs ♦ go to sea ♦ put (out) to sea ♦ a sea change ♦ one's sea legs ♦ son of a sea biscuit ♦ There are plenty of (other) fish in the sea.

seal so's fate is sealed ♦ So's lips are sealed. ♦ My lips are sealed. ♦ seal a bargain ♦ seal so's fate ♦ seal the bargain ♦ sealed with a kiss ♦ signed, sealed, and delivered

seam burst at the seams ♦ come apart (at the seams) ♦ fall apart (at the seams) ♦ the seamy side of life

seamy the seamy side of life

search go out in search of so/sth ♦ in search of so/sth ♦ search high and low (for so/sth) ♦ Search me. ♦ search sth with a fine-tooth(ed) comb

season come into season ♦ in season ♦ off season ♦ open season (on so) ♦ open season (on some creature) ♦ out of season

seat by the seat of one's pants ♦ fly by the seat of one's pants ♦ grab a seat ♦ have a seat ♦ in the catbird seat ♦ in the driver's seat ♦ in the hot seat ♦ (Is) this (seat) taken? ♦ keep one's seat ♦ a kick in the (seat of the) pants ♦ on the edge of one's seat ♦ on the hot seat ♦ show so to a seat

♦ sit on the edge of one's seat ♦ take a backseat (to so/sth) ♦ This (seat) taken?

second come off second best ♦ get one's second wind ♦ have second thoughts (about so/sth) ♦ in a split second ♦ in (just) a second ♦ in one's second childhood ♦ in the second place ♦ on second thought ♦ play second fiddle (to so) ♦ second-guess so ♦ secondhand ♦ second nature to so ♦ second thoughts (about so/sth) ♦ second to none ♦ one's second wind ♦ second-rate ♦ a split second

secrecy cloak so/sth in secrecy

secret carry a secret to the grave ♦ in secret ♦ keep a secret ♦ make a secret of sth ♦ an open secret ♦ a trade secret

security lull so into a false sense of security

seduce seduce so from sth

see Am I glad to see you! ♦ as far as I can see ♦ as I see it ♦ begin to see daylight ♦ (begin to) see the light (at the end of the tunnel) ♦ can (just) see the wheels turning ♦ cannot see (any) further than the end of one's nose ♦ can't see a hole in a ladder ♦ can't see beyond the end of one's nose ♦ can't see one's hand in front of one's face ♦ can't see straight ♦ Come back and see us. ♦ first see the light of day ♦ have a look-see ♦ have seen better days ♦ Haven't I seen you somewhere before? ♦ Haven't seen you in a month of Sundays. ♦ It remains to be seen. ♦ (I've) seen better. ♦ (I've) seen worse. ♦ Let's see. ♦ Long time no see. ♦ a look-see ♦ not able to see the forest for the trees ♦ not to see the forest for the trees ♦ see a man about a dog ♦ see beyond sth ♦ see sth coming ♦ see double ♦ see eye to eye (about so/sth) (with so) ♦ see fit (to do sth) ♦ see so in hell first ♦ see into sth ♦ see one's name in lights ♦ see no further than the end of one's nose ♦ see red ♦ see (right) through so/sth ♦ see stars ♦ see the color of so's money ♦ see the error of one's ways ♦ see the (hand)writing on the wall ♦ see the last of so/sth ♦ see the light ♦ see the light (at the end of the tunnel) ♦ see the light (of day) ♦ see the sights ♦ see sth

through ♦ see so through sth ♦ see to so/sth
♦ see (to it) that sth is done ♦ see so to
the door ♦ see one's way (clear) (to do sth)
♦ See what the cat dragged in! ♦ see
which way the wind is blowing ♦ See you
in church. ♦ See you in the funny papers.
♦ See you later, alligator. ♦ seeing as
how . . . ♦ seeing that . . . ♦ so far as I
can see ♦ That remains to be seen. ♦ the
way I see it ♦ They must have seen you
coming. ♦ wait-and-see attitude ♦ What
you see is what you get. ♦ would not be
seen dead (doing sth)

seed go to seed ♦ run to seed

seek hide-and-(go-)seek ♦ much sought
after ♦ seek professional help

seize seize the day ♦ seize the opportunity
♦ seize up ♦ seize (up)on sth ♦ seized with
sth

sell hard sell ♦ sell so a bill of goods ♦ sell
so down the river ♦ sell sth for a song ♦
sell like hotcakes ♦ sell so on sth ♦ sell so
out ♦ sell out (to so) ♦ sell so/sth short ♦
sell one's soul (to the devil) ♦ sell the farm
♦ a selling point ♦ soft sell

send a big send-off ♦ give so a big send-off
♦ send so a message ♦ send one about
one's business ♦ send so away ♦ send so
flying ♦ send so from pillar to post ♦ send
so in for so ♦ Send so my love. ♦ send so on
a wild-goose chase ♦ send out a warrant
(on so) ♦ send so (out) on an errand ♦
send out the wrong signals ♦ send so
packing ♦ send one scratching one's head ♦
send one to one's death ♦ send so to glory
♦ send so to the locker room ♦ send so to
the showers ♦ send so/sth up ♦ send up a
trial balloon ♦ send so up (the river) ♦
send word to so

sense bring one to one's senses ♦ come to
one's senses ♦ have more luck than sense
♦ horse sense ♦ in a sense ♦ knock some
sense into so ♦ lull so into a false sense of
security ♦ make sense ♦ make (some)
sense (out) of so/sth ♦ out of one's senses ♦
a sense of humor ♦ shake some sense
into so ♦ a sixth sense ♦ take leave of one's
senses ♦ talk sense

sentence pass sentence on so

separate go their separate ways ♦
separate the men from the boys ♦
separate the sheep from the goats ♦
separate the wheat from the chaff

separation the separation of church and
state

serious dead serious ♦ Get serious!

serve Dinner is served. ♦ if my memory
serves (me correctly) ♦ serve as a guinea
pig ♦ serve notice (on so) ♦ serve so's
purpose ♦ serve so right ♦ serve time ♦
serve sth to so ♦ serve sth up

service at so's service ♦ Call my service. ♦
come into service ♦ go into service ♦ go
into the service ♦ in service ♦ of service
(to so) ♦ out of service ♦ pay lip service
(to sth) ♦ press so/sth into service ♦ put sth
in(to) service

session in session ♦ a jam session ♦ rump
session

set (all) set (to do sth) ♦ at a set time ♦ at
the outset ♦ dead set against so/sth ♦ from
the outset ♦ get one's ears set out ♦ have
a set-to (with so) ♦ have one's heart
(dead) set against sth ♦ have one's heart
set on sth ♦ have one's sights set on so/sth ♦
one's heart is (dead) set against sth ♦ one's
heart is set on sth ♦ not set foot some place
♦ on your mark, get set, go ♦ ready, set,
go ♦ set a precedent ♦ set a trap ♦ set
about doing sth ♦ set so/sth above so/sth ♦ set
sth against so/sth ♦ set sth aside ♦ set so
back (some amount of money) ♦ set one (back)
on one's feet ♦ set one back on one's heels ♦
set sth down ♦ set sth down in black and
white ♦ set so down (on(to) sth) ♦ set sth
down to sth ♦ set (enough) time aside (for
so/sth) ♦ set eyes on so/sth ♦ set fire to so/sth
♦ set foot in some place ♦ set for life ♦ set
forth on sth ♦ set a timepiece forward ♦ set
great store by so/sth ♦ set one's heart
against sth ♦ set one's heart on so/sth ♦ set
one's hopes on so/sth ♦ set one's house in
order ♦ set in ♦ set sth in some place ♦ set sth
in a typeface ♦ set in cement ♦ set in
concrete ♦ set sth in motion ♦ set in one's
ways ♦ set so's mind at ease (about so/sth)
♦ set one's mind to sth ♦ a set of pipes ♦ a
set of wheels ♦ set so off ♦ set sth off ♦ set
so on fire ♦ set some place on its ear ♦ set

out (on sth) ♦ set out on one's own ♦ set out to do sth ♦ set out to be sth ♦ set one's own house in order ♦ set one's own pace ♦ set pen to paper ♦ set sth right ♦ set sail (for some place) ♦ set one's sights on so/sth ♦ set so straight ♦ set sth straight ♦ set so's teeth on edge ♦ set the pace ♦ set the record straight ♦ set the scene for sth ♦ set the stage for sth ♦ set the table ♦ set the tone ♦ set the world on fire ♦ set to ♦ set to do sth ♦ set sth to music ♦ set so/sth to work ♦ set to work (on so/sth) ♦ set tongues (a)wagging ♦ set type ♦ set so up ♦ set sth up ♦ set up housekeeping ♦ set so up (in business) ♦ set up shop some place ♦ set sth up (with so) ♦ set upon so/sth ♦ think the sun rises and sets on so

setback suffer a setback

settle have a score to settle (with so) ♦ settle a score with so ♦ settle so's affairs ♦ settle down ♦ settle for sth ♦ settle so's hash ♦ settle in(to sth) ♦ settle (sth) (out of court) ♦ settle up with so ♦ settle (up)on sth ♦ when the dust settles

seven at sixes and sevens ♦ a seven-day wonder ♦ the seven-year itch

seventh in seventh heaven

sever sever ties with so

several have several irons in the fire

sew sew so/sth up ♦ sewed up

sex the opposite sex

shack shack up (with so)

shade have it made in the shade ♦ leave so in the shade ♦ shades of so/sth ♦ a shady character ♦ a shady deal

shadow afraid of one's own shadow ♦ beyond the shadow of a doubt ♦ in so's shadow ♦ in the shadow of so ♦ a shadow of oneself ♦ without a shadow of a doubt

shaft give so the shaft ♦ the shaft

shag shagged out ♦ a shaggy-dog story

shake (all) shook up ♦ a fair shake ♦ give so a fair shake ♦ in two shakes of a lamb's tail ♦ more so/sth than one can shake a stick at ♦ movers and shakers ♦ no great shakes ♦ on shaky ground ♦ shake a leg ♦ shake so down ♦ shake sth down ♦ shake (hands) on sth ♦ shake in one's boots ♦ Shake it (up)! ♦ shake a disease or illness off ♦ shake so/sth off ♦ shake

sth out ♦ shake some sense into so ♦ shake the foundations of sth ♦ shake the habit ♦ shake the lead out ♦ shake so up ♦ shake sth up ♦ shaken up ♦ shook up ♦ two shakes of a lamb's tail

shambles in (a) shambles

shame a crying shame ♦ For shame! ♦ hide one's face (in shame) ♦ put so to shame ♦ The shame of it (all)!

shank by shank's mare ♦ shank it ♦ shank's mare

shape bend so out of shape ♦ bent out of shape ♦ flexed out of shape ♦ in any way, shape, or form ♦ in bad shape ♦ in good shape ♦ in shape ♦ lick so/sth into shape ♦ out of shape ♦ shape up ♦ shape so up ♦ Shape up or ship out. ♦ take shape ♦ whip so/sth into shape

share the lion's share (of sth) ♦ share and share alike ♦ share so's pain ♦ share so's sorrow ♦ Thank you for sharing.

sharp at some time sharp ♦ bring so up sharply ♦ have a mind as sharp as a steel trap ♦ sharp as a razor ♦ sharp as a tack ♦ a sharp tongue ♦ a sharp wit

shave a close shave ♦ have a close shave ♦ little shaver

shebang the whole shebang

shed get shed of so/sth ♦ not shed a tear ♦ shed crocodile tears ♦ shed (some) light on sth

sheep the black sheep of the family ♦ separate the sheep from the goats ♦ a wolf in sheep's clothing

sheet both sheets in the wind ♦ four sheets in the wind ♦ three sheets in the wind ♦ two sheets to the wind ♦ white as a sheet

shelf off the shelf ♦ on the shelf

shell come out of one's shell ♦ drop a bomb(shell) ♦ explode a bombshell ♦ in a nutshell ♦ out of one's shell ♦ put sth in a nutshell ♦ shell out (an amount of money) ♦ walk on eggshells

shellacking a shellacking

shet get shet of so/sth

shift the graveyard shift ♦ shift for oneself ♦ shift gears ♦ shift into overdrive

shine come rain or (come) shine ♦ from sea to shining sea ♦ a knight in shining armor ♦ make hay (while the sun shines) ♦ Rise and shine! ♦ shine up to so ♦ take a shine to so/sth ♦ where the sun don't shine

Shinola know shit from Shinola ♦ tell shit from Shinola

ship abandon ship ♦ desert a sinking ship ♦ Don't give up the ship! ♦ jump ship ♦ leave a sinking ship ♦ Loose lips sink ships. ♦ run a taut ship ♦ run a tight ship ♦ Shape up or ship out. ♦ shipping and handling ♦ ships that pass in the night ♦ when one's ship comes in

shirk shirk one's duty

shirt give so the shirt off one's back ♦ keep one's shirt on ♦ lose one's shirt

shit beat the shit out of so ♦ full of shit ♦ get one's shit together ♦ know shit from Shinola ♦ not give a shit ♦ scare the shit out of so ♦ shoot the shit ♦ tell shit from Shinola ♦ treat so like shit ♦ up shit creek ♦ What the shit? ♦ when the shit hits the fan

shithouse built like a brick shithouse

shock get the shock of one's life ♦ the shock of one's life

shoe comfortable as an old shoe ♦ common as an old shoe ♦ drop the other shoe ♦ fill so's shoes ♦ have the shoe on the other foot ♦ in so else's shoes ♦ put oneself in so else's shoes ♦ step into so's shoes ♦ tough as (old) (shoe) leather ♦ wait for the other shoe to drop ♦ wouldn't want to be in so's shoes

shoestring get along (on a shoestring) ♦ on a shoestring

shoot as easy as shooting fish in a barrel ♦ like shooting fish in a barrel ♦ shoot so/sth (all) to hell ♦ shoot one's breakfast ♦ shoot one's cookies ♦ shoot daggers at so ♦ shoot sth down ♦ shoot so down in flames ♦ shoot for sth ♦ shoot for the sky ♦ shoot from the hip ♦ shoot oneself in the foot ♦ shoot one's mouth off ♦ shoot (some) hoops ♦ shoot one's supper ♦ shoot the breeze ♦ shoot the bull ♦ shoot the cat ♦ shoot the crap ♦ shoot the shit ♦ shoot the works ♦ shoot one's wad ♦ shot full of holes ♦ shot through with sth ♦ shot to hell ♦ shot to pieces ♦ straight shooter ♦

Sure as shooting! ♦ the whole shooting match

shop close up shop ♦ go window-shopping ♦ set up shop some place ♦ shop around (for sth) ♦ shopping list ♦ talk shop ♦ window-shopping

short at short notice ♦ be short with so ♦ bring so up short ♦ catch so up short ♦ caught short ♦ come short of sth ♦ cut a long story short ♦ a day late and a dollar short ♦ fall short ♦ fall short of one's goal(s) ♦ fall short of the goal(s) ♦ fall short of the record ♦ a few bricks short of a load ♦ a few cards short of a deck ♦ for short ♦ for the short haul ♦ get the short end (of the stick) ♦ in a short space of time ♦ in short ♦ in short order ♦ in short supply ♦ in the short haul ♦ in the short run ♦ keep so on a short leash ♦ life is too short ♦ (a little) short on one end ♦ the long and (the) short of it ♦ long story short ♦ make a long story short ♦ make short work of so/sth ♦ nothing short of some quality ♦ nothing short of sth ♦ on a short leash ♦ on short notice ♦ one sandwich short of a picnic ♦ over the short haul ♦ pull so up short ♦ run short (of sth) ♦ sell so/sth short ♦ short and sweet ♦ the short and (the) long of it ♦ the short end (of the stick) ♦ short for sth ♦ a short fuse ♦ short of sth ♦ short on sth ♦ (a) short shrift ♦ a short temper ♦ short with so ♦ stop short (of doing sth) ♦ stop short of some place ♦ Take a long walk off a short pier. ♦ thick as a short plank ♦ thick as two short planks

shot one's best shot ♦ call (all) the shots ♦ fire a shot across the bow ♦ give sth a shot ♦ a long shot ♦ not by a long shot ♦ off like a shot ♦ a shot at so ♦ a shot at sth ♦ shot full of holes ♦ a shot in the arm ♦ a shot in the dark ♦ shot through with sth ♦ shot to hell ♦ shot to pieces ♦ take a potshot at so/sth

shotgun a shotgun wedding

shoulder carry the weight of the world on one's shoulders ♦ a chip on one's shoulder ♦ cold shoulder ♦ the cold shoulder ♦ give so the cold shoulder ♦ have a chip on one's shoulder ♦ have a good head on one's

keep sight of so/sth ♦ know so by sight ♦ lose sight of so/sth ♦ love at first sight ♦ lower one's sights ♦ no end in sight ♦ on sight ♦ out of sight ♦ partially sighted ♦ raise one's sights ♦ a sad sight ♦ see the sights ♦ set one's sights on so/sth ♦ a sight for sore eyes ♦ a sorry sight ♦ train one's sights on sth

sign give so the high sign ♦ the high sign ♦ sign in ♦ sign one's life away ♦ a sign of the times ♦ sign off ♦ sign off on sth ♦ sign on ♦ sign on the dotted line ♦ sign on (with so/sth) (as sth) ♦ sign out ♦ sign one's own death warrant ♦ signed, sealed, and delivered

signal send out the wrong signals

significance take on a new significance

silence break silence ♦ break the silence

silent silent as the dead ♦ silent as the grave ♦ the strong, silent type

silk smooth as silk ♦ soft as silk

silly bored silly ♦ laugh oneself silly ♦ scared silly ♦ silly as a goose

silver born with a silver spoon in one's mouth ♦ cross so's palm with silver ♦ on a silver platter

simmer simmer down

simple plain and simple ♦ pure and simple ♦ simply not done

sin cover a multitude of sins ♦ hate so/sth like sin ♦ live in sin ♦ ugly as sin

since the greatest thing since indoor plumbing ♦ the greatest thing since sliced bread ♦ since day one ♦ since time immemorial

sing sing a different tune ♦ sing another tune ♦ sing from the same hymn book ♦ sing one's heart out ♦ sing so's/sth's praises ♦ singing the blues ♦ till the fat lady sings ♦ when the fat lady sings

single every single ♦ in (a) single file ♦ in a single stroke ♦ of a single mind (about so/sth) ♦ the last person (to single out for sth)

sink desert a sinking ship ♦ everything but the kitchen sink ♦ fall for sth hook, line, and sinker ♦ have a sinking feeling ♦ have a sinking feeling in the pit of one's stomach ♦ leave a sinking ship ♦ Loose lips sink ships. ♦ makes one's heart sink ♦

sink in ♦ sink sth in(to) so/sth ♦ sink into despair ♦ sink into oblivion ♦ sink or swim ♦ sink one's teeth into sth ♦ sink to (doing) sth ♦ a sinking feeling ♦ a sinking feeling in the pit of one's stomach ♦ swallow sth hook, line, and sinker

sinker fall for sth hook, line, and sinker ♦ swallow sth hook, line, and sinker

siphon siphon sth off (from sth)

sister weak sister

sit able to sit up and take (a little) nourishment ♦ at a sitting ♦ Come in and sit a spell. ♦ Come in and sit down. ♦ like a sitting duck ♦ sit at the feet of so ♦ sit back and let sth happen ♦ sit bolt upright ♦ sit for so ♦ sit for an exam ♦ sit for one's portrait ♦ sit idly by ♦ sit in (for so) ♦ sit in judgment (up)on so/sth ♦ sit in (on sth) ♦ sit on so/sth ♦ sit on one's ass ♦ sit on one's hands ♦ sit on its hands ♦ sit on the edge of one's seat ♦ sit on the fence ♦ sit right with so ♦ sit still for sth ♦ sit tight ♦ sit up and take notice ♦ sit well with so ♦ a sitting duck ♦ sitting on a gold mine ♦ sitting on a powder keg ♦ sitting on top of the world ♦ sitting pretty

situation make the best of a bad situation ♦ no-win situation

six at sixes and sevens ♦ deep-six so/sth ♦ eighty-six sth ♦ It's six of one, half a dozen of another. ♦ six feet under ♦ a sixth sense

sixty do a three-sixty ♦ the sixty-four-dollar question ♦ turn three hundred and sixty degrees

size cut so down to size ♦ pick on so your own size ♦ size so/sth up ♦ That's about the size of it. ♦ try sth (on) (for size) ♦ whittle so down to size

skate awkward as a cow on roller skates ♦ skate on thin ice

skeleton skeleton(s) in the closet

sketch sketch sth out ♦ a thumbnail sketch

skids grease the skids ♦ hit the skids ♦ on the skids ♦ put the skids on (sth)

skillet black as a skillet ♦ busy as popcorn on a skillet

skim skim sth off (of) sth ♦ skim over sth ♦ skim through sth

skin (all) skin and bones ♦ (almost) jump out of one's skin ♦ by the skin of one's teeth ♦ get under so's skin ♦ Give me (some) skin! ♦ jump out of one's skin ♦ knock so some skin ♦ make so's skin crawl ♦ nearly jump out of one's skin ♦ no skin off so's nose ♦ no skin off so's teeth ♦ nothing but skin and bones ♦ save so's skin ♦ skin so alive ♦ skin and bones ♦ Skin me! ♦ Slip me some skin! ♦ soaked to the skin ♦ There's more than one way to skin a cat. ♦ thick-skinned ♦ thin-skinned ♦ under one's skin

skinny skinny as a beanpole ♦ skinny dip

skip one's heart skips a beat ♦ a hop, skip, and a jump ♦ skip bail ♦ skip off (with sth) ♦ skip out (on so/sth)

skittle (all) beer and skittles ♦ beer and skittles

skull get sth through so's thick skull ♦ go out of one's skull ♦ out of one's skull

skunk drunk as a skunk

sky aim for the sky ♦ come out of a clear blue sky ♦ go sky-high ♦ high as the sky ♦ pie in the sky ♦ praise so/sth to the skies ♦ reach for the sky ♦ shoot for the sky ♦ The sky's the limit.

slack cut so some slack ♦ pick the slack up ♦ slack off ♦ take the slack up

slam slam dunk ♦ slam the brakes on ♦ slam the door in so's face

slap slap so down ♦ a slap in the face ♦ slap sth on ♦ a slap on the wrist ♦ slap so on the wrist

slash slash and burn

slate slated for sth ♦ slated to do sth ♦ start (off) with a clean slate ♦ start (over) with a clean slate ♦ wipe so's slate clean

slaughter like lambs to the slaughter

slave be a slave to sth ♦ a slave to sth ♦ work like a slave

sled hard sledding ♦ tough sledding

sleep cry oneself to sleep ♦ drift off to sleep ♦ drop off (to sleep) ♦ get off to sleep ♦ (I've) got to go home and get my beauty sleep. ♦ lose sleep over so/sth ♦ not sleep a wink ♦ put so/animal to sleep ♦ put so to sleep ♦ read oneself to sleep ♦ sleep around the clock ♦ sleep around (with so) ♦ sleep in ♦ sleep like a baby ♦ sleep like a log ♦ sleep sth off ♦ sleep on sth ♦ sleep

tight ♦ sleep together ♦ sleep with so ♦ a sleeping giant

sleeve have an ace up one's sleeve ♦ have one's heart on one's sleeve ♦ have sth up one's sleeve ♦ laugh up one's sleeve ♦ roll one's sleeves up ♦ wear one's heart on one's sleeve

slice the greatest thing since sliced bread ♦ It's been a slice! ♦ no matter how you slice it ♦ a slice of the action ♦ a slice of the cake

slick slick as a whistle

slicker city slicker

slide a landslide victory ♦ let so slide by ♦ let sth slide by ♦ let things slide

slim a slim chance

sling have (got) one's ass in a sling

slip give so the slip ♦ let sth slip by ♦ let sth slip (out) ♦ slip so a Mickey ♦ slip away ♦ slip between the cracks ♦ slip by ♦ slip so five ♦ Slip me five! ♦ Slip me some skin! ♦ slip one's mind ♦ a slip of the tongue ♦ slip out ♦ slip sth over (on so/sth) ♦ slip sth through (sth) ♦ slip through so's fingers ♦ slip through the cracks ♦ slip one's trolley ♦ slip up (on sth)

slippery slippery as an eel ♦ a slippery customer ♦ a slippery slope

slob slob up

slope a slippery slope

slough slough (off) ♦ slough sth off

slow do a slow burn ♦ slow as molasses in January ♦ slow but sure ♦ slow going ♦ slow off the mark ♦ slow on the draw ♦ slow on the uptake ♦ a slow study ♦ slower than molasses in January ♦ slowly but surely ♦ take it slow ♦ twist (slowly) in the wind

sluff sluff (off) ♦ sluff sth off

slug slug it out

slur slur over sth

sly on the sly ♦ do sth on the sly ♦ sly as a fox

smack smack (dab) in the middle ♦ smack so down ♦ a smack in the face ♦ smack one's lips ♦ smack of sth ♦ smack the road

small a big frog in a small pond ♦ small change ♦ a small fortune ♦ small fry ♦ the small hours (of the night) ♦ small potatoes ♦ small print ♦ small-time ♦

Thank God for small favors. ♦ thankful for small blessings

smart get smart (with so) ♦ smart ass ♦ smart at sth ♦ smart money ♦ smart mouth

smash a smash hit

smear a smear campaign (against so) ♦ smear so/sth with sth

smell come out smelling like a rose ♦ come up smelling like a rose ♦ smell a rat ♦ smell blood ♦ smell fishy ♦ smell like a rose ♦ smell to (high) heaven ♦ smell to high heaven ♦ smell sth up ♦ wake up and smell the coffee

smile be all smiles ♦ crack a smile ♦ Keep smiling. ♦ put a smile on so's face ♦ smile from ear to ear ♦ Smile when you say that. ♦ smiling like a Cheshire cat

smithereens blow so/sth to smithereens

smoke go up in smoke ♦ need a smoke ♦ Put that in your pipe and smoke it! ♦ a smoke ♦ smoke and mirrors ♦ smoke like a chimney ♦ smoke so/sth/animal out of sth ♦ smoke-filled room ♦ the smoking gun ♦ Where there's smoke, there's fire.

smooth smooth as glass ♦ smooth as silk ♦ smooth sth out ♦ smooth (so's) ruffled feathers ♦ smooth sailing

smother smother so/sth with sth

snag hit a snag

snail at a snail's pace

snake like fighting snakes ♦ snake in the grass

snakebite snakebite medicine

snap It's a snap. ♦ Make it snappy! ♦ snap at so ♦ snap at sth ♦ snap back (at so) ♦ snap one's cookies ♦ snap so's head off ♦ Snap it up! ♦ snap out of sth ♦ snap to (attention) ♦ Snap to it! ♦ snap sth up

snatch snatch sth up ♦ snatch victory from the jaws of defeat

snazz snazz sth up

sneak sneak around so/sth

sneeze nothing to sneeze at

sniff sniff at so/sth ♦ sniff so/sth out

snipe snipe at so/sth

snit in a snit

snorter rip snorter

snow do a snow job on so ♦ pure as the driven snow ♦ a snow job ♦ snow so/sth

under with sth ♦ snowed under ♦ white as snow ♦ white as the driven snow

snowball not have a snowball's chance in hell ♦ snowball into sth

snuff snuff so out ♦ up to snuff

snug snug as a bug in a rug

snuggle snuggle up (with a (good) book)

soak soak one's face ♦ soak sth up ♦ soaked to the skin

soap no soap ♦ soft soap

sob sob one's heart out ♦ sob story

sober cold sober ♦ sober as a judge ♦ sober so up ♦ stone (cold) sober

society pay one's debt (to society)

sock beat the socks off (of) so ♦ knock so's socks off ♦ Put a sock in it! ♦ sock sth away ♦ sock so/sth in ♦ sock it to so ♦ Stuff a sock in it!

soft have a soft spot (in one's heart) for so/sth/animal ♦ soft as a baby's backside ♦ soft as a baby's bottom ♦ soft as down ♦ soft as silk ♦ soft as velvet ♦ soft in the head ♦ soft money ♦ soft on so ♦ soft on sth ♦ soft pedal sth ♦ soft sell ♦ soft soap ♦ soft touch ♦ soften one's stance (on so/sth) ♦ soften the blow ♦ soften up ♦ soften so up ♦ walk soft

soil soil one's diaper(s) ♦ soil one's hands

solace take solace (in sth)

sold sold on so/sth ♦ sold out

solid have a (solid) grasp of sth ♦ solid as a rock ♦ a (solid) grasp of sth

Solomon wise as Solomon

some and then some ♦ at some length ♦ at some point (in the future) ♦ at some point (in the past) ♦ at some time or another ♦ bag some rays ♦ blow off (some) steam ♦ bust (some) suds ♦ Catch me some other time. ♦ catch some rays ♦ catch some Zs ♦ cause (some) eyebrows to raise ♦ cause (some) tongues to wag ♦ Come in and get some weight off your feet. ♦ cop some Zs ♦ crack some suds ♦ cut so some slack ♦ cut some Zs ♦ dig some dirt up (on so) ♦ get some shut-eye ♦ get (some) steam up ♦ Give me (some) skin! ♦ give so some lip ♦ give some thought to sth ♦ have enough and some to spare ♦ have some elbow room ♦ have (some) time to kill ♦ have to go some (to do sth) ♦ in some respects ♦ It takes (some) getting used to. ♦ It will take some doing. ♦ kick some ass (around) ♦ knock some heads together ♦ knock some sense into so ♦ knock so some skin ♦ lay some sweet lines on so ♦ let off (some) steam ♦ make (some) sense (out) of so/sth ♦ open some doors (for so) ♦ pop (some) tops ♦ pull (some) strings ♦ pump (some) iron ♦ put out (some) feelers (on so/sth) ♦ put some distance between so and oneself or sth ♦ put some sweet lines on so ♦ put some teeth into sth ♦ shake some sense into so ♦ shed (some) light on sth ♦ shoot (some) hoops ♦ Slip me some skin! ♦ some elbow room ♦ some loose ends ♦ (some) new blood ♦ some pumpkins ♦ some shut-eye ♦ take care of some loose ends ♦ take (some) names ♦ throw (some) light on sth ♦ to some extent ♦ turn some heads ♦ use some elbow grease

something Do you want to know something? ♦ (Do you) want to make something of it? ♦ Have I got something for you! ♦ something of the sort ♦ something or other ♦ Something's got to give. ♦ something's up ♦ something to that effect ♦ There is something to be said for sth. ♦ Want to know something? ♦ You want to make something of it?

sometime Drop in sometime. ♦ We all gotta go sometime.

somewhere Haven't I seen you somewhere before? ♦ somewhere along the line ♦ somewhere down the line

son every mother's son (of them) ♦ son of a bachelor ♦ son of a bitch ♦ son of a gun ♦ son of a sea biscuit

song buy sth for a song ♦ for a song ♦ go into a song and dance (about sth) ♦ go into one's song and dance ♦ go into the same old song and dance (about sth) ♦ sell sth for a song ♦ swan song

soon as soon as ♦ Don't speak too soon. ♦ had (just) as soon do sth ♦ had sooner do sth ♦ I spoke too soon. ♦ I'd (just) as soon (as) do sth ♦ No sooner said than done. ♦ no sooner than some time ♦ pretty soon ♦ soon as possible ♦ sooner or later ♦ The

sooner the better. ♦ speak too soon ♦ too much too soon ♦ would (just) as soon do sth

sore hit a sore point ♦ a sight for sore eyes ♦ stand out like a sore thumb ♦ stick out like a sore thumb ♦ touch a sore point ♦ touch a sore spot

sorrow drown one's sorrows ♦ share so's sorrow

sorry (Are you) sorry you asked? ♦ better safe than sorry ♦ sorry (a)bout that ♦ a sorry sight ♦ a sorry state of affairs ♦ Sorry you asked?

sort in bad sorts ♦ sth of sorts ♦ out of sorts ♦ something of the sort ♦ sort of sth ♦ sort oneself out ♦ sort sth out

sought much sought after

soul bare one's soul (to so) ♦ can't call one's soul one's own ♦ enough to keep body and soul together ♦ every living soul ♦ God rest so's soul. ♦ gripe one's soul ♦ heart and soul ♦ keep body and soul together ♦ not a living soul ♦ not tell a (living) soul ♦ pour one's heart (and soul) into sth ♦ pour out one's soul ♦ put one's heart (and soul) into sth ♦ sell one's soul (to the devil) ♦ with all one's heart (and soul)

sound safe and sound ♦ sound as a bell ♦ sound as a dollar ♦ sound asleep ♦ a (sound) grasp of sth ♦ sound like a broken record ♦ sound off (about sth) ♦ sound so out ♦ sound sth out ♦ sound the death knell

soup alphabet soup ♦ duck soup ♦ easy as duck soup ♦ everything from soup to nuts ♦ in the soup ♦ Soup's on! ♦ soup sth up ♦ thick as pea soup

sour go sour ♦ hit a sour note ♦ sour as vinegar ♦ sour grapes ♦ strike a sour note ♦ sweet and sour

South down South ♦ go South ♦ head South ♦ a mouth full of South

sow sow one's wild oats

space in a short space of time ♦ space out ♦ spaced (out) ♦ take up space ♦ a waste of space

spade black as the ace of spades ♦ call a spade a spade ♦ cocky as the king of spades ♦ in spades ♦ spade sth up

Spain build castles in Spain

span spick-and-span

spank brand spanking new

spar spar with so

spare and sth to spare ♦ have enough and some to spare ♦ have sth to spare ♦ in one's spare time ♦ not a moment to spare ♦ not spare any effort to do sth ♦ spare no effort to do sth ♦ spare no expense ♦ spare tire ♦ with sth to spare ♦ without a moment to spare

spark spark sth off

speak as we speak ♦ Don't speak too soon. ♦ (even) as we speak ♦ I spoke out of turn. ♦ I spoke too soon. ♦ in a manner of speaking ♦ know whereof one speaks ♦ not to speak of so/sth ♦ nothing to speak of ♦ on speaking terms (with so) ♦ so to speak ♦ speak as one ♦ speak at great length ♦ speak down to so ♦ speak for oneself ♦ speak for so/sth ♦ speak for itself ♦ speak highly of so/sth ♦ speak ill of so ♦ speak so's language ♦ speak one's mind ♦ speak of so/sth ♦ speak of the devil (and he appears) ♦ speak of the devil (and in he comes) ♦ speak off the cuff ♦ speak out of turn ♦ speak out (on sth) ♦ speak one's piece ♦ speak the same language ♦ speak to sth ♦ speak too soon ♦ speak up ♦ speak volumes ♦ speak with a forked tongue ♦ speak with so (about so/sth) ♦ speak with one voice ♦ spoken for ♦ strictly speaking ♦ to speak out of both sides of one's mouth

spear take the spear (in one's chest)

spec on spec

special Saturday night special

spectacle make a spectacle of so

speed at full speed ♦ get up to speed on so/sth ♦ pick up speed ♦ reach speeds of some number ♦ speeds of some number ♦ up to speed

spell break the spell ♦ Come in and sit a spell. ♦ Do I have to spell it out (for you)? ♦ dry spell ♦ have so in one's spell ♦ have so under a spell ♦ spell so (at sth) ♦ spell disaster ♦ spell sth out ♦ spell trouble ♦ under a spell

spend spend money like it's going out of style ♦ spend money like there's no tomorrow ♦ spending money ♦ tax-and-spend

spew spew one's guts (out)

spice spice sth up

spick spick-and-span

spiff spiff sth up ♦ spiffed out

spill cry over spilled milk ♦ spill one's guts ♦ spill (out) into sth ♦ spill the beans ♦ spill the works ♦ take a spill

spin for a spin ♦ go for a spin ♦ go into a tailspin ♦ go out for a spin ♦ make so's head spin ♦ put a spin on sth ♦ spin a yarn ♦ spin doctor ♦ spin in one's grave ♦ spin sth off ♦ spin one's wheels

spindle fold, spindle, or mutilate

spirit in good spirits ♦ spirit so/sth away (some place) ♦ That's the spirit!

spit mad enough to chew nails (and spit rivets) ♦ mad enough to spit nails ♦ the spit and image of so ♦ spit and polish ♦ spit sth out ♦ spit up ♦ spit sth up ♦ the spitting image of so ♦ within spitting distance

spite cut off one's nose to spite one's face ♦ in spite of so/sth ♦ out of spite

splash splash down

spleen vent one's spleen

split in a split second ♦ split a gut ♦ split hairs ♦ split people up ♦ a split second ♦ split one's sides (with laughter) ♦ split the difference ♦ split up (with so) ♦ a splitting headache ♦ vote a split ticket

spoil spoiled rotten ♦ spoiling for a fight

spoke I spoke out of turn. ♦ I spoke too soon.

spoken spoken for

sponge sponge sth off of so/sth ♦ throw in the sponge ♦ toss in the sponge

spook spook so/sth

spoon born with a silver spoon in one's mouth ♦ a greasy spoon ♦ spoon-feed so

sport a good sport ♦ the sport of kings ♦ sport with so/sth ♦ a sporting chance

spot have a soft spot (in one's heart) for so/sth/animal ♦ hit the high spots ♦ hit the spot ♦ in a (tight) spot ♦ Johnny-on-the-spot ♦ on the spot ♦ rooted to the spot ♦ spot so (sth) ♦ touch a sore spot ♦ X marks the spot

spotlight in the spotlight ◆ steal the spotlight

spout spout off (about so/sth) ◆ spout sth out

sprain sprain one's ankle

spread spread like wildfire ◆ spread the word ◆ spread oneself too thin ◆ spread one's wings (and fly)

spring no spring chicken ◆ spring for sth ◆ spring into action ◆ spring sth on so ◆ spring to attention ◆ spring to so's defense ◆ spring to one's feet ◆ spring to life ◆ spring to mind

sprout sprout wings

spruce (all) spruced up ◆ get (all) spruced up ◆ spruce so/sth up

spunk get enough spunk up (to do sth)

spur on the spur of the moment ◆ spur so on

square back to square one ◆ Be there or be square. ◆ call sth square ◆ do sth fair and square ◆ fair and square ◆ go back to square one ◆ square accounts (with so) ◆ a square deal ◆ square off (for sth) ◆ a square peg (in a round hole) ◆ square up to so/sth ◆ square up with so ◆ square with so ◆ square with sth ◆ squared away ◆ three squares (a day)

squat cop a squat

squawk squawk about sth

squeak squeak by (so/sth) ◆ squeak through (sth) ◆ squeak sth through

squeal squeal (on so) (to so)

squeeze put the squeeze on (so) ◆ squeeze sth from sth ◆ squeeze so out ◆ squeeze (themselves) up

squirm squirm out (of sth)

squirrel squirrel sth away

stab a stab at so ◆ a stab at sth ◆ stab so in the back

stack black as a stack of black cats ◆ blow one's stack ◆ the cards are stacked against so ◆ have the cards stacked against one ◆ have the deck stacked against one ◆ stack the cards (against so/sth) ◆ stack the deck (against so/sth) ◆ stack up to so/sth ◆ swear on a stack of Bibles

staff plain as a pikestaff

stag go stag

stage at this stage (of the game) ◆ boo so off the stage ◆ hiss so off ((of) the stage) ◆ hoot so off the stage ◆ in a stage whisper ◆ laugh so off the stage ◆ set the stage for sth ◆ take center stage ◆ take the stage

stain stain sth with sth

stake burn so at the stake ◆ have a stake in sth ◆ pull up stakes ◆ put so/sth at stake ◆ raise the stakes ◆ stake so/sth out ◆ stake (out) a claim to sth ◆ stake one's reputation on so/sth ◆ stake so to sth ◆ up stakes

stall stall so/sth off

stamp one's old stamping ground ◆ stamp so out ◆ stamp sth out

stance soften one's stance (on so/sth)

stand able to do sth standing on one's head ◆ as it stands ◆ as things stand ◆ cause so's hair to stand on end ◆ Don't stand on ceremony. ◆ feel one's hair stand on end ◆ feel the hair on the back of one's neck stand on end ◆ from where I stand ◆ have one's heart stand still ◆ one's heart stands still ◆ It (only) stands to reason. ◆ know where so stands (on so/sth) ◆ make a stand (against so/sth) ◆ make so's hair stand on end ◆ more than one can stand ◆ not able to stand so/sth ◆ not have a leg to stand on ◆ on the (witness) stand ◆ one-night stand ◆ stand so/sth ◆ stand a chance (of doing sth) ◆ stand and deliver ◆ stand apart (from so/sth) ◆ stand aside ◆ stand behind so/sth ◆ stand by ◆ stand by so ◆ stand corrected ◆ stand down ◆ stand for sth ◆ stand one's ground ◆ stand head and shoulders above so/sth ◆ stand idly by ◆ stand in awe (of so/sth) ◆ stand (in) back of so/sth ◆ stand in (for so) ◆ stand so in good stead ◆ stand so/sth off ◆ stand on ceremony ◆ stand on one's dignity ◆ stand on one's head ◆ stand sth on its head ◆ stand on one's (own) two feet ◆ stand out from the crowd ◆ stand out from the rest ◆ stand out like a sore thumb ◆ stand pat (on sth) ◆ stand still for sth ◆ stand tall ◆ stand the test of time ◆ stand there with one's bare face hanging out ◆ stand so to a treat ◆ stand to lose sth ◆ stand to reason ◆ stand together ◆ stand trial ◆ stand up ◆ stand so up ◆ stand up against so/sth ◆

stand up and be counted ♦ stand up before so ♦ stand up for so/sth ♦ stand up in court ♦ stand up to so/sth ♦ stand up (under sth) ♦ stand well with so ♦ stand with so ♦ a standing joke ♦ sure as I'm standing here ♦ take a (firm) stand on sth ♦ take a stand (against so/sth) ♦ take the stand ♦ time stands still ♦ the way things stand ♦ (with)stand the test of time

standard come up to so's standards

standby on standby

standstill bring sth to a standstill

star have stars in one's eyes ♦ see stars ♦ star as so/sth ♦ star in sth ♦ star-crossed lovers ♦ stars in one's eyes ♦ thank one's lucky stars ♦ think so hung the moon (and stars)

starch take the starch out of so

stare give so a blank stare ♦ stare so in the face ♦ stare sth in the face

stark stark raving mad

start by fits and starts ♦ Don't start (on me)! ♦ fits and starts ♦ for starters ♦ a fresh start ♦ from start to finish ♦ get a head start (on so) ♦ get one's start ♦ get so started (talking) ♦ give so a start ♦ a head start (on so) ♦ a head start (on sth) ♦ jump-start so/sth ♦ make a start on sth ♦ off to a bad start ♦ off (to a flying start) ♦ off to a good start (with so/sth) ♦ off to a running start ♦ (right) out of the (starting) blocks ♦ (right) out of the (starting) gate ♦ one's start ♦ start sth ♦ start a fire under so ♦ start from scratch ♦ start sth off ♦ start off on the wrong foot ♦ start (off) with a bang ♦ start (off) with a clean slate ♦ start on so/sth ♦ start (over) with a clean slate ♦ start the ball rolling

state a fine state of affairs ♦ in a (constant) state of flux ♦ keep so in (a state of) suspense ♦ lie in state ♦ a pretty state of affairs ♦ a sad state of affairs ♦ the separation of church and state ♦ a sorry state of affairs ♦ state of mind ♦ state of the art

static give so static

station busy as Grand Central Station ♦ station so at sth

stave stave so/sth off ♦ stave sth off

stay Come back when you can stay longer. ♦ have no staying power ♦ stay abreast of sth ♦ stay after so (about sth) ♦ stay ahead of the game ♦ stay clear of so/sth ♦ stay in touch (with so/sth) ♦ stay loose ♦ stay on sth ♦ stay on (after so/sth) ♦ stay on top of so/sth ♦ stay out (of sth) ♦ Stay out of my way. ♦ Stay out of this! ♦ stay the course

stead hold so in good stead ♦ in so's stead ♦ stand so in good stead

steady go (steady) with so ♦ steady as a rock

steal steal a base ♦ steal a march on so/sth ♦ steal so's heart ♦ steal over so/sth ♦ steal the show ♦ steal the spotlight ♦ steal so's thunder

steam blow off (some) steam ♦ full steam ahead ♦ get (some) steam up ♦ get up a (full) head of steam ♦ let off (some) steam ♦ pick up steam ♦ run out of steam ♦ steam across sth ♦ steam so's beam ♦ steam up ♦ steam so up ♦ steamed (up) ♦ steaming (mad) ♦ under one's own steam

steel have a mind as sharp as a steel trap ♦ nerves of steel ♦ steel so against so/sth ♦ steel oneself for sth ♦ a steely gaze ♦ true as steel

steep a little steep ♦ steep so in sth

steer a bum steer ♦ give so a bum steer ♦ kick like a steer ♦ steer clear of so/sth

stem from stem to stern ♦ stem from sth ♦ stem the flow (of so/sth) ♦ stem the tide (of so/sth)

step (Do) you want to step outside? ♦ fall in(to step) ♦ follow in so's footsteps ♦ in step (with so) ♦ in step (with so/sth) ♦ in step (with sth) ♦ keep one step ahead of so/sth ♦ lay sth at so's doorstep ♦ one step ahead of so/sth ♦ one step at a time ♦ out of step (with so/sth) ♦ overstep one's bounds ♦ overstep the bounds of good taste ♦ step aside (for so) ♦ step away from one's desk ♦ step back in time ♦ step by step ♦ step down (from sth) ♦ step forward ♦ step into so's shoes ♦ step in(to the breach) ♦ step off on the wrong foot ♦ step off (to the side) with so ♦ step on it ♦ step on the gas ♦ step on so's toes ♦ step out of line ♦ step out (on so) ♦ step outside ♦ step right up ♦ step sth up ♦

step up to the plate ♦ take a step in the right direction ♦ take steps (to prevent sth) ♦ watch one's step

stern from stem to stern

steven even steven

stew get (oneself) into a stew (over so/sth) ♦ in a stew (about so/sth) ♦ stew in one's own juice

stick get on the stick ♦ get the short end (of the stick) ♦ have sth stick in one's craw ♦ have sticky fingers ♦ make sth stick ♦ more so/sth than one can shake a stick at ♦ not hold a stick to so/sth ♦ on the stick ♦ the short end (of the stick) ♦ stick around (some place) ♦ stick by so ♦ stick by sth ♦ Stick 'em up! ♦ stick one's foot in one's mouth ♦ stick one's head in the sand ♦ stick in so's mind ♦ stick in the mud ♦ stick it to so ♦ stick man ♦ stick one's neck out (for so/sth) ♦ stick one's nose in (where it's not wanted) ♦ stick one's nose in(to sth) ♦ stick one's nose up in the air ♦ stick one's oar in ♦ stick sth out ♦ stick out a mile ♦ stick out like a sore thumb ♦ stick to so/sth ♦ stick to so's fingers ♦ stick to one's guns ♦ stick to one's ribs ♦ stick together ♦ stick so/sth up ♦ stick up for so/sth ♦ stick so with so/sth ♦ Stick with it. ♦ stuck on so/sth ♦ stuck with so/sth ♦ one's words stick in one's throat

sticky have sticky fingers

stiff bore so stiff ♦ bored stiff ♦ scare so stiff ♦ scared stiff ♦ stiff as a poker ♦ a working stiff

still bring sth to a standstill ♦ have one's heart stand still ♦ one's heart stands still ♦ hold still for sth ♦ The jury is still out (on so/sth). ♦ keep sth still ♦ sit still for sth ♦ so still you could hear a pin drop ♦ stand still for sth ♦ still as death ♦ time stands still

stink create a stink (about sth) ♦ kick up a stink (about sth) ♦ like stink ♦ make a (big) stink (about so/sth) ♦ make a stink (about sth) ♦ raise a (big) stink (about so/sth) ♦ raise a stink (about sth) ♦ run like stink ♦ stink on ice ♦ stink to high heaven ♦ stink sth up ♦ stinking rich ♦ stinking with sth

stir cause (quite a) stir ♦ go stir crazy ♦ stir crazy ♦ stir so up ♦ stir sth up ♦ stir up a hornet's nest

stitch in stitches ♦ keep so in stitches ♦ not have a stitch of clothes (on)

stock have sth in stock ♦ in stock ♦ laughingstock (of so/group) ♦ lock, stock, and barrel ♦ make oneself or sth a laughingstock ♦ make a laughingstock (out) of oneself or sth ♦ not put (a lot) of stock in sth ♦ out of stock ♦ play the (stock) market ♦ put no stock in sth ♦ stock in trade ♦ stock up on sth ♦ take no stock in sth ♦ take stock (of sth)

stoke stoke sth up ♦ stoked on so/sth ♦ stoked out

stomach butterflies in one's stomach ♦ cannot stomach so/sth ♦ can't stomach so/sth ♦ cast-iron stomach ♦ one's eyes are bigger than one's stomach ♦ get butterflies in one's stomach ♦ have a sinking feeling in the pit of one's stomach ♦ have no stomach for sth ♦ not able to stomach so/sth ♦ not have the stomach for sth ♦ the pit of one's stomach ♦ a sinking feeling in the pit of one's stomach ♦ turn so's stomach ♦ weak stomach

stomp stomp on so

stone bust (so's) stones ♦ carve sth in stone ♦ carved in stone ♦ cast the first stone ♦ engraved in stone ♦ hard as stone ♦ have a heart of stone ♦ keep one's nose to the grindstone ♦ kill two birds with one stone ♦ leave no stone unturned ♦ a milestone in so's life ♦ a millstone about one's neck ♦ put one's nose to the grindstone ♦ run into a stone wall ♦ stone (cold) sober ♦ stone dead ♦ a stone's throw away ♦ within a stone's throw (of sth) ♦ written in stone

stood should have stood in bed

stool fall between two stools ♦ stool (on so)

stoop stoop to some level

stop The buck stops here. ♦ a nature stop ♦ not stop at anything (to do sth) ♦ pull all the stops out ♦ put a stop to sth ♦ stop at nothing (to do sth) ♦ stop so cold ♦ stop (dead) in one's tracks ♦ stop so/sth dead in so's/sth's tracks ♦ stop, look, and listen ♦

stop on a dime ♦ stop short (of doing sth) ♦ stop short of some place ♦ stop-and-go

storage in cold storage ♦ in storage

store have sth in store (for so) ♦ in store (for so) ♦ lie in store (for so) ♦ mind the store ♦ set great store by so/sth ♦ watch the store

stork a visit from the stork

storm any port in a storm ♦ the calm before the storm ♦ the eye of the storm ♦ kick up a storm ♦ the lull before the storm ♦ ride out the storm ♦ risk of thunder(storms) ♦ storm at so/sth ♦ storm in(to some place) ♦ A storm is brewing. ♦ storm out (of some place) ♦ take so/sth by storm ♦ talk up a storm ♦ up a storm ♦ weather the storm

story break a story ♦ cock-and-bull story ♦ cut a long story short ♦ End of story. ♦ fish story ♦ the inside story ♦ long story short ♦ make a long story short ♦ the same old story ♦ a shaggy-dog story ♦ sob story ♦ tell its own story ♦ That's the story of my life. ♦ top story ♦ upper story ♦ a whole nother story

straddle straddle the fence

straight can't see straight ♦ get sth straight ♦ get the facts straight ♦ give it to so (straight) ♦ go straight ♦ go (straight) to the top ♦ have one's head screwed on straight ♦ have the facts straight ♦ keep a straight face ♦ keep people straight ♦ keep things straight ♦ keep to the straight and narrow (path) ♦ put sth straight ♦ set so straight ♦ set sth straight ♦ set the record straight ♦ the straight and narrow ♦ straight as an arrow ♦ the straight dope ♦ a straight face ♦ (straight) from the horse's mouth ♦ straight from the shoulder ♦ straight low ♦ straight man ♦ straight off the bat ♦ straight out ♦ straight shooter ♦ straight talk ♦ straight up ♦ straighten out ♦ straighten so out ♦ straighten sth out ♦ straighten up ♦ straighten so/sth up ♦ straighten up and fly right ♦ think straight ♦ vote a straight ticket

strain crack under the strain ♦ place a strain on so/sth ♦ put a strain on so/sth ♦ strain at the leash

strait in dire straits

stranger Don't be a stranger. ♦ no stranger to sth ♦ a perfect stranger ♦ a total stranger

strap strapped for sth

straw clutching at straws ♦ draw straws for sth ♦ grasping at straws ♦ the last straw ♦ a straw man ♦ the straw that broke the camel's back

streak be on a losing streak ♦ have a yellow streak down one's back ♦ a losing streak ♦ a lucky streak ♦ a mean streak ♦ a streak of bad luck ♦ a streak of good luck ♦ a streak of luck ♦ talk a blue streak ♦ a yellow streak (down so's back)

stream change horses in midstream ♦ change horses in the middle of the stream ♦ in the mainstream (of sth)

street down the street ♦ the man in the street ♦ on easy street ♦ on the street ♦ put sth on the street ♦ take it to the street ♦ a two-way street

strength at full strength ♦ by brute strength ♦ by main strength and awkwardness ♦ go from strength to strength ♦ main strength and awkwardness ♦ not know one's own strength ♦ on the strength of sth ♦ pillar of strength ♦ a tower of strength

stress lay stress on sth ♦ no stress

stretch at a stretch ♦ down the road a stretch ♦ in the (home)stretch ♦ make one's money stretch ♦ not by any stretch of the imagination ♦ stretch a point ♦ stretch one's legs ♦ stretch one's money ♦ stretch the point ♦ stretch the truth

stricken stricken with sth

strict strictly business ♦ strictly from hunger ♦ (strictly) on the level ♦ (strictly) on the up-and-up ♦ strictly speaking

stride attain one's stride ♦ break one's stride ♦ get into one's stride ♦ hit one's stride ♦ put one off one's stride ♦ reach one's stride ♦ take sth in (one's) stride

strike go (out) on strike ♦ have two strikes against one ♦ It strikes me that . . . ♦ out on strike ♦ strike a balance (between two things) ♦ strike a bargain ♦ strike a blow against so/sth ♦ strike a blow for so/sth ♦ strike a chord (with so) ♦ strike a deal ♦ strike a happy medium ♦ strike a match ♦ strike a pose ♦ strike a sour note ♦ strike so as sth ♦ strike sth down ♦ strike so's fancy ♦ strike so funny ♦ strike home with so ♦ strike it rich ♦ strike out ♦ strike sth out ♦ strike out on one's own ♦ strike pay dirt ♦ strike the right note ♦ strike up a conversation (with so) ♦ strike up a friendship (with so) ♦ strike up the band ♦ strike while the iron is hot ♦ two strikes against one ♦ within striking distance

string control the purse strings ♦ get along (on a shoestring) ♦ have so on the string ♦ hold the purse strings ♦ The latch string is always out. ♦ on a shoestring ♦ on a string ♦ play on so's heartstrings ♦ pull on so's heartstrings ♦ pull (some) strings ♦ string so along ♦ string along (with so) ♦ a string of bad luck ♦ a string of good luck ♦ string sth out ♦ string so up ♦ strings attached ♦ strung out ♦ tied to one's mother's apron strings ♦ tug at so's heartstrings ♦ without any strings attached

strip strip to sth

stroke at one stroke ♦ have a stroke ♦ in a single stroke ♦ stroke so's ego ♦ a stroke of genius ♦ a stroke of good fortune ♦ a stroke of luck

strong come on strong ♦ going strong ♦ strong as a bull ♦ strong as a horse ♦ strong as a lion ♦ strong as an ox ♦ the strong, silent type ♦ strong-arm tactics

struggle give up the struggle ♦ put up a struggle ♦ struggle to the death ♦ an uphill struggle

strung strung out

strut strut one's stuff

stub stub sth out

stuck stuck on so/sth ♦ stuck with so/sth

study a quick study ♦ a slow study

stuff beat the stuffing out of so ♦ Cut the funny stuff! ♦ get one's stuff together ♦ green stuff ♦ kid's stuff ♦ know one's stuff ♦ the right stuff ♦ rough stuff ♦ show so one's stuff ♦ strut one's stuff ♦ Stuff a sock in it! ♦ stuff and nonsense ♦ stuff sth down so's throat ♦ stuff one's face ♦ stuff so's head with sth ♦ stuff the ballot box

stumble stumble across so/sth ♦ a stumbling block

stump on the stump ♦ out stumping (some place) ♦ stump so ♦ stump for so ♦ You've got me stumped.

stunt pull a stunt (on so)

stupor in a stupor

style after the style of so/sth ♦ cramp so's style ♦ in style ♦ like it is going out of style ♦ out of style ♦ spend money like it's going out of style

sub sub for so/sth

subject change the subject ♦ Drop the subject! ♦ off the subject ♦ subject to sth

sublime from the sublime to the ridiculous

subscribe subscribe to sth

substance form and substance ♦ sum and substance

succeed succeed so as sth

success the key to success

such as such ♦ Like it's such a big deal! ♦ No such luck. ♦ such as it is ♦ There's no such thing as a free lunch.

suck suck so's hind tit ♦ suck so in ♦ suck sth in ♦ suck up to so ♦ teach one's grandmother to suck eggs ♦ That sucks.

sucker a sucker for so/sth ♦ a sucker for punishment ♦ sucker so into sth ♦ sucker list

sudden all of a sudden

suds bust (some) suds ♦ crack some suds

sue So, sue me! ♦ sue the pants off (of) so

suffer not suffer fools gladly ♦ not suffer fools lightly ♦ suffer a setback ♦ suffer an attack (of an illness) ♦ suffer the consequences

sufficiency an elegant sufficiency

sugar sweet as sugar

suggestive suggestive of sth

suit follow suit ♦ in one's birthday suit ♦ (It) suits me (fine). ♦ monkey suit ♦ suit one's actions to one's words ♦ suit so's fancy ♦ suit so to a T ♦ Suit yourself. ♦ suited for sth ♦ Suits me (fine).

suitcase live out of a suitcase

suite Tout suite!

sum sum and substance

summary in summary

sun everything under the sun ♦ make hay (while the sun shines) ♦ the sun belt ♦

think the sun rises and sets on so ♦ under the sun ♦ where the sun don't shine

Sunday Haven't seen you in a month of Sundays. ♦ in a month of Sundays ♦ in one's Sunday best ♦ Sunday best ♦ Sunday driver ♦ Sunday-go-to-meeting clothes

sundry all and sundry

sunny sunny-side up

sunset one's sunset years

sunshine a ray of sunshine

superhighway electronic superhighway ♦ information superhighway

supper shoot one's supper

supply in short supply

support pillar of support

suppose supposed to do sth

sure Don't be too sure. ♦ for sure ♦ make sure all the bases are covered ♦ slow but sure ♦ slowly but surely ♦ sure as eggs is eggs ♦ sure as fate ♦ sure as God made little green apples ♦ sure as hell ♦ sure as I'm standing here ♦ Sure as shooting! ♦ sure as you live ♦ a sure bet ♦ a sure thing ♦ swift and sure

surf surf and turf ♦ surf the Net

surface on the surface of the earth ♦ scratch the surface

surgery in surgery

surprise catch so by surprise ♦ come as no surprise ♦ take so by surprise ♦ take so/sth by surprise

survival the survival of the fittest

susceptible susceptible to sth

suspense keep so in (a state of) suspense

suspicion above suspicion ♦ under a cloud (of suspicion)

suspicious a suspicious character

swallow a bitter pill (to swallow) ♦ hard to swallow ♦ look like the cat that swallowed the canary ♦ swallow sth hook, line, and sinker ♦ swallow one's pride ♦ swallow so/sth up

swan graceful as a swan ♦ swan song

swap swap notes (on so/sth)

swath cut a big swath ♦ cut a wide swath

sway hold sway (among a group) ♦ hold sway (over so/sth) ♦ sway so to sth

swear swear by so/sth ♦ swear like a trooper ♦ swear (sth) off ♦ swear on a

stack of Bibles ♦ swear on one's mother's grave

sweat blood, sweat, and tears ♦ break out in a cold sweat ♦ by the sweat of one's brow ♦ in a cold sweat ♦ no sweat ♦ sweat blood ♦ sweat bullets ♦ sweat for sth ♦ sweat sth out ♦ sweat sth out of so ♦ sweat weight off ♦ work up a sweat ♦ work oneself (up) into a sweat

sweep a clean sweep ♦ make a clean sweep ♦ sweep so away ♦ sweep so into sth ♦ sweep one off one's feet ♦ sweep out of some place ♦ sweep sth under the carpet ♦ sweep sth under the rug

sweet all sweetness and light ♦ fresh and sweet ♦ have a sweet tooth ♦ lay some sweet lines on so ♦ put some sweet lines on so ♦ short and sweet ♦ sweet and sour ♦ sweet as honey ♦ sweet as sugar ♦ sweet nothings ♦ sweet on so ♦ sweeten the pot ♦ sweeten (up) the deal ♦ sweeter than honey ♦ sweet-talk so ♦ You bet your (sweet) life!

sweetheart sweetheart agreement ♦ sweetheart deal

swell swell with sth ♦ a swelled head

swift swift and sure ♦ swift as an arrow ♦ swift as lightning ♦ swift as the wind ♦ swift as thought

swim in the swim of things ♦ make so's head swim ♦ out of the swim of things ♦ sink or swim ♦ swim against the current ♦ swim against the tide ♦ swimming in sth

swine cast (one's) pearls before swine

swing come out swinging ♦ get in(to) the swing of things ♦ in full swing ♦ not enough room to swing a cat ♦ swing sth ♦ swing by ♦ swing into high gear

switch asleep at the switch ♦ bait and switch ♦ fall asleep at the switch ♦ switch gears ♦ switch off ♦ switch on ♦ switched on

swoop at one fell swoop ♦ in one fell swoop

sword cross swords (with so) ♦ a double-edged sword ♦ fall on one's sword ♦ a two-edged sword

sync out of sync

system All systems (are) go. ♦ beat the system ♦ buck the system ♦ get sth out of one's **system**

T

tab keep tab(s) (on so/sth) ♦ pick up the tab (for sth) ♦ run a tab ♦ tab so for sth

table bring sth to the table ♦ clear the table ♦ coffee-table book ♦ drink so under the table ♦ get so around the table ♦ lay one's cards on the table ♦ on the table ♦ put one's cards on the table ♦ set the table ♦ table a motion ♦ turn the tables (on so) ♦ under the table ♦ wait (on) tables

tack get down to brass tacks ♦ sharp as a tack ♦ tack sth onto sth

tactic strong-arm tactics

tag put a price (tag) on sth ♦ tag so out

tail bright-eyed and bushy-tailed ♦ come up tails ♦ freeze one's tail off ♦ get off so's tail ♦ get one's tail in gear ♦ have a tiger by the tail ♦ heads or tails ♦ hightail it out of some place ♦ in two shakes of a lamb's tail ♦ make heads or tails (out) of so/sth ♦ not able to make head or tail of sth ♦ on so's tail ♦ tail off ♦ the tail wagging the dog ♦ turn tail (and run) ♦ two shakes of a lamb's tail ♦ with one's tail between one's legs ♦ work one's tail off

tailspin go into a tailspin

take able to sit up and take (a little) nourishment ♦ able to take a joke ♦ able to take just so much ♦ able to take only so much ♦ as a duck takes to water ♦ as easy as taking candy from a baby ♦ can take it to the bank ♦ Come in and take a load off your feet. ♦ do a double take ♦ for the taking ♦ one's for the taking ♦ (free) for the taking ♦ Give one an inch and one will take a mile. ♦ give or take an amount ♦ give-and-take ♦ hard to take ♦ have (got) what it takes ♦ (Is) this (seat) taken? ♦ It takes all kinds (to make a world). ♦ (It) takes one to know one. ♦ It takes (some) getting used to. ♦ It will take some doing. ♦ it would take an act of Congress to do

sth ♦ (just) taking care of business ♦ let nature take its course ♦ like taking candy from a baby ♦ a lot of give-and-take ♦ more than one can take ♦ no offense taken ♦ not take no for an answer ♦ on the take ♦ so's point is well taken ♦ sit up and take notice ♦ take sth ♦ take a backseat (to so/sth) ♦ take a bath (on sth) ♦ take a beating ♦ take a bite out of sth ♦ take a bow ♦ take a break ♦ take a chance on so/sth ♦ Take a deep breath. ♦ take a dig at so ♦ take a dim view of so/sth ♦ take a dive ♦ take a drag (on sth) ♦ take a fall ♦ take a fancy to so/sth ♦ take a firm grip on so/sth ♦ take a (firm) stand on sth ♦ take a gander (at so/sth) ♦ take a hand in sth ♦ take a hard line (with so) ♦ take a hike ♦ take a hint ♦ take a jab at so ♦ take a leaf out of so's book ♦ take a leak ♦ take a liking to so/sth ♦ take a load off one's feet ♦ take a load off (of) so's mind ♦ take a long hard look at so/sth ♦ Take a long walk off a short pier. ♦ take a lot off (of) so's mind ♦ take a lot out of so ♦ take a nosedive ♦ take a page from so's book ♦ take a pass (on sth) ♦ take a poke at so ♦ take a pop at so ♦ take a potshot at so/sth ♦ take a powder ♦ Take a running jump (in the lake)! ♦ take a shine to so/sth ♦ take a spill ♦ take a stand (against so/sth) ♦ take a step in the right direction ♦ take a turn for the better ♦ take a turn for the worse ♦ take a walk ♦ take a whiff of sth ♦ take account of sth ♦ take action (against so/sth) ♦ take advantage of so ♦ take advantage of so/sth ♦ take after so ♦ take aim at so/sth ♦ take sth amiss ♦ take an interest in so/sth ♦ take an oath ♦ take so apart ♦ take sth apart ♦ take sth as Gospel ♦ take so aside ♦ take so/sth at face value ♦ take one at one's word ♦ take attendance ♦ take away from so/sth ♦ take sth away (from so/sth) ♦ take sth back ♦ take one back ((to) some time) ♦ take one's belt in (a notch) ♦ take so's blood pressure ♦ take so's breath away ♦ take so/sth by storm ♦ take so by surprise ♦ take so/sth by surprise ♦ take care of so ♦ take care of number one ♦ take care of some loose ends ♦ Take care (of yourself). ♦ take center

(against so/sth) ♦ take so up on sth ♦ take up residence some place ♦ take up room ♦ take up space ♦ take up the challenge ♦ take up (so's) time ♦ take up where one/sth left off ♦ take sth up (with so) ♦ take up with so ♦ take sth (up)on oneself ♦ take well to sth ♦ take sth with a grain of salt ♦ take sth with a pinch of salt ♦ take so's word for sth ♦ take so wrong ♦ take years off (of) so/sth ♦ take your chances ♦ taken aback ♦ taken for dead ♦ taken with so/sth ♦ take-off artist ♦ That takes care of that. ♦ That takes the cake! ♦ This (seat) taken? ♦ winner take all

takeoff do a takeoff on so/sth

tale fish tale ♦ an old wives' tale ♦ tale of woe ♦ tell its own tale ♦ tell tales out of school ♦ thereby hangs a tale

talent have a hidden talent

talk all talk (and no action) ♦ fast-talk so into sth ♦ fast-talk so out of sth ♦ get so started (talking) ♦ give so a (good) talking to ♦ give so sth to talk about ♦ a (good) talking to ♦ have a heart-to-heart (talk) ♦ know what one is talking about ♦ Let's talk (about it). ♦ like to hear oneself talk ♦ Look who's talking! ♦ money talks ♦ Now you're talking! ♦ straight talk ♦ sweet-talk so ♦ talk a blue streak ♦ talk a mile a minute ♦ talk about so/sth ♦ Talk about so/sth . . . ! ♦ talk around sth ♦ talk back (to so) ♦ talk big ♦ talk down to so ♦ talk so's ear off ♦ talk one's head off ♦ talk so's head off ♦ talk in circles ♦ the talk of some place ♦ talk oneself out ♦ talk out of turn ♦ talk over so's head ♦ talk sense ♦ talk shop ♦ talk the talk and walk the walk ♦ talk sth through ♦ talk through one's hat ♦ talk to so ♦ talk to hear one's own voice ♦ talk turkey ♦ talk until one is blue in the face ♦ talk so/sth up ♦ talk up a storm ♦ talk one's way out of sth ♦ talked out ♦ That's what I'm talking about!

tall stand tall ♦ a tall order ♦ tall timber(s) ♦ walk tall

tally tally with sth

tan tan so's hide

tandem in tandem

tangent off on a tangent

tangle tangle with so/sth (over so/sth)

tank tank up (on sth)

tantrum throw a (temper) tantrum

tap on tap ♦ tap dance like mad ♦ tap so (for sth) ♦ tap out ♦ tap sth out

tape cut through red tape ♦ red tape

tar beat the tar out of so ♦ tar and feather so ♦ tar so with the same brush ♦ tarred with the same brush ♦ whale the tar out of so

target (right) on target

task take so to task

taste acquire a taste for sth ♦ in bad taste ♦ in poor taste ♦ leave a bad taste in so's mouth ♦ overstep the bounds of good taste ♦ so bad one can taste it ♦ taste blood ♦ a taste for sth ♦ taste like more ♦ a taste of sth ♦ a taste of one's own medicine ♦ want sth so bad one can taste it

tat give so tit for tat

tater Hold your taters!

tatters in tatters

tattle going to tattle

tattoo screwed, blued, and tattooed

taut run a taut ship

tax Nothing is certain but death and taxes. ♦ tax so/sth with sth ♦ tax-and-spend ♦ write sth off (on one's taxes)

taxi hail a taxi

tea coffee, tea, or milk ♦ just one's cup of tea ♦ not one's cup of tea ♦ not for all the tea in China

teach teach so a lesson ♦ teach one's grandmother to suck eggs ♦ teach school ♦ the teacher's pet ♦ That'll teach so!

teacher the teacher's pet

teacup a tempest in a teacup

team make the team ♦ May the best team win. ♦ a team player

teapot a tempest in a teapot

tear all tore up (about sth) ♦ blood, sweat, and tears ♦ bore so to tears ♦ bored to tears ♦ break out in(to) tears ♦ burst into tears ♦ cry crocodile tears ♦ in tears ♦ move so to tears ♦ not shed a tear ♦ put wear (and tear) on sth ♦ shed crocodile tears ♦ tear so apart ♦ tear some place apart ♦ tear sth apart ♦ tear one's hair (out) ♦ tear one's heart out ♦ tear into so ♦ tear so/animal limb from limb ♦ tear so up ♦ That tears it!

♦ tore (up) ♦ torn (up) ♦ vale of tears ♦ wear and tear ♦ wear and tear (on sth)

tee tee off ♦ tee so off

telegraph telegraph one's punches

telephone on the (tele)phone

tell all told ♦ Do tell. ♦ going to tell ♦ How many times do I have to tell you? ♦ if I've told you once, I've told you a thousand times ♦ I'm here to tell you ♦ kiss and tell ♦ A little bird told me. ♦ No telling. ♦ No way to tell. ♦ not tell a (living) soul ♦ not tell which way the wind is blowing ♦ show and tell ♦ tell all ♦ tell so/sth by sth ♦ Tell it like it is. ♦ Tell it to the marines! ♦ tell its own story ♦ tell its own tale ♦ Tell me about it! ♦ Tell me another (one)! ♦ tell so off ♦ tell on so ♦ tell so on so ♦ tell shit from Shinola ♦ tell tales out of school ♦ tell the (whole) world ♦ tell time ♦ tell one to one's face ♦ tell so what to do with sth ♦ tell so where to get off ♦ tell which is which ♦ Time will tell. ♦ What can I tell you?

temper keep one's temper ♦ lose one's temper (at so/sth) ♦ a quick temper ♦ a short temper ♦ temper sth with sth ♦ throw a (temper) tantrum

temperature run a temperature ♦ take so's temperature

tempest a tempest in a teacup ♦ a tempest in a teapot

tempt tempt fate

ten first and ten ♦ hang ten ♦ I wouldn't touch it with a ten-foot pole. ♦ nine times out of ten ♦ not touch so/sth with a ten-foot pole ♦ wouldn't touch so/sth with a ten-foot pole

tender tender age ♦ the tender age of a number of years ♦ tender sth for sth

tent pitch a tent

tenterhooks keep so on tenterhooks

term come to terms (with so/sth) ♦ a contradiction in terms ♦ for the long term ♦ in glowing terms ♦ in no uncertain terms ♦ in terms of sth ♦ on bad terms (with so) ♦ on good terms (with so) ♦ on speaking terms (with so)

terminate terminate so

territory come with the territory ♦ cover the territory ♦ go with the territory ♦ unfamiliar territory

terror hold terror for so

test the acid test ♦ litmus test ♦ put so/sth to the test ♦ stand the test of time ♦ test out (of sth) ♦ test the water(s) ♦ (with)stand the test of time

testament last will and testament

thank no thanks to you ♦ Thank God for small favors. ♦ Thank goodness! ♦ Thank heavens! ♦ thank one's lucky stars ♦ Thank you. ♦ Thank you a lot. ♦ Thank you for sharing. ♦ thankful for small blessings ♦ thanks a bunch ♦ Thanks (a lot). ♦ Thanks a million. ♦ Thanks awfully. ♦ Thanks, but no thanks. ♦ Thanks loads. ♦ thanks to so/sth ♦ a vote of thanks

Thanksgiving busy as a cranberry merchant (at Thanksgiving)

then and then some ♦ (every) now and then ♦ (Good-bye) until then. ♦ now and then ♦ then and there

theory in theory

there all there ♦ as if there's no tomorrow ♦ Be there or be square. ♦ Been there(, done that). ♦ Getting there is half the fun. ♦ go there ♦ Hang in there. ♦ here and there ♦ here, there, and everywhere ♦ in there ♦ in there pitching ♦ It's a jungle out there. ♦ (I've) been there(, done that). ♦ Keep in there! ♦ like there's no tomorrow ♦ neither here nor there ♦ not all there ♦ spend money like there's no tomorrow ♦ stand there with one's bare face hanging out ♦ then and there ♦ There are plenty of (other) fish in the sea. ♦ There aren't enough hours in the day. ♦ There is a fine line between sth and sth else. ♦ There is a thin line between sth and sth else. ♦ there is no doing sth ♦ There is no love lost (between so and so else). ♦ (There is) no need (to). ♦ There is something to be said for sth. ♦ There will be hell to pay. ♦ There will be the devil to pay. ♦ There you are. ♦ There you go. ♦ There's a time and place for everything. ♦ There's more than one way to skin a cat. ♦ There's no flies on so. ♦ There's no such thing as a free lunch. ♦ There's no time like the present. ♦ There's no two ways about it. ♦ there's no use (doing sth) ♦ There's nobody home. ♦ (There's) nothing to it! ♦ There's the rub. ♦ Where there's smoke, there's fire. ♦ (You) can't get there from here.

thereby thereby hangs a tale

these between you and me and these four walls ♦ in these parts ♦ one of these days

thick get sth into so's (thick) head ♦ get sth through so's thick skull ♦ in the thick of sth ♦ lay it on thick ♦ The plot thickens. ♦ thick and fast ♦ thick as a short plank ♦ thick as pea soup ♦ thick as thieves ♦ thick as two short planks ♦ thick-skinned ♦ through thick and thin

thief thick as thieves

thin disappear into thin air ♦ on thin ice ♦ out of thin air ♦ pull sth out of thin air ♦ skate on thin ice ♦ spread oneself too thin ♦ There is a thin line between sth and sth else. ♦ thin-skinned ♦ through thick and thin ♦ vanish into thin air ♦ walk on thin ice ♦ wear thin

thing add up to the same thing ♦ all things being equal ♦ all things considered ♦ all things must pass ♦ all things to all men ♦ amount to the same thing ♦ any fool thing ♦ any old thing ♦ (Are) things getting you down? ♦ as things stand ♦ come to the same thing ♦ do one's (own) thing ♦ every fool thing ♦ first thing (in the morning) ♦ the first thing that comes into one's head ♦ First things first. ♦ Funny thing is that . . . ♦ get in(to) the swing of things ♦ the greatest thing since indoor plumbing ♦ the greatest thing since sliced bread ♦ a harbinger of things to come ♦ have a good thing going ♦ have a thing about so/sth ♦ have a thing going (with so) ♦ in the (great) scheme of things ♦ in the swim of things ♦ the in thing (to do) ♦ It's a funny thing, but . . . ♦ It's just one of those things. ♦ (I've) (got) better things to do. ♦ know a thing or two (about so/sth) ♦ the least little thing ♦ let things slide ♦ next best thing ♦ not know the first thing about so/sth ♦ not miss a thing ♦ one final thing ♦ one thing after another ♦

One thing leads to another. ♦ onto a good thing ♦ other things being equal ♦ out of the swim of things ♦ patch things up ♦ the real thing ♦ the same old thing ♦ a sure thing ♦ take things easy ♦ the way things stand ♦ There's no such thing as a free lunch. ♦ a thing of the past ♦ a thing or two (about so/sth) ♦ Things are looking up. ♦ Things getting you down? ♦ too much of a good thing ♦ the very thing ♦ a whole nother thing

think as one think(s) best ♦ bring so around (to one's way of thinking) ♦ cannot hear oneself think ♦ come to think of it ♦ Don't even think about (doing) it. ♦ Don't even think about it (happening). ♦ hardly have time to think ♦ put one's thinking cap on ♦ think a great deal of so/sth ♦ think a lot of so/sth ♦ think ahead of one's time ♦ think better of so/sth ♦ think better of sth ♦ Think big. ♦ think for oneself ♦ think so hung the moon (and stars) ♦ think inside the box ♦ think so is God's own cousin ♦ think little of so/sth ♦ think nothing of doing sth ♦ think nothing of so/sth ♦ Think nothing of it. ♦ think on one's feet ♦ think out loud ♦ think outside the box ♦ think straight ♦ think the sun rises and sets on so ♦ think the world of so/sth ♦ think twice about so/sth ♦ think twice (before doing sth) ♦ think under fire ♦ to my way of thinking ♦ Where do (you think) you get off? ♦ Who could have thought? ♦ Who would have thought? ♦ wishful thinking ♦ You (always) think you have all the answers! ♦ You can (just) think again. ♦ You've got another think coming.

third get the third degree ♦ go down for the third time ♦ the third degree

thirst get up a thirst ♦ have a thirst for sth ♦ thirst for sth ♦ thirsty for sth ♦ work up a thirst

thither hither and thither ♦ hither, thither, and yon ♦ thither and yon

Thomas doubting Thomas

thorn a thorn in so's flesh ♦ a thorn in so's side

those along those lines ♦ and those ♦ It's just one of those things. ♦ Those were the days.

thou holier-than-thou

thought collect one's thoughts ♦ deep in thought ♦ food for thought ♦ give so pause (for thought) ♦ give some thought to sth ♦ have second thoughts (about so/sth) ♦ immersed in thought ♦ lose one's train of thought ♦ lost in thought ♦ not give it a(nother) thought ♦ on second thought ♦ Perish the thought. ♦ school of thought ♦ second thoughts (about so/sth) ♦ swift as thought ♦ thoughts to live by ♦ so's train of thought ♦ Who could have thought? ♦ Who would have thought?

thousand if I've told you once, I've told you a thousand times ♦ one in a thousand

thrash thrash sth out

thread a common thread (to all this) ♦ hang by a thread ♦ lose the thread (of sth)

three a couple three ♦ didn't exchange more than three words with so ♦ do a three-sixty ♦ like a three-ring circus ♦ phony as a three-dollar bill ♦ queer as a three-dollar bill ♦ three sheets in the wind ♦ three squares (a day) ♦ turn three hundred and sixty degrees

threshold on the threshold (of doing sth)

thrill thrill so to death ♦ thrill so to pieces ♦ thrilled to death ♦ thrilled to pieces

throat at each other's throats ♦ by the throat ♦ clear one's throat ♦ cut one's (own) throat ♦ a frog in one's throat ♦ go for the throat ♦ have a frog in one's throat ♦ have a lump in one's throat ♦ jump down so's throat ♦ a lump in one's throat ♦ ram so/sth down so's throat ♦ shove so/sth down so's throat ♦ stuff sth down so's throat ♦ one's words stick in one's throat

throne on the throne ♦ the power behind the throne

throw don't have a pot to piss in (or a window to throw it out of) ♦ a stone's throw away ♦ throw so ♦ throw so a curve (ball) ♦ throw a fight ♦ throw a fit ♦ throw a game ♦ throw a (monkey) wrench in the works ♦ throw a party (for so) ♦ throw a punch ♦ throw a (temper) tantrum ♦ throw oneself at so ♦ throw oneself at so's feet ♦ throw oneself at the mercy of some authority ♦ throw caution to the wind ♦ throw cold water on sth ♦ throw doubt on so/sth ♦ throw down the gauntlet ♦ throw so for a loop ♦ throw so for a loss ♦ throw good money after bad ♦ throw one's hands up (in despair) ♦ throw one's hat in the ring ♦ throw in one's lot with so/sth ♦ throw in the sponge ♦ throw in the towel ♦ throw in with so ♦ throw oneself into sth ♦ throw sth in(to) so's face ♦ throw sth into the bargain ♦ throw sth in(to) the pot ♦ throw an amount of light on so/sth ♦ throw money at sth ♦ throw money down the drain ♦ throw so's name around ♦ throw sth off ♦ throw so off balance ♦ throw so off the scent ♦ throw so off the track ♦ throw so off the trail ♦ throw one out on one's ear ♦ throw sth out (to so/sth) ♦ throw (some) light on sth ♦ throw the baby out with the bath(water) ♦ throw the book at so ♦ throw the bull ♦ throw the crap ♦ throw so to the dogs ♦ throw so to the wolves ♦ throw up ♦ throw sth up ♦ throw sth up to so ♦ throw one's voice ♦ throw one's weight around ♦ throw one's weight behind so/sth ♦ within a stone's throw (of sth)

thrust thrust and parry

thumb all thumbs ♦ have a green thumb ♦ keep so under so's thumb ♦ a rule of thumb ♦ stand out like a sore thumb ♦ stick out like a sore thumb ♦ thumb a ride ♦ thumb one's nose at so/sth ♦ thumb through sth ♦ thumbs-down ♦ thumbs-up ♦ turn thumbs-down (on so/sth) ♦ turn thumbs-up (on so/sth) ♦ twiddle one's thumbs ♦ under so's thumb

thumbnail a thumbnail sketch

thump thump sth out (on the piano)

thunder steal so's thunder ♦ thunder across sth ♦ thunder sth out ♦ thunder past so/sth

thunderstorm risk of thunder(storms)

thunk Who would'a thunk (it)?

tick full as a tick ♦ tick so off ♦ tick sth off ♦ ticked (off) ♦ tight as a tick ♦ what makes so tick ♦ what makes sth tick

ticket buy so's wolf ticket ♦ get a ticket ♦ get one's ticket punched ♦ a hot ticket ♦ just the ticket ♦ round-trip ticket ♦ That's the ticket! ♦ vote a split ticket ♦ vote a straight ticket

tickle tickle so's fancy ♦ tickle so pink ♦ tickle the ivories ♦ tickle so to death ♦ tickle so to pieces ♦ tickled pink

tide go with the tide ♦ happy as a clam (at high tide) ♦ stem the tide (of so/sth) ♦ swim against the tide ♦ tide so over (until sth) ♦ the tide turned ♦ turn the tide

tidy tidy so/sth up

tie coat and tie ♦ fit to be tied ♦ so's hands are tied ♦ have one's hands tied ♦ sever ties with so ♦ tie so down ♦ tie so's hands ♦ tie one on ♦ tie the knot ♦ tie so to sth ♦ tie so/sth up ♦ tie sth up ♦ tie so (up) in knots ♦ tied down ♦ tied to one's mother's apron strings ♦ tied up ♦ with one hand tied behind one's back

tiger have a tiger by the tail

tight have one's head screwed on tight ♦ in a (tight) spot ♦ keep a tight grip on so/sth ♦ keep a tight rein on so/sth ♦ on a tight leash ♦ run a tight ship ♦ sit tight ♦ sleep tight ♦ tight as a drum ♦ tight as a tick ♦ tight as Midas's fist ♦ a tight race ♦ tighten one's belt ♦ tighten the screws on (so) ♦ tighten up

tightfisted tightfisted (with money)

tightrope walk a tightrope

till (Good-bye) till later. ♦ have one's finger(s) in the till ♦ have one's hand in the till ♦ It's not over till it's over. ♦ till kingdom come ♦ Till next time. ♦ till the bitter end ♦ till the cows come home ♦ till the fat lady sings ♦ Till we meet again.

tilt at full tilt ♦ tilt at windmills ♦ tilt toward so/sth

timber tall timber(s)

time ahead of time ♦ ahead of one's time ♦ (all) in good time ♦ all the time ♦ at a set time ♦ at all times ♦ at any one time ♦ at no time ♦ at one time ♦ at one time or another ♦ at some time or another ♦ at the appointed time ♦ at the present time ♦ at the same time ♦ at this point (in time) ♦ at times ♦ back in time ♦ a bad time ♦ bad times ♦ before one's time ♦ before so's time ♦ behind the times ♦ the best of times ♦ Better luck next time. ♦ bide one's time ♦ buy sth on time ♦ buy time ♦ Catch me some other time. ♦ change with the times ♦ a devil of a time ♦ difficult times ♦ do time ♦ down time ♦ every time one turns around ♦ fall on hard times ♦ fight against time ♦ find enough time to do sth ♦ find the time to do sth ♦ for old time's sake ♦ for the time being ♦ from time to time ♦ Give it time. ♦ go down for the third time ♦ (Good-bye) until next time. ♦ A good time was had by all. ♦ half the time ♦ happen before so's time ♦ a hard time ♦ hard times ♦ hardly have time to breathe ♦ hardly have time to think ♦ have a rare old time ♦ have a rough time (of it) ♦ have a tough time (of it) ♦ have a whale of a time ♦ have all the time in the world ♦ have an easy time of it ♦ have (some) time to kill ♦ have the time of one's life ♦ have (too much) time on one's hands ♦ Having a wonderful time; wish you were here. ♦ How many times do I have to tell you? ♦ if I've told you once, I've told you a thousand times ♦ (I'm) having a wonderful time; wish you were here. ♦ I'm having the time of my life. ♦ in a short space of time ♦ in due time ♦ in good time ♦ in less than no time ♦ in no time (at all) ♦ in no time flat ♦ in one's spare time ♦ in the course of time ♦ in the fullness of time ♦ in the interest of saving time ♦ in the meantime ♦ in the right place at the right time ♦ in the (very) nick of time ♦ in the wrong place at the wrong time ♦ in time ♦ in time (with sth) ♦ in times past ♦ in tune with the times ♦ (It's) about time! ♦ it's high time ♦ just in time (to do sth) ♦ keep good time ♦ keep time ♦ keep up with the times ♦ kill time ♦ lean times (ahead) ♦ leave ahead of time ♦ a legend in one's own (life)time ♦ live on borrowed time ♦ Long time no see. ♦ lose no time ♦ lose time ♦ make (enough) time (for so/sth) ♦ make good time ♦ make time (with so) ♦

make up for lost time ♦ many a time ♦ many (and many)'s the time ♦ mark time ♦ a matter of time ♦ the mists of time ♦ (My,) how time flies! ♦ nine times out of ten ♦ no time to lose ♦ not able to call one's time one's own ♦ not give so the time of day ♦ not have a lot of time for so/sth ♦ on one's own time ♦ on time ♦ once upon a time ♦ once-in-a-lifetime chance ♦ once-in-a-lifetime opportunity ♦ one at a time ♦ one day at a time ♦ one step at a time ♦ (only) a matter of time ♦ out of time (with so/sth) ♦ pass the time (of day) ♦ pass the time of day ♦ play for time ♦ pressed for time ♦ pushed for time ♦ quality time ♦ a question of time ♦ race against time ♦ right on time ♦ a rough time ♦ run out of time ♦ the sands of time ♦ save (enough) time (for so/sth) ♦ scarcely have time to breathe ♦ serve time ♦ set (enough) time aside (for so/sth) ♦ show up ahead of time ♦ a sign of the times ♦ since time immemorial ♦ small-time ♦ stand the test of time ♦ step back in time ♦ take the time to do sth ♦ take one's time ♦ take time out ♦ take up (so's) time ♦ tell time ♦ the time is ripe (for sth) ♦ There's a time and place for everything. ♦ There's no time like the present. ♦ think ahead of one's time ♦ Till next time. ♦ time after time ♦ Time flies! ♦ time flies (when you're having fun) ♦ time hangs heavy (on so's hands) ♦ so's time has come ♦ time in ♦ time so in ♦ Time is money. ♦ Time is of the essence. ♦ time is on so's side ♦ time is running out ♦ time is up ♦ one's time of life ♦ time off ♦ time off for good behavior ♦ Time (out)! ♦ time out ♦ time so out ♦ time stands still ♦ time was (that) . . . ♦ Time will tell. ♦ tough times ♦ trying times ♦ turn sth into a full-time job ♦ two-time so ♦ a two-time loser ♦ waste no time ♦ waste time ♦ (with)stand the test of time

tin busy as a cat on a hot tin roof ♦ a tin ear

tinker not give a (tinker's) damn

tiny the patter of tiny feet

tip from tip to toe ♦ have sth on the tip of one's tongue ♦ on the tip of one's tongue ♦

tip one's hand ♦ the tip of the iceberg ♦ tip the balance ♦ tip the scales ♦ tip the scales at sth

tiptoe on tiptoe

tire sick (and tired) of so/sth ♦ spare tire

tit cold as a witch's tit ♦ give so tit for tat ♦ suck so's hind tit ♦ tits and ass

tittle jot and tittle

tizzy in a tizzy

toad ugly as a toad

toast propose a toast ♦ the toast of some place ♦ warm as toast

toe (from) head to toe ♦ from tip to toe ♦ head to toe ♦ on tiptoe ♦ on one's toes ♦ step on so's toes ♦ toe the line ♦ toe the mark ♦ tread on so's toes ♦ turn up one's toes ♦ with bells on (one's toes)

together bring so together ♦ cup one's hands together ♦ enough to keep body and soul together ♦ get one's act together ♦ get one's head together ♦ get it (all) together ♦ get one's shit together ♦ get one's stuff together ♦ get sth together ♦ get sth together (for a particular time) ♦ get together (with so) (on so/sth) ♦ hang together ♦ have it all together ♦ keep body and soul together ♦ knock one's knees together ♦ knock some heads together ♦ knock sth together ♦ link so/sth and so/sth together ♦ lump so and so else together ♦ piece sth together ♦ pull oneself together ♦ pull sth together ♦ put people's heads together ♦ put sth together ♦ put two and two together ♦ put two and two together and come up with five ♦ scrape sth together ♦ sleep together ♦ stand together ♦ stick together

toilet go to the toilet

toing toing and froing (on sth)

token as a token (of sth) ♦ by the same token ♦ a token gesture

told all told ♦ if I've told you once, I've told you a thousand times ♦ A little bird told me.

tolerance zero tolerance

toll take (quite a) toll (on so/sth)

Tom any Tom, Dick, and Harry ♦ (every) Tom, Dick, and Harry ♦ Tom, Dick, and Harry

tomorrow as if there's no tomorrow ◆ like there's no tomorrow ◆ spend money like there's no tomorrow

ton like a ton of bricks ◆ tons of sth

tone set the tone

tong fight so/sth hammer and tongs ◆ go at it hammer and tongs

tongue bite one's tongue ◆ Cat got your tongue? ◆ cause (some) tongues to wag ◆ find one's tongue ◆ have sth on the tip of one's tongue ◆ hold one's tongue ◆ keep a civil tongue (in one's head) ◆ loosen so's tongue ◆ on everyone's tongue ◆ on the tip of one's tongue ◆ set tongues (a)wagging ◆ a sharp tongue ◆ a slip of the tongue ◆ speak with a forked tongue ◆ tongue-in-cheek ◆ a tongue-lashing

tool tool around (in sth) ◆ tools of the trade

toot darn tootin(g) ◆ toot one's own horn

tooth armed to the teeth ◆ bare one's teeth ◆ by the skin of one's teeth ◆ clean as a hound's tooth ◆ cut one's (eye)teeth on sth ◆ cut teeth ◆ dressed to the teeth ◆ drop one's teeth ◆ fight so/sth tooth and nail ◆ get one's teeth into sth ◆ give one's eyeteeth (for so/sth) ◆ gnash one's teeth ◆ a gnashing of teeth ◆ go at it tooth and nail ◆ go at one another tooth and nail ◆ go over sth with a fine-tooth(ed) comb ◆ go through sth with a fine-tooth(ed) comb ◆ grit one's teeth ◆ have a sweet tooth ◆ a kick in the teeth ◆ lie through one's teeth ◆ like pulling teeth ◆ long in the tooth ◆ no skin off so's teeth ◆ pull so's/sth's teeth ◆ put some teeth into sth ◆ scarce as hen's teeth ◆ scarcer than hen's teeth ◆ search sth with a fine-tooth(ed) comb ◆ set so's teeth on edge ◆ show one's teeth ◆ sink one's teeth into sth ◆ take the bit in one's teeth ◆ teething troubles

top at the top of one's game ◆ at the top of the hour ◆ at the top of one's voice ◆ blow one's top ◆ claw one's way to the top ◆ come out on top ◆ come (right) on top of sth ◆ feel on top of the world ◆ from the top ◆ from top to bottom ◆ get to the top (of sth) ◆ go (straight) to the top ◆ in top form ◆ keep on top (of so/sth) ◆ off the top of one's head ◆ on top of sth ◆ over the

top ◆ pop (some) tops ◆ (right) off the top of one's head ◆ scream (sth) from the rooftops ◆ shout (sth) from the rooftops ◆ sitting on top of the world ◆ stay on top of so/sth ◆ take it from the top ◆ top brass ◆ top notch ◆ the top of the heap ◆ the top of the ladder ◆ top sth off ◆ top story ◆ yell (sth) from the rooftops

topic off topic

torch carry a torch (for so) ◆ carry the torch ◆ pass the torch (on) to so

toss It's a toss-up. ◆ toss a salad ◆ toss and turn ◆ toss one's cookies ◆ toss (so) for sth ◆ toss one's hat into the ring ◆ toss in the sponge ◆ toss sth off ◆ toss sth out (to so/sth)

total in total ◆ a total stranger

totem high man on the totem pole ◆ low man on the totem pole

touch final touch(es) ◆ finishing touch(es) ◆ have the Midas touch ◆ I wouldn't touch it with a ten-foot pole. ◆ in touch (with so) ◆ Keep in touch. ◆ keep in touch (with so) ◆ lose one's touch (with so/sth) ◆ lose touch (with so) ◆ lose touch with reality ◆ not to touch a drop ◆ not touch so/sth with a ten-foot pole ◆ out of touch (with so/sth) ◆ put so in touch with so/sth ◆ put the touch on so (for sth) ◆ remain in touch (with so) ◆ remain in touch (with so/sth) ◆ soft touch ◆ stay in touch (with so/sth) ◆ touch a (raw) nerve ◆ touch a sore point ◆ touch a sore spot ◆ touch and go ◆ touch base (with so) ◆ a touch of sth ◆ touch so (up) for sth ◆ touch (up)on sth ◆ touched by so/sth ◆ touched (in the head) ◆ wouldn't touch so/sth with a ten-foot pole

tough get tough (with so) ◆ hang tough (on sth) ◆ have a tough time (of it) ◆ if the going gets tough ◆ a tough act to follow ◆ tough as an old boot ◆ tough as nails ◆ tough as (old) (shoe) leather ◆ a tough break ◆ a tough call ◆ a tough cookie ◆ tough cookies ◆ a tough customer ◆ tough going ◆ tough guy ◆ tough luck ◆ a tough nut to crack ◆ tough on so ◆ tough sth out ◆ a tough row to hoe ◆ tough sledding ◆ tough times ◆ when the going gets tough

tour on tour

tout Tout suite!

tow have so/sth in tow ♦ in tow ♦ with so/sth in tow

toward go a long way toward doing sth ♦ head toward so/sth ♦ lean toward doing sth ♦ lean toward so/sth ♦ tilt toward so/sth ♦ well disposed to(ward) so/sth

towel throw in the towel

tower in an ivory tower ♦ live in an ivory tower ♦ tower head and shoulders above so/sth ♦ a tower of strength

town all over town ♦ Get out of town! ♦ go to town ♦ hit town ♦ Look me up when you're in town. ♦ man about town ♦ a night on the town ♦ one-horse town ♦ the only game in town ♦ out of town ♦ out on the town ♦ paint the town (red) ♦ town-and-gown

toy like a kid with a new toy ♦ toy with so ♦ toy with sth

trace kick over the traces

track back on track ♦ cover so's tracks (up) ♦ drop in one's tracks ♦ follow in so's tracks ♦ get sth back on track ♦ get sidetracked ♦ get the inside track ♦ have a one-track mind ♦ the inside track ♦ jump the track ♦ keep so/sth on (the) (right) track ♦ keep track (of so/sth) ♦ lose track (of so) ♦ lose track (of sth) ♦ make tracks (for sth) ♦ off on a sidetrack ♦ off the beaten track ♦ off the track ♦ on the fast track ♦ on the right track ♦ on the track of so/sth ♦ on the wrong track ♦ on track ♦ one-track mind ♦ the other side of the tracks ♦ put so off the track ♦ sidetracked ♦ stop (dead) in one's tracks ♦ stop so/sth dead in so's/sth's tracks ♦ throw so off the track ♦ track so/sth down ♦ the wrong side of the tracks

trade jack of all trades ♦ know the tricks of the trade ♦ stock in trade ♦ take sth out in trade ♦ tools of the trade ♦ trade places (with so) ♦ a trade secret ♦ trade (up)on sth ♦ tricks of the trade

tradition break with tradition

traffic Go play in the traffic. ♦ traffic in sth ♦ a traffic jam

trail blaze a trail ♦ the end of the trail ♦ hit the trail ♦ hot on the trail (of so/sth/animal) ♦ leave a paper trail ♦ on the trail of so/sth ♦ a paper trail ♦ put so off the trail ♦ throw so off the trail ♦ trail away ♦ trail off

train have one's sights trained on sth ♦ lose one's train of thought ♦ ride the gravy train ♦ so's train of thought ♦ train one's sights on sth

transit in transit

translation a free translation ♦ a loose translation

trap build a better mousetrap ♦ fall into a trap ♦ fall into the trap of doing sth ♦ have a mind as sharp as a steel trap ♦ set a trap ♦ trap so in sth

travel travel at a good clip

travesty a travesty of justice

tread tread lightly (with so/sth) ♦ tread on so's toes ♦ tread water

treat Dutch treat ♦ How's the world (been) treating you? ♦ stand so to a treat ♦ treat so like dirt ♦ treat so like shit ♦ treat so like the scum of the earth ♦ treat so with kid gloves ♦ Trick or treat!

treatment the red-carpet treatment ♦ the royal treatment

tree bark up the wrong tree ♦ Go climb a tree! ♦ make like a tree and leave ♦ not able to see the forest for the trees ♦ not grow on trees ♦ not to see the forest for the trees ♦ tree so/animal ♦ up a tree

tremble in fear and trembling

trial bring so/sth to trial ♦ go to trial ♦ on trial ♦ send up a trial balloon ♦ stand trial ♦ trial and error ♦ trial balloon ♦ trials and tribulations

triangle the eternal triangle

tribulation trials and tribulations

tribute floral tribute ♦ pay tribute to so/sth

trick bag of tricks ♦ do the trick ♦ every trick in the book ♦ How's tricks? ♦ know a trick or two ♦ know the tricks of the trade ♦ miss a trick ♦ the oldest trick in the book ♦ play a trick on so ♦ play tricks on so ♦ pull a trick (on so) ♦ Trick or treat! ♦ trick sth out ♦ tricks of the trade ♦ turn a trick ♦ whole bag of tricks

trickle trickle down (to so/sth) ♦ trickle in(to sth) ♦ trickle out (of sth)

trigger quick on the trigger

trim fit and trim ♦ with all the trimmings

trip day-tripper ♦ Have a safe trip. ♦ lay a guilt trip on so ♦ lay a (heavy) trip on so ♦ on a power trip ♦ round-trip ticket ♦ (a trip down) memory lane ♦ trip the light fantastic ♦ trip so up

triplicate in triplicate

trolley off one's trolley ♦ slip one's trolley

trooper swear like a trooper

trot trot sth out

troth plight one's troth to so

trouble ask for trouble ♦ borrow trouble ♦ buy trouble ♦ can't be troubled to do sth ♦ drown one's troubles ♦ fish in troubled waters ♦ foment trouble ♦ for (all) one's trouble ♦ go to the trouble (of doing sth) ♦ (Have you) been keeping out of trouble? ♦ in trouble ♦ look for trouble ♦ make trouble ♦ not trouble one's (pretty) (little) head about sth ♦ pour oil on troubled water(s) ♦ spell trouble ♦ teething troubles ♦ trouble so for sth ♦ trouble one's head about so/sth ♦ trouble oneself (to do sth) ♦ You been keeping out of trouble?

trowel lay it on with a trowel

truck have no truck with sth ♦ just fell off the turnip truck ♦ keep on trucking

trudge trudge through sth

true come true ♦ a dream come true ♦ hold true ♦ ring true ♦ show one's (true) colors ♦ too good to be true ♦ tried and true ♦ true as steel ♦ so's true colors ♦ true to form ♦ true to one's word ♦ twelve good men and true

trump play one's trump card ♦ trump sth up ♦ trumped up

trust in the trust of so ♦ place so/sth in the trust of so ♦ place one's trust in so/sth ♦ put one's trust in so/sth ♦ take sth on trust ♦ Trust me!

truth Ain't it the truth? ♦ economical with the truth ♦ the gospel truth ♦ a grain of truth ♦ the moment of truth ♦ the naked truth ♦ stretch the truth

try Don't quit trying. ♦ give sth a try ♦ Keep (on) trying. ♦ like trying to find a needle in a haystack ♦ Lord knows I've tried. ♦ a mere trifle ♦ old college try ♦ tried and true ♦ try as I may ♦ try as I might ♦ a try at so ♦ a try at sth ♦ try so back (again) ♦ try so for sth ♦ try one's hand (at sth) ♦ try one's

luck (at sth) ♦ Try me. ♦ try sth (on) (for size) ♦ try out (for sth) ♦ try so's patience ♦ try one's wings (out) ♦ trying times ♦ without half trying

tub tub of lard

tube down the tube(s) ♦ go down the tube(s)

tuck nip and tuck ♦ tuck sth away ♦ tuck into sth

tucker (all) tuckered out ♦ one's best bib and tucker ♦ tucker so out

tug tug at so's heartstrings

tumble rough and tumble

tune call the tune ♦ can't carry a tune in a bucket ♦ can't carry a tune (in a bushel basket) ♦ can't carry a tune in a paper sack ♦ change one's tune ♦ change so's tune ♦ dance to a different tune ♦ dance to another tune ♦ fine-tune sth ♦ in tune ♦ in tune with so/sth ♦ in tune with the times ♦ out of tune (with so/sth) ♦ sing a different tune ♦ sing another tune ♦ to the tune of some amount of money ♦ tune sth in ♦ tune in (on so/sth) ♦ tune out ♦ tune so/sth out ♦ tune up ♦ tune sth up ♦ tuned in ♦ turn on, tune in, drop out

tunnel (begin to) see the light (at the end of the tunnel) ♦ see the light (at the end of the tunnel) ♦ tunnel vision

turf surf and turf

turkey cold turkey ♦ go cold turkey ♦ talk turkey ♦ a turkey's nest

turn at every turn ♦ can (just) see the wheels turning ♦ done to a turn ♦ every time one turns around ♦ I spoke out of turn. ♦ in turn ♦ It's your turn. ♦ not know where to turn ♦ out of turn ♦ speak out of turn ♦ take a turn for the better ♦ take a turn for the worse ♦ take one's turn ♦ take turns (doing sth) ♦ talk out of turn ♦ the tide turned ♦ toss and turn ♦ turn a blind eye (to so/sth) ♦ turn a deaf ear (to so/sth) ♦ turn a profit ♦ turn a trick ♦ turn sth around ♦ turn one's back (on so/sth) ♦ turn back the clock ♦ turn belly up ♦ turn sth down ♦ turn one's hand to sth ♦ turn so's head ♦ turn in ♦ turn some place inside out ♦ turn sth into a career ♦ turn sth into a fine art ♦ turn sth into a full-time job ♦ turn one's nose up at so/sth ♦ a turn of fate

unison in unison
unknown an unknown quantity
unlikely in the unlikely event of sth
unpleasantness the late unpleasantness
unquote quote, unquote
unring can't unring the bell
unsaid better left unsaid
unseen buy sth sight unseen
unspeakable do the unspeakable
unsung unsung hero
unthinkable do the unthinkable
until (Good-bye) till later. ♦ (Good-bye) until later. ♦ (Good-bye) until next time. ♦ (Good-bye) until then. ♦ have not lived until one has done sth ♦ It's not over till it's over. ♦ make it (until sth) ♦ talk until one is blue in the face ♦ tide so over (until sth) ♦ till kingdom come ♦ Till next time. ♦ till the bitter end ♦ till the cows come home ♦ till the fat lady sings ♦ Till we meet again. ♦ until all hours ♦ (un)til hell freezes over ♦ (un)til the cows come home ♦ Until we meet again.
untimely come to an untimely end
unto a law unto oneself
unturned leave no stone unturned
unwashed the great unwashed
uphill an uphill battle ♦ an uphill struggle
upper on one's uppers ♦ upper crust ♦ the upper hand (on so) ♦ upper story
upright sit bolt upright
uproar create an uproar ♦ Don't get your bowels in an uproar! ♦ make an uproar
ups so's ups and downs
upset upset the apple cart
upshot the upshot of sth
upside get upside down ♦ turn some place upside down ♦ turn so/sth upside down ♦ upside down
upstairs nothing upstairs
uptake quick on the uptake ♦ slow on the uptake
use come in useful ♦ have (a) use for so/sth ♦ have no use for so/sth ♦ in use ♦ It takes (some) getting used to. ♦ it's no use (doing sth) ♦ lose the use of sth ♦ not as young as one used to be ♦ put sth into use ♦ put sth to (good) use ♦ there's no use (doing sth) ♦ They don't make them like they used to. ♦ use one's head ♦ use one's

noggin ♦ use one's noodle ♦ use some elbow grease ♦ use so up ♦ Use your head! ♦ Use your noggin! ♦ Use your noodle! ♦ used to do sth ♦ used to so/sth ♦ user friendly
useful come in useful
usher usher so in ♦ usher sth in
usual as usual ♦ business as usual
utter not utter a word

V

vacation on vacation
vacuum in a vacuum
vain do sth in vain ♦ vain as a peacock
vale vale of tears
value take so/sth at face value
vanish vanish into thin air
vapor running on vapor
veg veg out ♦ vegged out
vein go for the jugular (vein)
velvet rule with a velvet glove ♦ soft as velvet
vengeance with a vengeance ♦ wreak vengeance (up)on so/sth
vent give vent to sth ♦ vent one's spleen ♦ vent sth (up)on so/sth
venture Nothing ventured, nothing gained. ♦ venture forth
verdict bring a verdict in
verge on the verge of doing sth
verse chapter and verse
very at the very least ♦ at the (very) outside ♦ in the (very) nick of time ♦ (right) under so's (very) nose ♦ under so's (very) nose ♦ the (very) picture of sth ♦ the very thing
vest keep one's cards close to one's vest ♦ play one's cards close to one's vest ♦ a vested interest in sth
vested a vested interest in sth
vicinity in the vicinity (of some amount)
vicious in a vicious circle
victim fall victim to so/sth
victory a landslide victory ♦ snatch victory from the jaws of defeat
view a bird's-eye view ♦ from my point of view ♦ in view of sth ♦ on view ♦ point of

view ◆ take a dim view of so/sth ◆ with a view to doing sth

vigor vim and vigor

villain the villain of the piece

vim vim and vigor

vine wither on the vine

vinegar sour as vinegar

violet a shrinking violet

virtual virtual reality

virtue by virtue of sth

vision tunnel vision

visit pay (so/sth) a visit ◆ pay a visit to so/sth ◆ pop around (for a visit) ◆ pop by (for a visit) ◆ pop in (for a visit) ◆ a visit from the stork ◆ visit the plumbing ◆ visit sth (up)on so

visually visually impaired

vogue in vogue

voice at the top of one's voice ◆ give voice to sth ◆ have a voice (in sth) ◆ lower one's voice ◆ raise one's voice against so/sth ◆ raise one's voice (to so) ◆ speak with one voice ◆ talk to hear one's own voice ◆ throw one's voice ◆ a voice crying in the wilderness ◆ a voice (in sth)

void fill a void ◆ null and void

volume speak volumes

vomit vomit sth out

vote cast one's vote ◆ put sth (up) to a vote ◆ vote a split ticket ◆ vote a straight ticket ◆ vote sth into law ◆ a vote of confidence ◆ a vote of thanks ◆ vote with one's feet ◆ vote with one's wallet

vouch vouch for so/sth

voyage maiden voyage

wad shoot one's wad

wade wade in(to sth) ◆ wade through sth

wag cause (some) tongues to wag ◆ set tongues (a)wagging ◆ the tail wagging the dog ◆ wag one's chin

wage freeze so's wages

wagon fall off the wagon ◆ fix so's wagon ◆ off the wagon ◆ on the wagon

wait hurry up and wait ◆ (just) can't wait (for sth (to happen)) ◆ lie in wait (for so/sth)

◆ the moment everyone has been waiting for ◆ on the wait list ◆ on the waiting list ◆ wait for the next wave ◆ wait for the other shoe to drop ◆ Wait (just) a minute! ◆ wait on so hand and foot ◆ wait (on) tables ◆ wait one's turn ◆ wait (up)on so ◆ wait-and-see attitude ◆ waiting in the wings

wake in the wake of sth ◆ wake the dead ◆ wake up and smell the coffee ◆ wake up on the wrong side of bed ◆ wake up to sth

walk all walks of life ◆ cock of the walk ◆ every walk of life ◆ get one's walking papers ◆ Take a long walk off a short pier. ◆ take a walk ◆ talk the talk and walk the walk ◆ walk a tightrope ◆ walk all over so/sth ◆ walk arm in arm ◆ walk away from so/sth ◆ walk away with sth ◆ walk so's feet off ◆ walk off the job ◆ walk off with sth ◆ walk on air ◆ walk on eggshells ◆ walk on thin ice ◆ walk out (on so) ◆ walk out (on sth) ◆ walk (right) into sth ◆ walk soft ◆ walk tall ◆ walk the extra mile ◆ walk the floor ◆ walk the plank ◆ walk through sth ◆ walk so through sth ◆ one's walking papers ◆ worship the ground so walks on

wall bang one's head against a brick wall ◆ beat one's head against the wall ◆ between you and me and these four walls ◆ climb the wall(s) ◆ drive so to the wall ◆ drive so up the wall ◆ force so to the wall ◆ go to the wall (on sth) ◆ have one's back against the wall ◆ have one's back to the wall ◆ a hole in the wall ◆ knock one's head (up) against a brick wall ◆ nail so('s hide) to the wall ◆ off-the-wall ◆ over the wall ◆ press so to the wall ◆ push so to the wall ◆ read the handwriting on the wall ◆ run one's head against a brick wall ◆ run into a stone wall ◆ see the (hand)writing on the wall ◆ up against the wall ◆ up the wall ◆ wall-to-wall sth

wallet vote with one's wallet

wallop pack a wallop

waltz waltz around sth ◆ waltz in(to some place) ◆ waltz off ◆ waltz off (with sth) ◆ waltz through sth ◆ waltz up (to so)

wane on the wane ◆ wax and wane

want Do you want to know something? ♦ (Do you) want to make something of it? ♦ (Do) you want to step outside? ♦ I don't want to wear out my welcome. ♦ know when one is not wanted ♦ not want to catch so doing sth ♦ put one's nose in (where it's not wanted) ♦ stick one's nose in (where it's not wanted) ♦ Want a piece of me? ♦ want for sth ♦ want for nothing ♦ want sth so bad one can taste it ♦ Want to know something? ♦ What do you want me to say? ♦ wouldn't want to be in so's shoes ♦ (You) want a piece of me? ♦ You want to make something of it?

war an act of war ♦ all-out war ♦ go to war (over so/sth) ♦ make war (on so/sth)

warhorse an old warhorse

warm like death warmed over ♦ warm as toast ♦ warm body ♦ warm the bench ♦ warm the cockles of so's heart ♦ warm up to so/sth ♦ warmed over

warpath on the warpath

warrant put out a warrant (on so) ♦ send out a warrant (on so) ♦ sign one's own death warrant

wart warts and all

wash chief cook and bottle washer ♦ come out in the wash ♦ It won't wash! ♦ It'll all come out in the wash. ♦ wash one's dirty linen in public ♦ wash sth down (with sth) ♦ wash one's hands of so/sth ♦ wash out ♦ wash so out of sth ♦ wash over so ♦ washed out ♦ washed up

washer chief cook and bottle washer

waste Don't waste your breath. ♦ go to waste ♦ lay sth to waste ♦ lay waste to sth ♦ waste so ♦ waste one's breath ♦ waste no time ♦ a waste of space ♦ waste time

watch bear watching ♦ clock watcher ♦ exciting as watching (the) paint dry ♦ keep a close watch on so/sth ♦ keep watch on so/sth ♦ keep watch over so/sth ♦ on the watch for so/sth ♦ on so's watch ♦ watch one's back ♦ watch so/sth like a hawk ♦ Watch my lips! ♦ Watch out! ♦ watch one's Ps and Qs ♦ watch one's step ♦ watch the store

water as a duck takes to water ♦ a big drink of water ♦ blow so/sth out of the water ♦ bread and water ♦ come hell or

high water ♦ Come on in, the water's fine! ♦ cut so's water off ♦ dash cold water on sth ♦ dead in the water ♦ dull as ditchwater ♦ fish in troubled waters ♦ get one's head above water ♦ hold one's head above water ♦ in deep water ♦ in hot water ♦ in hot water (with so) (about so/sth) ♦ keep one's head above water ♦ like a fish out of water ♦ like water off a duck's back ♦ make so's mouth water ♦ make water ♦ muddy the water(s) ♦ not hold water ♦ of the first water ♦ pour cold water on sth ♦ pour oil on troubled water(s) ♦ test the water(s) ♦ through hell and high water ♦ throw cold water on sth ♦ tread water ♦ turn so's water off ♦ water sth down ♦ water over the dam ♦ water under the bridge ♦ watering hole ♦ won't hold water

waterfront cover the waterfront

Waterloo meet one's Waterloo

waterworks turn on the waterworks

wave catch the next wave ♦ make waves ♦ wait for the next wave

wavelength on the same wavelength

wax mind your own beeswax ♦ None of your beeswax! ♦ wax and wane ♦ wax angry ♦ wax eloquent ♦ wax poetic ♦ wax wroth ♦ the whole ball of wax

way all the way ♦ all the way live ♦ (Are you) going my way? ♦ bluff one's way in(to sth) ♦ bluff one's way out (of sth) ♦ bring so around (to one's way of thinking) ♦ buy one's way in(to sth) ♦ buy one's way out (of sth) ♦ by the way ♦ by way of sth ♦ change one's ways ♦ claw one's way to the top ♦ Clear the way! ♦ cry all the way to the bank ♦ cut both ways ♦ downhill all the way ♦ ever(y) which way ♦ feel one's way ♦ find (sth) out the hard way ♦ from way back ♦ get so across (in a good way) ♦ get out of the way ♦ get sth under way ♦ go a long way toward doing sth ♦ go all the way (with so) ♦ go back a long way ♦ go back quite a way(s) ♦ go out of one's way (to do sth) ♦ go the way of the dodo ♦ go the way of the horse and buggy ♦ go their separate ways ♦ Going my way? ♦ have a way with so/sth ♦ have a way with words ♦ have come a long way ♦ have it both

ways ♦ Have it your way. ♦ have one's way
with so ♦ hold one's mouth the right way ♦
in a bad way ♦ in a big way ♦ in a family
way ♦ in a way ♦ in any way, shape, or
form ♦ in harm's way ♦ in the way ♦ in the
way of sth ♦ in the worst way ♦ in so's/sth's
way ♦ It cuts two ways. ♦ Keep out of my
way. ♦ keep so/sth out of the way ♦ know
one's way around ♦ laugh all the way to
the bank ♦ lead the way ♦ learn (sth) the
hard way ♦ look the other way ♦ make
headway ♦ make way ♦ make way (for
so/sth) ♦ make one's way in the world ♦
marry one's way out of sth ♦ mend one's
ways ♦ No way! ♦ No way, José! ♦ No way
to tell. ♦ not tell which way the wind is
blowing ♦ on one's way ((to) some place) ♦
one way or another ♦ the only way to go ♦
the other way (a)round ♦ out of harm's
way ♦ out of the way ♦ a parting of the
ways ♦ pave the way (for so/sth) (with sth)
♦ pay one's own way ♦ pay so's way ♦ pick
one's way along (sth) ♦ pick one's way
through sth ♦ put so across (in a good way)
♦ put another way ♦ put so out of the way
♦ the right-of-way ♦ rub so's fur the wrong
way ♦ rub so the wrong way ♦ see the
error of one's ways ♦ see one's way (clear)
(to do sth) ♦ see which way the wind is
blowing ♦ set in one's ways ♦ Stay out of
my way. ♦ take the coward's way out ♦
take the easy way out ♦ take sth the
wrong way ♦ talk one's way out of sth ♦
That ain't the way I heard it. ♦ (That's
the) way to go! ♦ There's more than one
way to skin a cat. ♦ There's no two ways
about it. ♦ to my way of thinking ♦ to put
it another way ♦ turn the other way ♦ a
two-way street ♦ under way ♦ the way I
see it ♦ the way it plays ♦ way off (base)
♦ way out ♦ the way things stand ♦ Way to
go! ♦ work (one's way) into sth ♦ work (one's
way) through sth ♦ works both ways ♦
worm (one's way) in(to sth) ♦ worm (one's
way) out (of sth) ♦ yield the right-of-way

wayside drop by the wayside ♦ fall by the
wayside

weak have a weakness for so/sth ♦ weak as
a baby ♦ weak as a kitten ♦ the weak link

(in the chain) ♦ weak sister ♦ weak
stomach
wealth a wealth of sth
wear Don't let the bastards wear you
down. ♦ I don't want to wear out my
welcome. ♦ none the worse for wear ♦
put wear (and tear) on sth ♦ wear and tear
♦ wear and tear (on sth) ♦ wear one's heart
on one's sleeve ♦ wear more than one hat
♦ wear on so ♦ wear out one's welcome ♦
wear the britches (in the family) ♦ wear
the pants (in the family) ♦ wear thin ♦
wear so to a frazzle ♦ the worse for wear
weasel weasel out (of sth)
weather fair-weather friend ♦ Fine
weather for ducks. ♦ keep one's weather
eye open ♦ Lovely weather for ducks. ♦
under the weather ♦ weather permitting ♦
weather the storm
weave weave sth from sth ♦ weave sth into
sth
wed dance at so's wedding ♦ a shotgun
wedding ♦ wedded to sth
wedlock born out of wedlock
wee the wee hours (of the night)
week by the week ♦ for (some) weeks
running ♦ inside a week ♦ week in, week
out ♦ weeks running
weep read it and weep ♦ weep for joy
weigh weigh (up)on so ♦ weigh so's words
weight carry (a lot of) weight (with so/sth)
♦ carry one's (own) weight ♦ carry the
weight of the world on one's shoulders ♦
carry weight (with so) ♦ Come in and get
some weight off your feet. ♦ give weight
to sth ♦ have a weight problem ♦ pull one's
(own) weight ♦ put on weight ♦ put
weight on ♦ throw one's weight around ♦
throw one's weight behind so/sth ♦ a weight
off one's mind ♦ work some weight off ♦
worth its weight in gold
welcome I don't want to wear out my
welcome. ♦ wear out one's welcome ♦
welcome so with open arms
well alive and well ♦ (all) well and good ♦
as well ♦ clean up well ♦ cold as a well
digger's ass (in January) ♦ cold as a well
digger's ears (in January) ♦ cold as a well
digger's feet (in January) ♦ go over (well)
♦ hail-fellow-well-met ♦ have so/sth (well)

in hand ♦ know full well ♦ know sth only too well ♦ leave well enough alone ♦ let well enough alone ♦ may as well ♦ mean well ♦ might as well ♦ play one's cards well ♦ so's point is well taken ♦ sit well with so ♦ stand well with so ♦ take well to sth ♦ Two can play (at) this game (as well as one). ♦ well and good ♦ well disposed to(ward) so/sth ♦ well done ♦ well in hand ♦ well into sth ♦ well up in years ♦ well up (inside so) ♦ well-fixed ♦ well-heeled ♦ well-off ♦ well-to-do

West out West

wet all wet ♦ get one's feet wet ♦ mad as a wet hen ♦ wet behind the ears ♦ a wet blanket ♦ wet one's whistle

whack out of w(h)ack ♦ a whack at sth ♦ whacked (out)

whale have a whale of a time ♦ whale the tar out of so

whammy a double whammy

what and what have you ♦ come what may ♦ Do what? ♦ get what's coming to one ♦ give so what for ♦ go above and beyond (what is expected) ♦ good for what ails you ♦ Guess what! ♦ have (got) what it takes ♦ if one knows what's good for one ♦ if you know what's good for you ♦ Is that some quality or what? ♦ just what the doctor ordered ♦ know one for what one is ♦ know what one is talking about ♦ know what's what ♦ Look (at) what the cat dragged in! ♦ not know what hit one ♦ not know what to make of so/sth ♦ Practice what you preach! ♦ recognize sth for what it is ♦ Say what? ♦ See what the cat dragged in! ♦ So (what)? ♦ (So) what else is new? ♦ tell so what to do with sth ♦ That's just what you need. ♦ That's what I'm talking about! ♦ What are you driving at? ♦ What can I say? ♦ What can I tell you? ♦ What do you know? ♦ What do you want me to say? ♦ What one doesn't know won't hurt one. ♦ what for ♦ What I wouldn't give for a sth! ♦ what so/sth is cracked up to be ♦ what makes so tick ♦ what makes sth tick ♦ What on earth? ♦ What price sth? ♦ What so said. ♦ What say? ♦ What the devil? ♦ What the fuck? ♦ What the heck! ♦ What the hell? ♦ What the

shit? ♦ what with sth ♦ What you see is what you get. ♦ What's coming off? ♦ what's coming to one ♦ What's cooking? ♦ What's eating so? ♦ What's going down? ♦ What's got(ten) into so? ♦ what's more ♦ What's the (big) idea? ♦ What's the catch? ♦ What's the damage? ♦ What's the drill? ♦ What's the world coming to? ♦ You and what army? ♦ You are what you eat.

whatever for what(ever) it's worth ♦ whatever comes down the pike ♦ whatever comes into one's head (first) ♦ Whatever floats your boat. ♦ Whatever turns you on.

wheat separate the wheat from the chaff

wheel asleep at the wheel ♦ at the wheel ♦ behind the wheel ♦ can (just) see the wheels turning ♦ die behind the wheel ♦ a fifth wheel ♦ have one's shoulder to the wheel ♦ keep one's shoulder to the wheel ♦ like hell on wheels ♦ put one's shoulder to the wheel ♦ reinvent the wheel ♦ a set of wheels ♦ spin one's wheels ♦ wheel and deal

when Come back when you can stay longer. ♦ cross that bridge when one comes to it ♦ It'll be a cold day in Hell when sth happens. ♦ know when one is not wanted ♦ Look me up when you're in town. ♦ Say when. ♦ Smile when you say that. ♦ time flies (when you're having fun) ♦ when all is said and done ♦ when so's back is turned ♦ when one is good and ready ♦ when it comes right down to it ♦ when it comes to sth ♦ when it comes to the crunch ♦ when it gets down to the crunch ♦ when least expected ♦ when push comes to shove ♦ when one's ship comes in ♦ when the chips are down ♦ when the dust settles ♦ when the fat lady sings ♦ when the going gets tough ♦ when the shit hits the fan ♦ When they made so/sth, they broke the mold. ♦ when you get a chance ♦ when you get a minute

where from where I stand ♦ hit one where one lives ♦ know where all the bodies are buried ♦ know where one is coming from ♦ know where it's at ♦ know where so stands (on so/sth) ♦ let the chips fall (where they may) ♦ not know where to turn ♦ put one's nose in (where it's not wanted) ♦ Put your money where your mouth is! ♦ stick one's nose in (where it's not wanted) ♦ take up where one/sth left off ♦ tell so where to get off ♦ This is where I came in. ♦ Where do (you think) you get off? ♦ where so's head is at ♦ where one is coming from ♦ Where on (God's green) earth? ♦ Where's the beef? ♦ Where's the fire? ♦ where the action is ♦ where the sun don't shine ♦ Where there's smoke, there's fire.

wherefore the whys and wherefores of sth

whereof know whereof one speaks

wherewithal have the wherewithal (to do sth) ♦ the wherewithal (to do sth)

whet whet so's appetite

whether not know whether one is coming or going ♦ not know whether to laugh or cry

whiff catch a whiff of sth ♦ take a whiff of sth ♦ a whiff of sth

whip went out with the buggy whip ♦ whip so/sth into shape ♦ whip sth off ♦ whip sth up ♦ a whipping boy

whirl give sth a whirl

whirlwind whirlwind courtship

whisker by a whisker

whisper in a stage whisper

whistle bells and whistles ♦ blow the whistle (on so/sth) ♦ can (just) whistle for sth ♦ clean as a whistle ♦ not just whistling Dixie ♦ slick as a whistle ♦ wet one's whistle ♦ whistle in the dark ♦ you ain't (just) whistlin' Dixie

whit didn't care a whit

white black and white ♦ bleed so white ♦ get sth down (in black and white) ♦ get sth in black and white ♦ in black and white ♦ a little white lie ♦ put sth down in black and white ♦ set sth down in black and white ♦ white as a ghost ♦ white as a sheet ♦ white as snow ♦ white as the driven snow ♦ a white elephant ♦ white knuckle sth ♦ white-collar

whittle whittle so down to size

whiz whiz (right) through sth

who don't care who knows it ♦ Look who's talking! ♦ many is the person who . . .

♦ Says who? ♦ show so who's boss ♦ Who could have thought? ♦ Who would have thought? ♦ Who would'a thunk (it)? ♦ You and who else?

whole as a whole ♦ go whole hog ♦ make a (whole) production out of sth ♦ make sth up out of whole cloth ♦ on the whole ♦ tell the (whole) world ♦ whole bag of tricks ♦ the whole ball of wax ♦ the whole enchilada ♦ a (whole) hell of a lot ♦ the whole kit and caboodle ♦ a (whole) new ball game ♦ the whole nine yards ♦ a whole nother story ♦ a whole nother thing ♦ the whole shebang ♦ the whole shooting match ♦ the whole wide world ♦ the whole works

whom to whom it may concern

whoop whoop it up

why the whys and wherefores of sth

wicked No rest for the wicked.

wide all wool and a yard wide ♦ blow sth wide open ♦ bust sth wide open ♦ come from far and wide ♦ crack sth (wide) open ♦ cut a wide swath ♦ far and wide ♦ give so/sth a wide berth ♦ lay oneself (wide) open for sth ♦ leave oneself (wide) open for sth ♦ leave oneself (wide) open to sth ♦ scattered far and wide ♦ the whole wide world ♦ wide awake ♦ wide of the mark ♦ wide open ♦ (wide) open to sth ♦ a wide place in the road ♦ with (one's) eyes (wide) open

widow grass widow

wife an old wives' tale

wig flip one's wig

wiggle wiggle out of sth

wilco Roger (wilco).

wild be wild about so/sth ♦ go hog wild ♦ go wild ♦ hog wild ♦ run wild ♦ send so on a wild-goose chase ♦ sow one's wild oats ♦ wild and woolly ♦ a wild-goose chase

wilderness a voice crying in the wilderness

wildfire spread like wildfire

will at will ♦ if you will ♦ ill will ♦ It will be your ass! ♦ It will take some doing. ♦ last will and testament ♦ Like hell you will! ♦ of one's own free will ♦ put sth in will-call ♦ That will do. ♦ There will be hell to pay. ♦

There will be the devil to pay. ♦ Time will tell. ♦ will be the death of so/sth (yet) ♦ will not hear of sth ♦ with a will ♦ with the best will in the world

willing God willing. ♦ God willing and the creek don't rise. ♦ Lord willing and the creek don't rise. ♦ ready, willing, and able

win Can't win them all. ♦ May the best man win. ♦ May the best team win. ♦ no-win situation ♦ Win a few, lose a few. ♦ win all the marbles ♦ win by a nose ♦ win so's heart ♦ win the day ♦ win the heart of so ♦ winner take all ♦ (You) can't win them all.

wind both sheets in the wind ♦ break wind ♦ catch wind of sth ♦ four sheets in the wind ♦ get one's second wind ♦ get wind of sth ♦ gone with the wind ♦ in the wind ♦ knock the wind out of so's sails ♦ like the wind ♦ not tell which way the wind is blowing ♦ out of wind ♦ run like the wind ♦ one's second wind ♦ see which way the wind is blowing ♦ swift as the wind ♦ take the wind out of so's sails ♦ three sheets in the wind ♦ throw caution to the wind ♦ twist (slowly) in the wind ♦ two sheets to the wind ♦ whirlwind courtship ♦ wind so up ♦ wind sth up ♦ wind up some place ♦ wind up somehow ♦ wind up (by) doing sth

windmill tilt at windmills

window crack the window (open) ♦ don't have a pot to piss in (or a window to throw it out of) ♦ go window-shopping ♦ out the window ♦ a window of opportunity ♦ window-shopping

wine wine and dine so

wing a candidate for a pair of wings ♦ clip so's wings ♦ come in on a wing and a prayer ♦ on a wing and a prayer ♦ on the wing ♦ spread one's wings (and fly) ♦ sprout wings ♦ take so under so's wing(s) ♦ try one's wings (out) ♦ under so's wing(s) ♦ waiting in the wings ♦ wing it

wink catch forty winks ♦ forty winks ♦ have forty winks ♦ hoodwink so into sth ♦ hoodwink so out of sth ♦ in the wink of an eye ♦ not sleep a wink ♦ quick as a wink ♦ take forty winks ♦ wink at sth

winter winter over (some place)

wipe wipe so/sth from the face of the earth ♦ wipe sth off (one's face) ♦ wipe so/sth off the face of the earth ♦ wipe out ♦ wipe so out ♦ wipe sth out ♦ wipe so's slate clean ♦ wipe the floor up with so

wire down to the wire ♦ have one's wires crossed ♦ Hold the wire(, please). ♦ under the wire ♦ wired into so/sth

wisdom in so's infinite wisdom

wise get wise to so/sth ♦ none the wiser ♦ not any the wiser ♦ sadder but wiser ♦ wise as an owl ♦ wise as Solomon ♦ wise to so/sth ♦ wise so up (about so/sth) ♦ wise up (to so/sth) ♦ a word to the wise

wish have a death wish ♦ Having a wonderful time; wish you were here. ♦ (I'm) having a wonderful time; wish you were here. ♦ wish list ♦ wish so the best of luck ♦ wishful thinking

wit at one's wit's end ♦ frighten one out of one's wits ♦ keep one's wits about one ♦ live by one's wits ♦ match wits (with so) ♦ scare one out of one's wits ♦ scare the wits out of so ♦ a sharp wit ♦ to wit ♦ one's wits about one

witch cold as a witch's caress ♦ cold as a witch's tit

wither wither on the vine

withstand (with)stand the test of time

witness bear witness to sth ♦ on the (witness) stand

woe tale of woe ♦ Woe is me!

wolf buy so's wolf ticket ♦ cry wolf ♦ cut one's wolf loose ♦ keep the wolf from the door ♦ The wolf is at the door. ♦ throw so to the wolves ♦ wolf sth down ♦ a wolf in sheep's clothing

woman make an honest woman of so ♦ woman to woman

women God's gift (to women)

wonder a nine days' wonder ♦ no wonder ♦ a seven-day wonder ♦ wonder at so/sth ♦ work wonders (with so/sth)

wonderful Having a wonderful time; wish you were here. ♦ (I'm) having a wonderful time; wish you were here.

woo pitch (the) woo

wood a babe in the woods ♦ in some neck of the woods ♦ knock on wood ♦ out of the woods ♦ the woods are full of so/sth

woodwork crawl out of the woodwork ◆ out of the woodwork

wool all wool and a yard wide ◆ dyed-in-the-wool ◆ pull the wool over so's eyes ◆ wild and woolly ◆ wool-gathering

word as good as one's word ◆ at a loss (for words) ◆ beyond words ◆ break one's word ◆ by word of mouth ◆ didn't exchange more than three words with so ◆ a dirty word ◆ Don't breathe a word of this to anyone. ◆ eat one's words ◆ famous last words ◆ the final word ◆ from the word go ◆ get a word in edgewise ◆ get the word ◆ get word (from so/sth) ◆ go back on one's word ◆ grateful beyond words ◆ hang on (so's) every word ◆ have a way with words ◆ have a word with so (about sth) ◆ have the last word ◆ have words (with so) (over so/sth) ◆ a household word ◆ in a word ◆ in other words ◆ in so many words ◆ (just) say the word ◆ keep one's word ◆ the last word ◆ the last word in sth ◆ leave word for so to do sth ◆ leave word (with so) ◆ lost for words ◆ a man of few words ◆ a man of his word ◆ mark my word(s) ◆ mince (one's) words ◆ Mum's the word. ◆ not breathe a word (about so/sth) ◆ not utter a word ◆ one final word ◆ or words to that effect ◆ put in a good word (for so) ◆ put sth into words ◆ put words in(to) so's mouth ◆ send word to so ◆ spread the word ◆ suit one's actions to one's words ◆ take one at one's word ◆ Take my word for it. ◆ take the words out of so's mouth ◆ take so's word for sth ◆ Them's fighting words! ◆ too funny for words ◆ true to one's word ◆ twist so's words (around) ◆ weigh so's words ◆ word by word ◆ word for word ◆ word (from so/sth) ◆ one's word is one's bond ◆ so's word is final ◆ so's word is good ◆ so's word is law ◆ so's word of honor ◆ a word to the wise ◆ a word with so (about sth) ◆ one's words stick in one's throat ◆ words to live by

work all in a day's work ◆ at work ◆ close enough for government work ◆ crawl out of the woodwork ◆ dirty work ◆ do one's homework ◆ Does it work for you? ◆ The dog ate my homework. ◆ domestic worker ◆ fancy footwork ◆ get down to

work ◆ get worked up (over sth) ◆ give so a (good) working over ◆ give so the works ◆ good enough for government work ◆ a (good) working over ◆ grunt work ◆ gum the works up ◆ have one's work cut out for one ◆ in the works ◆ (It) works for me. ◆ Keep up the good work. ◆ leg work ◆ a lick of work ◆ make fast work of so/sth ◆ make short work of so/sth ◆ off (work) ◆ out of the woodwork ◆ out of work ◆ pile the work on so ◆ put in a hard day at work ◆ set so/sth to work ◆ set to work (on so/sth) ◆ shoot the works ◆ spill the works ◆ take off from work ◆ throw a (monkey) wrench in the works ◆ the whole works ◆ work one's ass off ◆ work one's buns off ◆ work one's butt off ◆ work some fat off ◆ work one's fingers to the bone ◆ work hand in glove (with so) ◆ work so/sth into sth ◆ one's work is cut out for one ◆ work its magic on so/sth ◆ work itself out ◆ work like a beaver ◆ work like a charm ◆ work like a horse ◆ work like a mule ◆ work like a slave ◆ work of art ◆ work sth off ◆ work on so ◆ work out ◆ work out for the best ◆ work so over ◆ work one's tail off ◆ work through channels ◆ work oneself up ◆ work up a sweat ◆ work up a thirst ◆ work oneself (up) into a lather ◆ work oneself (up) into a sweat ◆ work oneself up (to sth) ◆ work up to sth ◆ work (one's way) into sth ◆ work (one's way) through sth ◆ work some weight off ◆ work wonders (with so/sth) ◆ worked up (over sth) ◆ working at cross purposes ◆ a working stiff ◆ the works ◆ works both ways ◆ Works for me.

world all over the world ◆ bring so into the world ◆ carry the weight of the world on one's shoulders ◆ come down in the world ◆ come into the world ◆ come up in the world ◆ dead to the world ◆ do a world of good (for so/sth) ◆ feel on top of the world ◆ for all the world ◆ from all corners of the world ◆ have all the time in the world ◆ have the worse of both worlds ◆ How's the world (been) treating you? ◆ in a world of one's own ◆ It takes all kinds (to make a world). ◆ make a world of difference (in so/sth) ◆ make a

X, Y, Z

yack yack one's head off

yard all wool and a yard wide ♦ the graveyard shift ♦ the whole nine yards

yarn spin a yarn

ye Oh, ye of little faith. ♦ Ye gods (and little fishes)!

year advanced in years ♦ (all) year round ♦ along in years ♦ by the year ♦ for (some) years running ♦ frighten so out of a year's growth ♦ get on (in years) ♦ on in years ♦ put (some) years on so/sth ♦ ring in the new year ♦ ring out the old (year) ♦ scare so out of a year's growth ♦ the seven-year itch ♦ one's sunset years ♦ take years off (of) so/sth ♦ twilight years ♦ up in years ♦ well up in years ♦ year in, year out ♦ year round ♦ years running

yell yell bloody murder ♦ yell (sth) from the rooftops ♦ yell one's guts out ♦ yell one's head off

yellow have a yellow belly ♦ have a yellow streak down one's back ♦ a yellow streak (down so's back)

yesterday I need it yesterday. ♦ need sth yesterday ♦ not born yesterday

yet will be the death of so/sth (yet)

yield yield the right-of-way

yoke a yoke around so's neck

yokel local yokel

yon hither, thither, and yon ♦ thither and yon

yore of yore

York in a New York minute ♦ a New York minute ♦ quicker than a New York minute

young not as young as one used to be ♦ You are only young once. ♦ young at heart

zenith at the zenith of sth

zero zero in (on so/sth) ♦ zero tolerance

ziggety Hot ziggety!

zip Zip (up) your lip!